The LaTeX Graphics Companion

Second Edition

Addison-Wesley Series on
Tools and Techniques for Computer Typesetting

This series focuses on tools and techniques needed for computer typesetting and information processing with traditional and new media. Books in the series address the practical needs of both users and system developers. Initial titles comprise handy references for LaTeX users; forthcoming works will expand that core. Ultimately, the series will cover other typesetting and information processing systems, as well, especially insofar as those systems offer unique value to the scientific and technical community. The series goal is to enhance your ability to produce, maintain, manipulate, or reuse articles, papers, reports, proposals, books, and other documents with professional quality.

Ideas for this series should be directed to the editor: mittelbach@aw.com.
Send all other comments to the publisher: awprofessional@aw.com.

Series Editor

Frank Mittelbach
Manager LaTeX3 Project, Germany

Editorial Board

Jacques André
Irisa/Inria-Rennes, France

Barbara Beeton
Editor, TUGboat, USA

David Brailsford
University of Nottingham, UK

Tim Bray
Textuality Services, Canada

Peter Flynn
University College, Cork, Ireland

Leslie Lamport
Creator of LaTeX, USA

Chris Rowley
Open University, UK

Richard Rubinstein
Human Factors International, USA

Paul Stiff
University of Reading, UK

Series Titles

Guide to LaTeX, Fourth Edition, by Helmut Kopka and Patrick W. Daly

The LaTeX Companion, Second Edition, by Frank Mittelbach and Michel Goossens with Johannes Braams, David Carlisle, and Chris Rowley

The LaTeX Graphics Companion, Second Edition, by Michel Goossens, Frank Mittelbach, Sebastian Rahtz, Denis Roegel, and Herbert Voß

The LaTeX Web Companion, by Michel Goossens and Sebastian Rahtz

Also from Addison-Wesley:

LaTeX: A Document Preparation System, Second Edition, by Leslie Lamport

The Unicode Standard, Version 5.0, by the Unicode Consortium

The LaTeX Graphics Companion

Second Edition

Michel Goossens
Frank Mittelbach
Sebastian Rahtz
Denis Roegel
Herbert Voß

✦✦Addison-Wesley

Upper Saddle River, NJ • Boston • Indianapolis • San Francisco
New York • Toronto • Montreal • London • Munich • Paris • Madrid
Capetown • Sydney • Tokyo • Singapore • Mexico City

Many of the designations used by manufacturers and sellers to distinguish their products are claimed as trademarks. Where those designations appear in this book, and Addison-Wesley was aware of a trademark claim, the designations have been printed with initial capital letters or in all capitals.

The authors and publisher have taken care in the preparation of this book, but make no expressed or implied warranty of any kind and assume no responsibility for errors or omissions. No liability is assumed for incidental or consequential damages in connection with or arising out of the use of the information or programs contained herein.

The publisher offers discounts on this book when ordered in quantity for bulk purchases and special sales. For more information, please contact:

U.S. Corporate and Government Sales
(800) 382-3419
corpsales@pearsontechgroup.com

For sales outside of the United States, please contact:

International Sales
international@pearsoned.com

Visit Addison-Wesley on the Web: www.awprofessional.com

Library of Congress Cataloging-in-Publication Data

```
The LaTeX Graphics companion / Michel Goossens ... [et al.]. -- 2nd ed.
       p. cm.
  Includes bibliographical references and index.
  ISBN 978-0-321-50892-8 (pbk. : alk. paper)
 1.  LaTeX (Computer file) 2.  Computerized typesetting. 3.  PostScript
(Computer program language) 4.  Scientific illustration--Computer programs.
5.  Mathematics printing--Computer programs. 6.  Technical
publishing--Computer programs.  I. Goossens, Michel.
    Z253.4.L38G663 2008
    686.2'2544536-dc22                                    2007010278
```

Pearson Education, Inc.
Rights and Contracts Department
75 Arlington Street, Suite 300
Boston, MA 02116
Fax: (617) 848-7047

ISBN 10:   0-321-50892-0
ISBN 13:   978-0-321-50892-8

Text printed in the United States on recycled paper at Courier in Westford, Massachusetts.

First printing, July 2007

We dedicate this book to the hundreds of LaTeX developers
whose contributions are showcased in it,
and we salute their enthusiasm and hard work.

We would also like to remember with affection and thanks
Daniel Taupin, whose MusiXTeX system is described in
Chapter 9, and who passed away in 2003, a great loss to our community.

Rhapsodie

pour piano

Composé partiellement vers 1975, terminé en août 2002

Daniel TAUPIN

Music composed by Daniel Taupin and typeset with MusiXTEX

Contents

List of Figures

Color Plates

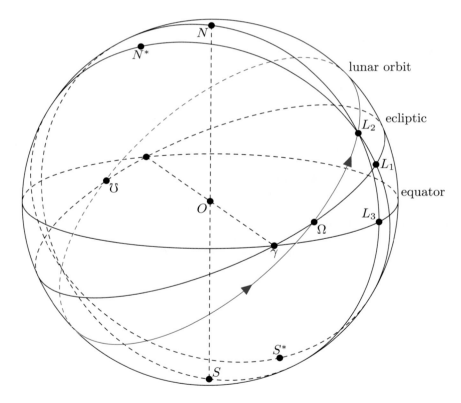

Lunar orbit on the celestial sphere with METAPOST

List of Tables

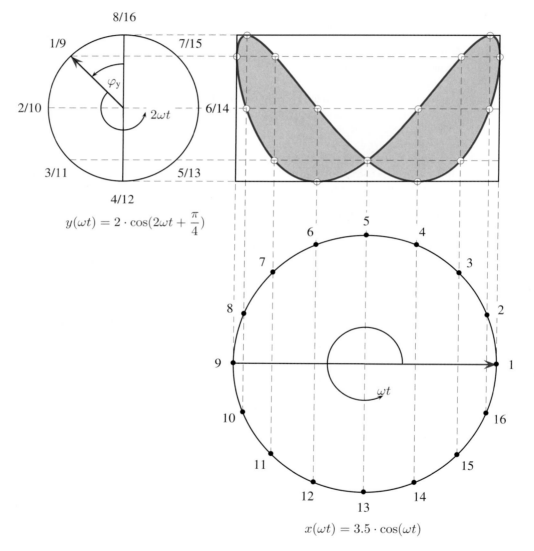

$$y(\omega t) = 2 \cdot \cos(2\omega t + \frac{\pi}{4})$$

$$x(\omega t) = 3.5 \cdot \cos(\omega t)$$

A Lissajous example with PSTricks (idea by Jürgen Gilg)

Preface

More than a decade has passed since the publication of the first edition of *The LaTeX Graphics Companion*, and there have been many changes and new developments since 1996.

The second edition has seen a major change in the authorship: Frank, Michel and Sebastian have been joined by Denis and Herbert as authors, enriching the book with their knowledge and experience in individual subject areas.

As in the first edition, this book describes techniques and tricks of extended LaTeX typesetting in the area of graphics and fonts. We examine how to draw pictures with LaTeX and how to incorporate graphics files into a LaTeX document. We explain how to program pictures using METAFONT and METAPOST, as well as how to achieve special effects with small fragments of embedded PostScript. We look in detail at a whole range of tools for building graphics in TeX itself.

TeX is the world's première markup-based typesetting system, and PostScript (on which PDF is based) is the leading language for describing the printed page. We describe how they can produce even more beautiful results when they work together. TeX's mathematical capability, its paragraph building, its hyphenation, and its programmable extensibility can cooperate with the graphical flexibility and font-handling capabilities of PostScript and PDF to provide a rich partnership for both author and typesetter.

To be able to do justice to the graphics packages that have been further developed since the first edition, we decided to omit a description of PostScript and PDF tools, and of font technologies, from the printed version of this book. This material, which was covered in Chapters 10 and 11 of the first edition, has been substantially expanded and is now freely available (see http://xml.cern.ch/lgc2). It covers DVI-to-PostScript drivers, the free program ghostscript to view PostScript and PDF files, tools for manipulating PostScript and PDF files, and suggestions on how to combine the latest font technologies (PostScript Type 1 and OpenType) with LaTeX.

This volume is not a complete consumer guide to packages. In trying to teach by example, we present hundreds of self-contained code samples of the most useful types of solutions, based on proven and well-known implementations. But, given the space available, we cannot provide a full manual for every package. Our aim is simply to show how easy it is to use a given package and to indicate whether it seems to do what is required—not to dwell on the precise details of syntax or options. Nevertheless, we have described in more detail a few selected tools that we consider especially important.

We assume you know some LaTeX; you cannot read this book by itself if you have never used TeX before. We recommend that you start with *LaTeX: A Document Preparation System, Second Edition* [78], or the *Guide to LaTeX, Fourth Edition* [76], and continue with *The LaTeX Companion, Second Edition* [83], to explore some of the many (non-graphical) packages available.

Why LaTeX, and why PostScript?

This book is about LaTeX, graphics, PostScript, and its child PDF. We believe that the structured approach of a system like LaTeX is the best way to use TeX, and LaTeX is by far the most widely used TeX format. This means that it attracts contributors who develop new packages, and thus some of what we describe works only in LaTeX. We apologize in advance for our LaTeX bias to those who appreciate the elegance of the original plain TeX format and its derivatives, and we promise them that most of the packages will work well with any TeX dialect: the delights of systems such as METAPOST, PSTricks, Xy-pic, and MusiXTeX are open to all.

We also want to explain why we talk about PostScript so much. This language has been well established for almost two decades as an extremely flexible page-description language, and it remains the tool of choice for professional typesetters. Among the features that make it so attractive are these:

- The quantity, quality, and flexibility of Type 1 fonts

- The device-independence and portability of files

- The quality of graphics and the quantity of drawing packages that generate it

- The facilities for manipulating text

- The mature color-printing technology

- The encapsulation conventions that make it easy to embed PostScript graphics

- The availability of screen-based implementations (e.g., ghostscript/ghostview)

PostScript has spawned an enterprising child, the PDF (*Portable Document Format*) language, used by Adobe Acrobat and now well established as an exchange format for documents on the Web. Designed for screen display with hypertext features, PDF offers a new degree of portability and efficiency. Although not the main subject of this book, we nevertheless mention that LaTeX can also produce "rich" PDF documents, and versions of TeX (e.g., pdflatex) that produce PDF directly are available.

Again, we apologize to those of you who are disappointed not to read about LaTeX's association with Mac's QuickDraw, or the Windows GDI, HPGL, PCL, etc., but with so many packages available, we had to make a choice.

Please note that the absence of a given package or tool in this book in no way implies that we consider it less useful or of inferior quality. We do think, though, that we have included a representative set of tools and packages, and we sincerely hope that you will find here one or more subjects to entertain you.

How this book is arranged

This book is subdivided in two basic ways: by application area and by technique. We suggest that all readers look at Chapter 1 before going any further, because it introduces how we think about graphics and summarizes some techniques developed in later chapters. We also suggest that you read Chapter 2, which covers the LaTeX standard **graphics** package, since the tools for including graphics files will be needed often. Chapter 2 also covers **pict2e**, a package that reimplements LaTeX's `picture` environment using PostScript, and a further extension **curve2e**. Together these packages not only do away with most of the limitations inherent in the standard version of LaTeX's `picture`, but also offer new and powerful commands to draw arcs and curves with mininal effort.

Basic information in Chapters 1 and 2

We have tried to make it possible to read each of the other chapters separately; you may prefer to go straight to the chapters that cover your subject area or look at those that describe a particular tool. Two chapters each are dedicated to the generic systems METAPOST and PSTricks.

3 METAFONT and METAPOST: TeX's Mates   shows how to exploit the power of TeX's META languages (Knuth's METAFONT and its PostScript-based extension META-POST). After introducing the basic functions, the basic METAPOST libraries are described, as well as available TeX interfaces and miscellaneous tools and utilities.

4 METAPOST Applications   introduces the METAPOST toolkit, and explains how to use METAPOST's unparalleled expressive power for describing many types of graphs, diagrams, and geometric constructs. Applications in the areas of science and engineering, 3-D representations, posters, etc. conclude the overview.

5 Harnessing PostScript Inside LaTeX: PSTricks   walks the reader through the various components of the PSTricks language, looking at such things as defining the coordinate system, lines and polygons, circles, ellipses and curves, arrows, labels, fill areas, and much more.

6 The Main PSTricks Packages   takes you even deeper into the world of PSTricks. Armed with the knowledge gained in Chapter 5, the reader will find here detailed descriptions of the most common PSTricks packages—in particular, **pst-plot** for plotting functions and data; **pst-node** for mastering nodes and their connections; **pst-tree** for creating tree diagrams; **pst-fill** for filling and tiling areas; **pst-3d** for creating 3-D effects, such as shadows and tilting; and **pst-3dplot** for handling 3-D functions and data sets. The chapter ends with a summary of PSTricks commands and keywords.

The next four chapters discuss problems in special application areas and survey more packages:

7 The Xy-pic Package   introduces a package that goes to great lengths to define a notation for many kinds of mathematics diagrams and implements it in a generic and portable way.

8 Applications in Science, Technology, and Medicine   looks at chemical formulae and bonds, applications in bioinformatics, Feynman diagrams, timing diagrams, and electronic and optics circuits.

9 Preparing Music Scores   first describes the principles of the powerful MusiXTEX package. Then several preprocessors providing a more convenient interface are introduced: abc for folk tunes, PMX for entering polyphonic music, and M-Tx (an offspring of PMX) for dealing with multi-voice lyrics in scores. We also take a short look at LilyPond, a modern music typesetter written in C++, and say a few words about TEX*muse*.

10 Playing Games   is for those who use LaTeX for play as well as for work. It shows you how to describe chess games and typeset chess boards (the usual and oriental variants). This chapter also describes how to handle Go, backgammon, and card games. We conclude with crosswords in various forms and Sudokus, including how to typeset, solve, and generate them.

Our last chapter addresses an area of general interest: color, and some of its common uses in LaTeX.

11 The World of Color   starts with a short general introduction to color. Next comes an overview of the xcolor package and the colortbl package, that is based on xcolor. The final part discusses the beamer class for producing color slides with LaTeX.

Appendix A describes ways to generate PDF from LaTeX. Appendix B introduces CTAN and explains how to download the LaTeX packages described in this book.

As mentioned earlier, material about PostScript and PDF tools, as well as information about how to use PostScript and OpenType fonts with LaTeX, is available as supplementary material (see http://xml.cern.ch/lgc2), which covers the following subjects:

PostScript Fonts and Beyond   describes the ins and outs of using PostScript fonts with LaTeX. It also looks at the latest developments on how to integrate OpenType fonts by creating TEX-specific auxiliary files (TEX metrics, virtual fonts, etc.) or by reading the font's characteristics directly in the OpenType source.

PostScript and PDF Tools   starts with a short introduction to the PostScript, PDF, and SVG languages. It then describes some freely available programs, in particular dvips and pdflatex to generate PostScript and PDF, ghostscript and ghostview to manipulate and view PostScript and PDF, plus a set of other tools that facilitate handling PostScript and PDF files and conversions.

Typographic conventions

It is essential that the presentation of the material conveys immediately its function in the framework of the text. Therefore, we present below the typographic conventions used in this book.

Throughout the text, LaTeX command and environment names are set in mono-spaced type (e.g., \includegraphics, sidewaystable, \begin{tabular}), while names of package and class files are in sans serif type (e.g., **graphicx**). Commands to be typed by the user on a computer terminal are shown in monospaced type and are underlined (e.g., This is user input). *Commands, environments, packages,...*

The syntax of the more complex LaTeX commands is presented inside a rectangular box. Command arguments are shown in italic type: *Syntax descriptions*

$$\boxed{\texttt{\char`\\includegraphics*} \; [\textit{llx},\textit{lly}] \; [\textit{urx},\textit{ury}] \; \{\textit{file}\}}$$

In LaTeX, optional arguments are denoted with square brackets and the star indicates a variant form (i.e., is also optional), so the above box means that the \includegraphics command can come in six different incarnations:

```
\includegraphics{file}
\includegraphics[llx,lly]{file}
\includegraphics[llx,lly][urx,ury]{file}
\includegraphics*{file}
\includegraphics*[llx,lly]{file}
\includegraphics*[llx,lly][urx,ury]{file}
```

In case of **PSTricks** the syntax is not as straight forward and optional arguments may have other delimiters than brackets. For this reason they are shown with a gray background as in the following example:

$$\boxed{\texttt{\char`\\pstriangle*} \; \textit{[settings]} \; (x_M,y_M) \; (\textit{dx,dy})}$$

Lines containing examples with LaTeX commands are indented and are typeset in a monospaced type at a size somewhat smaller than that of the main text: *Code examples...*

```
\fmfdotn{v}{4}
\fmfv{decor.shape=circle,decor.filled=full,
    decor.size=2thick}{v1,v2,v3,v4}
```

However, in the majority of cases we provide complete examples together with the output they produce side by side: *... with output...*

```
\usepackage{feyn}
$\feyn{fglf}$ \qquad $\Feyn{fglf}$
```

Example
0-0-1

Note that the preamble commands are always shown in blue in the example source.

… with several pages …   In case several pages need to be shown to prove a particular point, these are usually framed to indicate that we are showing material from several pages (this setup is repeatedly used in Section 11.4, where the beamer class for producing color slides with LaTeX, is described), as shown here.

Example 0-0-2

The Declaration of Independence of the Thirteen Colonies.

by Thomas Jefferson et al.

July 4, 1776

Self-evident truths.

We hold these truths to be self-evident,
- **that** all men are created equal,
- **that** they are endowed by their Creator with certain inalienable rights,
- **that** among these are Life, Liberty and the Pursuit of Happiness.
- **That**, to secure these rights, Governments are instituted among Men, deriving their just powers from the consent of the governed.
- **That**, when any form of government becomes destructive of these ends, it is the Right of the People to alter or abolish it.

```
\documentclass{beamer}
\title{The Declaration of Independence of
        the Thirteen Colonies.}
\author{by Thomas Jefferson et al.}
\date{July 4, 1776}
\frame{\maketitle}

\section{The unanimous Declaration}
\begin{frame}
 \frametitle{Self-evident truths.}
 We hold these truths to be self-evident,
 \begin{itemize}
  \item \textbf{that} all men are created equal,
  \item \textbf{that} they are endowed by their
         Creator with certain inalienable rights,
  \item \textbf{that} among these are Life,
         Liberty and the Pursuit of Happiness.
  \item \textbf{That}, to secure these rights,
Governments are instituted among Men, deriving
their just powers from the consent of the governed.
  \item  \textbf{That}, when any form of government
becomes destructive of these ends, it is the Right
... further code omitted ...
```

… with large output …   For large examples, where the input and output cannot be shown conveniently alongside each other, the following layout is used:

```
\usepackage{feyn}
\begin{eqnarray}
\feyn{fcf} &=& \feyn{faf} + \feyn{fpf} + \cdots \\
   &=& \sum_{n=0}^\infty \feyn{fsafs ( pfsafs)}^n
 \end{eqnarray}
```

Example 0-0-3

Depending on the example content, some additional explanation might appear between input and output.

All of these examples are "complete" if, for the LaTeX examples, you mentally add a \documentclass line (with the **article** class[1] as an argument) and surround the body of the example with a document environment. In fact, this is how all the examples in this book were produced. When processing the book, special LaTeX commands take the source lines for an example and write them to an external file, thereby automatically adding the \documentclass or the relevant lines needed to run the example. This turns each example into a small but complete source document, which can then be externally processed (using a mechanism that runs each example as often as necessary; see also the next section on how to use the examples). The result is converted into small EPS graphics, which are then loaded in the appropriate place the next time LaTeX is run on the whole book. The implementation is based on the **fancyvrb** package, and is described in more details in *The LaTeX Companion* [83] (Section 3.4.3, in particular pages 162–163).

In some cases input for the examples may get very lengthy without providing additional insight to the reader. In that case some of it is replaced by the line "... further code omitted ..." to save space, as shown in Example 0-0-2. Technically this is achieved by placing the command \empty on a line by itself into the example code (where you will find it in the online version of the examples). When the example is processed to produce the output graphic this command is ignored, but when the code is read verbatim to show the input in the book, it serves as marker to end the code display. *Omitting example code*

Throughout the book, blue notes are sprinkled in the margin to help you easily find certain information that would otherwise be hard to locate. In a few cases these notes exhibit a warning sign, indicating that you should probably read this information even if you are otherwise only skimming through the particular section. *Watch out for these*

Using the examples

Our aim when producing this book was to make it as useful as possible for our readers. For this reason the book contains nearly 1200 complete, self-contained examples illustrating the main aspects of the packages and programs covered in the book.

We have put the source of the examples on CTAN (Comprehensive TeX Archive Network—see Appendix B) in the directory info/examples/lgc2. The examples are numbered per section, and each number is shown in a small box in the inner margin (e.g., 2-1-1 for the Example 2-1-1 on page 26). These numbers are also used for the external file names by appending a filetype that corresponds to the source. Most files are in LaTeX source format (with an extension of .ltx for a single page, or .ltxb for generating several pages when giving examples of the use of the **beamer** class). There are also plain TeX files (extension .ptx), METAPOST source files (extension .mp), MusiXTeX preprocessor source files (extensions .abc, .abcplus, .pmx, .mtx, and .ly), pic files (extension .pic), and m4 sources (extension .m4). For each of these types of sources there is a corresponding Unix script (runabc, runabcpl, runltx, runltxb, runly, runm4, runmp, runmtx, runpic, runpmx, runptx), which can be used as an example of how to run the given source file on a system where all the needed packages and software, as described in this book, are available. *Online example sources*

---

[1] Except for examples in Chapter 11 that require the **beamer** class.

To reuse any of the examples it is usually sufficient to copy the preamble code (typeset in blue) into the preamble of your document and, if necessary, adjust the document text as shown. In some cases it might be more convenient to place the preamble code into your own package (or class file), thus allowing you to load this package in multiple documents using \usepackage. If you want to do the latter, there are two points to observe:

- Any use of the \usepackage command in the preamble code should be replaced by \RequirePackage, which is the equivalent command for use in package and class files (see e.g., Section A.4.5 of *The LATEX Companion* [83]).
- Any occurrence of \makeatletter and \makeatother *must* be removed from the preamble code. This is very important because the \makeatother would stop correct reading of such a file.

So let us assume you wish to reuse the code from the following (rather complex) example:

```
\usepackage{pstricks,pst-xkey}

\makeatletter                          % '@' now normal "letter"

\newif\ifHRInner
\def\psset@HRInner#1{\@nameuse{HRInner#1}}
\psset@HRInner{false}
\def\psHexagon{\pst@object{psHexagon}}
\def\psHexagon@i{\@ifnextchar({\psHexagon@ii}%
                              {\psHexagon@ii(0,0)}}
\def\psHexagon@ii(#1)#2{%
  \begin@ClosedObj%                      closed object
    \pst@@getcoor{#1}%                   get center
    \pssetlength\pst@dimc{#2}%           set radius to pt
    \addto@pscode{%                      PostScript
      \pst@coor T %                      xM yM new origin
      \psk@dimen CLW mul %               set line width
      /Radius \pst@number\pst@dimc\space % save radius
        \ifHRInner\space 3 sqrt 2 div div \fi def % inner?
      /angle \ifHRInner 30 \else 0 \fi def % starting angle
      Radius angle PtoC moveto %         go to first point
      6 { %                              6 iterations
        /angle angle 60 add def %        alpha = alpha+60
        Radius angle PtoC L %            line to next point
      } repeat
      closepath %                        closed object
    }%
    \def\pst@linetype{3}%                set linetype
    \showpointsfalse%                    do not show base points
  \end@ClosedObj%                        end
  \ignorespaces}%                        swallow spaces

\makeatother                 % '@' is restored as "non-letter"
```

```
\psset{unit=7mm}
\begin{pspicture}(-3,-3)(3,3)
  \psHexagon[linewidth=3pt,linecolor=red]{2.5}
  \pscircle[linestyle=dashed,linecolor=red]{2.5}
%
  \psHexagon[linewidth=3pt,linecolor=blue,HRInner=true]{2.5}
  \pscircle[linestyle=dashed,linecolor=blue]{2.17}
\end{pspicture}
```

Example
0-0-4

You have two alternatives: You can copy the preamble code (i.e., code colored blue) into your own document preamble or you can place that code—but without the `\makeatletter` and `\makeatother` and with `\usepackage` replaced by `\RequirePackage`—in a package file (e.g., `myhexagon.sty`) and afterwards load this "package" in the preamble of your own documents with `\usepackage{myhexagon}`.

Finding all those packages and programs

All of the packages and programs described in this book are freely available in public software archives; a few are in the public domain, but most are protected by copyright and available to you under an open-source license. Some programs are available only in source form or work only on certain computer platforms, and you should be prepared for a certain amount of "getting your hands dirty" in some cases. We also cannot guarantee that later versions of packages or programs will give results identical to those in our book. Many of these packages and programs remain under active development, and new or changed versions appear several times a year; we completed this book in spring 2007, and tested the examples with the versions current at that time.

In Appendix B we give full details on how to access CTAN sites and how to download files using the Internet. You can also purchase the *TEX Collection* DVD from one of the TEX Users Groups. This DVD contains implementations of TEX for various systems, many packages and fonts, in particular it provides you with all the LATEX packages described in this book and *The LATEX Companion, Second Edition*. Some programs (such as the ones described in the music chapter) are not available on CTAN (or the DVD) and must be downloaded from the location indicated in the text.

Acknowledgments

We gratefully recognize all of our many colleagues in the TEX world who develop LATEX packages—not only those described here, but also the hundreds of others that help users typeset their documents faster and better. Without the continuous effort of all these enthusiasts, TEX would not be the magnificent and flexible tool it is today.

We have many people to thank. Our primary debt, of course, is to the authors of the programs and packages we describe. Every author whom we contacted to discuss problems provided us with practical help in the spirit of the TEX community, and often gave us permission to reuse examples from their documentation.

We are greatly indebted to Eric Beitz, Ulrich Dirr, Ulrike Fischer, Federico Garcia, Uwe Kern, Claudia Krysztofiak, Aaron Lauda, Susan Leech O'Neale, Ross Moore, Janice Navarria, Han-Wen Nienhuys, Ralf Vogel, and Damien Wyart, for their careful reading of sections of the manuscript. Their numerous comments, suggestions, corrections, and hints have substantially improved the quality of the text. Special thanks go to Hubert Gäßlein, who greatly helped us at all stages of preparation, verification, and typesetting.

As he did with *The LATEX Companion, Second Edition*, Richard Evans of Infodex Indexing Services in Raleigh, North Carolina, undertook the groundwork for the comprehensive indexes in the back of the book—thank you, Dick.

On the publishing side, we wish to thank Peter Gordon, our editor at Addison-Wesley, who gave us much-needed support and encouragement over the three years duration of this project. When it came to production, Elizabeth Ryan was unfailingly patient with our idiosyncrasies and steered us safely to completion. Jill Hobbs edited our dubious prose into real English; we greatly appreciate their work.

*   *   *

Our families and friends have lived through the preparation of this book over several years, and we thank them for their patience and moral support.

Feedback

To Err is Human We would like to ask you, dear reader, for your collaboration. We kindly invite you to send your comments, suggestions, or remarks to any of the authors. We shall be glad to correct any mistakes or oversights in a future edition, and are open to suggestions for improvements or the inclusion of important developments we may have overlooked. Any mistake or oversight found in this book and reported represents a gain for all readers. The latest version of the errata file (with contact details) can be found on the LATEX project site at `http://www.latex-project.org/guides/lgc2.err` where you will also find an online version of the index and other extracts from the book.

Michel Goossens
Frank Mittelbach
Sebastian Rahtz
Denis Roegel
Herbert Voß
June 2007

CHAPTER 1

Graphics with LaTeX

The phrase "A picture paints a thousand words" seems to have entered the English language thanks to Frederick R. Barnard in *Printer's Ink*, 8 December 1921, retelling a Chinese proverb.[1] However, while LaTeX is quite good at typesetting words in a beautiful manner, LaTeX manuals usually tell you little or nothing about how to handle graphics. This book attempts to fill that gap by describing tools and TEXniques that let you generate, manipulate, and integrate graphics with your text.

In these days of the multimedia PC, graphics appear in various places. With many products we get ready-to-use collections of clipart graphics; in shops we can buy CD-ROMs with "the best photos" of important places; and so forth. As we shall see, all such graphics can be included in a LaTeX document as long as they are available in a suitable format. Fortunately, many popular graphic formats either are directly supported or can be converted via a program that allows transformation into a supported representation.

If you want to become your own graphic artist, you can use stand-alone dedicated drawing tools, such as the freely available dia (www.gnome.org/projects/dia) and xfig (www.xfig.org/userman) on Linux, or the commercial products Adobe Illustrator (www.adobe.com/illustrator) or Corel Draw (www.corel.com/coreldraw) on a Mac or PC. Spreadsheet programs, or one of the modern calculation tools like Mathematica

---

[1] Paul Martin Lester (commfaculty.fullerton.edu/lester/writings/letters.html) states that the literal translation of the "phony" Chinese proverb should rather be "A picture's meaning can express ten thousand words". He, rightly, emphasizes that pictures cannot and should not replace words, but both are complementary and contribute equally to the understanding of the meaning of a work.

(`www.wolfram.com/mathematica`), Maple (`www.maplesoft.com/maple`), and MAT-LAB (`www.mathworks.com/matlab`), or their freely available GNU variant Octave (`www.octave.org`) and its plotting complements Octaviz (`octaviz.sourceforge.net`) and Octplot (`octplot.sourceforge.net`), can also produce graphics by using one of their many graphical output representations. With the help of a scanner or a digital camera you can produce digital photos, images of hand-drawn pictures, or other graphics that can be manipulated with their accompanying software. In all these cases it is easy to generate files that can be directly referenced in the LATEX source through the commands of the **graphics** package described in Chapter 2.

If needed, LATEX can also offer a closer integration with the typesetting system than that possible by such programs. Such integration is necessary if you want to use the same fonts in text and graphics, or more generally if the "style" of the graphics should depend on the overall style of the document. Close integration of graphics with the surrounding text clearly requires generation of the graphic by the typesetting system itself, because otherwise any change in the document layout style requires extensive manual labor and the whole process becomes very error-prone.

*   *   *

This chapter considers graphic objects from different angles. First. we look at the requirements that various applications impose on graphic objects. Next, we analyze the types of drawings that appear in documents and the strategies typically employed to generate, integrate, and manipulate such graphics. Then, we discuss the interfaces offered by TEX for dealing with graphic objects. Armed with this knowledge, we end the chapter with a short survey of graphics languages built within and around TEX. This overview will help you select the right tool for the job at hand. In fact, the current chapter also gives some examples of languages and approaches not covered in detail elsewhere in the book. Thus this survey should provide you with enough information to decide whether or not to follow the pointers and obtain such a package for a particular application.

1.1 Graphics systems and typesetting

When speaking about "graphic objects", we should first define the term. One extreme position is to view everything put on paper as a graphic object, including the characters of the fonts used. This quite revolutionary view was, in fact, adopted in the design of the page description language PostScript, in which characters can be composed and manipulated by exactly the same functions as other graphic objects (we will see some examples of this in Chapters 5 and 6, which describe PSTricks and its support packages).

Most typesetting systems, including TEX, do not try to deploy such a general model but instead restrict their functional domain to a subset of general graphic objects—for example, by providing very sophisticated functions to place characters, resolve ligatures, etc., but omitting operators to produce arbitrary lines, construct and fill regions, and so forth. As a result the term "graphics" for most LATEX users is a synonym for "artwork", thereby ignoring the fact that LATEX already has a graphics language—the `picture` mode.

When discussing the graphical capabilities of an ideal typesetting system, we must remember that different applications have different, sometimes conflicting requirements:

- One extreme is the need for complete portability between platforms; another is to take into account even differences in the way printers put ink onto paper.

- A graphic might need to be correctly scaled to a certain size depending on factors of the visual environment created by the typesetting system, e.g., the measure of the text.

- It is also possible that parts of the graphic should not scale linearly. For example, it might be important for readability to ensure that textual parts of a graphic do not become smaller or larger than some limit. It might also be required that, when a graphic is scaled by, say, 10% to fit the line, any included text must stay the same, so as to avoid making it larger than the characters in the main document body.

- It might be required that the graphical object be closely integrated with the surrounding text, such as by using the same fonts as in other parts of the document or more generally by containing objects that should change their appearance if the overall style of the document is changed. (The latter is especially important if the document is described by its logical content rather than by its visual appearance, with the intention of reusing it in various contexts and forms.)

As LaTeX is a general-purpose typesetting system used for all types of applications, the preceding requirements and more might arise in various situations. As we will see throughout this book, a large number of them can be handled with grace, if not to perfection. In some cases an appropriate solution was anything but obvious and developing the mature macro packages and programs we now have took a decade or more of work.

1.2 Drawing types

The typology of graphics at the beginning of this chapter focused on the question of the integration with the LaTeX system, and divided the graphics into externally and internally generated ones. A different perspective would be to start from the types of graphics we might encounter in documents and discuss possible ways to generate and incorporate them.

A first class of graphics to be included are treated by LaTeX as a single object, a "black box", without an accessible inner structure. LaTeX, via its **graphics** package (described in Chapter 2), is interested only in the rectangular dimensions of the graphic image, its "bounding box". The graphics will be included in the output "as is", possibly after some simple manipulation, such as scaling or rotation. On top of that LaTeX can also produce a caption and legend to allow proper referencing from within the document. The main categories are as follows:

1. *Free-hand pictures* drawn without a computer, such as the drawing of a glass bead in Figure 1.1. For use in LaTeX, such a graphic must to be transformed into a digital image, using, for example, a scanner.

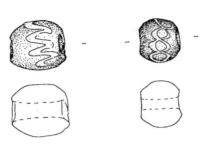

Figure 1.1: Pen and ink drawing of a bead

Figure 1.2: Bitmap drawing output created with GIMP

2. *"Art" graphics* drawn with bitmap tools on a computer, such as the example in Figure 1.2, which are to some extent the computer equivalents of pen and ink drawings. This drawing was created with GIMP, the GNU Image Manipulation Program (`www.gimp.org`), using a deliberately crude technique. The distinctive characteristic of this type of drawing is that the resolution chosen in the generation process cannot easily be changed without loss of quality (or alternatively without a lot of manual labor). In other respects such a picture is like a free-hand drawing: there is generally no desire to integrate the drawing with the text or to worry about conformity of typefaces.

3. *Photographs* either created directly using a digital camera or scanned like hand-drawn pictures. In the latter case the continuous tones of the photograph are converted into a distinct range of colors or gray levels (black-and-white photographs treated in this way are known as half-tones). Full-color reproduction requires sophisticated printing techniques, but this issue arises at the printing stage and does not normally affect the typesetting. Figure 1.3 shows how LATEX can distort the image.

A second class of graphics is the "object-oriented" type, where the information is stored in the form of abstract objects that incorporate no device-dependent information (unlike bitmap graphics, where the storage format just contains information about whether a certain spot is black or white, making them resolution-dependent). This device independence makes it easy to reuse the graphic with different output devices and allows us to manipulate individual aspects of the graphic during the design process.

There are essentially three types of such graphics systems: one in which LATEX mainly remains passive (it just takes into account the bounding box of the picture), and two others that relate to graphics that contain more complex text, in particular formulae. For the latter types it is important to use LATEX to typeset text within the graphic because the symbols in formulae and their typeset form carry a precise semantic meaning. Therefore one must take great care to ensure that their visual representation is identical in both text and associated graphics.

1. *Self-contained object-oriented graphics.* The ducks of Figure 1.4, which was produced with Adobe Illustrator, were created by drawing one object in terms of curves and then

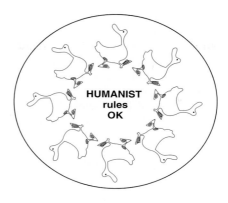

Figure 1.3: Digitally transformed image (vertically stretched)

Figure 1.4: Object-oriented drawing

copying and rotating it many times. This type of drawing often also contains textual annotations comparable to typeset text. Although it is usually possible to add text to the graphic with external tools such Illustrator, it is not in general possible to use LaTeX to typeset this text (although psfrag provides a solution in some circumstances).

2. *Algorithmic display graphics* (e.g., histograms, graphs). These drawings are created without human interaction but often contain text that should match the document text. The scale and distance between elements is an essential characteristic of the drawing. Extensive plotting and diagram facilities are provided by many LaTeX packages building on the picture mode, by generic TeX packages such as PiCTeX [139], DraTex [39], and tikz [115]; and by PSTricks (see Chapters 5 and 6). All these solutions let us deploy the full power of LaTeX's typesetting functions within textual parts of the graphic and thus integrate it perfectly with surrounding document elements.

3. *Algorithmic structural graphics*, which can be derived from a textual representation. Unlike with the previous category, often merely the spatial relationship between elements is important with these graphics, not the elements' exact position or size. Examples are category diagrams, chemical formulae, trees, and flowcharts. Such graphics are natural candidates for generation by graphics languages internal to LaTeX that provide high-level interfaces which focus on objects and relationships and decide final placement and layout automatically.
   Of the general-purpose languages, the METAPOST system (Chapters 3 and 4) is perhaps the most flexible one for this type of graphics, although PiCTeX, Xy-pic (Chapter 7), PSTricks (Chapters 5 and 6), and DraTex are also suitable. They are based on different paradigms, and differ greatly in approach, focus, and user interface, but they all have found their place in the LaTeX world. We describe small specialized languages tailored for specific application domains such as physics, chemistry or electronics diagrams (Chapter 8), music (Chapter 9), and games (Chapter 10). For special applications such as tree drawing, many other LaTeX languages are available as well (see [13], for instance).

As we see, many types of graphics exist, each with its own requirements. The first three types essentially present themselves as black boxes to LaTeX and thus their use within a LaTeX document involves no more than their inclusion and in some cases their manipulation as a whole. The necessary functionality is discussed in detail in Chapter 2.

In scientific texts, the other types of graphics are by far the more common. Examples include maps [119], chemical structures, or commutative diagrams. They are for the most part based on an object-oriented approach, specifying objects and their relations in an abstract way using a suitable language. Close integration with the surrounding text can be achieved, if needed, by choosing one of the graphics languages described in this book.

In some cases interactive drawing programs can be instructed to output their results in one of the graphics languages built directly on top of LaTeX's picture mode. Widely used examples under Linux are dia and xfig, whose pictures, although externally produced, can be influenced by layout decisions within the document. Note, however, that such mechanically produced LaTeX code is normally not suitable for further manual editing and manipulation is practically limited to layout facilities implemented by the chosen graphics language. Nevertheless, in certain situations this approach can offer the best of two worlds.

1.3 TeX's interfaces

To understand the merits of the different approaches to graphics as implemented by various packages, it is helpful to consider yet another point of view: the interfaces provided by TeX for dealing with them. Describing the methods by which graphics can be generated, included, or manipulated will give you some feeling for such important issues as portability, quality, and resource requirements of individual solutions. We assume that the reader has a reasonable understanding of how TeX works—that is, the progression from source file to a DVI file that is processed by a driver to produce printed pages. Of course, the DVI stage can be skipped when using pdflatex, but the various ways of including the graphics material are still identical.

In the following we first look at ways of including externally generated graphics (i.e., those that appear as black boxes to TeX) and methods to manipulate them. Then we consider interfaces provided to build graphics languages within TeX.

1.3.1 Methods of integration

TeX offers two major facilities for integrating graphics as a whole: one involving the \special command, and the other using the font interface.

Using \special commands

The TeXbook [70] does not describe ways to directly include externally generated graphics. The only command available is the \special command, which by itself does nothing, but does enable us to access capabilities that might be present in the post-processor (DVI driver or pdflatex). To quote Knuth [70, page 229]:

> The \special command enables you to make use of special equipment that might be available to you, e.g., for printing books in glorious TeXnicolor.

Saying it differently, Knuth saw that there might be a need to enrich the TₑX language but was reluctant to provide primitives for further graphical operators and data structures or, in case of the inclusion of external graphics, a well-defined interface.

Thus `\special` allows us to access *special* features of a driver program that translates the DVI output of TₑX into a language understood by the output device. If this driver has mechanisms to include external graphics, then we can import such graphics.[1] In principle, the price that must be paid is non-portability, since source files will contain calls to a non-standard interface—and, indeed, originally, authors of different drivers had implemented different conventions. However, in 1993 Leslie Lamport, Frank Mittelbach, and Chris Rowley designed a high-level interface for LATEX that abstracts from the underlying low-level syntax understood by the individual drivers. This interface was implemented in 1994 by David Carlisle and Sebastian Rahtz in LATEX 2ₑ's **graphics** package [15], which is discussed in detail in Chapter 2. That chapter also introduces the **pict2e** package, which reimplements LATEX's `picture` environment and eliminates many of its limitations. In a similar manner the use of `\special` commands to address the color capabilities of some drivers was made transparent with the high-level interface provided by the **xcolor** package described in Chapter 11.

By offering a set of high-level commands, the dependency on the idiosyncrasies of the driver used is effectively eliminated from the document. The only place where one has to change a document using such commands is a single line in the preamble that controls how the commands are implemented (by loading a driver-specific control file).

Using fonts or half-tones

External graphics can also be included using TₑX's font mechanism. A font is described to TₑX by its external name and by a TFM file that contains the metric information about the glyphs in the font. The shape of the character is irrelevant as far as TₑX is concerned since the actual printing of the glyph is the task of the DVI driver program, which uses the standard PK font format. This technique is effective and portable but it has the drawback that scaling cannot easily be performed without going back to the original artwork to produce a font at a different resolution. Moreover, TₑX has a limit on the number of fonts it can load.

Figure 1.5: Scanned cartoon converted to font

Figure 1.5 is a cartoon by Duane Bibby that was scanned, saved as a bitmap graphic file, converted into PBM,[2] and finally turned into a single character PK font, called `lion`, with the help of Angus Duggan's **pbmtopk**.[3] It was included with a declaration like `\font\lion=lion` to load the font followed by `{\lion A}` at the point where it should appear.

---

[1] When using **pdflatex** the DVI intermediate step is skipped, since the **pdflatex** processor itself handles the inclusion of the graphics in the PDF output file. In this case PNG, JPEG, and PDF files can be included natively, but EPS cannot.

[2] The PBM (portable bitmap) format is an intermediate graphic format for transforming one format into another. The **netpbm** Project (`netpbm.sourceforge.net/doc/index.html`) has more than 200 programs to convert between graphics formats. The **ImageMagick** Project (`www.imagemagick.org`) also supports more than 90 different formats and allows conversions between them.

[3] See CTAN: `graphics/pbmtopk`. Friedhelm Sowa has developed a more sophisticated program, **bm2font**, that also accepts other graphics formats, such as PCX, GIF, and TIFF, and produces one or more PK and their corresponding TFM files. See `gnuwin32.sourceforge.net/packages/bm2font.htm` for more details.

Half-tone drawings can be included by making up a font that consists of gray-level blocks and combining them together in the normal TEX way. Both Donald Knuth [75] and Adrian Clark [17] (see also CTAN: `fonts/halftone`) have demonstrated this technique. The drawing can be scaled, but it is not easy to put text within the picture boundary, and one is dependent on the original resolution.

Half-toning can also be achieved directly in PostScript, a rather less cumbersome method than TEX half-toning, albeit at the cost of device independence and flexibility.

1.3.2 Methods of manipulation

The facilities in TEX for manipulating graphics (e.g., scaling or rotating) provided by one of the previously mentioned methods appear at first glance to be relatively poor. If the graphic is included as one or more font characters, then scaling is in principle possible, since TEX can load fonts at any size. At the printing stage, however, the driver program will probably complain that it cannot find the font at the appropriate size, which means that one has to regenerate it at the size requested, a task that is (to say the least) time-consuming.

The only alternative is to resort to the `\special` capabilities of the driver via the graphics package interface mentioned earlier and include the image as a bitmap.

The situation is slightly different when the half-tone approach is chosen, as then the fonts in question are METAFONT fonts and can be generated automatically at the requested size by a modern driver, assuming that their sources are available.

1.3.3 TEX's graphics hooks

Graphics are not always around in some form just waiting to be included—often we have to produce them in the first place. In the following sections we explore the facilities available in the TEX world for generating graphics.

Using TEX's built-in commands

As already observed, TEX does not provide a rich set of graphic primitives. What we find are built-in functions that let us draw horizontal or vertical lines of arbitrary thickness—even sloped lines are lacking. In addition, TEX allows us to position objects with high accuracy anywhere on the page. The only other functions offered are primitives for placing objects in matrix structures where the exact placement is determined automatically by the size of the objects (e.g., the `tabular` and `array` environments in LATEX).

But even with this minimal set it is possible to define powerful graphics languages, especially if we consider the character "." as a building block, since arbitrary lines and curves can be drawn by placing hundreds of tiny dots next to each other.

Using fonts

Instead of using a "." character as an individual graphic object, Leslie Lamport provided LATEX with a basic set of picture-drawing macros that use special fonts containing line segments at various angles and circle and curve fragments at various sizes.

These macros have allowed programmers to produce surprisingly sophisticated output, beyond the quite respectable uses to which the `picture` environment of basic LaTeX can be put. The Xy-pic package (see Chapter 7) follows a similar approach and has its own set of fonts for arrowhead styles.

The approach of using fonts is not limited to working with technical drawing fragment fonts created with METAFONT. Music, chess, and Go fonts, which allow you to typeset musical scores, chessboards, and Go boards using TEX as a layout engine, are available as well; these are described in Chapters 9 and 10.

Using `\special` commands

We have already seen that the `\special` command can be used to access graphics inclusion capabilities provided by DVI drivers. Drivers' extended drawing capabilities can be accessed in the same way.

To understand how the `\special` command works, you can think of it as producing an invisible space annotated in some way with the text of its argument. Depending on where in the source the `\special` command was encountered, this "invisible space" appears somewhere on the typeset page, just as a word in the source finally appears somewhere in a paragraph. Thus, after typesetting a document with TEX, each `\special` command is associated with a position on a page.

When a driver encounters such an "invisible space" produced by a `\special`, it knows its position on the current page. It then reads the annotation (i.e., the argument of the `\special` command) and (if it understands it) carries out the action requested. Therefore, if the driver offers such capabilities, it is possible to denote points and regions for special treatment, ranging from drawing a line between two points to rotating an area after typesetting by TEX. This is the mechanism by which some of the more complicated graphic functions of some packages described in this book are implemented. Back in 1982 Knuth wrote about using the `\special` command and conventions for the syntax within its argument [70, page 229]:

> [...] the author anticipates that certain standards for common graphic operations will emerge in the TEX user community, after careful experiments have been made by different groups of people; then there will be a chance for some uniformity in the use of the `\special` extensions.

Unfortunately, such a standard never emerged despite various efforts. Today, for graphics inclusion, we have a high-level interface that abstracts from the underlying driver facilities. The situation with respect to other drawing capabilities of driver programs via the `\special` command is less satisfactory, as there exists neither a standard nor a high-level interface that hides the capabilities of different drivers. However, as these capabilities depend so strongly on the target language of the driver, it may be that useful standardization cannot be achieved. Given the dominance of PostScript in the printer and typesetting market, standardization of `\special` primitives for PostScript drivers is probably the most useful thing to do. In effect, this is the route taken by PSTricks (see Chapters 5 and 6).

1.4 Graphics languages

A number of distinct ways of producing graphics exist, each with its own advantages and disadvantages in terms of ease of generation, flexibility, device independence, and ability to include arbitrary TEX text. With the help of LATEX's graphics package it is possible to manipulate a graphic object as a whole using a variety of standard operations, such as scaling, rotation, and so forth. However, to manipulate individual parts of a graphic these parts need to be addressable in a suitable manner—i.e., the source of the graphic must be in some abstract graphic language.

After a short description of the general-purpose device- and resolution-independent graphics languages PostScript, PDF, SVG, and CGM, the remainder of this section presents a "roadshow" of graphics languages, explaining how they make use of the interfaces provided by TEX or, in the case of external graphics languages, how they can interact with the LATEX system to produce impressive documents. Several of these languages are discussed in detail in later chapters; the others are included here to provide a first-level introduction.

1.4.1 Generic graphics languages

The current section describes important features of generic languages that are most often used to store graphics information today. On medium- and high-volume printers most LATEX output is nowadays translated into PostScript or PDF for high-quality printing or viewing. On the Web, SVG has become an important player for all kinds of graphics, especially graphic arts applications while WebCGM is available for more technical applications.

PostScript

PostScript [5] is a device- and resolution-independent, general-purpose, programming language. PostScript programs describe a complete "output page" and are written in the form of ASCII source that can be viewed on a computer display with a previewer, such as ghostview (www.cs.wisc.edu/~ghost/gv), and printed on a small laser printer or a high-resolution phototypesetter.

In the PostScript language the following can be freely combined [1, 2, 16]:

- Arbitrary shapes, which can be constructed from lines, arcs, and cubic curves. The shapes may self-intersect and contain disconnected sections and holes.

- Painting primitives, which permit shapes to be outlined with lines of any thickness, filled with any color, or used as a clipping path to crop any other graphic.

- A general coordinate system, which supports all combinations of linear transformations, including scaling, rotation, reflection, and skewing. These transformations apply uniformly to all page elements, including text, graphical images, and sampled images.

- Text characters, which are treated as graphical shapes that may be operated on by any of the language's graphics operators. This is fully true for PostScript Type 3 fonts, where character shapes are defined as ordinary PostScript language procedures. In contrast, Adobe's PostScript Type 1 format defines a special smaller language where character shapes are defined by using specially encoded procedures for efficiency of rendering.

- Images (such as photographs or synthetically generated images), which can be sampled at any resolution and with a variety of dynamic ranges, so that their rendering on the output device can be closely controlled.

- Several color models (device-based: RGB, HSB, CMYK; standard-based: CIE) and conversion functions from one model to another.

- Compression filters, such as JPEG and LZW.

All current implementations of TEX include a DVI-to-PostScript driver or generate PostScript or PDF directly. Commercial or shareware solutions include **Textures** (`www.bluesky.com/products/textures.html`) on Macintosh and *Personal TEX*'s **PCTeX** (`www.pctex.com`) and Michael Vulis's **VTeX** (*Visual TEX*; see `www.micropress-inc.com`). In addition, for more than a decade Tom Rokicki's **dvips** driver has been rightly regarded as the standard by which other drivers are measured, and nowadays **dvips** is part of almost all TEX distributions. It is highly configurable and lets the user specify almost all settings to control output devices in configuration files or on the command line. **dvips** will also automatically generate missing fonts, if needed.

To view PostScript files, one can use Aladdin **ghostscript** (`www.cs.wisc.edu/~ghost`) a freely available PostScript interpreter written by L. Peter Deutsch. It can be used to prepare output for various printing devices, to convert PostScript into raster formats, and to manipulate PostScript (e.g., calculating the bounding box of an EPS file). The program also handles PDF (see below).

The Portable Document Format

Adobe's Portable Document Format (PDF) [6] is a direct descendant of the PostScript language. Whereas PostScript is a full-blown programming language, PDF is a second-generation, more light-weight graphics language optimized for faster download and display. Most of the advantages of PostScript remain: PDF guarantees page fidelity, down to the smallest glyph or piece of white space, while being portable across different computer platforms. For these reasons, PDF is being used ever more frequently in the professional printing world as a replacement for PostScript. Moreover, all present-day browsers will embed or display PDF material, alongside HTML, using plug-in technology. The latest versions of PDF (1.4 and later) have added many new features that are especially useful for multimedia applications. However, to ensure that files can be handled with minimal problems by different applications and printers, it is advisable to limit functions to those offered by PDF 1.4, or even PDF 1.3.

The main characteristics of PDF, as compared to PostScript, are:

- PDF offers full page independence by clearly separating resources from page objects.

- PDF, in contrast to PostScript, is not a programming language, i.e., PDF cannot calculate values, although a small set of *function objects* allow for some simple arithmetic.

- PDF files are compact and fully searchable. Markup annotations and interactive hyperlinks make PDF files easy to navigate.

- PDF's security features allow PDF documents to have special access rights and digital signatures applied.

- Font outlines can be subsetted or font substitution can even completely eliminate the need for font inclusion (although this feature should be handled with great care, especially with TEX fonts, which use many nonstandard characters, for example, in its mathematics fonts).

- PDF has advanced compression features to keep the size of PDF files small. PNG and JPEG images can be inserted directly.

- PDF offers a transparent imaging model (PostScript uses an opaque model) and features multimedia support.

- Tagged PDF—a stylized form of PDF that contains information on content and structure, lets applications extract and reuse page data (text, graphics, images). For instance, tagged PDF allows text to reflow for display on handheld devices, such as Palm OS or Pocket PC systems or portable phones.

PDF can be viewed and printed on many different computer platforms by downloading and installing **Adobe Reader**.[1] Other free PDF viewers are ghostscript (`www.cs.wisc.edu/~ghost`), evince (`www.gnome.org/projects/evince`), and xpdf (`www.foolabs.com/xpdf/home.html`). Various ways of generating PDF from LATEX are described in Section A.

Scalable Vector Graphics

As the Web grew popularity and complexity, users and content providers sought ever better, more precise, and, above all, scalable graphical rendering. As a complement to PDF, which provides a mostly static and high-quality page image, the World Wide Web Consortium developed SVG,[2] an open-standard vector graphics language for describing two-dimensional graphics using XML syntax, which lets you produce Web pages containing high-resolution computer graphics. Tim Berners-Lee, the inventor of the World Wide Web, wrote (`www.w3.org/Graphics/SVG/About.html`):

> [...] SVG: at last, graphics which can be rendered optimally on all sizes of device.

As an XML instance, SVG consists of Unicode text enclosed in *graphics elements*:

- Graphics paths consisting of polylines, Bézier curves, which can be simple or compound, closed or open, (gradient) filled or stroked; they can be used for clipping and for building common geometric shapes.

- Patterns, markers, templates, and symbol libraries.

- Transformations, which can be nested.

- Direct inclusion of bitmap or raster images (PNG, JPEG).

---

[1] Freely downloadable from `www.adobe.com/products/acrobat/readermain.html`.

[2] SVG stands for *Scalable Vector Graphics*. The W3C Web site (`www.w3.org/Graphics/SVG`) is a good first source of information on SVG and has a lot of pointers to other sites. The current specification (version 1.1) of the SVG language is available at `www.w3.org/TR/SVG11`.

- Clipping, filter, and raster effects; alpha masks.
- Animations, scripts, groupings and styles.
- SVG fonts, which can be independent from the fonts installed on the system [36].

To fully exploit the possibilities of LaTeX on the Web, several DVI drivers can generate SVG: Adrian Frischauf's dvi2svg (`www.activemath.org/~adrianf/dvi2svg`), Rudolf Sabo's dvisvg (`dvisvg.sourceforge.net`), and Martin Gieseking's dvisvgm (`dvisvgm.sourceforge.net`).

CGM and WebCGM

CGM (Computer Graphics Metafile) is an ISO standard [54] for defining vector and composite vector and raster pictures. CGM is important in the fields of technical illustration, interactive electronic documentation, geophysical data visualization, automotive engineering, aeronautics, and the defense industry. It is specifically optimized for technical graphics with long life cycles, very complex illustrations needing large file sizes, re-authoring capabilities, interoperability (lots of data exchange), and compliance with industry standards.

As a complement to the more general-purpose SVG language the W3C, together with the CGM-Open Consortium (`www.cgmopen.org`), developed WebCGM (`www.cgmopen.org/technical/webcgm_svg.htm`). Technically speaking, WebCGM is a reasonably full profile of CGM optimized for use on the Web. It features a rich set of graphics elements, text strings defined as Unicode UTF-8 or UTF-16, complex paths, poly-symbols, smooth curves defined as piecewise cubic Bézier elements, and a large set of color models. In addition WebCGM can integrate PNG and JPEG elements inside vector components.

Many commercial graphics tools provide CGM output; xfig (`www.xfig.org`) is a free tool where CGM can be obtained with the help of Brian Smith's transfig (CTAN: `graphics/transfig`).

1.4.2 TeX-based graphics languages

Several graphics languages that use the hooks provided by TeX have been developed over the years. They differ in their approach and focus and thus offer a wide range in portability, resource usage, and flexibility.

Character-based diagrams and pictures

Pictures built from fonts with fixed-width characters can be produced on any machine with nearly every editor and are easily incorporated into LaTeX using the `verbatim` environment. However, they have the disadvantage of being crude, very limited, and rather cumbersome to generate.

PiCTeX

A hybrid approach to drawing pictures without any new fonts is available through Michael Wichura's brilliant PiCTeX [138, 139], which implements a complete plotting language mainly by setting a myriad of dots taken from a standard TeX font. Its main drawback is the large computation and memory overhead (pictures can take several minutes to process on smaller machines, and it is not at all easy to use PICTEX with other packages without running out of TEX "dimension" variables[1]). It has the advantage of scalability and ease of inserting plain TEX text, and the complexity of the drawing language is more a design feature than a necessary concomitant to the approach.

```
\usepackage{rawfonts,pictex}
\beginpicture \normalgraphs \longticklength=3pt
\setcoordinatesystem units <.02in,.01in>
\setplotarea x from 1780 to 1990, y from 0 to 220
\axis bottom label {decade} ticks numbered from 1780 to 1980 by 20 /
\axis left label {\stack {No.,of,burials}}
              ticks withvalues 20 40 60 80 100 120 140 160 180 200 /
              from 0 to 200 by 40 /
\setbars <-2pt,0pt> breadth <0pt> baseline at y = 0
\linethickness=4pt    \plot "decade.wom"
\setbars < 2pt, 0pt> breadth <4pt> baseline at y = 0
\linethickness=.25pt \plot "decade.men"
\endpicture
```

Example 1-4-1

This example shows a histogram with the number of burials for men (white entries) and women (black entries) per decade in the Protestant Cemetery in Rome [95]; the authors' input is shown above the picture.

Advantages of a system like PICTEX are that annotations (e.g., the title, the labels on the axes) are typeset by LATEX, and can thus include maths formulae, and that parts of the graphic can be shaded, rotated, and colored using standard LATEX packages. This flexibility gives the user considerable power to improve the graphic's appearance while retaining compatibility with TEX fonts.

---

[1] This should no longer be a problem when using etex or pdftex. You can also try Andreas Schnell's pictexwd package, which reimplements PICTEX with fewer dimension registers.

The DraTex and AlDraTex packages

A later addition to the TEX-based graphic languages was a drawing package developed by Eitan M. Gurari [39] that allows one to draw most common diagrams in a convenient way. It has two levels: one for basic drawing commands (in the DraTex package) and another for higher-level constructs (in the AlDraTex package). Both are implemented largely using TEX primitives, but do use the LaTEX circle fonts on occasion. A simple example of a piechart follows:

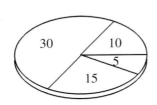

```
\usepackage{DraTex,AlDraTex}
\Draw
    \Scale(1,0.6)
    \PieChartSpec(1,50,25)()
    \PieChart(10 & 30 & 15 & 5)
    \Move(0,-6)
    \DrawOvalArc(50,50)(180,360)
\EndDraw
```

Example
1-4-2

Building on the picture environment

LaTEX's `picture` mode provides a basic graphics language that is fully portable among different installations. Although not always easy to use, it has allowed generations of LaTEX users to produce diagrams of surprising complexity.

Various extensions to the LaTEX picture macros exist; the most widely used is Sunil Podar's epic [94], whose commands enhance the graphic capabilities of LaTEX and provide a friendlier and more powerful user interface by reducing the calculations needed to specify the layout of objects. The epic package, Joachim Bleser's bar macros for drawing bar charts, and Ian Maclaine-cross's curves package are described in [83].

The disadvantages of the limited facilities of the LaTEX picture fonts are clear, even when the enhancements in epic are used. Circle sizes and line angles are in a fixed range or appear jagged (because they are built from small line segments), and there is no facility for shading or coloring areas. On the positive side, the method is very portable and is well integrated with the rest of the text.

One important addition to LaTEX's `picture` mode is the pict2e package, which reimplements the `picture` macros to be device-dependent by mapping them directly to PostScript \specials, thus doing away with the limited range of circle sizes and line angles. The pict2e package is considered part of the standard LaTEX, although it is currently packaged and distributed separately. Paul Gastin's gastex package (http://www.lsv.ens-cachan.fr/~gastin/gastex/gastex.html) is an extension to LaTEX's picture environment using PostScript \specials that offers a simplified way of drawing nets and automata diagrams.

Several approaches to building higher-level interfaces to the `picture` mode are possible. The first approach is typified by some of the board-game packages described in Chapter 10. Here each symbol needed (e.g., a chess piece) is defined with a LaTEX command.

The second and by far the most common approach is to define a little language entirely in LaTEX. For instance, Johannes Braams's nassflow package for drawing flowcharts and Nassi-Shneiderman diagrams is implemented using the `picture` environment. Several other examples of such an approach appear in later chapters of this book.

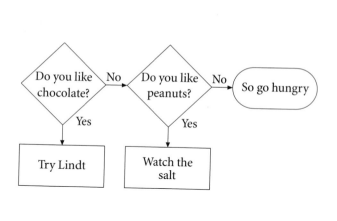

```
Right
Choice . . No Yes
   Do you like
   chocolate?
Tag
Choice . . No Yes
   Do you like
   peanuts?
Tag
Right
Oval
   So go hungry
ToTag
Down
Box
   Try Lindt
ToTag
Down
Box
   Watch the salt
```

Figure 1.6: Example of flow language

A third approach is to define a specialized external language together with a preprocessor program that converts input in that language to TEX primitives. A sophisticated example is the gpic program described below. Many smaller examples also exist, e.g., the flow program by Terry Brown that translates simple flowchart description files into commands of the LATEX picture environment. The language allows variously framed boxes to be joined together with arrows, with a choice of direction. Multiple directions are supported by setting "tags" on a stack and reverting to them. An example is shown in Figure 1.6.

XY-pic

XY-pic is a language for typesetting graphs and diagrams with TEX originally developed by Kristoffer H. Rose, with the help of Ross Moore. The system in its default setup uses standard TEX and METAFONT, i.e., it makes use of the font approach by supplying its own arrow fonts, etc., but output for a specific driver (like dvips) can be generated. It can typeset complicated diagrams in several application areas, including category theory, automata theory, algebra, neural networks, and database theory. The system is built around an object-oriented *kernel drawing language*. Each "object" in a picture has a "method" describing how it should be typeset, stretched, etc. A set of enhancements to the kernel have also been built, called *extensions*. XY-pic is reviewed in detail in Chapter 7.

PSTricks

PSTricks takes advantage of the extremely powerful PostScript page-description language used to drive most printers and typesetters. It uses \special commands to embed fragments of PostScript in TEX's DVI output, which are passed on by conforming drivers (including **dvips, dvipsone,** and **Textures**). This allows for effects ranging from line drawing through color, shading, and character transformation (such as setting text on a curve) and right up to pseudo-3-D pictures. **PSTricks** offers most of the power of PostScript in the familiar TEX syntax and extends the low-level functionality with a range of high-level packages for trees and graphs, for example. **PSTricks** is reviewed in detail in Chapters 5 and 6.

1.4.3 External graphics languages and drawing programs

There are many commonly used graphics languages and interactive packages, ranging from the very low-level to the extremely specialized. Translators have been written to convert some of them to forms TEX can handle, whether a LATEX picture, commonly used `\special` sets, or even METAFONT. We look at a selection of them here, but our catalog is by no means exhaustive. Many ad hoc programs exist for converting between formats. Figure 1.7, for example, was generated by converting plotter output from **AutoCAD** (`www.autodesk.com`) into METAFONT; the detailed contour lines on this plan of the Comoran island of Moheli consist of about 10,000 line segments. The widely used drawing or drafting packages all come with a range of output formats, some of which can be converted to TEX-compatible forms, so the possibilities are numerous. Programs such as **Adobe Photoshop** (`www.adobe.com/photoshop`), **GIMP**, and the **ImageMagick** library (`www.imagemagick.org`) provide a huge range of conversions (largely but not exclusively to do with bitmaps).

gnuplot—A plotting package

gnuplot (by Thomas Williams, Colin Kelley, and others; see `www.gnuplot.info`) is a general-purpose 2-D (and 3-D) plotting program that has its own language for describing graphs and plots. It comes with drivers for many output devices, including **pic**, LATEX (using emTEX `\special` commands), METAFONT, PostScript, **PSTricks**, TEXdraw, and **eepic**. A typical graph, again using the data introduced with Example 1-4-1, is presented in Figure 1.8, with the simple **gnuplot** commands that generated it shown above.

The pic language

Those who used to typeset in traditional Unix will be familiar with the **troff** program and Brian Kernighan's low-level picture language *pic* with its preprocessor (**pic**) to translate files written in that language into statements understood by **troff**. The **pic** and **troff** programs were reimplemented by James Clark as part of work for the Free Software Foundation. Within this suite of programs, **gpic**, unlike the original **pic**, can be instructed to output TEX code containing `\special` commands using the "tpic" syntax (**gpic** should be called with the option `-t` or `-c` in this case).

The **gpic** program reads a TEX file and leaves all lines unchanged until it encounters a line containing only the statement `.PS`. From that point on, it assumes that statements in the **pic** language follow, and translates them until it finds a line containing a `.PE` statement.

The **pic** language defines basic graphics objects such as `line`, `box`, `arc`, `arrow`, `ellipse`, `circle`, `spline`, and text strings. Named blocks can be created for a higher-

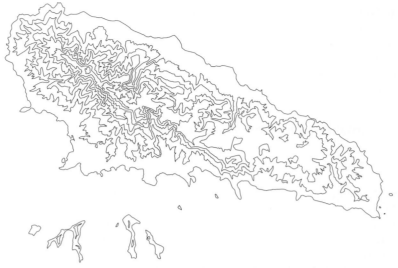

Figure 1.7: AutoCAD plotter output converted to METAFONT

```
set terminal latex
set xlabel "Protestant Cemetery decades"
set ylabel "Number \\of \\burials"
plot 'decade.wom' with lines, 'decade.men' with linespoints
```

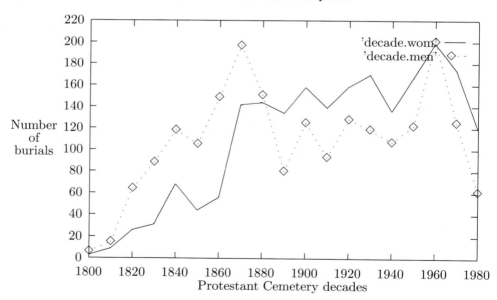

Figure 1.8: Graph generated by **gnuplot** using LaTeX picture commands

level construct than the simpler objects. Looping, conditionals, variables, and elementary functions (e.g., sin, cos, atan, sqrt, and rand) are also part of the language. The position of an object can be given by absolute location or relative to previously specified objects or locations. A current location and drawing direction are defined at all times. To demonstrate the effect, consider the following lines of code:

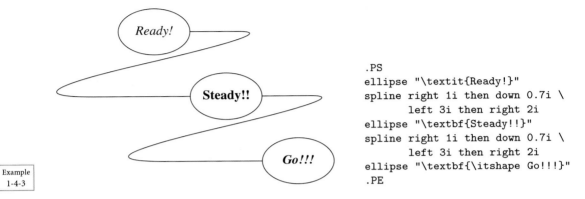

```
.PS
ellipse "\textit{Ready!}"
spline right 1i then down 0.7i \
      left 3i then right 2i
ellipse "\textbf{Steady!!}"
spline right 1i then down 0.7i \
      left 3i then right 2i
ellipse "\textbf{\itshape Go!!!}"
.PE
```

Example
1-4-3

The ellipses are drawn at the current default position, but the lines joining them are given an explicit direction and size; the text can contain arbitrary LaTeX code. A second example builds a graph through relations between its objects.

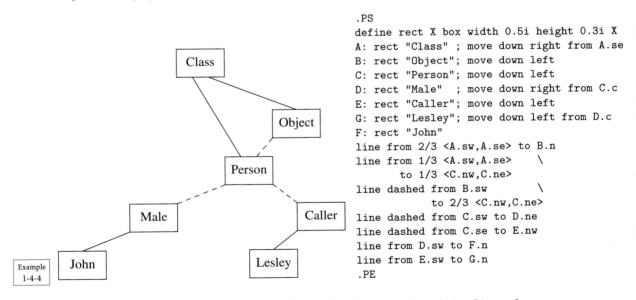

```
.PS
define rect X box width 0.5i height 0.3i X
A: rect "Class" ; move down right from A.se
B: rect "Object"; move down left
C: rect "Person"; move down left
D: rect "Male"  ; move down right from C.c
E: rect "Caller"; move down left
G: rect "Lesley"; move down left from D.c
F: rect "John"
line from 2/3 <A.sw,A.se> to B.n
line from 1/3 <A.sw,A.se>      \
      to 1/3 <C.nw,C.ne>
line dashed from B.sw          \
            to 2/3 <C.nw,C.ne>
line dashed from C.sw to D.ne
line dashed from C.se to E.nw
line from D.sw to F.n
line from E.sw to G.n
.PE
```

Example
1-4-4

The **pic** language has an intuitive way of expressing simple graphic relationships and in this respect is superior to using, say, the `picture` environment. However, the problems with the **gpic** approach are threefold. First, it requires a preprocessing stage, i.e., a separate

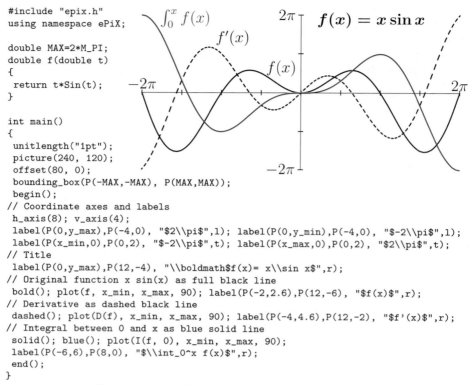

```
#include "epix.h"
using namespace ePiX;

double MAX=2*M_PI;
double f(double t)
{
 return t*Sin(t);
}

int main()
{
 unitlength("1pt");
 picture(240, 120);
 offset(80, 0);
 bounding_box(P(-MAX,-MAX), P(MAX,MAX));
 begin();
// Coordinate axes and labels
 h_axis(8); v_axis(4);
 label(P(0,y_max),P(-4,0), "$2\\pi$",l); label(P(0,y_min),P(-4,0), "$-2\\pi$",l);
 label(P(x_min,0),P(0,2), "$-2\\pi$",t); label(P(x_max,0),P(0,2), "$2\\pi$",t);
// Title
 label(P(0,y_max),P(12,-4), "\\boldmath$f(x)= x\\sin x$",r);
// Original function x sin(x) as full black line
 bold(); plot(f, x_min, x_max, 90); label(P(-2,2.6),P(12,-6), "$f(x)$",r);
// Derivative as dashed black line
 dashed(); plot(D(f), x_min, x_max, 90); label(P(-4,4.6),P(12,-2), "$f'(x)$",r);
// Integral between 0 and x as blue solid line
 solid(); blue(); plot(I(f, 0), x_min, x_max, 90);
 label(P(-6,6),P(8,0), "$\\int_0^x f(x)$",r);
 end();
}
```

Figure 1.9: Example of ePiX program (source and result)

compiled program for the computer platform where it is used. Second, it uses the "tpic" \specials, which not all drivers support; and third, the preprocessor knows nothing about how text is typeset and so cannot, for example, fit boxes accurately around formulae.

ePiX: a structured drawing language

Another example of a small application-specific language is Andrew D. Hwang's ePiX [51] (see also CTAN: graphics/epix). It comprises a collection of command-line utilities for creating mathematically accurate, two- and three-dimensional figures and animations in LaTeX and provides a bridge between the powerful numerical capabilities of C++ and high-quality typesetting. A logically structured input file is prepared with a text editor, then compiled into eepic code that can be included into a LaTeX document.

As the program is closely integrated with LaTeX's picture environment (via the eepic package), it is easy to annotate parts of the graphics with LaTeX commands. Figure 1.9 shows an example of an ePiX program written in the C++ language. One can see how LaTeX labels and annotations are defined (the backslash for the LaTeX commands has to be doubled so that it is transmitted to the output file by the C++ processor).

METAFONT and METAPOST

TEX has a companion font-creation program, METAFONT. While METAFONT was designed for producing beautiful character shapes in fonts, it can also be used very successfully to create drawings for TEX. It offers very powerful techniques and data structures well suited to many types of drawing, and has the advantages that it is available anywhere that TEX is and that its output (PK fonts after conversion) is understood by practically all DVI drivers. It has two disadvantages, but both have solutions:

1. The syntax of METAFONT is completely different from TEX, and some users find it hard to learn. An ingenious "wrapper" solution is available in the **mfpic** LATEX package, which lets you describe your picture in familiar LATEX syntax and have it written out in METAFONT form to generate the picture.

2. The bitmap font output of METAFONT is awkward to handle in some drivers and requires regeneration for each different output device; it renders very badly in the popular **Adobe Acrobat** program. METAFONT also lacks support for some basic building blocks like color. A nice solution is METAPOST, a reimplementation by John Hobby of METAFONT to produce device-independent PostScript output. Hobby's version also added support for color and provided some high-level graph-drawing support.

METAFONT, **mfpic**, and METAPOST are explored in Chapters 3 and 4.

1.5   Choosing a package

Most people do not choose a graphics program or macro package on the basis of the method TEX adopts to handle the output. Usually the *type* of picture to be produced is a more important consideration than the *way* it is created. Excellent, often commercial, interactive tools exist to address the particular needs of a user in a given subject area. Examples include **AutoCAD** for architects and engineers, **ChemDraw** (`www.cambridgesoft.com/software/ChemDraw`) for chemists, **Adobe Illustrator** for graphic artists, **SPSS** (`www.spss.com`) for statisticians, **Mathematica** for mathematicians, **GRASS** (Geographic Resources Analysis Support System; see `grass.itc.it`) for geographers, **xfig** for computer scientists, and **Excel** (`www.microsoft.com/excel`) and **calc** (`www.openoffice.org/product/calc.html`), its free **openoffice** counterpart, for business people. However, sometimes creating graphics by describing them in a special notation comes more naturally.

If you *can* make a completely free choice about which package to use, you might consider the following points:

- The basic decision you make depends on the relationship between the picture and the text. If the picture is a "black box", then generate it separately and include it at the printing stage. If its contents should have the same style as the text, then investigate drawing packages integrated with TEX.

- How important is *total* portability in the TEX world to you? If it is vital, use the packages that draw pictures using tiny dots or TEX fonts. You could also choose the portability provided by common (but not standard) \special primitives, portability provided by PostScript, or portability using black-box bitmap graphics. The future use intended affects your choice of package.

- If you want to do "art" graphics, which need interactive drawing or painting, then choose a package that suits your subject area and that can drive the printer of your choice. If you have a TEX driver for a printer, then it will probably allow you to automatically include files destined for the same printer. In practice, the most flexibility is offered by the huge array of software written for the Macintosh and Microsoft Windows, but it is sensible to choose a package that can write encapsulated PostScript or PDF, because these are the most widely portable formats for publishing.

- If you want to include PostScript pictures, use the standard graphics package discussed in Chapter 2, so that your documents are not dependent on the vagaries and syntax of a particular driver.

- If you have nondigital photographs to reproduce, you can easily scan them and include them in TEX. Scan them at the highest resolution you can afford (in terms of equipment and disk storage), but be sure that you understand the issues of scaling bitmaps—scanning at 1200 dpi and then printing at 1270 dpi can produce unpleasant results due to the tiny scaling that has to be performed.

- If you want to plot data in relatively simple ways, the choice of software will depend on your normal working environment. If your data is in a spreadsheet, then you probably have adequate facilities there. If you use a database, it might be easier to write retrieval programs that generate pictures in a TEX-world plotting language such as PSTricks or METAPOST.

- If you are creating algorithmic pictures in which the *layout* is determined by your data rather than the *contents*, and if the output includes a lot of textual material (particularly mathematics or non-Roman scripts), then you need to look at the macro packages that implement drawing directly in TEX, so that your text is processed by TEX.

In this book we will show you the good points of many programs and LATEX macro packages, but we cannot tell you which one is right for your needs. We hope that the variety and quantity of pictures in the following chapters demonstrate that graphics in LATEX is alive and well and can meet almost any need.

CHAPTER 2

Standard LaTeX Interfaces

Since the introduction of LaTeX 2_ε in 1994, LaTeX has offered a uniform syntax for including every kind of graphics file that can be handled by the different drivers. In addition, all kinds of graphic operations (such as resizing and rotating) as well as color support are available.

These features are not part of the LaTeX 2_ε kernel, but rather are loaded by the standard, fully supported color, graphics, and graphicx extension packages. Because the TeX program does not have any direct methods for graphic manipulation, the packages must rely on features supplied by the "driver" used to print the dvi file. Unfortunately, not all drivers support the same features, and even the internal method of accessing these extensions varies among drivers. Consequently, all of these packages take options, such as dvips, to specify which external driver is being used. Through this method, unavoidable device-dependent information is localized in a single place, the preamble of the document.

In this chapter we start by looking at graphics file inclusion. LaTeX offers both a simple interface (graphics), which can be combined with the separate rotation and scaling commands, and a more complex interface (graphicx), which features a powerful set of manipulation options. The chapter concludes with a discussion of the pict2e package, which implements the driver encapsulation concept for line graphics and with a brief description of the curve2e package, which is not part of the "standard LaTeX interface" but nevertheless represents an interesting extension to pict2e. Color support is covered in Chapter 11.

2.1 Inclusion of graphics files

The packages graphics and graphicx can both be used to scale, rotate, and reflect LaTeX material or to include graphics files prepared with other programs. The difference between

Table 2.1: Overview of color and graphics capabilities of device drivers

Option	Author of Driver	Features
dvips	T. Rokicki	All functions (reference driver; option also used by xdvi)
dvipdf	S. Lesenko	All functions
dvipdfm	S. Lesenko	All functions
dvipsone	Y&Y	All functions
dviwin	H. Sendoukas	File inclusion
emtex	E. Mattes	File inclusion only, but no scaling
pdftex	Hàn Thế Thành	All functions for pdftex program
pctexps	PCTeX	File inclusion, color, rotation
pctexwin	PCTeX	File inclusion, color, rotation
pctex32	PCTeX	All functions
pctexhp	PCTeX	File inclusion only
truetex	Kinch	Graphics inclusion and some color
tcidvi	Kinch	TrueTeX with extra support for Scientific Word
textures	Blue Sky	All functions for Textures program
vtex	Micropress	All functions for VTeX program

the two is that **graphics** uses a combination of macros with a "standard" or TEX-like syntax, while the "extended" or "enhanced" **graphicx** package presents a key/value interface for specifying optional parameters to the \includegraphics and \rotatebox commands.

2.1.1 Options for graphics **and** graphicx

When using LATEX's graphics packages, the necessary space for the typeset material after performing a file inclusion or applying some geometric transformation is reserved on the output page. It is, however, the task of the *device driver* (e.g., dvips, xdvi, dvipsone) to perform the actual inclusion or transformation in question and to show the correct result. Given that different drivers may require different code to carry out an action, such as rotation, one has to specify the target driver as an option to the graphics packages—for example, option dvips if you use one of the graphics packages with Tom Rokicki's dvips program, or option textures if you use one of the graphics packages and work on a Macintosh using Blue Sky's Textures program.

Some drivers, such as previewers, are incapable of performing certain functions. Hence they may display the typeset material so that it overlaps with the surrounding text. Table 2.1 gives an overview of the more important drivers currently supported and their possible limitations. Support for older driver programs exists usually as well—you can search for it on CTAN.

The driver-specific code is stored in files with the extension .def—for example, dvips.def for the PostScript driver dvips. As most of these files are maintained by third parties, the standard LATEX distribution contains only a subset of the available files and not necessarily the latest versions. While there is usually no problem if LATEX is installed as part of a full TEX installation, you should watch out for incompatibilities if you update the LATEX graphics packages manually.

It is also possible to specify a default driver using the `\ExecuteOptions` declaration in the *configuration* file `graphics.cfg`. For example, `\ExecuteOptions{dvips}` makes *Setting a default driver* the **dvips** drivers become the default. In this case the graphics packages pick up the driver code for the **dvips** TEX system on a PC if the package is called without a driver option. Most current TEX installations are distributed with a ready-to-use `graphics.cfg` file.

In addition to the driver options, the packages support some options controlling which features are enabled (or disabled):

`draft`   Suppress all "special" features, such as including external graphics files in the final output. The layout of the page will not be affected, because LATEX still reads the size information concerning the bounding box of the external material. This option is of particular interest when a document is under development and you do not want to download the (often huge) graphics files each time you print the typeset result. When `draft` mode is activated, the picture is replaced by a box of the correct size containing the name of the external file.

`final`   The opposite of `draft`. This option can be useful when, for instance, "draft" mode was specified as a global option with the `\documentclass` command (e.g., for showing overfull boxes), but you do not want to suppress the graphics as well.

`hiresbb`   In PostScript files, look for bounding box comments that are of the form `%%HiResBoundingBox` (which typically have real values) instead of the standard `%%BoundingBox` (which should have integer values).

`hiderotate`   Do not show the rotated material (for instance, when the previewer cannot rotate material and produces error messages).

`hidescale`   Do not show the scaled material (for instance, when the previewer does not support scaling).

With the **graphicx** package, the options `draft`, `final`, and `hiresbb` are also available locally for individual `\includegraphics` commands, that is, they can be selected for individual graphics.

2.1.2 The `\includegraphics` **syntax in the** graphics **package**

With the **graphics** package, you can include an image file by using the following command:

> `\includegraphics*[`*llx,lly*`] [`*urx,ury*`] {`*file*`}`

If the [*urx,ury*] argument is present, it specifies the coordinates of the upper-right corner of the image as a pair of TEX dimensions. The default units are big (PostScript) points; thus [`1in,1in`] and [`72,72`] are equivalent. If only one optional argument is given, the lower-left corner of the image is assumed to be located at [`0,0`]. Otherwise, [*llx,lly*] specifies the coordinates of that point. Without optional arguments, the size of the graphic is determined by reading the external *file* (containing the graphics itself or a description thereof, as discussed later).

```
%!PS-Adobe-2.0
%%BoundingBox:100 100 150 150
100 100      translate % put origin at 100 100
  0   0      moveto    % define current point
 50  50      rlineto   % trace diagonal line
 50 neg 0    rlineto   % trace horizontal line
 50  50 neg  rlineto   % trace other diagonal line
stroke                 % draw (stroke) the lines
  0   0      moveto    % redefine current point
/Times-Roman findfont  % get Times-Roman font
 50          scalefont % scale it to 50 big points
             setfont   % make it the current font
(W) show               % draw an uppercase W
```

Figure 2.1: The contents of the file w.eps

The starred form of the \includegraphics command "clips" the graphics image to the size of the specified bounding box. In the normal form (without the *), any part of the graphics image that falls outside the specified bounding box overprints the surrounding text.

The examples in the current and next sections use a small PostScript program (in a file w.eps) that paints a large uppercase letter "W" and a few lines. Its source is shown in Figure 2.1. Note the BoundingBox declaration, which stipulates that the image starts at the point 100, 100 (in big points), and goes up to 150, 150; that is, its natural size is 50 big points by 50 big points.

In the examples we always embed the \includegraphics command in an \fbox (with a blue frame and zero \fboxsep) to show the space that LATEX reserves for the included image. In addition, the baseline is indicated by the horizontal rules produced by the \HR command, defined as an abbreviation for \rule{1em}{0.4pt}.

The first example shows the inclusion of the w.eps graphic at its natural size. Here the picture and its bounding box coincide nicely.

```
\usepackage{graphics,color}
\newcommand\HR{\rule{1em}{0.4pt}}
\newcommand\bluefbox[1]{\textcolor{blue}{%
   \setlength\fboxsep{0pt}\fbox{\textcolor{black}{#1}}}}
left\HR \bluefbox{\includegraphics{w.eps}}\HR right
```

Example
2-1-1

Next, we specify a box that corresponds to a part of the picture (and an area outside it) so that some parts fall outside its boundaries, overlaying the material surrounding the picture. If the starred form of the command is used, then the picture is clipped to the box (specified as optional arguments), as shown on the right.

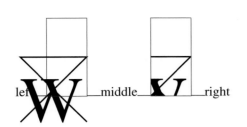

```
\usepackage{graphics,color}
% \bluefbox and \HR as before
left\HR
 \bluefbox{\includegraphics
          [120,120][150,180]{w.eps}}%
\HR middle\HR
 \bluefbox{\includegraphics*
          [120,120][150,180]{w.eps}}%
\HR right
```

Example
2-1-2

In the remaining examples we combine the \includegraphics command with other commands of the **graphics** package to show various methods of manipulating an included image. (Their exact syntax is discussed in detail in Section 2.2.) We start with the \scalebox and \resizebox commands. In both cases we can either specify a change in one dimension and have the other scale proportionally, or specify both dimensions to distort the image.

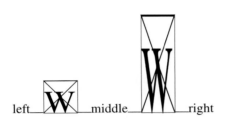

```
\usepackage{graphics,color}
% \bluefbox and \HR as before
left\HR
  \bluefbox{\scalebox{.5}{%
    \includegraphics{w.eps}}}%
\HR middle\HR
  \bluefbox{\scalebox{.5}[1.5]{%
    \includegraphics{w.eps}}}%
\HR right
```

Example
2-1-3

```
\usepackage{graphics,color}
% \bluefbox and \HR as before
left\HR
  \bluefbox{\resizebox{10mm}{!}{%
    \includegraphics{w.eps}}}%
\HR middle\HR
  \bluefbox{\resizebox{20mm}{10mm}{%
    \includegraphics{w.eps}}}%
\HR right
```

Example
2-1-4

Adding rotations makes things even more interesting. Note that in comparison to Example 2-1-1 on the facing page the space reserved by LaTeX is far bigger. LaTeX "thinks" in rectangular boxes, so it selects the smallest size that can hold the rotated image.

```
\usepackage{graphics,color}
% \bluefbox and \HR as before
left\HR
  \bluefbox{\rotatebox{25}{%
    \includegraphics{w.eps}}}%
\HR right
```

Example
2-1-5

2.1.3 The \includegraphics syntax in the graphicx package

The extended graphics package **graphicx** also implements \includegraphics but offers a syntax for including external graphics files that is somewhat more transparent and user-friendly. With today's TEX implementations, the resultant processing overhead is negligible, so we suggest using this interface.

\includegraphics*[*key/val-list*] {*file*}

The starred form of this command exists only for compatibility with the standard version of \includegraphics, as described in Section 2.1.2. It is equivalent to specifying the clip key.

The *key/val-list* is a comma-separated list of *key=value* pairs for keys that take a value. For Boolean keys, specifying just the key is equivalent to *key*=true; not specifying the key is equivalent to *key*=false. Possible keys are listed below:

bb The bounding box of the graphics image. Its value field must contain four dimensions, separated by spaces. This specification will overwrite the bounding box information that might be present in the external file.[1]

hiresbb Makes LATEX search for %%HiResBoundingBox comments, which specify the bounding box information with decimal precision, as used by some applications. In contrast, the normal %%BoundingBox comment can take only integer values. It is a Boolean value, either "true" or "false".

viewport Defines the area of the graphic for which LATEX reserves space. Material outside this will still be print unless trim is used. The key takes four dimension arguments (like bb), but the origin is with respect to the bounding box specified in the file or with the bb keyword. For example, to describe a 20 bp square 10 bp to the right and 15 bp above the lower-left corner of the picture you would specify viewport=10 15 30 35.

trim Same functionality as the viewport key, but this time the four dimensions correspond to the amount of space to be trimmed (cut off) at the left-hand side, bottom, right-hand side, and top of the included graphics.

natheight,natwidth The natural height and width of the figure, respectively.[2]

angle The rotation angle (in degrees, counterclockwise).

origin The origin for the rotation, similar to the origin parameter of the \rotatebox command described on page 40.

width The required width (the width of the image is scaled to that value).

---

[1]There also exists an obsolete form kept for backward compatibility only: [bbllx=a, bblly=b, bburx=c, bbury=d] is equivalent to [bb = a b c d], so the latter form should be used.

[2]These arguments can be used for setting the lower-left coordinate to (0 0) and the upper-right coordinate to (natwidth natheight) and are thus equivalent to bb=0 0 w h, where w and h are the values specified for these two parameters.

`height`   The required height (the height of the image is scaled to that value).

`totalheight`   The required total height (height + depth of the image is scaled to that value). This key should be used instead of `height` if images are rotated more than 90 degrees, because the height can disappear (and become the `depth`) and LaTeX may have difficulties satisfying the user's request.

`keepaspectratio`   A Boolean variable that can have a value of either "`true`" or "`false`" (see above for defaults). When it is `true`, specifying both the `width` and `height` parameters does not distort the picture, but the image is scaled so that neither the width nor height *exceeds* the given dimensions.

`scale`   The scale factor.

`clip`   Clip the graphic to the bounding box or the rectangle specified by the keys `trim` or `viewport`. It is a Boolean value, either "`true`" or "`false`".

`draft`   Locally switch to draft mode. A Boolean-value key, like `clip`.

`type`   The graphics type; see Section 2.1.5.

`ext`   The file extension of the file containing the image data.

`read`   The file extension of the file that is "read" by LaTeX to determine the image size, if necessary.

`command`   Any command to be applied to the file.

If the size is given without units for the first four keys (`bb` through `trim`), then TeX's "big points" (equal to PostScript points) are assumed.

The first six keys (`bb` through `natwidth`) specify the size of the image. This information needs to be given in case the graphic is in a format that the TeX engine cannot read (this can differ for different TeX variants), the file contains incorrect size information, or you wish to clip the image to a certain rectangle.

The next seven keys (`angle` through `scale`) deal with scaling or rotation of the included material. Similar effects can be obtained with the graphics package and the `\includegraphics` command by placing the latter inside the argument of a `\resizebox`, `\rotatebox`, or `\scalebox` command (see the examples in Section 2.1.2 and the in-depth discussion of these commands in Section 2.2).

It is important to note that keys are read from left to right, so that [`angle=90, totalheight=2cm`] means rotate by 90 degrees and then scale to a height of 2 cm, whereas [`totalheight=2cm, angle=90`] would result in a final *width* of 2 cm.

By default, LaTeX reserves for the image the space specified either in the file or in the *key/val-list*. If any part of the image falls outside this area, it will overprint the surrounding text. If the starred form is used or the `clip` option is specified, any part of the image outside this area is not printed.

The last four keys (`type`, `ext`, `read`, `command`) suppress the parsing of the file name. When they are used, the main *file* argument should have no file extension (see the description of the `\DeclareGraphicsRule` command on page 34).

Next, we repeat some of the examples from Section 2.1.2 using the syntax of the **graphicx** package, showing the extra facilities offered by the extended package. In most cases the new form is easier to understand than the earlier version. In the simplest case without any optional arguments, the syntax for the \includegraphics command is identical in both packages.

If we use the draft key, only a frame showing the bounding box is typeset. This feature is not available in the **graphics** package on the level of individual graphics.

```
\usepackage{graphicx}
% \HR as before
left\HR
 \includegraphics[draft]{w.eps}%
\HR right
```

Example
2-1-6

The effects of the bb, clip, viewport, and trim keys are seen in the following examples. Compare them with Example 2-1-2 on page 27.

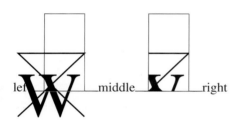

```
\usepackage{graphicx,color}
% \bluefbox and \HR as before
left\HR\bluefbox{\includegraphics
    [bb=120 120 150 180]{w.eps}}%
\HR middle\HR
 \bluefbox{\includegraphics
    [bb=120 120 150 180,clip]{w.eps}}%
\HR right
```

Example
2-1-7

Using viewport or trim allows us to specify the desired result in yet another way. Notice that trimming by a negative amount effectively enlarges the space reserved for the picture.

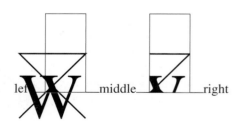

```
\usepackage{graphicx,color}
% \bluefbox and \HR as before
left\HR\bluefbox{\includegraphics
    [viewport=20 20 50 80]%
    {w.eps}}%
\HR middle\HR
\bluefbox{\includegraphics
    [trim= 20 20 0 -30,clip]{w.eps}}%
\HR right
```

Example
2-1-8

The scale key applies a scale factor to the image. With this key, however, you can only scale the picture equally in both directions.

```
\usepackage{graphicx,color}
% \bluefbox and \HR as before
left\HR \bluefbox{\includegraphics[scale=.5]{w.eps}}\HR right
```

Example
2-1-9

To make the dimensions of an image equal to a given value, use the `width` or `height` key (the other dimension is then scaled accordingly). If you use both keys simultaneously, you can distort the image to fit a specified rectangle, as shown in the following example:

```
\usepackage{graphicx,color}
% \bluefbox and \HR as before
left\HR \bluefbox{\includegraphics
    [width=15mm]{w.eps}}%
\HR middle\HR
  \bluefbox{\includegraphics
    [height=15mm,width=25mm]{w.eps}}%
\HR right
```

To ensure that the aspect ratio of the image itself remains intact, use the `keepaspectratio` key. LaTeX then fits the image as best it can to the rectangle you specified with the `height` and `width` keys.

```
\usepackage{graphicx,color}
% \bluefbox and \HR as before
left\HR \bluefbox{\includegraphics
    [height=15mm,width=25mm]{w.eps}}%
\HR middle\HR
  \bluefbox{\includegraphics[height=15mm,
    width=25mm,keepaspectratio]{w.eps}}%
\HR right
```

Rotations using the `angle` key add another level of complexity. The reference point for the rotation is the reference point of the original graphic—i.e., the lower-left corner if the graphic has no depth. By rotating around that point, the height and depth change, so the graphic moves up and down with respect to the baseline, as can be seen in the next examples.

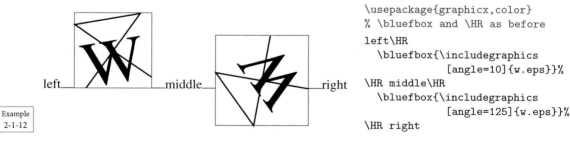

```
\usepackage{graphicx,color}
% \bluefbox and \HR as before
left\HR
  \bluefbox{\includegraphics
            [angle=10]{w.eps}}%
\HR middle\HR
  \bluefbox{\includegraphics
            [angle=125]{w.eps}}%
\HR right
```

The real fun starts when you specify both a dimension and a rotation angle for an image, since the order in which they are given matters. The **graphicx** package interprets the keys *from left to right*. You should pay special attention to the keys' order if you plan to rotate images and want to set them to a certain height. The next example shows the difference between specifying an angle of rotation before and after a scale command. In the first case, the picture is rotated and then the result is scaled. In the second case, the picture is scaled and then rotated.

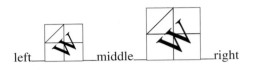

```
\usepackage{graphicx,color}
% \bluefbox and \HR as before
left\HR\bluefbox{\includegraphics
       [angle=45,width=10mm]{w.eps}}%
\HR middle\HR
\bluefbox{\includegraphics
       [width=10mm,angle=45]{w.eps}}%
\HR right
```

Example
2-1-13

LaTeX considers the height and the depth of the rotated bounding box separately. The height key refers only to the height; that is, it does not include the depth. In general, the total height of a (rotated) image should fit in a given space, so you should use the totalheight key (see Figure 2.2 on page 41 for a description of the various dimensions defining a LaTeX box). Of course, to obtain special effects you can manipulate rotations and combinations of the height and width parameters at will. Here we show some key combinations and their results:

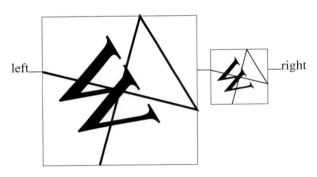

```
\usepackage{graphicx,color}
% \bluefbox and \HR as before
left\HR\bluefbox{%
   \includegraphics[angle=-60,%
                    height=15mm]%
   {w.eps}}\HR
\bluefbox{%
   \includegraphics[angle=-60,%
                    totalheight=15mm]%
   {w.eps}}\HR right
```

Example
2-1-14

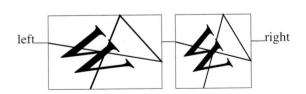

```
\usepackage{graphicx,color}
% \bluefbox and \HR as before
left\HR\bluefbox{\includegraphics
       [angle=-60,totalheight=20mm,%
       width=30mm]{w.eps}}\HR
\bluefbox{\includegraphics
       [angle=-60,totalheight=20mm,%
       width=30mm,keepaspectratio]%
       {w.eps}}\HR right
```

Example
2-1-15

2.1.4 Setting default key values for the graphicx package

Instead of specifying the same set of key/value pairs over and over again on individual \includegraphics commands, you can specify global default values for keys associated with such commands. To do so, you use the \setkeys declaration provided by the keyval package, which is automatically included when **graphicx** is used.

> \setkeys{*identifier*}{*key/val-list*}

The *identifier* is an arbitrary string defined by the macro designer. For example, for \includegraphics the string Gin was chosen. The *key/val-list* is a comma-separated list of key/value pairs.

As an example, consider the case where **graphicx** is used and all figures are to be scaled to the width of the line. Then you would specify the following:

```
\setkeys{Gin}{width=\linewidth}
```

All images included with the \includegraphics command will then be automatically scaled to the current line width. (Using \linewidth in such a case is generally preferable to using \columnwidth, as the former changes its value depending on the surrounding environment, such as quote.)

You can specify defaults in a similar way for any key used with the \rotatebox command (the other command that has a key/value syntax when **graphicx** is used; see Section 2.2.3). It has the *identifier* Grot. Thus

```
\setkeys{Grot}{origin=ct}
```

specifies that ct should be used for the origin key on all \rotatebox commands unless locally overwritten.

2.1.5 Declarations guiding the inclusion of images

While key/value pairs can be set only when the **graphicx** package is used, the declarations described in this section can be used with both the **graphics** and the **graphicx** packages.

By default, LaTeX looks for graphics files in the same directories where it looks for other files. For larger projects, however, it might be preferable to keep the image files together in a single directory or in a set of directories. A list of directories where LaTeX should search for graphics files can be specified with the command \graphicspath; its argument is a list of directories, with each directory being placed inside a pair of braces {} (even if the list contains only one directory). For example,

Where to find image files

```
\graphicspath{{./eps/}{./tiff/}}
```

causes LaTeX to look in the subdirectories eps and tiff of the current directory.

The \DeclareGraphicsExtensions command lets you specify the behavior of the system when no file extension is given in the argument of the \includegraphics command. Its argument {*ext-list*} is a comma-separated list of file extensions. Full file names are constructed by appending each extension of the list *ext-list* in turn until a file corresponding to the generated full file name is found.

Defining the file extension search order

When the \includegraphics command is used with a file name without an extension, the algorithm tests for the existence of a graphics file to determine which extension to use. Hence the graphics file must exist at the time LATEX is run. However, if a file extension *is* specified, such as \includegraphics{gr.eps} instead of \includegraphics{gr}, then the graphics file need not exist at the time of the LATEX run.[1] LATEX needs to know the size of the image, however, so it must be specified in the arguments of the \includegraphics command or in a file that is actually read by LATEX. (This file can be either the graphics file itself or another file specified with the read key or constructed from the list of file extensions. In the latter case the file must exist at the time LATEX is run.)

With the declaration shown below, the \includegraphics command will first look for the file file.ps and then, if no such file exists, for the file file.ps.gz:

```
\DeclareGraphicsExtensions{.ps,.ps.gz}
  \includegraphics{file}
```

If you want to make sure that a full file name must always be specified, then you should use the following declaration. In the cases shown below, the size of the (bitmap) image is specified explicitly on the \includegraphics command each time.

```
\DeclareGraphicsExtensions{{}}
  \includegraphics[1in,1in]{file.pcx}
  \includegraphics[75pt,545pt][50pt,530pt]{file.pcx}
  \includegraphics[bb=75 545 50 530]{file.pcx}
```

The action that has to take place when a file with a given extension is encountered is controlled by the following command:

\DeclareGraphicsRule{*ext*}{*type*}{*read-file*}{*cmd*}

Any number of these declarations is allowed. The meaning of the arguments is as follows:

ext The extension of the image file. It can be specified explicitly or, if the argument to \includegraphics does not have an extension, it can be determined from the list of extensions specified in the argument *ext-list* of the \DeclareGraphicsExtensions command. A star (*) can be used to specify the default behavior for all extensions that are not explicitly declared. For example,

```
\DeclareGraphicsRule{*}{eps}{*}{}
```

causes all undeclared extensions to be treated as EPS files, and the respective graphics files are read to search for a %%BoundingBox comment.

type The "type" of the file involved. All files of the same type are input with the same internal command (which must be defined in the corresponding driver file). For example,

---

[1] For instance, it can be created on the fly with a suitable \DeclareGraphicsRule declaration.

all files with an extension of `.ps`, `.eps`, or `.ps.gz` should be classified as being of type `eps`.

read-file   The extension of the file that should be read to determine the size of the graphics image. It can be identical to *ext* but, in the case of compressed or binary images, which cannot be interpreted easily by LaTeX, the size information (the bounding box) is normally put in a separate file. For example, for compressed gzipped PostScript files characterized by the extension `.ps.gz`, the corresponding readable files could have an extension of `.ps.bb`. If the *read-file* argument is empty (i.e., `{}`), then the system does not look for an external file to determine the size, and the size must be specified in the arguments of the command `\includegraphics`. If the driver file specifies a procedure for reading size files for *type*, then that procedure is used; otherwise, the procedure for reading `.eps` files is used. Therefore, in the absence of any other specific format, you can select the size of a bitmap picture by using the syntax for PostScript images (i.e., with a `%%BoundingBox` line).

cmd   The command to be inserted in the `\special` argument instead of the file name. In general *cmd* is empty, but for compressed files you might want to uncompress the image file before including it in the file to be printed if the driver supports such an operation. For instance, with the dvips driver, you could use

```
\DeclareGraphicsRule{.ps.gz}{eps}{.ps.bb}{`gunzip #1}
```

where the argument `#1` denotes the full file name. In this case the final argument causes dvips to use the gunzip command to uncompress the file before inserting it into the PostScript output.

The system described so far can present some problems if the extension *ext* does not correspond to the *type* argument. One could, for instance, have a series of PostScript files called `file.1`, `file.2`, ... Neither the graphics nor the graphicx package can automatically detect that these are PostScript files. With the graphicx package, this situation can be handled by using a `type=eps` key setting on each `\includegraphics` command. As explained earlier, you can also define a default type by using a `\DeclareGraphicsRule` declaration for a type `*`.

2.1.6   A caveat: encapsulation is important

It is important at this point to emphasize that PostScript is a page description language that deals with the appearance of a *complete printed page*. This makes it difficult for authors to include smaller PostScript pictures created by external tools into their electronic (LaTeX) documents. To solve this problem Adobe has defined the *Encapsulated PostScript* file format (EPS or EPSF), which complies with the *PostScript Document Structuring Conventions Specification* [4] and the *Encapsulated PostScript File Format Specification* [3].

The EPS format defines standard rules for importing PostScript-language files into different environments. In particular, so as not to interfere destructively with the PostScript page being built, EPS files should be "well behaved". For instance, they must not contain certain PostScript operators, such as those manipulating the graphics state, interpreter stack, and global dictionaries.

Most modern graphics applications generate an EPS-compliant file that can be used without difficulty by LATEX. Sometimes, however, you may be confronted with a bare PostScript file that does not contain the necessary information. For use with LATEX, a PostScript file does not have to conform strictly to the structuring conventions mentioned previously. If the file is "well behaved" (see above), it is enough that the PostScript file contains the dimensions of the box occupied by the picture. These dimensions are provided to LATEX via the PostScript comment line %%BoundingBox, as shown below:

```
%!
%%BoundingBox: LLx LLy URx URy
```

The first line indicates that we are dealing with a nonconforming EPS file. Note that the %! characters *must* occupy the first two columns of the line. The second line, which is the more important one for our purpose, specifies the size of the included picture in PostScript "big" points, of which there are 72 to an inch. Its four parameters are the x and y coordinates of the lower-left corner (LLx and LLy) and the upper-right corner (URx and URy) of the picture. For instance, a full A4 page (210 mm by 297 mm) with zero at the lower-left corner would need the following declaration:

```
%!
%%BoundingBox: 0 0 595 842
```

If your picture starts at $(100, 200)$ and is enclosed in a square of 4 inches (288 points), the statement would be

```
%!
%%BoundingBox: 100 200 388 488
```

A PostScript display program, such as ghostview, lets you easily determine the bounding box of a picture by moving the cursor on its extremities and reading off the corresponding coordinates. In general, it is good practice to add one or two points to make sure that the complete picture will be included, because of the potential for rounding errors during the computations done in the interpreter.

2.2 Manipulating graphical objects

In addition to the \includegraphics command, the graphics and graphicx packages implement a number of graphical manipulation commands.

With the exception of the \rotatebox command, which also supports a key/value pair syntax in the graphicx package, the syntax for these commands is identical in both packages.

2.2.1 Scaling a LaTeX box

The \scalebox command lets you magnify or reduce text or other LaTeX material by a scale factor.

\scalebox{*h-scale*}[*v-scale*]{*material*}

The first two arguments (*h-scale* and *v-scale*) specify the factors by which the *material* is to be scaled in the horizontal and vertical dimensions, respectively. However, if the optional second argument is omitted, the first one applies to both dimensions, as demonstrated in the following example.

This text is normal.

This text is large.

This text is tiny.

```
\usepackage{graphics} % or graphicx
\noindent This text is normal.    \\
\scalebox{2}{This text is large.}\\
\scalebox{0.5}{This text is tiny.}
```

Example
2-2-1

The effect of the optional argument is demonstrated in the following example, which also shows how multiple lines can be scaled by using the standard LaTeX \parbox command.

America
&
Europe

America
&
Europe

```
\usepackage{graphics} % or graphicx
\fbox{\scalebox{1.5}{%
  \parbox{.5in}{America \&\\Europe}}}
\fbox{\scalebox{1.5}[1]{%
  \parbox{.5in}{America \&\\Europe}}}
```

Example
2-2-2

\reflectbox{*material*}

This command is a convenient abbreviation for \scalebox{-1}[1]{*material*}, as seen in the following example:

America?America?
America?America?

```
\usepackage{graphics} % or graphicx
\noindent America?\reflectbox{America?}    \\
        America?\scalebox{-1}[1]{America?}
```

Example
2-2-3

More interesting special effects are also possible. Note, in particular, the use of the zero-width \makebox commands, which hide their contents from LaTeX and thus offer the possibility of fine-tuning the positioning of the typeset material.

America?
America?
America?
America?
America?
America?

```
\usepackage{graphics} % or graphicx
\noindent America?\scalebox{-1}{America?}    \\
        America?\scalebox{1}[-1]{America?}\\
        America?\makebox[0mm][r]{%
            \scalebox{-1}{America?}}\\
        \makebox[0mm][l]{America?}%
            \scalebox{1}[-1]{America?}
```

Example
2-2-4

2.2.2 Resizing to a given size

It is possible to specify that LᴬTEX material should be typeset to a fixed horizontal or vertical dimension:

```
\resizebox*{h-dim}{v-dim}{material}
```

When the aspect ratio of the material should be maintained, then it is enough to specify one of the dimensions, replacing the other dimension with a "!" sign.

```
\usepackage{graphics} % or graphicx
\fbox{\resizebox{5mm}{!}{%
    \parbox{14mm}{London,\\ Berlin \&\\ Paris}}}
\fbox{\resizebox{!}{10mm}{%
    \parbox{14mm}{London,\\ Berlin \&\\ Paris}}}
```

Example
2-2-5

When explicit dimensions for both *h-dim* and *v-dim* are supplied, then the contents can be distorted. In the following example the baseline is indicated by a horizontal rule drawn with the \HR command.

Köln   Lyon   Oxford
— Rhein   Rhône   Thames —

Köln   Lyon   Oxford
— Rhein   Rhône   Thames —

```
\usepackage{graphics} % or graphicx
\HR\begin{tabular}{lll}
    K\"oln & Lyon   & Oxford \\
    Rhein  & Rh\^one & Thames
    \end{tabular}\HR\par\bigskip
\HR\resizebox{2cm}{.5cm}{%
    \begin{tabular}{lll}
    K\"oln & Lyon   & Oxford \\
    Rhein  & Rh\^one & Thames
    \end{tabular}}\HR
```

Example
2-2-6

As usual with LᴬTEX commands involving box dimensions, you can refer to the natural lengths \depth, \height, \totalheight, and \width as dimensional parameters:

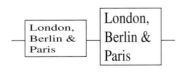

```
\usepackage{graphics} % or graphicx
\HR\fbox{\resizebox{\width}{.7\height}{%
    \parbox{14mm}{London,\\ Berlin \&\\Paris}}}\HR
\fbox{\resizebox{\width}{.7\totalheight}{%
    \parbox{14mm}{London,\\ Berlin \&\\Paris}}}\HR
```

Example
2-2-7

The unstarred form \resizebox bases its calculations on the height of the LᴬTEX material, while the starred \resizebox* command takes into account the total height (the depth plus the height) of the LaTeX box. The next `tabular` examples, which have a large depth, show the difference.

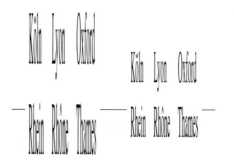

```
\usepackage{graphicx}
\HR\resizebox{20mm}{30mm}{%
    \begin{tabular}{lll}
      K\"oln & Lyon    & Oxford \\
      Rhein  & Rh\^one & Thames
    \end{tabular}}\HR
\HR\resizebox*{20mm}{30mm}{%
    \begin{tabular}{lll}
      K\"oln & Lyon    & Oxford \\
      Rhein  & Rh\^one & Thames
    \end{tabular}}\HR
```

2.2.3 Rotating a LaTeX box

LaTeX material can be rotated through an angle with the `\rotatebox` command. An alternative technique that is useful with environments is described in Section 2.2.4.

`\rotatebox{`*angle*`}{`*material*`}`

The *material* argument is typeset inside a LaTeX box and rotated through *angle* degrees counterclockwise around the reference point.

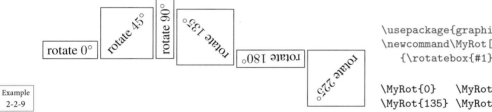

```
\usepackage{graphics} % or graphicx
\newcommand\MyRot[1]{\fbox
    {\rotatebox{#1}{rotate
                    $#1^\circ$}}}
\MyRot{0}    \MyRot{45}  \MyRot{90}
\MyRot{135}  \MyRot{180} \MyRot{225}
```

To understand where the rotated material is placed on the page, we need to look at the algorithm employed. Below we show the individual steps carried out when rotating `\fbox{text}` by 75 degrees.   *The rotation algorithm*

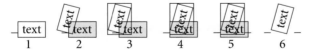

Step 1 shows the unrotated text; the horizontal line at the left marks the baseline. First the *material* (in this case, `\fbox{text}`) is placed into a box. This box has a reference point around which, by default, the rotation is carried out. This is shown in step 2 (the original position of the unrotated material is shown as well for reference purposes). Then the algorithm calculates a new bounding box (i.e., the space reserved for the rotated material), as shown in step 3. Next the material is moved horizontally so that the left edges of the new and the old bounding boxes are in the same position (step 4). TeX's typesetting position is then advanced so that additional material is typeset to the right of the bounding box in its new position, as shown by the line denoting the baseline in step 5. Step 6 shows the final result, again with the baseline on both sides of the rotated material.

For more complex material it is important to keep the location of the reference point of the resulting box in mind. The following example shows how it can be shifted by using the placement parameter of the \parbox command.

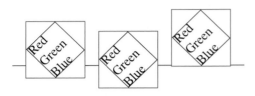

```
\usepackage{color,graphics} % or graphicx
\HR\bluefbox{\rotatebox{45}{%
    \fbox{\parbox{3em}{Red\\Green\\Blue}}}}%
\HR\bluefbox{\rotatebox{45}{%
    \fbox{\parbox[t]{3em}{Red\\Green\\Blue}}}}%
\HR\bluefbox{\rotatebox{45}{%
    \fbox{\parbox[b]{3em}{Red\\Green\\Blue}}}}\HR
```

Example
2-2-10

The extended graphics package **graphicx** offers more flexibility in specifying the point around which the rotation is to take place by using *key/val* pairs.

\rotatebox[*key/val-list*] {*angle*}{*material*}

The four possible keys are `origin`, `x`, `y`, and `units`. The possible values for the `origin` key are shown in Figure 2.2 on the next page (one value can be chosen for each of the horizontal and vertical alignments), as are the actual positions of these combinations with respect to the LaTeX box produced from *material*.

Strange result with optional argument
Note that without an optional argument, the rotation is carried out around the *reference point*, whereas the *center point* is used by default as soon as an optional argument is present. This somewhat idiosyncratic behavior can lead to unexpected results, e.g., when only `units=-360` is specified to achieve clockwise rotation.

Possible combinations for the `origin` key when applied to an actual LaTeX box are shown below, where two matrices of the results are shown for 90-degree and 45-degree rotated boxes. To better appreciate the effects, the unrotated text is shown against a grey background.

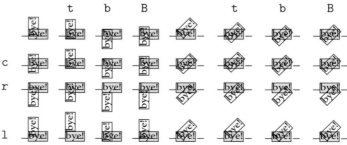

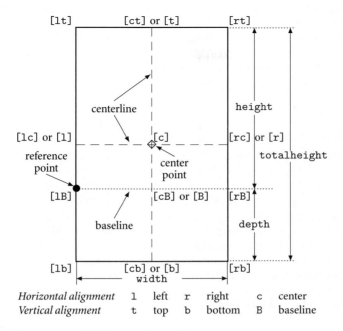

Figure 2.2: A L^AT_EX box and possible `origin` reference points

If the specification of the `origin` is not enough, you also can supply the x and y coordinates (relative to the reference point) for the point around which the rotation is to take place. For this purpose, use the keys x and y and the format x=*dim*, y=*dim*. A matrix showing some sample values and their effect on a box rotated by 70 degrees follows.

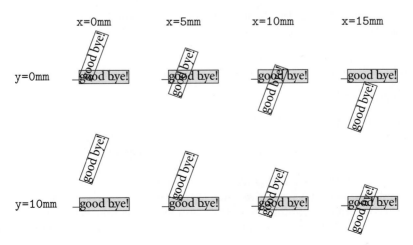

The interpretation of the *angle* argument of \rotatebox can be controlled by the units keyword, which specifies the number of units counterclockwise in a full circle. The default is 360, so using units=-360 would mean that angles are specified clockwise. Similarly, a setting of units=6.283185 changes the degree specification to radians. Rather than changing the units key on individual \rotatebox commands, you should probably set up a default interpretation using the \setkeys declaration as described in Section 2.1.4.

2.2.4 The epsfig and rotating packages

Sebastian Rahtz's LATEX 2.09 packages epsfig and rotating have been rewritten as interfaces to the graphicx package, so that users of those packages can continue to use the syntax with which they are familiar. For new documents, it is normally advisable to use LATEX's native graphics commands directly as described in this chapter. Nevertheless, the rotating package offers some supplementary high-level functionality, such as the sidewaystable and sidewaysfigure environments, that are not provided in the standard graphics packages.

The functionality of rotating is implemented in this package through the environments turn and rotate; the latter environment generates an object that occupies no space. Using environments has the advantage that the rotated material can contain \verb commands. The extended syntax of the \rotatebox command is not supported, however, so in most cases the latter command is preferable.

Turning   a bit.

```
\usepackage{rotating}
Turning \begin{rotate}{-90}\Huge\LaTeX\end{rotate}%
        \begin{rotate}{-20}\Large\LaTeX\end{rotate}%
        \begin{turn}{20}\verb=\LaTeX=\end{turn} a bit.
```

Example
2-2-11

The rotating package lets the user control the direction of rotation with the package options clockwise (the default) and counterclockwise.

2.3 Line graphics

As part of its kernel, LATEX offers the picture environment, which allows for the creation of line graphics from a number of fairly basic constructs. Surprisingly complex graphics can be produced, as can be seen in Chapter 8, which covers a number of "languages" that have been built using the picture environment as a basis.

Nevertheless, as the building blocks for generating lines, vectors, and circles in the picture environment are effectively tiny characters in specially designed fonts, this approach has naturally severe limitations. There are only a finite (and, in fact, small) number of different characters in these fonts and thus only a small number of different slopes for lines, a smallest circle and a largest circle, and so on. For instance, the next example generates two warnings and three errors and shows the defects quite drastically.

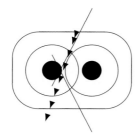

```
\begin{picture}(0,0)
  \put(0,0) {\circle{80}} \put(0,0) {\circle*{24}}
  \put(30,0){\circle{40}} \put(30,0){\circle*{16}}
  \put(15,0){\oval(90,60)}
  \put(0,12){\line(15,-2){30}} \put(0,-12){\line(15,2){30}}
  \thicklines
  \put(-5,-40){\vector(2,6){25}}
\end{picture}
```

Example
2-3-1

These restrictions were supposed to be lifted by the **pict2e** package described in the second edition of Lamport's "LATEX: A Document Preparation System" [78]. But until its real release in 2004 by Hubert Gäßlein and Rolf Niepraschk [28], the package merely produced an apologetic error message.

Applying this package to our previous example, we can clearly identify some of the limitations of the font-based solution.

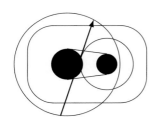

```
\usepackage{pict2e}
\begin{picture}(0,0)
  \put(0,0) {\circle{80}} \put(0,0) {\circle*{24}}
  \put(30,0){\circle{40}} \put(30,0){\circle*{16}}
  \put(15,0){\oval(90,60)}
  \put(0,12){\line(15,-2){30}} \put(0,-12){\line(15,2){30}}
  \thicklines
  \put(-5,-40){\vector(2,6){25}}
\end{picture}
```

Example
2-3-2

2.3.1 Options for pict2e

Similar to the packages from the graphics bundle, the **pict2e** package supports a number of different output devices. Thus it is not surprising that the majority of the package options are options to select the back-end driver—`dvipdfm`, `dvips`, `oztex`, `pdftex`, `vtex`, and `xdvi` at the time of this book's writing. In comparison to the graphics bundle, a smaller number of output drivers are supported, although that may change in the future. Like a lot of other packages (e.g., **graphics** and **color**), **pict2e** tries to detect which driver is needed; only in some special cases must an explicit option be given on the \usepackage command.

If supplied with an unknown option name, the package automatically uses the option `original` instead. This default is mainly intended to handle driver option names that are not yet implemented for **pict2e**. Unfortunately, however, it also means that misspelling an option name has the surprising effect of turning off all features instead of producing an error message.

 The danger of misspelled options

Setting the arrow style The options `ltxarrows` and `pstarrows` determine the arrow style used by the `\vector` command. There is no document-level declaration that would allow to mix both styles in one document. The default form used by LaTeX has a more or less triangular tip:

```
\usepackage[ltxarrows]{pict2e}
\begin{picture}(170,50)
  \put(0,25){\vector(2,1){100}}
  \linethickness{10\unitlength}
  \put(0,25){\vector(1,0){100}} \put(170,25){\vector(1,0){0}}
\end{picture}
```

Example
2-3-3

In contrast, the arrows modeled after those in PSTricks are much more like barbed hooks, with their tips also pointing backwards. To better show the different forms both examples display the arrows at normal size as well as 10 times magnified.

```
\usepackage[pstarrows]{pict2e}
\begin{picture}(170,50)
  \put(0,25){\vector(2,1){100}}
  \linethickness{10\unitlength}
  \put(0,25){\vector(1,0){100}} \put(170,25){\vector(1,0){0}}
\end{picture}
```

Example
2-3-4

2.3.2 Standard LaTeX and pict2e compared

Looking more closely at pict2e, we find the following features in comparison to the LaTeX's standard `picture` environment and the commands used therein:

- The enhanced commands can draw lines and arrows at any slope (no limitation on the allowed values for slopes) and with an arbitrary line thickness (i.e., not limited to two values) and produce circles with any diameter.

- It is possible to specify the radius used in ovals. In standard `picture`, this value is calculated automatically.

- Support for cubic Bézier curves is implemented as part of the package.

> $\backslash$`line`$(\Delta x, \Delta y)$ *{length}* $\backslash$`vector`$(\Delta x, \Delta y)$ *{length}*

In standard LaTeX, the slope arguments $(\Delta x, \Delta y)$ are severely restricted (integers in a very small range with no common divisors). With pict2e, this restriction has been more or less lifted: one has to satisfy only the condition $(-1000, -1000) \leq (\Delta x, \Delta y) \leq (1000, 1000)$ to avoid arithmetic overflow. Due to the font-based implementation in standard LaTeX, there was a minimal line segment and thus a minimal length for a line or vector. With pict2e, lines and vectors can be drawn at any length. Furthermore, the `\linethickness` declaration now affects lines and vectors at any slope and arrowheads can be drawn at any size.

> \circle{*diameter*}   \circle*{*diameter*}

The standard LaTeX \circle macro has restrictions on the values of the possible diameters: only a fixed set of sizes are available, with the largest value being approximately 40 points for circles and 15 points for filled disks. With **pict2e**, a circle or disk of any positive size can be drawn. Obviously, specifying negative values is still impossible and will be flagged as an error. Furthermore, the circle lines are now affected by \linethickness, while in standard LaTeX only two values (\thinlines and \thicklines) are supported.

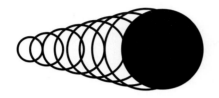

```
\usepackage{multido,pict2e}
\begin{picture}(118,60)(-45,-30)
   \linethickness{1.6pt}
   \multido{\iA=-30+10,\iB=15+5}{8}
         {\put(\iA,0){\circle{\iB}}}
   \put(50,0){\circle*{50}}
\end{picture}
```

Example
2-3-5

The amount of improvement provided by **pict2e** can be clearly seen by comparing the above example with the result produced by standard LaTeX:

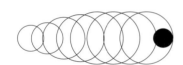

```
\usepackage{multido}
\begin{picture}(118,60)(-45,-30)
   \linethickness{1.6pt}
   \multido{\iA=-30+10,\iB=15+5}{8}
         {\put(\iA,0){\circle{\iB}}}
   \put(50,0){\circle*{50}}
\end{picture}
```

Example
2-3-6

> \oval[*radius*] ($\Delta x, \Delta y$) [*part*]   \maxovalrad

Without using the package **pict2e**, the user can control only the size of an oval but not its shape, since its corners would always consist of the "quarter circles of the largest possible radius less than or equal to *radius*" [78, page 223]. The original definition therefore has only one optional argument (for specifying which *part* of the oval to typeset).

With **pict2e**, an additional optional argument for specfying the *radius* is available. Its default value is the command \maxovalrad, which defaults to 20 pt. The **pict2e** package will "auto-detect" whether its argument is a length value or a number (in which case \unitlength is used as the unit).

In the following example, the oval halves on the left are specified without the optional *radius* argument, thus using the default of 20 pt for the maximum. Consequentially, the inner halves show half-circles that turn into ovals once the size exceeds 20 pt. This more or less would be the result one gets without the **pict2e** package, except that the font-based solution can render only a limited number of quarter-circles. Thus even the inner lines may not be perfect half-circles in that case. On the right side, an explicit value of 5 is used, so that real ovals appear from the third \oval on (which has a vertical size of 15).

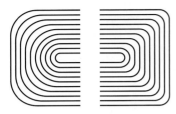

```
\usepackage{multido,pict2e}
\begin{picture}(100,80)
  \thicklines
  \multido{\iA=25+5,\iB=5+5}{10}
          {\put(45,40){\oval(\iA,\iB)[l]}}
  \multido{\iA=25+5,\iB=5+5}{10}
          {\put(55,40){\oval[5](\iA,\iB)[r]}}
\end{picture}
```

Example
2-3-7

The next example experiments with different values for \maxovalrad. On the left we decrease it from 10 to 1 (inside to outside), so that the rounded corners get smaller and smaller. Of course, we could have used those values directly in the optional *radius* argument; in real life \maxovalrad will normally be used to set the default once. On the right we increase the *radius* as we move outwards (this time using the optional argument): for the top corners by 1 pt each time and on the bottom corners by 1 (\unitlength). As our picture is typeset with a \unitlength of 2 pt, the quarter-circles grow faster than the top ones. The example also proves that \oval obeys changes to the \linethickness.

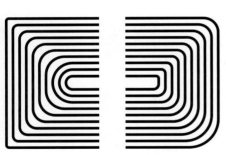

```
\usepackage{multido,pict2e}
\setlength\unitlength{2pt}
\linethickness{2pt}
\begin{picture}(100,80)
  \multido{\iA=25+5,\iB=5+5,\iM=10+-1}{10}
          {\renewcommand\maxovalrad{\iM}
           \put(45,40){\oval(\iA,\iB)[l]}}
  \multido{\iA=25+5,\iB=5+5,\dM=2pt+1pt,\iM=2+1}{10}
          {\put(55,40){\oval[\dM](\iA,\iB)[rt]}
           \put(55,40){\oval[\iM](\iA,\iB)[rb]}}
\end{picture}
```

Example
2-3-8

```
\qbezier[n] (a_x, a_y) (b_x, b_y) (c_x, c_y)
\qbeziermax
\cbezier[n] (a_x, a_y) (b_x, b_y) (c_x, c_y) (d_x, d_y)
```

The \qbezier command draws a quadratic Bézier curve using the three control points given as mandatory picture arguments. In the standard LATEX implementation, the curve is plotted using a number of small square dots (less or equal to \qbeziermax or specified explicitly in the optional argument). As those dots are implemented in TEX and not as font characters, this is one of the few commands in the basic implementation that obeys changes to \linethickness. The example shows the middle control point as a small circle.

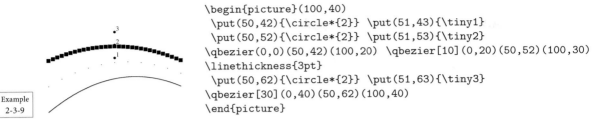

```
\begin{picture}(100,40)
 \put(50,42){\circle*{2}} \put(51,43){\tiny1}
 \put(50,52){\circle*{2}} \put(51,53){\tiny2}
\qbezier(0,0)(50,42)(100,20) \qbezier[10](0,20)(50,52)(100,30)
\linethickness{3pt}
 \put(50,62){\circle*{2}} \put(51,63){\tiny3}
\qbezier[30](0,40)(50,62)(100,40)
\end{picture}
```

Example
2-3-9

With the pict2e package, the optional argument is ignored and the curve is always plotted in a smooth manner using the graphics capability of the back-end output driver. In the standard implementation, that would be possible only by plotting with a large number of dots, which may exceed TeX's internal memory. The next example first repeats the curves in the previous example but this time using pict2e. In addition, we added a cubic Bézier curve with four control points, not available with standard LaTeX.

```
\usepackage{pict2e}
\begin{picture}(100,80)
 \put(50,42){\circle*{2}} \put(51,43){\tiny1}
 \put(50,52){\circle*{2}} \put(51,53){\tiny2}
\qbezier(0,0)(50,42)(100,20)\qbezier[10](0,20)(50,52)(100,30)
\linethickness{3pt}
 \put(50,62){\circle*{2}} \put(51,63){\tiny3}
\qbezier[30](0,40)(50,62)(100,40)
% cubic bezier
 \put(30,80){\circle*{2}} \put(31,81){\tiny4}
 \put(70,0){\circle*{2}}  \put(71,1){\tiny5}
\cbezier(0,0)(30,80)(70,0)(100,20)
\end{picture}
```

Example
2-3-10

2.3.3   Slightly beyond standard graphics: curve2e

Claudio Beccari developed the package **curve2e**. This extension to **pict2e** includes ideas from David Carlisle's **pspicture** and Ian Maclaine-cross's **curves** packages. Compared to pict2e, curve2e enhances the syntax of the \line command and introduces two new commands: \Line, which allows the user to specify the relative x and y displacements from the current point, and \LINE, which has two absolute coordinates as its arguments. Similarly, \Vector and \VECTOR are defined and extend the \vector command. Claudio also defines a \polyline command for drawing polylines between two (minimum) or more vertices that are specified as arguments, as well as a \Curve command for drawing third-order Bézier curves. This macro needs a series of nodes on the curve together with the tangent at each node. Finally, he introduces an \Arc command and some variants for drawing circular arcs of any radius and any angular aperture.

The first example shows sine and cosine-like functions that are defined as Bézier curves whose values and tangents are specified at four points between 0 and 2π. Note how we use LaTeX's standard \vector command to draw the vertical axis and the extension command \Vector to draw the horizontal axis.

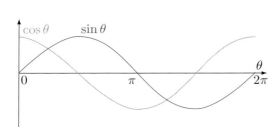

```
\usepackage{xcolor,pict2e,curve2e}
\setlength\unitlength{1cm}
\begin{picture}(6.6,3)(0,-1.5)
  \put(0,-1.5){\vector(0,3){3}}
  \put(0,0){\Vector(6.6,0)}
  \put(6.3,0.1){$\theta$}
  \put(0.05,-0.3){$0$}% 0
  \put(2.9,-0.3){$\pi$}% pi
  \put(6.23,-0.3){$2\pi$}% 2 pi
  \color{red}\put(0.1,1.1){$\cos\theta$}
  \Curve(0,1)<1,0>(1.570796,0)<1,-1>%
  (3.1415924,-1)<1,0>(6.283185,1)<1,0>%
  \color{blue}\put(1.65,1.1){$\sin\theta$}
  \Curve(0,0)<1,1>(1.570796,1)<1,0>%
  (4.712389,-1)<1,0>(6.283185,0)<1,1>%
\end{picture}
```

Example
2-3-11

A more complex example of the use of the \Curve command is the following heart figure. Note how we make use of the variants \line, \Line, and \LINE for drawing the sides of the square.

```
\usepackage{xcolor,pict2e,curve2e}
\setlength\unitlength{1cm}
\begin{picture}(5,5)(0.,0.)
  \Curve(2.5,0)<0,1>(5,3.5)<0,1>%
  (2.5,3.5)<-.5,-1>[-.5,1]%
  (0,3.5)<0,-1>(2.5,0)<0,-1>
  \color{blue}
  \thinlines
  \put(0,0){\line(0,5){5}}
  \put(0,0){\line(5,0){5}}
  \put(5,0){\Line(0,5)}
  \LINE(0,5)(5,5)
\end{picture}
```

Example
2-3-12

The following example shows in more detail how we can control the tangent on the incoming (triangular brackets) and outgoing sides, if different (square brackets). For instance, for the rightmost node (5.0,2.5), the tangent of the curve arriving at the node, <1,0>, points along the positive x direction, whereas the tangent of the curve leaving the node, [-1,0], points along the negative x direction.

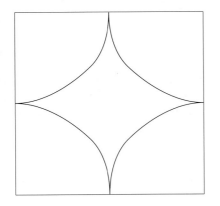

```
\usepackage{xcolor,pict2e,curve2e}
\setlength\unitlength{1cm}
\begin{picture}(5,5)(0.,0.)
  \Curve(2.5,0.0)<0,1>(3.0,1.5)<1,1>%
  (5.0,2.5)<1,0>[-1,0](3.0,3.5)<-1,1>%
  (2.5,5.0)<0,1>[0,-1](2.,3.5)<-1,-1>%
  (0.0,2.5)<-1,0>[1,0](2.,1.5)<1,-1>%
  (2.5,0.0)<0,-1>
  \color{blue}
  \thinlines
  \put(0,0){\line(0,5){5}}\put(0,0){\line(5,0){5}}
  \put(5,0){\Line(0,5)}    \LINE(0,5)(5,5)
\end{picture}
```

Example
2-3-13

The **curve2e** package implements vector calculus in the two-dimensional plane, which is useful to represent complex numbers. The following example of a five-pointed star shows some of the advantages of this approach. The `\DivideE` command implements long division and lets us define an angle of 72 degrees, which the `\DirFromAngle` command translates into a vector direction. We first move to the top node of the graph at the point (0,2.5), to which we assign the vector coordinates `\Vone`. We then define the vector coordinates `\Vtwo`, `\Vthree`, `\Vfour`, and `\Vfive` of the other nodes as the previous vector multiplied by `\Dir` (i.e., rotated by 72 degrees). Finally, the first `\polyline` command draws the sides of the pentagon, while the second `\polyline` command draws the sides of the five-pointed star. For completeness we add the circumscribing circle.

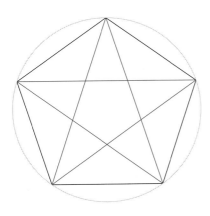

```
\usepackage{xcolor,pict2e,curve2e}
\setlength\unitlength{1cm}
\begin{picture}(5,5)(-2.5,-2.5)
  \DivideE 360pt by 5pt to\Fifth
  \DirFromAngle\Fifth to\Dir
  \CopyVect 0,2.5 to\Vone
  \MultVect\Vone by\Dir to\Vtwo
  \MultVect\Vtwo by\Dir to\Vthree
  \MultVect\Vthree by\Dir to\Vfour
  \MultVect\Vfour by\Dir to\Vfive
  \polyline(\Vone)(\Vtwo)(\Vthree)%
          (\Vfour)(\Vfive)(\Vone)
  \color{blue}
  \polyline(\Vone)(\Vfour)(\Vtwo)%
          (\Vfive)(\Vthree)(\Vone)
  \color{green}\thinlines
          \put(0,0){\circle{5.}}
\end{picture}
```

Example
2-3-14

We end our short overview of the **curve2e** package with instances of commands for drawing circular arcs. If we want an arc with an opening angle of 30 degrees, we first define that angle (\Twelfth) and turn it into a vector direction (\Dir). Using \Dir, the \MultVect command lets us construct several circular arcs, that are 30 degrees apart: two in the positive (counterclockwise) direction (\Vone and \Vtwo) and two in the negative (clockwise) direction (\Vmone and \Vmtwo).[1] The arcs are drawn with the \Arc command, where the first point specifies the center of the arc, the second the start point on the arc, and the third the opening angle (in degrees, positive means counterclockwise). The variants \VectorArc and \VectorARC draw an arrow at the end point, and at both start and end points of the arc, respectively. The \VECTOR command, in analogy with the \LINE command, draws a vector by specifying the absolute coordinates of its start and end points.

```
\usepackage{xcolor,pict2e,curve2e}
\setlength\unitlength{1cm}
\begin{picture}(2.5,5)(-2.5,-2.5)
  \DividE 360pt by 12pt to\Twelfth
  \DirFromAngle\Twelfth to\Dir
  \CopyVect -2.5,0 to\Vzero
  \MultVect\Vzero by\Dir to\Vone
  \MultVect\Vone by\Dir to\Vtwo
  \Arc(0.0,0.0)(\Vzero){30}
  \Arc(0.0,0.0)(\Vone){30}
  \VectorArc(0.0,0.0)(\Vtwo){-30}
  \color{blue}\MultVect\Vzero by*\Dir to\Vmone
            \MultVect\Vmone by*\Dir to\Vmtwo
            \Arc(0.0,0.0)(\Vzero){-30}
            \Arc(0.0,0.0)(\Vmone){-30}
            \VectorARC(0.0,0.0)(\Vmtwo){30}
  \color{green}\thinlines
            \VECTOR(0,0)(\Vzero)
            \VECTOR(0,0)(\Vone)\VECTOR(0,0)(\Vmone)
            \VECTOR(0,0)(\Vtwo)\VECTOR(0,0)(\Vmtwo)
\end{picture}
```

Example
2-3-15

---

[1] If the keyword "by" of the \MultVect command is followed by a star, the complex conjugate of the specified direction is used to define the resulting vector.

CHAPTER 3

METAFONT and METAPOST: TeX's Mates

In designing the TeX typesetting system, Donald Knuth soon realized that he would also have to write his own font design program. He devised METAFONT, a language for describing shapes, and a program to interpret that language and turn the shapes into a pattern of dots for a printing or viewing device. The result of Knuth's work was TeX, METAFONT, and the extensive Computer Modern font family written in METAFONT. METAFONT has also been used to create special-purpose symbol fonts and some other font families.

The development of METAFONT as a font description language paralleled to some extent that of the PostScript language, which also describes character shapes very elegantly. PostScript's strategy, however, is to leave the rendering of the shape until the final printing stage, whereas METAFONT seeks to precompute the bitmap output and print it on a fairly dumb printing device.

Font design is a decidedly specialist art, and one that most of us are ill equipped to tackle. METAFONT, however, defines a very powerful language that can cope with most graphical tasks. A sibling program, METAPOST, was developed that uses essentially the same language but generates PostScript instead of bitmaps. Together, the two provide an excellent companion facility with which (LA)TEX users can illustrate their documents, particularly when they want pictures that graphically express some mathematical construct; this is not surprising, given that Knuth's aim was to describe font shapes mathematically. Applications vary from drawing Hilbert or Sierpiński curves (described in Section 4.4.3) to plotting data in graphs and expressing relationships in graphical form.

In this chapter we consider how to use both METAFONT and METAPOST (henceforth we use META to mean "both METAFONT and METAPOST") to draw pictures and shapes other than characters in fonts.

Our coverage of META is divided into six parts. We start with a brief look at the META language basics; our aim is to give readers new to META some ideas of its facilities and the level at which pictures can be designed. We try to explain commands as they are used, but some examples may contain META code that is not explicitly described.

We next consider in some detail the extra facilities of the METAPOST language, in particular the inclusion of text and color in figures.

The third section examines how the META programs are run and how resulting figures can be included in a LATEX document. The following section describes the general-purpose METAPOST libraries, covering in particular boxing macros and the METAOBJ package.

We then look at programs that write META commands for you, concentrating on the mfpic (LA)TEX package. We conclude with an overview of miscellaneous tools and utilities related to METAPOST.

For some applications, such as drawing of graphs, diagrams, geometrical figures, and 3-D objects, higher-level macro packages have been developed, which define their own languages for the user. These packages are described in Chapter 4.

3.1 The META language

The full intricacies of METAFONT are described in loving detail in [72]; the manual for METAPOST [47] not only describes the differences between the two systems, but is itself a good introduction to META. Alan Hoenig's book *TEX Unbound* [49] provides a wealth of material on METAFONT techniques. Articles over many years in the journal *TUGboat* are also vital reading for those who want to delve deeply into METAFONT and METAPOST.

The job of the META language is to describe shapes; these shapes can then be filled, scaled, rotated, reflected, skewed, and shifted, among other complex transformations. Indeed, META programs can be regarded as specialized equation-solving systems that have the side effect of producing pictures.

META offers all the facilities of a conventional programming language. Program flow control, for example, is provided by a `for ... endfor` construct, with the usual conditionals. You can write parameterized macros or subroutines, and there are facilities for local variables and grouping to limit the scope of value changes. Some of these features are described with more detail in the METAPOST section, although they are also available in METAFONT.

Because a lot of the work in writing META programs deals with describing geometrical shapes, the numeric support is extensive. For instance, Pythagorean addition (++) and subtraction (+-+) are directly supported. Useful numeric functions include `length` x

(absolute value of x), sqrt x (square root of x), sind x (sine of x degrees), cosd x (cosine of x degrees), angle (x, y) (arctangent of y/x), floor x (largest integer $\leq$ x), uniformdeviate x (uniformly distributed random number between 0 and x), and normaldeviate (normally distributed random number with mean 0 and standard deviation 1).

A variety of complex data types are defined, including boolean, numeric, pair, path, pen, picture, string, and transform. Here we can look at some of these in more detail:

pair "Points" in two-dimensional space are represented in META with the type pair. Constants of type pair have the form (x, y), where x and y are both numeric constants. A variable p of type pair is equal to the pair expression (xpart p, ypart p).

path A path is a continuous curve, which is composed of a chain of *segments*. Each segment has a shape determined by four *control points*. Two of the control points, the *key* points, are the segment's end points; very often we let META determine the other two control points.

pen Pens, a distinctive feature of META, are filled convex shapes that are moved along paths and affect the way lines are drawn in the result. Two pens are initially present in META: nullpen and pencircle. nullpen is the single point $(0, 0)$; it contains no pixels and can be used to fill a region without changing its boundary. By contrast, pencircle is circular, with the points $(\pm 0.5, 0)$ and $(0, \pm 0.5)$ on its circumference. Other pens are constructed as convex polygons via makepen c, where c is a closed path; the key points of c become the vertices of the pen. Pens themselves can be transformed.

picture A picture is a data type that can be used to store a sequence of META drawing commands; the result of a complete META program is often built up from the interaction of a set of pictures. The meaning of $v + w$ in METAFONT, for example, is a picture in which each pixel is the sum of the two pixels occupying the same position in pictures v and w, respectively.

transform Affine transforms are the natural transformations of Euclidean geometry— that is, the linear transformations augmented by translation. META can construct any affine transform and provides seven primitive ones [72, p. 141]: *shifted, scaled, xscaled, yscaled, slanted, rotated,* and *zscaled*. The effect of most of the operations is self-evident; the last one, *zscaled*, uses a pair of numbers, interpreted as a complex number in Cartesian coordinates (i.e., complex multiplication).

Finally, META is famous for its ability to solve linear equations, including equations that involve points. In particular, you can define a point in terms of other points. For example, z3=1/2[z1,z2] defines z3 as the point in the middle of the line from z1 to z2.

3.1.1 First examples of META programs

Let us first look at some examples of META code, all drawn using METAPOST. You should have little difficulty making these examples run under METAFONT as well, except that you may encounter problems with high-resolution output devices, as METAFONT can run out of memory when composing large pictures—remember that METAFONT generates a bitmap output. This book was typeset at 2400 dpi, and some METAFONT examples were impossible to run at this resolution. Your only recourse is to work at a lower resolution (e.g., 300 dpi) or to break your picture into separate "characters" in a font and join them together in LaTeX. It is almost certainly easier to use METAPOST, as it generates PostScript that can be rendered directly by many printers or turned into PDF.

We do not show the "wrapper" code that is always necessary to turn these examples into a self-contained document. See the notes in Section 3.3.1 on page 68 for information on how METAFONT creates a character and Section 3.3.2 on page 71 for more on how METAPOST creates a figure.

The simplest statement in META is `draw`, which takes a sequence of points separated by `..` and connects them with curves:

```
draw (0,0)..(50,20)..(40,30)..(30,20);
```

Example
3-1-1

The default unit here is a PostScript point (1/72 inch, TEX's "big point"). To close a object smoothly between its last and first points, the sequence can be terminated by `cycle`:

```
draw (0, 50)..(0,0)..
     (60,40)..(60,10)..cycle;
```

Example
3-1-2

Straight lines are drawn by putting `--` instead of `..` between the points (the lines are actually implemented as specially constrained curves):

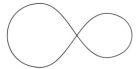

```
draw (0,0)--(50,20)--(40,60)--(30,20);
```

Example
3-1-3

There are several ways of controlling curves: one can vary the angles at the start and end of the curve with `dir`, the points that are to be the extremes (the upmost, the leftmost, and so forth), and the inflection of the curve (with `tension` and `curl`). Thus the following code draws a crude coil by judicious use of `dir`. Instead of the default units, we express all dimensions in terms of a unit of 2.5 cm, defined at the start:

```
u=2.5cm;
path p;
p= (0,0) {dir 130}..
    {dir -130}(0.25u,0){dir 130}..
    {dir -130}(0.5u,0){dir 130}..
    {dir -130}(0.75u,0){dir 130}..
    {dir -130}(u,0);
draw p rotated -90;
```

Example
3-1-4

The next example shows the effect of `curl`. Here a straight line is drawn between three points and then a curve is drawn between the same points, with `curl` values:

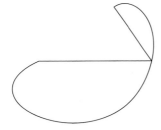

```
path p,q;
u=.5cm;
q=(0u,0u)--(6u,0u)--(4u,3u);
draw q;
p=(0u,0u){curl 4000}..(6u,0u)
    ..{curl 4000}(4u,3u);
draw p;
```

Example
3-1-5

To demonstrate META's unusual "pens", we approximate a spiral drawn with a strange "nib". A colored version of this drawing appears in Color Plate I(a).

```
pickup pencircle scaled 3pt
    yscaled .2pt rotated 60;
n:=5;
for i := (n*20) step -(n) until (n):
 draw ((i,0)..(0,i)..(-i,0)
    ..(0,-(i-n))..(i-n,0)) scaled 0.7;
endfor
```

Example
3-1-6

A very characteristic technique with META is creating a path and then using it several times with different transformations. The following code is an extract from a drawing of a kite's tail. Note that shapes can be made solid by using `fill` instead of `draw`:

```
u=1cm;
path p[];
p1:=(.5u,.5u)--(1.5u,.5u)--(.5u,1.5u)
 --(1.5u,1.5u)--(.5u,.5u)--cycle;
fill (p1 shifted (0,2.5u))
 rotatedaround ((u,3.5u),90);
draw p1 shifted (u,4u);
fill p1 shifted (3.5u,3u);
p2 =(2u,2u)..(u,3.5u)..(2u,5u)
 ..(4.5u,4u)..(7u,5u);
pickup pencircle scaled 4pt;
draw p2;
```

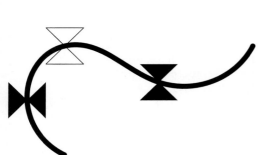

Example
3-1-7

A more complicated picture, courtesy of Alan Hoenig from his book *TEX Unbound* [49], demonstrates looping commands. Boxes of gradually decreasing size are drawn alternately white and black, with each one being rotated slightly with respect to the previous box.

```
boolean timetofillbox; timetofillbox := true;
partway := 0.9; l := .45in; u := 1.05in;
n := 4; theta := 360/n; z1 = (0,u);
for i := 2 upto n:
  z[i] = z1 rotated ((i-1)*theta);
endfor
forever:
  path p;    p := z1
  for j := 2 upto n: --z[j] endfor   --cycle;
  if timetofillbox:
    fill p;  timetofillbox := false;
  else:
    unfill p;  timetofillbox := true;
  fi
  pair Z[];
  for j := 1 upto n:
    Z[j] := partway[z[j-1],z[j]];
  endfor
  Z1 := partway[z[n],z1];
  for j := 1 upto n:
    x[j] := xpart Z[j]; y[j] := ypart Z[j];
  endfor
  if not timetofillbox: l := abs(z1); fi
  exitif l < .05u;
endfor
```

Example
3-1-8

Finally, a pleasing side effect of META's curve-drawing abilities is it makes for a nice artist's tool. Kees van der Laan demonstrates[1] in Figure 3.1 how METAPOST lends itself to moving into 3-D description on the one hand, and art on the other hand, with a picture modeled on Naum Gabo's constructivist art.

3.1.2 Defining macros

META supports the definition of macros, the full intricacies of which are described in [72]. Here we give only a brief overview of their definition.

Macros

Essentially two kinds of macros exist. The first kind is defined with def, the second with vardef. The latter makes it possible to define macros with variable names. Here we will give an insight into only the first kind. In its simplest form, a macro is merely an abbreviation. For example,

```
def circle=
   fullcircle scaled 1cm
enddef;
```

defines circle as a new METAPOST abreviation for a circle centered at the origin with a diameter of 1 cm. A more useful definition would make use of parameters. For example,

```
def circle(expr c,r)=
   fullcircle scaled 2r shifted c
enddef;
```

defines circle(c,r) as a circle with radius r and centered on c. It can be used with a call such as draw circle((3cm,2cm),2cm);, which draws a circle with a diameter of 2 cm, offset from the origin 3 cm in the x-axis and 2 cm in the y-axis.

Macros can have any of three kinds of parameters, each of which is identified by a specific keyword. The expr keyword denotes parameters that are evaluated, such as numerical values, points, colors, and strings. The suffix keyword denotes a type that represents a name, rather than a value. Suffixes are used, for instance, in packages such as boxes. In the next example, b1 is a suffix representing a box around the letter A:

```
boxit.b1(btex $A$ etex);
```

The third and last keyword is text. It represents non-evaluated text, similar to macro parameters in TEX.

Another important feature of METAPOST is its ability to evaluate strings with scantokens. Strings can be constructed, and these strings can represent macros or other pieces of code. The METAPOST code can therefore be dynamically modified, depending on the values of some parameters, for instance.

---

[1] The code for this picture can be found on CTAN with the other examples from this book.

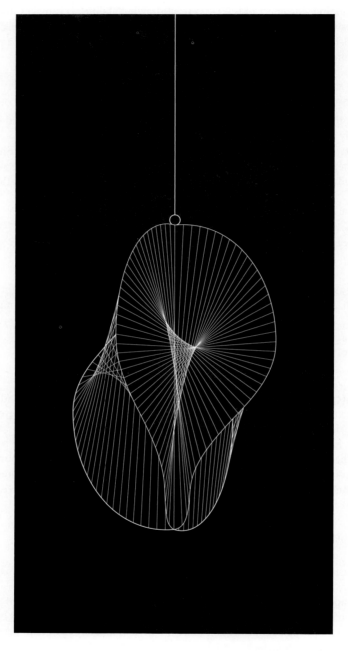

Figure 3.1: META picture after Naum Gabo, by Kees van der Laan

It is sometimes desirable to have macros with default behaviors and optional argu-
ments. The easiest way to achieve this is to use a trailing `text` parameter, as in the following   *Options mechanisms*
example:

```
def optarg text arg=
  for i=arg:
    message "arg=" & i;
  endfor;
enddef;

optarg "a", "b", "c";

optarg ;
```

whose sole output is

```
arg=a
arg=b
arg=c
```

This is a very simple example, meant only to convey the basic idea. `arg` is a possibly empty
comma-separated list of arguments. In our example, all the parameters are strings, but, in
fact, the parameters could be of different types. The loop traverses the list and does some
action. The last call to `optarg` doesn't produce any output, because the `for` loop is never
entered.

A more elaborate scheme is the use of a "*key*/value" syntax. The METAOBJ package
was among the first METAPOST packages to provide such a syntax. It did so by enclosing
each key/value pair in a string, as in the following example:

```
ncline(a)(b) "linewidth(1mm)","linestyle(dashed evenly)";
```

Many LaTeX packages follow the well-known "*key*=value" syntax; Jens-Uwe Morawski
showed how such a syntax can be used in METAPOST. His latexMP package defines a
macro for coping with lists of "*key*=value" pairs. As it seems to us a good idea for package
writers to use this syntax, we give here a complete example showing how short and simple
its usage is:

```
vardef executekeyval(text k)=
  save _equals;
  let _equals= =;
  tertiarydef _ll_ _assign _rr_ =
    hide(_ll_ _equals _rr_ ) 1
  enddef;
  save =;
  let = _equals _assign ;
  for _xx_ _equals k:endfor;
enddef;
```

```
vardef testkv text kv=
  save a,b,c,s,t; %key names
  pair c;string s,t;
  executekeyval(kv);
  A:=a;B:=b;
  message "a=" & decimal a;
  message "b=" & decimal b;
  if known t:message "t=" & t;fi;
enddef;

testkv a=8*4,b=a+7,c=(1,2),s="hello",t=(s&" Bob!");
message "A=" & decimal A;
message "B=" & decimal B;

testkv b=a+7,a=8*4;
message "A=" & decimal A;
message "B=" & decimal B;
```

This code produces the following output:

```
a=32
b=39
t=hello Bob!
A=32
B=39
a=32
b=39
A=32
B=39
```

The user macro, called `testkv`, takes an optional list of comma-separated arguments. The evaluation of this list is performed by the `executekeyval` macro, which is adapted from Jens-Uwe Morawski's code. The user macro defines variables a, b, c, s, and t for the *keys*. These variables are local, but in cases where the parameters need to be saved, they can be assigned to global variables (A and B in the previous example). This example shows that certain equations between arguments are possible.

3.2 Differences between METAPOST and METAFONT

3.2.1 Color

Color in METAPOST is represented by a triple defining a color in terms of red, green, and blue or, alternatively, in terms of one of the constants `black`, `white`, `red`, `green`, or `blue`. The `color` triple is three real numbers between 0 and 1 for each of the red, green, and blue values. It can be used in expressions just like `pair`, which makes possible color specifications like `.3blue` and `(.4,.2,.5) - (.9,.7,.3)`. If the resulting color component exceeds 1 or becomes less than 0, it is automatically brought back to a legal value.

Some METAPOST packages, such as **metafun**, provide other color models, including CMYK.

3.2.2   Adding text to pictures

One of the great advantages of METAPOST relative to METAFONT is that you can annotate your pictures with text. That is, METAPOST can typeset text with ordinary PostScript fonts, or you can tell it to use TeX to handle the formatting. This text handling can be quite intricate, so we delay discussing some of it to the next section.

The most common way to add text is the `label` command.

`label`*.suffix* (*string expression, pair expression*)

The *string expression* is printed at the position specified by the *pair expression* (i.e., a coordinate). The *suffix* is optional and can be one of `lft` (*left*), `rt` (*right*), `top` (*top*), `bot` (*bottom*), `ulft` (*upper left*), `urt` (*upper right*), `llft` (*lower left*), or `lrt` (*lower right*); it specifies the relative position of the label to the *pair expression*. The distance from the point to the label is set by the variable `labeloffset`.

The *string expression* can take either of two forms:

1. If it is a META string (i.e., delimited by double quotes in the simplest case), then META-POST sets the text directly in PostScript using the font specified by the `defaultfont` variable (usually set to be `cmr10`). This font must have a TeX font metric available; note that ligatures and kerning in the `.tfm` file are *not* used.

2. If you surround the text (but do not put it in quotes) with `btex ... etex`, it is passed to TeX for typesetting. This approach lets you use any TeX or LaTeX commands, enter math mode, and so on.

In either form, the variable `defaultscale` (default 1) is applied to the basic font size (normally 10 pt). There is also a special form of `label` that prints a dot at the coordinate as well as the label.

`dotlabel`*.suffix* (*string expression, pair expression*)

We demonstrate these commands with the following example:

Example
3-2-1

```
u=1.5pt;
labeloffset:=10pt;
defaultfont:="ptmb8r";
dotlabel.ulft ("upper left",(100u,100u));
label.urt (btex upper right etex,(100u,100u));
label.llft ("lower left",(100u,100u));
label.lrt (btex $x_1,y_1$ etex,(100u,100u));
draw (50u,100u)--(150u,100u);
draw (100u,125u)--(100u,75u);
```

upper left   upper right

lower left x_1, y_1

Two of the labels are META strings and are set in the font "ptmb8r" (converted to Times-Bold), and the other two are passed to TeX and set in the default Computer Modern.

There is also a command `dotlabels` that can be used to label a set of points which you have just created.

> `dotlabels`.*suffix* (*pair*$_1$,...,*pair*$_n$)

In this case a dot is printed at each point in the list, labeled with the name of the point variable, and placed according to the *suffix*. This command is used in the next example.

A label defined by a string has a default font and size; however, the label can also be passed to TEX for typesetting with the format `btex` *typesetting commands* `etex`. If the latter form is used, the output is no longer completely portable, as it relies on a special structured comment in the PostScript output that only a few `dvi` drivers understand (**dvips** is the reference implementation for this support).

To save the label in a META "picture" variable, you can use the command `thelabel`; it lets you use the same label several times, with different transformations. Another useful technique is to apply the `bbox` command to a saved label, which returns the rectangular path enclosing a META picture. The following example uses this method to draw white text on a green box and shows some of the other transformations you might need; it also shows how to apply `bbox` to the picture we are drawing, as an easy way of framing it:

```
defaultscale:=1.4;    u=1pt;
picture p,q;          gap:=18u;
for i := 0 upto 6:
 z[i]=(0u,i * gap * u);
endfor;
draw z0--z6;
dotlabels.lft(0,1,2,3,4,5,6);
q=thelabel.urt(btex Poly\TeX etex ,z0);
draw q;
draw q reflectedabout(z0,z0+(2u,0));
draw q shifted(0,gap) withcolor red;
fill bbox q shifted(0,2*gap*u)
            withcolor green;
draw q shifted(0,2*gap*u)
        withcolor white;
draw q scaled 2 shifted(0,5*gap*u);
p=q rotatedabout(z0,45);
draw p shifted(10u,3*gap*u);
draw bbox currentpicture
            withcolor green;
```

Example
3-2-2

3.2.3 Adding text—some gory details

In the previous section we passed text to TEX using `btex ... etex`. "TEX" in this case was plain TEX, not LATEX. In this section we examine the process in more detail and see how to use LATEX; we also look carefully at font handling.

When METAPOST first meets `btex`, it calls a script **makempx**. This script runs a program called **mptotex** that scans the `.mp` file and extracts all the `btex...etex` fragments into a temporary file, surrounding them by appropriate macros, so that each fragment is a "page" in this TeX file. It then calls TeX to typeset the material and passes the `.dvi` file to another program (**dvitomp**) that rewrites it into an `.mpx` file, which METAPOST can read back in. When METAPOST continues after **makempx** has finished, it inserts a picture expression read from the `.mpx` file for each `btex...etex` fragment.

Any text between the commands `verbatimtex` and `etex` is written to the external file, but not used to generate a picture; this lets you define macros, set up LaTeX document *Macros* class or package loading, or change defaults. In particular, if the first TeX environment of a METAPOST file starts with "`%&latex`", it tells METAPOST to call LaTeX and not TeX.

When the script runs behind the scenes, it looks for an environment variable called TEX to work out which program to run (e.g., `tex`, `latex`, `amstex`); you must *Environment* set this appropriately if, for instance, you have used `verbatimtex ...etex` to write `\documentclass{article}` to the file. Generally it is a better idea to write explicitly in your code (with "`%&latex`") which format is used, as the resulting code is more portable. Certain users use only the LaTeX format and forget to specify the format, making it difficult for others to use TeX sometimes and LaTeX at other times.

As an example, suppose you want to typeset some complex equations, which need the $\mathcal{AMS}$-LaTeX math package, as a METAPOST "label";[1] the following picture shows what to do. When the fragment is run through LaTeX, it is in *horizontal mode*, so we cannot simply type in the displayed equation. Instead we put it inside a `minipage`:

```
verbatimtex
\documentclass{article}
\usepackage{times,amsmath}
\begin{document}
etex;
picture p; path q;
p:=thelabel(btex \Large
\begin{minipage}{4in}
\begin{gather}
\iint\limits_A f(x,y)\,dx\,dy\qquad
\iiint\limits_A f(x,y,z)\,dx\,dy\,dz\\
\iiiint\limits_A f(w,x,y,z)\,dw\,dx\,dy\,dz
\qquad\idotsint\limits_A f(x_1,\dots,x_k)
\end{gather}
\end{minipage}
etex,(0,0));
q:=fullcircle scaled 2.5in;
draw q;
clip p to q;
draw p rotated 90;
```

This example also demonstrates how the shape of one picture can be used as a clipping path for another (we see only the portion of the equation that falls within the circle).

---

[1] Of course, the equation numbers and labels are *not* visible from the main LaTeX file that includes this picture.

You do not need to add \end{document}, as METAPOST takes care of this task for you. Before running METAPOST, the environment variable TEX must be set to "latex" or the special "%&latex" comment must be added as explained earlier.

The TEX package

The small package TEX provides a TEX command that, when called on a string, returns a picture containing the application of TEX to this string.

For LaTEX labels, there are two packages based on the same principles. Both packages are much faster than TEX because they store all labels in one LaTEX file—there is not a separate LaTEX file for each label. In both cases the METAPOST file needs to be run twice to produce the correct results.

The latexMP package

- The latexMP package, by Jens-Uwe Morawski, provides a flexible interface for LaTEX labels. It defines a setupLaTeXMP command that can be used, among other things, to set the LaTEX class, its options, and additional packages to be loaded. latexMP also has special provisions for the handling of color and transparency in METAPOST labels, but these features are accessible only with PDFLaTEX. The following minimal example uses the textext function:

$i = 5$
$i = 4$
$i = 3$
$i = 2$
$i = 1$

```
input latexmp;

for i=1 upto 5:
  label(textext("$i=" & (decimal i) & "$"),(0,10*i));
endfor
```

Example 3-2-4

The next example includes color labels:

```
input latexmp;
beginfig(1);
setupLaTeXMP(textextlabel=enable,multicolor=enable);
color Qcolor; Qcolor:=(0.8,0.4,0.7);
color Lcolor; Lcolor:=(0.2,0.9,0.2);
  label(
    "\parbox{5cm}{\color{blue}The \textcolor{Qcolor}{quick}"
    & " \textcolor[rgb]{0.6,0.4,0}{brown fox}"
    & " jumps over \textcolor[Hsv]{30,0.5,0.9}{the"
    & " \textcolor{Lcolor}{lazy} dog}.}",(200,100));
```

The quick brown fox jumps over the lazy dog.

Example 3-2-5

The latex.mp package

- A similar, but simpler, package latex, by José Luis Díaz, requires a first call to initlatex for setting up the LaTEX packages to load (even if no LaTEX package is loaded).

The prologues variable

You can set a METAPOST variable prologues to determine how fonts are handled. With the value 0, the output is dependent on an application (e.g., dvips) that can resolve references to TEX fonts that have to be downloaded and included in the output file. If the value is greater than 0, METAPOST tries to generate free-standing PostScript output using either troff (1) or TEX (any value greater than 1).

When `prologues` is set to 0, METAPOST does not try to write self-contained Post-Script, but inserts special comments for each font in the output that give the name and size needed, like this:

```
%*Font: ptmr8r 9.96265 9.96265 28:c06
%*Font: cmsy10 9.96265 9.96265 01:8
%*Font: cmr7 6.97385 6.97385 31:8
```

When the picture is included in a LaTeX document, the `.dvi`-to-PostScript program needs to read these commands and supply the fonts requested, either as bitmaps or in PostScript Type 1 form. Currently, only Tom Rokicki's **dvips** understands this convention.

To ask METAPOST to write PostScript that can be included by any application or edited by programs such as **Adobe Illustrator**, set `prologues` to 2 (avoid 1; this value is for **troff**). Now each time you use a font (either as a META string or in a TeX fragment), METAPOST looks it up in **dvips**'s `psfonts.map` control file to find the real PostScript font name and writes the PostScript file accordingly. It does *not* embed the font in the output, so unless your fonts are built into your printer, you will have to supply them explicitly with your job. If you use Type 1 Computer Modern fonts, you must ensure that they are listed in `psfonts.map` and downloaded to the printer.

The drawback of this approach is that you cannot control the font encoding when using PostScript fonts. For instance, the entry for "ptmb8r" in `psfonts.map` has instructions for re-encoding it differently from the standard encoding. The METAPOST setup currently ignores these instructions, however, so any characters outside the standard ASCII range are likely to be wrong. If you want the METAPOST output to work with non-ASCII characters, we recommend that you use font names and TeX font metrics that are set up to use Adobe Standard Encoding for text fonts. For mathematics, you have to make sure that no re-encoding is required. Using Alan Jeffrey's LaTeX package **mathptm** helps, but it still uses Computer Modern (e.g., for square root signs). As a last resort, you can create genuinely free-standing PostScript files by including the picture in a LaTeX document that is otherwise empty and running that document to PostScript.

3.2.4 Internal structures

Introductions to METAPOST often present it as a technical drawing tool. In reality its power goes beyond the ability to define points and draw curves, fill surfaces, or label objects.

Of course, the ability to use equations as a geometrical aid is very convenient, but the great strength of METAPOST is that it keeps its current drawing in memory until the figure is closed with `endfig`. As a consequence, it becomes possible to reflect on past drawing instructions, either for introspection or as a basis for new drawings.

We give here a flavor of the latent power under the hood. When drawing commands are issued, they are actually stored in the special picture variable `currentpicture`. This variable, like any `picture` variable, has a tree-like structure, where nodes are operators that apply to leaves.

The `currentpicture` can at any time be saved or even reset. The following example first draws a circle, saves it in a `picture` variable, and then produces two reduced copies of the same drawing, after having reset it (using `nullpicture`):

```
draw fullcircle scaled 2cm;
picture savepic;
savepic=currentpicture;
currentpicture:=nullpicture;
draw savepic scaled .5;
draw savepic scaled .5 shifted (3cm,0);
```

Example
3-2-6

A picture is usually made of paths, and paths can be manipulated. New pictures can be created by applying changes to a path's components. For instance, we can remove one end point of a path:

```
path p,q;
p=(0,0)..(1cm,0)..(2cm,1cm)..(3cm,3cm);
q=subpath(1,3) of p;
```

It is also possible to traverse a picture using the `for..within` construction and identify its components. In the following example, two paths are drawn, but only the longest is overdrawn in blue:

```
draw (0,0)..(1cm,0)..(2cm,1cm)..(3cm,3cm);
draw (0,0)--(3cm,3cm);
picture p;
p=currentpicture;
for i within p:
  if stroked i:
    if length(pathpart i)>2:
      draw pathpart i withcolor blue;
    fi
  fi
endfor;
```

Example
3-2-7

The fact that METAPOST keeps the drawing structure at hand, and doesn't output it immediately, makes it possible to maintain firm control over the drawing. Intersections can be computed within METAPOST and the results of those computations can be used to influence other parts of the figure, without the need to run METAPOST several times.

A very interesting application of the introspection `for..within` loop are Anthony Phan's macros implementing transparency in METAPOST (see Section 4.1.6).

Another interesting application is a macro that determines when two pictures are closest. It is, for instance, fairly easy to write a macro that puts two paths in tangent contact, assuming one path is fixed and the other rotates around a point, no matter how the paths are shaped, because METAPOST has access to the paths. By contrast, if the paths were output immediately, extra calculations—either in METAPOST or in another language—would be needed to achieve the same result. Only METAPOST's intersection capabilities are used in the straightforward solution.

The following macro summarizes all the introspection capabilities available using
within. Each object is tested with the functions stroked, filled, textual, bounded,
and clipped to see what type it is. The macro can be used on any picture variable. It merely
traverses the variable and performs the draw, fill, or clip, and sets bounds as needed. This
should produce a copy of the picture given as an argument.

```
vardef reconstruct(expr p)=
  for i within p:
    if stroked i:
      draw pathpart i withpen penpart i
           withcolor (redpart i,greenpart i,bluepart i)
           dashed dashpart i;
    elseif filled i:
      fill pathpart i withcolor (redpart i,greenpart i,bluepart i);
    elseif textual i:
      save T;
      transform T;
      xpart  T=xpart  i;ypart  T=ypart  i;
      xxpart T=xxpart i;xypart T=xypart i;
      yxpart T=yxpart i;yypart T=yypart i;
      draw (textpart i infont fontpart i) transformed T
           withcolor (redpart i,greenpart i,bluepart i);
    elseif bounded i:
      reconstruct(i);
      setbounds currentpicture to pathpart i;
    elseif clipped i:
      reconstruct(i);
      clip currentpicture to pathpart i;
    fi;
  endfor;
  if length(p)=1: % special case
    %  (bounded and clipped are ignored above when
    %   the picture contains only one component)
    if bounded p:setbounds currentpicture to pathpart p;fi;
    if clipped p:clip currentpicture to pathpart p;fi;
  fi;
enddef;
```

3.2.5   File input and output

METAPOST files can be organized as modules and loaded with the familiar input command.

It is also possible to read individual lines from a file by using readfrom. However, a file
read with this command stays open unless the end of file has been reached. As this can sometimes be a problem, Ulrik Vieth wrote a short macro called closefrm (CTAN: graphics/
metapost/contrib/macros/misc) that attempts to close a file by reading until its end.

The `readfrom` command reads a whole line and returns a string. This string can then be analyzed by the user. Suppose a file `data.txt` contains two lines: one with the numerical value 3, and the other with the pair (7,2). These two lines can be read into METAPOST variables as follows:

```
numeric val;
pair p;
val=scantokens readfrom "data.txt";
p=scantokens readfrom "data.txt";
```

where `scantokens` is used to convert a string into the data it represents.

METAPOST can also be used to write output either to the terminal or to a file. Writing to the terminal can be done with `message`, which is useful for debugging. For instance, the following example shows how the value of the `time` variable can be output on the terminal:

```
message "The current value of time is:" & decimal time;
```

In general, writing to a file is done with the `write` command, as shown in the following examples:

```
write "hello" to "tmp1";
write "How are you?" to "tmp1";
write EOF to "tmp1"; % close the tmp1 file
write "a=17;" to "tmp2";
write EOF to "tmp2"; % close the tmp2 file
input tmp2;
message "a=" & decimal a;
end
```

Several packages use this feature—for instance, the **3d** package when it outputs a shell script.

3.3 Running the META programs

3.3.1 Running METAFONT

To some extent METAFONT is like TEX; it has a low-level language on top of which you can write user-level macros. Most users do not start from scratch but rather load a prebuilt library of useful commands ("base" files), such as the "plain" base written by Donald Knuth. When a system implements "METAFONT", you can normally assume that the "plain" library is installed.

Each character, or object, in a METAFONT file is created by enclosing the code in a `beginchar...endchar` group. The `beginchar` has four parameters: the name of the letter being produced, the width, the height, and the depth. The following code, which consists of a very simple line, creates a "letter" at position "X" in the font:

```
beginchar ("X", 50, 50, 0);
draw (0,0)..(50,50)..(50,0);
```

```
endchar;
end
```

You write a font source simply by creating a METAFONT file with a set of characters defined. You must then run the program on it to create the bitmap .gf format output. An interactive session with METAFONT to run a font file might look like this (on a Unix machine):

```
> mf
This is METAFONT, Version 2.71828 (Web2C 7.5.3)
**\mode=qms;input logo10
(/local/tex2004/texmf-dist/fonts/source/public/mflogo/logo10.mf
(/local/tex2004/texmf-dist/fonts/source/public/mflogo/logo.mf [77] [69]
[84] [65] [70] [80] [83] [79] [78]) )
Font metrics written on logo10.tfm.
Output written on logo10.300gf (9 characters, 1124 bytes).
Transcript written on logo10.log.
```

The line with the "∗∗" prompt tells us that METAFONT is waiting for input. At that point we indicate the device for which we want to generate bitmapped fonts by using the mode command, and we ask METAFONT to read a font source file and generate a bitmap font. Now the resulting .gf file is transformed to .pk format for use with a previewer or printer driver (although it is possible to use it directly):

```
> gftopk -verbose logo10.300gf
This is GFtoPK, Version 2.3 (Web2C 7.5.3)
'METAFONT output 2006.05.01:1412'
1124 bytes packed to 512 bytes.
```

You can also ask METAFONT to preview the character it is creating on the screen as it goes along.

The *mode* is very important; it is here that you tell METAFONT about your printer or screen. Because the software is creating bitmaps, it needs to know how many pixels there are to an inch and how they are made. There is, for instance, a considerable difference between printers that (conceptually!) start with a white sheet of paper and put black dots on it and printers that start with a black sheet and remove the areas that should be white. Mode descriptions for a large number of devices are available in a special METAFONT file called modes.mf that is maintained by Karl Berry (available with most METAFONT distributions and on CTAN). Typical names are "cx" (the Canon 300 dpi laser printer engine used in many machines), "ljfour" (HP LaserJet IV at 600 dpi), and "linoone" (Linotronic typesetter at 1270 dpi). The setup for each device provides values for a number of METAFONT internal variables, as this example for a LaserJet IV shows:

```
mode_def ljfour =
  mode_param (pixels_per_inch, 600);
  mode_param (blacker, .25);
```

```
      mode_param (fillin, 0);
      mode_param (o_correction, 1);
      mode_common_setup_;
   enddef;
```

This is explained in [72, pages 90–93]. After setting the mode, you should normally execute the command `mode_setup`, which initializes the internal setup appropriately for the mode.

The *dpi* (dots per inch) parameter in the mode description is used to name the output file in conjunction with the magnification. METAFONT's bitmap output is a `.gf` (*generic font*) file, which can be compressed into an equivalent `.pk` (*packed*) format by the auxiliary program **gftopk**. If users specify an unknown mode or no mode at all, they will obtain file names with the extension `.2602gf`. This behavior invokes METAFONT's "proof" mode, used by font designers to get a magnified view of their fonts at a resolution of 2601.72 dpi— 36 pixels per point (hence the 2602 file extension).

If we run METAFONT again, this time with the mode for a Linotronic typesetter at medium resolution, the output file has a different name and the `.gf` file is three times larger:

```
 > mf
This is METAFONT, Version 2.71828 (Web2C 7.5.3)
**\mode=linoone;input logo10
(/local/tex2004/texmf-dist/fonts/source/public/mflogo/logo10.mf
(/local/tex2004/texmf-dist/fonts/source/public/mflogo/logo.mf [77] [69]
[84] [65] [70] [80] [83] [79] [78]) )
Font metrics written on logo10.tfm.
Output written on logo10.1270gf (9 characters, 3900 bytes).
Transcript written on logo10.log.
 > gftopk -verbose logo10.1270gf
This is GFtoPK, Version 2.3 (Web2C 7.5.3)
'METAFONT output 2006.05.01:1415'
3900 bytes packed to 1552 bytes.
```

Besides the `.gf` file, METAFONT usually creates a metric file (extension `.tfm`). The metric file should always be the same, regardless of the mode or magnification selected. Although TEX can scale the information in the `.tfm` files, the glyphs in the bitmap files cannot be scaled. If you need a bigger character, you must run METAFONT again to generate the bitmap images at the correct size and resolution.

Because TEX font sizes increase in geometric ratios ("magsteps", which go in steps of 1.2), you can specify values for those magsteps to METAFONT and create larger characters. For example:

```
 > mf
This is METAFONT, Version 2.71828 (Web2C 7.5.3)
**\mode=cx; mag=magstep(1); input logo10;
(/local/tex2004/texmf-dist/fonts/source/public/mflogo/logo10.mf
(/local/tex2004/texmf-dist/fonts/source/public/mflogo/logo.mf [77] [69]
[84] [65] [70] [80] [83] [79] [78]) )
```

```
Font metrics written on logo10.tfm.
Output written on logo10.360gf (9 characters, 1280 bytes).
Transcript written on logo10.log.
```

The mag=magstep(1) means that, starting from the resolution defined in the mode (300 dpi in this case), a font of 1.2×300 dpi is created (i.e., .360gf).

There is a difference between a font of letters 10 points high (e.g., cmr10) run through METAFONT with a magnification of 1.2 so as to create letters 12 points high, and a font of letters 12 points high (e.g., cmr12) run through METAFONT without magnification. In the former case, the 10-point design is simply scaled up, while the latter has a real design for the larger size. In the context of drawing pictures, however, rather than fonts, this distinction is seldom made; pictures are usually created at the "right" size by specifying the scale in METAFONT.

A picture created with METAFONT can be included as a font character in the following way:

```
\font\test=drawing
{\test A}
```

In this example, drawing is the name of a font containing METAFONT characters, and the font is loaded under the name \test. The character at position 65 (A) in this font is then selected, assuming there is such a character in the font.

3.3.2 Running METAPOST

Derived by John Hobby from the source of METAFONT, METAPOST understands a language almost identical to that of METAFONT but generates PostScript files instead of .gf files. These output files can be included as figures in a LaTeX document with the standard graphics package. METAPOST is designed not for creating fonts, but rather for drawing general pictures and graphs. It differs from METAFONT in some important ways:

1. Since the output is not a bitmap but PostScript code, it is *not* device-dependent and you need not be concerned with *modes*.

2. The program is intended as a general tool, so it allows incorporation of normal LaTeX code in the picture for labels, captions, and so forth.

3. Color support has been added.

The METAPOST manual [47] details the differences between the METAFONT and METAPOST languages. Almost all drawing commands that work in METAFONT also work in METAPOST, but the latter has extra commands.

METAPOST does not create high-quality PostScript Type 1 fonts from METAFONT sources, unfortunately, although it can be used to create the less sophisticated Type 3 font format (see, for instance, [14]).

Input structure Unlike METAFONT programs, which usually consist of beginchar...endchar pairs, a METAPOST file usually consists of pairs of beginfig and endfig and an end statement after the final pair. The beginfig has a parameter that is the extension of the output file corresponding to each figure. You need not specify the size of the picture: METAPOST works that out and inserts the correct %%BoundingBox line in the output. The default units are PostScript points (what TEX calls "big points"—72 to the inch rather than 72.27), though explicit lengths can of course be given. The following very simple METAPOST program draws a one-inch square:

```
beginfig(1);
draw (0,0)--(0,72)--(72,72)--(72,0)--cycle;
endfig;
end
```

If this program is named test.mp and run through METAPOST, it produces the PostScript file test.1, which looks like this:

```
%!PS
%%BoundingBox: -1 -1 73 73
%%Creator: MetaPost
%%CreationDate: 2005.11.21:2155
%%Pages: 1
%%EndProlog
%%Page: 1 1
 0 0.5 dtransform truncate idtransform setlinewidth pop [] 0 setdash
 1 setlinejoin 10 setmiterlimit
newpath 0 0 moveto
0 72 lineto
72 72 lineto
72 0 lineto
 closepath stroke
showpage
%%EOF
```

Graphics inclusion with LATEX and PDFLATEX This output is a normal EPS file[1] that can be included in your LATEX document with the **graphics** package or any other application. If you use text labels, however, matters can become more complicated (see Section 3.2.3).

When creating a PDF file with PDFLATEX, it is necessary to tell PDFLATEX that the file is a METAPOST file. Otherwise, one runs into an error message like this:

```
! LaTeX Error: Unknown graphics extension: .1.
```

One solution is to rename the METAPOST EPS files with the extension .mps. In that case, PDFLATEX knows that the files are METAPOST files and processes them correctly.

---

[1] Notice that the bounding box is larger than you might expect, due to the width of the line drawing the box.

Another possibility is to tell PDFLᴬTEX that graphics files are METAPOST by default. This is done by writing

```
\DeclareGraphicsRule{*}{mps}{*}{}
```

in the preamble of the LᴬTEX file.

3.3.3 Previewing

When preparing a drawing, there is often a trial-and-error phase in which the drawing is designed incrementally. It is therefore useful to be able to preview such a drawing, which can be done in several ways. For example, a drawing can be included in a LᴬTEX file and the file can be converted into a PostScript or PDF file. But there are at least three other ways to do previewing, which make it much simpler to see the drawings being produced.

mptopdf (by Hans Hagen) is a Perl script that is part of ConTEXt. When called on a METAPOST file, it produces a PDF file for each beginfig/endfig environment. These *The mptopdf program* files are useful for previewing or can be included as PDF graphics in a PDFLᴬTEX run. There are certain METAPOST constructions—for instance, those in metafun—that are under-stood only by mptopdf, but the result can nevertheless be included in LᴬTEX documents.

mproof is a set of TEX macros providing a minimal wrapper around a METAPOST file. *The mproof package* It is used as follows, on one or more METAPOST outputs:

```
$ tex mproof lens.1
This is TeX, Version 3.141592 (Web2C 7.5.4)
(/usr/share/texmf-tetex/tex/plain/mproof/mproof.tex
(/usr/share/texmf-tetex/tex/generic/epsf/epsf.tex
This is 'epsf.tex' v2.7k <10 July 1997>
))
lens.1: BoundingBox: llx = 413 lly = -317 urx = 823 ury = 142
lens.1: scaled width = 411.53275pt scaled height = 460.71593pt
[1]
Output written on mproof.dvi (1 page, 400 bytes).
Transcript written on mproof.log.
```

The DVI file can be converted to PostScript and previewed or printed. mproof has several minor limitations: it cannot be used with PDFTEX, and the input file names cannot contain underscores. These two problems are solved when using the mpsproof macros.

mpsproof (by Daniel H. Luecking) is based on mproof. It is used as follows, with TEX or *The mpsproof package* PDFTEX:

```
$ pdftex mpsproof diopter.1 diopter.2
This is pdfeTeX, Version 3.141592-1.21a-2.2 (Web2C 7.5.4)
entering extended mode
(./mpsproof.tex (/usr/share/texmf-tetex/tex/context/base/supp-pdf.tex
(/usr/share/texmf-tetex/tex/context/base/supp-mis.tex
loading : Context Support Macros / Miscellaneous (2004.10.26)
)
```

```
loading : Context Support Macros / PDF (2004.03.26)
)) [MP to PDF] (./diopter.1) [MP to PDF] (./diopter.2) [1{/var/lib/texm
f/fonts/map/pdftex/updmap/pdftex.map}] [2]</usr/share/texmf-tetex/fonts
/type1/bluesky/cm/cmr10.pfb></usr/share/texmf-tetex/fonts/type1/bluesky
/cm/cmr7.pfb></usr/share/texmf-tetex/fonts/type1/bluesky/cm/cmtex10.pfb>
Output written on mpsproof.pdf (2 pages, 13626 bytes).
Transcript written on mpsproof.log.
```

mpsproof also improves upon **mproof** by allowing file names to contain underscores and by allowing the syntax: `tex mpsproof \\noheaders pic.1`, which omits all added text. This is useful when creating an EPS or PDF file containing just the figure.

3.4 Some basic METAPOST libraries

3.4.1 The metafun **package**

Only a few general packages other than the **plain** macros are supplied with METAPOST. The **metafun** package is a good supplement to **plain** that offers a variety of useful constructions. It is primarily designed for use with ConTEXt, but a number of its features can also be used in plain METAPOST and LATEX. We give here a few examples of interesting features that **metafun** adds to the **plain** macros. The **metafun** package is loaded with

```
input metafun
```

In addition to `fullcircle` and `unitsquare`, **metafun** provides `unitcircle`, `fullsquare`, `unitdiamond`, and `fulldiamond`:

```
input metafun
draw fulldiamond scaled 1cm withcolor blue;
```

Example
3-4-1

There are also macros for quartercircles: `llcircle`, `lrcircle`, `urcircle`, and `ulcircle`. Half-circles are obtained with `tcircle`, `bcircle`, `lcircle`, and `rcircle`. Four triangle corners are also provided: `lltriangle`, `lrtriangle`, `ultriangle`, and `urtriangle`.

There are several operators in **metafun** for changing paths. `randomized` and `squeezed` produce the following results:

```
input metafun
draw unitsquare scaled 1.5cm
                randomized (1mm,2mm);
draw unitsquare scaled 1.5cm
                squeezed (1mm,5mm)
                shifted (3cm,0);
```

Example
3-4-2

The smoothed operator introduces round corners:

Example
3-4-3

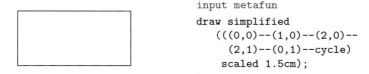

```
input metafun
draw unitsquare scaled 1.5cm smoothed 2mm;
```

Paths can also be simplified, with simplified:

```
input metafun
draw simplified
    (((0,0)--(1,0)--(2,0)--
      (2,1)--(0,1)--cycle)
    scaled 1.5cm);
```

Example
3-4-4

metafun extends the color capabilities of plain and allows the use of CMYK colors, transparency, and various operations such as greying. Most of these features will work properly only when ConTEXt is used as the TEX engine. If you want to use them in a LATEX document, the METAPOST files can be converted to PDF files with mptopdf and then included in LATEX using the standard graphics package.

For more details on metafun, consult its excellent manual [43].

3.4.2 The boxes package

When METAPOST was first made public, only two general-purpose macro libraries were available: the boxes and graph packages, both written by John Hobby. Since then, many other packages have been introduced—some of them very general, others more specialized.

In this section, we describe the boxes package; in the next section, we examine META-OBJ, which extends boxes. The main application packages, some of them with boxing capabilities, are described in Chapter 4.

One motivation for developing METAPOST was to provide tools comparable to those available to troff users. One of the best troff tools is the pic language (see Section 1.4.3 on page 17, and [67]), which is often used for drawing and linking boxes. John Hobby's boxes library of METAPOST macros combined with standard METAPOST facilities can do a similar job.

The boxes package is loaded with the following command:

```
input boxes
```

The idea behind the package is that drawings consist of four types of statements:

1. Creating named boxes (META pictures)

2. Expressing relationships among boxes

3. Asking the system to place the boxes

4. Joining the boxes with lines and arrows

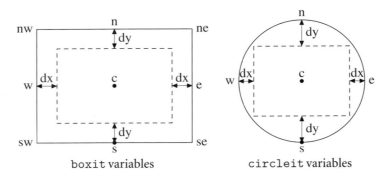

boxit variables   circleit variables

Figure 3.2: Cardinal points in boxit and circleit

This means that you need not specify exact positions for objects, but only their relationship to other objects.

There are two basic **boxes** commands to create boxes and circles:

> boxit.*name*(*picture*)   circleit.*name*(*picture*)

These commands draw rectangular and circular frames around the *picture*. An additional package, rboxes, provides another command, rboxit, that draws a rectangular frame with rounded corners. The result of these commands is an object *name*, and you have access to a set of variables *name*.c, *name*.e, *name*.n, and so forth, which are the coordinates of the object's cardinal points (see Figure 3.2). The variables dx and dy are the gap between the picture and the surrounding box; you can either set these explicitly or allow METAPOST to use the values defaultdx and defaultdy, respectively. The circmargin variable (default 2 points) determines the minimum gap around the text in circleit.

The relationships between boxes are specified as a set of equation statements:

> boxjoin(*equations*)

Within the equations, you describe the relationships between notional boxes *a* and *b* by reference to their cardinal points; these are applied to successive calls of boxit. You can also explicitly write equations to specify the relationship between any boxes.

Once you have created a series of boxes, you can commit them to the page with the following commands:

> drawboxed(*box*₁,*box*₂,…*box*ₙ)   drawunboxed(*box*₁,*box*₂,…*box*ₙ)
> drawboxes(*box*₁,*box*₂,…*box*ₙ)   pic(*box*)

These commands simply require a list of objects defined with boxit or circleit. The first draws the boxes and their contents, the second draws just the contents, and the third draws just the boxes. The fourth command returns the drawn box as a META "picture" that can be rendered with draw or fill in the usual way.

You can now join the boxes with normal META lines or curves. Two useful standard METAPOST macros make lines with arrowheads at one or both ends:

```
drawarrow path        drawdblarrow path
```

The *path* specifications can use the special coordinates available for each box. For example, `drawarrow one.n--two.s` draws a line between the top of box "one" and the bottom of box "two". The `dir` qualifier is useful for drawing curved lines to connect boxes, as these examples demonstrate:

Example 3-4-5

```
input boxes
boxjoin(a.se=b.nw);
boxit.one("One");  boxit.two("Two");
drawboxed(one,two);
drawarrow one.n{up}..two.n;
```

Example 3-4-6

```
input boxes
boxjoin(a.se=b.nw-(10,-10));
boxit.one("One");  boxit.two("Two");
drawunboxed(one,two);
drawarrow one.n{dir 45}..two.n;
```

Often one wants to draw lines that conceptually link the center points of two boxes but stop at their boundaries. This can be accomplished with three useful standard METAPOST macros:

```
bpath box name        cutafter path        cutbefore path
```

bpath produces the bounding rectangle of a box as a path. When `cutafter` and `cutbefore` follow a drawing command, they control its interaction with their following *path*. Thus, in the next example, we say that the line joining the center of two boxes should start upon leaving the bounding rectangle of the first box and stop when it reaches the bounding rectangle of the second.

Example 3-4-7

```
input boxes
boxjoin(a.n=b.s-(20,60));
boxit.one("One");circleit.two("Two");
drawboxes(one,two);
drawarrow one.c--two.c
 cutbefore bpath one cutafter bpath two;
boxjoin();
boxit.three("Three");three.w=one.e+(20,0);
fill bpath three withcolor blue;
draw bpath three;draw pic(three) withcolor white;
```

We also show here how to specify the position of the third box in absolute relation to the first box: the default rules are turned off with an empty `boxjoin` equation.

Labeling the boxes is usually easy; but what about labeling the lines joining the boxes? Here we can use the `point` macro:

> `point` *distance* of *path*

This macro returns a coordinate of a point *distance* along *path*. It can be used, with the macro `length` to compute the length of a path, as the parameter for `label`:

```
input boxes
boxjoin(a.e=b.w-(30,0));
boxit.one("One");
circleit.two("Two");
drawboxed(one,two);
label.lft("1.",one.w);
label.rt("2.",two.e);
label.top("a.",
  point .5*length  (one.c{dir 45}..two.c)
    of (one.c{dir 45}..two.c) );
draw one.c{dir 45}..two.c
  cutbefore bpath one
  cutafter bpath two;
```

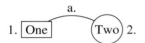

Example
3-4-8

A more elegant version of this example puts both tasks—drawing the line and calculating the label coordinate—into a META `vardef` macro (borrowed from the METAPOST graph documentation). This contains two statements, separated by `;`. The first draws the connecting line, and the second generates a coordinate that is returned as the value of the overall macro. Judicious use of `tension` and variations in direction make the joining curve a little more interesting.

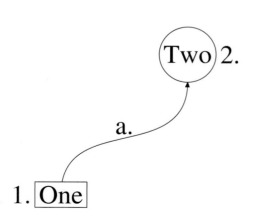

```
input boxes
vardef labelarrow
  (suffix BoxA,BoxB) expr Line =
    drawarrow Line
    cutbefore bpath BoxA
    cutafter bpath BoxB;
    point (.5*length Line) of Line
enddef;
defaultscale:=2;
boxjoin(a.e=b.w-(.75in,1.5in));
boxit.one("One");  circleit.two("Two");
drawboxed(one,two);
label.lft("1.",one.w);
label.rt("2.",two.e);
label.top("a.",labelarrow(one,two)
  one.c{dir90}..tension0.8..{dir90}two.s);
```

Example
3-4-9

We conclude this section with an extended example showing how to use the **boxes** package for typical computer science diagrams. This output is also printed in (rather arbitrary) color in Color Plate I(b) to show some of the ways to use color with the **boxes** package. The same diagram is drawn with the XY-pic TEX package on page 485; comparison of the code is interesting for those who need to produce this sort of picture.

Example
3-4-10

```
input boxes
defaultfont:="ptmb8r";
vardef labelarrow
 (suffix BoxA,BoxB) expr Line =
  drawarrow Line
  cutbefore bpath BoxA
  cutafter bpath BoxB;
  point (.5*length Line) of Line
enddef;

color yellow,orange;
yellow:=red+green;   orange:=red+(green/2);
boxjoin(a.n=b.s-(0,.5in));
defaultscale:=1.5; circmargin:=4pt;
circleit.In("in"); circleit.One("1"); circleit.Two("2");
circleit.Three("3"); circleit.Four("4");
boxjoin(); circmargin:=16pt; circleit.X(""); X.c=Four.c;
drawunboxed(One,Two,Three,Four,In,X);
drawarrow In.n--One.s;
label.rt("a",labelarrow(One,Two) One.c--Two.c)
  withcolor red;
label.rt("b",labelarrow(Two,Three) Two.c--Three.c)
  withcolor green;
label.rt("b",labelarrow(Three,Four) Three.c--Four.c)
  withcolor green;
label.rt("a",labelarrow(Four,Two) Four.c{dir335}..
  {dir205}Two.c)  withcolor red;
label.lft("a",labelarrow(Three,Two) Three.c{dir205}..
  {dir335}Two.c)  withcolor red;
label.lft("b",labelarrow(Four,One) Four.c{dir180}..
  tension2..One.c)   withcolor green;
label.rt("b",labelarrow(One,One) One.c{dir45}..One.c+(40,0)
  ..{dir120}One.c) withcolor green;
label.rt("a",labelarrow(Two,Two) Two.c{dir65}..Two.c+(40,0)
  ..{dir100}Two.c)  withcolor red;
fill bpath One withcolor blue;
fill bpath Two withcolor yellow;
fill bpath Three withcolor orange;
draw bpath Four;   draw pic Two;
draw pic One withcolor white;
draw pic Three withcolor white;
pickup pencircle scaled 2pt;
draw bpath X dashed evenly withcolor (1 , .75, .8);
```

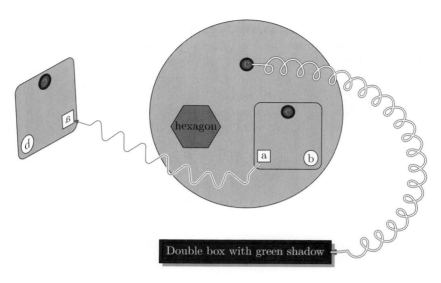

Figure 3.3: A complex example produced by METAOBJ

3.5 The METAOBJ package

METAOBJ (Denis Roegel, [40, 100, 102]) is a system for high-level object-oriented drawing based on METAPOST. The name METAOBJ is short for "METAPOST Objects".

METAOBJ can be viewed as an approximate extension of the **boxes** package, but one in which structured objects can easily be built and manipulated. A standard library of objects is provided: basic objects, basic containers, box alignment constructors, recursive objects, trees, proof trees, and matrices. In addition, METAOBJ can connect objects with links inspired by those found in the **PSTricks** package.

METAOBJ is normally available in standard installations of METAPOST and is loaded using `input metaobj`. It can be a very resource-intensive package and may require you to increase the resources defined in the METAPOST configuration file.

A complex drawing created by METAOBJ is given in Figure 3.3 and reproduced in Color Plate IV(b). The source code for this example goes beyond the scope of this book but can be found in the documentation of the package [102].

Loading METAOBJ   All of the following examples assume that METAOBJ has been properly loaded and that each figure is given in a `beginfig/endfig` pair.

3.5.1 Underlying principles

METAOBJ was created with some important principles in mind, following John Hobby's **boxes** package, but also other TₑX-related packages such as **PSTricks**:

- An object should be a structure with a shape and possibly a contents.

- Objects should be created with constructors.

- It should be possible to have "floating" objects as it makes their positioning as easy as in the **boxes** package.

- It should be possible to transform objects—for instance, by rotations.

- There should be a simple mechanism that allows specification of default behaviors, which can be overriden.

- It should be possible to make composite objects—for instance, to put a square within a circle.

METAOBJ meets all of these requirements, and it also provides means to define new classes of objects.

However, METAOBJ also has its limits. It is not fully object-oriented, there is, for instance, no inheritance mechanism. Another limitation is the syntax, which is not as flexible as a TEX syntax.

3.5.2 METAOBJ concepts

Objects have names, like boxes in the **boxes** package. Internally, an integer is associated with an object, and this number is used to access the object in certain circumstances. The `Obj` *Object names* command can be used to find out the object name from the object number, as discussed later.

Objects are created with constructors, such as `newBox`. Constructor variants, such as `new_Box` and `new_Box_`, are available for special purposes that are not covered here, although they may be used in certain examples. Once an object has been created, it cannot normally be reassigned, except by clearing it beforehand with `clearObj`.

Both objects and connection commands can have options. These options are usually given as a comma-separated list of strings, where each string has the syntax *key(value)*. The *Options* following command, for instance, has two options with values "s" for both keys *posA* and *posB*.

```
ncline(a)(b) "posA(s)","posB(s)";
```

METAOBJ provides linear transformations on objects. The next example shows how a double ellipse is scaled and rotated. The frames, contents, and cardinal points follow the *Operations on objects* operations.

```
input metaobj
newDEllipse.a(btex some text etex);
scaleObj(a,1.7);
rotateObj(a,45);
a.c=origin;
drawObj(a);
```

Example
3-5-1

Table 3.1: Options for EmptyBox and RandomBox

Option	Type	Default	Description
filled	boolean	false	whether filled
fillcolor	color	black	the fill color
framed	boolean	false	default for EmptyBox
		true	default for RandomBox
framewidth	numeric	.5bp	the frame thickness
framecolor	color	black	the color of the frame
framestyle	string	""	the style of the frame
shadow	boolean	false	whether there is a shadow
shadowcolor	color	black	the color of the shadow

3.5.3 Basic objects

METAOBJ defines a set of basic objects that are not containers of other objects, but appear at the leaves of a structure hierarchy.

> newEmptyBox.*name*(*wd*, *ht*) options

An empty box is a rectangle with a given size. Its options are shown in Table 3.1. It can be framed or not. However, the frame is visible only when show_empty_boxes is set to true. An empty box cannot contain anything—it is simply a frame. The bounding box is as expected, with nw at the upper-left corner, sw at the lower-left corner, ne at the upper-right corner, and se at the lower right corner.

```
input metaobj
show_empty_boxes:=true;

newEmptyBox.a(2cm,1cm) "framed(true)";
a.c=origin;
drawObj(a);
```

Example
3-5-2

METAOBJ defines Tn as a shortcut for new_EmptyBox(0,0) for compatibility with PSTricks.

EmptyBox shortcut

> newHRazor.*name*(*wd*) options   newVRazor.*name*(*ht*) options

An HRazor object is a degenerated empty box, where the height is 0. There is, therefore, only one size parameter. An HRazor is really an EmptyBox. The object can be framed or not, and the frame is visible only when show_empty_boxes is set to true. When not visible, an HRazor can be used as an horizontal strut in a variety of contexts. The width can also be negative. The bounding box is like the one for EmptyBox, except that the left corners are located at the same place, and the right corners are also located at the same place.

```
input metaobj;
show_empty_boxes:=true;
```

Example
3-5-3

```
show_empty_boxes:=true;
newHRazor.a(3cm) "framed(true)";
a.c=origin; drawObj(a);
```

There is also a similar `newVRazor` constructor. A VRazor is also a EmptyBox.

| newRandomBox.*name*(*wd,ht,dx,dy*) options |

A `RandomBox` is also an empty object, but the frame is slightly random. There are four parameters. The first two are the normal frame and are similar to the parameters of `EmptyBox`. The last two parameters are the maximum horizontal and vertical deviations. The deviations are computed randomly using a uniform random generator. The options and defaults are the same as those for `EmptyBox` (see Table 3.1 on the facing page), except that the `framed` option is `true` by default.

```
input metaobj;
show_empty_boxes:=true;
```

Example
3-5-4

```
newRandomBox.a(2cm,1cm,2mm,-1mm) "framed(true)";
a.c=origin; drawObj(a);
```

The cardinal points are now no longer identical to a rectangular bounding box and coincide with the corners of the visible box.

The thickness of the frame can be modified as follows:

```
input metaobj
newRandomBox.a(2cm,1cm,2mm,-1mm)
        "framed(true)", "framewidth(1mm)";
a.c=origin; drawObj(a);
```

Example
3-5-5

A random box can also be filled with a given color:

```
input metaobj
newRandomBox.a(1cm,5mm,2mm,-1mm)
   "framed(true)",  "framewidth(1mm)",
   "framecolor(green)",
   "filled(true)",
   "fillcolor(red)";
a.c=origin; drawObj(a);
```

Example
3-5-6

3.5.4 Connections

METAOBJ provides extensive support for connections. A connection is a high-level means to connect several objects or points of an object. METAOBJ implements connections similar (but not identical) to those available in PSTricks. The PSTricks connection commands are \ncline, \nccurve, and so forth, and METAOBJ uses exactly the same names. In addition to these standard connection commands, METAOBJ provides special variants of ncline, such as tcline and mcline.

All of the connection commands except nccircle connect two points or two objects. They can take as parameters either objects or points. Points must be given as pair variables. Objects can be given by their name or by a shortcut given to an object with the *name* option. If an object is given by its number and not its name, the Obj command can be used. For instance, if a and b are objects, we can write either ncline(a)(b) or

```
an=a; % store the object number in 'an'
bn=b; % store the object number in 'bn'
ncline(Obj(an))(Obj(bn));
```

Moreover, a connection is either *immediate* or *deferred*. An immediate connection is not part of an object and is drawn immediately. A deferred connection is stored in an object and drawn later. The syntax for both cases is the same, except that the object name, when present, is given as a suffix to the connection command. For instance, ncline.A(a)(b) is a deferred connection command connecting the objects a and b (assuming these are objects) and the connection is stored as part of the object A. If we write ncline(a)(b), we get an immediate connection between a and b.

Each of the connection commands has many options—for example, to change the style of the connection, the thickness of the line, and the point where the line starts. The options have types and default values. The main options are listed in Table 3.2 on the next page.

The default values can be changed with setCurveDefaultOption:

> setCurveDefaultOption(*key*, *value*)

For instance, the default value for *arrows* is "drawarrow", but it can be changed to "draw" using:

```
setCurveDefaultOption("arrows","draw");
```

We might also have written setCurveDefaultOption("arrows","-"); because METAOBJ provides several shortcuts for the kind of arrows. Currently the following shortcuts are implemented: "-" produces draw, "->" stands for drawarrow, and "<-" stands for rdrawarrow. Any other sequence of symbols is equivalent to "-".

Several of the options come in two flavors, one for each end of the connection. This is the case for *posA* and *posB*; special shortcuts are provided, so that *pos* is a shortcut option setting both *posA* and *posB*. For instance,

```
ncline(a)(b) "pos(s)";
```

Table 3.2: Options for connections (shortcuts are not shown)

Option	Type	Default	Description
posA	string	`"ic"`	where the connection starts
posB	string	`"ic"`	where the connection ends
name	string		connection name
linestyle	string	`""`	connection style; this can take values such as "dashed evenly" or "dashed withdots"
linewidth	numeric	`.5bp`	line thickness
linecolor	color	`black`	line color
arrows	string	`"drawarrow"`	name of a draw command such as `draw`, or `drawarrow`, or the shortcut of such a command
angleA	numeric		angle
angleB	numeric		angle
arcangleA	numeric	`10`	angle
arcangleB	numeric	`10`	angle
border	boolean	`0pt`	whether there is a border around the connection
bordercolor	color	`white`	color of the border
nodesepA	numeric	`0pt`	node separation at start (except for `ncbox` and `ncarcbox`)
nodesepB	numeric	`0pt`	node separation at end (except for `ncbox` and `ncarcbox`)
loopsize	numeric	`0.25cm`	parameter for `ncloop`
boxsize	numeric	`5mm`	parameter for `ncbox` and `ncarcbox`
boxheight	numeric	`-1pt`	parameter for `ncbox` and `ncarcbox`
boxdepth	numeric	`-1pt`	parameter for `ncbox` and `ncarcbox`
linearc	numeric	`0cm`	rounding of corners in connections
linetensionA	numeric	`1`	line tension used by `nccurve`
linetensionB	numeric	`1`	line tension used by `nccurve`
armA	numeric	`5mm`	connection arm at start
armB	numeric	`5mm`	connection arm at end
doubleline	boolean	`false`	whether the line is doubled
doublesep	numeric	`1pt`	separation between the two lines if *doubleline* is true
visible	boolean	`true`	whether the connection is visible
offsetA	pair	$(0,0)$	offset at the start of a connection
offsetB	pair	$(0,0)$	offset at the end of a connection
coilarmA	numeric	`5mm`	parameter for coils and zigzags
coilarmB	numeric	`5mm`	parameter for coils and zigzags
coilwidth	numeric	`1cm`	parameter for coils and zigzags
coilheight	numeric	`1`	parameter for coils and zigzags
coilaspect	numeric	`45`	parameter for coils and zigzags
coilinc	numeric	`90`	parameter for coils and zigzags
pathfilled	boolean	`false`	whether the path must be filled (none of the standard connections uses this option)
pathfillcolor	color	`black`	path fill color

is equivalent to

```
ncline(a)(b) "posA(s)","posB(s)";
```

These shortcuts can also be used with `setCurveDefaultOption` and passed to a `Tree` constructor. The shortcuts currently supported are *pos*, *coilarm*, *linetension*, *offset*, *arm*, *angle*, *arcangle*, and *nodesep*.

> `ncline(`*po1*, *po2*`)` options

`ncline` is the simplest of all connection commands. It connects either two points or two objects by a straight line. If two objects are connected, the line is cut before the bounding path of the first object and after the bounding path of the second object.

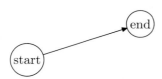

```
input metaobj
newCircle.a(btex start etex);
newCircle.b(btex end etex);
a.c=origin;
b.c-a.c=(3cm,1cm);
ncline(a)(b);  drawObj(a,b);
```

Example 3-5-7

In Example 3-5-7, the two circled objects are produced with the commands listed in blue. The first commands create circle objects "a" and "b", each framing the labels "start" and "end". The first object is centered at the origin, and the second is shifted from the first by (3cm,1cm). This code is used in most of the following examples.

If `ncline` is used to connect two object points (such as `a.c` and `b.c`), the bounding paths of the objects are not taken into account:

```
input metaobj
% Circles produced as before

drawObj(a,b);
ncline(a.c)(b.c);
```

Example 3-5-8

The thickness and the style of the line can easily be changed with the *linewidth* and *linestyle* options:

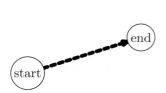

```
input metaobj
% Circles produced as before

ncline(a)(b)
  "linewidth(1mm)",
  "linestyle(dashed evenly)";
drawObj(a,b);
```

Example 3-5-9

The position where the line starts can be set with the *posA* option. Similarly, the position where the line ends can be set with the *posB* option. It must be one of the cardinal points of the object. The default positions are the `ic` points—that is, the centers of the internal interface (see the METAOBJ manual for more details). In the next example, `posA(n)` causes the line to start at a.n. In addition, we have changed the direction of the arrow with arrows(<-).

```
input metaobj
% Circles produced as before

ncline(a)(b) "posA(n)","arrows(<-)";
drawObj(a,b);
```

The starting point can also be offset by a vector with the *offsetA* option, and the end point by a similar *offsetB* option. These options differ from those found in PSTricks, where *offsetA* and *offsetB* are numerical values, not vectors.

```
input metaobj
% Circles produced as before

ncline(a)(b) "offsetA((1cm,0))";
drawObj(a,b);
```

A line can be doubled with *doubleline*, and the arrow style of the line can be changed with the *arrows* option. This option takes a name of a draw function such as draw or drawarrow as a parameter. A gap can be introduced at either end of the connection with the *nodesepA* and *nodesepB* options.

```
input metaobj
% Circles produced as before

ncline(a)(b) "doubleline(true)",
   "nodesepB(10mm)", "arrows(draw)";
drawObj(a,b);
```

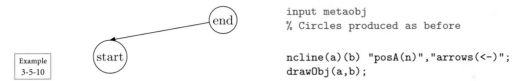

nccurve(*po1, po2*) **options**

nccurve draws a Bézier curve between the nodes. The default angles at which the curve leaves or reaches the nodes are those obtained when a straight line connects the nodes. Hence, without options, nccurve behaves like ncline. The two angles can be changed with the *angleA* and *angleB* options.

```
input metaobj
% Circles produced as before

nccurve(a)(b) "angleA(0)";
drawObj(a,b);
```

In the next example, more parameters are modified—namely, the *linecolor*, the *linewidth*, and *linestyle*—and the line is drawn double with *doubleline*.

```
input metaobj
% Circles produced as before

nccurve(a)(b) "angleA(-30)", "angleB(80)",
  "linecolor(blue)","linewidth(1mm)",
  "doubleline(true)", "linestyle(dashed withdots)";
drawObj(a,b);
```

Example
3-5-14

The tension of the line (in METAPOST's sense) can be modified with the *linetensionA* and *linetensionB* options (or with the *linetension* shortcut). This allows for control similar to that provided by PSTricks' ncurvA and ncurvB parameters. The default tensions are 1.

```
input metaobj
% Circles produced as before

nccurve(a)(b) "angleA(-30)", "angleB(80)",
  "linecolor(blue)","linewidth(3pt)",
  "linestyle(dashed withdots)",
  "linetension(2)";
drawObj(a,b);
```

Example
3-5-15

ncarc(*po1*, *po2*) options

ncarc connects the two nodes with an arc. The angle between the arc and the line between the two nodes is *arcangleA* at the beginning and −*arcangleB* at the end. Default values draw a curved connection, as shown below in red and green.

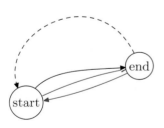

```
input metaobj
% Circles produced as before

ncarc(a)(b) "linecolor(blue)";
ncarc(b)(a) "linecolor(blue)";
ncarc(a)(b) "arcangleA(50)";
ncarc(b)(a) "arcangleA(-90)","arcangleB(-110)",
            "linestyle(dashed evenly)";
drawObj(a,b);
```

Example
3-5-16

ncbar(*po1*, *po2*) options

ncbar draws a line from the first node leaving at angle *angleA*. The line reaches the second node with the same angle (*angleB* is ignored). These two lines are connected with a line at right angles, and each end line is at least as long as *armA* or *armB* (the length being measured to the center of the objects). In this example, we also set the color with *linecolor*.

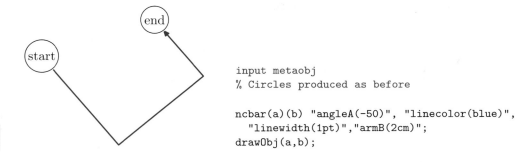

Example
3-5-17

```
input metaobj
% Circles produced as before

ncbar(a)(b) "angleA(-50)", "linecolor(blue)",
    "linewidth(1pt)","armB(2cm)";
drawObj(a,b);
```

ncangle(*po1, po2*) options

ncangle draws three segments, though in certain cases the third segment has no length. The two extreme segments are at angles defined by the *angleA* and *angleB* options. The point on the last segment at a distance *armB* from the node is connected to node A with a right angle. *armA* is not taken into account.

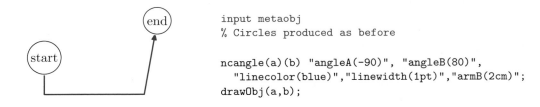

Example
3-5-18

```
input metaobj
% Circles produced as before

ncangle(a)(b) "angleA(-90)", "angleB(80)",
    "linecolor(blue)","linewidth(1pt)","armB(2cm)";
drawObj(a,b);
```

ncangles(*po1, po2*) options

ncangles is similar to ncangle, but the length of arm A (measured from the node) is fixed by the *armA* option. Arm A is connected to arm B by two line segments that meet arm A and each other at right angles. The angle at which they join arm B, and the length of the connecting segments, depend on the positions of the two arms. ncangles generally draws a total of four line segments.

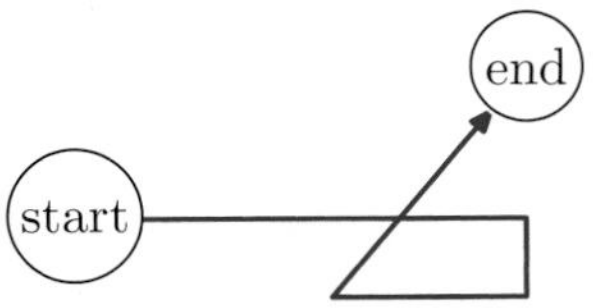

Example
3-5-19

```
input metaobj
% Circles produced as before

ncangles(a)(b) "angleA(0)", "angleB(50)",
    "linecolor(blue)","linewidth(1pt)",
    "armA(3cm)","armB(2cm)";
drawObj(a,b);
```

In the next example, the start of the line is offset by $(0, 1\text{cm})$, resulting in the line passing behind one of the objects because the objects are here drawn last.

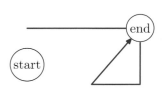

```
input metaobj
% Circles produced as before

ncangles(a)(b) "angleA(0)", "angleB(50)",
  "linecolor(blue)","linewidth(1pt)",
  "armA(3cm)","armB(2cm)","offsetA((0,1cm))";
drawObj(a,b);
```

Example
3-5-20

ncdiag(*po1*, *po2*) options

ncdiag draws an arm from each node at angle *angleA* or *angleB*, and with a length of *armA* or *armB* (from the centers of the nodes). Then the two arms are connected by a straight line, so that the whole line has three line segments.

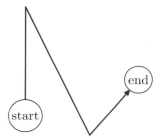

```
input metaobj
% Circles produced as before

ncdiag(a)(b) "angleA(90)", "angleB(50)",
  "linecolor(blue)","linewidth(1pt)",
  "armA(3cm)","armB(2cm)";
drawObj(a,b);
```

Example
3-5-21

ncdiagg(*po1*, *po2*) options

ncdiagg is similar to ncdiag, but only the arm for node A is drawn. The end of this arm is then connected directly to node B. *armB* is not used.

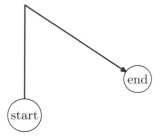

```
input metaobj
% Circles produced as before

ncdiagg(a)(b) "angleA(90)", "angleB(50)",
  "linecolor(blue)","linewidth(1pt)",
  "armA(3cm)";
drawObj(a,b);
```

Example
3-5-22

ncloop(*po1*, *po2*) options

ncloop is in the same family as ncangle and ncangles, but now typically five line segments are drawn. Hence ncloop can reach around to opposite sides of the nodes. The lengths of the arms (from the centers of the nodes) are fixed by *armA* and *armB*. Starting at arm A, `ncloop` makes a 90-degree turn to the left, drawing a segment of length *loopsize*. This segment connects to arm B in the same way arm A connects to arm B with `ncangles`; that is, two more segments are drawn, which join the first segment and each other at right angles, and then join arm B.

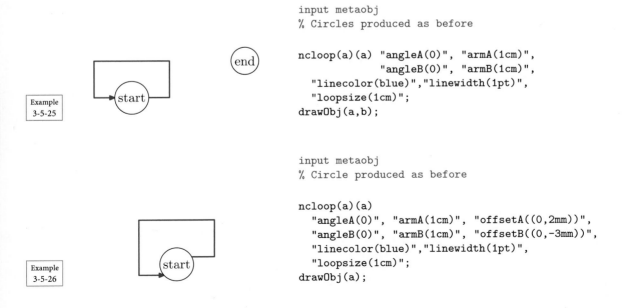

```
input metaobj
% Circles produced as before

ncloop(a)(b) "angleA(0)", "armA(2cm)",
             "angleB(180)", "armB(1cm)",
   "linecolor(blue)","linewidth(1pt)";
drawObj(a,b);
```

```
input metaobj
% Circles produced as before

ncloop(a)(b) "angleA(0)", "armA(2cm)",
             "angleB(-100)","armB(1cm)",
   "linecolor(blue)","linewidth(1pt)";
drawObj(a,b);
```

The two last examples have only one node. Notice that the parameters for the b node are set up but not used.

```
input metaobj
% Circles produced as before

ncloop(a)(a) "angleA(0)", "armA(1cm)",
             "angleB(0)", "armB(1cm)",
   "linecolor(blue)","linewidth(1pt)",
   "loopsize(1cm)";
drawObj(a,b);
```

```
input metaobj
% Circle produced as before

ncloop(a)(a)
   "angleA(0)", "armA(1cm)", "offsetA((0,2mm))",
   "angleB(0)", "armB(1cm)", "offsetB((0,-3mm))",
   "linecolor(blue)","linewidth(1pt)",
   "loopsize(1cm)";
drawObj(a);
```

`nccircle(`*po*`)` options

`nccircle` draws a circle, or part of a circle, that if complete, would pass through the center of the node counterclockwise, at an angle of *angleA*. The *angleB* option is not used.

```
input metaobj
% Circle produced as before

nccircle(a) "angleA(0)",
  "linecolor(blue)","linewidth(1pt)";
drawObj(a);
```

Example
3-5-27

`ncbox(`*po1*`,` *po2*`)` options

`ncbox` and `ncarcbox` do not connect the nodes with an open curve, but rather enclose the nodes in a box or curved box. The depth of the box is determined by the size of the objects within it, or twice *boxsize*. The dimensions of the box can also be set explicitly with the *boxheight* and *boxdepth* options. The ends of the boxes extend beyond the nodes by *nodesepA* and *nodesepB*.

    Two of the sides of the `ncbox` box are parallel to the line connecting the two node centers. No angle is taken into account by `ncbox`.

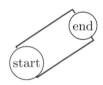

```
input metaobj
% Circles produced as before

ncbox(a)(b)
  "linecolor(blue)","linewidth(1pt)";
drawObj(a,b);
```

Example
3-5-28

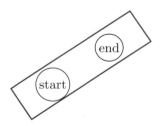

```
input metaobj
% Circles produced as before

ncbox(a)(b)
  "linecolor(blue)","linewidth(1pt)",
  "nodesepA(1cm)","nodesepB(1cm)";
drawObj(a,b);
```

Example
3-5-29

The corners can be rounded with the *linearc* option, as shown below:

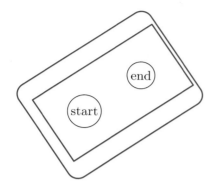

```
input metaobj
% Circles produced as before

ncbox(a)(b)
  "linecolor(blue)","linewidth(1pt)",
  "nodesepA(1cm)","nodesepB(1cm)",
  "boxsize(1cm)";
ncbox(a)(b)
  "linecolor(blue)","linewidth(1pt)",
  "nodesepA(1.3cm)","nodesepB(1.1cm)",
  "boxsize(1.5cm)","linearc(3mm)";
drawObj(a,b);
```

Example
3-5-30

---

ncarcbox(*po1, po2*) options

ncarcbox is similar to ncbox. It encloses the nodes in a curved box that is *arcangleA* away from the line connecting the two nodes. PSTricks seems to count that angle clockwise, whereas it is counted counterclockwise in ncarc. We decided for consistency to count the angle counterclockwise in both cases. The *arcangleB* option is not used.

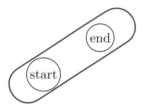

```
input metaobj
% Circles produced as before

ncarcbox(a)(b) "arcangleA(0)",
  "linecolor(blue)","linewidth(1pt)",
  "nodesepA(5mm)","nodesepB(5mm)";
drawObj(a,b);
```

Example
3-5-31

The second example shows the effect of changing the angle of the box. The value of the *arcangleA* option is used symmetrically for both objects. The box is made parallel to an imaginary arc drawn here with dashes.

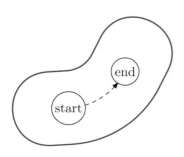

```
input metaobj
% Circles produced as before

ncarcbox(a)(b) "arcangleA(-30)",
  "linecolor(blue)","linewidth(1pt)",
  "nodesepA(5mm)","nodesepB(5mm)",
  "boxsize(1cm)";
ncarc(a)(b)
  "arcangleA(-30)", "arcangleB(-30)",
  "linestyle(dashed evenly)";
drawObj(a,b);
```

Example
3-5-32

```
nczigzag(po1, po2) options        nccoil(po1, po2) options
```

These connections draw a coil or zigzag whose width (diameter) is *coilwidth*, with the distance along the axes for each period (360 degrees) being equal to *coilheight* × *coilwidth*. nccoil draws a "3-D" coil, which is projected onto the xz-axes. The center of the "3-D" coil lies on the yz-plane at angle *coilaspect* to the z-axis. The coil is drawn by joining points that lie at angle *coilinc* from each other along the coil. The coil is drawn as a Bézier curve (not as a succession of segments, as with **PSTricks**), and it should always be smooth. However, decreasing *coilinc* may produce a better-looking coil, especially when *coilaspect* is near 0.

nczigzag does not use the *coilaspect* and *coilinc* parameters.

nczigzag and nccoil connect two points or two objects starting and ending with straight-line segments of length *coilarmA* and *coilarmB*.

All the usual connection modifiers can be used on coils or zigzags. However, in certain cases, strange effects can be produced—for instance, if *coilwidth* is too small with respect to *linearc*.

The path_size parameter of METAPOST might potentially overflow if *coilinc* is small and the coils have many turns. In that case, you should increase *coilinc* or enlarge the dimensions of the coil.

```
input metaobj
% Circles produced as before

nczigzag(a)(b);
nczigzag(a)(b)
  "angleA(-90)","angleB(120)",
  "linetension(0.8)", "coilwidth(2mm)",
  "linearc(.1mm)";
drawObj(a,b);
```

Example 3-5-33

```
input metaobj
% Circles produced as before

nccoil(a)(b) "coilwidth(5mm)";
drawObj(a,b);
```

Example 3-5-34

The next example shows various combinations of options, including the use of symbolic shortcuts for the kind of arrow.

```
input metaobj
% Circles produced as before

nccoil(a)(b)
  "doubleline(true)","coilwidth(2mm)",
  "angleA(0)", "arrows(-)", "linewidth(1pt)";
drawObj(a,b);
```

Example 3-5-35

Table 3.3: Options for connection labels ("/" means that there are no default values)

Option name	Type	Default	Description
labpic	`picture`	/	a picture variable
labdir	`string`	/	direction of a label
labpos	`numeric`	0.5	position on a path
labangle	`numeric`	0	rotation angle of a label with respect to the path tangent
labdist	`numeric`	1	distance ratio for the label

Connections can also have labels, but those labels must be stored in a `picture` variable and you may have to give the location of the labels on the connection. The main recognized options are listed in Table 3.3. The simplest case is the following:

Connection labels

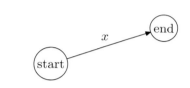

```
input metaobj
% Circles produced as before

picture lab;
lab=btex $x$ etex;
ncline(a)(b) "labpic(lab)","labdir(top)";
drawObj(a,b);
```

Example
3-5-36

3.5.5 Containers

All of the basic containers take a picture or an object and provide a frame for it. A picture can be given in the TeX notation (`btex...etex`) or obtained in other ways—for instance, with the `image` command of METAPOST.

newBox.*name*(*contents*) `options`

`Box` is the simplest of the containers. It is similar to `EmptyBox` but is a container. By default, the frame is visible. The size of the box is adapted to its contents. The options of this class are given in Table 3.4 on the next page.

Example
3-5-37

some text

```
input metaobj
newBox.a(btex some text etex);
a.c=origin;
drawObj(a);
```

By default, the frame fits the contents. With the `fit(false)` option, it is no longer required to do so. The frame is then a square.

some text

Example
3-5-38

```
input metaobj
newBox.a(btex some text etex)
   "fit(false)";
a.c=origin;
drawObj(a);
```

Table 3.4: Options for Box

Option	Type	Default	Description
dx	numeric	3bp	horizontal clearance left and right of the box
dy	numeric	3bp	vertical clearance above and below the box
filled	boolean	false	whether filled
fillcolor	color	black	fill color
fit	boolean	true	whether the box fits its contents
framed	boolean	true	whether framed
framewidth	numeric	.5bp	the width of the frame
framecolor	color	black	the color of the frame
framestyle	string	""	the style of the frame
picturecolor	color	black	the color that will override the color of the contents
shadow	boolean	false	whether there is a shadow
shadowcolor	color	black	the shadow color
rbox_radius	numeric	0	radius of round corners

In addition, we can specify horizontal and vertical margins to the contents with the dx and dy options. If the content is empty and we want a solid 4 mm × 4 mm square, we can write the following code:

```
input metaobj
newBox.a("") "filled(true)",
             "dx(2mm)", "dy(2mm)";
a.c=origin;
drawObj(a);
```

Example 3-5-39

We can obtain round corners by specifying a radius. If the radius is too large, the clearance (*dx* and *dy*) may have to be increased (it is also possible to call the newRBox constructor, which creates a Box with a default value of 1 mm for *rbox_radius*).

```
input metaobj
newBox.a(btex This is an ovalbox etex)
  "rbox_radius(2mm)";
a.c=origin;
drawObj(a);
```

Example 3-5-40

Box shortcuts   METAOBJ defines a few shortcuts for **PSTricks** compatibility:

- Tr_(*name*) is equivalent to new_Box_(*name*)("framed(false)");

- Tf is equivalent to new_Box_("")("filled(true)").

newPolygon.*name*(*contents,n*) options

The newPolygon constructor builds polygons. The options of this class are given in Table 3.5 on the facing page. Polygons are containers. The number of sides is specified with

Table 3.5: Options for `Polygon`

Option	Type	Default	Description
polymargin	`numeric`	`2mm`	clearance
angle	`numeric`	`0`	angle of the first vertex
filled	`boolean`	`false`	whether filled
fillcolor	`color`	`black`	fill color
fit	`boolean`	`true`	whether the polygon fits its contents
framed	`boolean`	`true`	whether framed
framewidth	`numeric`	`.5bp`	the width of the frame
framecolor	`color`	`black`	the color of the frame
framestyle	`string`	`""`	the style of the frame
picturecolor	`color`	`black`	the color that will override the color of the contents
shadow	`boolean`	`false`	whether there is a shadow
shadowcolor	`color`	`black`	the shadow color

n, and we can decide if the polygon fits the contents. By default, it does. Here is a pentagon:

Example 3-5-41

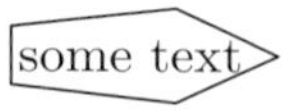


```
input metaobj
newPolygon.a(btex some text etex,5);
a.c=origin;
drawObj(a);
```

Some clearance can be added by changing the *polymargin* option:

Example 3-5-42

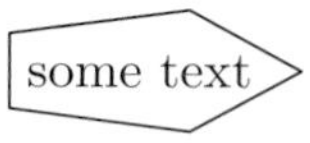


```
input metaobj
newPolygon.a(btex some text etex,5)
  "polymargin(3mm)";
a.c=origin;
drawObj(a);
```

The cardinal points are those of the rectangle bounding the ellipse on which the vertices are located.

A heptagon that does not fit its contents is shown here:

Example 3-5-43

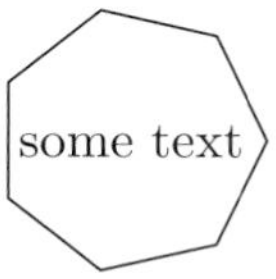


```
input metaobj
newPolygon.a(btex some text etex,7)
  "fit(false)", "polymargin(3mm)";
a.c=origin;
drawObj(a);
```

A `Polygon` can also be rotated.

Table 3.6: Options for `Ellipse` and `Circle`

Option	Type	Default	Description
circmargin	numeric	2bp	clearance
filled	boolean	false	whether filled
fillcolor	color	black	fill color
fit	boolean	true	whether the `Ellipse` fits its contents
framed	boolean	true	whether framed
framewidth	numeric	.5bp	the width of the frame
framecolor	color	black	the color of the frame
framestyle	string	""	the style of the frame
picturecolor	color	black	the color that will override the color of the contents
shadow	boolean	false	whether there is a shadow
shadowcolor	color	black	the shadow color

`newEllipse.`*name*`(`*contents*`)` options

The `newEllipse` constructor builds an ellipse that is a container. This ellipse can contain text, by default, it fits the text. The options are given in Table 3.6.

```
input metaobj
newEllipse.a(btex some text etex);
a.c=origin;
drawObj(a);
```

Example 3-5-44

When the option `"fit(false)"` is given, the ellipse doesn't fit the contents vertically, but only horizontally. Thus we get a circle:

```
input metaobj
newEllipse.a(btex some text etex)
   "fit(false)";
a.c=origin;
drawObj(a);
```

Example 3-5-45

It is possible to build an ellipse with no content and to specify a "margin" with the *circmargin* option. Moreover, the ellipse can be filled with the `filled(true)` option. The following example shows a disk with a 2-mm radius:

```
input metaobj
newEllipse.a("")
   "filled(true)","circmargin(2mm)";
a.c=origin;
drawObj(a);
```

Example 3-5-46

Ellipse shortcuts   METAOBJ provides `Toval_` as a shortcut for `new_Ellipse` for compatibility with PSTricks.

Table 3.7: Options for `DBox` and `DEllipse`

Option	Type	Default	Description
dx	numeric	3bp	horizontal clearance on each side of the content and inside the inner frame (only for DBox)
dy	numeric	3bp	vertical clearance on each side of the content and inside the inner frame (only for DBox)
circmargin	numeric	2bp	circular clearance (only for DEllipse)
filled	boolean	false	whether the object is filled (in which case the double frame is not very useful)
fillcolor	color	black	fill color
framed	boolean	true	whether the object is framed
fit	boolean	true	whether the box fits its content, both horizontally and vertically; if false, the contents fits only horizontally
framewidth	numeric	.5bp	width of the frame
framecolor	color	black	color of the frame
framestyle	string	""	style of the frame (e.g., dashed)
picturecolor	color	black	color of the picture if there is a picture inside the object
hsep	numeric	1mm	horizontal separation between the two frames
vsep	numeric	1mm	vertical separation between the two frames
shadow	boolean	false	whether there is a shadow (*framed* too must be true)
shadowcolor	color	black	shadow color

`newCircle.`*name*(*contents*) options

The `newCircle` constructor produces a circle. The options are given in Table 3.6 on the facing page. The *circmargin* option can be used to change its size.

Example
3-5-47

```
input metaobj
newCircle.a(btex some text etex);
a.c=origin;
drawObj(a);
```

`newDBox.`*name*(*contents*) options

A DBox is similar to a Box (see Table 3.7 for a table of its options), but the frame is doubled. By default, it fits its contents. For instance:

Example
3-5-48

```
input metaobj
newDBox.a(btex some text etex);
a.c=origin;
drawObj(a);
```

The cardinal points are located on the outside frame. As usual, we can specify that the box should *not* fit its contents with the *fit* option:

```
input metaobj
newDBox.a(btex some text etex)
  "fit(false)";
a.c=origin;
drawObj(a);
```

Example
3-5-49

Empty double boxes can also be defined, and the dimensions can be specified with the *dx* and *dy* options. To have a box with internal dimensions of 2 cm×2 cm, for example, we can write the following code:

```
input metaobj
newDBox.a("") "dx(1cm)", "dy(1cm)";
a.c=origin;
drawObj(a);
```

Example
3-5-50

> newDEllipse.*name*(*contents*) options

The newDEllipse constructor is to newEllipse as the newDBox constructor is to newBox. See Table 3.7 on the preceding page for a list of its options. The following example shows three objects built with newDEllipse. The first is an ellipse with a double frame, the second is a circle, and the third is a filled circle.

```
input metaobj
newDEllipse.a(btex some text etex);
newDEllipse.b(btex other text etex) "fit(false)";
newDEllipse.c("")
  "filled(true)","circmargin(2mm)";
a.c=origin;
a.c-b.c=(0,2cm);
c.c-a.c=(2cm,0);
drawObj(a,b,c);
```

Example
3-5-51

3.5.6 Box alignment constructors

Two constructors to align other objects exist: HBox and VBox. Their names have been chosen with analogy to the \hbox and \vbox primitives of TEX, respectively.

> newHBox.*name*(*obj1*,*obj2*,...,*objn*) options

The newHBox constructor provides horizontal alignment of objects. Its options are given in Table 3.8 on the next page. By default, the objects are aligned on the bottom and they appear

Table 3.8: Options for HBox, VBox, and Container

Option	Type	Default	Description
dx	numeric	0	horizontal clearance around the object
dy	numeric	0	vertical clearance around the object
hbsep	numeric	1mm	horizontal separation between elements in HBox
vbsep	numeric	1mm	vertical separation between elements in VBox
elementsize	numeric	−1pt	if non-negative, all the objects are assumed to have this width (for HBox) or height (for VBox)
align	string	"bot"	(only for HBox) "top" and "center" are the other possible values
		"left"	(only for VBox) "right" and "center" are the other possible values
framed	boolean	false	whether the object is framed
filled	boolean	false	whether the box is filled
fillcolor	color	black	fill color
framewidth	numeric	.5bp	width of the frame
framecolor	color	black	color of the frame
framestyle	string	""	style of the frame (e.g., dashed)
flip	boolean	false	whether to reverse the order of the components (only HBox and VBox)
shadow	boolean	false	whether there is a shadow (*framed* too must be true)
shadowcolor	color	black	shadow color

from left to right. The following example shows three boxes (created with newBox) of different sizes and contents. The boxes are put in one larger box, which can then be manipulated like a simple object.

```
input metaobj
newBox.a(btex Box A etex);
newBox.b(btex Box B etex scaled \magstep3);
newBox.c(btex Box C etex scaled \magstep2);
newHBox.h(a,b,c);
h.c=origin;
drawObj(h);
```

The cardinal points may lie outside the contained object. In Example 3-5-52, they happen to coincide with the bottom left and right corners of two boxes, but that is only because the boxes are aligned on the bottom and because the component objects are rectangular boxes.

To change the alignment, the *align* option can be given as either bot, top, or center. Here is an alignment at the top, with the same objects:

```
input metaobj
newBox.a(btex Box A etex);
newBox.b(btex Box B etex scaled \magstep3);
newBox.c(btex Box C etex scaled \magstep2);
newHBox.h(a,b,c) "align(top)";
h.c=origin;
drawObj(h);
```

The next example shows objects that are centered vertically:

```
input metaobj
newBox.a(btex Box A etex);
newBox.b(btex Box B etex scaled \magstep3);
newBox.c(btex Box C etex scaled \magstep2);
newHBox.h(a,b,c) "align(center)";
h.c=origin;
drawObj(h);
```

Box A | Box B | Box C

Example 3-5-54

A default horizontal separation appears between objects, which we can change with the *hbsep* option:

```
input metaobj
newBox.a(btex Box A etex);
newBox.b(btex Box B etex scaled \magstep3);
newBox.c(btex Box C etex scaled \magstep2);
newHBox.h(a,b,c)
  "align(center)","hbsep(3mm)";
h.c=origin;
drawObj(h);
```

Box A   Box B   Box C

Example 3-5-55

In the following example, not all of the components are boxes, but rather are polygons, a box, and a razor. The razor's function is to create a wide horizontal gap. It is similar to \kern in TEX.

```
input metaobj
newPolygon.a(btex Box A etex,5)
  "fit(false)","polymargin(5mm)";
newBox.b(btex Box B etex
        scaled \magstep3);
newHRazor.ba(1cm);
newPolygon.c(btex Box C etex
            scaled \magstep2,11)
  "polymargin(3mm)";
newHBox.h(a,b,ba,c)
  "align(center)","hsep(3mm)";
h.c=origin;
drawObj(h);
```

Example 3-5-56

newVBox.*name*(*obj1,obj2,...,objn*) options

A VBox is the vertical equivalent of an HBox. Its options are given in Table 3.8 on the preceding page. The boxes are piled up from bottom to top, which is unlike the behavior of \vbox in TeX, where the components would start at the top. By default, the components are aligned to the left, as in \vbox. A right alignment is obtained with the align(right) option:

```
input metaobj
newBox.a1(btex Box A1 etex);
newBox.b1(btex Box B1 etex scaled \magstep3);
newBox.c1(btex Box C1 etex scaled \magstep2);
newVBox.v1(a1,b1,c1);
newBox.a2(btex Box A2 etex);
newBox.b2(btex Box B2 etex scaled \magstep3);
newBox.c2(btex Box C2 etex scaled \magstep2);
newVBox.v2(a2,b2,c2) "align(right)";
v1.c=origin;
v2.c-v1.c=(3cm,0);
drawObj(v1,v2);
```

The components can be centered, and the separation between components can be changed with the *vbsep* option:

```
input metaobj
newBox.a1(btex Box A1 etex);
newBox.b1(btex Box B1 etex scaled \magstep3);
newBox.c1(btex Box C1 etex scaled \magstep2);
newVBox.v1(a1,b1,c1) "align(center)";
newBox.a2(btex Box A2 etex);
newBox.b2(btex Box B2 etex scaled \magstep3);
newBox.c2(btex Box C2 etex scaled \magstep2);
newVBox.v2(a2,b2,c2) "align(center)";
v1.c=origin;
v2.c-v1.c=(3cm,0);
drawObj(v1,v2);
```

We can potentially use any kind of object, not just boxes:

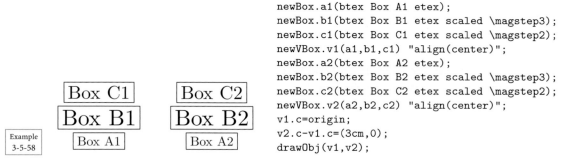

```
input metaobj
newPolygon.a(btex Box A etex,5)
  "fit(false)","polymargin(5mm)";
newBox.b(btex Box B etex scaled \magstep3);
newVRazor.ba(1cm);
newPolygon.c(btex Box C etex scaled \magstep2,11)
  "polymargin(3mm)";
newVBox.v(a,b,ba,c)
  "align(center)","vbsep(3mm)";
v.c=origin;
drawObj(v);
```

newContainer.*name*(*obj1,obj2,...,objn*) options

Finally, a special Container class creates a new object by enclosing a list of objects in a frame. The options recognized by this class are given in Table 3.8 on page 101.

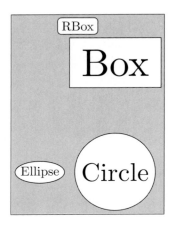

```
input metaobj
numeric u;
u=1cm;
newEllipse.A(btex Ellipse etex);
newCircle.B(btex Circle etex);
scaleObj(B,2);
newBox.C(btex Box etex);
scaleObj(C,3);
newRBox.D(btex RBox etex);
A.c=origin;
B.c-A.c=(2u,0);
C.c-B.c=(0,3u);
D.c-C.c=(-u,u);
newContainer.ct(A,B,C,D)
  "framed(true)", "framecolor(blue)",
  "filled(true)","fillcolor((.8,.8,.8))",
  "dx(1mm)", "dy(1mm)";
drawObj(ct);
```

Example
3-5-60

3.5.7 Recursive objects and fractals

METAOBJ provides several standard objects to define recursive objects.

newRecursiveBox.*name*(*n*) options

This is one of the simplest kinds of recursive objects. Such a box contains a box slightly rotated, which itself contains such a box, and so on. The depth of the recursion is a parameter of the constructor. The options recognized by the RecursiveBox objects are shown in Table 3.9 on the facing page.

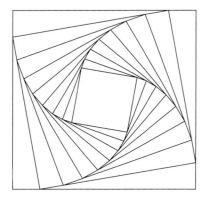

```
input metaobj
newRecursiveBox.a(8);
scaleObj(a,.3);
a.c=origin;
drawObj(a);
```

Example
3-5-61

Table 3.9: Options for `RecursiveBox`

Option	Type	Default	Description
filled	`boolean`	`false`	whether the object is filled
fillcolor	`color`	`black`	fill color
framed	`boolean`	`true`	whether the object is framed
framewidth	`numeric`	`.5bp`	thickness of the frame
framecolor	`color`	`black`	frame color
framestyle	`string`	`""`	frame style
dx	`numeric`	`5cm`	object width
dy	`numeric`	`5cm`	object height
rotangle	`numeric`	`10`	angle by which an internal object is rotated before inserting it into an outer object
shadow	`boolean`	`false`	whether there is a shadow (*framed* too must be true)
shadowcolor	`color`	`black`	shadow color

`newVonKochFlake.`*name*`(`*n*`)`

The Von Koch flake is a well-known fractal curve that is obtained by recursively replacing a side of a triangle by four smaller segments. A Von Koch flake of a given depth can easily be obtained with the `VonKochFlake` object. This class does not take any options.

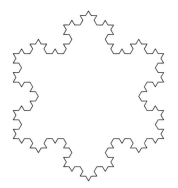

```
input metaobj
newVonKochFlake.a(3);
scaleObj(a,.4);
a.c=origin;
drawObj(a);
```

Example
3-5-62

3.5.8 Trees

The standard library provides a general tree constructor, `newTree`, and a more specialized one for proof trees, `newPTree`.

`newTree.`*name*`(`*root*`)(`*leaf1*`,`*leaf2*`,...,`*leafn*`)` options

Trees are generic, and the constructor takes a root and a list of subtrees. The root and the subtrees can be any objects having a standard interface. The tree is built recursively, so that

Table 3.10: Options for `Tree`

Option	Type	Default	Description
treemode	string	"D"	direction in which the tree develops; there are four possible values: "D" (default), "U", "L", and "R"
treeflip	boolean	false	whether to reverse the order of the subtrees
treenodehsize	numeric	−1pt	if non-negative, all nodes are assumed to have this width
treenodevsize	numeric	−1pt	if non-negative, all nodes are assumed to have this height
dx	numeric	0	horizontal clearance around the tree
dy	numeric	0	vertical clearance around the tree
hsep	numeric	1cm	for a horizontal tree, this is the separation between the root and the subtrees
vsep	numeric	1cm	for a vertical tree, this is the separation between the root and the subtrees
hbsep	numeric	1cm	for a vertical tree, this is the horizontal separation between subtrees; the subtrees are actually put in an HBox and the value of this option is passed to the HBox constructor
vbsep	numeric	1cm	for an horizontal tree, this is the vertical separation between subtrees; the subtrees are actually put in a VBox and the value of this option is passed to the VBox constructor
hideleaves	boolean	false	whether to take the subtrees into account in the bounding box
edge	string	"ncline"	name of a connection command
framed	boolean	false	whether the tree is framed
filled	boolean	false	true if the tree is filled
fillcolor	color	black	fill color
framewidth	numeric	.5bp	thickness of the frame
framecolor	color	black	color of the frame
framestyle	string	""	style of the frame
Dalign	string	"top"	vertical alignment of subtrees for trees that go down (the root on the top); the other possible values are "center" and "bot"
Ualign	string	"bot"	vertical alignment of subtrees for trees that go up (the root on the bottom); the other possible values are "center" and "top"
Lalign	string	"right"	horizontal alignment of subtrees for trees that go left (the root on the right); the other possible values are "center" and "left"
Ralign	string	"left"	horizontal alignment of subtrees for trees that go right (the root on the left); the other possible values are "center" and "right"
shadow	boolean	false	whether there is a shadow (*framed* too must be true)
shadowcolor	color	black	shadow color

the root and the subtrees given as arguments are not changed, but merely assembled by the `Tree` constructor. This, of course, is not always adequate and can leave a lot of unnecessary blank space, but it is the default behavior. Because the whole `Tree` object is memorized and can be traversed, it is actually possible to reformat such an object completely and implement any tree layout algorithm. The reader who is interested in pursuing such an endeavor is encouraged to consult the METAOBJ manual for further details. Trees support a large number of options, which are summarized in Table 3.10.

We start with a first tree. By default, a tree is constructed with the root at the top.

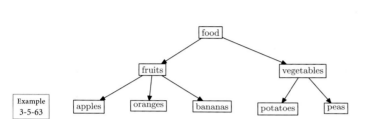

```
input metaobj
newBox.a(btex apples etex);
newBox.b(btex oranges etex);
newBox.c(btex bananas etex);
newBox.d(btex potatoes etex);
newBox.e(btex peas etex);
newBox.f(btex fruits etex);
newBox.v(btex vegetables etex);
newBox.fo(btex food etex);

newTree.fruits(f)(a,b,c);
newTree.vegetables(v)(d,e);
newTree.food(fo)(fruits,vegetables);
scaleObj(food,.7);
food.c=origin;drawObj(food);
```

Example
3-5-63

In this example, the leaves are aligned on the top, and the baselines of the labels are not aligned, because the labels have different heights.

In the next example, the left subtree is aligned on the bottom with the *Dalign* option. This was not sufficient to align all the baselines, because the word "bananas" has no descenders. We therefore added a \strut in the TEX part of the labels; this command adds an invisible vertical line that forces the box to have the size of ascenders and descenders. The right subtree is aligned on the center.

These new box definitions are also used in later examples.

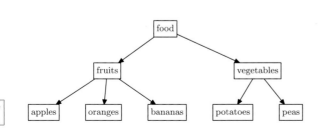

```
input metaobj
newBox.a(btex apples\strut etex);
newBox.b(btex oranges\strut etex);
newBox.c(btex bananas\strut etex);
newBox.f(btex fruits\strut etex);
newBox.d(btex potatoes\strut etex);
newBox.e(btex peas\strut etex);
newBox.v(btex vegetables\strut etex);
newBox.fo(btex food\strut etex);

newTree.fruits(f)(a,b,c) "Dalign(bot)";
newTree.vegetables(v)(d,e)
   "Dalign(center)";
newTree.food(fo)(fruits,vegetables)
   "hbsep(1cm)";
scaleObj(food,.7);
food.c=origin;drawObj(food);
```

Example
3-5-64

The next example shows how the tree can be drawn toward the left with the *treemode* option. The fruits are aligned on the left edge and the vegetables are centered.

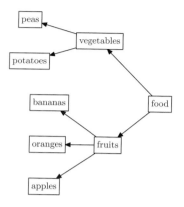

```
input metaobj
% Boxes as previously defined
newTree.fruits(f)(a,b,c)
   "Lalign(left)", "treemode(L)";
newTree.vegetables(v)(d,e)
   "Lalign(center)", "treemode(L)";
newTree.food(fo)(fruits,vegetables)
   "hsep(1cm)", "treemode(L)";
scaleObj(food,.7);
food.c=origin;drawObj(food);
```

Example
3-5-65

This tree is not very pleasing, because the fruits and vegetables are not aligned. This problem is solved in the next tree. Here, all five boxes on the left are extended to the right so that their width is 3 cm. This is done with `extendObjRight`, but it is not sufficient to align the five boxes. We also need to make sure that the "fruits" are as large as the "vegetables". Therefore, the "fruits" box is extended to the left with `rebindrelativeObj` so that its width is exactly that of the "vegetables" box. We might also have called `extendObjLeft` with the appropriate value.

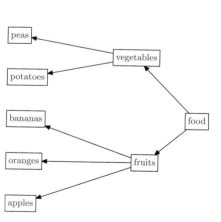

```
input metaobj
% Boxes as previously defined
extendObjRight.a(3cm);extendObjRight.b(3cm);
extendObjRight.c(3cm);extendObjRight.d(3cm);
extendObjRight.e(3cm);

rebindrelativeObj(f)
   (0,0,0,-xpart(v.e-v.w-f.e+f.w));
newTree.fruits(f)(a,b,c)
   "Lalign(left)", "treemode(L)";
newTree.vegetables(v)(d,e)
   "Lalign(center)", "treemode(L)";
newTree.food(fo)(fruits,vegetables)
   "hsep(1cm)", "treemode(L)";
scaleObj(food,.7);
food.c=origin;drawObj(food);
```

Example
3-5-66

A tree can also be drawn toward the right:

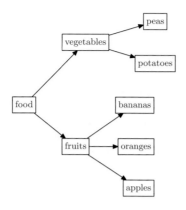

```
input metaobj
% Boxes as previously defined
newTree.fruits(f)(a,b,c)
    "Ralign(right)", "treemode(R)";
newTree.vegetables(v)(d,e)
    "Ralign(center)", "treemode(R)";
newTree.food(fo)(fruits,vegetables)
    "hsep(1cm)", "treemode(R)";
scaleObj(food,.7);
food.c=origin;drawObj(food);
```

For the next tree, the "fruits" box is extended to the right with `rebindrelativeObj`; its width now matches the width of the "vegetables" box. We could also have used `extendObjRight`. This is sufficient to align the five leaves on the left.

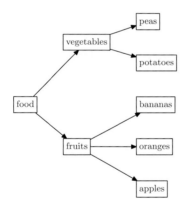

```
input metaobj
% Boxes as previously defined
rebindrelativeObj(f)
    (0,0,xpart(v.e-v.w-f.e+f.w),0);
newTree.fruits(f)(a,b,c)
    "Ralign(left)", "treemode(R)";
newTree.vegetables(v)(d,e)
    "Ralign(left)", "treemode(R)";
newTree.food(fo)(fruits,vegetables)
    "hsep(1cm)", "treemode(R)";
scaleObj(food,.7);
food.c=origin;drawObj(food);
```

We now develop the tree toward the top:

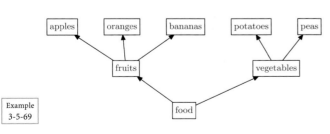

```
input metaobj
% Boxes as previously defined
newTree.fruits(f)(a,b,c)
    "Ualign(bot)", "treemode(U)";
newTree.vegetables(v)(d,e)
    "Ualign(center)", "treemode(U)";
newTree.food(fo)(fruits,vegetables)
    "hsep(1cm)", "treemode(U)";
scaleObj(food,.7);
food.c=origin;drawObj(food);
```

In the following example, the *treeflip* option is set to `true` and the order of subtrees is reversed.

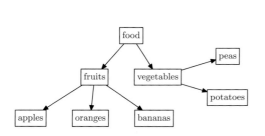

```
input metaobj
% Boxes as previously defined
setObjectDefaultOption
   ("Tree")("treeflip")(true);
newTree.fruits(f)(a,b,c)
   "Ualign(bot)", "treemode(U)";
newTree.vegetables(v)(d,e)
   "Ualign(center)", "treemode(U)";
newTree.food(fo)(fruits,vegetables)
   "hsep(1cm)", "treemode(U)";
scaleObj(food,.7);
food.c=origin;drawObj(food);
```

Example
3-5-70

Two different directions can be mixed. In this case, we have decided to ignore the space used by the subtrees by using the *hideleaves* option.

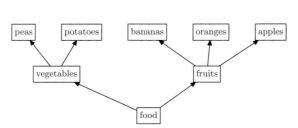

```
input metaobj
% Boxes as previously defined
newTree.fruits(f)(a,b,c)
   "Dalign(bot)", "hideleaves(true)";
newTree.vegetables(v)(d,e)
   "Ralign(center)", "hideleaves(true)",
   "treemode(R)";
newTree.food(fo)(fruits,vegetables)
   "hbsep(1cm)";
scaleObj(food,.7);
food.c=origin;drawObj(food);
```

Example
3-5-71

We can even mix three different directions:

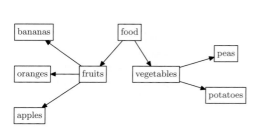

```
input metaobj
% Boxes as previously defined
newTree.fruits(f)(a,b,c)
   "Lalign(left)", "hideleaves(true)",
   "treemode(L)", "vsep(3mm)";
newTree.vegetables(v)(d,e)
   "Ralign(center)", "hideleaves(true)",
   "treemode(R)";
newTree.food(fo)(fruits,vegetables)
   "hbsep(1cm)";
scaleObj(food,.7);
food.c=origin;drawObj(food);
```

Example
3-5-72

In the next tree, the two subtrees overlap because the *hideleaves* option is set to true. The "potatoes" cover the "bananas".

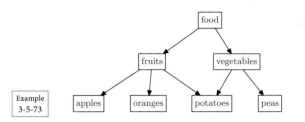

```
input metaobj
% Boxes as previously defined
newTree.fruits(f)(a,b,c)
   "Dalign(bot)", "hideleaves(true)";
newTree.vegetables(v)(d,e) "Dalign(center)";
newTree.food(fo)(fruits,vegetables)
   "hsep(1cm)";
scaleObj(food,.7); food.c=origin;drawObj(food);
```

Trees can be separated even when the leaves are hidden using *hbsep*:

```
input metaobj
% Boxes as previously defined
newTree.fruits(f)(a,b,c)
   "Dalign(bot)", "hideleaves(true)";
newTree.vegetables(v)(d,e)
   "Dalign(center)", "hideleaves(true)";
newTree.food(fo)(fruits,vegetables)
   "hbsep(5cm)";
scaleObj(food,.7);
food.c=origin;drawObj(food);
```

The same constructions can be made with different types of objects. First the tree is built with the following code:

```
input metaobj
newPolygon.a(btex apples\strut etex,5);
newPolygon.b(btex oranges\strut etex,6);
newPolygon.c(btex bananas\strut etex,7);
newPolygon.f(btex fruits\strut etex,8);
newEllipse.d(btex potatoes\strut etex);
newDEllipse.e(btex peas\strut etex);
newDBox.v(btex vegetables\strut etex);
newPolygon.fo(btex food\strut etex,12);

newTree.fruits(f)(a,b,c)
   "Lalign(left)", "hideleaves(true)",
   "treemode(L)", "vsep(3mm)";
newTree.vegetables(v)(d,e)
   "Ralign(center)", "hideleaves(true)",
   "treemode(R)";
newTree.food(fo)(fruits,vegetables)
   "hsep(1cm)";
scaleObj(food,.7);
food.c=origin;drawObj(food);
```

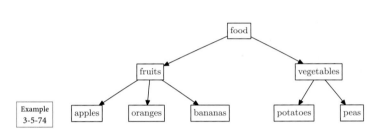

If we frame the tree, we get a frame that extends only to the root and the two leaves of the root, but not to the other nodes, because the bounding box of the tree was changed by the use of the *hideleaves* option.

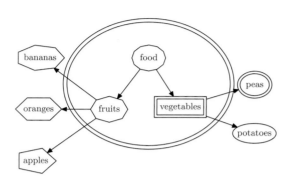

```
input metaobj
% Polygons etc. as previously defined
newTree.fruits(f)(a,b,c)
  "Lalign(left)", "hideleaves(true)",
  "treemode(L)", "vsep(3mm)";
newTree.vegetables(v)(d,e)
  "Ralign(center)", "hideleaves(true)",
  "treemode(R)";
newTree.food(fo)(fruits,vegetables)
  "hsep(1cm)";
scaleObj(food,.7);food.c=origin;
newDEllipse.ff(food);
ff.c=origin;drawObj(ff);
```

Example
3-5-76

To frame the whole tree, we can change the bounding box and set it to the visible part of the tree with `rebindVisibleObj`:

```
input metaobj
% Polygons etc. as previously defined
newTree.fruits(f)(a,b,c)
  "Lalign(left)", "hideleaves(true)", "treemode(L)", "vsep(3mm)";
newTree.vegetables(v)(d,e)
  "Ralign(center)", "hideleaves(true)", "treemode(R)";
newTree.food(fo)(fruits,vegetables) "hsep(1cm)";
scaleObj(food,.7);food.c=origin;
rebindVisibleObj(food);
newDEllipse.ff(food);drawObj(ff);
```

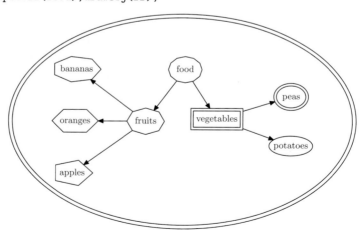

Example
3-5-77

The next example shows that we can build a new tree having as a leaf the object with a double elliptic frame. The root of the tree is typeset larger because it is not in the scope of scaleObj.

```
input metaobj
% Polygons etc. as previously defined
newTree.fruits(f)(a,b,c)
  "Lalign(left)", "hideleaves(true)", "treemode(L)", "vsep(3mm)";
newTree.vegetables(v)(d,e)
  "Ralign(center)", "hideleaves(true)", "treemode(R)";
newTree.food(fo)(fruits,vegetables) "hsep(1cm)";
scaleObj(food,.7);food.c=origin;
rebindVisibleObj(food); newDEllipse.ff(food);
newEllipse.xx(btex This is a new root etex) "circmargin(2mm)";
newTree.x(xx)(ff) "vsep(6mm)";drawObj(x);
```

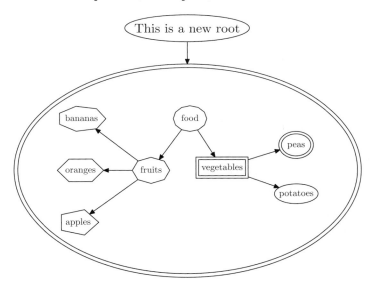

Example
3-5-78

A Tree constructor also accepts connection options (see Section 3.5.4 for an example), which are useful to modify the way standard tree connections are displayed.

METAOBJ defines a few useful shortcuts for trees: _T, T, and T_ stand for new_Tree, newTree, and new_Tree_, respectively.   *Tree shortcuts*

When we introduced the Tree class, we said that the root and the subtrees can be any objects. Most of these objects can also be used in a non-tree context. For instance, we can   *HFan and VFan* use a circle not just as a leaf of a tree, but also elsewhere, outside a tree. Two objects, however, are meant to be used only as part of a Tree structure: the HFan and VFan objects. These objects were borrowed from **PSTricks**. HFan represents an horizontal fan, where one of the fan segments is horizontal. VFan represents a vertical fan.

> newHFan.*name*(*wd,ht*) options   newVFan.*name*(*wd,ht*) options

Both HFan and VFan objects take a width and a height, as well as options. The height of an HFan (and the width of a VFan) will usually be small, often 0. These two classes are quite similar to HRazor and VRazor, but they are classes in their own right. They differ from ordinary boxes in the way they are connected to the root node. The connection takes the appearance of a fan. The following example is inspired by a **PSTricks** example:

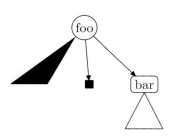

```
input metaobj
setObjectDefaultOption("Tree")
      ("hideleaves")(true);
t:=T_(new_Circle(btex foo etex))
      (new_HFan_(1cm,0)("filled(true)"),
        Tf,
        _T(new_RBox(btex bar etex))
          (new_HFan(1cm,0))
      )
      ("Dalign(center)");
Obj(t).c=origin;
draw_Obj(t);
```

Example
3-5-79

Here we build a tree with a `Circle` root node and three subtrees. The first subtree is an HFan of width 1 cm and height 0; this fan is filled. The second subtree is a black square obtained with `Tf`, which is a shortcut for `newBox` with certain options. The third subtree is a tree with a rounded-corner box (`newRBox`) at its root and with one leaf, which is an HFan. All of the leaves of the main tree are vertically centered, which creates the nice alignment; the leaf of the third subtree is actually hidden, because *hideleaves* is set to `true`. The two fans are "pointed", which means that the top end reaches the bounding path. If the *pointedfan* option is set to `false`, the top end of the fan is at the center of the root node.

The color of a fan can be changed with the *fillcolor* option, its style can be changed with the *fanlinestyle* option, and the rounding of its corners can be modified with the *fanlinearc* option.

A root node can also be a fan, as demonstrated in the following example:

```
input metaobj
t:=_T(new_Circle(btex foo etex))
      (_T(new_HFan_(1cm,0)
            ("filled(true)",
             "fillcolor(blue)",
             "fanlinearc(1mm)"
            )
      )
      (TC,new_HFan_(1cm,0)
            ("fanlinestyle(dashed evenly)")));
Obj(t).c=origin;
draw_Obj(t);
```

Example
3-5-80

Table 3.11: Options for HFan and VFan

Option	Type	Default	Description
filled	boolean	false	whether filled
fillcolor	color	black	fill color
edge	string	"yes"	"yes" or "none", depending on whether edges should be drawn
pointedfan	boolean	true	whether the fan is "pointed"
fanlinestyle	string	""	style of the fan frame
fanlinearc	numeric	0	radius of round corners

Here the red fan is the root of a subtree. The top of the black disk is aligned with the bottom of the fan, because descending trees are by default aligned on the top, and the fan is considered an horizontal line and its top is the same as its bottom. This wouldn't have been the case if the second parameter of new_HFan_ had not been set to 0.

The two classes have exactly the same options (Table 3.11). Most of these options have been explained earlier. The *edge* option is a string, which by default is "yes", meaning that the fan edges must be drawn. In certain cases we may want fans to skip levels; one way of achieving this effect is to set *edge* to "none".

3.5.9 Matrices

A special Matrix class provides a combination of horizontal and vertical boxes. A matrix is constructed with newMatrix by specifying a number n of rows and a number m of columns, and then a list of $n \times m$ objects, given row by row. Table 3.12 on the next page shows all options supported by the Matrix class.

newMatrix.*name*(*nrows,ncolumns*)(*matrix elements*)

Here is a first matrix with one row and one column. The matrix contains the object m1, which is a framed box.

Example
3-5-81

```
input metaobj
newBox.m1(btex A etex);
newMatrix.mat(1,1)(m1);
mat.c=origin;
drawObj(mat);
```

The second matrix contains two rows and one column:

Example
3-5-82

```
input metaobj
newBox.m2(btex B etex) "dx(1cm)";
newBox.m3(btex C etex) "dy(1cm)";
newMatrix.mata(2,1)(m2,m3);
mata.c=origin;
drawObj(mata);
```

Table 3.12: Options for `Matrix`

Option	Type	Default	Description
dx	`numeric`	`0`	horizontal clearance around the matrix
dy	`numeric`	`0`	vertical clearance around the matrix
hsep	`numeric`	`1mm`	horizontal separation between columns
vsep	`numeric`	`1mm`	vertical separation between rows
matrixnodehsize	`numeric`	`−1pt`	if non-negative, all the nodes are assumed to have this width
matrixnodevsize	`numeric`	`−1pt`	if non-negative, all the nodes are assumed to have this height
halign	`string`	`"c"`	a string where each character corresponds to one column and specifies the horizontal alignment within that column
valign	`string`	`"c"`	a string where each character corresponds to one row and specifies the vertical alignment within that row
framed	`boolean`	`false`	whether the matrix is framed
filled	`boolean`	`false`	whether the matrix is filled
fillcolor	`color`	`black`	fill color
framewidth	`numeric`	`.5bp`	frame thickness
framecolor	`color`	`black`	frame color
framestyle	`string`	`""`	frame style
shadow	`boolean`	`false`	whether there is a shadow (*framed* too must be true)
shadowcolor	`color`	`black`	shadow color

The next matrix has three rows and two columns, but only five elements. The last element of the first line is empty. This is shown in the `newMatrix` call with an `nb` value—a special value meaning "null box".

```
input metaobj
newBox.m4(btex Element 4 etex);
newBox.m5
   (btex D$\displaystyle\int_0^\infty
                {1\over 1+x^2}dx$ etex);
newBox.m6(btex Bb etex);
newBox.m7(btex C etex);
newBox.m8(btex D etex);
newMatrix.matc(3,2)
     (m4,nb,m5,m6,m7,m8)
      "halign(ew)", "valign(sns)";
matc.c=origin-(0,10cm);
drawObj(matc);
```

Example
3-5-83

By default, matrix elements are centered, both horizontally and vertically. It is possible to specify different alignments for each column and each line with the *halign* and *valign* options. In the preceding example, *halign* has a string of two letters as arguments and specifies that the left column is aligned to the right (e = east) and the right column is aligned to the left (w = west). *valign* has a string of three letters as parameters. The first and third letters are "s" (south) and mean that the first (top) and last lines are aligned to the bottom; the second letter is "n" (north) and means that the second line is aligned to the top.

The whole matrix can be duplicated, and we can see that the empty slot is duplicated, too. The matrix object can be scaled as well.

```
input metaobj
newBox.m4(btex Element 4 etex);
newBox.m5
  (btex D$\displaystyle\int_0^\infty
              {1\over 1+x^2}dx$ etex);
newBox.m6(btex Bb etex);
newBox.m7(btex C etex);
newBox.m8(btex D etex);
newMatrix.matc(3,2)
     (m4,nb,m5,m6,m7,m8)
     "halign(ew)", "valign(sns)";
matc.c=origin-(0,10cm);
duplicateObj(matd,matc);
scaleObj(matd,2);
matd.c=origin-(0,15cm);
drawObj(matd);
```

$$\boxed{\text{Element } 4}$$

$$\boxed{D\int_0^\infty \frac{1}{1+x^2}dx} \quad \boxed{Bb}$$

$$\boxed{C}\ \boxed{D}$$

Example
3-5-84

Multispan columns are not implemented. However, it is possible to obtain multispan-like results by changing the bounding box of a component, as explained in the METAOBJ manual.

3.5.10 Tree and matrix connection variants

When tree nodes or matrix nodes have to be connected, it is cumbersome to access the nodes, even though they are accessible. Therefore, we provide variants of all the connection commands for trees and matrices. The variants have a "t" and an "m" instead of the leading "n" in the names of the connection commands. Instead of an object, they take as parameters the position of the object within the tree or within the matrix. For instance, a curve connection between the roots of the second and third subtrees of tree gt can be drawn with the following code:

```
tccurve.gt(2)(3) "posA(e)","posB(n)", "angleA(0)","angleB(-90)",
  "linecolor(blue)", "linetension(1.75)";
```

The second and third parameters (after gt, the name of the tree) are lists of integers. If we had written

```
tccurve.gt(2,1)(3,2) "posA(e)","posB(n)", "angleA(0)","angleB(-90)",
  "linecolor(blue)", "linetension(1.75)";
```

we would have connected the node at position 2,1 (first subtree of second subtree of gt) with the node at position 3,2 (second subtree of third subtree of gt).

All other connection commands are similarly adapted: `tcline`, `tcangle`, `tcangles`, `tcarc`, `tccurve`, `tcdiag`, `tcdiagg`, `tcloop`, `tccircle`, `tcbox`, and `tcarcbox`.

Variants for matrices are also available with the names `mcline`, `mcarc`, `mccurve`, `mcangle`, `mcangles`, `mcdiag`, `mcdiagg`, `mcloop`, `mccircle`, `mcbox`, `mcarcbox`, `mczigzag`, and `mccoil`. Instead of an object identification, these commands take a pair of integers representing the position of the object within the matrix. For instance, a dashed line can be drawn between the objects at positions $(1, 1)$ and $(2, 2)$ in matrix `mat2` with the following code:

```
mcline.mat2(1,1)(2,2) "linestyle(dashed evenly)";
```

If a component of a matrix is itself a matrix, this notation cannot be used. Instead, special access commands must be used, such as `matpos` (or `mpos`), which are described in the META-OBJ manual.

There are also "reverse" variants of certain connection commands. These reverse variants can be useful for tree connections. The reverse connections are `rncline`, `rnccurve`, `rncangle`, `rncangles`, `rncarc`, `rncdiag`, `rncdiagg`, `rncbar`, `rncloop`, `rncbox`, `rncarcbox`, `rnczigzag`, and `rnccoil`.

There are no "reverse" variants of the tree and matrix variants of the connection commands.

3.5.11 Labels

Labels can be added to an object. The main command is `ObjLabel`. This command has as parameters an object, a label, and a list of options.

```
input metaobj
t:=T_(Tc)(TC,TC,Tc)
    ("treemode(R)","arrows(draw)",
     "hsep(2cm)");
Obj(t).c=origin;
ObjLabel.Obj(t)(btex below etex)
    "labpathid(1)", "labdir(bot)";
ObjLabel.Obj(t)(btex above etex)
    "labpathid(2)", "labdir(top)";
ObjLabel.Obj(t)(btex above etex)
    "labpathid(3)", "labdir(top)";
draw_Obj(t);
```

Example
3-5-85

In this example, three labels have been added to the tree `t`. This tree is given by a number, and the real tree object is obtained when `Obj` is called on `t`. `ObjLabel` takes `Obj(t)` as its first (suffix) parameter; the labels are given as TEX pictures. The options indicate where the labels will be put. The *labpathid* option determines on which connection the label goes. In a tree, each standard connection has a number ranging from 1 to n, the number of subtrees. This value can be given as parameter to *labpathid*. If it had been the only option, the

Table 3.13: Options for labels ("/" means that there are no default values)

Option name	Type	Default	Description
labpathid	numeric	/	path identifier
labdir	string	/	direction of a label
labrotate	numeric	0	rotation angle of a label with respect to its normal position
labangle	numeric	/	rotation angle of a label with respect to the path tangent
labpos	numeric	0.5	position on a path
labshift	pair	$(0,0)$	shift of a label
labcolor	color	black	label color
laberase	boolean	false	true if the label erases what lies below it
labpoint	string	"ic"	object point
labcard	string	/	object point
labpathname	string	/	name of a path

labels in the preceding example would have come out over the connections. The *labdir* option is used to shift the label with respect to the normal point where it would have been positioned. *labdir* takes options similar to those taken by the standard METAPOST label command.

Table 3.13 shows the list of all options recognized by the ObjLabel command.

ObjLabel puts a label either somewhere along a path or somewhere near a point of an object. Two options help specifying the relevant path:

labpathid: This option takes a path number as parameter. It is seldom used, except in cases where the path numbers are well known—for instance, in the example given previously.

labpathname: When a path is created (with a connection command such as ncline), the path can be given a name (with the *name* option); this name can be given as parameter to *labpathname*.

On a given path, a position can be specified with *labpos*. This option is a numerical value between 0 and 1, where 0 represents the beginning of the path (if the path starts at the bounding path of an object, this is also the 0 position) and 1 represents the end of the path. The default value is 0.5.

By default, a label is set horizontally, no matter what the slope of the path at the label position. The label can be set parallel to the path direction by specifying the *labangle* option with the value 0. Other values rotate the label with respect to the path tangent.

A label can also be set with respect to an object point with the *labpoint* option. For instance,

```
ObjLabel.g(btex hello! etex) "labpoint(po1)";
```

writes "hello!" over point po1 of object g.

A label can also be set in an object, with respect to a cardinal point with the *labcard* option. Like *labpoint*, *labcard* takes an object point as parameter; however, the label is not put over the point but rather beyond the label point, in a direction determined by the line joining the center of the object and the point. For instance, to put the label $(-10, 10. - 10)$ below (south) of the object at position $(2, 1, 1)$ of the tree Obj(t), we can write

```
ObjLabel.ntreepos(Obj(t))(2,1,1)(btex $(-10,10.-10)$ etex)
    "labcard(s)";
```

The ntreepos command used above takes an object and a tree position as parameters, and returns the node at that position.

Four additional options apply in both cases (labels on a path or next to a point):

labrotate: With this option, a label can be rotated with respect to its normal position.

labshift: With this option, a label can be shifted in a way similar to the *offsetA* and *offsetB* connection options.

labcolor: This option determines the color of the label.

laberase: This option determines whether the label erases what lies beneath it.

3.6 TEX interfaces: getting the best of both worlds

Although META produces beautiful pictures, it is not an easy language for a casual user who wants relatively simple diagrams. There are three ways to deal with this complexity:

1. Use of high-level libraries of META code, as described in Chapter 4

2. Use of an interactive drawing package that can generate META output

3. Use of a LATEX package that generates the necessary META code

One of the most sophisticated LATEX packages that writes METAFONT is Thorsten Ohl's **feynmf**, discussed in detail in Section 8.4 on page 555. **feynmf** was designed to create the Feynman diagrams used by high-energy physicists and is a good example of a very specialized language that was carefully designed to solve one problem well. Its sibling package, **feynmp**, uses METAPOST instead of METAFONT.

The following sections describe other ways to use METAPOST within TEX. The most straightforward method is to use the **emp** package, which provides one environment for every picture but stays with the METAPOST syntax. Alternatively, **mfpic** is a package that hides METAPOST and provides LATEX macros for specific tasks. Finally, a seamless integration of TEX and METAPOST is achieved in ConTEXt, but a description of that package is beyond the scope of this book.

3.6.1 The emp **package**

The **emp** package by Thorsten Ohl is a simple package for embedding METAPOST diagrams within a LATEX source document. This approach offers several benefits. For instance, the code for figures appear with the text, and there is no need to devise names for METAPOST files. Moreover, an emp environment can be included in other graphical environments, in particular within a picture environment. Here is an example mixing \includegraphics and the emp and the picture environments:

```
\begin{empfile}
\begin{figure}[htbp]
\begin{picture}(5,8.25)
\put(...){\includegraphics{...}}
\begin{emp}(10,10)
 s = 1;
 for d := 36 step -2 until 0:
   draw origin withpen pencircle scaled d withcolor s*white;
   s := 1 - s;
 endfor
\end{emp}
\end{picture}
\end{figure}
\end{empfile}
```

The emp package provides the following environments:

> \begin{empfile} [*file*]   ...   \end{empfile}

The empfile environment is used to contain METAPOST code that will go into one METAPOST file. It normally contains other environments such as emp, as in the preceding example, and merely indicates the scope of the METAPOST file. If no *file* is given, the default name for the METAPOST file is \jobname.mp.

> \begin{emp} [*name*] (*width,height*)   ...   \end{emp}

The emp environment contains the code of a figure that will be placed where the environment appears. The *width* and *height* are mandatory. They are expressed in units of \unitlength and are available within METAPOST as w and h, respectively. The optional *name* argument can be used to give a name to the drawing for future reuse with \empuse.

> \begin{empdef} [*name*] (*width,height*)   ...   \end{empdef}

The empdef environment is similar to emp, but the figure is not drawn immediately. It can be drawn later using its name.

> \begin{empcmds}   *METAPOST commands*   \end{empcmds}

The empcmds environment writes METAPOST commands to the current file (defined by empfile) outside of a figure.

> `\begin{empgraph}` *[name]* (*width,height*)   ...   `\end{empgraph}`

The empgraph environment contains the description of a graph. The user must include the graph package using `\empprelude`.

An example of code for such an inline graph follows:

```
\usepackage{emp}
...
\empprelude{input graph;}
\begin{empfile}
\begin{empgraph}(250,150)
  pickup pencircle scaled 1pt;
  path p;
  for x=-20 step 0.2 until -0.2:
    augment.p (x, sind(x*180/3.14159)/x);
  endfor;
  augment.p (0, 1);
  for x=0.2 step 0.2 until 20:
    augment.p (x, sind(x*180/3.14159)/x);
  endfor;
  glabel.lrt(btex $\displaystyle\frac{\sin(x)}{x}$ etex,(-20,1));
  gdraw p;
\end{empgraph}
\end{empfile}
```

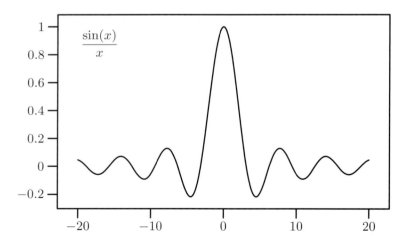

Example
3-6-1

3.6.2 **The** mfpic **package**

The mfpic package was designed and implemented by Thomas E. Leathrum and is now maintained and enhanced by Geoffrey Tobin and Daniel H. Luecking. It consists of a TEX package (usable with LATEX) and a supporting library of METAFONT and METAPOST macros. This section details the use of mfpic with LaTeX and describes the version current in July 2006. As mfpic provides equivalent methods to many METAPOST constructions, their complete description would amount to much repetition. For this reason, only a survey of the package is given here.

How a drawing is processed

mfpic's LaTeX macros write code to an external file and read in the resulting drawing either as a character in a special font (this requires two passes of LaTeX when the picture dimensions change and a run of METAFONT if the picture contents change at all) or as a METAPOST drawing. When the output is processed with METAFONT, each picture is a single META-FONT character. When it is processed with METAPOST, each picture is a stand-alone EPS file.

The advantage of this system is that the LaTeX user has access to all the power of META-FONT or METAPOST as a drawing package without having to learn a new language. Type-setting of labels and text is handled transparently by the LaTeX macros, solving a major problem associated with using METAFONT (METAPOST is an easier system to use for this reason).

METAFONT mode

This mode is the default. A simple example of function plotting shows the clarity of mfpic markup:

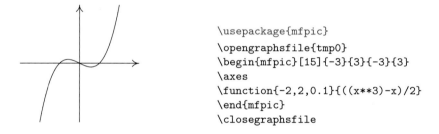

```
\usepackage{mfpic}
\opengraphsfile{tmp0}
\begin{mfpic}[15]{-3}{3}{-3}{3}
\axes
\function{-2,2,0.1}{((x**3)-x)/2}
\end{mfpic}
\closegraphsfile
```

Example
3-6-2

One of the main drawbacks of mfpic in METAFONT mode is that you must be confident about running METAFONT on the "font" file that is generated and putting the results where TEX can find them. You also have to worry about METAFONT capacity, which can easily be exceeded at high resolution. Likewise, you must keep track of whether the pictures have changed and whether the font needs rerunning after each pass of LaTeX; this is comparable, however, to running BibTEX or makeindex as part of the LaTeX process and can be hidden in intelligent batch files.

When using mfpic in METAFONT mode, you must remember that you are dealing with a *font*. Thus you cannot have more than 255 pictures in a single font. In addition, you must watch your TEX implementation, which usually has a limit on how many fonts it can load. If you have several thousand pictures to create, you have to open a series of font files and keep a sharp eye on the font memory.

METAPOST **mode**

This mode is selected by loading **mfpic** with the option "metapost" or by writing \usemetapost in the LaTeX preamble.

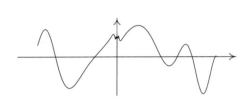

```
\usepackage[metapost]{mfpic}
\opengraphsfile{tmp}
\begin{mfpic}[15]{-5}{6}{-2}{2}
\axes
\function{-4,5,0.011}
        {sin(x)*cos(1/(2x))+cos(x*x/2)}
\end{mfpic}
\closegraphsfile
```

Example
3-6-3

The options of the package

The **mfpic** package can be loaded with several options:

metapost, \usemetapost: This option selects METAPOST as the figure processor. The command must appear before the \opengraphsfile command; if the **babel** package is used, **mfpic** should be loaded and \usemetapost (if used) declared before **babel** is loaded. There is also a (default) *metafont* option.

mplabels, \usemplabels, \nomplabels: This option causes all label creation commands to write their contents to the output file. In this case, labels are handled by METAPOST and can be rotated. The user is responsible for adding the appropriate verbatimtex header to the output file if necessary. This can be done with \mfpverbtex, but is usually necessary only when LaTeX macros are called. Care must also be taken that LaTeX, and not TeX, is called in this case.

overlaylabels, \overlaylabels, \nooverlaylabels: With this option (or after the command \overlaylabels), text labels are saved in a separate place from the rest of a picture. When a picture is completed, the labels that were saved are added on top of it.

truebbox, \usetruebbox, \notruebbox: This option causes **mfpic** to use the normal METAPOST bounding box instead of the bounding box given in the mfpic environment.

clip, \clipmfpic, \noclipmfpic: This option removes all parts of the figure outside the rectangle specified by the \mfpic command.

centeredcaptions, \usecenteredcaptions, \nocenteredcaptions: this option causes multiline captions created by \tcaption to have all lines centered.

debug, \mfpicdebugtrue, \mfpicdebugfalse: This option causes **mfpic** to write debug information to the .log file.

clearsymbols, \clearsymbols, \noclearsymbols: **mfpic** has two commands, \point and \plotsymbol, that place a small symbol at each of a list of points.

The first command can place either a small filled disk or an open disk, with the choice being dictated by the setting of the Boolean `\pointfilltrue` or `\pointfillfalse`. The behavior of `\point` in the case of `\pointfillfalse` is to erase the interior of the disk in addition to drawing its circumference.

The command `\plotsymbol` can place a variety of shapes—some open, some not. Its behavior until now was simply to draw the shape without erasing the interior. Two other commands that placed these symbols, `\plotnodes` and `\plot`, had the same behavior. If you use the *clearsymbols* option, `\plotsymbol` and `\plotnodes` will erase the interior of the open symbols before drawing them. Thus `\plotsymbol{SolidCircle}` still works just like `\pointfilltrue\point`, and now with this option `\plotsymbol{Circle}` behaves the same as `\pointfillfalse\point`. The `\plot` command is unaffected by this option.

draft, final, nowrite, `\mfpicdraft`, `\mfpicfinal`, `\mfpicnowrite`: These options are useful when you are debugging figures that contain errors and you want to continue with the processing of correct figures. Refer to the **mfpic** manual for more information on these options.

The syntax of drawings

The section of a document that is to use **mfpic** must be surrounded by macros to open and close a META file containing the pictures to be included:

> `\opengraphsfile{`*file*`}` ... `\closegraphsfile`

The name of the file will be ⟨*file*⟩`.mf` or ⟨*file*⟩`.mp`; the extension should not be specified. A typical input file, with several drawings, would appear like this:

```
\opengraphsfile{tmp}
\begin{mfpic}...
...
\end{mfpic}

\begin{mfpic}...
...
\end{mfpic}

\begin{mfpic}...
...
\end{mfpic}
\closegraphsfile
```

You would normally have just one file per document. If you are using METAFONT and there are more than 255 pictures, however, you must start a new file. You may prefer to have a separate drawing file for each section.

Normally, `\mfpic` assigns the number 1 to the first `mfpic` environment, after which the number is increased by one for each new `mfpic` environment. This number is used internally to include the picture. In METAFONT this number becomes the position of the character in the font file; in METAPOST it is the extension of the graphics file that is output. The command

> \mfpicnumber{*num*}

tells **mfpic** to ignore this sequence and number the next `mfpic` picture with *num* (and the one after that *num*+1, and so forth).

All picture drawing takes place inside an `mfpic` environment:

> \begin{mfpic}[x_{scale}] [y_{scale}] {x_a}{x_b}{y_a}{y_b}　　　…　　　\end{mfpic}

The parameters give the picture's coordinate system and size:

x_{scale}　*x*-scale of the coordinate system, in multiples of the length \mfpicunit (the default value of which is 1 pt).

y_{scale}　*y*-scale of coordinate system. If no y_{scale} is given, it is the same as the x_{scale}.

x_a　Lower bound for *x*-axis coordinates.

x_b　Upper bound for *x*-axis coordinates.

y_a　Lower bound for *y*-axis coordinates.

y_b　Upper bound for *y*-axis coordinates.

The four mandatory parameters set the size of the picture, and the two optional arguments allow it to be scaled. Like LATEX's `picture` environment, the **mfpic** package does not verify whether elements of the drawing fall within the limits specified; they may well overlap the surrounding text.

mfpic supports a number of primitive drawing commands, a set of object modifiers, and some higher-level macros for drawing functions and performing special transformations. By default, each of the simple drawing commands draws a self-contained line or shape, but these elements can be combined to make more complex shapes:

> \begin{connect}　　　…　　　\end{connect}

Inside a `connect` environment you can join objects together; extra line segments are drawn from the end point of one object to the start of the next. Even if the objects are closed, like circles, the joining lines are still (unfortunately) drawn.

The default is to render objects with lines. You can change this behavior with the \setrender command:

> \setrender{*commands*}

This is a switch; all objects within the (LATEX scope) of this command will be rendered using *commands*. This allows a more succinct notation. For instance, to draw a series of shapes in the same style, the single command `\setrender{\gfill}` causes all subsequent closed objects to be filled.

All coordinates and distances are normally expressed in TEX point dimensions; angles are expressed in degrees counterclockwise. The behavior of the drawing primitives depends on a set of variables that you can set globally; these are mostly length commands, which are changed with `\setlength`. mfpic also has a set of commands that can be used at any point in a drawing to affect subsequent commands.

Many of mfpic's simple drawing commands and some of the modifiers are demonstrated in the following example. The last line has *multiple* modifiers (`\gfill` and `\bclosed`).

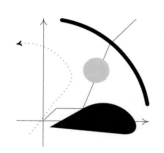

```
\usepackage[metapost]{mfpic}
\opengraphsfile{tmp}
\begin{mfpic}[1]{-20}{80}{-20}{80}
\pen{.3pt}\axes
\lines{(1,1),(10,10),(30,10),(50,60),(70,80)}
\pen{3pt}
\arc[p]{(0,0),10,80,80}
\pen{1pt}
\shade\circle{(40,40),10}
\arrow\dotted
 \curve{(-10,-10),(5,10),(20,40),(-20,60)}
\gfill\bclosed\lines{(60,-10),(5,-5),(30,10)}
\end{mfpic}
\closegraphsfile
```

Example
3-6-4

Color

When METAPOST is used, drawings can be colored. mfpic adds some support for color in the form of two main commands:

  `\drawcolor[`*model*`]{`*colorspec*`}`

This command sets the default color for drawing elements.

  `\fillcolor[`*model*`]{`*colorspec*`}`

This command sets the default color for filling.

The optional *model* may be one of `rgb`, `RGB`, `cmyk`, `gray`, and `named`:

rgb   Three numbers in the range 0 to 1 separated by commas.

RGB   Three numbers in the range 0 to 255 separated by commas.

cmyk   Four numbers in the range 0 to 1 separated by commas.

gray   One number in the range 0 to 1, with 1 for white and 0 for black.

named   A METAPOST color variable name either predefined by mfpic or defined by the user.

New color names may be defined as follows:

\mfpdefinecolor{*name*}{*model*}{*colorspec*}

This command defines a new color name.

METAFONT offers only limited support for color, and colored areas are approximated by gray areas.

Basic drawing commands

\arc[*c*]{$(x,y),(x_1,y_1),\theta$}

Draw an arc with center at (x,y), starting at point (x_1,y_1), over θ degrees.

\arc[*a*]{$(x,y),r,\theta_a,\theta_b$}

Draw an arc with center at (x,y) and a radius r, between the angles θ_a and θ_b.

\arc[*s*]{$(x_0,y_0),(x_1,y_1),\theta$}

Draw an arc from the point (x_0,y_0) to the point (x_1,y_1), at an angle of θ degrees.

\arc[*t*]{$(x_0,y_0),(x_1,y_1),(x_2,y_2)$}

Draw an arc that passes through the three points.

\axis[*hlen*]{*one-axis*}

Draw an axis. The parameter *one-axis* can be x or y to produce an x- or y-axis; or it can be l, b, r, or t to produce an axis on the border of the picture.

\doaxis[*hlen*]{*axis-list*}

This command is like \axis, but takes a list of any or all of the six letters.

\axes

Draw axes to span the current picture. An arrowhead of length \axisheadlen is drawn at the end of each axis. There are also \xaxis and \yaxis commands. These three commands are retained only for compatibility.

\circle[*format*]{*specification*}

\circle[p]{$(x,y),r$}

\circle[c]{$(x,y),(x_1,y_1)$}

\circle[t]{$(x_1,y_1),(x_2,y_2),(x_3,y_3)$}

\circle[s]{$(x_1,y_1),(x_2,y_2),\theta$}

Draw a circle. The circle can be specified in four different ways: by its center and radius (case p), by its center and a point (case c), by three points (case t), or by two points and an angle (case s).

\curve[*tension*]{$(x_0,y_0),(x_2,y_2),\ldots,(x_n,y_n)$}

Draw a Bézier path through the points. The optional parameter influences how smooth the path is. It should be greater than 0.75; its default value is 1.

\cyclic{$(x_0,y_0),(x_1,y_1),\ldots,(x_n,y_n)$}

Draw a Bézier curve through the points, and join the last and first points to create a closed object.

\ellipse[θ]{$(x,y),r_x,r_y$}

Draw a centered ellipse (x,y) with a "width" of r_x and a "height" of r_y. If θ is given, rotate the ellipse by that amount.

\fcncurve[*tension*]{$(x_0,y_0),(x_2,y_2),\ldots,(x_n,y_n)$}

Draw a curve through the specified points. If the points are listed with increasing (or decreasing) x coordinates, the curve will also have increasing (or decreasing) x coordinates. The tension should be greater or equal to 1.

\grid[*ptsize*]{*xsep,ysep*}

Draw a dot at every point for which the first coordinate is an integer multiple of *xsep* and the second coordinate is an integer multiple of *ysep*.

\lines{$(x_0, y_0),(x_1, y_1),\ldots,(x_n, y_n)$}

Draw line segments between points. \polylines is an alias for \lines.

\point[*ptsize*]{$(x_0, y_0),(x_1, y_1),\ldots,(x_n, y_n)$}

Draw small filled circles centered at the points. If the optional argument *ptsize* is present, it determines the diameter of the disks, which otherwise equals the TEX dimension \pointsize.

\plotsymbol[*size*]{*symbol*}{$(x_0, y_0),(x_1, y_1),\ldots,(x_n, y_n)$}

Draw small symbols centered at the points (x_0, y_0), (x_1, y_1), and so on. The symbols must be given by name, and the available symbols are Asterisk, Circle, Diamond, Square, Triangle, Star, SolidCircle, SolidDiamond, SolidSquare, SolidTriangle, SolidStar, Cross, and Plus.

\pointdef{*name*}(x, y)

Define a symbolic name \name for (x, y). \name$x$ is defined to be x and \name$y$ is defined to be y.

\polygon{$(x_0, y_0),(x_1, y_1),\ldots,(x_n, y_n)$}

Draw a closed polygon with vertices at the points.

\regpolygon{*num*}{*name*}{*eqn$_1$*}{*eqn$_2$*}

Draw a regular polygon with *num* sides. The second argument is a symbolic name that can be used to refer to the vertices later. The last two arguments should be equations that position two of the vertices or one vertex and the center. The center is refered to by *name*0 and the vertices by *name*1, *name*2, and so forth, going anticlockwise. *name* itself will be a variable assigned the value of *num*.

\rect{$(x_0, y_0),(x_1, y_1)$}

Draw a rectangle with corners at (x_0, y_0) and (x_1, y_1).

\turtle{$(x, y),(x_1, y_1),(x_2, y_2),\ldots$}

Draw a line segment starting at (x, y), and then draw line segments (x, y) to $(x + x_1, y + y_1)$, $(x + x_1, y + y_1)$ to $(x + x_1 + x_2, y + y_1 + y_2)$, and so forth.

\sector{$(x, y),r,\theta_1,\theta_2$}

Draw a wedge of a circle from θ_1 to θ_2 centered at (x, y) with radius r.

\xmarks[*len*]{*numberlist*}
\ymarks[*len*]{*numberlist*}
\tmarks[*len*]{*numberlist*}
\bmarks[*len*]{*numberlist*}
\lmarks[*len*]{*numberlist*}
\rmarks[*len*]{*numberlist*}
\axismarks{*axis*}[*len*]{*numberlist*}

Place marks on x, y, top, bottom, left, or right axes at the coordinates specified in the list. The length of the marks is is *len* and defaults to \hashlen. \axismarks{x} is equivalent to \xmarks, and so on. *numberlist* can also be replaced by the sequence "-2 step 1 until 2", which is equivalent to "-2,-1,0,1,2".

Bar charts and pie charts

mfpic also provides a command to draw bar or pie charts:

> \barchart [*start,sep,r*] {*h-or-v*}{*list*}

The macro \barchart computes a bar chart or a Gantt chart. It does not draw the bars, but merely defines their rectangular paths, which the user may then draw or fill, or both, using the \chartbar macros. *h-or-v* should be v if the ends of the bars should be measured vertically from the x-axis, or h if they should be measured horizontally from the y-axis. *list* should be a comma-separated list of numbers and/or pairs giving the coordinates of the end(s) of each bar. A number c is interpreted as the pair $(0, c)$; a pair (a, b) is interpreted as an interval giving the ends of the bar. The parameters *start*, *sep*, and *r* affect how the bars are positioned and make it easy to superimpose several series of bars.

> \chartbar{*n*}

This command draws bar n, where n is an element in the list given as an argument to \barchart.

The following example shows how \barchart and \chartbar can be used with two sets of adjoining and differently colored bars.

```
\usepackage[metapost]{mfpic}
\newcommand{\greenbar}[1]{%
   \gfill[green]\chartbar{#1}\chartbar{#1}}
\newcommand{\redbar}[1]{%
   \gfill[red]\chartbar{#1}\chartbar{#1}}


\opengraphsfile{tmp}
\begin{mfpic}[10][10]{0}{11}{0}{7}
\axes
\barchart[1,1,-.4]{v}{1,2,3,4,5,4,3,2,1}
\redbar{1}\redbar{2}\redbar{3}
\redbar{4}\redbar{5}\redbar{6}
\redbar{7}\redbar{8}\redbar{9}


\barchart[1,1,.4]{v}{2,1,5,3,6,3,6,4,3}
\greenbar{1}\greenbar{2}\greenbar{3}
\greenbar{4}\greenbar{5}\greenbar{6}
\greenbar{7}\greenbar{8}\greenbar{9}


\end{mfpic}
\closegraphsfile
```

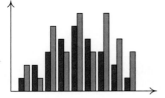

Example
3-6-5

> \piechart [*dir angle*] {*c, r*} {*list*}

Like \barchart, this command doesn't draw anything, but computes the \piewedge regions described next. The first part of the optional parameter, *dir*, is a single letter that may be either c or a, which stand for clockwise and anticlockwise, respectively. *angle* is the starting angle (90 degrees by default). The data is entered as a comma-separated *list* of positive numbers. c is the center, and r is the radius of the pie chart.

> \piewedge [*spec trans*] {*num*}

This command draws the wedge corresponding to data *num*. *spec* can be x (exploded), s (shifted), or m (move to) and allows the wedge to be drawn at a different position. x is followed by a distance in graph units, s by a pair of relative coordinates, and m by a pair of absolute coordinates.

An example of the use of \piechart and \piewedge is given below.

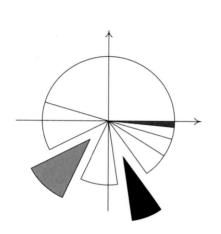

```
\usepackage[metapost]{mfpic}
\opengraphsfile{tmp}
\begin{mfpic}[10][10]{-7}{7}{-7}{7}
\axes
\piechart[c 0]{(0,0),5}{1,2,3,4,5,6,7,8,30}
\gfill[red]\piewedge{1}\piewedge{1}
\piewedge{2}
\piewedge{3}
\piewedge{4}
\gfill[blue]\piewedge[x 3]{5}\piewedge[x 3]{5}
\piewedge{6}
\gfill[green]\piewedge[x 2]{7}\piewedge[x 2]{7}
\piewedge{8}
\piewedge{9}
\end{mfpic}
\closegraphsfile
```

Example
3-6-6

Drawing parameters

\dashlen (default 4pt)
  Length of dashes.

\dashspace (default 4pt)
  Gap between dashes.

\hashlen (default 4pt)
  Length of hash marks on the axes.

\shadespace (default 1pt)
  Gap between dots drawn by \shade.

\hatchspace (default 3pt)
  Gap between lines drawn by \hatch.

`\mfpicunit` (default 1pt)
> Basic unit length for pictures.

`\pointsize` (default 2pt)
> Diameter of circle for `\point` macro.

`pointfilled` (default true)
> Boolean variable determining whether circles drawn by `\point` are filled.

`\headlen` (default 3pt)
> Length of arrowhead.

`\axisheadlen` (default 5pt)
> Length of arrowhead on `\axes`.

Global modifier commands

`\headshape{`*ratio*`}{`*tension*`}{`*filled*`}`
> Set the arrowheads shape. The arguments are: the *ratio* of the width of the arrowhead to its length (default 1); the *tension* of the Bézier curves used to draw the arrowhead (default 1); and *filled* is a Boolean that determines whether arrowheads are filled (default true).

`\pen{`*pensize*`}`
> Set the width of the drawing pen (the default is 5pt).

`\dashlineset`
> Set `\dashlen` and `\dashspace` to 4pt.

`\dotlineset`
> Set `\dashlen` to 1pt and `\dashspace` to 2pt.

`\darkershade`
> Make shading denser by multiplying `\shadespace` by a factor of $5/6$.

`\lightershade`
> Make shading lighter by multiplying `\shadespace` by a factor of $6/5$.

Figure modifier commands

Any object drawn with one of the simple commands, or a composite object created using `connect`, can be modified with one or more *prefix* commands. These commands apply just to the next object and are mostly used for closed objects such as circles, ellipses, and so on. The filling commands do *not* draw an outline for the object and must come first if there is more than one modifier.

`\arrow[l`*length*`] [r`θ`] [b`*distance*`]`
> Draw an arrowhead at the last specified point of an object. The three optional parameters let you change the shape: the length of the arrowhead is set by *length* (default is `\headlen`), the angle by θ, and the distance from the end point by *distance* (this lets you draw double arrowheads). The optional parameters can occur in any order but must be preceded by the special key characters.

`\bclosed, \lclosed, \sclosed, \cbclosed`
> Close an open object by joining the end points; `\lclosed` draws a straight line, `\bclosed` draws a Bézier curve, `\sclosed` draws a smooth curve, and `\cbclosed` draws a cubic B-spline.

\dotted[*dash*] [*gap*]
  Draw dotted or dashed object lines. The length of dashes is set by \dashlen, but it can be
  overridden by *dash*. Similarly, the space between dashes can be set with *gap* (the default
  is \dashspace).

\draw
  Draw an outline for an object; this is needed if you want to draw *and* fill a object.

\gclear
  Erase everything inside a closed object.

\gfill
  Fill a closed object.

\hatch[*distance*]
  Draw cross-hatched shading to fill a closed object. The default gap between lines is
  \hatchspace, but it can be overridden with the optional *distance* parameter. A variety
  of other hatching commands are also defined.

\reverse
  Reverse the orientation of an object. This command is useful in changing the sequence of
  points inside a connect environment so that a different end point is used.

\rotatepath{(x,y),θ}
  Rotate an object by θ degrees around (x,y).

\shade[*distance*]
  Fill a closed object with dots. The default gap between dots is \shadespace, but it can
  be overridden with the optional *distance* parameter.

Analytical curves and functions

A common requirement in scientific data analysis is plottting functions and parametric
curves. METAFONT and METAPOST are very suitable for this sort of work, and mfpic
has five general commands. Each of them has an optional first parameter that can have the
value s, meaning that the plot is drawn with a smooth Bézier curve, or p, meaning that it is
drawn with straight lines. The default is s except for \btwnfcn and \plrregion.

Each command has a mandatory parameter to express the minimum and maximum
values for the function and the step. The other parameters are function(s) passed to META-
FONT or METAPOST to evaluate.

\function[*type*]{*minimum,maximum,step*}{*expr*}
  Plot *expr*.

\parafcn[*type*]{*minimum_t,maximum_t,step*}{(*expr_1,expr_2*)}
  Plot the parametric path $(x(t), y(t)) = (expr_1, expr_2)$.

\plrfcn[*type*]{*minimum,maximum,step*}{*expr*}
  Plot the polar function *expr*.

\btwnfcn[*type*]{*minimum,maximum,step*}{*expr_1*}{*expr_2*}
  Draw the region between functions $f(x) = expr_1$, and $g(x) = expr_2$, where the region
  is bounded also by the vertical lines at *minimum* and *maximum*. By default, the function
  is drawn as a set of line segments.

\plrregion[*type*]{*minimum,maximum,step*}{expr}

Plot the polar region determined by $r =$ expr(θ). The θ values are angles (measured in *degrees*) between *minimum* and *maximum*. By default, the function is drawn as a set of line segments.

Annotating drawings

Two commands for annotating drawings are processed entirely in LaTeX and pass nothing to the METAFONT or METAPOST file.

\tlabel[*pos*](x,y){*text*}

This command labels a graph with *text* at (x,y). By default, the text is positioned with its lower-left corner at (x,y), but the optional position parameter *pos* can also be used. *pos* is similar to the placing parameters for boxes in the `picture` environment. It specifies the relative placement of the label with respect to the reference point: the first character is for the *vertical* placement (t for top, c for center, and b for bottom), and the second character is for the horizontal placement (l for left, c for center, and r for right).

\tcaption[*maxwidth,linewidth*]{*text*}

This command centers a caption underneath your drawing. You can specify how a long caption will be broken into lines with the optional parameters. If the caption is wider than *maxwidth* × the width of the drawing, then the text is typeset in a paragraph with a line length of *linewidth* × the width of the drawing. The default is [*1.2,1.0*].

Examples

We conclude our description of **mfpic** with some examples; these are designed not to show all the features of the package but rather to demonstrate some typical applications.

A repetitive drawing can take advantage of LaTeX's programmability. Below we define a macro to draw a flower petal and then call it several times with different modifiers. This example uses an affine transformation (see Section 3.6.2) to allow cumulative rotation.

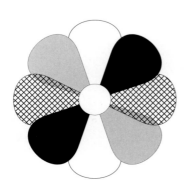

```
\usepackage[metapost]{mfpic}
\opengraphsfile{tmp}
\begin{mfpic}[1.2]{-50}{50}{-50}{50}
 \pen{.3pt}
 \newcommand\petal{\bclosed\lines{(30,10),(0,0),(10,30)}}
 \newcommand\halfflower
    {\begin{coords}
        \gfill\petal \turn{45}\petal\turn{45}
        \shade\draw\petal\turn{45}\hatch\draw\petal
     \end{coords}}
 \halfflower\turn{180}\halfflower
 \gclear\draw\circle{(0,0),10}
\end{mfpic}
\closegraphsfile
```

Example 3-6-7

Our next picture, a simple data plot, demonstrates the use of labels; again, we use a LaTeX macro to parameterize how these are drawn. Because the values in the x direction have a much greater range than those in the y direction, the optional y scaling of the mfpic environment is convenient. This also shows how a drawing as a whole can be manipulated with the standard rotation macros.

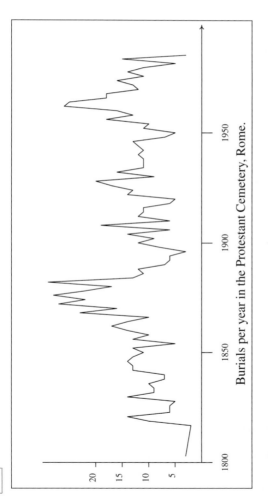

Example
3-6-8

```
\usepackage[metapost]{mfpic}
\usepackage{graphicx}

\opengraphsfile{tmp}
\rotatebox{90}{\fbox{%
\begin{mfpic}[1.7][4]{-10}{200}{-5}{35}
\newcommand\XmyLabel[2]{%
 \tlabel[bc](#1,-5){{\scriptsize#2}}
   \lines{(#1,0),(#1,-2)}}
\newcommand\YmyLabel[1]{%
 \tlabel[br](-5,#1){{\scriptsize#1}}
   \lines{(0,#1),(-2,#1)}}
\XmyLabel{0}{1800}\XmyLabel{50}{1850}
\XmyLabel{100}{1900}\XmyLabel{150}{1950}
\YmyLabel{5}\YmyLabel{10}
\YmyLabel{15}\YmyLabel{20}
\arrow\lines{(0,30),(0,0),(200,0)}
\lines{(03,3), (17,2), (19,10), (21,14),
  (23,6), (26,6), (28,5), (30,14), (32,9),
  (34,9), (36,10), (38,7), (40,7), (42,13),
  (44,13), (46,14), (48,13), (50,11),
  (52,13), (54,5), (56,13), (58,10),
  (60,14), (62,17), (64,14), (66,10),
  (68,23), (70,16), (72,27), (74,22),
  (76,28), (78,22), (80,17), (82,29),
  (84,13), (86,11), (88,12), (90,7),
  (92,6), (94,6), (96,3), (98,8), (100,12),
  (102,9), (104,14), (106,6), (108,19),
  (110,6), (112,12), (114,11), (116,11),
  (118,6), (120,5), (122,14), (124,13),
  (126,17), (128,20), (130,9), (132,16),
  (134,11), (136,11), (138,11), (140,12),
  (142,11), (144,12), (146,13), (148,7),
  (150,5), (152,11), (154,10), (156,18),
  (158,13), (160,16), (162,26), (164,25),
  (166,18), (168,18), (170,12), (172,13),
  (174,16), (176,11), (178,14), (180,11),
  (182,5), (184,15), (186,3)}
\tcaption[.8,.75]{Burials per year in the
Protestant Cemetery, Rome.}
\end{mfpic}}}
\closegraphsfile
```

A useful tool in these circumstances is the standard LaTeX **ifthen** package, which lets us perform routine looping:

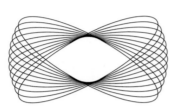

```
\usepackage[metapost]{mfpic}
\usepackage{ifthen}
\opengraphsfile{tmp}
\newcounter{mfcntA}
\begin{mfpic}[1.5]{-30}{40}{-25}{25}
\setcounter{mfcntA}{-30}
  \whiledo{\themfcntA<31}{%
    \ellipse[\themfcntA]{(0,0),40,12}
    \addtocounter{mfcntA}{6}}%
\end{mfpic}
\closegraphsfile
```

Example
3-6-9

Another use of looping is to draw a spiral, using the same technique as on page 55. This is not necessarily the "correct" way to draw such a shape, which might be better expressed using the \parafcn command:

```
\usepackage[metapost]{mfpic}
\usepackage{ifthen}

\opengraphsfile{tmp}
\begin{mfpic}[1.5]{-40}{50}{-48}{50}
\newcounter{mfcntA}
\newcounter{mfcntB}
\setcounter{mfcntA}{50}
\setcounter{mfcntB}{48}
\whiledo{\themfcntA>1}{%
  \expandafter\curve{(\themfcntA,0),
    (0,\themfcntA),
    (-\themfcntA,0),
    (0,-\themfcntB),
    (\themfcntB,0)}
  \addtocounter{mfcntA}{-2}%
  \addtocounter{mfcntB}{-2}%
}
\end{mfpic}
\closegraphsfile
```

Example
3-6-10

Going further

mfpic defines a set of affine transformations (rotation, reflection, translation, scaling, and skewing) described in detail in the package documentation. We used one of these (\turn) in the "flower" example given earlier, to keep turning the current drawing state. All the transformations are cumulative, but their effect can be conveniently limited with the coords environment (as demonstrated in the "flower" example).

Users who want to build new facilities can use commands to write METAFONT or METAPOST directly to the output file, to store and use METAFONT or METAPOST paths directly, and to develop sophisticated fill patterns for objects.

3.6.3 The mft and mpt pretty-printers

METAFONT and METAPOST sources can be pretty-printed with mft and mpt. Donald Knuth's mft is a program for pretty-printing METAFONT programs. Ulrik Vieth's mpt (CTAN: `graphics/metapost/contrib/misc`) is a script that processes METAPOST sources with mft.

Other TeX formats, such as ConTeXt, also provide means to pretty-print METAPOST sources within a document [42].

3.7 From METAPOST **and to** METAPOST

A variety of command-line and interactive drawing tools are available that produce META-POST, and a variety of ways to manipulate its output.

gnuplot Can generate METAPOST output.

pstoedit Can generate METAPOST from PostScript or PDF vector graphics. It can also generate a variety of outputs, such as SVG, from the PostScript output of METAPOST.

xfig Can export its drawings to METAPOST.

In general, graphical editors that can open PostScript files (such as **Adobe Illustrator**) should be able to cope with METAPOST output. Figure 3.4 shows a map drawn in **Auto-CAD** and converted to METAFONT; Figure 3.5 shows the same map converted to **Adobe Illustrator** from METAPOST output and colored using **Corel Draw**. While it would be possible to do the coloring with METAPOST, it is often more convenient to work on a map such as this in an interactive program.

Unfortunately, because most interactive drawing packages keep a rather simplistic internal representation of their pictures, META versions of their output are of limited use. Thus we could use **gnuplot** or **AutoCAD**, save the result as HPGL, and convert it to META, but the code would hardly be editable. A map of East Africa (Figure 3.4) drawn with **AutoCAD** and converted to METAFONT creates lines of code like this:

```
pickup pencircle scaled 0.1mm;
draw (10.732mm,11.563mm)--(10.651mm,11.517mm)--(10.592mm,11.505mm)--
(10.545mm,11.493mm)--(10.487mm,11.493mm)--(10.440mm,11.505mm)--
(10.405mm,11.540mm)--(10.346mm,11.563mm)--(10.299mm,11.599mm)--
(10.264mm,11.622mm)--(10.217mm,11.645mm); draw (10.217mm,11.645mm)--
(10.159mm,11.680mm)--(10.100mm,11.727mm)--(10.065mm,11.751mm)--
(10.007mm,11.786mm)--(9.960mm,11.798mm)--(9.913mm,11.821mm)--
(9.714mm,11.868mm)--(9.667mm,11.868mm);
```

Figure 3.4: **AutoCAD** map converted to METAFONT

Figure 3.5: METAFONT drawing enhanced using **Corel Draw**

This sort of code could hardly be edited by hand to shade the countries with different colors, as we have done in Figure 3.5.

A better result can be achieved with an elegant package called **mftoeps**, written by Bogusław Jackowski, Piotr Pianowski, and Marek Ryćko [58]. This METAFONT program intercepts drawing commands and rewrites them to the log file as Encapsulated PostScript; utility programs are provided to extract this code, and the result can be directly edited by **Corel Draw** and **Adobe Illustrator**.

3.8 The future of METAPOST

Most META drawings are rather self-contained and don't interact much with the surrounding text. Drawings may use text labels and other fragments, but then these labels and fragments are usually quasi-autonomous. They will influence the drawing in only one way.

In some cases, however, a drawing may have to interact with text in subtler ways—for instance, if text elements are supposed to belong at the same time to a flow of text (a paragraph) and be elements in a drawing. For such examples, a more elaborate communication between TEX and METAPOST is needed, such that a drawing can use positioning information from TEX while TEX uses the drawing. Post-processing the METAPOST output appropriately and using multiple TEX runs provide a solution. For an elaborate implementation of such a scheme, the reader should consult the manual for **metafun** by Hans Hagen.

Currently, METAPOST has a relatively small base of packages, whereas **PSTricks** comes equipped with packages for many applications. This doesn't mean, of course, that METAPOST cannot achieve some of the results achieved by packages like **PSTricks**. It is therefore important to distinguish what is easy in METAPOST, what can be added to METAPOST without much trouble, and what is more difficult to achieve.

The most important feature of METAPOST, in our view, is not the ability to solve linear equations, but rather the flexibility and the ability to manipulate complex objects and to take them apart. For instance, one can compute the intersections of curves *within* META-POST and use those intersections to build new curves. Curves can also be split into their control points, which can then be used to build new objects. The fact that a picture can be viewed as a tree of simple objects allows for a great variety of operations, most of which have not yet been explored. However, this advantage is also a drawback: the whole drawing remains in memory until the drawing is finished, which imposes some limits to the complexity of a drawing.

The main disadvantages of METAPOST lie in the deferment of certain operations—not only the memory problem just mentioned, but also the fact that operations such as clipping are not done at the METAPOST level but rather at the PostScript level. It is sometimes useful to manipulate a clipped path within METAPOST, but this isn't easily achieved. PSTricks has the same problem. This does not mean that there is no solution, but rather that more elaborate schemes must involve either macros (or extensions to METAPOST) that clip paths before outputting them to PostScript or an advanced communication between the METAPOST source and the PostScript output, so that during a second run METAPOST can use some of the information collected during the first run.

A lesser disadvantage of METAPOST is its syntax, which is not as flexible as TeX's syntax. Many complex packages still have a cumbersome way of dealing with optional arguments, but fortunately it is possible to rewrite or extend these packages to make use of a natural and TeX-friendly *key=value* syntax. TeX interfaces (which can be written for META-POST) alleviate such problems. Such a TeX interface does exist—namely, the **mfpic** package described in this chapter—but it does not cover the full range of METAPOST's applications.

CHAPTER 4

METAPOST **Applications**

Chapter 3 gave a general overview of METAFONT and METAPOST, as well as an extensive description of two multipurpose structuring packages, **boxes** and METAOBJ. However, as is the case for LATEX, solutions to many problems can often be found by using existing high-level packages. Sometimes several different METAPOST packages are aimed at the same tasks, and these packages come with both advantages and drawbacks.

Unfortunately, the perfect package is seldom at hand. It is therefore useful to have a general idea of what can be achieved in METAPOST, and to have some kind of toolbox for problem solving. Understanding a number of basic tricks will enable the beginner to supplement existing packages and achieve the desired results.

In this chapter, we start with a review of a number of basic problems and show how these problems can be solved. Then we describe some standard applications of META-POST, ranging from geometry to physics.

4.1 A drawing toolkit

This section is devoted to a number of advanced features, which are located somewhere between low-level METAPOST code and full application packages. We like to consider all these features as a kind of toolkit, which can be used with benefit in wider applications.

4.1.1 Text along a curve

It is sometimes necessary to write text along curves, and more generally along a META-POST path. This is possible, but achieving the desired results is rather more complex than writing text on an horizontal line.

The main problem is that the text characters must be appropriately spaced from each other, must be correctly rotated, and must align well. This is especially true when text is written in lowercase, as many letters go below the baseline.

Santiago Muelas defined a general macro **txp** (*text on path*) [86], which provides a good solution. It is available from CTAN: `graphics/metapost/contrib/macros/txp`.

For proper positioning of each character of a string, Muelas stores metric information obtained from the TFM files in METAPOST libraries, and loads this metric information when necessary.

We give here a simplified version of Muelas's code, which works properly only for upper-case text, but may nevertheless prove useful. The `stxp` (*simple text to path*) macro takes a string and a path, then writes the text along the curve, centering each character on the curve. The macro spaces or compresses the text as necessary to fit the path length. An example of use of this macro is given below. For more complex text, the full macro by Santiago Muelas should be used.

```
vardef stxp(expr s,p)=
  save len,prefix,car,lab,xpos,cpos,ratio;
  numeric len[];
  string prefix,car;
  picture lab;
  len0=0;
  for i:=length s step -1 until 1:
    prefix:=substring(0,i) of s;
    lab:=thelabel(prefix,(0,0));
    len[i]=2*(xpart(urcorner lab));
  endfor;
  ratio=arclength(p)/len[length s];

  for i=0 upto (length s)-1:
    car:=substring(i,i+1) of s;
    if car<>" ":
      xpos:=((len[i]+len[i+1])/2)*ratio;
      cpos:=arctime xpos of p;
      lab:=thelabel(car,(0,0));
      draw lab rotated (angle (direction cpos of p))
              shifted (point cpos of p);
    fi;
  endfor;
enddef;
path p;
p=((0,0)..(4cm,7cm)..(5cm,3cm)..(3cm,2cm)) yscaled .5;
draw p withcolor red;
stxp("IN PRINCIPIO CREAVIT DEUS CÆLUM ET TERRAM.",p);
```

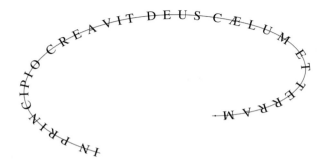

Example
4-1-1

4.1.2 Gradients

Gradients are areas where the color changes gradually, according to some specified rule. An easy way to produce such gradients is to draw a number of lines or curves with varying color. The code below provides two such kinds of gradients, circular and parallel. Circular gradients are obtained by drawing a number of concentric circles. Parallel gradients use a number of parallel lines with different colors.

Such an approach is rather resource-consuming, but still sufficient for most cases. For more elaborate applications, the gradient features of PostScript could be used through the **metafun** package (see Section 3.4.1). Some of **metafun**'s facilities for gradients are used by other packages, such as **piechartMP**.

```
def PARALLEL = 0 enddef;
def CIRCULAR  = 1 enddef;
def max(expr a,b)= (if a>b: a else: b fi) enddef;
def f(expr x)=((1+sind(2x*360))/2) enddef;
def g(expr x)=(x*x) enddef;

% f:   gradient function; a,b: interval for f
% n:   steps;             ca,cb: colors 1 and 2
% p:   path
% c:   center of gradient (CIRCULAR) or direction (PARALLEL)
vardef gradient(text f)(expr a,b,n,ca,cb,type)(expr p,c)=
  save A,B,C,D,pic,rp,r;
  pair A,B,C,D;picture pic;path rp;
  if type=PARALLEL:rp=p rotated (-angle(c));else:rp=p;fi;
  A=llcorner(rp);C=urcorner(rp);
  B=(xpart C,ypart A);D=(xpart A,ypart C);
  if type=PARALLEL:
    A:=A rotated angle(c);B:=B rotated angle(c);
    C:=C rotated angle(c);D:=D rotated angle(c);
  fi;
  if type=CIRCULAR:
    r=max(arclength(c--A),arclength(c--B));
    r:=max(r,arclength(c--C));r:=max(r,arclength(c--D));
```

```
      fi;
      pic=nullpicture;
      if type=PARALLEL:
        for i:=0 upto n-1:
          addto pic
            contour ((i/n)[A,B]--((i+1)/n)[A,B]
                      --((i+1)/n)[D,C]--(i/n)[D,C])--cycle
            withcolor ((f(i/n))[ca,cb]);
          endfor;
      elseif type=CIRCULAR:
        for i:=n step -1 until 1:
          addto pic
            contour fullcircle scaled (2*(i/n)*r) shifted c
            withcolor ((f(i/n))[ca,cb]);
          endfor;
      fi;
      clip pic to p;draw pic;
    enddef;

    def parallelgradient(text f)(expr a,b,n,ca,cb)(expr p,d)=
      gradient(f)(a,b,n,ca,cb,PARALLEL)(p,d);
    enddef;

    def circulargradient(text f)(expr a,b,n,ca,cb)(expr p,c)=
      gradient(f)(a,b,n,ca,cb,CIRCULAR)(p,c);
    enddef;
```

```
% parallelgradient as defined above
numeric u;
u=1cm;
path p;
p=fullcircle scaled 3u;
parallelgradient(f)(0,1,100,red,blue)(p,(1,1));
```

Example
4-1-2

```
% circulargradient as defined above
numeric u;
u=1cm;
path p;
p=fullcircle xscaled 4u
             yscaled 2u
             shifted (0,-4u);
circulargradient(g)(0,1,100,green,red)
             (p,center p+(2u,0));
```

Example
4-1-3

4.1.3 Hidden lines

It is sometimes useful to hide parts of a path, but achieving proper results can be cumbersome. The macro `hiddenpath`, while not absolutely general, provides a very simple means to achieve this purpose in most cases. The macro works as follows: A path that should be partly hidden is first drawn completely in the usual way. This will take care of all the non-hidden parts. Next, for every part of a path hidden by another one, the `hiddenpath` macro first erases the hidden part and then redraws it with dashed lines. This works even if some paths are hidden by several other paths, as in the example below.

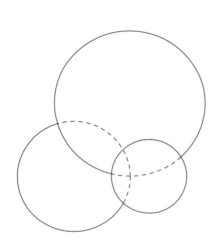

```
vardef hiddenpath(expr under,over)=
  save p,q;
  picture p,q;
  p=image(draw under);clip p to over;
  undraw p;
  q=image(draw under dashed evenly);
  clip q to over;
  draw q;
enddef;
path p[];
p1=fullcircle scaled 3cm;
p2=fullcircle scaled 2cm shifted (2cm,0);
p3=fullcircle scaled 4cm shifted (1.5cm,2cm);
draw p1; % we draw the three circles totally
draw p2;
draw p3;
hiddenpath(p1,p2); % p1 hidden by p2
hiddenpath(p1,p3); % p1          p3
hiddenpath(p3,p2); % p3          p2
```

Example
4-1-4

In certain cases, the order of operations will be meaningful. Nevertheless, the previous macro should, with minor alterations, fit almost all hidden line problems. A more complex example using this technique is given in Section 4.5.2.

The `hiddenpath` command in Example 4-1-4 illustrates METAPOST's `clip` command. With this command, a picture can be clipped with a path. However, contrary to appearances, METAPOST does not go to the trouble of actually cutting the various components of a picture; rather, it simply issues the appropriate PostScript orders. As a consequence, it is not easy to obtain the contours of the clipped paths within METAPOST, if for some reason these paths are needed.

METAPOST does not provide such advanced clipping features, but they could nevertheless be added on the macro level, using the following representation for multipaths.

4.1.4 Multipaths and advanced clipping

A multipath is an "interrupted path"—that is, a path that cannot be drawn with a single stroke. Such paths can be represented as lists of paths. It is not necessary to introduce a new data structure, as METAPOST already provides a most appropriate option—namely, picture. A `picture` can store any sequence of drawings, and in particular all the strokes that make up a multipath. However, it is up to us to define how such a multipath is used. For instance, if a picture contains a list of closed paths, those closed paths with a positive turning number could be considered as holes in the other closed paths. A useful feature would then be to produce a set of closed paths covering the original closed paths, minus their holes. To our knowledge, this work has not yet been tackled in METAPOST, but as an incentive for future work, we show here how basic multipaths could be manipulated.

We define two macros: one for drawing a multipath, and another to build a multipath by adding a path. In both cases, the p parameter is of type `picture`. An example of the use of these macros is given below.

```
% p=picture
def draw_multipath(expr p) text options=
  for i within p:
    draw i options;
  endfor;
enddef;

vardef addto_multipath(text p)(expr pa,thickness) text options=
  save savepen;
  pen savepen;
  savepen=currentpen;
  pickup pencircle scaled thickness;
  addto p also image(draw pa options;);
  currentpen:=savepen;
enddef;
numeric u;u=10mm;
path p[];picture pic;
p0=origin..(2u,0)..(4u,u)..(3u,2u)
    ...(2u,-u)..tension2..(u,3u);
n=20;
for i=1 upto n:
  p[i]=subpath(((i-1)/n)*length(p0),
               (i/n)*length(p0)) of p0;
endfor;
pic=nullpicture;
for i=1 upto n:
  if odd i:
    addto_multipath(pic)(p[i],2pt*i/n)
      withcolor ((i/n)*red+(1-i/n)*blue);
  else:
    addto_multipath(pic)(p[i],3pt*(1-i/n))
      withcolor ((i/n)*green+(1-i/n)*blue);
  fi;
endfor;
draw_multipath(pic);
```

Example
4-1-5

4.1.5 Patterns, hatchings, and tilings

Hatching and tiling are special cases of more general repeating patterns. Such drawings are based on a pattern that is repeated a number of times and then usually constrained to some area.

A grid is also this kind of drawing. Moreover, it serves as a good illustration of the many ways such a drawing can be created. For example, a grid can be produced either by repeating the horizontal and vertical lines:

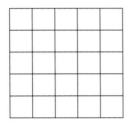

```
for i=0 upto 5:
   draw (0,i*6mm)--(3cm,i*6mm);
endfor;
for i=0 upto 5:
   draw (i*6mm,0)--(i*6mm,3cm);
endfor;
```

or by replicating squares:

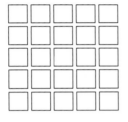

```
def square=(unitsquare scaled 5mm) enddef;
for i=0 upto 4:
  for j=0 upto 4:
    draw square shifted (i*6mm,j*6mm);
  endfor;
endfor;
```

Sometimes there are several base patterns—for instance, a square and a circle:

```
def square=(unitsquare
    shifted (-.5,-.5) scaled 3mm)
enddef;
def circle=(fullcircle scaled 3mm) enddef;
for i=0 upto 4:
  for j=0 upto 4:
    if odd(i+j):
      draw square shifted (i*6mm,j*6mm);
    else:fill circle shifted (i*6mm,j*6mm);
    fi
  endfor;
endfor;
```

Numerous applications of these ideas are possible. We refer the reader especially to articles on tilings, such as those by Kees van der Laan [125] (who compares many tiling examples in PostScript and METAFONT), and works on the Truchet tiling [21]. The Web site `http://melusine.eu.org/syracuse/metapost` has several good tiling examples, in particular on Escher's tilings.

Celtic artwork can also be viewed as a tiling problem, and Alun Moon has written METAPOST macros to produce such drawings [84]. He deals in particular with knots and defines a macro producing the list of intersections that a path has with a list of other paths; "keypatterns" (tilings) and spirals are also considered.

The mpattern package by Piotr Bolek provides macros to define and fill patterns [12].

Hatching

Hatching can be obtained by a combination of regular patterns and clipping to a specific area. The following macro, which is adapted from one written by Christophe Poulain, shows a straightforward example. The hatch macro takes a closed path and three parameters used to define the hatching style. The background hatching is drawn, but only insofar that the lines intersect with the path to fill. Once all the lines have been drawn, they are clipped to the argument path.

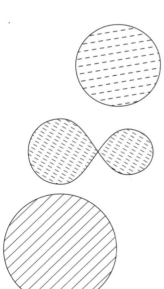

```
vardef hatch(expr pth, angle, shift, trace)=
  save pic,support,st;
  picture pic;
  path support;
  pair st;
  st=shift*dir(angle+90);
  support=((37cm*left)--(37cm*right)) rotated angle;
  if trace=1:drawoptions(dashed evenly);fi;
  pic=image(
    for j=-200 upto 200:
      if ((support shifted (j*st))
            intersectiontimes pth) <> (-1,-1):
        draw support shifted (j*st);
      fi
    endfor;
    );
  clip pic to pth;
  drawoptions();
  pic
enddef;

path p,q,r;
p=fullcircle scaled 3cm;
draw hatch(p,45,2mm,0) withcolor red;
draw p;
q=(p scaled .75) shifted (1.5cm,5cm);
draw hatch(q,10,2mm,1);
draw q;
r=(0,100)..(0,50)..(60,90)..(60,60)..cycle;
draw hatch(r,150,1mm,1) withcolor blue;
draw r;
```

Example
4-1-9

Bogusław Jackowski's **hatching** package provides a more elaborate way to achieve hatching patterns, by redefining the `withcolor` primitive in such a way that it represents hatching parameters when the blue component of the color is negative. The following examples illustrate this principle.

```
input hatching;
path p;
p:=unitsquare xscaled 30mm yscaled 15mm;
hatchfill p withcolor red
            withcolor (45,2mm,-.5bp)
            withcolor (-45,2mm,-.5bp);
```

The next three examples use a special closed path shaped as a star, defined by the `star` macro:

```
input hatching;
vardef star(expr n) =
 for i_:=0 upto 2n-1:
  if odd i_: 1/2 fi (right rotated (180*(i_/n))) --
 endfor cycle
enddef;
interim hatch_match:=0;
path p;
p:=star(10) xscaled 30mm
            yscaled 20mm
            rotated 20;
hatchfill p withcolor (0,1,.5);
draw image(hatchfill p
        withcolor (45,3bp,-.5bp)
        withcolor (-45,3bp,-.5bp);
     ) withcolor red dashed evenly;
```

```
input hatching;
% star macro defined as above
path p;
p:=star(10) xscaled 30mm
            yscaled 20mm
            rotated 20;
interim hatch_match:=0;
hatchoptions(withcolor blue
            dashed evenly scaled 2);
hatchfill p withcolor .75white
            withcolor (20,6bp,-.5bp);
hatchoptions(withcolor (blue+green)
            dashed evenly
            shifted (3/2bp,0));
hatchfill p withcolor (110,6bp,-.5bp);
```

The last example illustrates special effects obtained by redefining the macro `draw_hatched_band` that is normally responsible for drawing a strip component of a hatched line.

```
input hatching;
% star macro defined as above
path p;
p:=star(10) xscaled 20mm yscaled 20mm;
save draw_hatched_band;
vardef draw_hatched_band(expr za,zb,a,l,d) =
  save n_; n_:=length(za-zb)/l;
  for i_:=0 upto ceiling n_:
    fill star(10) xscaled 2/5l yscaled 2/5l
      shifted (i_/n_)[za,zb]
      withcolor (i_/n_)[green,blue];
  endfor
enddef;
hatchfill p withcolor (red+green)
             withcolor (45,10bp,-1bp);
```

Example
4-1-13

4.1.6 Transparency

Understanding transparency

The normal `fill` operation is opaque in METAPOST, with one color overriding the ones drawn before. It is, however, possible to find out which parts of a picture are below a given path and to change the color of the new area in accordance with the underlying parts and a transparency factor. The keys to the solution are the iterator `for...within` and the operators `redpart`, `greenpart`, `bluepart`, and `pathpart`. (See Section 3.2.4 for another example of use of these commands.) We give below the slightly adapted code written by Anthony Phan.

```
picture alphapict_; alphapict_=nullpicture;
vardef alphafill(expr c,col,transparency)=
  alphapict_:=nullpicture;
  alphafill_(currentpicture,c,col,transparency);
  addto currentpicture also alphapict_;
enddef;
def alphafill_(expr p,c,col,transparency)=
  begingroup
    save p_,xmax_,xmin_,ymax_,ymin_; picture p_;
    p_=nullpicture;
    (xmin_,ymin_)=llcorner c;(xmax_,ymax_)=urcorner c;
    addto p_ contour c withcolor transparency[background,col];
    for p__ within p:
      numeric xmin__,xmax__,ymin__,ymax__;
      (xmin__,ymin__)=llcorner p__;
      (xmax__,ymax__)=urcorner p__;
```

```
      if (xmax__<=xmin_) or (xmin__>=xmax_):
      else:
        if (ymax__<=ymin_) or (ymin__>=ymax_):
        else:
          if (not clipped p__) and (not bounded p__):
            addto p_ also p__ withcolor
            transparency[(redpart p__,greenpart p__,bluepart p__),col];
          else:
            begingroup save alphapict_;
              picture alphapict_; alphapict_ = nullpicture;
              alphafill_(p__,pathpart p__,col,transparency);
              addto p_ also alphapict_;
            endgroup;
          fi
        fi
      fi
    endfor
    clip p_ to c;  addto alphapict_ also p_;
  endgroup;
enddef;
```

An example of this macro's usage follows:

```
% alphafill as defined above
numeric u;
u=4cm;
fill unitsquare scaled u
               shifted (u,.5u+2u)
               withcolor blue;
unfill unitsquare
       scaled .8u
       shifted (.1u+u,.1u+.5u+2u);
alphafill (unitsquare scaled u
  shifted (u-.2u,2u),(.8,0,.5),.5);
alphafill (fullcircle shifted (.5,.5)
  xscaled .75u  yscaled 1.5u
  shifted (u+.5u,1.75u+.5u),(1,1,0),.5);
fill unitsquare scaled .5u
       shifted (.25u+u,.25u+.5u+2u)
       withcolor green;
alphafill (unitsquare scaled .5u
       shifted (.15u+u,.35u+.5u+2u),(0,.4,.5),.5);
```

Example
4-1-14

Transparent labels the easy way

An easy way to use transparent colors in labels is to use the latexMP package in conjunction with the metafun package. In this case, a PDF file should be produced and later included with \includegraphics.

4.1.7 Blurred effects

Blurred lines can be obtained by overlaying several versions of the line with slightly different positions and lighter or darker shades. If a path must be blurred, it is a straightforward matter to draw the path with different thicknesses, where the thickest is the palest. The example below illustrates a square, a star, and a circle with blurred edges.

```
vardef star(expr n) =
 for i_:=0 upto 2n-1:
  if odd i_: 1/2 fi (right rotated (180*(i_/n))) --
 endfor cycle
enddef;

vardef blur(expr p,w,col)=
  for i:=10 downto 1:
    pickup pencircle scaled ((i*i/100)*w);
    draw p withcolor ((i/10)[col,white]);
  endfor;
enddef;

blur (unitsquare scaled 3cm,.5mm,red);
blur (fullcircle scaled 4cm,1mm,blue);
blur (star(10) xscaled 30mm yscaled 20mm
                 rotated 20,2mm,black);
```

./EX/4-1-15

Example
4-1-15

4.1.8 Morphing

A path can be transformed into another path using the `interpath` command from the standard library. This command simply interpolates the control points of the paths to create a new intermediate path. An example is given below:

```
numeric u;
u=5mm;
path p[];
p1=fullcircle scaled 5u;
p2=unitsquare scaled 3u shifted (0,5u);
draw p2;
draw p1 withcolor red;
draw interpath(.1,p1,p2) withcolor .25[red,green];
draw interpath(.25,p1,p2) withcolor .5[red,green];
draw interpath(.5,p1,p2) withcolor green;
draw interpath(.75,p1,p2) withcolor .5[green,black];
draw interpath(.9,p1,p2) withcolor .7[green,black];
```

Example
4-1-16

The **metafun** package has a macro `interpolate` for the same purpose.

4.1.9 Turtle graphics

Even within the realm of METAPOST, drawings can be done in different ways or in different styles. Depending on the application, some approaches may be more suitable than others.

Classical style

The normal approach is first to define points and then to join these points. For instance, we can draw a rectangle using this approach:

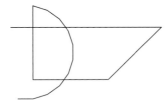

```
numeric u;
u=1cm;
z0=origin;z1-z0=(2u,0);
z2-z1=z3-z0=(0,u);
draw z0--z1--z2--z3--cycle;
```

Example
4-1-17

Equations can be given differently, and sometimes more elaborate operations such as intersections will be used to obtain new points. Nevertheless, the basic idea remains the same: Define points explicitly and then to use them for a drawing. Of course, in the preceding example, the `unitsquare` macro could have been used, but this is not true in general.

Turtle style

In certain cases, it is extremely cumbersome to define dozens of points, and a more natural way to produce these drawings is to use a "turtle style", as in the Logo language. For instance, suppose we write the following code:

```
pair _cp;        _cp=(0,0); % current point
numeric _tdir;   _tdir=0;   % turtle direction

def tdraw(expr d) text options=
  draw _cp--(_cp+d*dir(_tdir)) options;
  _cp:=_cp+d*dir(_tdir);
enddef;
def trotate(expr a)= _tdir:=_tdir+a;  enddef;
```

We then have at our disposal two commands: `tdraw`, which draws a segment of some length in the current direction, and `trotate`, which changes the current direction. Other commands could be added straightforwardly.

Using only these two commands, we can produce complex drawings in a very simple manner:

```
% tdraw and trotate as defined above
numeric u; u=4cm;
for i=1 upto 10:
  tdraw(.1u); trotate(18);
endfor;
trotate(90); tdraw(.5u); trotate(90); tdraw(.5u);
trotate(45); tdraw(.5u); trotate(135); tdraw(1u);
```

Example
4-1-18

This approach can be combined with a stack of positions, and possibly paths can be memorized on the fly, in case they are needed later. The following example illustrates how PUSH/POP operations can be defined. They can easily be adapted for some 3-D drawings (e.g., axonometric drawings). However, more elaborate examples have to take care of such complex features as dashed lines.

```
pair _cp;                % current point
pair _cps[];             % stack of current points
numeric _ncps; _ncps=0;

def PUSH = _cps[_ncps]:=_cp; _ncps:=_ncps+1; enddef;
def POP =
  if _ncps>0:  _ncps:=_ncps-1; _cp:=_cps[_ncps];
  else:  message "YOU CAN'T POP HERE"; stophere
  fi;
enddef;

def initdrawing=_cp:=origin; enddef;
def mv(expr d,a)=_cp:=_cp+d*dir(a);enddef;
def lineto(expr d,a) text options=
  draw _cp--(_cp+d*dir(a)) options;mv(d,a);enddef;

def mvright(expr d)=mv(d,0);enddef;
def mvleft(expr d)=mvright(-d);enddef;
def mvup(expr d)=mv(d,90);enddef;
def mvdown(expr d)=mvup(-d);enddef;
def lineright(expr d) text options=lineto(d,0) options;enddef;
def lineleft(expr d) text options=lineright(-d) options;enddef;
def lineup(expr d) text options=lineto(d,90) options;enddef;
def linedown(expr d) text options=lineup(-d) options;enddef;
numeric u; u=1cm;
initdrawing;
lineright(3u);lineup(2u);
PUSH
  lineto(1.5u/cosd(30),150);
  lineto(1.5u/cosd(30),210);
POP
lineleft(3u);linedown(2u);
mvright(u);
lineup(1.5u);lineright(u);linedown(1.5u);
```

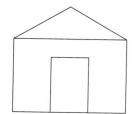

Example
4-1-19

The same ideas can be used to display L-systems and other fractals (see Section 4.4.3 for more examples of fractals and Color Plate IV(a)). An L-system, or Lindenmayer (after Aristid Lindenmayer) system, is a set of rules that can be used to model the growth of plants and other similar structures.

4.1.10 Using literal PostScript

Literal PostScript commands can be issued from within METAPOST with the `special` command. This command takes a string and outputs its value in the PostScript file. However, all special commands appear together before the code produced by the usual METAPOST commands. This structure somewhat restricts the application of `special`, but it can still be useful for matters of postprocessing or if the entire output is produced with `specials`.

The next simple examples demonstrate that the normal METAPOST output can be obtained by using only `special` commands, plus a command for setting the bounding box. The two examples are identical, and the PostScript output differs by only the three additional comments of the first figure.

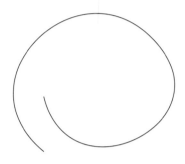

```
numeric u;
u=3cm;
special("(this is a PostScript comment!)");
z0=origin;
z1-z0=(u,u);
z2-z1=(-u,-.5u);
draw z0..z1{dir-50}..z2;
special("(this is another PostScript comment!)");
special("(z2 will be located at ("
   & decimal x2 & "," & decimal y2 & "))");
```

Example
4-1-20

```
numeric u;
u=3cm;
special("0 0.5 dtransform truncate " &
        "idtransform setlinewidth pop []");
special("0 setdash");
special("1 setlinecap 1 setlinejoin ");
special("10 setmiterlimit");
special("newpath 0 0 moveto");
special("-67.28128 56.4566 28.58275 " &
        "152.32063 85.03935 85.03935 curveto");
special("138.11453 21.78784 18.75612 " &
        "-37.89137 0 42.51967");
special("curveto stroke");
setbounds currentpicture
    to ((-24,-1)--(256,-1)
        --(256,109)--(-24,109)--cycle);
```

Example
4-1-21

The **exteps** package written by Palle Jørgensen (CTAN: graphics/metapost/contrib/macros/exteps) is a module for inclusion of external EPS figures into META-POST figures. It is written solely in METAPOST and does not require any post-processing of the METAPOST output. An example is given below:

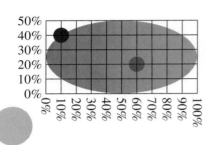

```
input exteps
begineps "gradient.eps";
  base := (25,25);
  clipping:=true;
  grid:=true;

  epsdrawdot(10pct,40pct)
    withpen pencircle scaled 10pct
    withcolor blue;
  epsdrawdot(60pct,20pct)
    withpen pencircle scaled 10pct
    withcolor red;
endeps;
draw origin withpen pencircle scaled 30
                withcolor blue+green;
```

Example
4-1-22

This package makes use of METAPOST's `special` command, with the problem noted earlier that the PostScript code must appear at the beginning of the PostScript figure code. It is therefore difficult to overlay normal METAPOST parts with included figures or to have a tighter interaction between them.

4.1.11 Animations

Drawings can be parameterized and an animation obtained by producing a series of drawings with varying values for the parameters. A simple example is given below, where a square is rotated in 90 steps of one degree.

```
def square(expr i)=
  beginfig(100+i);
    draw unitsquare shifted (-.5,-.5) scaled 2cm rotated i;
    setbounds currentpicture
              to (unitsquare shifted (-.5,-.5) scaled 4cm);
  endfig;
enddef;

for a:=0 upto 90: square(a); endfor;

end
```

In this example, the parameter is the argument to `beginfig`. When METAPOST is applied to the source file, 91 files are produced having extensions 100 to 190. We chose to start the numbering at 100, so that all extensions are properly sorted, something that is essential if the files are to be post-processed. These 91 files could, for instance, be transformed into bitmaps, and then combined to obtain a small MPEG film.

When proceeding this way, the bounding box must be very carefully set. In the previous example, the rotation of the square would normally cause the bounding box to change, and the center of the square of one figure would not coincide with the center of another square. This is why we have explicitly set the bounding box to a square containing all the rotated squares. In principle, it would suffice to find the maximal bounding box, but this may necessitate a first run through all the figures.

Some presentation packages, such as beamer, allow the user to include a sequence of METAPOST files and then to use those files as overlays.

PDF files with real animations based on METAPOST can also be produced. Such animations are self-standing and not advanced by the user. This is discussed in detail in [50].

4.2   Representing data with graphs

4.2.1   The graph package

METAPOST's author, John Hobby, wrote a high-level library of METAPOST macros [48] to provide a sophisticated package for drawing graphs, comparable to grap [see 11]. We can draw a simple graph (using data from the Protestant Cemetery, Rome—see [95]) with METAPOST's graph package:

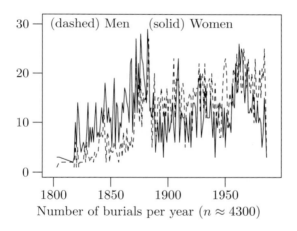

Number of burials per year ($n \approx 4300$)

Example
4-2-1

```
input graph
draw begingraph(2.5in,1.75in);
gdraw "yearm.dat" dashed evenly;
gdraw "yearw.dat";
glabel.lft
  (btex (solid) Women etex, 1960,30);
glabel.lft
  (btex (dashed) Men etex ,1870,30);
glabel.bot
  (btex Number of burials per year
  ($n \approx 4300$) etex,OUT);
endgraph;
```

The graph package provides the commands for plotting data from external data files and labeling that you would expect. It also offers the following features:

- Automatic scaling of data
- Automatic generation and labeling of tick marks or grid lines
- Multiple coordinate systems in the same picture
- Linear and logarithmic scales

- Plotting with arbitrary symbols

- Handling multiple columns in the same data file, with user-specified procedures

You start by inputting the **graph** macro package. Next you surround each plot with a
`begingraph`...`endgraph` pair; this returns a picture that you can render with `draw` (and
on which you can perform other transformations such as rotation). `begingraph` takes parameters (x and y dimensions separated by a comma) giving the size of the graph; the data
is scaled to fit automatically with special "g"-prefixed forms of `draw` and `fill`. `gdraw` has
the extra characteristic that, when followed by a file name, it draws the path created by reading coordinate pairs from the file. It can be followed by normal META qualifiers such as
`withpen` or METAPOST's `withcolor` and `dashed`. There are also "g" variants of other
commands: `glabel`, `gdotlabel`, `gdrawarrow`, and `gdrawdblarrow`.

`gdraw` can also be followed by a `plot` command with a parameter of a METAPOST
"picture" to be plotted at each coordinate. This can be typeset by TEX, as the following variation shows:

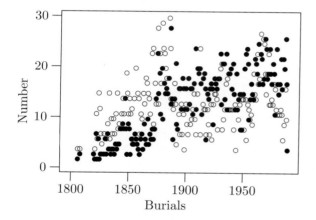

```
input graph
draw begingraph(2.5in,1.75in);
gdraw "yearm.dat"
 plot btex $\bullet$ etex;
gdraw "yearw.dat"
 plot btex $\circ$ etex;
glabel.bot
 (btex Burials etex,OUT);
glabel.lft
 (btex Number etex rotated 90,OUT);
endgraph;
```

Example
4-2-2

Notice that the `glabel` command has a special form of the position parameter, OUT, meaning that the text is to be placed outside the graph (it is normally used to place axis labels).
For this graph we also added a label to the y-axis, rotated by 90 degrees.

Frames, ticks, grids, and scales

By default, graphs have a frame on all sides, no grid, and tick marks on the bottom and
left. The frame can be altered with the `frame` command, which has the same set of optional
suffixes as `label` (see page 61). Grid lines and ticks are controlled with `autogrid`:

> `autogrid(`*x specification,y specification*`)`

The specifications can have the value `grid`, `itick`, or `otick`, which produce grid lines, inner ticks, or outer ticks, respectively. They can be suffixed with `.top` or `.bot` for the x-axis

and .lft and .rt for the y-axis, as the following example shows:

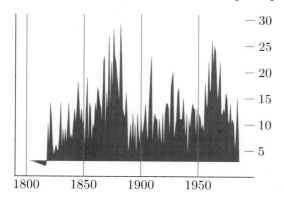

```
input graph
draw begingraph(2.5in,1.75in);
gfill "yearw.dat" withcolor red;
autogrid(grid.bot,itick.rt)
  withcolor .5white;
frame.llft;
endgraph;
```

Example
4-2-3

To override **graph**'s choice of where to put tick marks and how to write labels, you can add explicit ticks with `itick` or `otick` and grid lines with `grid`. These have the same suffixes as `autogrid` and are followed by a METAPOST picture variable containing a label or a `format` command, plus a coordinate. The `format` command is used to control how numbers are printed:

format(*specification,number*)

The *specification* consists of an optional initial string, a percent sign, an optional number indicating precision (default 3), a conversion letter (e, f, or g), and an optional final string. The conversion letter determines whether scientific notation is used; %g will use decimal format for most numbers. How the scientific notation used by `format` is typeset depends on a METAPOST macro called `init_numbers` (see the manual); since this uses the `btex...etex` system, you may need to look at it carefully if you are concerned about precisely which fonts are used.

The following graph shows both types of explicit labeling. Remember to turn off the normal marks at the end!

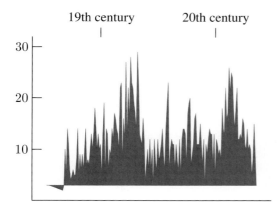

```
input graph
draw begingraph(2.5in,1.75in);
gfill "yearw.dat" withcolor red;
for y=10,20,30:
  itick.lft(format("%g",y),y);
endfor
otick.top("19th century",1850);
otick.top("20th century",1950);
frame.llft;
autogrid(,);
endgraph;
```

Example
4-2-4

> setcoords(*x style,y style*)

The labeling can be changed by `setcoords`. The parameters for x and y can be set to `log`, `-log`, `linear`, or `-linear`.

> setrange(*min,max*)

While the program's scaling of data to fit the graph usually gives the right results, it can be overridden with `setrange`. To do so, you need to supply the minimum and maximum coordinates. The special constant `origin` is a useful shorthand for (0,0). To leave any value to be figured out by METAPOST, specify `whatever`. If you specify no range at all, META-POST works it out from the data values and adds a small border.

Reading data files

Although the `gdraw` and `gfill` commands are often sufficient, we can get more control over the data read from a file by using `gdata`:

> gdata(*filename, variable, commands*)

The *commands* are executed for every line of data in *filename*, with the values for each column available as, e.g., $c1, c2, \ldots, cn$ for the variable name c. *filename* is a META string, so simple names should be enclosed in quotes (file names can also be computed from META variables). Using some more data from the Protestant Cemetery, in which each line consists of a person's age at death, we can show the distribution of mortality by age by accumulating data in an array and using it to create a path:

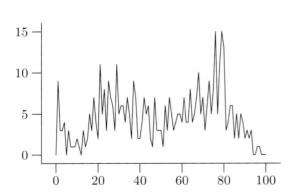

```
input graph
draw begingraph(2.5in,1.5in);
numeric p[];
path r;
for j := 0 upto 100:
  p[j]:=0;
endfor
gdata ("ages.dat",y, age:=(scantokens y1);
  p[age]:=p[age] + 1;);
r:=(0,0)
  for j := 1 upto 100: --(j,p[j]) endfor;
gdraw r;
frame.llft;
endgraph;
```

Example
4-2-5

The only complications are the need to initialize the array and the conversion of the string representation read from the data file into a numeric value with `scantokens`.

In the preceding example, the path created has straight edges. Sometimes it is desirable to have a smooth path connecting the different values; in such a case the definition of the path can readily be changed [109].

For every line in the data file, gdata actually separates the line into tokens using the space as a delimiter. Different lines need not have the same number of tokens. If a data file has different types of lines, however, the commands in gdata should take that fact into account, either by using a special token (for instance the first) as a selector for the others or by checking whether a given token has been defined. gdata can therefore be used for reading files in a flexible way, without outputting any graph.

When gdata reads data files, it stops when it reaches a blank line or end of file; if you start gdata again with the same file name, it carries on reading another set of data. This allows you to put all your data sets in one file—but use this command with care. One problem is that data files remain open if there is a blank line at the end, since METAPOST thinks some more data might follow. If you have many small data files, this situation can cause a METAPOST error—check the end of your files.

The display in Example 4-2-5 is not very readable; it might be better to accumulate data per decade of death from the file. As this gets a little more complicated, we abstract the job into a METAPOST macro called by the gdata command, as demonstrated in the next example:

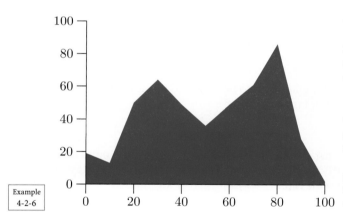

Example
4-2-6

```
input graph
draw begingraph(2.5in,1.75in);
setrange(origin,(100,100));
numeric p[]; path r;
for j := 0 step 10 until 100: p[j]:=0; endfor
def check(expr age) =
 if age < 100: xage:=round(age/10) * 10;
               p[xage]:=p[xage] + 1; fi
enddef;
gdata ("ages.dat",y, check((scantokens y1)););
r:=(0,0) for j := 0 step 10  until 100:
                  --(j,p[j]) endfor --(100,0);
gfill r -- cycle withcolor blue;
frame.llft;
endgraph;
```

It is often useful to accumulate points on a path for each line read from the data file; the macro augment is provided for this purpose. Given a suffix of a variable name of type "path" and a parameter of a coordinate, augment creates the path if it does not exist or adds the point to an existing path. We use this command to show the gravestone data again, this time processed to provide separate figures of deaths per decade for women (column 2) and men (column 3):

```
1800  3  6
1810  9  15
1820  26  64
1830  31  88
. . .
```

For each decade, we keep track of the last point reached and augment separate paths for male and female deaths; these are then shaded in different colors (this drawing also appears as Color Plate I(c)) to show how the male and female patterns vary over time. We need to know the last decade to establish a sensible corner for the filled shape. The female pattern appears as a dotted line on top of the male shading.

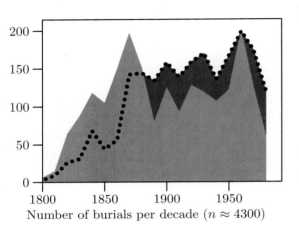

Number of burials per decade ($n \approx 4300$)

```
input graph

path m,w,last;
draw begingraph(2.5in,1.75in);
setrange((1800,0),(whatever,whatever));
gdata ("decade.dat",y,
  last:=((scantokens y1),0);
    augment.w(y1,y2);augment.m(y1,y3););
gfill (1800,0)--w--last--cycle
        withcolor red;
gfill (1800,0)--m--last--cycle
        withcolor green;
pickup pencircle scaled 3pt;
gdraw w dashed withdots;
pickup pencircle scaled .75pt;
glabel.bot (btex Number of burials per
    decade ($n \approx 4300$) etex,OUT);
endgraph;
```

Example
4-2-7

The example demonstrates that the graph macros return a META picture that can then be drawn and possibly transformed (for instance, rotated).

Different graph types

With a little effort, **graph** can draw bar charts. To demonstrate this ability, we copy a chart from [83] that was made with the LaTeX **bar** package. Our technique is to make a single path out of all the bars and fill the result at the end:

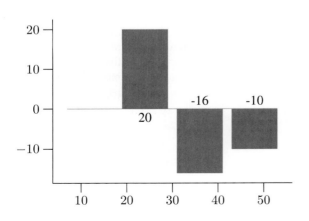

```
input graph

path s; numeric x,y;
draw begingraph(2.5in,1.75in);
gdata ("students.dat",c,
 x:=(scantokens c1) * 12;
 y:=(scantokens c2);
 augment.s((x-5,0)--
 (x-5,y)-- (x+5,y)--
 (x+5,0));
 if y < 0: glabel.top(c2,(x,0)); fi
 if y > 0: glabel.bot(c2,(x,0)); fi
 );
gfill s--cycle withcolor .5white;
frame.llft;
endgraph;
```

Example
4-2-8

We explicitly work out the corners of each bar and allow for their width by multiplying the x values by 12. The bars themselves span 5 units on either side of the data point, so there is a gap of 2 units between each one.

A similar technique is used in the next chart (also printed in Color Plate I(d)), which shows the number of pages in each chapter of the first edition of this book at one stage in its production. This time we draw each bar separately, so that the bars can be shaded according to their values. The work is delegated to a macro, which also prints a rotated label for each bar. Because explicit x labels are supplied, labeling of the x-axis is suppressed.

```
input graph
path m; numeric n,width;
width:=20; defaultscale:=0.6; n:=0;
def bar(expr name,value) =
 gfill(n,0)--(n,value)--(n+width,value)--(n+width,0)--cycle
   withcolor (value/100,value/100,value/100);
 picture p;
 p = name infont defaultfont scaled defaultscale rotated 90;
 glabel.rt(image(unfill bbox p; draw p),(n,10));
 n:=n+width;
enddef;
draw begingraph(2.5in,1.75in);
setrange((0,0),(11*width,100));
autogrid(,otick.lft);
gdata("chap.dat",c,bar(c1,(scantokens c2)););
endgraph;
```

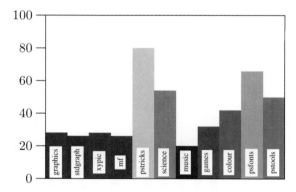

Example
4-2-9

The string value read from the first data column is put into a METAPOST picture variable by using the low-level command `infont`. This lets us use the `bbox` technique to give the extent of the text, which is made white with `unfill`. `image` is a useful macro that yields the picture resulting from a sequence of drawing commands; we use that as a label. The data for this graph starts as follows:

```
graphics 28
stdgraph 26
```

```
xypic 28
mf 26
pstricks 80
science 54
...
```

We can also present our earlier "decade" data as a dual bar chart, with male and female figures side by side. To do this, we maintain two separate paths; we fill one and leave the other as an outline:

```
input graph
path m[],w[];
def wcheck(expr decade,value) =
 augment.w1(decade,0);augment.w1(decade,value);
 augment.w1(decade+5,value);augment.w1(decade+5,0);
enddef;
def mcheck(expr decade,value) =
 augment.m1(decade+5,0);augment.m1(decade+5,value);
 augment.m1(decade+10,value);augment.m1(decade+10,0);
enddef;
draw begingraph(3.75in,2in);
gdata ("decade.dat",y,
  wcheck((scantokens y1),(scantokens y2));
  mcheck((scantokens y1),(scantokens y3)););
gfill m1--cycle;
gdraw w1;
glabel.bot (btex Number of burials per decade
     ($n \approx 4300$) etex,OUT);
frame.llft;
endgraph;
```

Number of burials per decade ($n \approx 4300$)

Example
4-2-10

With care, we can even draw pie charts using similar ideas. The following example reads data about gravestones in the Protestant Cemetery in the following form:

```
Romanian 1 0.02796420582
Czech 2 0.05592841163
.....
Italian 391 10.93400447
German 508 14.20581655
unknown 599 16.75055928
English 1462 40.8836689
```

Here the second column is the number of gravestones per nationality and, to make the code less complicated, the third column is the percentage of the total. For each pie wedge, we use the `buildcycle` macro to find the smallest enclosed shape from the union of a whole circle and two lines extending from the center at the starting and closing angles of the segment. The fill color of the wedge is derived from the percentage.

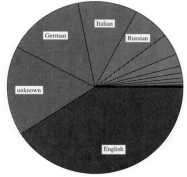

Example
4-2-11

```
input graph
numeric r,last; path c,w;
r:=5; c:=fullcircle scaled 2r; last:=0.0;
def wedge (expr lang,value,perc) =
  numeric current,n,half,xoff,yoff;picture p;
  n:=perc*3.6;
  current:=last+n; half:=last+(n/2);
  w:=buildcycle((0,0)--(2r,0) rotated last,c, (2r,0)--(0,0)
                                        rotated current);
  gfill w withcolor (0,0.8-(perc/100),0);
  gdraw w;
  if perc > 5: p=lang infont defaultfont scaled defaultscale;
    glabel(image(unfill bbox p; draw p),3/4r*dir(half));
  fi;
  last:=current;
enddef;
draw begingraph(3in,3in);
  defaultscale:=0.7;
  gdata ("langs.dat",c, wedge(c1, (scantokens c2),
                                  (scantokens c3)););
  autogrid(,);
  frame withcolor white;
endgraph scaled 0.7;
```

The placement of the labels in the pie chart bears a little examination; they are placed in the center of each wedge, three quarters of the way along the radius. An alternative algorithm to work out these coordinates would be

```
((r*3*cosd(half))/4,(r*3*sind(half))/4))
```

using META's sine and cosine functions.

Another type of graph has a linear x-scale and uses the y-axis simply to compare sets of data. The next graph uses our cemetery data to show the first and last occurrences of each type of gravestone. The code is straightforward, except that we draw the lines with a different-sized pen (with square ends) and revert to a thin line to draw the scale and frame (only on the bottom, since the y-axis is not linear).

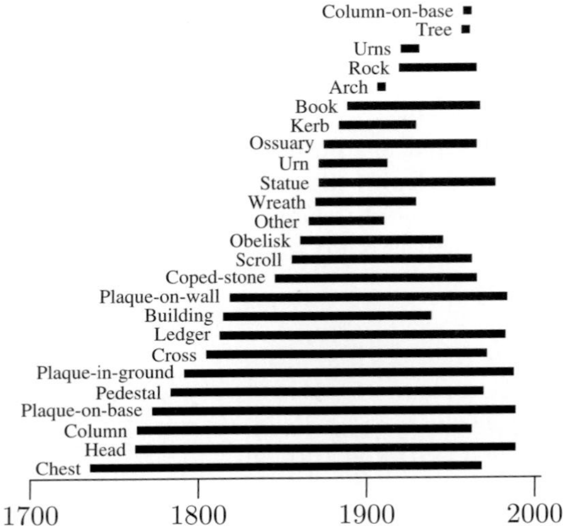

```
input graph
draw begingraph(2.5in,2.5in);
n:=10;
defaultscale:=0.7;
pickup pensquare scaled 3pt;
setrange((1700,0),(whatever,whatever));
gdata("stones.dat", s,
gdraw ((scantokens s2),n)--
  ((scantokens s3),n);
glabel.lft(s1,(scantokens s2)-3,n);
n:=n+16;);
pickup pensquare scaled .5pt;
frame.bot;
autogrid(otick.bot,);
endgraph;
```

Example
4-2-12

The data, ranked in order of first occurence, starts like this:

```
Chest 1738 1966
Head 1765 1986
Column 1766 1960
Plaque-on-base 1775 1986
Pedestal 1786 1967
Plaque-in-ground 1794 1985
```

Our last example is more unusual: we want to plot data from a survey grid and shade each grid square according to its data value. In the data file, the first two columns are the coordinates of the lower-left corner of the grid square, the third column is the absolute data value, and the fourth column is a percentage version:

```
2 1 102 85
2 2 10 98
2 3 110 84
2 4 112 83
2 5 114 83
...
```

The text is printed in white or black depending on the percentage.

```
input graph
def sq(expr x,y,num,perc) =
 gfill(x,y)--(x+10,y)--(x+10,y+10)--(x,y+10)--cycle
    withcolor (perc/100,perc/100,perc/100);
 glabel(num,(x+5,y+5)) if perc < 50: withcolor white  fi;
enddef;
defaultscale:=0.7;
draw begingraph(70mm,24mm);
  setrange((20,10),(110,40));
  autogrid(,);
  gdata ("pot.dat",c,
    sq((scantokens c1)*10,(scantokens c2)*10, c3, (scantokens c4)););
endgraph;
```

110	135	162	199	27	39	506	64	80
10	130	160	197	275	35	48	636	7
102	12	15	193	24	34	47	634	79

Example
4-2-13

Additional utilities

Two small packages by Ulrik Vieth provide useful additional functionality to the **graph** package:

- **gpdata** (CTAN: `graphics/metapost/contrib/macros/misc`). This file modifies the `Grdln_` routine of the METAPOST **graph** package, so that it can parse and ignore comment lines in data files starting with a "#" sign, similar to the conventions in Gnuplot.

- **interpol** (CTAN: `graphics/metapost/contrib/macros/misc`). This file declares a new internal quantity `interpolating` and modifies the `augment` and `Mreadpath` routines of the METAPOST **graph** package to construct a path from data points using Bézier curves instead of polygons (line segments) when `interpolating` is set positive.
  Andreas Scherer has also shown how paths created with the `augment` macro can be made smoother [109].

Finally, graphs can also be inserted inline in LaTeX, using the **emp** package (see Section 3.6.1).

The **matlab** (CTAN: `graphics/metapost/contrib/macros/matlab`) package by *matlab package* Yang Yang is a METAPOST package for plotting 2-D data. It extends the **graph** package (which it loads) by providing a Matlab-like syntax, making it easier to use for Matlab users.

4.2.2 Curve drawing

Given METAPOST's arithmetic limitations, and since METAPOST is not a specialized plotting program, it is not surprising that METAPOST does not provide facilities for automatic function drawing. However, if a function has been tabulated and is given by a set of points, we can use the **graph** package to draw the set of points in different ways.

If we want to use METAPOST with the function itself, we can either draw each point separately or join points of the curve. Depending on the drawing mode, we may have to take care of overflows and the way in which points should (or should not) be joined. If the function is simple, this is easy; if the function has idiosyncrasies, however, plotting it may take more work.

We will show several examples—one where the function is drawn as a set of points, and others where the points are linked.

First, the sine curve is a typical example of a curve drawn point by point. The only problem that can happen with such an approach is an arithmetic overflow.

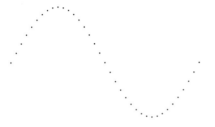

```
numeric u; u=5mm;
pickup pencircle scaled 1pt;
for i:=0 step 10 until 360:
   draw ((i/360)*10u,3u*sind(i));
endfor;
pickup pencircle scaled .5;
```

Example
4-2-14

The same sine curve can also be drawn with segments. The curve here is made of 36 segments, which are quite noticeable.

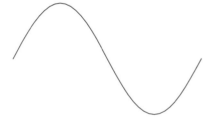

```
numeric u; u=5mm;
for i:=0 step 10 until 350:
   draw ((i/360)*10u,3u*sind(i))--
        (((i+10)/360)*10u,3u*sind(i+10));
endfor;
```

Example
4-2-15

The same sine curve can also be drawn by by smoothly joining 17 of its points:

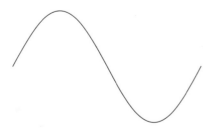

```
def f(expr a)=sind(a) enddef;
numeric u; u=5mm;
path p;
numeric n; n=16;
p=(0,f(0))
for i:=1 upto n:
   .. ((i/n)*10u,3u*f(i*(360/n)))
endfor;
draw p;
```

Example
4-2-16

Such curves can also easily be produced using the **graph** package, as shown below and in Section 3.6.1.

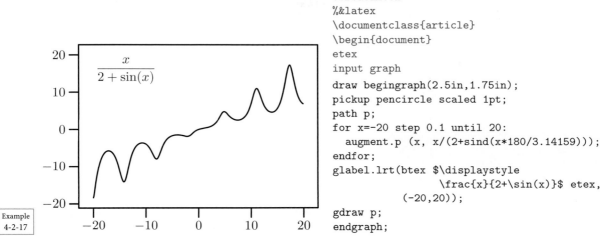

```
verbatimtex
%&latex
\documentclass{article}
\begin{document}
etex
input graph
draw begingraph(2.5in,1.75in);
pickup pencircle scaled 1pt;
path p;
for x=-20 step 0.1 until 20:
  augment.p (x, x/(2+sind(x*180/3.14159)));
endfor;
glabel.lrt(btex $\displaystyle
                \frac{x}{2+\sin(x)}$ etex,
          (-20,20));
gdraw p;
endgraph;
```

Example 4-2-17

Curves in polar coordinates can be drawn with the following custom definition of `polcurve`. The polar equation of the curve is given by the `r` definition.

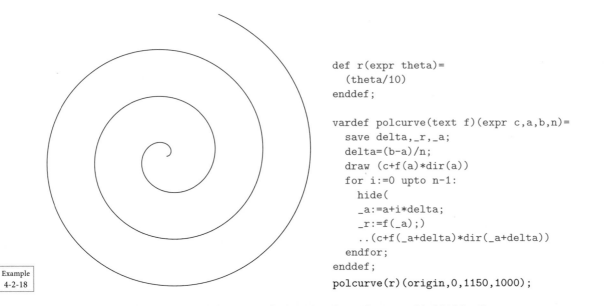

```
def r(expr theta)=
  (theta/10)
enddef;

vardef polcurve(text f)(expr c,a,b,n)=
  save delta,_r,_a;
  delta=(b-a)/n;
  draw (c+f(a)*dir(a))
  for i:=0 upto n-1:
    hide(
    _a:=a+i*delta;
    _r:=f(_a);)
    ..(c+f(_a+delta)*dir(_a+delta))
  endfor;
enddef;
polcurve(r)(origin,0,1150,1000);
```

Example 4-2-18

Curves in space are also rather easy to achieve using these ideas, provided hidden lines are not removed. 3-D surfaces based on curves can also be contemplated, and it is not too difficult to extend curve drawings to surface drawings for functions such as $z = f(x, y)$.

4.2.3 Pie charts

Introduction The **piechartMP** package by Jens-Uwe Morawski is an easy way to draw pie charts with METAPOST [85]. With this package, a pie chart is a graphical representation of sets of data called "segments". We start with a typical pie chart. Each segment is defined with the Segment command, of which there are five in this example:

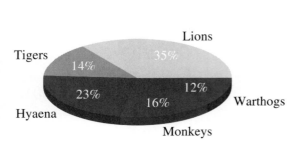

```
input piechartmp
SetupPercent(this,"%");
Segment(15,"Lions",auto);
Segment(6,"Tigers",auto);
Segment(10,"Hyaena",auto);
Segment(7,"Monkeys",auto);
Segment(5,"Warthogs",auto);
PieChart(2.5cm,0.1,65,0,0);
Label(0)(percent)(inwards,0)
   withcolor white;
Label.auto(0)(name)(outwards,0);
```

Example
4-2-19

The SetupPercent command specifies that the values are appended with "%." The two Label commands specify where the segment labels and value labels are located. Finally, the PieChart command draws the pie chart.

> Segment(*value*, *name, fillstyle, altvalue*)

A segment is declared with four arguments:

value   is the numerical data represented by the segment.

name   is a string representing the name that will appear next to a segment.

fillstyle   can be either a numerical value representing a pattern for filling, a color, or the value auto, which lets **piechartMP** calculate the segment color.

altvalue   is an alternative value that will be displayed. It is useful if the *value* had to be scaled down because of METAPOST's numerical limitations.

> SetupPercent(*PreString, PostString*)

This command specifies how percent labels are typeset. The *PreString* is attached before the string of the percent value, and the *PostString* is attached after it. this represents the current value, but SetupPercent(this,this) does not print the value twice. The usual way to call this command is with

```
SetupPercent(this,"%");
```

Special care should be taken if labels are typeset with TEX. In this case, the command should be

```
SetupPercent(this,"\%");
```

PieChart(*Radius, Height, Observation, Rotation, Offset*)

The pie chart itself is obtained with the PieChart command. The meaning of the parameters is as follows:

Radius is the radius of the pie chart.

Height is the ratio between the height and the radius.

Observation is an angle in degrees specifying how the pie chart is viewed. Valid values are from 0 (2-D chart) to 89.

Rotation is the angle by which the pie chart is rotated around its center. Valid values are from 0 to 359.

Offset is an offset applied to all segments in a pie chart. 0 represents no offset, 1 represents a full radial offset, and a different value represents an intermediate displacement. The offset can be greater than 1, but the segments look very scattered. The offset should not be negative. To offset only some of the segments, the SegmentState command should be used.

Thus our first example displayed a pie chart with radius of 2.5 cm, a height of 2.5 mm (2.5 cm × 0.1), an observation angle of 65 degrees, and no rotation; the segments were not offset.

The same example, with the same values for the PieChart parameters but no labels, looks like this:

Example
4-2-20

```
input piechartmp;
Segment(15,"Lions",auto);
Segment(6,"Tigers",auto);
Segment(10,"Hyaena",auto);
Segment(7,"Monkeys",auto);
Segment(5,"Warthogs",auto);
PieChart(3cm,0.1,50,0,0);
```

Other values for the PieChart parameters produce the following pie charts:

Example
4-2-21

```
input piechartmp;
Segment(15,"Lions",auto);
Segment(6,"Tigers",auto);
Segment(10,"Hyaena",auto);
Segment(7,"Monkeys",auto);
Segment(5,"Warthogs",auto);
PieChart(1cm,0,0,0,0);
```

and

```
input piechartmp;
Segment(15,"Lions",auto);
Segment(6,"Tigers",auto);
Segment(10,"Hyaena",auto);
Segment(7,"Monkeys",auto);
Segment(5,"Warthogs",auto);
PieChart(2.5cm,0.4,70,0,0);
```

Example
4-2-22

```
input piechartmp;
Segment(15,"Lions",auto);
Segment(6,"Tigers",auto);
Segment(10,"Hyaena",auto);
Segment(7,"Monkeys",auto);
Segment(5,"Warthogs",auto);
PieChart(1.5cm,0.1,30,120,0);
```

Example
4-2-23

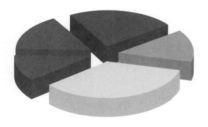

```
input piechartmp;
Segment(15,"Lions",auto);
Segment(6,"Tigers",auto);
Segment(10,"Hyaena",auto);
Segment(7,"Monkeys",auto);
Segment(5,"Warthogs",auto);
PieChart(2cm,0.3,60,220,0.2);
```

Example
4-2-24

SegmentState(*SegmentID*, *State*, *Offset*)

This command specifies the state of a given segment.

SegmentID   is the identifier of the segment to which this command applies. The identifier is 1 for the first segment declared, 2 for the second, and so on.

State   can be normal (the segment is visible), invisible (the segment is invisible, but space is inserted), hidden (the segment is ignored), or this (when the offset is changed, but not the state).

Offset   is the offset for this segment, and has the same meaning as the *Offset* parameter in the PieChart command. This offset is added to the global offset and can therefore be used to offset all segments but one.

The following example illustrates this command, with the second segment being invisible and the fourth segment offset by 0.3. Moreover, segments are defined with an alternative value for display. Finally, the colors are changed with `SetupColors` (discussed later in this section).

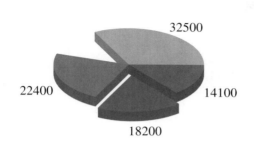

```
input piechartmp
SetupColors((0.7,0.7),this,this);
Segment(32.5,"Lions",auto,"32500");
Segment(12.8,"Tigers",auto,"12800");
Segment(22.4,"Hyaena",auto,"22400");
Segment(18.2,"Monkeys",auto,"18200");
Segment(14.1,"Warthogs",auto,"14100");
SegmentState(2,invisible,this);
SegmentState(4,this,0.3);
PieChart(2cm,0.15,60,0,0);
Label.auto(0)(value)(outwards,0);
```

Example 4-2-25

`Label`.*Alignment* (*Segments*)(*Data*) (*SegmentPoint,Shift*)

Labels are drawn with the `Label` command, where

Alignment   specifies the alignment of the label, which can be the usual METAPOST label position suffixes (`top`, `urt`, etc.), or the alignment `auto`, which enables the calculation of a placement according to the specific situation.

Segments   specifies for which segments a label should be created. It can be a comma-separated list of segment numbers, or the value 0 for all visible segments.

Data   is a string or a predefined value. A string is used to set a specific label. The predefined values are `value` (the segment values), `percent` (the calculated percent values), and `name` (the segment names). A comma-separated list of any such values can be used and will produce a concatenation of its values.

SegmentPoint   is a pair specifying the location of the label in a segment-specific system of coordinates; (X, Y) corresponds to a label at a fraction X of the radius from the center, and at an angular fraction Y of the segment from the beginning of the segment, counterclockwise. There are two predefined values: `inwards`, equal to $(0.7, 0.5)$, and `outwards`, equal to $(1.1, 0.5)$.

Shift   is either a pair used for shifting the label from the position set by the *SegmentPoint* parameter (in which case a line is also drawn) or the value 0 when shifting (and drawing the line) is disabled.

Our first example had the following calls:

```
Label(0)(percent)(inwards,0) withcolor white;
Label.auto(0)(name)(outwards,0);
```

which draw the percent values in white within the segments and keep the segment names outside. No shifting occurs.

A more elaborate example appears below. The 8% corresponds to 10 being 8% of $50 + 30 + 10 + 20 + 20$.

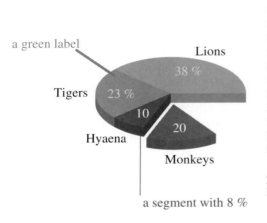

a green label

Lions

Tigers

Hyaena

Monkeys

a segment with 8 %

```
input piechartmp
SetupColors((.7,.7),this,this);
SetupPercent(this, " %");
Segment(50,"Lions");   Segment(30,"Tigers");
Segment(10,"Hyaena");  Segment(20,"Monkeys");
Segment(20,"Warthogs");
SegmentState(4,this,0.3);
SegmentState(5,invisible,this);
PieChart(2cm,0.15,60,0,0);
Label.auto(0)(name)(outwards,0);
Label(3,4,5)(value)(inwards,0) withcolor white;
Label(1,2)(percent)(inwards,0) withcolor (1,1,0);
Label.lrt(3)("a segment with ",percent)
                ((0.9,0.8),(0,-2cm)) withcolor .8red;
pickup pencircle scaled 2pt;
Label.auto(2)("a green label")
                ((0.9,0.1),(-1cm,7mm)) withcolor .8green;
```

Example
4-2-26

This example has labels with spaces and needs a font with spaces—hence the `defaultfont` declaration. This is not a problem when we are using TEX labels.

`SetupNumbers(`*precision,delimiter*`)`

Setup commands   In addition to the `SetupPercent` commands, several other setup commands are available. The first, `SetupNumbers`, sets the accuracy and delimiter used. `SetupNumbers(2,",")` will, for instance, round at two places and use a comma delimiter.

`SetupColors(`*auto-SV,shading-SV,grayscale*`)`

This command specifies the colors used for segments. The three arguments are as follows:

auto-SV   is a pair (S, V), where S is the saturation and V is the value in the HSV model. The hue H is taken from the position of the segment.

shading-SV   is a pair giving the maximum values of (S, V) for shaded areas in segments. The default is (0.4,0.3).

grayscale   is a Boolean that, when set to `true`, switches the colors to grayscale.

`SetupText(`*Mode,TeXFormat,TeXSettings*`)`

This command sets up how text is handled, using three arguments:

Mode   is an integer specifying the way labels are typeset: 0 is for string-based typesetting (default); 1 is for external TEX-based typesetting using *TeXFormat* and *TeXSettings*; 2 is like 1, except that `\documentclass{minimal}` and `\begin{document}` are automatically added; and 3 is like 2, but with *TeXFormat* defaulting to `%&latex`.

TeXFormat   is a string representing the TEX format to be used, and is written on top of the external `verbatimtex` block. The default is an empty string. Certain systems support `"%&latex"` for LATEX.

TeXSettings   is a string including TEX commands, which will be written after the TEX format in the external file.

For example, the command

```
SetupText(2, "%&latex", "\usepackage[latin1]{inputenc}");
```

uses a minimal LATEX class, selects the LATEX format (assuming the system supports the `%&latex` directive), and loads the standard package for Latin-1 input encoding.

SetupValue(*PreString,PostString*)

This command is similar to `SetupPercent`, but applies to the segment values. It might be used, for example, when segment values are in millions of euros and a special currency symbol needs to be used:

```
SetupValue(this, "million \EUR");
```

SetupName(*PreString,PostString*)

This command is also similar to `SetupPercent` and `SetupValue`, but applies to segment names.

DefinePattern(*ID,Method,FillColor, PatternColor,Dimen*)

Segments can be filled in with either a solid color or a pattern fill. In both cases, colors can be either chosen automatically or set explicitly. Patterns are defined with the `DefinePattern`   *Patterns* command, where

ID   is an integer identifying the pattern. It is best to number patterns starting with 1.

Method   is an integer specifying the pattern method. There are 10 predefined methods (1..10), and the value 0 selects a private pattern (see below).

FillColor   is a color for the pattern background.

PatternColor   is a color for the pattern foreground.

Dimen   is a pair (S, W) specifying the spacing S between pattern elements, and the linewidth W.

An example of pattern definition and its use in a segment follows:

```
DefinePattern(1,9,red,green,(5mm,2pt));
Segment(50,"Lions",1);
```

We can also create patterns other than the predefined ones. When the pattern method is 0, piechartMP calls the `PrivatePattern` macro, which must be defined by the user. The prototype of the definition is

```
vardef PrivatePattern (expr ulc, lrc, spc, lwd)=
  save pic; picture pic;
  ...
  pic
enddef;
```

This macro is called with a rectangular area given by an upper-left corner `ulc` and a lower-right corner `lrc`, plus the spacing and line width, which are embedded in the last parameter of `DefinePattern`. The `PrivatePattern` macro must provide a picture and should not modify the `currentpicture` variable. It can use the `image` or `addto` commands.

More advanced examples—in particular, mixing colors in strings—are shown in the piechartMP documentation.

Piecharts in presentations

When pie charts are used in presentations, and different versions of the same pie chart design are used, it may be important to align properly all the pie charts. This can be achieved by setting the `PiechartBBox` variable to 1 before loading the package:

```
PiechartBBox:=1;
input piechartmp;
```

piechartMP requires two runs for the bounding boxes to become right.

Incremental presentations can be simplified by applying the general principles on animations, described in Section 4.1.11. The piechartMP documentation gives examples using this technique.

4.3 Diagrams

Diagrams are a general class of drawings loosely covering objects that are interconnected with lines or arrows. In this section, we consider a number of such diagrams.

4.3.1 Graphs

Small graph theory diagrams can be drawn with plain METAPOST or with a few additional definitions. The example in Figure 4.1 on the facing page shows a Cayley graph produced in a simple way, taking advantage of the many symmetries [98].

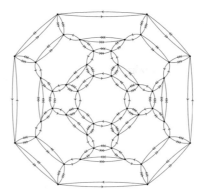

Figure 4.1: A Cayley graph drawn with METAPOST

More complex graphs (or trees) should probably be produced with dedicated tools, which can try to optimize the layout of these graphs. Computer algebra packages may also have the ability to export METAPOST code.

4.3.2 Flowcharts

Flowchartsare another kind of diagram that is not too difficult to achieve with **boxes**, METAOBJ, and other similar packages. The following example shows a simple METAOBJ flowchart:

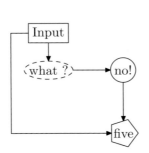

```
input metaobj
newBox.a(btex Input etex);
a.c=origin;
newEllipse.b(btex what ? etex)
   "framestyle(dashed evenly)";
a.s-b.n=(0,5mm);
newCircle.c(btex no! etex);
c.w-b.e=(1cm,0);
newPolygon.d(btex five etex,5)
   "fit(false)", "polymargin(2mm)";
c.s-d.n=(0,1cm);
ncbar(a)(d) "angleA(180)", "armA(1cm)";
drawObj(a,b,c,d);ncline(a)(b);
ncline(b)(c);ncline(c)(d);
```

The **expressg** package can also be used for flowcharts; see Section 4.3.4 for an example.

4.3.3 Block drawing and Bond graphs

The **blockdraw** (CTAN: `graphics/metapost/contrib/macros/blockdraw_mp`) package (Henrik Tidefelt) is a set of simple METAPOST macros for the creation of block

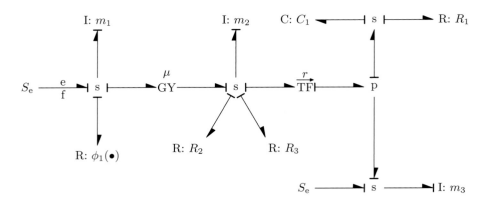

Figure 4.2: An example of Bond graph done with the `bondgraph` package

diagrams and bond graphs. Bond graphs are a graphical tool for capturing the common energy structure of systems. Figure 4.2 shows an example of Bond graph.

4.3.4 Box-line diagrams: the `expressg` package

EXPRESS-G is a standard graphical notation for information models. It is a useful companion to the EXPRESS language for displaying entity and type definitions, relationships, and cardinality. For information on the EXPRESS-G notation, consult Annex B of the EXPRESS Language Reference Manual (ISO 10303-11).

The `expressg` package by Peter Wilson provides a number of basic constructions covering this graphical notation. In this section, we give an overview of the package and some examples.

Data types `expressg` provides macros for a variety of data types, such as Booleans, and integers. These macros are as follows, all with similar graphical representations. The suffix is used to position the data type name. The integer 5, for instance, refers to the position $z5$, and so on. These coordinates must be defined before the data types are drawn.

`drawBINARY(`*suffix*`)`	`drawBOOLEAN(`*suffix*`)`
`drawCOMPLEX(`*suffix*`)`	`drawEXPRESSION(`*suffix*`)`
`drawGENERIC(`*suffix*`)`	`drawINTEGER(`*suffix*`)`
`drawLOGICAL(`*suffix*`)`	`drawNUMBER(`*suffix*`)`
`drawREAL(`*suffix*`)`	`drawSTRING(`*suffix*`)`

An exampleof such a data type is given below:

INTEGER

```
input expressg
z5=(0,0);
drawINTEGER(5);
```

Example
4-3-2

```
drawcirclebox(suffix,diameter)(name)
drawovalbox(suffix,length,height)(name)
drawroundedbox(suffix,length,height,radius)(name)
drawdashellipse(suffix,length,height)
drawdashcircle(suffix,diameter)
```

Circles, ovals, and rounded boxes are obtained with the above macros, whose parameters
are self-explanatory.

Circle and oval boxes

```
input expressg
verbatimtex
\def\stack#1{\vbox{\halign{\hfil##\hfil\cr#1\crcr}}}
etex

z0=origin;z1-z0=z2-z1=(3cm,0);z0-z3=z1-z4=z2-z5=(0,1.5cm);
drawovalbox(0, 2cm, 1cm)(btex \stack{This is\cr a number} etex);
drawcirclebox(3, 1.5cm)(btex circular etex);
drawdashcircle(4, 2cm);label(btex phantom? etex,z4);
drawroundedbox(2, 1.5cm, 1cm, 2mm)("rounded");
drawroundedbox(5, 1.5cm, 1cm, 0mm)(btex \stack{not\cr rounded} etex);
drawNUMBER(1);
```

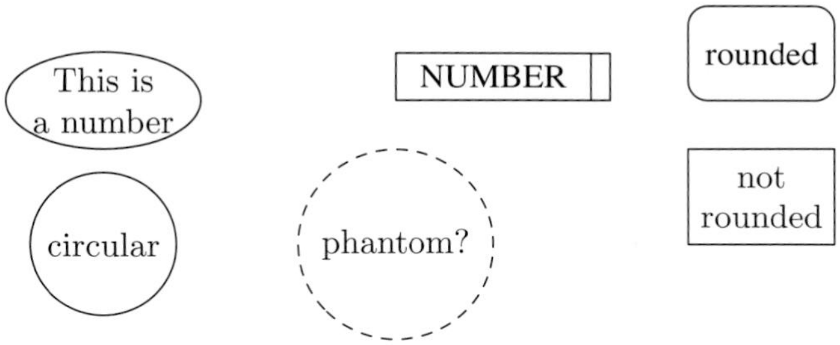

Example
4-3-3

```
drawLEVENT(suffix,length,height)(name)
drawGEVENT(suffix,length,height)(name)
```

Slanted rectangles can be used for events:

Slanted rectangles

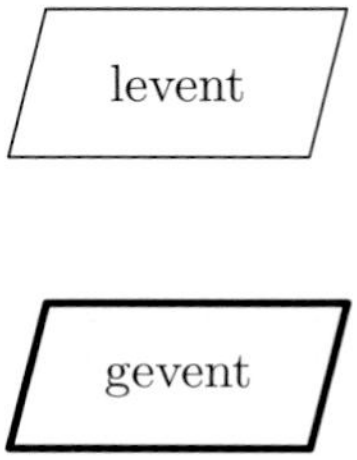

Example
4-3-4

```
input expressg
z1=(0,0);
drawLEVENT(1, 2cm, 1cm)(btex levent etex);
z2=(0,-2cm);
drawGEVENT(2, 2cm, 1cm)(btex gevent etex);
```

```
drawcardbox(suffix,length,height,fold)(name)
drawdiamondbox(suffix,length,height)(name)
drawindexbox(suffix,length,height,length2,height2)(name)
```

Other boxes
There are also card boxes (with a folded corner of size *fold*), diamond boxes, and index boxes (with additional dimensions for the top rectangle).

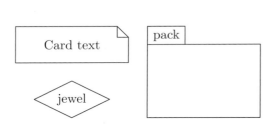

```
input expressg
z0=origin;
drawcardbox(0, 3cm, 1cm, 3mm)
            (btex Card text etex);
z1=(1.5cm,-1cm);
drawdiamondbox(1, 2cm, 1cm)
              (btex jewel etex);
z2=(3.5cm,-1.5cm);
drawindexbox(2, 3cm, 2cm, 1cm, 5mm)
            (btex pack etex);
```

Example
4-3-5

```
drawdash0(begin,end)          drawthick0(begin,end)
drawnormalD(begin,end)        drawnormalCA(begin,end)
drawnormalOA(begin,end)       drawnormalF(begin,end)
drawdashA(begin,end)          drawdashOA(begin,end)
drawnormalOD(begin,end)       drawnormalCD(begin,end)
drawnormalDCA(begin,end)
```

Relations
Finally, objects can be connected with relations. In this case, a relation takes two suffixes referring to coordinate variables.

```
input expressg
z1=(0,0);z101-z1=(3cm,0);
for i=2 upto 12:
  z1-z[i]=z101-z[100+i]=(0,(i-1)*5mm);
endfor;

drawdash0(1, 101); % open circle
drawthick0(2,102); % open circle
drawnormalD(3, 103); % black dot
drawnormalCA(4, 104); % closed arrowhead
drawnormalOA(5, 105); % open arrowhead
drawnormalF(6, 106); % fanin
draw z7--z107 dashes;

drawdashA(8, 108);       % arrow
drawdashOA(9, 109);      % open arrowhead
drawnormalOD(10, 110); % open diamond
drawnormalCD(11, 111); % closed diamond
% double closed arrowhead
drawnormalDCA(12, 112);
```

Example
4-3-6

A simple nonsensical flowchart, showing the use of individual points of an object, is given in the next example. `z1c` is the middle of the LEVENT object set at point 1, `z2bm` is the bottom middle of the diamond box object, etc. However, `z3`—and not `z3c`—is the middle of the oval box object, and it would not work to set `z3c=(0,-4cm)`. More details on the handles available for each kind of object can be found in the **expressg** package manual.

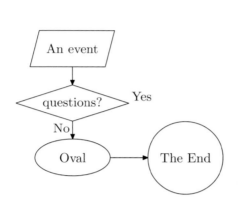

```
input expressg
z1c=(0,0);
drawLEVENT(1, 2cm, 1cm)(btex An event etex);
z2c=(0,-1.5cm);
drawdiamondbox(2, 3cm, 1cm)
               (btex questions? etex);
z3=(0,-3cm);
drawovalbox(3, 2cm, 1cm)(btex Oval etex);
z4c=z3+(3cm,0);
drawcirclebox(4, 2cm)(btex The End etex);
drawarrow z1bm--z2tm;
drawarrow z2bm--z3tm;
drawarrow z3mr--z4ml;
label.llft(btex No etex,z2bm);
label.urt(btex Yes etex,z2mr);
```

Example
4-3-7

More complex connections can be produced, as shown in Figure 4.3 on the next page (courtesy of Peter Wilson).

4.3.5 UML diagrams—MetaUML

METAPOST is a natural candidate for UML diagrams. Plain METAPOST can be used for making such diagrams, but there have also been several attempts at developing general packages. Here we confine ourselves to the description of the basic features of MetaUML (CTAN: `graphics/metapost/contrib/macros/metauml`). This package was developed by Ovidiu Gheorghieş [30].

MetaUML provides constructors for a variety of boxes and a variety of ways to connect these boxes. There are many features common to this package and other packages of the boxes family.

`Class.`*name*(*ClassName*)(*ListOfAttributes, ListOfMethods*)

The main command `Class` defines a class, and its arguments are as follows: *name* is the name of a `Class` object representing a UML class; *ClassName* is a string representing the class; *ListOfAttributes* is a comma-separated list of strings representing the attributes; and *ListOfMethods* is a comma-separated list of strings representing the list of methods.

The following example defines an instance of `Class`, which is identified as A. This name will be used only internally and will not be displayed. The visible name of the instance

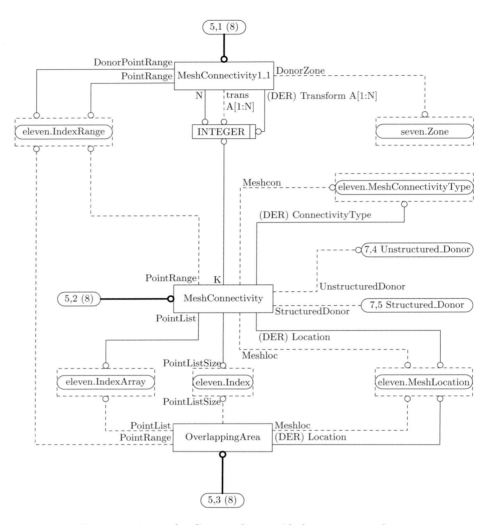

Figure 4.3: A complex diagram drawn with the **expressg** package

is MyClass, the attributes are `attr1` and `attr2`, and the methods are `method1` and `method2`.

MyClass
🔒 attr1: int
🔒 attr2: int
🔒 method1(): void
🔒 method2(): void

```
input metauml
Class.A("MyClass")
  ("attr1: int", "attr2: int")
  ("method1(): void", "method2(): void");
A.nw=(0,0);
drawObject(A);
```

Example
4-3-8

The location of the instance is set with a familiar command:

```
A.nw=(0,0);
```

It is drawn with

```
drawObject(A);
```

Each of the strings representing an attribute or a method may begin with a visibility marker: "+" for public, "#" for protected (default), or "–" for private. MetaUML uses these markers to render the appropriate locks.

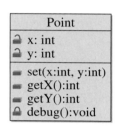

```
input metauml
Class.A("Point")
  ("#x: int", "#y: int")
  ("+set(x:int, y:int)",
  "+getX():int",
  "+getY():int",
  "-debug():void");
A.nw=(0,0);
drawObject(A);
```

classStereotypes.*name*(*ListOfStereotypes*)

This function is used to define stereotypes, where *name* is the object name of a previously created class, and *ListOfStereotypes* is a comma-separated list of strings. An example of its use follows:

```
input metauml
Class.A("User")()();
classStereotypes.A
  ("<<interface>>","<<home>>");
A.nw=(0,0);
drawObject(A);
```

ClassTemplate.*name*(*ListOfTemplates*) (*class-object*)

The macro `ClassTemplate` is the most convenient way of typesetting a class template. This macro creates a visual object that is appropriately positioned near the class object it adorns. It takes three arguments: *name* is the name of the template object, *ListOfTemplates* is a comma-separated list of strings, and *class-object* is the name of a class object. An example of its use follows:

```
input metauml
Class.A("Vector")()();
ClassTemplate.T("T","size: int")(A);
A.nw=(0,0);
drawObjects(A,T);
```

Template.*name*(*ListOfTemplates*)

This macro is used to create template objects independently of class objects.

link(*how-to-draw-information*)(*path*)

Several kinds of relations between classes are possible, which are represented using the link macro. This macro takes two arguments: *how-to-draw-information* is either association (bidirectional association), associationUni (unidirectional association), inheritance (inheritance), aggregation (aggregation), aggregationUni (unidirectional aggregation), composition (composition), compositionUni (unidirectional composition), or transition (transition); and *path* is a METAPOST path.

A simple example with an inheritance link between two class instances follows:

```
input metauml
Class.A("A")()(); Class.B("B")()();
B.e=A.w+(-20,0);
drawObjects(A,B);
link(inheritance)(B.e--A.w);
```

Example
4-3-12

The link macro is powerful enough to draw relations following arbitrary paths.

| pathManhattanX(*start,finish*) | pathManhattanY(*start,finish*) |
| pathManhattanX(*start,finish*) | rpathManhattanY(*start,finish*) |

"Manhattan" paths provide rectangular paths, like in a big city with parallel streets. The four macros take the same arguments *start* and *finish*, which are the starting and finishing points of the paths, respectively. The pathManhattanX and rpathManhattanX macros first draw a horizontal line, and then a vertical line, whereas pathManhattanY and rpathManhattanY first draw a vertical line, and then an horizontal one. The "r"-prefixed macros reverse the orientation of the paths. An example follows:

```
input metauml
Class.A("A")()(); Class.B("B")()();
B.sw=A.ne+(10,10);
drawObjects(A,B);
link(aggregationUni)
     (rpathManhattanX(A.e,B.s));
link(inheritance)
     (pathManhattanY(A.n,B.w));
```

Example
4-3-13

pathStepX(*start,finish,delta*)   pathStepY(*start,finish,delta*)

Stair-like paths are obtained with pathStepX and pathStepY, where *start* is the beginning of the path, *finish* is the end of the path, and *delta* is the amount by which the horizontal line (when pathStepX is used) or vertical line (when pathStepY is used) extends in the opposite direction before returning toward the end point.

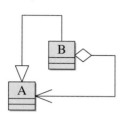

```
input metauml
Class.A("A")()();
Class.B("B")()();
B.sw=A.ne+(10,10);
drawObjects(A,B);
stepX:=60;
link(aggregationUni)
    (pathStepX(A.e,B.e,stepX));
stepY:=20;
link(inheritance)
    (pathStepY(B.n,A.n,stepY));
```

Example
4-3-14

pathHorizontal(*pA,untilX*)	pathVertical(*pA,untilY*)
rpathHorizontal(*pA,untilX*)	rpathVertical(*pA,untilY*)

Horizontal and vertical lines are also provided with these four macros, which draw a line from *pA* until the coordinate *untilX* or *untilY* is reached. The "r" versions reverse the paths.

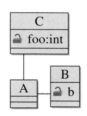

```
input metauml
Class.A("A")()();
Class.B("B")("b")();
Class.C("C")("foo:int")();
B.sw=A.e+(10,-10);
C.sw=A.nw+(0,20);
drawObjects(A,B,C);
untilX:=B.left;
link(association)
    (pathHorizontal(A.e,untilX));
untilY:=C.bottom;
link(association)
    (pathVertical(A.n,untilY));
```

Example
4-3-15

pathCut(*objA,objB*)(*path*)

Paths can also be drawn between objects, using `pathCut` to get a correct contact at the borders. The *path* argument is the path to be defined between the two objects *objA* and *objB*. An example of its use follows:

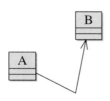

```
input metauml
Class.A("A")()();
Class.B("B")()();
B.sw=A.ne+(30,10);
drawObjects(A,B);
z=A.se + (30,-10);
link(transition)
    (pathCut(A,B)(A.c--z--B.c));
```

Example
4-3-16

$\boxed{\texttt{clink}(\textit{style})(\textit{objA},\textit{objB})}$

Direct paths between object centers can be obtained quickly with `clink`, where *style* is
`inheritance` or any other drawing style.

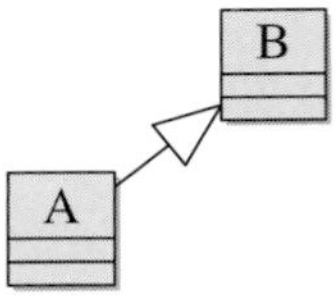

```
input metauml
Class.A("A")()();
Class.B("B")()();
B.sw=A.ne+(20,10);
drawObjects(A,B);
clink(inheritance)(A,B);
```

Example
4-3-17

$\boxed{\texttt{item}.\textit{aName}(\textit{iAssoc})(s)(\textit{equ})}$

Associations are drawn using the `item` macro, where *aName* is the name of the association
and will represent the string *s*, *s* is a string to adorn the association, and *equ* is an equation
specifying where the string *s* should be located. An example follows:

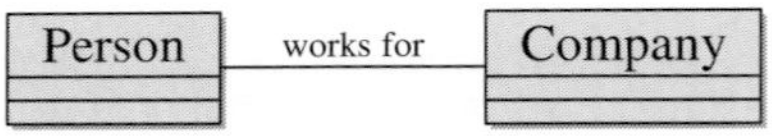

| Person | works for | Company |

```
input metauml
Class.P("Person")()();
Class.C("Company")()();
P.e=C.w+(-50,0);
drawObjects(P,C);
draw P.e--C.w;
item.aName(iAssoc)("works for")
            (aName.s=.5[P.e,C.w]);
```

Example
4-3-18

$\boxed{\texttt{Usecase}.\textit{name}(\textit{ListOfLines})}$

This macro creates a "use case", where *name* is the name of an object and *ListOfLines* is a
comma-separated list of strings, which are placed on top of each other and surrounded by
the appropriate visual UML notation.

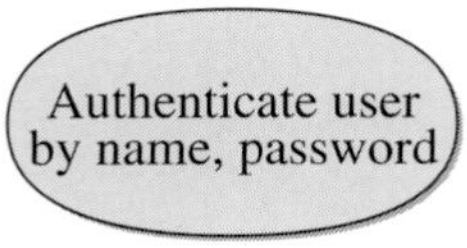

    Authenticate user
    by name, password

```
input metauml
Usecase.U("Authenticate user",
          "by name, password");
U.c=(0,0);
drawObject(U);
```

Example
4-3-19

Actor.*name*(*ListOfLines*)

This macro creates an actor, where *name* is the name of the object and *ListOfLines* is a comma-separated list of strings representing the actor's name.

Example
4-3-20

User

```
input metauml
Actor.A("User");
A.c=(0,0);
drawObject(A);
```

Begin.*beginName*
End.*endName*

These macros define the beginning and end of an activity diagram. An example follows:

Example
4-3-21

```
input metauml
Begin.b;
End.e;
b.nw=(0,0);
e.nw=(20,20);
drawObjects(b,e);
```

Activity.*name*(*ListOfStrings*)

This macro constructs an activity, where *name* is the name of the activity and *ListOfStrings* is a comma-separated list of strings representing the activity.

Example
4-3-22

Learn MetaUML -
the MetaPost UML library

```
input metauml
Activity.A("Learn MetaUML -",
           "the MetaPost UML library");
drawObject(A);
```

State.*name*(*state-name*)(*substates-list*)

This macro defines a state, where *name* is the name of the state, *state-name* is a string or a comma-separated list of strings representing the state's name, and *substates-list* specifies the substates of this state as a comma-separated list of objects. A simple state is obtained with

Example
4-3-23

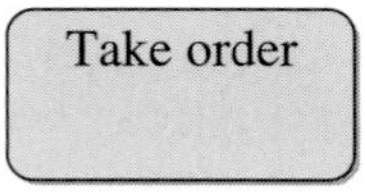

Take order

```
input metauml
State.s("Take order")();
drawObject(s);
```

Composite states are defined by enumerating the inner states at the end of the constructor.

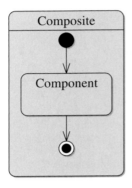

```
input metauml
Begin.b;
End.e;
State.c("Component")();
State.composite("Composite")(b,e,c);
b.midx = e.midx = c.midx;
c.top = b.bottom - 20;
e.top = c.bottom - 20;

composite.info.drawNameLine := 1;
drawObject(composite);

link(transition)(b.s -- c.n);
link(transition)(c.s -- e.n);
```

Example
4-3-24

stateTransitions.*name*(*transitions-list*)

This macro is used to specify internal transitions, where *name* is the state object and *transitions-list* is a comma-separated list of strings.

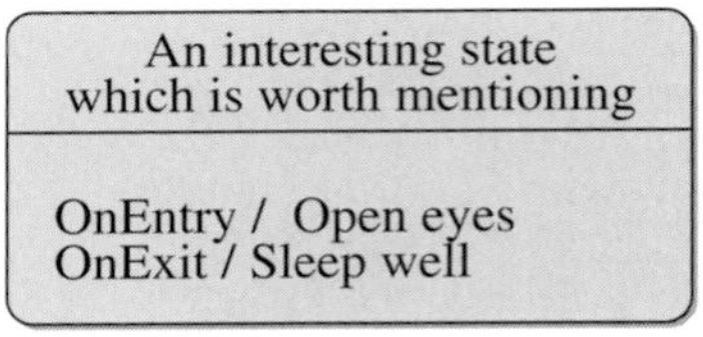

```
input metauml
State.s("An interesting state",
        "which is worth mentioning")();
stateTransitions.s(
  "OnEntry /  Open eyes",
  "OnExit / Sleep well");
s.info.drawNameLine := 1;
drawObject(s);
```

Example
4-3-25

> An interesting state
> which is worth mentioning
>
> OnEntry / Open eyes
> OnExit / Sleep well

History.*name*
ExitPoint.*name*
EntryPoint.*name*
Terminate.*name*

Finally, four kinds of special states exist. These macros define *name* to be either a history state, an exit point state, an entry point state, or a terminate state.

4.3.6 CM arrows utility

The **cmarrows** package by Tommy Ekola (CTAN: `graphics/metapost/contrib/macros/cmarrows`) contains macros to draw arrows and braces in the CM style. The recognized arrow styles are given in Table 4.1.

To use an arrow style, we give the command `setup_cmarrows` with the appropriate parameters, after loading the package. In the next example, we first define three

Table 4.1: CM arrow styles

	Bigbrace		lefthalfarrow
	Biggbrace		righthalfarrow
	bigbrace		parallelarrows
	biggbrace		paralleloppositearrows
	extensiblebrace		paralleloppositerighthalfarrows
	doublearrow		paralleloppositelefthalfarrows
	twoheadarrow		mapstoarrow
	twowayoldarrow		oldtexarrow
	twowayarrow		shortaxisarrow
	twowaydoublearrow		texarrow
	hookrightarrow		tailarrow
	hookleftarrow		tripplearrow

Example
4-3-26

new arrow styles. These definitions create the macros `drawtripple`, `drawbrace`, and `drawparallel`, which can be used like `draw` or `drawarrow`:

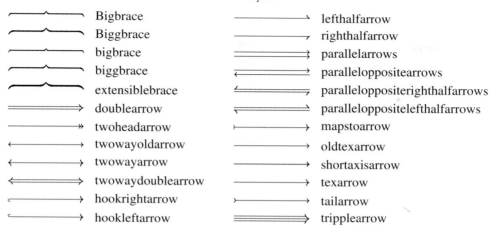

```
input cmarrows
setup_cmarrows(arrow_name = "tripplearrow";
              parameter_file = "cmr10.mf";
              macro_name = "drawtripple");
setup_cmarrows(arrow_name = "extensiblebrace";
              parameter_file = "cmr10.mf";
              macro_name = "drawbrace");
setup_cmarrows(arrow_name =
              "paralleloppositelefthalfarrows";
              parameter_file = "cmr10.mf";
              macro_name = "drawparallel");
numeric u; u=7mm; z0=origin;
z1-z0=(2u,0); z2-z1=(3u,2u);
drawtripple z0..z1..{dir-120}z2;
draw z0{up}..z2;
drawbrace z1{up}..z2;
drawbrace z1{down}..z0;
drawparallel z0{dir-150}..{up}z2;
```

Example
4-3-27

4.4 Geometry

METAPOST is particularly well suited for 2-D geometry, and its automatic resolution of linear equations makes drawing geometrical figures very natural. Intersections, symmetries, and various other geometrical properties can easily be specified.

4.4.1 Plane geometry

In its handling of linear equations, METAPOST defines a special, nameless, variable whatever representing an unknown numerical value. It is, for instance, possible to write

```
10=whatever*5;
```

This will automatically set the (nameless) variable to 2. However, because this variable is nameless, the resulting value is not accessible, so this feature may seem useless. For the above, we could as well have written

```
10=a*5;
```

and then the variable a could have been used for other purposes.

To appreciate better the power of the (nameless) whatever, we have to go a bit further. If we have two points A and B, finding the intersection between AB and Oy can be done as follows:

```
pair A,B,I;
A=...; B=...;
I=whatever[A,B]; xpart(I)=0;
```

But we can do more—we can use whatever twice:

```
pair A,B,I;
A=...; B=...;
I=whatever[A,B]=whatever[origin,(0,1)];
```

In the latter example, the two occurrences of whatever represent different variables, which usually get different values. The values themselves are not needed, however; only the intersection I is needed. Hence, whatever can be used very conveniently in such cases where linear constraints have to be specified, but where the factors themselves are not explicitly involved in other calculations.

A more complex example showing how whatever is applied to the classical geometrical problem of constructing the "nine points circle" of a triangle is given next [99]. It uses a straightforward definition, not given here, that draws all labels and dots.

```
numeric u;u=1cm;
pair A,B,C,D,E,F,G,H,I,J,K,L,N,X;
A=origin;B-A=(0,5u);C-A=(-7u,u); % A,B,C
D-A=B-D;E-B=C-E;F-A=C-F; % middles D,E,F
% then, the three heights:
G=whatever[B,C]=whatever[A,A+((C-B) rotated 90)]; % G
H=whatever[A,C]=whatever[B,B+((C-A) rotated 90)]; % H
I=whatever[A,B]=whatever[C,C+((B-A) rotated 90)]; % I
% then, the orthocenter X
X=(A--G) intersectionpoint (C--I);
% and the middles J, K and L of AX, BX and CX
```

```
J=.5[A,X];K=.5[B,X];L=.5[C,X];
% the center of the nine points circle
N=whatever[.5[D,I],(.5[D,I]+((D-I) rotated 90))]
 =whatever[.5[D,H],(.5[D,H]+((D-H) rotated 90))];
% circle radius
r=arclength(I--N);
draw A--B--C--cycle;draw A--G;draw B--H;draw C--I;
draw fullcircle scaled 2r shifted N;
NinepointsLabelsAndDots;
```

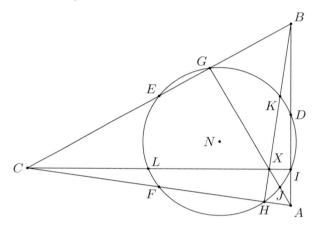

Example
4-4-1

The next example shows construction of an ellipse inscribed in a parallelogram:

```
pair O,A,B,C,D,E,F,G,K,M[],N[],P[];path parallelogram,X;
O=origin;B-O=O-A=3cm*dir(120);D-O=O-C=4cm*dir(180);
P1=A+D-O;P2=B+D-O;P3=B+C-O;P4=A+C-O;
draw A--B dashed evenly withcolor blue;
draw C--D dashed evenly withcolor blue;
parallelogram=P1--P2--P3--P4--cycle;
draw parallelogram;
E-D=arclength(O--B)*(unitvector(B-A) rotated -90);
draw D--E;draw O--E;F=.5[O,E];
X=fullcircle scaled arclength(O--E) shifted F;
draw X;
G=(F--D) intersectionpoint X;K=(F--(F+(F-D))) intersectionpoint X;
draw D--K;
N1-O=O-N2=arclength(D--G)*unitvector(O-K);
M1-O=O-M2=arclength(D--K)*unitvector(O-G);
draw N1--N2 dashed evenly;draw M1--M2 dashed evenly;
a:=arclength(M1--O);b:=arclength(N1--O);an:=angle(M1-O);
draw fullcircle xscaled 2a yscaled 2b rotated an shifted O withcolor red;
draw E--(E+(E-D)) dashed evenly;
EllipseLabelsAndPoints; % not shown
```

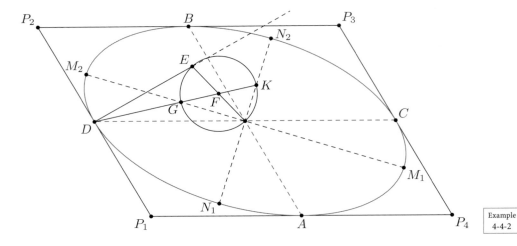

Example
4-4-2

Figure 4.4 (adapted from Coxeter: *The Golden Section, Phyllotaxis, and Wythoff's Game*, 1953) is another example of geometrical construction, where the construction provides a means to find the golden ratio. The value shown in the figure is slightly wrong, because it is the value measured by METAPOST after the construction was done, and there were rounding errors.

Plane fractals can also be constructed. The example in Figure 4.5 on the facing page shows the Apollonian gasket obtained from the three circles centered at C_1, C_2, and C_3 [101].

As a final goody, here is the **geometriesyr16** package by Christophe Poulain, which can produce hand-drawn geometrical figures:

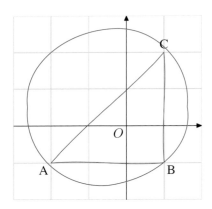

```
input geometriesyr16
figuremainlevee(0,0,5u,5u);
    trace grille(1) withcolor gris;
    origine((3,2));
    trace axes;
    pair A,B,C;
    A=placepoint(-2,-1);
    B=placepoint(1,-1); C=placepoint(1,2);
    trace polygone(A,B,C) withcolor rouge;
    trace cercles(A,B,C) withcolor bleu;
    nomme.llft(A);  nomme.lrt(B);
    nomme.top(C);
finmainlevee;
```

Example
4-4-3

4.4.2 Space geometry

METAPOST can also be used with great profit for space geometry applications. More detail can be found in Section 4.6.3 about 3-D extensions.

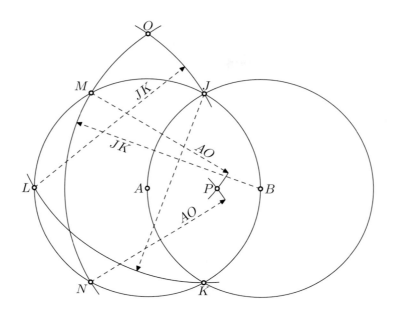

$$\frac{AP}{PB} \approx 1.61806 = \phi = \frac{1+\sqrt{5}}{2}$$

Figure 4.4: Pipping's construction for the golden number

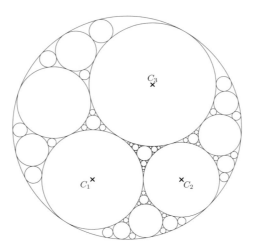

Figure 4.5: The Apollonian gasket

4.4.3 Fractals and other complex objects

METAPOST has been used for fractals as well. One example is the Von Koch flake (Section 3.5.7); another is the Apollonian gasket [101]. Still other examples include L-systems, which we saw earlier when discussing turtle-style graphics (see Section 4.1.9).

Hilbert's curve   Another fractal is Hilbert's curve, adapted from code written by Urs Oswald. The main macro is `hilbertPath`:

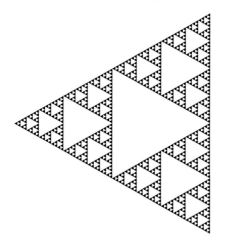

```
vardef hilbertPath(expr s, n) =
  save pa,pb,pc,A,B,C,shift,hilb,h;
  path pa,pb,pc,hilb,h; pair A,B,C,shift;
  if n=0:  hilb=origin;
  else:     shift=(s, 0);
    h=hilbertPath(s, n-1);
    pa=h reflectedabout(origin,(1, -1));
    A=point length(pa) of pa;
    pb=h shifted (A+shift);
    B=point 0 of pb;
    hilb=pa & A--B & pb;
    C=B shifted ((A+.5shift) rotated -90);
    pc=reverse hilb reflectedabout(C,C+right);
    hilb:=hilb & point length(hilb) of
            hilb--point 0 of pc  & pc;
  fi
  hilb
enddef;
side=5cm; n=5;
onestep=side/(2**n);
draw hilbertPath(onestep, n);
draw unitsquare scaled side
      shifted (-.5onestep,.5onestep-side);
```

Example
4-4-4

Sierpiński's curve   Sierpiński's curve is even easier (after Martin Geisler):

```
def sierpinski(expr a,b,n)=
  if n=0:
    fill a--(b rotatedabout(a,60))--b--cycle;
  else:
    sierpinski(a,0.5[a,b],n-1);
    sierpinski(0.5[a,b],b,n-1);
    sierpinski(0.5[a,b rotatedabout(a,60)],
            0.5[a rotatedabout(b,-60),b],n-1);
  fi
enddef;
sierpinski((0,0),(0,6cm),6);
```

Example
4-4-5

Verhulst diagrams are not much more complex to produce (after Jean-Michel Sarlat): *Bifurcation diagrams*

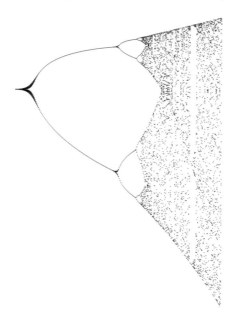

```
numeric r,pr,x,rmin,rmax,ur,ux;
rmin=1.9;
rmax=3;
ur=5cm;
ux=6cm;
r:=rmin;
pr:=(rmax-rmin)/250;
for i=1 upto 250:
  x:=.3;
  for j=1 upto 50:
    x:=(1+r)*x-r*x*x;
  endfor;
  for j=1 upto 50:
    x:=(1+r)*x-r*x*x;
    draw (r,x) xscaled ur yscaled ux;
  endfor;
  r:=r+pr;
endfor;
```

Example
4-4-6

4.4.4 Art

Simple combinations of scaling, rotations, and iterations sometimes produce impressive effects. Here is an example, also from Jean-Michel Sarlat:

```
numeric psi,iter,c,r,t,cv;
path p;
psi=137.6;
iter=200;
c=5;
r=0;
for i=iter downto 1:
  t:=sqrt(i);
  r:=(r+psi) mod 360;
  cv:=cosd((i/iter)*90);
  p:=((0,0)--(t,1)--
      (t+1,0)--(t,-1)--cycle)
    rotated r;
  fill p scaled c withcolor (1,cv,0);
  draw p scaled c;
endfor;
```

Example
4-4-7

See Color Plate III for examples of artwork producing optical illusions.

4.5 Science and engineering applications

4.5.1 Electrical circuits

There are two main METAPOST packages for drawing electrical circuits: makecirc and mpcirc. We will give a detailed description of the first package.

The makecirc package by Gustavo S. Bustamante Argañaraz provides a library containing various electrical symbols to be used in building circuit diagrams [10]. Like boxes, expressg, METAOBJ, MetaUML, and other packages, it is a package of the "box-line" type.

The package is loaded with

```
input makecirc
initlatex("");
```

The additionnal `initlatex` command is necessary only when labels are to be typeset with LaTeX. `initlatex` is provided by the latex package (by José Luis Díaz), which is automatically loaded by makecirc. This command takes a string representation of the LaTeX preamble. It must be issued whenever LaTeX is used, even if no package is loaded, as in Example 4-5-1 below.

When the labels are done in TEX or LaTeX, METAPOST has to be called twice on each file. The first run collects the labels, while the second run typesets them. This speeds up processing, as only one TEX or LaTeX file is created.

makecirc can handle all the common elements of electrical circuits. Example 4-5-1 shows the main ideas of this package. It needs LaTeX implicitly, because makecirc defines `\ohm` as an abbreviation for `\ensuremath{\Omega}` and `\ensuremath` is a LaTeX command. The three objects depicted are a resistor R, an inductor L, and a capacitor C.

```
input makecirc;
initlatex("");
resistor.a(origin,normal,90,"R","10\ohm");
inductor.a(R.a.r+(2cm,0),Up,-90,"L","");
centreof.A(R.a.r,L.a.l,cap);
capacitor.a(c.A,normal,phi.A,"C","");
wire(R.a.r,C.a.l,nsq);wire(C.a.r,L.a.l,nsq);
wire(L.a.r,R.a.l,udsq);
```

Example
4-5-1

The main elements at our disposal are listed and demonstrated in Table 4.2 and 4.3 on the next page (only one type for each element is shown).

Before going into more detail on these elements, it is useful to analyze the example. Suppose a resistor is set at the origin, rotated 90 degrees counterclockwise, and has the value 10Ω. The name of the resistor is "a". Once the resistor is in place, the locations of its two pins are R.a.l and R.a.r. The latter is used to position the inductor, which is also named "a" but could have been named differently. The inductor is rotated clockwise by 90 degrees and its spires are put on the "Up" side (before rotation). Then, the capacitor is positioned midway between the resistor and the inductor. The `centreof` command specifies that a capacitor type element (cap; see Table 4.2) is to be positioned between R.a.r and L.a.l. It accordingly sets c.A and phi.A to the location of the origin pin of the capacitor and to

Table 4.2: Elements and their abbreviations

Element	Abbreviation	Element	Abbreviation
Inductor	ind	Capacitor	cap
Motor	mot	Generator	gen
Transformer	tra	Battery	bat
AC source	sac	DC source	sdc
Current source	si	Voltage source	sv
Resistor	res	Diode	dio
Transistor	bjt	Measurement insttrument	ins
Impedance	imp	Lamp	lam
Switch	swt	Current	cur

Table 4.3: The main components of a circuit

```
input makecirc;
initlatex("");

means.a((0cm,11.5cm),volt,0,"Volt");
junction((3.5cm,11.5cm),"junction")(top);

rheostat.a((0cm,10.5cm),Rrheo,-90);
diode.a((3cm,10.5cm),normal,0,pinA,"D_1","");

transistor.a((0cm,9cm),pnp,0);
ground.a((3.5cm,9cm),simple,0);

battery.a((0cm,7.5cm),0,"Battery","");
transformer.a((3cm,7.5cm),normal,-90);

lamp.a((0cm,6cm),0,"Lamp","");
current.a((3.5cm,6cm),0,"Current","");

generator.a((0cm,4.5cm),0,"Generator","");
impedance.a((3cm,4.5cm),0,"Impedance","");

switch.a((0cm,3cm),NO,0,"NO","");
motor.a((3cm,3cm),0,"Motor","");

inductor.a((0cm,1.5cm),Up,0,"L","");
source.a((3cm,1.5cm),AC,0,"AC","");

resistor.a(origin,normal,0,"R","10\ohm");
capacitor.a((3cm,0),normal,0,"C","");
```

Example
4-5-2

its angle, respectively. These two values are then used to set the capacitor (also called "a"). Finally, wires are drawn between the resistor and the capacitor, between the capacitor and the inductor, and between the inductor and the capacitor. The last parameter of the `wire` command defines how the lines are drawn, whether as a straight line or as several cut lines.

Every **makecirc** element type has an abbreviation (Table 4.2). These abbreviations are used in macros such as `centreof` or `centerto`.

The first example showed how to center the capacitor, but the resistor and inductor were not centered. This can be achieved with the `centerto` command:

```
input makecirc;
initlatex("");
resistor.a(origin,normal,90,"R","10\ohm");
centerto.A(R.a.l,R.a.r,2cm,ind);
inductor.a(A,Up,90,"L","");
centreof.B(R.a.r,L.a.r,cap);
capacitor.a(c.B,normal,phi.B,"C","");
wire(R.a.r,C.a.l,nsq);wire(C.a.r,L.a.r,nsq);
wire(L.a.l,R.a.l,nsq);
```

Example 4-5-3

In this example, A (the origin of inductor "a") is defined as a point 2 cm away from the middle of [R.a.l,R.a.r] and at right angle with this segment. Note that `centerto.A` defines A as a point, but `centreof.B` defines c.B as a point. As a consequence, the resistor and the inductor are correctly centered and the capacitor is between them, but the capacitor is tilted and the wires are not parallel.

To overcome these problems, an additional point z1 can be introduced, at the right of the capacitor and above the inductor, using `xpart` and `ypart`:

```
input makecirc;
initlatex("");
resistor.a(origin,normal,90,"R","10\ohm");
centerto.A(R.a.l,R.a.r,2cm,ind);
inductor.a(A,Up,90,"L","");
z1=(xpart L.a.r, ypart R.a.r);
centreof.B(R.a.r,z1,cap);
capacitor.a(c.B,normal,phi.B,"C","");
wire(R.a.r,C.a.l,nsq);wire(C.a.r,L.a.r,nsq);
wire(L.a.l,R.a.l,nsq);
```

Example 4-5-4

The capacitor is now horizontal, and only the wiring needs to be improved.

The exact syntax of the `wire` command is as follows:

```
wire(pin1, pin2, type)
```

The wiring type indicates how the lines are drawn, and in particular whether they first go up or down (type "udsq") or first right or left (type "rlsq"). The "nsq" type is for straight lines ("no square"). Changing the types, the correct output is obtained as follows:

```
input makecirc;
initlatex("");
resistor.a(origin,normal,90,"R","10\ohm");
centerto.A(R.a.l,R.a.r,2cm,ind);
inductor.a(A,Up,90,"L","");
z1=(xpart L.a.r, ypart R.a.r);
centreof.B(R.a.r,z1,cap);
capacitor.a(c.B,normal,phi.B,"C","");
wire(R.a.r,C.a.l,udsq);wire(C.a.r,L.a.r,rlsq);
wire(L.a.l,R.a.l,udsq);
```

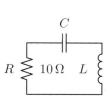

Example
4-5-5

We now give the syntax of all the commands:

resistor.*a*(*z, type, angle, name, value*)	capacitor.*a*(*z, type, angle, name, value*)
inductor.*a*(*z, type, angle, name, value*)	source.*a*(*z, type, angle, name, value*)
switch.*a*(*z, type, angle, name, value*)	

In most cases, the syntax is self-explanatory. Each element's name is indicated by the symbol *a*, except in the case of a mesh current (imesh—see below), which does not have a name. The first parameter *z* of most of the macros is the element's center. In the earlier examples, the centers were origin, A, and c.B.

Several elements are available in different kinds, or *type*s. Sometimes the type merely serves to indicate how an element is drawn, as for the Up and Down versions of inductors. At other times the type corresponds to real differences in the elements, such as for PNP, NPN, and other transistors.

An element can also have a name and a value (for instance, a resistor R_1 of value 200Ω).

Except for junctions, which are represented by dots, elements are also positioned using an angular value *angle*.

motor.*a*(*z, angle, name, value*)	generator.*a*(*z, angle, name, value*)
impedance.*a*(*z, angle, name, value*)	lamp.*a*(*z, angle, name, value*)
current.*a*(*z, angle, name, value*)	battery.*a*(*z, angle, name, value*)
transformer.*a*(*z, type, angle*)	transistor.*a*(*z, type, angle*)
ground.*a*(*z, type, angle*)	rheostat.*a*(*z, type, angle*)
diode.*a*(*z, type, angle, pin, name, value*)	means.*a*(*z, type, angle, text*)
junction.*a*(*z, text*)(*pos*)	imesh(*center, width, height, sense, angle, name*)

A measurement instrument (means) and a junction will also have a text label, and a junction will have a positioning argument *pos* for this label. Diodes have an additional parameter *pin* indicating which pin—the anode (pinA) or the cathode (pinK)—is placed on the *z* position. Finally, mesh currents (imesh) are also given a center position, a width, a height, and a direction (clockwise or counterclockwise).

The values of both the parameters and the pins are given in Table 4.4.

Table 4.4: Possible types, pins, and positioning pins for each element

Elements	Types	Pins	Positioning Pins
Inductor	Up, Down	$L.\alpha.l | L.\alpha.r$	$L.\alpha.l$
Capacitor	normal, variable, electrolytic, variant	$C.\alpha.l | C.\alpha.r$	$C.\alpha.l$
Resistor	normal, variable	$R.\alpha.l, R.\alpha.r$	$R.\alpha.l$
Source	AC, DC, V, I	$S.\alpha.n, S.\alpha.p$	$S.\alpha.n$
Switch	NO, NC	$st.\alpha.l, st.\alpha.r$	$st.\alpha.l$
Motor	/	$M.\alpha.D, M.\alpha.B$	$M.\alpha.D$
Generator		$G.\alpha.D, G.\alpha.B$	$G.\alpha.D$
Impedance		$Z.\alpha.l, Z.\alpha.r$	$Z.\alpha.l$
Lamp		$La.\alpha.l, La.\alpha.r$	$La.\alpha.l$
Current		$i.\alpha.s, i.\alpha.d$	$i.\alpha.s$
Battery		$B.\alpha.n, B.\alpha.p$	$B.\alpha.n$
Transformer	normal, mid, Fe, auto	$tf.\alpha.pi, \ tf.\alpha.ps, \ tf.\alpha.si, \ tf.\alpha.ss, tf.\alpha.m$	$tf.\alpha.pi$
Transistor	pnp, npn, cpnp, cnpn	$T.\alpha.B, T.\alpha.C, T.\alpha.E$	$T.\alpha.B$
Ground	simple, shield	$gnd.\alpha$	$gnd.\alpha$
Rheostat	Lrheo, Rrheo	$rh.\alpha.i, rh.\alpha.s, rh.\alpha.r$	$rh.\alpha.i$
Diode	normal, zener, LED	$D.\alpha.A, D.\alpha.K$	$D.\alpha.A$ (pin=pinA), $D.\alpha.K$ (pin=pinK)
Measurement instrument	volt, ampere, watt	$mi.\alpha.l, mi.\alpha.r, mi.\alpha.p$	$mi.\alpha.l$

`wireU(`*pin1*, *pin2*, *dist*, *type*`)`

This command is used when two pins need to be connected but with three segments, like the "U" shapes connecting the resistor G_ϕ to the inductor B_ϕ in Example 4-5-6. The *type* has the same meaning as for the `wire` command, except that it should not be "nsq". The absolute value of the *dist* parameter gives the distance by which the connection leaves the pins, and the sign of *dist* indicates the direction.

`ctext.`*pos* `(`*pin1*, *pin2*, *text*, *type*`)`

This command is used to center *text* between two pins, *pin1*, and *pin2*. Two types are available: `witharrow` and `noarrow`. Morover, the text can be positioned using the optional argument *pos*, which is identical to the optional argument of the `label` command.

The following examples illustrate some of the capabilities of this package.

```
input makecirc;
initlatex("\usepackage{amsmath,amssymb}");
junction.a(origin,"1b")(lft);junction.b((0,4cm),"1a")(lft);
resistor.a((1cm,4cm),normal,0,"R_1","0,82\ohm");
inductor.a(R.a.r,Up,0,"X_{L1}","0,92 H");
centerto.A(J.a,J.b,4cm,res);
```

```
resistor.b(A,normal,90,"G_{\phi}","0,41\ohm");
centerto.B(J.a,J.b,7cm,ind);
inductor.b(B,Down,90,"B_{\phi}","2,24 H");
inductor.c(L.a.r+(3.6cm,0),Up,0,"X'_{L2}","0,9 H");
resistor.c(L.c.r,normal,0,"R'_2","0,8\ohm");
junction.c(R.c.r+(1cm,0),"2a")(rt);
junction.d(R.c.r+(1cm,-4cm),"2b")(rt);
wire(J.a,J.d,nsq);wire(J.b,R.a.l,nsq);
wireU(R.b.r,L.b.r,3mm,udsq);wireU(R.b.l,L.b.l,-3mm,udsq);
wire(L.a.r,(5.5cm,ypart R.b.r + 3mm),rlsq);
wire((5.5cm,ypart R.b.l - 3mm),(5.5cm,0),nsq);
wire(R.c.r,J.c,nsq);wire(L.c.l,(5cm,ypart L.c.l),nsq);
ctext(J.a,J.b,"$V_1$",noarrow);ctext(J.c,J.d,"$V'_2$",noarrow);
```

```
input makecirc;
initlatex("\usepackage{amsmath,amssymb}");

transistor.a(origin,pnp,0);junction.B(T.a.B,"B")(top);
junction.E(T.a.E,"E")(llft);junction.C(T.a.C,"C")(top);
resistor.C(T.a.C+(2cm,-5mm),normal,-90,"R_C","");
source.CC(R.C.r,DC,-90,"V_{CC}","");
resistor.B(T.a.B+(-2cm,0),normal,-90,"R_B","");
source.EE(R.B.r,DC,-90,"V_{BB}","");
capacitor.a(T.a.B+(-3cm,0),normal,-180,"C_a","");
junction.a(C.a.r+(-1cm,0),"")(top);
junction.b((xpart J.a,ypart S.EE.p-5mm),"")(bot);
wire(T.a.C,R.C.l,rlsq);wire(T.a.B,C.a.l,nsq);
wire(C.a.r,J.a,nsq);wireU(S.EE.p,S.CC.p,-5mm,udsq);
wire(J.b,S.EE.p+(0,-5mm),nsq);
wire(T.a.E,(xpart T.a.E,ypart S.EE.p-5mm),nsq);
current.E(T.a.E+(0,-1cm),90,"I_E","");current.C(T.a.C+(5mm,0),0,"I_C","");
current.B(J.B+(-5mm,0),-180,"I_B","");
ctext.lft(J.a,J.b,"$E_1$",witharrow);
wire(R.C.l,R.C.l+(1cm,0),nsq);wire(R.C.r,R.C.r+(1cm,0),nsq);
```

```
ctext.rt(R.C.l+(1cm,0),R.C.r+(1cm,0),"$E_2$",witharrow);
```

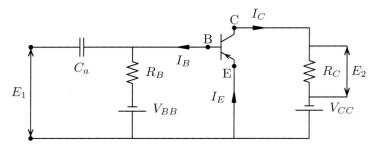

Example
4-5-7

```
input makecirc;
initlatex("\usepackage{amsmath,amssymb}");

source.a(origin,AC,90,"v","");
junction.a(S.a.p+(3cm,1cm),"")(top);
diode.a(J.a,normal,-45,pinA,"D_1","");
diode.b(D.a.K,normal,-135,pinK,"D_2","");
diode.c(D.b.A,normal,135,pinK,"D_3","");
diode.d(D.c.A,normal,45,pinA,"D_4","");
junction.b(D.b.A,"")(bot);
centerto.A(S.a.n,S.a.p)(5cm,imp);
impedance.a(A,90,"Z_L","");
wireU(S.a.p,D.a.A,1.5cm,udsq);
wireU(S.a.n,D.b.A,-1.5cm,udsq);
wire(D.a.K,Z.a.r,rlsq);
wire(Z.a.l,Z.a.l+(0,-4mm),nsq);
wireU(Z.a.l+(0,-4mm),D.d.A,-4cm,rlsq);
```

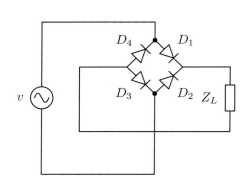

Example
4-5-8

```
input makecirc;
initlatex("\usepackage{amsmath,amssymb}");

transformer.a(origin,mid,0);
diode.a(tf.a.ss+(5mm,1cm),normal,0,pinA,"D_1","");
diode.b(tf.a.si+(5mm,-1cm),normal,0,pinA,"D_2","");
impedance.a(D.a.K+(2cm,-4mm),-90,"Z_L","300\ohm");
wire(tf.a.ss,D.a.A,udsq);wire(tf.a.si,D.b.A,udsq);
wire(D.a.K,Z.a.l,rlsq);wire(Z.a.r,tf.a.m,udsq);
wire(D.b.K,D.a.K+(5mm,0),rlsq);
junction.a(D.a.K+(5mm,0),"")(top);
centerto.A(tf.a.pi,tf.a.ps)(-15mm,sac);
source.a(A,AC,90,"220 V","v");
wire(S.a.p,tf.a.ps,udsq);wire(S.a.n,tf.a.pi,udsq);
centreof.A((xpart S.a.p,ypart tf.a.ps),tf.a.ps,cur);
current.a(c.A,phi.A,"i(t)","5 A");
imesh(tf.a.ss+(1cm,0),15mm,1cm,cw,0,"I_{cc}");
```

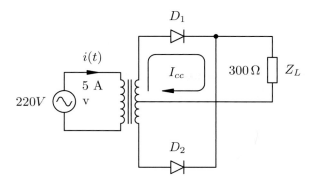

Example
4-5-9

At least one other pure METAPOST package for drawing electrical circuits exists: *Other circuit packages*
mpcirc by Tomasz Cholewo, available from `http://ci.uofl.edu/tom/software/`
`LaTeX/mpcirc`. In addition, tools are available that can take non-METAPOST input and
produce METAPOST output for electrical circuits. An example of such a tool is the M4
`Circuit_macros` by Dwight Aplevich [8] and described in Section 8.6.2 on page 583. This
tool also uses DPIC with a variety of output formats, in particular **PSTricks**.

4.5.2 Mechanics and engineering

METAPOST is very well suited for engineering drawings, and in particular drawings representing mechanical components, as demonstrated in Figure 4.6. This figure makes use of
the macros described in Section 4.1.3 for drawing hidden lines.

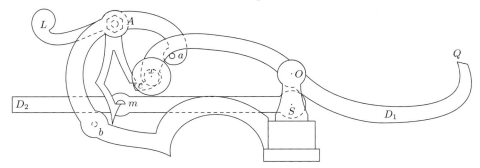

Figure 4.6: A drawing in mechanical engineering, making use of the macros for hidden lines

4.5.3 Simulation

The random number generators of METAPOST can be used to produce various random
walks for simulation purposes, as shown in the following example:

```
vardef randomwalk(expr C,wd,ht,n,l,f,r)=
  save A,B,a,b;pair A,B;a=0;
```

```
draw ((wd,-ht)--(wd,ht)--(-wd,ht)--(-wd,-ht)--cycle) shifted C;
A=C;
for i=1 upto n:
  forever:
    b:=a*f+((uniformdeviate 2)-1)*180r;
    B:=A+l*(uniformdeviate 1)*dir(b);
    if (abs(xpart(B-C))>= wd) or  (abs(ypart(B-C))>= ht):
      B:=A+l*(uniformdeviate 2)*dir(b+180);
    fi;
    exitif (abs(xpart(B-C))< wd) and  (abs(ypart(B-C))< ht);
  endfor;
  draw A--B;A:=B;a:=b mod 360;
endfor;
enddef;
randomwalk(origin,2.5cm,2.5cm,1000,10mm,0,1);
randomwalk((6cm,0),2.5cm,2.5cm,3000,4mm,1,0.3);
```

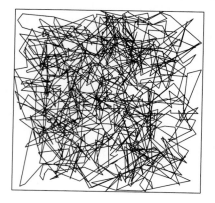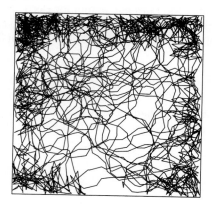

Example
4-5-10

4.5.4 Optics

There are no general-purpose METAPOST packages for optical drawing, although META-POST is very well suited for this purpose.

We give here a minimal example demonstrating the capabilities of METAPOST for tracing rays through diopters or rays reflected on mirrors. The macro `reflectray` takes a ray source, an angle, and a path representing a surface. The `refractray` macro takes two refraction indices. A ray is followed by computing its intersection with the surface, computing the normal at the intersection, and computing the refracted or reflected angles. These macros are very much simplified in that they will work for only certain surfaces, as the computation of the intersection is not robust enough and does not handle cases where there are several intersections in a given ray direction. A more elaborate package would identify each side of the diopter and ensure that refracted rays are, indeed, refracted. The main reason for our interest in these macros is their current simplicity and versatility with respect to the diopter surface.

A natural extension to these macros would be to associate several diopters and produce lenses. It would be desirable to have a data structure for each optical object so that rays could be followed in some transparent way, independent of the nature of the optical object.

```
vardef reflectray(expr s,a,p)=
  save tI,tn,ia,I,J;pair I,J;
  tI=xpart(p intersectiontimes (s--(s+30cm*dir(a))));
  if tI>=0:
    I=point tI of p;draw s--I;
    tn=angle(direction tI of p)+90;
    %drawarrow I--(I+dir(tn)*3cm); % normal
    %drawarrow I--(I+dir(180+tn)*3cm);
    ia=tn-angle(s-I);J=I+dir(tn+ia)*2cm;
    draw I--J withcolor blue;
  fi;
enddef;
numeric u;u=3mm;path p;
p=((5u,-6u)..(4u,-2u)..(4.5u,0)..(5u,5u)) rotated 90;
z0=origin;
for a=40 step 5 until 140: reflectray(z0,a,p); endfor;
draw p withcolor red;
```

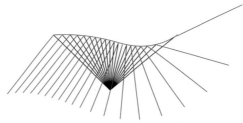

Example
4-5-11

```
vardef refractray(expr s,a,p,na,nb)=
  save tI,tn,ia,ib,I,J,sib;pair I,J;
  tI=xpart(p intersectiontimes (s--(s+30cm*dir(a))));
  if tI>=0:
    I=point tI of p;draw s--I;tn=angle(direction tI of p)+90;
    %drawarrow I--(I+dir(tn)*3cm); % normal
    %drawarrow I--(I+dir(180+tn)*3cm);
    ia=tn-angle(s-I);
    % we have na*sind(ia)=nb*sind(ib)
    sib=na*sind(ia)/nb;ib=-angle(1+-+sib,sib);
    J=I+dir(tn+180+ib)*2cm;draw I--J withcolor blue;
  fi;
enddef;
numeric u;u=3mm;path p;
p=((5u,-6u)..(4u,-2u)..(4.5u,0)..(5u,5u)) rotated 90;
z0=origin;
```

```
for a=-40 step 5 until 140:refractray(z0,a,p,1,1.5);endfor;
draw p withcolor red;
```

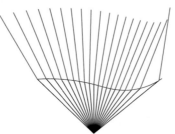

Example
4-5-12

It is possible, to some extent, to provide a lens-like feature over a picture, by clipping part of this picture and scaling it appropriately. An example is given below, where the text is stored in a METRPOST picture variable.

Lenses over a document

```
vardef magnify(expr pic,p,c,f)=
  save A;picture A;
  A=pic;clip A to p;
  unfill (p shifted -c scaled f shifted c);
  draw A shifted -c scaled f shifted c;
  draw p shifted -c scaled f shifted c;
enddef;

picture pic[];
% ptext=btex ... etex; % image with text not shown
pic0=ptext scaled 0.4;label(pic0,origin);pic1=thelabel(pic0,origin);
path p[];
p1=fullcircle xscaled 1.2cm yscaled .8cm shifted (0,1cm);
magnify(pic1,p1,center p1,2.5);
p2=unitsquare shifted (-.5,-.5) xscaled 2.5cm yscaled 1cm shifted (-2cm*up);
magnify(pic1,p2,center p2,2);
```

Proposition LX. Theorem XXIII.
If two bodies s *bodies, as* er with forces recip-
rocally proport revolve about
their comm *to the principal* axis of the
ellipsis u is motion
about th s, which
the sam *describe in the sam* e about
the othe S + P to
the first *nt, as the sum of* h and the
other body
For if th n other, their
periodic times by *roportional* n a subduplicate
ratio of the body S to the sum of the bodies S + P. Let the periodic time in the latter ellipsis be diminished in that ratio, and the
periodic times will become equal; but, by Prop. XV, the principal
axis of the ellipsis will be diminished in a ratio sesquiplicate to the
former ratio; that is, in a ratio to which the ratio of S to S + P is
triplicate; and therefore that axis will be to the principal axis of
described round the immovable as S + P
proportionals between $S + P$ and S. Q.
n, *The mathematical principles of natura*
y Andrew Motte, 1848.)

Example
4-5-13

4.6 3-D extensions

4.6.1 Introduction

METAPOST was written with an implicit 2-D structure: Curves are made of pairs, two-dimensional closed paths can be filled, etc. These constraints are unsurprising, as the final output was supposed to be a printed page or a screen.

METAPOST can be extended in several directions, with the same 2-D output, using "shallow" or "deep" techniques.

In the "shallow" model, 3-D capabilities are added as METAPOST macros. This type of extension has been explored by several packages—in particular, Denis Roegel's **3d** package and Nobre's **featpost** package.

"Deep" extensions involve changes to the source of METAPOST itself. In this case, extensions may break compatibility with the standard METAPOST. Examples of such extensions include 3DLDF (see Section 4.6.3) and, to a lesser extent, Asymptote [46].

Genuine 3-D extensions provide natural means to manipulate 3-D data and ease the task of projecting points on a reference surface representing a screen. The removal of hidden parts, the computation of visual intersections, and the integration of text labels on 3-D objects, while at the same time aiming at a vector output, are challenging tasks. It is therefore no surprise that no 3-D METAPOST package or extension provides a full solution.

None of the 3-D extensions go beyond output on a 2-D surface (screen or page), although it would be conceivable to have a 3-D extension to METAPOST output data for a 3-D printer.

4.6.2 Requirements for a 3-D extension

Before comparing the various 3-D extensions written for METAPOST, it is useful to consider the requirements for such an extension. In our mind, a reasonable 3-D extension to METAPOST should at least provide a solution to the following problems:

1. there should be a type for points in space, and this type should be subject to easy handling;

2. for mere perspective drawing, an observer, a screen, and an orientation should be defineable;

3. a projection routine should be available, so that a point can be projected on the screen, and several kinds of projections could be provided;

4. lines or surfaces should be defineable, and projectable, with the removal of their hidden parts;

5. complex objects—mainly bounded areas such as polyhedra—should be defineable;

6. there should be a good integration with TEX; and

7. vector graphics output should be available.

Some of these features are actually standard, whereas others exist in only some of the extensions developed so far. Some features, such as objects, are defined in METAOBJ, but not in the context of a 3-D environment. And some of the 3-D extensions go beyond this point—trying, for instance, to compute the intersections of the projections of various objects.

4.6.3 Overview of 3-D packages

This section gives a brief overview of the various 3-D extensions written for, or based on, METAPOST.

3d/3dgeom

The **3d** package by Denis Roegel was among the first packages to address 3-D issues in METAPOST [97]. This package provides basic functionalities for setting up a perspective projection and defining basic objects such as convex polyhedra. Its notion of an "object" (a set of points and methods to draw them) is flat, and there can be no composed objects. This package was specifically created for the animation of convex polyhedra; as such, it provides a framework for the generation of GIF animations based on METAPOST drawings. However, there is no provision for hidden parts removal, other than in the simple case of convex polyhedra.

Here are two figures produced with the **3d** package:

The **3d** package has been extended with the **3dgeom** package aimed at basic space geometry [99]. With the **3dgeom** package, it becomes possible to handle different kinds of projections, to manipulate abstract objects such as lines and planes, and to compute their intersections.

Here is a figure produced with the **3dgeom** extension:

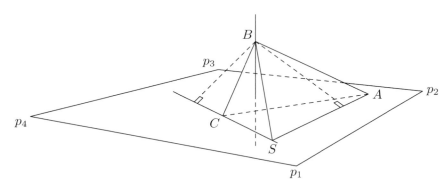

m3d

Anthony Phan's **m3d** (CTAN: `graphics/metapost/contrib/macros/m3D`) is another 3-D extension to METAPOST. It can also produce animations, following the footsteps of the **3d** package. See Color Plate II for some nice drawings made with this package.

Metagraf

Metagraf (`http://w3.mecanica.upm.es/metapost/metagraf.php`) is a WYSI-WYG interface for METAPOST created by Santiago Muelas. **Metagraf** outputs a META-POST file, which can then be run through normal METAPOST. The program is written in Java and is platform-independent.

Featpost

The **featpost** package, by Luís Nobre Gonçalves, also provides basic 3-D functionalities and is geared toward physics diagrams [32, 33]. The `color` type is used to represent points in space. Like the **3d** package, **featpost** does not handle the removal of hidden parts; it also does not have any notion of complex objects.

Here, we illustrate some of **featpost**'s features, without describing all the commands in detail.

globes   The `tropicalglobe` macro draws a globe in perspective, with its parallels. The meridians are obtained with the `spatialhalfcircle` macro. The position of the camera is specified in the `viewcentr` variable.

```
input featpost3Dplus2D
color gammacnt;
numeric newradius,radius,aux,i,numc,foc,lc;
path conepath, latpath;
pen thickp;

f:= (2,3,4);
viewcentr:= 1.5*(1,1,1);
Spread:= 200;
Shifts:= 300;
radius= 0.5;
numc= 9;
thickp= pencircle scaled .5;

pickup thickp;
tropicalglobe(numc,black,radius,blue);
for i=1 upto numc: % longitudes
  aux:= (i-1)*180/numc;
  gammacnt:=(cosd(aux),sind(aux),0);
  draw spatialhalfcircle
        (black,gammacnt,radius,true);
endfor;
```

hexagonal meshes   Given a function $z = f(x, y)$, a hexagonal mesh can be obtained with the hexagonaltrimesh macro.

```
input featpost3Dplus2D
def zsurface( expr xc, yc ) =
        cosd(xc*57)*cosd(yc*57)
        +4*mexp(-(xc**2+yc**2)*6.4)
enddef;


f := 7*(4,1,5);
Spread := 35;
LightSource := 10*(4,-3,4);
SubColor := 0.4background;


numeric np, ssize;
path chair;
np = 20;
ssize = 5;


hexagonaltrimesh( true,np,ssize,zsurface);
```

Example
4-6-2

cubes   The kindofcube macro produces a cube in an orientation depending on its parameters. In this example, each cube erases what has been drawn under it, so that it gives the illusion of the removal of hidden parts.

```
input featpost3Dplus2D
Spread := 30;
f := 5.4*(1.5,0.5,1);
numeric gridstep, sidenumber,
        i, j, coord, aa, ab, ac;
color pa;
gridstep = 0.7;
sidenumber = 4;
coord = 0.5*sidenumber*gridstep;
for i=0 upto sidenumber:
  for j=0 upto sidenumber:
    pa := (-coord+j*gridstep,-coord+i*gridstep,0);
    aa := uniformdeviate(360);
    ab := uniformdeviate(180);
    ac := uniformdeviate(90);
    kindofcube(false, false,
              pa, aa, ab, ac, 0.4, 0.4, 0.9 );
  endfor;
endfor;
```

Example
4-6-3

labels in space   The next example shows how labels can be drawn in space using the `labelinspace` macro.

```
input featpost3Dplus2D
verbatimtex
%&latex
\documentclass{article}
\begin{document}
etex


f := 1.1*(2,1,0.5);
ParallelProj := true;
kindofcube(false,true,(0,-0.5,0),
           90,0,0,1.2,0.1,0.4);
kindofcube(false,true,(0,0,0),
           0,0,0,0.5,0.1,0.8);
labelinspace(false,(0.45,0.1,0.65),
             (-0.4,0,0),(0,0,0.1),
      btex \framebox{\textsc{Label}} etex);
```

Example
4-6-4

projected segments   The last example shows how points can be defined in space, and `pathofstraightline` used to draw a segment joining the projections of these points.

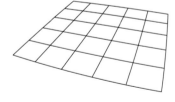

```
input featpost3Dplus2D
SphericalDistortion := true;
Spread := 50;
f := 0.4*(1.5,0.5,1);
numeric gridstep, sidenumber, i, coord;
color pa, pb, pc, pd;
gridstep = 0.1;
sidenumber = 5;
coord = 0.5*sidenumber*gridstep;
for i=0 upto sidenumber:
  pa := (-coord,-coord+i*gridstep,0);
  pb := (coord,-coord+i*gridstep,0);
  pc := (-coord+i*gridstep,-coord,0);
  pd := (-coord+i*gridstep,coord,0);
  draw pathofstraightline( pa, pb );
  draw pathofstraightline( pc, pd );
endfor;
```

Example
4-6-5

3DLDF

Laurence D. Finston's ambitious extension to METAPOST, 3DLDF (`http://www.gnu.org/software/3dldf/LDF.html`) is written in C++ using CWEB. 3DLDF (the author's initials) takes an input similar to METAPOST and outputs pure METAPOST code. The package currently computes the intersections of various projected curves, and the author plans to implement the removal of hidden parts.

3DLDF provides a number of classes for points, paths, pictures, transforms, focuses, ellipses, circles, regular polygons, rectangles, cuboids, tetrahedra, dodecahedra, icosahedra, etc.

A small piece of code defining a dodecahedron, and then rotating and scaling it, reads as follows (courtesy of Laurence D. Finston). The default units are centimeters.

```
beginfig(1);

pickup pencircle scaled (.75mm, .75mm, .75mm);

point p[];
p0 := (2, 0, 10);
polyhedron d;
d := unit_dodecahedron rotated (15, 15, 15) scaled 5 shifted p0;
draw d;
dotlabel.top("$p_0$", p0);
endfig;

verbatim_metapost "end";

end;
```

Processing this code with **3DLDF** yields some low-level METAPOST code looking like this:

```
beginfig(1);
draw (5.603746cm, -8.422028cm) -- (7.585488cm, -4.963817cm)
   -- (3.597142cm, -3.619159cm) -- (-0.630485cm, -5.034796cm)
   -- (-0.788186cm, -8.115661cm)
   -- cycle
withcolor (0.000000, 0.000000, 0.000000)
withpen pencircle transformed begingroup; save T; transform T;
 xxpart T = 0.075000cm; xpart T = 0.000000cm; xypart T = 0.000000cm;
 ...
```

If this is then processed with METAPOST we obtain the following graphic:

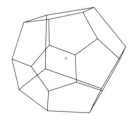

CHAPTER 5

Harnessing PostScript Inside LaTeX: PSTricks

As we saw in Chapter 1, one way of drawing graphics with LaTeX is to embed low-level picture drawing primitives for the target device into LaTeX macros, so that full typesetting information is available and we can work in a familiar macro programming environment. When the target device is something as rich as the full PostScript language, this can result in a very powerful system. While many macro packages have implemented access to some parts of PostScript for this purpose, the most complete is undoubtedly **PSTricks**. In the next two chapters, we survey its capabilities and demonstrate some of the power that results from combining LaTeX and PostScript.

We do not attempt to describe absolutely every **PSTricks**-related macro, nor do we give examples of all the possible combinations and tricks, as this would require a large book of its own, e.g., [135]. We have, however, tried to describe and give examples of all the important features of the basic packages. You'll find a lot of useful information on the official **PSTricks** Web site at `http://PSTricks.tug.org/`.

Because there are a great many commands and especially keywords in **PSTricks**, we provide a summary description at the end of the next chapter (Section 6.8 on page 459). **PSTricks** and its related packages are extremely powerful, and their facilities may take some time to understand. It is also documented in the individual packages and [127, 135], and its implementation is described in [126].

5.1 The components of PSTricks

The **PSTricks** project was started by Timothy Van Zandt a long time ago and is one of the oldest TeX packages still in use.

> I started in 1991. Initially I was just trying to develop tools for my own use. Then I thought it would be nice to package them so that others could use them. It soon became tempting to add lots of features, not just the ones I needed. When this became so interesting that it interfered with my "day job", I gave up the project "cold turkey", in 1994.
>
> [Timothy Van Zandt]

After Timothy Van Zandt stopped working on the project, Denis Girou took over the task to care for **PSTricks**, mainly fixing bugs and writing some more new packages; nowadays this job is done by Herbert Voß. Several developers are working on existing and new packages, which is the reason why the number of these additional packages, which depend on the basic **PSTricks**, is still increasing. A selection of them is discussed in Chapter 6, and the full list is available at the official Web site at `http://PSTricks.tug.org`.

5.1.1 The kernel

The basic **PSTricks** package file is `pstricks.tex`, which provides the basic unit handling, and basic graphic macros like dots, lines, frames, and so on. For some historical reason the packages **pstricks**, **pst-plot**, **pst-node**, and **pst-tree** build the core of **PSTricks** and are all available on CTAN in the directory `CTAN:/graphics/pstricks/base/generic/`. Each **PSTricks** package has a corresponding LaTeX style file, and the basic ones are stored in `CTAN:/graphics/pstricks/base/latex/`. In general, the style files do nothing other than load the TeX file via the `\input` macro.

The basic **PSTricks** packages consist of a core of picture-drawing primitives implemented by `\special` commands that pass PostScript code to a driver, mainly dvips. The packages also contain a set of higher-level macros for particular applications, like **pst-plot** or **pst-node**. With it you can

- Draw lines, polygons, circles, and curves.

- Place and manipulate TeX text.

- Plot data records and math functions with complicated labeled axes.

- Draw nodes and connectors (including trees).

- Color lines and fill objects.

- Define new graphical commands.

The packages rely on the ability of a dvi driver to pass through literal PostScript code and know that it will interact with the TEX text in a controlled way. The **dvips** driver is the reference implementation, but the package works with many other drivers as well. The **PSTricks** installation guide explains what functionality the driver has to provide and how to set it up.

PSTricks is not a tool for drawing just one type of diagram well, unlike many of the other packages described in this book. It is a programming environment for as close a combination of TEX and PostScript as is possible with existing software; its strength is its modularity, extensibility, and ability to access all the power of PostScript, and it is more or less easy to write some extensions to the code.

Nearly all **PSTricks** packages depend on other **PSTricks**-related packages, which will be loaded internally and are listed in the logfile. In the descriptions that follow, we do *not* normally indicate which file needs to be loaded for a particular function, since it is usually obvious. However, each example of code shows the necessary \usepackage commands. Be sure that you have the latest version of pstricks.sty installed when you are using LaTeX with colors; it replaces the old and now-obsolete **pstcol** package. This is important to make **pstricks** work with other packages that also use colors.

New modules for **PSTricks** may be released, as the packages are still under development. The material in this chapter was all tested with the files available in 2007.

5.1.2 Loading the basic packages

PSTricks packages are loaded into the document in the usual way:

```
\usepackage{pstricks}
```

Since **PSTricks** was originally written for plain TEX, almost all **PSTricks** packages are provided as files with extension .tex. In most cases the appropriate LaTeX packages (.sty files) basically do nothing other than load the corresponding .tex file. An exception is the core package **pstricks**: pstricks.sty performs several tests for the color management, then loads pstricks.tex, and modifies some of the TEX code afterwards. Thus the new version of the **pstricks** package (version 0.32) supersedes the use of the now-obsolete package **pstcol**.

There are two options for pstricks.sty available, which make sense only in some compatibility situations and are normally unimportant for LaTeX users.

noxcolor   Instead of loading **xcolor** (default), use the old **color** package.

plain   No color package is loaded and only **PSTricks**'s internal color handling is available.

Table 5.1: The predefined gray and color names of **PSTricks**

Gray	`black, darkgray, gray, lightgray, white`
Color	`red, green, blue, cyan, magenta, yellow`

All other options are passed to the **xcolor** package or, when using the `noxcolor` option, to the **color** package.

For historical reasons there exists a **pst-all** package, which loads all the so-called basic packages of **PSTricks** (pst-plot, pst-tree, pst-node, pst-3d, pst-grad, pst-coil, pst-text, pst-eps, pst-fill, multido). However, it is usually better to load the necessary packages individually with \usepackage. This makes it much easier to find and to fix errors, because one can comment out single packages or change the order.

5.1.3 Using colors

Since TEX itself does not provide any color handling, several packages have been developed in the past that implement color handling by means of a set of private color commands. Unfortunately, in most cases those packages cannot be used simultaneously without giving rise to conflicts with other such packages. As it was originally written for plain TEX, **PSTricks** also provides its own color handling rather than using LATEX's standard **color** package. It uses the PostScript internal syntax, and defines five shades of gray and six basic colors (see Table 5.1).

These colors can be used without any additional package within **PSTricks**. However, the corresponding simple macros (such as \blue) are obsolescent and their use is deprecated, even though they are still supported (for backwards compatibility) by all **PSTricks**-related packages. Instead, LATEX users are advised to select colors in the standard way, e.g., \color{*blue*} or \textcolor{*blue*}{...}.

Out of the blue you can become red, but this isn't advisable.

```
\usepackage{pstricks}

Out of the {\blue blue} you can become
{\red red}, but this isn't advisable.
```

Example
5-1-1

Always load the **pstricks** *package first*

PSTricks also provides its own commands for defining additional colors, but again it is better to define new colors through the standard LATEX interfaces of the **color** or **xcolor** package. In fact, **pstricks** nowadays loads one of these standard packages and then internally redefines the old declarations to use the modern interfaces. To avoid problems with the color management in **PSTricks** (that attempts to maintain both old and new syntax), it is important to always load the **pstricks** package prior to any other **PSTricks**-based package.

The **xcolor** package, which is loaded by default by **pstricks**, is an extended version of the older standard LATEX **color** package. It offers full support for **PSTricks** and should be the preferred color package for LATEX users, if possible. **xcolor** allows us to specify almost any color, be it a single one or a series of colors. Furthermore, the package allows us to convert color specifications between various color models and provides color separation. These topics are covered in detail in Chapter 11 and in the package documentation [68].

5.2 Setting keywords, lengths, and coordinates

PSTricks makes intensive use of the "key/value" interface provided by the package xkeyval (see Section 5.15.5 on page 310), which is an extended version of the standard keyval package. A special adaption for PSTricks, called pst-xkey, offers an interface between the old stand-alone key setting mechanism of the basic PSTricks packages and the corresponding mechanism of newer packages, such as pst-3dplot and pst-asr (see Section 5.15.3). These new packages allow a specific key setting by a so-called family name (Section 5.15.5 on page 310).

> \psset [*family*] {*key₁=value₁,key₂=value₂,...*}

The optional argument is used only for newer packages that define the keyword inside a family ("namespace") to prevent clashes with a keyword of the same name in another package. Without an optional argument, all keywords of that name in all families are set. For details on the *family* for a package, consult the package documentation.

PSTricks knows two more ways of passing key/value specifications to the macros. This may be confusing, because all such settings might also be achieved by means of \psset. First, nearly all macros have an optional argument for passing key/value options to the macro itself.

> ⟨*command*⟩ * [*settings*] ...

All changes to parameters set by the optional argument are kept local to the current macro, whereas those set by \psset are valid for all subsequent material and are subject to TEX's grouping mechanism. Hence, the following first two declarations are equivalent and the third one is valid for all following macros:

```
\psline[linewidth=5pt](3,3)          % valid for the macro (local)
{\psset{linewidth=5pt}\psline(3,3)}  % local inside {...} group
\psset{linewidth=5pt}                % global for the following macros
\psline(3,3)
\pscircle(0,0){1cm}
```

Second, for some historical reason PSTricks knows one more optional argument, enclosed in braces, for the end arrows of the so-called open objects, like lines and curves.

> ⟨*command*⟩ * [*settings*] {*arrowA−arrowB*} (...) (...)

This is indeed confusing for LATEX users, as it does not match the LATEX conventions (optional arguments in [], mandatory arguments in {}).

5.2.1 Lengths and units

PSTricks provides two macros for setting and changing the values of length registers.

```
\pssetlength{length register}{value[unit]}
\psaddtolength{length register}{value[unit]}
```

The difference between these commands and the corresponding LaTeX commands is that the length unit may be omitted. If no *unit* is specified, the one previously defined is used. If none was given previously, the default unit of 1cm is used. It can be changed for the x- and y-axes separately or together with one keyword (see Table 5.2).

Table 5.2: Lengths and their register names in PSTricks

Keyword	Meaning	Default	Length Register
unit	all together	1cm	\psunit
xunit	x-axis	1cm	\psxunit
yunit	y-axis	1cm	\psyunit
runit	radius (radians)	1cm	\psrunit

Specifying \psset{*xunit=1cm,yunit=1cm,runit=1cm*} is equivalent to setting \psset{*unit=1cm*}. PSTricks—in contrast to TeX or LaTeX—allows us to use a length with or without a unit. A missing unit is always replaced by the current one (if set by \psset) or the predefined value of 1cm. Thus a consecutive use of two \psset{*unit=0.5*} commands defines the current unit as 0.25cm. Defining the units before a pspicture environment also affects the coordinates of that environment. In the following examples the first unit setting is done inside the pspicture environment and the second one outside this environment. Hence, the \psline command has the same coordinate values in both cases, but the dimensions for the two pspicture environments have to be specified differently.

```
\usepackage{pstricks}
\begin{pspicture}(2,1)
  \psset{xunit=0.5mm,yunit=1mm}
  \psline{->}(20,10)
\end{pspicture}\\[0.75cm]
\psset{xunit=0.5mm,yunit=1mm}
\begin{pspicture}(20,10)
  \psline{->}(20,10)
\end{pspicture}
```

Example
5-2-1

5.2.2 Angles

The angles in polar coordinates (and other arguments) are specified in degrees (counter-clockwise) by default. Since the predefined value of 360 degrees for a full circle is not the best choice for all applications, you may change it with the following commands.

```
\degrees [units in a full circle]      \radians
```

The \degrees command lets you specify the number of units in a full circle; the optional argument defaults to 360, so \degrees is the same as \degrees[*360*]. If you prefer to specify angles clockwise, use \degrees[*-360*]. If you want to draw a pie chart, a setting of 100 units in a full circle makes it easier to use percentage values: \degrees[*100*]. Finally, the argument need not be an integer value; e.g., \radians is just a shortcut for \degrees[*6.28319*].

5.2.3 Coordinates

For the packages supporting three-dimensional views, coordinates are triplets of values (x, y, z). In all other situations they consist of pairs of values (x, y). In either case each value may be given with or without a unit. If no unit is specified explicitly, then the current default units are used, as explained in Section 5.2.1 on page 217. There is no restriction in mixing values with different units and/or without a unit. For example, in

> \psline(0.05,1in)(3mm,300pt)

the first value depends on the current unit (default 1 cm); the other ones use explicit units. PSTricks converts all of them into TeX's internal unit (pt).

\SpecialCoor	\NormalCoor

By default, (\NormalCoor) PSTricks supports only Cartesian coordinates, which have to be given as comma-separated values. After specifying \SpecialCoor you can use several other powerful systems of coordinate specification. PSTricks will analyze each coordinate argument and determine from its structure the input coordinate system. For example, polar coordinates are specified by separating the values with a semicolon; a full list of supported coordinate systems is given in Section 5.14 on page 296.

   When running LaTeX it takes some extra time to test for the different special coordinates, but with the power of today's hardware one can normally use \SpecialCoor throughout without any noticable effect. However, if one plots a function with more than 2000 points in Cartesian notation on a slow machine, a \NormalCoor may be useful.

5.2.4 Commands

Almost all the commands have the same (complex) structure. They need some or all of the following arguments, each of which has its consistent delimiters: obligatory arguments are surrounded by braces, like {arg}; optional settings, controlled by the key/value interface, are in square brackets, like [par1=val1, ...]; coordinates are in parentheses, like (x,y). Because PSTricks macros can get very complex with lots of different arguments, the summary macro descriptions here have a gray shading behind the optional arguments. The general syntactical form of most commands is

⟨*command*⟩ * [*settings*] {*arrows/arguments*}(coordinates)

For all macros, except the ones beginning with the letter q (as an indication for "quick"), there exists a star version, which basically is nothing else than an inverse representation of the object, filled with the current linecolor (the other changed options are shown in Table 5.3). The starred form of the command generally means that the object being drawn

Table 5.3: Meaning of the starred form

linewidth	0pt	fillcolor	\pslinecolor
fillstyle	solid	linestyle	none

is to be solid rather than an outline. This is programmed in a rather algorithmic way; e.g., \psline* is not very useful at all. The optional *settings* in square brackets consist of a set of key/value pairs that override, for the current object, PSTricks's drawing defaults as discussed below.

The existence of a starred form follows only some formal reasons in using PostScript code. However, for some macros it is rather pointless to use this option, such as \psline with only one line segment.

5.3 The pspicture environment

In most cases a PSTricks graphic object is put into a box of its own and not drawn overlapping the text, although this is possible: the following line appears here →⊾ PSTricks takes TEX's current point into account and draws the object, but doesn't insert any horizontal or vertical space; hence TEX's current point is left unchanged. The pspicture environment is simply a box command—it saves horizontal and vertical space for the drawing and has the following syntax:

```
\begin{pspicture *} [settings] (xMin,yMin) (xMax,yMax)
...
\end{pspicture *}
```

The box that is produced by pspicture is placed by default with its lower-left corner at the current baseline of the text, which can readily be seen in the next example.

```
\usepackage{pstricks,pst-plot}
Here we place a \texttt{pspicture} environment in the middle of a paragraph.
\psframebox[boxsep=0pt,framesep=0pt,linestyle=dashed]{%
  \begin{pspicture}(-1,-0.5cm)(1.5,10mm)
    \psaxes[labels=none]{->}(0,0)(-10mm,-5mm)(1.5cm,1)
  \end{pspicture}} By placing objects outside the box boundaries one can
achieve overprinting of surrounding text.
```

Here we place a pspicture environment in the mid-

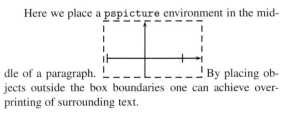

dle of a paragraph. By placing objects outside the box boundaries one can achieve overprinting of surrounding text.

Example
5-3-1

Its **internal** origin depends on the given PSTricks coordinates and can also be placed outside of the box. In the example above the origin is at point $(1, 0.5)$, measured from the lower left of the box. The area taken up by the box is $2.5 \,\mathrm{cm} \times 1.5 \,\mathrm{cm}\, ((x_2 - x_1) \times (y_2 - y_1))$. Obviously, using a `pspicture` environment within normal text is usually a bad idea, as its size will affect the line spacing. It is therefore usually deployed within a display environment such as `center`.

The `pspicture` environment complies with the following rules to determine missing values in the setup:

- In case all coordinates are missing, PSTricks sometimes generates a low-level error. However, it may also silently produce incorrect output!

- In the case of only one given pair of coordinates, PSTricks always chooses $(0, 0)$ (x, y) for the box. Negative values for (x, y) are no problem, but the lower left is always on the baseline (see Example 5-3-2).

- PSTricks does not check if the values supplied make sense.

- Values without a unit are interpreted in PSTricks's internal units (see Section 5.2.1 on page 217).

- The coordinates define the space reserved for the picture. It is still possible to draw outside of this box, in which case the drawing may potentially overprint other material (also shown in the Example 5-3-2).

- The starred form of `pspicture` clips everything around the given box. It uses `\pstVerb` and `\pstverbscale` for the clipping operation (see Section 5.15.2 on page 305).

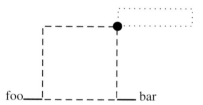

```
\usepackage{pstricks}
foo\rule{5mm}{1pt}%
\begin{pspicture}(-2,-2)% => (0,0)(-2,-2)
    \psdot*[dotscale=2](0,0)
    \psframe[linestyle=dashed](-2,-2)
    \psframe[linestyle=dotted](2,0.5)
\end{pspicture}\rule{5mm}{1pt} bar
```

Example
5-3-2

5.3.1 Keywords for the `pspicture` environment

There are only two special keywords for the `pspicture` environment. All other parameters are set but have no meaning for this environment itself; yet the values provided affect other macros used within the environment. With the `shift` keyword the PSTricks box can be   *The* `shift` *key* shifted relative to the text baseline in any vertical direction. A value of $0.5\,\mathrm{cm}$ shifts the box down. (This keyword's effect is similar to that of the LaTeX-macro `\raisebox`.)

```
\usepackage{pstricks}
\small\rule{5mm}{1pt}%
```

```
\begin{pspicture}[shift=0.5cm](-0.6,-0.5)(0.6,0.75)
  \psframe[linecolor=blue](-0.5,-0.5)(0.6,0.75)\rput(0,0){0.5cm}
\end{pspicture}%
\rule{5mm}{1pt}\hspace{1cm}\rule{5mm}{1pt}%
\begin{pspicture}(-0.6,-0.5)(0.6,0.75)
  \psframe[linecolor=blue](-0.6,-0.5)(0.6,0.75)\rput(0,0){none}
\end{pspicture}%
\rule{5mm}{1pt}\hspace{1cm}\rule{5mm}{1pt}%
\begin{pspicture}[shift=-0.5cm](-0.6,-0.5)(0.6,0.75)
  \psframe[linecolor=blue](-0.6,-0.5)(0.6,0.75)\rput(0,0){$-$0.5cm}
\end{pspicture}%
\rule{5mm}{1pt}
```

Example
5-3-3

When using the `pspicture` environment inside a text line, it often makes sense to put the internal **PSTricks** x-axis on the height of the text baseline. The current y unit is saved in the macro `\psyunit`, which can be used to shift the box up or down. In the following example the first arrow is placed 0.3 unit above the baseline, while the second arrow is shifted down to the baseline by referring to the current unit with [`shift=-0.3\psyunit`]. When you use the `shift` keyword without a unit, **PSTricks** takes as usual the currently active unit into account, which is by default 1 cm.

```
\usepackage{pstricks}
\rule{20pt}{.1pt}gg%
\begin{pspicture}(-0.25,-0.3)(0.25,0.25)
  \psline{<->}(-0.25,0)(0.25,0)
\end{pspicture}gg\rule{20pt}{.1pt}gg%
\begin{pspicture}[shift=-0.3\psyunit](-0.25,-0.3)(0.25,0.25)
  \psline{<->}(-0.25,0)(0.25,0)
\end{pspicture}gg\rule{20pt}{.1pt}
```

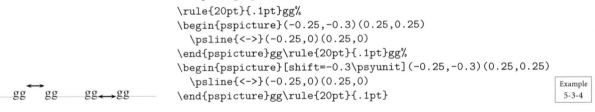

Example
5-3-4

The showgrid *key*   The Boolean-valued `showgrid` key enables (or disables — the default) the drawing of a grid with the predefined **PSTricks** style `gridstyle`. This option is often useful when an object should be placed somewhere inside a `pspicture` environment; with a plotted grid it is easier to get the coordinates right.

The layout of the grid can be overwritten by using other values than the following default ones:

`\newpsstyle{`*gridstyle*`}{`*subgriddiv=0,gridcolor=lightgray,griddots=10,gridlabels=8pt*`}`

For the `\newpsstyle` declaration, see Section 5.13 on page 279. Grids in general and the keywords controlling their layout, as well as solutions for creating special grids, are treated in Section 5.5 on the following page.

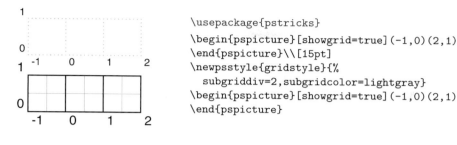

```
\usepackage{pstricks}
\begin{pspicture}[showgrid=true](-1,0)(2,1)
\end{pspicture}\\[15pt]
\newpsstyle{gridstyle}{%
    subgriddiv=2,subgridcolor=lightgray}
\begin{pspicture}[showgrid=true](-1,0)(2,1)
\end{pspicture}
```

Example
5-3-5

```
\usepackage{pstricks}
\newpsstyle{gridstyle}{}
\begin{pspicture}[showgrid=true](-1,0)(2,1)
\end{pspicture}\\[15pt]
\begin{pspicture}(-1,0)(2,1)
    \psgrid
\end{pspicture}
```

Example
5-3-6

5.3.2   White space between commands

Inside the pspicture environment, any white space between commands is ignored. Outside of this environment, every **PSTricks** object is like a single character and white space is not removed. The latter can be toggled by the switches \KillGlue and \DontKillGlue (see Section 5.15.2 on page 303). This compability may be of some interest when **PSTricks** macros are used in other environments, e.g., the picture environment of standard LaTeX, where the removal of white space is the expected behavior.

5.4   The coordinate system

As with PostScript, a Cartesian coordinate system is the basic system for **PSTricks**. The origin of the coordinates, as determined by the choice of the pspicture environment's size arguments (see Section 5.3 on page 220), can fall inside or outside of the box thus defined.

As seen in the following example, the origin pertaining to the coordinate system for the dashed line is $(0.25, -0.5)$. Both parabolas are defined with the same coordinate arguments, but with a different origin. There is one important fact: this keyword setting works only for *real* **PSTricks** graphic objects. A graphic object is a macro that is internally defined by the \pst@object macro (see Section 5.15.3 on page 307). Note that the coordinate pair specified as values for the origin keyword must be given *without* parentheses. Instead, to prevent the comma from being misinterpreted as one separating entries in the key/value list, braces have to be used, as shown in Example 5-4-1. (As usual, the coordinate values   *The origin key* may have an explicit measure; if it is missing, then the corresponding current default one is used.)

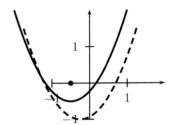

```
\usepackage{pstricks,pst-plot}
\begin{pspicture}(-1,-1)(2,2)
  \psaxes{->}(0,0)(-1,-1)(2,2)
  \psset{linewidth=1.5pt}
  \parabola(1,2)(-0.5,-0.5)
  \parabola[origin={0.25,-0.5},
    linestyle=dashed](1,2)(-0.5,-0.5)
  \qdisk(-0.5, 0){2pt}
\end{pspicture}
```

Example
5-4-1

The swapaxes *key*   The keyword `swapaxes` comes in handy for plotting mathematical functions if the calculation of the inverse can be realized easier, such as when PostScript supports only the inverse function. In the following example, the `swapaxes=true` setting is used to plot the function $y = \arccos x$ in an easy way by simply plotting the cosine with swapped axes. Thus there is no need to perform mathematical conversions; only the given interval is to be kept in mind. The **PSTricks** package **pst-math** offers support for mathematical functions for which there is no direct support in PostScript [64].

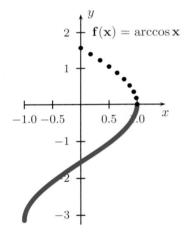

```
\usepackage{pstricks,pst-plot}
\psset{xunit=1.5,plotpoints=200,plotstyle=dots}
\begin{pspicture}(-1.1,-3.25)(1.5,2.6)
  \psaxes[Dx=0.5]{->}(0,0)(-1,-3.25)(1.5,2.5)
  \uput[-90](1.5,0){$x$}
  \uput[0](0,2.5){$y$}
  \rput[l](0.2,2){$\mathbf{f(x)=\arccos x}$}
  \psset{yunit=1.5,xunit=0.666667,swapaxes=true}
  \pstVerb{/rad {180 3.141592654 div mul} def}
  \psplot[linecolor=blue]{-3.141592654}{0}{x rad cos}
  \psplot[plotstyle=dots,plotpoints=10]%
    {0}{1.570796327}{x rad cos}
\end{pspicture}
```

Example
5-4-2

5.5 Grids

PSTricks offers a wide range of Cartesian coordinate grids; through a set of keywords many characteristics can be adjusted according to your requirements. Further variants are provided by the **pstricks-add** package, especially concerning logarithmic axis graduations and decimal labels.

$$\boxed{\texttt{\textbackslash psgrid}\,[\textit{settings}]\ (x_0, y_0)\ (x_1, y_1)\ (x_2, y_2)}$$

The \psgrid macro is a very powerful tool for drawing coordinate grids. The syntax is easy to use, but is valid only for Cartesian coordinate systems.

When no coordinates have been specified, \psgrid takes the ones defined by the enclosing pspicture environment or, if not inside such an environment, a 10×10 rectangle in the current units is assumed. If only one coordinate pair is given, it is taken to denote one corner and (0,0) is established as the opposite corner. When using two coordinate pairs, any two opposite corners of the grid should be specified. With three coordinate pairs given, the first pair determines the intersection point of the lines to be labeled and the other two pairs are interpreted as in the previous case.

In short: (x_0, y_0) defaults to (x_1, y_1); the default for the latter is (0,0), and (outside of a pspicture environment) the default for (x_2, y_2) is (10,10).

The labels are positioned along the two lines that intersect at (x_0, y_0), on the side of the line pointing away from (x_2, y_2), and shifted slightly horizontally or vertically towards the latter coordinate so they won't interfere with other lines. In the next example, \psgrid has no arguments, so it takes all coordinates from the surrounding pspicture environment. The keywords used in this and the following examples are discussed in detail in Section 5.5.1 on the following page.

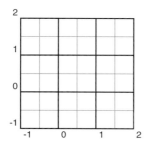

```
\usepackage{pstricks}
\psset{griddots=0,gridlabels=7pt,subgriddiv=2}
\begin{pspicture}(-1,-1)(2,2)
  \psgrid
\end{pspicture}
```

With only one pair of coordinates, \psgrid assumes that (0,0) is the opposite corner. Exchanging the order of the coordinate pairs, as in the second figure, changes the position of the labels from the left and bottom sides to the right and top sides of the rectangle, respectively. (See also the last example below with three pairs of coordinates.)

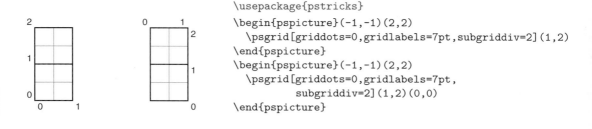

```
\usepackage{pstricks}
\begin{pspicture}(-1,-1)(2,2)
  \psgrid[griddots=0,gridlabels=7pt,subgriddiv=2](1,2)
\end{pspicture}
\begin{pspicture}(-1,-1)(2,2)
  \psgrid[griddots=0,gridlabels=7pt,
          subgriddiv=2](1,2)(0,0)
\end{pspicture}
```

By selecting any two opposite corners of the rectangle as (x_1, y_1) and (x_2, y_2), the labels can be positioned on any desired pair of adjacent sides.

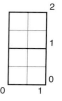 

```
\usepackage{pstricks}
\begin{pspicture}(-1,-1)(2,2)
   \psgrid[griddots=0,gridlabels=7pt,subgriddiv=2](1,0)(0,2)
\end{pspicture}
\begin{pspicture}(-1,-1)(2,2)
   \psgrid[griddots=0,gridlabels=7pt,subgriddiv=2](0,2)(1,0)
\end{pspicture}
```

Example
5-5-3

In the next example three pairs of coordinates have been specified; hence the labels no longer appear at the edges of the grid. In most applications (x_0, y_0) will be $(0,0)$, but as the second figure depicts, other values may be chosen as well.

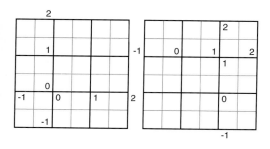

```
\usepackage{pstricks}
\psset{griddots=0,gridlabels=7pt,subgriddiv=2}
\begin{pspicture}(-1,-1)(2,2)
   \psgrid(0,0)(-1,-1)(2,2)
\end{pspicture}
\quad
\begin{pspicture}(-1,-1)(2,2)
   \psgrid(1,1)(2,2)(-1,-1)
\end{pspicture}
```

Example
5-5-4

5.5.1 Keywords of the \psgrid command

Table 5.4 shows all keywords that are only valid for the \psgrid command. They are individually discussed in the following examples.

The gridwidth *key*   The gridwidth keyword determines the width of the main grid lines and should be chosen rather too small than too big, at least wider than the sub-lines (subgridwidth).

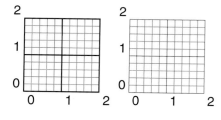

```
\usepackage{pstricks}
\begin{pspicture}(2,2)
   \psgrid% default is .8pt
\end{pspicture}\hspace{2em}
\begin{pspicture}(2,2)
   \psgrid[gridwidth=0.1pt]
\end{pspicture}
```

Example
5-5-5

The gridcolor *and* griddots *keys*   The keyword gridcolor determines the color of the main grid lines and can be used for highlighting. The griddots keyword determines the number of dots if a dotted main grid line should be drawn instead of a continuous line. This is especially of interest when the grid itself should stay in the background. Keep in mind that the dots can be seen only

Table 5.4: Summary of keywords for setting grids

Name	Value Type	Default
gridwidth	value[unit]	0.8pt
gridcolor	color	black
griddots	value	0
gridlabels	value[unit]	10pt
gridlabelcolor	color	black
subgriddiv	value	5
subgridwidth	value[unit]	0.4pt
subgridcolor	color	gray
subgriddots	value	0

if `subgriddiv` is set to 0 or 1; otherwise, the dots would be overlaid by the lines of the sub-grid.

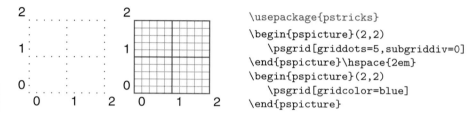

```
\usepackage{pstricks}
\begin{pspicture}(2,2)
    \psgrid[griddots=5,subgriddiv=0]
\end{pspicture}\hspace{2em}
\begin{pspicture}(2,2)
    \psgrid[gridcolor=blue]
\end{pspicture}
```

Example 5-5-6

The keyword `gridlabels` sets the font size of the labels, which can be set by a value given with or without a unit. In the latter case, the current **PSTricks** unit is taken into account. In many cases the default size of 10 pt is too large, as such labels are better set in a font size smaller than the running text. The `gridlabelcolor` keyword determines the font color of the labels, which may be useful for Web publishing.

The `gridlabels` *and* `gridlabelcolor` *keys*

```
\usepackage{pstricks}
\begin{pspicture}(2,2)
    \psgrid[gridlabelcolor=blue]
\end{pspicture}\hspace{2em}
\begin{pspicture}(2,2)
    \psgrid[griddots=5,gridlabels=7pt,subgriddiv=0]
\end{pspicture}
```

Example 5-5-7

The keyword `subgriddiv` determines the number of subdivisions between two main divisions. To calculate the divisions, the values for `xunit` and `yunit` are taken into account. This may cause massive problems when a small unit has been defined and `\psgrid` is called with large absolute values, as the unit determines the distance between main divisions. For instance, given a unit of 1 pt, a `\psgrid(10cm,10cm)` command might give rise to trouble, as there are about 280 main divisions and 1400 sub-divisions. Depending on the version of **PSTricks**, the maximum number of divisions is limited (in the current version, to about 500).

The `subgriddiv` *and* `subgridwidth` *keys*

Such problems can be avoided by locally switching to some unit of comparable magnitude: `\psgrid[`*`unit=1cm`*`]` (*10cm,10cm*).

The keyword `subgridwidth` determines the width of the sub-grid lines and should be chosen rather too small than too big and above all smaller than the superior main grid lines.

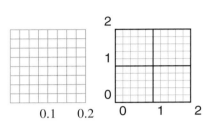

```
\usepackage{pstricks}

{\psset{unit=10}% local setting
\begin{pspicture}(0.2,0.2)
  \psgrid[gridlabels=0pt,subgriddiv=40]
  \uput[-90](0.1,0){0.1}
  \uput[-90](0.2,0){0.2}
\end{pspicture}}\hspace{2em}
\begin{pspicture}(2,2)
  \psgrid[subgridwidth=0.01pt]
\end{pspicture}
```

Example 5-5-8

The `subgridcolor` *and* `subgriddots` *keys*

The key `subgridcolor` determines the color of the sub-grid lines and can be used for highlighting. The key `subgriddots` determines the number of dots if a dotted sub-grid line should be drawn instead of a continuous line. This is especially of interest when the grid itself should stay in the background.

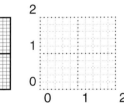

```
\usepackage{pstricks}

\begin{pspicture}(2,2)
  \psgrid[subgriddiv=10,gridlabels=0,
    gridwidth=1pt,subgridwidth=0.1pt,
    subgridcolor=blue]
\end{pspicture}\hspace{2em}
\begin{pspicture}(2,2)
  \psgrid[griddots=10,subgriddots=5]
\end{pspicture}
```

Example 5-5-9

5.5.2 Defining and using new grid commands

There is only one predefined command to draw grids: `\psgrid`. If you need to use some settings of its numerous options consistently, you may want to define some abbreviations for them. Of course, one way to achieve this is with standard LATEX macros, such as

```
\newcommand\myGrid{\psgrid[subgriddiv=0,griddots=10,gridlabels=7pt]}
```

However, PSTricks offers two more elegant ways to accomplish this task:

```
\newpsstyle{dotGrid}{subgriddiv=0,griddots=5,gridlabels=7pt}
\psgrid[style=dotGrid]
\newpsobject{myGrid}{psgrid}{subgriddiv=0,griddots=5,gridlabels=7pt}
\myGrid
```

The first method is to define a new style (named `dotGrid` in the code above) that can be used together with the `style` key to set all stored options in one go. (Styles are explained in detail in Section 5.13 on page 279.) The second method is to create a new **PSTricks** object (named in the code above), which essentially is a command that is based on `\psgrid` with a specific key setting.

5.5.3 Embellishing pictures with the help of grids

We often want to add a remark, measure, label, or some other description to a pre-existing external graphic included in a document. Here we describe how **PSTricks**'s macros can be applied to tackle this task.

As our first step, we want to determine the final overall size to be specified with the `pspicture` environment. To this end, the graphic is saved in a private box called `\IBox` with `\sbox`. This enables us to refer to the size of the imported graphic easily by using TEX's low-level `\wd` (width) and `\ht` (height) operators. Since in our example we want to put denotions and measures at the left and upper sides of the graphic, we allocate some extra space there by specifying (-2,0) as the lower-left corner and using a factor of 1.4 with the graphic's height in the size arguments of the `pspicture` environment (also, a small margin of 10 % of the graphic's width is inserted to the right).

To keep coordinate specifications simple, we choose the alignment parameter value `lb` for the `\rput` command, whereby we assign the lower-left corner of the graphic to the origin of the `pspicture` environment.

To facilitate the positioning of the individual items, we lay a coordinate grid over the graphic by means of `\psgrid` (see Section 5.5 on page 224) temporarily. (This will be removed in the end.)

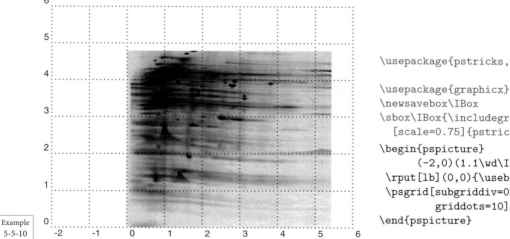

```
\usepackage{pstricks,pst-node}

\usepackage{graphicx}
\newsavebox\IBox
\sbox\IBox{\includegraphics
   [scale=0.75]{pstricks/overlay50-2}}
\begin{pspicture}
      (-2,0)(1.1\wd\IBox,1.2\ht\IBox)
\rput[lb](0,0){\usebox\IBox}
\psgrid[subgriddiv=0,gridlabels=7pt,
        griddots=10]
\end{pspicture}
```

Example
5-5-10

After these preliminaries it is relatively easy for us to position the labels as desired by applying the appropriate **PSTricks** macros, again referring to the width and height of the box containing the imported graphic. Note also how we use the \pnode command to define symbolic node names for use with the \ncline and (implicitly) \ncput commands.

```
\usepackage{pstricks,pst-node}    % graphic defined as before
\begin{pspicture}(-2,0)(1.1\wd\IBox,1.2\ht\IBox)
  \rput[lb](0,0){\usebox\IBox}
    \psgrid[subgriddiv=0,gridlabels=7pt,griddots=10]
 \pnode(-0.5,0){A}\pnode(-0.5,\ht\IBox){B}
  \ncline{->}{A}{B}
  \ncput*[nrot=:U]{\small molecular weight}
  \rput[rC](-1,.3\ht\IBox){\small $13$\,db}
  \rput[rC](-1,.65\ht\IBox){\small $38$\,db}
  \rput[rC](-1,.8\ht\IBox){\small $76$\,db}
  \pnode(0,1.05\ht\IBox){A}\pnode(\wd\IBox,1.05\ht\IBox){B}
  \ncline{->}{A}{B}
  \ncput*{\small molecular weight in the complex}
  \rput[rC]{-90}(0.1\wd\IBox,1.1\ht\IBox){\small $-100$\,kDa}
  \rput[rC]{-90}(0.8\wd\IBox,1.1\ht\IBox){\small $-800$\,kDa}
  \psline[linewidth=0.1pt,arrowscale=2]{|-|}(4,1)(5,1)
  \uput[-90](4.5,1){\small $1$\,$\mu$m}
\end{pspicture}
```

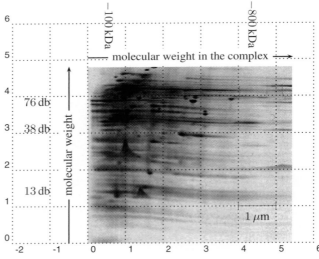

Example
5-5-11

Of course, the size chosen for the margins used in the example and thus the values required for the arguments of the pspicture environment are specific to our particular application. If annotations are to be placed only within the actual area of the graphic, we would simply set these values equal to the size of the graphic.

Finally, as all desired labels are in place, we can delete (or comment out) the \psgrid command to obtain the finished graphic. (In practice, such an ancillary instruction is often commented out, as it might become necessary to modify the labels later on.)

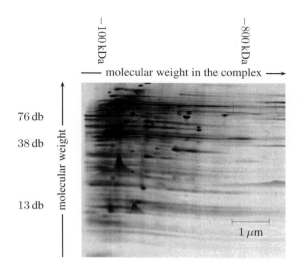

5.6 Lines and polygons

Lines represent a main feature in any graphical software, and PSTricks is no exception. It provides an extensive number of keywords that let you influence the appearance of lines; these are discussed in Section 5.6.2 on page 234. Here we deal with the basic commands that draw lines and some derived shapes.

$\texttt{\textbackslash psline} * [\textit{settings}] \{\langle \textit{arrow type} \rangle\} (x_0, y_0) (x_1, y_1) \dots (x_n, y_n)$

A series of points given by the coordinate pair arguments is connected by straight lines. If there is only one coordinate pair specified with \psline, a line is drawn from the current point to the specified point. However, inside a pspicture environment the current point is first reset to the origin of the coordinate system.

The starred form leads to a closed polygon by connecting the last point to the first one. Then the whole area is **filled** with the line color. This doesn't really make sense for lines with only one segment.

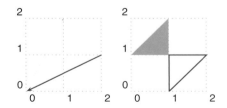

```
\usepackage{pstricks}
\begin{pspicture}[showgrid=true](2,2)
  \psline*[linecolor=red]{->}(1,2)
  \psline[linecolor=blue]{<-}(2,1)
\end{pspicture}\hspace{2em}
\begin{pspicture}[showgrid=true](2,2)
  \psline*[linecolor=red](0,1)(1,2)(1,1)
  \psline[linecolor=blue](1,0)(1,1)(2,1)(1,0)
\end{pspicture}
```

$$\boxed{\texttt{\textbackslash qline}(x_1,y_1)\,(x_2,y_2)}$$

This is the simplified version of \psline, because no local key setting via an optional argument is possible and exactly two points must be given (only one line segment). However, all keys set with \psset are respected by \qline and can be local when grouping this setting by putting it into parentheses, as seen in the example.

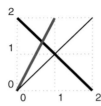

```
\usepackage{pstricks}
\begin{pspicture}[showgrid=true](2,2)
  { \psset{linewidth=2pt} % key is valid and local!
    \qline(0,2)(2,0)
    \psset{linecolor=blue}
    \qline(0,0)(1,2) }
  \qline(0,0)(2,2)
\end{pspicture}
```

Example
5-6-2

$$\boxed{\texttt{\textbackslash pspolygon} * \; [settings] \; (x_0,y_0)\,(x_1,y_1)\,(x_2,y_2)\,\ldots\,(x_n,y_n)}$$

In contrast to \psline, the command \pspolygon represents by default a closed line, as seen in the following examples, where the first and last points are not the same. When only two points are given, (0,0) is used as both starting point and end point. If the end point is not identical to the starting point, a line is drawn from the end point to the starting point to close the polygon. The asterisk version fills the inside of the polygon with the current line color and the current fill pattern.

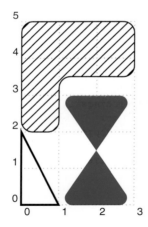

```
\usepackage{pstricks}
\begin{pspicture}[showgrid=true](3,5)
  \pspolygon[linewidth=1.5pt](0,2)(1,0)
  \pspolygon*[linearc=.2,linecolor=blue,
    swapaxes=true](0,1)(0,3)(3,1)(3,3)
  \pspolygon[fillstyle=hlines,
    linearc=0.3](0,2)(0,5)(3,5)(3,3.5)(1,3.5)(1,2)
\end{pspicture}
```

Example
5-6-3

$$\boxed{\texttt{\textbackslash psframe} * \; [settings] \; (x_1,y_1)\,(x_2,y_2)}$$

\psframe draws a horizontal rectangle, which is given by two opposite points. If only one point is given, (0,0) is taken as the second one automatically. The starred form fills the inside of the rectangle with the current line color and the current fill pattern, as seen in the

following example. For the rectangle the special keywords framearc and cornersize are
recognized.

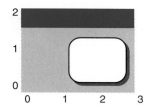

```
\usepackage{pstricks}
\begin{pspicture}[showgrid=true](3,2)
  \psframe*[linecolor=lightgray,shadow=true,shadowcolor=blue,
      shadowangle=90,shadowsize=15pt](3,1.75)
  \psframe[fillcolor=white,fillstyle=solid,
      framearc=0.5,shadow=true](1.25,0.25)(2.8,1.5)
\end{pspicture}
```

Example
5-6-4

$\boxed{\texttt{\textbackslash psdiamond} * \; [\textit{settings}] \; (x_M, y_M) \; (dx, dy)}$

\psdiamond draws a horizontal lozenge, which is given by its center and its perpendicular
diagonals. dx and dy specify only half of the lengths. If only one point is given, (0,0) is
taken as the center automatically. The asterisk version fills the inside of the lozenge with the
current line color and the current fill pattern, as seen in the following example. With the
keyword setting gangle=*angle*, the lozenge can be rotated arbitrarily.

```
\usepackage{pstricks}
\begin{pspicture}(3,3)
  \psdiamond*[linecolor=blue](1.5,1.5)(1.5,1)
  \psdiamond*[linecolor=red,gangle=45](1.5,1.5)(0.5,0.75)
  \psdiamond[fillstyle=solid,fillcolor=blue!60,
      gangle=-45](1.5,1.5)(0.25,0.5)
\end{pspicture}
```

Example
5-6-5

$\boxed{\texttt{\textbackslash pstriangle} * \; [\textit{settings}] \; (x_M, y_M) \; (dx, dy)}$

\pstriangle draws an isosceles triangle, which is given by the center of the baseline, the
length of this line, and the corresponding height. dx and dy specify the full length and base
height, respectively. If only one point is given, (0,0) is taken as the center of the baseline
automatically. The starred form fills the inside of the triangle with the current line color
and the current fill pattern. With the keyword setting =*angle*, the triangle can be rotated
arbitrarily, as seen in the following example.

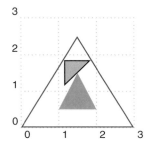

```
\usepackage{pstricks}
\begin{pspicture}[showgrid=true](3,3)
  \pstriangle[linecolor=blue](1.5,0)(3,2.5)
  \pstriangle*[linecolor=red](1.5,0.5)(1,1)
  \pstriangle[fillstyle=solid,fillcolor=cyan,
      gangle=45](1.5,1.5)(1,0.5)
\end{pspicture}
```

Example
5-6-6

5.6.1 Extensions to lines

The setlinejoin *command*

When lines are joined, **PSTricks** has to be told how the lines should be connected. As the following example shows, three variants are supported. The corresponding PostScript function is *value* setlinejoin, with valid values of 0, 1, and 2. The default value specified by PostScript is 0. The easiest way to change this PostScript value is to use the \pscustom command (see Section 5.13.1 on page 280). The \pstVerb can also be used (see Section 5.15.2 on page 305). Both have been applied in the examples below. The package **pst-3dplot** supports the drawing of lines through a separate key linejoin, thereby easing the process considerably (see Section 6.6.3 on page 412).

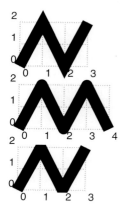

```
\usepackage{pstricks}
\psset{linewidth=3mm,unit=0.6}
\begin{pspicture}[showgrid=true](3,2)
    \psline(0,0)(1,2)(2,0)(3,2)
\end{pspicture}\\[3ex]
\begin{pspicture}[showgrid=true](4,2)
    \pstVerb{ 1 setlinejoin }
    \psline(0,0)(1,2)(2,0)(3,2)(4,0)
\end{pspicture}\\[3ex]
\begin{pspicture}[showgrid=true](3,2)
    \pscustom{\code{2 setlinejoin}
            \psline(0,0)(1,2)(2,0)(3,2)}
\end{pspicture}
```

Example
5-6-7

5.6.2 Keywords for lines and polygons

Table 5.5 on the next page lists all keywords that are of interest in the context of lines. The major part can also be used for other macros—for instance, for \pscircle.

Next, we give an example for each listed keyword, using the same order as in Table 5.5. A description of the keywords for fill options can be found in Section 5.9 on page 253.

The linewidth *key*

In theory, any desired line width can be chosen, e.g., 1 sp or 10 cm. However, both the biggest and the smallest widths depend on the PostScript driver, about which TEX and PostScript do not have any information. Thus no decision can be made about sense or nonsense of the line width at this point. Keep in mind that you may experience problems with very thin lines when viewing the PostScript output on the screen, given the screen resolution sets limits here.

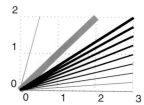

```
\usepackage{pstricks,multido}
\begin{pspicture}[showgrid=true](3,2)
    \psline[linewidth=0.01pt](0.5,2)
    \psline[linewidth=5pt,linecolor=red](2,2)
    \multido{\rA=0.0+0.25}{9}{%
        \psline[linewidth=\rA pt](3,\rA)}
\end{pspicture}
```

Example
5-6-8

Table 5.5: Summary of keywords for lines and polygons

Name	Value Type	Default
linewidth	value[unit]	0.8pt
linecolor	color	black
linestyle	line style	solid
dash	value[unit] value[unit]	5pt 3pt
dotsep	value[unit]	3pt
doubleline	Boolean	false
doublesep	value[unit]	1.25\pslinewidth
doublecolor	color	white
dimen	dimen refpoint	outer
arrows	arrow type	–
showpoints	Boolean	false
linearc	value[unit]	0pt
framearc	value	0
cornersize	relative|absolute	relative
gangle	angle	0
border	value[unit]	0pt
bordercolor	color	white
shadow	Boolean	false
shadowsize	value[unit]	3pt
shadowangle	angle	-45
shadowcolor	color	darkgray
linetype	value	0
liftpen	0|1|2	0

As mentioned in Section 5.1.3, PSTricks knows 11 predefined colors. Additional ones can be defined by the user with the command \definecolor from the color or xcolor package. *The* linecolor *key*

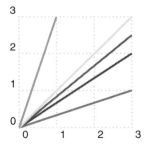

```
\usepackage{pstricks}
\begin{pspicture}[showgrid=true,linewidth=1.5pt](3,3)
    \psline[linecolor=black!50](3,1)
    \psline[linecolor=red](3,2)
    \psline[linecolor=magenta](3,2.5)
    \psline[linecolor=yellow](3,3)
    \definecolor{LColor}{rgb}{0.1,1,0.1}
    \psline[linecolor=LColor](1,3)
\end{pspicture}
```

Example
5-6-9

The keyword linestyle can have one of the following values: solid, dashed, dotted, or none. A line with the given line style none is not plotted, as can be gathered *The* linestyle *key* from the example. Such a behavior is especially of interest when, for instance, we are filling areas without border lines or setting the end points (nodes) of a line without having them drawn.

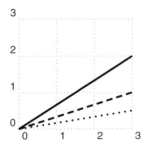

```
\usepackage{pstricks}
\begin{pspicture}[showgrid=true,linewidth=1.5pt](3,3)
  \psline[linestyle=none](3,3)% <-- no line!
  \psline[linestyle=solid](3,2)
  \psline[linestyle=dashed](3,1)
  \psline[linestyle=dotted](3,0.5)
\end{pspicture}
```

Example
5-6-10

The dash *and* dotsep *keys*   The keyword dash defines the structure of a dashed line in an order of "black–white" sequences, consisting of at least 1 sequence and a maximum of 11. The dotsep keyword is similiar to dash and is enabled by the line style dotted. The size of the individual dots depends on the specification of linewidth and is independent of the keywords dotsize and dotscale, which refer to the \psdot macro (discussed later).

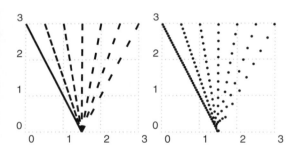

```
\usepackage{pstricks,multido}
\begin{pspicture}[showgrid=true](3,3)
  \psset{linewidth=1.5pt,linestyle=dashed}
  \multido{\rA=0.0+1.5,\rB=0.0+0.5}{7}{%
      \psline[dash=5pt \rA pt](1.5,0)(\rB,3)}
\end{pspicture}\hspace{1.5em}
\begin{pspicture}[showgrid=true](3,3)
  \psset{linewidth=2pt,linestyle=dotted}
  \multido{\rA=0.0+1.5,\rB=0.0+0.5}{7}{%
      \psline[dotsep=\rA pt](1.5,0)(\rB,3)}
\end{pspicture}
```

Example
5-6-11

The doubleline, doublesep, *and* doublecolor *keys*   The keywords doublecolor and doublesep refer to the "inner part" of the double line; the line color and line width itself can be changed with the keywords linecolor and linewidth, respectively. The double line can be enabled by the keyword doubleline.

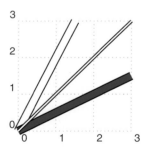

```
\usepackage{pstricks}
\begin{pspicture}[showgrid=true,
                  doubleline=true](3,3)
  \psline[doublesep=5pt](1.5,3)
  \psline[doublesep=5pt,doublecolor=blue](3,1.5)
  \psline(3,3)
\end{pspicture}
```

Example
5-6-12

When a straight line is drawn, it is actually a filled rectangle. The question is how this "rectangle" is positioned with respect to the given coordinates of the line. PSTricks allows a special setting for macros with closed lines, like \psframe, \pscircle, and \psellipse. For \pswedge, the dimen key applies to the radius only and doesn't affect the behavior at the center point (which will always be located in the middle of the line). The key dimen determines what the specified coordinates refer to: either the inner edge, the outer edge (default), or the middle of the line. The following example demonstrates the effect of drawing three rectangles and three circles with the same size specified, but with different settings of dimen.

The dimen *key*

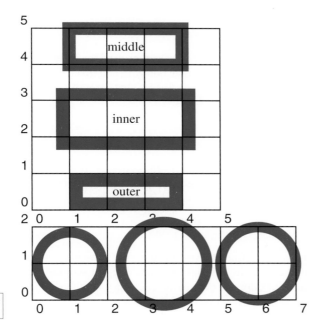

```
\usepackage{pstricks}
\begin{pspicture}[linewidth=10pt,
                  linecolor=blue](5,5)
  \psframe[dimen=outer](1,0)(4,1)
  \rput(2.5,0.5){outer}
  \psframe[dimen=inner](1,2)(4,3)
  \rput(2.5,2.5){inner}
  \psframe[dimen=middle](1,4)(4,5)
  \rput(2.5,4.5){middle}
  \psgrid[subgriddiv=0,linecolor=black]
\end{pspicture}

\bigskip

\begin{pspicture}[linewidth=8pt,
                  linecolor=blue](7,2)
  \pscircle[dimen=outer](1,1){1}
  \pscircle[dimen=inner](3.5,1){1}
  \pscircle[dimen=middle](6,1){1}
  \psgrid[subgriddiv=0,linecolor=black]
\end{pspicture}
```

Example
5-6-13

PSTricks comes equipped with a large variety of predefined arrows and line end markings (summarized in Table 5.12 on page 261). These arrows can be requested via the key-/value interface or with the special option, e.g., for the \psline macro:

The arrows *key*

> \psline∗ *[arrows=⟨arrow type⟩,...]* (x_0, y_0) (x_1, y_1) ... (x_n, y_n)
> \psline∗ *[settings]* {⟨*arrow type*⟩} (x_0, y_0) (x_1, y_1) ... (x_n, y_n)

If the line consists of several segments, the arrow specification refers to the beginning (first segment) and the end (last segment) of the line set. By definition, \pspolygon creates closed lines by connecting the last point to the first point, so that arrow specifications make little sense here.

The keyword showpoints can be used with Bézier curves (and other curve-drawing macros) to illustrate the position of the current control points. In some cases it is also useful

The showpoints *key*

with straight lines. The size of the dots can be changed through the keywords `dotsize` and `dotscale`, described in Section 5.8 on page 249.

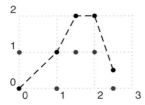

```
\usepackage{pstricks}
\begin{pspicture}[showgrid=true](3,2)
  \psline[showpoints=true,linestyle=dashed]%
      (0,0)(1,1)(1.5,2)(2,2)(2.5,0.5)
  \psline[showpoints=true,linestyle=none,linecolor=blue]%
      (0,1)(1,0)(1.5,1)(2,1)(2.5,0)
\end{pspicture}
```

Example
5-6-14

The linearc *key*

The keywords `linearc`, `framearc`, and `cornersize` can be used to create sophisticated lines. However, they are of use only with line sets (like polygons). In first example, the value for `linearc` denotes the radius of the circle that the line is "bent" around.

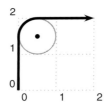

```
\usepackage{pstricks}
\begin{pspicture}[showgrid=true](2,2)
  \pscircle[linecolor=red](0.5,1.5){0.5}\psdot(0.5,1.5)
  \psline[linearc=0.5,linewidth=2pt]{->}(0,0)(0,2)(2,2)
\end{pspicture}
```

Example
5-6-15

If the beginning and the end of a set of straight lines drawn by `\psline` have the same coordinates, they won't be connected by an arc. In contrast, `\pspolygon` assumes closed lines by definition and produces an arc. (Compare the two figures at the top of the following example.)

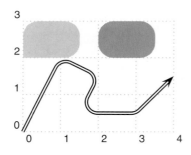

```
\usepackage{pstricks}
\begin{pspicture}[showgrid=true](4,3)
  \psline*[linecolor=green,linearc=0.4]%
      (0,2)(1.5,2)(1.5,3)(0,3)(0,2)
  \pspolygon*[linecolor=red,linearc=0.4]%
      (2,2)(3.5,2)(3.5,3)(2,3)(2,2)
  \psline[linearc=0.3,doubleline=true]{->}%
      (0,0)(1,2)(2,1.5)(1.5,0.5)(3,0.5)(4,1.5)
\end{pspicture}
```

Example
5-6-16

The framearc *key*

The keyword `framearc` is similar to `linearc`; the difference is that it refers to closed lines (frames) created by `\psframe` or `\pspolygon`. In contrast to `linearc`, the `framearc` key can take only values between 0 and 1, where 1 refers to the half of the short-est edge. With a value of 1, a square will turn into a circle.

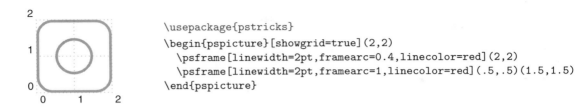

```
\usepackage{pstricks}
\begin{pspicture}[showgrid=true](2,2)
    \psframe[linewidth=2pt,framearc=0.4,linecolor=red](2,2)
    \psframe[linewidth=2pt,framearc=1,linecolor=red](.5,.5)(1.5,1.5)
\end{pspicture}
```

Example
5-6-17

To cause all area-shaped structures to show the same behavior at the edges, one can choose either `relative` or `absolute` for the `cornersize`. With `relative`, the `framearc` key determines the radius of the rounded corners, as described above (and hence the radius depends on the size of the frame). With `absolute`, the `linearc` keyword deter-mines the radius of the rounded corners (and hence the radius is of constant size).   *The* `cornersize` *key*

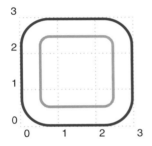

```
\usepackage{pstricks}
\begin{pspicture}[showgrid=true](3,3)
    \psframe[linewidth=2pt,linearc=0.25,
        cornersize=absolute,linecolor=red](0.5,0.5)(2.5,2.5)
    \psframe[linewidth=2pt,framearc=0.5,linecolor=blue](3,3)
\end{pspicture}
```

Example
5-6-18

With the keyword `bordercolor`, the crossings of lines can be shown easily when the line on top has a border in a different color. The width of the surrounding border is set by the keyword `border`.   *The* `border` *and* `bordercolor` *keys*

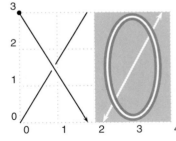

```
\usepackage{pstricks}
\begin{pspicture}[showgrid=true](4,3)
    \psline(0,0)(1.8,3)\psline[border=2pt]{*->}(0,3)(1.8,0)
    \psframe*[linecolor=lightgray](2,0)(4,3)
    \psset{linecolor=white}
    \psline[linewidth=1.5pt]{<->}(2.2,0)(3.8,3)
    \psellipse[linewidth=1.5pt,
        bordercolor=gray,border=2pt](3,1.5)(.7,1.4)
\end{pspicture}
```

Example
5-6-19

Shadow effects primarily serve the purpose of highlighting certain regions. The key-word `shadow` enables the shadow effect, and the keywords `shadowsize`, `shadowangle`, and `shadowcolor` set the style of the shadow. The size of the shadow should be chosen   *The* `shadow,` `shadowsize,` `shadowangle,` *and* `shadowcolor` *keys*

especially carefully. This feature is useful only with closed curves or polygons. More information on how PSTricks achieves this shadow effect can be found in Section 5.13.1 on page 289.

```
\usepackage{pstricks}
\begin{pspicture}(2,1.5)
 \pspolygon[linearc=2pt,shadow=true,shadowangle=45]%
   (0,0)(0,1.1)(0.2,1.1)(0.2,1.2)(0.8,1.2)(0.8,1.05)(2,1.05)(2,0)
\end{pspicture}
```

Example
5-6-20

The linetype *key*   The linetype keyword is only of interest to developers who write their own macros
depending on PSTricks. The line styles dashed and dotted can connect to existing paths
(lines or curves) with or without gaps only when they know something about the current
state of the path or the type of the line/curve, which has previously been drawn. With the
linetype keyword, the line type (see Table 5.6) can be passed to PostScript.

Table 5.6: Possible values for linetype

Value	Type
0	open curve without arrows
−1	open curve with arrow at the beginning
−2	open curve with arrow at the end
−3	open curve with arrow at the beginning and the end
1	closed curve with different elements
$n>1$	closed curve with n similar elements

The liftpen *and*   The keyword liftpen controls the behavior when drawing open curves, which is es-
labelsep *keys*   pecially of interest for \pscustom (see Section 5.13.1 on page 281; examples can be found
there). The keyword labelsep specifies the distance between specified coordinates and a
label set by one of the \?put macros (see Section 5.11 on page 265; examples can be found
there). The value of labelsep can be queried through the length register \pslabelsep.

5.7 Circles, ellipses, and curves

In PSTricks's terms, everything that is not part of a polygon is regarded as a curve. This class
of objects also includes circles and ellipses, and parts thereof. (Although a circle is mathematically a special case of the ellipse, PSTricks distinguishes between the two.) Both shapes
may be drawn in their entirety or as segments or sectors. For all macros of this group, the
center point defaults to TEX's current point or (0,0). The starred form of these commands
fills the interior of the respective shape (in the case of arcs, the area made up by connecting
the ends of the arc with a chord) using the current line color and the current fill pattern.
The keyword setting \showpoints=true, when used with \psarc or \pselliptarc,
causes dashed lines to be drawn from the center to the starting point and the end point of
the arc.

> \pscircle * [*settings*] (x_M, y_M) {*radius*}

If no circle center is specified, then the default (0,0) is used. The starred form fills the inside of the circle with the current line color and the current fill pattern.

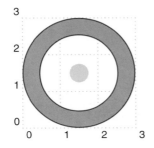

```
\usepackage{pstricks}
\begin{pspicture}[showgrid=true](3,3)
  \pscircle[linecolor=blue,doubleline=true,
      doublecolor=red,doublesep=12pt](1.5,1.5){1.5}
  \pscircle*[linecolor=green](1.5,1.5){0.25}
\end{pspicture}
```

Example
5-7-1

> \qdisk(x_M, y_M) {*radius*}

\qdisk is a simplified variant of the starred form of the circle macro; it is always filled with the current line color. Keywords may only be set with \psset, and both the center and the radius have to be specified.

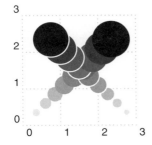

```
\usepackage{multido,pstricks}
\begin{pspicture}[showgrid=true](3,3)
  \multido{\rA=0.1+0.25,\rB=0.05+0.05,
    \rC=3.0+-0.25,\nA=0+10}{10}{%
      {\psset{linecolor=black!\nA}\qdisk(\rA,\rA){\rB}}
      \pscircle[linecolor=white,fillcolor=black!\nA,
        fillstyle=solid](\rC,\rA){\rB}}
\end{pspicture}
```

Example
5-7-2

> \psarc * [*settings*] {*arrow type*} (x_M, y_M) {*radius*}{*angleA*}{*angleB*}
> \psarcn * [*settings*] {*arrow type*} (x_M, y_M) {*radius*}{*angleA*}{*angleB*}

These commands draw arcs and sectors, when the filling function is used. The difference between the two is that \psarc draws the arc in the mathematically positive sense (i.e., counter-clockwise) and \psarcn draws it in the mathematically negative sense (i.e., clockwise). Note that the latter behavior is different from using \psarc with the angle specifications swapped, as the arc would still be drawn counter-clockwise. This is especially useful in applications of `\pscustom`, which deals with drawing closed lines (among other things).

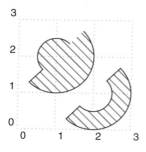

```
\usepackage{pstricks}
\begin{pspicture}[showgrid=true](3,3)
\pscustom[linecolor=blue,fillstyle=vlines,hatchcolor=gray]{
    \psarc(1,2){.5}{45}{225}
    \psarc(1,2){1}{225}{45}}
\pscustom[linecolor=blue,fillstyle=vlines,hatchcolor=gray]{
    \psarc(2,1){.5}{225}{45}
    \psarcn(2,1){1}{45}{225}
    \closepath}
\end{pspicture}
```

Example
5-7-3

Note that the center point is not really optional. Although the *{arrow type}* and (x_M, y_M) arguments are both marked as optional, the latter may be omitted only if the former has been given. Otherwise, TEX will mistake the *{radius}* argument for the *{arrow type}*.

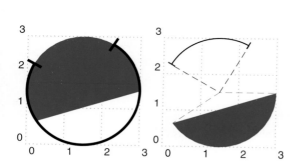

```
\usepackage{pstricks}
\begin{pspicture}[showgrid=true](3,3)
    \psarcn*[showpoints=true,linecolor=blue]%
        (1.5,1.5){1.5}{215}{0}
    \psarcn[linewidth=2pt]{|-|}%
        (1.5,1.5){1.5}{60}{150}
\end{pspicture}\hspace{1.5em}
\begin{pspicture}[showgrid=true](3,3)
    \psarc*[showpoints=true,linecolor=blue]%
        (1.5,1.5){1.5}{215}{0}
    \psarc[showpoints=true]%
        {|-|}(1.5,1.5){1.5}{60}{150}
\end{pspicture}
```

Example
5-7-4

> `\pswedge` ∗ *[settings]* (x_M, y_M) *{radius}{angleA}{angleB}*

`\pswedge` draws a sector starting at the first angle clockwise to the second angle. If no circle center is specified, `(0,0)` is taken by default. The starred form fills the interior of the sector with the current line color and the current fill pattern.

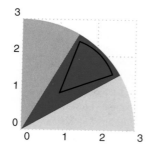

```
\usepackage{pstricks}
\begin{pspicture}[showgrid=true](3,3)
    \pswedge*[linecolor=black!15]{3}{0}{30}
    \pswedge*[linecolor=blue]{3}{30}{60}
    \pswedge*[linecolor=black!30]{3}{60}{90}
    \pswedge(1,1){1.5}{20}{70}
\end{pspicture}
```

Example
5-7-5

| $\verb|\psellipse*|$ *[settings]* (x_M,y_M) (a,b) |

In contrast to a circle, an ellipse needs an extended radius specification. As is common practice in mathematics, the two semi-axes are used, given in parentheses like a coordinate pair:
(a,b). If no ellipse center is given, $(0,0)$ is used. The starred form fills the interior of the
ellipse with the current line color and the current fill pattern.

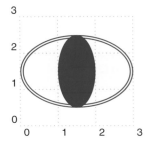

```
\usepackage{pstricks}
\begin{pspicture}[showgrid=true](3,3)
  \psellipse[linecolor=blue,doubleline=true]%
     (1.5,1.5)(1.5,1)
  \psellipse*[linecolor=blue](1.5,1.5)(0.5,1)
\end{pspicture}
```

| $\verb|\psellipticarc*|$ *[settings]* *{arrow type}* (x_M,y_M) (a,b) *{angleA}{angleB}* |
| $\verb|\psellipticarcn*|$ *[settings]* *{arrow type}* (x_M,y_M) (a,b) *{angleA}{angleB}* |

These commands are similar to their "circular" counterparts in that they are able to draw
not only elliptic arcs, but also elliptic sectors, if the fill function is used. Again, the only
difference between \psellipticarc and \psellipticarcn is that the former draws the
arc in the mathematically positive sense (i.e., counter-clockwise) and the latter draws it in
the mathematically negative sense (i.e., clockwise). Note that this different behavior cannot
be achieved by simply swapping the two angle specifications. \psellipticarcn can be
very useful when we are applying the \pscustom command to create a closed path around
an area.

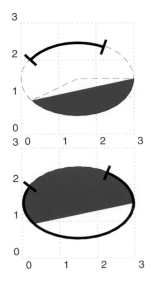

```
\usepackage{pstricks}
\begin{pspicture}[showgrid=true](3,3)
  \psellipticarc*[showpoints=true,linecolor=blue]%
     (1.5,1.5)(1.5,1){215}{0}
  \psellipticarc[linewidth=2pt]{|-|}%
     (1.5,1.5)(1.5,1){60}{150}
  \psellipse[linestyle=dashed,linewidth=0.1pt]%
     (1.5,1.5)(1.5,1)
\end{pspicture}\\[10pt]
\begin{pspicture}[showgrid=true](3,3)
  \psellipticarcn*[showpoints=true,linecolor=blue]%
     (1.5,1.5)(1.5,1){215}{0}
  \psellipticarcn[linewidth=2pt]{|-|}%
     (1.5,1.5)(1.5,1){60}{150}
  \psellipse[linestyle=dashed,linewidth=0.1pt]%
     (1.5,1.5)(1.5,1)
\end{pspicture}
```

$$\boxed{\texttt{\textbackslash psellipticwedge} * \; [\textit{settings}] \;\; (x_M, y_M) \; (a,b) \{\textit{angleA}\}\{\textit{angleB}\}}$$

This macro is similar to \pswedge (discussed on page 242), with the only difference being that an elliptic sector is drawn instead of a circular one.

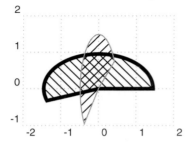

```
\usepackage{pstricks}
\begin{pspicture}[showgrid=true](-2,-1)(2,2)
  \psellipticwedge[fillstyle=vlines,
    linewidth=0.1](0,0)(1.5,1){0}{200}
  \psellipticwedge[fillstyle=hlines,
    linecolor=red](0,0)(0.5,1.5){30}{220}
\end{pspicture}
```

Example
5-7-8

5.7.1 General curves

PSTricks provides a variety of commands for drawing smooth curves according to a specified set of points. With some of these commands, the curve will go through all points given; other commands need some auxiliary points that determine the shape of the curve. Bézier curves always operate on a limited number of points (four with cubic Bézier curves), while the second-order polynomial functions applied by other macros allow for any number of points (above a certain minimum) to be connected. The starred form of most curve macros connects the end point of the curve to the starting point and fills the area thus obtained with the current line color and the current fill pattern. Whether this ability is useful depends on the particular application.

$$\boxed{\texttt{\textbackslash psbezier} * \; [\textit{settings}] \; \{\textit{arrow type}\} \;\; (x_0, y_0) \; (x_1, y_1) \, (x_2, y_2) \, (x_3, y_3)}$$

Since Bézier curves are an important method of drawing nonlinear curves, PostScript has a corresponding internal instruction, and \psbezier simply calls that procedure. It needs four points: the starting point and the end point of the curve, and two intermediate control points, which determine how the curve is bent.

However, \psbezier makes the first point optional. If it is not given, it is determined as follows: inside a \pscustom command, the PSTricks current point is used. Inside a pspicture environment, the origin (0,0) is taken. Elsewhere (i.e., outside of pspicture mode) TeX's current point is chosen.

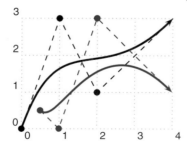

```
\usepackage{pstricks}
\begin{pspicture}[showgrid=true](4,3)
  \psbezier[linewidth=1.5pt,
    showpoints=true]{->}(1,3)(2,1)(4,3)
  \psbezier[linewidth=1.5pt,linecolor=blue,
    showpoints=true]{->}(0.5,0.5)(1,0)(2,3)(4,1)
\end{pspicture}
```

Example
5-7-9

As seen in the next example, the starred form always leads to a filled area with a straight connection between the last and first point.

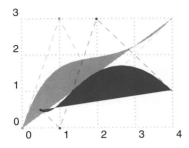

```
\usepackage{pstricks}
\begin{pspicture}[showgrid=true](4,3)
  \psbezier*[linewidth=1.5pt,linecolor=red,
    showpoints=true]{->}(1,3)(2,1)(4,3)
  \psbezier*[linewidth=1.5pt,linecolor=blue,
    showpoints=true]{->}(0.5,0.5)(1,0)(2,3)(4,1)
\end{pspicture}
```

Example 5-7-10

$\boxed{\texttt{\textbackslash parabola} * \;\textit{[settings]}\; \textit{\{arrow type\}}\; (x_P, y_P)(x_A, y_A)}$

This macro requires the specification of the vertex $AP(x_A, y_A)$ and an arbitrary curve point $P(x_P, y_P)$ to be able to draw the parabola. The starred form fills the area from the vertex to $y = y_P$ with the current line color and the current fill pattern.

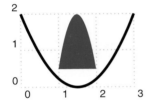

```
\usepackage{pstricks}
\begin{pspicture}[showgrid=true](3,2)
  \parabola*[linecolor=blue](1,0.5)(1.5,2)
  \parabola[linewidth=2pt](3,2)(1.5,0)
\end{pspicture}
```

Example 5-7-11

$\boxed{\texttt{\textbackslash pscurve} * \;\textit{[settings]}\; \textit{\{arrow type\}}\; (x_1, y_1)(x_2, y_2) \ldots (x_n, y_n)}$

\pscurve draws a smooth curve through a given list of points. It expects at least three points, because otherwise no interpolating second-degree polynomial can be created—PSTricks needs this expression to connect the points. Bear in mind that PSTricks does not give an error message when fewer than three coordinate pairs are specified! (The outcome will depend on the dvi driver and PostScript interpreter used.)

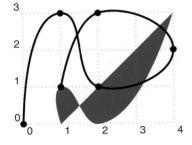

```
\usepackage{pstricks}
\begin{pspicture}[showgrid=true](4,3)
  \pscurve*[linecolor=blue,linewidth=1.5pt]%
    (1,0)(1,1)(2,0)(4,3)
  \pscurve[linewidth=1.5pt,
    showpoints=true](0,0)(1,3)(2,1)(4,2)(2,3)(1,1)
\end{pspicture}
```

Example 5-7-12

> \psecurve * [*settings*] {*arrow type*} $(x_1, y_1)(x_2, y_2) \ldots (x_n, y_n)$

The "*e*" in the name of \psecurve stands for "end point". This command is a variation of
the command that uses the first and last of the specified coordinate pairs as control points,
like those for a Bézier curve. These points are taken into account to determine the curve gradient but are not displayed; the curve starts at the second point and ends at the penultimate
point. This may be useful to let the curve start and end with a specific gradient. Hence, the
curve can be given a defined behavior at the "visible" end points, which is not possible with
\pscurve.

Note that it is not meaningful to give fewer than four coordinate pairs, because
\pscurve draws $n - 2$ points. PSTricks does not raise an error message when too few
coordinate pairs are specified! (The outcome will depend on the dvi driver and PostScript
interpreter used.)

In the following example, a \psecurve is used together with a corresponding
\pscurve (which omits the "invisible" starting point and end point) for comparison.

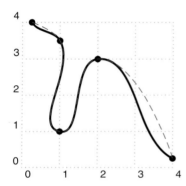

```
\usepackage{pstricks}
\begin{pspicture}[showgrid=true](4,4)
  \psecurve[showpoints=true,
     linewidth=1.5pt](.125,6)(.25,4)(1,3.5)%
     (1,1)(2,3)(4,.25)(8,.125)
  \pscurve[linecolor=blue,linewidth=0.5pt,
     linestyle=dashed](.25,4)(1,3.5)(1,1)(2,3)(4,.25)
\end{pspicture}
```

Example
5-7-13

> \psccurve * [*settings*] {*arrow type*} $(x_1, y_1)(x_2, y_2) \ldots (x_n, y_n)$

The name of the \psccurve command is an abbreviation for "closed curve"—it draws a
smooth curve through a given list of points and will also connect the last point to the first
point by a smooth curve. Like \pscurve, this command needs at least three points. Note
that PSTricks does not give an error message when too few coordinate pairs are specified!
(The outcome will depend on the dvi driver and PostScript interpreter used.)

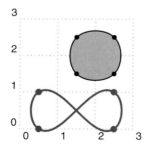

```
\usepackage{pstricks}
\begin{pspicture}[showgrid=true](3,3)
  \psccurve*[linecolor=cyan]%
     (1.5,1.5)(2.5,1.5)(2.5,2.5)(1.5,2.5)
  \psccurve[showpoints=true]%
     (1.5,1.5)(2.5,1.5)(2.5,2.5)(1.5,2.5)
  \psccurve[showpoints=true,linecolor=red,
     linewidth=1.5pt](.5,0)(2.5,1)(2.5,0)(.5,1)
\end{pspicture}
```

Example
5-7-14

Table 5.7: Summary of keywords for circles, ellipses and curves

Name	Value Type	Default
arcsep	*value[unit]*	0pt
arcsepA	*value[unit]*	0pt
arcsepB	*value[unit]*	0pt
curvature	*value1 value2 value3*	1 0.1 0

5.7.2 Keywords for curves

Table 5.7 lists all keys that are relevant to circles, ellipses, and curves. The keys displayed in Table 5.5 on page 235 also apply, insofar as they refer to filling and lines in general. In this section, examples are given for every keyword specified, according to the order given in Table 5.7.

The `arcsep` key is simply an abbreviation for the simultaneous setting of `arcsepA` (point A) and `arcsepB` (point B). These keywords are needed when line segments should not end in the center of another line or in another point, but rather exactly at the outer edge of that object. This is especially important when the line or curve ends with an arrow, as it should not normally overlap another line or point with its tip. As can be seen in the following example, this feature unfortunately does not work correctly in all cases: the upper arc does not end at the edge of the circle.

The arcsep, arcsepA, *and* arcsepB *keys*

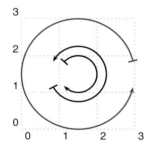

Example
5-7-15

```
\usepackage{pstricks}
\SpecialCoor
\begin{pspicture}[showgrid=true](3,3)
  \psset{linewidth=1pt}
  \psarc[arcsep=20pt,
    linecolor=blue]{|->}(1.5,1.5){1.5}{0}{360}
  \psarc[arcsep=20pt]{|->}(1.5,1.5){0.75}{180}{-180}
  \psarcn[arcsep=20pt]{|->}(1.5,1.5){0.5}{180}{-180}
\end{pspicture}
```

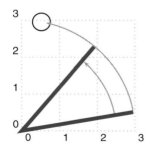

Example
5-7-16

```
\usepackage{pstricks}
\SpecialCoor
\begin{pspicture}[showgrid=true](3,3)
  \psline[linewidth=3pt,linecolor=blue](3;50)(0,0)(3;10)
  \psarc[arcsep=3pt,linecolor=red]{->}{2.5}{10}{50}
  \pscircle(3;80){0.25}
  \psarc[arcsepA=3pt,arcsepB=0.25cm,linecolor=red]
    {->}{3}{10}{80}
\end{pspicture}
```

The curvature key controls the appearance of all curves except Bézier curves (where the control points are part of the curve specification). The other curves are determined by an interpolating second-degree polynomial ($y = ax^2 + bx + c$), and the curvature can be influenced by the curvature key. The default values satisfy most needs, but can lead to insufficient results with curves that have to "steeply stub" the middle point (see Section 6.1.2 on page 333). A curve from A over C to B is drawn by "stubbing" point C in such a way that the tangent in this point is perpendicular to the bisecting line of the angle ACB.

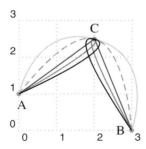

```
\usepackage{pstricks}
\begin{pspicture}[showgrid=true](3,3)
  \pscurve[showpoints=true,linecolor=red,
     linewidth=1.5pt](0,1)(2,2.5)(3,0)
  \pspolygon[linewidth=0.3pt](0,1)(2,2.5)(3,0)
  \rput[lC]{-105.7}(2,2.5){
    \psset{linewidth=0.2pt}
    \psline[linestyle=dashed](0,-1)(0,1)
    \psline[linestyle=dashed](0,0)(1.5,0)
    \psarc(0,0){0.25}{0}{90}}
  \uput[-75](0,1){A}\uput[135](3,0){B}\uput[45](2,2.5){C}
\end{pspicture}
```

Example
5-7-17

The bisecting line is displayed dashed in this example. This behavior is independent of the scale as well as the choice of the values of the curvature parameters. The values for the three parameters must be chosen from the range $[-1; +2]$. The *first parameter* determines the gradient of the curve in such a way that for values smaller than 0, the starting gradient is smaller than the gradient of the line $\overline{AC}$. For values larger than 0, the inverse is true and the gradient is larger than that of the line $\overline{AC}$. The following example demonstrates this for the values $[2; 1; 0; -0.5; -1]$. For the value 0, the curve corresponds to a straight line; for negative values, a loop has to be inserted, because otherwise the aforementioned gradient condition in point C cannot be fulfilled.

```
\usepackage{pstricks}
\begin{pspicture}[showgrid=true](3,3)
  \pscurve[showpoints=true,linecolor=red,
     linestyle=dashed](0,1)(2,2.5)(3,0)
  \pscurve[linecolor=green,curvature=2 0.1 0](0,1)(2,2.5)(3,0)
  \pscurve[linecolor=blue,curvature=0.0 0.1 0](0,1)(2,2.5)(3,0)
  \pscurve[linecolor=gray,curvature=-0.5 0.1 0](0,1)(2,2.5)(3,0)
  \pscurve[linecolor=black,curvature=-1.0 0.1 0](0,1)(2,2.5)(3,0)
  \uput[-75](0,1){A}\uput[180](3,0){B}\uput[90](2,2.5){C}
\end{pspicture}
```

Example
5-7-18

The *second parameter* influences the gradient right and left of the adjacent point, but only when the gradient $\overline{AC}$ with respect to $\overline{BC}$ is larger than $45°$. To show this effect, the middle point C has been raised in the following example. As can be seen, the result is symmetrical around the middle point.

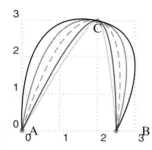

```
\usepackage{pstricks}
\begin{pspicture}[showgrid=true](3,3)
  \pscurve[showpoints=true,linecolor=red,
    linestyle=dashed](0,0)(2,3)(2.5,0)
  \pscurve[linecolor=green,curvature=1 2.0 0](0,0)(2,3)(2.5,0)
  \pscurve[linecolor=blue,curvature=1 1 0](0,0)(2,3)(2.5,0)
  \pscurve[linecolor=gray,curvature=1 -0.5 0](0,0)(2,3)(2.5,0)
  \pscurve[linecolor=black,curvature=1 -1.0 0](0,0)(2,3)(2.5,0)
  \uput[0](0,0){A}\uput[0](3,0){B}\uput[90](2,2.5){C}
\end{pspicture}
```

Example
5-7-19

The *third parameter* of the `curvature` keyword influences the gradient in every point. For the value 0, the result is as described above. For the value -1, the tangent at point C is parallel to the straight line $\overline{AB}$. Contrary to the second parameter, changes to the third parameter result in asymmetric effects in relation to the middle point: relocating the curve upwards on the left side causes it to move downwards on the right, and vice versa. For more information about the behavior of the `curvature` keyword, see [135].

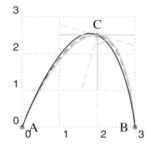

```
\usepackage{pstricks}
\begin{pspicture}[showgrid=true](3,3)
  \pscurve[showpoints=true,linecolor=red,
    linestyle=dashed](0,0)(2,2.5)(3,0)
  \pscurve[linecolor=green,curvature=1 0.1 -1](0,0)(2,2.5)(3,0)
  \pscurve[linecolor=blue,curvature=1 0.1  2](0,0)(2,2.5)(3,0)
  \PlotLines  % defined in preamble
  \uput[0](0,0){A}\uput[180](3,0){B}\uput[90](2,2.5){C}
\end{pspicture}
```

Example
5-7-20

5.8 Dots and symbols

For **PSTricks** a dot is everything that can be defined by the `dotstyle` key. This may be a dot (i.e., filled circle) or a symbol such as ready-made character from a font or a little graphic created with a PostScript subroutine. The symbols of the `Zapf Dingbats` font are especially easy to use because the font is already present inside PostScript. Such symbols can be defined as new "dots". The definition of dot style and size has direct influence on the key `showpoints` discussed in Section 5.6.2 on page 237.

The "singular" variant `\psdot` takes at most one point argument (which defaults to the "current" point), whereas the "plural" form `\psdots` must have at least one point but may take as many points as desired. As depicted in Table 5.9 on page 252, the starred version of \psdot produces filled symbols, if available.

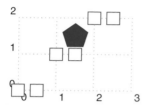

```
\usepackage{pstricks}
\begin{pspicture}[showgrid=true](3,2)
  \psset{linecolor=blue}
  \psdot*[dotstyle=pentagon,dotscale=5](1.5,1.5)
  \psdots[dotsize=.4cm,dotstyle=square]%
       (0,0)(0.5,0)(1,1)(1.5,1)(2,2)(2.5,2)
\end{pspicture}
```

Example
5-8-1

> \newpsfontdot{*name*} [*xW xS yS yW xO yO*] {*font name*}{*glyph number*}

The \newpsfontdot declaration allows you to define your own dot symbols. First you have to choose a *name* that you later use with the dotstyle key (see example below). Next comes a transformation specification that will be applied to the glyph. Although it is given in square brackets, this argument is *not* optional! It conforms to the usual PostScript representation of transformation matrices and comprises six numbers: *xW* and *yW*—the values for the horizontal and vertical scale factors; *xS* and *yS*—the values for the shearing factors in both dimensions; and *xO* and *yO*—the values for the offsets in the x and y directions. Then comes the *font name*, which must be a valid PSTricks internal or PostScript font designation, followed by the *glyph number*, which is the slot position of the character (given as a hexadecimal number enclosed in angle brackets). Which PostScript fonts will be available depend on the driver used on the one hand and on the character sets built into the printing device on the other hand. Alternatively, the PSTricks internal "font" can be used, where the characters are defined in the header file pst-dots.pro.

In the following example, we define three new symbols called CircPlus, CircMultiply, and Flower (plus a few variants of these). The first two symbols are part of the Symbol font, and the third symbol comes from the Zapf Dingbats font of PostScript with the numbers 196, 197, and 96.

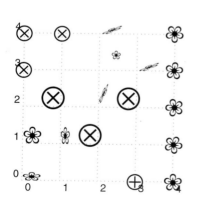

```
\usepackage{pstricks}
\newpsfontdot{CircMultiply}[2 0 0 2 -.78 -.7]{Symbol}{<C4>}
\newpsfontdot{CircPlus}[2 0 0 2 -.78 -.7]{Symbol}{<C5>}
\newpsfontdot{CircPlus45}[2 2 -2 2 -.78 -.7]{Symbol}{<C5>}
% ... other definitions see example code ...
\begin{pspicture}[showgrid=true](4,4)
  \psset{dotscale=2.5}            \psdot[dotstyle=Flower](4,0)
  \psdot[dotstyle=Flower45](4,1) \psdot[dotstyle=Flower90](4,2)
  \psdot[dotstyle=Flower135](4,3)\psdot[dotstyle=Flower180](4,4)
  \psdots[dotstyle=hFlower](0,0) \psdot[dotstyle=vFlower](1,1)
  \psdot[dotstyle=hvFlower](0,1) \psdot[dotstyle=xsFlower](2,2)
  \psdot[dotstyle=ysFlower](3,3) \psdot[dotstyle=dxyFlower](2,3)
  \psdot[dotstyle=ysFlower](2,4) \psdot[dotstyle=CircPlus](3,0)
  \psdots[dotstyle=CircPlus45](3,2)(1,2)(2,1)
  \psdots[dotstyle=CircMultiply](0,3)(0,4)(1,4)
\end{pspicture}
```

Example
5-8-2

To find suitable values for the transformation specification often requires some hand-work in the end, which is admittedly easier with axis-symmetrical glyphs.

5.8.1 Dot keywords

Table 5.8 shows the possible options for the dot macros.

Table 5.8: Summary of keywords for dot display

Name	Value Type	Default
dotstyle	*style name*	*
dotsize	*value[unit] [value]*	2pt 2
dotscale	*value1 [value2]*	1
dotangle	*angle*	0

A large number of predefined styles to set dots exist, which are summarized in Table 5.9 on the following page, in which the right column shows examples with an additional `fillcolor` key setting. For better reading the symbols have been set with `dotscale=1.5` (see below). Additional symbols can be defined using `\newpsfontdot` as explained on the facing page.

The size of a dot symbol is determined by two keywords. The `dotsize` key takes a size specification and an optional number as values; the latter is treated as a multiple of the `linewidth` value (see Section 5.6.2 on page 234). The default value is *2*pt *2*, making the dot size depend on the width used for drawing lines (a feature useful with `showpoints`). If need arises, you can use fixed dot sizes by using a factor of 0 (which is the default value, if omitted). In the case of circles, the value specified with the `dotsize` key refers to the diameter. *The* `dotsize` *and* `dotscale` *keys*

```
\usepackage{pstricks,pst-node}
\psdot[dotsize=0pt 10,dotstyle=square](0,0)%
\psdot[dotsize=0pt 10,dotstyle=square](2,0)%
\pcline[nodesep=5\pslinewidth,linewidth=10\pslinewidth](0,0)(2,0)
```

The other key affecting the size of dot symbols is `dotscale`, which takes one or two numbers as values. If two numbers are given, they specify the scaling factor in the horizontal and vertical directions, respectively; a single number applies to both directions. The default value is 1 (hence no additional scaling takes effect).

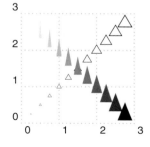

```
\usepackage{multido,pstricks}
\begin{pspicture}[showgrid=true](3,3)
\multido{\rA=0.25+0.25}{11}{%
  \psdot[dotscale=\rA,dotstyle=triangle](\rA,\rA)}
\multido{\rA=0.25+0.25,\rB=2.75+-0.25,\nB=0+9}{11}{%
  \psdot*[dotscale=\rA\space 4,dotstyle=triangle,
    linecolor=black!\nB](\rA,\rB)}
\end{pspicture}
```

Table 5.9: Summary of dot styles

Name	\psdot	\psdot*	Name	\psdot	\psdot*
*	● ● ● ●	● ● ● ●	o	○ ○ ○ ○	● ● ●
Bo	○ ○ ○ ○	● ● ● ●	x	× × × ×	× × × ×
+	+ + + +	+ + + +	B+	+ + + +	+ + + +
Add	+ + + +	+ + + +	BoldAdd	+ + + +	+ + + +
Oplus	⊕ ⊕ ⊕ ⊕	● ● ● ●	BoldOplus	⊕ ⊕ ⊕ ⊕	● ● ●
SolidOplus	⊕ ⊕ ⊕ ⊕	● ● ● ●	Hexagon	○ ○ ○ ○	● ● ●
BoldHexagon	○ ○ ○ ○	● ● ● ●	SolidHexagon	● ● ● ●	● ● ● ●
asterisk	＊ ＊ ＊ ＊	＊ ＊ ＊ ＊	Basterisk	＊ ＊ ＊ ＊	＊ ＊ ＊ ＊
Asterisk	✳ ✳ ✳ ✳	✳ ✳ ✳ ✳	BoldAsterisk	✳ ✳ ✳ ✳	✳ ✳ ✳ ✳
SolidAsterisk	⊛ ⊛ ⊛ ⊛	● ● ● ●	oplus	⊕ ⊕ ⊕ ⊕	⊕ ⊕ ⊕ ⊕
otimes	⊗ ⊗ ⊗ ⊗	⊗ ⊗ ⊗ ⊗	Otimes	⊗ ⊗ ⊗ ⊗	● ● ● ●
BoldOtimes	⊗ ⊗ ⊗ ⊗	● ● ● ●	SolidOtimes	⊗ ⊗ ⊗ ⊗	● ● ● ●
Mul	× × × ×	× × × ×	BoldMul	× × × ×	× × × ×
|	| | | |	| | | |	B|	| | | |	| | | |
Bar	| | | |	| | | |	BoldBar	| | | |	| | | |
Bullet	● ● ● ●	● ● ● ●	Circle	○ ○ ○ ○	● ● ● ●
BoldCircle	○ ○ ○ ○	● ● ● ●	square	□ □ □ □	■ ■ ■ ■
Bsquare	□ □ □ □	■ ■ ■ ■	square*	■ ■ ■ ■	■ ■ ■ ■
Square	□ □ □ □	■ ■ ■ ■	BoldSquare	□ □ □ □	■ ■ ■ ■
SolidSquare	■ ■ ■ ■	■ ■ ■ ■	diamond	◇ ◇ ◇ ◇	◆ ◆ ◆ ◆
Bdiamond	◇ ◇ ◇ ◇	◆ ◆ ◆ ◆	diamond*	◆ ◆ ◆ ◆	◆ ◆ ◆ ◆
Diamond	◇ ◇ ◇ ◇	◆ ◆ ◆ ◆	BoldDiamond	◇ ◇ ◇ ◇	◆ ◆ ◆ ◆
SolidDiamond	◆ ◆ ◆ ◆	◆ ◆ ◆ ◆	triangle	△ △ △ △	▲ ▲ ▲ ▲
Btriangle	△ △ △ △	▲ ▲ ▲ ▲	triangle*	▲ ▲ ▲ ▲	▲ ▲ ▲ ▲
Triangle	△ △ △ △	▲ ▲ ▲ ▲	BoldTriangle	△ △ △ △	▲ ▲ ▲ ▲
SolidTriangle	▲ ▲ ▲ ▲	▲ ▲ ▲ ▲	pentagon	⬠ ⬠ ⬠ ⬠	⬟ ⬟ ⬟ ⬟
Bpentagon	⬠ ⬠ ⬠ ⬠	⬟ ⬟ ⬟ ⬟	pentagon*	⬟ ⬟ ⬟ ⬟	⬟ ⬟ ⬟ ⬟
Pentagon	⬠ ⬠ ⬠ ⬠	⬟ ⬟ ⬟ ⬟	BoldPentagon	⬠ ⬠ ⬠ ⬠	⬟ ⬟ ⬟ ⬟
SolidPentagon	⬟ ⬟ ⬟ ⬟	⬟ ⬟ ⬟ ⬟	Hexagon	○ ○ ○ ○	● ● ● ●
BoldHexagon	○ ○ ○ ○	● ● ● ●	SolidHexagon	● ● ● ●	● ● ● ●

The dotangle *key*   After the application of the other keywords, like dotsize and dotscale, the symbol is rotated by the angle dotangle. The direction of the rotation is counter-clockwise.

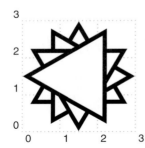

```
\usepackage{multido,pstricks}
\begin{pspicture}[showgrid=true](3,3)
  \multido{\nA=0+30}{12}{%
    \psdot[dotsize=2.25cm,dotstyle=triangle,
       dotangle=\nA](1.5,1.5)}
\end{pspicture}
```

Example
5-8-5

Table 5.10: Summary of the keywords used to fill areas

Name	Value Type	Default
fillstyle	none | solid | vlines | vlines* | hlines | hlines* | crosshatch | crosshatch*	none
fillcolor	color	white
hatchwidth	value[unit]	0.8pt
hatchwidthinc	value[unit]	0pt
hatchsep	value[unit]	4pt
hatchsepinc	value[unit]	0pt
hatchcolor	color	black
hatchangle	value	45
addfillstyle	none | solid | vlines | vlines* | hlines | hlines* | crosshatch | crosshatch*	none

5.9 Filling areas

Each "real" **PSTricks** graphic object command (that is, the commands internally defined through the macro \pst@object), except the commands starting with a "q", has also a starred variant that creates an object filled with the current linecolor. Other colors or patterns can be achieved by using the various keywords for filling areas.

Only areas with a closed path can be filled with a color or pattern. If a path is not defined by a closed polygon or curve, PostScript will connect the last point with the first point by a line to create a closed path. This may sometimes produce an unexpected result. In this section we describe only the basic keys for the standard fill option of the main package **pstricks**. Other fill styles require the package **pst-grad** for gradients or **pst-fill** for filling with patterns or tiles (see Section 6.4).

5.9.1 Filling keywords

The basic fill styles are solid with a defined color or with lines of different width, separation, angle, and color.

Several standard filling styles exist: none, solid, vlines, vlines*, hlines, hlines*, none, crosshatch, crosshatch*, and boxfill. The starred forms first fill *The* fillstyle *key* the background with the color specified by the fillcolor keyword, and then work similar to the unstarred forms. The fill style none fills an area with "no" style, which may seem to be useless, but actually suppresses and deactivates selected fillings of partitions. This also fillstyle=none provides an easy way to test and debug complex **PSTricks** figures. Simply changing the fill style to none disables the filling but leaves the current line path unchanged.

The value solid must be used for the fillstyle key when filling the complete area with the current fill color. This corresponds to the starred form of the used command, when fillstyle=solid the line color is set to the fill color.

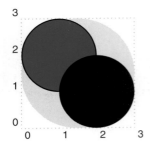

```
\usepackage{pstricks}
\begin{pspicture}[showgrid=true](3,3)
  \pscircle*[linecolor=black!10](1.5,1.5){1.5}
  \pscircle[fillstyle=solid,fillcolor=blue](1,2){1}
  \pscircle*(2,1){1}
\end{pspicture}
```

Example
5-9-1

`fillstyle=vlines`

`fillstyle=vlines*`

The key values `vlines` and `vlines*` are abbreviations for "vertical lines", and they fill the complete area with vertical lines of the current fill color. One must keep in mind that the `hatchangle` is set to 45 degrees by default but must be set to 0 degrees to get true vertical lines. While the `vlines` key value produces a transparent filling, the starred form `vlines*` first fills the background with the color specified by `fillcolor` and only then repaints with the "normal" `vlines` style.

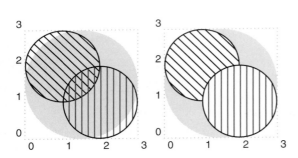

```
\usepackage{pstricks}
\begin{pspicture}[showgrid=true](3,3)
  \pscircle*[linecolor=black!10](1.5,1.5){1.5}
  \pscircle[fillstyle=vlines](1,2){1}
  \pscircle[fillstyle=vlines,%
    hatchcolor=blue,hatchangle=0](2,1){1}
\end{pspicture}\hspace{2em}%
\begin{pspicture}[showgrid=true](3,3)
  \pscircle*[linecolor=black!10](1.5,1.5){1.5}
  \pscircle[fillstyle=vlines*](1,2){1}
  \pscircle[fillstyle=vlines*,%
    hatchcolor=blue,hatchangle=0](2,1){1}
\end{pspicture}
```

Example
5-9-2

`fillstyle=hlines`
and `hlines*`

The fill styles `hlines` and `hlines*` (for "horizontal lines") work similar to their vertical counterparts `vlines` and `vlines*`, respectively.

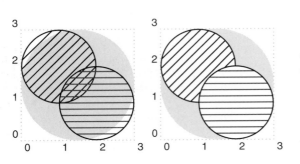

```
\usepackage{pstricks}
\begin{pspicture}[showgrid=true](3,3)
  \pscircle*[linecolor=black!10](1.5,1.5){1.5}
  \pscircle[fillstyle=hlines](1,2){1}
  \pscircle[fillstyle=hlines,%
    hatchcolor=blue,hatchangle=0](2,1){1}
\end{pspicture}\hspace{2em}%
\begin{pspicture}[showgrid=true](3,3)
  \pscircle*[linecolor=black!10](1.5,1.5){1.5}
  \pscircle[fillstyle=hlines*](1,2){1}
  \pscircle[fillstyle=hlines*,%
    hatchcolor=blue,hatchangle=0](2,1){1}
\end{pspicture}
```

Example
5-9-3

The fill styles `crosshatch` and `crosshatch*` (crossed lines) represent a combination of the above two styles and work analogously to them.

fillstyle=crosshatch and crosshatch*

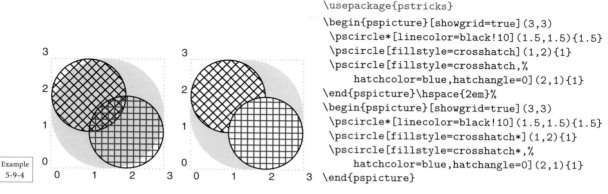

```
\usepackage{pstricks}
\begin{pspicture}[showgrid=true](3,3)
   \pscircle*[linecolor=black!10](1.5,1.5){1.5}
   \pscircle[fillstyle=crosshatch](1,2){1}
   \pscircle[fillstyle=crosshatch,%
      hatchcolor=blue,hatchangle=0](2,1){1}
\end{pspicture}\hspace{2em}%
\begin{pspicture}[showgrid=true](3,3)
   \pscircle*[linecolor=black!10](1.5,1.5){1.5}
   \pscircle[fillstyle=crosshatch*](1,2){1}
   \pscircle[fillstyle=crosshatch*,%
      hatchcolor=blue,hatchangle=0](2,1){1}
\end{pspicture}
```

Example 5-9-4

The `boxfill` style from the package **pst-fill** plots an object specified by `\psboxfill` repeatedly to fill the specified area. It is used in the next example and described in more detail in Section 6.4.

fillstyle=boxfill

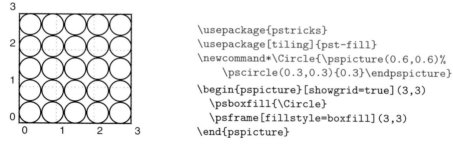

```
\usepackage{pstricks}
\usepackage[tiling]{pst-fill}
\newcommand*\Circle{\pspicture(0.6,0.6)%
   \pscircle(0.3,0.3){0.3}\endpspicture}
\begin{pspicture}[showgrid=true](3,3)
   \psboxfill{\Circle}
   \psframe[fillstyle=boxfill](3,3)
\end{pspicture}
```

Example 5-9-5

The keyword `fillcolor` determines the fill color for the fill styles `solid`, `vlines*`, `hlines*`, and `crosshatch*`.

The fillcolor *key*

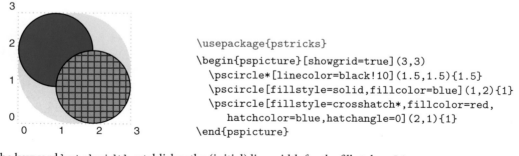

```
\usepackage{pstricks}
\begin{pspicture}[showgrid=true](3,3)
   \pscircle*[linecolor=black!10](1.5,1.5){1.5}
   \pscircle[fillstyle=solid,fillcolor=blue](1,2){1}
   \pscircle[fillstyle=crosshatch*,fillcolor=red,
      hatchcolor=blue,hatchangle=0](2,1){1}
\end{pspicture}
```

Example 5-9-6

The keyword `hatchwidth` establishes the (initial) line width for the fill styles `vlines`, `hlines`, and `crosshatch` (including their starred forms). In the following example, the two "incomplete" curves are completed with a line from the end point to the starting point

The hatchwidth *and* hatchwidthinc *keys*

by PSTricks, resulting in a definite area to fill. The keyword `hatchwidthinc` determines the increment of the line width for the fill styles `vlines`, `hlines`, and `crosshatch` (the starred forms included). PSTricks tries to hold the amount of white space between two lines as constant. This is possible only when changing the value for the keyword `hatchsep`. Only the start value for `hatchsep` can be set.

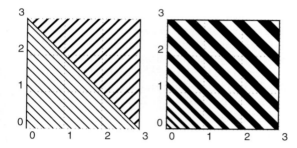

```
\usepackage{pstricks}
\begin{pspicture}[showgrid=true](3,3)
  \psline[fillstyle=vlines](0,0)(0,3)(3,0)
  \psline[fillstyle=hlines,hatchwidth=1.5pt]%
    (3,3)(3,0)(0,3)
\end{pspicture}\hspace{2em}%
\begin{pspicture}[showgrid=true](3,3)
  \psframe[fillstyle=vlines,
    hatchsep=1pt,hatchwidthinc=0.5pt](3,3)
\end{pspicture}
```

Example
5-9-7

The `hatchsep` *and* `hatchsepinc` *keys*

The keyword `hatchsep` sets up the (initial) size of the separation between the lines for the fill styles `vlines`, `hlines`, and `crosshatch` (and the starred forms). We call this the line distance. Again, the two "incomplete" curves of `\psline` have been completed with a line from the end point to the starting point by PSTricks to obtain a definite filling area. The keyword `hatchsepinc` determines the size of the increment for the separation between the lines for the fill styles `vlines`, `hlines`, and `crosshatch`, as well as the corresponding starred forms.

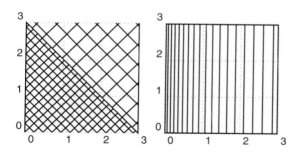

```
\usepackage{pstricks}
\begin{pspicture}[showgrid=true](3,3)
  \psline[fillstyle=crosshatch](0,0)(0,3)(3,0)
  \psline[fillstyle=crosshatch,hatchsep=10pt]%
    (3,3)(3,0)(0,3)
\end{pspicture}\hspace{2em}%
\begin{pspicture}[showgrid=true](3,3)
  \psframe[fillstyle=vlines,hatchangle=0,
    hatchsep=1pt,hatchsepinc=0.175pt](3,3)
\end{pspicture}
```

Example
5-9-8

The `hatchcolor` *and* `hatchangle` *keys*

With the `hatchcolor` key, you can choose the line color for the fill styles `vlines`, `hlines`, and `crosshatch`, including their starred forms. In the example the two "incomplete" curves of `\psline` are completed with a line from the end point to the starting point by PSTricks, making up a definite fill area. The keyword `hatchangle` determines the gradient of the lines for the fill styles `vlines`, `hlines`, and `crosshatch`, and their starred forms. Because of problems with rounding errors, not all angles are possible. In the next example the two "incomplete" curves of \psline are completed with a line from the end point to the starting point by PSTricks to form a closed path for a definite fill area.

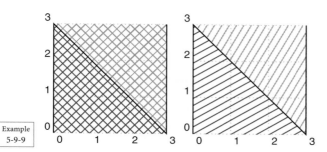

```
\usepackage{pstricks}
\begin{pspicture}[showgrid=true](3,3)
    \psline[fillstyle=crosshatch,
        hatchcolor=blue](0,0)(0,3)(3,0)
    \psline[fillstyle=crosshatch,
        hatchcolor=red](3,3)(3,0)(0,3)
\end{pspicture}\hspace{2em}%
\begin{pspicture}[showgrid=true](3,3)
    \psline[fillstyle=hlines,hatchcolor=blue,
        hatchangle=30](0,0)(0,3)(3,0)
    \psline[fillstyle=hlines,hatchcolor=red,
        hatchangle=60](3,3)(3,0)(0,3)
\end{pspicture}
```

Example
5-9-9

The package **pst-fill** allows you to define your own fill styles. Sometimes, however, it may be easier to use two existing styles and print them one over the other. The keyword addfillstyle determines such an additional fill style, so that especially in combination with the fill type boxfill there are manifold ways to fill areas. When you use this way of filling, you must assign the boxfill style to the addfillstyle key; the other way round doesn't work.

The addfillstyle *key*

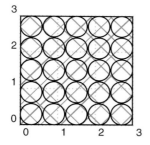

```
\usepackage{pstricks}
\usepackage[tiling]{pst-fill}
\newcommand*\Circle{\pspicture(0.6,0.6)
    \pscircle(0.3,0.3){0.3}\endpspicture}
\begin{pspicture}[showgrid=true](3,3)
    \psboxfill{\Circle}
    \psframe[fillstyle=crosshatch,addfillstyle=boxfill,
        hatchsep=10pt,hatchcolor=red](3,3)
\end{pspicture}
```

Example
5-9-10

5.9.2 More fill styles

Transparencies are not possible in PostScript level 2, which is the standard for PostScript printers these days; level 3 supports an alpha channel to create real transparencies. However, we can define a fill style with lines, where the separation and the line width are very small; the naked eye cannot perceive the difference between a solid filled area and such a hatch style. This makes sense only for printing or on-screen output, when the viewer doesn't zoom into such a "color".

In the next example we define a command \defineTColor with two arguments; one for the name of this new fill style and one for the basic color. (The **pstricks-add** package comes equipped with this command.) We print first the text and then the two rectangles, each with the special fill style. The result looks like we are using real transparency colors.

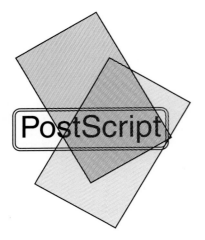

```
\usepackage{pstricks}
\newcommand*\defineTColor[2]{% transparent "colors"
  \newpsstyle{#1}{%
     fillstyle=vlines,hatchcolor=#2,
     hatchwidth=0.1\pslinewidth,hatchsep=1\pslinewidth}}
\defineTColor{tBlack40}{black!40}
\defineTColor{tBlack80}{black!80}

\begin{pspicture}(0,-1)(5,6)
\rput(2.5,2.5){\psframebox[doubleline=true,framearc=0.3]
                    {\Huge\textsf{PostScript}}}
\rput{-30}(1,1){\psframe[style=tBlack40](2.5,4)}
\rput{30}(2.5,1){\psframe[style=tBlack80](2.5,4)}
\end{pspicture}
```

Example
5-9-11

Remember that so-called Moiré effects may occur, when lines of the two fill styles have nearly the same gradient. In such a case one could select other angles for the lines, or choose the fill style crosshatch as an alternative.

Color gradients Circular color gradients can be constructed easily, for example, by using the \multido command. By default, the **pstricks** package loads the **xcolor** package, which is the reason why no explicit loading of a color package is seen in the examples.

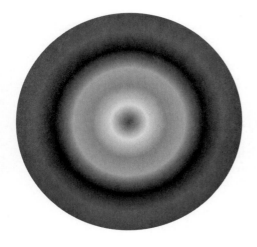

```
\usepackage{multido,pstricks}
\begin{pspicture}(-3,-3)(3,3)
\psset{unit=3}
\multido{\nHue=0.01+0.01}{100}{%
  \definecolor{MyColor}{hsb}{\nHue,1,1}
  \pscircle[linewidth=0.01,
            linecolor=MyColor]{\nHue}}
\end{pspicture}
```

Example
5-9-12

The next example could be defined as a macro and used as a fill style in conjunction with `psclip` environment (see Section 5.12.4 on page 275).

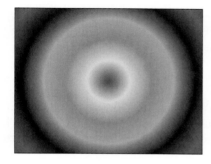

```
\usepackage{multido,pstricks}
\newcommand\circularFill[1]{%
  \psset{unit=#1}
  \begin{pspicture}(-1,-1)(1,1)
    \multido{\nHue=0.01+0.01}{100}{%
      \definecolor{MyColor}{hsb}{\nHue,1,1}
      \pscircle[linewidth=0.01,
                linecolor=MyColor]{\nHue}}
  \end{pspicture}}
\begin{pspicture}(5,4)
 \begin{psclip}{\psframe(5,4)}
   \rput(2.5,2){\circularFill{3.5}}
 \end{psclip}
\end{pspicture}
```

5.10 Arrows

PSTricks has a large choice of predefined "arrows", which are listed in Table 5.12. By "arrows", we mean a variety of line terminations (either beginning or ending), which are often actual arrows. These "arrows" can be set either by means of the key/value interface or by using the special optional {*arrow*} argument provided by many macros (see Section 5.6.2 on page 237). A specification through \psset is also possible (Section 5.2 on page 217).

Arrows may be used not only for lines, but for all "open" curves. The property of being open, in this context, refers to the way the curve is defined, not the resulting geometry. A polygon that starts and ends at the same point, for example, would be open in the required sense, when using the \psline command. In contrast, the \pspolygon command always yields a closed path. This implies that arrows make no sense for such a command. In this section, when we refer to line terminations, we implicitly include not only lines proper, but also other curves that are open in the relevant sense.

The next lines of code show the three ways to add a line termination to a line produced with the \psline command. All three possibilities for setting arrows are equivalent, except that the declaration with \psset must be put inside a group if the scope of its effect is intended to be local. The first line declares arrows=-> locally; it is valid only for the current graphic object. The same holds for the second line, where the special optional argument for line termination is used. The third line then applies the \psset command, but it is used together with the \psline command inside a group, delimited by the outer two curly braces; thus it is also local.

```
\psline[arrows=->](3,3)
\psline{->}(3,3)
{ \psset{arrows=->}\psline(3,3) }
```

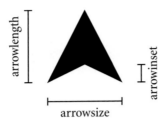

Figure 5.1: Dimensions of an arrow

5.10.1 Keywords for arrows

The keywords for arrows determine the style, size (see Figure 5.1), and shape of line terminations. In the keyword names, *length* is the dimension in the direction of the line, which is obvious for `arrowlength` but not for `bracketlength`; *size* is the dimension perpendicular to the line.

The `arrows` *key*   The predefined styles for line terminations that are set by the keyword `arrows` are shown in Table 5.12. The ways to use them will become clear from the examples that follow. Many mixed combinations of line beginnings and endings are possible, some of which are illustrated in the following example. Be careful when you use the arrow types "`-]`" and "`]-`" in optional argument declarations: you must put these types in curly braces to prevent the closing bracket from being misinterpreted as the one terminating the key/value list!

```
\usepackage{pstricks}
\psset{linecolor=blue,arrowscale=1.5}
\psline{->}(0,1ex)(1,1ex)    \psline{>-}(2,1ex)(3,1ex)   \\
\psline{<<-|}(0,1ex)(1,1ex)  \psline{[-<<}(2,1ex)(3,1ex)\\
\psline{]-|}(0,1ex)(1,1ex)   \psline{[->}(2,1ex)(3,1ex)  \\
\psline{]-o}(0,1ex)(1,1ex)
```

Example
5-10-1

Line terminations can also be affected by three additional `arrows` settings: c, cc, and C. The effects are shown in the next example. c and cc round the line end, with the difference

Table 5.11: Summary of keywords for arrows

Name	Value Type	Default
arrows	*style*	–
arrowsize	*value[unit] value*	1.5pt 2
arrowlength	*value*	1.4
arrowinset	*value*	0.4
tbarsize	*value[unit] value*	2pt 5
bracketlength	*value*	0.15
rbracketlength	*value*	0.15
arrowscale	*value1 [value2]*	1

Table 5.12: List of arrow tips

Value	Example	Code	Explanation
–		`\psline{-}(1.3,0)`	none
<->		`\psline{<->}(1.3,0)`	arrows
>-<		`\psline{>-<}(1.3,0)`	inverse arrows
<<->>		`\psline{<<->>}(1.3,0)`	double arrows
>>-<<		`\psline{>>-<<}(1.3,0)`	inverse double arrows
|-|		`\psline{|-|}(1.3,0)`	cross strut, flush with end point
|*-|*		`\psline{|*-|*}(1.3,0)`	cross strut, centered at end point
[-]		`\psline{[-]}(1.3,0)`	square brackets
]-[		`\psline{]-[}(1.3,0)`	inverse square brackets
(-)		`\psline{(-)}(1.3,0)`	round brackets
)-(		`\psline{)-(}(1.3,0)`	inverse round brackets
o-o		`\psline{o-o}(1.3,0)`	circle, centered at end point
-		`\psline{*-*}(1.3,0)`	disc, centered at end point
oo-oo		`\psline{oo-oo}(1.3,0)`	circle, flush with end point
-		`\psline{**-**}(1.3,0)`	disk, flush with end point
|<->|		`\psline{|<->|}(1.3,0)`	cross strut and arrow
|>-<|		`\psline{|>-<|}(1.3,0)`	cross strut and inverse arrow
c-c		`\psline{c-c}(1.3,0)`	rounded corners
cc-cc		`\psline{cc-cc}(1.3,0)`	rounded corners, flush with end point
C-C		`\psline{C-C}(1.3,0)`	squared end point

being that one centers the rounding disk at the nominal line end and the other centers the disk so that the line is not extended. C extends the line the same distance that c does, but keeps the end square. The effect of these settings becomes more important as the line width increases.

c-c cc-cc C-C

Example
5-10-2

```
\usepackage{pstricks}
\begin{pspicture}(3,3)
  \psset{linewidth=0.5cm}
  \psline(0.25,0.25)(0.25,2.25)\rput(0.25,-0.25){-}
  \psline{c-c}(1,0.25)(1,2.25)\rput(1,-0.25){c-c}
  \psline{cc-cc}(1.75,0.25)(1.75,2.25)\rput(1.75,-0.25){cc-cc}
  \psline{C-C}(2.5,0.25)(2.5,2.25)\rput(2.5,-0.25){C-C}
\end{pspicture}
```

The keyword `arrowsize` expects a *dimension* (with or without a unit) and optionally a *factor* as its value from which the width of the arrow is calculated as follows:

The `arrowsize` key

$$width = dimension[unit] + factor * \text{\texttt{\textbackslash pslinewidth}}$$

If the *dimension* is 0, then the arrow width depends on the current line width (set by the keyword `linewidth`). If the *factor* is 0 or not present, then the arrow width is independent of the current line width.

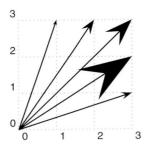

```
\usepackage{pstricks}
\begin{pspicture}[showgrid=true](3,3)
  \psline{->}(1,3)
  \psline[arrows=->,arrowsize=0pt 10](2,3)
  \psline[arrows=->,arrowsize=15pt](3,3)
  \psline[arrows=->,arrowsize=1](3,2)
  \psline[arrows=->,arrowsize=.2cm](3,1)
\end{pspicture}
```

Example
5-10-3

The arrowlength *key*   The keyword `arrowlength` sets the length of an arrow as a multiple of the arrow width. The ratio of arrow length to width is therefore preserved when a change of the `unit` value alters the scale.

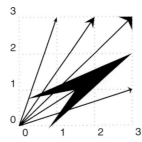

```
\usepackage{pstricks}
\begin{pspicture}[showgrid=true](3,3)
  \psset{arrows=->}
  \psline(1,3)
  \psline[arrowsize=0pt 10,arrowlength=1](2,3)
  \psline[arrowsize=15pt,arrowlength=0.5](3,3)
  \psline[arrowsize=1,arrowlength=3](3,2)
  \psline[arrowsize=.2cm,arrowlength=0.5](3,1)
\end{pspicture}
```

Example
5-10-4

The arrowinset *key*   The keyword `arrowinset` sets the depth of the notch of the arrow as a multiple of the arrow length (key `arrowlength`). The ratio of the notch depth to the arrow length is therefore preserved when a change of the `unit` value alters the scale.

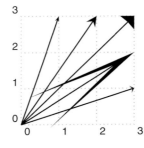

```
\usepackage{pstricks}
\begin{pspicture}[showgrid=true](3,3)
  \psset{arrows=->}
  \psline(1,3)
  \psline[arrowsize=0pt 10,arrowlength=1](2,3)
  \psline[arrowsize=15pt,arrowlength=0.5,arrowinset=0.1](3,3)
  \psline[arrowsize=1,arrowlength=3,arrowinset=0.8](3,2)
  \psline[arrowsize=.2cm,arrowlength=0.5,arrowinset=0.5](3,1)
\end{pspicture}
```

Example
5-10-5

The tbarsize *key*   The key `tbarsize` sets the width of a strut, square bracket, or round bracket line termination in the form of the dimension plus a multiple of the line width (key `linewidth`). This allows the width to depend on the current line width or not, as desired. Like the width of the arrow, this keyword accepts a *dimension* and an optional *factor* as its value using the following formula:

$$tbarsize = dimension[unit] + factor * \backslash pslinewidth$$

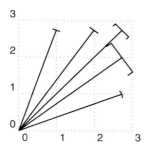

```
\usepackage{pstricks}
\begin{pspicture}[showgrid=true](3,3)
  \psline{-|}(1,2.75)
  \psline[arrows=-|,tbarsize=0pt 10](2,2.75)
  \psline[arrows={-]},tbarsize=15pt](2.75,2.75)
  \psline[arrows={-]},tbarsize=1](2.75,2)
  \psline[arrows=-),tbarsize=0.2cm](2.75,1)
\end{pspicture}
```

<table><tr><td>Example
5-10-6</td></tr></table>

The keyword `bracketlength` sets the length of a square bracket as a multiple of the bracket width.

The key
`bracketlength`

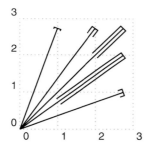

```
\usepackage{pstricks}
\begin{pspicture}[showgrid=true](3,3)
  \psline{{-]}}(1,2.75)
  \psline[arrows={-]},bracketlength=1](2,2.75)
  \psline[arrows={-]},bracketlength=5](2.75,2.75)
  \psline[arrows={-]},bracketlength=10](2.75,2)
  \psline[arrows={-]},bracketlength=0.5](2.75,1)
\end{pspicture}
```

<table><tr><td>Example
5-10-7</td></tr></table>

The keyword `rbracketlength` sets the length of a round bracket as a multiple of the bracket width.

The key
`rbracketlength`

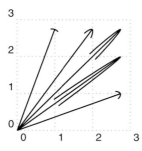

```
\usepackage{pstricks}
\begin{pspicture}[showgrid=true](3,3)
  \psline{{-)}}(1,2.75)
  \psline[arrows=-),rbracketlength=1](2,2.75)
  \psline[arrows=-),rbracketlength=5](2.75,2.75)
  \psline[arrows=-),rbracketlength=10](2.75,2)
  \psline[arrows=-),rbracketlength=0.5](2.75,1)
\end{pspicture}
```

<table><tr><td>Example
5-10-8</td></tr></table>

The keyword `arrowscale` sets a scaling factor, which scales all requested "arrows". The first value scales the width of the arrows, and second value the length (height). If only

The `arrowscale` *key*

one number is given, it applies to both the width and the height, which are then scaled equally.

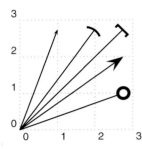

```
\usepackage{pstricks}
\begin{pspicture}[showgrid=true](3,3)
  \psline{{->}}(1,2.75)
  \psline[arrows=-),arrowscale=2](2,2.75)
  \psline[arrows={-]},arrowscale=2 3](2.75,2.75)
  \psline[arrows=->,arrowscale=3 5](2.75,2)
  \psline[arrows=-o,arrowscale=3](2.75,1)
\end{pspicture}
```

Example
5-10-9

5.10.2 Creating your own arrow types

The arrow types can be extended arbitrarily. If, for example, one wants to use the symbols defined in Section 5.8 on page 250 as "arrows", only the following additional definitions in the preamble are necessary. The new arrows are referred to as "cm" and "cp" and used in the conventional manner. The definitions are quite low level, which is the reason why they must be enclosed in \makeatletter … \makeatother (see the example).

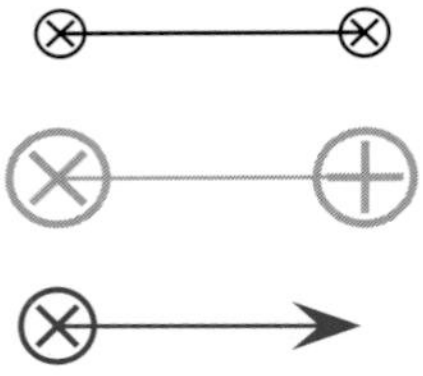

```
\usepackage{pstricks}
\makeatletter   % C4=196 and  C5=197
\newpsfontdot{CircleMultiply}[2 0.0 0.0 2 -0.78 -0.7]{Symbol}{<C4>}
\newpsfontdot{CirclePlus}[2 0.0 0.0 2 -0.78 -0.7]{Symbol}{<C5>}
\@namedef{psas@cm}{\psk@dotsize \psds@CircleMultiply 0 0 Dot}
\@namedef{psas@cp}{\psk@dotsize \@nameuse{psds@CirclePlus} 0 0 Dot}
\makeatother
\begin{pspicture}(3,2)
  \psline[arrowscale=2]{cm-cm}(0,2)(2,2)
  \psline[arrowscale=4,linecolor=red]{cm-cp}(0,1)(2,1)
  \psline[arrowscale=3,linecolor=blue]{cm->}(2,0)
\end{pspicture}
```

Example
5-10-10

In case existing characters from a font are not sufficient and it is necessary to draw the needed symbols, the task is a bit more complicated and computationally expensive. This scenario is illustrated below with a rectangle, which is symbolically assigned the arrow sign "B" for "Box".

```
% Definition of the new "arrow" type B-B
\makeatletter
\edef\pst@arrowtable{\pst@arrowtable,B-B} % add to existing arrow table
\def\tx@ABox{ABox } %                       internal PostScript name ABox
\@namedef{psas@B}{%                         internal macro name
  /ABox { %                                 PostScript procedure
    CLW mul add dup CLW sub 2 div %heed line width
    /x ED mul %                             save x value
```

```
    /y ED %                          y as well
    /z CLW 2 div def %               reserve
    x neg y moveto %                 starting point
    x neg CLW 2 div L %              lineto
    x CLW 2 div L  %                 lineto
    x y L  %                         lineto
    x neg y L  %                     lineto
    closepath %                      close the corner
    stroke 0 y moveto %              draw and go to line end
  } def
  \psk@bracketlength \psk@tbarsize \tx@ABox % width height ABox
}
\makeatother
```

At the PostScript level, it is important that the comment character % not be used immediately after a PostScript command or value. We need at least one space between two tokens.
As is well known from TeX preceding spaces have no meaning. When defining PostScript
code within a TeX document, therefore, it is important to keep in mind the different conventions of these two languages regarding white space and comments. While PostScript treats
comments as white space separating two tokens, TeX ignores comments altogether as well
as white space at the beginning of the line. Therefore one must be careful that the comment
character % doesn't follow immediately behind a PostScript command or value, but rather is
preceded by some white space; that way TeX will recognize the white space token and transfer it to the generated PostScript code.

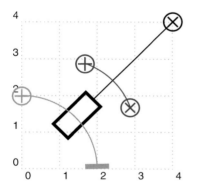

```
\usepackage{pstricks}
% cm, and cp arrows as defined in previous example
% B arrow as defined above
\begin{pspicture}[showgrid=true](4,4)
  \psset{arrowscale=3,arrows=B-cp}
  \psline[bracketlength=2](1,1)(4,4)
  \psarc[linecolor=red](0,0){2}{0}{90}
  \psarc[arrowsize=2mm,linecolor=blue]
     {cm-cp}(1,1){2}{20}{70}
\end{pspicture}
```

Example
5-10-11

5.11 Labels

The names of all **PSTricks** commands that place a label or an arbitrary object end in the
letters put. However, most of these commands have both their own syntax and their own
interpretation of their arguments.

There is only one special keyword for use with labels: `labelsep` of type *value[unit]* and   *The* `labelsep` *key*
a default of 5pt. It defines the distance between the reference point (the lower left) and the

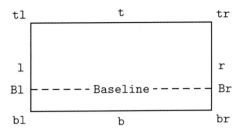

Figure 5.2: Reference point specification of a box

actual placement of the object for most label-placing commands (it doesn't affect \rput). It is also available for \psaxes and related commands from the **pst-plot** package (see Section 6.1 on page 313).

5.11.1 Reference points

Every object has a certain width, height and depth. To position it at a certain point you must specify the coordinates for this point and the reference point of the object that should be positioned there. By default, the reference point is the center of the object (box). This can be changed by specifying a letter for the horizontal and vertical alignments. **PSTricks** uses the usual shortcuts for the reference point: l for left, r for right, t for top, b for bottom, and B for baseline. Horizontal and vertical specifications can be used individually or combined as shown in Figure 5.2.

5.11.2 Rotation angle

For the specification of the rotation angle, the wind directions may be given in the form of abbreviations, summarized in Table 5.13. Those may be taken for certain angular values for simplicity's sake.

Table 5.13: Defined short forms for the rotation angles

Letter	Meaning	Counterpart
U	up	0
L	left	90
D	down	180
R	right	270
N	north	*0
W	west	*90
S	south	*180
E	east	*270

All rotation angles that have an asterisk as prefix make **PSTricks** ignore all superior rotations and execute only those rotations with an asterisk.

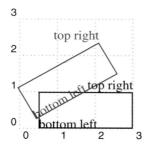

```
\usepackage{pstricks}
\begin{pspicture}[showgrid=true](3,3)
  \psframe(0.5,0)(3,1)
  \rput[lb](0.5,0){bottom left}
  \rput[br]{*0}(3,1){top right}
  \rput{30}(0,0){%
    \psframe[linecolor=blue](0.5,0)(3,1)
    \rput[lb](0.5,0){\color{blue} bottom left}
    \rput[br]{*0}(3,1){\color{blue} top right} }
\end{pspicture}
```

5.11.3 Commands to set labels or objects

> \rput * *[reference point]* *{rotation angle}* (x, y) *{object}*

\rput is a frequently used command, because it has all the properties one expects of a command that puts an arbitrary object at an arbitrary position in the coordinate system. Although a wealth of applications for this command exist, only one example is shown here.

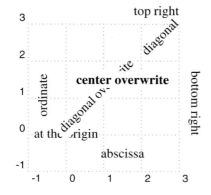

```
\usepackage{pstricks}
\begin{pspicture}[showgrid=true](-1,-1)(3,3)
  \rput[lb]{L}(-0.5,0.5){ordinate}
  \rput(1.5,-0.5){abscissa}
  \rput{*0}(0,0){at the origin}
  \rput[rB](3,3.25){top right}
  \rput[rb]{R}(3.25,0){bottom right}
  \rput*[lb]{45}{diagonal overwrite}
  \rput[rB]{45}(3,3){diagonal}
  \rput*(1.5,1.5){\textbf{center overwrite}}
\end{pspicture}
```

The starred form makes overwriting possible (see the example). The specification of a *reference point* and *rotation* angle can be omitted, in which case the center of the *object* is used as the reference point and a rotation angle of zero is selected.

> \multirput * *[reference point]* *{rotation}* (x, y) *(dx,dy)* *{n}* *{object}*

\multirput is based on \rput; executes the rotation n times, with the current point being shifted each time by (dx,dy) starting with the point (x,y). With \multirput, axis marks—including labels—can be readily placed.

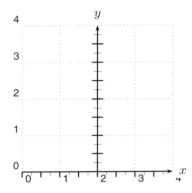

```
\usepackage{pstricks}

\begin{pspicture}[showgrid=true](4,4)
  \multirput(0,0)(0.25,0){16}{%
    \psline[linewidth=0.1pt](0,-0.1)}
  \multirput(2,0)(0,0.25){16}{%
    \psline[linewidth=0.1pt](-0.1,0)(0.1,0)}
  \multirput(0,0)(0.5,0){8}{\psline(0,-0.15)}
  \multirput(2,0)(0,0.5){8}{\psline(-0.15,0)(0.15,0)}
  \uput*[0](4,0){$x$}\uput*[90](2,4){$y$}
  \psline{->}(4,0)  \psline{->}(2,0)(2,4)
\end{pspicture}
```

Example
5-11-3

\uput ∗ *{distance}* [*direction*] *{rotation}* (x,y) {*object*}

For some applications the adjustments provided by \rput are not suitable, e.g., labeling coordinate axes or certain points in a graphic with explanatory information. Here \uput comes in handy owing to its different set of arguments: It allows you to place an *object* relative to a certain point (x,y) and optionally apply *rotation* to it, by specifying a direction *angle* and a distance (*labelsep*). The distance may also be set with the labelsep key. For often-used direction angles, mnemonic abbreviations have been predefined; these are summarized in Table 5.14.

In contrast to the LATEX conventions, the [*direction*] argument, although in square brackets, is mandatory, whereas the {*labelsep*} and {*rotation*} arguments are optional, despite their curly bracket syntax.

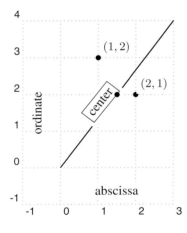

```
\usepackage{pstricks}

\begin{pspicture}[showgrid=true](-1,-1)(3,4)
  \uput{0.5}[180]{90}(0,1.5){ordinate}
  \uput*{0.5}[-90](1.5,0){abscissa}
  \psline(3,4)
  \uput*{0}[180]{52}(1.5,2){\fbox{center}}
  \qdisk(1.5,2){2pt}
  \qdisk(1,3){2pt}\uput[45](1,3){\small $(1,2)$}
  \qdisk(2,2){2pt}\uput*[45](2,2){\small $(2,1)$}
\end{pspicture}
```

Example
5-11-4

Table 5.14: Defined short forms for directions

Character	Meaning	Counterpart
r	right	0
u	up	90
l	left	180
d	down	270
ur	up-right	45
ul	up-left	135
dl	down-left	225
dr	down-right	315

`\cput` **∗** *[settings]* *{rotation}* (x,y) *{object}*

`\cput` combines the macros `\pscirclebox` (see Section 5.12.2 on page 272) and `\rput`. It always uses the center of the *object* as reference point.

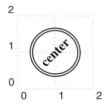

```
\usepackage{pstricks}
\begin{pspicture}[showgrid=true](2,2)
  \cput[doubleline=true]{45}(1,1){\textbf{center}}
\end{pspicture}
```

Example
5-11-5

`\multips` *{rotation}* (x,y) *(dx,dy)* *{n}* *{object}*

`\multips` is like `\multirput` except that the reference point is always the center and no starred form exists.

```
\usepackage{pstricks}
\def\myCoil{\pscurve(-0.5,0.5)(-0.1,0.45)(0.3,0)%
    (0,-0.5)(-0.3,0)(0.1,0.45)(0.5,0.5)}
\begin{pspicture}(2,0.5)
  \psset{unit=0.5,linewidth=1.5pt}
  \multips(0,0)(1,0){4}{\myCoil}
\end{pspicture}
```

Example
5-11-6

5.12 Boxes

Quite a number of **PSTricks** macros have an argument for text that is processed in restricted horizontal mode (known as LR mode in LaTeX parlance). In this mode, the argument, consisting of characters and other boxes, is concatenated to a single more or less long line. A line break is impossible with this mode, as are display formulas and vertically oriented environments, e.g., `center` and `itemize`. However, this is not really a restriction, because a `\parbox` or `minipage` can be inserted easily, so that relatively few commands cannot be used within the argument of an LR box in the end.

5.12.1 Keywords for box commands

The commands for framing boxes put their argument into an `\hbox` and place a frame around it at the PostScript level (they are analogous to LaTeX's `\fbox` command). Thus they are composite objects rather than pure graphics objects. In addition to the keys for `\psframe`, these commands use the keys listed in Table 5.15. Also, most of the line and fill keywords can still be used (see Table 5.5 on page 235).

Table 5.15: Summary of keywords for boxes

Name	Value	Default
framesep	*value[unit]*	3pt
boxsep	false|true	true
trimode	U|*U|D|*D|R|*R|L|*L	U

The `framesep` *key*   The `framesep` keyword defines the distance between the margin of the box and the inner object, similar to `\fboxsep` from standard LaTeX.

```
\usepackage{pstricks}
\psframebox{nothing}
\psframebox[framesep=10pt]{much}
\psframebox[framesep=0pt]{really}
```

Example
5-12-1

The boxsep *key*   The `boxsep` keyword determines whether the size of the final box is that of the inner object or includes the frame. It is applicable only to the commands `\psframebox`, `\pscirclebox`, and `\psovalbox`. For all others, it is always the outer frame.

When the size of the box refers to the inner object, the frame is automatically transparent to TeX, because it is not part of the box. This is especially useful when something within text or a figure should be highlighted through framing (see also Example 5-12-8 on page 273).

```
\usepackage{pstricks}
\psset{boxsep=false}
\psframebox{nothing}
\psframebox[framesep=10pt]{much}
\psframebox[framesep=0pt]{really}
```

Example
5-12-2

The trimode *key*   When using a triangle as a frame, one needs to specify how it should be oriented; the keyword `trimode` determines which direction the "tip" of the triangle points to: "U" (up), "D" (down), "R" (right), or "L" (left).

In the basic (unstarred) versions, an isosceles triangle (of minimum area) is produced, while the starred forms ("*U", "*D", "*R", and "*L") generate an equilateral triangle.

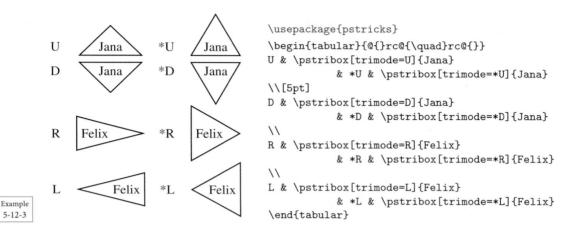

```
\usepackage{pstricks}
\begin{tabular}{@{}rc@{\quad}rc@{}}
U & \pstribox[trimode=U]{Jana}
          & *U & \pstribox[trimode=*U]{Jana}
\\[5pt]
D & \pstribox[trimode=D]{Jana}
          & *D & \pstribox[trimode=*D]{Jana}
\\
R & \pstribox[trimode=R]{Felix}
          & *R & \pstribox[trimode=*R]{Felix}
\\
L & \pstribox[trimode=L]{Felix}
          & *L & \pstribox[trimode=*L]{Felix}
\end{tabular}
```

Example
5-12-3

5.12.2 Commands for setting boxes

As mentioned earlier, the **PSTricks** box commands discussed in this section all format their arguments in LR mode and place a frame around these arguments. They differ only in the type and form of this frame.

\psframebox * [*settings*] {*contents*}

\psframebox is the simplest of all available boxes. Its starred form, in contrast to all those previously discussed, does not paint the background with the `linecolor`, but uses the `fillcolor` instead. This ability can be used to create labels with a white background very easily.

```
\usepackage{pstricks}
\begin{pspicture}(3,2)
  \pspolygon[fillcolor=lightgray,fillstyle=crosshatch,
    hatchsep=5pt](0,0)(3,0)(3,2)(1,2)
  \rput[b](1.5,0){\psframebox*[framearc=0.3]
    {\footnotesize bottom}}
  \rput[t](2,2){%
    \psframebox*[framearc=0.3]{\footnotesize top}}
\end{pspicture}
```

Example
5-12-4

\psdblframebox * [*settings*] {*contents*}

As opposed to \psframebox, the command \psdblframebox shows a double frame.

Note that with very large values for `framearc` the frame may overlap with the text, as its size is based on the *rectangular* box and frame measures.

This is an ordinary \psdblframebox*, which has line breaks because a \parbox was used!

```
\usepackage{pstricks}

\psdblframebox[framearc=0.25,framesep=10pt]{%
  \parbox{3.5cm}{\raggedright This is an ordinary
  \texttt{\textbackslash psdblframebox*}, which has
  line breaks because a \texttt{\textbackslash parbox}
  was used!%
}}
```

Example
5-12-5

\psshadowbox * *[settings]* *{contents}*

The command \psshadowbox is equivalent to \psframebox with the `shadow` key set to `true`.

\psshadowbox   \psframebox

```
\usepackage{pstricks}
\psshadowbox{\texttt{\textbackslash psshadowbox}}
\quad
\psframebox[shadow=true]
          {\texttt{\textbackslash psframebox}}
```

Example
5-12-6

\pscirclebox * *[settings]* *{contents}*

The command \pscirclebox normally creates a very big radius for a circle, because the inner, rectangular box is taken as a measure. Particularly when using the \parbox and \fbox commands or a `tabular` environment, the margins `framesep` and \fboxsep (as well as \fboxrule) or \tabcolsep, respectively, contribute to the final size of the circle. Note that using the @{} specification in the preamble argument of a `tabular` environment to avoid insertion of extra space at the outer edges of a table may have a considerable effect on the resultant size of the circle, as depicted in the next example.

A big circle   A big circle

```
\usepackage{pstricks}
\_ \pscirclebox{\rule{1pt}{1cm}} \_
\pscirclebox{\begin{tabular}{@{}c@{}}
    A big \\ circle \end{tabular}} \_
\pscirclebox{\begin{tabular}{c}
    A big \\ circle \end{tabular}} \_
```

Example
5-12-7

\cput is an alternative to \pscirclebox, if the contents should go to a particular spot (see Section 5.11.3 on page 269).

\psovalbox * *[settings]* *{contents}*

In contrast to standard LATEX's \oval command, which draws rectangles with rounded corners (and is therefore comparable to the frames generated by \psframebox), the

\psovalbox command creates a true oval (i.e., an ellipse). Again, this border may become too large when circumscribing some \parbox commands or a tabular environment (see the discussion of \pscirclebox on the facing page).

Example
5-12-8

```
\usepackage{pstricks}

\parbox{4cm}{The advertising price for this book is just
    \psovalbox[boxsep=false,linecolor=darkgray]{19.99\pounds},
    which is a very good price!}
```

\psdiabox * [settings] {contents}

\psdiabox produces a diamond-shaped frame, where the width is twice the height.

Example
5-12-9

```
\usepackage{pstricks}
\psdiabox[shadow=true]{\Large Jana}
```

\pstribox * [settings] {contents}

\pstribox puts its argument inside a triangle (isosceles or equilateral). It has already been discussed in the context of the special keyword trimode (see Section 5.12.1 on page 270).

Example
5-12-10

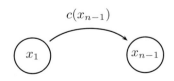

```
\usepackage{pstricks}
\pstribox[shadow=true,trimode=R]{\Large Jana}
```

5.12.3 Box size

In the box commands discussed so far, the resulting size is always determined by the box contents; i.e., different contents produce different box sizes, an effect not always desired. Only with \cnode (Section 6.2 on page 334) can equally sized circles be achieved, as shown in the next example.

$$c(x_{n-1})$$

$$x_1 \qquad x_{n-1}$$

Example
5-12-11

```
\usepackage{pstricks}
\usepackage{pst-node}
\begin{pspicture}(-0.25,-0.25)(3.25,0.5)
    \psset{nodesep=3pt,shortput=nab}
    \cnode(0,0){0.5cm}{A}\rput(0,0){$x_1$}
    \cnode(3,0){0.5cm}{B}\rput(3,0){$x_{n-1}$}
    \ncarc[arcangle=40]{->}{A}{B}^{$c(x_{n-1})$}
\end{pspicture}
```

For all other commands, one can embed the *contents* inside a \parbox, whose optional arguments allow one to adjust both its width and height. Alternatively, \makebox can be used if only the width has to be kept constant. Both commands are deployed in the following examples.

```
\usepackage{pstricks}
\newcommand\bBox[2]{\makebox[#1]{#2}}
\psframebox{\bBox{2cm}{Only constant}}
\psframebox{\bBox{2cm}{width}}
```

Example
5-12-12

The next example uses the same value for the height and the width. Alternatively one could define such commands with three arguments to allow different values.

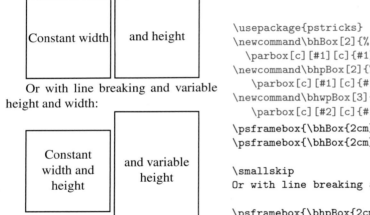

```
\usepackage{pstricks}
\newcommand\bhBox[2]{%
  \parbox[c][#1][c]{#1}{\makebox[#1]{#2}}}
\newcommand\bhpBox[2]{%
  \parbox[c][#1][c]{#1}{\centering #2}}
\newcommand\bhwpBox[3]{%
  \parbox[c][#2][c]{#1}{\centering #3}}
\psframebox{\bhBox{2cm}{Constant width}}
\psframebox{\bhBox{2cm}{and height}}

\smallskip
Or with line breaking and variable height and width:

\psframebox{\bhpBox{2cm}{Constant width and height}}
\psframebox{\bhwpBox{2cm}{3cm}{and variable height}}
```

Example
5-12-13

5.12.4 Clipping commands

As mentioned earlier, the starred form of the pspicture environment clips the picture along the nominal boundaries given by the environment's arguments. In this section we discuss other support for clipping.

\clipbox[*distance*]{*contents*}

This command puts arbitrary material into a horizontal box and chops off all "overlapping" parts a constant distance outside the nominal boundaries of the material. The extra *distance* is specified in the optional argument and defaults to 0pt. The following example demonstrates a somewhat complicated way to implement the functionality of the `pspicture*` environment.

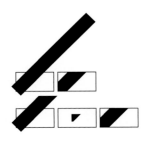

```
\usepackage{pstricks}
\newcommand*\exa[1][0pt]{%
   \fbox{\clipbox[#1]{%
      \begin{pspicture}(1,0.5)\psline(2,2)
      \end{pspicture}}}}
\psset{linewidth=10pt}
\fbox{\begin{pspicture}(1,0.5)\psline(2,2)\end{pspicture}}
\exa\\[12pt]
\exa[10pt] \exa[-10pt]
\fbox{\begin{pspicture*}(1,0.5)\psline(2,2)\end{pspicture*}}
```

```
\begin{psclip}{boundary}
... material ...
\end{psclip}
```

With this environment, arbitrary material can be clipped along the *boundary* specified as an argument. This can be any closed path; i.e., it may be built by various parts of different lines or curves, but either it should start and end at the same point or the individual segments should at least have intersection points. Otherwise, one gets unexpected results because Post-Script itself closes the path with a straight line from the last point to the first one.

In the following simple example, the closed curve is produced by a `\pscircle` command.

```
\usepackage{pstricks}
\newsavebox\TBox \savebox\TBox{\parbox{4cm}{%
The PSTricks project was started by Timothy Van Zandt long time
ago and is one of the oldest \TeX\ packages still in use.  `I
started in 1991. Initially I was just trying to develop tools
for my own use. Then I thought it would be nice to package them
so that others could use them. It soon became tempting to add
lots of features, not just the ones I needed. When this became
so interesting that it interfered with my day ``job'', I gave
up the project ``cold turkey'', in 1994.' --- Timothy Van Zandt
Other people who where involved in this project are Denis Girou,
Sebastian Rahtz, and Herbert Vo\ss}}
\begin{pspicture}(-2,-2)(2,2)
\begin{psclip}{\pscircle[linestyle=none]
                (0.5\wd\TBox,-0.15\ht\TBox){2cm}}
  \usebox\TBox
\end{psclip}
\end{pspicture}
```

em so that
ld use them. It s
ecame tempting to ad
ots of features, not just
the ones I needed. When
this became so interest-
ng that it interfered wit
· day "job", I gave
·oject "cold t"

Very often, a certain area between different mathematical functions must be marked. This can be achieved with the `\pscustom` macro and a subsequent filling of a clipping path.

The x values of the intersection points are not important here, because PostScript uses only the inner closed part of the boundary. A setting of `linestyle=none` is often useful for the clipping path, because then it doesn't affect the default drawing of the curves.

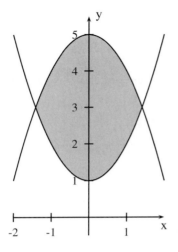

```
\usepackage{pstricks}
\usepackage{pst-plot}
\begin{pspicture}(-2,-0.5)(2,5.5)
 \begin{psclip}{%
  \pscustom[linestyle=none]{%
     \psplot{-2}{2}{x dup mul 1 add}}
  \pscustom[linestyle=none]{%
     \psplot{2}{-2}{x dup mul neg 5 add}}}
  \psframe*[linecolor=lightgray](-2,0)(2,5)
 \end{psclip}% <- % is important here
 \psaxes{->}(0,0)(-2,-0.5)(2,5.5)
 \psplot{-2}{2}{x dup mul 1 add}
 \psplot{2}{-2}{x dup mul neg 5 add}
 \uput[-90](2,0){x} \uput[0](0,5.5){y}
\end{pspicture}
```

Example
5-12-16

The clipping commands are not really robust. One troublesome situation may occur if the `psclip` environment is used in mid-text (i.e., outside some box or `pspicture` environment), and the positions of its start and end points happen to become separated by a page break. Very complicated clipping paths with a lot of different curves and placement of one clipping path inside another may also give rise to problems. In such cases, one can try to use the `\AltClipMode` declaration; this (essentially) causes an additional gsave and grestore pair to be inserted in the generated PostScript code, wrapping the clipping operation, so that the previous graphics state gets resurrected.

5.12.5 Rotating and scaling

There are three different macros to rotate LR mode material. They can be used much like the standard LATEX box commands (e.g., \mbox).

| `\rotateleft{`*contents*`}` | `\rotateright{`*contents*`}` | `\rotatedown{`*contents*`}` |

```
\usepackage{pstricks}
\Large\rotateleft{\Large Left}
\rotatedown{\Large Down}
\rotateright{\Large Right}
```

Example
5-12-17

PSTricks also defines three environments to rotate LR mode material, corresponding to the above commands. They can be used much like the standard LATEX `lrbox` environment.

```
\begin{Rotateleft} ...\end{Rotateleft}
\begin{Rotateright}...\end{Rotateright}
\begin{Rotatedown} ...\end{Rotatedown}
```

The environment forms have the advantage that one can use the verbatim mode (`\verb` and `verbatim` environment) inside their body, which is not allowed within the arguments of commands. For example, while `\rotatebox{90}{\verb/foo/}` causes an error, the form `\begin{Rotateleft}\verb/foo/\end{Rotateleft}` is permitted.

Question: Which macro creates a new page?
Answer:
\clearpage and \newpage.

Example
5-12-18

```
\usepackage{pstricks}
Question: Which macro creates a new page?\\
Answer:\\
\begin{Rotatedown}
\verb+\clearpage+ and \verb+\newpage+.%
\end{Rotatedown}
```

```
\psscalebox{scale}{contents}
\psscaleboxto(x,y){contents}
```

There are two macros to scale arbitrary content. The first one works in a way similar to the `\scalebox` command known from the standard LaTeX graphics bundle, albeit with a different syntax: if the *scale* argument consists of two numbers, the first one applies to the horizontal direction and the second to the vertical; if there is only one number, it is used for both directions, which are then scaled equally. For example, a specification of `\psscalebox{-1 1}{word}` corresponds to the `\reflectbox` command of the graphics package; it yields a horizontally mirrored image: bɹow .

By contrast, `\psscaleboxto` does not scale the material by a given factor, but rather to a target size specified in the form of a (Cartesian) coordinate pair (x, y) . If either of the values is 0, the other one is used for both dimensions.

```
\begin{Scalebox}{scale}  ...\end{Scalebox}
\begin{Scaleboxto}(x,y)...\end{Scaleboxto}
```

As in the case of rotation, there are corresponding environments for scaling, too. Hence it is possible to use the verbatim mode in the same way as shown above.

Since the contents of all these rotation and scaling environments are processed in LR mode, the spaces after the beginning and before the end are *not* ignored by PSTricks. Hence comment characters "%" must be used if such space is undesired (as shown in the examples above and below).

```
\usepackage{pstricks}
\begin{pspicture}[showgrid=true](4,1)
 \begin{Scalebox}{4} \verb+Jana+ \end{Scalebox}% <- these spaces show!
\end{pspicture}
\begin{pspicture}[showgrid=true](4,1)
```

```
\begin{Scaleboxto}(4,1)\verb+Jana+\end{Scaleboxto}
\end{pspicture}
```

Example
5-12-19

5.12.6 Math and verbatim boxes

If one desires to frame a part of a formula in math mode, TEX enters text mode beginning with `\fbox`, so that within this LR box, one needs to switch back to math mode, e.g., `$f(x)=\fbox{$x^2_3$}$`. In contrast, **PSTricks** frame boxes by default typeset their argument in math mode if they are used inside a formula.

> `\psmathboxtrue`   `\psmathboxfalse`

With `\psmathboxtrue` one can transparently use the command `\psframebox` in math mode—the default, as shown on the first line of the next example. This behavior can be switched off with `\psmathboxfalse`, from which point on those boxes would again typeset their argument in LR mode, requiring additional $ signs to reenter math mode.

$f(x) = \boxed{x_3^2}$ but $f(x) = \boxed{x_3^2}$

```
\usepackage{pstricks}
$ f(x) = \psframebox{x^2_3} $ but
\psmathboxfalse
$ f(x) = \psframebox{$x^2_3$} $
```

Example
5-12-20

However, there is the problem with inline math mode (in contrast to display math mode), in that limits are not displayed with certain operator symbols. This can be remedied by explicitly switching to `\displaystyle` whenever such a box is typeset.

> `\everypsbox{`*code*`}`

This declaration can be used to execute special *code* whenever a **PSTricks** box is typeset — e.g., `\displaystyle` in the next example. Conceivably there might be other applications for this command that are unrelated to math mode.

$f(x) = \boxed{\int_a^b \frac{x^2}{3}\,dx}$

Or with display style:

$f(x) = \boxed{\int_a^b \frac{x^2}{3}\,dx}$

```
\usepackage{pstricks}
\psmathboxtrue
$ f(x) = \psframebox{\int_a^b \frac{x^2}{3}\,dx} $

Or with display style:

\everypsbox{\displaystyle}
$ f(x) = \psframebox{\int_a^b \frac{x^2}{3}\,dx} $
```

Example
5-12-21

In the previous section, we demonstrated by several examples how to use "verbatim" material within LR mode by means of the environments provided by **PSTricks**. Analogous to the Boolean switch regarding math mode that was discussed earlier, another such switch controls the behavior with respect to verbatim material as argument for other boxes.

`\psverbboxtrue`   `\psverbboxfalse`

With `\psverbboxtrue` set, it is possible to use `\verb` inside the argument of "normal" box macros, such as `\psframebox`. It's no longer necessary to resort to using one of the environments.

Example
5-12-22

$$\boxed{\texttt{\textbackslash psframebox}}$$

```
\usepackage{pstricks}
\psverbboxtrue
\Large\psframebox{\verb+\psframebox+}
```

This behavior can be switched off with `\psverbboxfalse`, which would cause the example to raise an error message.

5.13 User styles and objects

PSTricks supports the definition of new styles to save time, and of new commands that can fill and clip arbitrary areas in a simple way. When one frequently uses a specific combination of keyword settings (Section 5.2 on page 217), one can define a named style to invoke them in one go.

`\newpsstyle{`*name*`}{`*key/value list*`}`

This declaration defines a new style that can be passed to a command by its *name* using the keyword `style`.

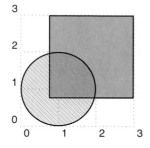

Example
5-13-1

```
\usepackage{pstricks}
\newpsstyle{TransparentMagenta}{%
    fillstyle=vlines,hatchcolor=magenta,
    hatchwidth=0.1\pslinewidth,hatchsep=1\pslinewidth}
\begin{pspicture}[showgrid=true](3,3)
    \psframe[fillstyle=solid,fillcolor=cyan](0.75,0.75)(3,3)
    \pscircle[style=TransparentMagenta](1,1){1}
\end{pspicture}
```

Another interesting application for `\newpsstyle` for the implementation of transparency was given in Section 5.9.2 on page 257.

Styles, can be applied to any object, and the resulting combination can be assigned to a command. This creates a new object with a custom style.

> \newpsobject *{name}* *{object name}* *{key/value list}*

In the example below, a new object called \dashedV is obtained by applying a particular style to the object \psline.

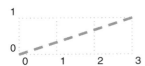

```
\usepackage{pstricks}
\newpsobject{dashedV}{psline}{linecolor=red,
    linestyle=dashed,dash=7pt 5pt,linewidth=2pt}
\begin{pspicture}[showgrid=true](3,1)   \dashedV(3,1)
\end{pspicture}
```

Example
5-13-2

Be aware that unlike the standard LATEX \new... commands, the \newpsstyle and \newpsobject commands of **PSTricks** do not warn you in case of name clashes, but simply replace the old definition with the new one.

5.13.1 Customizations with \pscustom

PSTricks provides a multitude of tools for creating graphic objects. Sometimes, however, none of the existing commands does the right job. In that case, \pscustom may be of help.

> \pscustom * [*settings*] *{arbitrary code}*

The \pscustom command expects the (almost) *arbitrary code* in its argument to produce some path. It then applies the drawing or filling operations requested in its *settings* argument (or some default operations) to that path. As usual, the starred form also fills the background with the current line color. (Whether an open path is treated as open or closed depends on the current graphic operation.) In other words, the path obtained can be rendered (i.e., stroked or filled or parqueted) in addition to or replacing what the commands generating the path already have specified.

PSTricks provides an interface to some low-level PostScript instructions through a set of special commands. This has the advantage of saving the user from having to resort to the explicit use of TEX's \special instructions. These additional commands can *only* be used in the argument of \pscustom. All of them are described in this section.

The commands introduced here interfere (practically all outside the control of **PSTricks**) with the PostScript output and should, therefore, be used only by users with a basic knowledge of the PostScript programming language. Although most of these commands are pretty low-level, they still adhere to the **PSTricks** conventions; i.e., the current point and the current units are taken into account if necessary. Within the scope of \pscustom, the coordinate system is scaled so that one unit is equal to one TEX point (1 pt) instead of one PostScript point (1 bp in TEX's terms). This fact has to be kept in mind when inserting raw PostScript code by means of the \code and \file commands.

The \pscustom command uses \pstverb (Section 5.15.2 on page 305), which writes \special instructions on the dvi file. The permissible length of the argument of \pscustom is system dependent. Problems may arise when many smaller curves are put together inside \pscustom, because they are all collected in the argument of a single \special instruction.

Since \pscustom creates only one closed path, any style keywords used must refer to that path. In the following example, \psline is executed outside and inside \pscustom. As seen from the coordinates, \psline inside \pscustom is intended to fill the lower triangle, but this does not happen because the fill keywords linewidth, linecolor, and fillstyle do not have an effect inside \pscustom. There are a few exceptions, such as when setting arrows, which are pointed out separately in the following examples.

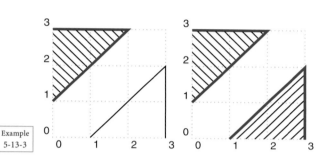

```
\usepackage{pstricks}
\begin{pspicture}[showgrid=true](3,3)
  \psline[linewidth=2pt,linecolor=blue,
    fillstyle=vlines](0,1)(2,3)(0,3)
  \pscustom{%
    \psline[linewidth=2pt,linecolor=blue,
      fillstyle=hlines](1,0)(3,2)(3,0)}
\end{pspicture}\qquad
\begin{pspicture}[showgrid=true](3,3)
  \psline[linewidth=2pt,linecolor=blue,
    fillstyle=vlines](0,1)(2,3)(0,3)
  \pscustom[linewidth=2pt,linecolor=blue,
    fillstyle=hlines]{\psline(1,0)(3,2)(3,0)}
\end{pspicture}
```

Example
5-13-3

As a rule, it is not a good idea to use keywords on commands within \pscustom. This is the reason why the left example is wrong.

The line styles dashed and dotted can cause problems, because they do not know anything about an existing path in the first place. In those cases, one of the line types from Table 5.6 on page 240 should be passed to \pscustom as a key value.

Some keywords are not available for use with \pscustom,—namely, shadow, border, doubleline, and showpoints. The keywords origin and swapaxes influence only \pscustom itself.

PSTricks distinguishes between closed curves and open curves. Since \pscustom is supposed to build a single curve, it does not make sense to use already-closed curves within \pscustom. The principal use of \pscustom is the concatenation of open curves. It helps to remember that, in general, a straight line is drawn from the end point of the previous line or curve to the start of the next one. However, a connecting line will not be drawn if the next line or curve possesses a start arrow. This can clearly be seen from the following example, where a straight connection is drawn from the end of the first arc to the start of the second arc only in the first case, which has an end arrow, and not in the second case, which has a start arrow.

Open and closed curves

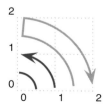

```
\usepackage{pstricks}
\begin{pspicture}[showgrid=true](2,2)
  \psset{linewidth=1.5pt,arrowscale=2}
  \pscustom[linecolor=red]{%
    \psarc(0,0){1.5}{5}{85} \psarcn{->}(0,0){2}{85}{5}}
  \pscustom[linecolor=blue]{%
    \psarc(0,0){0.5}{5}{85} \psarcn{<-}(0,0){1}{85}{5}}
\end{pspicture}
```

Example
5-13-4

Table 5.16: Meaning of the `liftpen` keyword

Value	Meaning
0	If a new line or curve does not start at the current point, a line from there to the beginning of the line or curve starts the path (default behavior).
1	The current point is not called upon with incomplete coordinates, but instead the origin of ordinates is taken. The paths are connected by a straight line.
2	Single lines or curves are treated as independent units; they do not use the current point as a beginning (with incomplete coordinates) and no line from the current point to the beginning of the next object is drawn.

The above example assumes that the arrow is specified locally, since it applies only to a single curve here. Keep in mind that the commands \psline, \pscurve, and \psbezier start with the current point when their list of arguments is "incomplete". The current point is always set to the origin of coordinates outside \pscustom by **PSTricks**. In the following example, a set of lines is created this way. Without \pscustom, three independent lines, each starting at the origin of coordinates, would have been drawn.

```
\usepackage{pstricks}
\begin{pspicture}[showgrid=true](3,2)
  \pscustom[linecolor=red,linewidth=1.5pt]{%
    \psline(1,2) \psline(2,0) \psline(3,2)}
\end{pspicture}
```

Example
5-13-5

Some graphic objects are *not* available inside\pscustom: the commands \psgrid, \psdots, \qline, and \qdisk. Closed lines or curves should *not* be used inside the argument of \pscustom; otherwise, unexpected side effects may occur.

The `liftpen` *key*   The keyword `liftpen` controls the behavior of \pscustom when several line or curve parts are to be connected by \pscustom itself. The different values possible are shown in Table 5.16.

The following example is identical to the previous one, except that now the \psline macros use `liftpen=1` as a keyword value. Therefore all lines use the origin of the coordinate system for the missing coordinate and not the current point, as they would with `liftpen=0`.

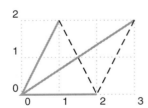

```
\usepackage{pstricks}
\begin{pspicture}[showgrid=true](3,2)
  \pscustom[linecolor=red,linewidth=1.5pt]{%
    \psline(1,2)
    \psline[liftpen=1](2,0)
    \psline[liftpen=1](3,2)}
  \psline[linestyle=dashed](1,2)(2,0)(3,2)
\end{pspicture}
```

Example
5-13-6

To clarify this somewhat complicated fact, we give another example.

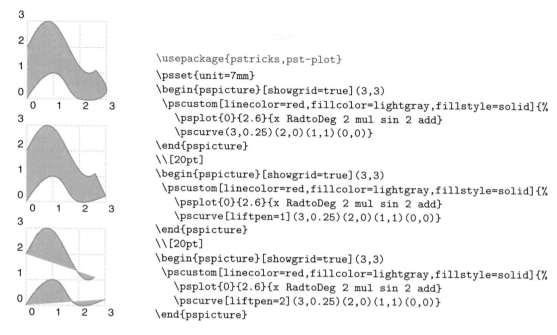

```
\usepackage{pstricks,pst-plot}
\psset{unit=7mm}
\begin{pspicture}[showgrid=true](3,3)
 \pscustom[linecolor=red,fillcolor=lightgray,fillstyle=solid]{%
    \psplot{0}{2.6}{x RadtoDeg 2 mul sin 2 add}
    \pscurve(3,0.25)(2,0)(1,1)(0,0)}
\end{pspicture}
\\[20pt]
\begin{pspicture}[showgrid=true](3,3)
 \pscustom[linecolor=red,fillcolor=lightgray,fillstyle=solid]{%
    \psplot{0}{2.6}{x RadtoDeg 2 mul sin 2 add}
    \pscurve[liftpen=1](3,0.25)(2,0)(1,1)(0,0)}
\end{pspicture}
\\[20pt]
\begin{pspicture}[showgrid=true](3,3)
 \pscustom[linecolor=red,fillcolor=lightgray,fillstyle=solid]{%
    \psplot{0}{2.6}{x RadtoDeg 2 mul sin 2 add}
    \pscurve[liftpen=2](3,0.25)(2,0)(1,1)(0,0)}
\end{pspicture}
```

Example 5-13-7

In the left example (`liftpen=0`), the end of the first curve (`\psplot`) is used as the starting point for the following curve (`\pscurve`). In the middle example (`liftpen=1`), the end of the first curve (`\psplot`) is *not* used as the starting point for the following curve (`\pscurve`), but a connecting straight line is drawn between those two points. In the right example (`liftpen=2`), neither the end of the first curve (`\psplot`) is used as the starting point for the second curve (`\pscurve`) nor a connecting line drawn, so two independent entities arise.

$\boxed{\texttt{\textbackslash moveto}(x, y)}$

This command is a direct interface to PostScript's `moveto` operator; it moves the current point to the new coordinates (x,y) without drawing a line.

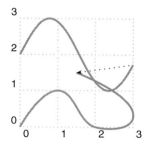

```
\usepackage{pstricks,pst-plot}
\SpecialCoor
\begin{pspicture}[showgrid=true](3,3)
  \pscustom[linecolor=red,linewidth=1.5pt]{%
     \psplot{0}{3}{x 180 mul 1.57 div sin 2 add}
     \moveto(1.5,1.5)  \pscurve(3,0.25)(2,0)(1,1)(0,0) }
  \psline[linestyle=dotted]{->}%
       (! 3 dup 180 mul 1.57 div sin 2 add)(1.5,1.5)
\end{pspicture}
```

Example 5-13-8

\newpath

The use and effect of this command are the same as for PostScript's corresponding `newpath` operator: the current path is deleted and a new one is started. All information about the old path is lost. Hence the first curve is not drawn in the following example.

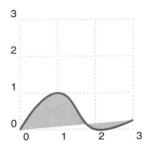

```
\usepackage{pstricks,pst-plot}
\begin{pspicture}[showgrid=true](3,3)
  \pscustom[linecolor=black!60,fillcolor=black!20,
      fillstyle=solid,linewidth=1.5pt]{%
    \psplot{0}{3}{x 180 mul 1.57 div sin 2 add}
    \newpath
    \pscurve(3,0.25)(2,0)(1,1)(0,0)}
\end{pspicture}
```

Example
5-13-9

\closepath

This is the counterpart of PostScript's `closepath` operator. The current path is closed by connecting the end point to the starting point. (Several disconnected parts can be drawn using \moveto, which will be treated independently.) The starting point is made the current point. In the following example, the starting point $(0,2)$ is made the new current point after \closepath, and consequently the following curve gets a completely different shape.

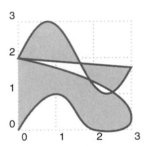

```
\usepackage{pstricks,pst-plot}
\begin{pspicture}[showgrid=true](3,3)
  \pscustom[linecolor=black!60,fillcolor=black!20,
      fillstyle=solid,linewidth=1.5pt]{%
    \psplot{0}{3}{x 180 mul 1.57 div sin 2 add}
    \closepath
    \pscurve(3,0.25)(2,0)(1,1)(0,0)}
\end{pspicture}
```

Example
5-13-10

\stroke [*settings*]

This command is *not* simply equivalent to PostScript's operator of the same name. Rather, it performs that operation non-destructively, i.e., within a pair of `gsave` and `grestore` operators, and obeying the current line drawing parameters. This means that the path just drawn is still available afterwards for further use. Hence it is possible to apply the \stroke command more than once to the same (partial) path within the body of a \pscustom macro and pass it different parameter settings each time. This fact comes in handy in special applications like the following example, where we demonstrate how lines consisting of multiple colors can be created in a simple manner: by overprinting with varying colors and decreasing line widths. While the starred form of \pscustom initializes parameters with values suitable for filling, the `linestyle` key has to be specified locally to make `\stroke` effective.

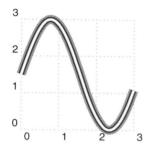

```
\usepackage{pstricks,pst-plot}
\begin{pspicture}[showgrid=true](3,3)
  \pscustom[linecolor=white,linewidth=1.5pt]{%
    \psplot{0}{3}{x 180 mul 1.57 div sin 1.5 mul 1.5 add}
    \stroke[linecolor=red,linewidth=7pt]
    \stroke[linecolor=blue,linewidth=4pt]
    \stroke[linecolor=green,linewidth=2pt]
  }
\end{pspicture}
```

Example
5-13-11

`\fill` *[settings]*

This command is *not* simply equivalent to PostScript's operator of the same name. Just as `\stroke` does, it rather performs that operation non-destructively, i.e., within a pair of `gsave` and `grestore` operators, and obeying the current filling parameters. This means that the path just filled is still available afterwards for further use. Hence it is possible to apply the `\fill` command more than once to the same (partial) path within the body of a `\pscustom` macro and pass it different parameter settings each time. In the admittedly somewhat contrived example below, we exploit this fact to apply various fillings in one go. As the operations specified with `\pscustom` itself are always applied last, the white line and light hatch pattern overprint the blue line generated by the `\stroke` command. While the unstarred form of `\pscustom` initializes parameters with values suitable for stroking, the `fillstyle` key has to be specified in order to make `\fill` effective. However, as the starred form of `\pscustom` will fill the area with the current line color and fill style at the end anyway, overprinting any previous filling, the use of `\fill` is pointless in this case.

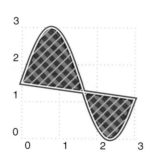

```
\usepackage{pstricks,pst-plot}
\begin{pspicture}[showgrid=true](3,3)
  \pscustom[fillstyle=hlines,hatchcolor=lightgray,
            hatchwidth=1pt,linecolor=white,linewidth=1pt]
  {\psplot{0}{3}{x 180 mul 1.57 div sin 1.5 mul 1.5 add}
    \closepath
    \fill[fillstyle=solid,fillcolor=darkgray]
    \fill[fillstyle=vlines,hatchcolor=gray,hatchwidth=3pt]
    \stroke[linecolor=blue,linewidth=3pt]
  }
\end{pspicture}
```

Example
5-13-12

`\gsave`   `\grestore`

With `\gsave` it is possible to save the current state of the PostScript stack that covers the graphical output (e.g., path details, color, line width, origin of ordinates). `\grestore` returns the graphics state to what it was when `\gsave` was called. The commands `\gsave`

and \grestore must always be used in pairs! (In addition to applying the corresponding
PostScript operators, they make up a group at the TEX level.) In the following examples, these
commands are used to fill an area without having a visible line drawn at the margin.

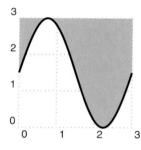

```
\usepackage{pstricks,pst-plot}
\begin{pspicture}[showgrid=true](3,3)
   \pscustom[linewidth=1.5pt]{%
      \psplot{0}{3}{x 180.0 mul 1.5 div sin 1.5 mul 1.5 add}
      \gsave
         \psline(3,3)(0,3)% is _not_ drawn
         \fill[fillcolor=lightgray,fillstyle=solid]
      \grestore }
\end{pspicture}
```

Example
5-13-13

Unlike in the earlier examples, now an area between two functions is filled. The path is built
by the sequence of function–line–function, where the last one is plotted from right to left.

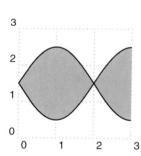

```
\usepackage{pstricks,pst-plot}
\SpecialCoor
\begin{pspicture}[showgrid=true](3,3)
   \pstVerb{/rad {180.0 mul 2 div} def}
   \pscustom[plotpoints=200]{%
      \psplot{0}{3}{x rad sin 1.5 add}
      \gsave
      \psline(! 3 dup rad sin 1.5 add)%
             (!3 dup rad sin neg 1.5 add)
      \psplot{3}{0}{x rad sin neg 1.5 add}
      \fill[fillcolor=lightgray,fillstyle=solid]
      \grestore
      \psplot[liftpen=2]{3}{0}{x rad sin neg 1.5 add} }
\end{pspicture}
```

Example
5-13-14

$\boxed{\texttt{\textbackslash translate}(x,y)}$

\translate sets the origin of ordinates to (x,y) for all subsequent graphics operations.
(This is a low-level interface to the PostScript operator of the same name.)

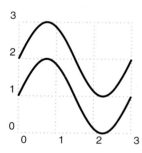

```
\usepackage{pstricks,pst-plot}
\begin{pspicture}[showgrid=true](3,3)
   \pscustom[linewidth=1.5pt]{%
      \translate(0,1)
      \psplot{0}{3}{x 180.0 mul 1.5 div sin}
      \translate(0,1)
      \psplot[liftpen=2]{0}{3}{x 180.0 mul 1.5 div sin}}
\end{pspicture}
```

Example
5-13-15

$\boxed{\texttt{\textbackslash scale\{\textit{factor} \fbox{\textit{v-factor}}\}}}$

\scale changes the size and/or proportions for all following \pscustom objects. (This is a low-level interface to the PostScript operator of the same name.) As is common practice with **PSTricks**'s scaling, the argument comprises one or two numbers. If only one *factor* is given, scaling is done proportionally; if there are two factors, they apply to the horizontal and vertical direction, respectively. Negative values result in scaling as well as reflection about the corresponding axis, as shown in the example.

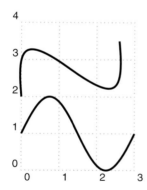

```
\usepackage{pstricks,pst-plot}
\begin{pspicture}[showgrid=true](3,3)
  \pscustom[linewidth=1.5pt]{%
    \scale{1 0.5}    \translate(0,1)
    \psplot{0}{3}{x 180.0 mul 1.5 div sin}
    \translate(0,1) \scale{1 -0.5}
    \psplot[liftpen=2]{0}{3}{x 180.0 mul 1.5 div sin}}
\end{pspicture}
```

Example
5-13-16

$\boxed{\texttt{\textbackslash rotate\{\textit{angle}\}}}$

This command rotates all following objects by the specified *angle*, which has to be given in degrees (as understood by PostScript). (This is a low-level interface to the PostScript operator of the same name.)

```
\usepackage{pstricks,pst-plot}
\begin{pspicture}[showgrid=true](3,4)
  \pscustom[linewidth=1.5pt]{%
    \translate(0,1)
    \psplot{0}{3}{x 180.0 mul 1.5 div sin}
    \translate(0,1)    \rotate{30}
    \psplot[liftpen=2]{0}{3}{x 180.0 mul 1.5 div sin}}
\end{pspicture}
```

Example
5-13-17

$\boxed{\texttt{\textbackslash swapaxes}}$

An example using \swapaxes was given in Section 5.4 on page 223, where it was used as a keyword. This command swaps the x- and y-axes, which is equivalent to

    \rotate{-90}\scale{-1 1}

This is also demonstrated in the next example.

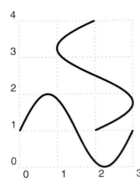

```
\usepackage{pstricks,pst-plot}
\begin{pspicture}[showgrid=true](3,4)
  \pscustom[linewidth=1.5pt]{%
    \translate(0,1)
    \psplot{0}{3}{x 180.0 mul 1.5 div sin}
    \translate(2,0)
    \swapaxes
    \psplot[liftpen=2]{0}{3}{x 180.0 mul 1.5 div sin}}
\end{pspicture}
```

Example
5-13-18

\msave   \mrestore

With this pair of macros, the currently valid coordinate system may be saved and restored, respectively. In contrast to what happens with \gsave and \grestore pairs, all other values such as line type, thickness, etc., will remain unaffected. The \msave and \mrestore commands must be used in pairs! They can be nested arbitrarily both with themselves and with \gsave and \grestore. Care must be taken to ensure that this nesting is pairwise balanced.

The next example plots the first sine function with the origin of ordinates set by \translate(0,1.5). Thereafter, the state of the coordinate system is saved, a new origin is set with \translate(1,2)[1], and another sine function is plotted. Following that, the old state is restored with \mrestore and the origin of ordinates is back at (0,1.5) again. The later cosine function is plotted with this origin.

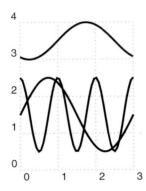

```
\usepackage{pstricks,pst-plot}
\begin{pspicture}[showgrid=true](3,4)
  \pscustom[linewidth=1.5pt]{%
    \translate(0,1.5)
    \psplot{0}{3}{x 180.0 mul 1.5 div sin}
    \msave
      \translate(1,2)
      \scale{1 0.5}
      \psplot[liftpen=2]{-1}{2}{x 180.0 mul 1.5 div sin}
    \mrestore
    \psplot[liftpen=2]{0}{3}{x 180.0 mul 0.5 div cos}}
\end{pspicture}
```

Example
5-13-19

---

[1]Referring to the current origin (0,1.5) a \translate(1,2) corresponds to the absolute coordinates (1,3.5).

\openshadow [settings]

The \openshadow command creates a copy of the current path, using the specified shadow
key values (see page 239). Whether the shadow path thus obtained is stroked or filled depends on the parameter settings supplied with \openshadow itself and/or \pscustom, as
can be seen in the example.

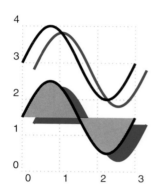

```
\usepackage{pstricks,pst-plot}
\begin{pspicture}[showgrid=true](3,4)
  \pscustom[linewidth=2pt]{%
    \translate(0,3)
    \psplot{0}{3}{x 180.0 mul 1.5 div sin}
    \openshadow[shadowsize=10pt,shadowangle=-30,
                 shadowcolor=blue]}
  \pscustom[linewidth=2pt,fillcolor=red,
             fillstyle=solid]{%
  \translate(0,1.5)
  \psplot{0}{3}{x 180.0 mul 1.5 div sin}
  \openshadow[shadowsize=10pt,shadowangle=-30,
               shadowcolor=blue]}
\end{pspicture}
```

Example
5-13-20

\closedshadow [settings]

The \closedshadow command *always* creates a filled shadow of the region enclosed by the
current path, as if it were a non-transparent environment.

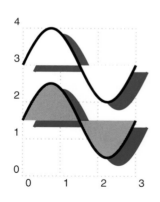

```
\usepackage{pstricks,pst-plot}
\begin{pspicture}[showgrid=true](3,4)
  \pscustom[linewidth=2pt]{%
    \translate(0,3)
    \psplot{0}{3}{x 180.0 mul 1.5 div sin}
    \closedshadow[shadowsize=10pt,shadowangle=-30,
                   shadowcolor=blue]}
  \pscustom[linewidth=2pt,fillcolor=red,
             fillstyle=none]{% <-- no effect!
  \translate(0,1.5)
  \psplot{0}{3}{x 180.0 mul 1.5 div sin}
  \closedshadow[shadowsize=10pt,shadowangle=-30,
                 shadowcolor=blue]}
\end{pspicture}
```

Example
5-13-21

The method used for producing the shadow should be noted. PSTricks simply creates a copy of the closed path, translates it according to the demands of shadowsize
and shadowangle, fills it with shadowcolor, and then refills the original path with
fillcolor, which is white by default. The \openshadow macro doesn't fill the original

path with the current `fillcolor`, so that the underlying shadow copy is visible (and in this example, not filled). The `\closedshadow` fills the original path, so that the underlying copy looks like a real shadow.

```
\usepackage{pstricks}
\begin{pspicture}(0,-0.25)(5,2)
\pscustom[fillstyle=none,shadowcolor=lightgray,fillcolor=blue]{%
  \psbezier(0,0)(1,1)(1,-1)(2,0) \psbezier(2,0)(3,1)(1,1)(2,2)
  \closepath
  \openshadow[shadowsize=10pt,fillcolor=white,shadowangle=30]}
\rput(2.5,0){%
\pscustom[fillstyle=none,shadowcolor=lightgray,fillcolor=blue]{%
  \psbezier(0,0)(1,1)(1,-1)(2,0) \psbezier(2,0)(3,1)(1,1)(2,2)
  \closepath
  \closedshadow[shadowsize=10pt,fillcolor=white,shadowangle=30]}}
\end{pspicture}
```

Example
5-13-22

This strategy is to be kept in mind when specifying, with the keyword `\pscustom`, a `fillcolor` that differs from `white`: in such cases the macro `\closedshadow` has to be given the correct fill color.

`\movepath(`dx, dy`)`

The `\movepath` command shifts the current path by (dx, dy). If the original path is needed later on, the `\movepath` operation has to be encapsulated within a `\gsave`/`\grestore` pair.

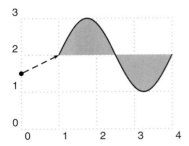

```
\usepackage{pstricks,pst-plot}
\begin{pspicture}[showgrid=true](4,3)
  \pscustom[fillcolor=lightgray,fillstyle=solid]{%
    \translate(0,1.5)
    \psplot{0}{3}{x 180.0 mul 1.5 div sin}
    \movepath(1,0.5)}
  \psline[linestyle=dashed]{*->}(0,1.5)(1,2)
\end{pspicture}
```

Example
5-13-23

$\boxed{\texttt{\textbackslash lineto}(x, y)}$

`\lineto` corresponds to `\psline(`x, y`)`, but always draws a line from the current point (which therefore has to exist) to (x,y). (This is a low-level interface to the PostScript operator of the same name.)

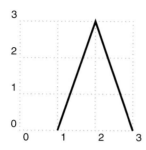

```
\usepackage{pstricks}
\begin{pspicture}[showgrid=true](3,3)
  \pscustom[linewidth=1.5pt]{%
      \psline(1,0)(2,3)
      \lineto(3,0)}
\end{pspicture}
```

$\boxed{\texttt{\textbackslash rlineto}(dx, dy)}$

`\rlineto` is similar to `\lineto(`x, y`)`, except that the coordinate pair is interpreted relative to the current point. (This is a low-level interface to the PostScript operator of the same name.)

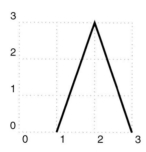

```
\usepackage{pstricks}
\begin{pspicture}[showgrid=true](3,3)
  \pscustom[linewidth=1.5pt]{%
      \psline(1,0)(2,3)
      \rlineto(1,-3)}
\end{pspicture}
```

$\boxed{\texttt{\textbackslash curveto}(x_1, y_1)\,(x_2, y_2)\,(x_3, y_3)}$

This command corresponds to `\psbezier(`x_1, y_1`)(`x_2, y_2`)(`x_3, y_3`)`, where the current point is taken as the starting point for the Bézier curve. The command expects three pairs of coordinates; otherwise, the curve can't be drawn. (This is a low-level interface to the Post-Script operator of the same name.)

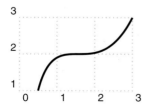

```
\usepackage{pstricks}
\begin{pspicture}[showgrid=true](0,1)(3,3)
  \pscustom[linewidth=1.5pt]{%
      \moveto(0.5,1)
      \curveto(1,3)(2,1)(3,3)}
\end{pspicture}
```

> $\texttt{\textbackslash rcurveto}(dx_1, dy_1)\,(dx_2, dy_2)\,(dx_3, dy_3)$

$\texttt{\textbackslash rcurveto}$ works like $\texttt{\textbackslash curveto}(x_1, y_1)\,(x_2, y_2)\,(x_3, y_3)$, except that all coordinate pairs are interpreted relative to the current point. The command expects three pairs of coordinates; otherwise, the curve can't be drawn. (This is a low-level interface to the PostScript operator of the same name.)

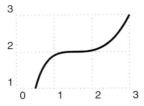

```
\usepackage{pstricks}
\begin{pspicture}[showgrid=true](0,1)(3,3)
  \pscustom[linewidth=1.5pt]{%
    \moveto(0.5,1)
    \rcurveto(0.5,2)(1.5,0)(2.5,2)}
\end{pspicture}
```

Example
5-13-27

> $\texttt{\textbackslash code}\{\textit{PostScript code}\}$

$\texttt{\textbackslash code}$ inserts the *PostScript code* specified as an argument directly into the PostScript output. This macro is identical to the internal macro $\texttt{\textbackslash addto@pscode}$ and should be preferred to directly using $\texttt{\textbackslash special}$ in any case. Note that setting $\texttt{linewidth}$ in the next example has no effect whatsoever, as the line width is explicitly overwritten inside the PostScript code later on.

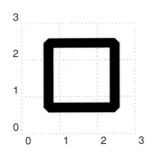

```
\usepackage{pstricks}
\begin{pspicture}[showgrid=true](3,3)
  \pscustom[linewidth=1cm]{%
    \code{
      newpath
      20 20 moveto    0 50 rlineto
      50 0 rlineto    0 -50 rlineto
      -50 0 rlineto
      closepath
      2 setlinejoin
      7.5 setlinewidth
      stroke}%
    }
\end{pspicture}
```

Example
5-13-28

> $\texttt{\textbackslash dim}\{\textit{length}\}$

$\texttt{\textbackslash dim}$ converts a *length* given in **PSTricks** terms (i.e., $\texttt{\textbackslash psunit}$ is used if necessary) into TEX's pt; the result is appended to the generated PostScript code (pushed on the stack) as a mere number. (Recall that within the scope of \pscustom, the PostScript coordinate system is scaled so that one unit is equal to one TeX point.)

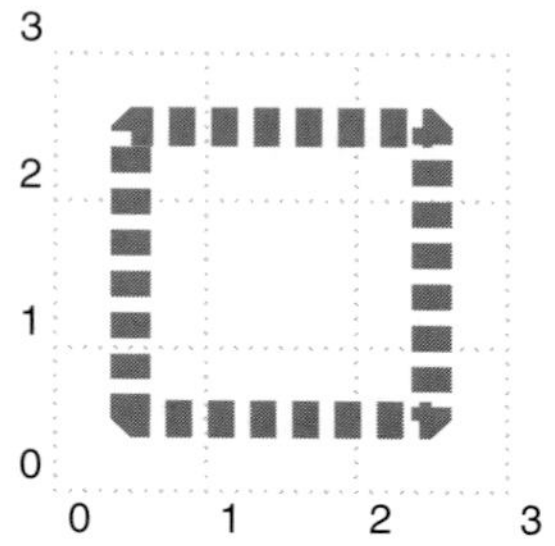

```
\usepackage{pstricks}
\begin{pspicture}[showgrid=true](3,3)
  \pscustom{%
     \code{newpath}
     \dim{0cm}\dim{-2cm} \dim{2cm}\dim{0cm}
     \dim{0cm}\dim{2cm}  \dim{0.5cm}\dim{0.5cm}
     \code{
        moveto rlineto rlineto rlineto
        closepath
        2 setlinejoin
        7.5 setlinewidth
        0.1 0.5 0.6 0.2 setcmykcolor
        [5 3] 0 setdash
        stroke}%
     }
\end{pspicture}
```

Example 5-13-29

\coor$(x_1,y_1)$ (x_2,y_2) ... (x_n,y_n)

\coor converts the specified coordinates from PSTricks terms (as usual, the current internal units are used if necessary) into TeX's pt; the results are appended to the generated PostScript code (pushed on the stack) as mere numbers. (Recall that within the scope of \pscustom, the PostScript coordinate system is scaled so that one unit is equal to one TeX point.) The use of \coor has a clear advantage over the use of \dim with several coordinates.

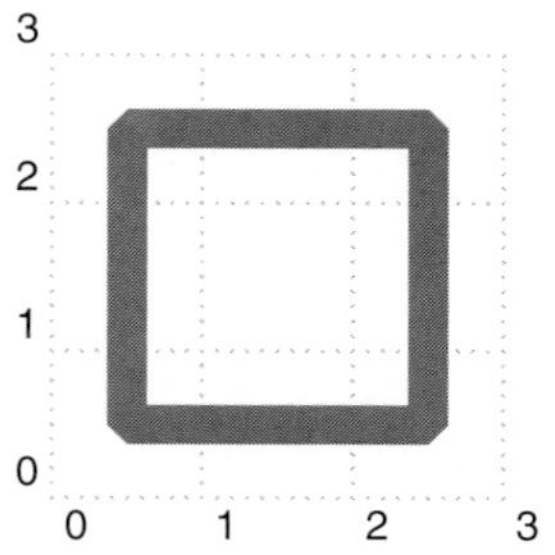

```
\usepackage{pstricks}
\begin{pspicture}[showgrid=true](3,3)
  \pscustom{%
     \code{newpath}
     \coor(0,-2)(2,0)(0,2)(0.5,0.5)
     \code{
         moveto  % 0.5 0.5
         rlineto % +0x +2y
         rlineto % +2x +0y
         rlineto % +0x -2y
         closepath % back to 0.5 0.5
         2 setlinejoin
         7.5 setlinewidth
         0.1 0.5 0.6 0.2 setcmykcolor
         stroke}%
     }
\end{pspicture}
```

Example 5-13-30

$$\boxed{\texttt{\textbackslash rcoor}(dx_1, dy_1)\ \colorbox{lightgray}{(dx_2, dy_2)}\ \dots\ (dx_n, dy_n)}$$

\rcoor is virtually identical to \coor, except that the coordinates are placed in reverse order on the stack (reverse \coor).

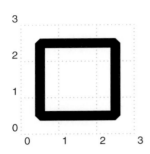

```
\usepackage{pstricks}
\begin{pspicture}[showgrid=true](3,3)
  \pscustom{%
    \code{newpath}
    \rcoor(0.5,0.5)(0,2)(2,0)(0,-2)
    \code{
      moveto rlineto rlineto rlineto
      closepath
      2 setlinejoin 7.5 setlinewidth
      stroke}}
\end{pspicture}
```

Example
5-13-31

$$\boxed{\texttt{\textbackslash file}\{\textit{file name}\}}$$

\file inserts the contents of a file (as PostScript code) without any expansion. Only comment lines starting with "%" are ignored. The following example first writes and then reads the contents of the file LGCfile.ps.

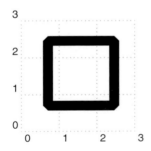

```
\usepackage{pstricks}
\begin{filecontents}{LGCfile.ps}
% demo for \file  hv 2006-05-13
newpath
20 20 moveto    0 50 rlineto
50 0 rlineto    0 -50 rlineto
-50 0 rlineto
closepath
2 setlinejoin 7.5 setlinewidth
stroke
% end
\end{filecontents}
\begin{pspicture}[showgrid=true](3,3)
  \pscustom{\file{LGCfile.ps}}
\end{pspicture}
```

Example
5-13-32

$$\boxed{\texttt{\textbackslash arrows}\{\textit{arrow type}\}}$$

\arrows defines the type of the line or curve start and line or curve end, respectively, to insert. Internally, the PostScript procedures ArrowA and ArrowB are both used, which are called as follows:

```
x2 y2 x1 y1 ArrowA
x2 y2 x1 y1 ArrowB
```

Both draw an arrow from (x_2, y_2) to (x_1, y_1). `ArrowA` sets the current point to the end of the arrowhead (where a line or curve connects) and leaves (x_2, y_2) on the stack. In contrast, `ArrowB` does not change the current point but leaves the four values (x_2, y_2, x_1', y_1') on the stack, with (x_1', y_1') being the point where a line or curve connects. The example shows that the "invisible" points are taken into account when calculating the arrow direction.

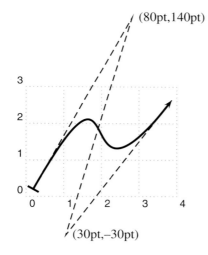

```
\usepackage{pstricks}
\SpecialCoor
\begin{pspicture}[showgrid=true](4,3)
 \pscustom[linewidth=1.5pt]{%
  \arrows{|->}
  \code{
    80 140 5 5 ArrowA     % leaves 80 140 on stack
    30 -30 110 75 ArrowB % leaves 30 -30 105.41 68.986
    curveto}}             % curve for three points
\psline[linestyle=dashed]%
  (5pt,5pt)(80pt,140pt)(30pt,-30pt)(110pt,75pt)
\uput[0](80pt,140pt){(80pt,140pt)}
\uput[0](30pt,-30pt){(30pt,--30pt)}
\end{pspicture}
```

\setcolor{color}

`\setcolor` sets the current color. Only previously defined color names can be used in the argument.

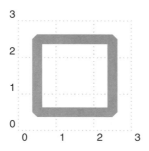

```
\usepackage{pstricks}
\begin{pspicture}[showgrid=true](3,3)
  \pscustom[linewidth=1.5pt]{%
    \code{newpath}
    \rcoor(0.5,0.5)(0,2)(2,0)(0,-2)
    \setcolor{red}
    \code{
      moveto rlineto rlineto rlineto
      closepath
      2 setlinejoin 7.5 setlinewidth
      stroke}}
\end{pspicture}
```

5.14 Coordinates

PSTricks provides Cartesian coordinates in its default setup. If the need arises, however, you can turn on the parsing of coordinate arguments to allow a number of variants for coordinate specification; these variants are distinguished by their syntax.

In general, one can switch back and forth between "normal" (i.e., Cartesian) and "special" coordinates within a document or, more precisely, even within a pspicture environment.

\SpecialCoor	\NormalCoor

If \SpecialCoor is activated, an internal analysis is carried out for each coordinate argument to find out what form of coordinate specification is being used. When processing complex pictures with Cartesian coordinates, \NormalCoor will speed things up considerably. However, given the power of today's computers, speed is rarely an issue, so in most circumstances the global activation of \SpecialCoor is quite feasible. The various syntax forms that are recognized when \SpecialCoor is in effect are presented in Table 5.17.

For the specification of angles in arguments (i.e., usually within curly braces), the activation of \SpecialCoor enables further syntax variants, too. These are summarized in Table 5.18.

5.14.1 Polar coordinates

(*radius*; *angle*): As is common practice in mathematics, polar coordinates specify a point by a *radius* (i.e., its distance from the origin) and an *angle* (its direction relative to the positive x-axis; counter-clockwise by default). The default unit for the *radius* is given by the value of the runit keyword in effect. The *angle* is always a mere number; its interpretation depends on the unit specified by means of a \degrees [*full circle*] command, as explained in Section 5.2.2 on page 218. In either case, PSTricks's built-in default applies if there hasn't been a declaration earlier.

```
\usepackage{pstricks,multido}
\SpecialCoor
\begin{pspicture}[showgrid=true](-1,-1)(1,1)
  \psdots[linecolor=blue](1;0)(1.414;45)(.5;90)
    \multido{\iAngle=18+18}{19}{\psdot(1;\iAngle)}
\end{pspicture}
```

Example
5-14-1

5.14.2 Coordinates calculated with PostScript

(!*ps*): The PostScript expression *ps* has to leave a pair of values ($x\ y$) on the stack (without a comma). These coordinates refer to the scale specified by the keywords xunit and yunit,

Table 5.17: Possible coordinate forms with enabled \SpecialCoor

Syntax	Explanation	Example
(x,y)	Cartesian coordinates (default).	(2,-3)
$(r;\alpha)$	Polar coordinates.	(2;-60)
$(!\,PostScript\ code)$		(! 2 sin -20 cos)
	The arbitrary PostScript code is expected to leave two values for x and y on the stack, given in terms of **PSTricks**'s current xunit and yunit, respectively.	
$(coord\,1\,|\,coord\,2)$		(2;35|3,-4)
	The x value is taken from the first coordinate specification and the y value is taken from the second specification, where any of the other forms supported may be used. (In this example the polar coordinates "{2;35}" are converted to Cartesian coordinates first.)	
$(node\ name)$		(A)
	The geometrical center of an arbitrary previously defined node.	
$(\,[parameters]\ node\ name)$		([nodesep=-1]A)
	The coordinates are determined relative to the geometrical center of the node and translated according to the specifications given by the parameters, which refer to the angle, a horizontal (nodesep), and a vertical (offset) translation (see the example).	
$(\,[parameters]\,\{node\,2\}node\,1)$		([nodesep=-1]BA)
	The coordinates are determined relative to the geometrical center of *node 1* and translated according to the specifications given by the parameters, which refer to the angle, a horizontal (nodesep, Xnodesep, and Ynodesep), and a vertical (offset) translation, which is given by the virtual line from *node 2* to *node 1* (see the example).	

Table 5.18: Possible angle specifications with enabled \SpecialCoor

Syntax	Explanation	Example
angle	A numerical value is given in units as established by the \degrees declaration (default).	{90}
!*PostScript code*		{! 1 -2 atan}
	The arbitrary PostScript code is expected to leave a single value α on the stack. (Here, too, **PSTricks**' current angle unit is taken into account.)	
(x,y)	A coordinate pair represents a vector pointing in the direction that corresponds to the angle satisfying $\tan\alpha = y/x$.	{(3,-4)}

respectively. The following example shows the conversion of a given polar coordinate specification to an $x\ y$ number pair.

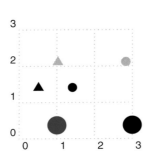

```
\usepackage{pstricks,pst-node}
\SpecialCoor
\begin{pspicture}[showgrid=true](3,3)
  \psset{dotscale=2,xunit=2,yunit=1.5} \psdot(2;45)
  \psdot[linecolor=cyan](! 2 45 cos mul 2 45 sin mul)
  \psset{dotstyle=triangle*}            \psdot(1.5;70)
  \psdot[linecolor=cyan](! 1.5 70 cos mul
                           1.5 70 sin mul)
  \pnode(0.5,0.25){A}\pnode(1.5,0.25){B}
  \psset{dotscale=4}
  \psdot[dotstyle=*,linecolor=blue](A)
  \psdot*[dotstyle=o](B)
\end{pspicture}
```

Example
5-14-2

In the next example PostScript's `rand` function is used twice to generate a sample of
coordinates at random and then a third time to determine the print color for each dot individually. This routine produces a random integer, which is then converted by the following
operations into a real number limited to a certain interval: $[0, 3]$ in the case of the coordinates and $[0, 1]$ for the color.

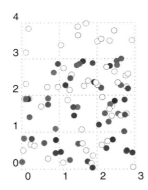

```
\usepackage{pstricks}
\SpecialCoor
\begin{pspicture}[showgrid=true](3,4)
 \psset{dotscale=1.25}
 \multips(0,0){50}{%
  \psdot(! rand 301 mod 100 div
   rand 301 mod 100 div rand 101
   mod 100 div 0.6 0.1 0.1 setcmykcolor)
  \psdot[dotstyle=o](! rand 301 mod 100 div
   rand 401 mod 100 div rand 101
   mod 100 div 0.6 0.1 0.1 setcmykcolor)}
\end{pspicture}
```

Example
5-14-3

5.14.3 Double coordinates

(*point1 | point2*): The x coordinate is taken from the first point and the y coordinate from
the second. The ability to compose a coordinate pair from two given points is especially useful for intersections, where one does not necessarily know both coordinates. The following
simple example illustrates this behavior. Here, for instance, the coordinates of the nodes A
and B are unknown, since the positions of the centers of the two words "PSTricks" and "PS"

are not determined. Yet with the use of double coordinates, vertical lines that possess the relevant x coordinates can be drawn without further ado.

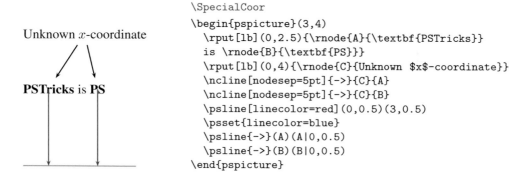

```
\usepackage{pstricks,pst-node}
\SpecialCoor
\begin{pspicture}(3,4)
  \rput[lb](0,2.5){\rnode{A}{\textbf{PSTricks}}
  is \rnode{B}{\textbf{PS}}}
  \rput[lb](0,4){\rnode{C}{Unknown $x$-coordinate}}
  \ncline[nodesep=5pt]{->}{C}{A}
  \ncline[nodesep=5pt]{->}{C}{B}
  \psline[linecolor=red](0,0.5)(3,0.5)
  \psset{linecolor=blue}
  \psline{->}(A)(A|0,0.5)
  \psline{->}(B)(B|0,0.5)
\end{pspicture}
```

Example
5-14-4

Alternatively, one could have defined new nodes to be able to use the nodesep keyword with \ncline (see Section 6.2.4 on page 350).

5.14.4 Relative translations

Using relative translations, it becomes possible to use points that make specified horizontal and vertical displacements from a target point. An explanation of the lines in Example 5-14-5 is given in Table 5.19 on page 301.

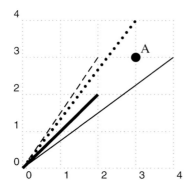

```
\usepackage{pstricks,pst-node}
\SpecialCoor
\begin{pspicture}[showgrid=true](4,4)
  \pnode(3,3){A}
  \psdot[dotscale=2](A)
  \uput[45](A){A}
  \psline([nodesep=1]A)
  \psline[linestyle=dashed]([nodesep=-1]A)
  \psline[linestyle=dotted,
    linewidth=0.08]([offset=1]A)
  \psline[linewidth=0.08]([nodesep=-1,
    offset=-1]A)
\end{pspicture}
```

Example
5-14-5

An additional effect can be achieved with the angle keyword, which rotates the coordinate system used at the target point prior to applying the nodesep and offset shifts.

The meanings of the arguments used in the next example are given in Table 5.20 on the next page.

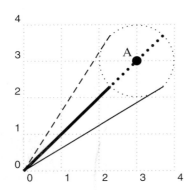

```
\usepackage{pstricks,pst-node}
\SpecialCoor
\begin{pspicture}[showgrid=true](4,4)
   \pnode(3,3){A}
   \psdot[dotscale=2](A)
   \uput[135](A){A}
   \pscircle[linestyle=dotted](A){1}
   \psline([nodesep=1,angle=-45]A)
   \psline[linestyle=dashed]([nodesep=-1,angle=-45]A)
   \psline[linestyle=dotted,linewidth=0.08]%
       ([offset=1,angle=-45]A)
   \psline[linewidth=0.08]([offset=1,angle=135]A)
\end{pspicture}
```

Example
5-14-6

The next example is a bit more complicated, since a third point is used to control the relative translation: the coordinate system used at the target point for the nodesep and offset shifts is rotated to make the positive x-axis point in the direction of the ancillary point. In contrast to this behavior, the Xnodesep and Ynodesep keywords refer to the original coordinate system. These features are especially useful to extend a line beyond a given end point or to locate a point somewhere on given line. Table 5.21 on the facing page gives additional explanations of the particular lines from Example 5-14-7.

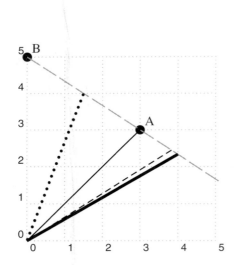

```
\usepackage{pstricks,pst-node}
\SpecialCoor
\begin{pspicture}[showgrid=true](5,5)
   \pnode(3,3){A}\psdot[dotscale=2](A)
   \uput[45](A){A}
   \pnode(0,5){B}\psdot[dotscale=2](B)
   \uput[45](B){B}
   \psline[linestyle=dashed,
       dash=0.4 0.1,linecolor=red]%
       (B)([nodesep=-2.5]{B}A)
   \psline(A)
   \psline[linestyle=dashed]([nodesep=-1]{B}A)
   \psline[linewidth=0.08]([Ynodesep=-1]{B}A)
   \psline[linestyle=dotted,linewidth=0.08]%
       ([Xnodesep=1]{B}A)
\end{pspicture}
```

Example
5-14-7

Table 5.19: Relative point translation in Example 5-14-5

Command	Explanation
`\psline([nodesep=1]A)`	Line from $(0,0)$ to $(x_A + 1, y_A)$.
`\psline[linestyle=dashed]([nodesep=-1]A)`	Line from $(0,0)$ to $(x_A - 1, y_A)$.
`\psline[linestyle=dotted,linewidth=0.08]([offset=1]A)`	Line from $(0,0)$ to $(x_A, y_A + 1)$.
`\psline[linewidth=0.08]([nodesep=-1,offset=-1]A)`	Line from $(0,0)$ to $(x_A - 1, y_A - 1)$.

Table 5.20: Relative point translation with angle specification in Example 5-14-6

Command	Explanation
`\psline([nodesep=1,angle=-45]A)`	Line from $(0,0)$ to $(1; -45°)$ with A as center.
`\psline[linestyle=dashed]` `([nodesep=-1,angle=-45]A)`	Line from $(0,0)$ to $(-1; -45°)$ with A as center.
`\psline[linestyle=dotted,linewidth=0.08]` `([offset=1,angle=-45]A)`	Line from $(0,0)$ to $(1; 45°)$ with A as center.
`\psline[linewidth=0.08]` `([offset=1,angle=135]A)`	Line from $(0,0)$ to $(1; -135°)$ with A as center.

Table 5.21: Relative point translation with reference to a third point in Example 5-14-7

Command	Explanation
`\psline[linestyle=dashed,dash=0.4 0.1,linecolor=red](B)([nodesep=-2.5]{B}A)`	
	Line from B to $(x_A + \Delta x, y_A + \Delta y)$, where $\sqrt{(\Delta x)^2 + (\Delta y)^2} = 2.5$ and the end point lies on the line $\overline{AB}$.
`\psline(A)`	"Normal" line from $(0,0)$ to (A).
`\psline[linestyle=dashed]([nodesep=-1]{B}A)`	
	Line from $(0,0)$ to $(x_A + \Delta x, y_A + \Delta y)$, where $\sqrt{(\Delta x)^2 + (\Delta y)^2} = 1$ and the end point lies on the line $\overline{AB}$.
`\psline[linewidth=0.08]([Ynodesep=-1]{B}A)`	
	Line from $(0,0)$ to $(x_A + \Delta x, y_A - 1)$, where Δx is chosen so that the end point lies on the line $\overline{AB}$.
`\psline[linestyle=dotted,linewidth=0.08]([Xnodesep=1]{B}A)`	
	Line from $(0,0)$ to $(x_A + 1, y_A + \Delta y)$, where Δy is chosen so that the end point lies on the line $\overline{AB}$.

5.14.5 Angle specifications

In the following example, {-1,1} is used for the first \psarc macro instead of an explicit angle specification; it corresponds to an angle of $\alpha = \arctan \frac{1}{-1} = 135$ degrees. The point P{-1,1} need not be part of the arc itself, as can clearly be seen in the example.

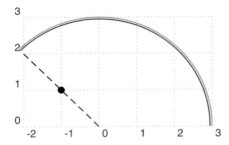

```
\usepackage{pstricks}
\SpecialCoor
\begin{pspicture}[showgrid=true](-2,0)(3,3)
  \psarc[linecolor=red](0,0){3}{0}{(-1,1)}
  \psarc[linecolor=blue](0,0){2.95}{0}{135}
  \psdot[dotscale=1.5](-1,1)
  \psline[linestyle=dashed](-2,2)
\end{pspicture}
```

Example
5-14-8

5.15 The PSTricks core

In this section, we discuss a few fundamental aspects of PSTricks, which will not necessarily be of importance to every user and which one normally encounters only when creating complex graphics. Those who want to develop PSTricks-related macros or packages of their own will find some vital information in this section.

5.15.1 Header files

In principle, a PostScript header (prologue) file is similar to a TEX macro file (e.g., a style or package file in LATEX terms), in that it contains application-specific definitions of routines, variables, and constants that can be referred to later, albeit at the PostScript level. The driver program will put a copy of the contents of each requested header file into the generated PostScript output, at the beginning of the file. The inclusion of such header files is demanded by means of TEX's \special primitive or with the PSTricks-specific \pstheader command, using the following syntax:

> \special{header=*header file*}
> \pstheader{*header file*}

Basically, a package writer is not forced to create a header file, although many authors of PSTricks packages choose to use this technique. It is advantageous in that one can put all definitions of PostScript routines in this separate file, thereby making the TEX package file more readable. At the same time, it reduces the processing overhead considerably, both at the TEX and at the driver stages, since otherwise those definitions would have to be passed on via \special commands.

PSTricks header files usually have the file name extension .pro. In a TEX system conforming to TDS, files in the PSTricks core are located in the $TEXMF/dvips/pstricks/ directory—e.g., pst-dots.pro, pst-node.pro, pstricks.pro.

In most cases the semantics of the PostScript code output via \special commands is determined only by the definitions contained in the header files. Thus these files represent the principal obstacle to processing TEX documents that contain PostScript-specific code with pdfTEX [126].

5.15.2 Special macros

```
\PSTricksOff
```

This macro turns off all **PSTricks**-specific output by redefining some low-level macros. The document can then be viewed with any dvi viewer. Also the creation of PDF files should be possible without problems. Especially with heavy use of **PSTricks** macros, this is only a temporary solution to get a quick overview over the plain text, because all the **PSTricks** output is suppressed. In particular, the following macros are changed into "no-ops" that "eat" their arguments: \pstheader, \pstverb, and \pstVerb. Additionally, \PSTricksfalse is set. A corresponding \PSTricksOn command does not exist.

```
\KillGlue        \DontKillGlue
```

Within a pspicture environment, all white space is removed between **PSTricks** objects. This—usually rubber—space is denoted as "glue" in the TEX terminology. Outside the pspicture environment, every object is treated as a single character, thus preserving white space. This outcome can sometimes be undesired — for example, within a LATEX picture environment. In such cases, white space can be ignored or preserved with the switch \KillGlue or \DontKillGlue, respectively.

<table>
<tr><td>Example
5-15-1</td><td></td><td>

```
\usepackage{pstricks}
\begin{pspicture}(3,2)
\KillGlue
\psframe*[linecolor=lightgray,shadow=true,shadowcolor=red,%
   shadowangle=90,shadowsize=15pt](3,1.75)
\quad% <---!!!!---
\psframe[fillcolor=white,fillstyle=solid,%
   framearc=0.5,shadow=true](1.25,0.25)(2.8,1.5)
\end{pspicture}
```

</td></tr>
<tr><td>Example
5-15-2</td><td></td><td>

```
\usepackage{pstricks}
\begin{pspicture}(3,2)
\DontKillGlue
\psframe*[linecolor=lightgray,shadow=true,shadowcolor=red,%
   shadowangle=90,shadowsize=15pt](3,1.75)
\quad% <---!!!!---
\psframe[fillcolor=white,fillstyle=solid,%
      framearc=0.5,shadow=true](1.25,0.25)(2.8,1.5)
\end{pspicture}
```

</td></tr>
</table>

`\pslbrace`   `\psrbrace`

The curly braces { and } play a vital role in the PostScript language, just as in (LA)TEX. Hence macro programmers need to send these characters to the PostScript output quite frequently. Sometimes it is difficult — if not a nuisance — to prevent them from being interpreted by TEX in its own way. The `\pslbrace` and `\psrbrace` macros come in handy to cope with this situation. They essentially represent curly braces "in disguise" — i.e., with a different category code that makes TEX treat them as ordinary characters (just like other punctuation symbols).

`\space`

This standard LATEX macro expands to a single space. (It has been part of the TEX folklore since the olden days of plain TEX.) Since TEX's parser ignores spaces after control words, macro programmers often need to (re)insert a space character after command names in an expansion context (i.e., inside `\edef`, `\write`, or `\special`). Such situations frequently arise when pieces of PostScript code are generated on the fly, as the PostScript syntax rules stipulate that tokens be separated by "white space" characters.

For instance, consider the following snippet of code, which might occur as a part of "special coordinates" (see Section 5.14.2 on page 296):

```
\psk@lineAngle abs 0 gt
```

Given the definition `\def\psk@lineAngle{20}`, TEX would yield the following expansion:

```
20abs 0 gt
```

To remedy this faulty PostScript instruction, one either has to supply a space with the macro being expanded (i.e., `\def\psk@lineAngle{20␣}`) or, if that is beyond the control of the programmer, employ the `\space` macro as follows:

```
\psk@lineAngle\space abs 0 gt
```

Either approach would produce the desired result:

```
20 abs 0 gt
```

`\altcolormode`

It has been pointed out several times (e.g., Section 5.1.3 on page 216) that the cooperation between (LA)TEX and the color packages color and xcolor on the one hand and PSTricks on the other hand is not without problems, because TEX does not have any built-in concept for coloring its output. In addition, the aforementioned packages and PSTricks do not use a unified syntax. Thus problems with color usage may arise when the user does not follow certain guidelines (see Section 5.1.3 on page 216). In some situations the `\altcolormode` declaration may resolve such conflicts. It redefines some internal macros so that they (among other things) take care of saving the PostScript graphics state with gsave prior to setting a color and restoring the state with grestore at the end of the TEX group. (However, with this variant of color setting, the scope of color commands should not reach beyond page boundaries.)

```
\addto@pscode{PostScript code}        \code{PostScript code}
\pstverb{PostScript code}             \pstVerb{PostScript code}
\pst@Verb{PostScript code}            \pstverbscale
```

Several macros can be used to contribute to the generated PostScript code.

\addto@pscode   This macro appends the *PostScript code* to the code accumulated for the current **PSTricks** object. It is used at various places by **PSTricks** internally and may also be useful to programmers for defining more involved macros.

\code   This macro may be used only within the argument of \pscustom; it is explained in Section 5.13.1 on page 292.

\pstverb   This macro sends the *PS code* directly to the PostScript output, but has the driver wrap it in a gsave/grestore pair and establish a standard PostScript coordinate system, albeit with the origin at TEX's *current point*.

\pstVerb   This macro, like the previous one, sends the PostScript *code* directly to the PostScript output, but does not change the current state of the graphical layer settings, such as origin, scale, etc. (With the **dvips** driver, this corresponds to TEX's coordinate system; i.e., the origin is located one inch down and right from the top-left corner of the paper, and one unit is equal to one pixel.)

\pst@Verb   This macro is like \pstVerb, but wraps the PostScript *code* so that the **PSTricks** dictionary (defined in pstricks.pro) is the current one.

\pstverbscale   When used within the argument of \pstVerb, this macro restores a standard PostScript coordinate system, albeit with the origin translated to TEX's *origin*. (It uses a special dictionary defined in special.pro.)

The following example demonstrates the use of these commands.

```
\usepackage{pstricks}
Theoretically, both macros should draw the same filled square, as the
absolute coordinates are the same. But two different squares are drawn,
appearing in different places on the page, the small dark blue one
(pstverb)\pstverb{newpath 20 -20 moveto
         40 0 rlineto  0 40 rlineto -40 0 rlineto 0 -40 rlineto
         0.8 setgray  fill }%
       \pstVerb{newpath 20 -20 moveto
         40 0 rlineto  0 40 rlineto -40 0 rlineto 0 -40 rlineto
         1 0.56 0 0 setcmykcolor fill }%
```

```
(pstVerb) outside of the text area and the big grey square amidst this
paragraph. The text ``(pstverb)(pstVerb)''{} is placed correctly at the
current text position.  However, the text afterwards is changed to blue
used in the book ($1\,0.56\, 0\, 0\,$ as CMYKa color).  Only a
\black\verb+black+ command switches this back here.  Additionally, two
different-sized squares are drawn, which is a problem with the
\verb+dvips+ program, because it does not reset all values properly.
With V\TeX{} both squares are of equal size, but on different positions.
```

Theoretically, both macros should draw the same filled square, as the absolute coordinates are the same. But two different squares are drawn, appearing in different places on the page, the small dark blue one (pstverb)(pstVerb) outside of the text area and the big grey square amidst this paragraph. The text "(pstverb)(pstVerb)" is placed correctly at the current text position. However, the text afterwards is changed to blue used in the book (1 0.56 0 0 as CMYKa color). Only a `black` command switches this back here. Additionally, two different-sized squares are drawn, which is a problem with the `dvips` program, because it does not reset all values properly. With VTEX both squares are of equal size, but on different positions.

Example
5-15-3

\pstVerb provides the ability to write **PSTricks**-compatible PostScript code to the PostScript output, while \pstverb exclusively writes local PostScript-compatible code, which is embedded within the gsave - grestore pair. Both macros correspond to the \special commands, e.g., for the **dvips** driver:

```
\pstverb → \special{" ...}
\pstVerb → \special{ps: ...}
```

In the following example, some of the trigonometrical constants are used. Instead of inserting them as number values or defining them within the argument of \psplot, we can write them with \pstVerb to the PostScript output prior to the \psplot command, locally inside the pspicture environment. This has the advantage that the constants are defined only once, and not for each and every calculated point. This would not work with \pstverb, because the values then declared as local would not be known to **PSTricks** after that command finished.

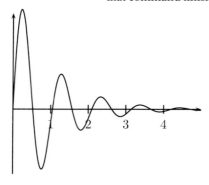

```
\usepackage{pstricks,pst-plot}
\psset{yunit=3.5,plotpoints=200}
\begin{pspicture}(-0.5,-0.75)(5,0.75)
  \pstVerb{%
    /euler 2.718281828 def
    /pi 3.141592654 def
    /rad {180 div pi mul } def
    /deg {pi div 180 mul } def }
  \psplot{0}{5}{euler x neg exp x 6 mul deg sin mul}
  \psaxes{->}(0,0)(0,-0.5)(5,0.75)
\end{pspicture}
```

Example
5-15-4

Table 5.22: Some basic PostScript procedures from `pstricks.pro`

Short Form	Definition
T	`/T /translate load def`
CLW	`/CLW /currentlinewidth load def`
PtoC	`/PtoC { 2 copy cos mul 3 1 roll sin mul } def`
L	`/L /lineto load def`

`\pst@def{`*name*`} < `*PS code*` >`

Although this macro is intended for internal use only, it is like an interface to PostScript. By contrast, the macro `\tx@`*name* is a synonym for a PostScript code sequence that can be used inside TEX when defining another PostScript-related code. These functions are normally addressed indirectly, by means of an internal TEX macro. This macro is then redefined by a `\pst@def` declaration, not the PostScript function itself. (Therefore this mechanism is less efficient than a redefinition at the PostScript level.) Example 6-1-34 on page 327 demonstrates how to employ the `\pst@def` macro.

5.15.3 "Low-level" macros

PSTricks recognizes four types of objects:

```
\begin@OpenObj    ... \end@OpenObj    % with arrows
\begin@AltOpenObj ... \end@OpenObj    % without arrows
\begin@ClosedObj  ... \end@ClosedObj
\begin@SpecialObj ... \end@SpecialObj
```

The names of these object macros indicate the type of path generated. Open objects come in two flavors: one for drawing paths with arrows and an alternative form for use without arrows. Special objects include the "quick" variants of some path-drawing commands, such as `\qline` and `\psgrid`.

We will now explore the structure of such an object with an example. To draw a hexagon with PSTricks is not a problem, as is generally known, yet several lines of code are required to do so. With repeated use of this code, the desire to define our own macro `\psHexagon` might arise. The only special (private) option in this case has to handle the question of whether the given radius refers to the inscribed circle or to the circumscribed one. Since this is a yes/no question, the obvious thing to do is to define a Boolean variable using the key/value interface. Thus our intention is to define a command `\psHexagon` with the following syntax:

`\psHexagon` ✳ [*settings*] (x, y) {*radius*}

The code needed to define this command is displayed below. Some PostScript procedures are used there, which are defined in the PSTricks header file `pstricks.pro`. They are listed in Table 5.22 and explained in more detail in [128].

```
\makeatletter
%------------ boolean key + its default --------------------
\newif\ifHRInner
\def\psset@HRInner#1{\@nameuse{HRInner#1}}
\psset@HRInner{false}
% ------------ pstricks object (command) --------------------
\def\psHexagon{\pst@object{psHexagon}}
\def\psHexagon@i{\@ifnextchar(%              center specified?
    {\psHexagon@ii}{\psHexagon@ii(0,0)}}
\def\psHexagon@ii(#1)#2{%
  \begin@ClosedObj%                          begin closed object
    \pst@@getcoor{#1}%                        get center
    \pssetlength\pst@dimc{#2}%                set radius to pt
    \addto@pscode{%                           PostScript
      \pst@coor T %                           xM yM new origin
      \psk@dimen CLW mul %                     set line width
      /Radius \pst@number\pst@dimc\space %    save radius
        \ifHRInner\space 3 sqrt 2 div div \fi % inner?
      def
      /angle \ifHRInner 30 \else 0 \fi def %  starting angle
      Radius angle PtoC moveto %               go to first point
      6 { %                                    6 iterations
          /angle angle 60 add def %              alpha = alpha+60
          Radius angle PtoC L %                  line to next point
        } repeat
      closepath }%                            closed object
    \def\pst@linetype{3}%                      set linetype
    \showpointsfalse%                          do not show base points
  \end@ClosedObj%                             end
  \ignorespaces}%                             swallow any spaces in input
\makeatother
```

PSTricks objects defined in this way can be used in the same way as other PSTricks objects. For instance, we can make use of standard keywords as shown in the next two examples.

```
\usepackage{pstricks}
% \psHexagon as defined above
\psset{unit=7mm}
\begin{pspicture}(-3,-3)(3,3)
  \psHexagon[linewidth=3pt,linecolor=red]{2.5}
  \pscircle[linestyle=dashed,linecolor=red]{2.5}
%
  \psHexagon[linewidth=3pt,linecolor=blue,%
    HRInner=true]{2.5}
  \pscircle[linestyle=dashed,linecolor=blue]{2.17}
\end{pspicture}
```

Example
5-15-5

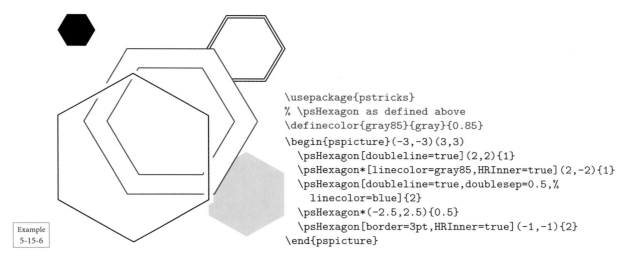

```
\usepackage{pstricks}
% \psHexagon as defined above
\definecolor{gray85}{gray}{0.85}

\begin{pspicture}(-3,-3)(3,3)
  \psHexagon[doubleline=true](2,2){1}
  \psHexagon*[linecolor=gray85,HRInner=true](2,-2){1}
  \psHexagon[doubleline=true,doublesep=0.5,%
    linecolor=blue]{2}
  \psHexagon*(-2.5,2.5){0.5}
  \psHexagon[border=3pt,HRInner=true](-1,-1){2}
\end{pspicture}
```

Example
5-15-6

5.15.4 "High-level" macros

"High-level" macros are understood to involve the application of existing "low-level" macros or other "high-level" macros to form a new macro. (Very often, the new macro will be a combination of those two.) The package **pst-circ** [63] is a very good example of this, because it does not define a single "low-level" macro but rather a large number of new "high-level" macros.

As an example, we will define a macro that determines the focal point of a given triangle and saves it in a node name. The focal point of a triangle is the point of intersection of the mediators. Suppose the triangle ABC is given by the coordinates of its corners (these can also be given by node names). (x_A, y_A) are the coordinates of A; likewise for B and C. Without proof (one can be found in any textbook on trigonometry), the coordinates of the focal point are the arithmetic mean of all three corners:

$$xS = (x_A + x_B + x_C)/3$$
$$yS = (y_A + y_B + y_C)/3$$

This result can be the basic information used to define a new macro.

```
\SpecialCoor
\makeatletter
\newif\ifPST@showFP                 % mark focal point?
\define@key[psset]{}{showFP}[true]{% "showFP" equals true
        \@nameuse{PST@showFP#1}%    use \ifPST@showFP
}
\psset{showFP=true}                 % default
%
\def\focalPoint{\pst@object{focalPoint}}
\def\focalPoint@i(#1)(#2)(#3)#4{{    % to keep everything local
  \pst@killglue                      %
```

```
\begingroup
\use@par
\pst@getcoor{#1}\pst@tempa%  point A       % get coordinates as x y
\pst@getcoor{#2}\pst@tempb%  point B       %  "
\pst@getcoor{#3}\pst@tempc%  point C       %  "
\pnode(!%                                   % set node
   \pst@tempa /YA exch \pst@number\psyunit div def
   /XA exch \pst@number\psxunit div def % x y in user coordinates
   \pst@tempb /YB exch \pst@number\psyunit div def
   /XB exch \pst@number\psxunit div def
   \pst@tempc /YC exch \pst@number\psyunit div def
   /XC exch \pst@number\psxunit div def
   XA XB XC add add 3.0 div                 % xFP
   YA YB YC add add 3.0 div                 % yFP
){#4}                                       % #5 = node name
\ifPST@showFP\qdisk(#4){2pt}\fi
\endgroup
}\ignorespaces}
\makeatother
```

The macro \pst@getcoor renders important services here. Above all, it performs the task of returning the coordinates in the normalized form used internally by PSTricks, i.e., as a pair of Cartesian coordinates, each terminated by a space. Recall that with \SpecialCoor activated, coordinates may be present in the input in a variety of forms (see Section 5.14 on page 296 and [128]).

The application of the macro is now easy, as demonstrated in the following example. The next section provides more information on the way the key/value interface is handled inside PSTricks.

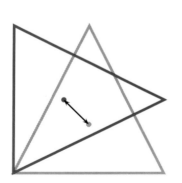

```
\usepackage{pstricks,pst-node,pst-xkey}
% \focalPoint as defined above
\begin{pspicture}(4,4)
  \psset{linewidth=2pt}
  \pspolygon[linecolor=red](0,0)(2,4)(4,0)%
  \focalPoint[showFP=true,linecolor=red](0,0)(2,4)(4,0){FP1}%
  \pnode(0,0){A}\pnode(0,4){B}\pnode(4,2){C}%
  \pspolygon[linecolor=blue](A)(B)(C)%
  \focalPoint(A)(B)(C){FP2}%
  {\psset{linecolor=blue}%
  \qdisk(FP2){2pt}}%
  \ncline[linewidth=1pt]{<->}{FP1}{FP2}%
\end{pspicture}
```

Example
5-15-7

5.15.5 The "key/value" interface

The package pst-xkey provides a specialization of the xkeyval package interface for PSTricks. It processes arguments in the key=value form—for instance, linecolor=red. The ac-

tual mechanism behind this is not of significance to **PSTricks** users, but it will help **PSTricks**
package authors in defining and setting keys for their packages. The main reason is the possibility of using multiple families in the \psset command, which allows each package to store
its keys in a well-chosen family, ensuring that no time needs to be spent checking whether
a particular key name has been used by another package. The **pst-xkey** package maintains a
list of the families used in a document that is using **PSTricks** packages and scans all of these
families when setting keys.

All **PSTricks** packages use the package name as family name as well—e.g., a definition   *family name=package*
from package **pst-blur**:   *name*

```
\define@key[psset]{pst-blur}{blurradius}{\pst@getlength{#1}\psx@blurradius}
\psset[pst-blur]{radius=1.5pt}
```

Actually, a single type of keyword would suffice to cover all cases; but **PSTricks** already has
the ability to validate keywords on input and make appropriate corrections. Therefore, it is
advisable to distinguish keywords by their meaning and define them accordingly.

The general syntax for defining new keywords provided by the **pst-xkey** package is

> \define@key[*prefix*] {*family*}{*key*} [*default*] {*function*}

For keys with Boolean values, a special interface will also declare the internal switch macro
on your behalf, using \newif.

> \define@boolkey[*prefix*] {*family*} [*macro-prefix*] {*key*} [*default*] {*function*}

Below are some examples that might be used with **PSTricks**. Note that psset must be used
as [*prefix*] (matching the name of the \psset command) and that the *family* is left empty
when the definition is not part or an extension of an existing package.

The *macro-prefix* (PST@ in our example) may be chosen quite arbitrarily, of course, but
serves to enforce a certain uniformity.

Boolean keys

The syntax of Boolean keys is as follows:

> \define@boolkey[psset]{} [PST@] {*name*} [true] {}

Let's review the Boolean switch from the example in the previous section.

```
\define@boolkey[psset]{}[PST@]{showFP}[true]{}% use \ifPST@showFP
\psset{showFP=false}            % set default value
```

Note that the specification of [true] does not establish a default value to be used when
the keyword is missing altogether, but rather the value to be taken when only the keyword
name is given in the input, without a value: for example, \focalPoint[showFP] will be
completed to \focalPoint[showFP=true] given the above definition. The *macro-prefix*

(PST@ in our example) may be chosen quite arbitrarily, of course, but serves to enforce a certain uniformity.

The **pst-xkey** package recognizes Boolean values regardless of their case (e.g., "True" and "FALSE" are valid), but will otherwise reject erroneous input.

Integer keys

The syntax for an integer keyword is as follows:

```
\define@key[psset]{}{name}{\pst@getint{#1}{\PST@name}}
```

Both the keyword value and the name of the macro, which is to save this value, are passed to \pst@getint. Note that if the number given as a value is not an integer but a real number, any fractional part is simply truncated. Otherwise, erroneous non-numeric input is treated as 0, with a low-level TEX error message being produced. (In either case, the rejected input will show up in TEX's output!)

Floating-point keys

The syntax for a floating-point keyword is as follows:

```
\define@key[psset]{}{name}{\pst@checknum{#1}{\PST@name}}
```

The \pst@checknum macro checks whether a valid value was input and saves it in the macro \PST@*name*. Erroneous input[1] is treated as 0, with an error message issued by PSTricks.

Dimension keys

The syntax for a length (dimension) keyword is as follows:

```
\define@key[psset]{}{name}{\pst@getlength{#1}{\PST@name}}
```

The \pst@getlength macro checks whether its first argument resembles a valid length value in PSTricks's terms (i.e., the current default unit is used if none has been given explicitly) and stores it in the macro whose name is given as the second argument. Erroneous non-numeric input is treated as 0, with a low-level TEX error message beeing produced. (As an implementation-dependent side effect, empty input is treated as 1, i.e., one PSTricks unit!)

String keys

The syntax for a string keyword is as follows:

```
\define@key[psset]{}{name}{\def\PST@name{#1}}
```

This is the simplest type. It simply saves the keyword value in the specified macro.

---

[1] Funny: redundant "+" signs are rejected!

CHAPTER 6

The Main PSTricks Packages

The "main" packages of **PSTricks** nowadays have this name only for historical reasons. **PSTricks** is used for those packages listed in the **pst-all** package. We do not follow this list here. Instead, we describe the most common ones (e.g., **pst-plot**, **pst-node**) in some detail. Section 6.7 then gives an overview of other packages, showing at least one characteristic example to help you understand the purpose of each package and approach that it takes.

6.1   pst-plot—**Plotting functions and data**

The base package **pstricks** provides some macros to plot function values and coordinates, as listed in Table 6.1. All of these macros accept an arbitrary number of coordinate pairs as arguments.

The **pst-plot** package provides improved commands for plotting external data and functions as well as coordinate axes [59, 60, 131]. It supports only two-dimensional data pairs. For plotting (x, y, z) data triplets or three-dimensional functions, you can use the **pst-3dplot** package discussed in Section 6.6, which supports a parallel projection of 3-D objects [132, 134].

Table 6.1: Plot macros included in the base package **pstricks**

\psdots	Section 5.8 on page 249
\psline	Section 5.6 on page 231
\pspolygon	Section 5.6 on page 232
\pscurve	Section 5.7.1 on page 245
\psecurve	Section 5.7.1 on page 246
\psccurve	Section 5.7.1 on page 246

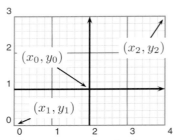

Figure 6.1: Reference points for plotting coordinate axes

6.1.1 The coordinate system—ticks and labels

Although you can use normal line commands to draw coordinate axes, this task is much more easily accomplished using \psaxes provided with **pst-plot**.

> \psaxes [*settings*] {*arrow type*} (x_0, y_0) (x_1, y_1) (x_2, y_2)

This command takes four optional arguments and one mandatory argument; i.e., at least one coordinate pair must be provided. The coordinates have to be given as Cartesian coordinates; you cannot use special coordinates as described in Section 5.14 on page 296. Figure 6.1 shows the relationship between the specified coordinate pairs and the plotted axes. The (x_1, y_1) and (x_2, y_2) arguments should specify any two opposite corners of the rectangle (see Figure 6.1). A missing (x_0, y_0) defaults to (x_1, y_1). If only one coordinate pair is given, the origin (0,0) is used for the first two. By default, no arrowheads are drawn. With the *arrow type* argument, you can specify the kind of arrow tip desired, as described in Section 5.10 on page 259.

Table 6.2 shows the keywords that are important for creating coordinate axes. They will be explained in detail on the following pages. The keyword labelsep, which was discussed in Section 5.11 on page 265, is important for labeling coordinate axes.

The axesstyle *key*   The keyword axesstyle can have the value axes, frame, or none. In the first case, two perpendicular lines are plotted, and the point of origin is placed at (x_0, y_0). The labels are positioned in relation to the axes' alignment. In the following example, (-0.5,-0.5)

Table 6.2: Keywords for \psaxes

Name	Value	Default
axesstyle	axes|frame|none	axes
Ox	*value*	0
Oy	*value*	0
Dx	*value*	1
Dy	*value*	1
dx	*value [unit]*	0pt
dy	*value [unit]*	0pt
labels	all|x|y|none	all
labelsep	*value [unit]*	5pt
showorigin	*Boolean*	true
ticks	all|x|y|none	all
tickstyle	full|top|bottom	full
ticksize	*value [unit]*	3pt

is chosen as the lower-left point of the surrounding box to prevent the axis labels from being placed outside the actual pspicture environment.

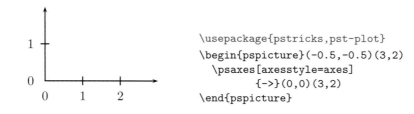

```
\usepackage{pstricks,pst-plot}
\begin{pspicture}(-0.5,-0.5)(3,2)
   \psaxes[axesstyle=axes]
          {->}(0,0)(3,2)
\end{pspicture}
```

Example
6-1-1

The next example shows how a third coordinate influences the placement of the axes. It also demonstrates that the placement of the labels depends on which corners of the rectangle are chosen.

```
\usepackage{pstricks,pst-plot}
\begin{pspicture}(-1,1)(3,-2)
   \psaxes[axesstyle=axes,linestyle=dashed]
          {(-]}(0,0)(-1,1)(3,-2)
\end{pspicture}
```

Example
6-1-2

For the axes style `frame`, the point of origin should be placed in a corner. Otherwise, it
`axesstyle=frame` would not really make sense to use this style.

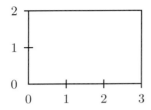

```
\usepackage{pstricks,pst-plot}
\begin{pspicture}(-0.5,-0.5)(3,2)
    \psaxes[axesstyle=frame]{->}(3,2)
\end{pspicture}
```
Example
6-1-3

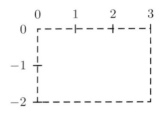

```
\usepackage{pstricks,pst-plot}
\begin{pspicture}(-0.5,0.5)(3,-2)
    \psaxes[axesstyle=frame,linestyle=dashed]{->}(3,-2)
\end{pspicture}
```
Example
6-1-4

On first glance the axes style `none` appears to be useless. However, since ticks and labels
`axesstyle=none` are still printed, it comes in handy when you are using manually designed axis lines. You can
hide labels and ticks in a similar fashion.

```
\usepackage{pstricks,pst-plot}
\begin{pspicture}(-0.5,-0.5)(3,2)
    \psaxes[axesstyle=none]{->}(2.5,2)
    \psline[linecolor=blue]{->}(3,0)
\end{pspicture}
```
Example
6-1-5

The keywords `Ox` and `Oy` allow you to specify arbitrary values for the axis origin (the
The `Ox` *and* `Oy` *keys* default is `(0,0)`). Although you can use any real number, you should keep in mind that
PSTricks uses the `\multido` command to create the axis labels and ticks. As `\multido` is
capable of only rudimentary floating-point arithmetics, some numbers may lead to inaccu-
rate results.

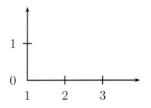

```
\usepackage{pstricks,pst-plot}
\begin{pspicture}(-0.5,-0.5)(3,2)
    \psaxes[Ox=1]{->}(3,2)
\end{pspicture}
```
Example
6-1-6

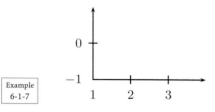

Example
6-1-7

```
\usepackage{pstricks,pst-plot}
\begin{pspicture}(-0.5,-0.5)(3,2)
    \psaxes[Ox=1,Oy=-1]{->}(3,2)
\end{pspicture}
```

The keywords Dx and Dy specify a scaling factor for the distance between consecutive labels. By default, the labels are placed one unit of measurement apart.   *The Dx and Dy keys*

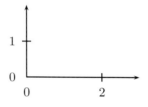

Example
6-1-8

```
\usepackage{pstricks,pst-plot}
\begin{pspicture}(-0.5,-0.5)(3,2)
    \psaxes[Dx=2]{->}(3,2)
\end{pspicture}
```

Example
6-1-9

```
\usepackage{pstricks,pst-plot}
\begin{pspicture}(-0.5,-0.5)(3,2)
    \psaxes[Dx=0.75,Dy=0.5]{->}(3,2)
\end{pspicture}
```

The keywords dx and dy define the physical distance between two consecutive labels. Thus they have a unit of measurement associated with them. If it is not explicitly given, the   *The dx and dy keys* current **PSTricks** unit is used. As you can see in Table 6.2, the keywords have the default value 0pt. Internally this value is replaced as follows:

$$dx = 0 \quad \rightarrow \quad dx = Dx \cdot psxunit$$
$$dy = 0 \quad \rightarrow \quad dy = Dy \cdot psyunit$$

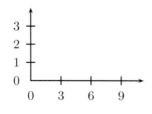

Example
6-1-10

```
\usepackage{pstricks,pst-plot}
\psset{unit=5mm}
\begin{pspicture}(-0.5,-0.5)(6,4)
    \psaxes[Dx=3,dx=8mm]{->}(6,4)
\end{pspicture}
```

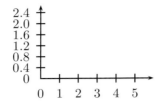

```
\usepackage{pstricks,pst-plot}
\begin{pspicture}(-0.5,-0.5)(3,2)
    \psaxes[Dx=1,dx=0.5cm,Dy=0.4,dy=0.3cm]{->}(3,2)
\end{pspicture}
```

Example
6-1-11

If these keywords are changed from their default, it is best to use values with an explicit unit of measurement. The two examples above also work without a unit. If you change the unit values with \psset, however, the labels may come out wrong.

The labels *key*   The labels keyword enables you to specify which axis is labeled. Possible values are all, x, y, or none. You can influence the distance between the axis and the label with the keyword labelsep (Table 6.2 on page 315). The label layout, however, can be changed only by redefining the macros for typesetting the vertical and horizontal axis labels. Their original definitions in the package are as follows:

```
\newcommand\pshlabel[1]{$#1$}
\newcommand\psvlabel[1]{$#1$}
```

If you want to typeset all labels in a small text font, simply precede the argument #1 with a command like \small or \tiny, as shown in the next examples. The package **pstricks-add** (see Section 6.7.1 on page 418) offers additional options with which to influence the label style.

labels=all   The value all is the default value for the keyword labels and has been used in all of
labels=x   the preceding examples; it ensures that both axes are labeled. If you set the keyword labels
labels=y   to the value x, only the x-axis is labeled, which is useful when the y-axis needs special labels that you cannot produce with the \psaxes command. The same is true for the y-axis with the value y. The following examples show the behavior of the keyword labels with the different values.

```
\usepackage{pstricks,pst-plot}
\renewcommand\pshlabel[1]{\small #1}
\begin{pspicture}(-0.5,-0.5)(3,2)
    \psaxes[labels=x]{->}(3,2)
\end{pspicture}
```

Example
6-1-12

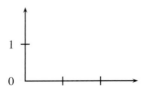

```
\usepackage{pstricks,pst-plot}
\renewcommand\psvlabel[1]{\small #1}
\begin{pspicture}(-0.5,-0.5)(3,2)
    \psaxes[labels=y]{->}(3,2)
\end{pspicture}
```

Example
6-1-13

With this value, all axes are plotted with ticks but without labels. This can be useful for   `labels=none`
special axis labels, e.g., logarithm values instead of decimal ones.

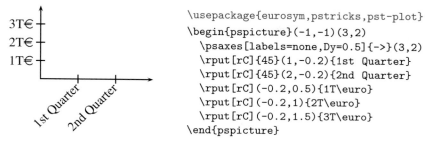

```
\usepackage{eurosym,pstricks,pst-plot}
\begin{pspicture}(-1,-1)(3,2)
    \psaxes[labels=none,Dy=0.5]{->}(3,2)
    \rput[rC]{45}(1,-0.2){1st Quarter}
    \rput[rC]{45}(2,-0.2){2nd Quarter}
    \rput[rC](-0.2,0.5){1T\euro}
    \rput[rC](-0.2,1){2T\euro}
    \rput[rC](-0.2,1.5){3T\euro}
\end{pspicture}
```

Example
6-1-14

You can use the keyword `showorigin` to hide the labels at the origin. In the following   *The* `showorigin` *key*
example, both axes have no label 0.

```
\usepackage{pstricks,pst-plot}
\begin{pspicture}(-0.5,-0.5)(3,2)
    \psaxes[showorigin=false]{->}(3,2)
\end{pspicture}
```

Example
6-1-15

With the keyword `ticks`, you can specify which axes are plotted with tick marks,
which are then positioned depending on the given values for the keywords dx and dy (see   *The* `ticks` *key*
page 317). Possible values for `ticks` are `all`, `x`, `y`, or `none`. The default key value is `all`,
as in the preceding examples; i.e., both axes get tick marks. With the value x, tick marks are
plotted only on the x-axis; with `ticks=y`, they are plotted only on the y-axis. With the key
value `none`, the axes are plotted with labels but without tick marks. This can be very useful
for plots of a more qualitative nature, which do not need tick marks.

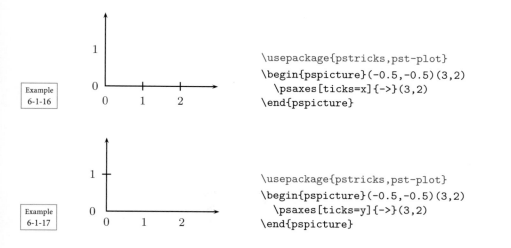

```
\usepackage{pstricks,pst-plot}
\begin{pspicture}(-0.5,-0.5)(3,2)
    \psaxes[ticks=x]{->}(3,2)
\end{pspicture}
```

Example
6-1-16

```
\usepackage{pstricks,pst-plot}
\begin{pspicture}(-0.5,-0.5)(3,2)
    \psaxes[ticks=y]{->}(3,2)
\end{pspicture}
```

Example
6-1-17

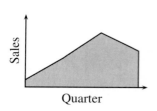

```
\usepackage{pstricks,pst-plot}
\begin{pspicture}(-0.5,-0.5)(3.25,2)
  \psaxes[ticks=none,labels=none]{->}(3.25,2)
  \uput[-90](1.5,0){Quarter}
  \uput[180]{90}(0,1){Sales}
  \pspolygon[fillcolor=lightgray,fillstyle=solid]
      (0,0)(0,0.2)(1,0.8)(2,1.5)(3,1)(3,0)
\end{pspicture}
```

Example
6-1-18

The tickstyle *key*

The keyword `tickstyle` defines the style of the tick marks. Possible values are `full`, `bottom`, or `top`. The default value for `tickstyle` is `full`; it has been used in all preceding examples. With the value `bottom`, the tick marks are placed only to the left of the y-axis and below the x-axis. When plotting negative axes, the ticks and labels are always outside of the plot area.

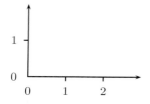

```
\usepackage{pstricks,pst-plot}
\begin{pspicture}(-0.5,-0.5)(3,2)
  \psaxes[tickstyle=bottom]{->}(3,2)
\end{pspicture}
```

Example
6-1-19

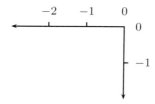

```
\usepackage{pstricks,pst-plot}
\begin{pspicture}(-3,0.5)(0.5,-2)
  \psaxes[tickstyle=bottom]{->}(-3,-2)
\end{pspicture}
```

Example
6-1-20

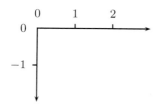

```
\usepackage{pstricks,pst-plot}
\begin{pspicture}(-0.5,0.5)(3,-2)
  \psaxes[tickstyle=bottom]{->}(3,-2)
\end{pspicture}
```

Example
6-1-21

With the value `top`, the tick marks are placed only to the right of the y-axis and above the x-axis. When plotting negative axes, the ticks are always inside and the labels always outside the plot area. The position of the ticks often has to be changed, when the direction of the axes changes.

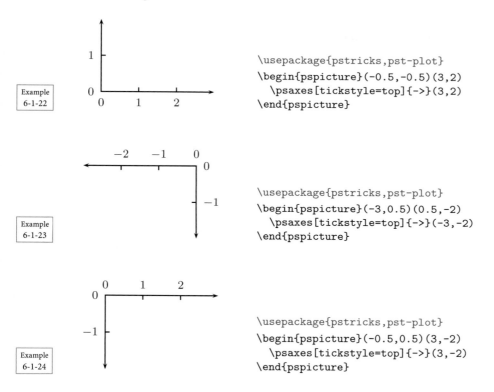

Example
6-1-22

```
\usepackage{pstricks,pst-plot}
\begin{pspicture}(-0.5,-0.5)(3,2)
  \psaxes[tickstyle=top]{->}(3,2)
\end{pspicture}
```

Example
6-1-23

```
\usepackage{pstricks,pst-plot}
\begin{pspicture}(-3,0.5)(0.5,-2)
  \psaxes[tickstyle=top]{->}(-3,-2)
\end{pspicture}
```

Example
6-1-24

```
\usepackage{pstricks,pst-plot}
\begin{pspicture}(-0.5,0.5)(3,-2)
  \psaxes[tickstyle=top]{->}(3,-2)
\end{pspicture}
```

The keyword `ticksize` defines the length of the tick marks (the default is 3 pt). A value without an explicit unit is interpreted in the current unit of measurement. You can easily use this keyword to fill the coordinate system with lines parallel to the coordinate axes, as shown in the next example.   *The* `ticksize` *key*

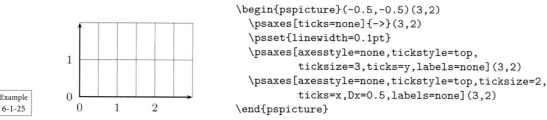

Example
6-1-25

```
\usepackage{pstricks,pst-plot}
\begin{pspicture}(-0.5,-0.5)(3,2)
  \psaxes[ticks=none]{->}(3,2)
  \psset{linewidth=0.1pt}
  \psaxes[axesstyle=none,tickstyle=top,
          ticksize=3,ticks=y,labels=none](3,2)
  \psaxes[axesstyle=none,tickstyle=top,ticksize=2,
          ticks=x,Dx=0.5,labels=none](3,2)
\end{pspicture}
```

By combining different values for `ticksize` and `labels`, interesting effects can be achieved. Note that we print the ticks first and then overprint them with the axes to ensure that the blue ticks do not run into the axes.

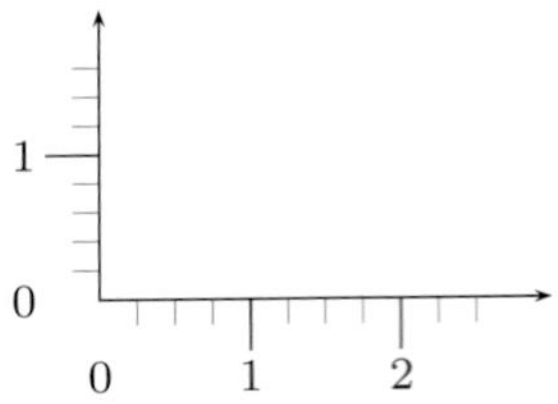

```
\usepackage{pstricks,pst-plot}
\begin{pspicture}(-0.5,-0.5)(3,2)
 \psset{linewidth=0.2pt,axesstyle=none,linecolor=blue,
        tickstyle=bottom,ticksize=5pt,labels=none}
 \psaxes[ticks=x,Dx=0.25](2.5,1.75)
 \psaxes[ticks=y,Dy=0.2](2.5,1.75)
 \psset{linewidth=0.4pt,ticksize=10pt,linecolor=black}
 \psaxes[ticks=x](2.5,1.75)
 \psaxes[ticks=y](2.5,1.75)
 \psaxes[axesstyle=axes,ticks=none,
        labels=all,labelsep=12pt]{->}(3,2)
\end{pspicture}
```

Example
6-1-26

Special labels
On many occasions, you may need to label axes with symbols or text, e.g., months of the year, instead of numbers. Example 6-1-14 on page 319 showed a way to achieve this effect. The package **arrayjob** offers further support for labeling axes by enabling customized alphanumeric labels. The TEX command \ifcase basically offers the same possibilities without the need to load an external package. The trick is to use it within a redefinition of the **PSTricks** macros \pshlabel and \psvlabel for labeling the axes, as shown in the next example.

```
\usepackage{pstricks,pst-plot}
\newcommand\Month[1]{%
  \ifcase#1\or January\or February\or March\or April\or May\or June\or%
    July\or August\or September\or October\or November\or December\fi}%
\newcommand\Level[1]{%
  \ifcase#1\or Low\or Medium\or High\fi}%
\renewcommand\psvlabel[1]{\footnotesize\Level{#1}}
\renewcommand\pshlabel[1]{\rput[rb]{30}{\footnotesize\Month{#1}}}
\psset{unit=0.8}
\begin{pspicture}(-0.5,-1)(13,4)
  \psaxes[showorigin=false]{->}(13,4)
\end{pspicture}
```

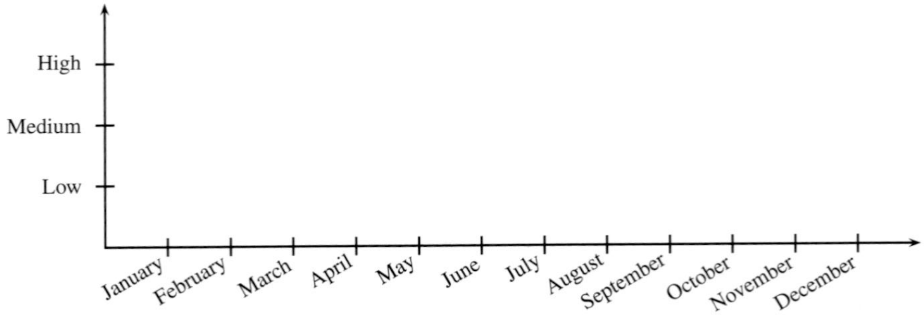

Example
6-1-27

A similar approach can be used for angular degrees by applying suitable (local) changes to the scaling factor. For example, plotting a sine function over the interval $[0; 3\pi]$ can be achieved by using 6 length units for 3π, resulting in a scaling factor of $\frac{\pi}{2}$. The resulting x-axis would then have a minimum length of $6 \cdot \frac{\pi}{2} \approx 9.4248\,\text{cm}$ if a measuring unit of 1 cm is used. The labels at each tick (one unit apart) should then show multiples of $\frac{\pi}{2}$.

This type of labeling of the axes can be easily achieved with the help of the packages ifthen and calc. Alternatively, the **pstricks-add** package provides a ready-made solution for trigonometric labels (see Section 6.7.1 on page 418).

```
\usepackage{pstricks,pst-plot,ifthen,calc}
\newcounter{temp}
\renewcommand\pshlabel[1]{\small%
  \ifthenelse{\isodd{#1}}{$\frac{#1}{2}\pi$}
             {\setcounter{temp}{#1/2}$\thetemp\pi$}}
\begin{pspicture}(-0.5,-1.25)(10,1.25)
  \psaxes[xunit=1.570796327,showorigin=false]{->}(0,0)(-0.5,-1.25)(6.4,1.25)
  \psplot[linecolor=blue,linewidth=1.5pt]{0}{9.424777961}{x RadtoDeg sin}
\end{pspicture}
```

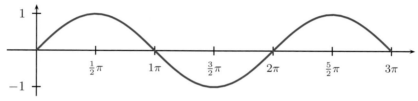

Here the command \psplot is invoked with the default scaling factor, allowing us to use the interval $[0; 3\pi]$ for this function.

6.1.2   Plotting mathematical functions and data files

The package **pst-plot** provides three plotting functions with two additional commands for loading and saving data files or data records.

```
\fileplot [settings] {file name}
\dataplot [settings] {macro name}
\listplot [settings] {macro name}
```

All three commands can create the same output, and it is not easy to see the differences between them, apart from the different syntax. If possible, \dataplot uses the "quick plot"; this approach is not feasible, if it internally calls \listplot. Various criteria are applied when making this decision. Here are two examples: the usage of the showpoints keyword and of the curve plot style. Neither is supported by "quick plots". Using \dataplot without these options, but with the default line key value for plotstyle, however, will result in a "quick plot". This method is completely different from what \listplot would use, and among other changes in its behavior it will not accept PostScript code inside the data. The definition of a "quick plot" depends on the PostScript behavior of handling data records. Normally, these details can be neglected when you are plotting external data files or data records.

Data structures for plotting data files External data must be arranged in pairs of numerical values using one of the four delimiters: space, comma, parentheses, or curly brackets.

```
x y
x,y
(x,y)
{x,y}
```

The data pairs do not have to appear in separate lines and you can combine the delimiters. A file with contents such as 1 2 3,4 (5,6) {7,8} will still be accepted by the plotting macros. You can considerably speed up processing by putting all numbers in square brackets[1] because PostScript can then read the data as an array. On the downside, there are device-specific limitations, regarding how many data records TeX can read during one run.

Tab characters Tab characters (\t or \009) are not allowed as delimiters. **PSTricks** does not recognize them, so their inclusion leads to a data reading error. A possible workaround is to replace the tab characters with spaces by means of an editor or other program, such as under U*X:

```
tr '\t' ' ' < inFile > outFile
```

Moreover, data files must not include symbols other than numeric values and the TeX comment character "%".

\fileplot You should use the command \fileplot whenever you wish to plot two-dimensional data that is saved in an external file. There are a few drawbacks when using \fileplot: the plot style curve is not allowed and the key settings for arrows, linearc, and showpoints are ignored.

Example 6-1-29 is a light absorption spectrum ($A = \lg \frac{I_0}{I}$ as a function of the wavelength). Example 6-1-30 shows the evolution of a population as a function of the breeding factor (known as a Feigenbaum or bifurcation diagram). The plotting style used here can be derived from the source code.

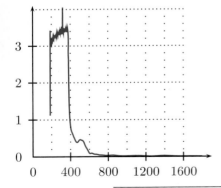

```
\usepackage{pstricks,pst-plot}
\psset{xunit=0.025mm}
\begin{pspicture}(-200,-0.5)(1900,4.25)
  \fileplot[plotstyle=line,linewidth=1pt,
    linecolor=blue]{pstricks/fileplot.data}
  \psaxes[dx=400,Dx=400]{->}(1900,4.1)
  \psgrid[griddots=5,subgriddiv=1,
        xunit=0.5cm,gridlabels=0pt](8,4)
\end{pspicture}
```

Example
6-1-29

---

[1] "[" has to be the first symbol in each line.

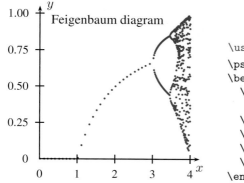

```
\usepackage{pstricks,pst-plot}
\psset{yunit=4cm}
\begin{pspicture}(-0.75,-0.5)(4.25,1.1)
  \fileplot[plotstyle=dots,dotsize=1.5pt,
      linecolor=blue]{pstricks/feigenbaum.data}
  \psaxes[Dy=0.25]{->}(4.25,1.05)
  \uput[-90](4.25,0){$x$}
  \uput[0](0,1.05){$y$}
  \rput[l](0.3,0.95){Feigenbaum diagram}
\end{pspicture}
```

Example
6-1-30

Just like \fileplot, the command \dataplot expects external data. Instead of re-
siding in a file, however, the data has to be saved in a macro in a special way. To achieve this,   \dataplot
we can use \readdata to read from an external data file and save the data in a macro as
follows:

```
\readdata{\bubble}{pstricks/bubble.data}
```

For details, see page 328. The size of the included data file(s) is limited only by the memory
constraints.

In addition, \dataplot supports plotting of simple overlays. The following example
shows two different data sets plotted on a single coordinate system:

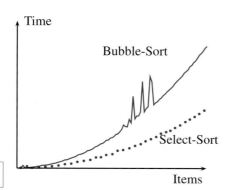

```
\usepackage{pstricks,pst-plot}
\psset{xunit=0.0005cm,yunit=0.004cm}
\begin{pspicture}(0,-50)(10000,1100)
  \readdata{\bubble}{pstricks/bubble.data}
  \readdata{\select}{pstricks/select.data}
  \dataplot[plotstyle=line,linecolor=blue]{\bubble}
  \dataplot[plotstyle=line,linestyle=dotted,
      linewidth=2pt,linecolor=blue]{\select}
  \psline{->}(0,0)(10000,0)\uput[-90](9000,0){Items}
  \psline{->}(0,0)(0,1000)  \uput[0](0,1000){Time}
  \rput[l](4500,800){Bubble-Sort}
  \rput[l](7500,200){Select-Sort}
\end{pspicture}
```

Example
6-1-31

From the user's point of view there are only small differences between \dataplot and
\fileplot. When working with large amounts of data, \dataplot offers faster processing, but uses more memory than \fileplot. Moreover, when it is called with optional
keywords, \dataplot internally invokes \listplot, which is described in detail below.
Consequently, \dataplot is best used for plotting polygons, for which it produces much
faster results. Given the overall performance of today's hardware, however, this argument
seems to lose its importance.

\listplot   In contrast to the preceding plot commands, the argument of \listplot is first expanded if it contains TeX macros; otherwise, it is passed to PostScript without change. In
the process, TeX macros are replaced with their corresponding replacement text. It is possible to include entire PostScript programs in the argument to \listplot, as shown in
Example 6-1-33.

The first example illustrates the Hénon attractor.

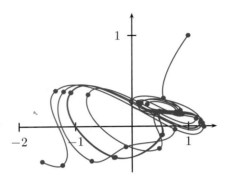

```
\usepackage{pstricks,pst-plot}
% definition of \henon with data points like this:
% \newcommand\henon{ 1.00000000   1.00000000
%                     0.56000000   0.31000000
%                          ... many more ...}

\psset{xunit=1.5cm, yunit=2.5cm}
\begin{pspicture}(-2,-0.5)(1.5,1.25)
  \psaxes{->}(0,0)(-2,-0.5)(1.5,1.25)
  \listplot[showpoints=true,plotstyle=curve,
    linecolor=blue]{\henon}
\end{pspicture}
```

Example
6-1-32

The second example includes the watermark "DRAFT", which was added to the original
data with additional PostScript code.

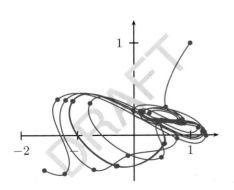

```
\usepackage{pstricks,pst-plot}
% \henon as in previous example
\newcommand{\dataA}{\henon
  gsave
  /Helvetica findfont 40 scalefont setfont
  45 rotate
  0.9 setgray
  -60 10 moveto (DRAFT) show
  grestore }
\psset{xunit=1.5cm, yunit=2.5cm}
\begin{pspicture}(-2,-0.5)(1.5,1.25)
  \psaxes{->}(0,0)(-2,-0.5)(1.5,1.25)
  \listplot[showpoints=true,linecolor=blue,
      plotstyle=curve]{\dataA}
\end{pspicture}
```

Example
6-1-33

Instead of modifying the data set passed to \listplot, you can redefine the
\ScalePoints macro in pst-plot. For example, if you wanted to exchange the x and y val-

ues and then rotate the whole plotted graphic, the redefinition would look like this:

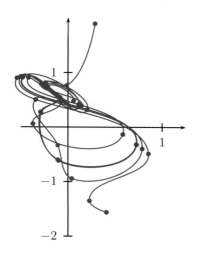

```
\usepackage{pstricks,pst-plot}
\makeatletter
\pst@def{ScalePoints}<%
   45 rotate % rotate all objects
   /y ED /x ED
   counttomark dup dup cvi eq not { exch pop } if
   /m exch def /n m 2 div cvi def
   n { exch % exchanges the last two stack elements
      y mul m 1 roll x mul m 1 roll
      /m m 2 sub def } repeat>
\makeatother
\psset{yunit=1.5cm, xunit=2.5cm}
\begin{pspicture}(-0.5,-2)(1.25,2.0)
   \psaxes{->}(0,0)(-0.5,-2)(1.25,2)
   \listplot[showpoints=true,linecolor=blue,%
            plotstyle=curve]{\henon}
\end{pspicture}
```

Example
6-1-34

Together \pscustom and the low-level macro \code enable you to perform virtually any kind of manipulation at the PostScript level without having to interfere with the
\listplot macro. The following example illustrates how to include the coordinate values
next to their corresponding data points *after* the data has been plotted.

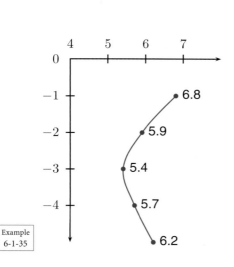

```
\usepackage{pstricks,pst-plot}
\makeatletter
\newcommand\plotValues[1]{\pscustom{\code{%
   /xOffset 5 def /yOffset -2 def
   /Helvetica findfont 10 scalefont setfont
   /Varray [ #1 ] def   /cnt 0 def
   Varray length 2 div cvi {
      /x Varray cnt get def   /y Varray cnt 1 add get def
      x \pst@number\psxunit mul xOffset add
      y \pst@number\psyunit mul yOffset add
      moveto x 10 string cvs show
      /cnt cnt 2 add def } repeat}}}
\makeatother
\begin{pspicture}(3.5,0.5)(8,-5)
   \psaxes[Ox=4]{->}(4,0)(8,-5)
   \newcommand*\dataV{ 6.8 -1 5.9 -2 5.4 -3 5.7 -4 6.2 -5 }
   \listplot[plotstyle=curve,showpoints=true,
      linecolor=blue]{\dataV}
   \plotValues{\dataV}
\end{pspicture}
```

Example
6-1-35

| \savedata{*file*} [*data points*]   \readdata [*settings*] {*macro*}{*file*} |

The implementation of the two commands for saving and loading data records is very straightforward: \savedata takes the *data points* and saves them in the *file*; \readdata expects a *macro* name and a *file* name as arguments. The latter command does not require data to be in pairs since it reads the data step by step, ignoring any existing structure in the file. This behavior can be useful for several types of user-defined additions. For instance, some user applications store not only data but also error values. In such cases, it would be nice to plot both the data and the corresponding errors. The macro \readdata reads **any** list of data records and saves the data as a sequence in a given macro as follows:

$$\sqcup D \sqcup value_1 \sqcup D \sqcup value_2 \sqcup D \sqcup value_3 \ldots$$

The character D is inserted to get rid of trailing spaces when reading the data file and is of no relevance for the standard use of the plot commands. At the PostScript level, the D is replaced by an empty subroutine: /D {} def. Consequently, the data can easily be manipulated in TEX **before** the data macro is sent to PostScript. With the command \@ifnextchar D, you can define a macro that checks whether there is another data value in the list. The following example shows how to do so using a data file (dataError.dat) with the structure *x y dmin dmax* and the following content:

```
-0.7    -0.4      -0.1   0.5
-0.43   3            0    0.4
 1       4.6      -0.5   0.2
 1.2     2.3      -0.2   0.2
 1.7     3.9      -0.1   1
 2.7    -1.1      -0.2   0.3
 3.98   -0.7      -0.4   0
 4.5     0.7539   -0.5   0.4
```

The maximum upper and lower measurement deviations are denoted by *dmax* and *dmin*, respectively, and use the same scale as the data values *x* and *y*. After reading the data from a file with \readdata{*dataError*}{\Data}, the macro \Data contains the complete data set in the following form:

```
D -0.7 D -0.4 D 0.1 D 0.5 D -0.43 D 3 D 0 D 0.4 D 1 D 4.6 D -0.5 D 0.2
D 1.2 D 2.3 D -0.2 D 0.2 D 1.7 D 3.9 D -0.1 D 1 D 2.7 D -1.1 D -0.2
D 0.3 D 3.98 D -0.7 D -0.4 D 0 D 4.5 D 0.7539 D -0.5 D 0.4
```

Instead of plotting only a single point, you now have to display a customized line such as \psline{|-|}(*x,y+dmax*)(*x,y+dmin*), which shows the error margins as a bar. We can read four values (separated by Ds) from the data stored in the macro \Data and process them, then check whether another D is present and repeat the process. This requires a low-level TEX definition (using \def) as we pick up the arguments with special delimiters:

```
\def\GetCoordinates#1{\expandafter\GetCoordinates@i#1}
% get rid of any preceding space if necessary:
\def\GetCoordinates@i#1{\GetCoordinates@ii#1}
% pick up four values separated by Ds:
\def\GetCoordinates@ii D #1 D #2 D #3 D #4 {\DoCoordinate{#1}{#2}%
```

```
\pserrorLine[linecolor=blue, linewidth=1.5pt](#1,#2){#3}{#4}%
% recurring if more data is coming up:
\@ifnextchar D{\GetCoordinates@ii}{}}
```

In the preceding code, \DoCoordinate typesets the data point itself and \pserrorLine handles the error margins around it. A possible definition for the latter macro—calculating the coordinates for the error bars directly within PostScript—is the following:

```
\def\pserrorLine{\pst@object{pserrorLine}}
\def\pserrorLine@i(#1)#2#3{\begingroup
  \use@par \pst@getcoor{#1}\pst@tempA
  \def\ps@errorMin{#2}\def\ps@errorMax{#3}%
  \psline{|-|}(! /yDot \pst@tempA exch pop \pst@number\psyunit div def
               /xDot \pst@tempA pop \pst@number\psxunit div def
               xDot yDot \ps@errorMin\space add )
            (! /yDot \pst@tempA exch pop \pst@number\psyunit div def
               /xDot \pst@tempA pop \pst@number\psxunit div def
               xDot yDot \ps@errorMax\space add)
\endgroup}
```

After putting these definitions together and providing a suitable definition for \DoCoordinate, we get the following result from the data in `dataError.dat`:

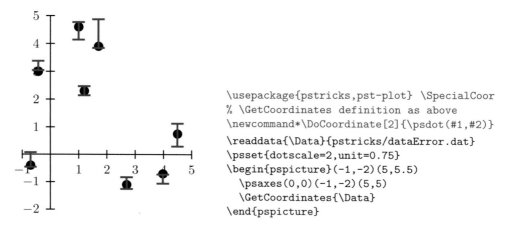

```
\usepackage{pstricks,pst-plot} \SpecialCoor
% \GetCoordinates definition as above
\newcommand*\DoCoordinate[2]{\psdot(#1,#2)}
\readdata{\Data}{pstricks/dataError.dat}
\psset{dotscale=2,unit=0.75}
\begin{pspicture}(-1,-2)(5,5.5)
  \psaxes(0,0)(-1,-2)(5,5)
  \GetCoordinates{\Data}
\end{pspicture}
```

Example
6-1-36

Internally PostScript uses the so-called stack system, which may be familiar to users of HP calculators (or the BIBTEX programming language). This system, which is also known as *Reverse Polish Notation* (RPN), represents the internal standard for all computers. The usual mathematical notation for multiplications "$a * b =$" becomes "$a\langle\text{ENTER}\rangle b\langle\text{ENTER}\rangle *$". Before a mathematical operation is performed, all parameters (variables) have to be put on the stack [with $\langle\text{ENTER}\rangle$]. The commands described here always refer to the highest or the two highest stack elements. Generally, if problems arise you can use an "Infix–Postfix" converter, which translates "usual" (Infix) mathematical expressions to RPN notation (Postfix) [93].

Plotting mathematical functions

When it comes to final printing, it is not always an advantage to directly use PostScript commands instead of programs such as **gnuplot** for illustrating mathematical contexts. Also, not every mathematical problem is easily solved using PostScript commands.

\psplot [*settings*] {x_{min}}{x_{max}}{*function* $y(x)$}
\parametricplot [*settings*] {t_{min}}{t_{max}}{*functions* $x(t)$ $y(t)$}

Here $[x_{min}; x_{max}]$ and $[t_{min}; t_{max}]$ denote the definition interval (beginning and end values). The special keywords for use with functions are plotpoints and plotstyle. The plotpoints keyword gives the number of data points plotted per interval, with the default beeing 50. Normally, all displayed values are connected by lines using plotstyle=lines, which may result in sharp polygon edges if we use too few interpolation points. For most applications, a value of 200 should be sufficient.

The default variable names for \psplot and \parametricplot are x and t, respectively. Although there is no easy way of altering these names, this does not pose any real limitations. Within a single expression, variables can be used as often as needed, since the second value coordinate is evaluated as being on top of the stack only after the closing parenthesis is applied. The only difference between these two commands is that \psplot takes the topmost stack value (y) as its single argument, whereas \parametricplot takes the two topmost stack values ($x; y$) as its arguments.

Special attention should be paid to the fact that neither command will detect incorrect input. This can be of importance when we are using mathematical functions whose domain is not within the domain of real numbers. A **single** false argument, such as $\sqrt{-1}$, will prevent the plot from being displayed! In such cases you should process the PostScript output with **ghostscript**, which reports such problems in an error message.

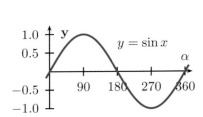

```
\usepackage{pstricks,pst-plot}
\psset{xunit=0.01cm,yunit=1cm}
\begin{pspicture}(-80,-1.25)(400,1.25)
  \psaxes[showorigin=false,
      Dx=90,Dy=0.5]{->}(0,0)(0,-1)(380,1.25)
  \uput{0.3}[90](360,0){$\mathbf{\alpha}$}
  \uput{0.3}[0](0,1){$\mathbf{y}$}
  \psplot[plotstyle=curve,linecolor=blue,
      linewidth=1.5pt]{-10}{370}{x sin}
  \rput[l](180,0.75){$y=\sin x$}
\end{pspicture}
```

Example
6-1-37

Example 6-1-38 shows a third-degree parabola and its inverse function. You do not have to choose an interval when using scientific notation, e.g., $y = x^{-\frac{1}{3}}$.

$$y^{-1}(x) = \begin{cases} +\sqrt[3]{|x|} & x > 0 \\ -\sqrt[3]{|x|} & x < 0 \end{cases}$$

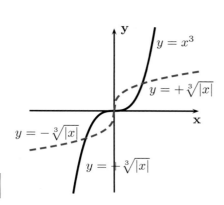

```
\usepackage{pstricks,pst-plot}
\psset{unit=0.75cm}
\begin{pspicture}(-3.25,-3)(3.25,3)
  \psaxes[linewidth=1pt,ticks=none,
    labels=none]{->}(0,0)(-3,-3)(3,3)
  \uput[-100](3,0){$\mathbf{x}$}
  \uput[-10](0,3){$\mathbf{y}$}
  \psset{linewidth=1.5pt}
  \psplot{-1.45}{1.45}{x 3 exp}
  \psset{linestyle=dashed,linecolor=blue}
  \psplot{0}{3}{x 0.333 exp}
  \psplot{-3}{0}{x -1 mul 0.333 exp -1 mul}
  \rput[l](1.5,2.5){$y=x^3$}
  \rput[l](-1,-2){$y=+\sqrt[3]{|x|}$}
  \rput[l](1.25,0.8){$y=+\sqrt[3]{|x|}$}
  \rput[r](-1.25,-0.8){$y=-\sqrt[3]{|x|}$}
\end{pspicture}
```

Example 6-1-39 shows a graphical representation of the relative mean power values of a power converter controlled by a pair of thyristors. The phase shift and delay angle (independent variable) are denoted as φ and α, respectively.

$$\frac{I(\alpha)}{I_0} = \begin{cases} \sqrt{1 - \frac{\alpha}{\pi} + \frac{1}{2\pi}\sin 2\alpha} & \varphi = 0 \\ \sqrt{\left(2 - \frac{2\alpha}{\pi}\right)(2 + \cos 2\alpha) + \frac{3}{\pi}\sin 2\alpha} & \varphi = \frac{\pi}{2} \end{cases}$$

PostScript expects the arguments of the trigonometric functions to be in degrees, which means we must convert relative angles to use this measurement unit. Therefore, we need to replace the expression $\frac{\alpha}{\pi}$ with $\frac{\alpha}{180}$.

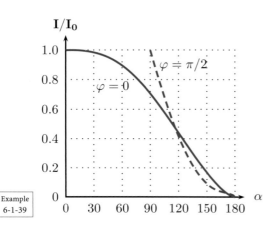

```
\usepackage{pstricks,pst-plot}
\psset{xunit=0.025cm,yunit=4cm}
\begin{pspicture}(-0.1,-0.25)(190,1.1)
  \psgrid[subgriddiv=0,griddots=5,
    gridlabels=0pt,xunit=30,yunit=0.2](6,5)
  \psaxes[linewidth=1pt,ticks=none,Dx=30,
    Dy=0.2]{->}(190,1.1)
  \uput{0.5}[0](180,0){$\mathbf{\alpha}$}
  \uput{0.5}[90](0,1){$\mathbf{I/I_0}$}
  \psset{linewidth=1.5pt,linecolor=blue}
  \psplot{0}{180}{1 x 180 div sub 1
    6.28 div x 2 mul sin mul add abs sqrt}
  \psplot[linestyle=dashed]{90}{180}{
    2 x 90 div sub x 2 mul cos 2 add mul x
    2 mul sin 3 3.15 div mul add abs sqrt}
  \rput(50,0.75){$\varphi=0$}
  \rput(125,0.9){$\varphi=\pi/2$}
\end{pspicture}
```

A typical application for equations in parametric form that frequently appear in physics and electrical engineering comprises the well-known Lissajous figures.

$$x = \sin 1.5t \qquad\qquad y = \sin\left(2t + \frac{\pi}{3}\right)$$

Because of the "length" of this plot, the `plotpoints` value was set to 200 to produce smooth polygons for the strong curvature at the plot "corners".

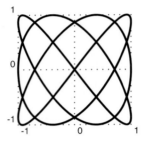

```
\usepackage{pstricks,pst-plot}
\psset{xunit=1.5cm,yunit=1.5cm}
\begin{pspicture}(-1.1,-1.1)(1.1,1.1)
  \psgrid[subgriddiv=0,griddots=10,
    gridlabels=7pt](-1,-1)(1,1)
  \parametricplot[plotstyle=curve,
    linewidth=1.5pt,plotpoints=200]{-360}{360}
    {t 1.5 mul sin t 2 mul 60 add sin}
\end{pspicture}
```

Example
6-1-40

The next example shows the following function plotted with three different values for the constant a.

$$x(t) = \frac{a\left(t^2 - 1\right)}{t^2 + 1} \qquad\qquad y(t) = \frac{at\left(t^2 - 1\right)}{t^2 + 1}$$

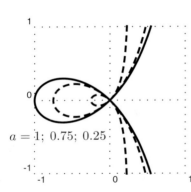

```
\usepackage{pstricks,pst-plot}
\psset{unit=2.0}
\newcommand\PSfunction[1]{t t mul 1 sub #1 mul t t mul 1 add div
  t t mul 1 sub t mul #1 mul t t mul 1 add div}
\begin{pspicture}(-1.1,-1.1)(1.1,1.1)
  \psgrid[subgriddiv=0,griddots=10,gridlabels=7pt]
  \psset{plotpoints=200,linewidth=1.5pt}
  \parametricplot{-1.85}{1.85}{\PSfunction{1}}
  \psset{linestyle=dashed}
  \parametricplot{-4.5}{4.5}{\PSfunction{0.25}}
  \parametricplot{-2.1}{2.1}{\PSfunction{0.75}}
  \rput[r](-0.05,-0.5){$a=1;\ 0.75;\ 0.25$}
\end{pspicture}
```

Example
6-1-41

There are only two special keywords for plotting functions and data. The keyword `plotstyle` can have a value of `dots`, `line`, `polygon`, `curve`, `ecurve`, `ccurve`, or `line`, just like the corresponding macro names without the preceding `ps`. The keyword `plotpoints` can be very important for plotting curves over a large x interval or curves with a great gradient. In both cases the predefined value of `plotpoints=50` may be too small.

The `plotstyle=line` setting is the default. The coordinates are connected with se- `plotstyle=line`
cants (lines) whose appearance can be altered with the keywords listed in Table 5.5 on
page 235.

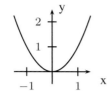

```
\usepackage{pstricks,pst-plot}
\begin{pspicture}(-1.5,0)(1.5,2.5)
   \psaxes{->}(0,0)(-1.5,-0.5)(1.5,2.5)
   \uput[-90](2,0){x} \uput[0](0,2.5){y}
   \psplot[plotstyle=line]{-1.5}{1.5}{x dup mul}
\end{pspicture}
```

With the `plotstyle=dots` setting, the coordinates are displayed as dots, and the display style can be changed with the keywords for dots given in Table 5.8 on page 251. You can `plotstyle=dots`
also define your own symbols (see Section 5.8 on page 250), e.g., if you wish to plot a lot of
different data sets.

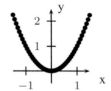

```
\usepackage{pstricks,pst-plot}
\begin{pspicture}(-1.5,0)(1.5,2.5)
   \psaxes{->}(0,0)(-1.5,-0.5)(1.5,2.5)
   \uput[-90](2,0){x} \uput[0](0,2.5){y}
   \psplot[plotstyle=dots]{-1.5}{1.5}{x dup mul}
\end{pspicture}
```

The `polygon` plot style shows a similar behavior as the `\pspolygon` command (Sec- `plotstyle=polygon`
tion 5.6 on page 232): it closes a curve at its end by plotting a line from the beginning to the
end point.

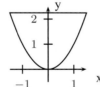

```
\usepackage{pstricks,pst-plot}
\begin{pspicture}(-1.5,0)(1.5,2.5)
   \psaxes{->}(0,0)(-1.5,-0.5)(1.5,2.5)
   \uput[-90](2,0){x} \uput[0](0,2.5){y}
   \psplot[plotstyle=polygon]{-1.5}{1.5}{x dup mul}
\end{pspicture}
```

As shown in the following examples, there is not much difference between the plot styles
curve, ecurve, and ccurve. This will generally be the case when we are plotting mathe- `plotstyle=curve`
matical functions with more than a few values. For details, see the discussion of the corre- `plotstyle=ecurve`
sponding commands in Section 5.7.1 on pages 245–246. When plotting very steep curves, `plotstyle=ccurve`
the key values curve, ecurve, and ccurve can lead to unique problems. A possible solution involves changing the value for the keyword `curvature` (Section 5.7.2).

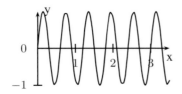

```
\usepackage{pstricks,pst-plot}
\begin{pspicture}(0,-1)(3.5,1)
   \psaxes{->}(0,0)(0,-1)(3.5,1)
   \uput[-90](3.5,0){x}   \uput[0](0,1){y}
   \psplot[plotstyle=curve,curvature=1 1 -1]
       {0}{3.5}{x 360 mul 0.6 div sin}
\end{pspicture}
```

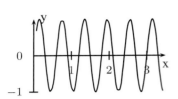

```
\usepackage{pstricks,pst-plot}
\begin{pspicture}(0,-1)(3.5,1)
  \psaxes{->}(0,0)(0,-1)(3.5,1)
  \uput[-90](3.5,0){x}
  \uput[0](0,1){y}
  \psplot[plotstyle=ecurve,curvature=1 1 -1]
       {0}{3.5}{x 360 mul 0.6 div sin}
\end{pspicture}
```

Example
6-1-46

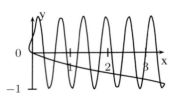

```
\usepackage{pstricks,pst-plot}
\begin{pspicture}(0,-1)(3.5,1)
  \psaxes{->}(0,0)(0,-1)(3.5,1)
  \uput[-90](3.5,0){x}
  \uput[0](0,1){y}
  \psplot[plotstyle=ccurve,curvature=1 1 -1]
       {0}{3.5}{x 360 mul 0.6 div sin}
\end{pspicture}
```

Example
6-1-47

The keyword `plotpoints` has a major influence on the appearance of all plots. The default value of 50 points per chosen interval is probably reasonable for most functions, but many functions will require more points to produce smooth curves. Modern computers can easily allow values of 5000 or more without forcing the user to get a coffee between each LaTeX run. Conversely, functions with a very shallow slope may produce good plots with fewer points. In this case, printer resolution might have to be adjusted accordingly.

`plotpoints=50`

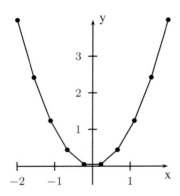

```
\usepackage{pstricks,pst-plot}
\begin{pspicture}(-2,-0.5)(2,4)
  \psaxes{->}(0,0)(-2,-0.5)(2,4)
  \uput[-90](2,0){x}
  \uput[0](0,4){y}
  \psplot[plotpoints=10,showpoints=true]{-2}{2}{x dup mul}
\end{pspicture}
```

Example
6-1-48

6.2 pst-node—**Nodes and connections**

While the base package **pstricks** provides some commands to draw arbitrary connecting lines, it lacks support for placing and saving nodes. By comparison, the package **pst-node** offers outstanding support for nodes and connections.

This section deals with the placement of nodes such as \rnode{B}{connections} in the section heading, and the creation of connecting lines such as the one from \rnode{A}{here} to the node placed in the heading. Since you can define a symbolic name for a node, you do not need to know its coordinates. **pst-node** saves the coordinates in a "dictionary", a two-column table mapping the symbolic node name to its coordinates.

Basically, there are no restrictions for node placement, except that all node connections that belong together *have to* be on the same TEX page, since information about the coordinates on a page is no longer available after that page has been completed.

A node name consists of a finite number of alphanumeric characters and should start with a letter. Since **PSTricks** adds the prefix N@ to the node names at the PostScript level, the restriction that names have to start with a letter is merely a precaution at the LATEX level, where command names may include only alphanumeric characters. As a rule, all node commands are fragile, so that they should be prefixed with \protect when used in headings, etc.

Node names

6.2.1 Setting nodes

PSTricks allows for a very large number of macros to be created for different node connections, and it isn't always easy to find the right node type with the right connection for a specific problem.

> \rnode `[reference point]` *{name}{object}*

This is the simplest form of a node command. It has a name similar to that of the \rput command because both refer to the same reference points. The center of a node is determined by the optional argument; if it is missing, the center of the surrounding box is taken as the default value. Other possible reference points are summarized in Table 5.2 on page 266.

```
\usepackage{pstricks,pst-node}
\begin{pspicture}(2,2)
\rput(0,0){\rnode{A}{\large G}}\rput(2,2){\rnode{B}{g}}
\ncline{A}{B}
\end{pspicture}
```

\rnode can be nested arbitrarily so that, for example, even for a single character, you can set four nodes into the corners of its surrounding box.

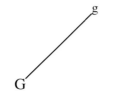

```
\usepackage{pstricks,pst-node}
\quad\rnode[lb]{A}{\rnode[rb]{B}{\rnode[rt]{C}{%
    \rnode[lt]{D}{\Huge g}}}}
\psset{nodesep=5pt}
\ncline{A}{B}\ncline{B}{C}\ncline{C}{D}\ncline{D}{A}
```

Example 6-2-2 can be extended to "encircle" arbitrary areas. For instance, with the definition in Example 6-2-3, you can choose four corner nodes for any area and interconnect them to a closed curve with the \psccurve command (see Section 5.7.1 on page 246). The corners are named #1-tl, #1-tr, #1-bl, and #1-br, where #1 has to be replaced by the basic node name, tl is top left, and so on. For this example, \SpecialCoor must be enabled (see Section 5.14 on page 296). With this "four-corner definition" of nodes, you can plot essentially any curve.

```
\usepackage{pstricks,pst-node}
\SpecialCoor
\newcommand\DefNodes[2]{%
  \rnode[tl]{#1-tl}{%
    \rnode[tr]{#1-tr}{%
      \rnode[bl]{#1-bl}{%
        \rnode[br]{#1-br}{#2}}}}}
\huge\[
\frac{\DefNodes{A}{A_1}+\DefNodes{B}{B_1}+C_1}
   {\DefNodes{D}{D_1}+\DefNodes{E}{E_1}+\DefNodes{F}{F_1}} \]
\psccurve[linecolor=blue,linestyle=dashed,%
  fillstyle=hlines,hatchcolor=black!20]
    (D-bl)(A-tl)(A-tr)([angle=-90,nodesep=0.1]B-bl)
    ([angle=-90,nodesep=0.1]B-br)(F-tr)(F-br)(F-bl)
    ([angle=90,nodesep=0.1]E-tr)([angle=90,nodesep=0.1]E-tl)
    (D-br)(D-bl)
```

$$\frac{A_1 + B_1 + C_1}{D_1 + E_1 + F_1}$$

Example
6-2-3

\Rnode [*settings*] {*name*}{*object*}

\Rnode differs from \rnode only in the way the center is specified: with \Rnode it is given relative to the baseline so that you can still obtain parallel lines when the actual center is different (see page 348).

```
\usepackage{pstricks,pst-node}
\Rnode{A}{\Large g}\hspace{2cm}\Rnode{B}{\Large G}
\ncline{A}{B}
```

```
\Rnode[vref=0pt]{A}{\Large g}\hspace{2cm}%
                    \Rnode[vref=0pt]{B}{\Large G}
\ncline{A}{B}
```

g————————G
g——————G

Example
6-2-4

\pnode (*x, y*) {*name*}

\pnode defines a node with a radius of zero, which is often used in normal line graphics. You can also set a node at any position within a text as shown in the section heading above (\section{... and \protect\rnode{B}{connections}}), but always keep in mind that `\protect` is necessary because the node commands are fragile. This method is illustrated on the first page of the current section (page 334), where a line was drawn with the following connection command:

```
\ncarc[arcangle=-100,linestyle=dashed,linewidth=0.5pt,
       arrowscale=2]{->}{A}{B}
```

If you specify coordinates by means of the optional argument, you can place nodes at locations that are arbitrarily independent of the current position. For instance, if you want to determine the center between two arbitrary points, you can easily locate it with `\pnode` when `\SpecialCoor` is set (see Section 5.14 on page 296).

With the special coordinate prefix "`!`", PSTricks identifies the coordinates as real PostScript code that, at the end of any calculation, must leave the two values x y on the stack. The following example shows a simple application of the newly defined macro `\nodeBetween`. Because of the coordinates argument there is no need to use `\rput` here, as was necessary in the first example for `\rnode`.

```
\usepackage{pstricks,pst-node}
\SpecialCoor
\makeatletter
\def\nodeBetween(#1)(#2)#3{%
  \pst@getcoor{#1}\pst@tempA \pst@getcoor{#2}\pst@tempB
  \pnode(!%
    \pst@tempA /YA exch \pst@number\psyunit div def
    /XA exch \pst@number\psxunit div def
    \pst@tempB /YB exch \pst@number\psyunit div def
    /XB exch \pst@number\psxunit div def
    XB XA add 2 div YB YA add 2 div){#3}}
\makeatletter
\begin{pspicture}[showgrid=true](-0.3,-0.45)(3,2)
  \psline[linestyle=dashed]{o-o}(0.25,0.33)(2.333,2)
  \nodeBetween(0.25,0.33)(2.333,2){center}
  \pscircle[linecolor=blue](center){3pt}
\end{pspicture}

\bigskip A node \rnode{B}{demonstration}.
\nccurve[arrows=->,linecolor=blue,nodesep=5pt]{B}{center}
```

A node demonstration.

`\cnode` * *[settings]* (x, y) *{radius}{name}*

In contrast to `\pnode`, `\cnode` creates a circular node with a defined radius, which again can be positioned within the running text, (`\cnode{1ex}{A}`), with the center of the node lying on the baseline. Keep in mind that `\cnode` does not reserve space in the running text, so that a box command such as `\makebox` should be used, e.g., `\makebox[3pt]{\cnode*{3pt}{B}}` As you can see, line connections inside the normal text are also possible.

> \Cnode * [*settings*] (*x, y*) {*name*}

The command \Cnode essentially corresponds to \cnode, except that the radius has to be set with the keyword radius. In large documents, this saves you from the trouble of specifying the radius for every single node, if all radii should have the same size anyway.

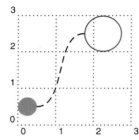

```
\usepackage{pstricks,pst-node}
\begin{pspicture}(3,3)
  \psgrid[subgriddiv=0,griddots=10,gridlabels=7pt]
  \Cnode*[linecolor=red](0.25,0.5){A}
  \Cnode[linecolor=blue,radius=0.5](2.25,2.5){B}
  \nccurve[linestyle=dashed,angleB=180]{A}{B}
\end{pspicture}
```

Example
6-2-6

> \circlenode * [*settings*] {*name*}{*object*}

\circlenode works like \pscirclebox, with the addition that the box serves as a node as well. The size of the circle is entirely determined by its contents.

```
\usepackage{pstricks,pst-node}
\psframe[fillcolor=lightgray,%
    fillstyle=solid](-0.1,1)(3.75,-0.5)
\circlenode[linecolor=blue]{A}{A}\hspace{2cm}%
\circlenode*{B}{\huge B}
\ncline[linestyle=dashed]{A}{B}
```

Example
6-2-7

> \cnodeput * [*settings*] {*angle*} (*x, y*) {*name*}{*object*}

\cnodeput essentially corresponds to \cput, which means a combination of \rput and \circlenode, i.e., \rput{*angle*}{\circlenode{*name*}{*object*}}. The starred form fills the circle with the current value of the fillcolor keyword.

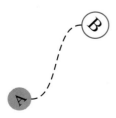

```
\usepackage{pstricks,pst-node}
\begin{pspicture}(3,3)
  \cnodeput*[fillcolor=red]{45}(0.25,0.5){A}{\large A}
  \cnodeput[linecolor=blue]{-45}(2.25,2.5){B}{\Large B}
  \nccurve[linestyle=dashed,angleB=180]{A}{B}
\end{pspicture}
```

Example
6-2-8

```
\ovalnode * [settings] {name}{object}
```

`\ovalnode` is like `\psovalbox` but the box serves as a node as well. The size of the oval is entirely determined by its contents.

```
\usepackage{pstricks,pst-node}
\psframe[fillcolor=lightgray,%
    fillstyle=solid](-0.1,1)(4,-0.5)
\ovalnode{A}{AA}\hspace{1.25cm}%
\ovalnode*{B}{\huge BB}%
\ncline[linestyle=dashed]{A}{B}%
```

```
\dianode * [settings] {name}{object}
```

`\dianode` essentially corresponds to `\psdiabox` but the box serves as a node as well. The size of the rhombus is determined entirely by its contents.

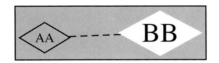

```
\usepackage{pstricks,pst-node}
\psframe[fillcolor=lightgray,%
    fillstyle=solid](-0.1,1)(5,-0.5)
\dianode{A}{AA}\hspace{1.25cm}%
\dianode*{B}{\huge BB}%
\ncline[linestyle=dashed]{A}{B}%
```

```
\trinode * [settings] {name}{object}
```

`\trinode` works like `\pstribox` (see Section 5.12.2 on page 273) but the box serves as a node as well. The size of the triangle is entirely determined by its contents.

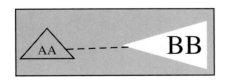

```
\usepackage{pstricks,pst-node}
\psframe[fillcolor=lightgray,%
    fillstyle=solid](-0.1,1.25)(5.2,-0.6)
\trinode{A}{AA}\hspace{1.25cm}%
\trinode*[trimode=L]{B}{\huge BB}%
\ncline[linestyle=dashed]{A}{B}%
```

```
\dotnode * [settings] (x,y) {name}
```

`\dotnode` essentially corresponds to `\psdot` but the box serves as a node as well. The size of the symbol is entirely specified by the given values for `dotsize` and `dotscale` (see Section 5.8 on page 251).

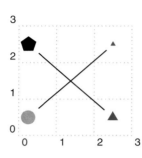

```
\usepackage{pstricks,pst-node}
\begin{pspicture}[showgrid=true](3,3)
  \rput(0.25,0.5){\dotnode[linecolor=red,%
         dotscale=3]{A}}
  \rput(2.5,2.5){\dotnode*[linecolor=blue,%
         dotstyle=triangle*]{B}}
  \ncline[nodesep=5pt]{A}{B}
  \rput(0.25,2.5){\dotnode[dotscale=3,%
         dotstyle=pentagon*]{A}}
  \rput(2.5,0.5){\dotnode[linecolor=blue,%
         dotscale=2,dotstyle=triangle*]{B}}
  \ncline[nodesep=5pt]{A}{B}
\end{pspicture}
```

Example
6-2-12

$\boxed{\texttt{\textbackslash fnode} * \; [\textit{settings}] \; (x,y) \; \{\textit{name}\}}$

`\fnode` essentially corresponds to `\psframe`, with the additional functionality of being a node. If no coordinate pair is specified, the center of the frame is set at the current coordinates; otherwise, it is set at the specified coordinates. The size of the frame can be modified with a keyword (see page 350).

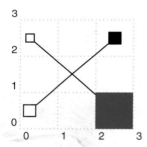

```
\usepackage{pstricks,pst-node}
\begin{pspicture}[showgrid=true](3,3)
  \fnode(0.25,0.5){A}
  \fnode*(2.5,2.5){B}
  \ncline{A}{B}
  \fnode[framesize=0.25](0.25,2.5){A}
  \fnode*[framesize=1,linecolor=blue](2.5,0.5){B}
  \ncline{A}{B}
\end{pspicture}
```

Example
6-2-13

6.2.2 `\nc` connections

All macros start with `\nc` and have the same syntax (where ???? is a placeholder):

$\boxed{\texttt{\textbackslash nc}\;\textit{????} * \; [\textit{settings}] \; \{\textit{arrows}\} \; \{\textit{nodeA}\}\{\textit{nodeB}\}}$

These macros draw a line or curve from node A to node B. Some of the connection commands may be a bit confusing, but you can easily discover the advantages of each particular connection type with a little experimentation. If relevant in the following examples, the names node A and node B always designate the order of the nodes. The starred form is not always useful, even where formally possible. The nc connections are always directed at the center of the node, while the values of the keyword nodesep and those for the angle specifications refer to the box frame.

> `\ncline` ***** *[settings]* *{arrows}* {nodeA}{nodeB}

The simplest of all connection types is `\ncline`, which just draws a straight line from one node to another.

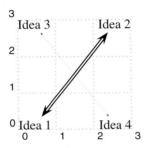

```
\usepackage{pstricks,pst-node}
\begin{pspicture}[showgrid=true](3,3)
  \rput[bl](0,0){\rnode{A}{Idea 1}}
  \rput[tr](3,3){\rnode{B}{Idea 2}}
  \ncline[nodesep=3pt,doubleline=true]{<->}{A}{B}
  \rput[lt](0,3){\rnode{A}{Idea 3}}
  \rput[rb](3,0){\rnode{B}{Idea 4}}
  \ncline*[nodesep=3pt,doubleline=true]{<->}{A}{B}
\end{pspicture}
```

Example
6-2-14

> `\ncarc` ***** *[settings]* *{arrows}* {nodeA}{nodeB}

`\ncarc` draws a curve whose gradient angle (in relation to the direct line) at the beginning of the first node equals `arcangle` (see page 351).

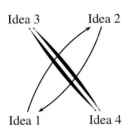

```
\usepackage{pstricks,pst-node}
\begin{pspicture}(3,3)
  \rput[bl](0,0){\rnode{A}{Idea 1}}
  \rput[tr](3,3){\rnode{B}{Idea 2}}
  \ncarc[nodesep=3pt,arcangle=20]{->}{A}{B}
  \ncarc[nodesep=3pt,arcangle=20]{->}{B}{A}
  \rput[lt](0,3){\rnode{A}{Idea 3}}
  \rput[rb](3,0){\rnode{B}{Idea 4}}
  \ncarc*[nodesep=3pt]{<->}{A}{B}
  \ncarc*[nodesep=3pt]{<->}{B}{A}
\end{pspicture}
```

Example
6-2-15

> `\ncdiag` ***** *[settings]* *{arrows}* {nodeA}{nodeB}

`\ncdiag` also draws a line, albeit one that consists of three segments. Thus this connection type is not useful for nodes that are positioned directly horizontally or vertically to each other. You can modify the length of each segment with the `arm` keyword (see page 351).

Example 6-2-16 illustrates that, as mentioned previously, the starred version of \ncdiag gives questionable results. Since the same is true for many of the examples, the starred version will be used only if it produces a usable effect in a particular case.

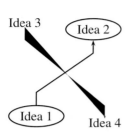

```
\usepackage{pstricks,pst-node}
\begin{pspicture}(3,3)
  \rput[bl](0,0){\ovalnode{A}{Idea 1}}
  \rput[tr](3,3){\ovalnode{B}{Idea 2}}
  \ncdiag[angleA=90,angleB=-90]{->}{A}{B}
  \rput[lt](0,3){\rnode{A}{Idea 3}}
  \rput[rb](3,0){\rnode{B}{Idea 4}}
  \ncdiag*[angleA=-90,angleB=90]{->}{A}{B}
\end{pspicture}
```

Example
6-2-16

In some cases, \ncdiag is more useful than \ncline, especially for connecting lines that are not directed at the center of a node. You can force a straight line with arm=0 and at the same time use the angle option to direct the line at a different point on the node.

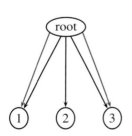

```
\usepackage{pstricks,pst-node}
\begin{pspicture}(2.75,3)
  \rput(1.5,2.8){\ovalnode{A}{root}}
  \rput[lb](0,0){\ovalnode{B}{1}}
  \rput[b](1.5,0){\ovalnode{C}{2}}
  \rput[rb](3,0){\ovalnode{D}{3}}
  \ncline{->}{A}{B}\ncline{->}{A}{C}\ncline{->}{A}{D}
\psset{linecolor=blue}
  \ncdiag[arm=0,angleA=80,angleB=-160]{<-}{B}{A}
  \ncdiag[arm=0,angleA=100,angleB=-20]{<-}{D}{A}
\end{pspicture}
```

Example
6-2-17

\ncdiagg ***** *[settings]* *{arrows}* {nodeA}{nodeB}

\ncdiagg resembles \ncdiag, with the sole difference between the two being that an "arm" (leg) is drawn only for the first node, so the connection consists of just two line segments. You might think that \ncdiag with armB=0pt would produce the same results, but this is not the case, as the following example illustrates. With \ncdiag, there is a third "arm"; even through this segment is of zero length, it affects the the place where the connection is made to the node (as this arm is directed to the center of the node with a default specification of angleB=0). To achieve a similar behavior we would need to add angleB=30 in the following example.

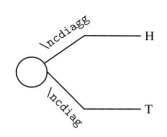

```
\usepackage{pstricks,pst-node}
\begin{pspicture}(-0.2,-1)(3,1)
  \cnode{12pt}{a}
  \rput[l](3,1){\rnode{b}{H}} \rput[l](3,-1){\rnode{c}{T}}
  \ncdiagg[angleA=180,armA=1.5,nodesepA=3pt]{b}{a}
  \nbput[nrot=:D,npos=1.3]{\texttt{\textbackslash ncdiagg}}
  \ncdiag[angleA=180,armA=1.5,armB=0,nodesepA=3pt]{c}{a}
  \naput[nrot=:D,npos=1.3]{\texttt{\textbackslash ncdiag}}
\end{pspicture}
```

Example
6-2-18

\ncdiagg may also be used to draw a single line that starts at a specific angle from the first node and is directed to the center of the second node.

\ncbar ***** *[settings]* *{arrows}* *{nodeA}{nodeB}*

\ncbar is similar to \ncdiag but the angles between the segments are always 90°. With differing arm lengths or a starting angle other than 90°, it produces a "slanting" connection. The angle can only be changed for both nodes together, and angleA and angleB must have the same value (see page 351).

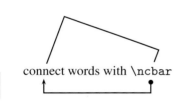

```
\usepackage{pstricks,pst-node}
\begin{pspicture}(0,-1)(3.5,2)
\rnode{A}{connect} words with %
    \rnode{B}{\texttt{\textbackslash ncbar}}
\ncbar[nodesep=3pt,angle=-90]{<-**}{A}{B}
\ncbar[nodesep=3pt,angle=70]{A}{B}
\end{pspicture}
```

Example
6-2-19

\ncangle ***** *[settings]* *{arrows}* *{nodeA}{nodeB}*

\ncangle is similar to \ncdiag, but arm lengths and angles are calculated from the specified values to ensure correct values are used.

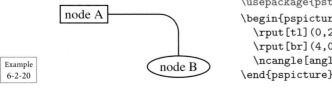

```
\usepackage{pstricks,pst-node}
\begin{pspicture}(4,3)
  \rput[tl](0,2){\rnode{A}{\psframebox{node A}}}
  \rput[br](4,0){\ovalnode{B}{node B}}
  \ncangle[angleB=90,armB=0,linearc=.5]{A}{B}
\end{pspicture}
```

Example
6-2-20

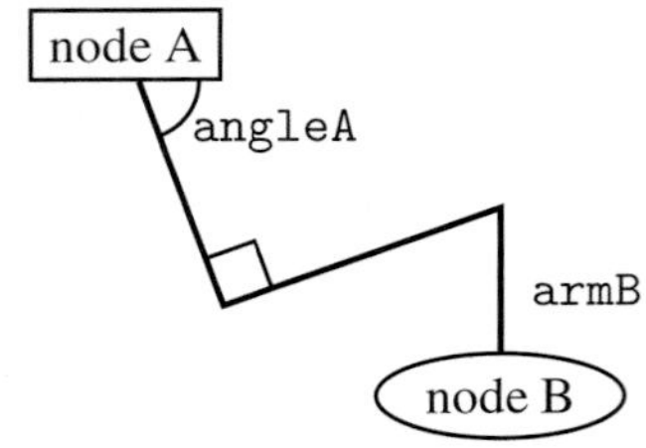

```
\usepackage{pstricks,pst-node}
% \showInfo defined in example code to display
% angle and arm info
\begin{pspicture}(4,3)
  \rput[tl](0,3){\rnode{A}{\psframebox{node A}}}
  \rput[br](4,0){\ovalnode{B}{node B}}
  \ncangle[angleA=-70,angleB=90,armB=1cm,
          linewidth=1.2pt]{A}{B}
  \showInfo % see example code
\end{pspicture}
```

Example
6-2-21

$\boxed{\texttt{\textbackslash ncangles} * \texttt{[settings]} \ \texttt{\{arrows\}} \ \{nodeA\}\{nodeB\}}$

\ncangles is a kind of "plural form" of \ncangle because it can represent up to four line segments. armA is connected to armB through two line segments, which are perpendicular to each other. The angle between armA and the middle segments is calculated as $90 + 2 \times$ angleA, and the angle between the middle segments and armB is then derived from the values of the other angles.

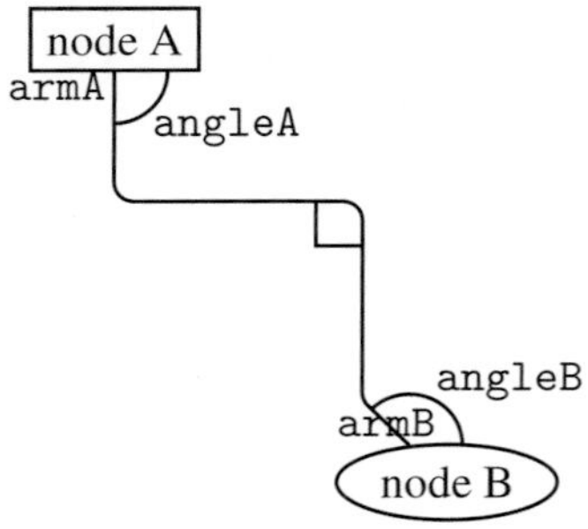

```
\usepackage{pstricks,pst-node}
% \showInfo defined in example code to display
% angle and arm info
\begin{pspicture}(4,4)
  \rput[tl](0,4){\rnode{A}{\psframebox{node A}}}
  \rput[br](4,0){\ovalnode{B}{node B}}
  \ncangles[angleA=-90,angleB=135,armA=1cm,armB=.5cm,
     linearc=.15]{A}{B}
  \showInfo % see example code
\end{pspicture}
```

Example
6-2-22

$\boxed{\texttt{\textbackslash ncloop} * \texttt{[settings]} \ \texttt{\{arrows\}} \ \{nodeA\}\{nodeB\}}$

\ncloop differs from the similar \ncangle and \ncangles commands in having a total of five line segments. The first and the last of these segments are determined by the armA and armB lengths and angleA and angleB angles as usual. The middle three segments connect to one another at angles of $90°$. The second line segment is always of length loopsize (see page 352).

All changes of direction occur counterclockwise, which determines whether the whole line is drawn above or below.

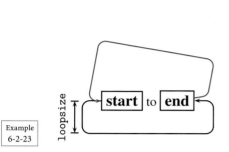

```
\usepackage{pstricks,pst-node}
\hspace*{0.5cm}\rnode{A}{\psframebox{%
    \large\textbf{start}}} to
\rnode{B}{\psframebox{\large\textbf{end}}}
\ncloop[angleA=180,loopsize=0.9,arm=0.5,%
    linearc=.2]{->}{A}{B}
\ncput[npos=1.5,nrot=:U]{%
    \psline{|<->|}(.45,-.2)(-.45,-.2)}
\nbput[npos=1.5,nrot=:D,labelsep=.35cm]%
    {\small\texttt{loopsize}}
\ncloop[angleA=10,angleB=180,%
    linecolor=blue,linearc=.2]{->}{B}{A}
```

You can close a loop by specifying the same node twice. For more circular loops, the use of \nccircle is recommended (see on the following page).

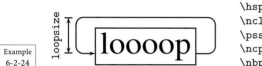

```
\usepackage{pstricks,pst-node}
\hspace*{0.5cm}\rnode[lB]{A}{\psframebox{\Huge loooop}}
\ncloop[angleB=180,loopsize=1,arm=.5,linearc=.2]{->}{A}{A}
\psset{npos=3.5}
\ncput[nrot=:U]{\psline{|<->|}(0.5,-0.2)(-0.5,-0.2)}
\nbput[nrot=:D,labelsep=.35cm]{{\small\texttt{loopsize}}}
```

You can also draw "railroad diagrams" with \ncloop by specifying appropriate angles. The connections will then touch both nodes from the same side.

```
\usepackage{pstricks,pst-node}
\large\rnode{A}{\psframebox{start}}\qquad
\rnode{M}{\psframebox{middle}}\qquad
\rnode{B}{\psframebox{end}}
\ncline{->}{A}{M}\ncline{->}{M}{B}
\ncloop[loopsize=0.9,arm=0.4,linearc=.2,angleB=180]
    {->}{A}{B}
```

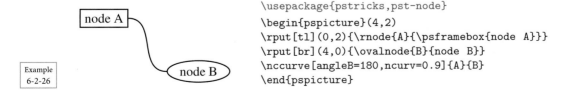

\nccurve creates a Bézier curve between two nodes. It can be modified through the two angles angleA and angleB and the curve keyword ncurv (see page 352).

```
\usepackage{pstricks,pst-node}
\begin{pspicture}(4,2)
\rput[tl](0,2){\rnode{A}{\psframebox{node A}}}
\rput[br](4,0){\ovalnode{B}{node B}}
\nccurve[angleB=180,ncurv=0.9]{A}{B}
\end{pspicture}
```

$\boxed{\texttt{\textbackslash nccircle} * \textit{[settings]} \ \textit{\{arrows\}} \ \{\textit{node}\}\{\textit{radius}\}}$

\nccircle refers to only one node, but requires two arguments. Technically, the circle runs through the center of the node and can be modified through angleA and the radius.

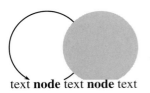

```
\usepackage{pstricks,pst-node}
\begin{pspicture}(5.5,2)
text \rnode{A}{\textbf{node}} text
\nccircle[nodesep=3pt]{->}{A}{1cm}\
\rnode{A}{\textbf{node}} text
\nccircle*[linecolor=lightgray,nodesep=3pt]{A}{1cm}
\end{pspicture}
```

text **node** text **node** text

Example
6-2-27

$\boxed{\texttt{\textbackslash ncbox} * \textit{[settings]} \ \textit{\{arrows\}} \ \{\textit{nodeA}\}\{\textit{nodeB}\}}$

With \ncbox, you must ensure that the node content is really enclosed in the box. The associated keywords boxsize (see page 353) and nodesep (see page 350) offer an easy way to do this. In the following example, the keyword border is used with \ncbox to illustrate the overlay effect (see also Section 5.6.2 on page 239). In contrast to the normal behavior of nc connections, no arrows are available for \ncbox (the *arrows* argument is ignored, as the example depicts).

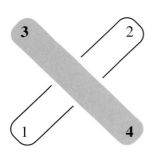

```
\usepackage{pstricks,pst-node}
\begin{pspicture}(3,3)   \large
  \psset{nodesep=3pt,linearc=0.3}
  \rput[bl](0,0){\rnode{A}{1}}
  \rput[tr](3,3){\rnode{B}{2}}
  \ncbox{A}{B}
  \rput[lt](0,3){\rnode{A}{3}}
  \rput[rb](3,0){\rnode{B}{4}}
  \ncbox*[border=4pt,linecolor=lightgray]{->}{A}{B}
  \rput[lt](0,3){\rnode{A}{\textbf{3}}}
  \rput[rb](3,0){\rnode{B}{\textbf{4}}}
\end{pspicture}
```

Example
6-2-28

$\boxed{\texttt{\textbackslash nccarcbox} * \textit{[settings]} \ \textit{\{arrows\}} \ \{\textit{nodeA}\}\{\textit{nodeB}\}}$

With \ncarcbox, you must also ensure that the node content is enclosed by the box. The associated keywords, boxsize (page 353) and nodesep (page 350), offer an easy way to accomplish this. In the following example, the keyword border is used with \ncarcbox to illustrate the overlay effect (see also Section 5.6.2 on page 239). Angles are counted clockwise.

```
\usepackage{pstricks,pst-node,textcomp}
\SpecialCoor
\begin{pspicture}(-0.5,0)(3,3) \large
  \psset{nodesep=3pt,linearc=0.3}
  \rput[bl](0,0){\rnode{A}{1}}
  \rput[tr](3,3){\rnode{B}{2}}
  \ncarcbox[arcangle=30]{A}{B}
  \pcline[linestyle=dashed](A)(B)
  \pcline[linestyle=dashed,nodesepB=-0.2](A)(3,0.8)
  \psarc{<->}(0,0){3.25}{15}{45}
  \rput(2.2,1.5){\small30\textdegree}
  \rput[lt](0,3){\rnode{A}{3}}
  \rput[rb](3,0){\rnode{B}{4}}
  \ncarcbox*[border=4pt,linecolor=lightgray,%
      arcangle=45]{A}{B}
  \rput[lt](0,3){\rnode{A}{\textbf{3}}}
  \rput[rb](3,0){\rnode{B}{\textbf{4}}}
\end{pspicture}
```

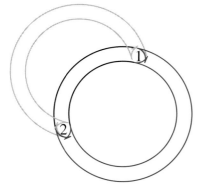

Example
6-2-29

The drawn arc is part of a circle with a line width of `boxsize`. A negative value for `arcangle`, e.g., -60, causes the arc to be drawn in the other direction when the nodes are reversed, resulting in a gradient angle of $60°$ (between line $\overline{AB}$ and the tangent at the starting point). However, in this case the nodes will not be enclosed by the drawn path.

```
\usepackage{pstricks,pst-node}
\begin{pspicture}(0.5,0)(4,3)   \large
  \psset{nodesep=3pt,linearc=0.3,boxsize=2mm}
  \rput(3,3){\rnode{A}{1}}
  \rput(1,1){\rnode{B}{2}}
  \ncarcbox[arcangle=60]                     {A}{B}
  \ncarcbox[arcangle=-60,linecolor=lightgray]{A}{B}
  \ncarcbox[arcangle=-60,linecolor=blue]     {B}{A}
\end{pspicture}
```

Example
6-2-30

6.2.3 \pc **connections**

All connection macros with a \pc prefix have a similar syntax and behavior as their \nc counterparts discussed in Section 6.2.2 on page 340. The only difference is that the \pc connections generally start and end at the node center, not at the surrounding box of the defined nodes. Primarily we are dealing with well-known line or curve macros here, which is the reason why the arguments also have to be inside round braces (). With the \SpecialCoor option (Section 5.14 on page 296) enabled, coordinates can still be passed as node names. Alternatively, you can refer to a node directly from a specific point.

> \pc ???? * [*settings*] {*arrows*} (*nodeA*) (*nodeB*)

This is the general syntax for all `pc` connections (where *????* is a placeholder). The available commands are \pcline, \pccurve, \pcarc, \pcbar, \pcdiag, \pcdiagg, \pcangle, \pcangles, \pcloop, \pcbox, and \pcarcbox.

The next two examples correspond to the discussion in Section 6.2.2 on page 341. With the help of the keyword nodesep, you can again extend (negative values) or shorten (positive values) the beginning and end of a connection.

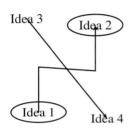

```
\usepackage{pstricks,pst-node}   \SpecialCoor
\begin{pspicture}(3,3)
  \rput[bl](0,0){\ovalnode{A}{Idea 1}}
  \rput[tr](3,3){\ovalnode{B}{Idea 2}}
  \pcdiag[angleA=90,angleB=-90,arm=1.25cm]{->}(A)(B)
  \rput[lt](0,3){\rnode{A}{Idea 3}}
  \rput[rb](3,0){\rnode{B}{Idea 4}}
  \pcdiag[angleA=-90,angleB=90,arm=0]{->}(A)(B)
\end{pspicture}
```

Example
6-2-31

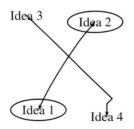

```
\usepackage{pstricks,pst-node}
\SpecialCoor
\begin{pspicture}(3,3)
  \rput[bl](0,0){\ovalnode{A}{Idea 1}}
  \rput[tr](3,3){\ovalnode{B}{Idea 2}}
  \pcarc{<->}(A)(B)
  \rput[lt](0,3){\rnode{A}{Idea 3}}
  \rput[rb](3,0){\rnode{B}{Idea 4}}
  \pcangles[angleA=-45,angleB=90]{->}(A)(B)
\end{pspicture}
```

Example
6-2-32

6.2.4 Node keywords

Table 6.3 on the facing page lists all valid keywords for the **pst-node** package. These keywords are discussed in more detail in the following examples.

The href *and* vref *keys*

The two keywords href and vref have meaning only for the \Rnode command, where, by definition, the node center is the middle of the baseline of the surrounding box. This center can be modified with these keywords. href moves the center by href multiplied with the half-width of the node box. Modifying href without also applying vref will yield no visible change when the connecting line runs horizontally. In contrast to href, vref determines this point with an absolute value relative to the baseline (vref=0pt). If relative

Table 6.3: Keywords for `pst-node`

Name	Value Type	Default	Name	Value Type	Default
href	*value*	0	angleB	*angle*	0
vref	*value [unit]*	0.7ex	arm	*value [unit]*	10pt
radius	*value [unit]*	0.25cm	armA	*value [unit]*	10pt
framesize	*value [unit] [value [unit]]*	10pt	armB	*value [unit]*	10pt
nodesep	*value [unit]*	0pt	loopsize	*value [unit]*	1cm
nodesepA	*value [unit]*	0pt	ncurv	*value*	0.67
nodesepB	*value [unit]*	0pt	ncurvA	*value*	0.67
Xnodesep	*value [unit]*	0pt	ncurvB	*value*	0.67
XnodesepA	*value [unit]*	0pt	boxsize	*value [unit]*	0.4cm
XnodesepB	*value [unit]*	0pt	offset	*value [unit]*	0pt
Ynodesep	*value [unit]*	0pt	offsetA	*value [unit]*	0pt
YnodesepA	*value [unit]*	0pt	offsetB	*value [unit]*	0pt
YnodesepB	*value [unit]*	0pt	ref	*reference*	c
arcangle	*angle*	8	nrot	*rotation*	0
arcangleA	*angle*	8	npos	*value*	{}
arcangleB	*angle*	8	shortput	none|nab|tablr|tab	none
angle	*angle*	0	tpos	*value*	0.5
angleA	*angle*	0	rot	*rotation*	0

units (e.g., ex or em) are used, the relation is also preserved with different font sizes.

```
\usepackage{pstricks,pst-node}\SpecialCoor
\ImgI\hspace{5mm}\ImgII\hspace{5mm}\begin{pspicture}[showgrid=true](6,4)
\rput[lb](0,0){\Rnode{A}{\Square}\hspace{1.4cm}\Rnode[href=4,vref=3]{B}{\Square}}
\psframe*[linecolor=black!20](3,3)(4,4)\psframe*[linecolor=black!20](5,3)(6,4)
\psline[arrows=->](3.5,3.5)(5.5,3.5) \uput[-90](4.5,3.5){href}
\pcline[linecolor=red,linestyle=dotted,linewidth=2pt](A)(B)
\ncline[linecolor=red,linewidth=2pt,arrowscale=2,arrows=->]{A}{B}
\pnode(3,0.7ex){C}
\ncline[linecolor=blue,linewidth=2pt,arrowscale=2,arrows=->]{A}{C}
\pcline{->}(3.5,0.5)(3.5,3.5)\uput[0](3.5,2){vref}
\pcline[linecolor=white](3.5,0.5)(3.5,1)
\end{pspicture}
```

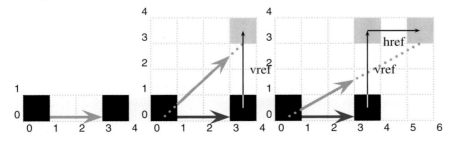

Example
6-2-33

The radius *key* The radius keyword is useful when you wish to show nodes as circles of equal size.

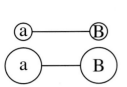

```
\usepackage{pstricks,pst-node}
\Cnode(0.5,0){A}\rput(0.5,0){\Large a}
\Cnode(2.5,0){B}\rput(2.5,0){\Large B}
\ncline{A}{B} \\[5mm]
\Cnode[radius=0.5cm](0.5,0){A}\rput(0.5,0){\Large a}
\Cnode[radius=0.5cm](2.5,0){B}\rput(2.5,0){\Large B}
\ncline{A}{B}
```

Example
6-2-34

The framesize *key* The framesize keyword only takes effect only when used in combination with \fnode (see Section 6.2.1 on page 340). If only one value is passed to this keyword, it is taken as the side length of a square.

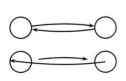

```
\usepackage{pstricks,pst-node}
\fnode(0.5,0){A}\fnode*(2.5,0){B}
\ncline{A}{B} \\[5mm]
\fnode[framesize=20pt](0.5,0){A}%
\fnode*[framesize=1 5pt](2.5,0){B}
\ncline{A}{B}
```

Example
6-2-35

The nodesep, nodesepA, *and* nodesepB *keys* Normally a connection touches the outer box of a node. With nodesep, you can modify this behavior at both ends of a connection. Thus the specifications for nodesep refer to both ends, while nodesepA refers to the end at the first node and nodesepB to the end at the second node.

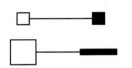

```
\usepackage{pstricks,pst-node}
\Cnode[radius=0.3cm](0.25,0){A}%
\Cnode[radius=0.3cm](2.5,0){B}
\ncarc{->}{A}{B}\ncarc{->}{B}{A} \\[5mm]
\Cnode[radius=0.3cm](0.25,0){A}%
\Cnode[radius=0.3cm](2.5,0){B}
\ncarc[nodesep=5pt]{->}{A}{B}%
\ncarc[nodesepA=-0.3cm,nodesepB=-0.6cm]{->}{B}{A}
```

Example
6-2-36

The Xnodesep *and* Ynodesep *keys and their variants* XnodesepA ... The values for [XY]nodesep do not refer to the direct connecting line to the center of the node. Instead, they determine the horizontal or vertical distance from the center of the node. In contrast, the values for nodesep determine the distance to the surrounding box (Section 5.14.4 on page 299). Example 6-2-37 shows connecting lines of different lengths.

These keywords are especially useful when you need to work with special coordinates.

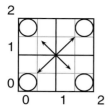

```
\usepackage{pstricks,pst-node}
\begin{pspicture}(2,2)\psgrid[subgriddiv=2]
    \cnode(0.25,1.75){0.25cm}{A}  \cnode(1.75,0.25){0.25cm}{B}
    \cnode(1.75,1.75){0.25cm}{C}  \cnode(0.25,0.25){0.25cm}{D}
    \ncline[nodesep=0.25]{<->}{A}{B}
    \ncline[Ynodesep=0.25]{<->}{C}{D}
\end{pspicture}
```

Example
6-2-37

The keyword `arcangle` defines the gradient angle of the connection at the two end points relative to the straight line. In Example 6-2-36, the connections are relatively close together, a result that can be modified with the keyword `arcangle`. The values for `arcangle` always refer to both nodes, those for `arcangleA` to the first node, and those for `arcangleB` to the second node. Thus, with an appropriate choice of angles, you can form the connections into virtually any curve shape.

The `arcangle`, `arcangleA`, *and* `arcangleB` *keys*

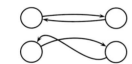

```
\usepackage{pstricks,pst-node}
\Cnode[radius=0.3cm](0.25,0){A}%
\Cnode[radius=0.3cm](2.5,0){B}
\ncarc{->}{A}{B}\ncarc{->}{B}{A}  \\[5mm]
\Cnode[radius=0.3cm](0.25,0){A}%
\Cnode[radius=0.3cm](2.5,0){B}
\ncarc[arcangle=30]{->}{A}{B}%
\ncarc[arcangleA=30,arcangleB=-60]{->}{B}{A}
```

Example
6-2-38

The keyword `angle` denotes the angle by which the connection reaches the nodes, relative to the horizontal line. The values for `angle` always refer to both nodes, while `angleA` refers to the first node and `angleB` to the second node. Thus, with an appropriate choice of angles, you can form the connections into virtually any curve shape.

The `angle`, `angleA`, *and* `angleB` *keys*

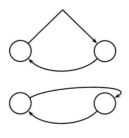

```
\usepackage{pstricks,pst-node}
\Cnode[radius=0.3cm](0.25,0){A}%
\Cnode[radius=0.3cm](2.5,0){B}
\ncangle[angleA=45,angleB=135]{->}{A}{B}%
\nccurve[angleB=-45,angleA=-135]{->}{B}{A}  \\[10mm]
\Cnode[radius=0.3cm](0.25,0){A}%
\Cnode[radius=0.3cm](2.5,0){B}
\nccurve[angle=30]{->}{A}{B}%
\nccurve[angleB=-45,angleA=-135]{->}{B}{A}
```

Example
6-2-39

The keyword `arm` defines the length of the straight line or arm, after which the connection is allowed to take another direction. Values for `arm` always refer to both nodes, while

The `arm`, `armA`, *and* `armB` *keys*

armA refers to the first node and armB to the second node. If no explicit value is given, a default of 10pt applies.

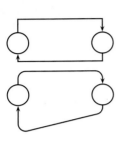

```
\usepackage{pstricks,pst-node}
\Cnode[radius=0.3cm](0.25,0){A}%
\Cnode[radius=0.3cm](2.5,0){B}
\ncbar[angle=90]{->}{A}{B}%
\ncbar[angle=-90,arm=0.2cm]{->}{B}{A} \\[10mm]
\Cnode[radius=0.3cm](0.25,0){A}%
\Cnode[radius=0.3cm](2.5,0){B}
\psset{linearc=0.2cm}
\ncdiag[angle=90]{->}{A}{B}%
\ncdiag[angle=-90,armA=0.2cm,armB=0.75cm]{->}{B}{A}
```

Example
6-2-40

The loopsize *key*   The keyword loopsize defines the "height" of a connection that is formed into a loop.

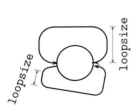

```
\usepackage{pstricks,pst-node}
\Cnode[radius=0.5cm](1.5,0){A}%
\ncloop[angleA=0,angleB=180,
    nodesepB=3pt,linearc=0.4cm]{<-<}{A}{A}
\psline[linewidth=0.1pt,tbarsize=5pt]{|<->|}(2.5,0)(2.5,1)
\uput[0]{90}(2.5,0.5){\textttt{loopsize}}
\ncloop[angleB=-10,angleA=-170,linearc=0.2cm,
    loopsize=0.5cm]{->}{A}{A}
\psline[linewidth=0.1pt,tbarsize=5pt]{|<->|}(0.4,-0.6)(0.5,-0.2)
\uput[180]{70}(.5,-0.25){\textttt{loopsize}}
```

Example
6-2-41

The ncurv, ncurvA, *and* ncurvB *keys*   The keyword ncurv influences the behavior of a Bézier curve connection formed with \nccurve. A small value for ncurv leads to a "tighter" curve that is closer to a line (Section 5.7.1 on page 244). As usual, ncurvA and ncurvB affect only the connection at the corresponding side.

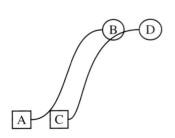

```
\usepackage{pstricks,pst-node}
\begin{pspicture}(4,3)
  \rput[bl](0,0){\rnode{A}{\psframebox{A}}}
  \rput[tr](3,3){\ovalnode{B}{B}}
  \nccurve[angleB=180]{A}{B}
  \rput[bl](1,0){\rnode{C}{\psframebox{C}}}
  \rput[tr](4,3){\ovalnode{D}{D}}
  \nccurve[angleB=180,ncurvA=0.3,ncurvB=1]{C}{D}
\end{pspicture}
```

Example
6-2-42

The keyword `boxsize` refers exclusively to the two connection types, `\ncbox` and `\ncarcbox`, for which it specifies the half-width.

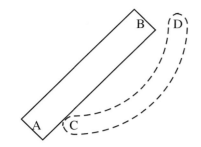

```
\usepackage{pstricks,pst-node}
\begin{pspicture}(4,3)
  \rput[bl](0,0){\rnode{A}{A}}
  \rput[tr](3,3){\rnode{B}{B}}
  \ncbox{A}{B}
  \rput[bl](1,0){\rnode{C}{C}}
  \rput[tr](4,3){\rnode{D}{D}}
  \ncarcbox[nodesep=5pt,linearc=0.3,linestyle=dashed,%
            boxsize=0.25cm,arcangle=45]{C}{D}
\end{pspicture}
```

Example
6-2-43

The keyword `offset` moves a connecting line to a position parallel to its original, which simplifies the process of drawing double straight lines. The values for `offset` always refer to both nodes, while `offsetA` refers to the connection at first node and `offsetB` to the connection on the second node. These keys are not available for `\ncarcbox` and `\pcarcbox`.

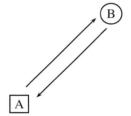

```
\usepackage{pstricks,pst-node}
\begin{pspicture}(3,3)
  \rput[bl](0,0){\rnode{A}{\psframebox{A}}}
  \rput[tr](3,3){\ovalnode{B}{B}}
  \psset{offset=0.2,nodesep=2pt}
  \ncline{->}{A}{B}
  \ncline{->}{B}{A}
\end{pspicture}
```

Example
6-2-44

The keyword `ref` refers to the reference points given in Table 5.2 on page 266 and is useful only for labels that are set with `\ncput`. This keyword determines how the label is set into the middle of a connecting line. For example, `rb` indicates that the lower-right corner is set exactly into the middle of the connecting line.

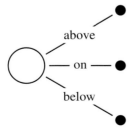

```
\usepackage{pstricks,pst-node}
\cnode(0.5,0){.5cm}{root}
\cnode*(3,1.5){4pt}{A}
\cnode*(3,0){4pt}{B}
\cnode*(3,-1.5){4pt}{C}
\psset{nodesep=3pt}
\ncline{root}{A}   \ncput*{above}
\ncline{root}{B}   \ncput*{on}
\ncline{root}{C}   \ncput*{below}
```

Example
6-2-45

```
\usepackage{pstricks,pst-node}
\cnode(0.5,0){.5cm}{root}
\cnode*(3,1.5){4pt}{A}
\cnode*(3,0){4pt}{B}
\cnode*(3,-1.5){4pt}{C}
\psset{nodesep=3pt}
\ncline{root}{A}    \ncput*[ref=rt]{above}
\ncline{root}{B}    \ncput*[ref=lb]{on}
\ncline{root}{C}    \ncput*[ref=lt]{below}
```

Example
6-2-46

The nrot key With the keyword nrot, you can rotate labels before placing them. The possible values for reference angles are given in Table 5.13 on page 266 and have to be specified in the form ": *angle/short-form*".

```
\usepackage{pstricks,pst-node}
\cnode(0.5,0){.5cm}{root}
\cnode*(3,1.5){4pt}{A}
\cnode*(3,0){4pt}{B}
\cnode*(3,-1.5){4pt}{C}
\psset{nodesep=3pt}
\ncline{root}{A}    \ncput*[nrot=:U]{above}
\ncline{root}{B}    \ncput*[nrot=:U]{on}
\ncline{root}{C}    \ncput*[nrot=:U]{below}
```

Example
6-2-47

```
\usepackage{pstricks,pst-node}
\cnode(0.5,0){.5cm}{root}
\cnode*(3,1.5){4pt}{A}
\cnode*(3,0){4pt}{B}
\cnode*(3,-1.5){4pt}{C}
\psset{nodesep=3pt}
\ncline{root}{A}    \ncput*[nrot=:L]{above}
\ncline{root}{B}    \ncput*[nrot=:R]{on}
\ncline{root}{C}    \ncput*[nrot=:D]{below}
```

Example
6-2-48

The npos key Every connection between two nodes consists of at least one segment (\ncline) and may include up to a maximum of five segments (\ncloop). With npos, you can specify the segments on which the label should appear. The real decimal value specifies both the segment number and the relative position within the segment. For example, a value of 1.6 places the label into the second segment with a distance of 60% from the beginning of the segment. Table 6.4 shows the number of segments possible with the different connection types, including the permissible value range for npos and the corresponding default values.

Table 6.4: Comparison of different node connections

Connection	*Segments*	*Range*	*Default*
\ncline	1	$0 \leq npos \leq 1$	0.5
\nccurve	1	$0 \leq npos \leq 1$	0.5
\ncarc	1	$0 \leq npos \leq 1$	0.5
\ncbar	3	$0 \leq npos \leq 3$	1.5
\ncdiag	3	$0 \leq npos \leq 3$	1.5
\ncdiagg	2	$0 \leq npos \leq 2$	0.5
\ncangle	3	$0 \leq npos \leq 3$	1.5
\ncloop	5	$0 \leq npos \leq 5$	2.5
\nccircle	1	$0 \leq npos \leq 1$	0.5

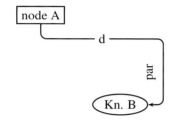

```
\usepackage{pstricks,pst-node}
\begin{pspicture}(3.5,3)
  \rput[tl](0,3){\rnode{A}{\psframebox{node A}}}
  \rput[br](3.5,0){\ovalnode{B}{Kn. B}}
  \ncangles[angleA=-90,arm=.4cm,linearc=.15]{->}{A}{B}
  \ncput*{d}
  \nbput[nrot=:D,npos=2.5]{par}
\end{pspicture}
```

The segments of closed connections such as \ncbox and \ncarcbox are counted clockwise starting from the lower side of the box.

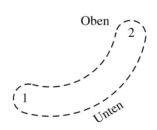

```
\usepackage{pstricks,pst-node}
\begin{pspicture}(3.5,2)
  \rput[bl](.5,0){\rnode{A}{1}}
  \rput[tr](3.5,2){\rnode{B}{2}}
  \ncarcbox[nodesep=.2cm,boxsize=.4,linearc=.4,%
    arcangle=50,linestyle=dashed]{<->}{A}{B}
  \nbput[nrot=:U]{Unten}
  \nbput[npos=2]{Oben}
\end{pspicture}
```

The keyword `shortput` allows short forms for setting labels. You are not required to use them, however, since all have corresponding "long forms". Possible key values are none, `nab`, `tablr`, and `tab`. They are discussed in turn below. The key value none disables `shortput`, which is the default setting; i.e., no short form characters are recognized.

The shortput *key*

shortput =none

Table 6.5 on the following page lists the short forms for placing the labels when using the key value `nab`. These short forms must follow *immediately after* a connection command, resulting in a simplified notation.

shortput =nab

Table 6.5: The short forms for `nab`			Table 6.6: The short forms for `tablr`	
Short Form	*Long Form*		*Short Form*	*Long Form*
`^{text}`	`\naput{text}`		`^{text}`	`\taput{text}`
`_{text}`	`\nbput{text}`		`_{text}`	`\tbput{text}`
			`<{text}`	`\tlput{text}`
			`>{text}`	`\trput{text}`

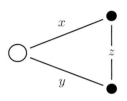

```
\usepackage{pstricks,pst-node}
\cnode(0.5,0){.25cm}{root}
\cnode*(3,1){4pt}{A} \cnode*(3,-1){4pt}{C}
\psset{nodesep=3pt,shortput=nab}
\ncline{root}{A}^{$x$}
\ncline{root}{C}_{$y$}
\ncline{A}{C}\ncput*{$z$}
```

Example
6-2-51

shortput=tablr   The short forms for the key value `tablr` are listed in Table 6.6. They must be placed *directly after* a connection to be recognized as short forms.

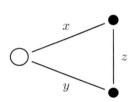

```
\usepackage{pstricks,pst-node}
\cnode(0.5,0){.25cm}{root}
\cnode*(3,1){4pt}{A}
\cnode*(3,-1){4pt}{C}
\psset{nodesep=3pt,shortput=tablr}
\ncline{root}{A}^{$x$}
\ncline{root}{C}_{$y$}
\ncline{A}{C}>{$z$}
```

Example
6-2-52

The key value `tab` is a simplified form of `tablr` that implements only the first two

shortput =tab   short forms in Table 6.6. It is only of historical interest, as there is no advantage to using `tab` rather than `tablr`.

The `tpos` *key*   The keyword `tpos` determines the relative position of a label within a line segment of a connecting line from the series of the `\t?put` macros.

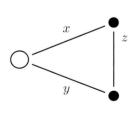

```
\usepackage{pstricks,pst-node}
\cnode(0.5,0){.25cm}{root}
\cnode*(3,1){4pt}{A}
\cnode*(3,-1){4pt}{C}
\psset{nodesep=3pt,shortput=tablr}
\ncline{root}{A}^{$x$}
\ncline{root}{C}_{$y$}
\ncline{A}{C}>[tpos=0.2]{$z$}
```

Example
6-2-53

The `rot` *key*   The keyword `rot` can take any value that is valid for `\rput` (Section 5.13 on page 266).

It works only in conjunction with the `\nput` command (see page 359).

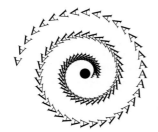

```
\usepackage{pstricks,pst-node,multido}
\begin{pspicture}(4.5,4.5)
  \cnode*(2,2){4pt}{A}
  \multido{\nA=0+10,\rB=0+0.5}{90}{%
    \nput[rot=\nA,%
        labelsep=\rB pt]{\nA}{A}{A}}
\end{pspicture}
```

Example
6-2-54

6.2.5   Putting labels on node connections

In Section 5.11 on page 265, we already discussed several commands that allow arbitrary placement of marks with respect to labels. In the context of connections, there are some special commands to consider. After a connection has been drawn, the coordinates of two points are stored temporarily until a new connection is drawn. This data may prove very useful for positioning the labels to be attached to such a connection. Of course, it also implies that label commands should come immediately after connection commands.

In Section 6.2.4 on page 348, which discussed the allowed keywords, you will find many examples of the placement of labels. In this section we will review the various commands once again.

`\ncput` * *[settings]* *{object}* `\naput` * *[settings]* *{object}* `\nbput` * *[settings]* *{object}*

The n label commands are always based on the visible length of a connection, without attention to the actual node centers. By default, the label is placed in the middle of this visible connection, which can be changed with the appropriate keyword. The letter c indicates *connected* (on the line), and a and b indicate *above* and *below* the line, respectively. The starred versions produce opaque material, which means you can overwrite lines with a label to gain increased visibility.

n labels

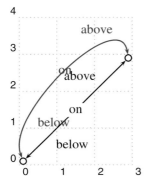

```
\usepackage{pstricks,pst-node}
\begin{pspicture}[showgrid=true](3,4)
  \cnode(0.1,0.1){0.1cm}{A}   \cnode(2.9,2.9){0.1cm}{B}
  \ncline{<->}{A}{B} \ncput*{on}
  \naput[npos=0.75]{above} \nbput[npos=0.25]{below}
  \nccurve[angleA=110,angleB=100,
    linecolor=blue]{<->}{A}{B}
  \ncput{\textcolor{blue}{on}}
  \naput[npos=0.75]{\textcolor{blue}{above}}
  \nbput[npos=0.25]{\textcolor{blue}{below}}
\end{pspicture}
```

Example
6-2-55

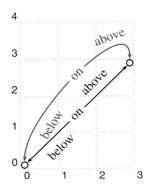

```
\usepackage{pstricks,pst-node}
\begin{pspicture}[showgrid=true](3,4)
  \cnode(0.1,0.1){0.1cm}{A}   \cnode(2.9,2.9){0.1cm}{B}
  \ncline{<->}{A}{B}   \ncput*[nrot=:U]{on}
  \naput[nrot=:U,npos=0.75]{above}
  \nbput[nrot=:U,npos=0.25]{below}
  \nccurve[angle=90,linecolor=blue]{<->}{A}{B}
  \ncput*[nrot=:U]{\textcolor{blue}{on}}
  \naput[nrot=:U,npos=0.75]{\textcolor{blue}{above}}
  \nbput[nrot=:U,npos=0.25]{\textcolor{blue}{below}}
\end{pspicture}
```

Example
6-2-56

Note that "above" and "below" refer to the default directions "from left to right". If the order of the nodes in the last example is reversed, the positions for "above" and "below" are reversed as well. This can, of course, easily be corrected by exchanging the angle specification :U (up) for :D (down).

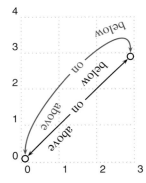

```
\usepackage{pstricks,pst-node}
\begin{pspicture}[showgrid=true](3,4)
  \cnode(0.1,0.1){0.1cm}{A}   \cnode(2.9,2.9){0.1cm}{B}
  \ncline{<->}{B}{A} \ncput*[nrot=:U]{on}
  \naput[nrot=:U,npos=0.75]{above}
  \nbput[nrot=:U,npos=0.25]{below}
  \nccurve[angle=90,linecolor=blue]{<->}{B}{A}
  \ncput*[nrot=:U]{\textcolor{blue}{on}}
  \naput[nrot=:U,npos=0.75]{\textcolor{blue}{above}}
  \nbput[nrot=:U,npos=0.25]{\textcolor{blue}{below}}
\end{pspicture}
```

Example
6-2-57

\tvput * [*settings*] {*object*}	\thput * [*settings*] {*object*}
\taput * [*settings*] {*object*}	\tbput * [*settings*] {*object*}
\tlput * [*settings*] {*object*}	\trput * [*settings*] {*object*}

The differences between the \t?put commands are as follows: \tvput places the label in the *vertical* center; and \thput in the *horizontal* center on the line. Placement *above* is done with \taput and *below* with \tbput; \tlput refers to **left**, and \trput to the **right** of the line.

The starred versions produce opaque material that overwrites lines to make labels more visible. In calculating positions, these commands refer to the node centers regardless of whether a connection is visible. The following example illustrates this difference: \thput puts the label lower than \ncput.

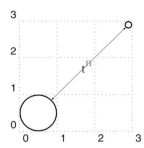

```
\usepackage{pstricks,pst-node}
\begin{pspicture}[showgrid=true](3,3)
  \cnode(0.5,0.5){0.5cm}{A}
  \cnode(2.9,2.9){0.1cm}{B}
  \ncline[linewidth=0.1pt]{<->}{A}{B}
  \ncput{\textcolor{red}{n}}
  \thput{\textcolor{blue}{t}}
\end{pspicture}
```

Example
6-2-58

The \t?put commands are primarily intended for trees and commutative diagrams.
For this reason there are the additional versions for left and right positions and horizontal
and vertical centering. In the following example, the nodes are defined with \Rnode; otherwise, we would not obtain horizontal lines (see Section 6.2.1 on page 336).

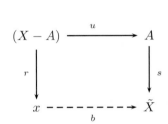

```
\usepackage{pstricks,pst-node}
\[
  \setlength\arraycolsep{1.1cm}
  \begin{array}{cc}
    \Rnode{a}{(X-A)} & \Rnode{b}{A} \\[1.5cm]
        \Rnode{c}{x} & \Rnode{d}{\tilde{X}}
  \end{array}
  \psset{nodesep=5pt,arrows=->}
  \everypsbox{\scriptstyle}
  \ncline{a}{c} \tlput{r}
  \ncline{a}{b} \taput{u}
  \ncline[linestyle=dashed]{c}{d} \tbput{b}
  \ncline{b}{d} \trput{s}
\]
```

Example
6-2-59

\nput * [*settings*] {*reference angle*} {*node name*}{*object*}

The command \nput is essentially identical to \uput (see Section 5.11.3 on page 268) but
refers to a node instead of a pair of coordinates.

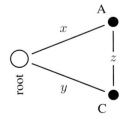

```
\usepackage{pstricks,pst-node}
\cnode(0.5,0){.25cm}{root}
\nput[rot=90]{-90}{root}{root}
\cnode*(3,1){4pt}{A}   \nput{130}{A}{A}
\cnode*(3,-1){4pt}{C}  \nput{-130}{C}{C}
\psset{nodesep=3pt,shortput=nab}
\ncline{root}{A}^{$x$}  \ncline{root}{C}_{$y$}
\ncline{A}{C}\ncput*{$z$}
```

Example
6-2-60

6.2.6 Multiple connections

Sometimes you may need several connections to start and stop at a particular node. With the `offset` key, you can very easily "separate" two connections of the same type.

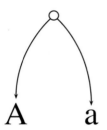

word1 to word2 to word3

```
\usepackage{pstricks,pst-node}
\rnode{A}{word1} to \rnode{B}{word2} %
    to \rnode{C}{word3}
\psset{angleA=-90,nodesep=3pt,%
    arm=0.4,linearc=0.2}
\ncbar[offsetB=4pt]{->}{A}{B}
\ncbar[offsetA=4pt]{->}{B}{C}
```

Example
6-2-61

If connections point to two objects with boxes of different size, naturally the connections do not end at the same height.

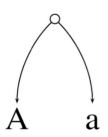

A   a

```
\usepackage{pstricks,pst-node}
\begin{pspicture}(-0.5,0)(3,3)   \Huge
  \cnode(1,3){4pt}{A}
  \rput[B](0,0){\Rnode{B}{A}}
  \rput[B](2,0){\Rnode{C}{a}}
  \psset{angleA=90,armA=1,nodesepA=3pt}
  \nccurve[angleB=-135]{<-}{B}{A}
  \nccurve[angleB=-45]{<-}{C}{A}
\end{pspicture}
```

Example
6-2-62

In this case, the `nodesep` key is not very helpful because you do not know the exact size difference between the lowercase letter and the uppercase letter. Since the lower nodes are defined with `\Rnode`, their centers are positioned at the same distance from the baseline (see also Section 6.2.1 on page 336). Instead of the `nc` connection, you can now use the `pc` version, which always refers to the node center. This way you obtain connections of equal lengths since both end at the same distance from the node centers.

```
\usepackage{pstricks,pst-node}
\SpecialCoor
\begin{pspicture}(3,3)
  \cnode(1,3){4pt}{A}
  \rput[B](0,0){\Rnode[vref=20pt]{B}{\Huge A}}
  \rput[B](2,0){\Rnode[vref=20pt]{C}{\Huge a}}
  \psset{angleA=90,nodesepB=4pt}
  \pccurve[angleB=-135]{<-}(B)(A)
  \pccurve[angleB=-45]{<-}(C)(A)
\end{pspicture}
```

A   a

Example
6-2-63

You can also use the `nc` commands in combination with the keyword Ynodesep, which specifies absolute distances from the center.

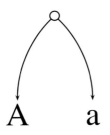

```
\usepackage{pstricks,pst-node}
\begin{pspicture}(-0.5,0)(3.5,3)    \Huge
  \cnode(1,3){4pt}{A}
  \rput[B](0,0){\Rnode{B}{A}}
  \rput[B](2,0){\Rnode{C}{a}}
  \psset{angleA=90,YnodesepA=1ex}
  \nccurve[angleB=-135]{<-}{B}{A}
  \nccurve[angleB=-45]{<-}{C}{A}
\end{pspicture}
```

Example
6-2-64

6.2.7 The `psmatrix` **environment**

As already demonstrated several times, you can position nodes at any place within a document, i.e., in running text or in a table or other object. You simply have to make sure the node connections refer to nodes defined on the same TeX page. Even connections from normal text to a floating environment are possible when this requirement is fulfilled.

This arbitrary placement of nodes allows you to realize larger projects on the basis of a matrix. Within this matrix the nodes are uniquely defined through the individual cells, which are specified by their row and column number as {row,column} instead of by a node name. Essentially, any LaTeX `tabular` or `array` type environment could be used, but `psmatrix` offers better support.

```
\begin{psmatrix} [settings]
    [cell-settings] ... & [cell-settings] ... ... \\ ...
\end{psmatrix}
```

The `psmatrix` environment is based on the math environment `array` but can be used in both math and text modes. For an upright font you must use the commands \mathrm or \text from the amsmath package.

Each cell can take an optional argument in square brackets to set keyword/value pairs for that cell. With the help of the keyword `name` (used in square brackets at the beginning of a cell), you can turn any cell into a node to obtain special forms. Although `psmatrix` can be nested, the node connections must be on the same nesting level as their respective nodes.

At the beginning of every row or column, hooks are executed if defined. This allows you to apply special settings to the cells in those rows or columns as described below.

```
\psspan{n}
```

`psmatrix` also supports a feature similar to LaTeX's \multicolumn. Here *n* denotes the number of columns to combine, and you have to place the command \psspan at *the end* of

Table 6.7: Keywords for `psmatrix`

Name	Value Type	Default
mnode	`R|r|C|f|p|circle|oval|dia|tri|dot|none`	R
emnode	`R|r|C|f|p|circle|oval|dia|tri|dot|none`	none
name	*name*	
nodealign	*Boolean*	false
mcol	`r|l|c`	c
rowsep	*value [unit]*	1.5cm
colsep	*value [unit]*	1.5cm
mnodesize	*value [unit]*	-1pt

the cell that is to be combined with the following $n - 1$ cells.

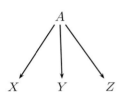

```
\usepackage{pstricks,pst-node}
$ \begin{psmatrix}[colsep=1cm]
    [name=A] A \psspan{3} \\[0pt]
    [name=X] X  & [name=Y] Y  & [name=Z] Z
  \end{psmatrix}
  \psset{nodesep=3pt,arrows=->}
  \ncline{A}{X} \ncline{A}{Y} \ncline{A}{Z} $
```

Example
6-2-65

`\psrowhook????`   `\pscolhook????`

You can specify that some code is to be executed for a particular row or column before that row or column is processed by placing the necessary definition before the actual `psmatrix` environment. To assign the code to the row or column, the command name is suffixed with the row or column number in the form of a lowercase Roman numeral (represented as *????* in the syntax). For example, valid command names include `\psrowhookii` for the second row and `\pscolhookxi` for the eleventh column. Note that counting starts with `i`—there is no Roman numeral for zero.

If both a row hook and a column hook are defined for a particular cell, the row hook is executed first. Thus the column hook may overwrite settings, as can be seen in the next example where the blue column wins over the gray row.

A B C

a b c

1 2 3

```
\usepackage{pstricks,pst-node}
\newcommand\psrowhookii{\color{lightgray}\huge}
\newcommand\pscolhookiii{\color{blue}}
$ \begin{psmatrix}[colsep=0.5cm,rowsep=0.5cm]
  A & B & C \\ a & b & c \\ 1 & 2 & 3
  \end{psmatrix} $
```

Example
6-2-66

Table 6.7 shows all valid special keywords for the `psmatrix` environment. They are discussed in the remainder of this section.

The keyword `mnode` defines the node type. It can be changed globally with `\psset`

The mnode *key*   or locally in the optional argument. The node names refer to the node types discussed in

Table 6.8: The keyword values for mnode and the corresponding commands

mnode	Node Type	Page	mnode	Node Type	Page
R	\Rnode	335	circle	\circlenode	338
r	\rnode	336	oval	\ovalnode	339
C	\Cnode	338	dia	\dianode	339
f	\fnode	340	tri	\trinode	339
p	\pnode	336	dot	\dotnode	339
none	*no node*				

Section 6.2.1. They are listed in Table 6.8, along with a reference to the page where their syntax is explained.

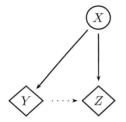

Example
6-2-67

```
\usepackage{pstricks,pst-node}
$\begin{psmatrix}[mnode=dia,colsep=1cm]
   & [mnode=circle] X \\ Y & Z
\end{psmatrix}
\psset{nodesep=3pt,arrows=->}
\ncline{1,2}{2,1} \ncline{1,2}{2,2}
\ncline[linestyle=dotted]{2,1}{2,2} $
```

The keyword emnode determines the node type for empty cells. It works only when it   *The* emnode *key*
is specified globally. Even then, you should be aware that empty cells in the last column of
the matrix are not necessarily recognized.

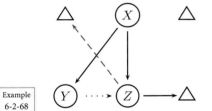

Example
6-2-68

```
\usepackage{pstricks,pst-node}
\psset{linestyle=solid}
$\begin{psmatrix}[mnode=circle,emnode=tri,colsep=1cm]
   & X & & \\ Y & Z &
\end{psmatrix}
\psset{nodesep=3pt,arrows=->}
\ncline{1,2}{2,1} \ncline{1,2}{2,2} \ncline{2,2}{2,3}
\ncline[linestyle=dotted]{2,1}{2,2}
\ncline[linestyle=dashed,linecolor=blue]{->}{2,2}{1,1}$
```

The keyword name allows you to assign a name to any cell. The name *must* be specified
in the optional argument at the beginning of the cell, which causes problems with the first   *The* name *key*
cell in a row when it is preceded by a line break. For example, the code

```
        ... & ... & ... \\
[name=K21] & ...
```

would appear to LaTeX as \\ [name=K21] and, consequently, [name=K21] would be interpreted as an optional line feed. This would produce an error message indicating an invalid value. A possible workaround is to write \\[0pt] or \\\space. The node names remain valid with their assigned coordinates until they are reassigned, even if a new `psmatrix` has been started.

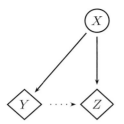

```
\usepackage{pstricks,pst-node}
$ \begin{psmatrix}[mnode=dia,colsep=1cm]
                    & [mnode=circle,name=X]  X \\[0pt]
         [name=Y]  Y & [name=Z]  Z
  \end{psmatrix}
  \psset{nodesep=3pt,arrows=->}
  \ncline{X}{Y} \ncline{X}{Z}
  \ncline[linestyle=dotted]{Y}{Z} $
```

Example
6-2-69

The `nodealign` *key*   Normally, the bottom of a node lies on the baseline. With `nodealign=true` you can put the node center on the base line. As a rule, this choice has little effect on `psmatrix` since the node content is generally represented by an entire cell.

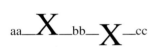

```
\usepackage{pstricks,pst-node}
aa\rule{1em}{0.5pt}\rnode{X}{\Huge X}\rule{1em}{0.5pt}bb%
\psset{nodealign=true}%
\rule{1em}{0.5pt}\rnode{X}{\Huge X}\rule{1em}{0.5pt}cc
```

Example
6-2-70

The `mcol` *key*   The keyword `mcol` specifies the horizontal alignment within cells. It can be used both globally and locally.

```
\usepackage{pstricks,pst-node}
$ \begin{psmatrix}[colsep=1cm,mcol=c]
     [name=A,mcol=r]  A & [name=X]  XxXxX \\[0pt]
     [name=Y]  YyYyY    & [name=Z]  Z
  \end{psmatrix}
  \psset{nodesep=3pt,arrows=->}
  \ncline{X}{Y}\ncline{X}{Z}\ncline{A}{Y}
  \ncline[linestyle=dotted]{Y}{Z} $
```

Example
6-2-71

The `rowsep` *and*   The keywords `rowsep` and `colsep` correspond to the dimension `\arraycolsep` and
`colsep` *keys*   the `\arraystretch` command. They specify additional vertical and horizontal space between cells and can take any value, including a negative one.

```
\usepackage{pstricks,pst-node}
$ \begin{psmatrix}[colsep=0pt,rowsep=0pt]
        a & b \\ c & d
  \end{psmatrix} $
```

Example
6-2-72

The `mnodesize` *key*   Usually, in `array`-like environments, the longest entry determines the width of a column. With `mnodesize` you can assign the same width to all columns, if the given value is sufficiently large for each column.

Example
6-2-73

$$111 \quad a \quad bbbb$$

$$2 \quad c \quad ddddd$$

```
\usepackage{pstricks,pst-node}
$ \begin{psmatrix}[colsep=0pt,rowsep=12pt,mnodesize=1cm]
  111 & a & bbbb \\ 2 & c & ddddd
\end{psmatrix}  $
```

6.2.8 TEX and PostScript: a one-way ticket

The relationship between TEX and PostScript is quite one-sided: you can pass information from TEX to PostScript at any time, but you cannot directly retrieve information from PostScript. This is possible only via intermediate steps, such as by having the PostScript driver write information to a file, which is then read when TEX is rerun, or by using the special TEX implementation VTeX, which incorporates a PostScript engine but prevents you from processing the document on other TEX installations.

When defining nodes whose precise coordinates are unknown (because they appear in the middle of a paragraph or are the result of some internal calculation), we may wish to know their values. With LATEX those values cannot be obtained directly. There are, however, possibilities when we are using PSTricks, as shown in the next example:

When defining nodes, such as ⊙ whose precise coordinates are unknown (because they appear in the middle of a paragraph or are the result of some internal calculation), we may wish to know their values. With LATEX those values cannot be obtained directly. There are, however, possibilities when we are using PSTricks.

```
\usepackage{pstricks,pst-node} \SpecialCoor \raggedright
When defining nodes, such as \ \cnode{3pt}{A}, whose precise
coordinates are unknown (because they appear in the middle of a
paragraph or are the result of some internal calculation), we may
wish to know their values.  With \LaTeX{} those values cannot be
obtained directly.  There are, however, possibilities when we are
using PSTricks.
  \begin{pspicture}(1,1)
    \psgrid[subgriddiv=0,griddots=10,gridlabels=7pt]
    \Cnode(0.5,0.5){B}
    \makeatletter
    \psline[arrowscale=2,linestyle=dashed]{->}(B)(!%
      tx@NodeDict begin
        /N@B load GetCenter % center of node B
        /yB ED /xB ED
        /N@A load GetCenter % center of node A
        /yA ED /xA ED
        xA xB sub 0.6 mul xB add \pst@number\psxunit div
        yA yB sub 0.6 mul yB add \pst@number\psyunit div
      end)
    \makeatother
  \end{pspicture}
```

Example
6-2-74

In this example, an arrow is drawn that points towards the node defined near the start of the paragraph. The length of the arrow line is 60% of the total distance between the two nodes. The arrow points exactly at node A. The PostScript code inside \psline uses the tx@NodeDict dictionary to call the needed procedures: ED (exchange and define variable) is an internally defined abbreviation for exch def and can be found in pstricks.pro. \psline has to be surrounded by \makeatletter...\makeatother because the Post-

Script code in its argument refers to internal **PSTricks** macros with @ signs in their names and is first evaluated by LaTeX before it is passed to PostScript.

6.3 pst-tree—**Typesetting trees**

The base packages **pstricks** and **pst-node** include some commands to draw frames, circles, ovals, and other shapes, which may then be connected with various lines. The package **pst-tree**, however, offers far better support for creating various kinds of trees. It is based on **pst-node** (see Section 6.2) and can be an excellent tool for creating trees.

\pstree *[settings]* {*root*}{*successors*}   \begin{psTree} *[settings]* {*root*}
                                            ... successors ...
                                            \end{psTree}

In terms of their content, there is no difference between these two versions. psTree is just the LaTeX "long" variant; it is defined as a longbox (see Section 5.12.5 on page 276). Both versions put the whole tree into a box with a baseline that runs through the center of the root.

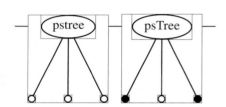

```
\usepackage{pstricks,pst-tree}
\psset{showbbox=true}%
\rule{1em}{0.5pt}%
\pstree[radius=3pt]{\Toval{pstree}}{
   \TC\TC\TC}%    the successors
\rule{1em}{0.5pt}%
\begin{psTree}[radius=3pt]{\Toval{psTree}}
   \TC*\TC\TC*
\end{psTree}\rule{1em}{0.5pt}
```

Example
6-3-1

The tree macros are not part of a pspicture environment. In some situations there may be a problem with the vertical line distance; in such a case you should either enclose the \pstree command or psTree environment in a pspicture environment or provide sufficient white space with \vspace. In the following examples, trees and tree connections will be denoted as tree objects. The root should be a single tree object, while a successor may be any arbitrary combination of tree objects. Subtrees are created recursively, and a successor consists of a new root.

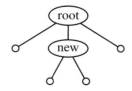

```
\usepackage{pstricks,pst-tree}
\pstree[radius=3pt,levelsep=0.9cm]{\Toval{root}}{%
   \TC%                    successor 1,1
   \pstree{\Toval{new}}{%  1,2 and new subroot
      \TC\TC}%             2,1    2,2
   \TC}%                   1,3
```

Example
6-3-2

In this example, you have to encode the tree in such a way that its tree structure can easily be recognized when you are creating complex trees. Otherwise, it will be very difficult to find any errors present.

6.3.1 Tree nodes, predecessors, and successors

Most of the node commands dealt with in Section 6.2 have counterparts here. Some nodes take an argument for material (e.g., a label), that is printed inside the node; others generate only fixed symbols. Commands that behave exactly like their peviously described counterparts will not be discussed in detail in this section.

```
\Tp * [settings]                      \Tcircle * [settings] {label}
\Tc * [settings] {value [unit]}       \TCircle * [settings] {label}
\TC * [settings]                      \Toval * [settings] {label}
\Tf * [settings]                      \Tdia * [settings] {label}
\Tdot * [settings]                    \Ttri * [settings] {label}
\Tr * [settings] {label}              \Tn [settings]
\TR * [settings] {label}
```

All tree command names have a preceding "T" and are derived from the corresponding node commands (except \Tn, which has no node equivalent): \Tp corresponds to \pnode, \Tc to \cnode, and so on. All tree node commands support an optional argument, even if the corresponding definition from Section 6.2 has none. There is no argument for a node name, nor are there coordinate specifications, as the tree nodes are placed automatically with their structure being defined through nesting. The next example shows all node types in action; later examples detail individual features of trees.

```
\usepackage{pstricks,pst-tree}
\newcommand\Lcs[1]{\small\texttt{\textbackslash #1}}
\psset{levelsep=2cm,labelsep=5pt}
\pstree[treemode=U,angleB=-90,angleA=90,treenodesize=0.7cm]{%
  \pstree[treemode=D,angleA=-90,angleB=90,treenodesize=0.3cm]{\Toval{Tree node}}{%
    \Tp~{\Lcs{Tp}}   \Tc{.5}~{\Lcs{Tc}}   \TC~{\Lcs{TC}}
    \Tn~{\Lcs{Tn}}   \Tf~{\Lcs{Tf}}       \Tr{\Lcs{Tr}}
    \TR{\Lcs{TR}}}}{%
  \TCircle{\Lcs{TCircle}} \Tcircle{\Lcs{Tcircle}} \Tdot~{\Lcs{Tdot}}
  \Toval{\Lcs{Toval}}     \Ttri{\Lcs{Ttri}}       \Tdia{\Lcs{Tdia}}}
```

In this example, the difference between the two node variants may not be obvious, so it will be reviewed here. Section 6.2.1 on page 336 explained the difference between \rnode and \Rnode on a node level: \rnode regards the geometric center of the box as being the node center, while \Rnode takes the baseline within the box as the center. Especially with vertical tree structures, it is better that all text around the same horizontal axis appears on the same baseline. In such cases only the application of \TR makes sense.

| \Tr * [settings] {label}   \TR * [settings] {label} |

Reference points for \Tr are set through the keyword ref.

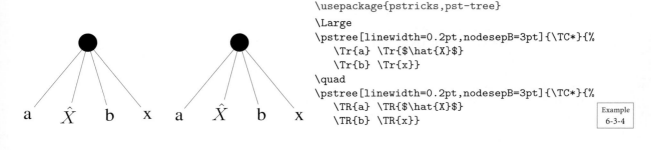

```
\usepackage{pstricks,pst-tree}
\Large
\pstree[linewidth=0.2pt,nodesepB=3pt]{\TC*}{%
    \Tr{a} \Tr{$\hat{X}$}
    \Tr{b} \Tr{x}}
\quad
\pstree[linewidth=0.2pt,nodesepB=3pt]{\TC*}{%
    \TR{a} \TR{$\hat{X}$}
    \TR{b} \TR{x}}
```

Example
6-3-4

| \Tn [settings] |

Whenever you wish to reserve space for a future node or simply make some room before the next group of nodes starts, you should use a "nil" node (not in list), which does nothing except occupy the space. Nevertheless, as the current point is moved to the nil node, you can add any material there, e.g., using \rput.

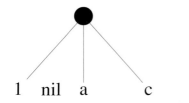

```
\usepackage{pstricks,pst-tree}
\Large
\pstree[linewidth=0.2pt,nodesepB=3pt]{\TC*}
    {\TR{1} \Tn\rput(0,0){nil} \TR{a} \Tn \TR{c}}
```

Example
6-3-5

| \Tfan * [settings] |

Another special node is \Tfan, which can, for instance, be used to symbolically continue the tree when the tree structure would be fanned out too far. \Tfan has no mandatory argument, \uput follows it directly to prevent trailing spaces. The current point after setting a tree node is (0,0), the center of the new root.

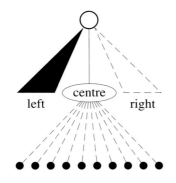

```
\usepackage{pstricks,pst-tree}
\pstree[treesep=0.2cm,linewidth=0.2pt,%
        radius=3pt]{\TC}
  {%
   \Tfan*\uput[-90](0,0){left}
   \pstree[linestyle=dashed]{\Toval{centre}}
     {%
      \TC*\TC*\TC*\TC*\TC*\TC*\TC*\TC*\TC*\TC*
     }
   \Tfan[linestyle=dashed]%
      \uput[-90](0,0){right}
  }
```

| \pssucc   \pspred |

After a new succeeding node has been defined, the command \pssucc contains its internal name. After a new node has been defined, the command \pspred contains the internal name of its precedessor.

| \tspace{*value[unit]*} |

For special cases, in which the methods described previously do not lead to the desired results, you can insert individual blank spaces with \tspace. The extra 10pt in the next example compensates for the fact that the left leaf node has only a short label.

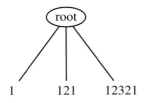

```
\usepackage{pstricks,pst-tree}
\begin{pspicture}(0,0.25)(0.5,-2)
\pstree[nodesepB=4pt]{\Toval{root}}{%
  \TR{1}
  \tspace{10pt}
  \TR{121}
  \TR{12321}}
\end{pspicture}
```

| \psedge{*nodeA*}{*nodeB*}{*connection macro*} |

The command \psedge was discussed in Section 6.3.2 on page 376, where you can also find some examples for it. For the sake of completeness, its syntax is shown here again. If you do not wish to have connecting lines, you can also define \psedge as empty: \renewcommand\psedge[2]{}. Its two nodes are generally determined by the two nodes \pssucc and \pspred.

Table 6.9: Keywords for `pst-tree`

Name	Value Type	Default
fansize	*value [unit]*	1cm
treemode	*tree mode value*	D
treeflip	*Boolean*	false
treesep	*value [unit]*	0.75cm
treefit	loose|tight	tight
treenodesize	*value [unit]*	-1pt
levelsep	*value [unit]*	2cm
edge	*macro*	\ncline
bbl	*value [unit]*	*empty*
bbr	*value [unit]*	*empty*
bbh	*value [unit]*	*empty*
bbd	*value [unit]*	*empty*
xbbl	*value [unit]*	0
xbbr	*value [unit]*	0
xbbh	*value [unit]*	*empty*
xbbd	*value [unit]*	*empty*
showbbox	*boolean*	false
thistreesep	*value [unit]*	*empty*
thistreenodesize	*value [unit]*	*empty*
thistreefit	*value [unit]*	*empty*
thislevelsep	*value [unit]*	*empty*

6.3.2 Keywords for tree nodes

Table 6.9 lists the special keywords for the **pst-tree** package. They are discussed in the following examples.

The fansize *key*   Sets of branches can be symbolized by a triangle, whose base side can be defined with `fansize`. You can move the triangle with the keywords `nodesep` (Section 6.2.4 on page 350) and `offset` (Section 6.2.4 on page 353).

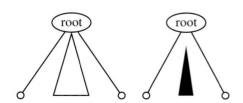

```
\usepackage{pstricks,pst-tree}
\pstree[radius=3pt]{\Toval{root}}{%
  \TC \Tfan \TC}
\quad
\pstree[radius=3pt]{\Toval{root}}{%
  \TC
  \Tfan*[fansize=0.4cm,nodesepA=10pt]
  \TC}
```

Example
6-3-8

The keyword `treemode` specifies the direction of the main tree and/or the following   *The* `treemode` *key*
subtrees: (D)own, (L)eft, (R)ight, (U)p.

```
\usepackage{pstricks,pst-tree}
\begin{pspicture}(-0.75,0.25)(0.75,-4)
  \pstree{\pstree[treemode=L]{\Toval{root}}{\TC*}}
    {\pstree[treemode=L]{\Toval{left}}{\TC\TC}
     \pstree{\Toval{new}}{\TC\TC}
     \pstree[treemode=R]{\Toval{right}}
       {\TC
         \pstree[treemode=U]{\Toval{right}}{\TC*\TC*}
       }
    }
\end{pspicture}
```

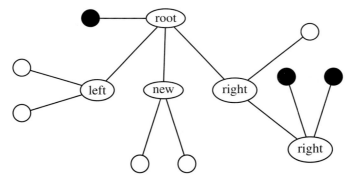

Normally, all nodes are arranged from left to right and from top to bottom. This or-
der can be changed with the keyword `treeflip` locally as well as globally. In the examples   *The* `treeflip` *key*
the use of this keyword becomes obvious wherever the sequence of the node ends is locally
reversed, because the order A-B is kept.

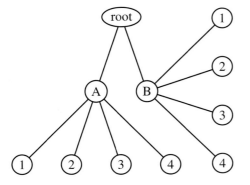

```
\usepackage{pstricks,pst-tree}
\pstree{\Toval{root}}
        {\pstree{\Tcircle{A}}
                {\Tcircle{1}   \Tcircle{2}
                 \Tcircle{3}   \Tcircle{4}
                }
         \pstree[treemode=R]{\Tcircle{B}}
                {\Tcircle{1}   \Tcircle{2}
                 \Tcircle{3}   \Tcircle{4}
                }
        }
```

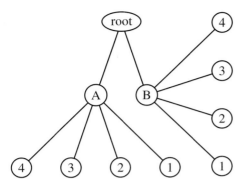

```
\usepackage{pstricks,pst-tree}
\pstree{\Toval{root}}{%
  \pstree[treeflip=true]{\Tcircle{A}}{%
    \Tcircle{1}   \Tcircle{2}
    \Tcircle{3}   \Tcircle{4}}%
  \pstree[treeflip=true,treemode=R]{%
  \Tcircle{B}}{%
    \Tcircle{1}   \Tcircle{2}
    \Tcircle{3}   \Tcircle{4}}}
```

Example
6-3-11

The treesep *and* thistreesep *keys*   You can define the distance between tree nodes with the keyword `treesep`. It automatically causes the whole tree to become narrower or smaller, which may be very welcome with larger tree structures.

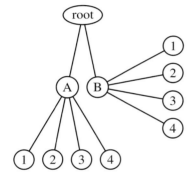

```
\usepackage{pstricks,pst-tree}
\pstree[treesep=0.2cm]{\Toval{root}}{
  \pstree{\Tcircle{A}}{%
    \Tcircle{1}   \Tcircle{2}
    \Tcircle{3}   \Tcircle{4}}%
  \pstree[treemode=R]{\Tcircle{B}}{%
    \Tcircle{1}   \Tcircle{2}
    \Tcircle{3}   \Tcircle{4}}}
```

Example
6-3-12

With `thistreesep`, changes may be restricted to a single level.

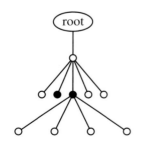

```
\usepackage{pstricks,pst-tree}
\pstree[levelsep=1cm,radius=3pt]{\Toval{root}}{%
  \pstree[thistreesep=0.2cm]{\TC}{%
  \TC\TC*
  \pstree{\TC*}{%
    \TC\TC\TC\TC}%
  \TC\TC}}
```

Example
6-3-13

The treefit *and* thistreefit *keys*   PSTricks determines the distance between end nodes with regard to their contents. This distance can be specified globally or locally with the keyword `treesep`, but you can also instruct PSTricks to generally make the distance a bit larger. With `treefit=tight` (default), the minimal distance between two nodes on the same level equals `treesep` and is modified only when node contents would overlap. With `treefit=loose`, the distance of the perpendiculars of *all* nodes is at least `treesep`. This may cause nodes of higher levels to be farther apart than nodes of lower levels. If *all* nodes are on the same level, there is no difference between `loose` and `tight`.

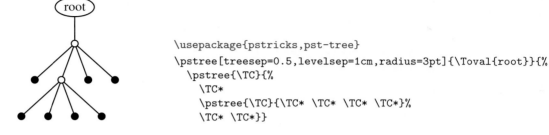

```
\usepackage{pstricks,pst-tree}
\pstree[treesep=0.5,levelsep=1cm,radius=3pt]{\Toval{root}}{%
  \pstree{\TC}{%
    \TC*
    \pstree{\TC}{\TC* \TC* \TC* \TC*}%
    \TC* \TC*}}
```

Local changes, referring to a subtree, may be achieved with the keyword `thistreefit`.

```
\usepackage{pstricks,pst-tree}
  \pstree[levelsep=1cm,radius=3pt]{%
    \Toval{root}}{\pstree[thistreefit=loose]{\TC}{%
      \TC\TC*
      \pstree{\TC*}{\TC\TC\TC\TC}%
      \TC\TC}
    \pstree[thistreefit=tight]{\TC}{%
      \TC\TC*
      \pstree{\TC*}{\TC\TC\TC\TC}%
      \TC\TC}}
```

If a tree level contains an odd number of nodes with contents of different width, the tree connection in the center often is not a perpendicular line, which is not really visually appealing. You can use the keyword `treenodesize` to set the box to a fixed width or, for vertical trees, to a fixed height and depth so that the structure becomes symmetrical with a perpendicular line in the middle. If this method does not yield the desired result, you can insert or

The `treenodesize` *and* `thistreenodesize` *keys*

remove (negative value) individual white space with \space (Section 6.3.1 on page 369).

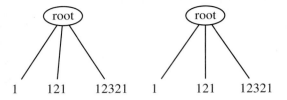

```
\usepackage{pstricks,pst-tree}
\pstree[nodesepB=4pt]{%
   \Toval{root}}{\TR{1} \TR{121} \TR{12321}}
\quad
\pstree[nodesepB=4pt,treenodesize=0.3cm]{%
   \Toval{root}}{\TR{1} \TR{121} \TR{12321}}
```

Example
6-3-16

You can use thistreenodesize to specify local changes that are valid only for subsequent trees.

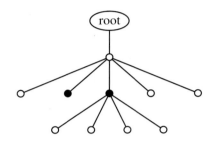

```
\usepackage{pstricks,pst-tree}
\pstree[levelsep=1cm,radius=3pt]{%
  \Toval{root}}{%
     \pstree[thistreenodesize=0.25cm]{\TC}{%
        \TC\TC*
        \pstree{\TC*}{%
           \TC\TC\TC\TC}%
        \TC\TC}}
```

Example
6-3-17

The levelsep *and* thislevelsep *keys*

The keys levelsep and thislevelsep refer to the vertical and horizontal distances between the centers of two levels, respectively. If the value of the keyword is prefixed with an asterisk, it refers to the distance from the bottom of the current box to the top of the successor's box; thus the distance can vary within levels.

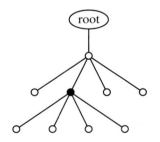

```
\usepackage{pstricks,pst-tree}
\pstree[levelsep=1cm,radius=3pt]{\Toval{root}}{%
  \pstree{\TC}{%
     \TC
     \pstree{\TC*}{%
        \TC\TC\TC\TC
     }%
     \TC\TC
  }}
```

Example
6-3-18

This method may enhance the appearance of trees—especially horizontal trees. The following example has been created with levelsep=3cm. The different name lengths produce unfavorable line lengths.

```
\usepackage{pstricks,pst-tree}      \SpecialCoor
   \psset{nodesep=5pt}
   \pstree[treemode=R,levelsep=3cm]{%
      \rnode{A}{}\Tr{\rnode{A}{}Friedrich Wilhelm}}{%
         \pstree{\Tr{Friedrich I.}}{%
            \Tr{\rnode{C}{}Friedrich Wilhelm I.}  \Tr{Friedrich}}}
```

```
    \pstree{\Tr{\rnode{B}{}Albrecht Friedrich}}{%
        \Tr{Wilhelm Heinrich}  \Tr{Friedrich}}}
\psset{arrowscale=2,linewidth=0.2pt}
\pcline[linestyle=dashed](A)(A|0,-1)    \pcline[linestyle=dashed](B)(B|0,-1)
\pcline[linestyle=dashed](C)(C|0,-1)
\pnode(A|0,-.8){A1}\pnode(B|0,-.8){A2} \ncline[arrows=<->]{A1}{A2}
\ncput*{\texttt{levelsep}}
\pnode(C|0,-.8){A3}  \ncline[arrows=<->]{A2}{A3}\ncput*{\texttt{levelsep}}
```

Example 6-3-19

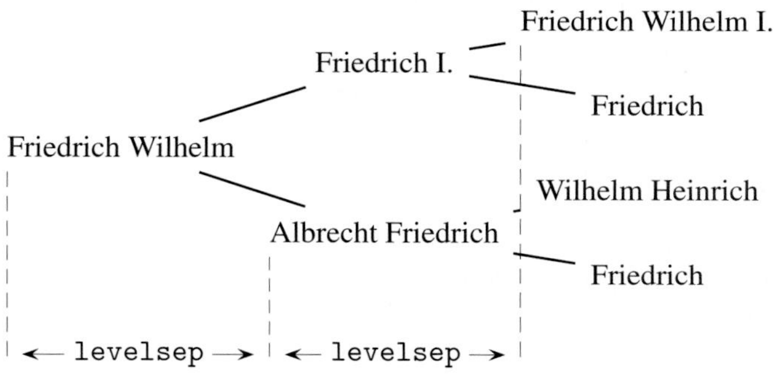

A value of `levelsep=*1cm` has a positive effect on this formation, so that the separation is between the end and beginning of two levels.

```
\usepackage{pstricks,pst-tree}    \SpecialCoor
  \pstree[treemode=R,levelsep=*1cm]{%
      \Tr{Friedrich Wilhelm\rnode{A}{}}}{%
          \pstree{\Tr{Friedrich I.}}{%
              \Tr{Friedrich Wilhelm I.}   \Tr{Friedrich}}
      \pstree{\Tr{\rnode{B1}{}Albrecht Friedrich\rnode{C}{}}}{%
          \Tr{\rnode{B2}{}Wilhelm Heinrich} \Tr{Friedrich}}}
  \psset{arrowscale=2,linewidth=0.2pt}
  \pcline[linestyle=dashed](A)(A|0,-1)    \pcline[linestyle=dashed](B1)(B1|0,-1)
  \pcline[linestyle=dashed](B2)(B2|0,-1) \pcline[linestyle=dashed](C)(C|0,-1)
  \psline{<->}(A|0,-.8)(B1|0,-.8)        \psline{<->}(B2|0,-.8)(C|0,-.8)
```

Example 6-3-20

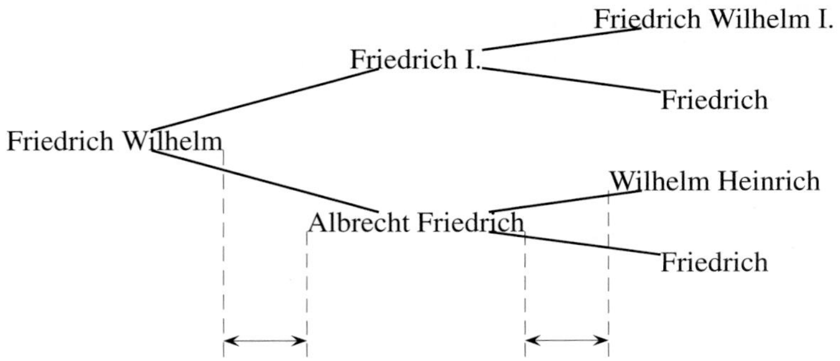

In contrast to the keyword `levelsep`, `thislevelsep` allows you to specify only the distance for the subtree.

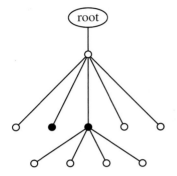

```
\usepackage{pstricks,pst-tree}
\pstree[levelsep=1cm,radius=3pt]{\Toval{root}}{%
  \pstree[thislevelsep=2cm]{\TC}{%
    \TC\TC*
    \pstree{\TC*}{%
      \TC\TC\TC\TC
    }%
    \TC\TC
}}
```

Example
6-3-21

PSTricks needs at least two (IA)TEX runs to calculate the correct distance. The values of the intermediate runs are saved in the aux file (LATEX) or in `\jobname.tmp`.

The edge *key* After a new tree node has been defined, `\pssucc` (successor) is set to the name of this new node and `\pspred` (predecessor) to that of its preceding node. Thus you can create an arbitrary line/curve between these two nodes as, for instance,

```
\ncline{\pspred}{\pssucc}
```

PSTricks offers a command for this case:

```
\psedge{\pspred}{\pssucc}
```

The command `\psedge` is identical to `\ncline`, unless it is redefined as in the following example, where curves are desired instead of simple lines. Such a redefinition takes effect globally for the whole tree. With the option edge you can use this command locally by passing a previously defined macro as its value, as also shown in the example.

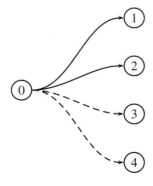

```
\usepackage{pstricks,pst-tree}
\renewcommand\psedge[2]{%
  \nccurve[angleA=0,angleB=180]{->}{#1}{#2}}
\newcommand\psedgeDash[2]{%
  \nccurve[angleA=0,angleB=180,%
    linestyle=dashed]{->}{#1}{#2}}

\pstree[treemode=R,levelsep=3cm]{\Tcircle{0}}{%
  \Tcircle{1}   \Tcircle{2}
  \Tcircle[edge=\psedgeDash]{3}
  \Tcircle[edge=\psedgeDash]{4}}%
```

Example
6-3-22

This strategy also enables you to improve the appearance of the last example from Section 6.3.2 on page 374 by using \ncdiagg (Section 6.2.2 on page 342) for the connections.

```
\usepackage{pstricks,pst-tree}
\SpecialCoor
\def\edgeRed#1#2{\ncdiagg[angleA=180,arm=0pt,nodesep=2pt,linecolor=red]{#2}{#1}}
\def\edgeBlue#1#2{\ncdiagg[angleA=180,arm=0pt,nodesep=2pt,linecolor=blue]{#2}{#1}}
  \pstree[treemode=R,levelsep=*1cm]{%
    \Tr{Friedrich Wilhelm\rnode{A}{}}}{%
      \pstree{\Tr[edge=\edgeRed]{Friedrich I.}}{%
        \Tr[edge=\edgeRed]{Friedrich Wilhelm I.}
        \Tr[edge=\edgeRed]{Friedrich}}
      \pstree{\Tr[edge=\edgeBlue]{%
        \rnode{B1}{}Albrecht Friedrich\rnode{C}{}}}{%
        \Tr[edge=\edgeBlue]{\rnode{B2}{}Wilhelm Heinrich}
        \Tr[edge=\edgeBlue]{Friedrich}}}
\psset{arrowscale=2,linewidth=0.2pt}
\pcline[linestyle=dashed](A)(A|0,-1)   \pcline[linestyle=dashed](B1)(B1|0,-1)
\pcline[linestyle=dashed](B2)(B2|0,-1)\pcline[linestyle=dashed](C)(C|0,-1)
\psline{<->}(A|0,-.8)(B1|0,-.8)        \psline{<->}(B2|0,-.8)(C|0,-.8)
```

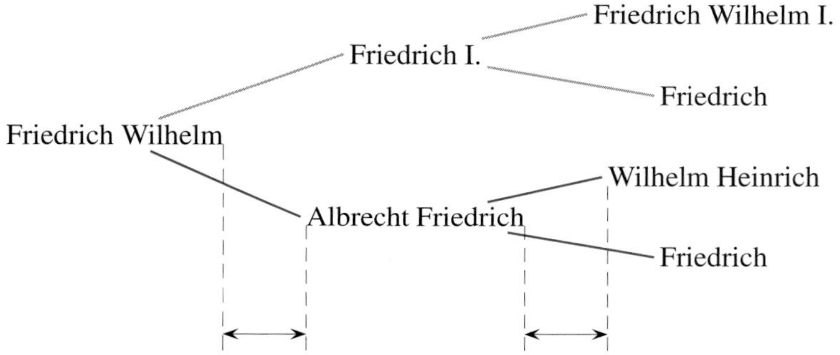

Example
6-3-23

If you do not want to define the macros outside \pstree, you can assign them directly to edge. If you wish to assign keywords to these macros as well, the entire definition has to be enclosed in {}.

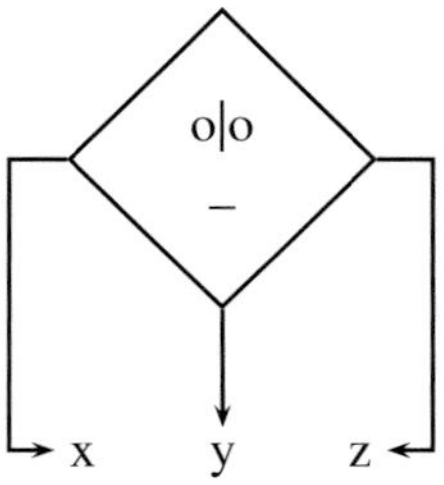

Example
6-3-24

```
\usepackage{pstricks,pst-tree,amsmath}
\pstree[nodesepB=3pt,arrows=->,levelsep=2cm]{%
  \Tdia{\begin{tabular}{c}o|o\\\_\end{tabular}}}{%
    \TR[edge={\ncbar[angle=180,armB=0.3cm]}]{x}
    \TR{y}
    \TR[edge={\ncbar[armB=0.3cm]}]{z}
}
```

In general, labels are placed without regard to the sizes of their respective boxes. There-
The showbox key fore, they may appear outside the regular box, causing `\psframebox` to produce a wrong
result, as you can see in the next example.

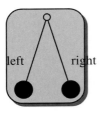

```
\usepackage{pstricks,pst-tree}
\psshadowbox[fillcolor=lightgray,fillstyle=solid,
    framearc=0.4]{
      \psset{tpos=.6}
      \pstree{\Tc{3pt}}{%
        \TC*^{left}
        \TC*_{right}}}
```

Example
6-3-25

You can show the frame of the current box with the key setting `showbox=true` and
then correct its dimensions with the box options. This usage is shown below for the same
example. In some of the earlier examples it was sometimes difficult to specify the size of the
The bounding box bounding box correctly. For this purposes, **pst-tree** provides eight keywords to influence the
keywords box surrounding a node.

bb *?* The bounding box is set to the specified values, where the question mark stands for
l, r, h, or d representing left, right, height, and depth, respectively. The distances are
measured from the object's origin.

xbb *?* The bounding box is increased or decreased by the specified values in the corresponding direction.

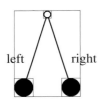 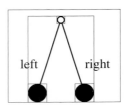

```
\usepackage{pstricks,pst-tree}
\psset{tpos=.6,showbbox=true}
\pstree{\Tc{3pt}}{%
  \TC*^{left} \TC*_{right}}
\qquad
\pstree[xbbl=15pt,xbbr=20pt,xbbh=5pt]
    {\Tc{3pt}}{\TC*^{left} \TC*_{right}}
```

Example
6-3-26

Having corrected the surrounding box, you can now use `\psshadowbox` successfully,
as shown in the next example.

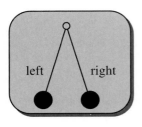

```
\usepackage{pstricks,pst-tree}
\psshadowbox[fillcolor=lightgray,
            fillstyle=solid,framearc=0.4]{%
  \psset{tpos=.6}
  \pstree[xbbl=15pt,xbbr=20pt,xbbh=5pt]{\Tc{3pt}}{%
    \TC*^{left}\TC*_{right}}}
```

Example
6-3-27

6.3.3 Labels

The connecting line from a predecessor to a new node (except for a root) is created immediately after the new node has been defined. The **pst-node** macros are used internally , so the coordinates of the two nodes \pssucc and \pspred are still available after the connection has been created. Therefore you can use the label macros discussed in Section 6.2 on page 334 to create labels. In particular, vertically or horizontally aligned labels are easily created with the \t?put variants.

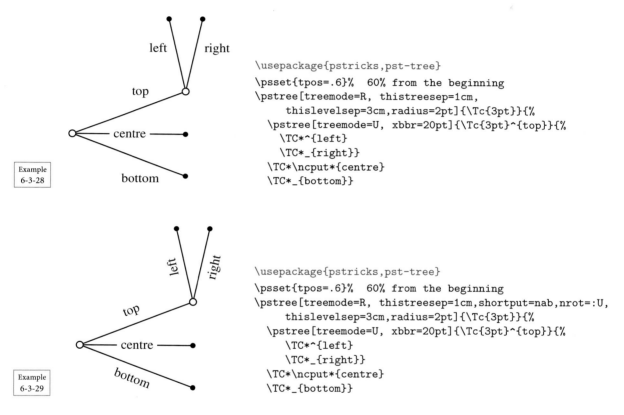

```
\usepackage{pstricks,pst-tree}
\psset{tpos=.6}%  60% from the beginning
\pstree[treemode=R, thistreesep=1cm,
     thislevelsep=3cm,radius=2pt]{\Tc{3pt}}{%
  \pstree[treemode=U, xbbr=20pt]{\Tc{3pt}^{top}}{%
    \TC*^{left}
    \TC*_{right}}
  \TC*\ncput*{centre}
  \TC*_{bottom}}
```

Example
6-3-28

```
\usepackage{pstricks,pst-tree}
\psset{tpos=.6}%  60% from the beginning
\pstree[treemode=R, thistreesep=1cm,shortput=nab,nrot=:U,
     thislevelsep=3cm,radius=2pt]{\Tc{3pt}}{%
  \pstree[treemode=U, xbbr=20pt]{\Tc{3pt}^{top}}{%
    \TC*^{left}
    \TC*_{right}}
  \TC*\ncput*{centre}
  \TC*_{bottom}}
```

Example
6-3-29

The macro \nput (Section 6.2.5 on page 359) is also available; it refers to a single node, which would always be \pssucc here. Furthermore, **pst-tree** defines the following special options:

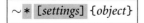

These options basically correspond to \nput, but are exclusively intended for tree connections here. You can use this short form in combination with other short or long forms to set two labels in one step. Just keep in mind that if the ~ variant is used in combination with other label macros, it must come immediately after the node macro.

The following example shows practically every possible combination of labels. The instruction `shortput=nab` replaces short forms with their `\n?put` long forms. The setting `nrot=:U` requests that all labels appear in parallel to their line.

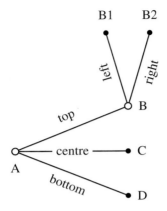

```
\usepackage{pstricks,pst-tree}
\psset{tpos=.6}%   60% from the beginning
\pstree[treemode=R, thistreesep=1cm,%
    shortput=nab,nrot=:U,thislevelsep=3cm,%
    radius=2pt]{\Tc{3pt}~{A}}{%
  \pstree[treemode=U, xbbr=20pt]{%
    \Tc{3pt}~{B}^{top}}{%
      \TC*~{B1}^{left}
      \TC*~{B2}_{right}}
    \TC*~{C}\ncput*{centre}
    \TC*~{D}_{bottom}}
```

Example
6-3-30

Table 6.10: Label keywords

Name	Value Type	Default
tnpos	l|r|a|b	\empty
tnsep	*value[unit]*	*empty*
tnheight	*value[unit]*	\ht\strutbox
tndepth	*value[unit]*	\dp\strutbox
tnyref	*number*	*empty*

The tnpos *key*   With the keyword `tnpos` you can arrange labels arbitrarily in the following ways: "(l)eft, (r)ight, (a)bove, (b)elow". Only the abbreviations l, r, a, and b are valid.

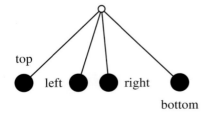

```
\usepackage{pstricks,pst-tree}
\pstree[treesep=0.3cm]{\Tc{3pt}}{%
    \TC*~[tnpos=a]{top}
    \TC*~[tnpos=l]{left}
    \TC*~[tnpos=r]{right}
    \TC*~[tnpos=b]{bottom}}
```

Example
6-3-31

The tnsep *key*   In general, **PSTricks** sets a distance of `labelsep` between the label and the box. If you specify any value for `tnsep`, this value is taken. If it is negative, the distance is measured starting from the node center—not from the node edge.

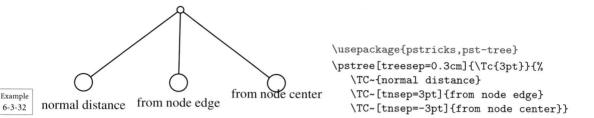

```
\usepackage{pstricks,pst-tree}
\pstree[treesep=0.3cm]{\Tc{3pt}}{%
  \TC~{normal distance}
  \TC~[tnsep=3pt]{from node edge}
  \TC~[tnsep=-3pt]{from node center}}
```

Example
6-3-32

In regard to horizontal alignment, all labels refer to the same baseline. Sometimes, however, you may wish to align them to the nodes. For this case you can use `tnheight=0pt` to eliminate the height of the label boxes, leaving them with only a depth, so that all labels are aligned at the same distance from the nodes. The same applies for `tndepth` if the tree is aligned vertically.

The `tnheight` *and* `tndepth` *keys*

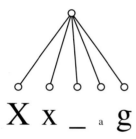

```
\usepackage{pstricks,pst-tree}
\Huge\pstree[treesep=0.3cm,radius=3pt]{\Tc{3pt}}{%
  \TC~{X}
  \TC~{x}
  \TC~{\_}
  \TC~{\footnotesize a}
  \TC~{g}}
```

Example
6-3-33

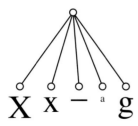

```
\usepackage{pstricks,pst-tree}
\Huge\pstree[treesep=0.3cm,radius=3pt,%
    tnheight=0pt]{\Tc{3pt}}{%
  \TC~{X}
  \TC~{x}
  \TC~{\_}
  \TC~{\footnotesize a}
  \TC~{g}}
```

Example
6-3-34

If this keyword is empty, which corresponds to {}, then `vref` is used for the vertical positioning of the label (page 348). The keyword `vref` denotes the vertical distance from the

The `tnyref` *key*

baseline to the top of the surrounding box. You can also specify a value of $0 < $ `tnyref` < 1 for this length.

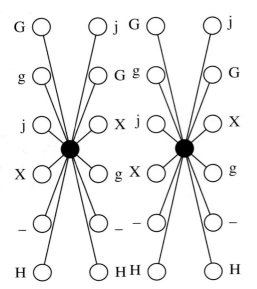

```
\usepackage{pstricks,pst-tree}
\psset{levelsep=.75cm,labelsep=5pt,%
    treenodesize=0.3}\large
\pstree[treemode=L,angleB=-90,angleA=90]{%
    \pstree[treemode=R,angleA=-90,%
        angleB=90]{\TC*}{
        \TC~{j}\TC~{G}\TC~{X}
        \TC~{g}\TC~{\_}\TC~{H}}%
}{ \TC~{G}\TC~{g}\TC~{j}
    \TC~{X}\TC~{\_}\TC~{H}}
%
\psset{tnyref=0.3}% <-----
\pstree[treemode=L,angleB=-90,angleA=90]{%
    \pstree[treemode=R,angleA=-90,%
        angleB=90]{\TC*}{
        \TC~{j}\TC~{G}\TC~{X}
        \TC~{g}\TC~{\_}\TC~{H}
    }%
}{ \TC~{G}\TC~{g}\TC~{j}
    \TC~{X}\TC~{\_}\TC~{H}}
```

Example
6-3-35

6.3.4 Skip tree levels

Usually, a connection leads from one level to the next. With the command `\skiplevel` and the environment `skiplevels`, you can skip single levels and establish connections to their pre-precedessors.

`\skiplevel` [*settings*] {*node or subtree*}	`\begin{skiplevels}` [*settings*] {*number*}
	nodes or subtrees
	`\end{skiplevels}`

The `skiplevels` environment may also be replaced by nested `\skiplevel` commands.

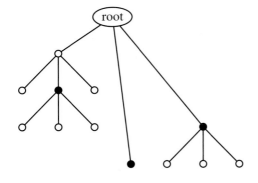

```
\usepackage{pstricks,pst-tree}
\pstree[levelsep=1cm,radius=3pt]{%
    \Toval{root}}{%
    \pstree{\TC}{%
        \TC
        \pstree{\TC*}{\TC\TC\TC}%
        \TC}
    \begin{skiplevels}{2}
        \skiplevel{\TC*}
        \pstree{\TC*}{\TC\TC\TC}%
    \end{skiplevels}}
```

Example
6-3-36

6.4   pst-fill—**Filling and tiling**

The package pst-fill optimizes the process of filling and tiling. The filling method covers a
plane with a color, color pattern, or picture pattern without offering control over the underlying coordinate system. By contrast, the tiling method takes the geometric structure of the
covered area into account—e.g., to achieve symmetry. Tiling or tesselation is a very old mathematical challenge and not at all an easy one [38, 111, 113]. The package pst-fill does not
claim to cover all aspects of tesselation but exclusively concentrates on monohedral tiling.
Monohedral tilings are composed of many copies of a single basic tile (prototile), whereas
n-hedral tilings consist of patterns that use different basic elements. Still, with \multido
(see Section 6.7.9 on page 458) or \multiput (Section 5.11.3 on page 267), you can create
individual basic patterns that then lead to monohedral tilings.

pst-fill has two different modes, a *manual* mode and an *automatic* mode. Both fill the
whole shape starting from one point and then clip tiles that are jutting out.

manual mode   To fill an area, a pattern is set n times and then written to the PostScript
output the same number of times.

automatic mode   To fill an area, a pattern is set n times but written only once to the Post-
Script output; the repetition is then handed over to PostScript. All data in the starting
point is lost in this process, so this method can be used only for filling with subsequent
clipping but not for tiling.

In principle, there are no urgent reasons to prefer the manual mode. The automatic
mode is achieved by loading pst-fill with the tiling option. Every fill object, such as a
PSTricks graphic or an external image, must be saved in the macro \psboxfill and the
fill style must be set to boxfill.

6.4.1   **Keywords for filling**

Table 6.11 lists the special keywords for the package pst-fill.

Unless indicated otherwise, the examples use one of the following defined tiles:
\FSquare and \FRectangle. This results in the following simple pattern:

```
\usepackage{pstricks} \usepackage[tiling]{pst-fill}
\newcommand\FSquare{\begin{pspicture}(0.5,0.5)
  \psframe[dimen=middle](0.5,0.5)\end{pspicture}}
\newcommand\FRectangle{\begin{pspicture}(0.5,0.75)
  \psframe[dimen=middle](0.5,0.75)\end{pspicture}}
```

```
\psboxfill{\FSquare}
\begin{pspicture}(2.1,2.1)
  \psframe[fillstyle=boxfill,fillloopadd=2](2,2)
\end{pspicture}\qquad
\psboxfill{\FRectangle}
\begin{pspicture}(2.1,2.1)
  \psframe[fillstyle=boxfill,fillloopadd=2](2,2)
\end{pspicture}
```

Example
6-4-1

Table 6.11: Keywords for `pst-fill`

Name	Value Type	Default
fillangle	*angle*	0
fillsep[1]	*value [unit]*	0pt
fillsepx[2]	*value [unit]*	0pt
fillsepy[2]	*value [unit]*	0pt
fillcycle	*value*	0
fillcyclex[2]	*value*	0
fillcycley[2]	*value*	0
fillmove	*value [unit]*	0pt
fillmovex[2]	*value [unit]*	0pt
fillmovey[2]	*value [unit]*	0pt
fillsize	auto$|\{(x_0, y_0)\,(x_1, y_1)\}$	auto
fillloopadd[2]	*value*	0
fillloopaddx[2]	*value*	0
fillloopaddy[2]	*value*	0
PstDebug[2]	0$|$1	0

[1] Without `tiling` option set to 2pt.
[2] Only available with `tiling` option.

The `fillangle` *key*   The keyword `fillangle` specifies by which angle the pattern is rotated with reference to the horizontal.

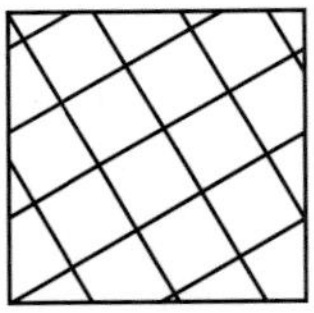

```
\usepackage{pstricks}
\usepackage[tiling]{pst-fill}
\psboxfill{\FSquare}
\begin{pspicture}(2.1,2.1)
  \psframe[fillstyle=boxfill,fillangle=30](2,2)
\end{pspicture}
```

Example
6-4-2

The `fillsep`, `fillsepx`, *and* `fillsepy` *keys*   The keyword `fillsep` specifies the distance between the single tiles. It can also have negative values, as shown in the following examples (the right one has a negative value resulting in some overlap). The keys `fillsepx` and `fillsepy` allow you to specify the separation along the axes individually.

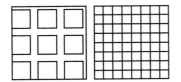

```
\usepackage{pstricks}
\usepackage[tiling]{pst-fill}
\psboxfill{\FSquare}
\begin{pspicture}(2.1,2.1)
  \psframe[fillstyle=boxfill,fillsep=0.2cm](2,2)
\end{pspicture}\
\begin{pspicture}(2.1,2.1)
  \psframe[fillstyle=boxfill,fillsep=-0.25cm](2,2)
\end{pspicture}
```

Example
6-4-3

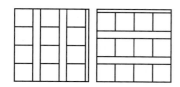

```
\usepackage{pstricks}
\usepackage[tiling]{pst-fill}
\psboxfill{\FSquare}
\begin{pspicture}(2.1,2.1)
  \psframe[fillstyle=boxfill,fillsepx=0.2cm](2,2)
\end{pspicture}\
\begin{pspicture}(2.1,2.1)
  \psframe[fillstyle=boxfill,fillsepy=0.2cm](2,2)
\end{pspicture}
```

The keyword `fillcycle` specifies the distance by which every second row and/or column is moved, while every first row remains at the original position. The specified value forms the denominator of the fraction by which the row/column is moved. A value of 2 means a movement of $\frac{1}{2} = 0.5$, or 50% of one tile width to the right. Again, negative values are possible.

The `fillcycle`, `fillcyclex`, *and* `fillcycley` *keys*

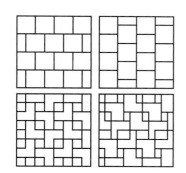

```
\usepackage{pstricks}
\usepackage[tiling]{pst-fill}
\psboxfill{\FSquare}
\begin{pspicture}(2.1,2.1)
  \psframe[fillstyle=boxfill,fillcyclex=2](2,2)
\end{pspicture}\
\begin{pspicture}(2.1,2.1)
  \psframe[fillstyle=boxfill,fillcycley=2](2,2)
\end{pspicture}\\
\begin{pspicture}(2.1,2.1)
  \psframe[fillstyle=boxfill,fillcycle=2](2,2)
\end{pspicture}\
\begin{pspicture}(2.1,2.1)
  \psframe[fillstyle=boxfill,fillcyclex=3,fillcycley=-2](2,2)
\end{pspicture}
```

The keyword `fillmove` specifies the distance by which the next row/column is displaced with regard to its predecessor. `fillmovex` affects only the horizontal axis, and `fillmovey` only the vertical axis. Negative values are also possible. Contrast this behavior with that of `fillcycle`, where every second row/column was displaced by the same value, while every first row/column remained at its original position. To make this difference more obvious here, a rectangle has been used as a tile.

The `fillmove`, `fillmovex`, *and* `fillmovey` *keys*

```
\usepackage{pstricks} \usepackage[tiling]{pst-fill}
\psboxfill{\FRectangle}
\begin{pspicture}(2.1,2.1)
  \psframe[fillstyle=boxfill,fillmovex=0.2](2,2)   \end{pspicture}
\begin{pspicture}(2.1,2.1)
  \psframe[fillstyle=boxfill,fillmovey=0.25](2,2)   \end{pspicture}
\begin{pspicture}(2.1,2.1)
  \psframe[fillstyle=boxfill,fillmove=0.25](2,2)   \end{pspicture}
```

```
\begin{pspicture}(2.1,2.1)
  \psframe[fillstyle=boxfill,fillmovex=0.2,fillmovey=-0.2](2,2)
\end{pspicture}
```

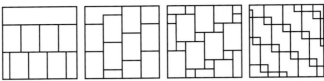

Example
6-4-6

The `fillsize` *key*   The keyword `fillsize` implicitly specifies the way of filling: if it is not present or is set to the value `auto`, filling is done in automatic mode. Otherwise, it defines the fill area in manual mode.

`auto`   The default value. In this case a plane of $(-15\,\text{cm}, -15\,\text{cm})(15\,\text{cm}, 15\,\text{cm})$ is tiled. The patterns are arranged in such a way that they appear symmetrical within the visible area.

$(x_0, y_0)\,(x_1, y_1)$ If only one pair of values is specified, (x_0, y_0) is set to the default value $(0,0)$ and the specified value defines (x_1, y_1).

The manual mode is recommended only for special cases, such as if you wish to form a pattern from an EPS graphic.

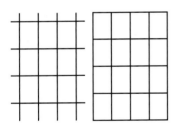

```
\usepackage{pstricks} \usepackage[tiling]{pst-fill}
\psboxfill{\FRectangle}
\begin{pspicture}(2.1,3.1)
  \psframe[fillstyle=boxfill,
           fillsize={(-0.25,-0.25)(4,4)}](2,3)
\end{pspicture}
\begin{pspicture}(2.1,3.1)
  \psframe[fillstyle=boxfill](2,3)
\end{pspicture}
```

Example
6-4-7

The `fillloopadd`,   The following keywords, which are only available in `tiling` mode, are useful for more
`fillloopaddx`, *and*   complex patterns where one or more rows are missing. With `fillloopadd` you can specify
`fillloopaddy` *keys*   the number of rows to add.

```
\usepackage{pstricks} \usepackage[tiling]{pst-fill}
\SpecialCoor
\newcommand\FHexagon{\def\HRadius{0.25}%
  \begin{pspicture}(0.433,0.375)%
    \pspolygon(\HRadius;30)(\HRadius;90)(\HRadius;150)%
       (\HRadius;210)(\HRadius;270)(\HRadius;330)% hexagon
  \end{pspicture}}
\psboxfill{\FHexagon}
\begin{pspicture}(2,2) \psframe[fillstyle=boxfill](2,2)
\end{pspicture}
```

```
\begin{pspicture}(2,2) \psframe[fillstyle=boxfill,fillcyclex=2](2,2)
\end{pspicture}
\begin{pspicture}(2,2) \psframe[fillstyle=boxfill,
                              fillcyclex=2,fillloopaddy=1](2,2)
\end{pspicture}
```

Example
6-4-8

PstDebug is not a real debugger but shows only the process of tiling, so that problems *The* PstDebug *key* with special patterns can be recognized more easily. The following examples are identical to the previous ones, but this time with the additional key setting PstDebug=1. To prevent rounding errors from changing the result, we might want to increase the coordinates of the enclosing pspicture environment a bit.

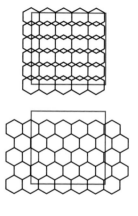

```
\usepackage{pstricks}
\usepackage[tiling]{pst-fill}
% \FHexagon as previously defined
\psboxfill{\FHexagon}
\begin{pspicture}(-0.5,-0.5)(2.5,2.5)
  \psframe[linecolor=blue,fillstyle=boxfill,PstDebug=1](2,2)
\end{pspicture}\\[-10pt]
\begin{pspicture}(-0.5,-0.5)(2.5,2.5)
  \psframe[linecolor=blue,fillstyle=boxfill,
          fillcyclex=2,PstDebug=1](2,2)
\end{pspicture}
```

Example
6-4-9

\psboxfill accepts everything as an argument (e.g., a graphic, which has to be scaled accordingly). Further examples can be found in the documentation on **pst-fill** [31].   *Filling with an image*

```
\usepackage{graphicx,pstricks}
\usepackage[tiling]{pst-fill}
\psboxfill{\includegraphics[scale=0.15]{figures/rose}}
\begin{pspicture}(2.1,2.1)
  \psframe[fillstyle=boxfill, fillloopadd=1](2,2)
\end{pspicture}\
\begin{pspicture}(2.1,2.1)
  \psframe[fillstyle=boxfill,fillcyclex=2,
                          fillloopadd=1](2,2)
\end{pspicture}
```

Example
6-4-10

6.5 pst-3d—Shadows, tilting, and three-dimensional representations

The base package **pstricks** contains a few commands for producing three-dimensional effects. In addition, several packages support the creation of three-dimensional objects or functions, as shown in Table 6.12. Although **pst-3d** is one of the older packages, it will be discussed here because it includes the preliminary stages of 3-D representations: shadows and tilting.

Table 6.12: Summary of 3-D packages

Package	Content
pst-3d	Basic three-dimensional operations
pst-3dplot	Three-dimensional plots
pst-fr3d	Three-dimensional framed boxes
pst-gr3d	Three-dimensional grids
pst-map3dll	Three-dimensional geographical projection
pst-ob3d	Three-dimensional basic objects
pst-vue3d	Three-dimensional views

6.5.1 Shadows

pst-3d defines the command \psshadow with the following syntax:

\psshadow *[settings]* *{material}*

The special keywords for this command are described on the following pages. The command also supports all other keywords that are useful for creating shadows. You can add shadows to any text-like material, text, rules, and mathematical expressions in inline mode.

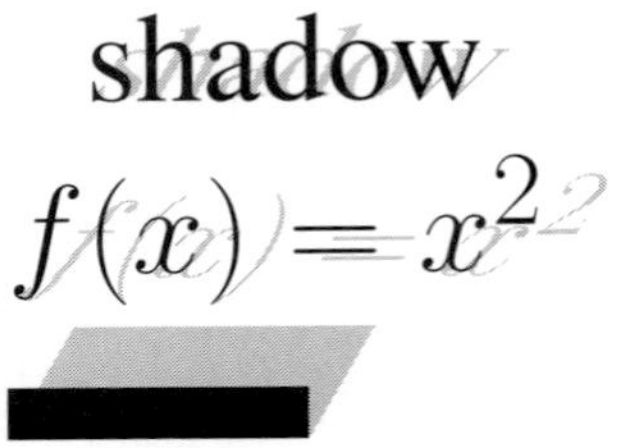

shadow

$$f(x) = x^2$$

```
\usepackage{pstricks,pst-3d}
\psshadow{\Huge shadow}\\[10pt]
\psshadow{\Huge $f(x)=x^2$}\\[15pt]
\psshadow[Tshadowsize=2.5]{%
    \rule{2cm}{10pt}}\\
```

Example 6-5-1

The Tshadowangle *key*   The keyword Tshadowangle defines the angle of the shadow with regard to the perpendicular of the paper plane. Therefore, the angle of the text itself is 90°. Negative angles cause the shadow to stand out from the paper plane. Shadow angles cannot take the value $0°$ or $180°$.

```
\usepackage{pstricks,pst-3d}
\psshadow{\Huge shadow}\\[5pt]
\psshadow[Tshadowangle=30]{\Huge shadow}\\[5pt]
\psshadow[Tshadowangle=70]{\Huge shadow}\\[5pt]
\psshadow[Tshadowangle=-30]{\Huge shadow}
```

The keyword `Tshadowcolor` is used to define the shadow color.   *The* `Tshadowcolor` *key*

```
\usepackage{pstricks,pst-3d}
\psshadow{\Huge shadow}\\[5pt]
\psshadow[Tshadowcolor=red]{\Huge shadow}\\[5pt]
\psshadow[Tshadowcolor=green]{\Huge shadow}\\[5pt]
\psshadow[Tshadowcolor=blue]{\Huge shadow}
```

The keyword `Tshadowsize` is used to determine the scaling factor of the shadow.   *The* `Tshadowsize` *key*

```
\usepackage{pstricks,pst-3d}
\psshadow{\Huge shadow}\\[5pt]
\psshadow[Tshadowsize=0.5]{\Huge shadow}\\[10pt]
\psshadow[Tshadowsize=1.5]{\Huge shadow}\\[20pt]
\psshadow[Tshadowsize=2.5]{\Huge shadow}
```

6.5.2   Tilting

By tilting objects you can simulate perspective views of three-dimensional objects. **pst-3d** defines two commands for this purpose:

$\backslash$pstilt *[settings]* *{angle}{object}* $\backslash$psTilt *[settings]* *{angle}{object}*

Figure 6.2 shows the difference between these two macros. In general, these macros can take any material as their argument and then tilt it. Vertical material, such as displays, may first have to be put into a \parbox (see the examples).

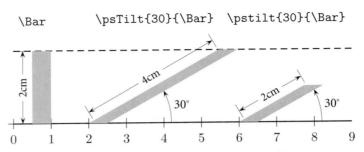

Figure 6.2: The difference between \pstilt and \psTilt

The command \pstilt tilts objects by rotating each point (x,y) by a given *angle*
\pstilt around its nadir point [the point $(x,0)$] while preserving the distance between the tilted
point and the nadir. In contrast, \psTilt keeps the vertical position of all tilted points. See
Figure 6.2 for a comparison.

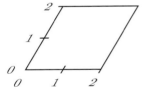

```
\usepackage{pstricks,pst-3d,multido}
\begin{pspicture}(5,2)
\newcommand*\Bar{\psframe(0,0)(0.25,2)}
\multido{\nA=15+15}{11}{\rput(2.5,0){\pstilt{\nA}{\Bar}}}
\end{pspicture}
```
Example
6-5-5

```
\usepackage{pstricks,pst-3d,multido}
\pstilt{60}{\parbox{0.5\linewidth}{%
    \[ f(x)=\int_1^{\infty}\frac{1}{x}\,dx=1 \]
}}
```
Example
6-5-6

```
\usepackage{pstricks,pst-3d,pst-plot,multido}
\pstilt{60}{%
  \begin{pspicture}(-0.5,-0.5)(2,2)
    \psaxes[axesstyle=frame](2,2)
  \end{pspicture}%
}
```
Example
6-5-7

```
\usepackage{graphicx,pstricks,pst-3d,multido}
\includegraphics[width=3cm]{pstricks/tiger}%
\pstilt{70}{%
  \includegraphics[width=3cm]{%
    pstricks/tiger}}
```
Example
6-5-8

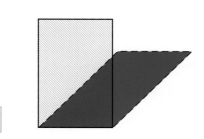

```
\usepackage{pstricks,pst-3d,multido}
\newpsstyle{TransparencyBlack}{%
  fillstyle=vlines,hatchwidth=0.1\pslinewidth,
  hatchsep=1.5\pslinewidth}
\begin{pspicture}(2,3)
  \rput[lb](0,0){\pstilt{45}{\psframe[linestyle=dashed,%
      fillstyle=solid,fillcolor=blue](2,3)}}
  \psframe[style=TransparencyBlack](0,0)(2,3)
\end{pspicture}
```

Example
6-5-9

The command \psTilt tilts objects in such a way that their vertical extension is preserved, while the horizontal extension grows as required so that, in theory, the object could   \psTilt
become infinitely wide (see Figure 6.2 on the facing page).

```
\usepackage{pstricks,pst-3d,multido}
\begin{pspicture*}(\linewidth,2)
  \newcommand*\Bar{\psframe(0,0)(0.25,2)}
  \multido{\nA=10+10}{17}{\rput(0.5\linewidth,0){\psTilt{\nA}{\Bar}}}
\end{pspicture*}
```

Example
6-5-10

Example
6-5-11

$$f(x) = \int_1^{\infty} \frac{1}{x}\,dx = 1$$

```
\usepackage{pstricks,pst-3d}
\psTilt{60}{\parbox{0.5\linewidth}{%
    \[ f(x)=\int_1^{\infty}\frac{1}{x}\,dx=1 \]
}}
```

Example
6-5-12

```
\usepackage{pstricks,pst-3d,pst-plot}
\psTilt{60}{%
  \begin{pspicture}(-0.5,-0.5)(2,2)
    \psaxes[axesstyle=frame](2,2)
  \end{pspicture}%
}
```

```
\usepackage{graphicx}
\usepackage{pstricks,pst-3d,pst-plot}
\includegraphics[width=3cm]{pstricks/tiger}%
\psTilt{70}{%
  \includegraphics[width=3cm]{%
    pstricks/tiger}}
```

Example
6-5-13

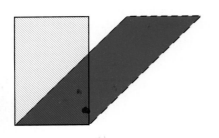

```
\usepackage{pstricks,pst-3d}
\newpsstyle{TransparencyBlack}{%
  fillstyle=vlines,hatchwidth=0.1\pslinewidth,
  hatchsep=1.5\pslinewidth}
\begin{pspicture}(2,3)
  \rput[lb](0,0){\psTilt{45}{\psframe[linestyle=dashed,%
    fillstyle=solid,fillcolor=blue](2,3)}}
  \psframe[style=TransparencyBlack](0,0)(2,3)
\end{pspicture}
```

Example
6-5-14

The package **rotating** provides macros to rotate text, e.g., to produce slanted table headings. The problem that arises when the text is surrounded by a frame is easily solved with \pstilt or \psTilt.

```
\usepackage{pstricks,pst-3d}
\newcommand*\tabA{\begin{tabular}{*{3}{|p{1em}}|}\hline
\rotateleft{column 1\ }&\rotateleft{column 2\ }&
  \rotateleft{column 3\ }
\end{tabular}}
\newcommand*\tabB{\begin{tabular}{*{3}{|p{1em}}|}\hline
 1 & 2 & 3 \\\hline  4 & 5 & 6 \\\hline
\end{tabular}}
\begin{tabular}{l}
  \pstilt{60}{\tabA}\\ \tabB
\end{tabular}\\[5pt]
\begin{tabular}{l}
  \psTilt{60}{\tabA}\\ \tabB
\end{tabular}
```

Example
6-5-15

6.5.3 Three-dimensional representations

pst-3d supports only parallel projections, so geometrical objects like spheres or cylinders are displayed with quite restricted options. Although **pst-3d** defines just a single macro for 3-D projection, the package is very efficient and serves as a basis for other packages [80, 134].

> \ThreeDput [*settings*] (*x,y,z*) {*object*}

The package **pst-3d** defines only this one macro. Nevertheless with the help of this macro, you can display virtually any linear or planar object within three-dimensional space. If no coordinates are specified, the default value for the origin is $(0,0,0)$. The *object* is anything that can be put into a box. If it is vertical material in the TEX sense, it first must be put into a \parbox command or minipage environment. To simplify the source code, we use the macro \IIIKOSystem in the following examples. This macro draws the coordinate axes with their grid and will not be explicitly mentioned again.

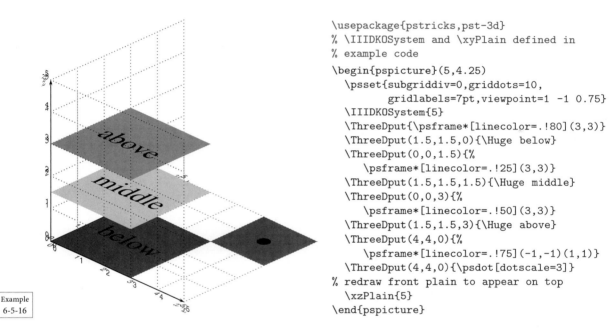

```
\usepackage{pstricks,pst-3d}
% \IIIDKOSystem and \xyPlain defined in
% example code
\begin{pspicture}(5,4.25)
  \psset{subgriddiv=0,griddots=10,
          gridlabels=7pt,viewpoint=1 -1 0.75}
  \IIIDKOSystem{5}
  \ThreeDput{\psframe*[linecolor=.!80](3,3)}
  \ThreeDput(1.5,1.5,0){\Huge below}
  \ThreeDput(0,0,1.5){%
      \psframe*[linecolor=.!25](3,3)}
  \ThreeDput(1.5,1.5,1.5){\Huge middle}
  \ThreeDput(0,0,3){%
      \psframe*[linecolor=.!50](3,3)}
  \ThreeDput(1.5,1.5,3){\Huge above}
  \ThreeDput(4,4,0){%
      \psframe*[linecolor=.!75](-1,-1)(1,1)}
  \ThreeDput(4,4,0){\psdot[dotscale=3]}
% redraw front plain to appear on top
  \xzPlain{5}
\end{pspicture}
```

The coordinates of \ThreeDput refer to the origin of the object, which does not necessarily have to be the visible geometrical center.

```
\psframe(2,2)%          origin bottom left (0,0)
\psframe(-1,-1(1,1)%    origin in the middle (0,0)
arbitrary text%         origin in the middle of the base line
```

In the preceding example, the smaller square with its center $(0,0)$ has been positioned exactly at the coordinates $(4,4,0)$. The macro \ThreeDput can be used in a variety of ways, especially in conjunction with the package **pst-vue3d** [80]. By specifying the normal vector $\vec{n}$ and a point $P(x,y,z)$ on a straight line and/or a plane, you can determine its exact position in space. Areas can be shaded in different levels of brightness to enhance the three-dimensional appearance.

```
\usepackage{pstricks,pst-3d}
\begin{pspicture}(-4.5,-3.5)(3,4.75)
\psset{subgriddiv=0,griddots=10,gridlabels=7pt,viewpoint=1 1.5 1}
\IIIDKOSystem[gridlabels=0pt]{5}
\ThreeDput[normal=0 0 1]
   {\psline[linewidth=3pt,linecolor=blue]{->}(4,4)(4,5.5)   % xy plane
    \uput[90](4,5.5){\rotateleft{\textcolor{blue}{$\vec{n}_A$}}}}
\ThreeDput[normal=0 -1 0]
   {\psline[linewidth=3pt,linecolor=green]{->}(4,0)(5.5,0) % xz plane
    \uput[90](5.5,0){\psscalebox{-1 1}{\textcolor{green}{$\vec{n}_B$}}}}
\ThreeDput[normal=1 0 0]
   {\psline[linewidth=3pt,linecolor=red]{->}(0,4)(0,5.5)    % yz plane
    \uput[0](0,5.5){$\vec{n}_{top}$}} % cube and axes
\ThreeDput[normal=0 0 1](0,0,4){ \psframe*[linecolor=.!50](4,4)
    \rput(2,2){\Huge\textbf{TOP}}}
\ThreeDput[normal=0 1 0](4,4,0){\psframe*[linecolor=.!75](4,4)
    \rput(2,2){\Huge\textbf{side A}}}
\ThreeDput[normal=1 0 0](4,0,0){\psframe*[linecolor=.!25](4,4)
    \rput(2,2){\Huge\textbf{side B}}}
% the small axes
\ThreeDput[normal=0 0 1](0,0,4){\psline(4,0)\uput[90](3,0){X$_{top}$}
    \psline(0,4)\uput[0](0,3){Y$_{top}$}}
\ThreeDput[normal=0 1 0](4,4,0){\psline(4,0)\uput[90](3,0){X$_{A}$}
    \psline(0,4)\uput[0](0,3){Y$_{A}$}}
\ThreeDput[normal=1 0 0](4,0,0){\psline(4,0)\uput[90](3,0){X$_{B}$}
    \psline(0,4)\uput[0](0,3){Y$_{B}$}}
\end{pspicture}
```

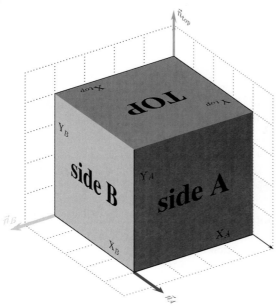

Example
6-5-17

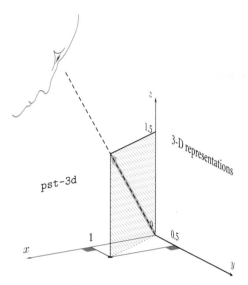

Figure 6.3: `viewpoint` definition

Table 6.13 shows the keywords that can be used to modify 3-D representations.

Table 6.13: Summary of 3-D keywords

Name	Value Type	Default
viewpoint	*valuex valuey valuez*	1 −1 1
viewangle	*angle*	0
normal	*valuex valuey valuez*	0 0 1
embedangle	*angle*	0

The direction from which you look at a 3-D object is essential for its representation. With `viewpoint` you specify the (x, y, z) coordinates, which then define the vector of the *The* `viewpoint` *key* viewing direction. In a parallel projection the length of this vector is unimportant, so that (1 0.5 1.5) and (2 1 3) yield the same representations. Figure 6.3 shows this representation. Naturally, you would look at the figure itself from a different angle; otherwise, you would look directly onto the vector.

For Figure 6.3, we defined a vector of `viewpoint=3 5 2`. If you would like to look at something from a larger distance along the y-axis, you could think of specifying `viewpoint=0 1 3`. That is, the viewer moves one unit in the y direction and three units in the z direction from the center (origin) and watches everything from there. However, zero values for `viewpoint` (along any axis) are not possible: they would result in a division by *Division* zero later on when displaying or printing the result. Instead, specify at least 0.001, which *by zero danger* prevents the division by zero problem while still essentially ignoring that direction.

A useful value for the viewpoint is `viewpoint=1 1 0.5`, which corresponds to a horizontal rotation by 45° and a vertical rotation by about 20°. Another useful point is

viewpoint=1.5 1 0.5, which corresponds to a horizontal rotation by 33° and the same
vertical rotation. Both are shown in the example below.

```
\usepackage{pstricks,pst-3d}
\psset{unit=.3cm}
\begin{pspicture}(-5,-3)(4,3)
  \psset{viewpoint=1 1 0.5}
  \ThreeDput[normal=0 0 1]{\psgrid(-3,-3)(6,6)}
  \ThreeDput[normal=-1 0 0](0,4,0){\psframe*[linecolor=blue](4,4)}
\end{pspicture}\hfill
\begin{pspicture}(-5,-3)(4,3)
  \psset{viewpoint=1.5 1 0.5}
  \ThreeDput[normal=0 0 1]{\psgrid(-3,-3)(6,6)}
  \ThreeDput[normal=-1 0 0](0,4,0){\psframe*[linecolor=blue](4,4)}
\end{pspicture}
```

Example
6-5-18

The next examples provide a view of a cube, using a viewpoint from each of the four
"top" corners:

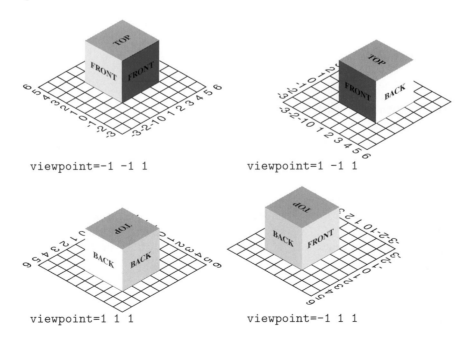

viewpoint=-1 -1 1   viewpoint=1 -1 1

viewpoint=1 1 1   viewpoint=-1 1 1

Example
6-5-19

It is important to realize that **PSTricks** does not check which side hides another side; the last drawn side wipes out those drawn earlier, even if it lies behind them in 3-D space. When drawing the different views, we must therefore draw the sides in an adequate order.

In addition to using `viewpoint`, you can rotate every object with the help of the keyword `viewangle`. You can also perform this manipulation with the `\rotatebox` command, but `viewangle` has some more advantages. Since it can sometimes be difficult to clearly identify front and back side in a three-dimensional coordinate system, a rectangle has been laid on the xy plane in the following examples.

The `viewangle` *key*

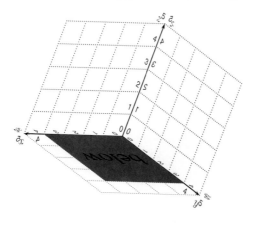

```
\usepackage{pstricks,pst-3d}
\begin{pspicture}(-3,-2.5)(-3,3)
  \psset{subgriddiv=0,griddots=10,gridlabels=7pt,
    unit=0.7,viewpoint=1 1 0.5,viewangle=20}
  \IIIDKOSystem{5}% see above
  \ThreeDput(0,0,0){\psframe*[linecolor=.!80](4,4)}
  \ThreeDput(2,2,0){\Huge below}
\end{pspicture}
```

Example
6-5-20

```
\usepackage{pstricks,pst-3d}
\begin{pspicture}(-4,-2.5)(-2,3)
  \psset{subgriddiv=0,griddots=10,gridlabels=7pt,
    unit=0.7,viewpoint=1 1.5 0.5,viewangle=-30}
  \IIIDKOSystem{5}% see above
  \ThreeDput(0,0,0){\psframe*[linecolor=.!80](4,4)}
  \ThreeDput(2,2,0){\Huge below}
\end{pspicture}
```

Example
6-5-21

The keyword `normal` denotes the direction of the normal vector, which is perpendicular to its corresponding plane. Therefore the normal vector can be used to clearly determine the position of an object in three-dimensional space.

The `normal` *key*

```
\usepackage{pstricks,pst-3d}
\begin{pspicture}(-3.5,-2.5)(-3,5)
  \psset{subgriddiv=0,griddots=10,gridlabels=7pt,viewpoint=1 1.5 0.5}
```

```
\IIIDKOSystem{5}
\ThreeDput(0,0,0){\psframe*[linecolor=.!50](4,4)}
\ThreeDput(2,2,0){\huge\rotatedown{xy-plane}}
\ThreeDput[normal=0 -1 0](0,0,0){\psframe*[linecolor=.!50](4,4)}
\ThreeDput[normal=0 1 0](2,0,2){\huge xz-plane}
\ThreeDput[normal=1 0 0](0,0,0){\psframe*[linecolor=.!75](4,4)}
\ThreeDput[normal=1 0 0](0,2,2){\huge yz-plane}
\ThreeDput[normal=0 0 1](0,0,0)
          {\psline{->}(0,0)(0,5)\psline{->}(0,0)(5,0)}% xy plane
\ThreeDput[normal=0 1 0](0,0,0){\psline{->}(0,0)(0,5)}% xz plane
\end{pspicture}
```

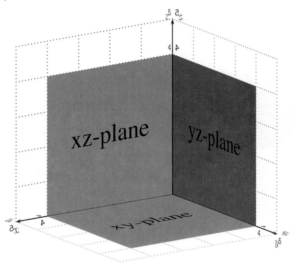

Example
6-5-22

Without the help of the normal vector, this example could not have been created so easily. Let us step through the code for a better understanding.

`\psset{viewpoint=1 1.5 0.5}` The `viewpoint` is placed at $P(1, 1.5, 0.5)$.

`\IIIDKOSystem{5}` First the coordinate system with the grid is drawn, so that axes and grid remain visible on the planes, which allows for a better visual orientation.

`\ThreeDput(0,0,0){\psframe*[linecolor=gray80](4,4)}` This puts the lower-left edge of a square with a side length of 4 at the origin of the coordinate system. Since no normal vector is specified here, the area is placed at the default position $\vec{n} = (0, 0, 1)$, in the first quadrant of the xy plane.

`\ThreeDput(2,2,0){\huge\rotatedown{xy-plane}}` This places text that is rotated by $180°$ in the `xy-plane`, centered on the point $(2, 2, 0)$.

`\ThreeDput[normal=0 -1 0](0,0,0){\psframe*[linecolor=gray85](4,4)}` This puts the lower-left edge of a square with a side length of 4 at the origin of the coordinate system. Since the normal vector here is the "negative" y-axis, the square is positioned in the first quadrant of the xz plane. With normal=0 1 0, it would have been in the second quadrant.

\ThreeDput[normal=0 1 0](2,0,2){\huge xz-plane} This places the text in the xy-plane centered on the point $(2, 0, 2)$. Since with regard to the viewpoint you look at the xz plane from the back, the normal vector for the area has to be reversed; otherwise, the text would be visible from the "back".

\ThreeDput[normal=1 0 0](0,0,0){\psframe*[linecolor=gray90](4,4)} This puts the lower-left edge of a square with a side length of 4 at the origin of the coordinate system. The normal vector is the "positive" x-axis, so the square is positioned in the first quadrant of the yz plane.

\ThreeDput[normal=1 0 0](0,2,2){\huge yz-plane} This places the text in the yz-plane centered on the point $(0, 2, 2)$. Since the text is written on the "positive" side of the area, the normal vector stays the same.

\ThreeDput[normal=0 0 1](0,0,0)   The coordinate axes have been covered by the three areas and are now redrawn, first the x- and y-axes.

\ThreeDput[normal=0 1 0](0,0,0)   Now the z-axis is redrawn.

With viewangle, you can rotate an object perpendicular to the plane of the viewer. With the keyword embedangle, you can rotate it perpendicular to the normal vector. The angles are counted mathematically (i.e., counterclockwise).   *The* embedangle *key*

```
\usepackage{pstricks,pst-3d}
\newcommand\tBlack[2]{\psframe[style=#2](2,2)
                      \rput(1,1){\textcolor{#1}{\textbf{PSTricks}}}}
\newpsstyle{SolidYellow}{fillstyle=solid,fillcolor=yellow}
\newpsstyle{TransparencyRed}{fillstyle=vlines,hatchcolor=red,
                       hatchwidth=0.1\pslinewidth,
                       hatchsep=1\pslinewidth}
\newpsstyle{TransparencyBlue}{fillstyle=vlines,hatchcolor=.!25,
                        hatchwidth=0.1\pslinewidth,
                        hatchsep=1\pslinewidth}

\begin{pspicture}(-1.2,-1.75)(4.8,3.7)
  \psset{subgriddiv=0,griddots=10,gridlabels=7pt}
  \ThreeDput{\psgrid[subgriddiv=0](-2,0)(4,3)} % embedangle=0
  \ThreeDput(-1,0,0){\tBlack{black}{SolidYellow}}
  \ThreeDput(2,0,0){\tBlack{black}{SolidYellow}}
  \ThreeDput[embedangle=50](-1,0,0){\tBlack{gray}{TransparencyRed}}
  \ThreeDput[embedangle=50](2,0,0){\tBlack{gray}{TransparencyBlue}}
% the normal vectors
  \ThreeDput[normal=0 1 0](-1,0,0)
          {\psline[linewidth=0.1,linecolor=red](0,4)}
```

```
    \ThreeDput[normal=0 1 0](2,0,0)
               {\psline[linewidth=0.1,linecolor=blue](0,4)}
\end{pspicture}
\quad
\psset{viewpoint=1 1 100}
\begin{pspicture}(-2.5,-4.5)(2.8,1.7)
  \ThreeDput{\psgrid[subgriddiv=0](-2,0)(4,3)} % embedangle=0
  \ThreeDput(-1,0,0){\tBlack{black}{SolidYellow}}
  \ThreeDput(2,0,0){\tBlack{black}{SolidYellow}}
  \ThreeDput[embedangle=50](-1,0,0){\tBlack{gray}{TransparencyRed}}
  \ThreeDput[embedangle=50](2,0,0){\tBlack{gray}{TransparencyBlue}}
% the normal vectors
  \ThreeDput[normal=0 1 0](-1,0,0)
             {\psline[linewidth=0.1,linecolor=red](0,4)}
  \ThreeDput[normal=0 1 0](2,0,0)
             {\psline[linewidth=0.1,linecolor=blue](0,4)}
\end{pspicture}
```

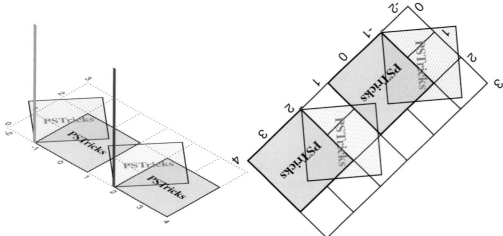

Example
6-5-23

6.6 pst-3dplot—3-D parallel projections of functions and data

The package **pst-3dplot** supports the representation of three-dimensional mathematical functions and three-dimensional data sets. It is based on the package **pst-plot** (see Section 6.1 on page 313) and has nearly the same syntax. Furthermore, **pst-3dplot** provides macros for the parallel projection of simple points, lines, curves, figures. and bodies into three-dimensional space. In contrast to the packages **pst-3d** and **pst-view3d** (see Section 6.5 on page 388), you do not need, and therefore cannot define, a viewpoint. The parallel projection simplifies the use of the commands, but also restricts their possibilities.

6.6.1 Commands for 3-D drawings

Three-dimensional coordinate axes are created with the following syntax:

> `\pstThreeDCoor` *[settings]*

If no settings are specified, the coordinate cross is drawn with the following default values:

  xMin=-1, xMax=4, yMin=-1, yMax=4, zMin=-1, zMax=4, Alpha=45, Beta=30

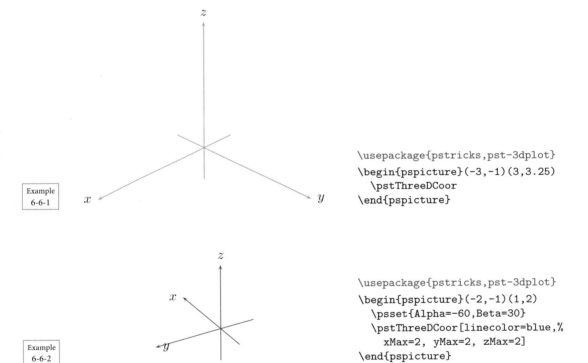

Example
6-6-1

```
\usepackage{pstricks,pst-3dplot}
\begin{pspicture}(-3,-1)(3,3.25)
  \pstThreeDCoor
\end{pspicture}
```

Example
6-6-2

```
\usepackage{pstricks,pst-3dplot}
\begin{pspicture}(-2,-1)(1,2)
  \psset{Alpha=-60,Beta=30}
  \pstThreeDCoor[linecolor=blue,%
    xMax=2, yMax=2, zMax=2]
\end{pspicture}
```

The angles `Alpha` and `Beta` influence the representation of all commands and should always be set globally with `\psset`.

> `\pstThreeDPut` *[settings]* *(x,y,z)* *{object}*

Internally `\pstThreeDPut` defines a two-dimensional node `temp@pstNode` and then uses the `\rput` command to place the object from its argument at these coordinates. The syntax is similar to `\rput`.

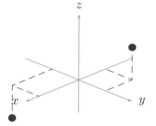

```
\usepackage{pstricks,pst-3dplot}
\begin{pspicture}(-2,-1)(1,2)
  \psset{ Alpha=-60,Beta=-30}
  \pstThreeDCoor[linecolor=blue, xMax=2,%
    yMax=2, zMax=2]
  \pstThreeDPut(1,0.5,2){\large TUGboat}
  \pstThreeDDot[drawCoor=true](1,0.5,2)
\end{pspicture}
```

Example
6-6-3

| \pstThreeDNode *[settings]* (*x,y,z*) {*node name*} |

Because (x, y, z) are saved internally as a two-dimensional node, these coordinates cannot be used to replace the coordinate triplet (x,y,z) for the purposes of the special coordinates used by PSTricks (Section 5.14 on page 296). If A and B are two nodes defined this way, then \psline{A}{B} draws a line from A to B.

| \pstThreeDDot *[settings]* (*x,y,z*) |

With this command dots can be defined and drawn together with their corresponding coordinates (dotted lines).

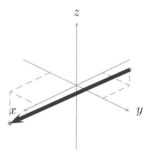

```
\usepackage{pstricks,pst-3dplot}
\begin{pspicture}(-2,-2)(2,2)
  \psset{xMin=-2,xMax=2,yMin=-2,yMax=2,zMax=2,Beta=25}
  \pstThreeDCoor
  \psset{dotstyle=*,dotscale=2,linecolor=blue,drawCoor=true}
  \pstThreeDDot(-1,1,1)
  \pstThreeDDot(1.5,-1,-1)
\end{pspicture}
```

Example
6-6-4

| \pstThreeDLine *[settings]* $(x_1,y_1,z_1)(x_2,y_2,z_2)$ |

All general keywords for lines can also be used for three-dimensional lines (see Section 6.1 on page 313).

```
\usepackage{pstricks,pst-3dplot}
\psset{xMin=-2,xMax=2,yMin=-2,yMax=2,zMin=-2,zMax=2}
\begin{pspicture}(-2,-2)(2,2.25)
  \pstThreeDCoor
  \psset{dotstyle=*,linecolor=red,drawCoor=true}
  \pstThreeDDot(-1,1,0.5)
  \pstThreeDDot(1.5,-1,-1)
  \pstThreeDLine[linewidth=3pt,%
    linecolor=blue,arrows=->](-1,1,0.5)(1.5,-1,-1)
\end{pspicture}
```

Example
6-6-5

> \pstThreeDTriangle [*settings*] $(x_1,y_1,z_1)(x_2,y_2,z_2)(x_3,y_3,z_3)$

A triangle is defined by its three corners. If the keyword `fillstyle` has a value different from `none`, then the triangle is filled in the usual way with the current fill color.

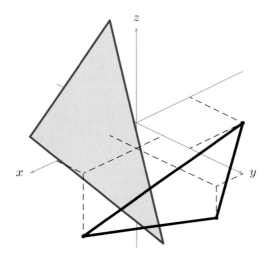

```
\usepackage{pstricks,pst-3dplot}
\begin{pspicture}(-3,-4)(3,3.25)
  \pstThreeDCoor[xMin=-4,xMax=4,yMin=-3,
               zMin=-4,zMax=3]
  \pstThreeDTriangle[
    fillcolor=yellow,fillstyle=solid,
    linecolor=blue,
    linewidth=1.5pt](5,1,2)(3,4,-1)(-1,-2,2)
  \pstThreeDTriangle[
    drawCoor=true,linecolor=black,
    linewidth=2pt](3,1,-2)(1,4,-1)(-2,2,0)
\end{pspicture}
```

Example
6-6-6

> \pstThreeDSquare [*settings*] $(x_o,y_o,z_o)(x_u,y_u,z_u)(x_v,y_v,z_v)$

The arguments of \pstThreeDSquare define the vectors $\vec{o}$, $\vec{u}$, and $\vec{v}$ with a relation as shown in the following example:

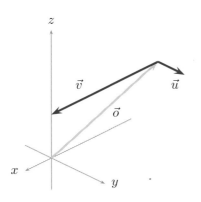

```
\usepackage{pstricks,pst-3dplot}
\begin{pspicture}(-1,-1)(4,4)
  \pstThreeDCoor[xMin=-3,xMax=1,yMin=-1,
             yMax=2,zMin=-1,zMax=4]
  \psset{arrows=->,arrowsize=0.2,linecolor=blue,
         linewidth=1.5pt}
  \pstThreeDLine[linecolor=green](0,0,0)(-2,2,3)
  \uput[45](1.5,1){$\vec{o}$}
  \pstThreeDLine(-2,2,3)(2,2,3)
  \uput[0](3,2){$\vec{u}$}
  \pstThreeDLine(-2,2,3)(-2,-3,3)
  \uput[180](1,2){$\vec{v}$}
\end{pspicture}
```

Example
6-6-7

Rectangles are simply closed polygons that start and end at the point P_o (support vector) and that are defined by their two direction vectors, which also specify the length of their respective sides. Rectangles can be filled with a color or pattern in the usual manner.

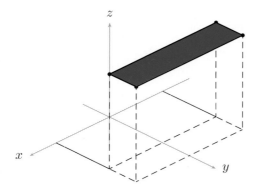

```
\usepackage{pstricks,pst-3dplot}
\begin{pspicture}(-2,-2)(4,3)
  \pstThreeDCoor[xMin=-3,xMax=3,yMax=4,zMax=3]
  \psset{fillcolor=blue,fillstyle=solid,
          drawCoor=true,dotstyle=*}
  \pstThreeDSquare(-2,2,3)(4,0,0)(0,1,0)
\end{pspicture}
```

Example
6-6-8

$$\boxed{\texttt{\textbackslash pstThreeDBox}\ [\textit{settings}]\ (x_o,y_o,z_o)(x_u,y_u,z_u)(x_v,y_v,z_v)(x_w,y_w,z_w)}$$

A box is based on rectangles, so this command has a syntax similar to that of the square command. Apart from the support vector $\vec{o}$ you have to specify the three direction vectors, which also determine the side lengths.

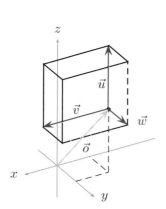

```
\usepackage{pstricks,pst-3dplot}
\begin{pspicture}(-1,-1)(3,4.25)
  \psset{Alpha=30,Beta=30}
  \pstThreeDCoor[xMin=-3,xMax=1,yMin=-1,yMax=2,zMin=-1,zMax=4]
  \pstThreeDBox(-1,1,2)(0,0,2)(2,0,0)(0,1,0)
  \pstThreeDDot[drawCoor=true](-1,1,2)
  \psset{arrows=->,arrowsize=0.2}
  \pstThreeDLine[linecolor=green](0,0,0)(-1,1,2)
  \uput[0](0.5,0.5){$\vec{o}$}
  \uput[0](0.9,2.25){$\vec{u}$}
  \uput[90](0.5,1.25){$\vec{v}$}
  \uput[45](2,1.){$\vec{w}$}
  \pstThreeDLine[linecolor=blue](-1,1,2)(-1,1,4)
  \pstThreeDLine[linecolor=blue](-1,1,2)(1,1,2)
  \pstThreeDLine[linecolor=blue](-1,1,2)(-1,2,2)
\end{pspicture}
```

Example
6-6-9

$$\boxed{\texttt{\textbackslash pstThreeDEllipse}\ [\textit{settings}]\ (cx,cy,cz)\ (ux,uy,uz)\ (vx,vy,vz)}$$

Here c is the center and u and v are the two vectors of the semi-axes.

Based on the two-dimensional form, the equation of an ellipse in three-dimensional space is

$$e : \vec{x} = \vec{c} + \cos\alpha \cdot \vec{u} + \sin\alpha \cdot \vec{v}, \qquad 0 \le \alpha \le 360$$

where $\vec{c}$ is the center of the ellipse and $\vec{u}$ and $\vec{v}$ are the perpendicular vectors of the semi-axes. Two keywords are used for creating an elliptic or circular arc:

```
beginAngle=0
endAngle=360
```

Ellipses and circles are created with the command \parametricplotThreeD (see Section 6.6.2 on page 407). The number of interpolation points for this command is set to 50. For very narrow ellipses, this value can lead to unfavorable curves, so that it has to be increased accordingly.

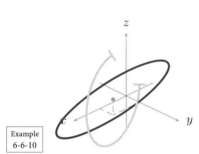

```
\usepackage{pstricks,pst-3dplot}
\psset{xMin=-1,xMax=2,yMin=-1,yMax=2,zMin=-1,zMax=2}
\begin{pspicture}(-2,-2)(2,2)
  \pstThreeDCoor
  \pstThreeDDot[linecolor=red,%
    drawCoor=true](1,0.5,0.5)% center
  \psset{linecolor=blue, linewidth=1.5pt}
  \pstThreeDEllipse(1,0.5,0.5)(-0.5,1,0.5)(1,-0.5,-1)
  % settings for an arc
  \psset{beginAngle=0,endAngle=270,linecolor=green,arrows=|-|}
  \pstThreeDEllipse(1,0.5,0.5)(-0.5,0.5,0.5)(0.5,0.5,-1)
\end{pspicture}
```

Example 6-6-10

A circle is a special ellipse where $|\vec{u}| = |\vec{v}| = r$ and $\vec{u} \cdot \vec{v} = \vec{0}$. The command \pstThreeDCircle basically is a synonym for \pstThreeDEllipse. The following circle was drawn with 20 points and the keyword setting showpoints=true.

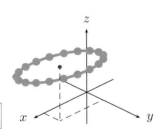

```
\usepackage{pstricks,pst-3dplot}
\begin{pspicture}(-2,-1)(2,2)
  \pstThreeDCoor[%
    xMin=-1,xMax=2,yMin=-1,yMax=2,zMin=-1,zMax=2,%
    linecolor=black]
  \psset{linecolor=red,linewidth=2pt,%
      plotpoints=20,showpoints=true}
  \pstThreeDCircle(1.6,+0.6,1.7)(0.8,0.4,0.8)(0.8,-0.8,-0.4)
  \pstThreeDDot[drawCoor=true,linecolor=blue](1.6,+0.6,1.7)
\end{pspicture}
```

Example 6-6-11

\pstThreeDSphere [*settings*] (x, y, z) {*radius*}

(x, y, z) is the center of the sphere and the segment color must be of the type CMYK, set as `SegmentColor={[cmyk]{0.1,0.5,0,0}}`. Before doing so, make sure that recent versions of **xcolor** and **pstricks** are installed.

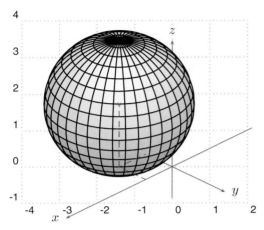

```
\usepackage{pstricks,pst-3dplot}
\begin{pspicture}[showgrid=true](-4,-1.25)(2,4.25)
  \pstThreeDCoor[xMin=-3,yMax=2]
  \pstThreeDSphere[%
    SegmentColor={[cmyk]{0.1,0.5,0,0}}](1,-1,2){2}
  \pstThreeDDot[dotstyle=x,%
    linecolor=red,drawCoor=true](1,-1,2)
\end{pspicture}
```

Example
6-6-12

6.6.2 Plotting mathematical functions and data

Analogous to the situation with **pst-plot**, two commands are available for creating mathematical functions, each of which depends on two variables $z = f(x, y)$.

$\boxed{\texttt{\psplotThreeD}\ [\textit{settings}]\ (x_{Min}, x_{Max})\ (y_{Min}, y_{Max})\ \{\textit{function term}\}}$

The plotpoints, xPlotpoints, *and* yPlotpoints *keys*

This command has a syntax different from the respective command in the **pst-plot** package, but it is used in the same manner. The function term has to be written in PostScript notation, as usual, and the only valid variable names are x and y. For example, `{x dup mul y dup mul add sqrt}` stands for the mathematical expression $\sqrt{x^2 + y^2}$. The plotpoints keyword is divided into xPlotpoints and yPlotpoints and, therefore, may as well be set separately. The option `hiddenLine` follows a rudimentary hidden-line algorithm by drawing the curve from the back to the front and filling it with the current fill color.

In several examples throughout this section, we plot the function described by the following equation:

$$z(x, y) = 10 \left(x^3 + xy^4 - \frac{x}{5} \right) e^{-(x^2 + y^2)} + e^{-((x-1.225)^2 + y^2)} \tag{6.1}$$

This function (`\func`) is defined in PostScript notation in the example below. Later examples just reuse it.

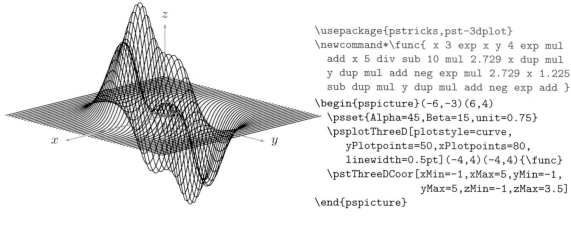

```
\usepackage{pstricks,pst-3dplot}
\newcommand*\func{ x 3 exp x y 4 exp mul
    add x 5 div sub 10 mul 2.729 x dup mul
    y dup mul add neg exp mul 2.729 x 1.225
    sub dup mul y dup mul add neg exp add }
\begin{pspicture}(-6,-3)(6,4)
    \psset{Alpha=45,Beta=15,unit=0.75}
    \psplotThreeD[plotstyle=curve,
        yPlotpoints=50,xPlotpoints=80,
        linewidth=0.5pt](-4,4)(-4,4){\func}
    \pstThreeDCoor[xMin=-1,xMax=5,yMin=-1,
                    yMax=5,zMin=-1,zMax=3.5]
\end{pspicture}
```

Example
6-6-13

The function is determined by two loops:

```
for (float y=yMin; y<yMax; y+=dy) {
    for (float x=xMin; x<xMax; x+=dx) {
        z=f(x,y); }}
```

Since the inner loop increases the x values, a closed curve can be created only in this direction; at the end of a partial curve in x direction, the current point is reset to the beginning. Therefore, too few yPlotpoints are not really a problem, but too few xPlotpoints produce a polygon-like shape.

> \parametricplotThreeD [*settings*] (*t1,t2*) {*function terms x y z*}
> \parametricplotThreeD [*settings*] (*t1,t2*) (*u1,u2*) {*function terms x y z*}

The only possible variable names are t and u; the definition interval is t1,t2 with respect to u1,u2. The sequence is not important, and u may be omitted if you are drawing a curve with no area in three-dimensional space.

$$x = f(t, u)$$
$$y = f(t, u) \tag{6.2}$$
$$z = f(t, u)$$

To create a helix, for example, you need the following functions in parameter notation:

$$x = r \cos t$$
$$y = r \sin t \tag{6.3}$$
$$z = t/600$$

The value of t is divided by 600 since PostScript needs angles specified in degrees.

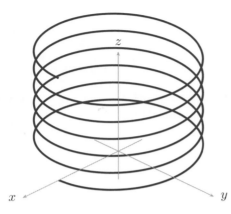

```
\usepackage{pstricks,pst-3dplot}
\psset{unit=0.9}
\begin{pspicture}(-3,-2)(3,5)
  \parametricplotThreeD[%
    xPlotpoints=200,linecolor=blue,%
    linewidth=1.5pt,plotstyle=curve](0,2160){%
        2.5 t cos mul
        2.5 t sin mul
        t 600 div}
  \pstThreeDCoor[zMax=3.5]
\end{pspicture}
```

Example
6-6-14

The data files have to be structured analogously to the ones specified in Section 6.1.2 on page 324. For example:

```
 0.0000   1.0000   0.0000
-0.4207   0.9972   0.0191
....
 0.0000,  1.0000,  0.0000
-0.4207,  0.9972,  0.0191
....
(0.0000,1.0000,0.0000)
(-0.4207,0.9972,0.0191)
....
{0.0000,1.0000,0.0000}
{-0.4207,0.9972,0.0191}
....
```

`\fileplotThreeD [`*settings*`] {`*file name*`}`

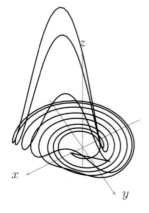

```
\usepackage{pstricks,pst-3dplot}
\psset{xunit=1.75mm,yunit=3mm,Alpha=30,Beta=30}
\begin{pspicture}(-6,-3)(6,10)
  \pstThreeDCoor[%
    xMin=-10,xMax=10,%
    yMin=-10,yMax=10,%
    zMin=-2,zMax=10]
  \fileplotThreeD[plotstyle=polygon]
                {data3D.Roessler}
\end{pspicture}%
```

Example
6-6-15

> \dataplotThreeD [*settings*] {*data macro*}
> \readdata{*macro name*}{*file name*}

In contrast to \fileplotThreeD, the command \dataplotThreeD needs a macro name, which holds all data, as an argument. With the command \readdata, external data files can be read and saved into a macro (see Section 6.1.2 on page 325).

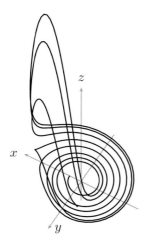

```
\usepackage{pstricks,pst-3dplot}
\psset{xunit=1.75mm,yunit=3mm,Alpha=-30,Beta=30}
\readdata{\dataThreeD}{data3D.Roessler}
\begin{pspicture}(-6,-2.25)(5,11)
  \pstThreeDCoor[xMin=-10,xMax=10,%
     yMin=-10,yMax=10,zMin=-2,zMax=10]
  \dataplotThreeD[plotstyle=line]{\dataThreeD}
\end{pspicture}
```

Example
6-6-16

> \listplotThreeD [*settings*] {*data macro*}

A user might perceive any real difference between the commands \listplotThreeD and \dataplotThreeD. With \listplotThreeD, however, you can easily transport additional PostScript code via TEX to PostScript. Example 6-1-33 on page 326 is an example of the use of this method.

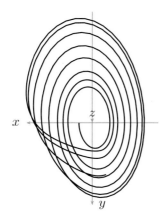

```
\usepackage{pstricks,pst-3dplot}
\psset{xunit=1.75mm,yunit=3mm,Alpha=-0,Beta=90}
\readdata{\dataThreeD}{data3D.Roessler}
\begin{pspicture}(-5,-4)(5,4.5)
  \pstThreeDCoor[xMin=-10,xMax=10,%
     yMin=-10,yMax=7.5,zMin=-2,zMax=10]
  \listplotThreeD[plotstyle=line]{\dataThreeD}
\end{pspicture}%
```

Example
6-6-17

Table 6.14: Keywords for the package `pst-3dplot`

Name	Value Type	Default	Name	Value Type	Default
Alpha	*angle*	45	endAngle	*angle*	360
Beta	*angle*	30	linejoin	*value*	1
xMin	*value*	−1	nameX	*label*	x
xMax	*value*	4	spotX	*angle*	180
yMin	*value*	−1	nameY	*label*	x
yMax	*value*	4	spotY	*angle*	0
zMin	*value*	−1	nameZ	*label*	x
zMax	*value*	4	spotZ	*angle*	90
drawing	*Boolean*	true	plane	*plane*	xy
xThreeDunit	*value*	1	origin	*refpoint*	c
yThreeDunit	*value*	1	hiddenLine	*Boolean*	false
zThreeDunit	*value*	1	drawStyle	*style*	xLines
xPlotpoints	*value*	25	visibleLineStyle	*line style*	solid
yPlotpoints	*value*	25	invisibleLineStyle	*line style*	dashed
beginAngle	*angle*	0	SpericalCoor	*Boolean*	false

6.6.3 Keywords for pst-3dplot

The Alpha *and* Beta *keys*   The keywords `Alpha` and `Beta` determine the rotation of the coordinate system in the horizontal and vertical directions.

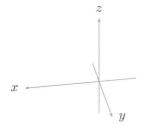

```
\usepackage{pstricks,pst-3dplot}
\begin{pspicture}(-2,-1)(1,2)
  \psset{Alpha=10,Beta=30,%
    xMax=2,yMax=2,zMax=2}
  \pstThreeDCoor
\end{pspicture}
```

Example
6-6-18

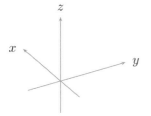

```
\usepackage{pstricks,pst-3dplot}
\begin{pspicture}(-2,-1)(1,2)
  \psset{Alpha=60,Beta=-30,%
    xMax=2,yMax=2,zMax=2}
  \pstThreeDCoor
\end{pspicture}
```

Example
6-6-19

The keys xMin, xMax, yMin, yMax, zMin, *and* zMax   These keywords define the visible part of the three-dimensional coordinate system and may be customized freely, as already shown in Section 6.6.2 on page 406. They have no further meaning. In particular, they do not depend on the given box size of the image, which is already defined by the values of the `pspicture` environment.

The keyword `drawing` can be used to suppress the plotting of coordinate axes even as important parameters are still calculated internally.

The `drawing` *key*

Example
6-6-20

```
\usepackage{pstricks,pst-3dplot}
\begin{pspicture}(-2,-1)(1,2)
  \psset{xMax=2,yMax=2,zMax=2}
  \pstThreeDCoor[drawing=false]
  \pstThreeDDot[drawCoor=true,dotscale=2](-1,-1,1)
\end{pspicture}
```

If you wish to change the scale of individual dimensions, you can do so by adjusting these key values accordingly. Just keep in mind that they are not available for spherical coordinates, so you cannot set `SphericalCoor=true` globally.

The `xThreeDunit,` `yThreeDunit,` *and* `zThreeDunit` *keys*

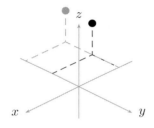

Example
6-6-21

```
\usepackage{pstricks,pst-3dplot}
\begin{pspicture}(-2,-1)(1,2)
  \psset{xMin=-2,xMax=2, yMin=-2.2,yMax=2,zMax=2}
  \pstThreeDCoor
  \psset{drawCoor=true,dotscale=2}
  \pstThreeDDot(-1.5,-1,1)
  \pstThreeDDot[linecolor=red,yThreeDunit=2](-1.5,-1,1)
\end{pspicture}
```

The keywords `xPlotpoints` and `yPlotpoints` strongly influence the appearance of a function. You have to find the correct values by trial and error.

The `xPlotpoints` *and* `yPlotpoints` *keys*

```
\usepackage{graphicx,pstricks,pst-3dplot}
% \func as defined in Example 6-6-13
\psset{unit=0.7}
\makebox[\linewidth]{%
\begin{pspicture}(-4,-3)(4,4)   \psset{Alpha=45,Beta=15}
  \psplotThreeD[plotstyle=curve,yPlotpoints=10,xPlotpoints=10,
    linewidth=0.5pt,hiddenLine=true](-3,3)(-3,3){\func}
  \pstThreeDCoor[xMax=5,yMax=5,zMax=3.5]
\end{pspicture}
\begin{pspicture}(-4,-3)(4,4)   \psset{Alpha=45,Beta=15}
  \psplotThreeD[plotstyle=curve,yPlotpoints=20,xPlotpoints=50,
    linewidth=0.5pt,hiddenLine=true](-3,3)(-3,3){\func}
  \pstThreeDCoor[xMax=5,yMax=5,zMax=3.5]
\end{pspicture}}
```

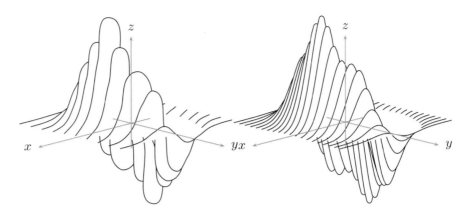

Example
6-6-22

The beginAngle *and*
endAngle *keys*

The two keywords beginAngle and endAngle support the three-dimensional presentation of elliptic and circular arcs.

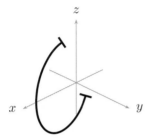

```
\usepackage{pstricks,pst-3dplot}
\begin{pspicture}(-2,-2)(2,2)
 \pstThreeDCoor[xMax=2,yMax=2,zMax=2]
 \pstThreeDEllipse[beginAngle=30,
    endAngle=270,arrows=|-|,linewidth=1.5pt]
    (1,0.5,0.5)(-0.5,0.5,0.5)(0.5,0.5,-1)
\end{pspicture}
```

Example
6-6-23

The linejoin *key*

Sometimes you may wish to modify the look of edges, especially in triangles with sharp edges. The key linejoin corresponds to the PostScript command setlinejoin and can take only the values 0 | 1 | 2.

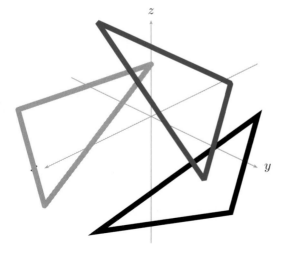

```
\usepackage{pstricks,pst-3dplot}
\begin{pspicture}(-3,-4)(3,3.25)
 \pstThreeDCoor[xMin=-4,xMax=4,
                yMin=-3,zMin=-4,zMax=3]
 \psset{linewidth=4pt}
 \pstThreeDTriangle[linejoin=0]
    (3,1,-2)(1,4,-1)(-2,2,0)
 \pstThreeDTriangle
    [linejoin=1,linecolor=red]
    (3,-1,-2)(1,-4,-1)(-2,-2,0)
 \pstThreeDTriangle
    [linejoin=2,linecolor=blue]
    (-1,1,-2)(-4,-1,-1)(-2,-4,0.5)
\end{pspicture}
```

Example
6-6-24

Normally, the axes are named x, y, and z as usual for Cartesian axes. With the nameX, *The* nameX, nameY,
nameY, and nameZ keywords you can change their names.   *and* nameZ *keys*

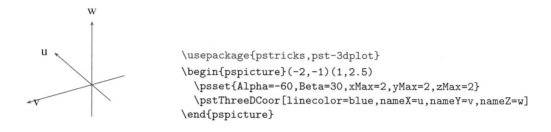

Example
6-6-25

```
\usepackage{pstricks,pst-3dplot}
\begin{pspicture}(-2,-1)(1,2.5)
  \psset{Alpha=-60,Beta=30,xMax=2,yMax=2,zMax=2}
  \pstThreeDCoor[linecolor=blue,nameX=u,nameY=v,nameZ=w]
\end{pspicture}
```

In the example above, the labels were not optimally positioned. You can modify their   *The* spotX, spotY,
positions with the spotX, spotY, and spotZ keywords, which define the angle by which a   *and* spotZ *keys*
label is rotated, analogous to the uput command (Section 5.11.3 on page 268).

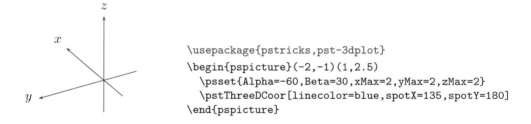

Example
6-6-26

```
\usepackage{pstricks,pst-3dplot}
\begin{pspicture}(-2,-1)(1,2.5)
  \psset{Alpha=-60,Beta=30,xMax=2,yMax=2,zMax=2}
  \pstThreeDCoor[linecolor=blue,spotX=135,spotY=180]
\end{pspicture}
```

The keyword plane specifies the plane the command \pstPlanePut can write to. Pos-   *The* plane *key*
sible values are xy | xz | yz.

Example
6-6-27

```
\usepackage{pstricks,pst-3dplot}
\begin{pspicture}(-2,-1)(1,2.5)
  \psset{xMax=2,yMax=2,zMax=2}
  \pstThreeDCoor
  \psset{pOrigin=lb}
  \pstPlanePut(1,0,0){\fbox{\Huge\red xy}}
  \pstPlanePut[plane=xz](0,1,0){\fbox{\Huge\blue xz}}
  \pstPlanePut[plane=yz](0,0,1){\fbox{\Huge\green yz}}
\end{pspicture}
```

The pOrigin *key*   The keyword pOrigin is the positioning key, which is passed to the command \rput. Its effects concern only \pstThreeDPut, and the default value is based on the defaults for \rput (see Section 5.11.1 on page 266).

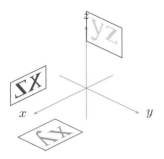

```
\usepackage{pstricks,pst-3dplot}
\begin{pspicture}(-2,-1)(1,2.5)
  \pstThreeDCoor[xMin=-1,xMax=2,yMin=-1,
             yMax=2,zMin=-1,zMax=2]
  \pstPlanePut[pOrigin=c](0,0,-1){\fbox{\Huge\red xy}}
  \pstPlanePut[plane=xz,pOrigin=rb](0,0,0)
             {\fbox{\Huge\blue xz}}
  \pstPlanePut[plane=yz,pOrigin=lb](0,0,1.5)
             {\fbox{\Huge\green yz}}
\end{pspicture}
```

Example
6-6-28

The hiddenLine *key*   The keyword hiddenLine enables a very simple "hidden-line algorithm": the lines are plotted with the command \pscustom and then filled with the predefined fill style hiddenStyle.

```
\newpsstyle{hiddenStyle}{fillstyle=solid,fillcolor=white}
```

You can overwrite this style as required. Just keep in mind that the curves must be built from the end to the beginning; otherwise, the hidden lines will be visible. For examples, see Section 6.6.2 on page 406.

The drawStyle *key*   The keyword drawStyle defines the manner in which the function is plotted. Possible key values are xLines, yLines, xyLines, and yxLines. The values refer to the plotting sequence; that is, xLines has the lines drawn in the x direction, whereas yxLines means that they are first drawn in the y direction and then in the x direction.

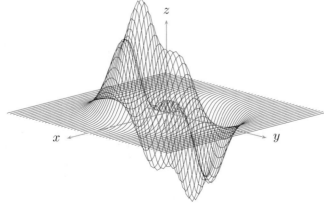

```
\usepackage{pstricks,pst-3dplot}
% \func as defined in Example 6-6-13
\begin{pspicture}(-6,-3)(6,4)
  \psset{Beta=15,unit=0.75}
  \psplotThreeD[plotstyle=line,
    drawStyle=xLines,
    yPlotpoints=50,xPlotpoints=50,
    linewidth=0.2pt](-4,4)(-4,4)
    {\func}
  \pstThreeDCoor[xMax=5,yMax=5,
             zMax=3.5]
\end{pspicture}
```

Example
6-6-29

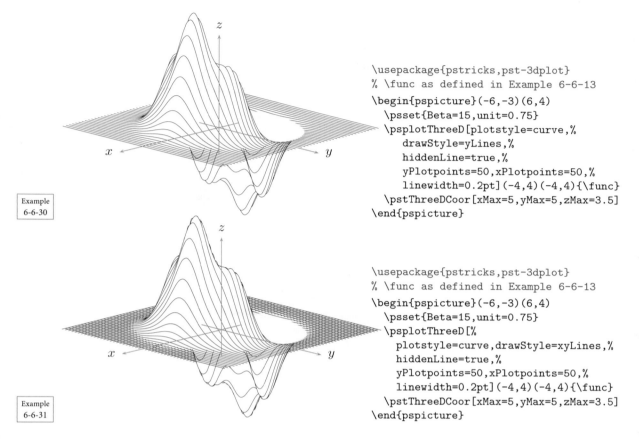

```
\usepackage{pstricks,pst-3dplot}
% \func as defined in Example 6-6-13
\begin{pspicture}(-6,-3)(6,4)
  \psset{Beta=15,unit=0.75}
  \psplotThreeD[plotstyle=curve,%
    drawStyle=yLines,%
    hiddenLine=true,%
    yPlotpoints=50,xPlotpoints=50,%
    linewidth=0.2pt](-4,4)(-4,4){\func}
  \pstThreeDCoor[xMax=5,yMax=5,zMax=3.5]
\end{pspicture}
```

Example
6-6-30

```
\usepackage{pstricks,pst-3dplot}
% \func as defined in Example 6-6-13
\begin{pspicture}(-6,-3)(6,4)
  \psset{Beta=15,unit=0.75}
  \psplotThreeD[%
    plotstyle=curve,drawStyle=xyLines,%
    hiddenLine=true,%
    yPlotpoints=50,xPlotpoints=50,%
    linewidth=0.2pt](-4,4)(-4,4){\func}
  \pstThreeDCoor[xMax=5,yMax=5,zMax=3.5]
\end{pspicture}
```

Example
6-6-31

The keywords `visibleLineStyle` and `invisibleLineStyle` refer to the drawing of bodies: the macro tries to identify hidden lines and draws them with the line style `invisibleLineStyle`, while drawing the visible ones with the style `visibleLineStyle`.

The `visibleLineStyle` *and* `invisibleLineStyle` *keys*

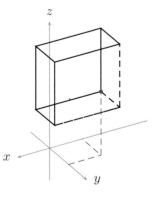

```
\usepackage{pstricks,pst-3dplot}
\begin{pspicture}(-1,-1)(3,3.25)
  \psset{Alpha=30}
  \pstThreeDCoor[xMin=-3,xMax=1,yMax=2,zMax=4]
  \pstThreeDBox(-1,1,2)(0,0,2)(2,0,0)(0,1,0)
  \pstThreeDDot[drawCoor=true,linecolor=blue](-1,1,2)
\end{pspicture}
```

Example
6-6-32

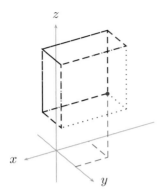

```
\usepackage{pstricks,pst-3dplot}
\begin{pspicture}(-1,-1)(3,3.25)
  \psset{Alpha=30,invisibleLineStyle=dotted,
    visibleLineStyle=dashed}
  \pstThreeDCoor[xMin=-3,xMax=1,yMax=2,zMax=4]
  \pstThreeDBox(-1,1,2)(0,0,2)(2,0,0)(0,1,0)
  \pstThreeDDot[drawCoor=true,linecolor=blue](-1,1,2)
\end{pspicture}
```

Example
6-6-33

The SphericalCoor
key   If the keyword SphericalCoor is set to true, all coordinate triplets are interpreted as spherical coordinates in the common notation $(raduis, theta, phi)$.

```
\usepackage{pstricks,pst-3dplot}
\begin{pspicture}(-6,-3)(6,5)
\psset{unit=3.4cm,drawCoor=true}
\newcommand\oA{\pstThreeDLine[linecolor=blue,
      linewidth=3pt,SphericalCoor=true,arrows=c->]
      (0,0,0)(1,60,70)}
\newcommand\oB{\pstThreeDLine[linecolor=red,
      linewidth=3pt,SphericalCoor=true,arrows=c->]
      (0,0,0)(1,10,50)}
\newcommand\oAB{\pstThreeDEllipse[beginAngle=58,
      endAngle=90,fillcolor=green,SphericalCoor=true]
      (0,0,0)(1,140,40)(1,10,50)}
\pstThreeDCoor[drawing=true,linewidth=1pt,
      linecolor=black,xMin=0,xMax=1.1,yMin=0,
      yMax=1.1,zMin=0,zMax=1.1]
\pstThreeDEllipse[beginAngle=0,endAngle=90,
      linestyle=dashed](0,0,0)(1,0,0)(0,1,0)
\pstThreeDEllipse[beginAngle=0,endAngle=90,
      linestyle=dashed](0,0,0)(1,0,0)(0,0,1)
\pstThreeDEllipse[beginAngle=0,endAngle=90,
      linestyle=dashed](0,0,0)(0,0,1)(0,1,0)
\psset{SphericalCoor=true}
\pstThreeDDot[dotstyle=none](1,10,50)
\pstThreeDDot[dotstyle=none](1,60,70)
\pscustom[fillstyle=crosshatch,hatchcolor=yellow,
          linestyle=none]{\oA\oB\oAB}
\oA \oB \oAB
\pstThreeDPut(1.1,60,70){\Large $\vec\Omega_1$}
\pstThreeDPut(1.2,10,50){\Large $\vec\Omega_2 \,$}
\pstThreeDPut(1,10,65){\Large $\gamma_{12}$}
\end{pspicture}
```

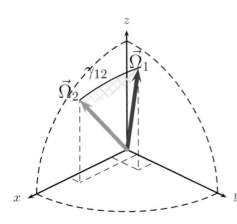

Example
6-6-34

6.7 Short overview of other PSTricks packages

It would be beyond the scope of this book to provide even a rudimentary discussion of all packages that are available for PSTricks. A more or less complete compilation can be found at the PSTricks site http://PSTricks.tug.org or in [135], especially all sources listed. Unfortunately, not every package has found its way into CTAN. Table 6.15 shows a list of all packages available on CTAN as of February 2007.

Table 6.15: List of PSTricks packages

Name	Purpose	Name	Purpose
pst-3d	basic three-dimensional operations	pst-3dplot	three-dimensional plots
pstricks-add	additional macros for pstricks/pst-node/pst-plot	pst-asr	linguistic: autosegmental representations
pst-bar	bar charts	pst-barcode	printing bar codes
pst-blur	blurred shadows	pst-calendar	calendars as tabular or on a dodecaeder
pst-circ	electrical circuits	pst-coil	drawing coils
pst-dbicons	ER diagrams	pst-eps	save environments as EPS files
pst-eucl	geometry for LaTeX with PSTricks	pst-fill	filling
pst-fr3d	three-dimensional framed boxes	pst-fractal	various types of fractals
pst-func	plotting special math functions	pst-geo	geographical objects
pst-gr3d	three-dimensional grids	pst-grad	gradient colors
pst-infixplot	math expressions in algebraic notation	pst-jtree	typesetting of trees common in linguistics
pst-labo	drawing various assemblies of chemical objects	pst-lens	using a lens to magnify parts of a text or a graphic
pst-light3d	three-dimensional light effects	pst-math	extended mathematical operators
pst-node	nodes	pst-ob3d	three-dimensional basic objects
pst-pdf	PostScript into PDF	pst-pdgr	medical pedigrees
pst-optic	optical systems with PSTricks	pst-osci	oscilloscopes with PSTricks
pst-plot	plotting functions and data records	pst-poly	polygons with PSTricks
pst-slpe	improved gradient fills	pst-spectra	draw continuum, emission, and absorption spectra
pst-stru	draw structural schemes in civil engineering analysis	pst-text	manipulating text and characters
pst-tree	trees	pst-uml	easily draw diagrams with UML notation
uml	another package to draw UML diagrams	pst-vue3d	three-dimensional views

— *Packages depending on or related to* PSTricks —

Name	Purpose	Name	Purpose
gastex	graphs and automata simplified	rrgtrees	linguistic tree diagrams for "role and reference grammar"
makeplot	plotting exported data records from Matlab	sfg	drawing signal flow graphs
multido	loops	vaucanson-g	drawing automata
psgo	draw Go diagrams (see Section 10.3)		

Table 6.16: Additional keywords of the package `pstricks-add`

Name	Meaning
ArrowInside	additional arrows inside a line or curve
ArrowFill	empty or filled arrows
lineAngle	\ncdiag and \pcdiag connections with constant angles
xyAxes	draw only one axis with \psaxes
xyDecimals	fixed numbers of decimals for the axis labels with \psaxes
comma	use a comma instead of a dot for decimals
nStepxStep	step value or number for plots
nStart,nEnd	
xStart,xEnd	
yStart,yEnd	start and end number or value for plots

We will discuss the **pstricks-add** package in some detail here, as it contains extensions and bug fixes for the core of PSTricks. For all other packages listed in Table 6.15 (except those that have been discussed in previous sections), we show a small example to promote better understanding of what the respective package can do. Further information can be found in the package documentation. These packages should be part of MiKTEX and the current TEX Live 2007 distribution. Missing packages can easily be installed in the usual way.

6.7.1 The pstricks-add **package**

This package contains several bug fixes for some base packages and summarizes everything that has been contributed on the PSTricks mailing list in the last few years, mainly by Denis Girou, to eventually solve problems. Detailed documentation for this package exists [133], but it is really dynamic, because all useful fixes or new commands in it should find their way into one of the other standard packages in due time.

The keywords added by **pstricks-add** are listed in Table 6.16. Their effects are explained throughout the examples found in this section.

Extended arrow options

In addition to the known arrow tips (Section 5.10.1), **pstricks-add** offers the arrows listed in Table 6.17. The length and width of an arrow of type H (hook left/right arrow) are set with the keywords `hooklength` and `hookwidth`, respectively, with the following default values:

    \psset{hooklength=3mm,hookwidth=1mm}

If a line or curve starts with a right hook, then it ends with a left hook, and vice versa.

Multiple arrows
When using one of the two arrow types << or >>, the additional keyword `nArrow` is available, which determines the number of arrows. If no key value is defined **pstricks-add** assumes the default behavior as described in Section 5.10.1 on page 260. There is no highest number; the maximum value depends on the length of the line or curve and has to be set by the user.

The `ArrowInside` *keys*
To support arrows inside of lines and curves, **pstricks-add** offers a number of keywords. Using the `ArrowInside` keyword alone draws one arrow inside a line or curve. The position can be set at a relative or absolute distance from the starting coordinates.

Table 6.17: Additional arrows defined by **pstricks-add**

Symbols	Example	Code
]-[	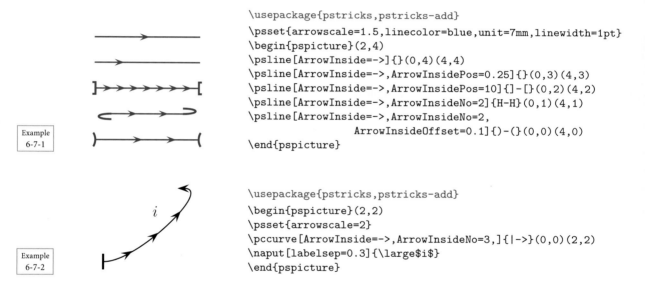	`\psline{]-[}(0,1ex)(1.3,1ex)`
)-(		`\psline{)-(}(0,1ex)(1.3,1ex)`
|>-<|		`\psline{|>-<|}(0,1ex)(1.3,1ex)`
H-H		`\psline{H-H}(0,1ex)(1.3,1ex)`

A value smaller than 1 for `ArrowInsidePos` means a relative distance; a value greater than 1 means an absolute distance measured in the default unit pt, which is then repeatedly used (e.g., `ArrowInsidePos=10` draws inside arrows at a distance of 10 pt each along the curve). With `ArrowInsideNo` the number of inner arrows can be fixed; with `ArrowInsideOffset` the first of them can be moved relative to the starting point of the curve.

```
\usepackage{pstricks,pstricks-add}
\psset{arrowscale=1.5,linecolor=blue,unit=7mm,linewidth=1pt}
\begin{pspicture}(2,4)
\psline[ArrowInside=->]{}(0,4)(4,4)
\psline[ArrowInside=->,ArrowInsidePos=0.25]{}(0,3)(4,3)
\psline[ArrowInside=->,ArrowInsidePos=10]{]-[}(0,2)(4,2)
\psline[ArrowInside=->,ArrowInsideNo=2]{H-H}(0,1)(4,1)
\psline[ArrowInside=->,ArrowInsideNo=2,
                 ArrowInsideOffset=0.1]{)-(}(0,0)(4,0)
\end{pspicture}
```

Example 6-7-1

```
\usepackage{pstricks,pstricks-add}
\begin{pspicture}(2,2)
\psset{arrowscale=2}
\pccurve[ArrowInside=->,ArrowInsideNo=3,]{|->}(0,0)(2,2)
\naput[labelsep=0.3]{\large$i$}
\end{pspicture}
```

Example 6-7-2

Generally, all arrows are implemented as filled polygons. However, the keyword setting `ArrowFill=false` produces "transparent", unfilled arrows with a borderline of width   *The* `ArrowFill` *key*
`\pslinewidth`, which is specified by the keyword `linewidth`.

```
\usepackage{pstricks,pstricks-add}
\begin{pspicture}(2,2)
\psset{arrowscale=3,ArrowFill=false}
\psline{<->}(0,0.5)(2,0.5)
\psline[arrowinset=0]{<->}(0,1.5)(2,1.5)
\psline[ArrowInside=->,ArrowFill=true]{|<->|}(1,0)(1,2)
\end{pspicture}
```

Example 6-7-3

Table 6.18: Examples of multiple arrows

Code	Example
`\psline{->>}(0,1ex)(2.3,1ex)`	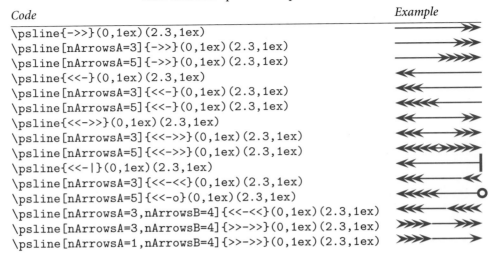
`\psline[nArrowsA=3]{->>}(0,1ex)(2.3,1ex)`	
`\psline[nArrowsA=5]{->>}(0,1ex)(2.3,1ex)`	
`\psline{<<-}(0,1ex)(2.3,1ex)`	
`\psline[nArrowsA=3]{<<-}(0,1ex)(2.3,1ex)`	
`\psline[nArrowsA=5]{<<-}(0,1ex)(2.3,1ex)`	
`\psline{<<->>}(0,1ex)(2.3,1ex)`	
`\psline[nArrowsA=3]{<<->>}(0,1ex)(2.3,1ex)`	
`\psline[nArrowsA=5]{<<->>}(0,1ex)(2.3,1ex)`	
`\psline{<<-|}(0,1ex)(2.3,1ex)`	
`\psline[nArrowsA=3]{<<-<<}(0,1ex)(2.3,1ex)`	
`\psline[nArrowsA=5]{<<-o}(0,1ex)(2.3,1ex)`	
`\psline[nArrowsA=3,nArrowsB=4]{<<-<<}(0,1ex)(2.3,1ex)`	
`\psline[nArrowsA=3,nArrowsB=4]{>>->>}(0,1ex)(2.3,1ex)`	
`\psline[nArrowsA=1,nArrowsB=4]{>>->>}(0,1ex)(2.3,1ex)`	

You can also draw unfilled "inside arrows", but they tend to produce a somewhat strange result, as the arrow is drawn first and then the line, which is therefore not hidden by the arrow.

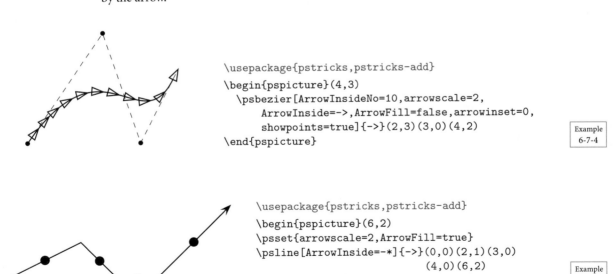

```
\usepackage{pstricks,pstricks-add}
\begin{pspicture}(4,3)
  \psbezier[ArrowInsideNo=10,arrowscale=2,
      ArrowInside=->,ArrowFill=false,arrowinset=0,
      showpoints=true]{->}(2,3)(3,0)(4,2)
\end{pspicture}
```

Example
6-7-4

```
\usepackage{pstricks,pstricks-add}
\begin{pspicture}(6,2)
\psset{arrowscale=2,ArrowFill=true}
\psline[ArrowInside=-*]{->}(0,0)(2,1)(3,0)
                        (4,0)(6,2)
\end{pspicture}
```

Example
6-7-5

New commands and environments

```
\begin{psgraph} [settings] (xMin,yMin) (xMax,yMax) {width}{height}
...
\end{psgraph}
```

In some cases it is not easy to get the right values for coordinate units. If possible, the environment psgraph calculates them internally and determines the values \psxunit and \psyunit depending on the physical width and height of a box, respectively. TEX does not support numerical calculations for floating-point numbers, so some problems may arise when using psgraph, especially for very small or very large values. (*xMin,yMin*) and (*xMax,yMax*) are the logical coordinates of the image, and *width* and *height* are the physical dimensions of the image. If no unit is given, the current PSTricks unit is taken as default. Calculating the right scaling values requires floating-point division, which is a bit tricky in TEX; as a consequence, very small or large scalings are likely to cause problems. In such cases one should use local xunit and yunit values and pass them in the optional *settings* argument to the environment. For more information, see the package documentation [133].

```
\usepackage{pstricks,pstricks-add}
\readdata{\data}{pstricks/demo2.dat}%
\readdata{\dataII}{pstricks/demo3.dat}%
\pstScalePoints(1,1){1989 sub}{}
\psset{llx=-0.5cm,lly=-1cm, xAxisLabel=Year,yAxisLabel=Whatever,%
    xAxisLabelPos={2in,-0.4in},yAxisLabelPos={-0.4in,1in}}
\begin{psgraph}[axesstyle=frame,Dx=2,Ox=1989,subticks=2](0,0)(12,6){4in}{2in}%
  \listplot[linecolor=red,linewidth=2pt]{\data}
  \listplot[linecolor=blue,linewidth=2pt]{\dataII}
  \listplot[linewidth=1pt,yunit=0.5]{\dataII}
\end{psgraph}
```

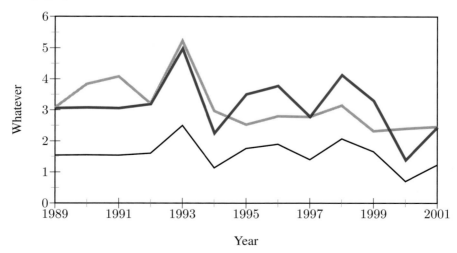

Example
6-7-6

$\boxed{\texttt{\textbackslash psMatrixPlot}\ \boxed{\textit{settings}}\ \{\textit{rows}\}\{\textit{columns}\}\{\textit{data file}\}}$

The command \psMatrixPlot draws a visual representation of a given $m \times n$ matrix (defined in PostScript) containing only the values 0 and 1.

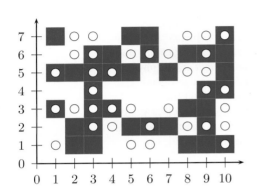

```
\begin{filecontents}{LGCmatrix.dat}
/dotmatrix [ 0 1 1 0 0 0 0 1 1 1
0 1 1 0 1 1 1 0 1 0  1 0 1 1 0 0 0 1 1 0
0 0 1 0 0 0 0 0 1 1  1 1 1 1 0 1 0 1 0 0 1
0 0 1 1 0 1 0 1 1 1  1 0 0 0 1 1 0 0 0 1 ] def
\end{filecontents}
\usepackage{pstricks-add}
\begin{pspicture}(-0.5,-0.75)(6,6)
 \psaxes[dx=0.5cm,dy=0.5cm]{->}(5.5,4)
 \psMatrixPlot[unit=0.5,dotsize=0.55cm,
          dotstyle=square*,linecolor=blue]
          {7}{10}{LGCmatrix.dat}
 \psMatrixPlot[unit=0.5,dotsize=.25cm,dotstyle=o,
          ChangeOrder]{7}{10}{LGCmatrix.dat}
\end{pspicture}
```
Example 6-7-7

$\boxed{\texttt{\textbackslash psforeach}\{\textit{macro name}\}\{\textit{value list}\}\{\textit{object}\}}$

This command implements a loop with an individual increment. It is a modified version of TEX's \loop command. The loop variable must be a TEX valid name. The object, which is executed n times, can be of any type (e.g., the \psdot command).

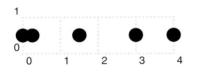

```
\usepackage{pstricks-add}
\begin{pspicture}[showgrid=true](4,1)
 \psforeach{\nA}{0, 0.25, 1.5, 3, 4}{%
    \psdot[dotscale=3](\nA,0.5)}
\end{pspicture}
```
Example 6-7-8

\psforeach takes anything as a value for the list, so you can use the \SpecialCoor feature to calculate the coordinates with all available PostScript commands. In the following example the dots are set at a horizontal distance of sqrt(\nA). The "!" character invokes the PostScript mode. At the end of any calculation, a pair of coordinates must be on top of the stack.

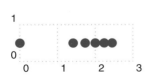

```
\usepackage{pstricks-add}
\SpecialCoor
\begin{pspicture}[showgrid=true](3,1)
 \psforeach{\nA}{0 0.5, 2 sqrt 0.5, 3 sqrt 0.5,
    4 sqrt 0.5, 5 sqrt 0.5, 6 sqrt 0.5}{%
    \psdot[linecolor=blue,dotscale=2](!\nA)}
\end{pspicture}
```
Example 6-7-9

$$\boxed{\texttt{\textbackslash psStep} \textit{ [settings]} \texttt{ \{}x_1, x_2\texttt{\}\{}\textit{steps}\texttt{\}\{}\textit{function}\texttt{\}}}$$

Step functions are useful to show the meaning of an integral. The macro supports lower, upper, and Riemann step types. See also Color Plate VIII(a).

```
\usepackage{pstricks-add}
\psset{unit=1.25cm}
\begin{pspicture}[plotpoints=200](-0.5,-3)(10,2.5)
  \psStep[algebraic,fillstyle=solid,fillcolor=yellow]
         (0.001,9.5){40}{2*sqrt(x)*cos(ln(x))*sin(x)}
  \psStep[algebraic,StepType=Riemann,fillstyle=solid,fillcolor=blue]
         (0.001,9.5){40}{2*sqrt(x)*cos(ln(x))*sin(x)}
  \psaxes{->}(0,0)(0,-2.75)(10,2.5)
  \psplot[algebraic,linecolor=white,labelFontSize=\footnotesize]
         {0.001}{9.75}{2*sqrt(x)*cos(ln(x))*sin(x)}
  \uput[90](6,1.2){$f(x)=2\cdot\sqrt{x}\cdot\cos{(\ln{x})}\cdot\sin{x}$}
\end{pspicture}
```

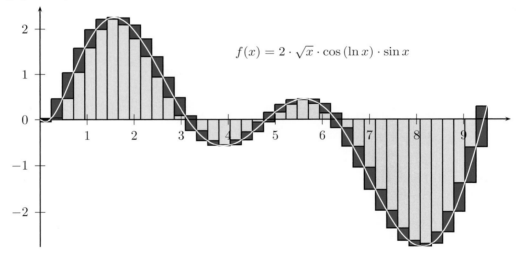

Example
6-7-10

$$\boxed{\texttt{\textbackslash psplotDiffEqn} \textit{ [settings]} \texttt{ \{}x_0\texttt{\}\{}x_1\texttt{\}\{}\textit{start values}\texttt{\}\{}\textit{differential equations}\texttt{\}}}$$

The \psplotDiffEqn command allows us to solve a differential equation or a system of differential equations. The author of this part of the package is Dominique Rodriguez. Possible numerical methods are the ones from Runge-Kutta and from Adams. The following example shows the "Cornu spiral", which is based on the Fresnel integrals. The keyword algebraic allows us to write the equations in the usual algebraic notation. For a system of differential equations, the delimiter between the equations is the bar character.

$$x = \int_0^t \cos\frac{\pi t^2}{2}\mathrm{d}t \quad y = \int_0^t \sin\frac{\pi t^2}{2}\mathrm{d}t \quad \text{with} \quad \dot{x} = \cos\frac{\pi t^2}{2} \quad \dot{y} = \sin\frac{\pi t^2}{2}$$

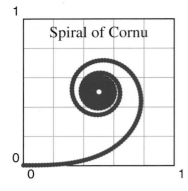

```
\usepackage{pstricks-add}
\psset{unit=4}
\begin{pspicture}(1,1)\psgrid[subgriddiv=5]
  \psplotDiffEqn[whichabs=0,whichord=1,
    method=rk4,algebraic,%
    linecolor=blue,plotpoints=500,
    showpoints=true]{0}{10}{0 0}%
        {cos(Pi*x^2/2)|sin(Pi*x^2/2)}
  \rput(0.5,0.9){\large Spiral of Cornu}
\end{pspicture}
```

Example
6-7-11

```
\resetOptions
```

Sometimes it is difficult to know which keywords were changed in a long document. With \resetOptions you can reset all keywords depending on pstricks, pst-plot, pst-node, and pstricks-add itself.

6.7.2 Linguistics

Three packages have been developed to cover different aspects of linguistics. These packages all refer to trees.

The pst-asr package

This package is designed to assist **PSTricks** in typesetting "autosegmental representations". **pst-asr** makes it fairly easy to design the complex structures that a linguist needs for a submitted paper or a handout for a presentation. The author of this package is John Frampton.

```
\usepackage{pstricks,pst-asr} \tiershortcuts
\newtier{nuclear,rhyme,coda,onset}
\psset{xgap=2.5em,yunit=2em,phB=-1,nuclear=.9 (lg),
  coda=1.2 (dg),rhyme=2.3 (hy),onset=1.8 (tg),syB=3.5}
\DefList{\onsetpos{.5},\nuclearpos{2.5},\rhymepos{3.25}}
\asr dri:m
|\@(\nuclearpos,nuclear){nuclear} \-(2,ts) \-(3,ts)
\@(4,coda){coda} \-(4,ts)
\@(\onsetpos,onset){onset} \-(0,ts) \-(1,ts)
\@(\rhymepos,rhyme){rhyme} \-(4,coda)
    \-(\nuclearpos,nuclear)
\@(2,sy){$\sigma$} \-(\onsetpos,onset)\-(\rhymepos,rhyme)
|\endasr
```

Example
6-7-12

The rrgtrees package

This package by D. J. Gardner supports the "role and reference grammar for human language" and is an interface to the **PSTricks** basic package **pst-tree** (see Section 6.3 on page 366).

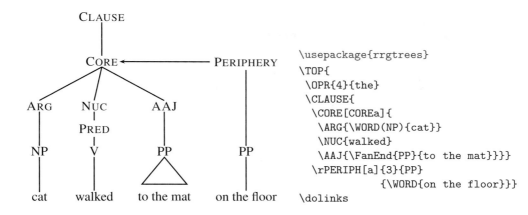

```
\usepackage{rrgtrees}
\TOP{
 \OPR{4}{the}
 \CLAUSE{
  \CORE[COREa]{
   \ARG{\WORD(NP){cat}}
   \NUC{walked}
   \AAJ{\FanEnd{PP}{to the mat}}}}
 \rPERIPH[a]{3}{PP}
                {\WORD{on the floor}}}
\dolinks
```

The pst-jtree package

The **pst-jtree** package is another package by John Frampton that is designed to assist **PSTricks** in typesetting the kinds of trees that are common in linguistics, but different than the trees created by the previously mentioned packages.

```
\usepackage{pstricks,pst-jtree}
\jtree[dirA=(1:-1),nodesepA=0,nodesepB=.8ex,xunit=2.2em,yunit=1em,style=arrows2]
\! =  :!a {\rnode{K1}{knew}}.   \!a = :!b {\rnode{O1}{owned}}.
\!b = :!c {\rnode{C1}{cats}}.
\!c = :\jtlong !d [scaleby=1.8] :{and}() [scaleby=2.4]
                                :{he}() @K2 <left>\jtjot !e .
\!d = :{she}() @K3 <left>\jtjot !f .
\!e = :{a woman}[labeloffset=-1ex] :{who}() @O2 <left>@C2 <left>{four}.
\!f = :{a man} :{who}() @O3 <left>@C3 <left>{three}.
\psset{linestyle=dashed,arrows=<-}
\nccurve[angleB=-10,ncurvB=2,ncurvA=1.2]{O2}{O1}
\nccurve[angleB=-90,ncurvA=1.4]{O3}{O1}
\nccurve[angleB=-10,ncurvB=1.8,ncurvA=1.6]{K2}{K1}
\nccurve[angleB=-90,ncurvA=1.4]{K3}{K1}
... further code omitted ...
```

6.7.3 Mathematics

The base packages pstricks and pst-plot support only basic mathematical functions; the following packages enhance them.

The pst-eucl package

This package by Dominique Rodriguez supports Euclidean geometry and offers the advantage that one defines only the physical coordinates of a triangle or any other object and then uses logical node names for all other special lines, circles, etc. In the following example only the three points A, B, and C have physical coordinates; all other coordinates are internally calculated from them. The user needs only the node names for additional lines, curves, or circles. A similar example is printed as Color Plate VIII(b).

```
\usepackage{pstricks,pst-eucl}
\psset{unit=1.5}
\begin{pspicture}(-2.5,-1.75)(2.75,2.5)
\pstTriangle[PosAngleA=180, PosAngleC=0](-2,-1){A}(1,2){B}(2,-1){C}
{ \psset{linestyle=none, PointSymbolB=none}
  \pstMediatorAB{B}{A}{I}{IP}
  \pstMediatorAB[PosAngleA=-40]{A}{C}{J}{JP}
  \pstMediatorAB[PosAngleA=75]{B}{C}{K}{KP}      }
\pstInterLL[PointSymbol=square, PosAngle=-170]{I}{IP}{J}{JP}{O}
{ \psset{nodesep=-.8,linecolor=green}
  \pstLineAB{O}{I}\pstLineAB{O}{J}\pstLineAB{O}{K}  }
\psdot[dotstyle=square](O)
\pstProjection[PosAngle=95]{B}{A}{C}{C'}\pstProjection{B}{C}{A}{A'}
\pstProjection[PosAngle=-90]{A}{C}{B}{B'}
\psset{linecolor=blue}\ncline{A}{A'}\ncline{C}{C'}\ncline{B}{B'}
\pstInterLL[PointSymbol=square]{A}{A'}{B}{B'}{H}
\psset{linecolor=magenta}\ncline{A}{K}\ncline{C}{I}\ncline{B}{J}
\pstMiddleAB[PointSymbol=o, PointName=\omega]{O}{H}{omega}
\pstCircleOA[linecolor=cyan, linestyle=dashed, dash=5mm 1mm]{omega}{B'}
... further code omitted ...
```

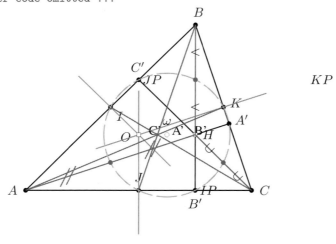

Example
6-7-15

The pst-func **package**

This package supports plotting of a variety of special mathematical functions:

- Polynomials with their derivatives and zeros
- Fourier curves
- Bessel curves
- Normal (Gauss), binomial, or Poisson distributions
- Gauß integrals
- Sine and cosine integrals
- Lamé curves
- Implicitly defined functions

The following examples first show the Poisson distribution and then an implicitly defined function, which is an example from fluid dynamics. A binominal distribution is shown on Color Plate VII(a).

```
\usepackage{pstricks,pst-func}
\psset{xunit=0.75cm,yunit=20cm}
\begin{pspicture}(-1,-0.05)(14,0.25)
\uput[-90](14,0){$k$}  \uput[90](0,0.2){$P(X=k)$}
\psPoisson[markZeros,fillstyle=solid,
  fillcolor=black!30,printValue,valuewidth=20]{13}{6}
\psaxes[Dy=0.1,dy=0.1\psyunit]{->}(0,0)(-1,0)(14,0.2)
\end{pspicture}
```

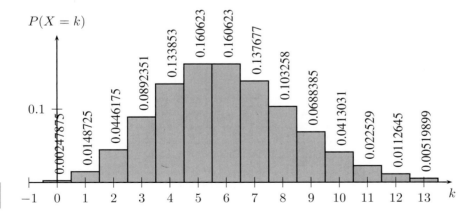

Example 6-7-16

```
\usepackage{pstricks-add,pst-func}
\begin{pspicture*}(-5,-2.2)(5.5,3.5)
\psaxes{->}(0,0)(-5,-2)(5.2,3)
```

```
\multido{\rA=0.01+0.2}{5}{%
  \psplotImp[linewidth=1pt,linecolor=blue,polarplot](-6,-6)(5,2.4)
          {r dup mul 1.0 r div sub phi sin dup mul mul \rA\space sub }}
\uput*[45](0,2){$f(r,\phi)=\left(r^2-\frac{1}{r}\right)\cdot\sin^2\phi=0$}
\pscircle[linewidth=1pt](0,0){1}
\end{pspicture*}
```

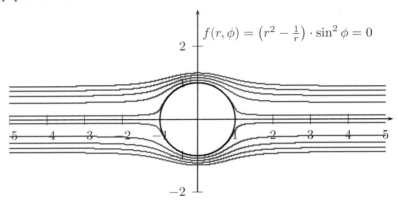

Example
6-7-17

The pst-math package

This package defines extensions to the PostScript basic math functions, all of which are listed
in Table 6.19. The style file just loads the PostScript header file to make all these extensions
available on the PostScript level. The package author is Christophe Jorssen.

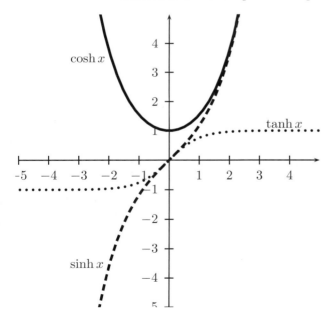

```
\usepackage{pstricks,pst-plot}
\usepackage{pst-math}
\psset{unit=0.8}
\begin{pspicture*}(-5,-5)(5,5)
  \psaxes{->}(0,0)(-5,-5)(5,5)
  \psset{linewidth=2pt}
  \psplot{-5}{5}{x COSH}
    \uput[0](-3.5,3.5){$\cosh x$}
  \psplot[linestyle=dashed]{-5}{5}
        {x SINH}
    \uput[0](-3.5,-3.5){$\sinh x$}
  \psplot[linestyle=dotted]{-5}{5}
        {x TANH}
    \uput[0](3,1.25){$\tanh x$}
\end{pspicture*}
```

Example
6-7-18

Table 6.19: PostScript math functions, supported by the **pst-math** package

Stack	Operator	Result	Description
num	COS	real	return cosine of num radians
num	SIN	real	return sine of num radians
num	TAN	real	return tangent of num radians
num	COSH	real	return hyperbolic cosine of num
num	SINH	real	return hyperbolic sine of num
num	TANH	real	return hyperbolic tangent of num
num	ACOSH	real	return reciprocal hyperbolic cosine of num
num	ASINH	real	return reciprocal hyperbolic sine of num
num	ATANH	real	return reciprocal hyperbolic tangent of num
num	EXP	real	return exponential of num
num_1 num_2 num_3	GAUSS	real	return Gaussian of num_1 with mean num_2 and standard deviation num_3
num	SINC	real	return cardinal sine of num radians
num	GAMMALN	real	return logarithm of Γ function of num

The pst-infixplot package

By default, mathematical expressions have to be defined in the postfix (PostScript) notation, but with this package they can be written in the usual infix (algebraic) notation (e.g., `pi x mul RadtoDeg sin 2 div` versus `sin(Pi*x)/2`). The package authors are Jean-Côme Charpentier and Christophe Jorssen.

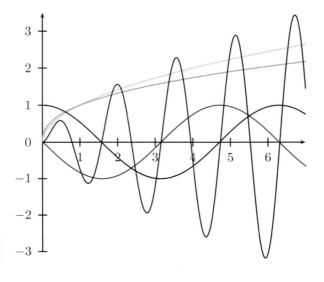

```
\usepackage{pstricks,pst-plot}
\usepackage{pst-infixplot}
\begin{pspicture}(0,-3)(7,4)
\psset{plotpoints=500}
\psaxes{->}(0,0)(0,-3)(7,3.5)
\psPlot[linecolor=green]{0}{7}
                       {sqrt(x)}
\psPlot[linecolor=red]{0}{7}{x^0.4}
\psPlot[linecolor=blue]{0}{7}%
     {sin(-x*180/3.1415)}
\psplot{0}{7}{x RadtoDeg cos}
\psPlot{0}{7}{sin(4*x*57)*x^0.65}
\end{pspicture}
```

Example
6-7-19

This package comes with another style file **infix-RPN**, which can be used to convert an infix expression to reverse polish notation (RPN). This may be useful for packages that support only the RPN notation.

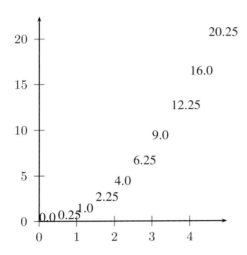

```
\usepackage{pstricks-add,infix-RPN}
\usepackage{pst-func}
\SpecialCoor
\psset{yunit=0.25}
\begin{pspicture}(-0.25,-2)(5,22.5)
  \infixtoRPN{x*x}
  \multido{\rx=0.0+0.5}{10}{\rput(!
    /x \rx\space def
    \RPN\space x exch )%
    {\psPrintValue{\RPN}}}
  \psaxes[dy=5,Dy=5]{->}(5,22.5)
\end{pspicture}
```

Example 6-7-20

The makeplot package

This package by Jose-Emilio Vila-Forcen is intended for plotting external data files created by **matlab** (http://www.mathworks.com) with nearly the same look as in **matlab** itself. The exported **matlab** data must have an x-y structure, with the values beeing separated by spaces. You can produce the values with **matlab** by saving the data in text (ASCII) format: save *file*.dat values -ascii.

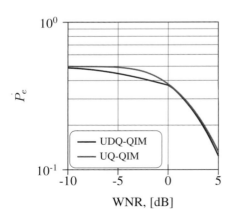

```
\usepackage[color]{makeplot}
\begin{makeplot}[startX=-10,endX=5,
                 startY=-1,endY=0,
                 Dx=5,width=40,
                 heightFactor=1,
                 ylogBase=10,logLines=y,
                 subticks=10,xsubticks=1]
                {$P_e$}{WNR, [dB]}
  \plotFileA{pstricks/data1.mat}
  \plotFileB{pstricks/data2.mat}
  \legendDL{24.5}{2}
  \legendAf{UDQ-QIM}
  \legendBf{UQ-QIM}
\end{makeplot}
```

Example 6-7-21

The pst-poly **package**

This package allows you to draw various kinds of polygons with several optional customization parameters. The package author is Denis Girou.

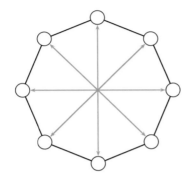

```
\usepackage{pstricks,pst-poly}
\providecommand{\PstPolygonNode}{%
    \psdots[dotstyle=o,dotsize=0.2](1;\INode)
    \psline[linecolor=red]{->}(0.9;\INode)}
\PstPolygon[unit=2,PolyNbSides=8]
```

```
\usepackage{pstricks,pst-poly,multido}
\multido{\nA=3+1}{7}{\pspolygonbox[PolyNbSides=\nA,framesep=2mm,doubleline=true]{Text}~}
```

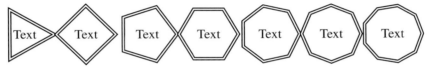

6.7.4 Sciences

The pst-pdgr **package**

This package supports the creation of medical pedigrees complying with the recommendations for standardized human pedigree nomenclature. The results are similar to genealogical trees but have a more complex and special structure [130]. The package authors are Boris Veytsman and Leila Akhmadeeva.

```
\usepackage{pst-pdgr}
\begin{pspicture}(6,6)
 \psset{belowtextrp=t,armB=1}
 \rput(2.5,5.5){\pstPerson[male,deceased,belowtext=A:1]{A:1}}
 \rput(3.5,5.5){\pstPerson[female,deceased,belowtext=A:2]{A:2}}
 \pstRelationship[descentnode=A:1_2]{A:1}{A:2}
 \rput(1,3.5){\pstPerson[female,affected,belowtext=B:1]{B:1}}
 \pstDescent{A:1_2}{B:1}
 \rput(2,3.5){\pstPerson[male,belowtext=B:2]{B:2}}
 \pstRelationship[descentnode=B:1_2]{B:1}{B:2}
 \rput(3.5,3.5){\pstPerson[male, affected, belowtext=B:3]{B:3}}
 \pstDescent{A:1_2}{B:3}
 \rput(4.5,3.5){\pstPerson[female, belowtext=B:4]{B:4}}
```

```
\pstRelationship[descentnode=B:3_4]{B:3}{B:4}
\rput(5.5,3.5){\pstPerson[female,affected, deceased,proband,
                         belowtext=B:5]{B:5}}
\pstDescent{A:1_2}{B:5}
\rput(0.5,1.5){\pstPerson[female,belowtext=C:1]{C:1}}
\pstDescent{B:1_2}{C:1}
\rput(1.5,1.5){\pstPerson[female,belowtext=C:2]{C:2}}
\pstDescent{B:1_2}{C:2}
\rput(2.5,1.5){\pstPerson[female, deceased,
                   belowtext=\parbox{2cm}{\centering C:3\\4/52}]{C:3}}
\pstDescent{B:1_2}{C:3}
\rput(3.5,1.5){\pstPerson[female, affected,belowtext=C:4]{C:4}}
\pstDescent{B:3_4}{C:4}
\rput(4.5,1.5){\pstPerson[male, insidetext=?,belowtext=C:5]{C:5}}
\pstDescent{B:3_4}{C:5}
\end{pspicture}
```

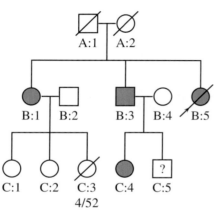

Example
6-7-24

The pst-spectra package

This package by Arnaud Schmittbuhl is based on the NASA lines database and allows you to draw continuum, emission, and absorption spectra of a variety of predefined chemical elements. A maximum of 16,880 visible lines from 99 chemical elements can be displayed. See also Color Plate VII(c).

```
\usepackage{pst-spectra,pstricks-add}
\psspectrum[element=Si](\linewidth,1)
\par
\renewcommand\pshlabel{\footnotesize\sffamily}
\begin{pspicture}(0,-0.5)(\linewidth,1.8) \psset{begin=650,end=450,gamma=1}
  \psspectrum[absorption,element=Ne](\linewidth,1.5)
  \psaxes[Ox=650,Dx=-10,dx=0.8999,yAxis=false,ticksize=0 1mm,
          ticks=x,subticks=0](\linewidth,0.01)
\end{pspicture}
```

```
\par
\begin{pspicture}(\linewidth,1.2)
  \psspectrum[absorption,lines={400,434.8,476.2,526.3,588.2,666.7},
              lwidth=0.1](\linewidth,1)
\end{pspicture}
```

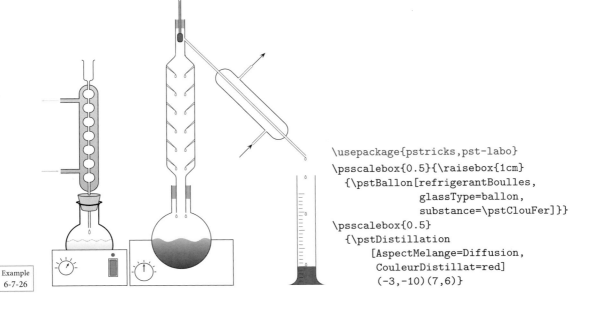

Example
6-7-25

The pst-labo **package**

This package by Manuel Luque provides macros for a collection of simple and complex
devices used mainly for chemical applications. The package comes with a variety of ready-
made chemical glasses, bottles, etc.

```
\usepackage{pstricks,pst-labo}
\psscalebox{0.5}{\raisebox{1cm}
  {\pstBallon[refrigerantBoulles,
              glassType=ballon,
              substance=\pstClouFer]}}
\psscalebox{0.5}
  {\pstDistillation
     [AspectMelange=Diffusion,
     CouleurDistillat=red]
     (-3,-10)(7,6)}
```

Example
6-7-26

The pst-optic **package**

This package by Manuel Luque and Herbert Voß is intended for optical systems with convergent and divergent lenses and mirrors with linear rays; it also supports lenses and mirrors for spherical optics. This package is mainly of interest for physics teachers in high schools.

```
\usepackage[cmyk]{pstricks} \usepackage{pst-optic}
\begin{pspicture*}(-7.5,-3)(7.5,3)
  \rput(0,0){%
    \lens[lensScale=0.6,XO=-4,nameF=F_1,nameA=A_1,nameB=B_1,
        nameFi=F'_1,nameAi={ },nameBi={},nameO=O_1,
        focus=1,OA=-2,lensGlass=true, lensWidth=0.5]}
  \pspolygon[style=rayuresJaunes,linestyle=none](B)(I)(B')(I')(B)
  \Transform
  \rput(0,0){%
    \lens[lensScale=1.2,XO=2,focus=2,nameA=A'_1,spotA=90,nameB=B'_1,
        spotB=270,nameO=O_2,nameAi=A'_2,spotAi=270,nameBi=B'_2,spotBi=90,
        nameF=F_2,nameFi=F'_2,lensTwo=true,lensGlass=true,lensWidth=0.5]}
  \pspolygon[style=rayuresJaunes,linestyle=none](B)(I)(B')(I')(B)
\end{pspicture*}
```

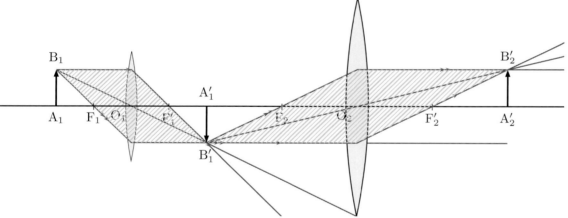

Example
6-7-27

The pst-osci **package**

This package by Manuel Luque and Christophe Jorssen simulates the output of a one- or two-channel oscilloscope. All switches on a real oscilloscope can be modified with special key settings. A y-x view is also possible, such as for Lissajous figures. See also Color Plate IX(b).

```
\usepackage{pstricks,pst-osci}
\psscalebox{0.5}{\Oscillo[amplitude2=1.5,period2=50,period1=10,
    combine=true,operation=add]}\qquad
\psscalebox{0.5}{\Oscillo[amplitude2=1.5,period2=50,period1=10,combine=true,
    operation=add,offset1=2,offset2=2]}
```

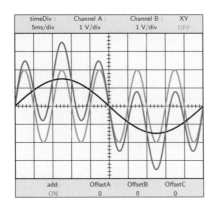
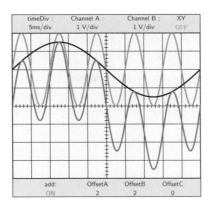

The pst-circ package

This package allows you to easily draw electric circuits. The authors are Christophe Jorssen and Herbert Voß. Most dipoles, tripoles, and quadrupoles used in classical electrical circuits are provided as graphical units, which can readily be interconnected to produce reasonably complex circuit diagrams. European logic symbols are also available.

```
\usepackage{pstricks,pst-circ}
\psset{unit=0.7}
\psset{intensitycolor=red,intensitylabelcolor=red,tensioncolor=green,%
       tensionlabelcolor=green,intensitywidth=3pt}
\begin{pspicture}(-1.25,0)(13.5,9)
  \circledipole[tension,tensionlabel=$U_0$,tensionoffset=-0.75,%
        tensionlabeloffset=-1,labeloffset=0](0,6)(0,0){\LARGE\textbf{=}}
  \wire[intensity,intensitylabel=$i_0$](0,6)(2.5,6)
  \diode[dipolestyle=thyristor](2.5,6)(4.5,6){$T_1$}
  \wire[intensity,intensitylabel=$i_1$](4.5,6)(6.5,6)
  \multidipole(6.5,7.5)(2.5,7.5)%
    \coil[dipolestyle=rectangle,labeloffset=-0.75]{$L_5$}%
    \diode[labeloffset=-0.75]{$D_5$}.
  \wire[intensity,intensitylabel=$i_5$](6.5,6)(6.5,7.5)
  \wire(2.5,7.5)(2.5,3)
  \wire[intensity,intensitylabel=$i_c$](2.5,4.5)(2.5,6)
  \qdisk(2.5,6){2pt}\qdisk(6.5,6){2pt}
  \diode[dipolestyle=thyristor](2.5,4.5)(4.5,4.5){$T_2$}
  \wire[intensity,intensitylabel=$i_2$](4.5,4.5)(6.5,4.5)
  \capacitor[tension,tensionlabel=$u_c$,%
    tensionoffset=-0.75,tensionlabeloffset=-1](6.5,4.5)(6.5,6){$C_k$}
  \qdisk(2.5,4.5){2pt}\qdisk(6.5,4.5){2pt}
  \wire[intensity,intensitylabel=$i_3$](6.5,4.5)(6.5,3)
  \multidipole(6.5,3)(2.5,3)%
    \coil[dipolestyle=rectangle,labeloffset=-0.75]{$L_3$}%
    \diode[labeloffset=-0.75]{$D_3$}.
  \wire(6.5,6)(9,6)\qdisk(9,6){2pt}
```

```
\diode(9,0)(9,6){$D_4$}
\wire[intensity,intensitylabel=$i_4$](9,3.25)(9,6)
\wire[intensity,intensitylabel=$i_a$](9,6)(11,6)
\multidipole(11,6)(11,0)%
  \resistor{$R_L$}
  \coil[dipolestyle=rectangle]{$L_L$}%
  \circledipole[labeloffset=0,tension,tensionoffset=0.7,%
                tensionlabel=$U_B$]{\LARGE\textbf{=}}.
\wire(0,0)(11,0)\qdisk(9,0){2pt}
\tension(12.5,5.5)(12.5,0.5){$u_a$}
\end{pspicture}
```

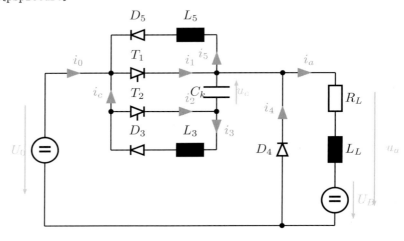

Example
6-7-29

The pst-stru package

The package **pst-stru** by Giuseppe Matarazzo can be very helpful for drawing bending moments and structural schemes for beams, portals, arches, and piles in civil engineering analysis.

```
\usepackage{pstricks,pst-stru}
\psset{arrowsize=0.8mm,arrowinset=0}
\begin{pspicture}(-1,-4)(9,2)
 \pnode(0,0){A}\pnode(2,0){B}\pnode(8,0){C}
 \rput{0}(C){\hinge}\rput{0}(B){\roller}
 \psline[linecolor=red,fillcolor=yellow,fillstyle=solid](0,0)(8,0)(8,1)(0,0)
 \multido{\nStart=1.00+0.025}{-37}{\psArrowCivil[RotArrows=0,
                  length=\nStart,start=\nStart,linecolor=magenta](A)(C){}}
 \rput(8.3,0.4){\large p}\rput(0,-0.4){\Large A}\rput(2,-1){\Large B}
 \rput(8.3,-0.6){\Large C}
 \pcline[offset=0,linecolor=blue]{|-|}(0,-3)(2,-3)
   \lput*{:U}{\bf $\frac{l}{3}$}
 \pcline[offset=0,linecolor=blue]{|-|}(2,-3)(8,-3)\lput*{:U}{\bf $l$}
 \def\MflettAB#1#2#3{#1 #2 div -.125 mul x mul x mul x mul #3 mul neg}
```

```
\pscustom[linecolor=blue,linewidth=1pt,fillstyle=hlines]{%
  \psplot[]{0}{2}{\MflettAB{6}{6}{0.15}}
  \psline[](2,0)(0,0)}
\def\TaglioAB#1#2#3{#1 #2 div -.375 mul x mul x mul #3 mul}
\pscustom[linecolor=green,linewidth=1pt,fillstyle=crosshatch]{%
  \psplot[]{0}{2}{\TaglioAB{6}{6}{0.15}}
  \psline[](2,0)(0,0)}
\def\MflettBC#1#2#3{#1 #2 div -.125 mul x mul x mul x mul
  #1 3.375 div #2 mul x mul add
  #1 10.125 div #2 mul #2 mul sub #3 mul neg}
\pscustom[linecolor=blue,linewidth=1pt,fillstyle=hlines]{%
  \psplot[]{2}{8}{\MflettBC{6}{6}{0.15}}
  \psline[](8,0)(2,0)}
\def\TaglioBC#1#2#3{#1 #2 div -.375 mul x mul x mul
                    #1 3.375 div #2 mul add #3 mul}
\pscustom[linecolor=green,linewidth=1pt,fillstyle=crosshatch]{%
  \psplot[]{2}{8}{\TaglioBC{6}{6}{0.15}}
  \psline[](8,0)(2,0)(2,1.4)}
\psline[linewidth=1.5pt](0,0)(8,0)  % Printing beam AC after diagrams BM/S
\rput(3,1.6){\em {\scriptsize Shear diagram (green boundary)}}
\rput[lb](0,-2.3){\em {\scriptsize Bending Moment diagram (blue boundary)}}
\rput[lb](0,-2.6){\scriptsize [assumed positive downwards]}
\rput(5,-1){\bf {\large +}}\rput(2.5,0.6){\bf {\large +}}
\rput(7.7,-1.3){\bf {\Large -}}
\end{pspicture}
```

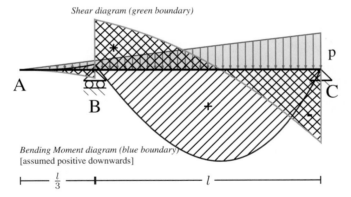

Shear diagram (green boundary)

Bending Moment diagram (blue boundary)
[assumed positive downwards]

$$\longmapsto \frac{l}{3} \longmapsto \longleftarrow l \longrightarrow$$

Example
6-7-30

The pst-geo **package**

This package is actually a bundle of four packages for plotting geographical representations in two- or three-dimensional views. The authors are Manuel Luque, Giuseppe Matarazzo, and Herbert Voß. The data is read on the PostScript level, so having a correct path is important. For some countries additional city data is available. The following projections are supported: Mercator, Lambert, Sanson-Flamsteed, Babinet, Collignon, Bonne, and a simple one. Two databases are available, one each for the two- and three-dimensional views.

The packages are called **pst-map2d**, **pst-map2dII**, **pst-map3d**, and **pst-map3dII**. The data is always read for the whole world, and the visible part is specified by the longitude and latitude for the 3-D view and by `pspicture` coordinates for the 2-D view.

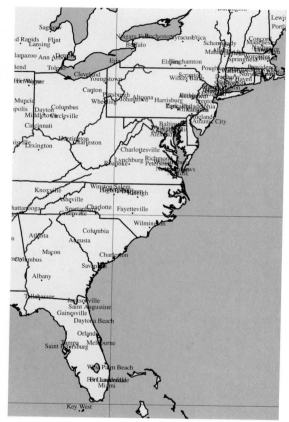

```
\usepackage{pstricks,pst-map2d}
% path to data files:
\psset{path=texmf/tex/latex/pstricks/data}

% select a larger unit value to make
% the map larger and more readable:
\psset{level=1,unit=9}

\begin{pspicture*}(-4.3,1.25)(-3.5,2.5)
  \WorldMap[rivers=true,USA=true,
            maillage=true]
  \def\psNodeLabelStyle{\tiny}
  \psset{mapCountry=USA,nodeWidth=0.2mm}
  \input{cities.tex}
\end{pspicture*}
```

Example 6-7-31

6.7.5 Information theory

An automaton is a mathematical model for a finite state machine. Given an input it jumps through a series of states according to a so-called transition function. This behavior can be described by a symbolic scheme.

The gastex package

This package by Paul Gastin is intended for graphs and automata. It is not a **PSTricks**-related package, but it uses the same way of passing graphical elements from LaTeX to PostScript. However, it is possible to combine any **PSTricks** command with **gastex** commands or to scale graphics in an easy way. Although no documentation comes with the package, it includes some quite self-explanatory examples.

```
\usepackage[dvipsnames]{pstricks}      \usepackage{gastex}
\psset{unit=2.5pt}
\begin{pspicture}(-35,-37)(85,15)
  \node[Nw=16,linecolor=Yellow,fillcolor=Yellow](A)(-20,0){initial}
  \imark[iangle=200,linecolor=Peach](A)
  \node[Nmr=0,Nw=14,fillgray=0.85,
        dash={1}0](B)(20,0){\textcolor{RedViolet}{final}}
  \fmark[flength=10,fangle=-30,dash={3 1 1 1}0](B)
  \node[Nadjust=wh,Nadjustdist=2,Nmr=3,Nmarks=r,linecolor=Green](C)(60,-20){%
    $\left(\begin{array}{ccc}
        2 & 1 & 0 \\
       -1 & 0 & 1 \\
        0 & -1 & 2
    \end{array}\right)$}
  \rmark[linecolor=Green,rdist=1.4](C)
  \drawedge[curvedepth=5,linecolor=Red](A,B){\textcolor{Cyan}{curved}}
  \drawedge[ELside=r,ELpos=35](A,B){straight}
  \drawedge[curvedepth=-25,ELside=r,dash={1.5}0](A,B){far}
  \drawloop[ELpos=75, loopangle=150, dash={0.2 0.5}0](A){loopCW}
  \drawloop[loopCW=n,ELside=r,loopangle=30,dash={3 1.5}{1.5}](B){loopCCW}
  \drawqbpedge[ELside=r,ELdist=0,dash={4 1 1 1}0](B,-90,C,180){qbpedge}
  \drawloop[ELpos=70,loopangle=0](C){$b / 01$}
  \drawloop[loopCW=n,ELpos=75,ELside=r,loopangle=-90,sxo=6](C){$a / 01$}
  \drawloop[ELpos=75,loopangle=-90,sxo=-6](C){$b / 10 $}
  \drawloop[loopangle=50](C){$b / 01$}
  \drawloop[ELpos=75,loopangle=148](C){$b / 01$}
\end{pspicture}
```

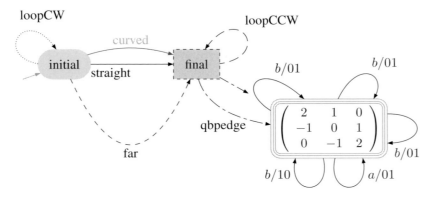

Example
6-7-32

The vaucanson-g package

The **vaucanson-g** package of macros allows you to draw automata and graphs within texts; it is the only package described here that is not is not yet available on CTAN. The authors are Sylvain Lombardy and Jacques Sakarovitch, and the package is available from their Web site.[1] They follow the philosophy that "simple" automata should be described with simple commands. The complexity of commands (or the number of things that must be remembered to use them) should gradually grow with the complexity of the figure composed by these commands.

The following example shows how a simple automaton can be drawn with commands, in which only the minimal information needed (position and label of states, shape and label of transitions) is made explicit. Except for the basic nodes, it also uses logical node names instead of physical coordinates.

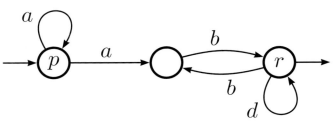

```
\usepackage{vaucanson-g}
\begin{VCPicture}{(0,-2)(6,2)}
\State[p]{(0,0)}{A} \State{(3,0)}{B}
\State[r]{(6,0)}{C}
\Initial{A} \Final{C}
\EdgeL{A}{B}{a} \ArcL{B}{C}{b}
\ArcL{C}{B}{b}
\LoopN{A}{a} \LoopS{C}{d}
\end{VCPicture}
```

Example
6-7-33

The authors provide a special file for the beamer class to make it easier to create a presentation. The hint on the Web site that one has to load beamer with the class option `xcolor=pst` is obsolete. The next example uses the macro `\resizebox` from the graphicx package, which can conveniently be used here to scale the output.

```
\usepackage{vaucanson-g,graphicx}
\resizebox{\linewidth}{!}{\begin{VCPicture}{(-11,-5)(11,12)}
 \PlainState\LargeState\ChgStateLabelScale{0.75}
 \StateIF[p,q]{(-10,-1)}{AB} \StateIF[q,r]{(-6,-1)}{BC}
 \StateIF[p,r]{(-8,-4.464)}{AC}
 \VCPut{(-5,-5)}{$\kappa=[2,0,0]$}
 \StateIF[p]{(8,1.536)}{A} \StateIF[q]{(6,5)}{B}
 \StateIF[r]{(10,5)}{C}
 \VCPut{(8,-0.5)}{$\kappa=[1,0,0]$}
 \StateIF[pq]{(-8,7.536)}{Ab} \StateIF[qr]{(-6,11)}{Bc}
 \StateIF[pr]{(-10,11)}{Ac}
 \VCPut{(-2,11)}{$\kappa=[0,1,0]$}
 \StateIF[p,qr]{(0,-1.464)}{ABc} \StateIF[q,pr]{(-2,2)}{BAc}
 \StateIF[r,pq]{(2,2)}{CAb}
 \VCPut{(3,-2)}{$\kappa=[1,1,0]$}
 \StateVar[pq,pr,qr]{(-8,3)}{AbAcBc}
 \VCPut{(-8,1)}{$\kappa=[0,3,0]$}
 \StateIF[pr,qr]{(2,8)}{AcBc} \StateIF[pq,pr]{(0,4.536)}{AbAc}
 \StateIF[pq,qr]{(-2,8)}{AbBc}
 \VCPut{(5,9)}{$\kappa=[0,2,0]$} %--- end physical coordinates
 \DimEdge \ChgEdgeLineStyle{dashed} \RstEdgeLineWidth
```

---

[1] http://igm.univ-mlv.fr/~lombardy/Vaucanson-G/

```
\EdgeR{Ab}{AbAc}{}       \EdgeR{Ab}{AbBc}{}      \EdgeR{Ac}{AbAc}{}      \EdgeR{Ac}{AcBc}{}
\EdgeR{Bc}{AbBc}{}       \EdgeR{Bc}{AcBc}{}      \EdgeR{AbAc}{AbAcBc}{} \EdgeR{AbAc}{A}{}
\EdgeR{AbBc}{AbAcBc}{}   \EdgeR{AbBc}{B}{}       \EdgeR{AcBc}{AbAcBc}{} \EdgeR{AcBc}{C}{}
\EdgeR{A}{ABc}{}         \EdgeR{B}{BAc}{}        \EdgeR{C}{CAb}{}
\EdgeR{AbAcBc}{ABc}{}    \EdgeR{AbAcBc}{BAc}{}   \EdgeR{AbAcBc}{CAb}{}
\EdgeR{ABc}{AB}{}        \EdgeR{ABc}{AC}{}       \EdgeR{BAc}{AB}{}
\EdgeR{BAc}{BC}{}        \EdgeR{CAb}{AC}{}       \EdgeR{CAb}{BC}{}
\RstEdge
\Initial{Ab}        \Final{Ab}        \Final[w]{Ac}      \Final{Bc}
\Initial{AbAc}      \Initial{AbBc}    \Final[s]{AbBc}    \Final{AbAc}      \Final{AcBc}
\Initial{AbAcBc}    \Final{AbAcBc}
\Initial{A}         \Initial{B}       \Final[s]{B}       \Final{C}
\Initial{ABc}       \Initial{BAc}     \Initial[s]{CAb}  \Final[s]{BAc}  \Final{CAb}
\Initial{AB}        \Initial{AC}      \Initial[s]{BC}
\Final{BC}
\EdgeR{Ab}{Bc}{a,b}    \EdgeR{Bc}{Ac}{a}      \EdgeR{Ac}{Ab}{a}
\EdgeL{AbAc}{AbBc}{a}  \EdgeL{AbBc}{AcBc}{a}  \EdgeL{AcBc}{AbAc}{a}
\LoopN{AbAcBc}{a}
\EdgeL{A}{B}{a} \EdgeL{B}{C}{a} \ArcL{A}{C}{b} \ArcL{C}{A}{a}
\LoopN{B}{b}
\EdgeL{ABc}{BAc}{a}  \EdgeL{BAc}{CAb}{a}  \EdgeL{CAb}{ABc}{a}
\EdgeL{AB}{BC}{a,b}  \EdgeL{BC}{AC}{a}    \EdgeL{AC}{AB}{a}
\end{VCPicture}}
```

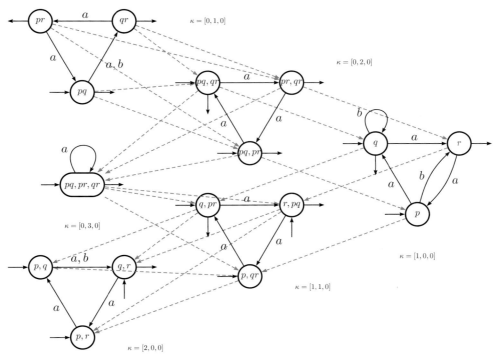

Example
6-7-34

The sfg package

This package by Hanspeter Schmid allows you to draw signal flow graphics. The "documentation" of the package can be found at the end of the style file.

```
\usepackage{sfg}
\sfgsetunit{0.5cm} \sfgsetsize{0.12}{0.4}{0.5}{0.3} \sfgsetcompass
\begin{picture}(27,4)    % branches related to node 2
  \put(6,2){\sfgbranch{3}{0}\S{$\frac{1}{R_1}$}}
  \put(9,2){\sfgbranch{3}{0}\N{\boldmath $Z_2$}}
  \put(18,2){\sfgcurve{-9}{0}{2}\S{$\frac{1}{R_2}$}}
  \put(24,2){\sfgcurve{-15}{0}{-2}\N{$sC_1$}} % branches related to node 3
  \put(12,2){\sfgbranch{3}{0}\N{$\frac{1}{R_2}$}}
  \put(15,2){\sfgbranch{3}{0}\N{\boldmath $Z_3$}}
  \put(0,2){\sfgcurve{6}{0}{2}\N{$1$}}% input, voltage gain, output
  \put(18,2){\sfgcurve{6}{0}{-2}\S{$\alpha_{\mathrm{V}}$}}
  \put(24,2){\sfgbranch{3}{0}\S{$1$}}
  \put(0,2){\sfgtermnode\S{$V_{\mathrm{in}}$}}    % nodes
  \put(3,2){\sfgnode\S{$I_1$}}   \put(6,2){\sfgnode\S{$V_1$}}
  \put(9,2){\sfgnode\S{$I_2$}}   \put(12,2){\sfgnode\S{$V_2$}}
  \put(15,2){\sfgnode\S{$I_3$}}  \put(18,2){\sfgnode\S{$V_3$}}
  \put(21,2){\sfgnode\S{$I_4$}}  \put(24,2){\sfgnode\S{$V_4$}}
  \put(27,2){\sfgtermnode\S{$V_{\mathrm{out}}$}}
\end{picture}
```

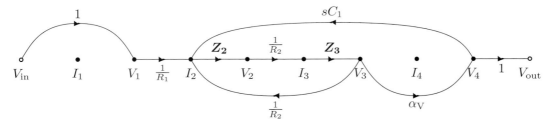

Example
6-7-35

6.7.6 UML and ER diagrams

Two different packages are available for creating Unified Modeling Language diagrams. They are incompatible with each other.

The pst-uml package

This package from Maurice Diamantini comes with a French documentation, but the examples are self-explanatory.

```
\usepackage{graphicx,pstricks,pst-uml}
\resizebox{12cm}{!}{%
\begin{pspicture}(18,15)
  \rput(3,13){\rnode{Class1}{\drawClassi}} \pnode(17.5,13){pnode1}
  \rput(9,10){\rnode{Class2}{\drawClassii}}
```

```
\rput(2,5){\rnode{Class3}{\drawClassiii}}
\rput(12,5){\rnode{Class4}{\drawClassiv}}\rput(5.5,5.5){\rnode{Class5}{\drawClassv}}
\rput(16,11){\rnode{Actor1}{\umlActor{Actor(s) 1}}}
\end{pspicture}
\ncline{Class1}{pnode1} \ncputicon[npos=0.7,nrot=:U]{umlV}
\naput{ncline}\naput[npos=1,ref=r]{Node "P1"}
\ncSXE[armA=11.5]{pnode1}{Class3} \nbput{SXE (armA=11.5)}
\ncputicon{umlV}\ncputicon[npos=1.9999,nrot=:U]{umlV}
\ncputicon[npos=2,nrot=:U]{umlV}\ncputicon[npos=5,nrot=:U]{umlV}
... further code omitted ...
```

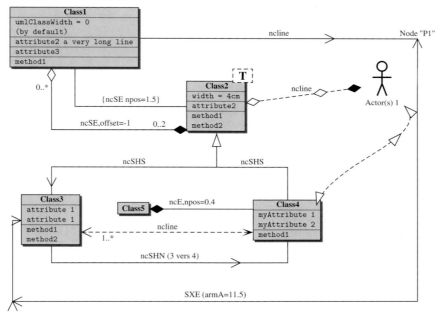

Example
6-7-36

The uml package

This package from Ellef Gjelstad is another one for Unified Modeling Language diagrams. It defines macros with the same name as pst-uml and should not be used together with that package.

```
\usepackage{uml}
\umlDiagram[box=,sizeX=11cm,sizeY=13.5cm,ref=ADTdiagram,grayness=0.92]{}% End of diagram
\umlSchema[pos=\umlTopRight{ADTdiagram},posDelta={-.5,-.5},refpoint=tr]{ADT}{% Attributes
  \umlAttribute[visibility,type=String]{name}}{}{}{}{}
\umlSchema[pos=\umlTopLeft{ADTdiagram},posDelta={.5,-1},refpoint=lt,abstract,
  ref=ADTexample]{ADT-example}{%
  \umlAttribute[visibility=-,
    type=\emph{\umlColorsArgument\umlColorsAdjust type},default=null]{firstNode}
  }{%Methods
```

```
}{%Arguments
  \umlArgument[type=Metaclass]{type}
}{%Constraints
}{%Structure
  \umlDiagram[box=,innerBorder=2mm,outerBorder]{%
    \umlClass[pos={.5,.5}, ref=adtNode,box=]{Node}{%
      \umlAttribute[visibility,
           type=\emph{\umlColorsArgument\umlColorsAdjust type}]{data}}{}%
      \umlAssociation[angleA=20, angleB=-20,arm=1em,arm=1em]{adtNode}{adtNode}%
  }\cr% End of Diagram
}% End of ADT-example
... further code omitted ...
```

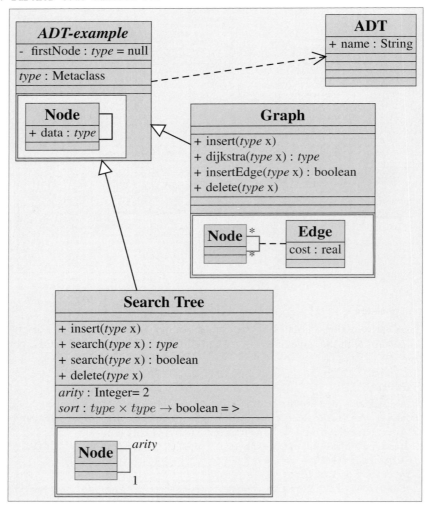

Example
6-7-37

The pst-dbicons **package**

This package from Wolfgang May allows you to create relationships between entities of a database model. The documentation comes with a very complex database example.

```
\usepackage{pst-dbicons}
\seticonparams{entity}{shadow=true,fillcolor=black!30,fillstyle=solid}
\seticonparams{attribute}{fillcolor=black!10,fillstyle=solid}
\seticonparams{relationship}{shadow=true,fillcolor=black!20,fillstyle=solid}
\setlength\attrdist{2.5em}
\entity{Person}\hspace{8cm}\entity{Company}
\attributeof{Person}{30}[key]{Name}  \attributeof{Person}{90}[mv]{Nickname}
\attributeof{Person}[4em]{150}{phone}[phone\_no]
\attributeof{Person}[2em]{270}[mv]{wt}[weight\_at]
\attributeof{wt}{240}{date}  \attributeof{wt}{300}{weight}
\relationshipbetween{Person}{Company}{worksat}[works\_at]
```

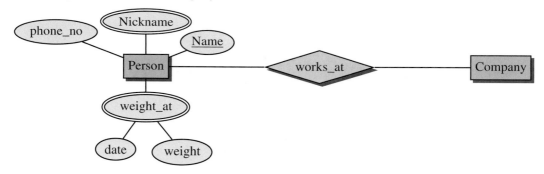

Example
6-7-38

6.7.7 3-D views

Table 6.12 on page 388 lists **PSTricks** packages available for three-dimensional views of text or graphical objects, and Sections 6.5 and 6.6 describe two of them.

The pst-vue3d **package**

This interesting package from Manuel Luque supports hidden lines or surfaces for 3-D objects and offers commands for almost all basic geometric objects, including planes, cones, pyramids, and spheres, among others. See also Color Plate IX(a).

```
\usepackage{pst-vue3d,multido}
\begin{pspicture}(-3.5,-2)(3,4.5)
\psset{THETA=5,PHI=40,Dobs=150,Decran=6.5,fillstyle=solid,linewidth=0.1mm}
{ \psset{normaleLongitude=0, normaleLatitude=90}
  \FrameThreeD[fillstyle=solid,fillcolor=black!15](0,0,0)(-50,0)(50,50)
  \FrameThreeD[fillstyle=solid,fillcolor=black!15](0,0,0)(-50,0)(50,-50)
  \QuadrillageThreeD(0,0,0)(-50,-50)(50,50)  }
\multido{\iCY=-45+90}{2}{\CylindreThreeD(-45,\iCY,0){5}{50}
                    \DemiSphereThreeD(-45,\iCY,50){5}}
```

```
\CylindreThreeD(0,0,0){10}{15}              \CylindreThreeD(0,0,15){20}{5}
\DemiSphereThreeD[RotX=180](0,0,35){20}
\SphereCreuseThreeD[RotX=180](0,0,35){20}
{ \psset{RotY=90,RotX=0,RotZ=30}   \CylindreThreeD(15,15,5){5}{20}   }
\multido{\iCY=-45+90}{2}{\CylindreThreeD(45,\iCY,0){5}{50}
                        \DemiSphereThreeD(45,\iCY,50){5}}

\end{pspicture}
```

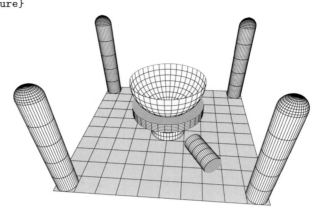

Example
6-7-39

The pst-ob3d package

This package allows you to draw basic three-dimensional objects such as cubes (which can be deformed to rectangular parallelepipeds) and dies. The package author is Denis Girou.

```
\usepackage{pst-ob3d}
\ThreeDput{\psframe[fillstyle=solid,fillcolor=black!15](6,6)
          \psgrid[subgriddiv=0,gridlabels=0,griddots=5](6,6)}
\psset{fillstyle=solid,dotscale=2,RandomFaces=true,Corners=true}
\randomi=123456 \PstDie[fillcolor=black!10](1,3,0)
\randomi=271354 \PstDie[fillcolor=black!20,viewpoint=1 0.3 1,
                  CornersColor=black!80](0.3,1.5,0)
\psset{linecolor=white}
\randomi=93850516 \PstDie[fillcolor=black!60,viewpoint=1 -0.5 1,
                    CornersColor=black!20](3,3,0)
\randomi=8873165  \PstDie[fillcolor=black!40,viewpoint=1 -0.2 1,
                    CornersColor=black!10](2,5,0)
```

Example
6-7-40

The pst-fr3d package

This package from Denis Girou is for drawing simple three-dimensional framed objects,
such as buttons.

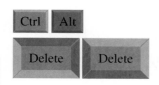

```
\usepackage{pstricks,pst-fr3d}
\PstFrameBoxThreeD{Ctrl}
\PstFrameBoxThreeD[FrameBoxThreeDColorHSB=0.1 0.9 0.5]{Alt}
\par\smallskip
\PstFrameBoxThreeD[FrameBoxThreeDOn=false,linewidth=0.1]{Delete}
\PstFrameBoxThreeD[FrameBoxThreeDOn=true,linewidth=0.1]{Delete}
```

The pst-light3d package

This is another package from Denis Girou for creating three-dimensional light effects on text
or graphical objects.

```
\usepackage{pstricks,pst-plot,pst-light3d}
\DeclareFixedFont{\Rmb}{T1}{ptm}{m}{n}{15mm}
\PstLightThreeDText[linestyle=none,fillstyle=solid,
                    fillcolor=black!20]{\Rmb PSTricks}

\psset{xunit=5cm,yunit=15mm,LightThreeDXLength=0.3,
       LightThreeDYLength=-0.3,plotpoints=500}
\begin{pspicture}(-0.1,-1.1)(1,1.3)
\psaxes[Dx=0.2,Dy=0.4]{->}(0,0)(0,-1)(1,1.2)
\PstLightThreeDGraphic[LightThreeDColorPsCommand=
            1.5 div 0.6 exch 0.8 0.2 setcmykcolor]
     {\psplot{0}{0.95}{x 40 mul RadtoDeg cos 2 div}}
\PstLightThreeDGraphic[LightThreeDColorPsCommand=
            1.5 div 0.05 exch 0.8 0.2 setcmykcolor]
     {\psplot{0}{0.95}{x 10 mul RadtoDeg sin}}
\rput(0.35,0.8){$\sin(10x)$}
\rput(0.2,-0.65){$\frac{1}{2}\cdot\cos(40x)$}
\end{pspicture}
```

The pst-gr3d package

This package allows you to create simple three-dimensional grids, such as a 3-D matrix. All
corners can be defined as nodes to create additional connections. The original author is
Denis Girou.

```
\usepackage{pst-gr3d}
\def\PstGridThreeDHookEnd{{\psset{PstPicture=false,gridwidth=0.1}
 {\def\PstGridThreeDHookNode{\PstGridThreeDNodeProcessor{blue}}%
  \PstGridThreeD[gridcolor=blue,GridThreeDZPos=3](0,7,0)}%
 {\def\PstGridThreeDHookNode{\PstGridThreeDNodeProcessor{red}}%
  \PstGridThreeD[gridcolor=red,GridThreeDXPos=1,GridThreeDZPos=1](0,3,1)}%
 {\def\PstGridThreeDHookNode{\PstGridThreeDNodeProcessor{green}}%
```

```
\PstGridThreeD[gridcolor=green,GridThreeDYPos=6](1,1,1)}}}
\PstGridThreeD[gridwidth=0.04,GridThreeDNodes=true](1,7,3)
\SpecialCoor
\rput([Rx=0.15,angle=140]Gr3dNode033){\psline[linecolor=blue]{<-}(0.8;150)}
\rput([Rx=0.95,angle=140]Gr3dNode033)
      {\shortstack{1d grid\\\footnotesize (X=8,Y=1,Z=1)}}
\rput([Rx=0.15,angle=-50]Gr3dNode121){\psline[linecolor=red]{<-}(1.2;-50)}
\rput([Rx=1.5,angle=-55]Gr3dNode121)
      {\shortstack{2d grid\\\footnotesize (X=4,Y=2,Z=1)}}
\rput([Rx=0.2,angle=-100]Gr3dNode160){\psline[linecolor=green]{<-}(0.8;-100)}
\rput([Rx=1.4,angle=-100]Gr3dNode160)
      {\shortstack{3d grid\\\footnotesize (X=2,Y=2,Z=2)}}
```

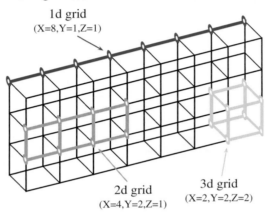

Example
6-7-43

6.7.8 Shapes and color gradients

Shapes and gradients are available for characters (text) or any other graphical objects. Characters must be typeset with the \pscharpath macro.

The pst-grad **package**

This package from Timothy Van Zandt is intended for linear color gradients having only two different colors.

```
\usepackage{pst-grad,pst-text}
\DeclareFixedFont{\RM}{T1}{ptm}{b}{n}{2cm}
```

```
\psset{fillstyle=gradient,gradbegin=black,gradend=white,cmyk}
\pscharpath[gradmidpoint=0.5,gradangle=90]{\RM PostScript}
```

$$PostScript$$

Example
6-7-44

The pst-slpe package

This package from Martin Giese is intended for extended linear, concentric, or radial color gradients. With its help you can fill any closed curve with any sequence of colors. See Color Plate IX(c) for a color version of the next example.

```
\usepackage{pst-slpe,pst-text}
\DeclareFixedFont{\RM}{T1}{ptm}{b}{n}{2cm}
\newcommand*\slpBox[1]{\makebox[4cm]{\rule[-1cm]{0pt}{2cm}\textttt{#1}}}
\begin{tabular}{@{}cc@{}}
  \psframebox[fillstyle=slope]{\slpBox{slope}}        &
  \psframebox[fillstyle=slopes]{\slpBox{slopes}}        \\[30pt]
  \psframebox[fillstyle=ccslope]{\slpBox{ccslope}}    &
  \psframebox[fillstyle=ccslopes]{\slpBox{ccslopes}}  \\[30pt]
  \psframebox[fillstyle=radslope]{\slpBox{radslope}} &
  \psframebox[fillstyle=radslopes]{\slpBox{radslopes}}
\end{tabular}

\medskip
\pscharpath[fillstyle=slopes]{\RM PostScript}
```

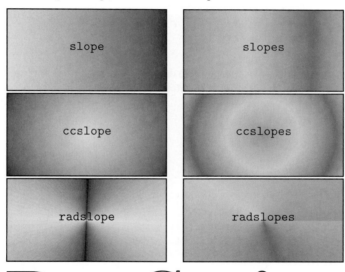

Example
6-7-45

The pst-blur package

This package produces blurred shadows for closed objects, such as curves. The package author is Martin Giese. Unlike with the default shadow option of PSTricks, a blurred shadow is more like a shadow gradient in **pst-blur**.

```
\usepackage{pst-text,pst-blur}
\psset{linewidth=0.5pt,blur=true,blurradius=0.1cm,shadow=true,
    shadowcolor=black!60,shadowsize=0.3cm}
\begin{pspicture}(10,3)
  \psframe(3,2)\fontfamily{ptm}\selectfont
  \rput(1.5,1){\pscharpath{\fontsize{30}{30}\selectfont blur}}
  \pscircle(4.5,1){1}\pscircle(4.5,1){0.25}
  \rput(6.5,1){\pscharpath{\fontsize{60}{60}\selectfont A}}
\end{pspicture}
```

Example
6-7-46

6.7.9 Miscellaneous packages

The pst-bar package

This package from Alan Ristow allows you to draw simple bar charts from external data files
with comma-separated data records. The output can be customized in several ways.

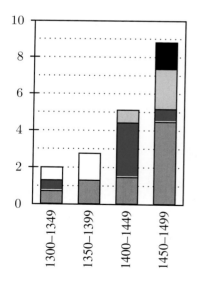

```
\usepackage{pstricks,pst-bar}
\psset{yunit=0.5}
\begin{pspicture}(-0.5,-1.75)(4,10)%
  \psgrid[xunit=4cm,gridlabels=0,%
    subgriddiv=0,griddots=30](0,0)(1,10)%
  \psaxes[axesstyle=frame,Ox=0,Dx=1,Dy=2,%
    labels=y,ticks=y](0,0)(4,10)%
  \psbarscale(0.75){}
  \readpsbardata{\data}{pstricks/data1.csv}%
  \psbarchart[barstyle={red,blue,green,%
    black,white},chartstyle=stack,%
    barlabelrot=90]{\data}%
\end{pspicture}
```

Example
6-7-47

The pst-text **package**

This package is for writing text along any path and for filling characters as you wish. The
original author is Timothy Van Zandt.

```
\usepackage{pst-plot,pst-text}
\newcommand*\textII{
  The PSTricks project was started by Timothy Van Zandt long time ago and is
  one of the oldest \TeX\ packages still in use. 'I started in 1991.
  Initially I was just trying to develop tools for my own use. Then I
  thought it would be nice to package them so that others could use them. It
  soon became tempting to add lots of features, not just the ones I needed.
  When this became so interesting that it interfered with my day ''job'', I
  gave up the project ''cold turkey'', in 1994.' --- Timothy Van Zandt
  Other people who where involved in this project are Denis Girou,
  Sebastian Rahtz and Herbert Vo\ss}
\DeclareFixedFont{\SF}{T1}{phv}{b}{n}{2.35cm}
\begin{pspicture}(-2.7,-2.2)(3.5,2.2)
\psset{linestyle=none}
\pstextpath[l](0,0){%
  \parametricplot[plotstyle=curve,plotpoints=500]{0}{3200}{%
      t 1000 div dup t sin mul exch t cos mul }}{\textII}
\end{pspicture}
\begin{pspicture*}(-2ex,-4ex)(0.3,4.5)
\pstextpath(0,-1ex){\pscharpath*[linestyle=none]{%
  \SF\shortstack{Van\\[20pt]Zandt}}}{\scriptsize\textII}
\end{pspicture*}
```

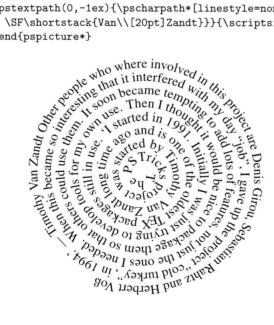

Example
6-7-48

The pst-lens package

This package from Denis Girou and Manuel Luque is for creating optical effects with a magnifier.

```
\usepackage{pst-lens}
\newcommand\Wishes{{\rput[lb](0,0){\Large\begin{minipage}{3cm}\centering
        \textbf{Jana},\\ all the best\\for this new year\\\Huge 2007!
   \end{minipage}}}}
\begin{pspicture}(0,-1.5)(3,4)
  \Wishes\PstLens[LensMagnification=2,cmyk](2,2){\Wishes}
\end{pspicture}\hfill
\begin{pspicture}(0,-1.5)(3,4)
  \Wishes\PstLens[LensMagnification=4,cmyk](1,2.4){\Wishes}
\end{pspicture}\hfill
\begin{pspicture}(0,-1.5)(3.5,4)
  \Wishes \PstLens[LensMagnification=0.5,cmyk](1,1){\Wishes}
  \PstLens[LensMagnification=-0.5,cmyk](2.5,3){\Wishes}
\end{pspicture}
```

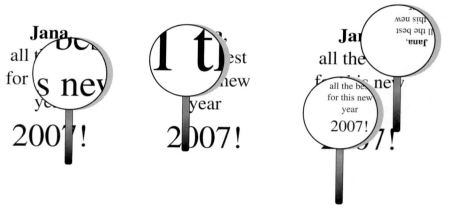

Example
6-7-49

The pst-calendar package

This package by Manuel Luque offers two different calendar macros, one for creating a calendar on a dodecahedron. All special national language support is up to the user.

```
\usepackage{pstricks,pst-calendar,graphicx}
\psset{Year=2007}
\resizebox{\linewidth}{!}{\begin{tabular}{cccc}
  \psCalendar[Month=3] & \psCalendar[Month=5] &
  \psCalendar[Month=7] & \psCalendar[Month=9]
\end{tabular}}

\psscalebox{0.25}{\psCalDodecaeder[style=february]} \hfill
\psscalebox{0.25}{\psCalDodecaeder[style=september]}
```

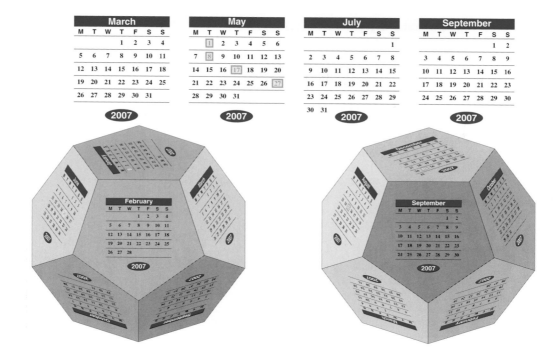

The pst-barcode **package**

This package supports the following bar codes: EAN-13 (JAN-13), EAN-8 (JAN-8), UPC-A,
UPC-E, EAN-5, EAN-2 (EAN/UPC add-ons), ISBN (including ISBN-13), Code 128 (A, B, C,
including EAN-128), Code 39 Extended, Code 93 Extended, Interleaved 2 of 5 (including
ITF-14), RSS-14, RSS Limited, RSS Expanded, Code 2 of 5, Code 11 (USD-8), Codabar, MSI,
Plessey, OneCode, PostNet, Royal Mail (RM4SCC), KIX (Dutch Postal), AusPost (FCC types
11, 59, 62), and USPS FIM symbols. The package authors are Terry Burton and Herbert Voß.

```
\usepackage{pst-barcode}
\resizebox{\linewidth}{!}{%
\begin{tabular}{p{1in}p{1.7in}p{0.9in}p{1.3in}}
  \psbarcode{01335583}{includetext guardwhitespace height=0.5 textsize=8}
           {ean8} &
  \psbarcode{0110197595}{includecheck includetext height=0.5 textsize=8}
           {interleaved2of5} &
  \psbarcode{0123456}{includetext height=0.5 textsize=8}{upce} &
  \psbarcode{231119496801}{includetext height=0.5 textsize=8}{ean13}\\[5pt]
  EAN-8 & Interleaved 2 of 5 & UPC-E & EAN-13
\end{tabular}}

\vspace{2cm}
\resizebox{\linewidth}{!}{%
```

```
\begin{tabular}{p{1.4in}p{1.7in}p{2in}}
  \psbarcode{78858101497}{includetext height=0.75 textsize=8}{upca} &
  \psbarcode{0123456789}{includetext height=0.75 textsize=8}{code11} &
  \psbarcode{^104^102Count^0991234^101!}
            {includetext height=0.75 textsize=8}{code128}\\[5pt]
  UPC-A & Code 11 & Code 128
\end{tabular}}

\vspace{2.5cm}
\resizebox{\linewidth}{!}{%
\begin{tabular}{p{2.1in}p{1.8in}p{1.2in}}
  \psbarcode{A0123456789B}{includecheck includetext textsize=8}
                          {rationalizedCodabar} &
  \begin{tabular}{p{1.7in}}
    \psbarcode[transy=1.5cm]{011075}{includetext textsize=8}
                            {postnet}\\[-1.4cm]
    Postnet\\[60pt]
    \psbarcode[transy=1.5cm]{LE28HS9Z}{includetext textsize=8}
                            {royalmail}\\[-1.4cm]
    Royal Mail
  \end{tabular} &
  \psbarcode{1-86074-271}{includetext textsize=8}{isbn}\\
  Rationalized Codabar &  & ISBN
\end{tabular}}
```

< 0133 5583 >
EAN-8

0 0 1 1 0 1 9 7 5 9 5
Interleaved 2 of 5

0 123456 5
UPC-E

2 311194 968013
EAN-13

7 88581 01497 4
UPC-A

0 1 2 3 4 5 6 7 8 9
Code 11

C o u n t 1234 !
Code 128

A 0 1 2 3 4 5 6 7 8 9 B
Rationalized Codabar

0 1 1 0 7 5
Postnet

L E 2 8 H S 9 Z
Royal Mail

ISBN 1-86074-271-8
9 781860 742712
ISBN

Example 6-7-51

The pst-coil **package**

This package from the **PSTricks** author Timothy Van Zandt is for creating coils and zigzag
lines or node connections.

```
\usepackage{pst-coil}
\newcommand\block{\psline[linewidth=.25pt](0,0)(.4,.6)(.5,.6)(.5,0)
      \pspolygon[linewidth=.25pt](-.1,0)(-.1,-.1)(5.4,-.1)(5.4,0)}
\begin{pspicture}(-.1,-.1)(5.4,5.6)
\psset{labelsep=2.5pt,fillstyle=solid,fillcolor=lightgray}
\footnotesize      % neutral spring
\rput(0,4){\rput(.5,.5){\psline{c-c}(0,0)(.125,0)
  \psCoil[coilaspect=0,coilwidth=.8,coilheight=.625,arrows=c-c]{90}{1890}
    \rput(2.625,0){\psline{c-c}(0,0)(.125,0)
      \rput(.125,0){\pspolygon[fillcolor=black!10](0,-.5)(0,.5)(1,.5)(1,-.5)
        \psdots(.5,0)
        \psline[linewidth=.25pt,linestyle=dashed,dash=2pt 1.5pt](.5,.75)(.5,-4.5)
        \uput[u](.5,.75){$x=0$}}}}\block}  % compressed spring
\rput(0,2){\rput(.5,.5){\psline{c-c}(0,0)(.125,0)
  \rput(.05,0){\psCoil[coilaspect=0,coilwidth=.8,coilheight=.375,arrows=c-c]{90}{1890}
    \rput(1.575,0){\psline{c-c}(0,0)(.125,0)\rput(.125,0){
        \pspolygon[fillcolor=black!10](0,-.5)(0,.5)(1,.5)(1,-.5)
        \uput[d](.65,0){$f$}\psline{*->}(.5,0)(.9,0)
        \uput[u](1,.6){$x<0$}\psline[linewidth=.5pt]{<-}(.5,.6)(1.5,.6)
        \psline[linewidth=.25pt](.5,.1)(.5,.7)}}}}\block}  % stretched spring
\rput(0,0){\rput(.5,.5){\psline{c-c}(0,0)(.125,0)
\rput(-.05,0){\psCoil[coilaspect=0,coilwidth=.8,coilheight=.875,arrows=c-c]{90}{1890}
    \rput(3.675,0){\psline{c-c}(0,0)(.125,0)
      \rput(.125,0){\pspolygon[fillcolor=black!10](0,-.5)(0,.5)(1,.5)(1,-.5)
        \uput[d](.3,0){$f$}  \psline{*->}(.5,0)(.1,0)
        \uput[u](0,.6){$x>0$}\psline[linewidth=.5pt]{<-}(.5,.6)(-.5,.6)
        \psline[linewidth=.25pt](.5,.1)(.5,.7)}}}}\block}
\end{pspicture}
```

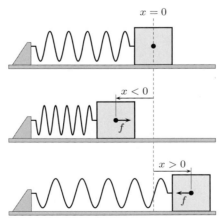

The pst-fractal **package**

This package provides several macros for fractals: Julia and Mandelbrot sets, Sierpinski triangle, Phyllotaxis, Fern, Koch flake, Apollonius circles, and Trees.

```
\psfractal [settings] (x_0,y_0) (x_1,y_1)
\psSier [settings] (x_0,y_0) (x_1,y_1) (x_2,y_2)
\psPhyllotaxis [settings] (x_0,y_0)
\psFern [settings] (x_0,y_0)
\psKochflake [settings] (x_0,y_0)
\psAppolonius [settings] (x_0,y_0)
\psPTree [settings] (x_0,y_0)
\psFArrow [settings] (x_0,y_0) {fraction}
```

\psfractal computes by default the Julia set; the Mandelbrot set is available by setting the optional keyword type=Mandel. Depending on the algorithmn and the iteration depth, the generation of the fractal will take some time. Every point is the result of an iteration with several calculations of complex numbers.

```
\usepackage{pst-fractal}
\psfractal[type=Mandel, xWidth=9.6cm, yWidth=7.8cm,
    dIter=15, baseColor=white](-2.5,-1.3)(0.7,1.3)
```

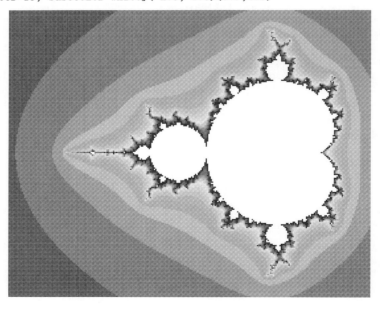

Example
6-7-53

　　The physical sizes of the fractal should be of the same ratio as the logical sizes. For the above example we have $9.6 = 3 \cdot (0.7 + 2.5)$ and $7.8 = 3 \cdot (1.3 + 1.3)$, i.e., both are of a factor 3 greater than the logical width and height.

The color for a point is produced by adding 400 to the number of iterations for this point and then interpreting this sum as the wavelength of the color to be used. To reduce the number of different colors in the output, you can set the keyword `dIter` to a value greater than one. In that case the algorithm changes the color only after `dIter` wavelength steps.

For the Phyllotaxis the size of the image depends to the iteration depth, which is set by default to 6 steps.

```
\usepackage{pst-fractal}
\begin{pspicture}(-3,-3)(3,3)
\psPhyllotaxis
\end{pspicture}
```

Example
6-7-54

An example of `\psPTree` is shown on Color Plate VII(b).

The pst-eps package

This package, also from Denis Girou, allows you to write the `pspicture` environment or a **PSTricks** object "on the fly" into an `.eps` file, which can then be read again into the LaTeX source in the same run. In the following example the macro `\PSTtoEPS` writes the **PSTricks** object into the external file `pstricks/frame.eps`, which is then read immediately. Using this package makes sense only for single images, because **pst-pdf** does a better job when you are dealing with a larger number of exported images.

```
\usepackage{pst-eps,graphicx}
\PSTtoEPS[bbllx=-0.5,bblly=-0.5,bburx=5.3,bbury=3.4,
  checkfile,headers=all,makeeps=all]{pstricks/frame.eps}{%
  \psgrid[subgriddiv=0](5,3)
  \psframe[linecolor=blue,linewidth=0.1](1,1)(4,2)%
}
\includegraphics[scale=0.5]{pstricks/frame}
```

Example
6-7-55

The pst-pdf package

As already mentioned, **PSTricks** is an abbreviation for PostScript tricks. It cannot be used directly with the **pdflatex** program, however. The package **pst-pdf** from Rolf Niepraschk and Hubert Gäßlein supports the transformation from PostScript to PDF in such a way that you can use **pdflatex**, at least in a last run. This is different from the way **dvips**→**ps2pdf** works, as it allows you to make use of features that are available only with **pdflatex**.

The **pst-pdf** package itself uses the **preview** package to intercept **PSTricks**-specific code (macros and environments) at the LaTeX level; anything else in the document is ignored. The resulting `dvi` file thus collects all **PSTricks**-related parts as code snippets. This code is converted to PostScript and then to PDF. This PDF file is an image container, which contains all the **PSTricks** graphics as single PDF pages that can then be read by **pdflatex**.

Preparing this image container requires four steps:

1. `latex file.tex` creates a special `dvi` file (**pst-pdf** is active).

2. `dvips -o file-pics.ps file.dvi` creates a PostScript file that collects all images as single pages.

3. `ps2pdf file-pics.ps file-pics.pdf` converts the image container to a PDF file.

4. `pdflatex file.tex` creates the documents by replacing the **PSTricks** parts in the document with the PDF images from the image container file (**pst-pdf** is inactive).

Unless the order or number of the images in the container changes, there is no need for a new LaTeX run when only the text part was edited. In such a case a single pdfLaTeX run is already sufficient. Scripts for different platforms are available on CTAN.

The only important consideration with this package is that **preview** takes the values of the `pspicture` environment for building the bounding box and then everything outside of this area is cut off.

The multido **package**

The **multido** package by Timothy Van Zandt is not actually a **PSTricks**-related package, but it is listed together with the other **PSTricks** packages for historical reasons. The package can be found at CTAN: `/macros/generic/multido`. To prevent problems caused by the identical macro names found in the **fp** package, you should at least use **multido** version 1.41. **multido** works best with integer values; it may cause problems when using real values due to rounding problems when using TeX arithmetics.

You should use the predefined prefixes from **multido** when declaring the counter variable names. **multido** knows the following prefixes:

Prefix	Meaning
d	length (dimension)
n	counter
i	integer number
r	real number

Valid values are `\dA,\nABC,\iAbCd`, and `\rAbCd`. Additional information is available in the package documentation [129]. The example shows 40 different curves of a so-called superellipse (Lamé curve) with `\multido{\rA=0.2+0.1,\iA=0+1}{40}{...}`.

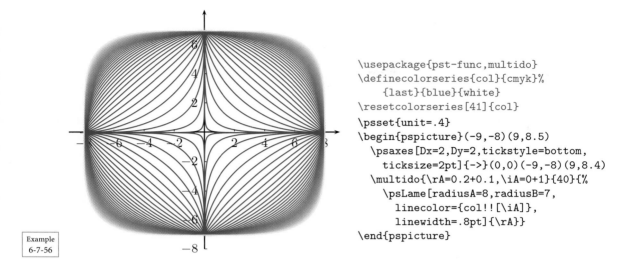

```
\usepackage{pst-func,multido}
\definecolorseries{col}{cmyk}%
    {last}{blue}{white}
\resetcolorseries[41]{col}
\psset{unit=.4}
\begin{pspicture}(-9,-8)(9,8.5)
  \psaxes[Dx=2,Dy=2,tickstyle=bottom,
    ticksize=2pt]{->}(0,0)(-9,-8)(9,8.4)
  \multido{\rA=0.2+0.1,\iA=0+1}{40}{%
    \psLame[radiusA=8,radiusB=7,
      linecolor={col!![\iA]},
      linewidth=.8pt]{\rA}}
\end{pspicture}
```

Example
6-7-56

6.8   Summary of PSTricks commands and keywords

Table 6.20: Alphabetical list of all environments of the basic **PSTricks** package

Name	Page	Name	Page
psclip	275	psgraph	421
psmatrix	361	pspicture	220

Table 6.21: Alphabetical list of all commands of the basic **PSTricks** package

Name	Page
\altcolormode	304
\arrows{*arrow type*}	294
\begin@AltOpenObj	307
\begin@ClosedObj	307
\begin@OpenObj	307
\begin@SpecialObj	307
\clipbox *[value[unit]]* *{object}*	274
\closedshadow *[settings]*	289
\closepath	284
\code{*PostScript code*}	292
\coor(x_1,y_1) (x_2,y_2) ... (x_n,y_n)	293
\cput * *[settings]* *{rotation}* (x,y){*object*}	269

Name	*Page*
\curveto$(x_1, y_1)$ (x_2, y_2) (x_3, y_3)	291
\degrees *[value for the full circle]*	218
\dim{*number unit*}	292
\DontKillGlue	303
\end@AltOpenObj	307
\end@ClosedObj	307
\end@OpenObj	307
\end@SpecialObj	307
\everypsbox{*code*}	278
\file{*file name*}	294
\fill *[settings]*	285
\grestore	285
\gsave	285
\KillGlue	303
\lineto$(x, y)$	291
\movepath$(dx,dy)$	290
\moveto$(x, y)$	283
\mrestore	288
\msave	288
\multips {*rotation*} (x, y) (dx,dy) {*n*}{*object*}	269
\multirput* *[reference point]* {*rotation*} (x, y) (dx,dy) {*n*}{*object*}	267
\newcmykcolor{*name*}{*value1 value2 value3 value4*}	216
\newgray{*name*}{*value*}	216
\newrgbcolor{*name*}{*value1 value2 value3*}	216
\newhsbcolor{*name*}{*value1 value2 value3*}	216
\newpath	284
\newpsfontdot{*name*} *[xW xS yS yW xO yO]* {*font name*}{*glyph number*}	250
\newpsobject{*name*}{*object name*}{*list of options*}	280
\newpsstyle{*name*}{*list of parameters*}	279
\NormalCoor	219,296
\openshadow *[settings]*	289
\parabola* *[settings]* {*arrow*} (x_P, y_P) (x_A, y_A)	245
\psaddtolength{*length register*}{*value[unit]*}	217
\psarc* *[settings]* {*arrow*} (x_M, y_M) {*radius*}{*angleA*}{*angleB*}	241
\psarcn* *[settings]* {*arrow*} (x_M, y_M) {*radius*}{*angleA*}{*angleB*}	241
\psbezier* *[settings]* {*arrow*} (x_0, y_0) (x_1, y_1) (x_2, y_2) (x_3, y_3)	244
\psccurve* *[settings]* {*arrow*} (x_1, y_1) (x_2, y_2) ... (x_n, y_n)	246
\pscircle* *[settings]* (x_M, y_M) {*radius*}	241
\pscirclebox* *[settings]* {*object*}	272
\pscurve* *[settings]* {*arrow*} (x_1, y_1) (x_2, y_2) ... (x_n, y_n)	245
\pscustom* *[settings]* *[arbitrary code]*	280
\psdblframebox* *[settings]* {*content*}	271
\psdiabox* *[settings]* {*object*}	273

Name	Page
\psdiamond* [*settings*] (x_M,y_M) (*dx,dy*)	233
\psdot* [*settings*] (x,y)	249
\psdots* [*settings*] (x_1,y_1) ... (x_n,y_n)	249
\psecurve* [*settings*] {*arrow*} (x_1,y_1) (x_2,y_2) ... (x_n,y_n)	246
\psellipse* [*settings*] (x_M,y_M) (*a,b*)	243
\psellipticarc* [*settings*] {*arrow*} (x_M,y_M) (*a,b*) {*angleA*}{*angleB*}	243
\psellipticarcn* [*settings*] {*arrow*} (x_M,y_M) (*a,b*) {*angleA*}{*angleB*}	243
\psellipticwedge* [*settings*] {*arrow*} (x_M,y_M) (*a,b*) {*angleA*}{*angleB*}	244
\psframe* [*settings*] (x_1,y_1) (x_2,y_2)	232
\psframebox* [*settings*] {*content*}	271
\pslbrace	304
\psline* [*settings*] {*arrow*} (x_1,y_1) (x_2,y_2) (...) (x_n,y_n)	231
\psmathboxtrue	278
\psmathboxfalse	278
\psovalbox* [*settings*] {*object*}	272
\pspolygon* [*settings*] (x_1,y_1) (x_2,y_2) (...) (x_n,y_n)	232
\psrbrace	304
\psscalebox{*value1 [value2]*}{*object*}	277
\psscaleboxto(x,y){*object*}	277
\psset{*par1=value1,par2=value2,...*}	217
\pssetlength{*length register*}{*value[unit]*}	217
\psshadowbox* [*settings*] {*object*}	272
\pst@def{*Code*}	307
\pstriangle* [*settings*] (x_M,y_M) (*dx,dy*)	233
\pstribox* [*settings*] {*object*}	273
\PSTricksOff	303
\pstVerb	305
\pstverb	305
\psverbboxtrue	279
\psverbboxfalse	279
\pswedge* [*settings*] (x_M,y_M) {*radius*}{*angleA*}{*angleB*}	242
\qdisk(x_M,y_M){*radius*}	241
\qline(x_1,y_1) (x_2,y_2)	232
\radian	218
\rcoor(*dx1,dy1*) (*dx2,dy2*) ... (*dxn,dyn*)	294
\rcurveto(*dx1,dy1*) (*dx2,dy2*) (*dx3,dy3*)	292
\rlineto(*dx,dy*)	291
\rotate{*angle*}	287
\rotatedown{*object*}	276
\rotateleft{*object*}	276
\rotateright{*object*}	276
\rput* [*ref point*] {*rotating angle*} (x,y) {*object*}	267
\scale{*num1 [num2]*}	287

Name	Page
\setcolor{*color name*}	295
\space	304
\SpecialCoor	219,296
\stroke [*settings*]	284
\swapaxes	287
\translate(x,y)	286
\uput * {*labelsep*} [*angle*] {*rotation*} (x,y) {*object*}	268

Table 6.22: Alphabetical list of all keywords

Name	Value	Default	Page
Alpha	*angle*	45	410
ArrowFill	*Boolean*	true	418
ArrowInside	*value*	*empty*	418
ArrowInsideNo	*value*	1	418
ArrowInsideOffset	*value*	0	418
ArrowInsidePos	*value*	*empty*	418
addfillstyle	*fillstyle*	none	257
angle	*angle*	0	351
angleA	*angle*	0	351
angleB	*angle*	0	351
arcangle	*angle*	8	351
arcangleA	*angle*	8	351
arcangleB	*angle*	8	351
arcsep	*value[unit]*	0pt	247
arcsepA	*value[unit]*	0pt	247
arcsepB	*value[unit]*	0pt	247
arm	*value[unit]*	10pt	351
armA	*value[unit]*	10pt	351
armB	*value[unit]*	10pt	351
arrowinset	*value*	0.4	262
arrowlength	*value*	1.4	262
arrows	*arrows*	–	260
arrowscale	*value1 [value2]*	1	263
arrowsize	*value[unit] value*	1.5pt 2	261
axesstyle	*framestyle*	axes	314
bbd	*value[unit]*	*empty*	378
bbh	*value[unit]*	*empty*	378
bbl	*value[unit]*	*empty*	378
bbr	*value [unit]*	*empty*	378
beginAngle	*angle*	0	412
Beta	*angle*	30	410
border	*value[unit]*	0pt	239

Name	Value	Default	Page
bordercolor	*color*	white	239
boxsize	*value[unit]*	0.4cm	353
bracketlength	*value*	0.15	263
cornersize	relative|absolute	relative	239
curvature	*value1 value2 value3*	1 0.1 0	248
dash	*value[unit] value[unit]*	5pt 3pt	236
Derivation	*value*	0	427
dimen	outer|inner|middle	outer	237
dotangle	*angle*	0	252
dotsize	*value[unit] value*	2pt 2	251
dotscale	*value1 [value2]*	1	251
dotsep	*value[unit]*	3pt	236
dotstyle	*style name*	*	251
doublecolor	*color name*	white	236
doubleline	*Boolean*	false	236
doublesep	*value[unit]*	1.25\pslinewidth	236
drawing	*Boolean*	true	411
drawStyle	xLines|yLines|xyLines|		
	yxLines	xLines	414
Dx	*value*	1	317
dx	*value[unit]*	0pt	317
Dy	*value*	1	317
dy	*value[unit]*	0pt	317
dZero	*value*	0.1	427
edge	*macro*	\ncline	376
embedangle	*angle*	0	399
endAngle	*angle*	360	412
epsZero	*value*	0.1	427
fansize	*value[unit]*	1cm	370
fillangle	*angle*	0	384
fillcolor	*color name*	white	255
fillcycle	*value*	0	385
fillcyclex	*value*	0	385
fillcycley	*value*	0	385
fillloopadd	*value*	0	386
fillloopaddx	*value*	0	386
fillloopaddy	*value*	0	386
fillmove	*value[unit]*	0pt/2pt	385
fillmovex	*value[unit]*	0pt/2pt	385
fillmovey	*value[unit]*	0pt/2pt	385
fillsep	*value[unit]*	0pt/2pt	384
fillsepx	*value[unit]*	0pt	384
fillsepy	*value[unit]*	0pt	384
fillsize	auto|{(x0,y0)(x1,y1)}	auto	386

Name	Value	Default	Page
fillstyle	*fillstyle*	none	253
framearc	*value*	0	238
framesep	*value[unit]*	3pt	270
framesize	*value[unit] [value[unit]]*	10pt	350
gangle	*angle*	0	233
gridcolor	*color*	black	226
griddots	*value*	0	226
gridlabelcolor	*color*	black	227
gridlabels	*value[unit]*	10pt	227
gridwith	*value[unit]*	0.8pt	226
hatchangle	*angle*	45	256
hatchcolor	*color name*	black	256
hatchsep	*value[unit]*	4pt	256
hatchsepinc	*value[unit]*	0pt	256
hatchwidth	*value[unit]*	0.8pt	255
hatchwidthinc	*value[unit]*	0pt	255
href	*value*	0	348
hiddenLine	*Boolean*	false	414
invisibleLineStyle	*line style*	dashed	415
labels	all|x|y|none	all	318
labelsep	*value[unit]*	5pt	265
levelsep	**value[unit]*	2cm	374
liftpen	0|1|2	0	282
linearc	*value[unit]*	0pt	238
linecolor	*color*	black	235
linejoin	0|1|2	1	412
linestyle	none|solid|dotted|dashed	solid	235
linetype	*value*	0	240
liftpen	0|1|2	0	240
linewidth	*value[unit]*	0.8pt	234
loopsize	*value[unit]*	1cm	352
nameX	*label*	x	413
nameY	*label*	y	413
nameZ	*label*	z	413
ncurv	*value*	0.67	352
ncurvA	*value*	0.67	352
ncurvB	*value*	0.67	352
nodesep	*value[unit]*	0pt	350
nodesepA	*value[unit]*	0pt	350
nodesepB	*value[unit]*	0pt	350
normal	*valuex valuey valuez*	0 0 1	397
npos	*value*	empty	354
nrot	*rotation*	0	354

Name	Value	Default	Page
offset	*value[unit]*	0pt	353
offsetA	*value[unit]*	0pt	353
offsetB	*value[unit]*	0pt	353
origin	*xvalue[unit],yvalue[unit]*	0pt,0pt	223
Ox	*value*	0	316
Oy	*value*	0	316
plane	xy|xz|yz	xy	413
plotpoints	*value*	50	334
plotstyle	dots|line|polygon|curve| ecurve|ccurve	line	333
pOrigin	*reference point*	c	414
radius	*value[unit]*	0.25cm	350
rbracketlength	*value*	0.15	263
ref	*reference*	c	353
rot	*rotation*	0	356
shadow	*Boolean*	false	239
shadowangle	*angle*	-45	239
shadowcolor	*color*	darkgray	239
shadowsize	*value[unit]*	3pt	239
shift	*value[unit]*	0pt	221
shortput	none|nab|tablr|tab	none	355
showbbox	*Boolean*	false	378
showgrid	*Boolean*	false	222
showpoints	*Boolean*	false	237
showorigin	*Boolean*	true	319
SphericalCoor	*Boolean*	false	416
spotX	*angle*	180	413
spotY	*angle*	0	413
spotZ	*angle*	90	413
subgridcolor	*color*	gray	228
subgriddiv	*value*	5	227
subgriddots	*value*	0	228
subgridwith	*value[unit]*	0.4pt	228
swapaxes	*Boolean*	false	223
tbarsize	*value[unit] value*	2pt 5	262
thistreefit	*value[unit]*	*empty*	372
thislevelsep	**value[unit]*	*empty*	374
thistreenodesize	*value[unit]*	*empty*	373
thistreesep	*value[unit]*	*empty*	372
ticks	all|x|y|none	all	319
ticksize	*value[unit]*	3pt	321
tickstyle	full|top|bottom	full	320
tndepth	*value[unit]*	\dp\strutbox	381
tnheight	*value[unit]*	\ht\strutbox	381

Name	Value	Default	Page
tnpos	*value[unit]*	*empty*	380
tnsep	*value[unit]*	*empty*	380
tnyref	*value*	*empty*	381
tpos	*value*	0.5	356
treeflip	*Boolean*	false	371
treefit	loose|tight	tight	372
treemode	D|U|R|L	D	371
treenodesize	*value[unit]*	-1pt	373
treesep	*value[unit]*	0.75cm	372
trimode	*U|D|R|L	U	270
Tshadowangle	*angle*	60	388
Tshadowcolor	*color*	lightgray	389
Tshadowsize	*value*	1	389
viewpoint	*valuex valuey valuez*	1 -1 1	395
viewangle	*angle*	0	397
visibleLineStyle	*line style*	solid	415
vref	*value [unit]*	0.7ex	348
xbbd	*value[unit]*	*empty*	378
xbbh	*value[unit]*	*empty*	378
xbbl	*value[unit]*	0	378
xbbr	*value[unit]*	0	378
xMin	*value*	-1	410
xMax	*value*	4	410
Xnodesep	*value[unit]*	0pt	350
XnodesepA	*value[unit]*	0pt	350
XnodesepB	*value[unit]*	0pt	350
XPlotpoints	*value*	25	411
xThreeDunit	*value*	1	411
yMin	*value*	-1	410
yMax	*value*	4	410
Ynodesep	*value[unit]*	0pt	350
YnodesepA	*value[unit]*	0pt	350
YnodesepB	*value[unit]*	0pt	350
yPlotpoints	*value*	25	411
yThreeDunit	*value*	1	411
zMin	*value*	-1	410
zMax	*value*	4	410
zThreeDunit	*value*	1	411

CHAPTER 7

The Xy-pic Package

Xy-pic is a general-purpose drawing package based on TeX. It works smoothly with most formats, including LaTeX, $\mathcal{AMS}$-LaTeX, $\mathcal{AMS}$-TeX, and plain TeX. It has been used to typeset complicated diagrams from numerous application areas, including category theory, automata, algebra, geometry, neural networks, and knot theory. Xy-pic's generic syntax lets you use a consistent mnemonic notation system that is based on the *logical* construction of diagrams by the combination of various elementary *visual* components. You can also write macros by combining these basic elements consistently to form higher-level structures specific to the intended application.

Xy-pic was originally written by Kristoffer Høgsbro Rose [105]. Later Ross Moore joined the development effort and the ensuing collaboration resulted in extensive revisions and extensions [104, 106].

7.1 Introducing Xy-pic

The Xy-pic system is built around an object-oriented drawing language called the *kernel*: this is a notation for composing "objects" with "methods" that correspond to the meaningful drawing operations on the object.

The kernel supports the following basic graphic notions (see Section 7.2):

- *Positions* can be specified in various formats. In particular, user-defined coordinates can be absolute or relative to previous positions, objects, object edges, or points on connections.

- *Objects* can have several forms—e.g., circular, elliptic, and rectangular—and can be adjusted in several ways, even depending on the *direction* of other objects. In particular, an object can be used to *connect* two other objects.

Enhancements to the kernel, called "options", have two main varieties: *extensions* (see Section 7.3) add more objects and methods to the repertoire (such as "curving" and "framing"), while *features* (see Section 7.4) provide notations for particular application areas (e.g., "arrows", "matrices", "polygons", "lattices", "knots"). In general, extensions provide visual components, whereas features add domain-specific notations for their logical composition.

This chapter gives examples of XY-pic's use in various application areas. Through this "teach by example" approach, it serves as a complement to the *XY-pic User's Guide* [106], which introduces the most used features, and the *XY-pic Reference Manual* [104], which describes the syntax of all XY-pic commands and their arguments. A study of our examples should put you in an excellent position to start drawing your own diagrams; we hope it will also convince you of the beauty, power, and flexibility of the XY-pic package.

A first example of XY-pic consists of various modules. If you are not sure which ones to load, it is probably
XY-pic code best to load "a large set", as follows:[1]

```
\usepackage[all]{xy}
```

Once you know enough about XY-pic to identify which functions you want to use, then you can specify only the extensions or features that are actually needed. For instance,

```
\usepackage[curve,arrow,cmactex]{xy}
```

loads the `curve` extension and `arrow` feature, which are tuned to produce `\special` commands understood by Thomas Kiffe's **CMacTeX** Macintosh port of TEX programs.

To get an idea of the philosophy on which XY-pic is based, let us first look at how we "construct" an XY-picture. To make things relatively easy, we consider a matrix-like diagram. As explained in more detail in Section 7.4.2, the principal way to create a diagram is with the command \xymatrix{*spec*}, where *spec* is the specification of the *matrix entries*, which, in general, are aligned in *rows* and *columns*. Just as in a `tabular` environment, entries inside a row are separated by ampersands and successive rows are separated by \\.

```
\usepackage[all]{xy}
\[
\xymatrix{
 A & *+[F]{\sum_{i=n}^m {i^2}} \\
   & {\bullet} & D \ar[ul]
}\]
```

Example
7-1-1

---

[1] For formats other than LATEX, use the command \input xy followed by \xyoption{all}. The all option loads the `curve`, `frame`, `tips`, `line`, `rotate`, and `color` extensions as well as the `matrix`, `arrow`, and `graph` features. Any other features or extensions needed must be loaded separately.

This example has two rows of three columns and shows a good deal about how XɣY-pic interprets commands.

- By default, entries inside XɣY-pic environments are typeset in mathematics mode, using "text style", and are centered.

- In many cases you may not start entries with a bare macro name—such names must be enclosed in braces or be otherwise "protected".

- As in a `tabular` environment, empty entries at the end of rows can be omitted if not referred to.

- Elements can be addressed by their *relative* ("logical") position in the diagram; thus `\ar[ul]` draws an arrow from the "current" position to the matrix cell "one up and one to the left".

- The *format* and *shape* of an element can be customized by specifying an "entry modifier" (e.g., "`[F]`" tells XɣY-pic to frame the entry).

If you have questions or need some help, you can address the XɣY-pic mailing list `xy-pic@tug.org`, to which you can subscribe by visiting the Web site `http://tug.org/mailman/listinfo/xy-pic`.

7.2 Basic constructs

A thorough knowledge of how XɣY-pic interprets the various commands will let you exploit its many functions fully. It will also help you understand the subtleties of the various extensions and features introduced in later sections.

A kernel XɣY-picture is enclosed in an xy environment:[1]

```
\begin{xy}...\end{xy}
```

The location at which an XɣY-pic object is being "dropped" is called its "position". In fact, in most cases only the coordinates or shape of the "current position" is set.

7.2.1 Initial positions

The simplest form of XɣY-pic position is called *absolute*, written $<X,Y>$. The coordinates X and Y are the offsets *right* and *above* the origin of the picture, which thus lies at $<0\mathrm{cm},0\mathrm{cm}>$. Simple arithmetic operators can be used to position the current point. A comma is used to separate one position from another:

$UL \quad UR$

$5,5$

$DL \quad DR$

```
\usepackage{xy}
\[\begin{xy}
  0*{DL}  ,+/r1cm/*{DR}
  ,<0cm,1cm>*{UL}  ,<1cm,1cm>*{UR}
  ,(5,5)*{5,5}
\end{xy}\]
```

Example
7-2-1

---

[1] When using XɣY-pic with formats other than LaTeX, use `\xy...\endxy`.

The above exampleillustrates various ways to specify coordinates.[1] In particular, 0 (zero) is a shorthand for the origin, and +/r1cm/ moves right by 1 cm. The next two points <0cm,1cm> and <1cm,1cm> are explicit X, Y coordinates. Finally, the middle point (5,5) uses the *default coordinate system* with units of 1 mm for usual Cartesian x- and y-axes starting from (0,0). We will say more about the "*" operator later.

In the next example, we define the units of the coordinate system explicitly by setting them to 5 mm in X and Y using the : operator. This means that all further dimensionless coordinate pairs refer to multiples of 5 mm. You can add or subtract lengths from a given position. In particular, for the right-hand part of the diagram below—starting on the third line of code—we first offset the coordinate with respect to the origin 0 by moving four units (i.e., 2 cm) to the right. We call this new location "NO" (for "new origin"—the quotation marks indicate that it is to be a name) using the "=" operator. We then use this name to calculate the location at which we want to drop the text object UR and name it "SUR" (for "saved upper right"). Finally, we use "SUR" twice, each time subtracting a coordinate specification, to obtain the locations at which the texts UL and DR are to be dropped.

```
\usepackage{xy}
\[\begin{xy} 0;<5mm,0mm>:
0*{DL} ,(2,0)*{DR} ,<0cm,1cm>*{UL} ,(2,2)*{UR}
,0+(4,0)="NO"*{\mathtt{DL}}
,"NO"+(2,2)="SUR"*{\mathtt{UR}}
,"SUR"-<1cm,0cm>*{\mathtt{UL}}
,"SUR"-(0,2)*{\mathtt{DR}}
\end{xy}\]
```

UL UR UL   UR

DL DR DL   DR

Example
7-2-2

7.2.2 Making connections

The effects of the *connect* operator, **, can be quite complex. To a first approximation, it "connects" the *current* and *previous* positions (c and p, respectively). As a simple example, let us connect some of the locations in an earlier diagram.

UL UR

DL DR

```
\usepackage{xy}
\[\begin{xy}
0*{DL};<1cm,1cm>*{UR}**@{-}
,<0cm,1cm>*{UL};<1cm,0cm>*{DR}**@{=}
\end{xy}\]
```

Example
7-2-3

Here the connection operation, **@{-}, typesets a connection using the special @{-} kernel object, which connects as a solid line. The Xᴚ-pic documentation lists the connections initially provided; new ones can be created with the command \newdir. Most have mnemonic names: @{.} connects with a dotted line, @{-} with a dashed line, @{=} with a double line, etc. Note the use of the semicolon operator, which *swaps* the positions p and c. Here it has the effect of moving the position in c (namely 0) into p; then c is immediately

---

[1] Note that the comma delimiter appears *before* the following item rather than *after* the preceding one. This is a particularly useful device in developing a picture, since whole lines can be easily "commented out" while retaining valid syntax overall.

overridden with a new position for the next object (remember that connections with the **
operator are drawn from *p* to *c*). The example also reveals that the drop operator * does not
place a default margin around objects. Rather, such space is created implicitly, by inserting
one or more + modifiers between the * and the brace opening the object—more on this later.

You can combine several drop operations. In addition, the question mark (?) operator
lets you specify the location where something is to be drawn "along" a just typeset connection in a coordinate-independent way:

```
\usepackage[frame]{xy}
\[\begin{xy}
  0*+[o][F]{DL};<2cm,1cm>*+[F]{UR}  **@{.}
  ?<*@{<<}  ?(0.5)*!/_3mm/{\Omega}  ?>>>*@{>}
\end{xy}\]
```

Example
7-2-4

The two objects are enlarged with the + modifier, and the [o] makes the *shape* of the
first object round instead of the default rectangular (we have added the [F] modifier, defined by the frame extension, to highlight this fact). On the second line, the ? operator lets
us position objects at a given place along the last "connection" (here the dotted line between
the circle and the frame). First, a left double arrow tip is placed at the starting end (?<),
i.e., the end given by the position *p* when the connection was made. Next, near the middle
(?(0.5)) and 3 mm above the line, we write an Ω (by shifting, as described later). Some
length units away from the finishing end of the line, i.e., at the position *c* when the connection was made, a right arrow tip is output (positioned by ?>>>). The > and < notations
accumulate, somewhat analogously to the +, ++, etc. operators that alter the object margin.

Finally, we calculate the intersection of two lines with the ?! operator:

```
\usepackage{xy}
\[\begin{xy}
  0*=+{l}="l"  ;<2cm,8mm>*=+{r}="r"  **@{-}
  ,<4mm,10mm>*+{ll}  ;<25mm,2mm>*+{rr}  **@{--}
  ?!{"r";"l"}*{\oplus}
\end{xy}\]
```

Example
7-2-5

First the two lines (l, r) and (ll, rr) are typeset and the end points are stored with
names "l" and "r", respectively. Using the syntax ?!{<XY1>;<XY2>} (where <XY1> and
<XY2> are two positions), the intersection with the last connection is computed as the place
to drop the LaTeX $\oplus$ symbol.

7.2.3 Dropping objects

We have already used *objects* in most of the examples in the previous section. More precisely,
objects are the arguments of the *drop* * and *connection* ** operators; they are usually the
elements that are actually output into the picture. Objects always include a brace pair {...}
specifying what is to be dropped. The part preceding the opening brace, called the *modifier*,
allows fine adjustments to specify exactly how the object is to be placed.

The "!" *shift* modifier lets you move the reference point of an object from its initial central position to somewhere else within the object's bounding box:

```
\usepackage[frame]{xy}
\[\begin{xy}
  (0,0)*@{o}*!UL{Box1}*\frm{-}*@{x}
  ,(20,0)*@{o}*!RD{Box2}*\frm{-}*@{x}
\end{xy}\]
```

Box1 *Box2*

Example
7-2-6

The first box has its upper-left corner (!UL) positioned at the current position (0,0), while the second box has its lower-right corner (!RD) at the current position (20,0). In either case, the location of *c* remains unchanged, since the times symbol (×, typeset with @{x}) and open circle (○, typeset with @{o}) overlap in the picture. This example also illustrates the use of the modifier @ to request a "directional" object from the kernel library, using the contents of the braces as a mnemonic abbreviation (a fact we have already used silently on several occasions).

Shifting an object can be compared to using the *skew* position operator, which also uses the "!" symbol but occurs after a dropped object or position specification:

```
\usepackage[frame,arrow,curve]{xy}
\[\begin{xy}
  (0,0)*@{*}*[F]{Box1}!UL="a",*@{x}
  ,(20,0)*@{*}*[F]{Box2}!RD*@{x}
  ,\ar@/^20pt/"a", \POS"a"!DR(.8)*@{+}
\end{xy}\]
```

Box1 *Box2*

Example
7-2-7

Here the current point *c* is translated to the location specified on the box [as can be seen by comparing the positions of *c before* (●) and *after* (×) applying the ! operator]. However, the "extents" of the position remain those of the box itself, as can be seen from where the curved arrow places its arrow tip. The difference between shifting and skewing highlights the essential difference between position operators and modifiers: only the former can change the current position, while the latter can be used to change the extents, adjustment, and other characteristics of the rendered object relative to the reference point at which the object is "anchored". Modifiers have no effect on the current position after the object has been dropped.

Several more commands are available to specify the vector amount of the shift or skew. We have already seen how to obtain a position based on the current object by using the vectors R (right), L (left), U (up), D (down), and combinations thereof. These vectors denote the offsets to the corners of the current (rectangular) object from the reference point; C is the offset to the center. These can be further refined using "factors"; e.g., !DR(.8) in the previous example specifies where to put the + sign (@{+}). Also useful is a specific distance in the *current direction*, as set by the most recent connection using **. The notation /3mm/ refers to the vector that is 3 mm long and oriented along the current direction. Similarly, the notation /_3mm/ has the same length but is oriented 90° clockwise of the current direction (this is how we positioned Ω in an earlier example), while /^3mm/ is the vector in the counterclockwise direction.

Among the object modifiers are some that change the size and shape of an object's bounding box (called the *edge* in Xy-pic jargon). Initially this box is the typeset size of the object itself, but it can be changed using the *grow* and *shrink* modifiers, "+" and "−". These operators add or subtract a fixed amount, called the *object margin*, to effectively create or reduce a margin of space around the object. The default value for the object margin is 3 pt, but it can easily be changed. The *set size* modifier, "=⟨*wid,ht*⟩", lets us set the width and height to any specified values. Without such a specific value, "=" is used to square the shape, i.e., equalize the width and height to the smaller of their existing values; similarly, "+=" equalizes the box size to the larger of these values. Modifiers are always interpreted sequentially, from left to right.

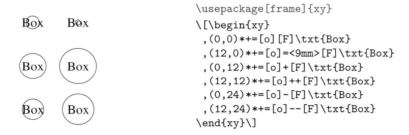

```
\usepackage[frame]{xy}
\[\begin{xy}
,(0,0)*+=[o][F]\txt{Box}
,(12,0)*+=[o]=<9mm>[F]\txt{Box}
,(0,12)*+=[o]+[F]\txt{Box}
,(12,12)*+=[o]++[F]\txt{Box}
,(0,24)*+=[o]-[F]\txt{Box}
,(12,24)*+=[o]--[F]\txt{Box}
\end{xy}\]
```

The bottom line above shows at the left the default equalized circle drawn around the object, and at the right a circle with radius set to 9 mm (more precisely, the height and width are both set to 9 mm, since <9mm> abbreviates <9mm , 9mm>). On the middle line we increase the circle's radius by the object margin, then by twice the object margin. Finally, on the top line we shrink the circle's radius by the same amounts.

7.2.4 Entering text in your pictures

The \txt object command facilitates entering text strings in Xy-pic pictures. It typesets text in centered paragraph mode, such that line breaks can be controlled with the \\ command. The syntax is

\txt ⟨*wid*⟩*sty*{*text strings*}

Both ⟨*wid*⟩, the declared width, and *sty*, the style to be used for typesetting, may be absent. Various possibilities are seen below; note the use of *opposite* vectors to obtain the same positioning by shifting and skewing. The example also illustrates how \newcommand declarations for one diagram should be made: before the xy environment, but within the outer math display, in order to ensure that those definitions have no effect on later diagrams.

```
\usepackage[frame]{xy}
\[
  \newcommand{\smbf}{\small\bfseries}  \newcommand{\smit}{\small\itshape}
  \begin{xy}
  0*=(22,14)!UR!(-10,-8)[F]\txt\smbf{center\\of box}="box";
```

```
  "box"+L*+!R\txt\small{Left\\side}
 ,"box"+R*+!L\txt\small{Right\\side}
 ,"box"+D*+!U\txt\small{Bottom side}
 ,"box"+U*+!D\txt\small{Top side}
 ,"box"+LD*@{*}*+!RU\txt<2cm>\smit{Lower left diagonal}
 ,"box"+RD*@{*}*+!LU\txt<2cm>\smit{Lower right diagonal}
 ,"box"+LU*@{*}*+!RD\txt<2cm>\smit{Upper left diagonal}
 ,"box"+RU*@{*}*+!LD\txt<2cm>\smit{Upper right diagonal}
 \end{xy}
\]
```

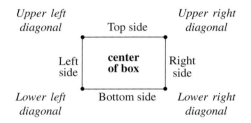

Example
7-2-9

7.3 Extensions

We have already used the frame extension, since that is where the [F] modifier is defined. By activating further extension options, other sophisticated graphics functions become available:

- The curve extension lets you draw *curves* and *splines* using quadratic or cubic Bézier curves and B-splines (see Section 7.3.1).

- The frame extension provides a convenient way to draw *frames*, *brackets*, and *filled regions* (see Section 7.3.2).

- The tips extension lets you choose the type of *arrow tip* (Computer Modern or Euler, in addition to the Xy-pic default "technical" style), while *line styles* are controlled by specifying the line extension.

- Both *rotation* and *scaling* are possible with the rotate extension. *Color* and *patterns* and *tiling* effects can be obtained using the color and tile extensions. Graphics images can be imported using the import extension.

Several of these extensions work fully only if your dvi driver supports them. By default, however, the Xy-pic package uses only standard TEX and METAFONT. Thus it produces completely standard dvi files containing references to the Xy-pic fonts. Output for a specific driver (e.g., **dvips**) can be generated by loading an appropriate *back end* option that "tunes" the output produced in the dvi file to the indicated driver (by using \special commands). This tuning does *not* extend the Xy-pic language. When no back end is available, Xy-pic tries to approximate what is requested by using, among other means, the special XY-pic fonts. In particular, the picture size is identical, so that the choice of back end can never affect the page count, or other aspects of the output.

As an example, consider the ps extension, which permits inclusion of PostScript code in XY-pictures whether or not the driver supports it (the included PostScript will work only if the driver supports it, of course). If the same file is to be LATEX'd on a different system, then the source file need not be changed (except to insert the declaration of which back end to use). With a PostScript-based back end, the XY-pic fonts are not used, since native Post-Script is generated to draw all arrows, tips, etc.[1] This improves the quality of the printed output, especially for dotted or dashed lines and curves; in addition, LATEX processing time is reduced. We do not discuss back ends further in this book; refer to the XY-pic documentation for details, including the current list of supported drivers.

7.3.1 Curves and splines

The curve extension makes it possible to draw spline curves. It allows calculation of curved connections along which objects may be dropped; when directional, the objects are aligned with the tangent direction. The basic syntax is

| \crv *setup*{*control-points*} |

where the argument *control-points* is a list of positions separated by & signs. The object really makes sense only with the connection operator **; as always, the previous and current points p and c, respectively, define the end points of the connection.

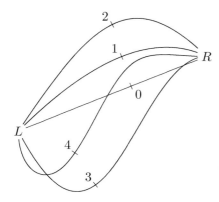

```
\usepackage[curve,frame]{xy}
\[\begin{xy}
  0*[o]+{L};(50,20)*[o]+{R}="R"
        **\crv{} ?(.6)*@{+}*^+!UL{0}
  ,"R" **\crv{(30,30)} ?*@{+}*^+!DR{1}
  ,"R" **\crv{(20,30)&(30,40)} ?*@{+}*^+!DR{2}
  ,"R" **\crv{(10,-20)&(25,-20)&(40,20)}
        ?(.4)*@{+}*^+!DR{3}
  ,"R" **\crv{(0,-10)&(12,-20)&(28,25)&(40,20)}
        ?(.4)*@{+}*^+!DR{4}
\end{xy}\]
```

Example
7-3-1

This example shows five curves, labeled from 0 to 4 to indicate the number of supplementary control points used. This number determines the type of Bézier curve used to

---

[1] The package also comes with a Type 1 version of the various XY-pic-specific fonts: these are used only when a PostScript driver is used on a dvi file produced *without* activating a PostScript back end!

connect the start (L) to the end (R) point. With one or two control points, a pure quadratic or cubic Bézier curve is drawn, with the tangents at L and R pointing along the lines connecting these points with the adjacent control point. When three or more control points are specified, then a cubic B-spline is constructed. Note the use of the ? operator to locate places along the connection; in addition to finding the correct location, it sets the "current direction" to be the tangent direction of the curve *at that point*. The small crosses, set with *@{+}, indicate that this directional object has been aligned appropriately.

It is quite simple to visualize the control points by using options along with the \crv objects.

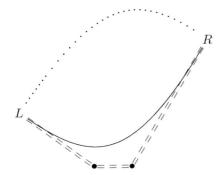

```
\usepackage[curve]{xy}
\[\begin{xy}
  0*+{L};(50,20)*+{R}
  **\crv{~*=<2mm>{.}(20,30)&(30,35)}
  **\crv~Lc{~**@{==}~*{\bullet}%
      (20,-15)&(30,-15)}
\end{xy}\]
```

Example
7-3-2

The first \crv has no optional part, but uses an object specifier ~* describing which objects should be drawn along the path. The second curve has the Lc option, specifying that the curve should be drawn together with the control points and the lines connecting them. Furthermore, the positional coordinates are preceded by connector (~**) and drop (~*) object specifiers; these determine how the control points are marked and which style to use for the connecting lines.

If you don't have a back end with built-in support for expressing curves, drawing curves can consume quite a lot of memory. In such cases it can be wise to use the command \SloppyCurves or to adjust the tolerance for typesetting the curves with the command \splinetolerance{*tol*}, whose only argument is a length *tol*. A curve is constructed as a series of closely spaced points. The value of *tol* is the minimum separation of points between which an intermediate point is not calculated—it is *not* the separation of the points themselves. This helps to explain the non-uniform spacing of objects on curves, especially dotted or dashed curves.

The minimum tolerance allowed is 0.2 pt, which is used for fine "solid" curves and is actually used if 0 pt is requested. Specifying \SloppyCurves changes *tol* to 0.8 pt.

7.3.2 Frames and brackets

The frame extension introduces commands of the type

\frm ⟨*dim*⟩{*spec*}

where *spec* is a frame specification and ⟨*dim*⟩ is an optional dimension. When the frame is "dropped" (with the * operator), then the object at the current point *c* is framed. When it is "connected" (with the ** operator), then the rectangle defined by the previous and current objects together is framed. A complete list of possible frames is given in the X~Y~-pic documentation.

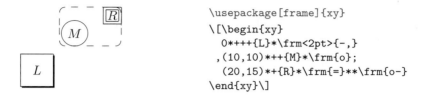

```
\usepackage[frame]{xy}
\[\begin{xy}
  0*+++{L}*\frm<2pt>{-,}
 ,(10,10)*+++{M}*\frm{o};
  (20,15)*+{R}*\frm{=}**\frm{o-}
\end{xy}\]
```

Example
7-3-3

In the picture above we drop the letter *L*, surrounding it with a rectangular shadow box of size increased by three times the object margin. At the coordinate point (10,10), we drop the letter *M* and surround it with a circular frame increased by twice the object margin. Then we transfer the current position to the *previous* position *p* (; operator) and set the current position *c* as the new coordinate (20,15). Here we drop the letter *R*, surrounded by a double rectangular frame increased by the object margin. Finally, with the connection operator **, we draw a rectangular dashed frame with rounded corners surrounding the covering rectangle defined by the objects at *c* and *p*.

```
\usepackage[frame]{xy}
\[\begin{xy}
  (0,0)*++++{L}="l";
  p+(15,10)*++++{M}**\frm{_)}% 1
              **\frm{\{}   % 2
            ;**\frm{\}}    % 3
 ,p+(15,10)*++++{R}**\frm{(} % 4
              **\frm{\}}    % 5
            ;"l"**\frm{^\}} % 6
\end{xy}\]
```

Example
7-3-4

When constructing braces using the `frame` extension, we must track the previous *p* and current *c* positions carefully. In the above example we drop the letter *L*, name the corresponding position "l", and store it as *p* (; operator). Then we use *p* to calculate the coordinates of a new object *M*. Next we link the objects *c* and *p* by a lower bracket (at "1") and a left-hand brace (at "2"). We then exchange *p* and *c* so that *M* becomes *p* and *L* becomes *c*. Next we draw the right-hand brace. Note in particular how the nibble of the brace is aligned for the cases "2" and "3". Next we move up to point *R*, which now becomes *c*, and we draw first a left-hand parenthesis (at "4") and then a right-hand brace (at "5") linking *M* and *R*. Once again using the ; operator, we make object *R* the "previous" *p* and retrieve the saved position "l" of *L*, which becomes "current" *c*. This lets us finally draw the top brace (at "6").

As a special convenience, rather than separately dropping a frame after an object via *\frm ⟨dim⟩{spec}, you can obtain the same effect using the object modifier [F spec:⟨dim⟩], or just [F spec] when no ⟨dim⟩ is specified. The simplest variant [F] corresponds to *\frm{-}, since this is the choice most frequently desired.

7.4 Features

The XY-pic package comes with an interesting and quite complete set of add-ons that extend XY-pic for particular application domains. These "features" must be loaded as needed. The present version of XY-pic provides functionality in the following areas:

- *Arrows.* Draw simple and segmented arrows with configurable marks and labels (Section 7.4.1).
- *Matrices.* Construct two-dimensional matrix-like layouts, in which an object may be addressed by its row and column identifier or by "hops" along the grid from another object (Section 7.4.2).
- *Graphs.* Draw directed graphs, flowcharts, trees, etc. (Section 7.4.3).
- *Two-cells.* Typeset "categorical two-cell" diagrams containing pairs of (labeled) curved arrows (Section 7.4.4).
- *Polygons.* Specify the positions of the vertices of regular polygons (Section 7.4.5).
- *Circles, ellipses, and arcs.* Construct (parts of) circles and ellipses with their minor and major axes aligned in any direction (Section 7.4.6).
- *Lattices and webs.* Draw objects on the regular arrangement of a two-dimensional lattice (Section 7.4.7).
- *Knots and links.* Draw and label knot-like and link-like structures (Section 7.4.8).

7.4.1 Arrows

The construction of "pretty"arrows was at the very heart of XY-pic's original development, as its author wrote [105]: "Our first task [with XY-pic] is to design an arrow such that it looks nice even when very long…"

The arrow feature is automatically loaded with the all option. In fact, many other extensions depend on this extension, so this feature is automatically loaded by them as well. Arrows are implemented as an extension of connections to permit an explicit *tail, stem,* and *head*. As arrows occur in many places, a simple and convenient syntax is available to typeset them, which is initiated by the \ar command. We limit ourselves here to a few simple examples. The versatility of the arrow feature will become more apparent later when we describe the matrix and knot features.

Generally speaking, the style of an arrow is customized with the help of the @ character. The braced part specifies the tail, stem, and head to be used. Preceding this, the characters ^, _, 0, 1, 2, and 3 stand, respectively, for the above, below, invisible, single, doubled, and tripled variants, as shown in the next example (note the absence in the center of the \ar@0 instance).

```
\usepackage[arrow]{xy}
\[\begin{xy}
  (0,-20)="a", (0,0)="b"
  \ar@{<.||}  @<24mm>  "a";"b" \ar@^{<.||} @<16mm>  "a";"b"
  \ar@_{<.||} @<8mm>   "a";"b" \ar@0{<.||}           "a";"b"
  \ar@1{<.||} @<-8mm>  "a";"b" \ar@2{<.||} @<-16mm> "a";"b"
  \ar@3{<.||} @<-24mm> "a";"b"
\end{xy}\]
```

The following example, combining syntax already introduced, shows several useful variations (the `curve` and `frame` extensions and the `arrow` feature must be loaded).

```
\usepackage[curve,arrow,frame]{xy}
\[\begin{xy} <1cm,0cm>:
              (0,0)*+@{*}="a"*+!DL{\mathrm{A}},"a"
\ar@(dr,dl)
\ar@{~>}      (2,0)*+@{*}="b"*+!DR{\mathrm{B}},"b"
\ar@(r,d)     "b";"b"
\ar@{<->}     "b";(2,2)*+@{*}="c"*+!UR{\mathrm{C}},"c"
\ar@(u,r)     "c";"c" |*=<2pt>[o][F]{}
\ar@(ul,dr)   "c"; (0,2)*+@{*}="d"*+!U{\mathrm{D}},"d"
\ar@(ul,ur)   "d";"d"
\ar@{.>}@`{(-0.8,1.5),(0.,1.0),(-0.8,0.5)} "d";
\end{xy}\]
```

After setting the coordinate system base unit to 1 cm and dropping the vertex A (named "a" using the = operator), we typeset several arrows. Like connections, arrows are typeset from *p* to *c* as determined by the position following the arrow. Both default to the current position *c* before the arrow: this is exploited by the first \ar command to draw a loop, i.e., an arrow leaving and reentering A. The outgoing and incoming directions of a loop are indicated using @(<dir>,<dir>), where <dir> represents a *direction*, combining at most one of d and u with at most one of l and r (other forms are described in the XY-pic documentation). Next we draw a "variant" arrow from A to a bullet at (2,0) with label B and name "b". Notice how the typesetting of the label relative to B is "hidden" with the comma operator so as explicitly to make the final *c* be "b" and not the label. We make a second loop arrow, this time from the explicitly specified "b" to itself, followed by a double arrow to C with yet another loop, this one "broken" in the middle by a 2 pt circle (typeset with *=<2pt>[o][F]{}). The next arrow, linking C to D at (0,2), is a "curved arrow" with specified tangent directions at either end. To finish, we draw another curved arrow, this time specifying control points explicitly, with the notation @`{cp, cp, ...}, where each cp is the position of a control point.

Parsing of the position specifying the arrow target (and, if ; is used, also the source), continues as long as possible. As in Example 7-4-2, the resulting current position *c* is the ultimate target, although other objects may have been typeset along the way; similarly, the resulting *p*, which defaults to the position before the arrow, is the ultimate source. The parser stops when it encounters a macro name such as \relax, \ar, \endxy, or \end, or at a label or break character (one of ^, _, or |), unless this character is absorbed as an argument of another operator (as in the \mathrm command in the example). After an \ar command is finished, however, what follows is *not* interpreted as a position. To achieve this the special \POS macro should be used, as we will see in later examples.

Finally, an arrow can be composed as a path of several segments, separated by ' or ' depending on whether they should be joined directly or by circle "turns". Each segment can have its own set of labels and breaks along the straight portion.

```
\usepackage[arrow]{xy}
\[\begin{xy} <6mm,0mm>:
  (0,0)*+\txt\small{Origin}="0"
  \ar@{.>>}
    'r  (3,2) *\dir{*}*+!DL{\mathrm{P_1}}  ^-1
    '     (-2,2)*\dir{*}*+!U{\mathrm{P_2}}  ^2
    '_dr(-2,0)*\dir{*}*+!U{\mathrm{P_3}}  _(.3)3
    'dr^r "0"                              _(.8)4
          "0"                             ^-(.2)5
\end{xy}\]
```

Example
7-4-3

In this example we start at the position labeled "Origin" (identifier "0"), set off to the right, and then turn towards point "P_1". Once XY-pic is given the point "P_2", it knows it is to move up and to the left (note the constructed quarter circles). Looking at the double arrow tips and the labels 1–5 shows the construction of the different line segments. To make things a little more interesting, we specify that we want to go back to the origin at "0" by going down and to the right—first turning clockwise (the three-quarter circle at the upper-left corner), and then going via "P_3" from the northwest to the east (right).

We have placed the labels using positioning "factors" that indicate the amount along the straight section where the label is to be dropped. In particular, "3" and "4" are placed 30% and 80% of the way along their respective straight sections. With no factor explicitly given, "2" uses the default 0.5. The minus sign in "1" and "5" is a useful device that tells XY-pic to calculate the label position as a factor along the "visible portion" of the straight segment, by excluding the edges of the source and target positions. Thus "5" is typeset 20% along the visible part of the final straight segment and "1" is halfway along its visible section—the default again is 0.5. Using the – sign is particularly appropriate when either the source or the target position is of significant size (as in Example 7-4-3).

7.4.2 Matrix-like diagrams

The matrix feature is a powerful tool for typesetting diagrams with a regular "matrix-like" structure (indeed, the initial release of XY-pic contained just the functionality of the arrow and matrix features). The format of the command is

> \xymatrix *setup*{*entries*}

The *setup* part can contain switches, shapes, decorations, and so on to be applied to every entry. The argument *entries* is the description of the text or objects to occupy the *cells* of the

matrix. These cells are positioned in *columns*, separated by &, and in *rows*, separated by \\.
Each cell can contain arbitrary Xy-pic decorations, with the current state c set to the matrix
entry in question. In particular, this means that the cell is the source for \ar commands
within that cell. The complete matrix is also an Xy-pic object with a reference point at the
top-left cell. Since * has a special function, the asterisk character must be entered between
curly braces {*} if it is to be the first character in a cell. The simple example in Section 7.1
illustrates most of these ideas.

Given that most of the *Xy-pic User's Guide* [106] describes the matrix feature, here we
merely look at examples that illustrate some finer points.

Commutative diagrams

The \xymatrix command is very useful for drawing commutative diagrams, a mathematical construct where arrows in different paths between two objects compose to the same
arrow. Many authors have developed ad hoc TEX packages for dealing with such diagrams.
James Milne gives an up-to-date list of the better-known packages.[1] It is a useful complement to the review article [123], where 10 different TEX packages for typesetting commutative diagrams are compared. We use here the first example of the Feruglio paper as the basis
of our own example.[2] The example assumes that both the tips extension and the arrow
feature are also loaded.

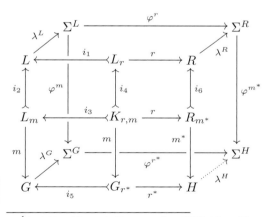

```
\usepackage[arrow,matrix,tips]{xy}
\[\UseTips
\newdir{ >}{!/-5pt/\dir{>}}
\xymatrix @=1pc @*[r] {
  & \Sigma^L \ar[rrrr]^{\varphi^r}
          \ar'[d]'[ddd]_{\varphi^m}[dddd]
  & & & & \Sigma^R \ar[dddd]^{\varphi^{m^*}}
  \\ L   \ar[ur]^{\lambda^L}
  & & L_r \ar@{ >->}[ll]_(.32){i_1} \ar[rr]^r
  & & R \ar[ur]_{\lambda^R}
  \\ \\ L_m \ar@{ >->}[uu]^{i_2} \ar[dd]_m
      & & K_{r,m} \ar@{ >->}[ll]_(.3){i_3}
          \ar@{ >->}[uu]_{i_4}
          \ar[dd]_<<<<m \ar[rr]^r
      & & R_{m^*} \ar@{ >->}[uu]_{i_6}
\ar[dd]_<<<<{m^*}
  \\ & \Sigma^G
          \ar'[r]'[rrr]_{\varphi^{r^*}}[rrrr]
      & & & & \Sigma^H
  \\ G \ar[ur]^(.7){\lambda^G}
      & & G_{r^*} \ar@{ >->}[ll]^{i_5}
          \ar[rr]_{r^*}
      & & H \ar@{.>}[ur]_{\lambda^H}
}\]
```

---

[1] See http://www.jmilne.org/tex/CDGuide.pdf.

[2] We recoded the Xy-pic version as given in his appendix, since his code was based on version 2 of Xy-pic. Our
code, based on version 3, is more readable and complete, and uses a more homogeneous notation.

First we add with \newdir a variant of the @{>} tip that is moved a bit so as to make a better arrow tail. The rest is just a matrix designed to have entries at all "interesting" locations. Note how the quote character ' is used to specify that an arrow should go via certain cells, passing "below" another arrow (without inserting "turns", as with the backquote character '). For instance, to produce the arrow pointing down from node Σ^L, we use that notation for the relative number of "hops" to refer to the nodes one ('[d]) and three ('[ddd]) rows below the current one. We use similar code to make the arrow to the right of Σ^G pass below the arrows at cells one ('[r]) and three ('[rrr]) hops to the right. The <<<< and (0.xx) notation lets you fine-tune the placement of the text associated with the arrows by specifying how far from the start point of the arrow the material should appear. The latter form is especially useful, since it allows you to take into account small differences in the lengths of the arrows due to slightly wider elements, so that the typeset material can be aligned with great precision. Also notice the three *setup* parameters: @=1pc forces the spacing *between* columns to be 1 pc; @*[r] imposes the adjustment [r] on all entries, which is aesthetically pleasing since all entries contain one uppercase letter with varying subscripts and superscripts.

Michael Barr has recently reimplemented his **diagram** package as an add-on to XY-pic. This new package, **diagxy**, builds on the \xymatrix construct but introduces a more uniform and higher-level syntax for many cases. The package introduces the arrow drawing function \morphism, which is used to define common diagram shapes (e.g., squares, triangles with a variety of orientations), and a few compound diagrams (e.g., cubes).

The general structure of a command in **diagxy** is as follows:[1]

> \morphism(*x,y*)|*placement*|/*shape*/<*dx,dy*>[*N'N;L*]

Only the last argument is required, and it corresponds to the source and target nodes of the arrow (before the semicolon) and its label. The argments *x* and *y* and *x+dx* and *y+dy* are the location of the source and target nodes (in units of, by default, 0.01 em). The *placement* argument is either a (above), b (below), l (left), r (right), or m (middle) and defines where the label is to be placed on the arrow. The *shape* argument describes the shape of the arrow (using XY-pic syntax).

Square diagrams are conveniently typeset with the \square command, as in the following example.

```
\usepackage{diagxy}
\[\bfig
  \square/>>'>'>' >->/[X_1'X_2'X_3'X_4;a'b'c'd]
  \morphism(500,500)|m|/.>/<-500,-500>[X_2'X_3;z]
\efig\]
```

Example 7-4-5

The various components of the geometric element—in this case the four vertices of the square—are separated by ' signs. The first part of the command specifies the shape of

---

[1] **diagxy** markup is set in math mode and bracketed inside \bfig and \efig commands, which are equivalent to being inside an xy environment.

the four arrows (using XY-pic conventions). Between the square brackets are the labels of the vertices and the sides. The \morphism command draws a dotted arrow from the upper-right corner ("X_2") to the lower-left corner ("X_3") and places the label "z"in its middle. Squares can be combined vertically and horizontally.

A square with different kinds of sides is readily drawn.

```
\usepackage{diagxy}
\[\bfig
  \square/@3{->}'`~)'=o`--x/[X_1`X_2`X_3`X_4;1`2`3`4]
  \place(400,100)[\twoar(-1,-1)]
  \place(100,400)[\twoar(1,1)]
  \morphism(500,500)||/{*}.{*}/<-500,-500>[X_2`X_3;]
\efig\]
```

The various kinds of arrows are specified in the first argument of the \square command. The \place command is similar to LATEX's \put and places its contents at the given coordinate. The \twoar command draws a double arrow with a slope indicated by its argument.

Annotations on vertices and sides are easily added with the \Square command, which figures out its own width. Hence only the vertical displacement dy (<350> in the example) needs to be specified.

```
\usepackage{diagxy,amsmath}
\DeclareMathOperator\Hom{Hom}
\DeclareMathOperator\Sub{Sub}
\[\bfig
  \Square/^{ (}->'>'>'^{ (}->/<350>%
    [\Hom(X,2^Y)`\Sub(X\times Y)`
     \Hom(X',2^{Y'})`\Sub(X'\times Y');
     \alpha(X,Y)```\alpha(X',Y')]
\efig\]
```

We note the use of `^{ (}->` in the first argument to construct the inclusion arrow, where we added some extra space before the hook. The amsmath package is loaded to define the math operators \Hom and \Sub in the preamble; we then use these operators in the diagram.

Various primitive commands for constructing trangle diagrams are available. The next example shows the combination of a pair of triangles in a "V" form.

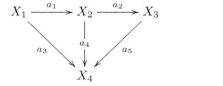

```
\usepackage{diagxy}
\[\bfig
  \Vtrianglepair[X_1`X_2`X_3`X_4;%
                 a_1`a_2`a_3`a_4`a_5]
\efig\]
```

Example 7-4-6

Example 7-4-7

Example 7-4-8

Squares and triangles can be easily combined to create more complex diagrams. A special kind of diagram is the "pullback", which is created as follows.

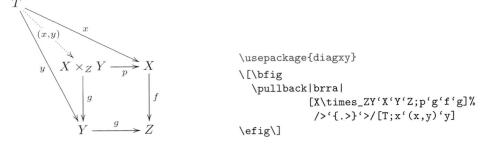

```
\usepackage{diagxy}
\[\bfig
  \pullback|brra|
           [X\times_ZY`X`Y`Z;p`g`f`g]%
           />`{.>}`>/[T;x`(x,y)`y]
\efig\]
```

Example
7-4-9

In homology one often encounters 3×3 and 3×2 diagrams. They are typeset with the \iiixiii and \iiixii commands, respectively, whose default behavior is displayed in the following examples. The usual order for the arrow parameters is first all horizontal arrows and then all vertical ones, left to right, and then top to bottom.

```
\usepackage{diagxy}
$\bfig \iiixiii[A`B`C`D`E`F`G`H`I; 1`2`3`4`5`6`7`8`9`10`11`12] \efig$
\quad
$\bfig \iiixii[A`B`C`D`E`F; 1`2`3`4`5`6`7] \efig$
```

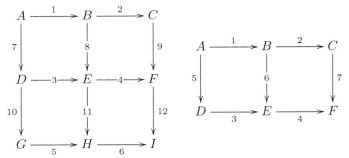

Example
7-4-10

A more interesting example of a 3×2 diagram is the following, where we add annotations (text and matrices) to the arrows. The placement of the arrow labels is specified with the first argument. Recall the order in which the arrow characteristics should be specified (see Example 7-4-10). We also load the amsmath package since we use the pmatrix environment.

```
\usepackage{diagxy,amsmath}
\[\bfig
 \iiixii|aaaalmr|<1000,800>
        [X`Y`Z`X\oplus X_0`Y\oplus X_0\oplus Z_0`Z\oplus Z_0;
         f_1`f_2`\begin{pmatrix}f_1&0\\0&1\\0&0\end{pmatrix}`
              \begin{pmatrix}f_2&0&0\\0&0&1\end{pmatrix}`
```

```
\begin{pmatrix}1\\0\end{pmatrix}`
\begin{pmatrix}1\\0\\0\end{pmatrix}`
\begin{pmatrix}1\\0\end{pmatrix}]
\efig\]
```

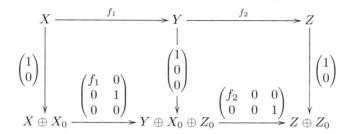

Example
7-4-11

Finite-state and stack diagrams

Finite-state diagrams can also be typeset in a straightforward way:

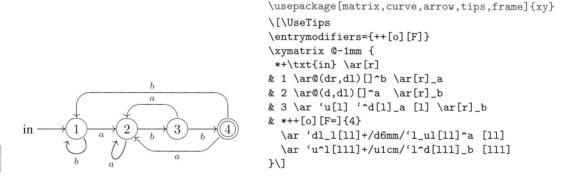

```
\usepackage[matrix,curve,arrow,tips,frame]{xy}
\[\UseTips
\entrymodifiers={++[o][F]}
\xymatrix @-1mm {
 *+\txt{in} \ar[r]
& 1 \ar@(dr,dl)[]^b \ar[r]_a
& 2 \ar@(d,dl)[]^a  \ar[r]_b
& 3 \ar `u[l] `^d[l]_a [l] \ar[r]_b
& *++[o][F=]{4}
  \ar `dl_l[ll]+/d6mm/`l_ul[ll]^a [ll]
  \ar `u^l[lll]+/u1cm/`l^d[lll]_b [lll]
}\]
```

Example
7-4-12

In this kind of diagram,[1] all states (elements) are enclosed in circles; here we use the `\entrymodifiers` command to specify the default modifier to realize this goal. To get nice arrowheads on the end of curves, we use Computer Modern tips. To keep the diagram a little more compact, we reduce the interelement spacing by 1 mm (`@-1mm` before the opening brace of the `\xymatrix` command). Starting an entry with an asterisk (i.e., using the form *⟨*object*⟩*) overrides the default settings from `\entrymodifiers`; this feature is used in the leftmost cell to eliminate the frame and in the rightmost cell to typeset a double circle. Note that in the latter case the complete modifier specification had to be given. The only other tricky bit is the use of displacements towards the exterior, which add 6 mm (for a) and 1 cm (for b) in establishing the locations of the turns.

---

[1] We based our example on the deterministic finite automaton diagram in [7, p. 136]; another representation of the same diagram can be found in [106, Section 3.4], and we also used it for Example 3-4-10 on p. 79.

As a final example, we draw stack diagrams with pointers.

```
\usepackage[matrix,arrow,frame]{xy}
\newcommand\topbar{\vrule height 0.4pt width 20mm}
\newcommand\previous{% turning-width of 15mm
  \save\ar'r[u]+/r15mm/'[u][u]\restore }
\newcommand\saved[2]{\txt{#1\\\emph{saved} $d[#2]$\\}}
\newcommand\bendto[2]{% creates a bendy arrow, offset 5mm
  \save c!C+/r5mm/\ar 'r#1!C+/l#2/ '^r#1!C #1!C\restore}
\newcommand\dinput[1]{% label-offset 11mm
  \save +/l11mm/*{d[#1]}\restore}
\[\begin{xy}
\xymatrix"R" @M=0mm @H=12mm @W=20mm @R=0mm @*[F] {%
 {\txt{\topbar\\s\\\\ }}    %1,1
\\ \saved{A}{2}             %2,1
\\ \saved{B}{2}\previous    %3,1
\\ \saved{C}{3}             %4,1
}\turnradius{2mm}\POS(-30,+4)
\xymatrix @M=0mm @H=5mm @W=12mm @R=0mm @*[F] {%
   \dinput{1}\bendto{"R1,1"}{15mm}   %1,1
\\ \dinput{2}\bendto{"R3,1"}{17mm}   %2,1
\\ \dinput{3}\bendto{"R4,1"}{19mm}   %3,1
}
\end{xy}\]
```

Example
7-4-13

We build up the picture using two \xymatrix commands, with text or labels on some entries. Arrows between entries are specified as *excursions* that use previously defined positions and are enclosed within \save...\restore pairs so as not to affect the layout of the subsequent matrix entries. Placing the right-hand stack first and assigning it the name "R" lets us access its cells as positions while the left-hand stack is being built; indeed, some of those cells are used as targets for arrows starting from the left-hand stack. For precise control on object positioning within each \xymatrix, we first kill the object margin (@M=0mm) and row separation (@R=0mm) as part of the matrix *setup*. Furthermore, we choose exact cell heights (@H=...) and widths (@W=...) appropriately and specify a frame (@*[F]) to appear around each entry.

Since the same types of structures are needed with different matrix entries, it is appropriate to define macros for these cases. Not only does this shorten the code by avoiding the repetition of long constructions, but it also facilitates making consistent changes if they are needed. In addition, macros help keep the main body of code tidy by shifting the details elsewhere; if chosen wisely, the macro name can signify its intent. Thus macro \saved places the contents of three cells from the right-hand stack, changing just two characters in each instance. The topmost cell is a little different, having an extra line created by expanding the macro \topbar. Also, the extra arrow from the third cell ("R3,1") to the second cell ("R2,1") is given as a \save...\restore excursion after expanding the macro \previous. The appearance of this turning arrow is controlled with the help of the 15 mm displacement in 'r[u]+/r15mm/.

Now we turn our attention to the left-hand stack, which is placed at the location with coordinates (-30,4). Reducing the \turnradius to 2 mm (from its default 10 pt) allows tighter turns. Again, sizes and margins are set as part of the matrix *setup*. The \dinput macro places each input label as an excursion translated a fixed amount to the left (+/111mm/). Each arrow to the right-hand stack is built by specifying its target cell (e.g., "R4,1") and a displacement from its center determining where the bends occur (e.g., 15 mm). The code of \bendto builds the appropriate arrow from this information.

7.4.3 Graphs

Flowcharts, directed graphs, trees, and other structured mathematical representations can be drawn with the graph feature, which implements a combinatorial drawing paradigm somewhat similar to the pic language. The graph feature depends on the arrow feature, which is always loaded with it. The syntax is

```
\xygraph{graphdesc}
```

where *graphdesc* describes the various components of the graph. The & operator puts objects into columns. Unlike with the matrix feature, there is no extra alignment or spacing of the objects.

The basic principle is to draw a line or arrow from a *current* node to a *target* node, after which the target becomes the current node. The basic operators are - and : for drawing a line and an arrow, respectively. These operators are followed by arrow, node, and label specifiers, if required. An example will make this clearer:

$$L \xleftarrow{\hspace{1cm}} M_1 \xrightarrow{\hspace{1cm}} M^2 \mid\cdots\cdots\!> R$$

```
\usepackage[graph,curve]{xy}
\[\xygraph{
[]L :@/_/ [r]{M_1} :@/^/ [r]{M^2}
    :@{|.>}[r]R    :@/_1em/"L"
}\]
```

We start by defining a point L and giving it a symbolic label "L", since we want to reference it later. Then, we construct three small arrows connecting the points L, M_1, M^2, and R with various types of arrows. Finally, we draw a long arrow pointing back from R to L, using the reference "L", which automatically refers to the most recent node containing just an L.

A convenient syntax for tree branching is ⟨*parent*⟩(⟨*child*⟩,...,...⟨*child*⟩): each ⟨*child*⟩ graph is typeset as if it came directly after ⟨*parent*⟩. The following example includes two lists, one at the top from node 1 and one at the second level from node 12.

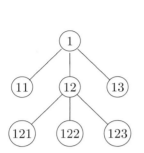

```
\usepackage[graph,frame]{xy}
\[\xygraph{
[] *+[o]+[F]{1}
  (-[dl] *+=[o]+[F]{11}
  ,-[d]  *+=[o]+[F]{12}
    (-[dl] *+=[o]+[F]{121}
    ,-[d]  *+=[o]+[F]{122}
    ,-[dr] *+=[o]+[F]{123}
    )
  ,-[dr] *+=[o]+[F]{13}
  )
}\]
```

Example
7-4-15

The example also shows that any Xy-pic object can be dropped at a node, as usual, by the * operator. Indeed, the ! escape makes it possible to introduce *any* Xy-pic kernel construction, placed in {}, after a given node; we use this technique in the following two examples. We present two "mini-packages" developed by the authors of the Xy-pic package for drawing neural networks and logic diagrams; together these illustrate most capabilities of the graph option. Both rely on the \newgraphescape command to define new types of objects, denoted !⟨*letter*⟩, in graphs.

Let us first look at Ross Moore's approach to typesetting neural network diagrams. He uses a structured-programming paradigm, guided by the principle that the higher-level objects the user must manipulate should look familiar. To illustrate this approach, we chose a simple diagram of the *feed-forward* type (so called because the neurons in each layer contribute to the input of the neurons in the next layer):

```
\usepackage[all,dvips]{xy}
\newcommand\Neuron[1]{\POS*+=<1em>[o]+[F]{#1}}
\newcommand\Link[1]{\ar @{-} "#1"}
\newcommand\Out{\ar +/r8mm/}
\newcommand\In{\save +/19mm/*{}\ar +/r5mm/\restore}
\newgraphescape{O}[1]{!{\Neuron{#1}="#1"\Out}}
\newgraphescape{H}[1]{!{\Neuron{#1}="#1"\Link{A}\Link{B}}}
\newgraphescape{I}[1]{!{\Neuron{#1}\In\Link{a}\Link{b}\Link{c}}}
\[\xygraph{!{0;<18mm,0mm>:<0mm,10mm>::}
  [] !O{A}        [d] !O{B}
  [dd]*[left]!U[F]\txt<12mm>{output\\layer}="T"
"A" [u(.5)l]!H{a}
     [d]!H{b}      [d]!H{c}
"T" [l] *[left]!U[F]\txt<12mm>{hidden\\layer}
```

```
"a" [ul]!I{t_1}     [d]  !I{t_2}     [d]  !I{t_3}
     [d]  !I{t_4}     [d]  !I{t_5}
"T"[ll]  *[left]!U[F]\txt<12mm>{input\\layer}
}\]
```

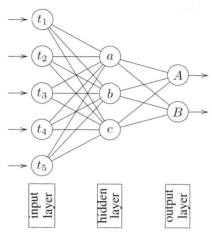

Example
7-4-16

First we define some macros, using names reminiscent of those for the actual neural networks being described. Use of these names in subsequent \xygraph allows us to specify the logical structure of the components in the diagram while hiding the details of the lower-level Xʏ-pic implementation. The command \newgraphescape permits new types of nodes to be recognized, following the ! character. These "node-macros" can even take arguments, as in Example 7-4-16.

After defining the unit vectors for the two base directions, we place the elements of the neural network. Moving from right to left, we first encounter object A on top of B (created by !O), both with a right arrow pointing away from the main part of the diagram. This is called the *output layer*. Then we have three objects a, b, and c (created by !H), all connected to A and B, in an intermediate layer called the *hidden layer*. Finally, we arrive at the *input layer* (using !I) with labels of type t_i.

When executing the code in Example 7-4-16, the two uses of the node macro !O define the labels "A" and "B", which are referenced by the three !H-nodes, which themselves define the labels "a", "b", and "c". These, in turn, are referenced by the five !I commands to draw links between all elements of the input and hidden layers. To typeset the text vertically, we use the [left] specifier, which is part of the rotate extension and requires a PostScript driver.

It should be evident from this description that these or similar commands can be used in a generic way to typeset all kinds of diagrams featuring neural circuits.

Our second mini-package is a command, \circuit, for typesetting logical circuit diagrams. The components we consider are nand (negated-and) and inverter gates, denoted by !N and !I, respectively. These are defined in the Xʏ-pic spirit of being *independent of the current direction*; however, only one direction, !R (for "right") is set up and used. A gate is placed with its output at the current location. It must have a name, which is used for later reference; in addition, the inputs are given names with suffixes a and b. Notice in the two sample circuits below how few of the gates are placed absolutely—this kind of specification is very modular.

```
\usepackage[graph,curve,arc]{xy}
\newgraphescape{N}[1]{!{\save-/4mm/-/4pt/;p+/4mm/:
    (-1,1);(-1,-1)**@{-} ?(.25)="N#1a" ?(.75)="N#1b",
    (-1,1);(0,1)**@{-} ; (0,-1),{\ellipse_{}} ; (-1,-1)**@{-},
    (0,0);(1,0)**{}*!E\cir<2pt>{}!C-E="N#1"\restore \POS"N#1"}}
\newgraphescape{I}[1]{!{\save-/4mm/-/2pt/;p+/4mm/:
    (-1,1);(-1,-1)**@{-} ?="I#1a",  (-1,1);(.667,0)**@{-};(-1,-1)**@{-},
    (0,0);**{}*!E\cir<2pt>{}!C-E="I#1"\restore \POS"I#1"}}
\newgraphescape{B}{!{*=0@{*}}}
\newgraphescape{R}{!{;p+/r4mm/**{};}}
\newgraphescape{p}[2]{[#1!{"#2";p+/^/}]}
\newcommand\circuit[1]{\xygraph{~{0;<10mm,0mm>:<0mm,9mm>::0}#1}}
\[\begin{array}{c}
\circuit{  []!R!N1 ("N1a"([l]x - ?), "N1b"([l]y - ?))
 [r]!I2 ("N1" - "I2a") - [r]{x\land y}}\\
\circuit{  []x
 [rrr]!R!I1 ("I1a"("x" - ?))
  [drr]!R!N1 ("I1" -'r[d]'"N1a""N1a", "N1b"!plx y - "N1b")
 "I1"[dddd]!R!I2 ("I2a"[l]!puy!B - 'd"I2a""I2a")
 "N1"[dd]!R!N2 ("I1a"[l(.5)]!pux!B -'d"N2a""N2a", "I2" -'r[u]'"N2b""N2b")
  [urr]!R!N3 ("N1" -'r[d]'"N3a""N3a", "N2" -'r[u]'"N3b""N3b")
  - [r]{x\mathrel{\textrm{xor}}y}}
\end{array}\]
```

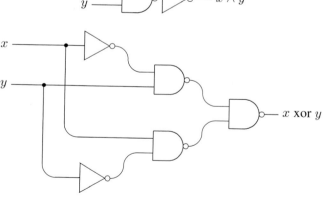

Example
7-4-17

We use a kernel code protected within \save...\restore to set up a local coordinate system reflecting the current direction when the gate is placed; we use the \ellipse command (see Section 7.4.6) to make the round part of nand gates independent of the chosen direction. Also notice that arrows with turns using ` are permitted.

Two packages have been developed for use on top of Xɏ-pic to generate diagrams that are often found in linguistics:[1] Ralf Vogel's **xyling** and Koaungli Un's **xytree**. Both packages let you draw syntactic and other trees. To give you a glimpse of the possibilities of those packages, we show a number of examples courtesy of the package authors. For in-depth information, consult the package documentation.

Graphs for linguistics

The first two trees are drawn with the **xyling** package, which provides a set of macros intended to facilitate the tree generation within the XɏY-pic framework. Note the possibility of highlighting parts of the tree in color.

```
\usepackage{xyling}
\Tree{ & & \K[5.2]{S}\Bkk{5.2,0}{0,0}{dl}\Bkk{5.2,0}{0,0}{drr}    \\
       &\NP\TRi                 &&       & \VP                     \\
       & \K{\emph{my beloved}}
         \Below{\emph{wife}}     &&\Vzero   &&\NP\TRi[2]           \\
       &                         &&\T{likes}&&\K{\emph{our old house}} }
\qquad
\Tree{ & \IP                                                       \\
   \NP  &         & \Ibar                                          \\
\T{John}&\Izero\D&        & \Kblue{VP}\Bblue{dl}\Bblue{dr}         \\
       &\Trace  &\Kblue{V$^{0}$}\Bblue{d}               && \Kblue{NP} \\
       &        &\Kblue[6]{V+INFL}\Linkblue[<-]{lu}&& \T{Mary}    \\
       &        &\T{loves}                            }
```

Example
7-4-18

Our next example is done with **xytree**. Connection lines are specified in the optional argument to `\xynode` and `\yynode` as relative moves from the current node to the nodes on the next level. At the left we reproduce the syntactical tree at the right of Example 7-4-18

---

[1] The Web page "Tree drawing in LʌTEX" (http://www.essex.ac.uk/linguistics/clmt/ latex4ling) maintained by Doug Arnold lists a number of excellent LʌTEX packages and other tools for linguists.

to show how this package approaches the task. At the right we construct a hierarchical tree. The optional argument [1,4] of the node grandparents connects to the row ma & pa directly under the current node and to the fifth row uncle & aunt (fourth row from the current node) with a line. Similarly, [1,2] connects the ma & pa node to the two following nodes.

```
\usepackage{xytree}
\xytree{
              & \xynode[1,-1]{IP}                                        \\
\xynode[0]{NP} &                    & \xynode[-1,1]{I$^\prime$}           \\
\xyterminal{John}
              & \xynode[0]{I$^0$} &           & \xynode[-1,1]{VP}        \\
              & \xynode{t$_i$}\xyconnect[->][_2pc](LD,L){1,1}
                                   & \xynode[0]{V$^{0}$}
                                   &       & \xynode[0]{NP}  \\
              &                   &\xynode[0]{V+INFL}
                                   &       & \xyterminal{Mary}\\
              &                   &\xyterminal{loves}
}
\qquad
\yytree{
\yynode[1,4]{grandparents}    \\
 & \yynode[1,2]{ma \& pa}     \\
 &   & \yynode{brother}       \\
 &   & \yynode{sister}        \\
 & \yynode[1]{uncle \& aunt}  \\
 &   & \yynode{cousin}
}
```

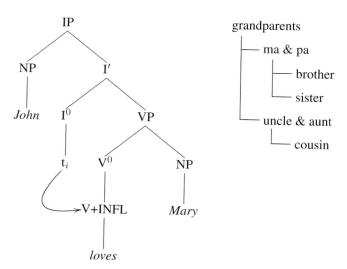

Example
7-4-19

7.4.4 Two-cell diagrams

In category theory, one often encounters "two-cell" morphisms that use pairs of curved arrows labeled on or between the arrows. The 2cell feature is available to typeset such diagrams.

The simplest two-cell diagram looks like this:

Example
7-4-20

$$L \overset{u}{\underset{d}{\Downarrow}} R$$

```
\usepackage[all,2cell]{xy}
\UseTwocells
\[
\xymatrix{L\rtwocell^u_d & R}
\]
```

Most category diagrams have an overall matrix-like structure, and hence we use the \xymatrix command. Since not all the commands available for typesetting two-cell components are always required, it is more efficient to load only those subsets that are actually needed. In particular, declaring \UseTwocells defines commands of the type \⟨cc⟩twocell; thus Example 7-4-20 uses \rtwocell to produce arrows pointing to the right. A maximum of three "hops" (l, r, u, and d) can be specified as part of the command name; beyond this the \xtwocell command is available (see Example 7-4-21).

In Example 7-4-20 we loaded only the commands associated with symmetric two-branch cells consisting of two curves. To typeset single-curve portions of two-cell diagrams, you should specify \UseHalfTwocells (defining commands of the type \⟨cc⟩uppertwocell and \⟨cc⟩lowertwocell). More complex (asymmetric) constructs are possible with the \UseCompositeMaps command (for commands of the type \⟨cc⟩compositemap). When you specify \UseAllTwocells, all available types are loaded. These commands need be issued only once, usually within the preamble to the LaTeX document. In the examples that follow, the \UseAllTwocells command is shown outside of the math display, to serve as a reminder only; it is not part of the diagram itself.

The next example illustrates the different commands and some of their options.

Example
7-4-21

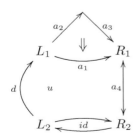

```
\usepackage[all,2cell]{xy}
\UseAllTwocells
\[
\xymatrix @=15mm {
  L_1 \rlowertwocell<-3>_{a_1}{<-1>}
      \rcompositemap<6>_{a_2}^{a_3}{\omit}
& R_1 \dtwocell<0>_{a_4}{""}
\\ L_2 \uuppertwocell_u^d{\omit}
      \rtwocell<2>{'id}
&  R_2
  }\]
```

As we want to exercise all possible forms of the two-cell diagram , we use the command \UseAllTwocells; we also set the row and column separations to 15 mm. The amount of curvature of the curved arrows is controlled using a "nudge" factor of the form *<nb>*, i.e., a number between triangular brackets. For the lower arrow (going from L_1 to R_1), the nudge factor <-3> reduces the curvature to about half the default. To position the double arrow correctly, we nudge it back by one unit (<-1>). Next we draw a composite arrow, going six units (<6>) higher than the default, and omit the central arrow (\omit). For the second cell R_1, we draw a vertical arrow downwards—the nudge factor zero (<0>) corresponds to a straight arrow and suppresses printing of the central double arrow. In this case, we have produced arrowheads pointing in both directions by specifying a double quote (") as the first character in the argument for the label text. Similarly, the end-quote character (') makes the arrows point in the clockwise direction, and the open-quote character (') in the counterclockwise direction; an exclamation point (!) suppresses the arrowheads altogether. Any text following one of these characters in the argument of the \rtwocell command is printed as the label for the two-cell diagram.

```
\usepackage[all,2cell]{xy}
\UseAllTwocells
\[
\renewcommand{\objectstyle}{\scriptstyle}
\renewcommand{\labelstyle}{\scriptstyle}
\xymatrix @=1pc {
&& \bullet \ar[2,2]
\\ \\
   \bullet \ar[-2,2]
        \rrtwocell {=}
        \xtwocell[0,4]{}\omit{^<-4>a}
&& x_b \ar[rr] \ar[dr]_{\mathrm{id}_x}
        \rrtwocell\omit{<1.5>}
&& \bullet
\\ &&& x_e \ar[ur]
}\]
```

Example
7-4-22

The diagram above illustrates a few more features available with two-cell diagrams. First we declare a smaller font size, by setting the style for the labels (\labelstyle) and objects (\objectstyle) to \scriptstyle. Also, we decrease the row and column spacing to one pica. Then we construct a matrix consisting of arrows (for the straight parts) and two-cell diagrams. Note the use of the equals sign (=) with the \rrtwocell command: this sets a double line (representing equality), instead of a double arrow. Putting \omit in that position would leave out this object altogether. To reverse the direction of the central double arrow so that it points counterclockwise, we can make the first character a caret (^), as in the \xtwocell command; the default is the clockwise direction (_).

The main purpose of the \xtwocell command is to allow "excursions" to link two distant cells more than three "hops" away. The first argument is the target (here, four cells to the right); next comes any displacement with respect to the center of the target cell (as this argument is empty, here we point to the center of cell "3,5" itself). The next token \omit signifies that we do not want the curved arrows, while the last argument specifies a negative nudge factor and a label a. This allows us to position the upper double arrow in a convenient way. The same applies to the rightmost double arrow: it is drawn with the \rrtwocell command with \omit as the first argument, also suppressing the curved arrows.

The two-cell feature can be combined with curved arrows to obtain the following interesting layout:

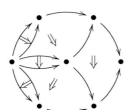

Example
7-4-23

```
\usepackage[all,2cell]{xy}

\UseTwocells
\[
\xymatrix @R=2.0pc @C=.8pc {
& \bullet \ar @/^1ex/ [rr]
&& \bullet \ar @/^1ex/ [dr]
\\ \bullet \urtwocell<2> \rrtwocell<2>
            \drtwocell<2> \xtwocell[1,3]{}\omit
            \xtwocell[-1,3]{}\omit
&& \bullet \ar @/_1ex/ [ur]
            \ar @/^1ex/ [dr]
            \rrtwocell\omit
&& \bullet
\\ & \bullet \ar @/_1ex/ [rr]
&&    \bullet \ar @/_1ex/ [ur]
}\]
```

The two \xtwocell commands produce the double arrows in the middle of the diagram, pointing towards and away from the central bullet. The rightmost double arrow is the only thing typeset by the final \rrtwocell command. The \omit on all three of these commands prevents typesetting of the curved arrows.

7.4.5 Polygons

Regular polygons are easy to construct with the poly feature. Moreover, one can draw several kinds of non-regular polygons by using a non-square coordinate system. This feature depends on the arrow feature, which it loads automatically.

The general form of the command for drawing polygons is

> \xypolygon⟨nb⟩"⟨pref⟩"{⟨swit⟩...}

The mandatory argument *nb* is the number of sides of the polygon. The other mandatory part, represented by the ellipsis (...) above, contains a description of the objects to be deposited at the vertices. The optional prefix "⟨pref⟩" provides an explicit name for the polygon so that you can address it from anywhere inside the xy environment. If the first character inside the curly braces is not the tilde character, then the material inside the braces is interpreted as an object to be dropped at each vertex. An argument starting with ~ signifies the presence of one or more switches that modify the form of vertices, sides, or spokes. A few examples will make this clearer.

```
\usepackage[all,poly]{xy}

\[\begin{xy} /r10mm/:
  ,     0     ,{\xypolygon6{}}
  ,+/r22mm/,{\xypolygon6{@{o}}}
  ,+/r22mm/,{*@{o}\xypolygon6{@{*}}}
\end{xy}\]
```

Example
7-4-24

Above we show three forms of a hexagon: the default (no ornaments), then with a simple object at the vertices, and finally with a small open circle in the middle (indicating that the reference point of the polygon lies at its center).

It is not very difficult to make a few variants on the preceding example by exploiting the switches. First, for the *vertices*, we can use ~*{*obj*} to drop an object and ~={*ang*} to indicate the angle of the first drawn vertex. By contrast, when we are typesetting the *spokes* (*sides*), directionals are specified with ~<{...} (~>{...}), arrow styles with ~<<{*arr*} (~>>{*arr*}), and labels and breaks with ~<>{...} (~><{...}).

Let us look at all this in practice.

```
\usepackage[all,poly]{xy}

\[\begin{xy} /r10mm/:
  ,     0     ,{*@{o}\xypolygon6{~*{\dir{*}}}}
  ,+/r22mm/,{\xypolygon6{~<{.}~>{}~={30}{\dir{*}}}}
  ,+/r22mm/,{\xypolygon6{~<{=}~>{:}{\dir{*}}}}
\end{xy}\]
```

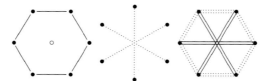

Example
7-4-25

By default, the object on a vertex is typeset in a box of zero size (see the third command of Example 7-4-25, where we wrote \xypolygon6{@{*}}). However, the first line above shows that, in the case of the switch ~*{...}, the object at each vertex takes into account the \objectmargin. On the second and third lines, we specify both the directionals for the spokes and the sides of the polygons; with an empty declaration (~>{}) no sides are drawn. Furthermore, on the second line the declaration ~={30} rotates the hexagon by 30 degrees. On the third line we specify the directionals for the spokes and the sides as ~<{=} and ~>{:}, respectively.

The vertices are automatically named "1", "2", ..., "nb", with the center being identified as "0". For typesetting labels, the command \xypolynode corresponds to the actual number of a side, spoke, or vertex at the moment the command is executed. Moreover, the command \xypolynum typesets the number of sides. Let us return to our hexagon and see what we can achieve with this knowledge.

```
\usepackage[all,poly]{xy}
\newcounter{node}
%
\[
\renewcommand{\objectstyle}{\scriptstyle}
\newcommand{\Letter}%
    {{\setcounter{node}%
      {\xypolynode}\Alph{node}}}
%
\begin{xy} /r11mm/:
  (2,4.8), {\xypolygon6{~*{\xypolynode}}}
 ,(2,2.5), {*{0}*\cir<5pt>{}
            \xypolygon6{~*{\xybox{%
              *{\xypolynode}*\cir<2mm>{}}}}}
 ,(2,0)  ,  {\xypolygon6{%
            ~><{@/_.5ex/}
            ~>>{_{\delta^{\xypolynode}
                    _{\xypolynum}}}
            ~<<{@{=}}
            ~<>{|\uparrow}
            ~*{\Letter}}}
\end{xy}
\]
```

After declaring that objects should be typeset in script style, we first define a command \Letter that translates a node number (1 through 6) into an uppercase letter. The top hexagon shows how node numbers can be typeset at the vertices. In the middle hexagon we circle the vertex numbers, but to achieve this we must specify the compound command sequence as an argument of an \xybox command. Finally, at the bottom we construct a rather more complex setup in which sides are curved arrows labeled with the Greek letter δ, with the node number and total number of sides as a superscript and a subscript, respectively. The spokes have a double line with an uparrow in the middle; the vertices have the uppercase letter corresponding to their number, as determined by the \Letter macro.

There is one more switch not yet described, namely ~:{...}. This notation allows scaling of the coordinate axes to build non-regular polygons. Perhaps more interestingly, this lets three-dimensional or perspective drawings be simulated, as in the following example.

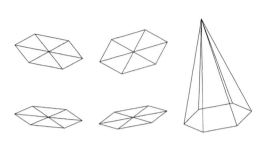

```
\usepackage[all,poly]{xy}
\[\begin{xy}/r9mm/:
  (0,0),{\xypolygon6{%
    ~:{(1,-.1):(0,.33)::}~<{-}}}
 ,(0,2),{\xypolygon6{%
    ~:{(1,-.2):(0,.5)::}~<{-}}}
 ,(2.5,0),{\xypolygon6{%
    ~:{(1,.2):(0,-.3)::}~<{-}}}
 ,(2.5,2),{\xypolygon6{%
    ~:{(1,.3):(0,-.6)::}~<{-}}}
 ,(5,0)="O",  +(-.5,3)="T","O"
 ,{\xypolygon6{~:{(1,0.2):(0,.4)::}
    ~<>{;"T"**@{-}}}}
\end{xy}\]
```

Example
7-4-27

At the left we show the effect of four different coordinate transformations on a hexagon. To understand the "colon" notation in the argument of the \xypolygon commands, consider the first hexagon, in which the new base's x-axis is set to the coordinate $(1, -.1)$ and the y-axis is set to $(0, .33)$ so as to generate the skewing effect. The drawing at the right, at position $(5, 0)$, defines an "origin" "O" and an apex "T" at position $(-.5, 3)$ with respect to that point. In drawing the hexagon, extra lines to "T" are drawn as a result of the ~<>{...} switch. This is achieved by the semicolon operator, which first loads the vertex position as "previous" object p, and then sets the "current" object c to the top "T", before finally drawing a connector **@{-} between them.

Another application is constructing a perspective drawing. The next example also shows how to use the prefixes to identify different polygons.

```
\usepackage[all,poly]{xy}
\[\begin{xy} /r1cm/:
  {\xypolygon4"F"{~:{(0,.6)::}}},+(.8,1.3)
 ,{\xypolygon4"B"{~:{(.7,0):(0,.7)::}}}
 ,"F1";"B1"**@{.}  ,"F2";"B2"**@{.}
 ,"F3";"B3"**@{.}  ,"F4";"B4"**@{.}
\end{xy}
\qquad
\begin{xy} /1cm/:
  {\xypolygon4"F"{~:{(0,.6)::}}},+(.8,1.3)
 ,{\xypolygon4"B"{~:{(.7,0):(0,.7)::}}}
 ,"F1";"B1"**@{.}  ,"F2";"B2"**@{.}
 ,"F3";"B3"**@{.}  ,"F4";"B4"**@{.}
\end{xy}\]
```

Example
7-4-28

In these two drawings, we first make the base asymmetric. For the front rectangle, the y-axis is scaled 60% with respect to the x-axis; for the back plane, the x-axis is scaled 70% and the y-axis a further 70%, to give an impression of perspective. Since we labeled the polygons "F" (front) and "B" (back), we can identify the various vertices with this prefix and their number. It is then easy to connect corresponding vertices on the rectangles to create the visual effect of a three-dimensional box.

A variant of the above allows the transition to nested polygons:

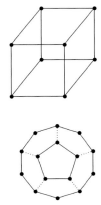

```
\usepackage[all,poly]{xy}
\[\begin{xy} /r10mm/:,
  {\xypolygon4"F"{\dir{*}}}
  ,+(.8,1.0),{\xypolygon4"B"{\dir{*}}}
  ,"F1";"B1"**@{-},"F2";"B2"**@{-}
  ,"F3";"B3"**@{-},"F4";"B4"**@{-}
  ,-(1.0,2.8)
  ,{\xypolygon10"O"{~={18}\dir{*}}}
  ,{\xypolygon5"I"{~:{(0.55,0):}
     ~={18}{\dir{*}}}}
  ,"O1";"I1"**@{.},"O3";"I2"**@{.}
  ,"O5";"I3"**@{.},"O7";"I4"**@{.}
  ,"O9";"I5"**@{.}
\end{xy}\]
```

Having learned above how to displace rectangles to give the impression of depth, it is now self-evident how to construct a cubical form: we just place two squares a certain distance from each other and then connect corresponding foreground ("F") and background ("B") vertices. In the lower part of the picture, we show that it is equally simple to draw a pentagon inside a decagon by merely positioning both at the same point. As we want the top vertices of both polygons to point up, we rotate them by 18 degrees. The inner polygon is scaled down (to 55% in our case) for aesthetics, and finally the vertices of the inner ("I") pentagon are connected to the appropriate vertices of the outer ("O") decagon.

We close this section on polygons by showing how to nest them. Here we draw a triangle at each of the vertices of a pentagon.

```
\usepackage[all,poly]{xy}
\[\renewcommand{\objectstyle}{\scriptscriptstyle}
\begin{xy}
\xypolygon5{~:{/r12mm/:}
  ~<>{\xypolygon3{~:{(0.45,0):}
     ~*{\xypolyname\xypolynode}
     ~={30}}}
  ~>{}
  ~<{.}
  =<3mm>[o]{\xypolynode}}
\end{xy}\]
```

Inside the "outer" pentagon are triangles at each of the vertices, scaled down 45% with respect to the dimensions of the pentagon. Each vertex of the triangle is labeled with its number but prefixed with \xypolyname, which corresponds to the vertex identifier of the enclosing polygon: labels of the type "4,2" identify the second vertex of the triangle positioned on the fourth vertex of the pentagon. All triangles are oriented at the same 30 degree angle (~={30}). Furthermore, we have turned off the drawing of the sides and connected the triangles to the center of the pentagon by a dotted line. At the center of each of the pentagon nodes we typeset its number inside an empty disk of radius 3 mm.

7.4.6 Arcs, circles, and ellipses

Circles and ellipses in many forms and styles are available with the arc feature. More generally, circular arcs can be specified that join two points or have a specified tangent at a given point. This feature is based on the curve extension discussed in Section 7.3.1, so you should ensure that it is also loaded. As explained there, drawing curves can overload TeX's memory quite rapidly, so you are advised to use a back end that directly supports the curve paradigm.

Simple circles and ellipses

Circles of arbitrary radius and line style, including curved arrows, are available with the \ellipse command. In its basic form \ellipse draws a "circle" at the current point. It has a variety of forms, as the next example shows.

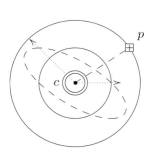

```
\usepackage[all,arc,dvips]{xy}
\[\begin{xy} /r12mm/:
  (0,0)*@{*}="c",*+++++!R{c}
  ,(1.2,.8)*+[][F]@{+}="p"
  ,*+++!LD{p},"p";"c"**@{--}
  ,{\ellipse<>{}}
  ,{\ellipse(0.8){}}
  ,0;(-1,1)::
  ,{\ar@{.>} 0;(1,0)}
  ,{\ar@{.>} 0;(0,1)}
  ,"p";"c",{\ellipse(.8){--}}
  ,{\ellipse<3mm>{=}}
\end{xy}\]
```

We start with a rectangular coordinate base of 12 mm in both directions. We choose a point p (for "previous") and a point c (for "current"); we position the latter at the origin for convenience. The simplest way to draw a circle is the first \ellipse command, which produces a circle with its center at the current point and radius $\overline{cp}$. As the argument between the curly braces is empty, the default style (a full line) is used to draw the curve. Note that the circle is not drawn through the object at p. The second \ellipse command draws a circle whose radius is expressed as a fraction of the current coordinate units (80% of 12 mm in our case). We now skew the coordinate system and draw the dotted coordinate axes. Then, with a command similar to the previous one but with a dashed line style, we draw an ellipse. While this shows clearly the effect of the introduction of the skewed base, the base has no effect on the drawing resulting from the last \ellipse command, where the radius is specified in angle brackets.

Since a non-square coordinate system is not always convenient, or even desirable, el-lipses can also be specified with other forms of the \ellipse command. For these figures you must in general specify the lengths of the minor and major axes and their alignment. As in Example 7-4-31, the current point *c* lies at the center of the ellipse and the vector connect-ing the previous point *p* with *c* provides the alignment of one of the axes.

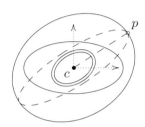

```
\usepackage[all,arc,dvips]{xy}
\[\begin{xy} 0;/r12mm/:
  {\ar@{.>} 0;(1,0)}
 ,{\ar@{.>} 0;(0,1)}
 ,(0,0)*@{*}="c",*+!RU{c}
 ,(1.2,0.8)*@{o}="p",*+!LD{p}
 ,"p";"c"**@{--}
 ,{\ellipse(1.1,.6){}}
 ,{\ellipse(,0.8){}}
 ,{\ellipse<6mm,4mm>{=}}
 ,{\ellipse<,5mm>{--}}
\end{xy}\]
```

Example
7-4-32

We begin with the same coordinate system as previously and choose the same points *c* and *p*, now of zero size. The syntax with parentheses before the argument uses the coor-dinate basis as the unit length. When numbers are explicitly given, both axes of the ellipse are aligned with the coordinate axes and their lengths are given as a fraction of the base vectors. When the number in front of the comma is absent, one of the axes of the ellipse is aligned with the line $\overline{cp}$ and the perpendicular axis is scaled by the number specified *after* the comma. Hence, in the preceding examples, the first ellipse is aligned with the coordinate system and has horizontal axis equal to 1.1 base units and vertical axis to 0.6 base unit. The second ellipse has an axis perpendicular to $\overline{cp}$ with a length of 0.8 base unit. The second basic syntax uses angle brackets in front of the curly braces; in this case, the actual dimen-sions of the axes are exactly specified as LaTeX lengths. With this syntax the ellipse is always aligned with the direction $\overline{cp}$. If the first dimension is absent, then (as in the parenthesized case) $\overline{cp}$ becomes one of the axes and the length specified after the comma is used for the perpendicular axis.

Constructing arcs

Often you are not interested merely in typesetting full circles or ellipses, but also in using circular or elliptical arcs. Generally speaking, two kinds of situations arise: (1) the end points are given but the radius is not determined; and (2) the radius is known but the end points are to be determined.

In fact, in most practical cases the end points are known. Yet, since an infinite number of circular (elliptical) arcs can be drawn through two points, more information is needed. For instance, to determine the arc uniquely, you can supply the tangent of the curve at one of its end points. This is implemented by taking the current direction at the point *p*—i.e., the direction determined by the latest connection or "up" when there has been no connection.

Let us look at an example.

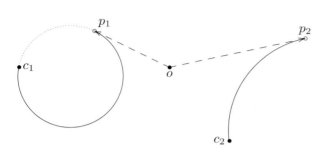

```
\usepackage[all,arc,dvips]{xy}
\[\begin{xy} 0;/r20mm/:
  (0,0)="o" ,*@{*} ,*+!U{o}
  ,(-1.0,0.5)="p"*@{o},*+!LD{p_1}
  ,{\ar @{-->} "o";"p"};
  (-2.,0.)="c",*@{*},*+!L{c_1}
  ,"c",{\ellipse_{}},{\ellipse^{.}}
  ,(1.8,0.4)="p",*@{o},*+!D{p_2}
  ,{\ar @{-->} "o";"p"};
  (0.8,-1)="c",*@{*},*+!R{c_2}
  ,"c",{\ellipse{}}
\end{xy}\]
```

Example
7-4-33

After defining the points "o" and "p" (at p_1), we draw an arrow, at the same time setting the direction $\overrightarrow{op}$; this arrow will be used as the tangent for the circular arc we will draw. We then define the current point (c_1) and draw the circle segment from p_1 to c_1 with the \ellipse command. Note that an underscore-tagged command draws the segment in the clockwise direction, while the form with the caret (^) draws it counterclockwise (the dotted circle segment). Similarly, we define points p_2 and c_2 and draw the circle segment to the right of the picture. Without further tags, the segments are drawn traversing the arc counterclockwise.

More generally, we can also base the drawing on the tangent at the end points or specify alternative types of curve, such as parabolic or cubic segments, "interpolating" Bézier splines, or "cuspidal" cubics (see [104] for more details).

7.4.7 Lattices and web structures

Two-dimensional lattices and other web-like structures can be handled with the web feature. At present its facilities are limited to dropping objects at the intersection points of an integer lattice. This lattice can be skew, such that its basis need not be rectangular; any coordinate basis setting defined with Xy-pic can be used.

The simplest command is \xylattice, whose four arguments are integers specifying which part of the lattice is to be drawn (in fact, they define the positions of the lattice points at the lower-left and upper-right corners as multiples of the base vectors).

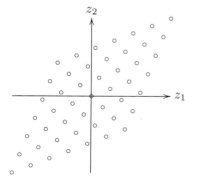

```
\usepackage[all,web]{xy}
\[\renewcommand{\latticebody}{\drop@{o}}
\begin{xy}
 *\xybox{0;<5mm,2mm>:<2mm,5mm>::
 ,0,{\xylattice{-3}{3}{-3}{3}}}="S"
 ,{"S"+L \ar "S"+R*+!L{z_1}}
 ,{"S"+D \ar "S"+U*+!D{z_2}}
\end{xy}\]
```

Example
7-4-34

The command \latticebody is expanded at each point of the lattice, so that it can be used to drop objects (\drop is like * but is a stand-alone command). In Example 7-4-34 we choose an open circle. The command \xybox isolates the coordinate base change needed to construct the lattice from the rest of the picture. We define the base vectors of the lattice as <5mm, 2mm> and <2mm, 5mm>, and then draw all lattice points from -3 to $+3$ in the directions of both unit vectors. The resulting box is stored as "S" so that we can reference its dimensions to draw the coordinate axes z_1 and z_2.

Sometimes we may want to drop objects at specific lattice points. To find the position of a lattice point, we use the commands \latticeA and \latticeB to give its "coordinate", and the commands \latticeX and \latticeY to return the x and y offsets (in points) with respect to the lattice origin. In addition, we can limit the size of the picture with the \croplattice variant, which has four arguments for specifying a cropping rectangle outside of which no lattice points are shown.

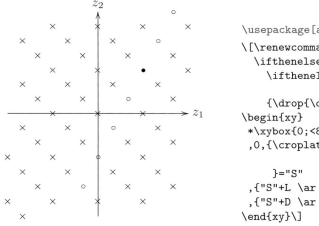

```
\usepackage[all,web]{xy}\usepackage{ifthen}
\[\renewcommand{\latticebody}{%
    \ifthenelse{\latticeA=1}{%
      \ifthenelse{\latticeB=1}{\drop{\dir{*}}}%
                             {\drop{\dir{o}}}}%
    {\drop{\dir{x}}}}
\begin{xy}
*\xybox{0;<8mm,4mm>:<4mm,8mm>::
,0,{\croplattice{-6}{6}{-6}{6}%
               {-3}{3}{-3.5}{3.5}}%
    }="S"
,{"S"+L \ar "S"+R*+!L{z_1}}
,{"S"+D \ar "S"+U*+!D{z_2}}
\end{xy}\]
```

Example 7-4-35

The four numbers defining the clipping rectangle need not be integers (as seen in the above code): they define the x and y ranges between which lattice points should be typeset as multiples of the lattice's unit vectors. When the object to be typeset at a given grid position depends on its x and y coordinates, then (as mentioned earlier) it is probably more convenient to use the commands \latticeX and \latticeY. Note that you need to load the ifthen package to use the \ifthenelse construction.

7.4.8 Links and knots

Research about strings has become very popular in many fields of physics and mathematics, and Xy-pic offers an interesting toolkit for constructing arrangements of different kinds of knots, string crossings, and links.

The knot feature provides two kinds of basic building blocks: "crossings," to pass one string above or below another string, and "joins," to connect strings at their endpoints. The knot feature uses the curve extension and arrow feature, so all three should be loaded together. Also, the processing of knot diagrams is the most time-consuming and memory-greedy application discussed so far, so that such diagrams must often be output on individual output pages or as separate Encapsulated PostScript files. Use of these files on subsequent LaTeX runs saves both time and memory.

Constructing crossings

Strings "cross" when they come close to each other without actually meeting. Therefore three types of crossings exist: a string can pass *above*, *below*, or *alongside* another string. These possibilities, in various configurations, are systematically summarized in the XY-pic reference manual; take care to separate the "h" and "v" categories of commands, which serve as building blocks for stacking in the *horizontal* (the current point moves to the top right) and *vertical* (the current point moves to the bottom left) directions.

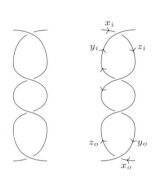

```
\usepackage[all,poly,knot,dvips]{xy}
\[\UseTips
\renewcommand{\objectstyle}{\scriptstyle}
\renewcommand{\labelstyle}{\scriptstyle}
\begin{xy} /r9mm/:
  \vover\vcross\vcross\vover-
\end{xy}
\hspace{1cm}
\begin{xy} /r9mm/:
  \vunder<><{x_i}|>|{y_i}>>>{z_i}%
  \vtwist|><<\vtwist
  \vunder-<><{x_o}|>|{y_o}>>>{z_o}%
\end{xy}\]
```

Example
7-4-36

    Some combinations of vertical crossings are drawn in this example. On the left we see the effect of the bare commands, while on the right we show how to add labels and arrow tips. Note that the \⟨*c*⟩twist and \⟨*c*⟩cross variants twist the strings in opposite directions. Note also that either end of the string can be the source or the target of a curved arrow—a distinction that becomes important when arrowheads and labels are to be placed in the string. Use of a hyphen (or minus sign) as the first character immediately following the name of any knot piece produces a mirror image of that piece. It may appear identical to another piece, but string orientations will be different (see the next example).

    Positioning of labels and arrows is controlled by the operators < and >, which should precede the object to be put on the initial and final portions of the crossed string. The operator | is used to specify material to be added to the crossing string. When the first character following the <, >, or | is another > (or <), then an arrow tip pointing in (against) the "natural" direction is typeset at a predetermined position. These placing operators can be repeated as many times as needed. Examine the code for Example 7-4-36 to see how each tip and label have been placed on the knot crossings, and see [104] for a complete listing of the pieces, their orientations, and the default label positions on each part.

    Horizontal rows of knot pieces can be combined in complete analogy with the "vertical" knot-building commands described previously. In the next example we show that the same knot configuration can be built by exchanging commands of the ..cross.. and ..twist.. series. However, from the labeled arrows, we can see that these visually identical curves actually have different orientations and label positions.

```
\usepackage[all,poly,knot,dvips]{xy}
\[\UseTips
\renewcommand{\labelstyle}{\scriptstyle}
\begin{xy} 0;/r8mm/:
  (0,0)
  ,{\hover\hcross<><{1}|>|{2}>>>{3}%
     \hcross<><{4}|>|{5}>>>{6}\hover-}
  ,(0,-3)
  ,{\hover\htwistneg<><{1}|>|{2}>>>{3}%
     \htwistneg<><{4}|>|{5}>>>{6}\hover-}
\end{xy}\]
```

Example
7-4-37

Adding joins

Ends of crossing strings can be connected by "joins"—in particular, *loops* and *caps*. The next two examples illustrate the use of joins with horizontal or vertical crossing commands of the types "..cross.." or "..twist..".

As with the crossing commands, labels and arrow tips can be placed on the joins. Now there is only one segment, so the | operator refers to the middle of the curve while < and > refer to places *before* and *after* the midpoint, respectively. A scale factor, given between square brackets immediately following the command name, can be introduced for each string segment. Moreover, the positions of the label and tip can be fine-tuned by specifying a value between 0 and 1 between the operator and the object to be typeset, or by adding/subtracting a small amount.

```
\usepackage[all,poly,knot,dvips]{xy}
\[\UseTips
\renewcommand{\labelstyle}{\scriptscriptstyle}
\begin{xy} /r9mm/:
  ,(0,0)
  ,{\hunder<><{1}|>|{2}>>>{3}%
     \htwist<<<{4}|>|{5}><>{6}%
     \hloop<><{7}|>|{8}>>>{9}}
  ,(0,-3)
  ,{\hunder<(+0.1)><{1}|>|{2}>>>{3}%
     \htwist<<<{4}|(-.2)>|(-.2){^{5}}><>{6}%
     \hloop<(+.1)><{7}|>|{8}>>>(-.1){9}}
\end{xy}\]
```

Example
7-4-38

Here we have combined two horizontal crossings and one join command. The top drawing shows the default positions for labels and tips; the lower one uses the fine-tuning parameters to position tips and labels. Positive values move along the curve in the "natural" direction.

Note the use of the ^ character in the first position of the label "5", which places the label "above" the arrow while the (default) _ character places it "below".

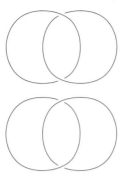

```
\usepackage[curve,knot,graph,dvips]{xy}
\[\xygraph{!{0;/r10mm/:}
            !{\vover}
        [u] !{\hcap[-2]}
        [d] !{\vover-}
        [ruu] !{\hcap[2]}
}\]
\[\begin{xy} 0;/r10mm/:
    ,\hcap[-2]\vunder\vunder-
    ,+(1,2),\hcap[2]
\end{xy}\]
```

Example
7-4-39

Since all knot crossings are, by default, bounded by a rectangle of one coordinate unit, and since loop and cap commands do not change the current point, it is convenient to use the graph feature to put together the various pieces of knot crossings and joins. This is shown in the top part of Example 7-4-39, where the \vover and \hcap commands position the elements by using "turtle" movements (up, down, left, right). The bottom part presents a variant diagram in which an explicit coordinate move was used to place the final \hcap. Note the use of the scaling factors, [2] or [-2].

Commands are also available to combine pieces in which the strings are basically at angles of 45 degrees, as in this next example.

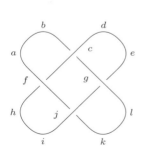

```
\usepackage[curve,knot,arrow,dvips]{xy}
\[\renewcommand{\labelstyle}{\scriptstyle}
\begin{xy} 0;/r8mm/:
    ,{\xcapv-|{a}}
    , +(0,1) ,{\xcaph|{b}\xunderh|{c}%
            \xcaph|{d}\xcapv|{e}}
    ,-(3,0),{\xoverh|{f}}
    ,+(1,0),{\xoverh|{g}}
    ,-(3,1),{\xcapv-|{h}\xcaph-|{i}}
    ,+(0,1),{\xunderh-|{j}}
    ,+(0,-1),{\xcaph-|{k}}
    ,+(0,1),{\xcapv|{l}}
\end{xy}\]
```

Example
7-4-40

The placement of the various pieces in this construction is easy to follow by looking at the labels.

There are also some "bendy" pieces that allow easy connection of these 45 degree pieces with the vertical and horizontal ones. However, even more general effects are obtained by using a non-square coordinate base.

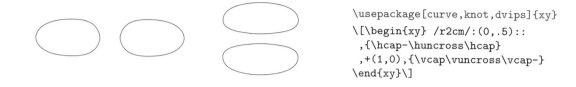

```
\usepackage[curve,knot,dvips]{xy}
\[\begin{xy} /r2cm/:(0,.5)::
  ,{\hcap-\huncross\hcap}
  ,+(1,0),{\vcap\vuncross\vcap-}
\end{xy}\]
```

Example 7-4-41

The greatest variety in the shape of knot pieces is obtained by setting the coordinate base for each piece individually, using the ~: switch. The remaining examples illustrate this technique in conjunction with the \xypolygon command from the poly option (in the form of the !P standout macro of the graph feature).

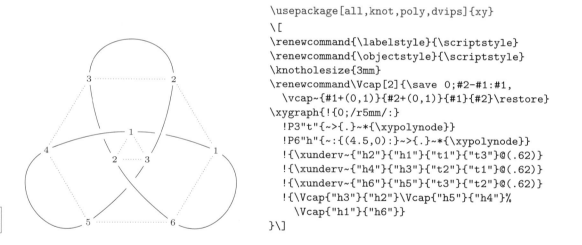

```
\usepackage[all,knot,poly,dvips]{xy}
\[
\renewcommand{\labelstyle}{\scriptstyle}
\renewcommand{\objectstyle}{\scriptstyle}
\knotholesize{3mm}
\renewcommand\Vcap[2]{\save 0;#2-#1:#1,
  \vcap~{#1+(0,1)}{#2+(0,1)}{#1}{#2}\restore}
\xygraph{!{0;/r5mm/:}
  !P3"t"{~>{.}~*{\xypolynode}}
  !P6"h"{~:{(4.5,0):}~>{.}~*{\xypolynode}}
  !{\xunderv~{"h2"}{"h1"}{"t1"}{"t3"}@(.62)}
  !{\xunderv~{"h4"}{"h3"}{"t2"}{"t1"}@(.62)}
  !{\xunderv~{"h6"}{"h5"}{"t3"}{"t2"}@(.62)}
  !{\Vcap{"h3"}{"h2"}\Vcap{"h5"}{"h4"}%
    \Vcap{"h1"}{"h6"}}
}\]
```

Example 7-4-42

This three-leaf figure is drawn with the help of the vertices defined by the inner (dotted) triangle (identified by "t") and the outer (dotted) hexagon (identified by "h"). To make explicit the different steps in the construction, we also show the number of each vertex. Three knot crossings of type \xunderv are used, and the ~ syntax permits their precise positioning between pairs of vertices of the triangle and the hexagon (see Section 7.4.5 for more details). To construct the outer caps we have to renormalize the coordinate base vector, since the \vcap command bridges one coordinate unit in the x direction. That is the reason for the base change inside the \Vcap command, which is isolated from the rest of the diagram with the \save...\restore pair. Note the scaling factor of 4.5 inside the hexagon specification and the fine-tuning of the position of the hole for the crossing with the @(.62) syntax and of its size with the `\knotholesize` command.

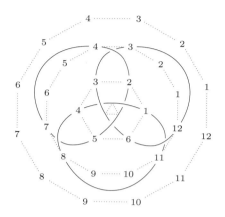

```
\usepackage[all,knot,poly,dvips]{xy}
\renewcommand{\labelstyle}{\scriptstyle}
\renewcommand{\objectstyle}{\scriptstyle}
\[\xygraph{!{0;/r2mm/:}
  !P3"t"{~>{.}}
  !P6"h"{~:{(4.5,0):}~>{.}~*{\xypolynode}}
  !P12"d"{~:{(9,0):}~>{.}~*{\xypolynode}}
  !P12"D"{~:{(13.,0):}~>{.}~*{\xypolynode}}
  !{\xoverv~{"h2"}{"h1"}{"t1"}{"t3"}@(.62)}
  !{\xoverv~{"h4"}{"h3"}{"t2"}{"t1"}@(.62)}
  !{\xoverv~{"h6"}{"h5"}{"t3"}{"t2"}@(.62)}
  !{\vover~{"d4"}{"d3"}{"h3"}{"h2"}}
          ,"d4"-@`{"D5","D6"}"d7",
  !{\vover~{"d8"}{"d7"}{"h5"}{"h4"}}
          ,"d8"-@`{"D9","D10"}"d11",
  !{\vover~{"d12"}{"d11"}{"h1"}{"h6"}}
          ,"d12"-@`{"D1","D2"}"d3"
}\]
```

Example
7-4-43

The drawing in Example 7-4-43 is a little more complex: it involves four polygons. The central triangle and hexagon are similar to those discussed earlier. Here, however, we add a second level of crossings defined by pairs of vertices of the hexagon and the inner dodecagon (identifier `"d"`). To close the ends of the open strings, we draw curves from the relevant vertices using control points on the *outer* dodecagon (identifier `"D"`) by means of the `@`` syntax discussed in Section 7.4.1.

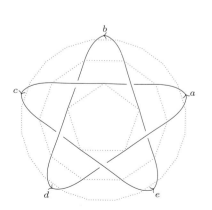

```
\usepackage[all,knot,poly,dvips]{xy}
\[
\UseTips
\knotholesize{2mm}
\xygraph{!{0;/r1cm/:}
  !P5"p"{~>{.}}
  !P10"d"{~:{(1.7,0):}~>{.}}
  !P20"D"{~={-9}~:{(2.2,0):}~>{.}}
  !{\xunderv~{"d3"}{"d2"}{"p2"}{"p1"}}
  !{\xunderv~{"d5"}{"d4"}{"p3"}{"p2"}}
  !{\xunderv~{"d7"}{"d6"}{"p4"}{"p3"}}
  !{\xunderv~{"d9"}{"d8"}{"p5"}{"p4"}}
  !{\xunderv~{"d1"}{"d10"}{"p1"}{"p5"}}
  !{\vloop~{"D3"}{"D2"}{"d2"}{"d1"}|>|{a}}
  !{\vloop~{"D7"}{"D6"}{"d4"}{"d3"}|>|{b}}
  !{\vloop~{"D11"}{"D10"}{"d6"}{"d5"}|>|{c}>}
  !{\vloop~{"D15"}{"D14"}{"d8"}{"d7"}|>|{d}}
  !{\vloop~{"D19"}{"D18"}{"d10"}{"d9"}|>|{e}}
}\]
```

Example
7-4-44

Finally, with the help of the 5-fold, 10-fold, and 20-fold symmetric polygons (shown with dotted lines), we construct the cinquefoil shown in Example 7-4-44. The inner pentagon is identified by "p", the middle decagon by "d", and the outer polygon by "D". The relative rotation angle of the vertices and the scaling factor of the polygons are defined inside braces following the !P.. specifier. Furthermore, the ~ syntax on the \xunderv and \vloop commands lets us precisely control the position and size of the crossing and joining elements. The loops of the foil can be made longer or shorter by tuning the scaling factor of the external polygon (a value of 2.2 is used here).

7.5 Further examples

The possibilities of XY-pic are many and go well beyond what has been shown in this chapter. A particularly valuable resource regarding what you can achieve with XY-pic is Aaron Lauda's XY-pic Web-site (`http://www.dpmms.cam.ac.uk/~al366/xytutorial.html`), which contains a tutorial with a large archive of examples. This marvelous site, whose contents is constantly enriched by its author, is certainly worth a visit! As an appetizer we show here a few instances of what is available. These examples, which are labeled with the category to which they belong, are reproduced with Aaron's kind permission.

Braids:

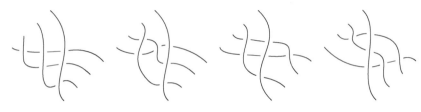

Example
7-5-1

Globular 3-morphisms in category theory:

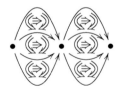

Example
7-5-2

A cobordism of Morse theory:

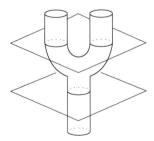

Example
7-5-3

A pentagonal sphere:

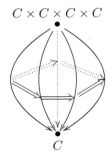

Example
7-5-4

A string diagram:

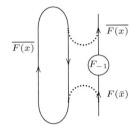

Example
7-5-5

Surfaces:

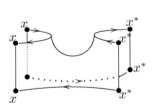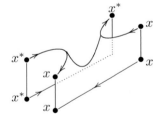

Example
7-5-6

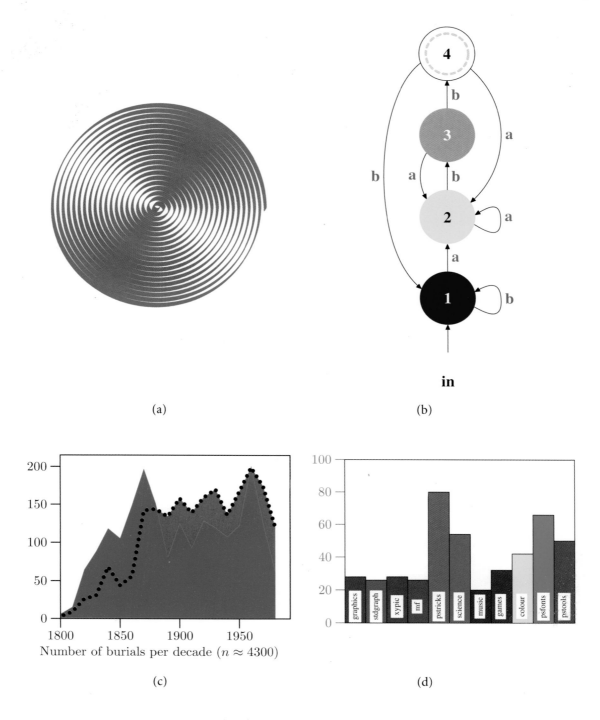

(a)

(b)

in

Number of burials per decade ($n \approx 4300$)

(c)

(d)

Color plate I: METAPOST examples

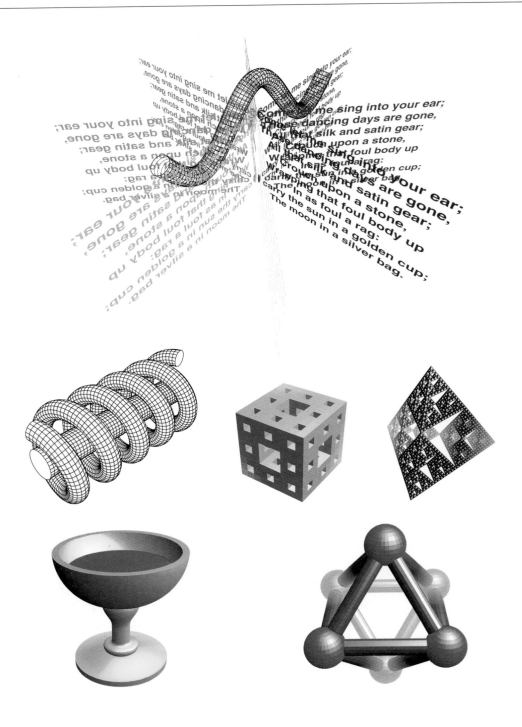

Color plate II: METAPOST examples: the m3d package (Anthony Phan)

(a) Moving circles (Maxime Chupin)

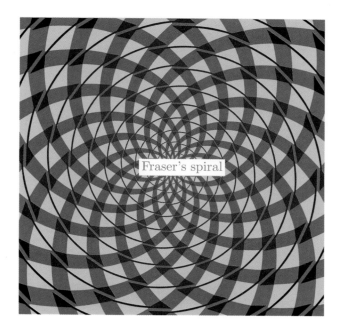

(b) Fraser's spiral

Color plate III: METAPOST examples: optical illusions

(a) L-Systems produced with a turtle-like approach (Jean-Michel Sarlat)

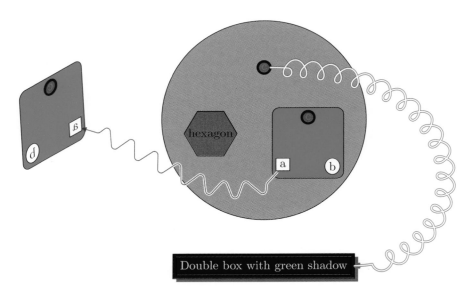

(b) A METAOBJ graphic

Color plate IV: METAPOST examples: turtle drawing and meta objects

(a) Colored lines

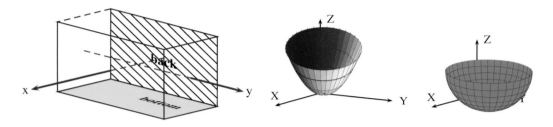

(c) 3-D objects in a parallel and central projection

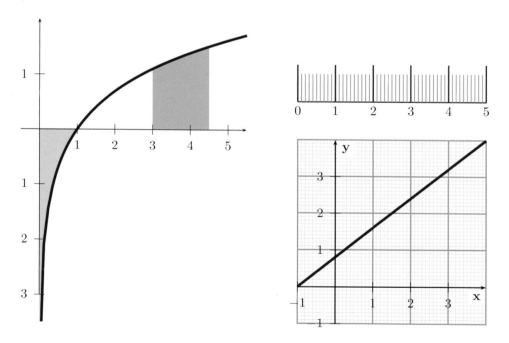

(b) Areas under a math function and special grids

Color plate V: **PSTricks** examples: lines, grids, and 3-D views

(a) Text along a path

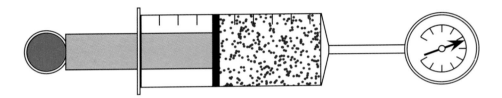

(b) Using basic PSTricks objects

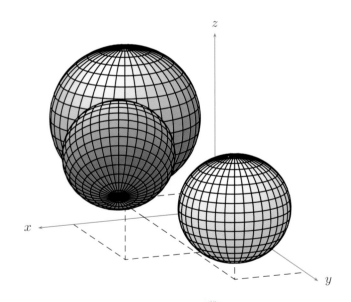

(c) Spheres in a 3-D coordinate system

Color plate VI: PSTricks examples: rotating text, using basic macros, and spheres

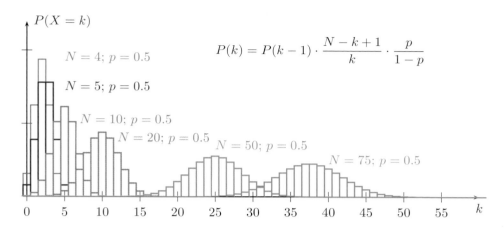

(a) Different binomial distributions

(b) A fractal tree

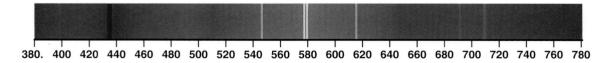

(c) Neon spectrum

Color plate VII: PSTricks examples: math and physics

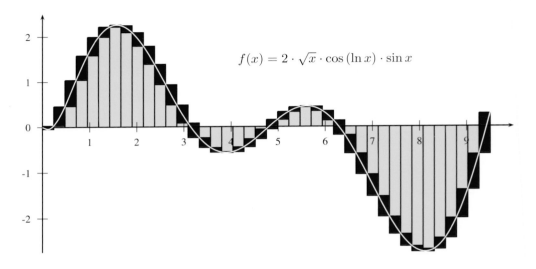

$$f(x) = 2 \cdot \sqrt{x} \cdot \cos\left(\ln x\right) \cdot \sin x$$

(a) Showing the Riemann squares

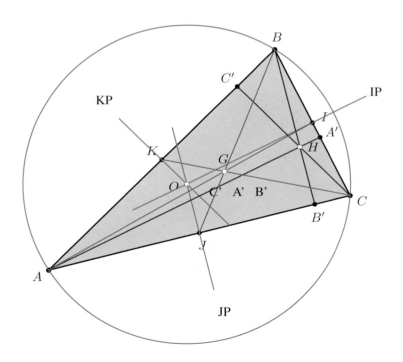

(b) Using **pst-eucl** for lines and points in a triangle

Color plate VIII: **PSTricks** examples: analysis and geometry

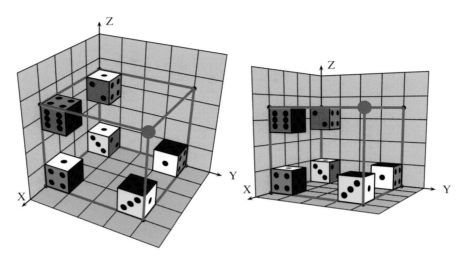

(a) 3-D view as a central projection

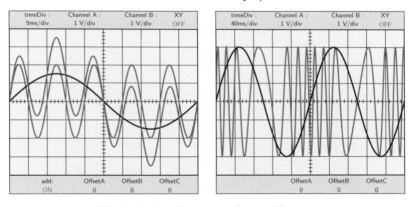

(b) Simulating the output of an oscilloscope

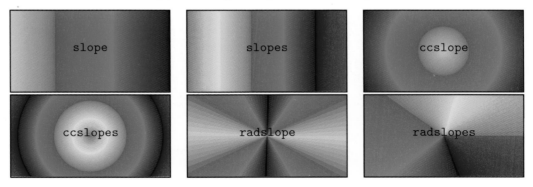

(c) Various color gradients

Color plate IX: **PSTricks** examples: 3-D views, oscilloscopes, and color gradients

```
138 GLGIEIIGTLQLVLCVLATTDR.RRRDLGG AQP1.PRO
130 AVTVELFLTMQLVLCIFASTDE.RRGDNLG AQP2.PRO
153 GFFDQFIGTAALIVCVLAIVDPYNNPVPRG AQP3.PRO
159 GLLVELIITFQLVFTIFASCDS.KRTDVTG AQP4.PRO
131 AMVVELILTFQLALCIFSSTDS.RRTSPVG AQP5.PRO
```

X acidic (−)
X aliphatic
X amide
X aromatic
X basic (+)
X hydroxyl
X imino
X sulfur

(a) Colored version of Example 8-3-4

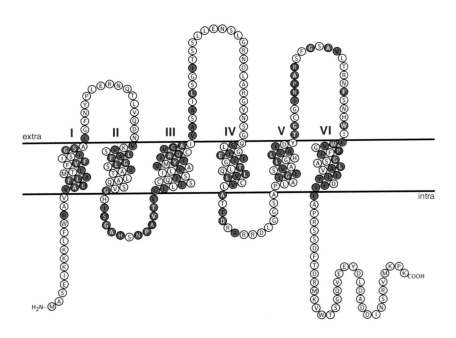

● similar positions
● conserved positions
● invariable positions

(b) Colored version of Example 8-3-8

Color plate X: Examples of the **texshade** and **textopo** packages

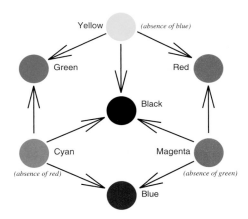

(a) The relation between the RGB and CMYK color models

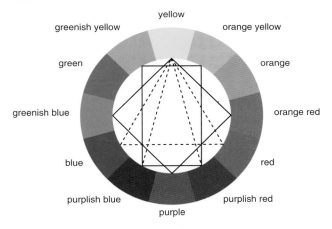

(b) Color harmonies and the chromatic circle [after 57]

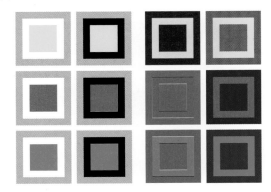

(c) Color harmony and the primary colors

Color plate XI: Color models and color harmonies

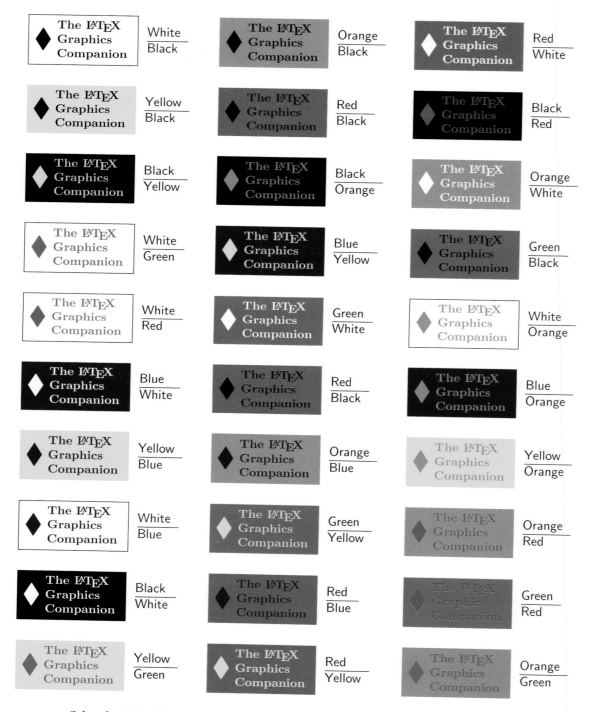

Color plate XII: Color contrasts for optimizing visibility and readability [after 19, p. 192]

Hue (H):   .0 .1 .2 .3 .4 .5 .6 .7 .8 .9
Saturation (S):   .0 .1 .2 .3 .4 .5 .6 .7 .8 .9
Brightness (B):   .0 .1 .2 .3 .4 .5 .6 .7 .8 .9

(a) The HSB model

Text starts off in green a little red nested blue text returning to green.

1. magenta cmyk black
2. predefined blue gray text

i. The current color changes.
ii. The current color changes.

Black text, green background, red frame

Teal text, lime background, magenta frame

White text, green background, red frame

Yellow text, orchid background, blue frame

Fun with color   Fun with color   Fun with color   Fun with color

Start with [black text] and [orange text], and return to black

Start in green, see [black text] and [orange text] and once again green

(b) Examples of LaTeX's xcolor package

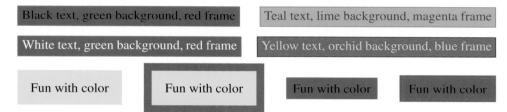

LONDON					Price
Sydney	OG4G	Thu Oct 10	Mon Oct 21 or 28	11 or 18 days	999 £
		Thu Oct 17	Mon Oct 21 or 28	4 or 11 days	999 £
	OG7A	Sun Oct 13	Mon Oct 21 or 28	8 or 15 days	999 £
		Sun Oct 20	Mon Oct 28	8 days	999 £

United Kingdom	London	Thames
France	Paris	Seine
Russia	Moscow	Moskva

(c) Colored tables

Color plate XIII: Examples of colored text

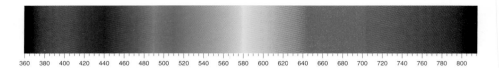

(a) Wave model (complete color spectrum)

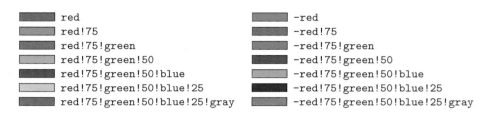

(b) Standard color expressions

(c) Base colors for `xcolor` (always available)

(d) Colors via the `dvipsnames` option for `xcolor`

Color plate XIV: Color expressions and color definitions with `xcolor`

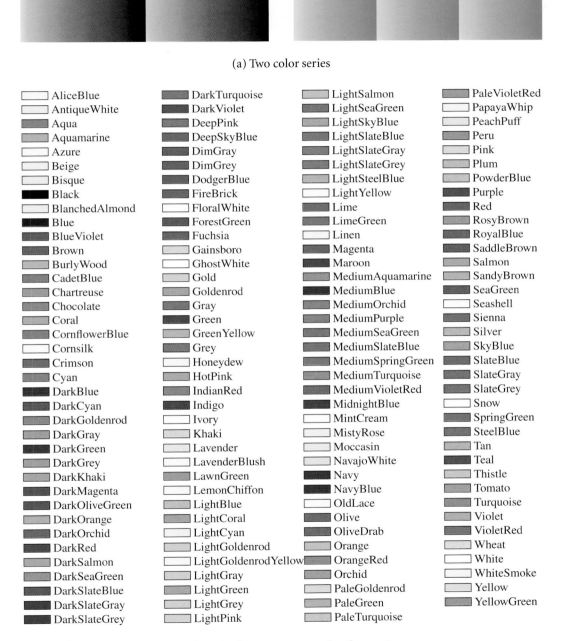

(a) Two color series

AliceBlue	DarkTurquoise	LightSalmon	PaleVioletRed
AntiqueWhite	DarkViolet	LightSeaGreen	PapayaWhip
Aqua	DeepPink	LightSkyBlue	PeachPuff
Aquamarine	DeepSkyBlue	LightSlateBlue	Peru
Azure	DimGray	LightSlateGray	Pink
Beige	DimGrey	LightSlateGrey	Plum
Bisque	DodgerBlue	LightSteelBlue	PowderBlue
Black	FireBrick	LightYellow	Purple
BlanchedAlmond	FloralWhite	Lime	Red
Blue	ForestGreen	LimeGreen	RosyBrown
BlueViolet	Fuchsia	Linen	RoyalBlue
Brown	Gainsboro	Magenta	SaddleBrown
BurlyWood	GhostWhite	Maroon	Salmon
CadetBlue	Gold	MediumAquamarine	SandyBrown
Chartreuse	Goldenrod	MediumBlue	SeaGreen
Chocolate	Gray	MediumOrchid	Seashell
Coral	Green	MediumPurple	Sienna
CornflowerBlue	GreenYellow	MediumSeaGreen	Silver
Cornsilk	Grey	MediumSlateBlue	SkyBlue
Crimson	Honeydew	MediumSpringGreen	SlateBlue
Cyan	HotPink	MediumTurquoise	SlateGray
DarkBlue	IndianRed	MediumVioletRed	SlateGrey
DarkCyan	Indigo	MidnightBlue	Snow
DarkGoldenrod	Ivory	MintCream	SpringGreen
DarkGray	Khaki	MistyRose	SteelBlue
DarkGreen	Lavender	Moccasin	Tan
DarkGrey	LavenderBlush	NavajoWhite	Teal
DarkKhaki	LawnGreen	Navy	Thistle
DarkMagenta	LemonChiffon	NavyBlue	Tomato
DarkOliveGreen	LightBlue	OldLace	Turquoise
DarkOrange	LightCoral	Olive	Violet
DarkOrchid	LightCyan	OliveDrab	VioletRed
DarkRed	LightGoldenrod	Orange	Wheat
DarkSalmon	LightGoldenrodYellow	OrangeRed	White
DarkSeaGreen	LightGray	Orchid	WhiteSmoke
DarkSlateBlue	LightGreen	PaleGoldenrod	Yellow
DarkSlateGray	LightGrey	PaleGreen	YellowGreen
DarkSlateGrey	LightPink	PaleTurquoise	

(b) Colors via the `svgnames` option for `xcolor`

Color plate XV: Color series and more color definitions with `xcolor`

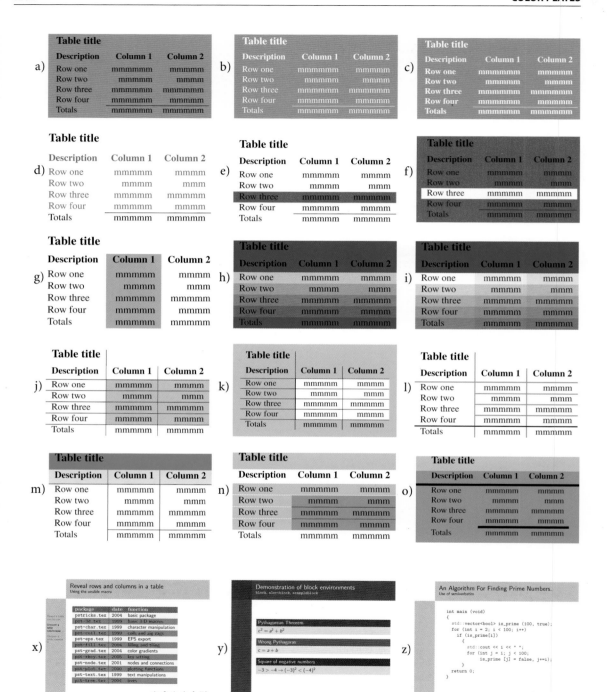

Color plate XVI: Examples of colored tables and the beamer class

Applications in Science, Technology, and Medicine

Because of its unsurpassed mathematical typesetting, TEX is widely used in the area of science, technology, and medicine (STM). It is not surprising, therefore, that the STM community has developed a number of packages to typeset the diagrams and schematics needed in their various disciplines. Chapter 8 of *The LATEX Companion, Second Edition* [83], describes in detail the $\mathcal{AMS}$-LATEX package, which makes marking up (higher) mathematics rather more convenient than with TEX's basic commands. Chapter 10 of that book mentions a few simple packages, such as **epic**, **eepic**, and **pspicture** (or the recently released **pict2e**), which complement LATEX's `picture` environment for drawing "simple" generic graphics. Of course, the general packages, such as METAPOST (Chapters 3 and 4) and **PSTricks** (Chapters 5 and 6), or even the slightly more directed XY-pic package (Chapter 7) may provide all the functionality you need to typeset even the most complex graphics. Nevertheless, the specific needs of a given user community are often better served by a more targeted approach; the packages covered in this chapter address such problem areas.

In scientific texts, precision and consistency are of the utmost importance. Therefore we start with a brief discussion of typographic conventions in scientific texts. The next two sections describe packages for typesetting chemical structures and complex biological protein topologies. Section 8.4 explores various ways of constructing Feynman diagrams, an important tool used by physicists. The last two sections turn to electronics and describe dedicated packages for drawing timing and circuit diagrams.

8.1 Typographical rules for scientific texts

In scientific texts the typographic representation of a symbol carries a semantic meaning. Authors working in these areas should, therefore, be aware of and adhere to these typographical conventions. A brief summary of the most important rules for composing scientific texts follows (see also [52, 53, 56, 69]).

The most important rule in all circumstances is *consistency*: a given symbol should always be presented in the same way, whether it appears in the text body, a title, a figure, a table, or a formula; on the main line or as a superscript or subscript. An important corollary for LaTeX users is this: always typeset a symbol in either math or text mode—never mix the two, even if the results appear to be the same. Indeed, with LaTeX, the final visual appearance may change substantially when using a different class file or after adding a new package. For example, when using PostScript fonts, digits in text are taken from the PostScript text face and can look quite different from those in formulae. Therefore, it is good practice to always typeset numbers that refer to a result or part of a formula in math mode—i.e., surrounded by $.

In scientific texts, many symbols are traditionally typeset as *Roman* (upright) characters[1] and may not be understood properly otherwise. The most important such symbols are described here:[2]

- *Units*—for example, g, cm, s, keV. Note that physical *constants* are usually set in italics, so that units involving constants are mixed Roman–italics, e.g., keV/c (where c is the speed of light, a constant). Unit symbols are never followed by a period (see Section 8.1.1).

- *Chemical elements*—for example Ne, O, Cu—and *elementary particle names*—for example, p, K, q, H. To help the typist produce typographically correct texts, packages that contain commands representing the various names have been developed. In particular, chemists can use **chemsym** (see Section 8.1.2), while the PEN (Particle Entity Notation) scheme has been proposed for high-energy physics [34].[3]

- Standard mathematical functions ($\sin$, $\det$, $\cos$, $\tan$, $\Re$, $\Im$, etc.), for which the built-in LaTeX functions should be used.

- Numbers.

---

[1] With LaTeX, Roman type in mathematics mode can be achieved by the \mathrm command.

[2] See http://physics.nist.gov/Document/typefaces.pdf for a convenient two-page overview.

[3] Andy Buckley's **heppennames** package is an implementation of the PEN notation. He also wrote **hepnicenames**, which complements **heppennames** by providing more "user-friendly" names for often-occurring particles. These packages do, however, allow you too much freedom by offering the possibility to define the output style for the particle names. For instance, you can typeset their symbols in italic, a style still often (wrongly) used in American physics journals, rather than in Roman, as mandated by the IUPAP rules [56] described here. See Section 8.4.2 for an example of how these packages are used in practice.

Table 8.1: The importance of typographic rules in scientific texts

Roman Type		Italic Type	
A	ampere (electric unit)	A	atomic number (variable)
e	electron (particle name)	e	electron charge (constant)
g	gluon (particle name)	g	gravitational constant
l	liter (volume unit)	l	length (variable)
m	meter (length unit)	m	mass (variable)
p	proton (particle name)	p	momentum (variable)
q	quark (particle name)	q	electric charge (variable)
s	second (time unit)	s	c.m. energy squared (variable)
t	tonne (weight unit)	t	time (variable)
V	volt (electric unit)	V	volume (variable)
Z	Z boson (particle name)	Z	atomic charge (variable)

- Names of waves or states (p-wave) and covariant couplings (A for axial, V for vector); names of monopoles (E for electric, M for magnetic).

- Abbreviations that are pieces of words (exp for experimental; min for minimum).

- The "d" in integrands (e.g., $\mathrm{d}p$).

Obeying these typesetting conventions helps the reader understand at first glance the meaning of a symbol. Table 8.1 shows a few examples in which the meaning of a symbol depends on its typographic representation.

8.1.1 Getting the units right

The importance of correctly typesetting units was recognized early, and several authors have developed packages to help users in this respect. Axel Reichert made a first step with his **units** and **nicefrac** packages. More recent and complete approaches are Patrick Happel's **unitsdef** package and Danie Els's **Slstyle** package. Both contain useful rules for expressing values of quantities.[1] **Slstyle** can be used together with Marcel Heldoorn's **Slunits** package. This package, which we shall describe next, is by far the more complete and provides full support for all units defined by the International System of Units (abbreviated SI[2]), the modern form of the metric system. It is the world's most widely used system of units, both in everyday com-

---

[1] The requirements for formatting and typesetting of SI units and numbers are described in the NIST (National Institute of Standards and Technology) document `http://physics.nist.gov/Document/sp811.pdf`. A very handy checklist for reviewing compuscripts is available from `http://physics.nist.gov/cuu/Units/rules.html`.

[2] From the French name *Système International d'Unités*. The SI was adopted by the "General Conference on Weights and Measures", which is also known under its French acronym CGPM (*Conférence Générale des Poids et Mesures*; see `http://www.bipm.fr/en/convention/cgpm/`). The CGPM meets in Paris once every four years, and the last CGPM was held in October 2003. The SI is a coherent system based on seven base units as defined in the CGPM 1960 and subsequent conferences. An overview of the SI system is available in the brochure `http://www1.bipm.org/utils/common/pdf/si_brochure_8_en.pdf` (eighth edition, 2006).

Table 8.2: SI base units, including their names, symbols, and their SIunits command names

Physical Quantity	Name	Symbol	Command
length	meter	m	\metre
mass	kilogram	kg	\kilogram
time	second	s	\second
electric current	ampere	A	\ampere
thermodynamic temperature	kelvin	K	\kelvin
amount of substance	mole	mol	\mole
luminous intensity	candela	cd	\candela

Table 8.3: Examples of SI-derived units, including their special names, symbols, and SIunits command names

Physical Quantity	Name	Symbol	Command
frequency	hertz	$Hz\,(s^{-1})$	\hertz
force	newton	$N\,(m\,kg\,s^{-2})$	\newton
pressure	pascal	$Pa\,(N\,m^{-2})$	\pascal
energy	joule	$J\,(N\,m)$	\joule
power	watt	$W\,(J\,s^{-1})$	\watt
electric charge	coulomb	$C\,(A\,s)$	\coulomb
potential difference	volt	$V\,(W\,A^{-1})$	\volt
capacitance	farad	$F\,(C\,V^{-1})$	\farad
electric resistance	ohm	$\Omega\,(V\,A^{-1})$	\ohm
magnetic flux	weber	$Wb\,(m^2\,kg\,s^{-2}\,A^{-1})$	\weber
magnetic flux density	tesla	$T\,(Wb\,m^{-2})$	\tesla
inductance	henry	$H\,(Wb\,A^{-1})$	\henry
Celsius temperature	celsius	$°C\,(K)$	\celsius
activity (of radionuclide)	becquerel	$Bq\,(s^{-1})$	\becquerel
absorbed dose	gray	$Gy\,(J\,kg^{-1})$	\gray
dose equivalent	sievert	$Sv\,(J\,kg^{-1})$	\sievert
catalytic activity	katal	$kat\,(s^{-1}\,mol)$	\kat

merce and in science. The SIunits package implements the basic standardization principles of the SI system:

1. It is based on seven well-defined "base units" that, by convention, are considered as dimensionally independent (Table 8.2).

2. It defines a set of "derived units", units that can be constructed by combining base units according to given algebraic relations. The names and symbols of such derived units can have their own special names and symbols (see Table 8.3 for examples).

3. Multiples and subdivisions of units are decimal only (see Table 8.4 on the facing page).

Table 8.4: SI prefixes, including their symbols, values, and Slunits command names

Name	Symbol	Factor	Command	Name	Symbol	Factor	Command
yocto	y	10^{-24}	\yocto	yotta	Y	10^{24}	\yotta
zepto	z	10^{-21}	\zepto	zetta	Z	10^{21}	\zetta
atto	a	10^{-18}	\atto	exa	E	10^{18}	\exa
femto	f	10^{-15}	\femto	peta	P	10^{15}	\peta
pico	p	10^{-12}	\pico	tera	T	10^{12}	\tera
nano	n	10^{-9}	\nano	giga	G	10^{9}	\giga
micro	µ	10^{-6}	\micro	mega	M	10^{6}	\mega
milli	m	10^{-3}	\milli	kilo	k	10^{3}	\kilo
centi	c	10^{-2}	\centi	hecto	h	10^{2}	\hecto
deci	d	10^{-1}	\deci	deca	dk	10^{1}	\deca

Many features of the Slunits package are controlled by package options. They can also be changed inside the body of the text with the \SIunits command (see Example 8-1-1).   *Package options*

Spacing between units   The option cdot typesets a \cdot between units, while the options thickspace, mediumspace, and thinspace typeset a thick, medium, and thin math space, respectively, between units.

Spacing between quantity and units   The options thickqspace, mediumqspace, and thinqspace typeset a thick, medium, and thin math space, respectively, between the numerical value(s) and the units (the numerical value is specified with the \unit command).

Typeset style of units   The textstyle option automatically prints units in the same typeface as the surrounding text.

Miscellaneous   A number of options exist to control the behavior of the Slunits package when its commands collide with those defined in other packages (such as amssymb, pstricks, or babel), or to activate extensions that augment the functions of the basic package. See the manual for details.

The following example shows how the spacing options operate. Note the use of the \usk command to typeset a unit spacing character between the units.

99 V · A	
99 V A	
99 V A	
99 V A	
99 V · A	

```
\usepackage[cdot,thickqspace]{SIunits}
\providecommand\test{\unit{99}{\volt\usk\ampere}}
\begin{flushleft}
\test\\ % default:            thickqspace, cdot
\SIunits[thickspace]\test\\ %     "        thickspace
\SIunits[mediumspace]\test\\%     "        mediumspace
\SIunits[thinspace]\test\\  %     "        thinspace
\SIunits[thinqspace,cdot]\test%thinqspace,cdot
\end{flushleft}
```

Example
8-1-1

We can combine several units, their multiples or subdivisions, their reciprocals, etc., as the following example shows.

2.2 A/s
3 Wm^{-3}
3.2 μJ/mol K
10 m^2
5 g/cm^2
6.022 10^{23} mol^{-1}

```
\usepackage[mediumspace,mediumqspace]{SIunits}
\begin{flushleft}
\unit{2.2}{\ampere\per\second}\\  \unit{3}{\watt\metre\rpcubed}
\unit{3.2}{\micro\joule\per\mole\usk\kelvin}\\
\unit{10}{\square\metre}\\  \unit{5}{\gram\per\centi\metre\squared}\\
\unit{6.022\,\power{10}{23}}{\reciprocal\mole}\\
\end{flushleft}
```

Example 8-1-2

More than 100 ready-to-use combinations of units (see the package documentation for a full list) are predefined. A few examples follow.

A m s
C m^{-3}
J kg^{-1} K^{-1}
kg s^{-1} m^{-3}
m^2 s^{-2}
W m^{-2} sr^{-1}

```
\usepackage{SIunits}
\begin{flushleft}
\amperemetresecond\\            \coulombpercubicmetrenp\\
\jouleperkilogramkelvinnp\\     \kilogrampersecondcubicmetrenp\\
\squaremetrepersquaresecondnp\\ \wattpersquaremetresteradiannp\\
\end{flushleft}
```

Example 8-1-3

Complementary user commands can be added in the SIunits.cfg configuration file, which is loaded at the end of the package.

Alternatively, such additional definitions can be grouped in a new package, dedicated to a given application area. For instance, Andy Buckley developed the **hepunits** package, which extends the original SIunits package with a set of units commonly used in high-energy physics. The following example shows the commands of the **hepunits** (and SIunits) packages in action. We also see that these commands can be used invariably inside text or mathematics mode, with the typeset result being correct in both cases. This feature makes these packages very convenient for authors since typographic rules are automatically taken care of.

5 MHz, 5 GHz, 5 THz
1.0 mrad, 1.0 G
Luminosity: 10^{32} cm^{-2} s^{-1},
10^{25} cm^{-2} s^{-1}
Cross-sections and event rates:
1 fb, 1 pb
3 fb^{-1}, 3 pb^{-1}
Energy and momenta:
3 meV, 3 GeV,
20 keV^{-1}, 20 TeV^{-1}
9 meV/c, 9 MeV/c
10 MeV/c^2, 10 TeV/c^2

```
\usepackage{hepunits}
\begin{flushleft}
\unit{5}{\MHz}, $\unit{5}{\GHz}$, \unit{5}{\THz} \\
\unit{1.0}{\mrad}, $\unit{1.0}{\gauss}$ \\
Luminosity: \unit{\power{10}{32}}{\lumiunits},
            $\unit{\power{10}{25}}{\lumiunits}$\\
Cross-sections and event rates: \\
\unit{1}{\femtobarn}, $\unit{1}{\picobarn}$ \\
\unit{3}{\invfemtobarn}, $\unit{3}{\invpicobarn}$ \\
Energy and momenta:\\
\unit{3}{\meV}, $\unit{3}{\GeV}$, \\
\unit{20}{\kineV}, $\unit{20}{\TineV}$\\
\unit{9}{\meVoverc}, $\unit{9}{\MeVoverc}$\\
\unit{10}{\MeVovercsq}, $\unit{10}{\TeVovercsq}$\\
\end{flushleft}
```

Example 8-1-4

8.1.2 Typesetting chemical symbols

Chemistry texts often contain the names of the elements. From the discussion in Section 8.1, we know that element names should be set in Roman type. Mats Dahlgren developed the **chemsym** package to ensure the typographic correctness of the element names. It provides commands for the 109 chemical elements, using the same names as those in the periodic table of the elements. Some supplementary commands handle chemical groups such as \OH, \COOH, and \CH, and the command \kemtkn lets you define further customized chemical symbols. As there are already LaTeX commands that use some of the element names, the **chemsym** package renames these commands as follows:[1]

\H → \h	Hungarian umlaut ű
\O → \OO	Danish and Norwegian Ø
\P → \PP	Paragraph sign ¶
\S → \SS	Section sign §
\Re → \re	Real part ℜ (math mode)
\Pr → \pr	Probability function Pr (math mode)

In addition, the Sb environment of the **amstex** package is renamed SB.

To simplify entering chemical formulae, LaTeX's superscript and subscript symbols ^ and _, respectively, are redefined to be available outside mathematics mode. For example,

```
2\H_2 plus \O_2 gives 2\H_2\O in an explosive reaction.
```

produces

2H$_2$ plus O$_2$ gives 2H$_2$O in an explosive reaction.

Some packages, however, rely on the original meaning of the ^ character—most notably those packages, like **longtable**, that use the ^^ syntax to handle control characters. In this case the redefinition results in chaos and should be turned off by specifying the collision option when loading **chemsym** with the \usepackage command.

A complex and interesting example of **chemsym** is Mats Dahlgren's file pertab.tex (Figure 8.1 corresponds to a slightly simplified version), which typesets the complete periodic table of the elements and is part of the **chemsym** distribution. For instance, the line starting with potassium (K) was entered as follows inside the tabular environment:

```
_{19}    & _{20}    & _{21}    & _{22}    & _{23}    &
_{24}    & _{25}    & _{26}    & _{27}    & _{28}    &
_{29}    & _{30}    & _{31}    & _{32}    & _{33}    &
_{34}    & _{35}    & _{36}                          \\
\K       & \Ca      & \Sc      & \Ti      & \V       &
\Cr      & \Mn      & \Fe      & \Co      & \Ni      &
```

[1] It should be noted that renaming of commands that depend on LaTeX's encoding, i.e., commands that might change internal meaning if the font encoding changes, such as \H or \O, can never be fully successful. To a certain extent these commands remember their old name; for example, they write that name into external files. This can produce surprises in the table of contents, for example.

```
\Cu        &   \Zn       &   \Ga        &   \Ge        &   \As       &
\Se        &   \Br       &   \Kr                                      \\
^{39.0983} & ^{40.078}   & ^{44.9559}   & ^{47.867}   &^{50.9415}&
^{51.9961} & ^{54.9380}  & ^{55.845}    & ^{58.9332}&^{58.6934}&
^{63.546}  & ^{65.39}    & ^{69.723}    & ^{72.61}    &^{74.9216}&
^{78.96}   & ^{79.904}   & ^{83.80}                              \\\hline
```

Typesetting isotope names

It is not straightforward to typeset isotopes correctly with LaTeX, since their notation uses superscripted and subscripted material in front of the symbol for positioning the atomic and nuclear numbers. One could use an ad hoc mathematical notation but in this case one can have problems with the alignment, as shown in the following example.

```
\usepackage{chemsym}
\begin{flushleft}
% pure math
$^{207}_{83}\mathrm{Bi}$ and $^{60}_{29}\mathrm{Co}$\\[1ex]
% math and chemsym package commands
$^{207}_{83}\Bi$ and $^{60}_{29}\Co$
\end{flushleft}
```

$^{207}_{83}$Bi and $^{60}_{29}$Co

$^{207}_{83}$Bi and $^{60}_{29}$Co

Example 8-1-5

Heiko Bauke's **isotope** package introduces the \isotope command, which is defined as follows:

> \isotope[*nuclear number*][*atomic number*]{*element name*}

One no longer has to use mathematics mode to get the correct typeset result. A command \isotopestyle lets you specify the style in which the isotope name and numbers are typeset, as the following example shows.

```
\usepackage{isotope}
\begin{flushleft}
\isotope[207][83]{Bi} and \isotope[60][29]{Co} \\[1ex]
\renewcommand{\isotopestyle}{\sf}% sans-serif
\isotope[207][83]{Bi} and \isotope[60][29]{Co}
\end{flushleft}
```

$^{207}_{83}$Bi and $^{60}_{29}$Co

$^{207}_{83}$Bi and $^{60}_{29}$Co

Example 8-1-6

8.2 Typesetting chemical formulae

Chemical diagrams are quite complex, and (LA)TEX has few utilities for typesetting them.[1] This is due in part to the fact that, although LaTeX's picture environment is quite adequate for drawing simple figures, a more structured set of macros is needed for chemical formulae.

The first attempts at special chemistry packages were ChemTEX by Roswitha T. Haas and Kevin C. Kane [41] and a plain TEX macro \structure by Michael Ramek [96]. These approaches represented a step forward, but it remained difficult to accommodate more than a few constituent groups in a systematic and transparent way. More recently,

---

[1]See [90] for an interesting overview of electronic publishing and chemical text processing.

Periodic Table of the Elements

Atomic number
Symbol
Relative atomic mass*

1 (I)	2 (II)	3	4	5	6	7	8	9	10	11	12	13 (III)	14 (IV)	15 (V)	16 (VI)	17 (VII)	18 (VIII)
1 H 1.00794																	2 He 4.00260
3 Li 6.941	4 Be 9.012182											5 B 10.811	6 C 12.011	7 N 14.0067	8 O 15.9994	9 F 18.9984	10 Ne 20.1797
11 Na 22.9898	12 Mg 24.3050											13 Al 26.9815	14 Si 28.0855	15 P 30.9738	16 S 32.066	17 Cl 35.4527	18 Ar 39.948
19 K 39.0983	20 Ca 40.078	21 Sc 44.9559	22 Ti 47.867	23 V 50.9415	24 Cr 51.9961	25 Mn 54.9380	26 Fe 55.845	27 Co 58.9332	28 Ni 58.6934	29 Cu 63.546	30 Zn 65.39	31 Ga 69.723	32 Ge 72.61	33 As 74.9216	34 Se 78.96	35 Br 79.904	36 Kr 83.80
37 Rb 85.4678	38 Sr 87.62	39 Y 88.9059	40 Zr 91.224	41 Nb 92.9064	42 Mo 95.94	43 Tc (98)	44 Ru 101.07	45 Rh 102.906	46 Pd 106.42	47 Ag 107.868	48 Cd 112.411	49 In 114.818	50 Sn 118.710	51 Sb 121.760	52 Te 127.60	53 I 126.904	54 Xe 131.29
55 Cs 132.905	56 Ba 137.327	La–Lu	72 Hf 178.49	73 Ta 180.948	74 W 183.84	75 Re 186.207	76 Os 190.23	77 Ir 192.217	78 Pt 195.08	79 Au 196.967	80 Hg 200.59	81 Tl 204.383	82 Pb 207.2	83 Bi 208.981	84 Po (209)	85 At (210)	86 Rn (222)
87 Fr (223)	88 Ra (226)	Ac–Lr	104 Db (261)	105 Sg (262)	106 Rf (263)	107 Bh (262)	108 Hs (265)	109 Mt (266)	**								

57 La 138.905	58 Ce 140.115	59 Pr 140.908	60 Nd 144.24	61 Pm (145)	62 Sm 150.36	63 Eu 151.965	64 Gd 157.25	65 Tb 158.925	66 Dy 162.50	67 Ho 164.930	68 Er 167.26	69 Tm 168.934	70 Yb 173.04	71 Lu 174.967
89 Ac (227)	90 Th (232.038)	91 Pa (231.036)	92 U (238.029)	93 Np (237)	94 Pu (239)	95 Am (243)	96 Cm (247)	97 Bk (247)	98 Cf (251)	99 Es (252)	100 Fm (257)	101 Md (258)	102 No (259)	103 Lr (262)

* Relative atomic mass based on $A_r(^{12}C) \equiv 12$ (after IUPAC "Atomic Weights of the Elements 1993", *Pure and Applied Chemistry*, **1994**,66(12), 2423-2444). For elements which lack stable isotope(s) is the mass number for the most stable isotope given in parentheses, or for Th, Pa and U the relative atomic mass given by IUPAC for the isotopic mixture present on Earth.

** Chemical symbols for elements 104–109 according to IUPAC "Names and Symbols of Transfermium Elements (IUPAC Recommendations 1997)", *Pure and Applied Chemistry*, **1997**, 69(12), 2471-2473.

Example 8-1-7

Figure 8.1: Periodic table of the elements typeset with LaTeX and the chemsym package

Shinsaku Fujita has developed the XꟙMTEX system, a set of LATEX packages for drawing a wide variety of chemical structural formulae; this system is described in Section 8.2.1.

Another approach to drawing chemical formulae is the PPCHTEX package written by Hans Hagen and A. F. Otten, which is the subject of Section 8.2.2.

8.2.1 The XꟙMTEX system

The commands of Shinsaku Fujita's XꟙMTEX package [23–26] offer a systematic approach for specifying arguments for substituent groups and their positions, endocyclic double bonds, and bond patterns, while an additional argument lets you specify heteroatoms on vertices of heterocycles. XꟙMTEX uses only LATEX's `picture` environment and in some cases the extension package epic, so it is highly portable. It consists of a set of package files, each specialized to treat a particular kind of chemical structure:

aliphat	aliphatic compounds
carom	vertical and horizontal carbocyclic compounds
ccycle	bicyclic compounds, etc.
chemstr	basic typesetting commands for atoms and bonds
lowcycle	carbocyles with five members or fewer
hcycle	pyranose and furanose derivatives
hetarom	vertical heterocyclic compounds
hetaromh	horizontal heterocyclic compounds
locant	helper package producing locant numbers and bond letters

The packages can be loaded individually using LATEX's `\usepackage` command, but the chemstr package is loaded automatically by any of the other packages. The xymtex package loads *all* packages in the XꟙMTEX bundle.

General conventions

The XꟙMTEX command names are based on the standard nomenclature used for organic compounds [55]. The invariant part of a structure—i.e., the base skeleton containing fixed bonds and atoms—is automatically printed with no designation, while the varying part—i.e., substituent groups, additional bonds and atoms—is specified by a set of arguments.

The commands can be subdivided into those for *general* and *specific* use. The specific commands offer convenient shortcuts for drawing a narrow range of structures in a particular category, while the general commands support a wider range at the cost of additional specification. This distinction is also reflected in the command names; e.g., specific commands for drawing certain N-heterocyles would be `\isoindolev` or `\purinev` (with the N atoms automatically typeset), while the name for the underlying general command would be `\nonaheterov` (i.e., describing the geometric structure of the base skeleton without any atoms in predefined positions).

Syntax for specific commands

For carbocycles and heterocycles we have the abstract syntax `\Com[opt]{subslist}` where `\Com` is a command name corresponding to the compound to be typeset. It is usually suffixed by either v or h, denoting a vertical or horizontal representation of the structure, respectively. If alternative orientations are possible, the name might be further suffixed with the letter i.

The preselected bond pattern can be modified by the argument *opt*, consisting of one or two letter combinations denoting a certain bond pattern. The values allowed and their exact meaning depend on the command; a detailed discussion appears in the manual [26].

The *subslist* argument lists substituents, with their bonds separated by semicolons if there is more than one bond–substituent pair. A bond is specified by a number giving the atom's position in the structure to which it is attached, optionally followed by a bond modifier (one or more letters) that classifies the type of bond to be used. The substituent is separated from this by two equals signs; e.g., `1D==O;3==OCH$_3$;`... means that the bond at the atom in position 1 takes an oxygen atom (O) through a double bond, the bond in position 3 takes a methoxy group through a single bond, and so on. Atom positions are numbered sequentially, usually in a clockwise fashion starting at the top for vertically oriented structures and on the left for horizontally oriented ones. Possible bond modifiers for the bond at an atom at position n are as follows:

nS   exocyclic single bond at n-atom (equivalent to specifying just n)

nD   exocyclic double bond

nA   alpha single bond represented as a dotted line

nB   beta single bond represented as a bold line

The nA modifier relies on the availability of the `\dottedline` command as defined by the **epic** or **eepic** package. If neither package is loaded, the bond appears as a single line of normal width; i.e., it looks the same as if n were specified.

If n is greater than 9, it must be surrounded by two braces; otherwise the commands fail to parse their *subslist* argument correctly. For example, while you can write `1D==O` to attach an O atom with a double bond to the first atom of a structure, you would specify `{{13}}D==O` to attach it to the thirteenth atom. Unfortunately, there is no error message— the only indication of a problem is an incorrectly drawn structure.

As a first example, let us look at the 1,4-dibromobenzene compound (also known as para-dibromobenzene or *p*-dibromobenzene). We can get several different representations by using the h and v suffixes on the command name and by specifying a bond pattern in the optional argument.

```
\usepackage{carom}
\bzdrh{1==Br;4==Br}      \bzdrv{1==Br;4==Br}
\bzdrv[l]{1==Br;4==Br} \bzdrv[c]{1==Br;4==Br}
```

The optional argument [l] designates a left-oriented set of double bonds (the default is [r]) and [c] specifies an aromatic circle. Other legal values for the optional argument for \bzdrv and \bzdrv are [pa] to [pc] for the three *p*-quinone variants (two examples are shown below) and [oa] to [of] for the six *o*-quinone variants.

Instead of letting the command decide on the handedness of a substituent, you can specify it explicitly using \rmoiety and \lmoiety commands, as shown in the following example with left-handed and right-handed methanesulfonimido groups:

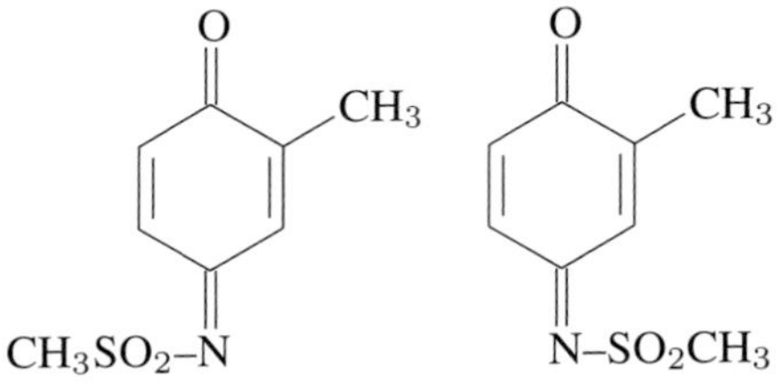

```
\usepackage{carom}
\bzdrv[pa]{1D==O;4D==%
    \lmoiety{CH$_{3}$SO$_{2}$--N};%
  2==CH$_{3}$}
\bzdrv[pa]{1D==O;4D==%
    \rmoiety{N--SO$_{2}$CH$_{3}$};%
  2==CH$_{3}$}
```

Example 8-2-2

Depending on the base structure, two bonds might also be possible at a locant. In that case the modifiers for a bond in position n are as follows:

n**SA**   alpha single bond represented as a dotted line

n**SB**   beta single bond represented as a bold line

n**Sa**   unspecified alpha single bond

n**Sb**   unspecified beta single bond

Again, the dotted line for the alpha bond requires the use of the **epic** or **eepic** package. As an abstract example we show below all bond modifiers in a single structure; real-life examples follow later on.

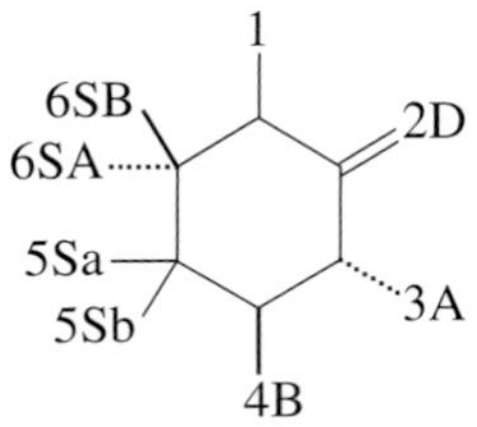

```
\usepackage{carom,epic}
\cyclohexanev{1==1;%
    2D==2D;%
    3A==3A;%
    4B==4B;%
    5Sa==5Sa;5Sb==5Sb;%
    6SA==6SA;6SB==6SB}
```

Example 8-2-3

Syntax for general commands

The general commands, such as \cyclohexanev in Example 8-2-3, are similar to the specific commands, but can have a variable set of skeletal heteroatoms so as to cover a wider range of compound structures. For carbocycles the general syntax is

\Com[*bondlist*]{*subslist*}

where, instead of an optional argument specifying a predefined bond pattern, we now have an optional *bondlist* argument that lets us specify double bonds individually. The possible double bonds of the structure are internally labeled as a, b, c, etc.; to make the desired bonds appear, you specify them in the *bondlist* argument. Aromatic cycles are usually labeled with uppercase letters A, B, etc., if the structure is large enough to permit more than one cycle, such as in the case of perhydro anthracene derivatives.

All of the specific commands are internally implemented as calls to the general forms with specific argument settings. For instance, one of our previous examples involving `\bzdrh` can also be typeset like this with the general command `\cyclohexaneh`:

Example
8-2-4

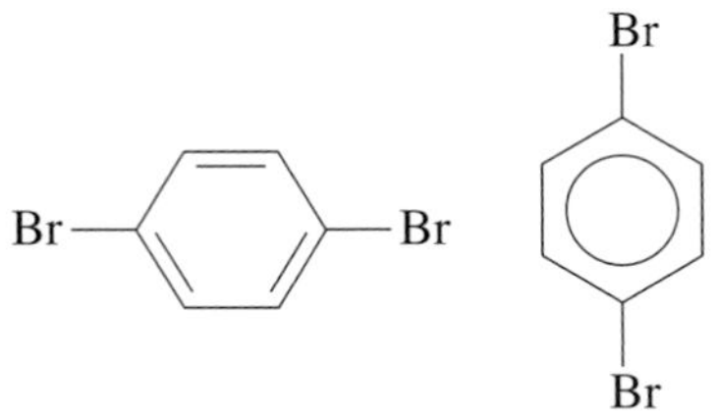

```
\usepackage{carom}
\cyclohexaneh
   [bdf]{1==Br;4==Br}
\cyclohexanev
   [A]{1==Br;4==Br}
```

The syntax is a little more complex for heterocycles because it must allow the user to specify individual atoms on the base skeleton:

`\Com` [*bondlist*] {*atomlist*}{*subslist*}

Endocyclic bonds are specified as before with the *bondlist* argument, as are the substituents, including their bonds, with the *subslist* argument. What is different for this type of command is the additional mandatory *atomlist* argument, in which the individual atoms on the base skeleton are specified if necessary. The argument syntax is comparable to that of the *subslist* argument: atom specifications are separated by semicolons and atom positions are denoted by a number, followed by a double equals sign, followed by the string denoting the atom.

Example
8-2-5

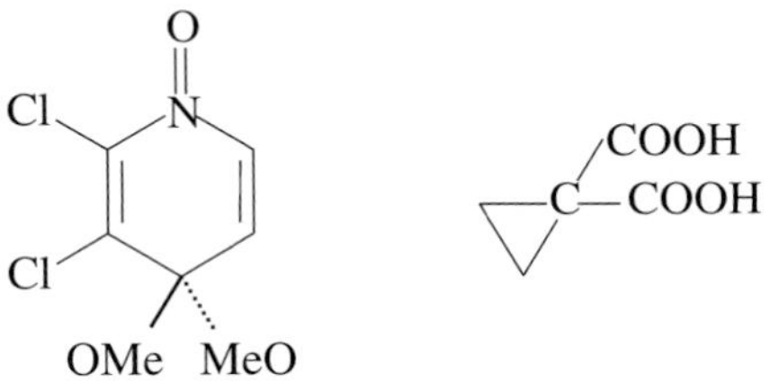

```
\usepackage{hetarom,epic}
\sixheterov[eb]{1==N}
   {1D==O;
    4SA==MeO;4SB==OMe;
    5==Cl;
    6==Cl}
\threehetero[H]{2==C}
   {2Sa==COOH;2Sb==COOH}
```

Charges on atoms

The charge on individual atoms of the base skeleton can sometimes be specified in the *opt* or *bondlist* argument, using the atom number followed by a plus sign and surrounded by a set of braces.

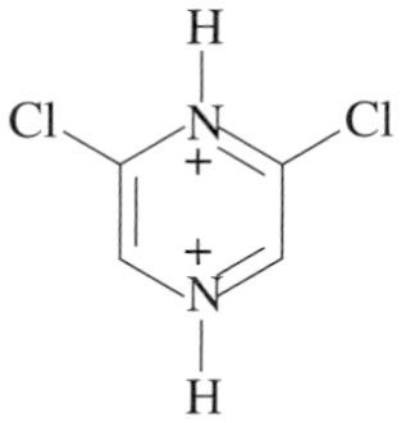

```
\usepackage{hetarom,epic}
\pyrazinev[1{1+}{4+}]
    {1==H;4==H;2==Cl;6==Cl}
```

Example
8-2-6

Having reviewed the design principles of the XꞂMTEX system, we are now ready to look in more detail at some of its packages for drawing chemical diagrams.

The carom package

XꞂMTEX's carom package allows you to draw a large variety of carbocyles (see Table 8.5 on the next page). We have already seen some examples of the \bzdrv and \bzdrh commands to draw benzene derivatives. General cyclohexane derivatives are available with the commands \cyclohexanev and \cyclohexaneh. Using the *bondlist* argument described earlier, you can introduce endocyclic double bonds at appropriate places.

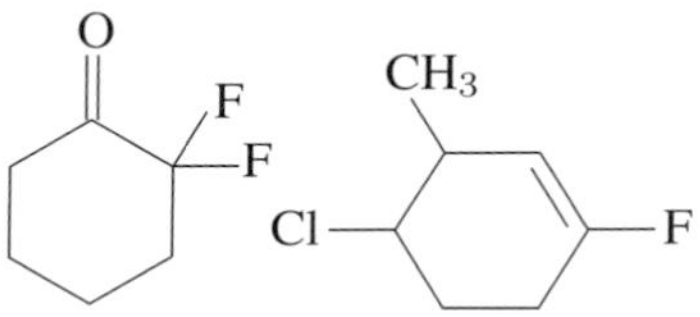

```
\usepackage{epic,carom}
\cyclohexanev
    {1D==O;2Sa==F;2Sb==F}
\cyclohexaneh[c]
    {1==Cl;4==F;2==CH$_{3}$}
```

Example
8-2-7

Fused rings, such as naphthalenes and naphthoquinones, are drawn with the \naphdrv set of commands. The *opt* argument for bond patterns supports all types of *o*-quinone variants as well as the aromatic circle.

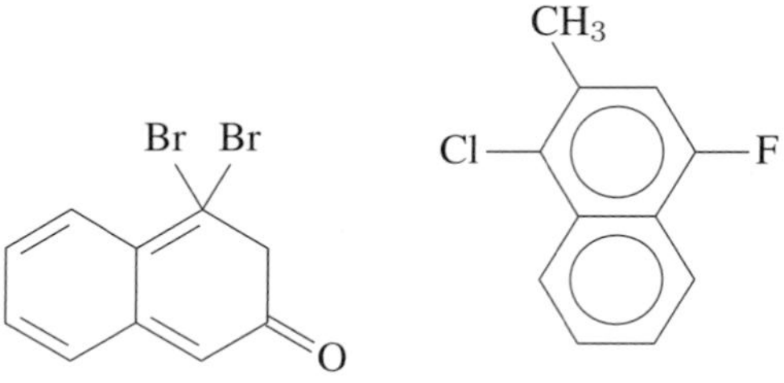

```
\usepackage{epic,carom}
\naphdrv[ob]
    {1Sb==Br;1Sa==Br;3D==O}
\naphdrh[A]
    {1==Cl;4==F;2==CH$_{3}$}
```

Example
8-2-8

Commands for other complex structures are available, such as tetraline derivatives (the \tetralinev and \tetralineh commands), decaline derivatives (\decalinev and \decalineh), tricyclic carbocycles such as anthracene derivatives (\anthracenev and \hanthracenv) and phenanthrene derivatives (\phenanthrenev and \hphenanthrenev), and steroid derivatives with and without side chains (\steroid and \steroidchain). These commands all employ the same general syntax, as outlined in the previous section, and are easy to use, although memorizing position numbers and

Table 8.5: Aromatic carbocycles commands (\command{1==a1 ; 2==a2 ; 3==a3})

Ring Size	Specific Commands			
6	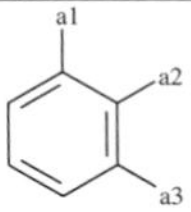 \bzdrv	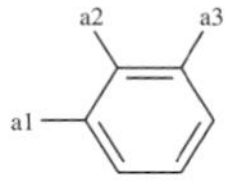 \bzdrh		
6,6	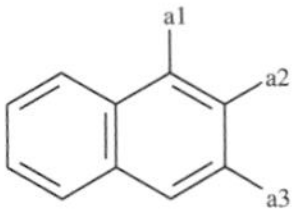 \naphdrv	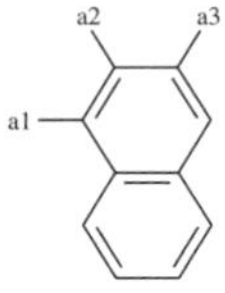 \naphdrh	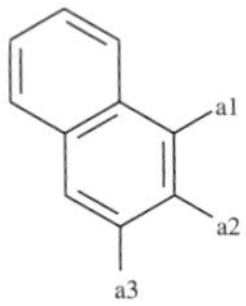 \naphdrvb	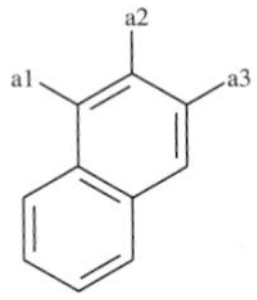 \naphdrvt
	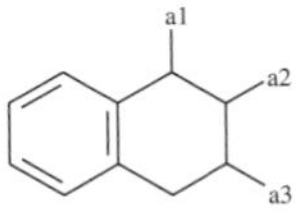 \tetralinev	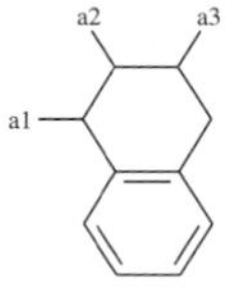 \tetralineh	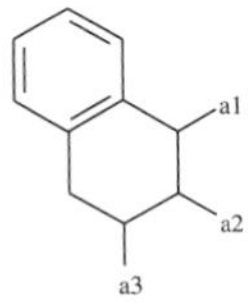 \tetralinevb	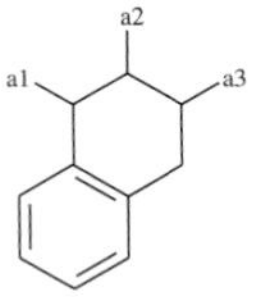 \tetralinevt
6,6,6	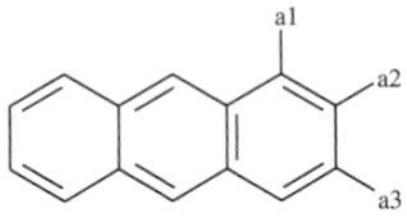 \anthracenev	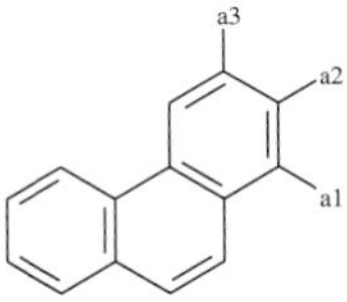 \phenanthrenev		

Example
8-2-9

bond letters might take some time. These are well documented both in the package files and in the extensive online manual (more than 120 pages of diagrams and examples), where they are shown in diagrams like the following:

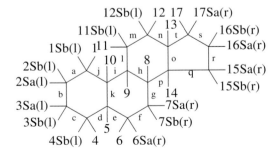

Example
8-2-10

By referring to these kinds of diagrams and tables listing the allowed values for the *opt* or *bondlist* argument, it is not too hard to produce formulae like

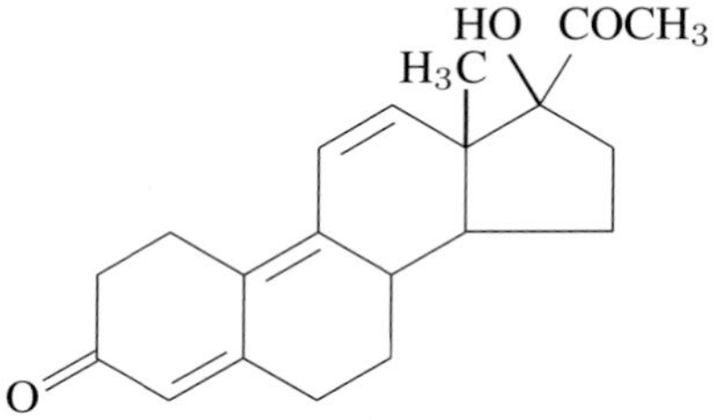

```
\usepackage{carom}
\steroid[dim]
  {3D==O;%
  {{13}B}==\lmoiety{H$_3$C};%
  {{17}SB}==HO;%
  {{17}SA}==COCH$_3$}
```

Example
8-2-11

The optional argument [dim] indicates the positions of the three endocyclic double bonds, and the command \lmoiety connects the right terminal carbon of the methyl to the corresponding bond at the fused 13-position.

The lowcycle **package**

Lower-order cycles (up to six carbon atoms in one of the cycles; see Table 8.6 on the facing page) are available by loading the **lowcycle** package. Five-member cycles can be drawn with the \cyclopentanev set of commands (all four suffix types). Below are a few examples.

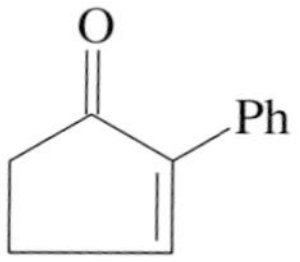

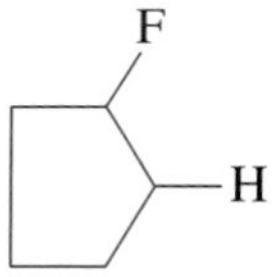

```
\usepackage{lowcycle}
\cyclopentanevi[b]{1D==O;%
  2==Ph}
\cyclopentaneh[H]{1==H;2==F}
```

Example
8-2-13

Beside putting charges on each atom, these structures support a charge in the center using {O+} or {O$-$}.

```
\usepackage{epic,lowcycle}
\cyclopentanev[A{O{$-$}}]{}
```

Example
8-2-14

Also provided by this package are indane derivatives (fused six- and five-member rings) with the \indanev set of commands; again, horizontal, vertical, and inverse forms exist.

Table 8.6: Carbocyclic compounds (*command*{1==a1;2==a2;3==a3})

Ring Size	Specific Commands			
3	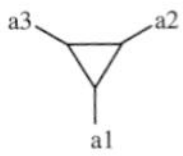 \cyclopropanev	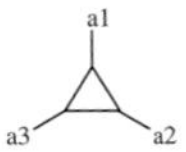 \cyclopropanevi	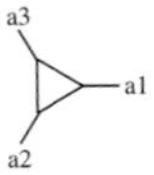 \cyclopropaneh	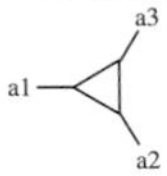 \cyclopropanehi
4	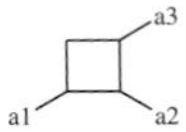 \cyclobutane			
5	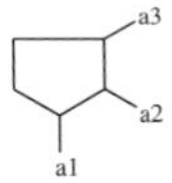 \cyclopentanev	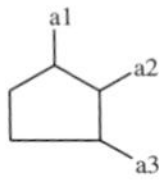 \cyclopentanevi	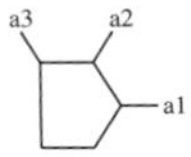 \cyclopentaneh	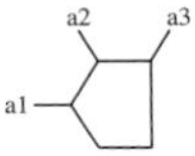 \cyclopentanehi
6	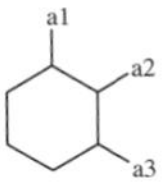 \cyclohexanev		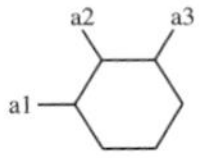 \cyclohexaneh	
5,6	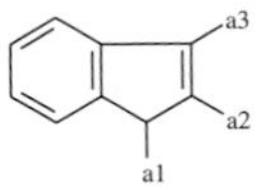 \indanev	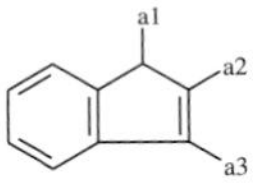 \indanevi	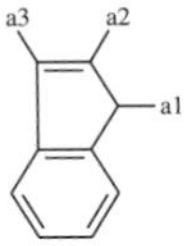 \indaneh	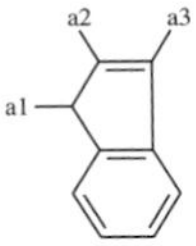 \indanehi
6,6	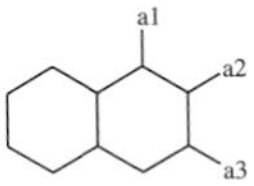 \decalinev	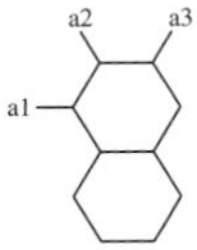 \decalineh	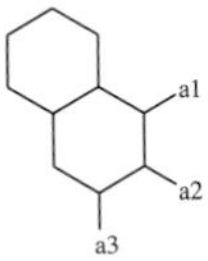 \decalinevb	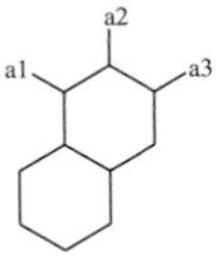 \decalinevt
6,6,6	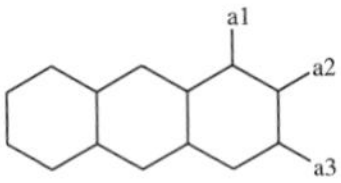 \hanthracenev	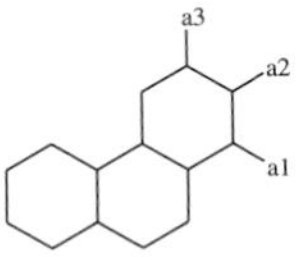 \hphenanthrenev		

Example
8-2-12

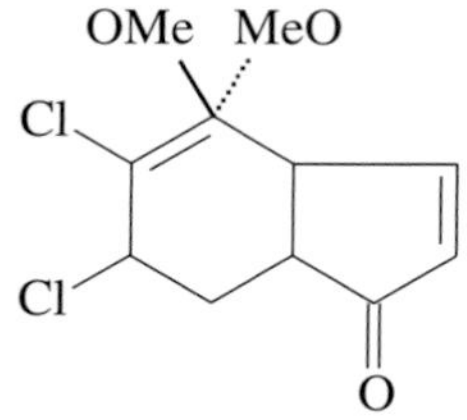

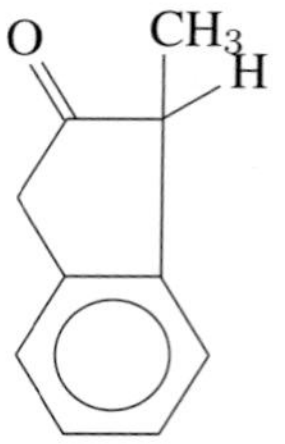

```
\usepackage{epic,lowcycle}
\indanev[eb]
  {1D==O;4SA==MeO;%
   4SB==OMe;5==Cl;6==Cl}
\indanehi[A]{2D==O;%
   3Sa==CH$_3$;3Sb==H}
```

Example
8-2-15

Finally, four- and three-member carbon cycles are supported through \cyclobutane and \cyclopropane, respectively. Not surprisingly, due to their geometric form, they do not have different suffix variants.

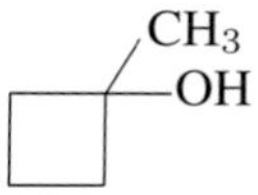

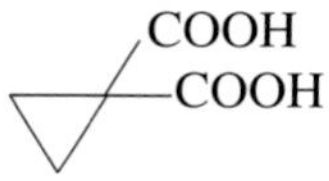

```
\usepackage{lowcycle}
\cyclobutane
  {3Sa==OH;3Sb==CH$_3$}
\cyclopropane{2Sa==COOH;%
   2Sb==COOH}
```

Example
8-2-16

The hetarom **and** hetaromh **packages**

Heterocyclic compounds—i.e., those in which one or more of the carbon atoms in the cyclic chain have been replaced with other atoms—are available by loading the **hetarom** package (vertical-form commands) or the **hetaromh** package (the corresponding horizontal forms).

General commands for three- to six-member heterocycles are available with predictable names like \sixheterov (see Table 8.7 on the next page). Here are some examples:

```
\usepackage{epic,hetarom}
\threehetero     {1==S}       {3Sa==H$_3$C;3Sb==H$_3$C}
\fourhetero      {1==O;2==O}{4Sa==COOH;4Sb==COOH}
\fiveheterov[eb] {1==N}       {1D==O;4SA==MeO;4SB==OMe;5==Cl}
\sixheterov [c]  {1==N}       {1==Cl;4==F;2==CH$_3$}
```

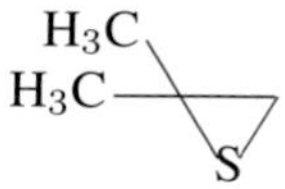

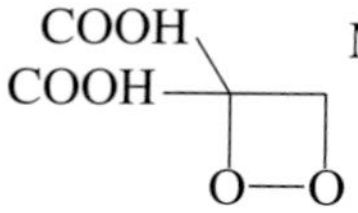

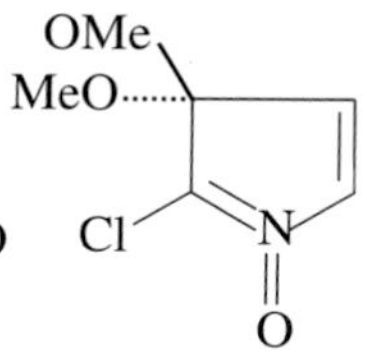

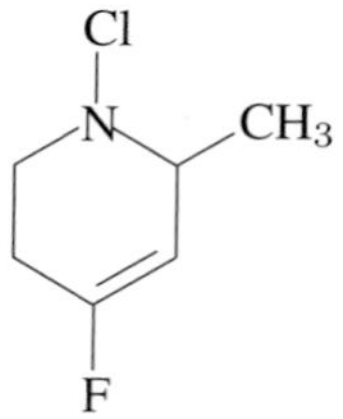

Example
8-2-18

Table 8.7: Heterocyclic compounds (\command{1==1}{2==a2;3==a3})

Ring Size	Generic Commands			
3	 \threeheterov	 \threeheterovi	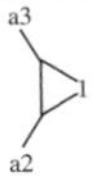 \threeheteroh	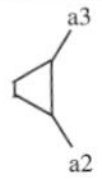 \threeheterohi
4	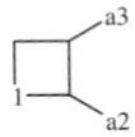 \fourhetero			
5	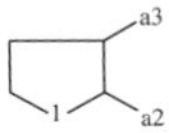 \fiveheterov	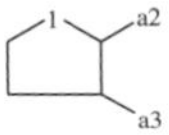 \fiveheterovi	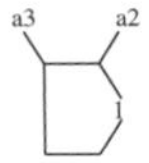 \fiveheteroh	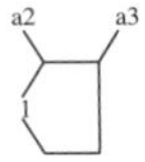 \fiveheterohi
6	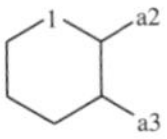 \sixheterov	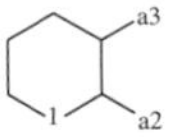 \sixheterovi	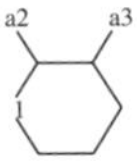 \sixheteroh	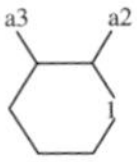 \sixheterohi
5,6	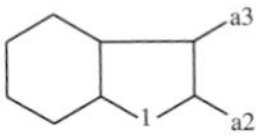 \nonaheterov	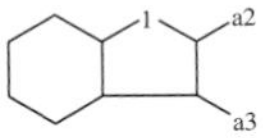 \nonaheterovi	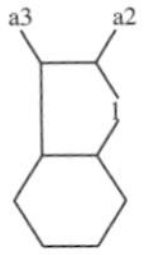 \nonaheteroh	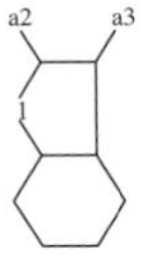 \nonaheterohi
6,6	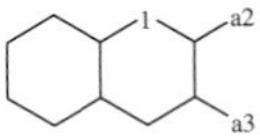 \decaheterov	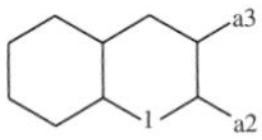 \decaheterovi	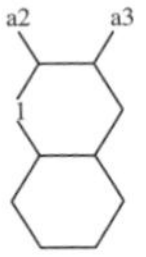 \decaheteroh	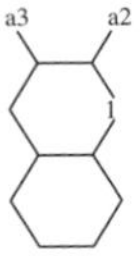 \decaheterohi
	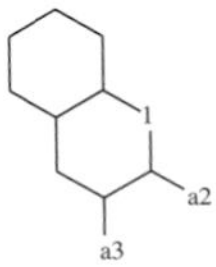 \decaheterovb	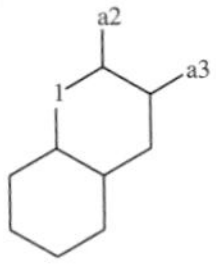 \decaheterovt		

Example
8-2-17

Table 8.8: Application commands of the hetarom package; corresponding horizontal forms are defined by the hetaromh package

Six-Member Heterocycles
\pyrazinev \pyridazinevi \pyridazinev \pyridinevi \pyridinev
\pyrimidinevi \pyrimidinev \triazinevi \triazinev

Five-Member Heterocycles
\imidazolevi \imidazolev \isoxazolevi \isoxazolev \oxazolevi
\oxazolev \pyrazolevi \pyrazolev \pyrrolevi \pyrrolev

Six-Six-Fused Heterocycles
\cinnolinevi \cinnolinev \isoquinolinevi \isoquinolinev \pteridinevi
\pteridinev \quinazolinevi \quinazolinev \quinolinevi \quinolinev
\quinoxalinev

Six-Five-Fused Heterocycles
\benzofuranevi \benzofuranev \benzoxazolevi \benzoxazolev \indolevi
\indolev \indolizinevi \indolizinev \isobenzofuranevi
\isobenzofuranev \isoindolevi \isoindolev \purinevi \purinev

In addition, fused six-member rings and fused five- and six-member rings are supported by general commands. They have horizontal and (where applicable) invariant forms.

```
\usepackage{eepic,hetarom}
\decaheterov[af]{4==O}
   {1==CH$_3$;6==H$_3$C;9A==H;%
      {{10}A}==\lmoiety{HOCH$_2$}}
\nonaheterov[bjge]{1==S;2==N}{3==Cl}
```

Example
8-2-19

Clearly, with this many general commands, it is easy to provide an even richer set of application commands, and indeed the two packages implement more than 80 of them (if we include all of the suffix variations for drawing the structures in different ways). This set includes pyridine derivatives and other six-member ring structures; for five-member rings we have pyrrole derivatives and others. As specializations of the general fused-ring commands \nonaheterov and \decaheterov, there are commands for drawing N,O-heterocycles such as indoles and isobenzofuranes (see Table 8.8) and N-heterocycles (see Table 8.9 on the next page)

The ccycle and hcycle packages

Use of stereochemical compounds is facilitated with commands for drawing cyclohexane chair forms, bicyclo[2.2.1]heptane, and adamantane derivatives, which are loaded with the ccycle package.

Table 8.9: Heterocycles containing nitrogen (\command{1==a1;2==a2;3==a3})

N	Specific commands			
1	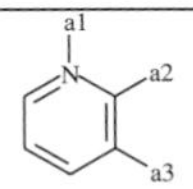 \pyridinev	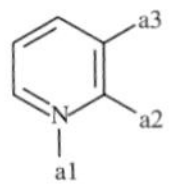 \pyridinevi	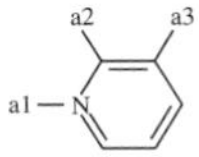 \pyridineh	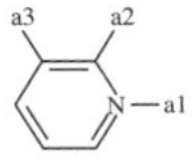 \pyridinehi
2,4	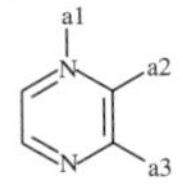 \pyrazinev		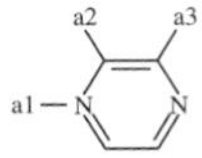 \pyrazineh	
1,3	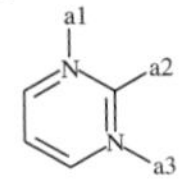 \pyrimidinev	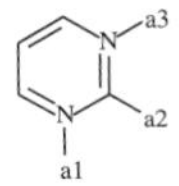 \pyrimidinevi	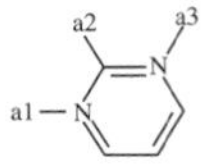 \pyrimidineh	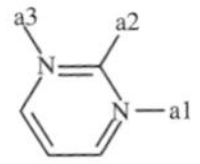 \pyrimidinehi
1,2	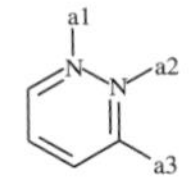 \pyridazinev	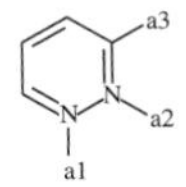 \pyridazinevi	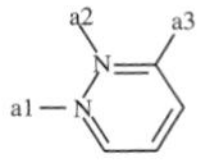 \pyridazineh	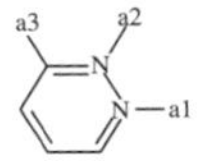 \pyridazinehi
1,3,5	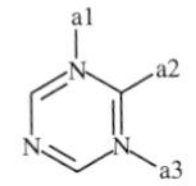 \triazinev	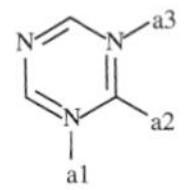 \triazinevi	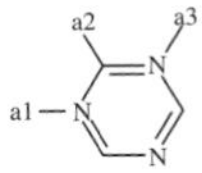 \triazineh	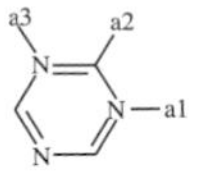 \triazinehi

Example 8-2-20

The \chair command uses nSe as a bond modifier to denote an equatorial single bond at the nth atom.

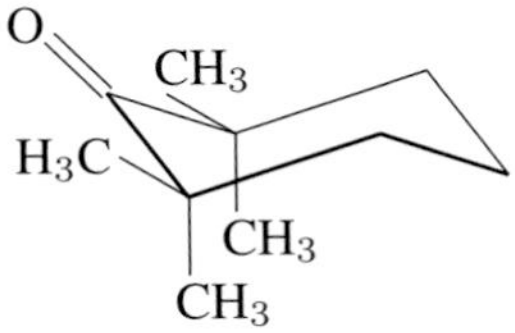

```
\usepackage{ccycle}
\chair{1D==O;%
  2Se==H$_3$C;2Sa==CH$_3$;%
  6Se==CH$_3$;6Sa==CH$_3$}
```

Example 8-2-21

The other commands follow the standard syntax, except that the handedness of substituents cannot be specified explicitly.

```
\usepackage{ccycle}
\bicychepv{2D==O}              \bicycheph[b]{2==OMe;3==OMe}
\bornane{3B==OH;2A==OH}        \adamantane{2D==O;6D==O;1==F;3==Cl}
```

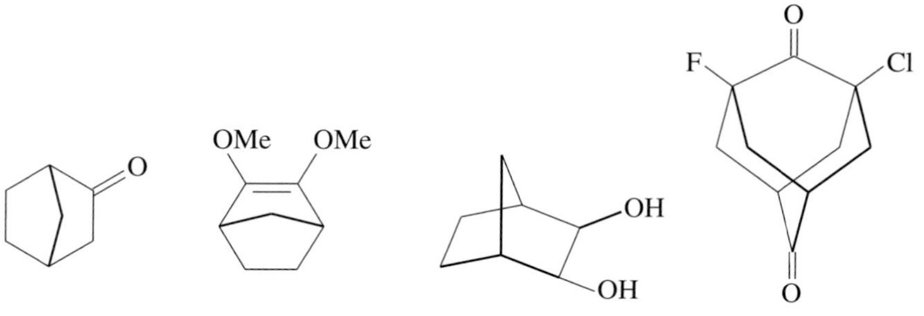

Example
8-2-22

The commands for drawing furanoses and pyranoses derivatives are defined in the hcycle package. Below are examples of both.

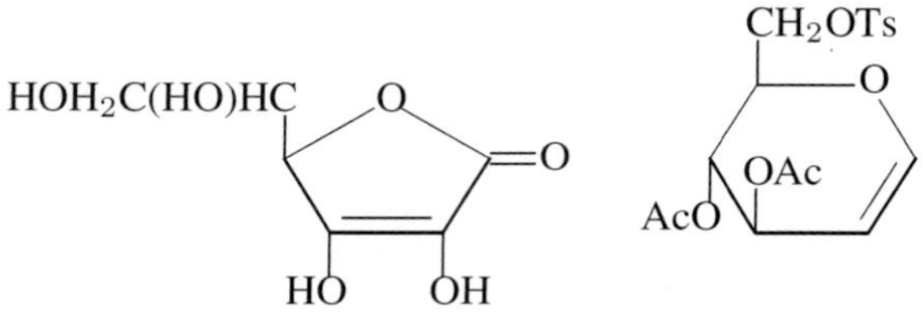

```
\usepackage{xymtex}
\furanose[b]{1D==O;2Sa==OH;%
   3Sa==\lmoiety{HO};%
   4Sb==HOH$_2$C(HO)HC}
\qquad
\pyranose[a]{3Sb==OAc;%
   4Sa==AcO;5Sb==CH$_{2}$OTs}
```

Example
8-2-23

The aliphat package

To draw tetrahedral and other aliphatic compounds you need the aliphat package. Given that the skeleton of tetrahedral or trigonal units consists only of a single atom, the commands for drawing them have no *bondlist* argument. They do, however, take an optional argument in which a charge for this atom can be specified, as seen below. Another advantage offered by this type of command is the possibility of assigning an atom symbol to the central position by specifying, e.g., O==C.

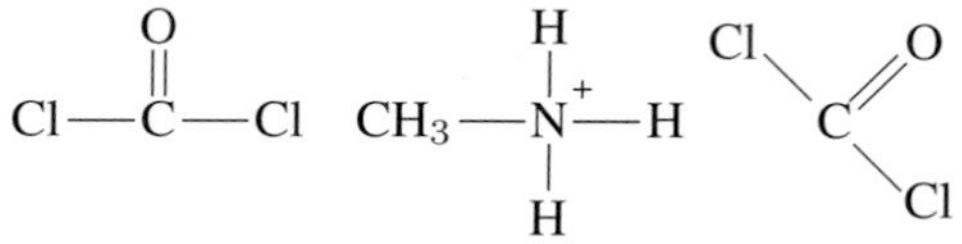

```
\usepackage{aliphat}
\tetrahedral{0==C;1D==O;2==Cl;%
   4==Cl}
\qquad
\tetrahedral[{0+}]{0==N;%
   1==H;2==CH$_3$;3==H;4==H}
\square{0==C;1D==O;2==Cl;4==Cl}
```

Example
8-2-24

There are six commands for drawing trigonal units. Those starting with an uppercase letter have an angle of 120° between the diagonal bonds, while the others are 90° apart.

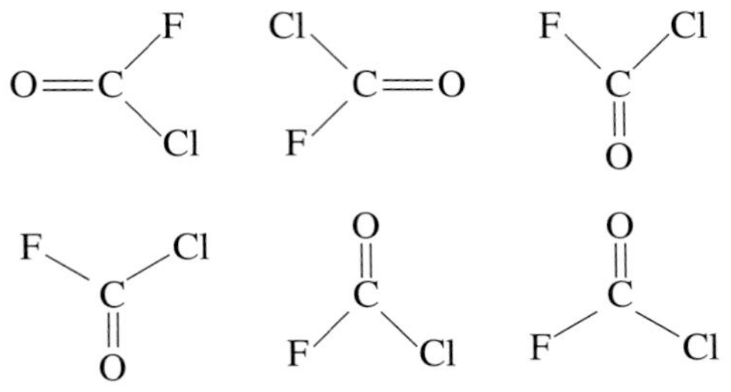

```
\usepackage{aliphat}
\begin{flushleft}
\rtrigonal{0==C;1D==O;2==Cl;3==F}\quad
\ltrigonal{0==C;1D==O;2==Cl;3==F}\quad
\utrigonal{0==C;1D==O;2==Cl;3==F}\\
\Utrigonal{0==C;1D==O;2==Cl;3==F}\quad
\dtrigonal{0==C;1D==O;2==Cl;3==F}\quad
\Dtrigonal{0==C;1D==O;2==Cl;3==F}
\end{flushleft}
```

Example 8-2-25

Drawing ethylene derivatives is supported with the \ethylene command (notice the missing suffix) and its vertical forms \ethylenev and \Ethylenev, the latter having the diagonal bonds 120° apart. Inner double and triple bonds are specified with d (default) and t in the optional argument.

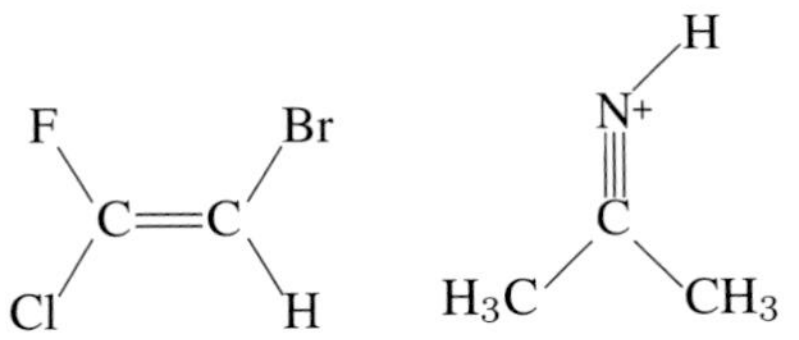

```
\usepackage{aliphat}
\ethylene{1==C;2==C}
   {1==F;2==Cl;3==H;4==Br}
\qquad
\ethylenev[t{2+}]{1==C;2==N}
   {1==H$_3$C;2==CH$_3$;3==H}
```

Example 8-2-26

Finally, the package supports the drawing of configurations of the tetrahedra carbon in different projections through the commands \tetrastereo and \dtetrastereo, and the configuration of ethane with the command \ethanestereo. Here the central atoms can be specified explicitly.

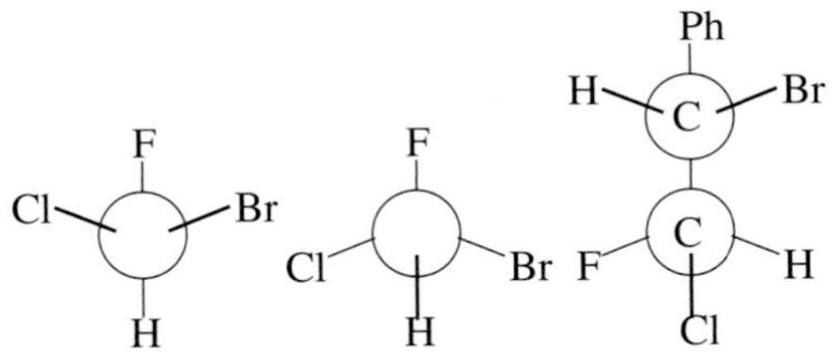

```
\usepackage{aliphat}
\setlength\unitlength{0.1pt}
\tetrastereo{1==F;%
   2==Cl;3==H;4==Br}
\dtetrastereo{1==F;%
   2==Cl;3==H;4==Br}
\ethanestereo{1==C;2==C}
   {1==F;2==Cl;3==H;4==Br;%
   5==Ph;6==H}
```

Example 8-2-27

Combining structures

The hetarom and hetaromh packages also support six- and five-member building blocks, which can be fused with other ring structures to produce new ring systems. Their syntax is comparable to that for general heterocycles but with one additional mandatory argument:

$$\text{\textbackslash Com}\,[\textit{bondlist}]\,\{\textit{atomlist}\}\{\textit{subslist}\}\{\textit{omit}\}$$

The *omit* argument specifies which bonds are to be deleted from the structure.

```
\usepackage{hetarom}
\sixunitv[b]{1==N}{1==H;2==F}{d}
\fiveunitv[b]{}{1D==O;2==Cl}{d}
\fiveunitvi[b]{}{1D==O;2==Cl}{d}
```

Example
8-2-28

The corresponding horizontal commands are defined in the hetaromh package.

Drawing complex structures

More complicated structural formulae can be constructed from the commands described in previous sections by combining two or more structures inside a picture environment. This technique is explained in detail in Chapter 14 (*Combining structures*) of the XΥMTEX manual for version 1.01. Moreover, Chapter 15 (*Large substituents*) explains how XΥMTEX commands can be used inside the argument of another.[1]

Since version 2 of XΥMTEX[2] the combination method mentioned in the previous paragraph has been conveniently extended by the introduction of the "yl" function. Almost all XΥMTEX commands can be converted into the corresponding substituent by adding the code (yl) together with a locant number; i.e., in the *subslist* argument we can write something like {n==(yl);...}, n to specify the locant at which the structure will be attached.

```
\usepackage{carom}
\bzdrh{1==a1;4==\bzdrh{1==(yl);3==a3}}
```

Example
8-2-29

Here the benzene ring at the right in converted into a substituent by specifying (yl) and is connected by its locant 1 to locant 4 of the benzene ring at the left. Nesting is possible,

---

[1]See http://imt.chem.kit.ac.jp/fujita/fujitas3/xymtex/xym101/xymdvi/xymtex.pdf.

[2]All versions of XΥMTEX—in particular the more recent ones—can be downloaded from the XΥMTEX home page at http://imt.chem.kit.ac.jp/fujita/fujitas3/xymtex/indexe.html. There you can also find the manuals for all versions as well as some recent journal articles describing XΥMTEX.

as the following example shows, where the various elements are added as substituents going from left to right.

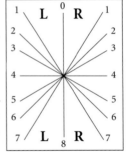

```
\usepackage{xymtex}
\naphdrh{1==HO;4==%
  \cyclohexaneh{1==(yl);4==%
    \tetrahedral{2==(yl);0==C;1D==O;4==%
      \bzdrh{1==(yl)}}}}
```

Example
8-2-30

In many cases the substituent is linked to a substitution site by an intervening unit (e.g., O, NH, SO$_2$). The commands \ryl and \lyl generate, respectively, a right-hand substituent and a left-hand substituent with a linking unit.

\lyl(*link*){*group*}   \ryl(*link*){*group*}

link Specifies the linking unit. The first element is an integer (0–8) indicating the slope of the incidental bond (L side of the boxed diagram for \ryl, R side for \lyl). The second element is the linking unit. Both elements are separated by a == delimiter.

group Specifies the substituent produced by a "yl" function. The first element is an integer (0–8) indicating the slope of the incidental bond (R side of the boxed diagram for \ryl, L side for \lyl). The second element is the substituent command. Both elements are separated by a == delimiter.

Consider the following example, which shows the \lyl and \ryl commands in action. Note how the slope parameters are used to specify the directions of the bonds.

```
\usepackage{xymtex}
\cyclohexanev[]{%
  1==\lyl(8==SO$\sb{2}$--HN){1==\bzdrh{5==(yl)}};%
  6==\lyl(5==SO$\sb{2}$--NH){4==\bzdrh{4==(yl)}};%
  5==\lyl(3==SO$\sb{2}$--NH){4==\bzdrh{4==(yl)}};%
  4==\lyl(0==SO$\sb{2}$--HN){7==\bzdrh{3==(yl)}}}
\quad
\cyclohexanev[]{%
  1==\ryl(8==NH--SO$\sb{2}$){1==\bzdrh{6==(yl)}};%
  2==\ryl(5==NH--SO$\sb{2}$){4==\bzdrh{1==(yl)}};%
  3==\ryl(3==NH--SO$\sb{2}$){4==\bzdrh{1==(yl)}};%
  4==\ryl(0==NH--SO$\sb{2}$){7==\bzdrh{2==(yl)}}}
```

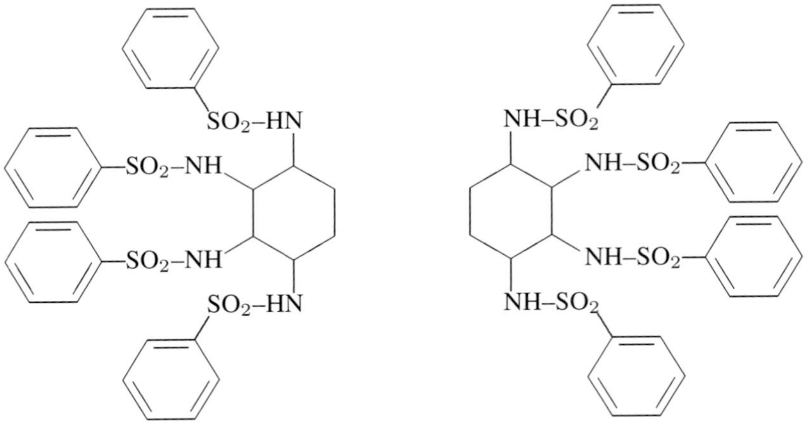

Example
8-2-31

A more complex example shows how we can control the layout of a formula in great detail.

```
\usepackage{xymtex}
\bzdrv{1==OH;5==CH$\sb{3}$;4==OC$\sb{16}$H$\sb{33}$;%
    2==\ryl(4==NH--SO$\sb{2}$){4==\bzdrh{1==(yl);%
        2==OCH$\sb{2}$CH$\sb{2}$OCH$\sb{3}$;%
        5==\ryl(2==NH--SO$\sb{2}$){4==\bzdrh{1==(yl);%
            5==\ryl(2==SO$\sb{2}$--NH){4==\naphdrh{1==(yl);5==OH;%
                8==\lyl(4==N=N){4==\bzdrh{4==(yl);1==NO$\sb{2}$;%
                    5==SO$\sb{2}$CH$\sb{3}$}}}}}}}}}
```

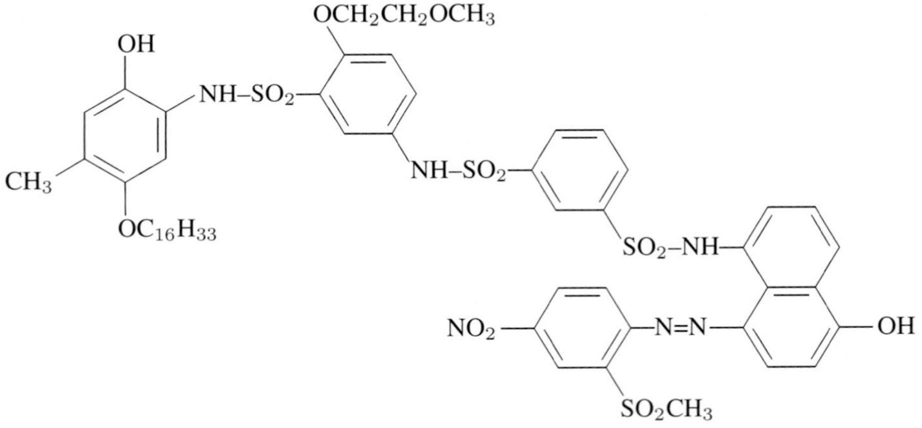

Example
8-2-32

We have already seen examples of predefined commands for fused rings (see the lower parts of Table 8.6 on page 527 and Table 8.7 on page 529). More generally, ring units can be

Table 8.10: Fusing skeleton commands

Ring Size	Fusing Skeleton			
3	\threefusev	\threefusevi	\threefuseh	\threefusehi
4	\fourfuse			
5	\fivefusev	\fivefusevi	\fivefuseh	\fivefusehi
6	\sixfusev	\sixfusevi	\sixfuseh	\sixfusehi

fused by using one of the commands in Table 8.10, which have the following general structure (note the presence of a third mandatory argument).

> \Com[*bondlist*]{*atomlist*}{*subslist*}{*fuse*}

The argument *fuse* identifies the bond to be used for the fusion—namely, a letter representing the bond to be omitted (see Chapter 5 of the XΥMTEX manual for version 1.01[1]). Example 8-2-38 on page 539 illustrates the use of ring fusion. Fuse commands can be nested.

Using PostScript output

Since 2004 (version 4.02 of the XΥMTEX package[2]), PostScript support has become fully integrated in XΥMTEX via the use of **PSTricks**, thus eliminating the limitations imposed by LATEX's `picture` environment. With respect to the package files present in version 1.0, as described on page 520, the following files have been added:

polymers   support for drawing polymers

fusering   support for drawing units for ring fusion (Table 8.10)

methylen   support for drawing zigzag polymethylene chains (Table 8.11 on the next page)

sizeredc   support for allowing size reduction (version 3 and above)

xymtx-ps   support for PostScript printing (This package reimplements several macros defined in the other XΥMTEX packages.)

There are also two utility packages: **xymtex**, which loads all packages except **xymtx-ps** (i.e., no PostScript support), and **xymtexps**, which loads all packages, including **xymtx-ps** (allowing full PostScript support). Furthermore, the **chemist** and **chmst-ps** packages define some specific chemical environments without and with PostScript support.

XΥMTEX now works in two modes. We have "TEX/LATEX-compatible mode" (uses **xymtex** with no PostScript support), which simulates stereochemistry effects with thick and dotted lines and reduces formulae with the help of **epic**, and "PostScript-compatible mode" (uses **xymtexps** providing PostScript support), which implements stereochemistry effects fully.

---

[1] See http://imt.chem.kit.ac.jp/fujita/fujitas3/xymtex/xym101/xymdvi/xymtex.pdf.

[2] The latest version of XΥMTEX and its full documentation are available from the XΥMTEX home page at http://imt.chem.kit.ac.jp/fujita/fujitas3/xymtex/indexe.html.

Table 8.11: Polymethylene commands (\command{1==1}{2==a2;3==a3})

Length	Generic Commands			
2 and 3	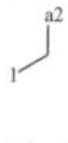 \dimethylene	\dimethylenei	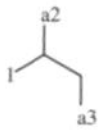 \trimethylene	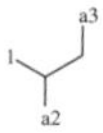 \trimethylenei
4 and 5	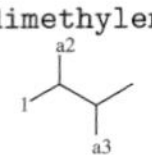 \tetramethylene	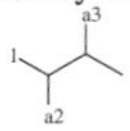 \tetramethylenei	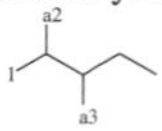 \pentamethylene	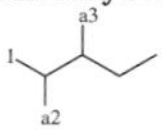 \pentamethylenei
6 and 7	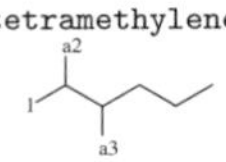 \hexamethylene	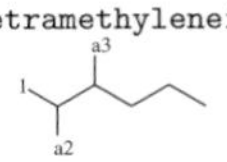 \hexamethylenei	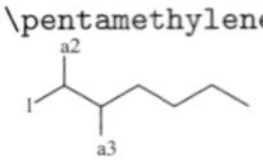 \heptamethylene	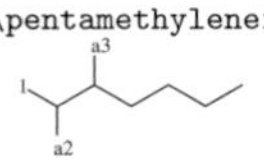 \heptamethylenei
8 and 9	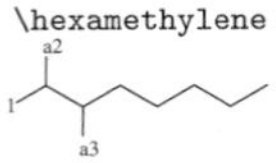 \octamethylene	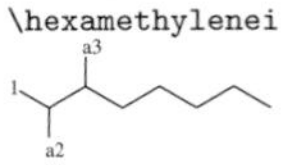 \octamethylenei	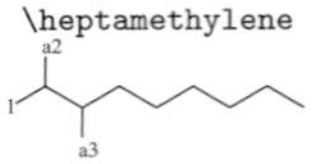 \nonamethylene	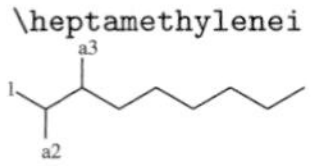 \nonamethylenei
10	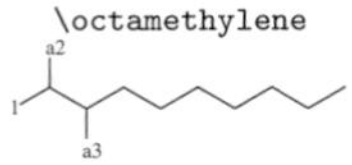 \decamethylene	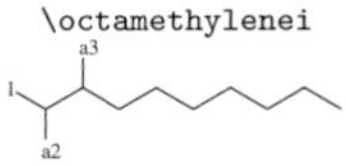 \decamethylenei		Example 8-2-33

The difference between these modes is seen in the following examples, where we first show
the standard (LATEX's `picture`) mode.

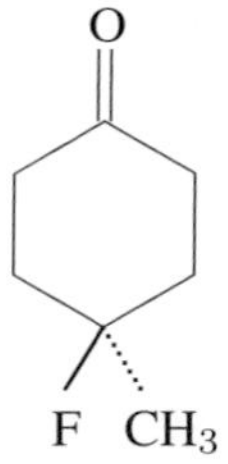

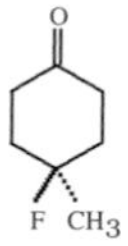

```
\usepackage{xymtex}
\begin{flushleft}
\reducedsizepicture
\cyclohexanev{1D==O;4SA==CH$\sb{3}$;4SB==F}
\changeunitlength{0.05pt}
\cyclohexanev{1D==O;4SA==CH$\sb{3}$;4SB==F}
\end{flushleft}
```

Example 8-2-34

With PostScript we can generate full stereochemistry effects with wedges and dashes.

```
\usepackage{xymtexps}
\wedgehashedwedge          \cyclohexanev{1D==O;4SA==CH$\sb{3}$;4SB==F}
{\changeunitlength{0.07pt}\cyclohexanev{1D==O;4SA==CH$\sb{3}$;4SB==F}}  \qquad
\dashhasheddash            \cyclohexanev{1D==O;4SA==CH$\sb{3}$;4SB==F}
\changeunitlength{0.05pt}\cyclohexanev{1D==O;4SA==CH$\sb{3}$;4SB==F}
```

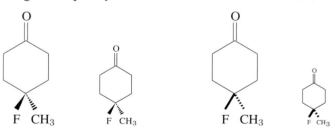

Example 8-2-35

The three types of derivations revisited

The three types of derivations used in XΥMTEX—namely, "substitution derivation" for nested substitution, "atom derivation" for generating spiro compounds, and "bond derivation" for ring fusion—can now be revisited with the PostScript mode turned on.

The structural formula of ribavirin, for example, can be obtained by the technique called "substitution derivation" using a "yl" function to turn a \fiveheterov command into a substituent, which is then attached to a furanose skeleton (\furanose command).

Example
8-2-36

```
\usepackage{xymtexps}
\changeunitlength{0.09pt}
\furanose{1Sa==H;2Sb==H;2Sa==OH;3Sb==H;%
3Sa==OH;4Sb==H;4Sb==HOC\rlap{H$\sb{2}$};%
1Sb==\fiveheterov[bd]{1==N;2==N;4==N}
{1==(yl);3==CONH$\sp{2}$}}
```

A substituent generated by a "yl" function can be declared in an atom list of a skeleton so as to generate the formula of a spiro compound, known as an "atom derivation". For instance, the three-member spiro ring of illudin S, an antibiotic, is obtained as follows.

Example
8-2-37

```
\usepackage{xymtexps}
\changeunitlength{0.09pt}
\wedgehashedwedge
\nonaheterovi[di]{%
5s==\cyclopropanev{2==(yl)}}%
{2SB==CH$\sb{3}$;2SA==CH$\sb{2}$OH;%
3B==OH;4==CH$\sb{3}$;6SB==CH$\sb{3}$;%
6SA==HO;7D==O}
```

Fused rings can be drawn using "bond derivation". An example is penicillin V, where the fusing command \fivefusevi (see Table 8.10 on page 537) is used. The five-member ring (\fiveheerovi) shares its bond edge labeled d with the bond edge labeled b of the four-member ring (\fourhetero). The command \lyl links the four-ring to the phenyl substituent via the group (OCH$_2$CONH).

Example
8-2-38

```
\usepackage{xymtexps}
\changeunitlength{0.09pt}
\wedgehashedwedge
\fourhetero[%
{b\fivefusevi{1==S;4==\null}%
{2Sa==CH$\sb{3}$;2Sb==CH$\sb{3}$;%
3A==COOH}{d}}]%
{2==N}{1D==O;3FA==H;4GA==H;4Su==%
\lyl(4==OCH$\sb{2}$CONH)%
{4==\bzdrh{4==(yl)}}}}
```

Configurations, conformations, and reaction schemes

Numerous configurations of tetrahedral molecules with wedged bonds can be drawn using variants of the command \tetrahedral. For instance, the following Fischer diagram, which shows the absolute configuration of the sugar D-glucose, uses four nested \tetrahedral commands.

```
CHO

H ► C ◄ OH

HO ► C ◄ H

H ► C ◄ OH

H ► C ◄ OH

CH₂OH
```

```
\usepackage{xymtexps}
\changeunitlength{0.09pt}
\tetrahedral{0==C;1A==CHO;%
             2B==H;4B==OH;3A==%
  \tetrahedral{0==C;1==(yl);%
               2B==HO;4B==H;3A==%
    \tetrahedral{0==C;1==(yl);%
                 2B==H;4B==OH;3A==%
      \tetrahedral{0==C;1==(yl);%
                   2B==H;4B==OH;3A==CH$\sb{2}$OH}}}}
```

Example
8-2-39

Finally, reaction schemes containing tetrahedral molecules with wedged bonds can also be handled. For instance, consider the Walden inversion reaction, which is drawn with the help of the chemeqn environment and the \reactrarrow command, both of which are defined in the chemist package (part of the X^Y^MTEX distribution).

```
\usepackage{xymtexps,chmst-ps}
\begin{chemeqn}
HO\sp{-}~+~
\raisebox{-28pt}{\ltetrahedralS{0==C;1==Cl;%
                  2==C$\sb{3}$H$\sb{7}$;%
                  3A==CH$\sb{3}$;4B==C$\sb{2}$H$\sb{5}$}}
\reactrarrow{0pt}{1cm}{}{}\qquad
\raisebox{-28pt}{\dtrigpyramid[{0{~~$\delta+$}}]%
                  {0==C;4A==HO$\sp{\delta-}$;%
                  5A==Cl$\sp{\delta-}$;%
                  1==C$\sb{3}$H$\sb{7}$;%
                  2A==CH$\sb{3}$;%
                  3B==C$\sb{2}$H$\sb{5}$}}
\quad\reactrarrow{0pt}{1cm}{}{}\quad
\raisebox{-28pt}{\rtetrahedralS{0==C;1==HO;%
                  2==C$\sb{3}$H$\sb{7}$;%
                  3A==CH$\sb{3}$;4B==C$\sb{2}$H$\sb{5}$}}
~+~Cl\sp{-} \label{myeqn}
\end{chemeqn}
```

$$(1)$$

Example
8-2-40

8.2.2 The ppchtex **package**

Hans Hagen and A. F. Otten are the developers of PPCHTₑX [44], a package for typesetting chemical formulae originally based on PₗCTₑX [138]. Presently, a PSTricks interface is available. You can use the PₗCTₑX interface by specifying the `pictex` option; you can choose the PSTricks interface by specifying the `pstricks` option (the latter is chosen for the examples). This PPCHTₑX package describes the chemical structures more by their graphical representation than their chemical significance. Unlike XꙮMTₑX, which relies on the LaTeX `picture` environment, this package can be used with both plain TₑX and LaTeX.

Rather than trying to explain the syntax in detail[1] we merely present some examples here, with the hope of giving you a feeling for the approach taken.

Structures

Chemical structure formulae are typeset with the help of four basic commands, all of which are used in the following example.

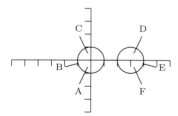

```
\usepackage[pictex]{m-ch-en}
\setupchemical
    [axis=on,border=on,scale=small,
     size=medium]
\startchemical
    \chemical[FIVE,B,R,RZ][1,2,3,4,5]
\stopchemical
```

`\setupchemical[`*typesetting-data*`]`	`\startchemical[`*typesetting-data*`]`

The `\setupchemical` command establishes various characteristics for setting the following chemical formulae. Its scope is limited to the current group. Typesetting instructions can also be specified on the `\startchemical` command itself, in which case the instructions remain valid only up to the corresponding `\stopchemical` command (i.e., for the current formula).

```
\usepackage[pictex]{m-ch-en}
\setupchemical[axis=on]
\startchemical
    [width=6000,scale=small,size=medium]
    \chemical[CARBON,CB1][A,B,C,D,E,F]
\stopchemical
```

---

[1] See `http://www.pragma-ade.com/general/manuals/mp-ch-en.pdf`, the PPCHTₑX manual, for a full description.

```
\chemical[structure] [atoms/molecule-list]
```

\chemical, the main command, can occur several times between the \startchemical
and \stopchemical commands that delimit a chemical formula. Its first argument defines
the *structure* that is filled with the data presented in the second (optional) argument. Any
text in the *atoms/molecule-list* is typeset in math mode (but with letters set properly in Roman). If the argument is missing, the command produces a skeleton with no atoms. There
are eight predefined base structures that can be used in the first argument *structure*:

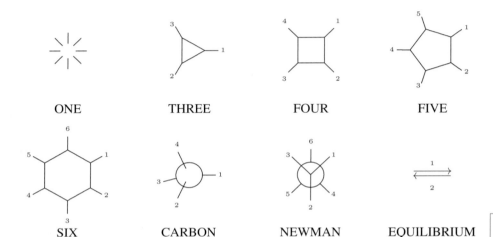

ONE   THREE   FOUR   FIVE

SIX   CARBON   NEWMAN   EQUILIBRIUM

Example
8-2-43

Chemical bonds between C atoms inside these structures are indicated, for example, by
the letter B and are referenced by numbers. Various representations are possible, as shown
below for a six-ring structure:

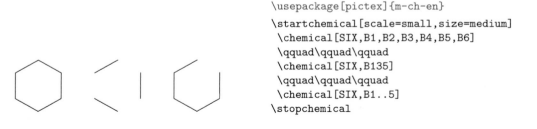

```
\usepackage[pictex]{m-ch-en}
\startchemical[scale=small,size=medium]
 \chemical[SIX,B1,B2,B3,B4,B5,B6]
 \qquad\qquad\qquad
 \chemical[SIX,B135]
 \qquad\qquad\qquad
 \chemical[SIX,B1..5]
\stopchemical
```

Example
8-2-44

Substructures can be added by the R tag, where the position on the ring again is indicated by a number. This tag merely draws bonds for subcomponents; the actual subcompo-
nent must be declared explicitly with a RZ tag, and its "value" (e.g., an atom), is then specified inside the second optional argument. When the second argument is omitted or doesn't

contain enough material, no text is placed and the corresponding RZ tags have no effect.

```
\usepackage[pictex]{m-ch-en}
\startchemical[scale=small,size=medium]
 \chemical[SIX,B1..6,R1..6]
 \qquad\qquad\qquad
  \chemical[SIX,B1..5,R12,RZ12][A]
 \qquad\qquad\qquad\qquad
  \chemical[SIX,B1..6,R1..6,RZ1..3]
    [CH_3,CH_3,OH]
\stopchemical
```

Definitions

It is straightforward to build a library of structures that can be used as building blocks of more complex components. For instance, you can define the string "sixring" as an unadorned six-ring by using the \definechemical command. With a definition like the one below, a simple six-ring without subconstituents can be typeset and the six substituents can be added by specifying them in the second argument:

```
\usepackage[pictex]{m-ch-en}
\definechemical[sixring]
   {\chemical[SIX,B,R,RZ]}
\startchemical[size=small]
 \chemical[sixring]
 \qquad\qquad\qquad\qquad\qquad
 \chemical[sixring]
    [R_1,R_2,R_3,R_4,R_5,R_6]
\stopchemical
```

More complex structures are possible; remember that the subconstituents in the second argument are placed according to the sequence specified in the first argument. An example with a slightly modified definition of sixring is

```
\usepackage[pictex]{m-ch-en}
\definechemical[sixring]
   {\chemical[SIX,B,R,RZ135]%
            [R_1,R_3,R_5]}
\startchemical[size=small]
 \chemical[sixring,SIX,RZ246]
            [A,B,C]
\stopchemical
```

Bonds

Different kinds of bonds can be used in structures in the PPCHTₑX package, as shown in Table 8.12 on the next page. The left-hand pair of columns corresponds to complete bonds, and the right-hand columns are for shortened variants. Bonds can be shortened on both

Table 8.12: Bond identifiers for **ppchtex**

Saturated bonds	B	bond	SB	single bond
			-SB	left single bond
			+SB	right single bond
Unsaturated bonds	EB	extra bond	DB	double bond
			TB	triple bond
Special bonds	S	shortcut	C	circle
Bonds to substituents	R	radical	SR	single radical
	-R	left radical	-SR	single left radical
	+R	right radical	+SR	single right radical
Double bonds to substituents	ER	extra radical	DR	double radical
Atoms and molecules (radicals)	Z	atom	RZ	radical atom
			-RZ	left radical atom
			+RZ	right radical atom

sides, on the left (−) or on the right (+). Shortened variants make it possible to attach atoms and molecules to a bond.

Bond specifiers can be followed by one or more numbers or a range (e.g., B1, B135, or B1..5). A specifier without numbers (e.g., B), applies to all bonds. Text to be linked to bonds is collected from the second optional argument of \chemical in the order given. Items are numbered clockwise. A text can be placed in the center of a structure with the Z0 ("Z-zero") specifier.

Combinations

Structures can be positioned or rotated to form complex compounds with the help of the following specifiers:

MOV (Move) move an identical structure in the direction of a bond

ADJ (Adjace) move two structures relative to each other in the x- or y-direction to make them share a common side

SUB (Substitute) move two structures relative to each other in the x- or y-direction and connect them via a bond

ROT (Rotate) rotate a structure

Note that these commands can have different effects for different structures. For instance, the rotation angle differs in the commands \chemical[FIVE,ROT1,B] and \chemical[SIX,ROT1,B]. A few examples are given below.

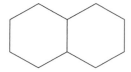

```
\usepackage[pictex]{m-ch-en}
\startchemical[size=small]
 \chemical[SIX,B,MOV1,B]
\stopchemical
```

Example
8-2-48

Here we can study the effects of the ROT tag:

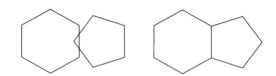

```
\usepackage[pictex]{m-ch-en}
\mbox{\startchemical[size=small]
  \chemical[SIX,B,ADJ1,FIVE,B]
\stopchemical\startchemical
  \chemical[SIX,B,ADJ1,FIVE,ROT3,B]
\stopchemical}
```

As you see, connected structures are built with the ADJ specifier. Often one of the two structures must be rotated with ROT to get a good connection. If there is a bond between the two structures, then use the SUB specifier. Rotations are specified in steps of 90 degrees clockwise, and displacements with ADJ and SUB are in the direction of one of the four axes.

```
\usepackage[pictex]{m-ch-en}
\startchemical
  \chemical[SIX,ROT2,B,R6,%
            SUB1,FIVE,B,R4]
\stopchemical
```

The preceding examples indicate that the sequence in which the tags are specified must follow a given order:

```
\chemical
  [structure & rotation,          % SIX, FIVE, ...
   bonds inside the structure,    % B, C, EB, ...
   bonds outside the structure,   % R, DR, ...
   locations of the atoms,        % Z
   locations of the subcomponents, % RZ, -RZ, ...
   connection,                    % MOV, ADJ, ...
   structure & rotation,          % SIX, FIVE, ...
   bonds inside the structure,    % B, C, EB, ...
   ...
  ]
  [atoms, subcomponents]
```

Chemical equations

Reaction equations can be typeset using symbols specially provided for this purpose, as the following example shows:

```
\usepackage[pictex]{m-ch-en}
\setupchemical[size=small,width=fit,height=5500,under=1500]
\mbox{%
    \startchemical
        \chemical[SIX,B,ER6,RZ6][O] \stopchemical
    \startchemical
        \chemical[SPACE,PLUS,SPACE] \stopchemical
```

```
\startchemical
     \chemical[FIVE,ROT4,B125,+SB3,-SB4,Z4,SR4,RZ4][N,H]
\stopchemical
\startchemical \chemical[SPACE,GIVES,SPACE][?] \stopchemical
\startchemical
     \chemical[SIX,B,EB6,R6,SUB4,FIVE,ROT4,B125,+SB3,-SB4,Z4][N]
\stopchemical
}
```

Example
8-2-51

The \mbox command ensures that the structures are typeset on a line; the symbols GIVES and PLUS are self-explanatory; and SPACE inserts a little extra space. An equilibrium can be shown with EQUILIBRIUM, and a text can be typeset above GIVES and EQUILIBRIUM (here a question mark).

Special features

With the ONE tag, Z0 can consist of more than one atom. If the reserved space is insufficient, bonds 1, 2, and 8 can be moved with the command OFF (for "offset"), as shown in the following example, where the offset is one extra character ("1"). In such complex constructs, rotations are best made last. The CRZ (for "centered radical atom") command is used to align an atom or a molecule with a bond.

```
\usepackage[pictex]{m-ch-en}
\startchemical[width=fit]
\chemical
   [SIX,B,C,ADJ1,FIVE,ROT3,SB34,
    +SB2,-SB5,Z345,DR35,SR4,CRZ35,
    SUB1,ONE,OFF1,SB258,Z0,Z28]
   [C,N,C,O,O,CH,COOC_2H_5,COOC_2H_5]
\stopchemical
```

Example
8-2-52

There are two other forms of the \chemical command:

\chemical{*formula*}   \chemical{*formula*}{*text*}

These forms typeset a formula inside a paragraph of text.

```
\usepackage[pictex]{m-ch-en}
\[ \chemical{2H_2}{}
   \chemical{PLUS}{}
   \chemical{O_2}{}
   \chemical{GIVES}{}
   \chemical{2H_20}{} \]
```

Example
8-2-53

$$2H_2 \quad + \quad O_2 \quad \longrightarrow \quad 2H_2O$$

Such a formula can also be typeset inside a paragraph in the running text where a smaller font size is chosen. Note that the same formula could have been obtained with either of the two (shorter) \chemical commands, in which everything is specified in the first argument:

```
\[\chemical{2H_2,PLUS,O_2,GIVES,2H_20}{}\]
\[\chemical{2H_2,+,O_2,->,2H_20}{}\]
```

The second argument *text* of the \chemical commands can be used to include explanatory text in the formula.

```
\usepackage[pictex]{m-ch-en}
\[ \chemical{2H_2}{hydrogen}
   \chemical{PLUS}{}
   \chemical{O_2}{oxygen}
   \chemical{GIVES}{violent}
   \chemical{2H_20}{} \]
```

Example
8-2-54

$$2H_2 \quad + \quad O_2 \quad \longrightarrow \quad 2H_2O$$
hydrogen   oxygen   violent

The package also supports other features, such as coloring parts of a formula.

8.3 Alignment and topology plots in bioinformatics

Preparing a clear visual representation of alignments of nucleotides and peptides for publication purposes is generally a rather complex two-step process. First, the alignment is calculated using a dedicated software program. Next, special relationships in the sequences are highlighted and positions or regions of interest labeled, which requires the use of another software program with high-level output capabilities. With standard word processing or graphics programs manipulation of sequence alignments often takes several hours. Moreover, even small changes in the input or different line breaks in the output imply that most of the work has to be repeated.

To help alleviate this problem, Eric Beitz developed his **texshade** and **textopo** packages[1] in the framework of the BioTEX-project. We will not describe these two packages in great detail, but simply show how they can handle complex graphical information for publication with LaTeX.

---

[1] Eric's home page at http://homepages.uni-tuebingen.de/beitz/txe.html contains the latest information.

8.3.1 Aligning and shading nucleotide and peptide sequences

The **texshade** package lets you align and shade multiple-nucleotide and -peptide sequences, which can be coded in several file formats used by the bioinformatics community (see the manual for more details). In addition to common shading algorithms, **texshade** provides special shading modes featuring functional aspects, such as charge or hydropathy, and several commands for controlling shading colors, text styles, labels, and legends. The user can also define completely new shading modes.

The **texshade** package provides a single new `texshade` environment, which is defined as follows.

```
\begin{texshade} [parameterfile] {alignmentfile}
    texshade commands, when needed
\end{texshade}
```

Since the package does not itself calculate aligments, the mandatory argument *alignmentfile* must contain the aligned nucleotide or peptide sequences in one of three common aligment input formats that **texshade** accepts (MSF, for *multiple sequence format*; ALN for *aligment format*; and FASTA, the format used by the `fasta` tools for biological sequence analysis). The optional argument, when specified, loads the file *parameterfile*, which contains definitions for the customized calculation of the consensus, special sequence features, labels, etc. Inside the environment itself, you can give even more **texshade** commands to replace or complete settings from the parameter file.

The examples that follow read the example alignment file `AQPpro.MSF`, which comes with the distribution. The first example shows a basic type of shading that is provided by almost any alignment program. All identical residues at a position are shaded if the number of matching residues is higher than a given threshold percentage.

```
 80   TLGLLLSCQISILRAVMYIIAQCVG   AQP1.PRO
 72   TVACLVGCHVSFLRAAFYVAAQLLG   AQP2.PRO
 80   TFAMCFLAREPWIKLPIYTLAQTLG   AQP3.PRO
101   TVAMVCTRKISIAKSVFYITAQCLG   AQP4.PRO
 73   TLALLIGNQISLLRAVFYVAAQLVG   AQP5.PRO
```

```
\usepackage[]{texshade}
\begin{texshade}{AQPpro.MSF}
 \setends{1}{80..104}
 \hideconsensus
\end{texshade}
```

Example 8-3-1

Positions where all residues are identical can be shaded in a special color and the consensus can be shown with or without shading according to the degree of conservation, as seen in the following example.

```
 80   TLGLLLSCQISILRAVMYIIAQCVG   AQP1.PRO
 72   TVACLVGCHVSFLRAAFYVAAQLLG   AQP2.PRO
 80   TFAMCFLAREPWIKLPIYTLAQTLG   AQP3.PRO
101   TVAMVCTRKISIAKSVFYITAQCLG   AQP4.PRO
 73   TLALLIGNQISLLRAVFYVAAQLVG   AQP5.PRO
      T.a.l....is.lravfY..AQ.lG   consensus
```

```
\usepackage[]{texshade}
\begin{texshade}{AQPpro.MSF}
 \allmatchspecial
 \setends{1}{80..104}
 \showconsensus[ColdHot]{bottom}
 \defconsensus{.}{lower}{upper}
\end{texshade}
```

Example 8-3-2

When you want to highlight differences rather than similarities, you can select the diversity mode. It is useful for comparing very similar sequences, such as species variants of a protein. One sequence is used as consensus. Matching residues in other sequences are blanked out, and mismatches are shown in lowercase. In this case the file AQP2spec.ALN is read.

```
\usepackage[]{texshade}
\begin{texshade}{AQP2spec.ALN}
  \seqtype{P}
  \shadingmode{diverse}
  \setends{1}{77..106}
  \featureslarge
  \feature{top}{1}{77..106}{}
           {AQP2 species variants}
  \namesrm\namesit
  \hidenumbering\showruler{top}{1}
  \shownames{left}
  \nameseq{1}{Bos taurus}
  \nameseq{2}{Canis familiaris}
  \nameseq{3}{Dugong dugong}
  \nameseq{4}{Equus caballus}
  \nameseq{5}{Elephas maximus}
  \frameblock{1}{82..82,106..106}
           {Red[1pt]}
\end{texshade}
```

AQP2 species variants

	80	90	100
Bos taurus	SFLRA	V	FYVAAQLLGAVAGAALLHE
Canis familiaris	. . . . .	a	. . . .
Dugong dugong	. . . . .	t	. .l . . . . .i . . .
Equus caballus	. . . . .	a	. . . .
Elephas maximus	. . . . .	t	. .l . . . .

AQP2 species variants

Bos taurus	ITPP|A|
Canis familiaris	. . . .|h|
Dugong dugong	. . . .|d|
Equus caballus	. . . .|d|
Elephas maximus	l . . .|d|

Example
8-3-3

Six functional shading modes are predefined.

charge   Residues that are charged at physiological pH (7.4) are shaded if their number at a position is higher than the threshold.

hydropathy   Discriminates between acidic and basic, polar uncharged and hydrophobic nonpolar residues.

structure   Displays the potential localization within the tertiary structure of the protein.

chemical   Residues are shaded according to the chemical properties of their functional groups.

standard area   Displays differences in surface area for the different amino acids' side chains.

accessible area   Uses the surface area accessed by solvent molecules as a basis for shading. Low accessibility means hydrophobic (i.e., strongly buried residues), whereas highly accessible side chains are hydrophilic.

Only one example of the chemical shading mode will be given here. The **texshade** manual gives examples of the other modes as well as how the package handles secondary protein structures (see also Color Plate Xa).

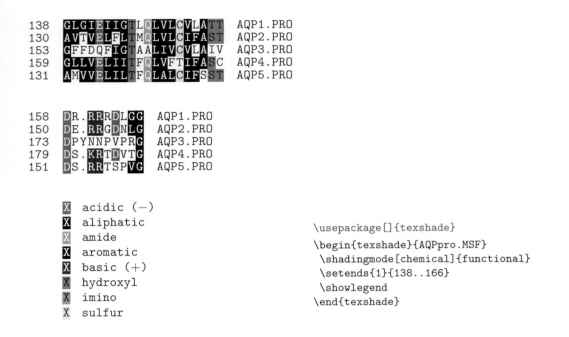

```
\usepackage[]{texshade}
\begin{texshade}{AQPpro.MSF}
 \shadingmode[chemical]{functional}
 \setends{1}{138..166}
 \showlegend
\end{texshade}
```

Example
8-3-4

To illustrate the flexibility of the package, we end the current section with an example of sequence fingerprints, which are obtained with the \fingerprint command. Fingerprints provide a convenient overview of sequence similarities or properties since one can display a complete sequence on one single line. Residues are presented as colored vertical lines. The higher the similarity, the darker the vertical lines. Sequence gaps are drawn as lines (the \gapchar command with a *rule* argument, although this argument can be left blank, the default).

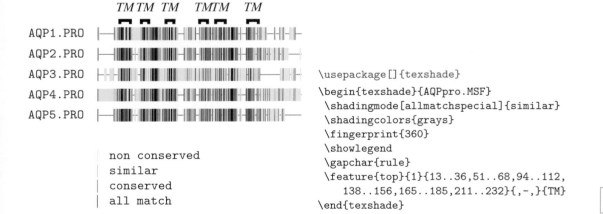

```
\usepackage[]{texshade}
\begin{texshade}{AQPpro.MSF}
 \shadingmode[allmatchspecial]{similar}
 \shadingcolors{grays}
 \fingerprint{360}
 \showlegend
 \gapchar{rule}
 \feature{top}{1}{13..36,51..68,94..112,
    138..156,165..185,211..232}{,-,}{TM}
\end{texshade}
```

Example
8-3-5

8.3.2 Membrane protein topology plots

Eric Beitz also wrote the **textopo** package, which provides a LaTeX interface to generate shaded membrane protein topology plots. This package provides two new environments, `textopo` and `helicalwheel`.

The `textopo` environment displays schematic topology plots of membrane proteins. It allows you to import sequence and topology data or alignment files in various formats. You can also manually enter the sequence and the positions of the membrane spanning domains within the environment. The package implementation will generate a basic layout from these data, which can be further adjusted by adding labels, special styles for the presentation of residues, automatic or manual shading, and annotations.

```
\begin{textopo}[parameterfile]
    textopo commands
\end{textopo}
```

The parameter file *parameterfile*, which is optional, can contain any command defined by the **textopo** package to specify user parameter settings. The `textopo` environment itself must contain at least one command to load the sequence and topology data for the protein that must be plotted (i.e., `\getsequence` or `\sequence` and `\MRs`, which specify the positions of the membrane regions).

The following example, which uses the file `AQP1.PHD`, comes with the distribution.

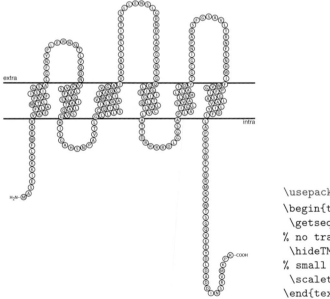

```
\usepackage[]{textopo}
\begin{textopo}
  \getsequence{PHD}{AQP1.phd}
% no transmembrane labels
  \hideTMlabels
% small font size (range 1-10)
  \scaletopo{2}
\end{textopo}
```

The second environment, `helicalwheel`, is in its functionality quite similar to `textopo`, but produces output that shows helical transmembrane spans as helical wheels or nets. All or a subset of the transmembrane domains as well as their order can be chosen. Different views of the cell membrane are possible.

```
\begin{helicalwheel}[parameterfile]{helixlist}
    further helicalwheel commands
\end{helicalwheel}
```

The parameter file, which is optional, is as described for `textopo`. The mandatory argument *helixlist* contains the list of the helices to be displayed.

The example shows helices 1 and 4 of an aquaporin and rotates helix 4 by 50 degrees.

```
\usepackage[]{textopo}
\begin{helicalwheel}{1,4[50]}
 \getsequence{PHD}{AQP1.phd}
\end{helicalwheel}
```

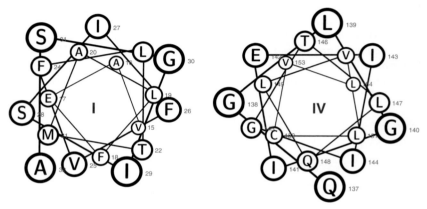

Example
8-3-7

The full functionality of **texshade** is available with **textopo**. For example, protein topology plots can be shaded automatically according to the functional properties of their amino acid residues or according to sequence conservation based on protein alignments. Thus most **texshade** commands can be used in addition to the commands provided by **textopo**.

A simple example of a topology plot with shading calculated according to protein alignment data follows. The sequence and topology data are read in one file, and shading is applied as calculated from alignment data read in a second file (see also Color Plate Xb).

```
\usepackage[]{texshade,textopo}
\begin{textopo}
 \getsequence{PHD}{AQP1.phd}
 \applyshading{similar}{AQPpro.MSF}
 \allmatchspecial
 \loopextent{15}
\end{textopo}
```

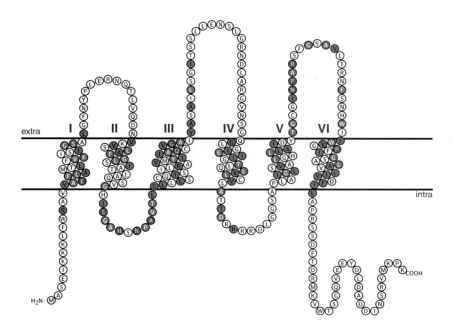

⊗ similar positions
⊗ conserved positions
⊗ invariable positions

A final annotated example shows how sequence data can be specified inline with the
\sequence command. The \loopextent commands set the number of residues allowed
in the straight sections (including the bends) for the loops in the structure. However, the
fifth loop in the example is very long; hence the \loopfoot command was used to control its layout. We let the loop go down in a straight line by 10 residues, then let it turn
left. From that point onwards, the parameters defined in the \loopextent argument apply (12 residues for each loop turn). The \labelstyle sets the style to be used for subsequent labels, which are associated to residue regions with the \labelregion commands.
These latter commands show the "neck" where the fifth loop descends and the role of the
\loopextent settings.

```
\usepackage[]{textopo}
\begin{textopo}
\sequence{%
  MNTSAPPAVS PNITVLAPGK GPWQVAFIGI TTGLLSLATV
  TGNLLVLISF KVNTELKTVN NYFLLSLACA DLIIGTFSMN
  LYTTYLLMGH WALGTLACDL WLALDYVASN ASVMNLLLIS
  FDRYFSVTRP LSYRAKRTPR RAALMIGLAW LVSFVLWAPA
  ILFWQYLVGE RTVLAGQCYI QFLSQPIITF GTAMAAFYLP
  VTVMCTLYWR IYRETENRAR ELAALQGSET PGKGGGSSSS
```

```
SERSQPGAEG SPETPPGRCC RCCRAPRLLQ AYSWKEEEEE
DEGSMESLTS SEGEEPGSEV VIKMPMVDPE AQAPTKQPPR
SSPNTVKRPT KKGRDRAGKG QKPRGKEQLA KRKTFSLVKE
KKAARTLSAI LLAFILTWTP YNIMVLVSTF CKDCVPETLW
ELGYWLCYVN STINPMCYAL CNKAFRDTFR LLLLCRWDKR
RWRKIPKRPG SVHRTPSRQC}

% position of the membrane regions
\MRs{25..47,62..82,100..121,142..164,187..209,367..387,402..421}
\Nterm{extra}% sets N-terminus

\loopfoot{5}{left[10]}% foot at 5th loop turns left after 10 residues
\loopextent{12}% maximum number of residues in straight sections of loop
\loopextent[C]{26}% for C-termini loop set to 26
\scaletopo{+1}
\labelstyle{black}{circ}{Black}{Black}{White}{}
\labelregion[E,7]{210..219}{black}{'neck'}
\labelregion[W,7]{237[NW]..248[SW]}{black}{'loopextent'}
\hidelegend
\end{textopo}
```

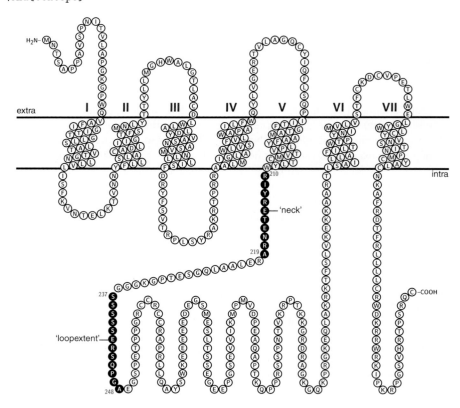

Example
8-3-9

8.4 Drawing Feynman diagrams

The graphical technique of Feynman diagrams was introduced by American physicist Richard Feynman in 1948 as a practical method for performing calculations in quantum field theory. In recognition for his work in quantum field theory. Feynman shared the 1965 Nobel Prize in physics with Julian Schwinger and Shin-Ichiro Tomonaga.

Originally the technique of Feynman diagrams was used to calculate scattering cross sections in particle physics. This implies summing the amplitudes of all possible intermediate (and possibly virtual) states. Each such state is represented by its Feynman diagram. The Feynman technique offers a convenient way to keep track of tortuous calculations by introducing a symbolic notation for the factors appearing in each term of the perturbation series. Feynman diagrams do not necessarily represent real processes. They nevertheless provide a deeper physical insight into the nature of particle interactions. For this reason they have found their way into other fields of physics, such as statistical mechanics (see `http://en.wikipedia.org/wiki/Feynman_diagram` for more).

Given their importance in physics, several authors have developed ways of creating Feynman diagrams. Michael Levine's **feynman** package [79] is an implementation on top of standard LaTeX's `picture` environment. This makes it completely portable, but the graphics output is less than perfect and complex graphs are often impossible to draw. **FeynArts** is a Mathematica package that includes procedures to calculate and draw Feynman diagrams [20]. We will not describe these packages any further.

Instead, we shall look in greater detail at the work of Norman Gray, who has developed a dedicated `feyn` font; Jos Vermaseren, whose **axodraw** package uses `\special` commands to directly access PostScript primitives; and Thorsten Ohl, whose **FeynMF** system uses METAFONT or METAPOST for drawing.

8.4.1 A special font for drawing Feynman diagrams

Norman Gray designed the font `feyn`, which allows users to typeset relatively simple Feynman diagrams inside equations or within text, in a size matching the surrounding text size.

The characters in the `feyn` font are accessed by the `\feyn` command, which must be used inside math mode. Given that in math mode spaces are ignored white space can be added to increase legibility.

All characters available in the `feyn` font are displayed in Table 8.13 on the following page in their `\textstyle` variant, together with their name and a short description. As seen in Table 8.13, almost all characters are obtained by typing a single letter or a couple of letters that form a ligature. The reference point of each character is indicated by the ○ sign. Characters that are marked with a † sign exist in two arrowed variants: an "A" variant for arrows pointing rightwards or upwards, and a "V" variant for arrows pointing leftwards or downwards. Unassigned positions in the `feyn` font are filled with a dummy character.

Example 8-4-2	

Arrows: ⟶ + ⌇⌇
Fermion: ⟶. Unknown:

```
\usepackage{feyn}
Arrows: $\feyn{fA + gV}$ \newline
Fermion: $\feyn{fs}$. Unknown: $\feyn{A}$.
```

Table 8.13: The `feyn` font: available symbols, with their names and descriptions

Symbol	Result	Description	Symbol	Result	Description
f		fermion[†]	fs		short fermion
fl		fermion loop[†]	fu		upward fermion[†] (45°)
fd		downward fermion[†]	fv		vertical fermion[†]
f0		spacer	fs0		short spacer
g		gluon/photon[†]	gl		gluon loop[†]
glB		gluon loop (big)[†]	glS		gluon loop (small)[†]
glu		gluon loop upsidedown[†]	g1		gluon loop, first quadrant (similar for 2, 3, 4[†])
gu		upward gluon[†] (45°)	gd		downward gluon[†]
gv		vertical gluon[†]	m		massive fermion[†]
ms		short massive fermion	h		ghost
hs		short ghost	hu		upward ghost (45°)
hd		downward ghost	x		counterterm vertex
p		proper vertex	c		complete vertex
a		arrow			

[†] *The symbol also exists in two arrowed variants; see the text.*

Example 8-4-1

The **feyn** package provides commands to conveniently use the characters defined in the `feyn` font. We describe the more often-used ones.

`\feyn, \Feyn` These commands are used inside math mode and typeset their argument using the `feyn` font in the `\displaystyle` and `\textstyle` variant. For example,

```
\usepackage{feyn}
$\feyn{fglf}$ \qquad $\Feyn{fglf}$
```

Example 8-4-3

`\momentum[`*pos*`]{`*ch*`}{`*text*`}` This command typesets character *ch* (can be a ligature) and puts *text* at the recommended annotation position for that character. The optional argument *pos* (possible values: `top`, `urt`, `lrt`, `bot`, `llft`, `ulft`) allows for a finer control of the placement. Note that the **feyn** package makes the "`!`" character active and defines it to be `\momentum`.

`\Diagram{...}` This command, which can be used to build more complex diagrams, takes one argument, which is structured like the contents of an `array` environment with its elements formulae separated by &'s and \\ symbols.

\vertexlabel{*p*}{*text*}   This command adds a label to a vertex. *p* can have only two
values: _, which places *text* below the vertex, and ^, which places *text* above the vertex.
For example,

```
\usepackage{feyn}
$\feyn{\vertexlabel_{b}g\vertexlabel^{a}}$
```

The next example shows a simple fermion propagator. We load David Carlisle's slashed
package to conveniently produce slashed symbols, which occur frequently in Feynman diagram calculations. The ! character serves as a shorthand for the \momentum command to
place the "p" above the arrowed fermion line.

$$a \xrightarrow{\;p\;} b \quad = \quad \frac{i\delta^{ab}}{\slashed{p} - m_0}$$

```
\usepackage{feyn,slashed}
$  \feyn{\vertexlabel^a
       !{fA}p \vertexlabel^b}
   = \displaystyle
       \frac{i\delta^{ab}}{\slashed{p}-m_0} $
```

The \Diagram command handles its argument as an array, as shown in the following
example, where two fermion lines join to form a gluon line, with three vertices labeled with
indices which are referenced in the formula on the right-hand side.

```
\usepackage{feyn}
$
\Diagram{\vertexlabel^a \\
         fd \\
       & g\vertexlabel_{\mu,c} \\
         \vertexlabel_b fu}
= \displaystyle ig\gamma_\mu (T^c)_{ab}
$
```

A fermion line with two gluon loops is shown next. The size effect of the \feyn as
compared to the \Feyn command is clearly seen.

and

```
$\feyn{fs f glu f gl f fs}$ and
$\Feyn{fs f glu f gl f fs}$
```

```
\usepackage{feyn}
```

Our final example shows how the feyn characters can be used as structural elements
of an equation.

```
\usepackage{feyn}
\begin{eqnarray}
\feyn{fcf} &=& \feyn{faf} + \feyn{fpf} + \cdots \\
    &=& \sum_{n=0}^\infty \feyn{fsafs ( pfsafs)}^n
  \end{eqnarray}
```

$$\qquad\qquad\qquad\qquad\qquad\qquad\qquad\qquad\qquad\qquad\qquad\qquad\qquad (1)$$

$$= \sum_{n=0}^{\infty} \qquad\qquad\qquad)^n \qquad\qquad (2)$$

Example
8-4-8

8.4.2 PostScript for drawing Feynman diagrams

Jos Vermaseren's axodraw package defines a set of drawing primitives that can be used for simple graphics. This package is particularly well suited for Feynman diagrams but can also be used for flowcharts. It uses PostScript to implement its drawing commands and is presently interfaced only to dvips.

The commands of axodraw should be executed inside a picture or figure environment. Inside such an environment, objects can be placed at arbitrary positions with text between them. We next give a one-line summary of each of these commands, without detailing their arguments. See the manual for details.[1]

\ArrowArc (\DashArrowArc)   counterclockwise (dashed) arrowed arc segment

\ArrowArcn (\DashArrowArcn)   clockwise (dashed) arrowed arc segment

\ArrowLine (\DashArrowLine)   (dashed) line with arrow in its middle

\BBox, \BBoxc   blanked-out box

\BCirc   blanked-out circle

\Boxc   box

\BText, (\B2Text)   blanked-out box with one (two) lines of text

\CArc (\DashCArc)   (dashed) counterclockwise arc segment

\CBox, \CBoxc   blanked-out colored box

\CCirc (\COval)   blanked-out colored circle (oval)

\CText (\C2Text)   blanked-out colored box with one (two) lines of text

\CTri   blanked-out colored triangle

\Curve (\DashCurve)   (dashed) curve through given points

\EBox   box

\ETri (\BTri)   (blanked-out) triangle

\GBox, \GBoxc   blanked-out grayscale box

\GCirc (\GOval)   blanked-out grayscale circle (oval)

\GlueArc   gluon on arc-segment

\Gluon   gluon between two points

\GText (\G2Text)   blanked-out grayscale box with one (two) lines of text

\GTri   blanked-out grayscale triangle

---

[1] The page http://www.nikhef.nl/~form/maindir/others/others.html gives access to the manual as well as the latest version of the package.

\LinAxis   axis with linear scale on a graph

\Line (\DashLine)   (dashed) line between two points

\LogAxis   axis with logarithmic scale on a graph

\LongArrow   line with arrow at its end

\LongArrowArc   counterclockwise arc segment with arrow at end

\LongArrowArcn   clockwise arc segment with arrow at end

\Oval   oval

\Photon   photon between two points

\PhotonArc   photon on arc-segment

\SetColor   sets color for next commands

\SetPFont   sets PostScript font

\SetScale   sets scale for PostScript graphics

\SetOffset   adds offset to all coordinates at LaTeX level

\SetScaledOffset   adds offset to all coordinates at PostScript level

\SetWidth   sets line width for graphics operations

\Text, (\PText,\rText)   places (PostScript, rotated) text

\Vertex   fat dot ("vertex")

\ZigZag   zigzag line between two points

The following example shows how the different elementary building blocks (arrows, text, and zigzag line) are placed at specific coordinates as defined by the picture environment. Note the use of the \mathrm commands to ensure that particle names are typeset in Roman.

Feynman rule for the vertex $\nu_\mathrm{e}\mathrm{e}\mathrm{W}$

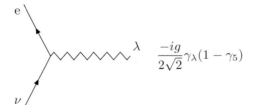

```
\usepackage{axodraw}
Feynman rule for the vertex
$\nu_\mathrm{e}\mathrm{eW}$
\begin{center}
\begin{picture}(160,100)(0,0)
  \ArrowLine(30,50)(10,90)
  \Text(5,85)[]{$\mathrm{e}$}
  \ArrowLine(10,10)(30,50)
  \Text(5,15)[]{$\nu$}
  \ZigZag(30,50)(90,50){3}{6}
  \Text(95,58)[]{$\lambda$}
  \Text(110,50)[l]
  {$\displaystyle\frac{-ig}{2\sqrt{2}}
   \gamma_{\lambda}(1 - \gamma_{5})$}
\end{picture}
\end{center}
```

Example
8-4-9

This second example introduces the construction of an arc segment (\CArc) with a vertex dot (\Vertex) in its middle).

```
\usepackage{axodraw}
The normal charged-current leptonic decay
of the positive kaon:
\begin{center}
  \begin{picture}(150,50)(0,0)
   \ArrowLine(70,30)(20,30)
   \ArrowLine(20,20)(70,20)
   \CArc(70,25)(5,-90,90)
   \Vertex(75,25){2}
   \ZigZag(75,25)(115,25){2}{5}
   \ArrowLine(125,50)(115,25)
   \ArrowLine(115,25)(125,0)
   \Text(17,25)[r]{$\mathrm{K}^{+}$}
   \Text(130,45)[l]{$\mu^{+}$}
   \Text(130,5)[l]{$\nu$}
   \Text(25,35)[b]{$\mathrm{\bar{s}}$}
   \Text(25,15)[t]{$u$}
  \end{picture}
\end{center}
```

The normal charged-current leptonic decay of the positive kaon:

Example 8-4-10

The next example shows a simple quark loop diagram for calculating quantum corrections to the Standard Model predictions for the mass of the W boson. It introduces two arcs with arrows (\ArrowArc) to draw the loop. Note the reference we make to the **heppennames** package (mentioned in Section 8.1) to typeset the particle names. The equivalent command to get the same typeset result in math mode is appended as a comment in each case, amply demonstrating the convenience of the scheme.

```
\usepackage{axodraw,heppennames}
\begin{picture}(280,80)(0,0)
 \ZigZag(10,40)(50,40){2}{5}
 \ZigZag(75,40)(115,40){2}{5}
 \ArrowArc(62.5,40)(12.5,0,180)
 \ArrowArc(62.5,40)(12.5,180,360)
 \Text(62.5,58)[b]{{\large\Paqb}}%$\bar{\mathrm{b}}$
 \Text(62.5,22)[t]{{\large\Pqt}}%$\mathrm{t}$
 \Text(5,40)[r]{{\large\PWp}}%$\mathrm{W}^+$
 \Text(120,40)[l]{{\large\PWp}}%$\mathrm{W}^+$
\end{picture}
```

Example 8-4-11

Our final example adds a photon line (\Photon) between the neutrino scattering vertices. We also use Andy Buckley's **hepnicenames** package, which complements his **heppennames** package (mentioned in the previous example). The former package proposes somewhat more mnemonic and simpler names to designate the particle names.

```
\usepackage{axodraw,hepnicenames}
Neutrino scattering diagrams
\begin{picture}(240,100)(0,0)
  \ArrowLine(40,100)(70,75)   \ArrowLine(40,0)(70,25)
  \Photon(70,75)(70, 25)3 4  \Text(105,50)[r]{\PWpm}   \Text(95,85)[r]{\Pe}
  \Text(110,15)[r]{\Pnue}     \Text(40,15)[l]{\Pe}      \Text(40,85)[l]{\Pnue}
  \ArrowLine(70,75)(100,100) \ArrowLine(70,25)(100,0)
%
  \ArrowLine(170,100)(200,75) \ArrowLine(170,0)(200,25)
  \Photon(200,75)(200, 25)3 4 \Text(225,50)[r]{\PZzero}
  \Text(265,85)[r]{\Pnue, \Pnum, \Pnut}  \Text(265,15)[r]{\Pproton, \Pneutron, \Pe}
  \Text(140,15)[l]{\Pproton, \Pneutron, \Pe}  \Text(140,85)[l]{\Pnue, \Pnum, \Pnut}
  \ArrowLine(200,75)(230,100) \ArrowLine(200,25)(230,0)
\end{picture}
```

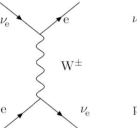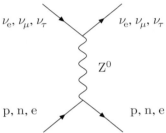

Example
8-4-12   Neutrino scattering diagrams

8.4.3 METAFONT **and** METAPOST **for drawing Feynman diagrams**

In this section we take a closer look at Thorsten Ohl's sophisticated FeynMF system [91, 92], which fully exploits the formal structure of Feynman graphs, thereby freeing the user from specifying the layout manually with low-level graphic primitives.

The aim of the FeynMF system is to provide a user interface so that the user need not specify graph layouts at the level of points and curves. The package was designed with the following goals:

- *Simplicity and conciseness* for common diagrams. For example, the Z-particle production diagram (very common in high-energy physics) can be specified with just eight LaTeX commands. The position of vertices is calculated automatically.

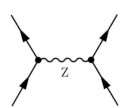

```
\usepackage{feynmp}
\begin{fmfgraph*}(100,70)
  \fmfleft{em,ep}
  \fmf{fermion}{em,Zee,ep}
  \fmf{photon,label=$\mathrm{Z}$}{Zee,Zff}
  \fmf{fermion}{fb,Zff,f}
  \fmfright{fb,f}
  \fmfdot{Zee,Zff}
\end{fmfgraph*}
```

Example
8-4-13

- *Expressiveness* and *extensibility* for complex diagrams.

- *Portability*. Only LATEX and METAFONT (or METAPOST) are needed.

- *Integration* with LATEX. All labels, including complex math expressions, are typeset by LATEX.

Two versions of the **FeynMF** package are available: **feynmf** uses METAFONT for drawing, whereas **feynmp** uses METAPOST and can add color to diagrams. Apart from this distinction, the programs differ little at the LATEX level. Just as in Chapter 3, we use the term META here if the explanation is valid for both programs.

The **FeynMF** system works by writing METAFONT or METAPOST code into an external file. The sequence of use is as follows:

1. Run LATEX; this writes METAFONT or METAPOST code for all the pictures into a file.

2. Run METAFONT or METAPOST; this generates either a set of PostScript files (METAPOST) or a font with a set of characters, one for each picture; in addition, an auxiliary file with labeling information is created.

3. Run LATEX again; this time the pictures or the font and the labeling information are used.

If the **FeynMF** code in the LATEX file does not change, there is no need to run METAFONT or METAPOST again every time you process the LATEX file.

The choice to use METAFONT or METAPOST is taken in the preamble of a document by loading either the **feynmf** or **feynmp** package. The commands defining your diagrams are then placed within the scope of an `fmffile` environment, which has an argument specifying the name of the file for intermediate METAFONT or METAPOST code. Thus the skeleton of a complete LATEX file might look like this:

```
\documentclass{article}
\usepackage{feynmf}
\begin{document}
\begin{fmffile}{fmpict}
    .... diagram commands ....
\end{fmffile}
\end{document}
```

Here we chose **feynmf**, so a METAFONT file called `fmpict.mf` is created in which each character represents one diagram.

To avoid a naming clash between the transcript files of TEX and METAFONT or METAPOST, all of which usually have the extension `.log`, the LATEX source file *cannot* have the same name as the **FeynMF** file specified as the argument on the `fmffile` environment (`fmpict` in the above example).

When a file like the one containing the diagram of Example 8-4-13 is run through LATEX for the first time, you see messages like the following:

```
This is pdfeTeXk, Version 3.141592-1.30.4-2.2 (Web2C 7.5.5)
%&-line parsing enabled.
```

```
entering extended mode
(./feynmfex.tex
LaTeX2e <2003/12/01>
(/texlive/2005/texmf-dist/tex/latex/base/article.cls
Document Class: article 2004/02/16 v1.4f Standard LaTeX document class
(/texlive/2005/texmf-dist/tex/latex/base/size10.clo))
(/texlive/2005/texmf-dist/tex/latex/feynmf/feynmf.sty
Package: 'feynmf' v1.0 (rev. 1.12) <1995/05/06> (ohl))
No file feynmfex.aux.
feynmf: Files fmpict.mf and fmpict.tfm not found:
feynmf: This job will create fmpict.mf, process it later with METAFONT
feynmf: and then reprocess this file. Don't worry about a harmless premature
feynmf: MakeTeXTFM that might have failed just a moment ago!
feynmf: Label file fmpict.t1 not found:
feynmf: Process fmpict.mf with METAFONT and then reprocess this file.
[1] (./feynmfex.aux) )
Output written on feynmfex.dvi (1 page, 232 bytes).
Transcript written on feynmfex.log.
```

The resulting file `fmpict.mf` must be processed by the METAFONT program to generate the TEX font metric file `fmpict.tfm` as well as a *generic font* `.gf` file. This file is then transformed with **gftopk** into a packed bitmap image of type `.pk` so that it can be used with a `dvi` driver:

```
> mf "\mode=localfont; \input fmpict"
This is METAFONT, Version 2.71828 (Web2C 7.5.5)
(fmpict.mf
(/texlive/2005/texmf-dist/metafont/feynmf/feynmf.mf)
:1:\fmfL(49.98672,41.08102,b){$\mathrm {Z}$}% [1] )
Font metrics written on fmpict.tfm.
Output written on fmpict.600gf (1 character, 4168 bytes).
Transcript written on fmpict.log.
> gftopk fmpict.600gf
```

When METAPOST rather than METAFONT is used to generate the images, the **FeynMF** system writes a METAPOST file called `fmpict.mp`. When the METAPOST program runs with this file as input, PostScript drawings in files named `fmpict.`*n* are created for each diagram in the input file (where *n* is the sequence number of the graph). These drawing files are automatically included in following LaTeX runs using the standard **graphics** package.

You can run **FeynMF** in two different modes, depending on how you want to tackle a particular problem:

- *Vertex mode*, in which the layout is determined automatically from the mathematical description of the graph (including its vertices and arcs); physical coordinates are not normally specified.

- *Immediate mode*, in which you can completely control all physical coordinates by coding in META.

Vertex mode and algorithmic layout

In vertex mode, everything can be specified at the LaTeX level and no knowledge of META is needed. For maximal flexibility, **FeynMF** accepts a *mathematical* description of a graph and

Table 8.14: **FeynMF** vertex and fill styles

	filled=-.5	filled=0	filled=.5	filled=1
circle	⊗	○	◍	●
square	▤	□	▨	■
triangle	◬	△	◭	▲
diamond	◈	◇	◈	◆
pentagon	⬠	⬠	⬠	⬠
hexagon	⬡	⬡	⬡	⬢
triagram	◬	△	◭	▲
tetragram	✦	✧	✦	✦
pentagram	☆	☆	☆	★
hexagram	✶	✶	✶	✶

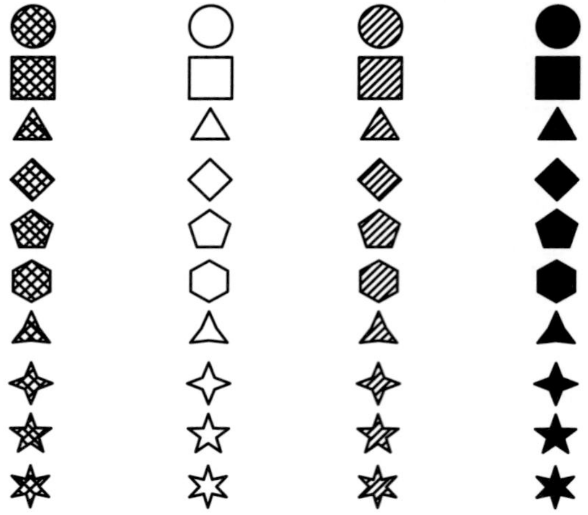

Example
8-4-15

creates the layout of the corresponding Feynman diagram automatically from that specification.

FeynMF includes commands to place external vertices along the sides of a diagram. To calculate optimal positions for the vertices, **FeynMF** minimizes a weighted sum of squared lengths for the internal vertices with the help of METR:

$$L(v_1, \ldots, v_n) = \frac{1}{2} \sum_{i,j} t_{ij}(v_i - v_j)^2$$

where i, j run over all combinations of vertices. The elements of the tension matrix t_{ij} are taken as 1 by default, but the user can specify other values to fine-tune the layout. The tension values can be viewed as rubber bands that let you pull together or push apart adjacent vertices, as shown in the following example:

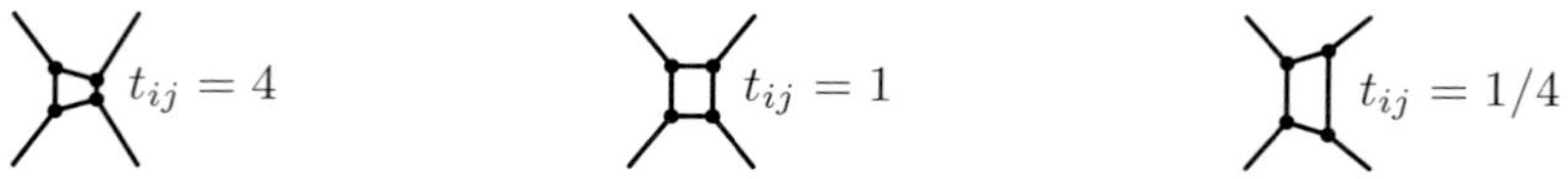

$t_{ij} = 4$ $t_{ij} = 1$ $t_{ij} = 1/4$

Example
8-4-14

Practice has shown that the most effective way to draw Feynman diagrams is a combination of step-by-step construction of subgraphs and, if necessary, adjustment of tensions. Often the default settings for the tensions give a quite satisfactory result straightaway, and only fine-tuning the tension of a single arc or loop is necessary.

A large choice of line, vertex, and fill styles are used by physicists, and **FeynMF** provides the most common styles (see Tables 8.14 and 8.15).

Table 8.15: FeynMF line styles

	: curly		: dbl_curly
– – – – –	: dashes	– – ▶ – –	: dashes_arrow
= = = = =	: dbl_dashes	= = ▶ =	: dbl_dashes_arrow
· · · · · · · · ·	: dots	· · · ▶ · · ·	: dots_arrow
◦◦◦◦◦◦◦◦◦	: dbl_dots	◦◦◦◀▶◦◦	: dbl_dots_arrow
	: phantom	▶	: phantom_arrow
————	: plain	———▶	: plain_arrow
═══════	: dbl_plain	═══▶═	: dbl_plain_arrow
∿∿∿	: wiggly	∿∿∿	: dbl_wiggly
⋁⋁⋁⋁⋁	: zigzag	⋀⋀⋀⋀⋀	: dbl_zigzag

Example
8-4-16

```
\fmfleft{v₁,...}        \fmfleftn{v}{n}
\fmfright{v₁,...}       \fmfrightn{v}{n}
\fmftop{v₁,...}         \fmftopn{v}{n}
\fmfbottom{v₁,...}      \fmfbottomn{v}{n}
\fmfsurround{v₁,...}    \fmfsurround{v}{n}
```

These are **FeynMF**'s basic commands in vertex mode; they place the set of external vertices $v_1,\ldots$ at the left, right, top, bottom, or surrounding the diagram. The right-hand form of the commands (with suffix n) places all vertices v from 1 to n, without the need to list them explicitly.

```
\fmfcurved     \fmfstraight
```

By default, the external vertices are put on a smooth curved path. When the `\fmfstraight` command is specified, they are put on a straight path from then on (i.e., `\fmfcurved` and `\fmfstraight` switch between both alternatives).

```
\fmf{lsty}{v₁,...}        \fmfn{lsty}{v}{n}
\fmfcyclen{lsty}{v}{n}    \fmfrcyclen{lsty}{v}{n}
```

The command `\fmf` connects a set of vertices $v_1,\ldots$ with line style *lsty* (see Table 8.15). This line style can be customized further by specifying a number of options (see Table 8.16). For instance,

```
\fmf{fermion,tension=.5}{vw,vn,ve,vs,vw}
```

connects the specified internal vertices with a "`fermion`" line using a "`tension`" keyword value of 0.5. The other commands `\fmfn`, `\fmfcyclen`, and `\fmfrcyclen` connect vertices v_1 to v_n normally, cyclically, or cyclically in reverse order, respectively.

Table 8.16: FeynMF line-drawing keywords

Keyword Name	Explanation
label	TEX text used for arc label
label.side	place label at "left" or "right"
label.dist	place label at given distance
left	draw half-circle on left
right	draw half-circle on right
straight	draw straight line (default)
tag	tag for disambiguating arc (if needed)
tension	draw tighter (> 1) or looser (< 1) arc
width	line width
foreground	foreground color (METAPOST only)
background	background color (METAPOST only)

$\boxed{\texttt{\textbackslash fmfpen}\{wgt\}}$

This command sets the thickness (weight) of the lines to *wgt*. Predefined sizes are `thin` and `thick`. To change the width of individual arcs, use the `width` keyword (see Table 8.16).

$\boxed{\texttt{\textbackslash fmfv}\{vopt\}\{v_1,\dots\} \quad \texttt{\textbackslash fmfvn}\{vopt\}\{v\}\{n\}}$

The command `\fmfv` declares the set of internal vertices $v_1,\dots$ with options *vopt* (`\fmfvn` does the same for vertices v_1 to v_n). Table 8.14 on page 564 shows some of the available vertex forms and fill styles, and Table 8.17 on the facing page shows possible values for the options associated with vertices.

$\boxed{\texttt{\textbackslash fmfdot}\{v_1,\dots\} \quad \texttt{\textbackslash fmfdotn}\{v\}\{n\}}$

This is a special case of the `\fmfv` command, in which a set of vertices is drawn as dots. For instance, the two following commands are equivalent:

```
\fmfdotn{v}{4}
\fmfv{decor.shape=circle,decor.filled=full,
      decor.size=2thick}{v1,v2,v3,v4}
```

$\boxed{\texttt{\textbackslash fmfblob}\{dia\}\{v_1,\dots\} \quad \texttt{\textbackslash fmfblobn}\{dia\}\{v\}\{n\}}$

Similarly, Thorsten Ohl has created a shorthand for drawing a "blob"; both commands below have the same result:

```
\fmfv{decor.shape=circle,decor.filled=shaded,
      decor.size=5mm}{vblob}
\fmfblob{5mm}{vblob}
```

Table 8.17: **FeynMF** vertex-drawing keywords

Keyword Name	Explanation
decoration.shape	shape of decoration
decoration.size	size of decoration
decoration.filled	fill, shade, or hatch decoration
decoration.angle	rotate decoration
label	TEX text used for vertex label
label.angle	place label at angle with respect to vertex
label.dist	place label at given distance
foreground	foreground color (METAPOST only)
background	background color (METAPOST only)

`\fmfpoly{vopt}{v₁,...}`   `\fmpolyn{vopt}{v}{n}`

Complex vertices are commonplace in solid-state physics. They can be constructed with polygons. The command `\fmfpoly` places the vertices $v_1,\ldots$ on a polygon using the argument *vopt* (`\fmpolyn` is similar for vertices v_1 to v_n). Possible keywords are listed in Table 8.18 on the next page.

`\fmffreeze`

A number of commands let you influence the automatic layout algorithms of **FeynMF**. Perhaps the most important is `\fmffreeze`, which calculates the diagram up to the current point and "freezes" it, so that arcs added later do not affect its positioning. This important technique of using skeletons in the construction of diagrams is described in detail in the manual [92] (see also Example 8-4-18).

METAPOST lets you use color in your diagrams (via the `foreground` and `background` specifiers in the line- and vertex-drawing keywords of Tables 8.16 and 8.17). The predefined colors are `white`, `black`, `red`, `green`, and `blue`; other colors can be specified as RGB (red, green, blue) triplets. For instance, `foreground=(1,,0,,1)`[1] and `foreground=red+blue` are equivalent. For arcs, the background color is used only for the interior between double lines. For example, the following command draws a red gluon line between the vertices `in` and `out`:

```
\fmf{gluon,fore=red}{in,out}
```

Note that keywords can be abbreviated to their shortest non-ambiguous form (e.g., `fore` for `foreground` in the previous example). This works for each dot-separated component of a keyword name; thus `l.d` is interpreted as `label.dist`.

FeynMF can calculate optimal positions for labels with the help of METAFONT. Since METAFONT can write only to its `.log` file, the positioning information needed to typeset

---

[1] Note the double commas "„", which are needed to disambiguate the comma as a keyword separator in the commands and inside the keyword values.

Table 8.18: FeynMF polygon keywords

Keyword Name	Explanation
empty	only outline drawn
fill	filled interior
filled	interior filled, shaded, or hatched
hatched	hatched interior
label	TEX text for labeling polygon
label.angle	place label at angle with respect to vertex
label.dist	place label at given distance
phantom	nothing is drawn
pull	edges pulled in (<0) or out (>0)
shade	shaded interior
smooth	corners are drawn smoothed
tension	tension used for edges
foreground	foreground color (METAPOST only)
background	background color (METAPOST only)

the labels with LATEX is written in that file, which is subsequently read and parsed by LATEX. By default, all labels are placed at the outside of the arc or vertex with which they are associated. Explicit user placement of labels is possible, of course, as described in the manual.

To get a flavor of how to specify Feynman diagrams in vertex mode, look at the diagram in Example 8-4-17. The environment fmfgraph contains the description of a single Feynman diagram. In analogy with LATEX's standard picture environment, the argument inside the parentheses specifies the width and height of the diagram in units of \unitlength. This environment does not allow labeling the diagram. To add labels—for instance, to label the central arc and the external vertices in our figure—we would use the starred version fmfgraph*.

```
\usepackage{feynmp}
1   \begin{fmfgraph*}(100,60)
2     \fmfleftn{i}{2} \fmfrightn{o}{4}
3     \fmflabel{$\mathrm{e}^-$}{i1}\fmflabel{$\mathrm{e}^+$}{i2}
4     \fmflabel{$\mu^+$}{o1}
5     \fmflabel{$\nu_{\mu}$}{o2}
6     \fmflabel{$\mathrm{s}$}{o3}
7     \fmflabel{$\bar\mathrm{c}$}{o4}
8     \fmf{fermion}{i1,v1,i2}
9     \fmf{boson,label=$\gamma,,\mathrm{Z}$}{v1,v2}
10    \fmf{boson}{v3,v2,v4}
11    \fmf{fermion}{o1,v3,o2}
12    \fmf{fermion}{o4,v4,o3}
13    \fmfdot{v1,v3,v4}\fmfblob{.12w}{v2}
14  \end{fmfgraph*}
```

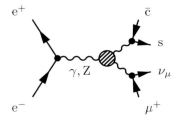

Line 2 declares two incoming particles (at the left of the diagram; \fmfleftn command) and four outgoing particles (at the right of the diagram; \fmfrightn command) and lines 3–7 assign them a label. The inner vertices are numbered v1 to v4 from left to right, so that line 8 connects the incoming fermions i1 and i2 with the first inner vertex v1. In line 9, this vertex is connected with a boson line style to the left of the "blob" (inner vertex v2), and a label is added. Line 10 draws the boson line between the internal vertices v2, v3, and v4; lines 11 and 12 connect these latter two inner vertices with outgoing fermion lines. Finally, on line 13, vertices v1, v3, and v4 get a dot, while a blob with a diameter equal to .12w (w being the total width of the diagram) is put at vertex v2.

Immediate mode

FeynMF's vertex mode operates on abstract vertices, and the result depends on how these vertices are connected. In most cases this "automatic" vertex mode suffices to obtain the desired layout. However, with minor exceptions, this mode can produce only straight lines. If you want curved arcs, you should use FeynMF's *immediate* mode instead. This mode also lets you control the positioning of the diagram elements more closely, since it acts on the vertex coordinates and the arcs connecting them.

Let us consider the loop diagrams in Example 8-4-18. The left-hand graph is drawn in vertex mode, while the right-hand version, which is created using immediate mode, has a more attractive appearance.

```
\usepackage{feynmp}
1   \fbox{\begin{fmfgraph}(100,40)
2     \fmfleft{w}\fmfright{e}
3     \fmf{boson}{w,vw}\fmf{boson}{ve,e}
4     \fmf{fermion,tension=.5}{vw,vn,ve,vs,vw}
5     \fmf{gluon}{vn,vs}
6     \fmffixed{(0,h)}{vn,vs}
7     \fmfdot{vw,vn,ve,vs}
8   \end{fmfgraph}}
9   \fbox{\begin{fmfgraph}(100,40)
10    \fmfleft{w}\fmfright{e}
11    \fmf{boson}{w,vw}\fmf{boson}{ve,e}
12    \fmf{phantom,left,tension=.4}{vw,ve,vw}
13    \fmfdot{vw,ve}
14    \fmffreeze
15    \fmfipath{pn,ps}\fmfipair{vn,vs}
```

```
16    \fmfiequ{pn}{vpath (__vw, __ve)}
17    \fmfiequ{ps}{vpath (__ve, __vw)}
18    \fmfiequ{vn}{point .5length(pn) of pn}
19    \fmfiequ{vs}{point .5length(ps) of ps}
20    \fmfi{fermion}{subpath (0,.5)*length(pn) of pn}
21    \fmfi{fermion}{subpath (.5,1)*length(pn) of pn}
22    \fmfi{fermion}{subpath (0,.5)*length(ps) of ps}
23    \fmfi{fermion}{subpath (.5,1)*length(ps) of ps}
24    \fmfi{gluon}{vn--vs}
25    \fmfiv{dec.sh=circle,dec.siz=2thick}{vn}
26    \fmfiv{dec.sh=circle,dec.siz=2thick}{vs}
27    \end{fmfgraph}}
```

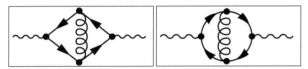

Example
8-4-18

For clarity, the vertices of both loop diagrams are named—going clockwise, vw, vn, ve, and vs (for west, north, east, and south, respectively). In the first diagram we observe on line 4 the use of the tension keyword to control the fermion loop. Line 6 has a \fmffixed command, which fixes the distance between subsequent vertices in the list. Here the distance between the top vertex and the bottom vertex is fixed to the height of the diagram h, 40 "units" (such a constraint is used in the METAFONT processing step for calculating the layout of the diagram). Without this command the loop would collapse.

Now look at the "improved" diagram. Lines 10 and 11, which correspond to the "external" lines, are identical to those in the previous diagram. The \fmffreeze command (line 14) ensures that this part of the diagram remains fixed (i.e., it cannot be influenced by subsequent FeynMF commands). From line 15 onwards we use FeynMF's *immediate* commands, all of which start with the four letters fmfi.[1] The \fmfipath and \fmfipair commands declare a META path and a coordinate pair, respectively. Lines 16–19 are assignments (*arg1=arg2*). Note the vpath commands, which get the META path between two vertices (after \fmffreeze). Note also that the vertices must be preceded by a double underscore (e.g., ve becomes __ve). The \fmfi commands on lines 20–24 draw a line in the given line style (first argument) along a path (second argument). Line 24 also shows META's -- operator, which forces a straight line (for the gluon). Finally, lines 25 and 26 draw a vertex with the \fmfiv command at the META coordinates specified as the second argument.

We end this section with a few more practical examples. The first one shows how LaTeX \parbox commands can be used to include Feynman diagrams in an equation. Further fine-tuning is possible with the help of \hspace commands.

```
\usepackage{feynmp}
\begin{equation}
\parbox{40mm}{%
```

---

[1] For a detailed understanding of these commands, you should have some familiarity with META's constructs, such as how they connect vertices using Bézier curves; see, for example, Knuth [72].

```
\begin{fmfgraph*}(100,90)
 \fmfleft{i}\fmfright{o}
 \fmf{photon}{i,v3}\fmf{photon}{v3,v1}
 \fmf{photon}{v4,v2}\fmf{photon}{v2,o}
 \fmf{fermion,left,tension=.3}{v1,v4,v1}
\end{fmfgraph*}}
=\frac{-i\eta^{\mu\alpha}}{q^2+i\epsilon}\left[\hspace*{-0.1cm}
\parbox{30mm}{%
 \begin{fmfgraph*}(60,60)
 \fmfleft{i}\fmfright{o}
 \fmf{phantom}{i,v1}\fmf{phantom}{v2,o}
 \fmf{fermion,left,tension=.3}{v1,v2,v1}
 \fmfdotn{v}{2}
 \fmflabel{$\alpha$}{v1}\fmflabel{$\beta$}{v2}
\end{fmfgraph*}}
\hspace*{-1cm}\right]
\frac{-i\eta^{\beta\nu}}{q^2+i\epsilon}\label{feyneq}
\end{equation}
```

$$= \frac{-i\eta^{\mu\alpha}}{q^2 + i\epsilon} \left[\alpha \qquad \beta \right] \frac{-i\eta^{\beta\nu}}{q^2 + i\epsilon} \qquad (1)$$

Example
8-4-19

Example 8-4-20 shows how textual labels can be placed in various positions on the diagram.

```
\usepackage{feynmp}

\begin{fmfgraph*}(90,70)
 \fmfleft{i1} \fmfright{o1,o2,o3}
 \fmf{fermion,label.side=right,label=$\mathrm{u}$}{i1,v1}
 \fmf{fermion,label.side=right,label=$\mathrm{d}$}{v1,o1}
 \fmf{photon,label.side=left,label.dist=1mm,
      label=$\mathrm{W}^{+}$,tension=0.5}{v1,v2}
 \fmf{fermion,label.side=left,label.dist=1mm,
      label=${\nu}_\mathrm{e}$,tension=0.5}{v2,o2}
 \fmf{fermion,label.side=right,
      label=$\mathrm{e}^{+}$,tension=0.5}{o3,v2}
\end{fmfgraph*}
```

Example
8-4-20

Finally, Example 8-4-21 displays a more complex cyclic diagram constructed with the \fmfcyclen command, using the tension keyword to control the appearance of arcs and edges.

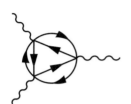

```
\usepackage{feynmp}

\begin{fmfgraph*}(90,70)
 \fmfleft{i1,i2}    \fmfright{o1}
 \fmf{photon,tension=4}{i1,v1} \fmf{photon,tension=4}{i2,v3}
 \fmf{photon,tension=4}{v2,o1}
 \fmfcyclen{fermion,tension=1}{v}{3}
 \fmf{fermion,tension=1,left=1.4/3}{v1,v3}
 \fmf{fermion,tension=1,left=2/3}{v3,v2}
 \fmf{fermion,tension=1,left=2/3}{v2,v1}
\end{fmfgraph*}
```

Example
8-4-21

8.4.4 Extending FeynMF

Sometimes it is necessary to go beyond **FeynMF**'s predefined facilities. In such a case, we can use META commands directly, either by inputting a META file or by exploiting **FeynMF**'s \fmfcmd command.

> \fmfcmd{*MFcmds*}

The \fmfcmd command enters the META commands *MFcmds* directly into the output file. This facility can be useful for defining new line styles. A META macro style_def is used to register the new style with **FeynMF** and to define a macro to be called whenever the new style is referenced—for instance, as the first argument in an \fmf command. Such functions are called *transformers* since they take a META path as their argument and return a transformed (embellished) path. This facility has already been used to obtain the various line styles given in Table 8.15 on page 565. For example, you can first transform a line into a wiggly line and then add an arrow with the help of the predefined style wiggly:

```
\fmfcmd{%
style_def charged_boson expr p =
draw (wiggly p);
fill (arrow p)
enddef;}
```

In general, all of META's path-related commands are available to extend **FeynMF**. To handle color (with METAPOST), you should use **feynmp**'s explicitly color-aware functions, such as cdraw and cfill.

8.5 Typesetting timing diagrams

Jens Leilich and Ludwig May wrote the **timing** package to typeset timing diagrams for digital circuits. They developed a METAFONT alphabet of symbols and used METAFONT's ligature mechanism to typeset logic transitions. Figure 8.2 on page 574 shows a complete example of the use of the **timing** package.

8.5.1 Commands in the `timing` environment

The commands described in this section can be used only inside the `timing` environment; it is an extension of LaTeX's `picture` environment, so that all `picture`-specific commands are available as well. The chosen `\unitlength` unit is `1sp`.

> `\begin{timing}` [*symbol-type*] {*label-width*} ... `\end{timing}`

The optional argument *symbol-type* specifies which of the four timing-symbol font variants is to be used. Its value can be `1`, `1s`, `2`, or `2s`, where the digit represents the width (about 1 or 2 mm) and the letter `s` selects oblique (rather than vertical) lines to connect the signal levels. By default, symbols of type 2 are used. Table 8.19 on page 575 shows all of the signal symbols with their representative letters and examples in all four font variants. The mandatory argument *label-width* gives the width of the widest label describing the signals. These labels are typeset to the left of the signal lines.

> `\til{`*y-pos*`}{`*symbols*`}`

A signal line in a timing diagram is typeset using the `\til` command; *y-pos* denotes the line position in the diagram. In most cases you should use consecutive integer values. The second argument *symbols* contains a combination of letters (see Table 8.19 on page 575) representing various signal states. Because of the way in which the symbol fonts are implemented, it is best to have at least two identical letters representing each state. Otherwise, the ligature mechanism that draws the state transitions may not work correctly.

The *symbols* argument can also contain one of following commands:

> `\timingcounter{`*separation*`}{`*Start-value*`}{`*End-value*`}{`*Interval*`}`
> `\conttimingcounter{`*separation*`}{`*Start-value*`}{`*End-value*`}{`*Interval*`}`

These commands typeset a scale of numbers representing timing values. The second form `\conttimingcounter`, for use after an interruption, also leaves the necessary space.

> `\tin{`*y-pos*`}{`*text*`}`

The `\tin` command describes the label of the signal line. By using the same *y-pos* value as in the corresponding `\til` command, the argument *text* is centered properly to the left of the line.

> `\tnote{`*y-pos*`}{`*x-pos*`}{`*text*`}`

The `\tnote` command lets you place annotations anywhere on a signal line. Again, the *y-pos* should correspond to the value in the `\til` command (you may want to add or subtract a bit to move the *text* vertically). The *x-pos* denotes the horizontal start position—that is, the width of the symbols produced by letters in the *symbols* argument of the `\til` command is used as a unit (e.g., a value of 5 denotes the position after LHHHL).

```
\usepackage{timing}
\begin{timing}[2s]{1.4cm}
 \tnote{0.5}{4}{$\mathrm{T}_1$}
 \tnote{0.5}{12}{$\mathrm{T}_2$}\tnote{0.5}{20}{$\mathrm{T}_i$}
 \tnote{0.5}{28}{$\mathrm{T}_1$}\tnote{0.5}{36}{$\mathrm{T}_2$}
 \tnote{0.5}{44}{$\mathrm{T}_i$}\tnote{0.5}{52}{$\mathrm{T}_1$}
%% Clock                ....1111....2222....iiii....1111....2222....iiii....1111
 \tin{1}{CLK}  \til{1}{HHHHLLLLHHHHLLLLHHHHLLLLHHHHLLLLHHHHLLLLHHHHLLLLHHHHLLLL}
%% Adresses line        ....1111....2222....iiii....1111....2222....iiii....1111
 \tin{2}{ADDR}  \til{2}{VVVVXVVVVVVVVVVVVVVVVXVVVVVVVXVVVVVVVVVVVVVVVVXVVVVVXVVVV}
 \tnote{1.85}{10}{Valid}\tnote{1.85}{22}{Invalid}%
 \tnote{1.85}{34}{Valid}\tnote{1.85}{46}{Invalid}
%% Adresses status      ....1111....2222....iiii....1111....2222....iiii....1111
 \tin{3}{ADS\#}  \til{3}{HHHHLLLLLLLLHHHHHHHHHHHHHHHHLLLLLLLLHHHHHHHHHHHHHHHHLLLL}
 %% Write/Read          ....1111....2222....iiii....1111....2222....iiii....1111
 \tin{4}{W/R\#}  \til{4}{HHHHLLLLLLLLLLLLLLLLFFFFFFFFHHHHHHHHHHHHHHHHFFFFFFFFLLLL}
%% Burst ready          ....1111....2222....iiii....1111....2222....iiii....1111
 \tin{5}{BRDY\#}\til{5}{UUUUUUUUUUUUUZZZZZZZZUUUUUUUUUUUUUUUUUZZZZZZZZUUUUUUUUUUUU}
%% Data lines           ....1111....2222....iiii....1111....2222....iiii....1111
 \tin{6}{DATA}  \til{6}{ZZZZZZZZZZZZZVVVVVVVVZZZZZZZZZZZZZZZZZVVVVVVVVZZZZZZZZZZZZ}
 \tnote{5.85}{14}{To CPU}\tnote{5.85}{37}{From CPU}
 \sline{0.6}{0}{6.}\sline{0.6}{8}{6.}\sline{0.3}{16}{5.5}\sline{0.6}{24}{1.5}
 \sline{2.1}{24}{6.}\sline{0.6}{32}{6.}\sline{0.3}{40}{5.5}\sline{0.6}{48}{1.5}
 \sline{2.1}{48}{6.}\sline{0.6}{56}{6.}
\end{timing}
```

Figure 8.2: Timing diagram of a memory read followed by a memory write

Table 8.19: Symbol combinations in all font variants

Letter	Symbol		Font Variants			
			1	1s	2	2s
L	Low level	HLLLLH →				
H	High level	LHHHHL →				
F	Floating line (unknown level)	LFFFFH →				
l	Low level with marks	hlllllh →				
h	High level with marks	lhhhhl →				
.	Empty line with marks	. . . . . . →				
V	Valid bus	ZVVVVU →				
X	Bus with change of state	VVVXVV →				
U	Invalid bus	ZUUUUV →				
Z	Tristate	VZZZZU →				
T	Top line with time mark	TtttTt →				
t	Top line without time mark	TtTtTt →				
B	Bottom line with time mark	BbbbBb →				
b	Bottom line without time mark	BbBbBb →				
–	Interruption sign	UUU–UU →				

Example 8-5-2

\rarw{*y-pos*}{*x-pos*}{*length*}{*text*}	\larw{*y-pos*}{*x-pos*}{*length*}{*text*}

These two commands produce horizontal arrows: \rarw points to the right, \larw points to the left. To position such an arrow over a signal line, make the *y-pos* a little smaller (e.g., 0.6) than the line value.

> `\sline{`*y-pos*`}{`*x-pos*`}{`*y2-pos*`}`

A vertical line is drawn with the `\sline` command, starting at *y-pos*/*x-pos* and going down to *y2-pos*/*x-pos*. The width of such lines can be influenced with LaTeX's `\linethickness` declaration.

8.5.2 Customization

A diagram can be further fine-tuned with the following commands:

> `\timescalefactor`

This command controls the separation between lines (the default value is 2, which means there is one empty line between two signal lines that are one vertical *y-pos* apart).

> `\timadjust`

This command adjusts the vertical lines (the default value is 0pt). It can be of help if the printer driver does not position the vertical lines properly in the middle of the state transitions.

Both these values are set using `\renewcommand`.

8.6 Electronics and optics circuits

As with Feynman diagrams (see Section 8.4), a variety of techniques can be used to typeset circuit diagrams. In this section we first look at the circ package, which uses dedicated fonts. Next we study the circuit_macros package, a series of macros written for the m4 macro processor. Finally we briefly mention the interactive XCircuit package, which generates PostScript output.[1]

8.6.1 A special font for drawing electronics and optics diagrams

The circ package (CTAN: `macros/generic/diagrams/circ`) by Sebastian Tannert and Andreas Tille can be used to typeset circuit and optics diagrams. This package provides a convenient way to draw diagrams containing not only resistors, capacitors, and transistors, but also lenses, mirrors, and the like. Symbols are coded in METAFONT, so that the output can be printed or viewed on any device.

The principles underlying the circ package are similar to those in a turtle system: all symbols and wires are drawn with respect to a "current" point that is advanced automatically, though if necessary the drawing position and direction can be set by hand. The package has commands to *draw*, *justify*, *link*, and *position* symbols and wires either absolutely or relatively.

---

[1] There is also the makecirc package by Gustavo S. Bustamante Argañaraz, a METAPOST library for drawing electric circuit diagrams, see the section on electrical circuits in Chapter 4.

Table 8.20: Electronic circuit symbols (`basic` option)

ground and junction	`\GND`	⊥	`\gnd`	⏚	`\.`		•
resistors and capacitor	`\R`	R_n ▭	`\Rvar`	▱	`\C`		C_n
capacitors and diode	`\Cvar`	C_n	`\Cel`	C_n	`\D`		D_n
various diodes	`\ZD`	D_n	`\LED`	D_n	`\Dcap`		D_n
sources	`\U`	U_n	`\Uvar`	U_n	`\I`		I_n
source and meters	`\Ivar`	I_n	`\V`	U_n	`\A`		I_n
coil, crystal	`\L`	L_n	`\xtal`	Q_n			
lamps, switch	`\La`	La_n	`\GasLa`	n	`\S`		S_n
(photo) transistors	`\npnEC`		`\pnp`		`\npnPH`		T_n
FET and VMOS	`\nfet`		`\pfet`		`\nvmos`		
VMOS	`\pvmos`		`\namos`		`\pamos`		

Example
8-6-1

The **circ** package is subdivided into several parts that can be specified separately as options to the `\usepackage` command:

`basic`   basic symbols, such as resistors, capacitors, switches, diodes, and transistors (see Table 8.20)

`box`   blackbox, oscilloscope, generator, and amplifier (see Table 8.22 on the next page)

`gate`   logical circuits (an `oldgate` option offers old-fashioned variants) (see Table 8.21 on the following page)

`ic`   integrated circuits, such as flip-flops (see Table 8.23 on page 579)

`optics`   optical elements, such as lenses and mirrors (see Table 8.24 on page 580)

`physics` Newtonian mechanics symbols (see Table 8.25 on page 580)

Table 8.21: Gate and trigger symbols (`gate` option)

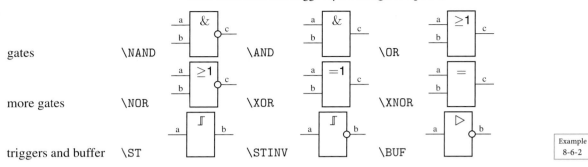

<table>
<tr><td>gates</td><td>\NAND</td><td></td><td>\AND</td><td></td><td>\OR</td></tr>
<tr><td>more gates</td><td>\NOR</td><td></td><td>\XOR</td><td></td><td>\XNOR</td></tr>
<tr><td>triggers and buffer</td><td>\ST</td><td></td><td>\STINV</td><td></td><td>\BUF</td></tr>
</table>

Example
8-6-2

Table 8.22: Electronic box symbols (`box` option)

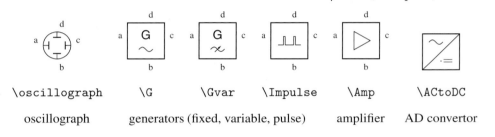

\oscillograph	\G	\Gvar	\Impulse	\Amp	\ACtoDC
oscillograph	generators (fixed, variable, pulse)			amplifier	AD convertor

Example
8-6-3

General circuit diagram commands

Every circuit diagram is enclosed inside a `circuit` environment.

```
\begin{circuit}{magstep}   ...   \end{circuit}
```

The argument *magstep* is an integer (in the interval 0 to 4) specifying the size of the symbols. Tables 8.20 through 8.25 show some of the commands available and associated symbols that can be used inside the `circuit` environment.

The general syntax of a drawing command is

```
\symbolname␣number␣label␣specs␣dir
```

The `basic` option offers more than 60 symbol commands from which to choose. The *number* argument is an additional identifier; i.e., the combination of \symbolname and *number* must be unique within one diagram, so that the various circuit elements can be connected unambiguously. The direction in which a symbol is drawn is specified with the argument *dir* (h for horizontal, v for vertical, l for left, etc.). Each symbol can be annotated by using the argument *label* (note the position of the symbol and its annotation with respect to the

Table 8.23: Integrated circuit symbols (`ic` option)

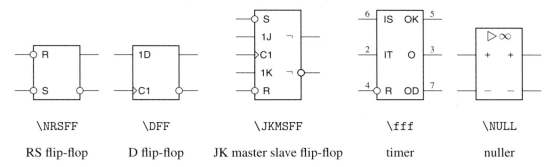

\NRSFF	\DFF	\JKMSFF	\fff	\NULL
RS flip-flop	D flip-flop	JK master slave flip-flop	timer	nuller

Example
8-6-4

current point in Tables 8.20–8.25). The optional argument *spec* specifies the pin position at the current drawing point (for variable resistors, transistors, etc.).

In addition to the inscription produced by *label*, the symbol is labeled automatically with an abbreviation indexed by *number*. The former can be suppressed by using \nv before the command, the latter by using \ln. In addition, the command \cc exchanges the positions of both labels.

\. *number*	\junction *number*

Junctions are made with the command \. (or, alternatively, \junction). The only argument is a *number* identifying the junction for further reference.

\- *len␣dir*	\wire *len␣dir*

Simple connections between symbols are drawn with the \- (\wire) command. The first argument *len* specifies the length in 2.5-mm steps, while the second argument *dir* indicates the direction (l for left, r for right, u for up, d for down). Thus \-␣8␣u draws a wire 8 units (2 cm) long upwards. Variants are \dashed, \bundle, and \wwire, which draw a dashed wire, a bundle, and a wire pair, respectively.

\htopin *pinref*␣	\vtopin *pinref*␣

The current position is connected horizontally or vertically to the x and y coordinates of a given pin by the commands \htopin and \vtopin, respectively, where the argument *pinref* is the symbolic identifer of a pin of some symbol. For example, if the resistor R2 was previously defined with an \R command, then the succession of commands

```
\vtopin R2r   \htopin R2r
```

draws a wire starting from the current position vertically to the y position and then horizontally to the x position of the right side of resistor R2.

Table 8.24: Optical symbols (`optics` option)

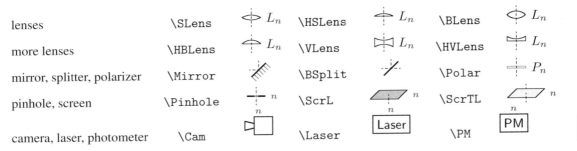

lenses	\SLens		L_n	\HSLens		L_n	\BLens		L_n
more lenses	\HBLens		L_n	\VLens		L_n	\HVLens		L_n
mirror, splitter, polarizer	\Mirror			\BSplit			\Polar		P_n
pinhole, screen	\Pinhole		n	\ScrL		n	\ScrTL		n
camera, laser, photometer	\Cam			\Laser	Laser		\PM	PM	

Example 8-6-5

Table 8.25: Newtonian mechanics symbols (`physics` option)

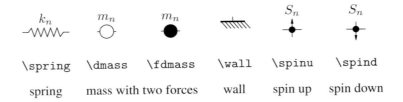

k_n	m_n	m_n		S_n	S_n
\spring	\dmass	\fdmass	\wall	\spinu	\spind
spring	mass with two forces		wall	spin up	spin down

Example 8-6-6

\at $x_\sqcup y_\sqcup$	\from $x_\sqcup y_\sqcup$
\moverel $x_\sqcup y_\sqcup$	\shift $x_\sqcup y_\sqcup$

The current drawing position can be changed with several commands. The first two in the syntax box set the current point to the absolute coordinate (x, y) in the circ coordinate system (in steps of 2.5 mm). In general, such absolute positioning is not desirable, since all diagrams are implicitly drawn with respect to the point $(0, 0)$ and introducing absolute coordinates destroys the logical structure. It is much better to issue the command \moverel (or \shift), which uses relative positioning to move the current points x units right and y units up.

\atpin *pinref*$_\sqcup$	\frompin *pinref*$_\sqcup$

You can move the drawing position with \atpin or, alternatively, \frompin. After executing this command, the drawing continues at the given pin position. For instance, the current point can be set to the down pin of the coil labeled L4 with the command \atpin$_\sqcup$L4d$_\sqcup$.

The previously described commands are only a few of the possibilities described in [114]. The circ package has commands to center objects horizontally or vertically with respect to other objects, commands to add text at the current drawing position, and a few more bells and whistles, most of which appear in the following examples.

Examples

Our first example is taken from the circ reference manual, which discusses in detail how the drawing is produced; it shows a circuit for measuring the current-amplifying characteristics of an npn transistor.

```
\usepackage[basic]{circ}
\begin{circuit}{0}
\npn1 {?} B l    % draw npn transistor
\frompin npn1C   % draw from collector
\- 1 u           % a little wire up
\nl\A1 {$I_C$} u % A-meter for collector current
\atpin npn1B     % next draw from base
\- 1 l           % a little wire left
\R1 {510 k$\Omega$} l % place resistor on base
\- 1 l           % add little wire left
\centerto A1     % align centered on first A-meter
\nl\A2 {$I_B$} u % draw second A-meter
\frompin A2b     % connect second A-meter to
\vtopin R1l      % resistor
\frompin A1t
\- 1 u \.1       % connection point
\frompin A2t
\vtopin .1
\htopin .1       % connect second A-meter to 1.
\- 1 u \cc\connection1
    {$U_b$} c u  % connect to voltage
\frompin npn1E   % connect emitter to
\- 1 d  \GND1    % ground
\end{circuit}
```

Another example from the reference manual is an experimental setup in optics, with a laser, a modulator, lenses, mirrors, a camera, and a screen:

```
\usepackage[basic,optics]{circ}
\begin{circuit}{0}
  \nl\Laser1 {} r                  % laser
  \oa 2 r                          % optical axis
  \Polar1 {} r                     % polarizer
  \oa 2 r
  \nl\OM1 P1 {} {} {} {} h         % optical modulator
  \atpin OM1P3
  \oa 4 r
  \cc\BLens1 {} r                  % first lens
  \oa 2 r
  \nl\Pinhole1 {} r                % pinhole
  \oa 7 r
  \cc\SLens2 {} r                  % second lens
```

Example
8-6-7

```
\oa 1 r
\Polar2 {} r                        % analyzer
\oa 3 r
\oa 3 r
\nl\BSplit1 {} + d                  % beam splitter
\atpin BSplit1+                     % continue drawing right
\oa 2 r
\nl\Cam1 {camera} . r               % camera
\atpin BLens1: \shift 0 2 \P3       % mark middle of first lens
\atpin Pinhole1: \shift 0 2 \P4     % mark middle of pinhole
\atpin SLens2: \shift 0 2 \P5       % mark middle of second lens
\Dtext{\small $f_1$} from P3 to P4 % f_1
\Dtext{\small $f_2$} from P4 to P5 % f_2
\atpin BSplit1.                     % second part of beam down
\oa 5 d
\Mirror1 {} * R                     % mirror
\oa 2 r
\nl\ScrL1 {screen} h                % white screen
\end{circuit}
```

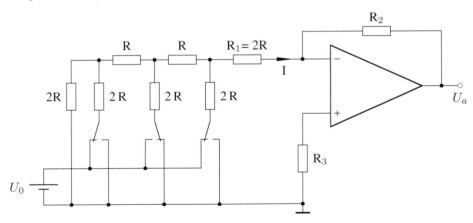

A more complex example (courtesy of the package authors) follows, given without code. It represents an operational amplifier.

8.6.2 Using the m4 macro processor for electronics diagrams

A procedure completely independent of TEX and METAFONT forms the basis of the cir-
cuit_macros package written by Dwight Aplevich. His approach uses a series of macros written for the m4 macro processor available on Unix systems. These macros generate code in
the pic language, which can be handled by a pic (gpic) interpreter generating TEX input in
the form of tpic \specials. Aplevich has developed a special tpic interpreter dpic that can
generate output for mfpic and PSTricks, as well as several other formats.[1]

Basic principles

The circuit_macros package has a number of m4 libraries, each containing a set of basic
macros, that let you construct complex electronic and flow diagrams. The IEEE Standard
315 of 1975 is followed for drawing the electronics and electrical elements.

Quite complex diagrams can be composed fairly easily (the distribution contains the
worked-out code of the complex example at the end of [81]). Here we merely show how to
obtain a simple circuit. The m4 code for our first example looks like this:

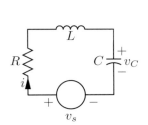

Example
8-6-10

```
.PS
cct_init
define('dimen_',0.6)
loopwid = 0.9; loopht = 0.7
  source(left_ loopwid); llabel(-,v_s,+)
  resistor(up_ loopht); llabel(,R,); b_current(i)
  inductor(right_ loopwid,L); rlabel(,L,)
  capacitor(down_ loopht,C); llabel(+,v_C,-); rlabel(,C,)
.PE
\usebox{\graph}
```

The macros .PS and .PE enclose each picture (these are the usual delimiters for the
pic program). The first macro command cct_init initializes some local variables for the
circuit package (global parameters, such as line widths, page size, and scaling factors). The
default value for the width of the picture is 0.5 inch. On the following two lines we set the
width of the body element (dimen_) and, since we want to draw a loop circuit, we specify its
width (loopwid) and height (loopht). Then we put a current source moving left and label
it with plus and minus signs and v_s, draw a resistor (going up), label it R, and add a current
arrow at i. This is followed by a self (inductor) at L. The loop is closed by a capacitor at C,
with an indication of the voltage V_C and the polarity of the charges on the plates. Note the
use of the llabel and rlabel commands to place texts to the left and right of the circuit
element, respectively.

Before we can use this input with LATEX, we must perform several translation steps. First
we have to translate the m4 instructions into pic code by executing m4 using the library
libcct.m4, which contains definitions for commonly used elements. This file is then run
through a pic-language interpreter like gpic to generate tpic \specials. The result can then
be processed by TEX and finally interpreted by a .dvi-reading program such as dvips. The

---

[1] The program dpic does not come with the distribution, but it can be downloaded from the author's Web site
at http://ece.uwaterloo.ca/~aplevich/dpic/.

command sequence for this precedure on a Unix machine would be similar to the following (depending on where the m4 files are stored):

```
m4 /usr/local/lib/m4/libcct.m4 cirexa.m4 > cirexa.pic
gpic -t cirexa.pic > cirexa.tex
```

This leaves us with a TEX file `cirexa.tex`, which contains only the tpic code for the example. To process it further, we could include it into a LATEX source using \input. This stores the picture in a box register named \graph, so we have to add a \usebox{\graph} statement into the document at the spot where we want it to appear.

Customizing the diagram

To show the flexibility of the `circuit_macros` approach, let us modify our example slightly to see how it behaves with an alternating current.

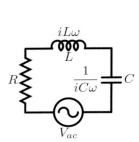

```
.PS
cct_init
linethick=1.6
define('dimen_',0.6)
loopwid = 0.9; loopht = 0.7
  source(left_ loopwid,AC); llabel(,V_{ac},)
  resistor(up_ loopht,5); llabel(,R,)
  inductor(right_ loopwid,W); rlabel(,L,); llabel(,iL\omega,)
  capacitor(down_ loopht,); llabel(,C,)
                  rlabel(,\displaystyle\frac{1}{iC\omega},)
.PE
\usebox{\graph}
```

Example 8-6-11

After specifying thick lines, we draw an alternating current (AC) source. The resistor is made a little bigger, and we specify a complex value for the impedance of the self and the capacitor. Note how we place text at either side of the element with the `llabel` and `rlabel` commands. As the label text is set in mathematics mode, you can freely use math symbols and other specific commands for math mode (e.g., \displaystyle to choose a larger type size for the capacitor's numerator and denominator).

Some authors prefer to draw their circuit elements using a grid. We can write an m4 macro `grid`, which has two arguments $1 and $2 that define the x and y coordinates at which the element is to be drawn.

```
.PS
cct_init
gridsize = 0.1
define('grid','(gridsize*'$1',gridsize*'$2')')
  source(left_ from grid(7,0) to grid(0,0),V); llabel(,V,)
  resistor(up_ from grid(0,0) to grid(0,5),4); llabel(,R,)
  inductor(right_ from grid(0,5) to grid(7,5),W); llabel(,L,)
  capacitor(down_ from grid(7,5) to grid(7,0)); llabel(,C,)
.PE
\usebox{\graph}
```

Example 8-6-12

In the next example we exploit the for loop construct of the **pic** language. The code below also shows how to scale a diagram by expressing movements and dimensions as functions of the lengths dimen_ (the body size of a two-terminal element, such as a resistor or a capacitor) and elen_ (the default length for an element). Both of these lengths are expressed as functions of the parameter linewid, which has a default value of 0.5 inch. As the code below shows, a variation of the latter parameter is reflected in a modification of both dimen_ (by default equal to linewid) and elen_ (by default equal to 1.5 dimen_).

```
.PS
cct_init

define('loop','[
 source(left_ elen_); llabel(,V,)
 resistor(up_ dimen_); llabel(,R,)
 inductor(right_ elen_); llabel(,L,)
 capacitor(down_ dimen_); llabel(,C,)
 ]')

for linewid = 0.2 to 0.4 by \
    *1.3 do { loop; move right }
.PE
\usebox{\graph}
```

Our last, somewhat more complex example (see the manual that comes with the package distribution for many more elaborate examples) also uses a for loop to replicate the same combination of elements several times. As previously, dimensions are expressed as functions of the lengths dimen_ and elen_. After defining the sresistor, sinductor, and tsection macros, the real work is done starting at the point labeled SW:. First a resistor "r" is placed. It is then connected to a succession of four tsection elements (an inductor "L" connected to a subcircuit consisting of a capacitor "C" and a resistor "R" in parallel, connected to a resistor "r"). Finally a dotted line is followed by another tsection element. The dot elements show the locations of the interconnections.

```
.PS
cct_init
hgt = elen_*1.5
ewd = dimen_*0.9

define('sresistor','resistor(right_ ewd); llabel(,r)')
define('sinductor','inductor(right_ ewd,W); llabel(,L)')

define('tsection','sinductor
  { dot; line down_ hgt*0.25; dot
    gpar_( resistor(down_ hgt*0.5); rlabel(,R),
           capacitor(down_ hgt*0.5); rlabel(,C))
    dot; line down_ hgt*0.25; dot }
  sresistor ')
```

```
SW: Here
  gap(up_ hgt)
  sresistor
  for i=1 to 4 do { tsection }
  line dotted right_ dimen_/2
  tsection
  gap(down_ hgt)
  line to SW
.PE
\usebox{\graph}
```

Example
8-6-14

8.6.3   Interactive diagram generation

For drawing electronics diagrams we can use one of the algorithmic approaches described in this chapter or one of the dedicated METAPOST or PSTricks packages. In addition, several commercial (e.g., Adobe's Illustrator) and free (e.g., xfig) tools exist for drawing diagrams in an interactive fashion on-screen.

For interactively designing circuit diagrams, Tim Edwards has written and maintains XCircuit.[1] This program runs on any Unix X-window system as well as on Microsoft Windows with an X-server. XCircuit considers circuits to be hierarchical structures and captures this interpretation in the form of a PostScript output instance. In fact, XCircuit defines a set of PostScript macros that can be used as building blocks for constructing complex circuit diagrams. Several libraries of fully editable circuit components are available. The use of Post-Script as an output format ensures that the electrical circuit schematic diagrams generated in this way will be of high quality. In comparison with more generic programs, such as xfig, XCircuit is particularly useful for drawings that require repeated instances of a standard set of graphical objects, making it, for instance, well suited to creating printed circuit board layouts. Good examples of the use of XCircuit in practice can be found in Tony Kuphaldt's series of Web books *Lessons In Electric Circuits*.[2]

---

[1] Freely downloadable from http://opencircuitdesign.com/xcircuit/.
[2] Freely downloadable from http://www.ibiblio.org/kuphaldt/electricCircuits/.

Preparing Music Scores

Preparing music scores of high quality is a complex task, since music notation can represent a huge amount of information about the structure and performance of a musical piece.[1] While reading a score for performing a music piece, musicians must gather all the information they need, including the pitch and the length of the notes, the rhythm, and the articulation. Depending on the instrument, the musical notation may span more than a single stave (e.g., three or more for the organ), so the amount of data to be processed concurrently can be quite large. This makes great demands on the musician's ability, especially when sight-reading a piece. The quality of the typeset score plays an important role in this process since it must clearly show the structure of the piece.

High-quality music typesetting requires a good eye and much experience. Until recently, this type of work has been done by highly trained music engravers who manage, according to Helene Wanske [136], no more than one or two pages per day. As in typesetting of text, a criterion of high quality is the overall look of the page, especially the distribution of black and white. Several texts about music notation practice have been published, but they cannot replace a practitioner when it comes to ensuring the aesthetic form of the score as a whole. The Production Committee of the Music Publisher's Association has pub-

---

[1] The Web site `http://www.music-notation.info/` provides a set of pointers to music notation languages, programs, fonts, etc.

lished a text that outlines a series of standards for music notation (http://www.mpa.org/notation/notation.pdf). *The Big Site of Music Notation and Engraving* (http://www.coloradocollege.edu/dept/MU/Musicpress/) intends to provide a helpful source for musicians, typesetters, students, publishers, and anyone else who is interested in music notation and engraving. See also Jean-Pierre Coulon's *Essay on the true art of music engraving* (http://icking-music-archive.org/lists/sottisier/sottieng.pdf).

In recent years several computer systems for writing scores have been developed. Encore (www.encoremusic.com), Finale (www.finalemusic.com), and Sibelius (www.sibelius.com) are examples of commercial products, while Rosegarden (http://www.rosegardenmusic.com/) and noteedit (http://developer.berlios.de/projects/noteedit) are freely available developments. All of these programs are of the WYSIWYG (What You See Is What You Get) type, and most of them have reached a genuine state of perfection. However, they cannot yet replace an experienced music engraver. All they can do to ensure high-quality typesetting is to create a "nice" draft: they contribute to a high-quality score only if they leave the aesthetic decisions to the *experienced* user.

This role is even more evident when one considers nonstandard situations, which are encountered in modern music, for which notational requirements are hard to standardize at all. Indeed, music, as a live art form, evolves continuously, and its current practice is often quite distinct from that of the 18th and 19th centuries, when the "standard" music notation was consolidated. Whereas standard notational practices are quite sufficient for popular and commercial music (and thus the favored target for commercial software), "modern" music goes well beyond this traditional form, in particular in its graphic representation. Moreover, musicology has notational needs (e.g., symbols for highlighting certain notes, unusual ties, superposition of staves) for the analysis of all kinds of music—classical and contemporary, western and oriental, ethnic from various peoples of the world—that go well beyond the possibilities of current professional typesetting applications. What is needed is a programmable system, and here TEX can be an important player.

In this chapter, after a short historical introduction (Section 9.1), we first consider MusiXTEX, a set of TEX macros that build a very powerful and flexible tool for typesetting scores. As MusiXTEX makes no aesthetic decisions—these choices must all be made by the typesetter—it is quite complex to use. Therefore several preprocessors have been developed to provide an easier interface. In Section 9.3, we introduce the abc language, which is in widespread use for folk tunes. In Section 9.5, we describe the PMX language, which makes entering polyphonic music more convenient. In Section 9.6, we have a look at the M-Tx language, an offspring of PMX, which adds, among other features, support for dealing with multi-voice lyrics in scores. In Section 9.7, we introduce LilyPond, a music typesetter written in C++, while Section 9.8 says a few words about TEX*muse*.

The *Werner Icking Music Archive* (http://icking-music-archive.org) contains a lot of material related to music software. In particular, it is the definitive archive of software related to MusiXTEX, including pointers to the latest developments of abc, PMX, M-Tx, and their brethren. It also contains hundreds of freely available music scores typeset with MusiXTEX, often with accompanying input files, so that it is an ideal source of examples.

This chapter is somewhat unusual as it contains little LaTEX: MusiXTEX is essentially low-level TEX, albeit with a LaTEX interface; some of the programs discussed to translate musical languages, such as abc, even bypass TEX altogether. We nevertheless believe that it is appropriate to introduce them here, as they can nicely work together with other LaTeX material and all have their origin in concepts developed in or for the TEX world.

9.1 Using TEX for scores—An overview

Early attempts to use TEX for score preparation were made by Andrea Steinbach and Angelika Schofer [110] and later by François Jalbert, who developed MuTEX [62]. It was Daniel Taupin, however, who really made a breakthrough by developing MusicTEX [117, 118, 120, 121]. For more than 10 years, until his untimely death in a climbing accident in August 2003, Daniel was a major driving force for promoting music typesetting with TEX.[1]

We dedicate this chapter to Daniel's memory

Daniel's main aim in developing the MusicTEX package was to typeset complex polyphonic orchestral or instrumental music. He first thought he could extend MuTEX to several staves, but soon decided to write a completely new set of macros, only adopting MuTEX's METAFONT code as a starting point. The resulting system (MusicTEX) was still inadequate, as its one-pass system did not compute an optimal spacing of the notes. Therefore, Daniel, together with Ross Mitchell and Andreas Egler, developed MusiXTEX, a new system derived from MusicTEX. It is backward-compatible with the earlier package, but uses a three-pass approach to optimize slurs and the spacing between the notes. Since the principles and commands for writing the source are to a large extent identical, differences in notation between MusicTEX and MusiXTEX are usually irrelevant to the ordinary user. For this reason, we shall describe only MusiXTEX here.

Beside the commands for handling a large number of instruments, and different kinds of clefs, notes, chords, beams, slurs, and ornaments, MusiXTEX has several extension libraries containing commands that are less frequently used or are necessary only for special kinds of music. The extension libraries cover such features as these:

- 128th notes
- Specialties for choral music
- Gregorian chant
- Guitar tablatures
- String instruments

The MusiXTEX system is not intended to translate standard music notation into TEX, nor does it attempt to include aesthetic considerations. The system typesets staves, notes, chords, beams, slurs, and ornaments by slavishly following the instructions of the typesetter (i.e., you). In the hands of a specialist, MusiXTEX is an extremely flexible and powerful tool and can generate very pleasing results.

Because MusiXTEX is quite complex, several preprocessors have been developed to provide an easier interface. These can, of course, cover only a subset of MusiXTEX's facilities. Each has its own main emphasis and input language.

---

[1] Being an very fine organ player himself, Daniel had a deep knowledge of music and was continuously improving his MusiXTEX system. As a tribute to his lasting contribution, the maintainers of the *Werner Icking Music Archive* have decided to keep his excellent work alive and current by assembling a new release of MusiXTEX, updating the manual and augmenting the distribution by adding some additional packages. See the *Icking Archive* for more details.

Several preprocessors are available that provide a text-based input language. abc2mtex (Section 9.3) uses the ASCII-format music-notation language abc as its input. This language, which was developed primarily for writing down tunes, is very intuitive to read and write. It is particularly suitable if only one stave is needed, but also handles guitar chords above a stave. The pmxab program supports another textual input language, Don Simons's PMX [112], which allows multi-stave input. Dirk Laurie's "Music from Text" (M-Tx) adds a level on top of PMX and provides a somewhat simpler interface, especially for handling lyrics.

In the next section, we introduce the main concepts of writing input for MusiXTEX. Because MusiXTEX is a very large system, only some of its features will be described here; you should consult the full documentation [116] for further details. The later sections of this chapter describe how to use the various preprocessors mentioned. Thus, if you are only interested in using one of the preprocessors, you can skip the next section on the first reading, as it is not necessary for understanding the preprocessors. Afterwards you should read at least Section 9.2.5 to learn how to run MusiXTEX, because you will need this information in all cases.

9.2 Using MusiXTEX

Let us start by looking at the score of a musical piece—specifically, bars 40–41 of a prelude by Johann Sebastian Bach (BWV 926).

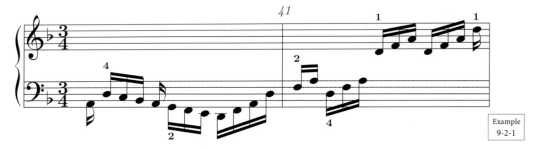

Example
9-2-1

This score contains important information that can be retrieved only with knowledge about the surrounding context.

- The pitch of a note. This cannot be determined from its position in relation to the lines of the stave only; it depends additionally on the clef and on accidentals valid for the note. The clef is normally found at the beginning of the line but may also appear anywhere else on the stave. When considering the accidentals, you must distinguish between local accidentals valid for the bar only and accidentals valid for a larger part of the piece; the latter are found at the beginning of the current bar or in one of the previous bars.

- The time at which a note should be played. This usually depends on the sequence of notes or rests in the same bar before the note, but may be obscured if a voice changes staves, as in Example 9-2-1.

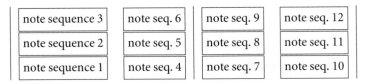

Figure 9.1: Sequence of score pieces coded in MusiXTeX

9.2.1 The structure of a MusiXTeX source

The MusiXTeX input specifies the structure and kind of information in scores. But the score of a piece of music with several staves has two dimensions: the x-axis represents the time and is divided by the bars, and the y-axis is used for the staves. To quote Daniel Taupin:

> The musician reads or thinks several consecutive notes (typically a long beat or a group of logically connected notes), then he goes [...] to the next instrument or voice and finally assembles the whole to build a sequence of music lasting roughly a few seconds. He then proceeds to the next bar or beat of this score.

Using this theory, Taupin implemented an input syntax that describes the score in small chunks starting with some notes in the bottom stave and then moving upwards (see Figure 9.1). The question of whether this bottom-up order is more natural than a top-down approach is a matter of debate in the music literature. Indeed, some of the preprocessors for MusiXTeX enter information into the staves from top to down.

The fundamental command of MusiXTeX is

```
\notes... &... &... \enotes
```

which describes one vertical row of note sequences. The character & separates note sequences that are to be typeset on one stave of the various voices or instruments, starting from the bottom. Multiple staves are separated by the | character: for instance, the score of a song for violin and piano would be coded using \notes... | ... & ... \enotes for each column of *groups of notes* considered a logical unit—not merely chords containing notes to be played simultaneously, but also small sequences of consecutive notes that build a musical phrase. Therefore the main part of a MusiXTeX source is determined by the \notes...\enotes commands. One or more of these commands is followed by the \bar command denoting the end of a bar. MusiXTeX provides a number of variant forms, such as \Notes and \NOtes (see Table 9.2 on page 595), that differ only in how they set the space between individual notes.

9.2.2 Writing notes

MusiXTeX provides many commands for typesetting score elements (Table 9.1 shows the most frequently used) that are the basis for work with this system. We concentrate here on some of the basic commands for writing notes to show the underlying principles.

Table 9.1: Overview of MusiXTEX commands (prepared by Daniel Taupin)

Specifying note pitches

The pitch of notes is denoted by letters (see Table 9.1 on the preceding page). It is important to note that this specification does not depend on the current clef. This is one deviation from the MusiXTEX principle that the representation of information about a musical piece is normally very similar to the way it is represented in the score itself. This feature exists so that you can change the clef for a few bars only, for example, without having to correct all the notes affected by it. The positions of the notes in the staves of the typeset score are automatically adjusted to the new clef.

Accidentals must be specified separately, for instance, to put a flat or sharp before a certain note; for example, with pitch c, you would write \fla c or \sh c, or simply _c or ^c, respectively. To define the key signature of the whole piece or a part of it, you use the command \generalsignature, which has a number as argument (positive for sharps and negative for flats).

Note symbols

To build a note, the pitch specification must be combined with a command specifying the duration of the note and the direction of the stem. The most frequently used note commands, which also set a single space after the note, are as follows:

\wh p :   whole note at pitch p

\hu p :   half note at pitch p with stem up

\hl p :   half note at pitch p with stem down

\ha p :   half note at pitch p, whose stem direction is chosen automatically according to the convention used for melodies; the stem points upwards if it is below the third line of the stave, but otherwise is presented stem down

\qu p :   quarter note at pitch p with stem up

\ql p :   quarter note at pitch p with stem down

\qa p :   quarter note at pitch p with automatic stem

\cu p :   eighth note at pitch p with stem up (The letter c in this and the following commands comes from the French word "croche", meaning eighth note; cc and ccc stand for "double croche" and "triple croche"; etc.)

\cl p :   eighth note at pitch p with stem down

\ca p :   eighth note at pitch p with automatic stem

\ccu p :   sixteenth note at pitch p with stem up

\ccl p :   sixteenth note at pitch p with stem down

\cca p :   sixteenth note at pitch p with automatic stem

\cccu p :   thirty-second note at pitch p with stem up

`\cccl `p`:`   thirty-second note at pitch p with stem down

`\ccccu `p`:`   sixty-fourth note at pitch p with stem up

`\ccccl `p`:`   sixty-fourth note at pitch p with stem down

We can use these commands to typeset a first simple example:

```
\usepackage{musixtex}
\begin{music}
\startextract
\Notes\qu c\cu d\cu e\ccu f\ccu g \ccu h\ccl i\enotes\bar
\Notes\cca j\cca i\cca h\cca g\ca f\ca d\qa c\enotes
\endextract
\end{music}
```

Example
9-2-2

As we are using LaTeX, everything must be placed into a `music` environment (if plain TeX is used, the wrapper is slightly different). The coding of the notes starts with the command `\startextract` and is ended by `\endextract`. If you are writing a whole piece, use `\startpiece` and `\endpiece` instead.

To get a dotted quarter with pitch c, you can write `\qu{.c}` or use the command `\pt` and write `\pt␣c\qu␣c`. For rests, the following commands are provided among others: `\pause` for a full bar rest, `\hpause` for a half-note rest, `\qp` for a quarter-note rest and `\ds` for an eighth-note rest.

The note symbol commands introduced earlier are not enough, however. To handle chords, you need commands that do *not* add a space after them, and to typeset chords with very small intervals, you need to be able to put the head of the note to the right or left side of the stem. For these purposes there is a set of non-spacing commands like the commands shown earlier but starting with `\z...`, and a set of commands for shifting note heads to the right or left starting with with `\r...` or `\l...`, respectively.

In typesetting chords, use non-spacing commands for all notes in the chord except the last. If the last note is stemmed, one stem for the chord is produced that links all of the simultaneous notes:

```
\usepackage{musixtex}
\begin{music}
\startextract
\Notes\zw c\zw e\zw g\wh j\enotes\bar
\Notes\zh c\zh f\zh h\hu j\zh d\rh f%
    \zh g\hu i\enotes\bar
\Notes\zw c\zw e\zw g\wh j\enotes
\endextract
\end{music}
```

Example
9-2-3

Table 9.2: Variant forms of the \notes command

Notation							Spacing		Suggested Use
\znotes	...	&	...	&	...	\enotes	0	\elemskip	special
\notes	...	&	...	&	...	\enotes	2.0	\elemskip	16th
\notesp	...	&	...	&	...	\enotes	2.5	\elemskip	dotted 16th
\Notes	...	&	...	&	...	\enotes	3.0	\elemskip	8th
\Notesp	...	&	...	&	...	\enotes	3.5	\elemskip	dotted 8th
\NOtes	...	&	...	&	...	\enotes	4.0	\elemskip	quarter
\NOtesp	...	&	...	&	...	\enotes	4.5	\elemskip	dotted quarter
\NOTes	...	&	...	&	...	\enotes	5.0	\elemskip	half
\NOTesp	...	&	...	&	...	\enotes	5.5	\elemskip	dotted half
\NOTEs	...	&	...	&	...	\enotes	6.0	\elemskip	whole

9.2.3 Note spacing

Positioning the notes in an aesthetically pleasing way is a complex matter. Within a column of notes the internote spacing is not necessarily constant, since it ideally depends on the duration of the shortest of the simultaneous notes. However, this is not an absolute rule, since spacing does not depend exclusively on the local notes, but also takes into account the context (at least in the same bar), and exceptions to the rule are easily found.

MusiXTEX, therefore, handles spacing in several steps. The first step is to specify the size of the spaces in the source. For this purpose, the sequence \notes ... \enotes is used. There is a set of variants on this command, all working in the same way but setting a different amount of space (\noteskip) between consecutive notes (see Table 9.2). In each of these variants, all typeset spaces are initially the same size. With the command \sk you get an extra space with a width equal to \noteskip between consecutive notes. By default, the length \noteskip increases linearly from \notes to \NOTEs. This can be changed to a geometric progression, in which \Notes is $\sqrt{2}$ wider than \notes, etc., by the command \geometricskipscale. In fact, both the basic spatial unit (\elemskip) and the note-specific spacing (\noteskip) can be freely adjusted, as explained in [116].

The second step is performed by the musixflx program, which takes the default value of \elemskip and computes for each line a new value that is then used for the typesetting. This step ensures that all lines are filled with bars and prevents a line from breaking in the middle of a bar. In Section 9.2.5 we take a closer look at this procedure.

To illustrate how the spacing commands work, here is the earlier example now typeset with proper spacing:

```
\usepackage{musixtex}

\begin{music}
\startextract
\NOtes\qu c\enotes \Notes\cu d\cu e\enotes \notes\ccu f\ccu g\ccu h\ccl i\enotes
\bar
\notes\cca j\cca i\cca h\cca g\enotes \Notes\ca f\ca d\enotes \NOtes\qa c\enotes
\endextract
\end{music}
```

Example
9-2-4

9.2.4 A moderately complete example

To present a few more concepts of MusiXTEX, we show below the first four bars of Bela Bartok's piano piece "Schweinehirtenlied". The beginning of the code contains some header information: if such information is missing, as in the previous examples, suitable defaults are assumed.

The header should probably contain the command \instrumentnumber, which sets the number of instruments in the piece. The instruments are numbered in a bottom-up fashion. An instrument whose score covers more than one stave is specified with the command \setstaffs.

Two type sizes are available: 20 pt per stave or 16 pt per stave. For the latter size, you would add \smallmusicsize in the header.

By convention, MusiXTEX users usually omit braces around command arguments whenever possible; e.g., they write \qb0g rather than \qb{0}{g}. To make the following example easier to understand, we have put braces around arguments denoting pitches of note-creating commands. Since it is a piano piece, the staves belong to one instrument. Thus | is used instead of & to separate note groups inside the \notes commands below:

```
\usepackage{musixtex}
\begin{music}
\instrumentnumber{1}         \setstaffs{1}{2}
\generalmeter{\meterfrac24}  \generalsignature{-2}
\setclef{1}{\bass}           \setclef{2}{\treble}
\startextract
\Notes  \isluru0g\ibl0e{-2}\qb0{g}\tslur0f\qb0{f}%
        \isluru0e\qb0{e}\tslur0{d}\tbl0\qb0{d}%
        |\isluru0n\ibl0m{-2}\qb0{n}\tslur0m\qb0{m}%
        \isluru0l\qb0{l}\tbl0\tslur0k\qb0{k}%
\enotes\bar
\Notes  \isluru0c\ibl0c0\qb0{c}\tslur0d\tbl0\qb0{d}%
        |\isluru0j\ibl0j0\qb0{j}\tslur0k\tbl0\qb0{k}%
\enotes
\NOtes  \zq{N}\ql{b}|\zq{g}\qu{i}\enotes\bar
\Notes  \isluru0N\ibl0N{-2}\qb0{N}\tslur0M\qb0{M}%
        \isluru0M\qb0{M}\tslur0L\tbl0\qb0{=L}%
        |\ibu0j0\zqb0{g}\rq{h}\qb0{j}\zqb0{g}\rq{h}\qb0{j}%
        \zqb0{g}\rq{h}\qb0{j}\tbu0\zqb0{g}\rq{h}\qb0{j}%
\enotes\bar
\NOtes \ql{K}\ql{K}|\zq{f}\zq{h}\qu{k}\zq{f}\zq{h}\qu{k}\enotes
\endextract
\end{music}
```

Example
9-2-5

The code for the above score looks quite complicated as a result of the slurs and beams. For each beam or slur, two commands are needed: one for the beginning (which must appear before the first note belonging to it) and one for the end (which must appear before the last note belonging to it).

For *slurs*, the most common opening command is `\isluru` *np* if the slur is to be above the notes and `\islurd` *np* if it is to be below them. The two parameters of this command specify the reference number of the slur[1] and the pitch to which the beginning of the slur belongs. The accompanying terminating command is `\tslur`, which takes as parameters the slur reference number and the pitch at which the slur is to terminate.

Frequently used opening commands for *beams* include `\ibu` for beams above the notes and `\ibl` for beams below them. To produce double, triple, or quadruple beams, just double, triple, or quadruple the number of b's in the command; e.g., use `\ibbu` for double beams above the notes. There are also commands for repeated beam patterns and semi-automatic beams whose slope is computed. It is even possible to print beams across bars.

These commands have three parameters: the reference number, the pitch to which the beginning of the beam belongs, and the slope (an integer in the range $[-9, 9]$ that creates a slope between -45% and 45%). The beam is drawn three lines above or below the line of the referenced pitch. To end a beam, the commands `\tbu` and `\tbl`, respectively, are provided, which take as an argument only the reference number.

The opening and terminating commands are not enough to create a beam: the notes belonging to it must be connected to the beam. The note command `\qb` performs this task; it works like `\qu` or `\ql` but has as an additional argument the reference number of the beam to which the stem is connected.

9.2.5 Running MusiXTEX

To produce its "beautiful scores", MusiXTEX adopts a three-step approach. As the first step, LaTEX or plain TEX[2] is run on the file containing the MusiXTEX source. This produces a file with the extension `.mx1` containing relevant information about the music piece, such as distances between notes. In the second step, the optimal between-note spacing is computed by the external program musixflx. This program reads the `.mx1` file and writes a new file with the extension `.mx2` containing the proper settings for `\elemskip` for every line of the

---

[1] The reference number is normally set to 0 if there is no more than one simultaneous slur in a stave.

[2] The choice of which TEX flavor to use depends on the content of the file. The examples in this section are set up to use the LaTEX interface; this is a sensible choice if music and text are to be mixed. However, if only scores are to be produced, the additional functionality of LaTEX is rarely needed, so most preprocessors produce files to be run with plain TEX, which is what we shall use in the remaining sections in this chapter.

score. As the third step, (LA)TEX is run again on the source file. This time MusiXTEX finds the corresponding .mx2 file and uses the information contained therein.

MusiXTEX might in the first step find an old .mx2 file from some previous run containing incorrect information. In such a case the .mx1 produced is incorrect, and thus the output after the third step will not be good, either. Thus, after changes are made to the source file, or when you get inscrutable error messages or unexpected output, you should delete all of the auxiliary files and start again.

To see how this works in practice, consider the MusiXTEX source of Example 9-2-6 on the next page. Let us process this file with LATEX for the first time.

```
> latex 7-2-6
(./7-2-6.tex
LaTeX2e <2003/12/01>
Babel <v3.8d> and hyphenation patterns for ...
(/TeX/texmf-dist/tex/latex/base/article.cls
Document Class: article 2004/02/16 v1.4f Standard LaTeX document class)
(/TeX/tex-dist/tex/generic/musixtex/musixtex.sty
 (/TeX/texmf-dist/tex/generic/musixtex/musixtex.tex
 MusiXTeX(c) T.112 <3 Jan. 2003>)
 (/TeX/texmf-dist/tex/generic/musixtex/musixltx.tex
 MusiXLaTeX T.61 <25 September 1996>))
No file 7-2-6.aux.
bar 1 bar 2 bar 3 bar 4 bar 5 bar 6 bar 7 bar 8
bar 9 bar 10 [6] (./7-2-6.aux))
Output written on 7-2-6.dvi (1 page, 2872 bytes).
Transcript written on 7-2-6.log.
```

This run yields the following output, with all lines containing equal (and thus incorrect) element spacing.

Next we process the generated `.mx1` file with musixflx.

```
> musixflx 7-2-6
 <<< musixflex 0.83/T.63dt+jh.2 >>>
 ... decoding command line
 ... open <7-2-6.mx1> for input
 ... testing versionnumber
 ... open <7-2-6.mx2> for output
 ... reading
 ... compute
 ... thats all, bye
```

Finally, as the third pass, we reprocess the source with LaTeX.

```
> latex 7-2-6
(./7-2-6.tex
LaTeX2e <2003/12/01>
Babel <v3.8d> and hyphenation patterns for ...
(/TeX/texmf-dist/tex/latex/base/article.cls
Document Class: article 2004/02/16 v1.4f Standard LaTeX document class)
(/TeX/tex-dist/tex/generic/musixtex/musixtex.sty
 (/TeX/texmf-dist/tex/generic/musixtex/musixtex.tex
 MusiXTeX(c) T.112 <3 Jan. 2003>)
 (/TeX/texmf-dist/tex/generic/musixtex/musixltx.tex
 MusiXLaTeX T.61 <25 September 1996>))
(./7-2-6.aux) (7-2-6.mx2)
< 1> bar 1 bar 2 bar 3 < 2> bar 4 bar 5 bar 6
< 3> bar 7 bar 8 bar 9 bar 10 [6] (./7-2-6.aux))
Output written on 7-2-6.dvi (1 page, 2772 bytes).
Transcript written on 7-2-6.log.
```

Note how the file `7-2-6.mx2` (the result of the musixflx run) is read by LaTeX so that its contents can be handled by the MusiXTEX macros to correct the spacing. As a final result, we obtain the following nice-looking typeset score (the first bars of Sonata Sesta for treble recorder and basso continuo by Francesco Maria Veracini):

```
\usepackage{musixtex}

\begin{music}
\instrumentnumber{1}
\generalmeter{\meterfrac34}
\nobarnumbers
\startpiece
\NOtes\qp\zcharnote N\f\ql{lm}\enotes\bar          %1
\NOtes\isluru0m\ql{m}\tslur0l\ql{l}\ql{p}\enotes\bar %2
\Notes\ibl0l0\qb0{p^np}\enotes
\notes\nbbl0\isluru0m\qb0{m}\tbl0\tslur0l\qb0{l}\enotes
\Notes\qb0p\tbl0\qb0k\enotes\bar%3
\NOtes\isluru0k\ql{k}\tslur0j\ql{j}\ql{o}\enotes\bar %4
\Notes\ibl0l0\qb0{mkpnr}\tbl0\qb0m\enotes\bar       %5
\NOtesp\qlp{l}\enotes
\Notes\ibl0n{-4}\qb0{nl}\tbl0\qb0j\enotes\bar       %6
```

```
\Notes\ibl0l0\qb0{omokr}\tbl0\qb0m\enotes\bar          %7
\NOtesp\qlp{p}\enotes
\Notes\cl{n}\enotes
\NOtes\itenu0r\ql{q}\enotes\bar                        %8
\Notes\ibl0q{-3}\tten0\qb0q\tbl0\qb0o\enotes
\NOtesp\Uptext{\it tr}\isluru0p\qlp{p}\enotes
\Notes\tslur0q\cl{q}\enotes\bar                        %9
\NOtes\ql{q}\enotes
\NOTes\hpause\enotes                                   %10
\endpiece
\end{music}
```

Example
9-2-6

9.3 abc2mtex—Easy writing of tunes

For writing music on a computer, most available music notation programs come with a *graphical* interface that displays staves on-screen. The user is supposed to position notes on these staves visually with the help of the mouse. Few music notation programs exist that allow you to enter music using a *textual* representation, by typing notes and other relevant symbols as symbols via the keyboard.

In this section we discuss the abc language (see http://abc.sourceforge.net), designed by Chris Walshaw[1] in the early 1990s. It uses an ASCII format and is particularly convenient to notate folk and traditional tunes of Western European origin (such as English, Irish, and Scottish) that can be written on one stave. More recently, several extensions of the abc language have been developed. Here we shall mention only abcPlus (http://abcplus. sourceforge.net), which can be used to typeset quite complex classical music scores.

Programs on most computer platforms are available to produce printed sheet music from abc or abcPlus sources or to perform them on your computer. Utilities also exist to let you search tune databases or analyze tunes in various ways.

Among the various textual notation systems, abc is one of the easiest to learn. After

---

[1] Many sites refer to Chris's home page for additional information but unfortunately give an obsolete link to its old place. The correct URL is http://abcnotation.org.uk.

a little practice, most users can play a tune directly from the **abc** notation (without generating sheet music output). Moreover, the simplicity and clarity of the notation make it a straightforward matter to notate tunes that are stored in a computer file. In addition, these files can be easily exchanged by e-mail, thus enabling dissemination and discussion of the music. In fact, the **abc** language has become the de facto standard among folk musicians, and thousands of tunes in **abc** notation are now available on the Internet (see, e.g., `http://abcnotation.org.uk/tunes.html`).

9.3.1 Writing an abc source

To see how an **abc** source is built up, consider the following example:

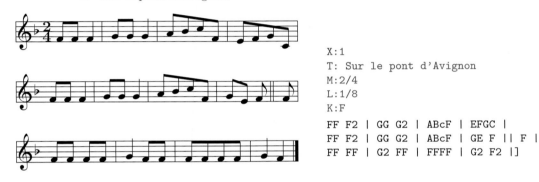

Example
9-3-1

```
X:1
T: Sur le pont d'Avignon
M:2/4
L:1/8
K:F

FF F2 | GG G2 | ABcF | EFGC |
FF F2 | GG G2 | ABcF | GE F || F |
FF FF | G2 FF | FFFF | G2 F2 |]
```

An **abc** source consists of two parts: a header and a body. The header (shown in blue in the examples) contains information fields, each starting with an uppercase letter to denote the kind of information, followed by a colon. The body consists of the music piece itself. Within the body, additional information fields can be inserted that are used for changes to the header information (e.g., the key, meter, or tempo).

Table 9.3 shows all possible information fields, most of which are optional. A few words about the more important ones follow.

- Musical information:

  - K: the key, consisting of a capital letter possibly followed by a # or b for sharp or flat, respectively. You can use major keys (e.g., K:Emaj) or minor keys (K:gmin), or specify other modes, such as Mixolydian (K:AMix) and Dorian modes (K:EDor).

  - L: the default note length (i.e., L:1/4 for a quarter note, L:1/8 for an eighth note, etc.). The default note length is also set automatically by the meter field M:.

  - M: the meter, such as M:3/4, M:C (common time), or M:C| (cut time).

Table 9.3: Overview of information fields in **abc** language tune files

Field and Usage	Example and Notes
A header	Area. `A:London`
B header	Book. `B:Groovy Songs`
C header	Composer. `C:Beethoven`
D header	Discography. `D:The piano sonatas`
E header, body	see comments below
F header	File name. `F:sonatas.abc`
G header	Group. `G:guitar`
H header	History. `H:This sonata was written...`
I header	Information. `I:lowered by a semitone`
K last in header	Key. `K:C`
L header, body	Note length. `L:1/4`, `L:1/8`
M header, body	Meter. `M:3/4`, `M:1/8`, `C`
N header	Notes. `N:See also...`
O header	Origin. `O:German`
P header, body	Part. `P:ABAC`, `P:A`, `P:B`
Q header, body	Tempo. `Q:1/4=66`
R header	Rhythm. `R:Reel`
S header	Source. `S:Collected in Bonn`
T second in header	Title. `T:First movement`
U header	User defined. `U:T=!trill!` (**abcm2ps** extension)
V header, body	Voice. `V:1` (**abcm2ps** extension)
W body	Lyrics at end. `W:some text...`
w body	Inline lyrics. `w:some text...` (**abcm2ps** extension)
X start of header	Reference number. `X:1`
Z header	Transcription notes. `Z:Copied from original`

- Q: tempo; can be used to specify the notes per minute (e.g., `Q:C3=40` would be 40 dotted quarter notes per minute). An absolute tempo can also be set (e.g., `Q:1/8=120` is 120 eighth notes per minute), irrespective of the default note length.

- Song information:

    - T: the title; second field in the header. It denotes the main title of the piece. It can be used several times in the header to indicate variant names (see Example 9-3-19 on page 608). It can also be used in the body to indicate sub-titles for parts of the piece (see Example 9-3-11 on page 606).

    - X: sequence number of the piece in the file; first field of the header.

- Technical information:

    - E: the value of `\elemskip` in MusiXTEX; used to manipulate the internote spacing in the output (see Section 9.2.3).

The order of the fields is not important except that X: must come first, T: must come second, and K: must come last since it denotes the start of the body. All three are mandatory (at least when used in conjunction with the **abc2mtex** program). However, to save space, we will normally omit X: and T: lines in the examples given in this book.

Note on the examples

Repeat/bar symbols

As Example 9-3-1 shows, *bars* are separated by |. More generally, *double bars* are denoted by || or |] (thin, thick). *Repeats* are generated by :| (left), :: (left-right), or |: (right). Finally, first and second repeats are obtained by additionally using [1 and [2.

Example
9-3-2

```
M:2/4
K:C

C8 | D8 || E8 | F8 |] G8 |: A8 :: \
D8 | E8 |[1 D8 | C8 :|[2 C8 |]
```

Note pitch and length

For each of the *notes* you write the letter used in music. Uppercase letters are used for low notes; lowercase letters are used for higher notes. A right quote (') is suffixed to a lowercase letter to represent the next higher octave, while suffixing the uppercase letters with a comma denotes the next lower octave. To obtain a rest, you use the letter z.

Example
9-3-3

```
M:C
L:1/4
K:C

C, D, E, F,|G, A, B, C|D E F G|A B c d|
e f g a    |b c' d' e'|f' g' a' z|]
```

The default note length depends on the meter specified. The sixteenth note is used if the meter represented as a decimal number is less than 0.75 and the eighth note otherwise; thus, for a 4/4 meter, the default note length is an eighth note. This default note length can be changed with the information field L:.

Notes of differing lengths are obtained by putting a multiplier after the letter. Thus, in 2/4, A or A1 is a sixteenth note, A2 an eighth note, A3 a dotted eighth note, A4 a quarter note, A6 a dotted quarter note, A7 a double dotted quarter note, A8 a half note, A12 a dotted half note, A14 a double dotted half note, A15 a triple dotted half note, and so on. In 3/4, A is an eighth note, A2 a quarter note, A3 a dotted quarter note, A4 a half note, and so on.

To get shorter notes or rests, either divide them—e.g., in 3/4, A/2 is a sixteenth note and A/4 is a thirty-second note—or change the default note length with the L: field.

```
M:C
K:C
L:1/16
A A2 A3 A4 A6 A7 A8 A12 A15 A16 z z2|]
L:1/8
A/2 A A2 A3 A4 A6 A7 A8 A12 A15 z/2 z|]
L:1/4
A/4 A/2 A A2 A3 A4 A6 A7 z/4 z/2 z|]
```

Example
9-3-4

As seen previously, the default note length changes with the meter. This is shown in the following example, which also displays how the use of \ lets you continue the music on the same line (by default, every source line produces one line in the output score).

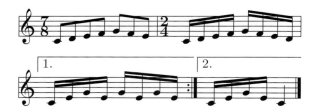

```
M:7/8
K:C
CDEF GFE  | \
M:2/4
CDEF GFED |[1 CEGE GEGE :|[2 CEGE C4 |]
```

Example
9-3-5

Broken rhythms

A common occurrence in traditional music is the use of a dotted or broken rhythm. For example, hornpipes music features dotted eighth notes followed by sixteenth notes. To support this, abc notation uses a > to mean "the previous note is dotted, the next note halved" and < to mean "the previous note is halved, the next note dotted". As a logical extension, >> means that the first note is double dotted and the second quartered, and >>> means that the first note is triple dotted and the length of the second divided by eight (and similarly for << and <<<).

```
M:6/4
K:C
A2>B2 c>d e>>f f2>>>g2  |
A2<G2 F<E D<<C B,2<<<C2 |]
```

Example
9-3-6

Accidentals

Accidentals are produced by prefixing a note with the symbol ^ (sharp), = (natural), or _ (flat), and double sharps and flats by ^^ and __, respectively.

```
M:2/4
L:1/8
K:C

^F<G ^^F<^G | ^G2>=G2 |
_A<<G __A<<_G | F2>>^F2 | G4 |]
```

Example
9-3-7

Doublets, triplets, quadruplets, etc.

These musical elements can be simply coded with the notation (2ab for a doublet, (3abc for a triplet, or (4abcd for a quadruplet, etc., up to (9. The musical meanings are as follows:

(2	2 notes in the time of 3	(3	3 notes in the time of 2
(4	4 notes in the time of 3	(5	5 notes in the time of n
(6	6 notes in the time of 2	(7	7 notes in the time of n
(8	8 notes in the time of 3	(9	9 notes in the time of n

If the time signature is compound (e.g., 3/8, 6/8, 9/8, 3/4), then n is 3, otherwise n is 2.

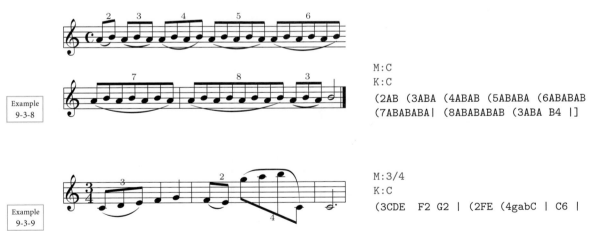

```
M:C
K:C

(2AB (3ABA (4ABAB (5ABABA (6ABABAB
(7ABABABA| (8ABABABAB (3ABA B4 |]
```

Example
9-3-8

```
M:3/4
K:C

(3CDE  F2 G2 | (2FE (4gabC | C6 |
```

Example
9-3-9

Beams

To group notes together under one beam, you should group them together without spaces. Thus, in 2/4, A2BC will produce an eighth note followed by two sixteenth notes under one beam, whereas A2␣B␣C will produce the same notes separated. The beam slopes and the choice of upper or lower stems are generated automatically.

```
M:C
K:C
A B c d AB cd|ABcd ABc2|]
```

Example
9-3-10

Changing key

The key can be changed by entering a new line with a K: field, as the following example shows. Some keys can be represented in more than one way. As shown in the example, the repeated use of T: inside the body produces sub-titles.

```
M:4/4
K:D
```

D = Dmajor = D maj

```
T:D = Dmajor = D maj
DEFG ABcd|\
K:Dmajor
DEFG ABcd|\
K:D maj
DEFG ABcd|]
```

D Lydian / D Ionian / D Mixolydian

```
T:D Lydian / D Ionian / D Mixolydian
M:2/4
K:D Lydian
DEFG ABcd|\
K:D Ionian
DEFG ABcd|\
K:D Mixolydian
DEFG ABcd|]
```

D Dorian / D Minor = Dm

```
T:D Dorian / D Minor = Dm
M:6/8
K:D Dorian
DEF/2G/2 ABc/2d/2|\
K:D Minor
DEF/2G/2 ABc/2d/2|\
K:Dm
DEF/2G/2 ABc/2d/2|]
```

D Phrygian / D Locrian

```
T:D Phrygian / D Locrian
K:D Phrygian
DEF/2G/2 ABc/2d/2|\
K:D Locrian
DEF/2G/2 ABc/2d/2|]
```

Example
9-3-11

Ties and slurs

You can tie two notes together either across or within a bar with a – symbol (e.g., abc-|cba or abc-cba). More general slurs can be put in with () symbols. Thus (DEFG) puts a slur over the four notes. Spaces within a slur are acceptable, as in (D␣E␣F␣G), but the open bracket should come immediately before a note (and its accents, accidentals, etc.) and the close bracket should come immediately after a note (and its octave marker or length). Thus (=b␣c'2) is acceptable but (␣=b␣c'2␣) is not.

Example
9-3-12

```
M:C
K:C
(AA) (A(A)A) ((AA)A) (A|A) \
A-A A-A-A A2-|A4|]
```

The next example shows beams, slurs, and ties as well as staccato marks (see Example 9-3-15 for details).

```
M:6/8
K:C
(g^f).e (ed)^c-| (^c3 d) z g-|
(g3-gec) | .B.c.A G3 |]
```

Example
9-3-13

Gracings and accents

Grace notes can be written by enclosing them in curly braces, {}. Grace notes have no time value, so expressions such as {a2} and {a>b} are illegal.

Example
9-3-14

```
M:6/8
K:C
{g}A3 A{g}AA|{gAGAG}A3 {g}A{d}A{e}A|]
```

A staccato mark (a small dot above or below the note head) can be generated by placing a dot before the note; e.g., a staccato triplet is written as (3.a.b.c.

The tilde symbol ~ represents the general gracing of a note, which, in the context of traditional music, can mean different things for different instruments—for example, a roll, cran, or staccato triplet.

For fiddlers, the letters u and v can be used to denote up-bow and down-bow, respectively (e.g., vAuBvA).

Example
9-3-15

```
M:C
K:C
~A ~c .A .c vA vc uA uc|]
```

Chords

Chords (i.e., more than one note head on a single stem) can be coded with [] symbols around the notes; e.g., [CEGc] produces the chord of C major. Chords can be grouped in beams (e.g., `[d2f2] [ce] [df]`) but there should be no spaces within a chord.

```
M:2/4
K:C
[C4E4G4c4] [C2G2] [CE][DF]| \
[D2F2] [EG] [FA]  [A4d4]|]
```

Example
9-3-16

Guitar chords

Guitar chords can be put in under the melody line by enclosing the chord in double quotes (e.g., `"Am7"A2D2`).

```
M:4/4
K:C
"A"A2 "Gm7"D/2E/2(F "Bb"F2) "F#"A2|]
```

Example
9-3-17

Order of symbols

The order of symbols for one note is ⟨*guitar chords*⟩, ⟨*accents*⟩ (e.g., roll, staccato marker, or up/down-bow), ⟨*accidental*⟩, ⟨*note*⟩, ⟨*octave*⟩, and ⟨*note length*⟩. Examples include `~^c'3` and even `"Gm7"v.=G,2`.

A tie symbol – should come immediately after a note group but may be followed by a space (e.g., `=G,2-␣`). Open and close chord symbols, `[]`, should enclose entire note sequences (except for guitar chords), as in `"C"[CEGc]` or `"Gm7"[.=G,^c']`, and open and close slur symbols, `()`, should do likewise, as in `"Gm7"(v.=G,2~^c'2)`.

```
M:4/4
L:1/4
K:G
"D"[FA] |"G"G4 |"D"[F4A4] | \
"Em"[(B/2E4]A/2 B)- B2|
```

Example
9-3-18

abc2mtex is a convenient tool for publishing music pieces with one voice. Here is a final example.

```
H:Example of an English tune
X:1                  % tune no 1
T:Dusty Miller, The  % title
T:Binny's Jig        % alternative title
O:English            % Mark as English
C:Trad.              % traditional
R:DH                 % double hornpipe
M:3/4                % meter
E:8                  % note spacing
I:speed 300          % speed for playabc
K:G                  % key
B>cd BAG|FA Ac BA|B>cd BAG|DG GB AG:|\
Bdd gfg|aA Ac BA|Bdd gfa|gG GB AG:|
```

```
BG G/2G/2G BG|FA Ac BA|BG G/2G/2G BG|DG GB AG:|
W:Hey, the dusty miller, and his dusty coat; He will win a shilling, or he spend a groat.
W:Dusty was the coat, dusty was the color; Dusty was the kiss, that I got frae the miller.
```

1. The Dusty Miller   *Trad.*

AKA Binny's Jig

Hey, the dusty miller, and his dusty coat; He will win a shilling, or he spend a groat.

Dusty was the coat, dusty was the color; Dusty was the kiss, that I got frae the miller.

Example
9-3-19

9.3.2 The abcPlus **extensions**

It is not our intention to describe in detail the various extensions that have been developed over the years for the abc language. In the present section we shall mention only abcPlus, which provides the following features:[1]

- Polyphonic scores
- Bass and alto clefs
- Vocals
- Sub-titles and inline information fields, which can be coded using [...]
- Multiple composer fields
- x acts like a rest but is invisible on the page
- Bagpipe mode for K:HP
- Predefined formats: standard, pretty, pretty2 (flag -p, -P)
- Pseudo-comments (lines starting with %% in the abc file), which provide for user control:
    - Page format (e.g., %%pagewidth, %%staffwidth, %%footer)
    - Text between tunes (e.g., %%begintext ... %%endtext, %%vskip)

---

[1] Guido Gonzato's very complete manual "Making Music with Abc Plus", available on the abcPlus Web site (http://abcplus.sourceforge.net), provides an excellent guide to the abcPlus language and its applications.

– Fonts (e.g., `%%titlefont,%%tempofont,%%vocalfont`)

– Spacing (e.g., `%%musicspace,%%vocalspace,%%slurheight`)

– Other commands (e.g., `%%deco,%%MIDI,%%beginps ... %%endps`)

This list shows, in particular, that one can embed MIDI commands and PostScript definitions in the files. These can later be used by programs that know how to handle them, such as **abc2midi**, which generates MIDI files, and **abcm2ps**, which directly generates PostScript without using TEX.

Next we give three examples of **abcPlus** source files containing short pieces of music, as well as the result as typeset with Jean-François Moine's **abcm2ps** program (`http://abcplus.sourceforge.net/#abcm2ps`).

Our first example is a piece by J. S. Bach in C minor. Note the use of `C:` and `Q:` and their representation in the output. Using a technique specific to **abcPlus**, the example defines two staves (RH and LH), whose notes are given after the lines `v:RH` and `V:LH`, respectively. The staff width is set to `14.5cm` to fit the book. There is also an indication for a MIDI interpreter (e.g., **abc2midi**), which is told to use instrument number 6 (a harpsichord) to perform the music.

```
X:1
T: Praeludium II (WT II)
C: J. S. Bach
M: C
L: 1/16
Q: 1/4=66
%%staves {RH LH}
%%staffwidth 14.5cm
%%MIDI program 6
K:Cm
V:RH
   zGFG AFEF GEDE FDCD       | E2c2F2c2 E2c2D2=B2                        |
V:LH
   C,2C2F,2C2 E,2C2D,2=B,2 | C,G,F,G, A,F,E,F, G,E,D,E, F,D,C,D, |
```

Praeludium II (WT II)

J. S. Bach

Example
9-3-20

The next example shows guitar chords (specified as strings between " signs, such as "Gm") and the use of vocals put below the staves (preceded by the "words" key w:). Normally one word corresponds to one note. If necessary, you can split words using a – or use _ to indicate that the word should be used for more than one note.

```
M: 2/4
L: 1/8
K: F
"Bb"d2 dd| d d3- | "Gm"d z z2 | "C7"z B dB | "F"c dA | c c3- | "C7"c z z2|
w: Guan-ta-na-me-ra,_ gua-ji-ra, guan-ta-na-me-ra_
"F"A2 Bc | "Bb"d4 | "Gm"c4- | "C7"c d BG | "F"F2 FE | "Bb"D4 | "C7"C4- | C4 |]
w: guan-ta-na-me-ra,_ gua-ji-ra, guan-ta-na-me-ra._
```

Example 9-3-21

As a final example of the possibilities of the **abcm2ps** program, we show how to define and use custom PostScript definitions. In this case we define commands for drawing a guitar diagram (guitar), drawing some auxiliaries (gdot, gx, go), and finally displaying some chords on the guitar diagram (Dm, Bb, C7). The interface with these PostScript definitions (specified between the %%beginps and %%endps pair of lines) is created with the help of the %%deco specifications just preceding the tune. They specify in this case that for each chord the corresponding PostScript instance has to be drawn with a height of 36 points. In the score, these commands are instantiated with !Dm!, etc.

```
% -- guitar diagrams
%%beginps
/SLW  {setlinewidth}!
/guitar{ gsave exch 10 sub exch 8 add T 1.5 SLW -0.3 24.6 M 20.6 0 RL stroke
 0.6 SLW 0 0 M 20 0 RL 0 6 M 20 0 RL 0 12 M 20 0 RL 0 18 M 20 0 RL 0 0 M
 0 24 RL 4 0 M 0 24 RL 8 0 M 0 24 RL 12 0 M 0 24 RL 16 0 M 0 24 RL 20 0 M
 0 24 RL stroke 0.5 SLW}!
/gdot{newpath 1.4 0 360 arc fill}!
/gx{28 M -1.3 -1.3 RM 2.6 2.6 RL 0 -2.6 RM -2.6 2.6 RL stroke}!
/go{28 newpath 1.5 0 360 arc stroke}!
/Dm{ guitar 0 gx 4 gx 8 go 20 21 gdot 12 15 gdot 16 9 gdot grestore}!
/Bb{ guitar 0 gx 20 gx 4 21 gdot 8 9 gdot 12 9 gdot 16 9 gdot grestore}!
/C7{ guitar 0 gx 20 go 16 21 gdot 8 15 gdot 4 9 gdot 12 9 gdot grestore}!
/F{ guitar 0 21 gdot 20 21 gdot 0.9 SLW 0 21 M 20 0 RL stroke
     12 15 gdot 4 9 gdot 8 9 gdot grestore}!
```

```
%%endps
% -- guitar chords
%%deco Dm 3 Dm 36 0 0
%%deco Bb 3 Bb 36 0 0
%%deco C7 3 C7 36 0 0
%%deco F  3 F  36 0 0
%%staffwidth 14.5cm
X:1
T:Defining customized decorations
M:C
K:C treble-8
"Dm"!Dm!e3/d/ d6 | "Bb"!Bb!z2 d/d3/ "C7"!C7!cB/A/- AG | "F"!F!F8 |
```

Defining customized decorations

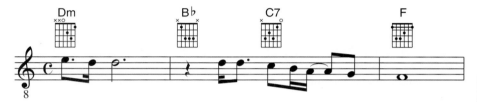

Example
9-3-22

Even without a deep understanding of PostScript, it should be a fairly easy task to provide additional chord diagrams. A complete set of definitions for base chords can be found at http://abcplus.sourceforge.net/deco-guitar.fmt. Instead of placing such declarations into the preamble before the tune (as we did in Example 9-3-22), you can store them in an external file with the extension .fmt. Such files can then be loaded using abcm2ps -f *deco-file tune-file*.

9.3.3 Easy inclusion of abc files in LaTeX documents

Enrico Gregorio wrote the **abc** package, which allows LaTeX users to include in their documents small excerpts of music written directly in ABC (Plus). The program defines the abc environment, which can be given several arguments, as the following example shows.

```
\documentclass{article}
\usepackage[generate,ps2eps]{abc}
\pagestyle{empty}
\begin{document}
An example of a very short piece of music follows.
\begin{abc}
X:1
M:6/8
K:C
(g^f).e (ed)^c-| (^c3 d) z g-| (g3-gec) | .B.c.A G3 |]
```

```
\end{abc}
The following piece of Bach is saved in the current
directory, as well as typeset.
\begin{abc}[name=Bach]
X:2
T: Praeludium II (WT II)
C: J.S. Bach
M: C
L: 1/16
Q:1/4=66
%%staves {RH LH}
%%MIDI program 6
K:Cm
V:RH
  zGFG AFEF GEDE FDCD      | E2c2F2c2 E2c2D2=B2                  |
V:LH
  C,2C2F,2C2 E,2C2D,2=B,2 | C,G,F,G, A,F,E,F, G,E,D,E, F,D,C,D, |
\end{abc}
Finally, we show how you can read a file from a directory and
typeset it (we reuse the file saved in the previous example).
\renewcommand{\abcwidth}{.8\linewidth}
\abcinput{Bach}
\end{document}
```

This LaTeX source file can be typeset with the following command (note the
-shell-escape command line option):

```
> latex -shell-escape abcexa
This is pdfeTeXk, Version 3.141592-1.30.4-2.2 (Web2C 7.5.5)
 \write18 enabled.
 %&-line parsing enabled.
entering extended mode
(./abcexa.tex
LaTeX2e <2003/12/01>
   ... lines deleted ...
(./abcexa.aux)abcm2ps-4.11.8 (October 12, 2005)
File out-abc.abc
Output written on out-abc.ps (1 page, 1 title, 17562 bytes)
 <out-abc.epsi>abcm2ps-4.11.8 (October 12, 2005)
File Bach.abc
Output written on Bach.ps (1 page, 1 title, 18396 bytes)
 <Bach.epsi>abcm2ps-4.11.8 (October 12, 2005)
File Bach.abc
Output written on Bach.ps (1 page, 1 title, 18396 bytes)
 <Bach.epsi> [1] (./abcexa.aux) )
Output written on abcexa.dvi (1 page, 788 bytes).
Transcript written on abcexa.log.
```

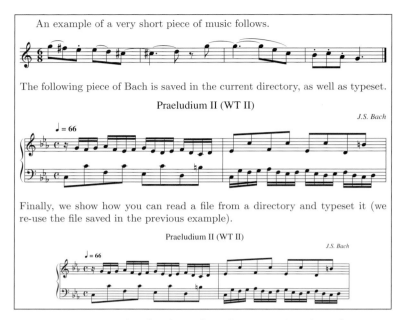

Figure 9.2: Using the **abc** package for typesetting **abc** code

```
> dvips abcexa -E -o abcexa.eps
This is dvips(k) 5.95b Copyright 2005 Radical Eye Software
  (www.radicaleye.com) ' TeX output 2006.04.23:1249' -> abcexa.eps
<tex.pro><texps.pro><special.pro>. <cmr10.pfb>[1<out-abc.epsi>
<Bach.epsi><Bach.epsi>]
```

You see that the **abcm2ps** program is run and that `.epsi` files are created, which are afterwards included by **dvips** to generate the typeset result `abcexa.eps`, which is shown in Figure 9.2. Alternatively, you could generate a PDF file directly by running **pdflatex** rather than **latex** on the source file `abcexa.tex`; in this case the **dvips** step is not needed.

The optional argument of the `abc` environment gives you some control over the use of the various programs that are invoked. For example,

```
\begin{abc}[name=Bach,options={...},postoption={...}]
...
\end{abc}
```

writes the file `Bach.abc` to the current directory, and then runs the program **abcm2ps** with the options specified on the `options` argument preceding the file name `Bach.abc` on the command line as well as those specified with the `postoptions` argument following this file name.

You can even run a different program than abcm2ps by specifying its name as argument of the `program` option. For instance,

```
\begin{abc}[name=Bach,program={myabcprog}]
...
\end{abc}
```

will run the program myabcprog (if it exists!) on the file Bach.abc. Finally, as seen in the source code of the example in Figure 9.2 on the preceding page, the code of an abc file that resides on an external file can be input and typeset with the help of the command `\abcinput`. Our example also shows how you can control the width of the typeset music piece by redefining the `\abcwidth` length. This is best done with respect to a known length, such as `\linewidth` (`\abcwidth` is set equal to `\linewidth` by default). A change to `\abcwidth` affects all subsequent music inclusions, subject to the usual scoping rules.

Package options

`shellescape` / `noshellescape`
> The option `shellescape` (default) means that LATEX calls external programs to typeset the music environments. If you do not want LATEX to run programs automatically, specify `noshellescape`. In this case, since LATEX by default uses the same file name for the .abc files that it writes, you should provide a different name for each abc environment to prevent overwriting. A shell command script `out-abc.sh` is produced to help you manage this situation.

`generate` / `nogenerate`
> The option `generate` (default) will process the .abc files by means of the external programs. In case you do not want this behavior (e.g., because the sources did not change), specify the `nogenerate` option. Similar to the previous case, you must then specify a different name with each of the abc environments.

`ps2eps` / `ps2epsi`
> The option `ps2eps` (default) specifies that the ps2eps Perl script must be used to generate the EPS files to be included. With the `ps2epsi` option, the ps2epsi program is used instead.

9.4   Preprocessors for MusiXTEX

MusiXTEX, which we described in Section 9.2, is undoubtedly one of the best programs for typesetting musical scores: it produces ready-to-print, high-quality output in PostScript and PDF format; it is stable; and it is freely available.

Nevertheless its use seems to be limited, with few exceptions, to musicians who have a scientific background. MusiXTEX is far from having an intuitive "look and feel". Indeed, it often uses terms that belong more to the everyday language of computer programmers than to the vocabulary of musicians. Moreover, coding a musical score in the MusiXTEX language remains a somewhat tedious process.

Fortunately, there exist two higher-level preprocessing languages, Don Simons's PMX and Dirk Laurie's M-Tx, which can significantly simplify the input process. As an illustration, let us consider the input that has to be coded for the first two bars of Mozart's *piano sonata KV 545* with MusiXTEX, PMX and M-Tx.

MusiXTEX *input*

```
\usepackage{musixtex}
\setname1{Piano}
\setstaffs12
\generalmeter{\meterfrac44}
\nobarnumbers
\startextract
\Notes\ibu0f0\qb0{cge}\tbu0\qb0g|\hl j\en
\Notes\ibu0f0\qb0{cge}\tbu0\qb0g|\ql l\sk\ql n\en
\bar
\Notes\ibu0f0\qb0{dgf}|\qlp i\en
\notes\tbu0\qb0g|\ibbl1j3\qb1j\tbl1\qb1k\en
\Notes\ibu0f0\qb0{cge}\tbu0\qb0g|\hl j\en
\endextract
```

Piano

Example
9-4-1

Now let's look at the same example in the PMX input language. If we ignore the preamble part (in blue), we end up with very few lines representing the notes, and it is almost possible to guess their meaning even without further explanation. But just like with MusiXTEX, the staves have to be entered in a bottom-up order, which is fairly unnatural for musicians.

PMX *input*

```
% PREAMBLE:
% nstaves ninstr mtrnuml mtrdenl mtrnump mtrdenp
2 1 4 4 4 4
% npickup nkeys npages nsystems musicsize fracindent
0 0 1 1 16 0.12
Piano
tt
./

% Bars 1-2
c8 g+ e g c- g+ e g | d g f g    c- g+ e g Rb /
c2+       e4      g | bd4-  c1 d c2            /
```

M-Tx *input*

The M-Tx language uses a somewhat more readable preamble and specifies the staves from top to bottom. The syntax for notes input is essentially the same as for PMX, which is not surprising given that M-Tx is a preprocessor language to PMX.

```
Style: piano
Piano: Voices RH LH; Clefs G G; Continuo
Name: Piano
Meter: 4/4
Size: 16

c2+         e4    g   | b4d-  c1 d c2            |
c8  g+ e g c- g+ e g | d g f g     c- g+ e g |
```

You will undoubtedly agree that the MusiXTEX variant seems less intuitive and more complicated than the other two. For further comparison, here is the same piece in abcPlus syntax as introduced earlier and processed by abcm2ps (i.e., without using TEX).

```
M: 4/4
%%staves {RH LH}
%%staffwidth 14.5cm
K:C
V:RH
   c4 e2 g2  | B3 c/2d/2 c4  |
V:LH
   CGEG CGEG | DGFG CGEG      |
```

Example
9-4-2

Using the right terms

In the next two sections of this chapter, we describe the PMX and M-Tx languages. To facilitate their discussion, we first define here a few technical terms rooted in the music vocabulary and explain how they are used in the framework of PMX and M-Tx.

- *Line*: text line of typed music
- *Word* or *symbol*: string of consecutive characters, separated by blanks from other words or symbols on the same line
- *Stave*: group of five closely spaced parallel lines on which music is written
- *Voice*: melodic strand of music, of which there can be one or two per stave
- *Instrument*: a single stave or a group of two or more adjacent staves linked together with a brace ({)—for instance, for a piano
- *System*: group of staves for noting the various voices that are played simultaneously

9.5 The PMX **preprocessor**

Before going into the details of Don Simons's **PMX** language, we describe the sequence of steps needed to go from the PMX source file to the typeset output "page".

1. The music piece is coded in the **PMX** language with the help of a text editor and is saved into a normal text file, which should have the suffix `.pmx` (e.g., `my-piece.pmx`).

2. This text file, `my-piece.pmx`, is run through the **PMX** processor, **pmxab**.[1] This produces (among others) the output file `my-piece.tex`. Whenever **pmxab** terminates due to a syntax error, the exit code is set to 1 (0 when there are no errors). Moreover, **pmxab** always writes a file `pmxaerr.dat` containing the line number in the `.pmx` file where the syntax error occurred (0 when the run was successful).

3. The file `my-piece.tex` is then processed with TEX to produce a `.dvi` output file. In fact, as already mentioned, this step is a three-pass procedure, consisting of (i) running TEX, (ii) running **musixflx**, and (iii) running TEX again (see Section 9.2.5).

4. The file `my-piece.dvi` can be viewed with a **DVI** viewer or can be translated into PostScript, such as with **dvips**. Of course, if in the previous step you had used **pdftex** rather than **tex**, you would have obtained PDF output directly.

As an example, we put the PMX file shown on page 616 through the various stages of this run procedure.

```
> pmxab my-piece.pmx
This is PMX, Version 2.506, 14 Nov 04
Opening my-piece.pmx
 Starting first PMX pass
  Bar 1  Bar 2
 Done with first pass
 Starting second PMX pass
  Bar 1  Bar 2
 Writing ./my-piece.tex
 Done with second PMX pass.  Now run TeX
> tex my-piece.tex
     ... [log output not shown]
> musixflx my-piece.tex
     ... [log output not shown]
> tex my-piece.tex
     ... [log output not shown]
> dvips -E -omy-piece.eps my-piece.dvi
This is dvips(k) 5.94b Copyright 2004 Radical Eye Software (www.radicaleye.com)
' TeX output 2005.03.29:1424' -> my-piece.eps
<tex.pro><texps.pro>. <cmbx12.pfb><musix20.pfb><cmr10.pfb><musixspx.pfb>[1]
```

[1] **pmxab** is a program written in Fortran. Its source and precompiled binaries for several computer platforms are available from the Icking Archive (`http://icking-music-archive.org/software/indexmt6.html`) under the heading "PMX".

9.5.1 General structure of a PMX score

A PMX music score always has two parts: a *preamble* followed by a *body*. The *preamble* contains musical as well as typographical specifications about the score. The *body* codes the music itself. It normally starts with a *header* followed by the bars for each of the instruments and voices from the bottom up. Comments can be introduced in the score by putting a "%" in the first column of a line. Such lines are ignored by the **pmxab** processor.

9.5.2 The preamble of a PMX file

To describe the structure of the preamble in detail, let us consider the first line of Mozart's Jupiter Symphony from page 644.

The numerical parameters

The first four lines of the score input are reproduced here.

```
% nstaves ninstr mtrnuml mtrdenl mtrnump mtrdenp
     11       11      4       4       0       6
% npickup nkeys npages nsystems musicsize fracindent
      0      0      1       1        16       .07
```

The first line(s) of the preamble (ignoring comment lines) must contain exactly 12 numerical parameters, separated by one or more spaces or newlines. In fact, the preceding is equivalent to this (much less readable) one-liner:

```
11 11 4 4 0 6 0 0 1 1 16 .07
```

A short explanation of each of these numbers follows (the names of these parameters are purely mnemonic and have no formal significance for **PMX**). The first eight numbers specify musical parameters. The ninth to twelfth numbers define the typographic layout.

nstaves (an integer ≤ 12) is the total number of staves per system (this limit of 12 staves can be increased). A *system* is a coherent set of staves to be played simultaneously. Moreover, *Number of staves* the number of voices in a stave may change as the piece progresses, but the total number of voices at any one time cannot exceed 12. Thus, when there are 12 staves, there can be only one voice per stave.

ninstr (an integer $\leq$ nstaves) is the number of *instruments*. Each instrument has a unique name (see below). If some instruments have more than one stave, they will have *Number of instruments* their staves joined with a curly bracket. In such a case the number of staves per instrument is assigned by preceding ninstr with a minus sign, and following it with the number of staves in each instrument in succession, in sequence *from the bottom one up*. Indeed, in a PMX input file, the first stave to be specified is the bottom one of the system as it appears in the final score, and the last stave specified is the top one. These numbers *must* add up to nstaves. For instance, 9 -7 1 1 1 1 2 2 1 means that there are nine staves, for a total of seven instruments, of which the second and third (from the bottom up) have two staves each, and the other five instruments have only one stave.

Meter specification `mtrnuml` and `mtrdenl` are a pair of numbers determining the *logical* meter of the piece. PMX uses these values to calculate the length of a bar, where `mtrnuml` is the numerator of the meter (the number of beats per measure), and `mtrdenl` is its denominator.

Meter representation `mtrnump` and `mtrdenp` are a pair of integers that are *not* used by PMX in its analysis of the timing. These numbers determine the appearance of the meter in the printed output. When `mtrnump` is positive, its value and that of `mtrdenp` are printed literally as the numerator and denominator of the time signature. If `mtrnump` is negative, the absolute values of `mtrnump` and `mtrdenp` will be used for the signature, which will be printed with a vertical slash through it. When `mtrnump` is zero, the value of `mtrdenp` determines the signature, as follows:

Example 9-5-1

Pickup bar length `npickup` is the number of beats in a pickup bar, if one is present. `npickup` need not be an integer, as the following example shows (the values of `npickup` are given under the stave).

Example 9-5-2

Key signature `nkeys` is the key signature. If `nkeys` is a positive integer, it specifies the integer for sharps; if negative, it specifies the number of flats. For instance, the previous example had `nkeys` set to −1.

Pages in the output `npages` is the total number of pages. If it is zero, the next parameter specifies the average number of bars per system.

Total number of systems `nsystems` is the total number of systems. When `npages` is zero, `nsystems` is interpreted as the average number of bars per system. In this case the PMX processor will calculate an optimal number of pages.

Stave height `musicsize` is the height of a stave, in points (only the values 16 and 20 are allowed).

First system indentation `fracindent` is the indentation of the first system from the left margin, expressed as a decimal fraction of the total line width (useful for specifying the instrument names).

The rest of the preamble

To describe the structure of the rest of the preamble, we display the start of the Mozart score from page 644.

```
 1   % nstaves ninstr mtrnuml mtrdenl mtrnump mtrdenp      10   Tp
 2       11      11      4       4        0      6          11   Tb (do)
 3   % npickup nkeys npages nsystems musicsize fracindent   12   Cr (do)
 4       0      0      1       1         16     .07         13   Fg
 5   Cb                                                     14   Ob
 6   Vc                                                     15   Fl
 7   Va                                                     16   bbattbttbtt
 8   Vl II                                                  17   ./
 9   Vl I
```

After the numerical parameters described in the previous section, we need 11 (`ninstr`) lines to specify the names of all instruments (lines 5–15 in our example), enumerated *from the bottom instrument up*. These names will be typeset within the indentation of the first system (`fracindent`). You *must* leave a blank line for each instrument for which no name has to be displayed.
Instrument names

Then, a separate line contains, as a single string, the clefs for each of the `nstaves` staves (as letters or numbers), again starting with the bottom stave. Possible choices are (Example 9-5-3) a (*alto* or 3), b (*bass*) or 6), f (*French violin* or 7), m (*mezzosoprano* or 2), n (*tenor* or 4), r (*baritone* or 5), s (*soprano* or 1), and t (*treble* or 0). Clef changes within the staves are displayed with slightly smaller symbols, so the following example shows only the treble key on the left in its natural size.
Clefs

Example
9-5-3

Let us look somewhat more closely at Example 9-5-36 on page 644, which shows a small fraction of Mozart's Jupiter symphony and its clefs definitions (line 16). Remembering that staves are specified from the bottom up, the first two staves (lines 5 and 6—the double bass, "Cb", and violoncello, "Vc") use the bass (b) clef, the third stave (line 7—the viola, "Va") uses the alto (a) clef, the two violin staves (lines 8 and 9—"V II" and "V I") use the treble (t) clef, and so on.

The last line of the preamble (line 17) contains the path name of the directory to which the **pmxab** program will write its output files—in particular, the `.tex` file. This is often the *current* directory, which on most systems is specified as `./` (on Windows it is `.\`). In any case, the path—and thus every **PMX** preamble—*must* terminate with a line ending in a slash or backslash (/ or \).
Output path

9.5.3 The body of a PMX file

The part following the preamble of a **PMX** input file is called the *body*. At its beginning, the body has a *header* where we can specify global options, one per line. Following the header, which can be empty, the actual music begins.

The music is specified using a *block* as the base unit. Each block consists of up to 15 complete bars. The input data for these bars are specified for each stave in turn, working from the bottom upwards, since the sequence of staves (and thus the instruments) is defined in the preamble. The data for each stave must start on a new line, can extend over as many lines as needed, and may include blank lines or comment lines, but it must end with a / (slash). If a stave contains more than one *voice*, these are separated by //. A block ends with the slash of the last stave of the last instrument (the top stave in the score).

For convenience, many users of PMX put only one bar per block. If you prefer to put more than one bar in a block, however, it is advisable (although not required) to separate bars with a | ("vertical stroke"). This provides visual separation in the input file and helps **pmxab** better diagnose input errors. It is also good practice to separate the blocks with comment lines that indicate which bar is being coded. A *pickup bar*, when present (pickup > 0), must be in a block with the first full bar.

Generally speaking, PMX input code comprises sequences of *symbols*, each one containing one or more adjacent characters, separated by one or more spaces or newlines. Thus several characters strung together without spaces are considered *one single* symbol.

9.5.4 Notation to describe a stave

In this section we describe the notation that is used to produce the material for individual staves, such as to obtain notes, rests, and chords. Section 9.5.5 on page 639 then discusses the notation that affects all voices of a system. To shorten the examples we will omit the header part of the examples if it doesn't contribute anything new.

Notes

A single note, characterized by its *pitch* and *duration*, is the basic input item of a music score. The pitch is specified using the traditional one-letter *lowercase* note name: c (do), d (re), e (mi), f (fa), g (sol), a (la), b (si). Possible *accidentals* are attached to the note name: s (sharp), f (flat), n (natural), ss (double sharp), ff (double flat).

The *basic duration* (i.e., exclusive of a possible dot) is specified by appending an unsigned digit following to the note name: 9 (double whole or breve), 0 (whole or semi-breve), 2 (half), 4 (quarter), 8 (eighth or quaver), 1 (sixteenth or semi-quaver), 3 (thirty-second), and 6 (sixty-fourth). For a sequence of notes with an equal duration, this number needs to be given explicitly only for the first note of the sequence, since subsequent, consecutive notes without explicit duration "inherit" their basic durations from the most recent note with an explicit duration.

Dotted or *doubly dotted* notes are specified by including a d or dd somewhere inside the note symbol following the note name. Dots are *never* inherited and, therefore, must be specified for every note in question.

The *octave* that is needed to fully qualify the pitch of a note can be specified by the second digit following the note name.[1] This digit indicates the octave to which the note belongs.

---

[1] Unlike the letters for accidentals and dots (and other letters to be explained later), the two digits for duration and pitch, if present, must always be given in this order. Specifically, if the duration digit is omitted (inherited duration), the octave can no longer be specified explicitly by an unsigned digit.

For reference, octave 4 runs from middle C to the B above, as seen in the following schema.

If we omit an explicit octave specifier, PMX will make the note "inherit" the pitch and assign it to the octave that makes it nearest to the most recent note *in the same voice*. Thus, for jumps of less than a fourth up or down, you need to enter only the note name to fully specify the pitch.

By contrast, for jumps of a fifth or more, you need to specify the octave either explicitly, as described above, or *relatively*, by adding a + or − to a note symbol, which moves it an octave higher or lower than it would otherwise be. Two consecutive plus signs will raise the pitch two octaves, and so forth, as seen in Example 9-5-5, where we also use the equivalent absolute notation for duration and pitch.

```
% PREAMBLE up to ./ omitted
c8  d   e   c+  b4  g-  |
c2++ g2-- | c0    Rb  /
% Or in absolute values
c84 d84 e84 c85 b44 g43 |
c26  g23  | c04    Rb  /
```

It is always good practice, though not strictly necessary, to specify for the first note of each line of music in a block not only the note name and a basic duration value but also the explicit octave. In later blocks, PMX will use the obvious inheritance rules from the end of the prior block. Nevertheless, it is safest to reset the octave at the start of a new block, especially if the number of voices in a stave has changed from the prior block. Note that duration is never inherited across block ends, so it must be reset at the start of each input block.

Stems and other note parameters

Although **pmxab** does a decent job when translating the PMX source into MusiXTEX, it is sometimes necessary to help **pmxab** generate TEX code that guarantees a better placement of some visual components defining a note. Therefore, PMX has several parameters that let you specify the display characteristics of a note in a printed score. Table 9.4 on page 625 gives an overview of the more important of these parameters. Practical instances of how one can characterize the form of a note according to these parameters are seen in Examples 9-5-6 to 9-5-9 on the next page.

Example
9-5-6

The positions of the dots for dotted notes can be adjusted by using + and − signs immediately following the letter d. The first value indicates a *vertical* displacement (in units of \internote, which is the vertical spacing of contiguous notes for the current instrument); the second value, when present, indicates a *horizontal* displacement (in multiples of note head widths). The following example shows how this works in practice.

Example
9-5-7

It is possible to modify the position of an accidental, but in this case we must introduce the values of both the vertical and horizontal displacements (e.g., +1+0). As in many other cases, only the horizontal position needs to be tuned. A special notation for left (<) and right (>) shifts is possible, where in each case these symbols are followed by a floating-point number. Examples of specifying the position of accidentals using both notations are given next.

Example
9-5-8

Pointed rhythms (having the value 3:1) can be easily entered using a "dot" symbol (.) *without* duration indicator, rather than with a d. For example, the first bar ("a" in Example 9-5-9) was coded e8.g c.a g.f; this is evidently much simpler than ed8 g1 cd8 a1 gd8 f1.

Similarly, ternary 2:1 rhythms can be coded using a comma (,). For instance, part "b" of the following example was coded e4+,d | c,e | d,b | cd; the full form would be e4+ d8 | c4 e8 | d4 b8 | cd4.

Example
9-5-9

Table 9.4: Note parameters

Accidentals	
s	sharp
f	flat
n	natural
ss	double sharp
ff	double flat
sc, ssc, fc, ffc, nc	cautionary accidental (accidental in parentheses)

Dotted Notes	
d	single **d**ot
dd	**d**ouble **d**ot
.	shorthand for 3:1 rhythm
,	shorthand for 2:1 rhythm

Stems	
u	force the stem **up**
l	force the stem down (**l**ower)

Shifts of Position	
e	shift note head **l**eft by note head's width
r	shift note head **r**ight by note head's width
<	left shift of accidental
>	right shift of accidental
+, −	general shift of accidental

Beam Inhibit	
a	stem **a**lone

Xtuplets	
x	(xtuplet)

Rests

Rests are coded with the letter r. Like notes, rests have a duration whose value is specified by a number. Identical inheritance rules apply to rests and notes, as the duration algorithm makes no distinction between the two. Thus any rest or note can inherit from the prior note or rest. Similarly, the same rules as those outlined for notes apply for generating rests with dotted values. Any rest (or sequence of rests) that occupies a full bar will, by default, be horizontally centered in the bar.

A few special notations exist for rests:

- rp: denotes a full-bar rest (whole rest), regardless of what the meter signature for the bar may be.

- rpo: typesets the rest horizontally off-center.

- rb: generates a *blank* rest—i.e., one that is *not typeset*. This option is useful when there are two voices in a stave, and one voice is silent for part of the current input bar.

- rm: generates a "multi-bar" rest, where the number of full bars is specified by appending an integer n. This will generate the multi-bar rest symbol with the number n typeset above it.

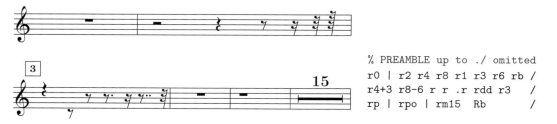

% PREAMBLE up to ./ omitted
r0 | r2 r4 r8 r1 r3 r6 rb /
r4+3 r8-6 r r .r rdd r3   /
rp | rpo | rm15 Rb   /

Example
9-5-10

Xtuplets

PMX checks that the sum of durations of all notes or rests in a bar add up to the total required by the bar's meter. For polyrhythmic music, PMX supports the traditional xtuplets—doublets, triplets, etc.—together with their usual notation.

Xtuplets can have from 2 to 24 notes (or rests) and, by default, all notes in an xtuplet have the same duration. Nevertheless, some can be dotted or have twice the basic duration. The following notation applies.

1. The symbol for the first note of an xtuplet begins exactly like a note symbol, with the name of the first note in the xtuplet (or r if it starts with a rest), and an optional duration digit. However, this duration, whether given explicitly or inherited from a previous note or augmented by a dot, is not the duration of the first note, but rather represents the *total* duration of the *whole* xtuplet.

2. Next, without space, comes x (for "xtuplet"), followed by a one- or two-digit integer, indicating the number of notes in the xtuplet. If the first note is to be dotted, add the usual d; if it is to have twice the basic duration, add a D or F (see below). The only options allowed after this begin with the letter n and control the printed appearance of the xtuplet:

   - If n is omitted, the xtuplet is printed in the standard way (e.g., for a triplet, a 3 is typeset above or below). By default, PMX prints a bracket only if the xtuplet notes are unbeamed; otherwise, just the xtuplet number is printed.

   - If n is followed by an *unsigned* integer, this integer is taken as the number to be printed instead of the natural (default) one.

   - If n is followed by the letter f (flip), the xtuplet number is flippped vertically from its default position.

   - The position of the xtuplet number can be adjusted in the usual way with one or two *signed numbers* following n: the first is a vertical shift (in units of \internote), and the second (optional) a horizontal shift (in note head widths), as explained with Example 9-5-7.

   - If n is given but followed by a space (thus ending the first-note symbol), *no number* will be printed.

3. The second through the last notes of the xtuplet are then each given by a separate note symbol, containing the meaningful subset of the parameters permitted for notes or rests:

   (a) The note name, which is required, as the first character. It can be an r (for a rest), except that PMX does not allow that the *last note of an xtuplet* be a rest.

   (b) An accidental.

   (c) An octave change (+ or −). The octave may also be given explicitly. This is the only digit allowed, since *no* explicit duration is allowed in symbols for the second through last members of the xtuplet, as their duration is determined by the first note.

   (d) A d (**d**ot). The next note after the dotted one is automatically shortened to half the normal value.

   (e) The character D in the note symbol for any note in an xtuplet doubles the duration of this note. As this accounts for two notes of the xtuplet, it will decrease the expected number of notes in the xtuplet by one. If used for the first note of an xtuplet, D goes *before* an optional n parameter.

   (f) The character F is a variant of D in which the doubled note will typeset as dotted, a notation sometimes used by Bach.

Beaming of xtuplets is done automatically. If it is to be inhibited, add the a ("alone" option; see Table 9.4) to the first-note symbol. Grace notes are not allowed in xtuplets.

Example 9-5-11 shows how xtuplets are built in practice (note the change of measure after the second bar—this notation is explained on page 640). By merely changing the specifier of the first note of the xtuplet (compare bars 1 and 2, or 3 and 5), the variant forms are obtained. Note that the first flip in bar 5 has been lowered even further due to the specifier cd4x2n-4f.

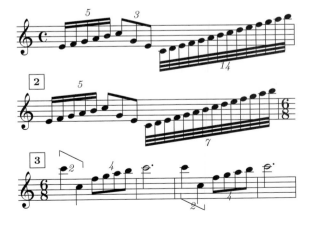

Example
9-5-11

```
% PREAMBLE up to ./ omitted
% Bar 1
e4x5   f g a b c4x3 g e c2x14
              d e f g a b c d e f g a b /
% Bar 2
e44x5n+1+1 f g a b c4x3n g e
c2x14n7-1 d e f g a b c d e f g a b /
% Bars 3-6
m6868
cd4x2    c- fd4x4   g a b | cd2    /
cd4x2n-4f c- fd4x4nf g a b | cd2 Rb /
```

To introduce a note with twice the duration of the other notes in the xtuplet (which reduces the total number of notes by one unit), you would use a D specifier (or F if you want the note dotted). Dotted notes inside an xtuplet are entered with the d specifier.

```
% PREAMBLE up to ./ omitted
c4x3D d e4x3F f gx3d a b cx3 gd e Rb /
```

Example 9-5-12

Chords

A *chord* consists of notes that share a common stem and have the same duration. In PMX a chord is characterized by its "main" or "first" note, which is coded specially, as well as by one or more supplementary notes, which are all separated by a space. The symbols of the supplementary notes of a chord all start with z, followed by the note name, an octave indicator (+ or −, if needed). Although PMX will try to avoid collisions between notes you might sometimes select to move the note head to the right or left, which is achieved by adding r or e, respectively. The example also shows how TEX code can be passed to MusiXTEX at the beginning of the body. More details on this behavior are found in Section 9.5.8 on page 646.

```
2 1 2 4 0 0 0 -1 1 2 16 0.0

bt
./
\\nobarnumbers\
w54m
% bars 1-3
f22 za zc zf | gf- zb zdf zgf | ef- zgn zb zef /
c2 zef zf za | df- zgf zb zdf | b- zdf zef zgn /
% bars 4-5
dn2- zbn+ zen | cs zes zgs zcs Rb /
bn2- zen zgs | es zgs zcs /
```

Example 9-5-13

The main note is written as usual and can have all kinds of modifiers, as described previously. In particular, you can specify its duration, which is inherited by all other notes of the chord. A dot on the main note is inherited, so that adding a d to the supplementary notes is redundant unless you want to shift the dot of the note in question. In this case the d *must* be specified, followed by the relevant shift parameters.

The position of accidentals is calculated automatically, but you can shift accidentals of chord notes manually with the techniques available for single notes. Note, however, that a manual shift of *any* accidental in a chord will disable automatic positioning of *all* accidentals in a chord, unless you preface the shift parameter with A (e.g., zcsA<.5), which will *add* the manual shift to that applied automatically by PMX.

The option Ao will typeset accidentals in the order specified in the input source. Each accidental is positioned as far to the right as it will go without crashing into a note head, stem, or another accidental.

The stem length and direction of a chord are controlled by the first note. The PMX default can be overridden with u or l in the first note symbol.

An *arpeggio*—notes of a chord that are played in rapid succession, and indicated by a vertical wavy line in front of the chord in a score—is specified by placing the symbol ? (question mark) following the symbols of both the first and last notes of the chord.

```
% PREAMBLE up to ./ omitted
% bars 1-2
e22f zgn zb  zef | dn2- zbn+ zen /
b24  zdf zef zgn | bn2- zen  zgs /
% bar 3
dn4- zbn<1.5+ zen dn- zbnA<0.5+ zen /
bn4- zen<1.5  zgs bn- zen<0.5  zgs /
% bar 4
f8-  ? za  zc zf ? gd4f- zb  zdf zgfd+0.5+2 /
cd4-   zef zf za    d8f- zgf zb  zdf         /
% bar 5
c4s- zes zgs zcs c4sAo zgs zes zbn Rb        /
es2-u zgs zcs                                /
```

Example
9-5-14

More complex chords showing various combinations of accidentals are seen in the following PMX code. The second bar is especially interesting, since it shows how to fine-tune the vertical and horizontal positions of dots and accidentals.

```
% PREAMBLE up to ./ omitted
c4 ze zg [u c8 za zfs zefd-2 zcd-2 .b+ zg zfn zd ] c4 zds zfs za zbf c ze zg zc /
% bar 2 with key change
Cb K+0+7 g22d-2 za zb zd zf zad+0+0.8ff<3.2 zbd+1+0.2ff<1.6 zcff r4 /
```

Example
9-5-15

Grace notes

The symbol for grace notes, which are usually entered before the note to which they relate, starts with a G and is followed by a combination of options.

- A single digit (default 1) for the number of notes in the grace

- m and a digit (for multiplicity), representing the number of flags or beams (default is 1; 0 is allowed)

- s (for slur) to join all notes of the grace to the main note (no s is needed in the main note symbol)
- x for a slash (only for single graces)
- l or u to force the direction of the stem(s) as desired

Next comes the only required character, the first grace note name. No time value must be entered, but, if one is needed, the relative octave or an accidental can be given as usual. Second and later notes must follow immediately in sequence, set apart by spaces, and likewise without any time value or any intervening symbols.

Graces that *follow* a note ("after"-graces) are entered as described above, but are followed (without space) by A (After) or W (Way-after). After-grace symbols are specified *after* the main note symbol.

```
% PREAMBLE up to ./ omitted
G3sm2g++ a b c4 f- G2slAe d c Gsxb+ c /
Ga- g4 Gfs- g c G13sm3d e f g a b c d e f g a b c /
c2- G3slWb a b c2 of Rb /
```

Example
9-5-16

Ornaments

Symbols for ornaments must follow the associated note symbol, separated by a space. Table 9.5 on the facing page shows the list of ornaments available with PMX. Instances of ornaments and their associated symbol are displayed in the following example.

Example
9-5-17

Most ornaments appear above the stave. Exceptions are staccato (o.) and tenuto (o_), which appear just above or below the note head, and down fermata (ofd), which appears below the stave. Parentheses (o(, o)) are typeset at the level of the note head.

Table 9.5: List of ornaments

+	o+	×	ox
accent	o>	breath	ob
caesura	oc	dubious accidental	oes?, oef?, oen?
dubious note	oe?	editorial accidentals	oes, oef, oen
fermata (upper, lower)	of, ofd	left parenthesis before note head	o(
mordent	om	ornament repetition	:
pizzicato	ou	right parenthesis after note head	o)
segno	og*x*	sforzando	o^
shake	ot	staccato	o.
strong pizzicato	op	tenuto	o_
trills	oT, oT*x*, oT0, oTt		

A segno symbol (og), which can be specified only for the first (lowest) voice, may be immediately followed by a positive or negative integer indicating the horizontal offset (in points). The segno will appear above every stave of the system.

A trill symbol (oT) extends by default until the next note. The second stave in Example 9-5-17 shows how appending a decimal number to specify the length of the wavy line (in units of \noteskips) allows you to vary the duration of trilling. For example, oT0 gives a *tr* without any wavy line, and oTt2 is a wavy line of two \noteskips without any *tr* symbol starting the wavy line (see Section 9.2.3, which deals with note spacing).

Most ornaments can be raised or lowered from their default positions by appending a signed integer to the symbol, giving the vertical offset (in units of \internotes). As seen at the beginning of the second stave in Example 9-5-17, caesura and breath are typeset horizontally offset to the right of the note they qualify. This position can be fine-tuned by adding a signed number, giving a horizontal shift in note head widths.

For notes in the same block, an ornament can be automatically repeated for consecutive notes by appending a : sign to the first ornament symbol. From there on, every note in the given voice has the same ornament until a note is followed by the repeat terminator (o:), as seen on the third stave in Example 9-5-17.

Beams

PMX usually automatically selects which notes are beamed together, calculating the necessary angle, direction, height, and *multiplicity* (the number of bars at top or bottom). If, for some reason, you want to override PMX's choice and define a *forced* beam, you should surround the note symbols to be beamed together with a pair of bracket symbols [and]. Moreover, a single note can be excluded from a beam by adding the option a to the note symbol ("beam inhibit" in Table 9.4 on page 625).

Certain aspects of a forced beam can be controlled by appending one or more option symbols to [. The direction of the beam can be made to go up (u), down (l), or opposite (flipped, f) with respect to PMX's selection. A horizontal beam is forced with h, and a j symbol joins beams between staves. The multiplicity of the beam is specified by m followed by a single digit (1, 2, 3, or 4). However, this option is probably of little use, as the internal counting doesn't take this change into account (as can be seen in bar 3 in Example 9-5-18).

Subgroups inside a forced beam can be specified with the] [symbol, which causes the multiplicity to decrease to unity and immediately increase to its natural value for the next note (see the first forced beam in bar 4). You can also interrupt the beam at a given point inside a forced beam by using the] – [symbol (see the second forced beam in bar 4).

Beam symbols can also contain one, two, or three consecutive *signed* integers (i.e., + signs must *always* be specified). The first integer determines the stem length of the first beamed note by indicating how its starting height is to be adjusted (in \internote units, allowed values are between –30 and 30). The second integer is for the slope adjustment (again in the range –30 to 30). The third integer is an additional adjustment to the starting height, given in units of the beam thickness (possible values are 1, 2, and 3); it can act only to increase the stem length. The first and third options can be combined for optimizing the result, as seen in bar 6 of the music sample in Example 9-5-18, which also shows other examples of specifying beam parameters.

The next example also shows how to use the Ab option to obtain bigger accidentals (other options of that kind are discussed in Section 9.5.6 on page 642).

```
% PREAMBLE up to ./ omitted
Ab
% bar 1
     f1s   c f a         c fs a c-       b g+ b g    [1+12-8 b-- g1++ b g ] Rd /
% bar 2
[1  f1s-  c f a ] [u  c fs a c- ] [f b g+ b g         b-- g1++ b g ] Rd /
% bar 3
[m3 f1s-  c f a ] [   c fs a c- ]  b g+ b g      [m1h b-- g1++ b g ] Rd /
% bar 4
   [ f1s-  c f a ][   c fs a c- ]  [ b g+ ]-[ b g      b-- g1++ b g ] Rd /
% bar 5
[ fs-4x3nf   c a+ c1 fs a c- ] b g+ b g b-- g1++ b g Rd /
% bar 6
m3434        cd84   c3 c6 c [+0+0+3 cd8 c3 c6 c ] [-1+0+3 cd8 c3 c6 c ] Rd /
```

Example
9-5-18

Example 9-5-19 shows other instances of fine-tuning beams with vertical and horizontal shifts as well as the effect of the X symbol for moving stems and the use of the Abp options to get big accidentals and to use PostScript K slurs (for more on both operations, see Section 9.5.6 on page 642).

```
% PREAMBLE up to ./ omitted
Abp
% bar 1-3
[1+13-8 a13 X.9 a++ s g3 a f1 s+1 ]   [u-13+8 a X-.7 a-- s b3 a g1 s ] /
[1+13-8 a13 a++ s g3 a f1 s+1 ]        [u-13+8 a a-- s b3 a g1 s ] /
[1+13-1 a X.9 a++ g3 a X-.7 a1-- ]     [u-12+7 a++ X-.7 a-- b3 a c1 ] /
% bar 4-6
[1+13-1 a a++ g3 a a1-- ]              [u-12+7 a++  a-- b3 a c1 ] /
[u-12+1 a++ X-.7 a-- b3 a X.9 a1++ ]   [u-12+7 a X-.7 a-- b3 a c1 ] /
[u-12+1 a++  a-- b3 a a1++ ]           [u-12+7 a  a-- b3 a c1 ] /
```

Example
9-5-19

The following points should be noted. Xtuplets have, by default, their own beam. If you want a beam to be shared between the notes of an xtuplet and other notes, you should include everything inside a forced beam. Rests that have a duration of less than a quarter note and are placed between the first and last notes under the beam can be included within forced beams.

If large jumps in pitch exist between notes inside a beam within a single stave, you may want to flip the direction of the beam between its beginning and end. This configuration can be initiated by forcing a beam with the appropriately up/down-ness, starting level, and slope.

Normally, beams cannot jump staves, although this behavior is sometimes needed, such as in piano scores. To obtain a stave-jumping beam, we start the beam in one voice as usual with [and terminate the part of the beam in the current voice with] j . The beam is resumed in the neighboring stave with [j and ends with] . Stave-jumping beams can have a single note inside one or both of the partial beams. Nevertheless, because each voice must have the right number of beats, it will often be necessary to adjust the durations with blank rests after the first members of the beam and before the second. Moreover, adjustments to beam height and slope will usually be required, and the direction of beam for the ending section must sometimes be overridden, using a u or l specifier. Example 9-5-20 shows how a stave-jumping beam can be constructed.

```
% PREAMBLE up to ./ omitted
Abdv
h35m
r4 | [ c8-- e c+ e c+ e- c a+ ]j stl | ald2 st ze ze+ r4 Rb /
c4+ zc+ su | bdf2 zbf- a4+ s za- | [ju c8- a+ c e ] c+ r+0 c4 zc- //
```

```
% second voice in top stave
rb4 | er0+ | rb0 /
```

Example
9-5-20

Slurs and Ties

In PMX a slur can be created by putting a (before the first note and a) following the last note of the slur from which they are separated by spaces (slurs to or from grace notes are created differently; see Example 9-5-16).

```
% PREAMBLE up to ./ omitted
( c45 g ) ( [ d85 c b a ] ) | (1 b4 [ a8 b ] ) c2 /
```

Example
9-5-21

Slurs can also be defined by using the "slur toggle": put an s *after* the first and last notes defining the slur. This s symbol turns a slur on or off, depending on its current state. Similarly, there exists a t toggle for creating ties. For all practical purposes, however, ties are indistinguishable from slurs, except with the K-package, which typesets true ties.

Because of the limitations of the fonts used by MusiXTEX for typesetting PMX scores, the slurs generated are not always of the required quality, as can be seen in the following example.

```
% PREAMBLE up to ./ omitted
(u cl4 c+ ) (u cl- g++ ) |
(u cl-- e++ ) (u cl-- e+++ ) Rb /
```

Example
9-5-22

Later in this section we will address this shortcoming with the help of supplementary packages. See Example 9-5-25 on page 636.

In complicated scores, where you have slurs inside slurs, PMX lets you identify each slur by appending a single digit or letter (0 to 9, A to Z) to the opening character ((, s, t) for the slur. Then the correct slur can be closed by specifying the identifying character following the closing symbol (), s, t) for the slur. Example 9-5-23, which includes part of a music piece by Ernest Bloch, shows how the six slurs were identified with letters from A to F.

```
% PREAMBLE up to ./ omitted
% bar 1
(A e4x3n g bff cf4x3n b g )A (B e4x3n bf e /
```

```
f8+ (C zf+ e- ze+ c4nc- zcnc+ (Dtl b- D< (Et zb+ /
% bar 2
g4x3n an g e4x3n b e g4x3n a g )B+0+0-8 Rb /
b4- )Dt D< zb+ )Et )C+0+0+4:24 dd4- D< (F+1 zd+ o_ e8- D< ze+ )F /
```

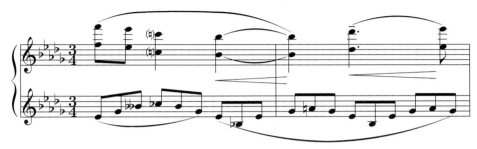

Example
9-5-23

Usually, PMX generates slurs that are quite acceptable, although sometimes we might want to optimize their visual appearance. Therefore, just after the closing symbol that defines the slur (including the identifier, if present), we can add u to instruct PMX to put the slur above the notes, or l or d to force it below. The start or end points of a slur can be shifted from their default positions by appending one or two explicitly signed numbers. The first one, which must be an integer, gives the vertical shift (\internote units); the second, which may be decimal, specifies the horizontal offset, in note head widths. These two numbers can be followed by a signed, nonzero integer to specify a vertical adjustment to the mid-height of the slur (again in \internote units). Finally, you can tune the slope by appending a : (colon) followed by two integers that specify the slope at the beginning and end of the slur, respectively (see the section on slurs and ties in the MusiXTEX manual for details). Instances of fine-tuning slur positions are seen at the end of the B and C slurs in Example 9-5-23.

Dotted (broken) slurs are obtained by adding the option b in the start symbol of the slur.

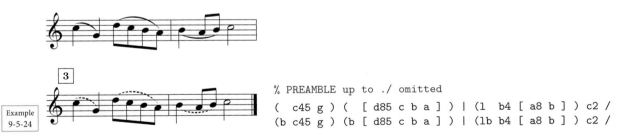

Example
9-5-24

```
% PREAMBLE up to ./ omitted
(  c45 g ) (  [ d85 c b a ] ) | (l  b4 [ a8 b ] ) c2 /
(b c45 g ) (b [ d85 c b a ] ) | (lb b4 [ a8 b ] ) c2 /
```

Additional packages for generating slurs

For typesetting slurs, PMX uses MusiXTEX's built-in, font-based slur mechanism. Generally, this approach works quite well, although for some ties for complicated layouts it lacks flexibility. For such cases users can turn to two packages that are based on PostScript slurs.

Invoking and using type K slurs

Stanislav Kneifl's PostScript *Slur Package K*[1] is directly supported by PMX. After installing the files of this package, you can activate it by adding the `Ap` symbol in the preamble of the PMX source file. To see the result of this package's action, we repeat here Example 9-5-22 from page 634, this time adding the `Ap` option in the header.

```
% PREAMBLE up to ./ omitted
Ap
(u cl4 c+ )  (u cl- g++ )  |
(u cl-- e++ )  (u cl-- e+++ )  Rb  /
```

Example
9-5-25

For type K slurs, some optional parameters can be used in the slur symbol to change the shape of the slur. Example 9-5-26 shows how an `f` option flattens the slur, while `h`, `H`, and `HH` increase the slur's curvature more and more, thereby raising (or lowering) its middle.

```
% PREAMBLE up to ./ omitted
Ap
( e44 g )  |  (f e g )  |  (h e g )  /
(H e g )  |  (HH e g )  /
```

Example
9-5-26

The behavior of slurs and ties—in particular, their appearance if they span lines—is controlled by the `A` specifier, which can appear either in the preamble (for global settings) or in the score (for local settings). The **PMX** manual has more details. Example 9-5-27 is the same as Example 9-5-23 from page 634 after adding `Ap` to the preamble to call the K slurs.

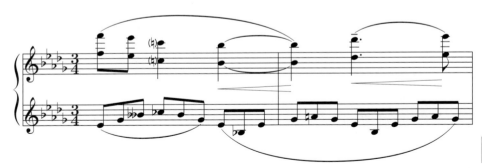

Example
9-5-27

---

[1] Available from `http://icking-music-archive.org/software/indexmt6.html` under the heading "Postscript Slur Package K".

Using type M slurs and ties

Hiroaki Morimoto's PostScript *Slur Package M*[1] is not directly interfaced to PMX. It is somewhat more flexible than the K package, but needs METAPOST to be installed and the files to be downloaded from the Icking Web site. Moreover, the musixpss preprocessor executable also needs to be available on the system. To call the M slur package, insert the command `\\input musixpss\relax\` in the header of your PMX source file, as shown here.

Example
9-5-28

```
% PREAMBLE up to ./ omitted
\\input musixpss\relax\
( c45 g ) (b [ d85 c b a ] ) |(l b4 [ a8 b ] ) c2 /
```

To process a file using M slurs, *three extra steps* are needed to produce a printed musical score, as seen in the sequence of commands shown below. After the second tex run, we execute the musixpss program, which reads a file (`my-piece.slu` in our case) that contains the slur characteristics and generates a METAPOST file (`my-piece.mp`). This file is then handled by the mpost program, which generates files with PostScript code to draw each slur. These files (`my-piece.1, my-piece.2, my-piece.3`) are read by tex (TEX), to take into account the slur's dimensions, and by dvips, to display them in the final PostScript file. The parts relevant to `musixpss` are shown in the following transcript.

```
> pmxab my-piece
> tex my-piece
> musixflx my-piece
> tex my-piece
> musixpss
MusiXTeX Extension: PostScript Slurs by MetaPost
Support Program version 0.50 <January 5, 2003>
file: musixpss
file: my-piece
Now processing my-piece.slu -> my-piece.mp
...
Completed. 3 slur(s) performed.
> mpost my-piece
This is MetaPost, Version 0.641 (Web2C 7.5.3)
(my-piece.mp
(/home/goossens/save/texlive2004/texmf-update/metapost/musixpss/musixpss.mp
MusiXTeX Extension: PostScript Slurs by MetaPost v0.50 <January 5, 2003>) [1]
[2] [3] )
3 output files written: my-piece.1 .. my-piece.3
Transcript written on my-piece.log.
> tex my-piece

    ... [lines deleted]

(/TeX/texmf/tex/generic/musixpss/musixpss.tex
  MusiXTeX Extension: PostScript Slurs by MetaPost v0.51 <February 21, 2004>)
  (my-piece.mx2) < 1> (my-piece.1) (my-piece.2) bar 1 (my-piece.3) bar 2 [1]
  Memory usage before: 970&26272; after: 204&26113; still untouched: 1493102)
```

---

[1] Available from `http://icking-music-archive.org/software/indexmt6.html` under the heading "Postscript Slur Package M".

```
Output written on my-piece.dvi (1 page, 808 bytes).
Transcript written on my-piece.log.
> dvips -E -omy-piece.eps my-piece
This is dvips(k) 5.94b Copyright 2004 Radical Eye Software (www.radicaleye.com)
' TeX output 2005.04.11:1437' -> my-piece.eps
<texc.pro><texps.pro><special.pro>.
<musix16.pfb>[1<my-piece.1><my-piece.2><my-piece.3>]
```

Examples 9-5-22 and 9-5-23 are repeated here, this time running them with type M slurs.

Example
9-5-29

Example
9-5-30

Dynamical Marks

It is straightforward to include dynamical marks by using the D ("dynamics") symbol, which comes in three types (plus, optionally, a positional shift specifier for vertical and horizontal adjustments). *Standard* marks (pppp, ppp, pp, p, mp, mf, f, ff, fff, ffff, sfz, fp) are generated by including D followed by any of these symbols. The *crescendo* and *diminuendo* passages are delimited by a pair of D< or D> symbols, respectively. Finally, arbitrary text can be added to a score by using the construct D"...", where ... can be anything (e.g., *molto cantabile*). The text will be typeset in italic, unless an explicit TEX font specification is given.

All dynamics symbols go *after* the note to which they refer; e.g., c Dmf will typeset a mezzo-forte c. Moreover, pairs of D> or D< must stay within the same input block. Example 9-5-31 shows instances of dynamical marks.

```
% PREAMBLE up to ./ omitted
Abp
% bar 1
r2 D"Adagio"+16 r4 e8-- Dpp-1 D< s f D< D>-1 s |
% bar 2
g4 D>-1 s f2 s D<-1 f8 s D<-1 Dp-1 g s D>-2 |
```

```
% bar 3
a4 s D>-2 D<-2 g2 s D<-2 g8 s Dmp-1 D<-1 a s |
% bar 4
b4 D<-1 D>-1 asd2 D>-1 D<-1 |
% bars 5-6
b0 st D<-1 Dsfz-1 D>-1 | b8 st D>-1 Dp-1 r r4 r2 Rb /
```

Example 9-5-31

Clef Changes

As explained in Section 9.5.2, the clef for each instrument of a score is specified in the preamble. To change the clef in the midst of the music, we can use a C followed by a single lowercase letter or a digit, as defined earlier. The next example shows how the key signatures defined in Example 9-5-3 on page 621 are used. Compared to the clef at the beginning of the stave, the inline clef symbols are slightly smaller in size.

```
% PREAMBLE up to ./ omitted
c | C1 c | C2 c | C3 c | C4 c | C5 c | C6 c | C7 c  | C0 c Rb /
```

Example 9-5-32

9.5.5 Notation that affects all voices

In Section 9.5.4, we described commands that were associated with a note or a group of notes. In this section we introduce commands that, unless specified otherwise, affect all staves in a score in the same way. Such commands must be entered in the first (lowest) voice of the first (lowest) stave only.

Bars and repeats

Keeping with general practice, by default **PMX** typesets no bar line at the beginning of a score, a single bar line at the beginning of each system after the first (except if there is only one stave per system), a single bar line at the end of each bar (except the last one of a movement or score), and a common ending bar line (thin-thick double bar line) as the last bar line of a movement or score.

Explicit bar symbols are obtained by using R symbols followed by one of the following in the lowest voice (see Example 9-5-33 on the following page).

b   single bar line

d   thin-thin double bar line

D   thin-thick double bar line

z   invisible bar

l   left repeat

r   right repeat

lr   left-right repeat

dl   thin-thin double bar followed by left repeat

Voltas

The end of repeated sections in music often come in two versions, called "volte". To denote the beginning and end of such a section and its shape, PMX uses the "V" symbol (for Volta). The start of the first volta is signaled by V followed by any text string that does not start with b or x (often V1 is used). The end of the first volta and the beginning of the second volta is signaled by Vb followed by a text string. Vx indicates the end of the volta—i.e., the first measure following the repeated section. This is shown on the second stave of the example.

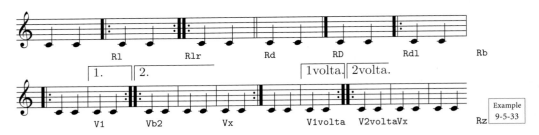

Example 9-5-33

Meter changes

The meter is changed with the m symbol. We can specify the meter two ways. First, we can use the four meter-defining numbers mtrnuml, mtrdenl, mtrnump, and mtrdenp for the new meter (the meaning of these numbers is explained in Section 9.5.2) separated by slashes (/). For instance, 1/8 is coded as m1/8/1/8, 12/8 as m12/8/12/8, and 2/1 as m2/0/2/1, since a whole tone is represented by 0.

    Alternatively, we can specify the meter by using the same four numbers, but entered consecutively (without spaces). In this case, to distinguish between one- and two-digit numbers, we would use the convention that the number "1" is represented by the letter o, while consecutive digits 11,..., 19 stand for themselves. Hence the previously mentioned examples of meters become in this case mo8o8, m128128, and m202o, respectively.

Key changes

We can change the key anywhere in a score by using a K symbol in the first voice, since it will automatically affect all other voices. In fact, since the K symbol is also used for transpositions (which are not described here), we should use the combination K+0, followed by the new key signature: a positive integer for sharps, a negative integer for flats.

```
% PREAMBLE up to ./ omitted
Ab
% bars 1+2
c8 d e f g a b c | K+0+2 d8-  e f g a b c d /
% bar 3
K+0+4 e- f g a b c d e /
% bars 4+5
K+0-4 f- g a b c dn en f /
K+0-2 g- a b c d en fs g Rb /
```

Example
9-5-34

Titles and text above/below a system

The header of a PMX score can contain a title block, consisting of three components (prefer-ably entered in the order shown here):

1. `Ti`: name of the instrument (typeset left justified)

2. `Tc`: name of the composer (typeset right justified)

3. `Tt`: title of the piece (typeset centered), optionally followed by a one- or two-digit num-ber indicating the space (in `\internote` units) to be left after the title

Each of these title symbols is followed by a text string to be contained on a single and sepa-rate line.

Text can be typeset below and above a system with the `l` and `h` symbols, respectively. As with the `T` symbols, the text string to be typeset is specified on a separate, single line.

The example that follows shows instances of how these symbols are used in practice.

```
% PREAMBLE up to ./ omitted
Ti
Oboe I
Tc
A. Vivaldi (1678--1741)
Tt
Concerto\\RV535\\(d min.)
h-2
~~~Largo
d45 a44 r4 | g44 f44 r4 | g45 a45 b45 | cs45 d45 r4 /
l
(continued)
fs45 g45 a45 | b45 r4 r4 | cs45 d45 e45 | f45 r4 r4 Rb /
```

Oboe I

Concerto RV535 (d min.)

A. Vivaldi (1678–1741)

Largo

(continued)

Example 9-5-35

Page layout parameters

By default, PMX does not typeset page numbers. Page numbering is turned on with the P symbol, which can be followed by a number (for the initial page number to be used) and by the letter l or r for putting the page number at the left or right of the page, respectively. By default, PMX starts page numbers with 1 and puts them at the top right on odd-numbered pages, and at the top left on even-numbered pages.

We can typeset a header on every page (except the first) by using c as the last option on the P symbol. The text to be typeset is specified between quotes. For instance, the string

```
P54lc"Title on every page"
```

will typeset "54" at the top left as the page number for the current page (and number subsequent pages as 55, 56, etc.), and put the text "Title on every page" as a centered title on all of these pages.

The layout of a score is determined by the parameters npages and nsystems, which are specified in the preamble (see Section 9.5.2). PMX attempts to distribute the music evenly over the number of systems, and then spread the systems evenly over the number of pages. This layout can be fine-tuned by specifying explicit line and page breaks.

In particular, Ln introduces a line break at the start of the nth system (n<nsystem). A page break can be specified only following a line break; e.g., L4P7 introduces a page break at the start of the fourth system on page 7.

9.5.6 Some general options and technical adjustments

Many of PMX's defaults for its layout parameters can be changed with the help of the A symbol (which is present in the header of many of the PMX examples). Table 9.6 on the next page displays a list of the available options. Options can be concatenated (e.g., AdI2.3p+hlbr).

The width and height of the page are specified by the symbols h[n][u] or w[n][u] in the header, where n is a decimal number for the new size, and u defines the units (i for inches, m for millimeters, and p for points).

Table 9.6: PMX global A options

Accidentals

Ab	make accidentals big
As	make accidentals small
Ar	switch accidentals to relative (needed for transpositions)

Layout Specifications

Aa[x]	set space before first note in bar to x\elemskip (see Section 9.2.3)
Ad	put dots in lower voices below the line
ASnnn	inform PMX that some staves have used a smaller font, where the mandatory *nnn* is a sequence of nstaves (total number of staves), – (for reduced) and 0 (for normal) symbols

Vertical Spacing

Ae	equalize inter-system space; by default, PMX distributes space according to what is occupied by the symbols in each stave
AI[x]	change default interstave spacing to x\interstaff for the complete score
Ai[x]	change default interstave spacing to x\interstaff for the current page only
Av	when there is too much space between staves PMX places them all at the top of a page; the toggle Av turns this behavior off so that systems are spread over all of an unfilled page

PostScript K Slurs and Ties

Ap	enable PostScript type K slurs
Ap[+,-]	active (or deactivate) automatic height adjustment
Ap[s,t,h]	previous function acts on slurs (s), ties (t), and half-ties (h)
Ap[l]	break every slur and tie automatically into separate ones at a line break (fine-tuning is possible on the individual symbols)

Although PMX usually generates adequate horizontal spacing, manual adjustments are sometimes needed. For this purpose you can use an X symbol, which allows you to shift a single element, a group of elements or all elements of a system. In particular, XS[x] adds horizontal space before the next note or rest, while X:[x], a group shift, adds space to everything up to the next X: symbol. Finally, X[x] introduces a hard space at the present point in all staves of a system. In all of these cases, x must be a positive or negative decimal number that specifies the desired shift in \notehead widths.

Example 9-5-19 on page 633 shows how the X symbol is used for fine-tuning note stems in beams. The global option Abp specifies that big accidentals (sharps in this case) and the PostScript K slur package should be used.

The minimal spacing between notes in PMX is 0.3 note head width. This value can be changed by specifying W.n, where n is a single digit going from 1 to 9. This sets the new minimal spacing to n-tenths of note head widths.

Table 9.8 on page 650 gives a convenient one-page overview of most of the PMX commands that have been described so far.

9.5.7 Two complete examples

```
% Mozart, Symphony No 41, in C K 551 "Jupiter"
% nstaves ninstr mtrnuml mtrdenl mtrnump mtrdenp
     11       11       4       4       0       6
% npickup nkeys npages nsystems musicsize fracindent
      0       0      1       1        16       .07
Cb
Vc
Va
Vl II
Vl I
Tp
Tb (do)
Cr (do)
Fg
Ob
Fl
bbattbttbtt
./
\\interstaff{12.}\
w120m
Abp
B
h
Allegro vivace
% Bars 1-2
c4- Df r8 g8x3 s a b c4 s r8 g8x3 s a b | c4 s r r2 /
c4- Df r8 g8x3 s a b c4 s r8 g8x3 s a b | c4 s r r2 /
c4 Df r8 g8x3 s a b c4 s r8 g8x3 s a b | c4 s r r2 /
c4 Df r8 g8x3 s a b c4 s r8 g8x3 s a b | c4 s r r2 /
c4 Df r8 g8x3 s a b c4 s r8 g8x3 s a b | c4 s r r r8 c+ o. /
c4- r c r | c r r2 /
c4 Df zc+ r c- zc+ r | c- zc+ r r2 /
c4 Df zc+ r c- zc+ r | c- zc+ r r2 /
c4- Df D"a2"+16 r8 g8x3 s a b c4 s r8 g8x3 s a b | c4 s r r2 /
c4+ Df D"a2"+16 r8 g8x3 s a b c4 s r8 g8x3 s a b | c4 s r r2 /
c4++ Df r8 g8x3 s a b c4 s r8 g8x3 s a b | c4 s r r2 /
% Bars 3-4
rp | rp Rb /
d2+ s c s | b t b4 t r /
g0+ t | g2 t t g4 t r /
f2 s e s | d t d4 t r /
c4 s .b d.c s | g2+ s f4 s r /
rp | rp /
rp | rp /
rp | rp /
rp | rp /
rp | rp /
rp | rp /
```

Example
9-5-36

```
% F. J. Haydn, Quartetto Op.76, n. 2, bb. 1--4
4 4 4  4 0 6  0 -1 1 1 16 .07
Vc
Va
Vl II
Vl I
batt
./
Abp
It92ivcvavlvl
w120m
% Bars 1-2
h
Allegro
d8-- Df o. d+ o. d o. d o. r d o. d o. d o. |r d o. d o. d o. r e o. e o. e o. /
f8- Df o. f o. f o. f o. r f o. f o. f o. |r g o. g o. g o. r g o. g o. g o. /
r8 a Df o. a o. a o. r a o. a o. a o. |r b o. b o. b o. r cs o. c o. c o. /
a2+ Df d- | e a- /
% Bars 3-4
f8 s e f cs s d4 a | b2 s a4 s o. r Rb /
a2 t a4 t .cs- | d8 s e f d s e4 o. r /
d8 s cs d e s e s d c s a1+ s g s | f s g f e s d8 o. d o. cs4 r /
d8 s cs d e s g s f e s a | d4- zd+ cn1 s b a gs s a4 o. r /
```

Example 9-5-37

9.5.8 Inline TₑX commands

In some of the examples you may have noticed inline TₑX commands entered in the PMX file. For instance, to change the default behavior of PMX, which places a bar number above the first bar of the top stave in every system, we must use a MusiXTₑX command. In this case we add in the PMX header \\nobarnumbers\ (to turn bar numbers off) or \\barnumbers\

(to add the bar number to every bar). Similarly, for loading the type M slurs package (see Example 9-5-28 on page 637), we need to use the command `\\input musixpss\relax\`.

Such doubly escaped commands (starting with `\\`) apply to the whole score and are moved by **pmxab** to the beginning of the generated TeX source. A normal TeX command (initiated with a single `\`) can be used for actions limited to the current music line (note, however, that (re)definitions of TeX commands are valid for the whole file). In any case, direct use of TeX commands should be limited to final adjustments of the score, where MusiXTeX fine-tuning turns out to be the only way to achieve the desired result. See the MusiXTeX and PMX manuals for more details.

9.5.9 Lyrics

PMX has no special provisions for lyrics. One way to include them is by using Rainer Dunker's **musixlyr.tex** extension package for MusiXTeX, whose commands are entered as inline TeX directly into the `.pmx` file.

Rather than use **musixlyr.tex** directly, it is often more appropriate to take advantage of Dirk Laurie's M-Tx program, which provides a convenient interface for lyrics, as explained in Section 9.6.3.

9.5.10 Creating parts from a score

Parts of a score can be split off into separate files with the help of the **scor2prt** program. By default, when specifying the name of a PMX source file, this program will create `noinst` (the number of instruments) separate `.pmx` files. Suppose we take Example 9-5-37 and run it through **scor2prt**.

```
> scor2prt haydn.pmx
This is scor2prt for PMX 2.501, 29 February 04
```

This generates, as expected, four files, `haydn1.pmx` through `haydn4.pmx`, each of which contains one of the instruments. The result of typesetting the contents of these files is shown in Figure 9.3 on the next page. We never need to edit the `.pmx` files of the parts separately since we can control the layout of the parts by embedding commands in the PMX source of the score (see the PMX manual for a list of these commands). This greatly simplifies the editing process, since both the score and the parts are always kept up-to-date, the latter by simply regenerating them from the modified score.

9.5.11 Making MIDI files

The Musical Instrument Digital Interface (MIDI) protocol[1] provides a standardized and efficient means of conveying musical performance information as electronic data. It was developed in the early 1980s and has since become widely accepted and utilized by musicians and composers. However, the characteristics of MIDI data make this protocol attractive not only for composers or performers, but also for computer applications that produce sound,

---

[1] See http://www.midi.org/, the home page of the MIDI Manufacturer's Association.

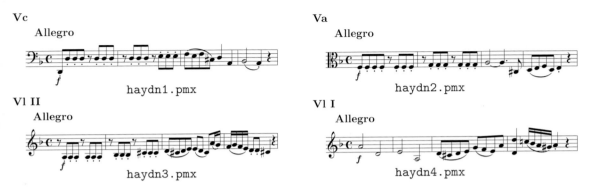

Figure 9.3: Individual voices created by scor2prt from a PMX score

such as multimedia presentations or computer games. The "standard MIDI file" is used to distribute music playable on MIDI players. Today practically all computer platforms can play such files, with hundreds of Web sites offering (free) downloads.

It is not surprising, then, that music editing systems, such as abcPlus and the abc2midi program (see Section 9.3.2), can handle MIDI files. Similarly, PMX offers a convenient way to generate MIDI output from the score.

Due to its lack of expressivity (rhythmic accents, dynamics, intonation, etc.), you should not expect the generated MIDI files to be of a quality that comes close to the performance by a human player. Moreover, the PMX MIDI processor ignores graces, ornaments, repeats, voltas, octaviation, etc. Only simple ties, coded as s or (, are recognized. Nevertheless, the generated MIDI files can be extremely useful as an acoustic check for detecting errors in the notes entered.

To produce a MIDI file concurrently with the MusiXTEX output, it is sufficient to enter the symbol I, plus a series of options in the header of the PMX file. This will generate a MIDI file with the extension .mid (an I symbol can also appear at the *beginning* of subsequent blocks). In most cases the order of the options matters—so it is advisable to adhere to the order in which they are given here.

1. t[x] sets the tempo to x quarter notes per minute (default 96). The tempo can be changed as often as needed at the start of an input block.

2. p[x] inserts a pause of x quarter notes for all instruments at the beginning of the input block.

3. i[$i1i2...in$] assigns the MIDI instrument names $i1, i2, ..., in$ to the staves of the respective PMX instruments. Table 9.7 on the facing page displays a list of recognized two-letter mnemonics, along with their corresponding identifiers in the range 1–128, as specified in the *General Midi* standard (see the PMX manual). In fact, numbers and mnemonics may be mixed, but consecutive pairs of numbers must be separated by : (colon).

Table 9.7: MIDI mnemonics and identifiers for instruments recognized by PMX

pi	Acoustic Grand Piano	(1)	tr	Trumpet	(57)
rh	Rhodes Piano	(5)	tb	Trombone	(58)
ha	Harpsichord	(7)	tu	Tuba	(59)
ct	Clavinet	(8)	fr	French Horn	(61)
ma	Marimba	(13)	so	Soprano Sax	(65)
or	Church Organ	(20)	al	Alto Sax	(66)
gu	Acoustic Nylon Guitar	(25)	te	Tenor Sax	(67)
ab	Acoustic Bass	(33)	bs	Baritone Sax	(68)
vl	Violin	(41)	ob	Oboe	(69)
va	Viola	(42)	ba	Bassoon	(71)
vc	Cello	(43)	cl	Clarinet	(72)
cb	Contrabass	(44)	fl	Flute	(74)
vo	Synth Voice	(55)	re	Recorder	(75)

With this option, it is important *all* instruments be specified. In particular, care is needed with multi-stave instruments: there must be one instrument name *per stave* (for instance, a sonata for violin and piano needs the instrument names entry ipipivl or, equivalently, i1:1:41, but not ipivl).

4. v[*i1*]:[*i2*]:[...]:[*in*] specifies the relative volume for *each* instrument. The *i* are integers between 1 and 127, separated by colons. When specified, the v option must contain exactly as many parameters as there are instruments. The default (no parameters given) is 127.

5. b[*m1*]:[*m2*]:[...]:[*mn*] sets the stereo balance for each instrument. The usage of this option is similar to that of the v option. The integers *m* must be in the range 1–128, with the default being 64, which represents the center. Smaller numbers increase the left stereo channel, larger ones the right.

6. g[*i*] sets the silence between notes in the MIDI rendering to *i*MIDI clock tics. This silence (default value is 10 tic units, equivalent to two-thirds of a sixty-fourth note), is inserted at the end of every note by decreasing the sounding duration by the same amount.

7. MR[*i*] starts recording MIDI macro number *i*.

8. M stops recording current MIDI macro (no nesting allowed).

9. IMP[*i*] plays back MIDI macro number *i*. MIDI macros are needed for repeats or dacapos; as explained earlier, the MIDI processor ignores such features when they are coded in the PMX score. Only one macro may be active at a time, either for recording or for playing, but not for both.

As an example, It92ivcvavlvl sets the MIDI tempo to 92 units (quarter notes) per minute and defines four instrument names (a cello, a viola, and two violins).

Table 9.8: Overview of PMX commands

644

Example
9-5-38

9.6 M-Tx—Music from TeXt

After describing the PMX language we now turn to Dirk Laurie's M-Tx language,[1] which adds a layer of convenience to PMX, making entering information—in particular, in the preamble—more intuitive. By its very conception, it offers also a straightforward way for adding words (lyrics) to the music.

Let us first have another look at Section 9.4 on page 615, especially the example comparing the coding of the first bars of the Mozart piece. One large difference between PMX and M-Tx coding is that, with M-Tx voice (instrument) lines are input *as they are printed* (i.e., from top to bottom), whereas with PMX they are entered last line first (i.e., from bottom to top).

```
Title: Riff in C
Composer: W. A. Mozart (1756--1791)
Style: piano
Name: Piano
Meter: 4/4
Size: 16
Indent: 0.18

%% w70m
c2+         e4      g   | b4d-   c1 d c2          |
c8 g+ e g c- g+ e g | d g f g      c- g+ e g |
```

Example
9-6-1

Example 9-6-1 was compiled by the M-Tx processor **prepmx**, which transforms the M-Tx input file into a PMX file to be run through the **pmxab** processor.

```
> prepmx 9-6-1
==> This is M-Tx 0.60 (Music from TeXt) <16 March 2005>
==>> Input from file 9-6-1.mtx
Writing to 9-6-1.pmx
instrumentNames = TRUE
PrePMX done.  Now run PMX.

> pmxab 9-6-1
 This is PMX, Version 2.506, 14 Nov 04
 Opening 9-6-1.pmx
 Starting first PMX pass
  Bar 1  Bar 2
 Done with first pass
 Starting second PMX pass
  Bar 1  Bar 2
 Writing ./9-6-1.tex
 Done with second PMX pass.
```

The **prepmx** processor has several options, all of which are described in the M-Tx manual.

---

[1] The M-Tx entry on the home page `http://icking-music-archive.org/software/indexmt6.html` of the Icking Music Archive provides pointers to the latest version of the distribution, manual, examples, and related utilities.

Table 9.9: M-Tx preamble elements with examples

`Bars/line: 4`	try to use four bars per typeset line
`Composer: Mozart`	name of composer (set flush right below title)
`Disable: unbeamVocal`	disables unbeamVocal feature
`Enable: pedanticWarnings`	enable pedanticWarnings feature
`Flats: 3`	key signature has three flats
`Indent: 0.10`	indent first system by 10% of music width
`Meter: 4/4`	meter for piece
`Name: Dietrich Gerald`	names of instruments, performers, etc.
`Octave: 4 4 3 3`	initial octaves for each stave
`Options: x`	uses x option for compilation
`Pages: 2`	typeset piece on two pages
`Part: Recorder`	part name (set flush left above title)
`Poet: Rilke`	name of poet (set flush left below title)
`PMX: w4i`	PMX command (obsolete—use %% feature)
`Sharps: 2`	key signature has two sharps
`Size: 16`	size of music (in points—default 20)
`Space: 6 0 3`	extra interlines of space below staves
`Start: @+1;@-3`	put specified items at start of voice lines
`Style: Singer Piano`	piece for singer accompanied by piano
`Systems: 11`	total of 11 systems to be used
`Title: Piano concerto`	title of piece

The preamble lines in this example are self-explanatory (see Table 9.9 for details). The line starting with %% at the top of the music paragraph passes information to PMX—in this case, "set the width to 70 millimeters".

9.6.1 The M-Tx preamble

Table 9.9 gives an example, with explanations, of built-in M-Tx preamble elements (case is ignored for element names). Most of the commands in this table have PMX equivalents, and their usage should be straightforward from the examples and the information given in the PMX section. The `Bars/line` declaration should be used only as long as `Pages` and `Systems` are not defined. In the following discussion we limit ourselves to the supplementary elements introduced in M-Tx.

The `Style` element

The `Style` line permits us to define the number and the type of the staves in a system. It may contain several style elements (e.g., instruments). Presently (version 0.6), M-Tx defines the following style elements:

```
SATB:    Voices S,A T,B; Choral; Clefs G F
SATB4:   Voices S A T B; Choral; Clefs G G G8 F
SINGER:  Voices S; Vocal; Clefs G
```

```
PIANO:    Voices RH LH; Continuo; Clefs G F
ORGAN:    Voices RH LH Ped; Continuo; Clefs G F F
SOLO:     Voices V; Clefs G
DUET:     Voices V1 Vc; Clefs G F
TRIO:     Voices V1 Va Vc; Clefs G C F
QUARTET:  Voices V1 V2 Va Vc; Clefs G G C F
QUINTET:  Voices V1 V2 Va Vc1 Vc2; Clefs G G C F F
SEXTET:   Voices V1 V2 Va1 Va2 Vc1 Vc2; Clefs G G C C F F
SEPTET:   Voices V1 V2 Va1 Va2 Vc1 Vc2 Cb; Clefs G G C C F F F
```

In these definitions, `Voices` gives the labels of the voices, which are later used to identify lyrics lines and out-of-sequence music lines (do not use labels such as L, U, C, 1 or L1 since they conflict with M-Tx labels for chords, lyrics, etc.). Labels separated by blanks belong to voices on different staves; labels separated by a comma, to voices on the same stave (SATB has four voices on two staves, SATB4 has them on four staves). The maximum number of voices is 15, written in up to 15 staves.

The `Clefs` part defines the clefs for each of the staves. You can use C (alto), F (bass), or G (treble), as well as any PMX key notation (see Example 9-5-3 on page 621). The symbol 8 or G8 indicates music written in the treble clef but sounding an octave lower (useful for the tenor voice in choral music; see the definition of the SATB4 style).

The `Vocal` specifier treats the voices as vocal for the purpose of beams and lyrics. `Continuo` staves belong to a single instrument, and are grouped together by braces. `Choral` means that all voices are vocal and belong to a choir; their staves will be grouped together by brackets. (Similarly, instrumental voices can be grouped together with brackets by using `Group` instead of `Choral` as a specifier.)

New styles can be readily defined. For instance, a piano score with four voices on two staves could be defined and then referenced as follows:

```
Piano4v: Voices RH1,RH2 LH1,LH2; Continuo; Clefs G F
Style: Piano4v
```

Given that the whole preamble is read, and new style elements saved, before any of the commands is interpreted, the order in which the commands occur in the input file is irrelevant. Note, however, that when an element is defined multiple times, the last instance will be used.

The `Space` and `Start` elements

In the final fine-tuning stage of a score, the `Start` element can be useful since it allows you to insert additional space after each voice. For instance, you can add space after each system of a quartet (after the fourth of the four voices) with `Space: 0 0 0 1`. By contrast, in a score for one vocal accompanied by piano, `Space: 2 0 0` (or simpler, `Space: 2`) will leave two lines (for the lyrics) after the first stave.

Global adjustments to the lyrics lines are introduced with the `Start` element, which uses @ symbols with a syntax like the one explained with Example 9-6-8.

The `Options` element

The string following an `Options:` element is transmitted to the M-Tx prepmx preprocessor, thus simplifying considerably the command-line sequence needed to run that program (see the M-Tx manual for more details).

9.6.2 The body of an M-Tx input file

Most PMX commands and symbols are also accepted by M-Tx or can be passed through to the PMX processor using the %% notation. For instance, global A options (see Table 9.6 on page 643) can be introduced, such as %%Abp.

Bars and meter changes

The notation for bars is mostly taken from Chris Walshaw's abc (see Example 9-3-2)—namely, | for a normal bar line, | | for a simple double bar (section separation), and |] for a thin-thick double bar (end of a movement). Repeats are generated by : | (left repeat), : : (left-right repeat), and | : (right repeat).

Normal bar lines, which are usually optional, correspond to actual bar separations, and their presence makes life easier. The double line and repeat signs may appear in mid-bar; they must appear in the bottom voice and are optional elsewhere, but for readability it is advisable to add them in all voices.

M-Tx handles a pickup as an incomplete "bar 0", which must be coded by a bar line in the first voice. When an incomplete bar appears at the end of a final paragraph, M-Tx automatically redefines the meter without printing a new time signature.

Your ability to vary the number of voices per stave and to change the meter is more restricted in M-Tx than in PMX; see the M-Tx documentation for details.

Beams and slurs

Like PMX, M-Tx constructs beams in instrumental voices automatically. In vocal music, it is customary to use beams only when the notes in question are sung to the same single syllable. Hence, when selecting a style like SATB or Singer that involves voices, M-Tx will ensure that notes will normally appear unbeamed, except those that appear under slurs. This feature can be overridden with PMX's "forced beam" construct (using [. . .]).

The slur notation is similar to forced beams, but uses parentheses.

```
Style: SATB
Sharps: 2
Meter: 3/4
Space: 9
Size: 16

%% w70m
%% As
f4 | e2  a4 | ( d4 c ) b | a2d |
d4 | b2  e4 | ( f4 e ) d | c2d |
L: O Lam van God, ek kom.
L: O Lam van God, ek kom.
L: O Lam van God, ek kom.
a4 | g2s a4 |   a2   g4s | a2d |
d4 | d2  c4 | ( b4 e ) e | a2d |
```

Example
9-6-2

Slurs can be nested, as in (`c8 d e` (`f g`) `f d b`) `c2`. Occasionally a slur ends at a note and the next one starts immediately. In this case you can use the slur continuation code) (as a single word after the note. For a tie, use braces { . . . } instead of parentheses, with a continuation tie being coded as }{.

With multi-verse lyrics, sometimes a slur should appear in one verse but not in another. In this case you can start the slur with (" or { ", which will produce a slur symbol that is no longer solid, but broken like a dotted line. The following example shows how to synchronize lyrics by using void syllables and extension rules.

```
Style: Singer
Meter: 3/4
Size: 16

%% w70m
%% As
e f g ( a2d a ) (" g8 f ) (" e4 e )
L: She is a dan-ge-rous wo-man
L: You'll get a bro--ken heart_
```

Example 9-6-3

The trailing underscore on "heart" takes the place of a syllable of lyrics, and on a longer note would produce a lyrics rule that extends to the end of the melisma. Very long melismas can be coded with multiple underscores, e.g., `Oh_____` or, more conveniently, `Oh_6`.

Conversely, when you want to make a melisma but without typesetting a visible slur, you can code a "blind" slur, which starts with (~ or { ~ and ends with) ~ or } ~. Its effect on the lyrics is identical to that of a normal slur.

```
Style: ST
ST: Voices S T; Choral; Clefs G G
Meter: C/
Size: 16
Pages: 1
Systems: 1
Space: 2 2
Name: {\it{Superius}} {\it{Tenor}}

%%Ab
%%w120m
% Superius
@+1 rp | rp | c0+ | d2 {~ ( e | e4 ) c }~ ( c2 | c ) f |
L: A-ve ve-rum cor-
% Tenor
@-2 f0 | g2 {~ ( a | a4 ) f }~ ( f2 | f ) {~ ( c+ | c4 ) [ bf8 a ] a4.f }~ | f0 |
L: A-ve ve-rum, ve-rum
```

Example
9-6-4

Chords

As a complement to PMX's z notation for representing chords (see Example 9-5-13 on page 628), M-Tx offers the possibility to have a basic melodic line immediately followed by a separate line (prefixed with C:) for the chordal notes.

The chordal notes are a concatenated sequence of note names in PMX notation, with the exception of t for "flat" and l for "note head left". The melodic (base) note cannot be shifted (i.e., have a displaced note head), and such notes can be present only on the chord line (e.g., the f in bar 1 and the e in bar 3 of the top stave are typeset to the right of the staff).

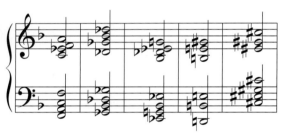

```
Style: Piano
Meter: m2400
Flats: 1

%%Ab
%%w70m
      c2   | df    | b        | bn    | es    |
C: etfra   gtbdt   dtertgn    engs    gscs
      f2-  | gf    | ef       | dn    | cs+   |
C: acf     bdtgt   gnbet      bn+en   esgscs
```

Example
9-6-5

With M-Tx, the pitch of the melodic line is determined by the base note only, which serves as frame of reference for the whole chord. This is different from the situation with PMX, where the pitch of each chordal note (using the z... notation) is determined by the previous note. The melodic structure of the piece (base line and chordal notes) are thus clearly identified, as can be seen in the coding of the introduction to Schubert's song *Der Tod und das Mädchen*, which also has two bass (F) clefs for the piano score.

```
Style: PianoBass
PianoBass: Voices RH LH; Clefs F F; Continuo
Meter: C/
Flats: 1
Pages: 1
Systems: 1
Size: 16

%%w110m
   f2 g4 e  | f2 a4   a | a2 f4 e |
```

```
C: ad bd gd+   ad gle+ f+   gle+ ad acs
   d2 d4 d  | d2 d4    a | a2   a4 a |
C: d- d- d-    d- d-   d   a-  a- a-

   f2 f4 e | f2 g4 e | f2 a4    a | a2   f4 e |
C: ad d+ gd+ ad bd gd+ ad gle+ f+   gle+ ad acs
   a2 d4 d | d2 d4 d | d2 d4    a | a2   a4 a |
C: d- d- d-  d- d- d-  d- d-   d   a-  a- a-
```

Example
9-6-6

Isolated melodic notes (i.e., without chordal notes) are noted by ~. A vertical bar | on the chord line signifies that all remaining notes in the current bar are isolated notes. Therefore, unless they have that meaning, bar separators should never be used on C: lines. Notes in chords can be tied with no need to close the tie, since M-Tx will tie the chordal note to the one at the next pitch in the next chord or generate an error otherwise.

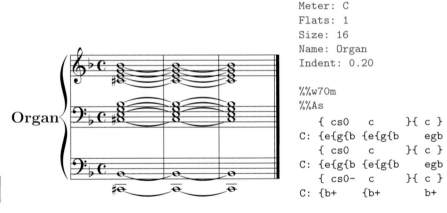

```
Style: Organ
Meter: C
Flats: 1
Size: 16
Name: Organ
Indent: 0.20

%%w70m
%%As
   { cs0    c      }{ c }
C: {e{g{b {e{g{b      egb
   { cs0    c      }{ c }
C: {e{g{b {e{g{b      egb
   { cs0-   c      }{ c }
C: {b+     {b+        b+
```

Example
9-6-7

Expression marks and other annotations

In PMX, dynamic and other annotations are marked up using the D notation (see Example 9-5-31 on page 638). M-Tx has a different system, using lines with a U: prefix. Such a U: line is normally placed *above* the music line to which it applies; otherwise, an identifying label must specify the voice name or number. Note that U: lines are synchronized after taking into account both notes and rests. The ~ and | signs, which have the same meaning as for chords, are available for the alignment of the text.

M-Tx recognizes most usual dynamic indications, such as *mp* and *sf*, and will typeset them in the correct MusiXTeX font. Unrecognized combinations are typeset in Roman. The font for the current voice can be set to bold (!bf) or italic (!it). Note that such font declarations remain in effect beyond the paragraph in which they appear. The same applies to the vertical and horizontal adjustment specifications that follow.

Vertical adjustments are obtained with the help of @ constructs, as follows:

- @v places the symbols below rather than above the stave.
- @^ places the symbols above the stave.
- @=*n* places the symbols precisely at *n*\internote units above or below the stave.
- @+*n* and @-*n* place the symbols *n*\internote units higher and lower, respectively, than the current default height. In other words, @+4 followed by @-2 will typeset the text 2\internote units above the default vertical position.

Horizontal adjustments are obtained with the help of @< (move left) and @> (move right). The default placement is to the right of a note, so that @< centers it on the note, and @< @< puts it to the left. To come back to the center or the right, you would use one or two @> symbols, respectively.

For a crescendo or decrescendo sign, type a < or > where the sign starts, and <. or >. where it ends. You can also explicitly specify the length of the sign in units of \elemskip by using <*n* or >*n*.

```
Style: Solo
Meter: 9/8
Sharps: 4
Size: 16
Pages: 1
Systems: 2
Space: 10
Name: Flute
```

Très modéré

```
%%Ab
%%B
%%It44ifl
%%w70m
%%\\nobarnumbers\
%%\\input musixpss\relax\
%%h+3
%% Tr\`es mod\'er\'e
U: @+1 < ~ ~ ~ ~ <.
[ c8 sA d g ] e4,g- bd4 sBt+0+.5 |

U: @+1  > ~ ~ >.
b8 sBt b c as4 sA-2+1+3 r8 r4 r8 ||
```

Example
9-6-8

Guitar chords can be entered on a U: line. For convenience, on such lines the characters # (sharp) and % (flat) can be entered as normal text.

9.6.3 Lyrics

PMX does not directly allow the inclusion of lyrics in a score. One of the major novelties that
Dirk Laurie introduced when developing M-Tx was a convenient interface to Rainer Dunker's
musixlyr.tex package for handling lyrics.

In M-Tx, each line of lyrics starts with the sequence L: followed by the text to be associated with the voice immediately preceding it in the input score. Syllables are indicated
by hyphens, and multiple notes that belong to a single syllable are handled by slurring or
beaming the notes together.

```
Style: SATB4
Meter: C
Sharps: 4
Size: 16
Pages: 1
Systems: 2
Space: 3 3 3 6
Name: {\it{S}} {\it{A}} {\it{T}} {\it{B}}
Indent: 0.15

%%\font\rx = cmr9   \rx

%%Asp
%%\\nobarnumbers\
%%It72ibatuclobb58:70:60:68T+0-12+0+0
%%w55m
% Bars 1-2
@+1 [ e8 f ] | g4 a b b | a g f of b |
L: 1. Durch dein Ge-f\"ang-nis Got-tes Sohn, ist
L: 2. Dein Ker-ker ist der Gna-den-thron, die
b4- | e e e e | [ e8 d ] e4 d of f |
L: 1. Durch dein Ge-f\"ang-nis Got-tes Sohn, ist
L: 2. Dein Ker-ker ist der Gna-den-thron, die
@+1 [ g8 a ] | b4 c dn [ c8 b ] | c4 b b of ds |
L: 1. Durch dein Ge-f\"ang-nis Got-tes Sohn, ist
L: 2. Dein Ker-ker ist der Gna-den-thron, die
@+2 e4 | e c g c | f [ g8 a ] b4 of b |
L: 1. Durch dein Ge-f\"ang-nis Got-tes Sohn, ist
L: 2. Dein Ker-ker ist der Gna-den-thron, die
```

Example
9-6-9

The @ symbols followed by a number in the music lines are used to fine-tune the height of the lyrics lines, whose global placing with respect to the music score is determined by the Space: 3 3 3 6 command in the preamble (the last number is larger since it also includes the distance between systems).

The example also shows that a number followed by a point and a blank at the start of a lyrics line is treated separately from the remaining text and will be printed to the left of the first lyrics syllable, which will be positioned as though the number was not there. We also see various TEX commands used to guide the typesetting, which demonstrates how M-Tx, PMX, MusiXTEX, and the TEX typesetter work closely together. Note, in particular, the font specification that sets the font size to nine points. Moreover, a MIDI output file is prepared by the line starting with %%I.

Instead of mixing the text of the lyrics with the music lines as in Example 9-6-9, we can group all the lyrics for a particular voice together in one paragraph by specifying a name for the group of lyrics in braces (e.g., {pA}). Afterwards, such lyrics paragraphs can be referenced on a lyrics line (e.g., L: {pA}), where the identifier must be unique to the input file (compare Examples 9-6-9 and 9-6-10).

```
Style: SATB
Meter: C
Sharps: 4
Size: 16
Pages: 1
Systems: 2
Space: 10
Name: {\it{S/A}} {\it{T/B}}

%%\font\rx = cmr9  \rx

{pA}
Durch dein Ge-f\"ang-nis, Got-tes Sohn, ist

{pB}
Dein Ker-ker ist der Gna-den-thron, die

%%Abp
%%\\nobarnumbers\
%%w60m
[ e8 f ] | g4 a b b | a g f of b |
L: {pA,pB}
b4- | e e e | [ e8 d ] e4 d f |
[ g8 a ] | b4 c dn [ c8 b ] | c4 b b ds |
Abp e4 | e c g c | f [ g8 a ] b4 ofd b |
```

Example
9-6-10

M-Tx offers several more possibilities to handle lyrics in a flexible way. For instance, you can have multiple voices on a single stave, and you can place lyrics lines above and below staves. This behavior, the full command set of the musixlyr.tex package, and a few more *dirty tricks*, are described in the M-Tx manual.

9.7   The music engraver LilyPond

In 1996, in the previous edition of this book, we described Jan Nieuwenhuizen's M$^{P}_{P}$ MusiXTEX preprocessor [89]. Since then, Jan and his colleague Han-Wen Nienhuys have abandoned that system and developed **LilyPond**,[1] an "automated engraving system that formats music beautifully and automatically and has a friendly syntax for its input files". They no longer use TEX as the basic typesetting engine but have developed a large C++ program (more than 6000 lines of code); they also use **Python** and **Scheme** code, as well as a specially designed font family (*feta*), which is available in various formats (PostScript Type 1, Open-Type, and SVG).

9.7.1   The LilyPond source language

To typeset one note, four kinds of information can be specified: *notename*, *octave*, *duration*, and *features*. Only the *notename* is mandatory. All this information is coded in the given order with no intervening spaces; a blank separates two notes.

Notes are denoted by lowercase letters. A comma (,) following the letter transposes the note one octave deeper, while a right quote (') makes it an octave higher. To generate different clefs, use the command \clef followed by either treble, alto, tenor, or bass. The following example shows some pitches and ways to generate different kinds of *bar lines*.

```
{c d   \bar "|" e f   \bar "|:" g c'        \bar "||"
d' e' \bar ":|" f' g' \bar ".|"  c' d'      \bar ".||." \break
e'' f'' g'' c'''       \bar ":|:"
d''' e''' f''' g'''    \bar "|." c' c c, c,, \bar ":"     }
```

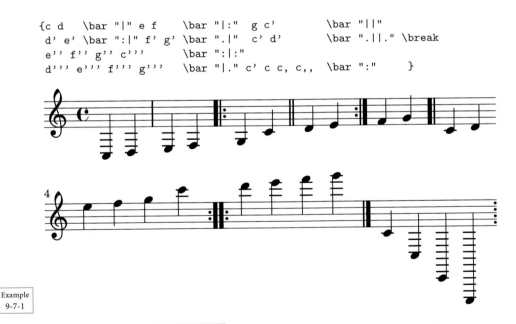

Example
9-7-1

---

[1] The LilyPond home page is at www.lilypond.org, where you can download the latest version of the system. There is also a tutorial, the reference guide, and much more. Of particular interest is the essay "What is behind LilyPond?", which explains the authors' views on problems in music notation (software) and their approach to solving them.

By default, LilyPond uses an absolute system to define the pitch of a note, thus making entering music quite tedious. You can also enter the music relative to a reference note, as the following example shows, where we reenter the second line in Example 9-7-1.

```
\relative c'
{c e' f g c \bar ":|:" d e f g \bar "|." c,,, c, c, c, \bar ":" }
```

Example
9-7-2

The pitch of a note in a sequence is determined based on the assumption that, without the modifier (' or ,), a note is less than one quarter away from its predecessor, where the first one is considered with respect to the absolute note indicated on the \relative command (c' by default). Note expecially in the last bar how we first descend by three octaves, and then three times by one more octave.

In contrast to the situation with **abc2mtex** and the other preprocessors, accidentals in LilyPond are denoted by extra *notenames*, such as gis or bes—not by prefixing the base note with a symbol.[1] The key of the piece is specified with the command \key.

```
\relative{\key a \major a cis c cis fis f g gis  a1 }
```

Example
9-7-3

As *durations*, whole, half, quarter, eighth, sixteenth, thirty-second, and sixty-fourth notes are provided; they are specified by placing the corresponding number after the note name (e.g., the whole note in the last example). For dotted notes, you would place a dot following this number. If a sequence is not specified, the last duration entered is used. The default duration for the first note, when unspecified, is a quarter. Our next example shows a sequence of ever shorter notes and rests. A certain amount of space can be skipped with the s notation, as shown on the second line just preceding the sixty-fourth rest at the end of

---

[1]The default names of the accidentals are based on the Dutch-German system: the suffix "is" indicates a sharped note (e.g., "cis" means "c sharp"), and the suffix "es" indicates a flatted note (e.g., "ges" is "g flat"). However, by loading a language unit you can use the usual note names in that language chosen. For instance, with english.ly (English) the preceding examples become "csharp" and "gflat", and with espanol.ly (Spanish) "dos" and "solb".

the bar. Note also the use of the \longa and \breve commands, and observe how LilyPond automatically keeps track of the correct number of bars.

```
#(set-global-staff-size 13)
\relative{c\breve c1 c2 c4 c8 c16 c32 c64 c64\break
  r\longa r\breve r1 r2 r4 r8 r16 r32 s64 r64 }
```

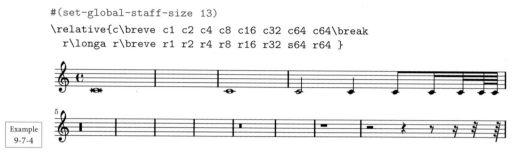

Example 9-7-4

This representation of note length has its limitations—namely, you cannot represent duplets, triplets, etc., in a natural way. However, as we see below, these can be specified by using a note-grouping mechanism.

Other information, such as typesetting details and accents or, more generally, subscript and superscripts, can be added to the end of the code for a note, as the following example shows.

```
{\key f \major \time 2/4 \autoBeamOff
  \acciaccatura f'8 f''--  \stemUp c''^-  \stemNeutral
a''-. \tiny { f'' c' } \normalsize a'-.
g'-- \small { g' } \tiny { g' } \normalsize g'4.          }
```

Example 9-7-5

The grace note at the beginning is typeset with the \acciaccatura command, while articulations are generated by appending the notation - or ^ to a note to place a sign below or on top of it, respectively. We can override the natural direction of the stem (equivalent to the command \stemNeutral, which corresponds to the direction automatically calculated by LilyPond) with the \stemUp and \stemDown commands.

A *beam* is created by appending [to the first note and] to the last note of the sequence of notes to be joined together (e.g., c8[d8 e8 f8]). Similarly, for connecting a sequence of notes with a *slur*, we append (to the first note of the sequence of notes and) to the last note (e.g., c8(d8 e8)). For *chords*, triangular brackets are used.

```
\relative c'' {\key bes \major \time 2/4
  g8[( f) es( d)]  c[( d) ] <g,-- bes>4
  <g a c>8[ <g a c> <g a c> <g a c>]
  <f-- a d>4 <f-- a d>          }
```

Example
9-7-6

Tuplets are constructed with the `\times` command, which is followed by a fraction and a music expression. The duration of the music expression is multiplied by the fraction, whose denominator will be printed over the beam or slur that connects the notes.

```
\relative c''' {\time 2/4
 \times 2/3 {c,8[( b a)]}  f4  \times 2/3 {f( a g)}
}
```

Example
9-7-7

LilyPond comes with many examples, which are well worth studying. The following example shows more of its functionality.

```
\relative c' {\time 3/4 \key f \major \clef alto
      \acciaccatura c'8\pp( \times 2/3 {bes)[( a) bes]} d4. bes8
\clef treble
    << {  a[ c f c f  c]} \\
       { f,2 r4 }                    >>
    << { d'2.( d4)   \setTextDecresc r4\> d4\! }\\
       { fis,2.( f2._> ) }         >>
\bar"||" \key as \major
     \times 2/3 {d'16[( g a)]}  \times 2/3 { g[( a b)]} b4 c,
}
```

Example
9-7-8

We change key and clef and introduce a second voice in bars 2, 3, and 4 (the stacked voices are contained inside `<<...>>` and are separated by the `\\` command). We also add some dynamics markers, the `\pp` command at the beginning, and the *decrescendo* in bar 4,

which is bracketed inside \> and \!, and typeset as the word *decr.*, as specified by the
\setTextDecresc command.

9.7.2 Running LilyPond

Files that contain LilyPond code are characterized by the extension .ly. Running them
through the program LilyPond will generate a PDF file by default. LilyPond has back ends
for PostScript, SVG, and TEX.

Our moderately complex example from Section 9.2.4 is much easier to write with Lily-
Pond, as shown in the next example. We have already developed the code for the upper staff
in Example 9-7-6, but we repeat it here, together with the code for the lower staff.

```
\new PianoStaff
<<
  \new Staff {
    \relative c''' {\key bes \major \time 2/4
        g8[( f) es( d)]   c[( d) ] <g,-- bes>4
        <g a c>8[ <g a c> <g a c> <g a c>]
        <f-- a d>4 <f-- a d>                        }}
  \new Staff {
    \relative c'' {\time 2/4 \key bes \major \clef bass
        g8[( f) es( d)] c[( d)] <g, bes-->4
        g8[( f) f( e)]   d4-- d--                    }}
>>
```

Example
9-7-9

Copy this example to a file and call it myexample.ly. You can then run it as follows.

```
lilypond myexample.ly
```

By default, LilyPond generates a PDF file. You can also get an EPS file as follows.

```
lilypond --backend=eps --ps myexample.ly
```

To see all options of the program, just type lilypond.

9.8 TEX*muse*—TEX and METAFONT **working together**

A promising new approach is Federico Garcia's TEX*muse* [27], where TEX and METAFONT work together to produce a score. First, TEX collects the information about the notes (their starting points, number of note heads, direction of the stems, possible accidentals or accents, stave in a polytonic piece on which the note occurs, etc.). With this information TEX builds a METAFONT program that does not consist only of single notes but rather combines *all* the notes of a vertical axis into one large character. Based on the characteristics of the next note, TEX figures out the shortest rhythmic value of the current character and determines the spacing, taking into account possible glue. A score is thus typeset as a single line of text with its words (vertical columns) automatically designed.

In summary, a LATEX run with TEX*muse* on a music piece typesets musical material by creating one *new* font for each page (consisting of "large" characters), on which META-FONT is run automatically to generate the `.tfm` and `.pk` instances. After a change to the score, these instances must be deleted so that TEX always uses the correct latest version generated on the fly.

At the time of writing (early 2007) "stage 1" of the program has been implemented.[1] This version can typeset the basic musical components of Bach's *Inventions*, pieces for piano featuring two staves with one voice per staff and needing only limited additional interpretative notation. These pieces are ideal material for testing this stage and for preparing further developments of TEX*muse*, where improvements for ties, line breaking, time signatures, rest typesetting, beam heights, etc., need to be addressed.

---

[1] The TEX*muse* home page `http://www.fedegarcia.net/TeX/TeXmuse.html` contains information about the current status of the system.

CHAPTER 10

Playing Games

Board and card games have a long history, and thousands of books in many languages have been dedicated to chess, Go, cards, and the like. These books almost always use diagrams to explain the rules or show the evolution of a game. In the present chapter we look at a number of examples showing how to prepare such graphical presentations with LaTeX.

Most game packages are concerned with making available either a special font for typesetting the right symbols or macros for producing nice examples of the state of play. The highly developed field of chess notation, however, lends itself well to an algorithmic typesetting system like LaTeX. The chess packages, with which we begin, keep track of the state of moves and allow various forms of output.

We move next to the rather similar games of Chinese chess and Go, followed by backgammon. We then look at cards, where the classic game of bridge has a special package, before concluding the chapter with the esoteric subject of crossword and Sudoku puzzles. Although crossword design is not a game, it has some similar typesetting problems, and LaTeX-using crossword makers will enjoy using the sophisticated package to help them. In the case of Sudoku, there is even a package that generates new puzzles or solves existing ones.

10.1 Chess

Two decades of history

Typesetting chess using TeX started in 1988, when Wolfgang Appelt developed a number of macros for this purpose [9]. This early attempt was done without a font containing chess figures, so Appelt denoted them with symbols like Ω. A little later, Zalman Rubinstein [107]) produced a first simple chess font with METAFONT. Nearly four years later, Piet Tutelaers, a Dutch chess enthusiast, designed a rather classical-looking chess font and developed an accompanying LaTeX package [122] that turned LaTeX for the first time into a mature typesetting system for chess journals.

Piet's chess package internally kept track of the positions of all pieces on the board so that it was easy to display the current board once in a while. For doing so, it used a somewhat uncommon and verbose notation: moves were denoted by always providing the start and end positions on the board (e.g., `\move g1f3 g8f6`) instead of allowing the use of Portable Game Notation (PGN; e.g., `1. Nf3 Nf6`). As an alternative, the chess package introduced a "tournament style" notation in which a | sign would signal notation in "chess mode", similar to the use of $ to indicate inline "math mode".

In the second decade

Following these early attempts, several people worked on improving the situation further. The first package to surface was skak by Torben Hoffmann. Just like the chess package, it internally keeps track of the board positions and supports displaying the board or parts of it at any point. In contrast to chess, it uses a subset of PGN as its input syntax. It comes with a new set of fonts that offers additional symbols needed for game analysis and provides a number of bells and whistles to customize layout and style. In addition, it offers import and export possibilities in the popular Forsyth-Edwards Notation (FEN) used by many programs, so that it becomes easy to professionally typeset boards and games.

In contrast, the texmate package by Federico Garcia concentrated on providing a compact and easy-to-use input syntax (based on the tournament style of the chess package). Unfortunately, its first implementation lacked the possibility to keep track of the board situation automatically, so that diagrams had to be set up manually.

Today's situation

Both packages were still confined to use the fonts provided with skak, making it very difficult to use any other chess fonts available via the Net. This situation prompted Ulrike Fischer to develop the chessfss package. This package provides a number of generic font switching and support commands that allows the user to switch between different chess fonts with ease, based on NFSS (New Font Selection Scheme) methods. Of course, as long as packages use hard-wired direct font calls, this isn't going to help. Thus the next step in the evolution was to modify existing packages to rely on chessfss rather than doing their own font setup. This became reality with skak version 1.4 (described in Section 10.1.3 on page 673) and texmate version 2. In fact, texmate did undergo an even larger set of modifications: it now uses skak to keep track of board positions and thus provides the features of all three packages together. The new texmate is described in Section 10.1.4 on page 680.

10.1.1 chessboard—**Coloring your boards**

Ulrike also developed the chessboard package, which allows you to produce sophisticated chessboard diagrams with ease, including colored boards. At the moment it works as a stand-alone package but perhaps we'll see a future version of this package forming the basis for board diagrams for skak and texmate. As chessboard is still being actively developed, it is not described in this book, but it might be worth checking out its documentation found on CTAN. As a teaser, here is an example prepared by Ulrike for this book. It uses chessboard version 1.3.

```
\usepackage[LSBC1,T1]{fontenc} \usepackage{chessboard}
\setchessboard{border=false,vlabellift=2.8ex,linewidth=0.01ex,padding=0.05ex,pgfborder,
 linewidth=0.1ex,padding=0.25ex,pgfborder,showmover=false,boardfontencoding=LSBC1}
\chessboard[
%% pieces
 setpieces={Ka8,qd7,kc6}, addpieces={ka1,Kb3,Rc3},
 addpieces={kh1,Nf3,Rg4}, addpieces={kh8,ph7,Rg6,Bg5},
%% lines between the four parts
 linewidth=0.1ex,padding=0pt,markstyle=leftborder,markfile=e,
 markstyle=topborder,markrank=4,
%% marks mating moves
 markstyle=straightmove, color=blue, linewidth=0.2ex,
 shortenstart=0.4em, arrow=to, markmoves={d7-b7,c3-c1,g4-g1,g5-f6},
%% coloring the mating figure
 piececolor=blue,coloremph, emphfields={d7,g5,c3,g4},
%% borders
 addpgf=\pgfsetdash{{0.1ex}{0.1ex}}{.05ex}, markstyle=border,
 linewidth=0.05ex, markfields={b7,a8,c1,b1,a1,g1,h1,f6,g7,h8}]
```

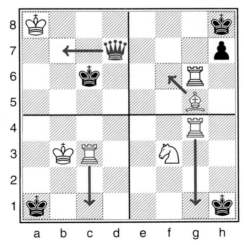

Example
10-1-1

10.1.2 chessfss—A generic font mechanism for chess

The chessfss package by Ulrike Fischer provides an interface for other packages to use a variety of chess fonts available on the Net. It uses the standard NFSS mechanisms, so that you can easily change the size, or switch to boldface or italic, provided the selected chess font family offers the corresponding series or shape. For this very reason you might see a lot of font substitution warnings if you make use of this feature, as most chess fonts come in only one shape and series, such that switching to bold generates such a warning.

To use a chess font family with NFSS, it needs to be made available in certain font encodings, which can be done by providing suitable virtual fonts or by reencoding the fonts by other means. For some freely available font families, this work has already been done (see the first block in the next example). For other fonts, the enpassant package documentation describes the recipe for doing the conversion to Type 1 fonts in the right encoding. The following example shows a number of available fonts; the commands used to access them are explained later.

skaknew	♛♕♖♗♘♙	♛♕♖♗♘♙
alpha		
berlin		
pirat		

Fonts that need conversion to Type 1 first

alfonso		
aventurer		
cases		
condal		
harlequin		
kingdom		
leipzig		
line		
lucena		
magnetic		
mark		
marroquin		
maya		
mediaeval		
merida		
millennia		
motif		

```
\usepackage{chessfss}
\newcommand\test[1]{\ttfamily #1&
 \setfigfontfamily{#1}\figfont KQRBNp&
 \setfigfontfamily{#1}\figfont\Large
   KQRBNp\\}
\begin{tabular}{lll}
 \test{skaknew}
 \test{alpha}
 \test{berlin}
 \test{pirat}
[3pt] % optional arg of \\ in \test
\multicolumn{3}{c}{\itshape Fonts that
   need conversion to Type 1 first}\\[4pt]
 \test{alfonso}
 \test{aventurer}
 \test{cases}
 \test{condal}
 \test{harlequin}
 \test{kingdom}
 \test{leipzig}
 \test{line}
 \test{lucena}
 \test{magnetic}
 \test{mark}
 \test{marroquin}
 \test{maya}
 \test{mediaeval}
 \test{merida}
 \test{millennia}
 \test{motif}
\end{tabular}
```

Example
10-1-2

When documenting chess games, various types of glyphs come into play. The chessfss package distinguishes three categories and provides standard encodings for each: figurine fonts (which are used to record games), board fonts (which show the pieces behind black and white fields), and informator fonts (which hold additional "information symbols" used to produce commented games). We will look at each group and its support separately.

\setfigfontfamily{*name*}   \figfont   \figsymbol{*glyph(s)*}

You can choose the font family to use for figurine symbols through the declaration \setfigfontfamily. Afterwards, you can use \figfont to select this family and the appropriate font encoding. The scope of the command has to be limited by a group; i.e., it behaves similarly to font commands like \ttfamily, except that it also switches the encoding. For situations where a command with one argument is more appropriate, you would use \figsymbol, which is comparable to \textsf. These commands can be combined with other font commands such as \bfseries and \small, and will yield the expected results, provided the chosen font family offers the corresponding variants. To address the figurine symbols in this way, the ASCII letters KQRBNp can be used.

In the previous example we saw that the fonts obey font size commands. Here we show the switch to boldface and italic. Note that skaknew doesn't have an *italic* variant, so NFSS substitutes an upright shape.

skaknew:

```
\usepackage{chessfss}\setlength\parindent{0pt}
\newcommand\test[1]{\setfigfontfamily{#1}%
 \texttt{#1}:\\
 \figsymbol{KQRBNp \LARGE KQRBNp\\[5pt]
     \textbf{KQRBNp} \textit{KQRBNp}}\par}

\test{skaknew}
\test{pirat}
```

Example
10-1-3

pirat:

\symking \symqueen \symrook \symbishop \symknight \sympawn

The main reason for the development of chessfss was to provide a standard interface to chess fonts that can be used by other packages. But, as we have seen already, it can be used on its own as well. The commands \symking, etc. support this stand-alone usage further: they can be used in normal text and produce the corresponding figurine glyph.

Example
10-1-4

The ♙ got promoted to ♘.

```
\usepackage{chessfss}
\setfigfontfamily{aventurer}

The \sympawn{} got promoted to \symknight.
```

In some situations, we don't want to use figurine symbols but rather normal characters to represent pieces in a game notation (for example, when teaching children). For this scenario, a similar set of commands is available.

\textking \textqueen \textrook \textbishop \textknight \textpawn

---

These commands produce letters, such as "K" for king. However, in contrast to the symbols, those characters are language specific, so we need a way to specify which characters to use for individual languages and a possibility to choose the target language.

```
\settextfigchars[language]{king}{queen}{rook}{bishop}{knight}{pawn}
\settextfiglanguage{language}
```

The `\settextfigchars` declaration specifies for a *language* (default `english`) the letters to use for the individual pieces. The package contains predefined values for several languages (using the **babel** naming conventions), and others are expected to follow in the future. Typical declarations would be

```
\settextfigchars[english]{K}{Q}{R}{B}{N}{P}
\settextfigchars[german]{K}{D}{T}{L}{S}{B}
```

To select a specific language, use `\settextfiglanguage` as shown in the next example. Of course, normally you would select only a single language per document.

```
                              \usepackage{chessfss}
Be1, Na1                                              \textbishop e1, \textknight a1 \par
Fe1, Ca1           \settextfiglanguage{french}  \textbishop e1, \textknight a1 \par
Le1, Sa1           \settextfiglanguage{german}  \textbishop e1, \textknight a1 \par
```

Example
10-1-5

So far we have seen two sets of commands for explicitly selecting figurine symbols or letters, but, in fact, there exists a third set that allows us to switch between the two representations for the chess pieces.

```
\king     \queen     \rook     \bishop     \knight     \pawn
\usetextfig          \usesymfig            \setfigstyle{style-commands}
```

By default, `\king`, `\queen`, etc. produce the figurine symbols. After issuing a `\usetextfig` declaration, however, they change to produce letters and `\usesymfig` switches back to figurine symbols. In addition, it is generally possible to set the style for both cases via `\setfigstyle` (in the example we use boldface and underline). The last of the macros defining the style is allowed to take an argument (e.g., `\underline`).

```
                    \usepackage{chessfss}
                    \setfigfontfamily{cases}
♗e1, ♘a1                           \bishop e1, \knight a1 \par
Be1, Na1            \usetextfig \bishop e1, \knight a1 \par
Be1, Na1            \setfigstyle{\bfseries\underline}
Be1, Na1                           \bishop e1, \knight a1 \par
♗e1, ♘a1            \usesymfig  \bishop e1, \knight a1 \par
```

Example
10-1-6

`\setboardfontfamily{`*name*`}`	`\boardsymbol{`*glyph(s)*`}`	`\boardfont`
`\setboardfontsize{`*size*`}`		
`\setinffontfamily{`*name*`}`	`\infsymbol{`*glyph(s)*`}`	`\inffont`

If you want to individually select the font family used for board symbols or informational symbols, a corresponding set of interface commands is available for this purpose. However, while using figurine fonts directly is an option for small documents, it is not really advisable to try building chess boards manually. This is better done through the interfaces provided by **skak**, **texmate**, or **chessboard**. Thus the three most important declarations to remember are `\setboardfontfamily` and `\setinffontfamily`, which can be used to direct the other packages to choose the specified font family, and `\setboardfontsize`, which allows you to specify the size of the board squares.

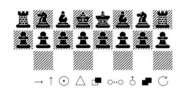

```
\usepackage{chessfss}
\setboardfontfamily{maya}
\setboardfontsize{15pt}

\noindent
{\boardfont rmblkans\\opopopop\\0Z0Z0Z0Z}

\infsymbol{A C D E o q r s t}
```

Example
10-1-7

In the previous example we accessed the informational symbols through their font positions. These are difficult to memorize and make the source document more or less unreadable. For that reason **chessfss** provides individual commands to access each symbol, as shown in Table 10.1 on the following page. When referring to these symbols, it is best to use these commands.

`\setchessfontfamily{`*name*`}`

It is also possible to set all three font encodings with a single `\setchessfontfamily` declaration. However, as most chess font families lack the information symbols, this will most likely result in a number of NFSS substitutions (the fallback family is `skaknew`).

The **chessfss** package offers a number of additional commands, including command versions for all board glyphs and several commands that are only of interest to package writers. One of the recent additions is the ability to produce colored boards (used by **chessboard**). For details, consult the package documentation.

10.1.3 skak—The successor to the chess package

The **skak** package by Torben Hoffmann allows you to document chess games, by intermixing details of the game with commentaries. This package internally keeps track of the board situation, so that it is possible to print the state of the board at any time during the game. Game positions can be stored and loaded from external files, using the popular Forsyth-Edwards Notation (FEN). The first distribution of this package contained a new set of chess fonts, written in METAFONT. Since then, these fonts have been further improved and converted to Type 1 by Ulrich Dirr; they are now available under the name `skaknew`. While earlier

Table 10.1: Informational symbols for chess

Symbol	Command	Font Position	Symbol	Command	Font Position
	\bbetter	g		\mate	m
	\bdecisive	i		\morepawns	S
	\betteris	b		\moreroom	U
	\bishoppair	a		\onlymove	F
	\bupperhand	e		\opposbishops	o
	\capturesymbol	X		\passedpawn	r
	\castlinghyphen	-		\qside	M
	\centre	I		\samebishops	s
	\checksymbol	+		\seppawns	q
	\chesssee	l		\timelimit	T
	\compensation	n		\unclear	k
	\counterplay	V		\unitedpawns	u
	\devadvantage	t		\wbetter	f
	\diagonal	G		\wdecisive	h
	\doublepawns	d		\weakpt	J
	\ending	L		\with	v
	\equal	j		\withattack	A
	\etc	P		\withidea	E
	\file	H		\withinit	C
	\kside	O		\without	w
	\markera	x		\wupperhand	c
	\markerb	y		\zugzwang	D

Example
10-1-8

releases of skak hard-wired the used fonts, the current release delegates the font setup to the chessfss package, thereby enabling the use of any chess font that is set up for use with chessfss.

Specifying and displaying the board

To enter a game, you first have to initialize the board—i.e., place all pieces in their appropriate position. This is normally done with \newgame , which places all pieces in their standard positions. Alternatively, you can set up an arbitrary position by using \fenboard.

\newgame   \fenboard{*FEN-notation*}

The \fenboard declaration expects the game state to be specified in FEN (Forsyth–Edwards Notation), a notation that can be generated by most chess programs. It is also possible to save and load positions from external files, as we will see later. No checks are made to validate the specified board situation, so it is up to you to ensure that everything is specified correctly. The \newgame declaration is, in fact, just an abbreviation for the following:

```
\fenboard{rnbqkbnr/pppppppp/8/8/8/8/PPPPPPPP/RNBQKBNR w KQkq - 0 1}
```

\showboard   \showinverseboard

Once the initialization is done, moves can be recorded and the board can be printed at any point in the game by issuing a \showboard or \showinverseboard command. The latter command shows the board with the white figures on top.

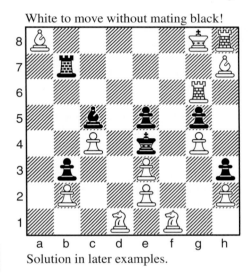

Solution in later examples.

```
\usepackage{skak}
\setboardfontfamily{maya}

White to move without mating black!

\fenboard{B5KR/1r5B/6R1/%
          2b1p1p1/2P1k1P1/%
          1p2P2p/1P2P2P/3N1N2
          w - - 0 12}
\showboard

Solution in later examples.
```

Example 10-1-9

As we see, the standard size of the printed board is fairly large. In some situations this may not be appropriate, so skak offers a number of commands and options to manipulate this display, including highlighting of fields or moves.

\setupboard{*field-size*}{*annotation-size*} \tinyboard \smallboard \normalboard \largeboard \notationOn \notationOff

To define the board size displayed by \showboard or \showinverseboard, you can use a \setupboard declaration. The *field-size* specifies the width of each field on the board, and the *annotation-size* defines the font size used for board annotations. A small number of board sizes are predefined and can be called up by \tinyboard, \smallboard, \normalboard, or \largeboard. Alternatively, the board size can be initialized through the options tiny, small, normal, or large. The default is the normal board size, which corresponds to \setupboard{20pt}{10pt}.

Board annotations (numbers on the left, letters at the bottom) are displayed by default. Through \notationOn and \notationOff or the options notationon and notationoff, they can be activated and deactivated, respectively.

ps *option needed* / *for highlighting*

The preceding possibilities are always available. In contrast, the highlighting commands offered by skak make use of PSTricks and, therefore, do not work out of the box if the target format is PDF. In that case, the solution is to use the pst-pdf package, which is described in Section A.2 on page 800.

```
\showmoverOn   \showmoverOff   \highlight[symbol]{field(s)}
\printarrow{start}{target}     \printknightmove{start}{target}
```

To indicate who moves next, issue a `\showmoverOn` declaration or load the package with the `mover` option. This will display an indicator to the right of the board. To prevent this behavior, use `\showmoverOff` or the option `moveroff` (the default).

Highlighting of fields is done with a `\highlight` declaration. The *field(s)* are given as a comma-separated list, and the form of highlighting is controlled by the optional argument *symbol*. Without the optional argument, a square is used; o or O produces a smaller or larger circle; and x or X produces a smaller or larger cross as shown in the next example. It is also possible to indicate movements by using `\printarrow` (for straight arrows) or `\printknightmove`. Note that the order of highlighting can be important: if you first print an arrow and then highlight the target field, the field symbol overprints the arrow as shown in the example.

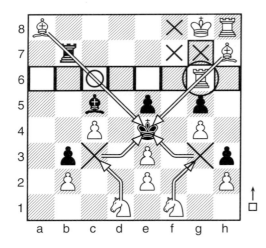

```
\usepackage[ps]{skak}
\fenboard{B5KR/1r5B/6R1/2b1p1p1/2P1k1P1/%
   1p2P2p/1P2P2P/3N1N2 w - - 0 12}
\showmoverOn
\showboard
\highlight{a6,b6,c6,d6,e6,f6,h6,g7}
\highlight[x]{f7,f8,g7}
\printknightmove{f1}{g3}
\printknightmove{g3}{e4}
\highlight[X]{c3,g3}
\printknightmove{d1}{c3}
\printknightmove{c3}{e4}
% order of highlighting is important
\highlight[O]{g6}    \printarrow{h7}{e4}
\printarrow{a8}{e4}  \highlight[o]{c6}
```

Example
10-1-10

```
\showonlyblack      \showonlywhite
\showonly{figures}  \showallbut{figures}   \showall
```

When discussing openings or complicated positions in the middle game, it is sometimes helpful to present only certain important pieces to clearly show lines of influence or other aspects of the game. For this purpose, skak offers four commands. With `\showonlyblack` and `\showonlywhite`, the figurines of only one color are shown. More granular control is available through `\showonly` and `\showallbut`. In their argument, the figurines that should (or should not) be shown are specified as a comma-separated list of the letters "K",

"Q", "R", "B", "N", and "P" (representing King, Queen, Rook, Bishop, kNight, and Pawn, with uppercase denoting white and lowercase denoting black figurines).

Once made, a selection will apply to all further diagrams until the point at which a new selection is made. To show all pieces again in the next diagram, specify \showall, which is a shorthand for \showonly with all necessary letters in the argument.

As can be seen in the last two diagrams of the next example, an empty argument to either \showonly or \showallbut gives a somewhat strange result in the current implementation—the opposite of what would be expected. It's better not to rely on this behavior, as it might get corrected one day.

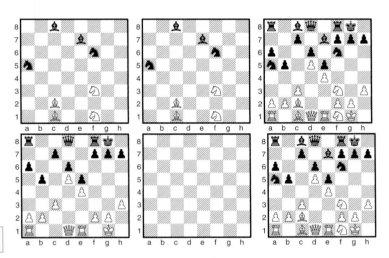

```
\usepackage{skak}
\tinyboard
\fenboard{r1bq1rk1/2p1bppp%
    /p2p1n2/np1Pp3/4P3/2P2N1P%
    /PPB2PP1/R1BQRNK1 w - - 0 1}
\showonly{B,N,b,n}%
              \showboard \quad
              \showboard \quad
\showall      \showboard

\showallbut{B,N,b,n}%
              \showboard \quad
% strange behavior:
\showallbut{}\showboard \quad
\showonly{}   \showboard
```

Example
10-1-11

Documenting a game

Once the board is initialized internally, you can record and print moves with \mainline, just record moves without printing by using \hidemoves, or discuss variations with \variation intermixed with textual comments.

\mainline{*move(s)*}   \variation{*move(s)*}   \hidemoves{*move(s)*}

All three commands take the same data in their argument. The differences between them are that the commands \mainline and \hidemoves update the board (while \variation does not) and that \mainline and \variation print the moves in different styles (by default, bold and regular typeface) to allow the reader to distinguish progress in the game and variations being discussed.

The *move(s)* in the argument of \mainline, \variation, and \hidemoves are given in a restricted form of PGN (Portable Game Notation), which is a big improvement   *Specifying moves* in comparison to the predecessor package chess. For one thing, it allows for more concise input. It also offers the possibility to comfortably enter the game in any chess editor that can store a game in this notation. The argument consists of one or more moves and has to start with the correct move number followed by a period (in case of a move by white) or with the move number followed by three periods (to denote a continuation move by black). Move numbers and individual moves are separated by blanks. Castling is denoted using the letter "O" not zero "0".

1 d4 ♘f6 2 c4 c5 3 d5 A possible continuation is the Benko Gambit. 3...b5 4 c×b5 a6 5 b×a6 ♗×a6 6 ♘c3 d6 7 e4. Here the game follows the Classical Benoni opening **3...e6 4 ♘c3 e×d5 5 c×d5 d6 6 e4 g6** leading after some additional moves ... to **9 O-O a6 10 a4 ♗g4.**

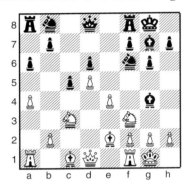

```
\usepackage{skak}
\smallboard
\setchessfontfamily{magnetic}

\newgame
\mainline{1. d4 Nf6 2. c4 c5 3. d5}
A possible continuation is the Benko
Gambit.
\variation{3... b5 4. cxb5 a6
        5. bxa6 Bxa6 6. Nc3 d6
        7. e4}.
Here the game follows the Classical
Benoni opening
\mainline{3... e6 4. Nc3 exd5
        5.cxd5 d6 6. e4 g6}
leading after some additional moves
\ldots\hidemoves{7. Nf3 Bg7 8. Be2 O-O}
to \mainline{9. O-O a6 10.a4 Bg4}.
\begin{center} \showboard \end{center}
```

Example 10-1-12

All three commands will analyze their input to some extent and reject obviously wrong moves (though not all mistakes are detected). With \mainline and \hidemoves, a correct move number must be given and the move must fit the internal state of the board. With \variation, it is required only that the argument is formally correct and that the moves are, in principle, possible (e.g., not a diagonally moving rook). The state of the board is not taken into account, however, so incorrect moves of that nature will not be detected.

PGN has a complex syntax and, as a result, the skak package is somewhat unforgiving in case of errors and currently does not support all syntax possibilities. In particular, you cannot use NAG (Numeric Annotation Glyphs) comments, text comments (denoted in PGN by braces), or variations (done in PGN by square brackets). NAGs are numbers that are prefixed with a dollar sign and represent symbolic comments (e.g., $13 stands for "unclear": ∞). Many of them can be represented by information symbol commands provided by chessfss; see Table 10.1 on page 674. However, you need to enter them as LaTeX commands and you must place them after the full or half moves and not *before* them (i.e., not following a blank), as this confuses skak's parsing algorithm. In a \variation you can place appropriate symbols, such as \betteris, before the move number, as the next example shows.

Here we see **1 e4 d6 2 d4 ZZ±Nf6 3 ♘c3 g6** incorrect output as the NAG symbol in the input was preceded by a space. Correct is **1 e4 d6 2 d4± ♘f6 3 ♘c3 g6** or in a variation ⌒3...

```
\usepackage{skak} \setfigfontfamily{line}
\newgame Here we see
\mainline{1. e4 d6 2.d4 \wbetter Nf6 3. Nc3 g6}
incorrect output as the NAG symbol in the input
was preceded by a space. \newgame Correct is
\mainline{1. e4 d6 2.d4\wbetter{} Nf6 3. Nc3 g6}
or in a variation \variation{\betteris 3... }
```

Example 10-1-13

The **skak** package only distinguishes between the main game (specified by `\mainline` and `\hidemoves` commands) and one level of variations. If a more detailed analysis is necessary, try the **texmate** package, which offers up to three levels of nested variations.

`\wmove{`*move*`}`   `\bmove{`*move*`}`   `\lastmove`

For commentaries, **skak** offers a few additional commands to typeset individual moves. The command `\lastmove` typesets the last move in the main game including its move numbers, while `\wmove` and `\bmove` typeset a single move notation (for white or black) without the number.

`\storegame{`*label*`}` `\restoregame{`*label*`}` `\savegame{`*name*`}` `\loadgame{`*name*`}`

Another way to document variations is to save the board position at a certain point and return to it later. This can be done in memory (using `\storegame`) or externally in a file (using `\savegame`). With `\storegame`, the current board situation is saved in memory and can be referenced through its *label*. Thus, to return to this position, you would use `\restoregame` with the same *label*.

The commands `\savegame` and `\loadgame` work in a similar manner but use the external file *name*`.fen` for storing or retrieving the game state. The current state of the game is stored in FEN notation, so this is the way to generate this notation from within **skak**.

Changing the style

The **skak** package offers three predefined styles for presenting the moves of a game. They can be selected with `\styleA`, `\styleB` (the default), and `\styleC`, respectively. Alternatively, or in addition, a default style for the whole document can be defined by giving one of the options `styleA`, `styleB`, or `styleC`.

As the package analyzes each move and splits it into its components, it is possible to provide highly granular control with respect to spacing, fonts, and punctuation characters. The next example shows the standard styles in action.

Style A: **1. e4, d6 2. d4,** ♘**f6 3.** ♘**c3** 3. f3, e5 4. d5, c6 5. c4, ♕b6

Style B: **1 e4 d6 2 d4** ♘**f6 3** ♘**c3** 3 f3 e5 4 d5 c6 5 c4 ♕b6

Style C:

1	e4	d6
2	d4	♘f6
3	♘c3	

3 f3 e5 4 d5 c6 5 c4 ♕b6

```
\usepackage{skak} \setchessfontfamily{condal}
Style A:  \styleA\newgame
  \mainline{1. e4 d6 2.d4 Nf6 3. Nc3}
\variation{3.f3 e5 4. d5 c6 5. c4 Qb6} \par
Style B:  \styleB\newgame
  \mainline{1. e4 d6 2.d4 Nf6 3. Nc3}
\variation{3.f3 e5 4. d5 c6 5. c4 Qb6} \par
Style C:  \styleC\newgame
  \mainline{1. e4 d6 2.d4 Nf6 3. Nc3}
\variation{3.f3 e5 4. d5 c6 5. c4 Qb6}
```

Example 10-1-14

Unfortunately, the package offers no user interface to define new styles or adjust existing ones—to do so you have to copy the definitions for, say, `\styleA` into the preamble or a separate package and adjust them there.

10.1.4 texmate—**The power of three**

The **texmate** package was developed by Federico Garcia because he was not satisfied with
the syntax and typesetting flexibility offered by early versions of **skak**. For a while, both packages were developed independently, focusing on different aspects of chess typesetting. When
chessfss became available and with it the ability to readily use different chess fonts, Federico
reimplemented **texmate** to make use of it. At this point he decided to delegate the task of
board management to the **skak** package so that all such commands, such as \showboard,
are available the moment **texmate** is loaded. In this respect the new **texmate** combines the
power of all three packages.

Move notations

The **texmate** package supports the PGN input notation (similar to the "tournament notation" developed for the **chess** package) to denote moves in a chess game. However, in contrast to the former package, it is more flexible in the supported syntax: Essentially it requires
only that moves are separated by spaces; the user is free to add punctuation marks and/or
move numbers at will. The input is given in "chess mode", which is entered and exited us-
ing a | sign, similar to the use of $ to indicate inline "math mode". In situations where
| should not indicate chess mode (e.g., in tabular environments), you can disable it via
\makebarother and then later reenable it with \makebarchess. As an alternative to this
short notation, you can use the environment texmate to denote chess mode.

  If move numbers are given, they are normally verified when **texmate** passes the input to
skak. In the next example, we have to explicitly disable that behavior with \SkakOff. After
all, the moves are nonsensical if they are considered to belong to a single game.

Input as **1. e4 c5 2. ♘f3 d6 3. d4 c×d4** or as
1. e4 c5 2. ♘f3 d6 3. d4 c×d4 or as **1. e4 c5 2. ♘f3
d6 3. d4 c×d4**

```
\usepackage{texmate}   \SkakOff
Input as |e4 c5 Nf3 d6 d4 cxd4|
or as    |1 e4 c5 2 Nf3 d6 3 d4 cxd4|
or as    |1. e4 c5 ; 2. Nf3 d6 ; 3. d4 cxd4|
```

Example
10-1-15

```
[move(s)]   \[ comments-in-chess-mode \]
```

Within chess mode, the notation [...] denotes a variation. The **texmate** package then expects it to contain an alternative move or sequence of moves. If no move numbers are given,
it will automatically label them accordingly, as can be seen in the next example. Such comments can be nested up to three levels. The formatting differs from level to level and can be
adjusted.

Some variants of the Italian game (Greco attack):
1. e4 e5 2. ♘f3 ♘c6 3. ♗c4 ♗c5 [Hungarian defence 3...♗e7 4. d4] **4. c3** [Canal variation 4. d3
♘f6 5. ♘c3 d6 6. ♗g5 (6. ♗e3)] **4...♘f6 5. d4
e×d4 6. c×d4 ♗b4+ 7. ♘c3**

```
\usepackage{texmate}
\setchessfontfamily{leipzig}

Some variants of the Italian game
(Greco attack):
|1. e4 e5 ; 2. Nf3 Nc6 ; 3. Bc4
 Bc5 [|Hungarian defence |Be7 d4] ;
4. c3 [|Canal variation |d3 Nf6 Nc3 d6
       Bg5 [ Be3]] Nf6 ;
5. d4  exd4 ; 6. cxd4 Bb4+ ; 7. Nc3 |
```

Example
10-1-16

$\backslash$ [*comments-in-chess-mode* $\backslash$]

For free commentaries that include text, the automatically produced punctuation symbols at either side are usually not necessary or wanted. For this case \[...\] is provided. The difference is that, by default, no parentheses or other punctuation is added on either side and it is left to the reader to provide whatever is necessary. The *comment* is still interpreted as a variation; i.e., moves within it will not be considered part of the game. In contrast, simply ending chess mode with |, typesetting the comment, and then restarting it would not work if moves are present within the comment.

The commentary is still parsed in chess mode, so if it should start out with normal text, you must cancel this mode inside via \[| and resume it at the end via |\] .

Accelerated Benoni Defense analysis:
1. d4 ♘f6 2. ♘f3 c5 3. d5 g6 4. ♘c3 ♗g7 5. e4 d6 6. ♗b5+ this is not very ambitious: the main goal is to set the trap 6... ♘bd7?! 7. a4a6 ♗e2 and white is quite strong. The right answer is **6... ♗d7! 7. a4!** The bishop exchange would ease black's development and going back with 7. ♗e2 is weak because of 7... b5!∓

```
\usepackage{texmate}
\setchessfontfamily{cases}
Accelerated Benoni Defense analysis: \\
| d4 Nf6 ; Nf3 c5 ; d5 g6 ; Nc3 Bg7 ; e4 d6 ;
Bb5+ \[| this is not very ambitious: the main
goal is to set the trap | \ahead Nbd7?! ; a4
a6 ; Be2 | and white is quite strong. The right
answer is |\]  Bd7! ; a4! \[| The bishop exchange
would ease black's development and going back
with | Be2 | is weak because of | b5!\bbetter \] |
```

Example
10-1-17

When a commentary is opened with either [or \[, it is assumed that a variation is discussed (i.e., an alternative move for the last move made). Therefore **texmate** temporarily undoes the last move on the board so that the first move inside the commentary will show the same move number as used outside the commentary. However, sometimes you might want to talk about developments that may come. For this **texmate** offers different possibilities.

\threat<*threat*>   \Threat<*numbered-move(s)*>

With \threat, simple threats can be denoted. The **texmate** package inserts a triangle (produced by \withidea) and typesets *threat* without a move number. Note the special way of denoting the argument to this command. In contrast, \Threat typesets a threatening variation including move numbers. In this case, neither the symbol \withidea nor any spaces are added automatically. If necessary, you can force a space with \␣ and typeset the symbol in front of the *numbered-move(s)*.

Steinitz – Walsh, London 1870:
1. e4 c5 2. ♘c3 ♘c6 3. ♘f3 h6 4. d4 c×d4 5. ♘×d4 ♕b6 6. ♗e3! ♕×b2 7. ♘db5 △♖b1! ♕b4 8. c7+ ♔d8 9. ♗d2 △♘d5+ ♖b8 10. ♖b1 ♕d4 11. ♗d3 ♘b4? 12. ♘3b5 ♘×d3+ 13. c×d3 ♕×d3 14. ♘e6+!!△15. ♗a5+ ... 16. ♕×d3 ♔e8 15. ♘bc7#

```
\usepackage{texmate}
\setchessfontfamily{cases}
Steinitz -- Walsh, London 1870: \\
| e4 c5 ; Nc3 Nc6 ; Nf3 h6 ; d4 cxd4 ; Nxd4 Qb6 ;
Be3! Qxb2 ; Ndb5 \threat<Rb1!> Qb4 ; c7+ Kd8 ;
Bd2 \threat<Nd5+> Rb8 ; Rb1 Qd4 ; Bd3 Nb4? ;
N3b5 Nxd3+ ; cxd3 Qxd3 ; Ne6+!! \Threat<\withidea
  Ba5+ \dummy\,\dots Qxd3> Ke8 ; Nbc7 \# |
```

Example
10-1-18

> \ahead   \dummy   \ddummy

It is, of course, also possible to talk about the next move in a commentary started with \[or
[: simply prefix the first move inside with\ahead.

If certain moves are irrelevant for the analysis you can use \dummy or \ddummy to ad-
vance the game state by one or two half-moves, respectively. This means that **skak** can't fol-
low the position on the board any longer, so **texmate** immediately disables this functionality
with \SkakOff upon encountering these commands for the remainder of the variation.

French Defense analysis:
**1. e4 e6 2. d4 d5 3. ♘c3 ♗d4 4. e×d5 e×d5 5. ♗d3
♘c6 6. a3 ♗e7 7. ♗f4!** [7…♘×d4?! 8. ♗b5+!
♘c6 9. ♘×d5 ♗d6 10. ♕e2+ ♘ge7 11. ♖d1 ♗d7
12. ♗×c6 ♗×c6 13. ♘×c7+!+−] **7…a6!** [7…♗e6
8. ♘f3 ♘f6 (8…♗g4 9. h3! ♗h5 10. ♘b5!♖c8
♗f5!+−) 9. ♘b5! ♖c8 10. ♘e5! ♘×e5 11. d×e5…
12. ♘×a7] **8. ♘f3!**

```
\usepackage{texmate}
\setchessfontfamily{leipzig}
French Defense analysis:\\
| e4 e6 ; d4 d5 ; Nc3 Bd4 ; exd5 exd5 ;
Bd3 Nc6 ; a3 Be7 ; Bf4! [ \ahead Nxd4?! ;
Bb5+! Nc6 ; Nxd5 Bd6 ; Qe2+ Nge7 ;
Rd1 Bd7 ; Bxc6 Bxc6 ; Nxc7+!\wdecisive ]
a6! [ Be6 ; Nf3 Nf6 [ Bg4 ; h3! Bh5 ; Nb5!
Rc8 ; Bf5!\wdecisive] ; Nb5! Rc8 ;
Ne5! Nxe5 ; dxe5 \dummy\,\dots Nxa7 ] Nf3! |
```

> Example
> 10-1-19

If there are multiple variations to discuss as alternatives at a certain point in the game,
you can use the `variations` environment or its starred form.

> \begin{variations}\var *variation*₁ \var *variation*₂ … \end{variations}

Inside the `variations` environment, each variation is introduced with a \var command.
This will typeset the first move of a variation in boldface and separate variations by a semi-
colon. Alternatively, you can use \var*, in which case no special formatting is applied. The
starred form `variations*` of the environment is equivalent to using \var* for all varia-
tions.

Mate in 3 moves by Bayersdorfer, 1888

   1. ♘d3!△2. ♕a8+ ♕d4 3. ♕a4# [**1…♘d4**
2. ♘c5+ ♔e5 (2…♔f4 3. ♕b8#) 3. ♕b8# ;
1…c×d2 2. ♘f5! △♕×e6# ♕d5 (2…♔×f5
3. ♕g6#) 3. ♕a8#]

```
\usepackage{texmate}
\setchessfontfamily{leipzig}

\position{4Q3/4N3/4np1K/8/4kNp1/1Pp5/3PP1b1/8}
\shortstack{\showboard\\
   Mate in 3 moves by Bayersdorfer, 1888}

| Nd3! \Threat<\withidea Qa8+ Kd4 Qa4 \#>
  [\ahead\begin{variations}
     \var  Nd4 Nc5+ Ke5 [Kf4 Qb8 \#] Qb8 \#
     \var cxd2 Nf5! \threat<Qxe6 \#>
        Kd5 [Kxf5 Qg6 \#] Qa8 \#
  \end{variations}] |
```

> Example
> 10-1-20

How the variations are formatted within the paragraph depends on whether the environment is used within `[` or `\[`. In short commentaries the variations are typeset inline, but within `\[` they are formatted as `itemize` environments. The environment can be nested and its formatting can be changed by using a `\VariationsEnvironment` as shown in the next example. Here we make use of the extended capabilities of the **paralist** package by specifying the format of items for the list.

Main variations in the Orang-Utang opening:

1. b4

a) 1...c6 2. ♘b2 ♛b6

b) 1...d5 2. ♘b2 ♛d6

c) 1...d5 2. ♘b2 ♘f6 3. g3

d) 1...d5 2. ♘b2 ♘f6 3. e3

e) 1...e5 2. a3

f) 1...d5 2. ♘b2 f6

g) 1...d5 2. ♘b2 ♘×b4 3. ♘×e5 ♘f6

```
\usepackage{texmate,paralist}
\setchessfontfamily{condal}
\VariationsEnvironment
    {\begin{enumerate}[a)]}{\end{enumerate}}
Main variations in the Orang-Utang opening:\\
| b4 \[ \ahead \begin{variations}
\var c6 ; Bb2 Qb6
\var d5 ; Bb2 Qd6
\var d5 ; Bb2 Nf6 ; g3
\var d5 ; Bb2 Nf6 ; e3
\var e5 ; a3
\var d5 ; Bb2 f6
\var d5 ; Bb2 Bxb4 ; Bxe5 Nf6
\end{variations} \] |
```

Example
10-1-21

Starting and ending a game

To start a new game in your document, you can use `\newgame`, as known from **skak**. As an alternative, **texmate** offers `\makegametitle`, which both initializes the board and typesets a title from previously specified information. This data is entered using the following commands (each taking one argument): `\whitename`, `\blackname`, `\chessevent`, `\ECO`, `\chessopening`, `\welo`, and `\belo`. If you document more than one game, you need to update this information (if necessary using an empty argument); otherwise, it will be carried forward from game to game.

To record the outcome of the game, you can place `\resigns` after the last move. This will show "0:1" or "1:0" depending on which player resigns (i.e., does not move).

☐ **Paul Morphy**	Paris 1858
■ **Duke Karl & Count Isouard**	

1. e4 e5 2. ♘f3 d6 3. d4 ♝g4 4. d×e5 ♝×f3 ♛×f3 5. d×e5 ♝c4 6. ♘f6 ♛b3 7. ♛e7 ♘c3c6 8. ♝g5 b5 9. ♘×b5 c×b5 10. ♝×b5+ ♘bd70-0-0 11. ♜d8 ♜×d7 12. ♜×d7 ♜d1 13. ♛e6♝×d7+ ♘×d7 14. ♛b8+ ♘×b8 15. ♜d8#

1 : 0

```
\usepackage{texmate}
\setchessfontfamily{condal}
\whitename{Paul Morphy}
\blackname{Duke Karl \& Count Isouard}
\chessevent{Paris 1858}

\makegametitle
|e4 e5 Nf3 d6 d4 Bg4 dxe5 Bxf3
Qxf3 dxe5 Bc4 Nf6 Qb3 Qe7 Nc3
c6 Bg5 b5 Nxb5 cxb5 Bxb5+ Nbd7
0-0-0 Rd8 Rxd7 Rxd7 Rd1 Qe6
Bxd7+ Nxd7 Qb8+ Nxb8 Rd8\# \resigns|
```

Example
10-1-22

Setting up position

As texmate loads skak, it should, in principle, be possible to directly use skak's \fenboard command to set up the board position. However, in that case texmate's mechanism for typesetting moves wouldn't know the current move number or who is next to play. For this reason texmate has its own implementation of \fenboard. It also offers a second command to set up the board in situations where detailed status information is not needed.

\fenboard{*FEN-notation*}   \position[*next*]{*board-setup*}

The \fenboard command expects a complete *FEN-notation*, analyzes that input to enable texmate's mechanisms, and then passes the data to skak to update the board position.

If it doesn't matter who can castle, where, etc. you can use the simpler \position command instead. This command also expects the *board-setup* in FEN notation, but to simplify the input you can leave out information on empty squares on the right of each line. The position can then be visualized with \showboard as usual. If moves following the position setup should be typeset, you need to inform texmate who is *next* by also specifying in the optional argument something like "b 9" (i.e., the color of the next player and the move number).

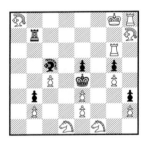

Solution to Example 10-1-9

```
\usepackage{texmate}
\setchessfontfamily{condal}
\position[w 1]{B5KR/1r5B/6R/%
              2b1p1p/2P1k1P/%
              1p2P2p/1P2P2P/3N1N}

\begin{center}
  \shortstack{\showboard \\[5pt]
     Solution to Example 10-1-9}
\end{center}
```

1. ♖**6c** [any other move results in immediate checkmate] **1...**♖×**7h**

```
| R6c [| any other move results
  in immediate checkmate |] Rx7h |
```

Example
10-1-23

There also exists a command called \diagram, which is a shorthand for \position followed by \showboard. It accepts the same arguments as \position.

Typesetting diagrams

As mentioned earlier, texmate uses the skak package to keep track of the position on the board. Thus, to typeset a diagram of the current situation on the board, \showboard or any other of the skak commands can be used. In addition, texmate offers commands to save the status for typesetting at a later stage (e.g., several diagrams in a float).

\toD{*move*} \toD*{*move*}	\preparediagram{*header*}{*footer*}
\makediagrams[*diagrams-to-print*]	\diagramcache{*diagrams-in-memory*}

The command \toD indicates that the status at this point will be shown in a diagram and then saves the board state in memory. It takes one argument which will be printed below[1] the board; normally it contains the last *move* made. In the game, this command typesets the content of \diagramsign (default "*(D)*"). The starred form \toD* has the same behavior but omits typesetting \diagramsign.

Another way to save the current state in memory is to call \preparediagram at the appropriate point. The difference between this approach and the use of \toD* is that the *header* and *footer* of the diagram are explicitly given as arguments and not automatically constructed from game data.

Diagrams saved in this way are eventually typeset by issuing \makediagrams. If the optional argument is given, only the first *diagrams-to-print* are typeset. Diagrams printed will be erased from memory so that you can print all diagrams held in memory by repeatedly calling \makediagrams with suitable values for its optional argument. By default, three diagrams can be held in memory. If this is not enough, issue a \diagramcache declaration in the preamble to specify the maximum *diagrams-in-memory* you need. The \makediagrams command is best used in a paragraph by its own or in a figure environment.

Larsen – Spassky, Belgrade 1970:
1. b3 e5 2. ♘b2 ♘c6 3. c4 ♘f6 4. ♘f3 e4 5. ♘d4 ♘c5 6. ♘×c6 d×c6! 7. e3 ♘f5 8. ♕c2 ♕e7 9. ♘e2 0–0–0 10. f4? *(D)* **♘g4! 11. g3 h5! 12. h3 h4!! 13. h×g4 h×g3 14. ♖g1** *(D)* **♖h1!!! 15. ♖×h1 g2 16. ♖f1 ♕h4+ 17. ♔d1 g×f1=D+** and White resigns.

```
\usepackage{texmate}
\setchessfontfamily{condal}
\tinyboard

  Larsen -- Spassky, Belgrade 1970: \\
| b3 e5 ; Bb2 Nc6 ; c4 Nf6 ; Nf3 e4 ;
  Nd4 Bc5 ; Nxc6 dxc6! ; e3 Bf5 ;
  Qc2 Qe7 ; Be2 0-0-0 ;
  f4? \toD{f4?} Ng4! ;
  g3 h5! ; h3 h4!! ; hxg4 hxg3 ;
  Rg1 \toD{Rg1} Rh1!!! ; Rxh1 g2 ;
  Rf1 Qh4+ ; Kd1 gxf1=D+ |
and White resigns.

\medskip \makediagrams
```

10. f4?   14. ♖g1

\nextdiagramtop{*text*}	\nextdiagrambottom{*text*}	\bname \wname

Instead of using \preparediagram to control the header and footer of the diagram, you can explicitly specify either of them for use with the next \toD or \toD* command. For this purpose, the commands \nextdiagramtop and \nextdiagrambottom are provided. These declarations have to be made outside of chess mode. Within their argument, you can

---

[1] This is customizable, as explained later on.

make good use of \bname and \wname, which hold the players' names as given in the title specification.

1. e4 e5 2. ♘f3 ♘c6 3. ♗c4 ♗c5 4. d3 ♘f6 5. ♗g5?! [5. ♘c3] **5...d6 6. 0–0?! h6 7. ♗h4**

Player X – Player Y

Position after
5. ♗g5

```
\usepackage{texmate}
\tinyboard
\nextdiagramtop{Player X -- Player Y}
\nextdiagrambottom{Position after}
| e4 e5 Nf3 Nc6 Bc4 Bc5 d3 Nf6 Bg5?!
\toD*{Bg5} [Nc3] d6 0-0?! h6 Bh4|

\medskip
\makediagrams
```

Example
10-1-25

Adjusting the layout

… of diagrams

The look and feel of the diagrams can be customized in a number of ways. By default, players' names are shown (black above, white below). The command \topdiagramnames places both names above, \bottomdiagramnames places them below, and \nodiagramnames omits them altogether. With \diagramnumber, the diagrams get numbers on top; the default (\nodiagramnumber) is to omit them. The last move is normally shown at the bottom (\diagrammove), but issuing \nodiagrammove will prevent its display. To indicate who is next to play, issue \leftdiagramturn or \rightdiagramturn. The default (\nodiagramturn) is to omit this information. The command \makediagramsfont holds the font setting used for the text around the diagram; it defaults to \small.

Diagrams that belong to a commentary—i.e., those saved within [and] or \[and \]—show the text stored in \analysistop (the default is "Analysis") on top and the last move at the bottom.

… of moves

The output formatting can be tailored by redefining one or more commands: \beforeno specifies the punctuation before the move number (default empty) and \afterno the one after the number (default .~). The command \afterw specifies the material between white's and black's moves (default \␣) and \afterb holds the material to place between complete moves (default \␣). The command \beforeb is placed before black's move when resuming the move after discussing a variation (default \the\move\dots).

Some variants of the Italian game (Greco attack): **1 e4 e5; 2 ♘f3 ♘c6; 3 ♗c4 ♗c5** [Hungarian defence 3...♗e7; 4 d4] **4 c3** [Canal variation 4 d3 ♘f6; 5 ♘c3 d6; 6 ♗g5 (6 ♗e3)] **4...♘f6; 5 d4 e×d4; 6 c×d4 ♗b4+; 7 ♘c3**

```
\usepackage{texmate}
\renewcommand\afterno{\,} % only small space
\renewcommand\afterb{; }  % semicolon + space
Some variants of the Italian game (Greco attack):
|e4 e5 ; Nf3 Nc6 ; Bc4
 Bc5 [|Hungarian defence |Be7 d4] ;
  c3 [|Canal variation |d3 Nf6 Nc3 d6 Bg5 [Be3]]
 Nf6 ; d4 exd4 ; cxd4 Bb4+ ; Nc3|
```

Example
10-1-26

The fonts used for the main game (level 1) and the three levels of commentaries can be adjusted by redefining the commands \ifont to \ivfont corresponding to the four levels. Similarly, there are a number of commands to produce the punctuation around the variant levels. For example, the default definitions for level 2 (first-order variants) are

... of fonts and of opening and closing punctuations

```
\newcommand\iiopen{[}   \newcommand\iiclose{\leavevmode\unskip]}
```

Note the use of \leavevmode\unskip to remove any preceding space on the line before typesetting the closing bracket. By redefining these commands other conventions can be implemented.

Some variants of the Italian game (Greco attack): **1. e4 e5 2. ♘f3 ♘c6 3. ♗c4 ♗c5** (Hungarian defence 3...♗e7 4. d4) **4. c3** (Canal variation 4. d3 ♘f6 5. ♘c3 d6 6. ♗g5 *6. ♗e3*) **4...♘f6 5. d4 e×d4 6. c×d4 ♗b4+ 7. ♘c3**

```
\usepackage{texmate}
\renewcommand\iiopen{(}
\renewcommand\iiclose{\leavevmode\unskip)}
\renewcommand\iiiopen{}   \renewcommand\iiiclose{}
\renewcommand\iiifont{\itshape}
Some variants of the Italian game (Greco attack):
|e4 e5 ; Nf3 Nc6 ; Bc4
 Bc5 [|Hungarian defence |Be7 d4] ;
 c3 [|Canal variation |d3 Nf6 Nc3 d6 Bg5 [Be3]]
 Nf6 ; d4 exd4 ; cxd4 Bb4+ ; Nc3|
```

Example
10-1-27

10.1.5 Online resources for chess

There are several chess-related databases containing complete games, such as ChessBase and NicBase. Information about these formats can be found on CTAN in support/ chesstools. That directory also contains some **Pascal** programs by Jürgen Lamers that can convert these formats to LaTeX. As the programs are quite old, they are intended to work with the **chess** package notation. They can, however, generate "short" notation that should be processable by **texmate** with little or no correction. These programs, together with some example databases, are available as binaries and source files on CTAN in support/chesstools.

Besides the material available on CTAN, there are a number of online resources for chess that contain free material (e.g., news items, theory discussions, fonts, games). An important source for news and games is http://www.chesscenter.com/twic/ twic.html. The site http://www.enpassant.dk/chess/homeeng.htm covers material for chess publishing, including the fonts used in this chapter. At http://pgn2ltx. sourceforge.net/ you will find the **pgn2ltx** program by Dirk Bächle to convert PGN into LaTeX. A free chess database with export to LaTeX is **scid**, see http://scid.sourceforge. net/. Its potential successor can be found at http://sourceforge.net/projects/ chessx/.

10.2 Xiangqi—Chinese chess

The Chinese chess game, xiangqi, has the same roots as the European chess game but shows extensive differences. For example, the two armies are separated by a river that some pieces cannot cross. Also interesting is the fact that the two armies have different pieces: the white

Table 10.2: Coding for xiangqi pieces in the cchess46 font

White		Black		Alternate Black		Common Names
k	帥	K	將	S	將	King, General
g	仕	G	士	T	士	Guard, Assistant
b	相	B	象	U	象	Bishop, Elephant
n	馬	N	馬	V	馬	Knight, Horse
r	車	R	車	W	車	Rook, Chariot, Car
c	炮	C	炮	X	炮	Cannon, Gun, Gunner
p	兵	P	卒	Y	卒	Pawn, Foot-soldier

Example
10-2-1

elephants are replaced by ministers on the opposite side; and while the white general is accompanied by advisors, the black commander has officers at his side. In European versions of this game in which the Chinese characters are replaced by pictograms, these differences are often ignored.

Jacques Richer[1] has written METAFONT code for the Chinese chess pieces that produces stones with traditional Chinese characters (shown in Table 10.2). This font, cchess46, has a set of black and white stones (uppercase letters denote black, lowercase denote white). The letters chosen correspond to the common names for comparable pieces of European chess; e.g., the general is accessible as the letter "k" for king. In addition, the font contains a third set of stones: an alternate set for black in which the characters also have a white background. This third set is useful in producing colored game diagrams—traditionally all stones are white with green and red characters.

The distribution originally did not offer a package with environments and commands to typeset games. But it did contain a LaTeX document called cchessboard.tex to produce a board with the stones in their initial positions, as shown in Figure 10.1 (except that we used the alternate set of stones for the black player).

Rearranging the code in this document, Frank Mittelbach produced a small package called cchess that displays arbitrary positions with the help of a position environment and the commands \piece and \textpiece.

\textpiece{*name*}

Within running text, the command \textpiece can be used. Possible values for *name* are the characters shown in Table 10.2. With this and, for example, the tabbing environment, one can easily document and annotate games.

---

[1]While we were preparing to go to press with this book, Stephan Weinhold announced that he is working on his xq package for typesetting xiangqi games. It contains METAFONT code for drawing the chess pieces as well as a support package called xq.sty.

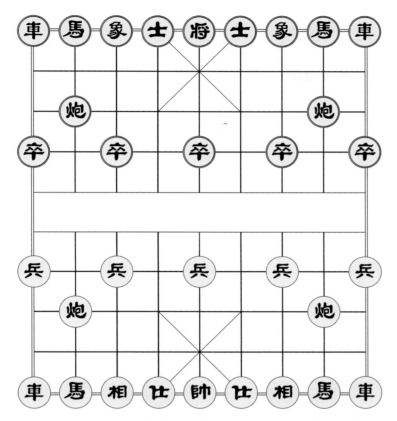

Figure 10.1: Initial setup of Chinese chess game (xiangqi)

The following listing, a mate situation after four moves, gives an example of the use of this command. The board situation after these four moves is shown in Example 10-2-4 on the following page.

```
\usepackage{cchess}
\newcommand\x{$\times$} % a shortcut to denote capture
\begin{tabbing}
1. \= \textpiece{c}h3--e3 \qquad
                        \=\textpiece{N}b0--a8 \\
2. \> \textpiece{c}e3\x e7 \>\textpiece{R}a0--a9 \\
3. \> \textpiece{c}b3--b5  \>\textpiece{N}h0--g8 \\
4. \> \textpiece{c}b5--e5 mates!
\end{tabbing}
```

1.　炮　h3–e3　　　馬　b0–a8

2.　炮　e3×e7　　　車　a0–a9

3.　炮　b3–b5　　　馬　h0–g8

4.　炮　b5–e5 mates!

The position environment draws a complete board. Within its body, the \piece command is used to place the individual pieces.

> \piece{*file*}{*rank*}{*name*}

The \piece command places a piece *name* at a certain file and rank (the horizontal and vertical position). The *file* argument can take a letter in the range from a to i (left to right), while the *rank* is specified by a number between 1 and 10 (bottom to top).

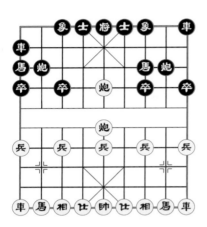

```
\usepackage{cchess}
\smallboard
\begin{position}
\piece{a}{1}{r}\piece{i}{1}{r}
\piece{b}{1}{n}\piece{h}{1}{n}
\piece{c}{1}{b}\piece{g}{1}{b}
\piece{d}{1}{g}\piece{f}{1}{g}
\piece{e}{5}{c}\piece{e}{7}{c}
\piece{a}{4}{p}\piece{c}{4}{p}
\piece{e}{4}{p}\piece{g}{4}{p}
\piece{i}{4}{p}\piece{e}{1}{k}
\piece{a}{9}{R}\piece{i}{10}{R}
\piece{a}{8}{N}\piece{g}{8}{N}
\piece{c}{10}{B}\piece{g}{10}{B}
\piece{d}{10}{G}\piece{f}{10}{G}
\piece{b}{8}{C}\piece{h}{8}{C}
\piece{a}{7}{P}\piece{c}{7}{P}
\piece{g}{7}{P}
\piece{i}{7}{P}\piece{e}{10}{K}
\end{position}
```

Example 10-2-4

In addition, the package offers the commands \largeboard, \normalboard, and \smallboard that specify the size of the board and pieces. Figure 10.1 on the previous page shows a normal-size board, whereas Example 10-2-4 uses \smallboard.

In the current implementation the cchess package uses \special commands for Post-Script drivers to place the pieces on the board without reconstructing the picture. But this is not the only way to program this behavior, as we will see in Section 10.3. Perhaps the future will bring us a new and extended implementation of this package that includes concepts used in the chess package to allow documenting of tournaments, annotated games, and analysis of this interesting Eastern game.

10.3 Go

Go, which is perhaps the most popular Asian game, is played by two players using black and white stones on the intersections of a 19×19 grid. Stones, after being placed, are never moved unless they are captured, so in documenting the course of a game you usually show a board with numbered stones. If more than one diagram is used to document a game, stones from earlier diagrams (i.e., stones placed in earlier parts of the game) are typically shown without numbers. An algebraic notation such as we saw for chess is normally not used.

In 1991, Hanna Kołodziejska developed a number of fonts and an accompanying pack- *Early attempts*
age go to typeset Go diagrams and document full or partial games. The fonts available in
the three sizes 10pt, 15pt, and 20pt contain numbered stones in the range 1–252, as well
as unnumbered stones, various symbols, and intersection and border lines to produce a display of the board. In addition, a font with a single character shows the traditional symbol for
the Go game.

```
\newfont\gosign{gosign50}
\begin{center}
  \fbox{\gosign\symbol{0}}
\end{center}
```

Example
10-3-1

In principle, more than 250 stones might potentially be used in a game, in which case
it could not be represented in a single diagram with the currently available fonts. However, since for readability it is usually best to put no more than 100 moves on a single diagram (and then restart the numbering), this theoretical limitation is not that important in
practice.

In 2001, Victor Bos developed the package psgo, which works on top of PSTricks instead
of deploying its own fonts. Compared to go, it uses a different, but similarly verbose input
syntax and offers a few additional possibilities for marking stones.

These early Go packages used a very verbose input syntax, which—while fairly *A newer package*
consistent—is somewhat painful to enter manually. In addition, at least the go package had
a number of technical problems and limitations, as it redefined commands already existing
in LaTeX, thus conflicting with other packages. To improve that situation, in 2003 Étienne
Dupuis developed the package igo, which built upon the existing fonts (with slight updates)
but provided a radically changed user interface with additional features. The remainder of
this section describes the igo package.

Like the chess package, igo has commands for board initialization, placement of stones
(which in this case are equivalent to moves), and display of the board or parts of the board.
The actual syntax, however, is quite different.

To place stones on the board, each line intersection is identified by a column label (a
lowercase letter in the set a, b, c, d, e, f, g, h, j, k, l, m, n, o, p, q, r, s, t, note the absence of
i!) and a row number (in the range 1–19), with the lower-left corner of the board being the
starting point. Stones are then added using the \black and \white commands.

\black[*mark*]{*intersection-list*}   \white[*mark*]{*intersection-list*}

The commands \black and \white add stones at each intersection point specified in
the comma-separated *intersection-list*. This list should contain no spaces and no trailing
comma; a single intersection point can also be used.

If the optional *mark* argument is a positive number or the command \igonone, then
all stones in the *intersection-list* will receive alternate colors and the command name simply

indicates the color of the first stone being placed. This method is most suitable to record games or longer sequences where the order of play needs to be indicated.

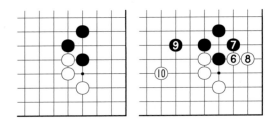

```
\usepackage{igo}
\white[\igonone]{q3,q5,p5,p6,p4,q7}
\showgoban[m1,t8]
\white[6]{r5,r6,s5,n6,m4}
\showgoban
```

Example
10-3-2

If \white or \black is used without an optional argument or if the optional argument is \igotriangle, \igosquare, \igocircle, or \igocross, then all stones typeset are of the same color and decorated with the respective glyph as specified by the optional argument. This input method is most suitable for documenting Go problems, where the order of stones placed previously is unimportant.

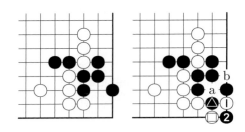

```
\usepackage{igo}
\white{o3,q2,q3,q4,r2,r5,r6,r7}
\black{p5,q5,r3,r4,s4,s5,t3}
\showgoban
\black[\igotriangle]{s2}
\white[\igosquare]{s1}
\gobansymbol{s3}{a}\gobansymbol{t4}{b}
\white[1]{t2,t1}
\showgoban
```

Example
10-3-3

```
\cleargobansymbols
```

Once the progress in a game has been shown in a diagram, it is customary to show the already placed stones in later diagrams without numbers, achieved by issuing a \cleargobansymbols command. This helps in identifying newly placed stones and makes the diagrams more readable. Whether numbering is continued is a matter of taste. Although igo supports sequentially numbered stones for a full game, for readability it is usually better to restart numbering when three-digit numbers are reached and you can afford to typeset more than a single diagram.

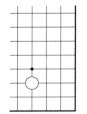
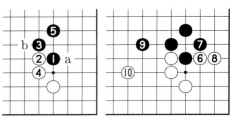

```
\usepackage{igo}
\white{q3}
\showgoban[p1,t8]
\black[1]{q5,p5,p6,p4,q7}
\gobansymbol{r5}{a}\gobansymbol{o6}{b}
\showgoban[n1,t8]\cleargobansymbols
\white[6]{r5,r6,s5,n6,m4}
\showgoban
```

Example
10-3-4

\gobansymbol{*intersection-point*}{*symbol*}

The previous examples showed the use of \gobansymbol to mark certain free intersection points with labels. Currently available are lowercase and uppercase letters (typically used for showing alternative moves when discussing problems or games) and digits (used to indicate points of various strength in teaching moves). Note that the second argument can receive only a single glyph.

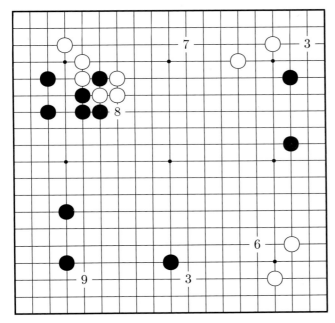

```
\usepackage{igo}
\igofontsize{12}

\black{d4,d7,k4,r11,r15,c13,%
       c15,e13,e14,f13,f15}
\white{q3,r5,d17,e15,e16,%
       f14,g14,g15,q17,o16}
\gobansymbol{e3}{9}
\gobansymbol{l3}{3}
\gobansymbol{p5}{6}
\gobansymbol{g13}{8}
\gobansymbol{l17}{7}
\gobansymbol{s17}{3}
\shortstack{\showfullgoban\\
           Best moves for Black}
```

Best moves for Black

Example
10-3-5

\gobansize{*number*}   \showfullgoban   \showgoban[*intersection-pair*]

The board onto which Go is played is called a goban; hence the command to display it is called \showgoban. Although the standard size is 19×19, smaller sizes (e.g., 13×13) are also common.

The igo package supports goban sizes up to 50×50 (by using capital letters for columns 26 to 50). The board size can be specified through \gobansize (default 19). While \showfullgoban displays the entire board, \showgoban presents only the part that has stones placed, to conserve space. More precisely, by default \showgoban displays one row/ column free of stones in each direction, unless that brings you too close to edge of the board. In the latter case the row/column at the edge of the board is also shown. If this doesn't give the appropriate results, it is possible to specify the part to display manually through an *intersection-pair* that marks the lower-left and upper-right corners of the display. For example, if we are interested only in the situation in the upper-left corner of the board shown in Example 10-3-5 on the preceding page, we can specify a12,h19. Note that stones or symbols placed outside the visible area are ignored and that hoshi points (the specially marked intersections where handicap stones can be placed) are shown only for standard goban sizes 9×9, 13×13, and 19×19.

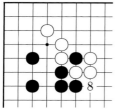

Upper left corner

```
\usepackage{igo}
\black{d4,d7,k4,r11,r15,c13,c15,e13,e14,f13,f15}
\white{q3,r5,d17,e15,e16,f14,g14,g15,q17,o16}
\gobansymbol{e3}{9}   \gobansymbol{l13}{3}
\gobansymbol{p5}{6}   \gobansymbol{g13}{8}
\gobansymbol{l17}{7} \gobansymbol{s17}{3}
\shortstack{\showgoban[a12,h19]\\[3pt]
           Upper left corner}
```

Example
10-3-6

Each diagram is internally ended by calling \igobreakafterdiagram, which does nothing by default. If desired, this command can be redefined to execute code (e.g., a line break) after each diagram. If the diagrams need a local caption, a simple way to produce them is to use \shortstack as shown in Example 10-3-6.

\igofontsize{*number*}   \smallgoban   \normalgoban   \largegoban

---

The goban can be presented in different sizes. Available font sizes are 5, 6, 7, 8, 9, 10, 11, 12, 15, and 20 points that can be given as a *number* to \igofontsize. Predefined commands include \smallgoban (10 points, the default), \normalgoban (15 points), and \largegoban (20 points).

\cleargoban[*intersection-pair*]   \clear{*intersection-list*}

Once a game or a problem (and perhaps its solution) has been presented, the goban needs to be cleared to allow new stones to be placed onto it. This is achieved by calling \cleargoban. Without the optional argument, the whole board is cleared; if an *intersection-pair* is specified, the rectangle spanned by it is cleared. Alternatively, it is possible to remove a certain set of stones by specifying their positions in the *intersection-list* given to the \clear command. This is sometimes useful when presenting problems with alternative solutions, shown one after another. You can also record a certain state in the game by making use of the copying features of the igo package.

\copytogoban{*number*}   \copyfromgoban{*number*}   \usegoban{*number*}

The igo package supports several gobans in parallel: the user can copy the goban state from one goban to another or change the currently active goban. This is useful for recording certain states in a game—e.g., to discuss a possible variation before returning to main game. Internally these gobans are numbered with the one active at the start of the package being labeled as 1. To copy the current goban state to another goban numbered *number*, use

\copytogoban. To copy a saved goban back into the current one, use \copyfromgoban.
Alternatively, you can change the current goban by using \usegoban.

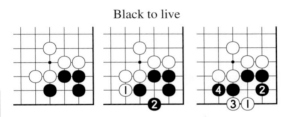

Example
10-3-7

```
\usepackage{igo}

\white{c4,e3}\black[1]{b4,c5,c3,d3,c2}
\showgoban \cleargobansymbols
\copytogoban{2}
\white[1]{d2,b2}
\showgoban \copyfromgoban{2}
\white[1]{b5,a3}
\showgoban
```

\rotategoban	\rotategobanleft	\rotategobanright
\hflipgoban	\vflipgoban	\mirrorgoban

The igo package offers commands to perform certain geometric transformations, such as
rotating the goban. In the next example, the problem was set up using the lower-left corner
and then flipped over to the right corner before displaying the board. Here the two possible
solutions were produced by backing up with the \clear command.

Black to live

Example
10-3-8

```
\usepackage{igo}

\shortstack{Black to live\\[4pt]
\black{b2,b3,c3,d2}\white{b4,c4,d5,d3,e3}
\hflipgoban \showgoban
\white[1]{p2,r1}
\showgoban \clear{p2,r1}
\white[1]{r1,s2,q1,p2}
\showgoban}
```

\whitestone[*mark*]	\blackstone[*mark*]

The commands \whitestone and \blackstone are available for typesetting individual
stones in running text—for example, in commentaries. They obey font size changes, so their
use in headings or footnotes is possible. Being fragile, they need \protection in moving
arguments.

Example
10-3-9

Unnumbered stones are typeset as ○
and ●; numbered stones as ⑯ and ⑧⑦
and special symbols as △, ◙, ◎, and
⊗. All are obeying font size changes: ⊗ ⑫③.

```
\usepackage{igo}

Unnumbered stones are typeset as \whitestone{} and
\blackstone{}; numbered stones as \whitestone[16] and
\blackstone[87] and special symbols as
\whitestone[\igotriangle], \blackstone[\igosquare],
\whitestone[\igocircle], and \blackstone[\igocross].
\footnotesize All are obeying font size changes:
\blackstone[\igocross] \whitestone[123].
```

10.4 Backgammon

Jörg Richter's package **bg** defines two LaTeX environments, `position` and `game`, to display backgammon games. The `position` environment draws a single board and is thus convenient for discussing a problem, while with the `game` environment you can enter each move individually. In the latter case the board positions are stored internally, allowing the "current" status to be drawn at any time.

By convention, the homes of both players are on the left-hand side, with white's home at the top and black's home at the bottom. Unlike in the other packages discussed so far, positions on the board are not denoted with absolute coordinates but rather are numbered as viewed by the party whose move is being placed (e.g., white's 24 corresponds to black's 1, and so on). Moves are always performed from high to low numbers, and the cube is always on the right-hand side of the board.

`\begin{position}...\end{position}`

The `position` environment initializes an empty board into which stones are placed by the commands described below. Some of these commands also allow you to customize some aspects of the board's layout. The board is printed when the `\end{position}` command is encountered. Example 10-4-1 shows the use of various commands of the `position` environment.

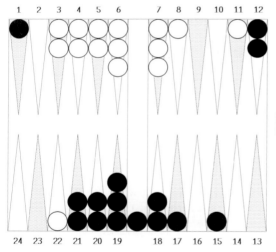

White to play 3–2

```
\usepackage{bg}
\begin{position}
\normalboard
\whitepoint{3}{2}    \whitepoint{4}{2}
\whitepoint{5}{2}    \whitepoint{6}{3}
\whitepoint{7}{3}    \whitepoint{8}{1}
\whitepoint{11}{1}   \whitepoint{22}{1}
\blackpoint{24}{1}   \blackpoint{13}{2}
\blackpoint{10}{1}   \blackpoint{8}{1}
\blackpoint{7}{2}    \blackpoint{6}{3}
\blackpoint{5}{2}    \blackpoint{4}{2}
\blackbar{1}
\shownumbers \middlecube{1} \showcube
\whiteonmove
\boardcaption{White to play 3--2}
\end{position}
```

Example 10-4-1

`\blackpoint{`*p*`}{`*n*`}`   `\whitepoint{`*p*`}{`*n*`}`

These two commands are used to place stones on the board; *n* denotes the number of stones to place and *p* denotes the point where they are positioned. It is important to remember that these points are numbered downwards from 24 relative to the home position of each player.

```
\blackbar{n}      \whitebar{n}
```

Captured stones are placed on the middle bar. This is done by using the commands \blackbar and \whitebar, where *n* gives the number of stones to put there.

```
\blackcube{n}     \whitecube{n}      \middlecube{n}
\showcube         \dontshowcube
```

These commands define the position and state of the cube. By default, the cube is in the middle position (i.e., not owned by any player). It can be moved to either side by using \whitecube or \blackcube with *n* as its current number. If \dontshowcube is used, the cube is not displayed.

```
\smallboard           \normalboard          \bigboard
\fullboard            \halfboard
\blackonmove          \whiteonmove
\shownumbers          \dontshownumbers      \togglenumbers
\boardcaption{text}
```

To denote the size of the board, three commands are available; the default is \normalboard. Normally a full board is produced. When discussing problems, however, it is sometimes useful to draw only half of it, which can be achieved using \halfboard. The next player to move can be specified, which changes the numbering of the board. Numbering of the board can be suppressed (\dontshownumbers) or toggled (i.e., shown from the view of the other player). In all cases you can give the board a caption with the \boardcaption command.

```
\begin{game}{Black}{White} ... \end{game}
```

The game environment is used to document the progress of a game. In contrast to the position environment, it is initialized not with an empty board but rather with the stones in their starting positions. Its two arguments can be used to specify information about the two players, such as their names or current scores.

```
\move{die}{moves}
\printboard           \rawboard
```

Moves are entered using the \move command. The values of the *die* are entered as a two-digit number. The *moves* are specified in the form x-y and separated by commas with x and y denoting the start and target points, respectively, and being numbered as viewed by the current player.

All moves are recorded and output is preceded by a small checker of the right color. At any time during the game, the \printboard command shows the current state of the board in a diagram centered with a caption, while \rawboard produces the board encapsulated in an \mbox without a caption—a version that can be used even in the middle of a text line.

> \textmove{*text*}   \takecube

The \textmove command outputs *text* instead of a move and then switches to the opposite player. It can, for example, be used for double/pass actions or in cases where one player is unable to move at all. The \takecube command passes the cube to the opposite player and doubles its value.

The following example documents the first moves in game showing several of the commands discussed above.

• Black   ∘ White

                                 1. ∘ 64 : 24–18, 18–14

1. • 55 : 6–1*, 6–1, 8–3, 8–3
                                 2. ∘ Doubles.

2. • Takes.

```
\usepackage{bg}
\begin{game}{Black}{White}
\smallboard
\whiteonmove
\move{64}{24-18, 18-14}
\move{55}{6-1,6-1,8-3,8-3}
\textmove{Doubles.}
\textmove{Takes.}
\takecube
\boardcaption
    {Black's turn 31}
\printboard
\end{game}
```

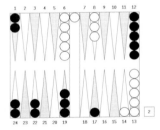

Black's turn 31

Example
10-4-2

> \fullincr   \indentwhite   \showmoves
> \halfincr   \dontindentwhite   \dontshowmoves

The output of the \move commands can be customized in several ways. By default, the move number is incremented after every move; if \halfincr is used, it is updated after every second move. The indentation of the moves by white can be suppressed if desired, and the output is fully suppressed if \dontshowmoves is used.

In addition to these commands, the customization commands of the position environment (e.g., \dontshowcube) are available.

10.5 Card games

The symbols ♣, ♠, ♡, and ♢ are already part of standard (LA)TEX: for some reason Donald Knuth included them into his mathematical fonts and made them accessible via the commands \clubsuit, \spadesuit, \heartsuit, and \diamondsuit. As these commands have long names and are available only in mathematical formulas, using them repeatedly in normal text is rather awkward. In such a case it might be best to define new commands to reduce the amount of typing:

```
\newcommand\club{\ensuremath{\clubsuit}}
\newcommand\diam{\ensuremath{\diamondsuit}}
\newcommand\heart{\ensuremath{\heartsuit}}
\newcommand\spade{\ensuremath{\spadesuit}}
```

These definitions can be used both in formulas and normal text, so \heart␣A produces ♡A. Adding a few more definitions like the ones in Example 10-5-1 enables you to document rules and annotate games for any game that uses standard playing cards.

♠ A
♡ A
◇ A 9
♣ Q

```
% card commands as defined above
\newcommand{\hand}[4]{%
 \begin{minipage}[t]{8em}
 \begin{tabbing}
   \spade{} \= #1\\ \heart \> #2\\
   \diam     \> #3\\ \club  \> #4
 \end{tabbing}
 \end{minipage}}
\hand{A}{A}{A 9}{Q}
```

Example
10-5-1

The above definition shows the cards in the order suitable for poker or bridge games. In other card games, ♣ is usually the highest color, in which case you should modify the definition accordingly.

10.5.1 Bridge

Using the ideas outlined in the previous section, Kees van der Laan developed LaTeX macros and a bidding environment for typesetting annotated bridge games in the fashion often found in bridge literature [124]. In the following sections we show the commands that can be found in the file bridge.tex and develop some additional commands for special situations.

Card deals

The distribution of cards among the players is often shown in bridge literature as a diagram that shows the position and the hand of each player. Players are traditionally designated by the four points of the compass N, E, S, and W in the center of the graphic that symbolizes a play table. Such a graphic can be produced by the \crdima command.

\crdima{*dealer*}{*info*}{*north*}{*west*}{*east*}{*south*}

The first parameter *dealer* provides information about dealer and vulnerability (e.g., N/None for "North" dealer and vulnerability "none"). The second parameter *info* is text describing the game. The final four parameters describe the hands of each player in the order N, W, E, S.[1] Usually they all contain a call to the \hand command, but it is also possible to put other or additional information into them.

Both commands together then produce diagrams like the one in Example 10-5-1—a start situation showing the hands of all players.

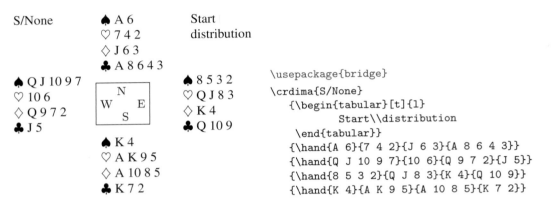

```
\usepackage{bridge}

\crdima{S/None}
   {\begin{tabular}[t]{l}
        Start\\distribution
    \end{tabular}}
   {\hand{A 6}{7 4 2}{J 6 3}{A 8 6 4 3}}
   {\hand{Q J 10 9 7}{10 6}{Q 9 7 2}{J 5}}
   {\hand{8 5 3 2}{Q J 8 3}{K 4}{Q 10 9}}
   {\hand{K 4}{A K 9 5}{A 10 8 5}{K 7 2}}
```

Example 10-5-2

When discussing defense play, two hands—your own and the hand of the dummy—are often shown. This data can be displayed with the \crdima command by using empty arguments for the hands to be omitted. The example below shows an early situation in the game in Example 10-5-1.

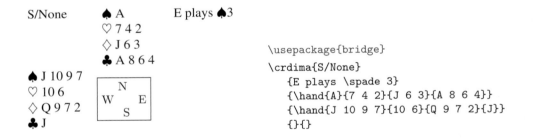

```
\usepackage{bridge}
\crdima{S/None}
   {E plays \spade 3}
   {\hand{A}{7 4 2}{J 6 3}{A 8 6 4}}
   {\hand{J 10 9 7}{10 6}{Q 9 7 2}{J}}
   {}{}
```

Example 10-5-3

An en dash (i.e., -- , which produces –) is customarily used to denote a void. Its use is shown in the next example, which documents the same game after some more cards have been played.

---

[1] In the original article [124], the order is described as clockwise (i.e., N, E, S, W), but the macros as stored on CTAN in the file bridge.tex use a different sequence.

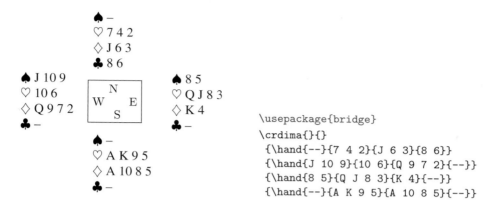

```
\usepackage{bridge}
\crdima{}{}
  {\hand{--}{7 4 2}{J 6 3}{8 6}}
  {\hand{J 10 9}{10 6}{Q 9 7 2}{--}}
  {\hand{8 5}{Q J 8 3}{K 4}{--}}
  {\hand{--}{A K 9 5}{A 10 8 5}{--}}
```

In discussing certain techniques of play, often only the card distribution in a single suit is shown. In that case it would be nice not to use the \hand command in the arguments of \crdima, but unfortunately the result is not quite what we would expect.

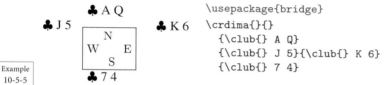

```
\usepackage{bridge}
\crdima{}{}
  {\club{} A Q}
  {\club{} J 5}{\club{} K 6}
  {\club{} 7 4}
```

In this case a solution using the `tabular` environment gives better results. The first argument specifies the suit of interest, and the other arguments correspond to the four players (with the same order as in the \crdima command). Note the use of the \multicolumn command to suppress the vertical lines in the first and last rows.

```
\usepackage{bridge}
\newcommand{\Crdexa}[5]{{\renewcommand\arraystretch{1.2}%
   \begin{tabular}{l|@{}c@{}|l}
     \multicolumn{1}{c}{} & \multicolumn{1}{c}{#1 #2} \\
     \cline{2-2}
                          &    N    &              \\
         #1 #3 &W\hfill\hfill E& #1 #4             \\
                          &    S    &              \\
     \cline{2-2}
     \multicolumn{1}{c}{} & \multicolumn{1}{c}{#1 #5} \\
   \end{tabular}}}
\Crdexa{\club}{A Q}{J 5}{K 6}{7 4}
```

Bidding

An important part of the bridge game is the initial bidding phase, in which the players decide who plays the contract. To document such a bidding sequence, Kees van der Laan introduced a `bidding` environment as an application of LaTeX's standard `tabbing` environment.

West	North	East	South
–	1♣	no	1♠
no	2♠	no	4♠
a.p.			

```
\usepackage{bridge}
\begin{bidding}
-- \> 1\club\> no \> 1\spade  \\
no \> 2\spade\> no \> 4\spade \\
a.p.
\end{bidding}
```

Example
10-5-7

In discussing the theory of bidding, the bridge literature often shows such a bidding sequence together with the hand of one player. This can be achieved as follows:

```
\usepackage{bridge}
\hand{3 2}{K J 10 8 5 2}
     {Q 6 3}{K 3}          \qquad
\begin{minipage}[t]{8em}
\begin{bidding}
-- \> 1\diam\> 1\heart \> no \\
2\heart
\end{bidding}
\end{minipage}
```

♠ 3 2
♡ K J 10 8 5 2
◇ Q 6 3
♣ K 3

West	North	East	South
–	1◇	1♡	no
2♡			

Example
10-5-8

An alternative form in which the bidding of only two partners is shown can be produced by defining a simple command \bid as follows. Here the \hand command shows one hand and the bidding sequence is maintained with a tabular environment, so that this time we must use & characters in the fifth argument.

```
\usepackage{bridge}
\newcommand\bid[5]{\hand{#1}{#2}{#3}{#4}%
       \qquad   \begin{tabular}[t]{ll}%
               self & partner \\ #5%
             \end{tabular}}
\bid{Q J 10 5}{A 10 9 6 3}{A 5 2}{3}
  { & 1\club \\ 1\heart & 1\spade \\  4\spade }
```

♠ Q J 10 5
♡ A 10 9 6 3
◇ A 5 2
♣ 3

self	partner
	1♣
1♡	1♠
4♠	

Example
10-5-9

10.6 Crosswords in various forms

In an article in *TUGboat* [45], Brian Hamilton Kelly introduced a set of LaTeX macros to draw crosswords. His system is conceived so as to ensure that the "grid" comes together correctly. For example, Figure 10.2 on the next page shows a crossword grid[1] to be completed from the clues given (the solution is found in Example 10-6-5 on page 706). To input the crossword, one specifies the clues, their placement, and their solution. The actual grid is then built and

---

[1] We thank Gerd Neugebauer for generating the puzzle from the index of this book. The clues (added by the authors) sometimes deliberately disguise this origin to increase the challenge.

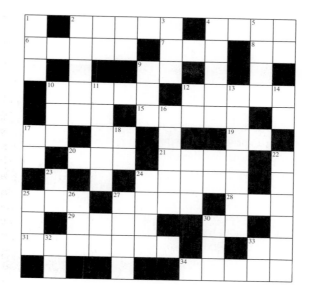

<table>
<tr><td colspan="2">

ACROSS

</td></tr>
</table>

2	Gap between tree node labels and the node in PSTricks (5)
4	Modern replacement for scissors and glue (4)
6	A Unicode TEX variant (5)
7	… you always wanted to know but never dared to ask (3)
8	A graphics key that needs four numbers (2)
10	Called bb in Karl Berry's font-naming schemes (5)
12	A way to make your pages into thumbnails (5)
15	You can do it to a box but it isn't proper LaTeX (5)
19	In LaTeX denotes $\wp$; in other circumstances might mean a word processor (2)
20	Result of a TEX run (3)
21	A language whose name should probably have five letters, but then it was developed for Unix (4)
24	It's not Intel (5)
25	A pointer misspelled (3)
27	Testing your LaTeX knowledge: $\prec$ (4)
28	Label for a signal line (3)
29	Another name for the LaTeX3 project team on c.t.t. (4)
30	One way to get a sharp in MusiXTEX (2)
31	A figure or plan intended to explain rather than represent actual appearance (7)
33	72.27 to an inch (2)
34	see **1d** (5)

DOWN

1 & a34	Grand wizard of TEX (3,5)
2	A ready-to-run TEX for Unix (5)
3	A novice golfer's dream (3)
4	LaTeX 2_ε name for document style (5)
5	Double beam above notes in MusiXTEX (4)
9	Either/or—mathematically speaking (3)
10	German beer (3)
11	Save your coordinates (PSTricks) (5)
12	Approximation of TEX's version number (2)
13	A PostScript operator (7)
14	Probability function (2)
16	A divine messenger misspelled (5)
17	How do you get an Å? (2)
18	ξ (2)
22	LaTeX has rigid and rubber ones (6)
23	Amor uses them and Xy-pic calls them (2)
24	Length of the line segment where the connector joins the first node (4)
25	Files containing LaTeX font-definition documentation (3)
26	η—don't say this is all Greek to you (3)
27	$\perp$, also the first letters of everlasting (4)
30	We plot it in Chapter 4 (3)
32	TEX's name for inch (2)
33	Lula is chief of (2)

Example 10-6-1

Figure 10.2: A sample crossword for you to fill in (done with crosswrd)

verified automatically. For example, the input for the first two clues from Figure 10.2 would be

```
\clue{2}{A}{3}{1}{TNSEP}{Gap between tree node labels and
                        the node in \textsf{PSTricks}}{5}
\clue{1 \& a34}{D}{1}{1}{DON}{Grand wizard of \TeX{}}{3,5}
```

The downside of this approach is that the input source does not show the actual layout of the crossword. To produce one, you have to translate back from a finished puzzle (on paper) into \clue statements like the above.

A different approach has been taken in the cwpuzzle package by Gerd Neugebauer, where the crossword puzzle is graphically represented in the source and the specification of clues is done in a separate step. This package supports classical crossword puzzles, number puzzles, and fill-in puzzles. (In number puzzles, all letters are replaced by numbers and the task is to figure out which number represents which letter; in fill-in puzzles, the list of clues is replaced by a list of all words in the puzzle and the task is to find the correct places for the words). In all cases the puzzle is constructed using the Puzzle environment.

`\begin{Puzzle}{`*columns*`}{`*rows*`}`

The arguments *columns* and *rows* specify the horizontal and vertical numbers of cells, respectively. Each line in the body of the environment describes the contents of the cells in one row. Cells are surrounded by vertical bars and the end of the line is marked with a dot. The contents of a cell can be a *, denoting a black box or a single character, possibly prefixed by a number in brackets, to denote the start of a clue. For number puzzles you would put such a number in each cell; for fill-in puzzles no such numbers are needed. For instance,

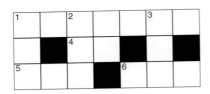

```
\usepackage{cwpuzzle}
\begin{Puzzle}{7}{3}
|[1]T | A |[2]B | U |   L |[3]A | R |.
|   A | * |[4]I | M |   * |   X | * |.
|[5]N | E |   G | * |[6]D |   E | T |.
\end{Puzzle}
```

Example
10-6-2

As a final possibility, you can put {} in a cell, in which case this cell is left completely empty and not even a frame is produced. This lets you produce non-rectangular puzzles or leave space for an ad or a picture in the middle of the puzzle. The latter output is produced using the \Frame command. As the name indicates it produces a frame and typesets material inside.

`\Frame{`*horizontal*`}{`*vertical*`}{`*width*`}{`*height*`}{`*content*`}`

The arguments *horizontal* and *vertical* specify the lower-left corner of the frame and *width* and *height* the extension towards the right and the top—all in units of crossword cells. The *content* can contain any material and is typeset as centered. If it is too large it will overlap with other elements of the puzzle.

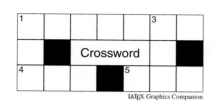

```
\usepackage{cwpuzzle}
\begin{Puzzle}{7}{3}
\Frame{2}{1}{3}{1}{\sffamily Crossword}
|[1]T | A |   B | U |   L |[3]A | R |.
|   A | * |  {} | {} |  {} |   X | * |.
|[4]N | E |   G | * |[5]D |   E | T |.
\put(7,-0.1){\makebox(0,0)[rt]{\tiny
                    \LaTeX{} Graphics Companion}}
\end{Puzzle}
```

As you may have guessed from the preceding description, the grid is internally typeset using a `picture` environment, with (0,0) indicating the lower-left corner and the unit length being the cell width. With a bit of care you can annotate it using standard `picture` commands, which is what we did in the previous example. The `\PuzzleHook` command also comes in handy if such annotations should be used for several crosswords.

Two commands determine how any following puzzles are typeset. The command `\PuzzleUnsolved` (the default) presents the empty grid together with the clues. The command `\PuzzleSolution` shows the puzzle with the words filled in and any clues (if present) suppressed. It takes an optional argument that determines whether clue numbers are shown (value `true`) or suppressed (value `false`, the default) in the filled-out grid. Example 10-6-5 on page 706 shows the result with the value being set to `true`.

10.6.1 Classical puzzles

For a classical crossword puzzle, the **cwpuzzle** package offers the `PuzzleClues` environment to typeset the list of clues. The individual clues are entered in the body using the command `\Clue`, as in the following example:

```
\usepackage{cwpuzzle}
\begin{Puzzle}{7}{3} |[1]T | A |[2]B | U |   L |[3]A | R |.
                     |   A | * |[4]I | M |   * |   X | * |.
                     |[5]N | E |   G | * |[6]D |   E | T |. \end{Puzzle}
\begin{PuzzleClues}{\textbf{Across:}}
  \Clue{1}{TABULAR}{environment to produce tables}  \Clue{4}{IM}{$\Im$}
  \Clue{5}{NEG}{$\neg$}   \Clue{6}{DET}{loglike function}
\end{PuzzleClues}
\begin{PuzzleClues}{\textbf{Down:}}
  \Clue{1}{TAN}{not the pin} \Clue{2}{BIG}{not small} \Clue{3}{AXE}{a British ax}
\end{PuzzleClues}
```

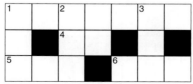

Across: 1 environment to produce tables 4 $\Im$ 5 $\neg$ 6 loglike function   **Down:** 1 not the pin 2 not small 3 a British ax

In contrast to the behavior of the **crosswrd** package, your input is *not* checked for correctness but rather is used only to typeset the clue list—in fact, the second argument of \Clue is currently not used at all. Technically, this means that it is not necessary to use that markup at all. If you do not like the way the clues are presented, you can typeset them manually instead. The only functionality you lose this way is that the clues are no longer suppressed by \PuzzleSolution.

For illustration purposes, the next example was created using **cwpuzzle** syntax (including the clues, which are suppressed by adding \PuzzleSolution), while the earlier presentation of this puzzle was marked up using the **crosswrd** package. The interested reader can compare both approaches on the source level by comparing the example files.

```
\usepackage{cwpuzzle}
\setlength\PuzzleUnitlength{18pt}
\renewcommand\PuzzleNumberFont{\sffamily\tiny}
\renewcommand\PuzzleClueFont{\scriptsize}
\PuzzleSolution[true]
\begin{Puzzle}{12}{12}
|[1] D| *   |[2]T |    N|   S|   E|[3] P| *   |[4] C|    L|[5] I|    P|.
|[6] O|   m|   E |    G|   A| *   |[7] A|    L|   L| *   |[8] B|   B|.
|   N| *   |   T | *   | *   |[9] L|   R| *   |   A| *   |   B| *   |.
| *   |[10]B|   E |[11]M|   B|   O| *   |[12]P|   S|[13]N|   U|[14]P|.
| *   |    I|   X |   S| *   |[15]R|[16]A|   I|   S|   E| *   |   R|.
|[17]A|    T| *   |   A|[18]X| *   |   N| *   | *   |[19]W|   P| *   |.
|   A| *   |[20]D|   V|   I| *   |[21]G|   R|   A|   P| *   |[22]L|.
| *   |[23]A| *   |   E| *   |[24]A|   L|   P|   H|   A| *   |   E|.
... further code omitted ...
```

Example
10-6-5

10.6.2 Fill-in puzzles

Fill-in puzzles are those where all "words" (even if they are not meaningful) are listed without any other clue where to place them. The task is then to determine the right placement through the word length and possible combinations at the intersections. Thus the actual puzzle grid is produced as usual, but without using the optional argument to add clue numbers. The "word" lists are generated by using the `PuzzleWords` environment as often as necessary. It takes one argument that specifies the word length in the current list and in its body the `\Word` command is used to enumerate all words of that length.

```
\usepackage{cwpuzzle}
\begin{minipage}{.38\textwidth}
\begin{Puzzle}{7}{3}
  | T | A | B | U | L | A | R |.
  | A | * | I | M | * | X | * |.
  | N | E | G | * | D | E | T |.
\end{Puzzle}\end{minipage}
\begin{minipage}{.6\textwidth}
\begin{PuzzleWords}{2} \Word{IM} \Word{UM} \end{PuzzleWords}
\begin{PuzzleWords}{3}
   \Word{AXE} \Word{BIG} \Word{DET}
   \Word{NEG} \Word{TAN}
\end{PuzzleWords}
\begin{PuzzleWords}{7}  \Word{TABULAR} \end{PuzzleWords}
\end{minipage}
```

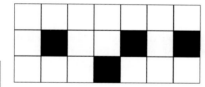

Words of length 2: IM UM
Words of length 3: AXE BIG DET NEG TAN
Words of length 7: TABULAR

To customize the generated text, you can redefine the command `\PuzzleWordsText`. It takes one argument, which receives the current word length (i.e., the argument given to the `PuzzleWords` environment). For example, a typical redefinition for the German language could look as follows:

```
\renewcommand\PuzzleWordsText[1]{W\"orter der L\"ange #1: }
```

10.6.3 Number puzzles

Number puzzles are crosswords in which each square is labeled with a number, and the task is to determine which number represents which letter. Again the puzzle grid is created using the `Puzzle` environment, this time using the bracket syntax all over the place to add the numbers.

In addition, the `\PuzzleLetters` declaration shows the list of all *letters* appearing in the puzzle (preferably in alphabetic order), while `\PuzzleNumbers` produces a list of boxes so that the reader can fill in the solution. The text generated by `\PuzzleLetters` can be customized by redefining `\PuzzleLettersText` as indicated.

```
\usepackage{cwpuzzle}
\begin{minipage}{.38\textwidth}
\begin{Puzzle}{7}{3}
  |[1]T | [2]A |[3]B | [4]U |[5]L |[2]A  |[6]R |.
  |[2]A |  *   |[7]I | [8]M |  * |[9] X |*    |.
  |[10]N| [11]E|[12]G| *    |[13]D|[11]E |[1]T |.
\end{Puzzle} \end{minipage}
\begin{minipage}{.6\textwidth}
  \renewcommand\PuzzleLettersText{Letters used: }
  \PuzzleLetters{ABDEGILMNRTUX} \medskip \PuzzleNumbers{TABULRIMXNEGD}
\end{minipage}
```

Letters used: ABDEGILMNRTUX

Example 10-6-7

10.6.4 General adjustments to the layout

Beside the customizations related to the clue representation, the cwpuzzle package offers a number of parameters and macros to influence the typesetting of the main puzzle grid.

Grid size and fonts The size of a grid cell is determined by the parameter `\PuzzleUnitlength`. It defaults to 20pt. If the cell size is changed, it is usually advisable to adjust the font size for clue numbers in the grid as well, by redefining the macro `\PuzzleNumberFont` (the default is `\sf\scriptsize`), and to modify the font size for letters in the solution display, by configuring through `\PuzzleClueFont` (the default is `\footnotesize`). For example, the grid displayed in Example 10-6-5 on page 706 was produced using the following settings:

```
\setlength\PuzzleUnitlength{18pt}
\renewcommand\PuzzleClueFont{\scriptsize}
\renewcommand\PuzzleNumberFont{\sffamily\tiny}
\PuzzleSolution[true]
```

The documentation also mentions a `\PuzzleFont`. It is defined but never used by the package, so don't expect any miracles from changing it.

Two other mildly interesting hooks are `\PuzzleBlackBox`, which defines the look and feel of cells marked as unusable (i.e., produced by a *), and `\PuzzleHook`, which stores `picture` commands that are executed when the grid is being built. Using these hooks is equivalent to issuing these commands within each `Puzzle` environment as shown in Example 10-6-3 on page 705.

10.6.5 External puzzle generation

One of the most popular puzzle formats of the Internet is the *Across Lite*® format from Literate Software Systems.[1] Many electronic versions of daily newspapers, such as the *New York Times* and *USA Today*, provide their puzzles in this format. On CTAN three small C programs are available (directory `AcrossLite`) to convert this format into **cwpuzzle** syntax for off-line printing.

10.7 Sudokus

The origins of Sudoku puzzles can be traced back to the Swiss mathematician Leonard Euler, who developed similar puzzles under the name "Latin Square". The modern form became popular in Japan in the 1980s, and in recent years it started to conquer the world, with Sudoku puzzles appearing in many newspapers. It comes as no big surprise that the first tool for typesetting Sudokus with LaTeX appeared in 2005.

Today's Sudoku puzzles usually consist of a table with nine rows and columns subdivided into nine 3×3 regions. Some of the cells are prefilled with numbers between 1 and 9. The player's task is to fill the remaining cells such that in each row, column, and region every number appears exactly once. Sometimes one sees Sudokus with 4×4 sub-regions so that 16 different symbols have to be placed. The puzzle derives its name from the Japanese words Su, meaning "number", and Doku, meaning "singular" or "solitary".

10.7.1 sudoku—Typesetting Sudokus

The first **sudoku** package that was published on CTAN in 2005 was written by Paul Abraham. It provides the environment `sudoku-block`, which allows for typesetting puzzles with a fairly natural syntax. Each puzzle row is represented by 10 vertical bars (indicating the grid lines) and followed by a dot. The cell content is entered between these bars, either as a space (empty cell) or as a number between 1 and 9.

```
\usepackage{sudoku}
\setlength\sudokusize{5cm}
\renewcommand\sudokuformat[1]{\textsf{#1}}
\begin{sudoku-block}
|4| | | | | | |1| |.
| | |2|6| | |4| | |.
|6|7| | | | | |9|2|.
| |2| | | |4| | | |.
| |1| |7| |9| |6| |.
| | | |3| | | |2| |.
|1|3| | | | | |7|9|.
| | |7| | |5|3| | |.
| | |8| | | | | |1|.
\end{sudoku-block}
```

---

[1]Software to solve such puzzles is available at `http://www.litsoft.com/across/alite/download.htm`.

The size of the grid can be adjusted by setting \sudokusize (the default value is 10cm), and the size and font for the numbers can be manipulated by redefining \sudokuformat as shown in Example 10-7-1. The default definition uses \Huge to fit the larger grid size. The package also offers the environment sudoku, which is simply an abbreviation for sudoku-block inside a center environment.

10.7.2 sudokubundle—Solving and generating Sudokus

In 2006, Peter Wilson published a bundle of three packages that not only typeset but also attempt to solve existing Sudokus or generate new ones. In contrast to the **sudoku** package, with Wilson's bundle the puzzles have to be stored in external files and require a somewhat different input syntax.

In these external files, only the first nine lines are relevant. Each must consist of nine characters, either a dot (representing an empty cell) or one of the numbers 1 to 9 (indicating prefilled cells). Any further lines can be used for comments and will not be read by LaTeX.

The **printsudoku** package provides the command \sudoku for typesetting such files. It also offers a \writepuzzle command to write external Sudokus into separate files, but for this purpose a filecontents* environment, as used in the next example, or a simple text editor is equally or even more suitable.

```
\usepackage{printsudoku}
\begin{filecontents*}{sample.sud}
..9....64
4........
1..36..72
..46....9
...9.3...
2....54..
92..57..8
........5
34....6..
A moderate challenge
\end{filecontents*}
\cluefont{\small}
\cellsize{1.2\baselineskip}
\sudoku{sample.sud}
```

Example
10-7-2

As seen in the previous example, the size of the puzzle and the numbers inside are controlled through \cluefont (default \Huge) and \cellsize (default 2.5\baselineskip), respectively. Note that compared to the **sudoku** package these are declarations, rather than length registers or macros, and thus are changed in a different way. For example, to get sans serif numbers, we would need to use \sffamily instead of using \textsf.

The **solvesudoku** package attempts to solve a given puzzle and prints the solution as far as it was able to produce it. Given that TeX isn't the best language in which to implement complicated algorithms, it does a surprisingly good job and is able to fully resolve most puzzles rated medium or higher. As a high-level command it offers \sudokusolve, which first prints the original puzzle in large size, then resolves it, and finally typesets the result in a smaller grid below. Rather than using this interface we use the more low-level commands for solving puzzles below and then print the result so that not so much space is taken up by the next example.

7	3	9	5	2	1	8	6	4
4	6	2	8	7	9	1	5	3
1	5	8	3	6	4	9	7	2
5	1	4	6	8	2	7	3	9
6	8	7	9	4	3	5	2	1
2	9	3	7	1	5	4	8	6
9	2	6	1	5	7	3	4	8
8	7	1	4	3	6	2	9	5
3	4	5	2	9	8	6	1	7

Example 10-7-3

```
\usepackage{solvesudoku}
% use previously defined sample.sud file

% produce the solution:
\getproblem{sample.sud}
\reduceallcells \keepreducing
\writegame
% print it (using printsudoku):
\cluefont{\small\sffamily}
\cellsize{1.2\baselineskip}
\sudoku{sud.out}
```

The third package in the bundle, **createsudoku**, can be used to generate new puzzles from existing ones. Its command \generategrid takes a solution file as its optional argument, randomly permutes an arbitrary number of rows and columns, and then removes a number of clues until it reaches a grid that cannot be solved any longer through the algorithm implemented by **solvesudoku**. The last valid puzzle is stored in \genfile (default gensud.sud) and then printed using \sudokusolve. If \generategrid is called without an argument, a puzzle solution defined within the package is used as a starting point.

To demonstrate we use the output from the previous example, sud.out, to generate a puzzle. As the output of \sudokusolve (showing puzzle and result) takes up a lot of space, we disable that once more and print the puzzle manually.

	5	8	6					
7			2		5	8		
4	6		7		8		3	5
	1	4				7		3
2		3				4		8
				2			7	1
		5			3			4
	7		3			2	5	

Example 10-7-4

```
\usepackage{createsudoku}
% previous example is needed as input

% Explicitly initialize the random
% generator to always get the same
% output. Comment out if you want to
% get different puzzles each time!
\setsudrandom{1682604876}
% do not typeset solution
\renewcommand\sudokusolve[1]{}
% produce the puzzle:
\generategrid[sud.out]
% print it (using printsudoku):
\cluefont{\small\sffamily}
\cellsize{1.2\baselineskip}
\sudoku{\genfile}
```

Since the permutation of rows and columns is created using a random generator that, by default, is initialized using the current date and time, a huge number of different puzzles can be generated from code like the above. Of course, the complexity of the puzzles is limited by the capabilities of the puzzle solver algorithm, but as the examples show it will produce reasonably difficult puzzles.

Besides explicitly initializing the random number generator (as we did in the previous example), the puzzle generation can be influenced by manipulating the initial selection of clues that are removed from the grid before the elimination algorithm starts; details can be found in the package documentation.

The World of Color

For many people, color is indispensable for effective graphics. All of the modern interactive drawing packages support coloring of lines, filling objects with color, etc., and all of the standard bitmap file formats such as GIF (Graphics Interchange Format), PNG (Portable Network Graphic), JPEG (Joint Photographic Experts Group), PBM (Portable Bitmap), TIFF (Tagged Image File Format), BMP (Windows Bitmap), SVG (Scalable Vector Graphic), and Encapsulated PostScript support color. Thus, if you generate a picture with a drawing package, and then import it into your LaTeX document using the packages described in Chapter 2, you should have no problems if your printing or viewing device supports color. However, you do have to know something about how color is represented and which color model you are using. We discuss these issues in the first part of this chapter.

If you prepare your graphics using LaTeX itself or simply want colored text, you need some special support from both LaTeX and your driver. The main body of this chapter describes the extended LaTeX xcolor package, which we believe is powerful enough to meet almost all needs and is capable of working with most other packages. xcolor extends the old color package with features such as color mixing, color sequences, and tabular shading.

LaTeX users often request color for use in presentations. The xcolor package can, of course, be used with old LaTeX slides classes, but we devote some space to explaining a more sophisticated class, beamer, and give lots of examples of its facilities.

As the book is printed in two colors, it is possible to show some color effects in examples. All other colors will appear in grayscale throughout the text. However, we repeat selected examples in the color plates. We indicate when the reader should refer to the full-color version. You can also take the example source code, run it through LaTeX or pdfLaTeX, and view the PostScript or PDF output.

11.1 An introduction to color

You should think about color in a document as being a tool, not a gadget to merely make the pages look "prettier". The French painter Eugène Delacroix wrote [19]:

> Color is above all that part of art which bestows the gift of magic; while subject, form, and line are concerned firstly with reasoning, color has no relationship with intelligence; it has power over feeling, and invades your senses.

This sentence summarizes perfectly the role that color plays in the construction of the visual image. By choosing the right color, the typographer or painter can add an affective value to the message, thus making it understood more clearly.

11.1.1 Color theories

Since prehistoric times, color has played an important role in visual communication, as the colored depictions of animals in the caves of Altamira or Lascaux clearly indicate. The Egyptians, Assyrians, and other ancient Middle East cultures, and later the Phoenicians, knew how to produce paint and dyes, and they loved colored stones. But it was the Greek philosopher Aristotle who first, in the 4th century B.C., tried to actually "understand" color by studying the mixing of colors in different-colored glass. To explain his observations he postulated that each color was a mixture of white and black, the dark colors being produced by the reflection of light by the medium. This interpretation, in which colors were ordered on a straight line from the lightest to the darkest, starting with white and ending with black, lasted for almost 2200 years. It was was only in the 17th century, thanks to Isaac Newton's experiments with glass prisms, that the spectral theory of light was discovered. Newton ordered the colors on a closed circular ring, a representation still in use today.

Gœthe at the beginning of the 19th century dedicated much of his life to the study of physics and chemistry, and he was particularly fascinated by color. Even though his color theory is no longer accepted today, his discussion of the matter served as the basis of some significant progress in the field. Thomas Young, an English doctor, introduced in 1801 the three-color theory of light; this concept was further developed by Hermann von Helmholtz, and their theory of three-color vision is called the *Young–Helmholtz* Law.

It was the work of Maxwell, Helmholtz and Grassmann that formed the basis of the science of colorimetry. The laws of mixing colored light were first formulated by Grassmann (1853), who was the first to show clearly the relationship between light and color. He summarized his findings in three theorems, called *Grassmann's laws*:

(a) Colors obtained by *additive* color mixing are completely determined by their three-color components and do not depend on their spectral composition (*color mixing* theorem).

(b) Three numbers are necessary and sufficient to fully describe a color (*additivity* theorem).

(c) In daylight conditions, color sensation does not depend on light intensity (*proportionality* theorem).

Recent studies and experiments have consolidated our knowledge in the field of color; see, e.g., [29, 87] for more details.

11.1.2 Color systems

Today we know that several representations may be used to describe colors, any of which can be chosen depending on the targeted application domain—for instance, additive or substractive color mixing, color perception theory, television, artwork, dyes, or gray levels. In particular, PostScript subdivides color spaces into three categories:

- *Device color spaces*: colors or gray levels are directly expressed in units that the output device understands. Examples of such models are RGB (*Red, Green, Blue*) and a variant for television YIQ, CMYK (*Cyan, Magenta, Yellow, Black*), and HSB, also called HSV (*Hue, Saturation, Brightness* or *Value*). See Color Plate XI a) and Color Plate XIII a) for demonstrations of the RGB and HSB models.

- *CIE color spaces*: colors are specified in a device-independent way. In 1931 the *Commission Internationale de l'Éclairage* (CIE) established a colormetric system defining all colors in an unambiguous and objective way. In 1964 (CIEUCS) and 1976 (CIELAB/ CIELUV), extensions were introduced in the CIE model to correct certain shortcomings of the original version.

- *Special color spaces*: these are used for special applications, such as patterns, color maps, and separations.

An introduction to the use of color with PostScript can be found in [77] and [82]. A detailed description of all the models and algorithms to transform colors from one space to another is beyond the scope of this book. More details can be found in [5, 22, 61, 108]; [29] classifies all the color models that have been proposed into groups; see also [87]. We deal simply with the RGB and CMYK models, since these are widely used in the printing and computer industries.

The additive RGB color space

In RGB space, all colors are obtained by the superposition (addition) of three *primary* components, defined by the CIE as red (700 nm), green (546.1 nm), and blue (435.8 nm). In this model the electrons of the cathode ray tube hit phosphorus elements that emit light of the right wavelength, and combine (add) to give the desired color (see Color Plate XI a).

The subtractive CMYK color space

The printing industry does not use the RGB primary colors, but rather their complements: cyan, magenta, and yellow. This is because inks "subtract" their complementary colors from the white light that falls on the surface; e.g., cyan ink absorbs the red component of white light and thus, in terms of the additive primaries, cyan is white minus red i.e., blue plus green. Similarly, magenta absorbs the green component and corresponds to red plus blue, while yellow, which absorbs blue, is red plus green (see Color Plate XI a). In practice, the printing industry uses a process called "undercolor removal" in which a fourth "color", black, is added so as to create a darker black than is available by mixing the three colored inks. This color

Table 11.1: Symbolic connotation of colors in different countries

	Red	Blue	Green	Yellow	White
China	happiness	sky, clouds	Ming dynasty, sky, clouds	birth, riches, power	purity, death
Egypt	death,	virtue, faith, truth	fertility, force	happiness, prosperity	joy
France	aristocracy	freedom, peace	criminality	worldliness	neutrality
India	creativity, life		prosperity, fertility	success	purity, death
Japan	anger, danger	infamy	future, youth, energy	nobility, grace	death
U.S.A.	danger	masculinity	security	cowardice	purity

model is called the CMYK model, where the final "K" stands for the black component. The effect of the black component is handled as follows:

- *Calculate black component*: it is the minimum of the components C, Y, and M, because this number corresponds to the value of which all three inks are superimposed to yield black: K=min(C,Y,M).
- *Undercolor removal*: subtract this black component K from the three components C, M, and Y to compensate for the amount of black introduced by the use of black ink: C = C-K; Y = Y-K; M = M-K.

11.1.3 Symbolic values of color

The significance of color, like symbols, varies greatly across cultures. Table 11.1 shows some cultural connotations for various colors (following [37]). For example, red means danger in the United States, as in most Western cultures, but it is a symbol for life and creativity in India. It is important to be aware of these differences when designing a poster, book cover, or computer interface.

To minimize ambiguity, international standards groups have chosen colors with generally understood significances. In the field of traffic signs, for instance, red is a sign for danger, while green indicates health services or says that the road is clear. Blue, white, and black are only secondary colors in such contexts, used for information on road surfaces, rest areas, etc. Similar standards have been developed for plumbing and electrical wiring.

A color with a generally recognized significance can help to reinforce an idea and can play an important psychological role in creating an atmosphere or conveying a cultural, religious, or political message. It should be noted, however, that every human activity, profession, and interest group, even within the same culture, has its own "color" jargon. Thus you should always be aware of possible side effects of using a color in any given context.

11.1.4 Color harmonies

Color harmonies are arrangements of color pleasing to the eye. Scores of books have been written on color harmony, and the conclusions of many of these works are often contradictory. Reasons for this disagreement are not hard to find [65]:

- Color harmony is a matter of individual emotional response, of likes and dislikes. Even the same person can change his or her mind about colors over time, since old combinations can become boring while frequent exposure to new combinations can make us appreciate them.

- Color harmony depends on the absolute size of the areas covered by the colors as well as on the design and the colors themselves. For instance, a nice-looking mosaic pattern can become quite unattractive when magnified by a factor of 10.

- Color harmony depends on the relative sizes of the areas as well as on their colors.

- Color harmony depends on the shape of the elements as well as on their colors.

- Color harmony depends on the meaning or interpretation of the design as well as on the colors. Clearly, color harmony for a portrait painter is quite a different matter from color harmony in abstract design or typography.

Nonetheless, it is still interesting to try to formulate a few principles for the construction of color harmonies.

- Color harmony results from the juxtaposition of colors selected on an orderly plan that can be recognized and emotionally appreciated.

- When comparing two similar sequences of color, observers choose the one most familiar as the most harmonious.

- Groups of colors that seem to have a common aspect or quality are considered to be harmonious.

- Colors are perceived as harmonious only if the combination of colors has a selection plan that is unambiguously recognizable.

It has been observed experimentally that the eye prefers combinations in which primary colors are in equilibrium with their complementary colors, and that our perception of a color changes in relation to its environment. Color Plate XI c shows the effects of *saturation* or *absorption* of the three primary colors with respect to white (leftmost column) and black (second column), and with respect to its complementary color (third column) and a gray tone of the primary color itself (rightmost column).

Itten [57] uses a model based on a harmonic color circle subdivided into 12 equal parts to explain his theory of colors (see Color Plate XI b). It contains the three primary colors yellow, red, and blue, 120 degrees apart. Their complementary colors purple, green, and orange, also called the secondary colors, are positioned diametrically opposite their respective primaries. The circle contains six more colors, intermediate between each primary and its adjacent secondaries. The harmonic color circle is merely a simplification. Indeed, all possible colors can be represented on the surface of a sphere that has the harmonic colors at its equator, white at the north pole, and black at the south pole. Thus moving from the equator towards the south (north) pole yields darker (lighter) variants of a given color. This also means that for each point on the color sphere, there exists a diametrically opposed point with complementary characteristics—e.g., light greenish blue is opposed to dark orange red. Centuries of artistic experience have shown that a few simple basic rules let artists construct effective color harmonies in their works. Following Itten, we discuss a few of them below.

Two-color harmonic combinations

Complementary colors lying at diametrically opposite points of the color circle (sphere) define two-color harmonies, like the 2-tuples (red, green) and (blue, orange), plus the almost infinite number constructed using possible combinations on the sphere.

Three-color harmonic combinations

When an equilateral triangle is constructed inside the color circle, the colors at each edge form a three-color harmony. The most fundamental 3-tuple (yellow, red, blue) is well known in all forms of art, publishing, and publicity for its effectiveness; it can be used in a wide variety of patterns and layouts, and in all kinds of light and dark combinations. The secondary color 3-tuple (purple, green, orange) has also a strong character and is frequently used. Other 3-tuples are also possible and you can construct harmonic 3-tuples by replacing the equilateral triangle by an isosceles triangle, or by working on the color sphere and combining light and dark variants. As a special case, you can put one edge of the triangle at the white point (north pole) to create the harmony (white, dark greenish blue, dark orange red), or on the black point (south pole) to create the harmony (black, light greenish blue, light orange red).

Four-color harmonic combinations

You can construct a four-color harmony by taking the colors lying on the edges of a square in the color circle—e.g., the 4-tuple (yellow, orange red, purple, greenish blue). It is also possible to use a rectangle combining two pairs of complementary colors.

Higher-order harmonies (like six-color) are equally easy to obtain using similar geometric models, on the color circle or the color sphere. Note, however, that each combination has its own character and set of basic laws, and only long experience can show which of the various sets of harmonies is most efficient for a given application.

11.1.5 Color and readability

The readability of a message or sign is closely linked to how our visual system processes the information presented to it. The following factors influence the visibility of colors:

- *Intensity*: pure colors of the spectrum have the highest intensity.
- *Contrast*: between the different colors.
- *Purity*: pure colors are more visible than graded variants, in which white has been added, making them fainter, or black, making them darker.

Color Plate XII shows some of the most effective color contrasts for maximum readability or visibility, e.g., on slides, road signs, or publicity leaflets.

11.2   Colors with LaTeX — The color and xcolor packages

When LaTeX 2_ε was released in 1994, it provided for the first time some abstraction layers for graphics (see Chapter 2) and color (in shape of the **color** package by David Carlisle).

LaTeX's color support is built around the idea of a system of *color models*. The color models supported by a driver may vary, but typically include the following:

rgb   *red green blue.* A comma-separated list of three real numbers between 0 and 1 (the color components in function of the additive RGB model).

cmyk   *cyan magenta yellow black.* A comma-separated list of four real numbers between 0 and 1 gives the components of the color according to the subtractive CMYK model used in most printers.

gray   *grayscale.* A single real number between 0 (black) and 1 (white).

hsb   *hue saturation brightness.* A comma-separated list of three real numbers between 0 and 1. This model is understood only by some drivers.

named   A name selected from a list of predefined colors is used. Here the actual color is defined in the driver, e.g., through special profiles; this method is supported by only some drivers.

When the named color model is available then the driver may predefine the color for each name according to one of the other color models, or refer to color names supported by the printer or page-description language like PostScript. The **dvips** driver, for example, offers 64 "Crayola" colors, as originally proposed by Jim Hafner in his **colordvi** and **foiltex** packages (see the file `colordvi.tex` coming with your TeX distribution for a list). It is important to realize that these colors are defined not according to fixed CMYK or RGB values in the document, but rather at the PostScript level in a replaceable header file that can be customized for different printers. The idea was to allow some independence from fixed CMYK or RGB values that may not look right on your device.

The abstraction layer provided by the **color** package hides the `\special` syntax that differs between device drivers, but otherwise passes color model information to the driver for execution. Therefore a document containing, for example, colors specified as CMYK values would only work with drivers supporting that color model, thereby reducing the device independence—in case of "named" colors, sometimes even to a single driver.

This "partial device" dependency asked for some future development—which happened in 2003 in the form of the package **xcolor** by Uwe Kern. Uwe's **xcolor** implements an upward-compatible version of the **color** user interface while adding a number of useful functions such as extended color model support. Thus documents written for use with the **color** package can be processed unmodified with the **xcolor** package (with additional functionality in the back end, such as outputting all colors in a certain color model regardless of the model specified on input).

Enter the xcolor package

In the opposite direction (though it is not normally necessary), documents written with **xcolor** can usually be processed with **color** with only some small declaration adjustments, unless heavy use of extended specification possibilities has been made in document commands rather than in declarations. The latter, while allowed, is discouraged, as it makes documents difficult to maintain.

Common features of both packages   We therefore discuss both packages together in this chapter, pointing out the differences as necessary as we go along. In summary, common to both packages are the following features:

- The basic document-level commands for selecting color in various circumstances, i.e., `\color`, `\textcolor`, `\colorbox`, `\fcolorbox`, and `\pagecolor`.
- The declaration `\definecolor` for specifying new colors. xcolor offers addition declarations here.
- The basic color models `rgb`, `cmyk`, `gray`, `hsb`, and `named`.

The additional xcolor features   The xcolor package also provides the following features:

- Support for an extended set of color models for specifying color input such as
  - Color notation as in HTML.
  - Defining colors by their wavelength.
- Converting any color from one color model into another one, e.g., from RGB to CMYK.
- documentwide transformation of all color definitions into one model e.g., always using the CMYK model without rewriting existing color definitions using other models.
- Extended color specification possibilities, such as
  - Choosing a proportional value of a given color definition e.g., 80% of an existing color.
  - Mixing colors or parts of them to a new one e.g., 80% of red with 20% of blue.
  - Using the complementary color of a given one.
- Coloring alternate tabular rows using the colortbl package.
- Full support of all PSTricks packages (see Chapter 5 on page 213).

Reason(s) for not choosing the xcolor package?   Are there any reason to use the color package at all? As far as the authors can see, there is only one: xcolor is still under active development, making it more likely that newly defined features or bug fixes may not be available everywhere. Of course, this also means that support for new drivers e.g., `xetex` becomes available more quickly than with the color package.

11.2.1 Options supported by color and xcolor

Options to specify the target device   As discussed in Section 2.1.1 with reference to the graphics commands, it is ultimately the output driver for your particular output device that paints the colors on the output medium. Therefore the driver must be declared as an option on the `\documentclass` or `\usepackage` commands or specified in the configuration file `color.cfg` (common to both color and xcolor), using, for instance, the command

```
\ExecuteOptions{dvips}
```

Use of a configuration file is the recommended method.

The following driver options are supported: dvipdfmx,[1] dvipdfm, dvipdf, dvipsone, dvips, dviwin, emtex, pctex32, pctexhp, pctexps, pctexwin, pdftex, tcidvi, textures, truetex, vtex, and xetex.[1]

A few options control the behavior of the named model. By default, the named color *Options for the named* model has no predeclared names; the dvipsnames option defines a set of 68 CMYK colors *model* (Color Plate XIV d) that are defined in the color prologue of dvips.[2] The xcolor package additionally offers a set of 147 RGB color names according to the SVG 1.1 specification and a set of 317 RGB color names according to Unix/X11 standards. These sets are made available by specifying the svgnames (Color Plate XV b) or x11names option respectively. Note that there is a certain overlap in the names of these sets, which makes it important to specify the right order if the sets should be used together. With xcolor the colors in the named model become immediately available when one of the previously mentioned options is given.[3]

There is an important difference between the **color** and **xcolor** packages regarding how the dvipsnames option is handled. The **color** package implicitly invokes the dvipsnames option with certain device drivers (**dvips** and others). This makes documents less portable, since the use of the corresponding color names without an explicit dvipsnames option will result in "unknown color" errors if the document is processed with a different driver such as **pdftex**. Therefore, **xcolor** always requires an explicit dvipsnames option to use these names—which then works in all cases.

With the **color** package the colors are passed unmodified to the output device (i.e., the target model corresponds to the input model). In this situation it is up to the driver to inter- *Options for the target* pret the color model specification; if that operation fails, the document cannot be printed *color model* on that particular device. With the **xcolor** package it is also possible to specify an explicit target color model through an option. If this is done, all color specifications are internally converted to the target model prior to passing them to the driver-specific code.[4] This way the document can effectively use any color model, yet still remains printable on any output device that supports at least one basic color model, such as rgb or cmyk. Target color models are rgb, cmy, cmyk, hsb, gray, RGB, HTML, HSB, and Gray (these color models are explained in Section 11.2.4 on page 728). The default pass-through can be explicitly requested using the option natural.

With both packages it is possible to turn off the effect of all color commands by speci- *Black and white* fying the monochrome option. This ability can be useful when you are previewing the docu- *requested* ment prior to printing it.

The remaining options are specific to the **xcolor** package. To provide support for other packages or extend them in a suitable way, there are currently two options available: *Miscellaneous options* hyperref enables support for the **hyperref** package and table loads the **colortbl** package.

By default (option showerrors), an undefined color results in an error. When using the option hideerrors, the color is replaced by black and only a warning is displayed.

When the prologue option is used, **xcolor** writes all color definitions into a PostScript prologue file with the extension .xcp. This feature can be useful in conjunction with the

---

[1] Not available with the **color** package.

[2] To use these with color commands from the **color** package, you have to specify the usenames option. Otherwise they are available only for definitions with \definecolor.

[3] If the option name is suffixed by a star, (e.g., svgnames*) the set is loaded without defining the names for use. In that case they have to be explicitly defined using \definecolors or a similar declaration.

[4] Section 11.2.4 on page 728 explains how this setting can be overridden at any point in a document.

named color model, where the actual color definitions are under the control of a device driver such as dvips. Details can be found in the package documentation.

11.2.2 Using colors within the document

The syntax for color changes is similar to that of font changes. It has two forms, one declarative and the other with arguments for local changes. The commands in this section are available with both color and xcolor.

Using predefined colors by name
The simplest and most portable way of using color is specifying it by name. With this approach, the user does not need to know the color model used. All drivers define the colors black and white; if they support the RGB model, they define red, green, and blue, and if they support the CMYK model, they also define cyan, magenta, and yellow.

Additional colors can be defined either through options (Section 11.2.1 on page 720) or through color declarations (Section 11.2.3 on page 726).

| \color{*color*}   \textcolor{*color*}{*text*} |

The first form, \color, is a state-changing command that sets colors to remain "active" until the end of the current (implicit or explicit) group. The second form, \textcolor, is a command suitable for short colored text fragments: \textcolor{*color*}{*text*} is equivalent to {\color{*color*}*text*}. This example is also printed in Color Plate XIII b.

Text starts off in green a little red
nested blue text returning to green.

```
\usepackage{color}
{\color{green} Text starts off in green
\textcolor{red}{a little red}
{\color{blue}nested blue text}
returning to green.}
```

Example
11-2-1

Using explicit color model values
If the predefined colors are not sufficient, you can specify a color explicitly with respect to a given color model.

| \color[*model*]{*specification*}   \textcolor[*model*]{*specification*}{*text*} |

Note that the meaning of the first mandatory argument (*specification*) to the \color and \textcolor commands changes when the option *model* is given; instead of a predefined color name, you supply the appropriate values for the model.

With xcolor the *specification* possibilities are further extended as explained in Section 11.2.5 on page 730.

The example in the previous section (with predefined colors) can be rewritten in terms of the RGB model as follows (see also Color Plate XIII b):

Text starts off in green a little red
nested blue text returning to green.

```
\usepackage{color}
{\color[rgb]{0,1,0} Text starts off in green
\textcolor[rgb]{1,0,0}{a little red}
{\color[rgb]{0,0,1}nested blue text}
returning to green.}
```

Example
11-2-2

Another example (also in Color Plate XIII b) that mixes predefined and local color specifications is the following list:

1. magenta cmyk black

2. predefined blue gray text

```
\usepackage{color}

\begin{enumerate}
\item \textcolor[cmyk]{0,1,0,0}{magenta cmyk} black
\item \color[gray]{0.5}
       \textcolor{blue}{predefined blue}
       gray text
\end{enumerate}
```

As the use of local color specifications throughout a document reduces its portability and makes updating it cumbersome, it is usually best to avoid using this feature. A better approach is to define your own colors in the preamble and then refer to them by name, as discussed in Section 11.2.3 on page 726.

Two commands similar to \fbox produce boxes with backgrounds shaded in a given color.   *Colored boxes*

$\boxed{\texttt{\textbackslash colorbox[}\textit{model}\texttt{] \{}\textit{background color}\texttt{\}\{}\textit{text}\texttt{\}}}$

The \colorbox command puts the *text* into a box and colors the background. This background extends \fboxsep in all four directions. If the optional *model* argument is given, the *background color* has to be specified in the syntax for this model, exemplified with the two levels of gray below.

Black text on blue background

Light background

Dark background

```
\usepackage{color}

\colorbox{blue}{Black text on blue background}
\par\colorbox[gray]{.80}{%
    \textcolor{blue}{Light background}}
\par\colorbox[gray]{.20}{%
    \textcolor{white}{Dark background}}
```

$\boxed{\texttt{\textbackslash fcolorbox[}\textit{model}\texttt{] \{}\textit{frame color}\texttt{\} [}\textit{background model}\texttt{] \{}\textit{background color}\texttt{\}\{}\textit{text}\texttt{\}}}$

The \fcolorbox command puts a frame (in the color specified) around the colored box (this example is also in Color Plate XIII b). If the *model* argument is used it applies to both the *frame color* and the *background color*; i.e., both need to be specified in the syntax for the given model. With xcolor it is possible to specify a separate *background model*.

Black text, green background, red frame

White text, green background, red frame

```
\usepackage{color}

\fcolorbox{red}{green}{Black text,
      green background, red frame}
\par\smallskip
\fcolorbox{red}{green}{\color{white}%
    White text, green background, red frame}
```

Some further examples (also in Color Plate XIII b) show how to control the exact form of the box with the \fbox parameters \fboxrule and \fboxsep, which specify the thickness of the rule and the size of the shaded area respectively.

```
\usepackage{color}
\setlength{\fboxrule}{6pt}%
\setlength{\fboxsep}{10pt}%
\colorbox{yellow}{Fun with color}\qquad
\fcolorbox{red}{yellow}{Fun with color}
\par\bigskip\par
\setlength{\fboxrule}{2pt}%
\setlength{\fboxsep}{5pt}%
\colorbox{green}{Fun with color}\qquad
\fcolorbox{red}{green}{Fun with color}
```

Example
11-2-6

Combining the use of PostScript fonts and color, you can construct lists with colorful elements; the \ding command is part of the **pifont** package described in [83, p. 378].

```
\usepackage{pifont,color}
\newenvironment{coldinglist}[1]
        {\begin{list}{\textcolor{blue}{\ding{#1}}}{}}
        {\end{list}}
\newcommand\OnThe[1]{On the \textcolor{blue}{#1} day of
                     Christmas my true love sent to me}
\begin{coldinglist}{113}
 \item \OnThe{first}
 \begin{coldinglist}{42}
    \item a partridge in a pear tree
 \end{coldinglist}
 \item \OnThe{second}
 \begin{coldinglist}{42}
    \item two turtle doves
    \item and a partridge in a pear tree
 \end{coldinglist}
 \item \OnThe{third}
 \begin{coldinglist}{42}
    \item three French hens
    \item two turtle doves
    \item and a partridge in a pear tree
 \end{coldinglist}
\end{coldinglist}
```

Example
11-2-7

❏ On the first day of Christmas my true love sent to me

☞ a partridge in a pear tree

❏ On the second day of Christmas my true love sent to me

☞ two turtle doves

☞ and a partridge in a pear tree

❏ On the third day of Christmas my true love sent to me

☞ three French hens

☞ two turtle doves

☞ and a partridge in a pear tree

More complicated color support can be obtained in the framework of the **colortbl** package, which allows you to produce colored tables (see Section 11.3) or the **beamer** class, which makes color slides (see Section 11.4).

> \pagecolor[*model*] {*background color*}

You can set *background color* of the whole page by using \pagecolor, which takes the same arguments as \color but sets the background color for the current and all subsequent pages. Since it is a global declaration, you must use \pagecolor{white} to return to a white background (the default setting) and it makes no sense to use it inside a mini-page.

Using colors from the named model

Using the named color model has certain advantages over using other color models. First, since the output file contains a request for a color by *name*, the actual mix of primary colors used to obtain the color requested can be tuned to the characteristics of a particular printer. In particular, the **dvips** driver uses an external header file color.pro that contains the definitions of the color names. To ensure constant colors when printing on different devices, you should ideally produce a different version of this file for each output device that is to be used.

Second, apart from the "process colors" which are produced by mixing primary colors during the print process, you may want to use "spot" or "custom" colors for which a particular color name refers not to a mix of primaries, but rather to a particular ink. The parts of the document using this color are printed separately with this named ink color.

Special concerns with color in LATEX

You need to be aware of some special situations relating to stored boxes in LATEX. The following example (also printed in Color Plate XIII b) shows that color is defined when the box is *created* with the \sbox command, not when it is *used* (i.e., the color characteristics are stored with the box and the surrounding color does not influence that color).

```
\usepackage{xcolor}
\newsavebox{\X}

\sbox{\X}{[black text] and
  \color[cmyk]{0,0.6,0.8,0}[orange text]}
```

Start with [black text] and [orange text], and return to black

```
Start with \usebox{\X}, and return to black
```

Example
11-2-8

Start in green, see [black text] and [orange text] and once again green

```
{\color{green}Start in green, see
  \usebox{\X} and once again green}
```

This parallels LATEX's handling of font attributes, which are also fixed when the box is created. However, the internal mechanisms used are quite different, which can lead to unpleasant surprises if new commands are not carefully designed.

When text is stored inside a box such as with the \sbox or the low-level \hbox command, each character carries with it a note about the font in which it is set. In contrast, color is handled by putting "start color" and "end color" messages into the output. Thus, if such a constructed box is decomposed with low-level TEX commands, the correspondence between color and text can be lost. As an example of the problems this can cause, consider a situation in which "red" starts at the bottom of one page and continues on the next; when a TEX format that is not aware of "color", such as plain TEX (but not LaTeX 2_ε), comes to format these pages, the footer and header on the page break in question are also printed in red. Similar situations arise when such a format handles lists (e.g., the item labels might be printed in the wrong color).

Standard LaTeX goes a long way to support color, and many of the potential problems are circumvented in the main LaTeX code (in practice you do not have to worry about coloring headers and footers by accident). Nevertheless, but you may get unexpected color effects if you use packages that were not written with the restrictions of color support in mind. These problems are discussed in detail in the document *LaTeX 2_ε for class and package writers* distributed with LaTeX, and in [103]. Unless you are a confident LaTeX programmer, it is sensible to confine your use of color to simple situations using official LaTeX rather than low-level TEX commands (e.g., \savebox instead of \setbox, \mbox rather than \hbox), so you can be sure to obtain the expected result.

11.2.3 Defining colors

When you use the color package, the colors black, white, red, green, blue, cyan, magenta, and yellow should be always available. With xcolor the colors orange, violet, purple, brown, darkgray, and lightgray are also predefined (see Color Plate XIV c). A lot of LaTeX packages define other colors.

Defining single colors

To define new colors yourself, you can use the \definecolor declaration, which is available with both the color and xcolor packages. If you use xcolor, a number of other declaration possibilities are available as well.

> \definecolor[*type*]{*name*}{*model*}{*color specification*}

The \definecolor declaration associates the *name* with a color *model* and a *color specification* so that it can be used afterwards in any color command.[1] The *name* should consist of letters and digits (even though certain other characters currently work). This avoids misunderstandings and ensures compatibility with future extensions of xcolor. Thus valid names include be red20 and LGC2blue.

The declaration is local to the current group (unless it is preceded by an \xglobal command). Thus, if the color should be available throughout the document, the declaration is best placed in the preamble.

The xcolor package offers additional declarations.

> \providecolor[*type*]{*name*}{*model*}{*color specification*}
> \colorlet{*name*}[*new model*]{*color*}

\providecolor works like \definecolor, except that it will not overwrite a color definition if it already exists.

---

[1]The optional *type* argument is available only with xcolor and enables you to define colors in the "named" model. This is of interest only in special circumstances; see the xcolor package documentation for details.

The \colorlet declaration takes an existing *color* name and assigns it to a new *name*. If the optional *new model* argument is present, the *color* is first transformed into that model and then saved under the new *name*; otherwise, this is a straight copy.

In the example below, five new colors are defined: MyOrange defines an orange color in the cmyk model; the next line translates that color into the rgb model and assigns it to MyRGBOrange; the third line "provides" a definition for blue (which would actually produce red due to the setting), but that declaration is ignored because there already exists a definition for blue; the fourth line defines a gray value; and the final definition makes the color Black from the named model available as MyBlack. Because of that declaration, xcolor must be loaded with the dvipsnames option. After these declarations the new colors can be used in addition to the built-in colors.

Example
11-2-9

```
\usepackage[dvipsnames]{xcolor}
\definecolor{MyOrange}{cmyk}{0,0.42,1,0}
\colorlet{MyRGBOrange}[rgb]{MyOrange}
\providecolor{blue}{rgb}{1,0,0}
\definecolor{MyGrey}{gray}{0.75}
\definecolor{MyBlack}{named}{Black}

\newcommand\blob[1]{{\color{#1}\rule{3cm}{5mm}}}
\blob{MyOrange} \\ \blob{MyRGBOrange}\\
\blob{blue} \\ \blob{MyGrey} \\ \blob{MyBlack}
```

Defining sets of colors

To simplify the declaration of several colors with the same color model (but otherwise independent), xcolor offers two declarations that are short forms for calling \definecolor or \providecolor multiple times. It also provides support for specifying color series where each color in the series is built according to some algorithm; this feature is covered in Section 11.2.6 on page 734.

\definecolorset[*type*]{*model*}{*prefix*}{*suffix*}{*set specification*}
\providecolorset[*type*]{*model*}{*prefix*}{*suffix*}{*set specification*}

The \definecolorset declaration defines a set of colors in a specified *model* according to the *set specification*. This specification consists of a semicolon-separated list of individual color definitions. Each such color definition consists of a *name* for the new color and a *color specification* in the chosen color *model* separated by a comma. For example,

```
\definecolorset{rgb}{}{}{red,1,0,0;green,0,1,0;blue,0,0,1}
```

defines the three rgb base colors red, green, and blue. The arguments *prefix* and *suffix* are used to make up the color name, so that it is possible to specify common name parts in them if so desired.

Table 11.2: Color models supported by xcolor

Name	Base Colors/Notions	Parameter Range	Default	Target model
rgb	*red, green, blue*	$[0,1]^3$		yes
cmyk	*cyan, magenta, yellow, black*	$[0,1]^4$		yes
hsb	*hue, saturation, brightness*	$[0,1]^3$		yes
gray	*gray*	$[0,1]$		yes
cmy	*cyan, magenta, yellow*	$[0,1]^3$		yes
HTML	*RRGGBB*	$\{000000,\ldots,FFFFFF\}$		HTML $\rightarrow$ rgb
RGB	*red, green, blue*	$\{0,1,\ldots,L\}^3$	$L=255$	RGB $\rightarrow$ rgb
Gray	*gray*	$\{0,1,\ldots,N\}$	$N=15$	Gray $\rightarrow$ gray
HSB	*hue, saturation, brightness*	$\{0,1,\ldots,M\}^3$	$M=240$	HSB $\rightarrow$ hsb
Hsb	*hue°, saturation, brightness*	$[0,H]\times[0,1]^2$	$H=360$	no
tHsb	*hue°, saturation, brightness*	$[0,H]\times[0,1]^2$	$H=360$	no
wave	*lambda* (nm)	$[363,814]$		no

L, M, and N are positive integers; H is a positive real number.

The \providecolorset declaration works in the same way, but uses the command \providecolor to set up the individual colors. Thus the colors will be defined only if there isn't already a definition for them.

```
\usepackage{xcolor}
\providecolorset{gray}{Gray}{}{9,0.9;6,0.6;3,0.3}
\newcommand\blob[1]{{\color{#1}\rule{3cm}{5mm}}}
\blob{Gray9}\\ \blob{Gray6}\\ \blob{Gray3}
```

Example
11-2-10

11.2.4 Color models with xcolor

As mentioned earlier, the color package copies the color specifications straight into the .dvi file, requiring the device driver to interpret this information correctly. Consequently, it can support only "base" color models that are supported at least by some driver, and a document using colors models will print only on output drivers supporting those models.

By contrast, xcolor can convert between different color models and decide which color model information to pass to the output driver, thereby allowing any document to print with any driver. In addition, it supports other models for input purposes only (e.g., specifying colors by their wavelength).

The models currently supported by xcolor are listed in Table 11.2 with an indication about their parameter ranges and whether they can serve as target models. Some models are only intermediate target models—e.g., specifying HTML results in all color specifications being converted into HTML and then afterwards into rgb.

The first four models—rgb, cmyk, hsb, and gray—are the ones directly supported by PostScript. The cmy model is a simple complement of rgb, mainly used internally for transformation purposes. HTML is a model derived from rgb to enable color specifications as used in CSS or Web pages.

```
\usepackage{xcolor}
\newcommand*\DANTE{%
   {\usefont{OT1}{dante}{m}{n}\selectfont DANTE}}
\colorbox[HTML]{E5E5E5}{%
   \color[HTML]{2B00F0}\Huge\DANTE}
```

RGB, Gray, and HSB correspond to the base models with the same names in lowercase, except that the input ranges are not in the range 0 to 1 but instead are discrete integer values in adjustable intervals (default values are shown in Table 11.2). Hsb and tHsb are variations of hsb where the *hue* value is represented by a range different from $[0, 1]$. With the default of H = 360, one can think of this model as representing the 360 degrees of a color wheel. The tHsb corresponds to Hsb after applying a set of piecewise linear transformations, a useful feature when you are working with different types of color wheels (for details, see the package documentation [68]). Finally, the wave model is an attempt to enter a color specification by its wavelength in the visible light spectrum. It is an input model only, with no conversions set up to transform any of the other models to this one.

The next example shows an application of the wave model displaying the entire spectrum by placing small vertical lines side by side, each of which is colored in the color corresponding to the wavelength of the position (also shown in Color Plate XIV a).

```
\usepackage{xcolor}
\newcounter{WL} \setlength\unitlength{.75pt}
\begin{picture}(460,60)(355,-10)
\sffamily \tiny \linethickness{1.25\unitlength}
\setcounter{WL}{360}
\multiput(360,0)(1,0){456}%
 {{\color[wave]{\theWL}\line(0,1){50}}\stepcounter{WL}}
\linethickness{0.25\unitlength}%
\setcounter{WL}{360}
\multiput(360,0)(20,0){23}%
 {\picture(0,0)
  \line(0,-1){5} \multiput(5,0)(5,0){3}{\line(0,-1){2.5}}
  \put(0,-10){\makebox(0,0){\theWL}}\addtocounter{WL}{20}
  \endpicture}
\end{picture}
```

So how do we specify the target color model? One possibility is to set it as a package option as described in Section 11.2.1 on page 720. Alternatively, it can be set using \selectcolormodel or \substitutecolormodel.

\selectcolormodel{*model*}

The \selectcolormodel declaration takes one of the *model* names suitable as a target model from Table 11.2 as its argument. From that point on, all color specifications will be converted into that model (or the corresponding base model as described earlier). The declaration is local to the current group.

A useful technique is to set cmyk as the target model, which is often required by printing houses. Another interesting technique is to use gray, as it allows you to simulate how your document looks on a black-and-white printer.

Transformation from one color model into another is not always 100% accurate, as some of the color models represent different color spaces. In addition, all the calculations performed by xcolor are done within the somewhat limited accuracy of the TEX engine. Thus, if you have a certain color specification in some model, it might be best to pass it on unchanged to the driver if that driver supports this model.

In the situation where your driver has a broken or nonexistent implementation of a certain model while other models are properly supported, you can use the command \substitutecolormodel to transform that one color model, leaving the handling of others unchanged.

\substitutecolormodel{*source model*}{*target model*}

The \substitutecolormodel declaration directs xcolor to transform any color specification given in the *source model* into the corresponding form in the *target model*. The declaration is local to the current group.

11.2.5 Extended color specification with xcolor

The advantages of xcolor over the old color package become obvious when you look at the color specification possibilities. With color you can only specify colors by giving their values in a some color model, but what happens if you don't have the right values available? In that case, a calculator, patience, and a good knowledge of the formulas behind the color models are required—the latter being something the average user will lack!

The xcolor package offers an extended specification syntax that allows you to perform many tasks without knowing these internal details. We will introduce this syntax first with a number of practical examples and only afterwards give the precise syntax and algorithm used. The examples use \color as the command for demonstration even though this syntax is available for all color commands—including the \colorlet declaration, where it is most useful.

Printing in two colors   If a document is printed in two colors (like the book you are currently reading), it may be possible to mix the second color with white or black at no extra cost (just as you are normally able to produce gray by mixing the black color with white). To mix white into a specific color (a process called tinting), you append an exclamation mark to the color name followed by a number. This number describes the percentage of this color to use in the mix, with the remainder being white.

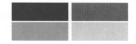

Example
11-2-13

```
\usepackage{xcolor}
\newcommand\blob[1]{{\color{#1}\rule{1.5cm}{5mm}}}
\blob{blue} \blob{blue!75} \\ \blob{blue!50} \blob{blue!25}
```

What we see in this example is actually an abbreviation of the more general syntax for mixing colors: if the second color in the mix is not white, you have to specify it as well by adding it to the right, again separated by an exclamation mark. The next example shows the mixing of blue with black (called adding tone) and gray (called shading). *Tone and shade*

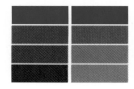

Example
11-2-14

```
\usepackage{xcolor}
\newcommand\blob[1]{{\color{#1}\rule{1.5cm}{5mm}}}
\blob{blue}              \blob{blue}\\
\blob{blue!75!black} \blob{blue!75!gray}\\
\blob{blue!50!black} \blob{blue!50!gray}\\
\blob{blue!25!black} \blob{blue!25!gray}
```

It is also possible to mix more than two colors in this way, but you have to understand how the algorithm works to do it successfully. Assume you have the three colors in individual buckets and some empty buckets for mixing. You mix the first two colors according to the specified percentage into a free bucket. That gives you a new color in that bucket. Then you use this color and mix it with the third color again into a free bucket, etc. *Colorful mix*

If you want to mix several colors with a specific percentage in the final mix, that can still be quite tricky. The next example reimplements the mix of blue and gray (which is a 50% mix of black and white) from the previous example. Here it is clearly simpler to first mix black and white and then blue to obtain the same results as before.

```
\usepackage{xcolor}
\newcommand\blob[1]{{\color{#1}\rule{1.5cm}{5mm}}}
\blob{blue}                          \blob{blue}           \\
\blob{white!50!black!25!blue} \blob{blue!75!gray}\\
\blob{white!50!black!50!blue} \blob{blue!50!gray}\\
\blob{white!50!black!75!blue} \blob{blue!25!gray}
```

Example
11-2-15

It is also possible to specify the complement of a color or color mix with this syntax, by putting a minus sign before the specification. The complement is the color that, if combined with the original color, yields white. However, in the example below, mixing the colors test and anti yields gray due to the fact that each of the colors in the mix consists of 50% white. Only the extended specification in the third row (explained afterwards) allows us to use 100% of each color, i.e., combine them.

```
\usepackage{xcolor}
\colorlet{test}{yellow!90} \colorlet{anti}{-test}
\newcommand\blob[1]{\fbox{\color{#1}\rule{1.5cm}{5mm}}}
\blob{test}                  \blob{anti}         \\
\blob{test!50!anti}      \blob{gray}         \\
\blob{rgb,1:test,1;anti,1}
```

Example
11-2-16

Mixing in the painters way As an alternative (or rather an extension as we will see), **xcolor** allows us to mix colors by adding defined portions of different colors in the mix. For instance, 2 parts blue plus 3 parts black and white should result in the color in the last line of the example. All colors participating in the mix are first converted into a specified *core model* (the next example uses `rgb`) and are then mixed according to the factor specified after each *color* and an optional divisor specified after the *core model* (as in the previous example).

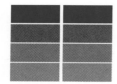

```
\usepackage{xcolor}
\newcommand\blob[1]{{\color{#1}\rule{1.3cm}{5mm}}}
\blob{blue}                        \blob{blue}              \\
\blob{rgb:blue,6;white,1;black,1} \blob{blue!75!gray}\\
\blob{rgb:blue,2;white,1;black,1} \blob{blue!50!gray}\\
\blob{rgb:blue,2;white,3;black,3} \blob{blue!25!gray}
```

Example
11-2-17

This example uses named colors in the mix. However, each *color* can be replaced by a color mix (as introduced in the earlier examples), allowing very flexible specifications.

Standard color expressions

The examples so far (see also Color Plate XIV b) have probably introduced the syntax of color expressions well enough for most practical situations. Here we formally define it and explain the algorithm that is used to produce the result color.

$$\langle prefix \rangle \; \langle color_0 \rangle \,!\, \langle value_1 \rangle \,!\, \langle color_1 \rangle \,!\, \ldots \,!\, \langle value_n \rangle \,!\, \langle color_n \rangle \; \langle postfix \rangle$$

The algorithm starts by extracting the color model and parameters from $\langle color_0 \rangle$ to define a temporary color $\langle temp \rangle$. If the $\langle postfix \rangle$ has the form `!!`[*num*], then the $\langle temp \rangle$ color will be the corresponding color $\langle num \rangle$ from the color series named $\langle color_0 \rangle$; see Section 11.2.6 on page 734 for details.

It then takes $\langle temp \rangle$, $\langle value_1 \rangle$, and $\langle color_1 \rangle$ to mix a new color by taking $\langle value_1 \rangle$% of $\langle temp \rangle$ and $(100 - \langle value_1 \rangle)$% of $\langle color_1 \rangle$, saving the result as the new $\langle temp \rangle$ color. If $\langle color_1 \rangle$ is defined in a different model than *temp*, it is first transformed into the latter model and then mixed. This step is then repeated for all remaining color pairs.

Finally, $\langle temp \rangle$ is changed to its complementary color if the $\langle prefix \rangle$ consists of an odd number of minus signs (–). At this point *temp* contains the result color, which is then either used or serves as input to other operations depending on the calling command.

The $\langle postfix \rangle$ can also take the form `!!` followed by zero or more + signs. This syntax is used in conjunction with color series (explained in Section 11.2.6 on page 734). It has no influence on the color produced.

Extended color expressions

Example 11-2-17 introduced the extended color expressions of **xcolor**. In this section we formally define them.

$$\langle core\ model \rangle \,,\, \langle div \rangle \,:\, \langle expr_1 \rangle \,,\, \langle fac_1 \rangle \,;\, \langle expr_2 \rangle \,,\, \langle fac_2 \rangle \,;\, \ldots \,;\, \langle expr_n \rangle \,,\, \langle fac_n \rangle$$

Each $\langle expr_i \rangle$ in the extended expression is a color expression as discussed earlier. These expressions are all evaluated according to the algorithm above and then converted into the specified ⟨*core model*⟩, resulting in a vector $\vec{c}_i$ in that model. Each color ⟨*expr_i*⟩ has an associated weight factor ⟨*fac_i*⟩. The result color is then calculated as

$$\langle result\ color\rangle = \sum_{i=1}^{n} \frac{\langle fac_i\rangle}{\langle div\rangle}\ \vec{c}_i$$

That is, each color vector from the first step is multiplied with a weight based on its ⟨*fac_i*⟩ value and then all the results are summed.

If ⟨*div*⟩ is not present, it is calculated automatically as $\langle div\rangle = \sum_{i=1}^{n}\langle fac_i\rangle \neq 0$ and required to be non-zero. In most cases ⟨*div*⟩ will probably be implicit; if explicitly given it is not required to equal the sum of all factors. Example 11-2-16 on page 731 used $1 = \langle div\rangle = \langle fac_i\rangle$ (adding each color at full strength to the mix) to superimpose a color and its complement.

The current color in color expressions

There also exists a reserved color name " . " (a dot) for use in color expressions. It is declared *implicitly* and denotes what PostScript calls the *current color*. This notation can be useful when calculating colors based on each other; e.g., in the next example the background color moves from dark towards white, while the text color changes in the opposite direction.

This effect is achieved by using an expression based on the current color inside the definition of \CBox: with every call to this command, the new current color is set to 80% of the old one (\color{.!80}). The following \colorbox then uses this color for the background and its complement for the text.

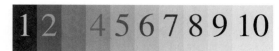

```
\usepackage{xcolor,multido}
\newcommand\CBox[1]{%
   \color{.!80}\colorbox{.}{{\color{-.}#1}}}
\multido{\iCol=1+1}{10}{%
   \CBox{\Huge\strut\iCol}}
```

Color expressions within PSTricks

Many commands in **PSTricks** support keywords to set the color of some part of the current object or to fill the background, for example. **PSTricks** loads xcolor by default and allows all the color-related keywords to take an xcolor expression instead of a previously declared color if so desired.

```
\usepackage{pstricks}
\psframebox[linecolor={[rgb]{0,0,1}},
           fillcolor=yellow!90!cyan,
           doublecolor=-yellow!90!cyan,
           fillstyle=solid,doubleline=true,
           doublesep=10pt,framesep=10pt]
          {\Huge Test\textcolor{red!75}{Test}}
```

The only potential problems you have to watch out for are that the square brackets around the color model might be mistaken for the end of the optional argument holding the key value list. Similarly, commas used in the extended color expressions might be mistaken for a comma separating the key/value pairs in the argument. In that case you have to surround the color expression with an extra set of braces, as we did for the `linecolor` value in the example above.

11.2.6 Support for color series

With the declarations given in Section 11.2.3 on page 726, it is possible to assign specific colors to names. Sometimes, however, a large number of different colors are needed, each built according to some algorithm. In this case it may be impractical to predeclare all color names individually. For this situation xcolor offers a color series declaration.

A color series declaration *defines* a base color and an algorithm for generating individual colors from this base. Once such an algorithm is defined with the command \definecolorseries, it has to be initialized with \resetcolorseries. From that point on it is possible to access the colors within the series using the standard color expression (page 732). By using a special postfix form in such an expression we can step through the series as well as explicitly access a specific component.

There is an important difference between a color series and a single color defined by the commands in Section 11.2.3: a color series is global for the document, whereas a color, when declared by \definecolor and friends, is local in its group.

\definecolorseries{*name*}{*core-model*}{*method*}
                          [*base-model*] {*base-spec*} [*step-model*] {*step-spec*}
\resetcolorseries[*divisor*]{*name*}

The algorithm and the base color for a color series are declared with the command \definecolorseries and associated with *name*. This has to happen exactly once per series and usually occurs in the document preamble. The initialization is done with \resetcolorseries. This command can appear as often as necessary to restart the series, such as with a different *divisor*.

\resetcolorseries initializes the series with the declared base color specified through the *base-model* and *base-spec* converted to the *core-model*. Furthermore, it calculates a step vector that defines, given one color within the series, how to obtain the next color. This step vector depends on the chosen *method* as well as on the arguments *step-model*, *step-spec*, and *divisor*. If the optional *divisor* argument is missing, it defaults to \colorseriescycle (which, in turn, has a default definition of 16). The available *method*s last, grad, and step are discussed below.

The last *method*   When last is specified in \definecolorseries, the arguments *step-model* and *step-spec* denote the last color in the series and the step vector $\vec{s}$ is calculated as

$$\vec{s} = \frac{1}{divisor}(\vec{\ell} - \vec{b}) \tag{11.1}$$

where $\vec{b}$ and $\vec{\ell}$ are the color vectors of the base and last colors, respectively, expressed in the *core-model*. Thus when stepping through the series, the color gradually transforms from the base color to the last color, with the amount of change depending on the size of *divisor*.

In the next example we transform black into white in 200 steps. Each of the color expressions explicitly requests a color in the sequence using the syntax !![*num*]. Later examples show different methods to access the colors in a color sequence.

```
\usepackage{xcolor,multido}
\definecolorseries{testA}
  {rgb}{last}{black}{white}
\resetcolorseries[200]{testA}% series of 200 col
\linethickness{0.005\linewidth}

\noindent
\multido{\nC=1+1}{200}{\color{testA!![\nC]}%
  \line(0,1){50}\hspace{0.005\linewidth}}
```

Example
11-2-20

With the grad method the step vector $\vec{s}$ is given by   *The* grad *method*

$$\vec{s} = \frac{1}{divisor}\overrightarrow{step\text{-}spec} \qquad (11.2)$$

In this case the optional argument *step-model* is ignored and the mandatory argument *step-spec* denotes a transformation vector in the *core-model*. Combining Equations (11.1) and (11.2), it follows that

$$\vec{\ell} = \vec{b} + \overrightarrow{step\text{-}spec}$$

In other words the last color in the color series is given by adding $\overrightarrow{step\text{-}spec}$ to its base color.

In the example below, two color series are defined: testB runs gradually from yellow ([rgb](1,1,0)) to black ([rgb](0,0,0)) defined by using the vector (-1,-1,0) and the method grad, and testC transforms yellow into cyan ([rgb](0,1,1)), again using grad and an appropriate transformation vector.

This time we use the !!+... syntax to step through the color series. With the postfix !! the current color in the series is chosen. Afterwards, for each +, one step in the color series is calculated. Thus testB!!+ selects each color in the series testB one by one, while testC!!+++ prints every third step. Whenever we reach the end of the series, the series restarts at the beginning. Thus testB is traversed twice (as the \multido has 200 steps but the series only 100) and testC three times (200 steps in the series but jumping ahead three steps each time). This is also printed on Color Plate XV(a).

```
\usepackage{xcolor,multido}
\definecolorseries{testB}{rgb}{grad}[rgb]{1,1,0}{-1,-1,0}
\definecolorseries{testC}{rgb}{grad}[rgb]{1,1,0}{-1,0,1}
\resetcolorseries[90]{testB}\resetcolorseries[180]{testC}
\linethickness{0.005\linewidth}

\noindent
\multido{\nC=1+1}{180}{\color{testB!!+}%
  \line(0,1){50}\hspace{0.005\linewidth}}\\[2pt]
\multido{\nC=1+1}{180}{\color{testC!!+++}%
  \line(0,1){50}\hspace{0.005\linewidth}}
```

Example
11-2-21

The step *method*   In contrast to `grad`, the `step` method interprets *step-spec* directly as the step vector and applies it each time.

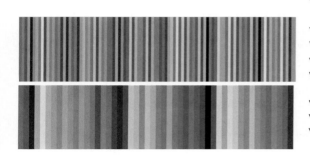

```
\usepackage{xcolor,multido}
\definecolorseries{testC}{rgb}{step}
    [rgb]{0.85,0.15,0.55}{0.37,0.47,0.17}
\resetcolorseries[100]{testC}
\linethickness{0.01\linewidth}
\noindent
\multido{\nC=1+1}{100}{\color{testC!!+}%
   \line(0,1){50}\hspace{0.01\linewidth}}
\\[2pt]
\linethickness{0.02\linewidth}
\multido{\nC=1+1}{50}{\color{testC!!++}%
   \line(0,1){50}\hspace{0.02\linewidth}}
```

Example
11-2-22

Obviously, when applying a step vector $(x_1, \ldots, x_n)$ such as $(0.37, 0.47, 0.17)$ multiple times, the resulting vector components will quickly go outside the $[0, 1]$ interval. To prevent this and ensure that each step results in a defined color vector in the *core-model*, the resulting vector is always remapped into the unit cube using the mapping

$$U(x_1, \ldots, x_n) = (u(x_1), \ldots, u(x_n)), \qquad u(x) = \begin{cases} 1 & \text{if } x = 1 \\ x - [x] & \text{if } x \neq 1 \end{cases}$$

The general algorithm is described in the xcolor package documentation.

In the last example of this section, we visualize the HSB (Hue, Saturation, Brightness) model, which is well suited for graphics artists. In this model colors are given by one number (the hue), and saturation and brightness can easily be varied, independently of the color. This model is also well suited to color calculations. In the example (also printed in Color Plate XIII a), we vary each of the three HSB parameters in turn, in 10 steps of 0 to 1 by defining a suitable color series. The numbers are printed with the complementary color, which is available by the minus sign: `\color{-testH!![\nColr]}`.

```
\usepackage{xcolor,multido}
\definecolorseries{testH}{hsb}{last}[hsb]{0,1,1}[hsb]{1,1,1}
\definecolorseries{testS}{cmyk}{last}[hsb]{.1,0,1}[hsb]{.1,1,1}
\definecolorseries{testB}{cmyk}{last}[hsb]{1,1,0}[hsb]{1,1,1}
\resetcolorseries[10]{testH} \resetcolorseries[10]{testS}
\resetcolorseries[10]{testB}
\newcommand\dotest[2]{\makebox[25mm][l]{#1:}
    \multido{\nColr=0+1}{10}{\colorbox{#2!![\nColr]}
            {\color{-#2!![\nColr]}\strut .\nColr}}}
\dotest{Hue (H)}{testH}           \\
\dotest{Saturation (S)}{testS} \\
\dotest{Brightness (B)}{testB}
```

11.2.7 Color blending and masking

The xcolor package offers an number of auxiliary features such as color blending and color masking. The process of color blending involves adding a certain color expression to all subsequent color commands. With color masking, a specified color is masked out from all following color specifications. A special application of this technique is color separation, in which all colors in the document are separated into the base colors of a specific color model (e.g., cmyk). Details can be found in the package documentation.

11.3 Coloring tables

Adding color to tables is not as straightforward as one might like. The basic problem is that color support for lines and cells cannot be provided at the TeX level but must be added in the code of the various packages. Table packages are complex and varied, and the standard ones do not directly provide color. LaTeX's color or (even better) the xcolor package can provide a standard interface to the color facilities of drivers, but a good deal of work must still be done on the internal commands of the table-building environment (tabular or array).

11.3.1 The colortbl package

The colortbl package was written by David Carlisle to provide basic facilities for coloring table cells and lines. It can be used with other LaTeX table add-on packages such as longtable, dcolumn, and hhline,[1] and loads the standard color and array packages to provide basic facilities.

To combine colortbl with xcolor (which offers some extended functionalities for tables), load xcolor with the option table, which then automatically loads colortbl and adds some additional commands for use in tables.

\columncolor[*color model*] {*color*} [*left overhang*] [*right overhang*]

This is the basic command of the colortbl package. It can be used *only* in the argument of a > column specifier, either in a table preamble or in the column specification of a \multicolumn. It provides a background color for that column or cell. The *color model* and *color* specifications are just as in normal use of the color/xcolor package. The "overhang" arguments determine how far the color spreads beyond the column contents; they default to the values of \tabcolsep (in tabular) or \arraycolsep (in array); i.e., the color fills the entire column.

---

[1] You can also use colortbl with tabular*, but see the documentation for examples of border conditions where this does not yield the expected results.

As our first example we show a multicolor table with interesting proposals for a few days' trip to Australia, also printed as Color Plate XIII c:

```
\usepackage{colortbl}
\setlength{\extrarowheight}{2mm}    \setlength{\tabcolsep}{2mm}
\begin{tabular}{l *{2}{>{\columncolor{yellow}}c c}
               >{\columncolor{red}\bfseries}c<{\,\textsterling}}
\hline
 \multicolumn{3}{>{\columncolor{red}}l}{\color{white}\textsf{LONDON}}
&\multicolumn{3}{>{\columncolor{red}}r}{\color{white}\textsf{Price}}
\\[1pt]
\hline
Sydney  & OG4G &Thu Oct 10 &Mon Oct 21 or 28 &11 or 18 days &999\\
        &      &Thu Oct 17 &Mon Oct 21 or 28 & 4 or 11 days &999\\
        & OG7A &Sun Oct 13 &Mon Oct 21 or 28 & 8 or 15 days &999\\
        &      &Sun Oct 20 &Mon Oct 28       & 8 days       &999\\
\hline
\end{tabular}
```

Example
11-3-1

Contrast this with the following simpler version, in which the \newcolumntype command defines a column with gray background and the colors cover only the text in the cells, not the white space on either side:

```
\usepackage{colortbl}
\setlength{\extrarowheight}{2mm}    \setlength{\tabcolsep}{2mm}
\newcolumntype{G}{>{\columncolor[gray]{0.8}[0pt][0pt]}c}
\begin{tabular}{l c G c G >{\bfseries}c<{\,\textsterling}}
\hline
  \multicolumn{3}{>{\columncolor[gray]{0.5}}l}{\textsf{LONDON}}
 &\multicolumn{3}{>{\columncolor[gray]{0.5}}r}{\textsf{Price}}
\\[1pt]
\hline
Sydney  & OG4G &Thu Oct 10 &Mon Oct 21 or 28 &11 or 18 days &999\\
        &      &Thu Oct 17 &Mon Oct 21 or 28 & 4 or 11 days &999\\
        & OG7A &Sun Oct 13 &Mon Oct 21 or 28 & 8 or 15 days &999\\
        &      &Sun Oct 20 &Mon Oct 28       & 8 days       &999\\
\hline
\end{tabular}
```

LONDON					Price
Sydney	OG4G	Thu Oct 10	Mon Oct 21 or 28	11 or 18 days	**999** £
		Thu Oct 17	Mon Oct 21 or 28	4 or 11 days	**999** £
	OG7A	Sun Oct 13	Mon Oct 21 or 28	8 or 15 days	**999** £
		Sun Oct 20	Mon Oct 28	8 days	**999** £

Example
11-3-2

This system is fine for vertically colored tables, but how do we handle tables where *rows* have alternate colors? Using \multicolumn would be very clumsy, so **colortbl** has an extra command.

```
\rowcolor[color model] {color} [left overhang] [right overhang]
```

This command can be used only at the start of a row; it overrides any current \columncolor specifications (in the preamble or \multicolumn specification), but its scope is limited to the current row as shown in the next example. Since all rows except the fourth use \rowcolor the blue color specified for the last column appears only on that line.

```
\usepackage{colortbl}
\setlength{\extrarowheight}{2mm}
\begin{tabular}{l c c c c >{\columncolor{blue}}c<{\,\textsterling}}
\hline \rowcolor[gray]{0.5}
\multicolumn{3}{l}{\textsf{LONDON}} & & & \textsf{Price}        \\[1pt]
\hline \rowcolor[gray]{0.9}
Sydney  & OG4G &Thu Oct 10 &Mon Oct 21 or 28 &11 or 18 days &999\\
\hline \rowcolor[gray]{0.7}
        &      &Thu Oct 17 &Mon Oct 21 or 28 & 4 or 11 days &999\\
\hline
        &OG7A  &Sun Oct 13 &Mon Oct 21 or 28 & 8 or 15 days &999\\
\hline \rowcolor[gray]{0.7}
        &      &Sun Oct 20 &Mon Oct 28       & 8 days        &999\\
\hline
\end{tabular}
```

LONDON					Price £
Sydney	OG4G	Thu Oct 10	Mon Oct 21 or 28	11 or 18 days	999 £
		Thu Oct 17	Mon Oct 21 or 28	4 or 11 days	999 £
	OG7A	Sun Oct 13	Mon Oct 21 or 28	8 or 15 days	999 £
		Sun Oct 20	Mon Oct 28	8 days	999 £

Example
11-3-3

While the \rowcolor command improves the input situation, it still takes a lot of effort to color the rows of a long table with alternate colors, and adding or deleting a row will then require major rearrangements. This situation is improved by extra commands currently offered through xcolor.

\rowcolors*[*commands*] {*start*}{*odd row color*}{*even row color*}
\hiderowcolors   \showrowcolors

These commands are provided by the xcolor *package*

The \rowcolors declaration has to appear outside the table. It applies *odd row color* to odd rows and *even row color* to even rows. An empty color argument means that the background is left uncolored.

The first row on which coloring starts is given by *start row*. By setting this value to anything other than 1, you can prevent the table header from being colored with \rowcolors. Later on in the table you can stop coloring for subsequent rows by \hiderowcolors and start it again with \showrowcolors.

The *commands* argument can contain commands like \hline that are applied to every row. In the starred form of \rowcolors, these commands are suppressed when \hiderowcolors is in effect; in the non-starred form, they are always applied.

```
\usepackage[table]{xcolor}
\setlength{\extrarowheight}{2mm}
\rowcolors[\hline]{2}{black!30}{black!10}
\begin{tabular}{l c c c >{\columncolor{blue}}c<{\,\textsterling}}
\rowcolor[gray]{0.5}
\multicolumn{3}{l}{\textsf{LONDON}} & & & \textsf{Price}        \\[1pt]
Sydney  & OG4G &Thu Oct 10 & Mon Oct 21 or 28 &11 or 18 days &999\\
        &      &Thu Oct 17 & Mon Oct 21 or 28 & 4 or 11 days &999\\
% \colomcolor ignored everywhere except in the next row:
\hiderowcolors
        &OG7A &Sun Oct 13 & Mon Oct 21 or 28 & 8 or 15 days &999\\
\showrowcolors
        &      &Sun Oct 20 & Mon Oct 28      & 8 days        &999\\
\end{tabular}
```

LONDON					Price £
Sydney	OG4G	Thu Oct 10	Mon Oct 21 or 28	11 or 18 days	999 £
		Thu Oct 17	Mon Oct 21 or 28	4 or 11 days	999 £
	OG7A	Sun Oct 13	Mon Oct 21 or 28	8 or 15 days	999 £
		Sun Oct 20	Mon Oct 28	8 days	999 £

Example
11-3-4

As coloring through \rowcolors or \rowcolor takes precedence over colors specified through \columncolor, the previous examples showed a uniform line appearance whenever a row color was used. To change the background color for individual cells in such lines (and elsewhere), the **colortbl** package offers \cellcolor.

\cellcolor[*color model*] {*color*}

This command takes the same arguments as \color and defines the background color for the current table cell. It takes precedence over any other background color specification (through \rowcolor or \columncolor). As can be seen in the next example it can appear anywhere in the cell.

```
\usepackage[table]{xcolor}
\setlength{\extrarowheight}{2mm}
\rowcolors[\hline]{2}{black!30}{black!10}
\begin{tabular}{l c c c c c<{\,\textsterling}}
\rowcolor[gray]{0.5}
\multicolumn{3}{l}{\textsf{LONDON}} & & & \textsf{Price}          \\[1pt]
Sydney  & OG4G &Thu Oct 10 & Mon Oct 21 or 28 &
                            \cellcolor{white} 11 or 18 days &999\\
        &      &Thu Oct 17 & Mon Oct 21 or 28 & 4 or 11 days &999\\
        &OG7A  &Sun Oct 13 & Mon Oct 21 or 28 &
                            8 or \cellcolor{white} 15 days &999\\
        &      &Sun Oct 20 & Mon Oct 28       & 8 days        &999\\
\end{tabular}
```

LONDON					Price £
Sydney	OG4G	Thu Oct 10	Mon Oct 21 or 28	11 or 18 days	999 £
		Thu Oct 17	Mon Oct 21 or 28	4 or 11 days	999 £
	OG7A	Sun Oct 13	Mon Oct 21 or 28	8 or 15 days	999 £
		Sun Oct 20	Mon Oct 28	8 days	999 £

Example
11-3-5

\arrayrulecolor[*color model*] {*color*}

To color the *lines* in a tabular environment, including \vline, \cline, and \hline, the **colortbl** package provides the \arrayrulecolor declaration, which has the same arguments as \color and colors all subsequent horizontal and vertical rules in tables. It can be set outside the table, at the start of a row, or in a > specification in a table preamble. Its effects are *not* limited to the current scope, but do not override specifications in the table preamble.

Thus, in the following table (also printed in Color Plate XIII c), the vertical rules are set to green at the start and are unaffected by the subsequent \arrayrulecolor commands:

```
\usepackage{colortbl}
\renewcommand{\arraystretch}{1.1}
\setlength{\arrayrulewidth}{2pt}
\arrayrulecolor{green}
\begin{tabular}{|l|c|r|}
\arrayrulecolor{black}\hline
    United Kingdom & London & Thames \\
\arrayrulecolor{blue}\hline
    France         & Paris  & Seine  \\
\arrayrulecolor{black}\cline{1-1}
\arrayrulecolor{red}\cline{2-3}
    Russia  & Moscow &   Moskva        \\
\hline
\end{tabular}
```

United Kingdom	London	Thames
France	Paris	Seine
Russia	Moscow	Moskva

Example
11-3-6

There is one problem: if colored rules are combined with colored cells, partial \cline rules are covered by the cell shading and thus are invisible. If necessary, you can use the more complicated hhline package with colortbl to achieve the desired effect.

> \doublerulesepcolor[*color model*]{*color*}

This declaration colors the remaining area that can be colored in tables—the gap between rules created by using || in a table preamble or \hline\hline in a table body. It works like \arrayrulecolor. Note, however, that when you color the space between two \hline commands in the longtable package, LATEX no longer allows a page break at this point. This is one of the situations in which adding color to your document may produce different page breaks.

11.3.2 Examples

Here we show how to color elements of tables by using the various coloring commands described above. Support of color with LATEX is not yet optimal, so that some complex constructs must sometimes be used to obtain a particular effect. These tables are reproduced in color in Color Plate XVI.

We invite our readers to study *Color for the Electronic Age* [137], an excellent book on many aspects of color, for ideas about how colors can add value to tabular material. In the chapter on charts and graphs, Jan White shows how to introduce variety in table presentations by using a single color in different ways. In the following variations, we implement some of his suggestions.

Let us start by looking at the generic table that will be the basis of our discussion (not reproduced on Color Plate XVI):

Table title

Description	Column 1	Column 2
Row one	mmmmmm	mmmmm
Row two	mmmmm	mmmm
Row three	mmmmmm	mmmmmm
Row four	mmmmmm	mmmmm
Totals	mmmmmm	mmmmmm

```
\usepackage{colortbl}
\begin{tabular}{lrr}
  \large\textbf{Table title}
\\[2mm]
  \textbf{Description}
          & \textbf{Column 1}
              & \textbf{Column 2}
\\[1mm]
  Row one   & mmmmmm & mmmmm   \\
  Row two   & mmmmm & mmmm    \\
  Row three& mmmmmm & mmmmmm \\
  Row four  & mmmmmm & mmmmm   \\
\cline{2-3}
  Totals    & mmmmmm & mmmmmm
\end{tabular}
```

Example 11-3-7

First, let us put the table completely inside a colored box—orange, say, by defining that color with \definecolor and then using the simple \colorbox command (see Color Plate XVI a):

Table title

Description	Column 1	Column 2
Row one	mmmmmm	mmmmm
Row two	mmmmm	mmmm
Row three	mmmmmm	mmmmmm
Row four	mmmmmm	mmmmm
Totals	mmmmmm	mmmmmm

```
\usepackage{colortbl}
\definecolor{orange}{cmyk}{0,0.61,0.87,0}
\colorbox{orange}{%
  \begin{tabular}{lrr}
    \large\textbf{Table title}
\\[2mm]
    \textbf{Description}
            & \textbf{Column 1}
                & \textbf{Column 2}
\\[1mm]
    Row one   & mmmmmm & mmmmm   \\
    Row two   & mmmmm & mmmm    \\
    Row three& mmmmmm & mmmmmm \\
    Row four  & mmmmmm & mmmmm   \\
  \cline{2-3}
    Totals    & mmmmmm & mmmmmm
  \end{tabular}%
}
```

Example 11-3-8

Not only does this not add much information to the table, but you may also feel that the text is too dark to read easily. We can, therefore, print the text in white (Color Plate XVI b):

Table title		
Description	**Column 1**	**Column 2**
Row one	mmmmmm	mmmmm
Row two	mmmmm	mmmm
Row three	mmmmmm	mmmmmm
Row four	mmmmmm	mmmmm
Totals	mmmmmm	mmmmmm

```
\usepackage{colortbl}
\colorbox[cmyk]{0,0.61,0.87,0}{\color{white}%
\begin{tabular}{lrr}
  \large\textbf{Table title}
\\[2mm]
  \textbf{Description}
          & \textbf{Column 1}
             & \textbf{Column 2}
\\[1mm]
  Row one  & mmmmmm & mmmmm  \\
  Row two  &  mmmmm & mmmm   \\
  Row three& mmmmmm & mmmmmm \\
  Row four & mmmmmm & mmmmm  \\
\cline{2-3}
  Totals   & mmmmmm & mmmmmm
\end{tabular}%
}
```

Example 11-3-9

This does not, of course, affect the color of the horizontal rule drawn with \cline.

Depending on the circumstances, you might or might not consider this an improvement. If you do want to set light text like this on a dark background then it is usually better to render the text in a heavier font, or the same font in bold (Color Plate XVI c):

Table title		
Description	**Column 1**	**Column 2**
Row one	mmmmmm	mmmmm
Row two	mmmmm	mmmm
Row three	mmmmmm	mmmmmm
Row four	mmmmmm	mmmmm
Totals	mmmmmm	mmmmmm

```
\usepackage{colortbl}
\colorbox[cmyk]{0,0.61,0.87,0}{%
\color{white}\bfseries%
\begin{tabular}{lrr}
  \large\textbf{Table title}
\\[2mm]
  \textbf{Description}
          & \textbf{Column 1}
             & \textbf{Column 2}
\\[1mm]
  Row one  & mmmmmm & mmmmm  \\
  Row two  &  mmmmm & mmmm   \\
  Row three& mmmmmm & mmmmmm \\
  Row four & mmmmmm & mmmmm  \\
\cline{2-3}
  Totals   & mmmmmm & mmmmmm
\end{tabular}%
}
```

Example 11-3-10

So far no elements of the table have been highlighted, so the color is only an embellishment, not a functional tool. Let us see how by coloring some elements we can focus the reader's attention (not reproduced on Color Plate XVI):

Table title

Description	Column 1	Column 2
Row one	mmmmm	mmmm
Row two	mmmm	mmm
Row three	mmmmm	mmmmm
Row four	mmmmm	mmmm
Totals	mmmmm	mmmmm

Example 11-3-11

```
\usepackage{colortbl}
\begin{tabular}{lrr}
  \color{blue}
      \large\textbf{Table title}\\[3mm]
  \textbf{Description}
          & \textbf{Column 1}
              & \textbf{Column 2}\\[1mm]
Row one   & mmmmm & mmmm  \\
Row two   &  mmmm & mmm   \\
Row three& mmmmm & mmmmm \\
Row four & mmmmm & mmmm  \\
\cline{2-3}
  \color{blue} Totals
          & \color{blue} mmmmm
              & \color{blue}mmmmm
\end{tabular}
```

The title and bottom line have been set in blue for emphasis. We can also invert the procedure by coloring the text you do *not* want to stress, thereby bringing out the black text elements (Color Plate XVI d):

Table title

Description	Column 1	Column 2
Row one	mmmmm	mmmm
Row two	mmmm	mmm
Row three	mmmmm	mmmmm
Row four	mmmmm	mmmm
Totals	mmmmm	mmmmm

Example 11-3-12

```
\usepackage{colortbl}
{\color{green}%
\begin{tabular}{lrr}
  \color{black}
      \large\textbf{Table title}\\[3mm]
  \textbf{Description}
    & \textbf{Column 1}
            & \textbf{Column 2}\\[1mm]
Row one   & mmmmm & mmmm  \\
Row two   &  mmmm & mmm   \\
Row three& mmmmm & mmmmm \\
Row four & mmmmm & mmmm  \\
\arrayrulecolor{black}\cline{2-3}
  \color{black} Totals
          & \color{black}mmmmm
              & \color{black}mmmmm
\end{tabular}%
}
```

Note the \arrayrulecolor command that colors in black the horizontal line separating the body from the last line.

To draw attention to individual rows of a table, we can put a band of color behind them (Color Plate XVI e):

Table title

Description	Column 1	Column 2
Row one	mmmmm	mmmm
Row two	mmmm	mmm
Row three	mmmmm	mmmmm
Row four	mmmmm	mmmm
Totals	mmmmm	mmmmm

```
\usepackage{colortbl}
\newcommand\panel[1]{\multicolumn{1}%
            {>{\columncolor{magenta}}#1}}
\begin{tabular}{lrr}
  \large\textbf{Table title}\\[2mm]
  \textbf{Description}
            & \textbf{Column 1}
                & \textbf{Column 2}\\[1mm]
  Row one & mmmmm & mmmm \\
  Row two &  mmmm & mmm  \\
  \panel{l}{Row three}
          & \panel{r}{mmmmm}
              & \panel{r}{mmmmm} \\
  Row four& mmmmm & mmmm  \\ \cline{2-3}
  Totals  & mmmmm & mmmmm
\end{tabular}
```

Example 11-3-13

But we can do even better: color the whole table, and leave the row to be emphasized with a white background (Color Plate XVI f):

Table title

Description	Column 1	Column 2
Row one	mmmmm	mmmm
Row two	mmmm	mmm
Row three	mmmmm	mmmmm
Row four	mmmmm	mmmm
Totals	mmmmm	mmmmm

```
\usepackage{colortbl}
\newcommand\panel[1]{\multicolumn{1}%
            {>{\columncolor{white}}#1}}
\colorbox{magenta}{%
\arrayrulecolor{black}
\begin{tabular}{lrr}
  \large\textbf{Table title}\\[2mm]
  \textbf{Description}
            & \textbf{Column 1}
                & \textbf{Column 2}\\[1mm]
  Row one & mmmmm & mmmm \\
  Row two &  mmmm & mmm  \\
  \panel{l}{Row three}
          & \panel{r}{mmmmm}
              & \panel{r}{mmmmm} \\
  Row four& mmmmm & mmmm \\ \cline{2-3}
  Totals  & mmmmm & mmmmm
\end{tabular}}
```

Example 11-3-14

This is completely analogous to the previous example except that the \columncolor command now uses the color white, while the \colorbox at the beginning makes the whole table magenta.

Now we look at ways to highlight columns rather than rows. We use the `\columncolor` command to specify the color of the columns (Color Plate XVI g):

Table title

Description	Column 1	Column 2
Row one	mmmmm	mmmm
Row two	mmmm	mmm
Row three	mmmmm	mmmmm
Row four	mmmmm	mmmm
Totals	mmmmm	mmmmm

Example
11-3-15

```
\usepackage{colortbl}
\definecolor{Bluec}{cmyk}{.60,0,0,0}
\begin{tabular}{l>{\columncolor{Bluec}}rr}
\large\textbf{Table title}\\[2mm]
\textbf{Description} & \textbf{Column 1}
          & \textbf{Column 2} \\[1mm]
Row one  & mmmmm & mmmm \\
Row two  &  mmmm &  mmm \\
Row three& mmmmm & mmmmm \\
Row four & mmmmm & mmmm \\
Totals   & mmmmm & mmmmm
\end{tabular}
```

Colored panels of this type are often used to highlight connected regions in a table. The blue shade (`Bluec`) is defined at the beginning with the standard `\definecolor` command, although we could also have combined it with `\columncolor` as

```
\columncolor[cmyk]{.60,0,0,0}
```

Another feature often encountered in color work is the color gradient (Color Plate XVI h). Here we use various levels of cyan defined at the start for successive rows. We use the extended mixing possibilities of **xcolor** to achieve this effect:

Table title

Description	Column 1	Column 2
Row one	mmmmm	mmmm
Row two	mmmm	mmm
Row three	mmmmm	mmmmm
Row four	mmmmm	mmmm
Totals	mmmmm	mmmmm

Example
11-3-16

```
\usepackage[table]{xcolor}
\definecolor{Cyan}{cmyk}{1,0,0,0.3}
\begin{tabular}{l rr}
\rowcolor{Cyan}\multicolumn{3}{l}
    {\large\textbf{\strut Table title}}\\[2mm]
\rowcolor{Cyan}
\textbf{Description} & \textbf{Column 1}
          & \textbf{Column 2} \\[1mm]
\rowcolor{Cyan!20}Row one  & mmmmm & mmmm \\
\rowcolor{Cyan!40}Row two  &  mmmm &  mmm \\
\rowcolor{Cyan!60}Row three& mmmmm & mmmmm\\
\rowcolor{Cyan!80}Row four & mmmmm & mmmm \\
\rowcolor{Cyan}  Totals   & mmmmm & mmmmm
\end{tabular}
```

Although this task requires specifying colors for each row, the result can be quite pleasing. This technique is certainly one of those most often used to produce attractive and easily readable tabular material.

One might expect to be able to achieve the same effect by defining a color series and stepping it through each row. However, as it turns out, this approach results in the color changing for every cell: due to the implementation, the color expression is evaluated each time (rather than once per row). Nevertheless, this also results in an interesting application (Color Plate XVI i).

```
\usepackage[table]{xcolor}
\definecolor{Cyan}{cmyk}{1,0,0,0.3}
\definecolorseries{XXX}{cmyk}{last}{white}{Cyan}
\resetcolorseries[20]{XXX}
\rowcolors{2}{XXX!!+}{XXX!!+}
\begin{tabular}{lrr}
\rowcolor{Cyan}\multicolumn{3}{l}
    {\large\textbf{\strut Table title}}\\[2mm]
\rowcolor{Cyan}
\textbf{Description} & \textbf{Column 1}
               & \textbf{Column 2} \\[1mm]
Row one   & mmmmm & mmmm \\
Row two   & mmmm  & mmm  \\
Row three & mmmmm & mmmmm\\
Row four  & mmmmm & mmmm \\
Totals    & mmmmm & mmmmm
\end{tabular}
```

Example
11-3-17

To emphasize the titles and headings, we can color fields we consider less important. To further guide the eye, we can add some vertical and horizontal lines (Color Plate XVI j):

```
\usepackage{colortbl}
\begin{tabular}{l
    *2{|>{\columncolor[cmyk]{.40,0,0,0}}r}}
\rowcolor{white}
\large\textbf{Table title}  \\[2mm]
\rowcolor{white}
\textbf{Description} & \textbf{Column 1}
               & \textbf{Column 2} \\[1mm]\hline
Row one   & mmmmm & mmmm \\\hline
Row two   & mmmm  & mmm  \\\hline
Row three & mmmmm & mmmmm\\\hline
Row four  & mmmmm & mmmm \\\hline
\rowcolor{white}
Totals    & mmmmm & mmmmm
\end{tabular}
```

Example
11-3-18

As already remarked, we can color the region containing the important text and leave the less important text region white. As we want the surrounding region to extend a bit beyond the table limits, we reset the \fboxsep width to 3 mm, and we choose a lightish blue tint as the background color. The rest is similar to the previous example, although here we used the approach in which we recolor individual cells with \cellcolor rather than using \rowcolor and \columncolor (to show a different coding approach, even though it is less efficient here). It is interesting to compare the examples to see which is better at getting the message across (Color Plate XVI k):

```
\usepackage{colortbl}
\newcommand{\panel}[1]{%
  \multicolumn{1}{|>{\cellcolor{white}}r}{#1}}
\setlength\fboxsep{3mm}
\colorbox[cmyk]{.40,0,0,0}{%
\begin{tabular}{l|r|r}
\multicolumn{1}{l|}
     {\large\textbf{Table title}}\\[2mm]
\textbf{Description} & \textbf{Column 1}
          & \textbf{Column 2} \\[1mm]\hline
Row one   & \panel{mmmmm} & \panel{mmmm} \\\hline
Row two   &  \panel{mmmm} &  \panel{mmm} \\\hline
Row three& \panel{mmmmm} & \panel{mmmmm}\\\hline
Row four & \panel{mmmmm} & \panel{mmmm} \\\hline
Totals    & mmmmm & mmmmm
\end{tabular}}
```

Table title		
Description	**Column 1**	**Column 2**
Row one	mmmmm	mmmm
Row two	mmmm	mmm
Row three	mmmmm	mmmmm
Row four	mmmmm	mmmm
Totals	mmmmm	mmmmm

Example 11-3-19

We need not always color the column cells themselves; coloring the rules inside the table can sometimes be enough to highlight the relevant information. We can do this with the **colortbl** facilities. First we replace the default black rules with colored ones; this is done with the \arrayrulecolor command and affects the vertical rules defined in the table preamble. After the preamble, we switch to a slightly different blue for all horizontal rules, but the rightmost part of the last rule is switched back to black with a new \arrayrulecolor declaration before the \cline (Color Plate XVI l):

```
\usepackage{colortbl}
\newcommand\rules{%
   \arrayrulecolor[cmyk]{.80,0,0,0}\cline{2-3}}
\setlength\arrayrulewidth{1pt}
\arrayrulecolor[cmyk]{.80,0,0,0}
\begin{tabular}{l|r|r}
\large\textbf{Table title}\\[2mm]
\textbf{Description} & \textbf{Column 1}
          & \textbf{Column 2} \\[1mm]
\hline
Row one  & mmmmm & mmmm  \\\rules
Row two  &  mmmm &  mmm  \\\rules
Row three& mmmmm & mmmmm \\\rules
Row four & mmmmm & mmmm  \\
     \arrayrulecolor{black}\hline
Totals   & mmmmm & mmmmm
\end{tabular}
```

Table title		
Description	**Column 1**	**Column 2**
Row one	mmmmm	mmmm
Row two	mmmm	mmm
Row three	mmmmm	mmmmm
Row four	mmmmm	mmmm
Totals	mmmmm	mmmmm

Example 11-3-20

Alternatively, we can go back to a blue-colored background for some rows, and draw only a few of the rules to guide the reader through the information (Color Plate XVI m):

```
\usepackage{colortbl}
\arrayrulecolor{black}
\begin{tabular}{l|r|r}
\multicolumn{3}{>{\columncolor[cmyk]{1,0,0,0}}l}
  {\large\textbf{Table title}}\\[2mm]
\rowcolor[cmyk]{0.2,0,0,0}
\textbf{Description} & \textbf{Column 1}
        & \textbf{Column 2} \\[1mm]\hline
Row one   & mmmmm & mmmm \\
Row two   &  mmmm & mmm \\
Row three& mmmmm & mmmmm \\
Row four & mmmmm & mmmm \\\cline{2-3}
Totals    & mmmmm & mmmmm
\end{tabular}
```

Table title		
Description	**Column 1**	**Column 2**
Row one	mmmmm	mmmm
Row two	mmmm	mmm
Row three	mmmmm	mmmmm
Row four	mmmmm	mmmm
Totals	mmmmm	mmmmm

Example 11-3-21

To construct a more complicated arrangement that subdivides the table into different regions, we can use a combination of row, column, and cell colors. As we noted on page 742, the standard method for creating partial horizontal rules does not work correctly with **colortbl**, so **hhline** is used in the following example (Color Plate XVI n):

```
\usepackage{colortbl,hhline}
\definecolor{Light}{cmyk}{.4,0,0,0} \definecolor{Dark}{cmyk}{.8,0,0,0}
\begin{tabular}{>{\columncolor{Light}}l >{\columncolor{Dark}}r
                    >{\columncolor{Dark}}r }
 \multicolumn{3}{>{\cellcolor{Light}}l}{\large\textbf{Table title}}\\[2mm]
\rowcolor{white}
 \textbf{Description} & \textbf{Column 1} & \textbf{Column 2}      \\[1mm]
\rowcolor{Light}
 Row one    & mmmmm & mmmm \\
\arrayrulecolor{white}\hline\arrayrulecolor{black}
 Row two    & mmmm  & mmm  \\\hhline{~--}
 Row three & mmmmm & mmmmm\\\hhline{~--}  Row four & mmmmm & mmmm\\
\rowcolor{white} Totals    & mmmmm & mmmmm
\end{tabular}
```

Table title		
Description	**Column 1**	**Column 2**
Row one	mmmmm	mmmm
Row two	mmmm	mmm
Row three	mmmmm	mmmmm
Row four	mmmmm	mmmm
Totals	mmmmm	mmmmm

Example 11-3-22

The interplay among the various styles of typesetting titles, coloring rules, and shades of the background color gives you a rich palette of possibilities for presenting complex data. As a last effect, we can consider altering the *width* of the rules; in the example below, a thick horizontal rule highlights the title and header lines (Color Plate XVI o).

Note the supplementary columns in the table to extend the color by one \quad to the left and right. Wider margins are not easy to achieve otherwise, as the \rowcolors declaration doesn't support explicit overhang of the background color.

```
\usepackage[table]{xcolor}
\definecolor{Light}{cmyk}{.40,0,0,0}
\definecolor{Dark}{cmyk}{.80,0,0,0}
\usepackage{hhline}
\setlength\arrayrulewidth{1mm}
\rowcolors{2}{Dark}{Dark}
\begin{tabular}{llrrl}
\rowcolor{Light}
\qquad & \multicolumn{3}{l}{\large
    \textbf{Table title}} &\qquad \\[2mm]
&\textbf{Description} & \textbf{Column 1}
        & \textbf{Column 2} & \\[1mm]
\hline
& Row one   & mmmmm & mmmm & \\
& Row two   &  mmmm & mmm  & \\
& Row three& mmmmm & mmmmm& \\
& Row four & mmmmm & mmmm & \\
\doublerulesepcolor{Dark}\hhline{~~--~}
&    Totals & mmmmm & mmmmm&\\[2mm]
\end{tabular}
```

Table title

	Description	Column 1	Column 2
Row one		mmmmm	mmmm
Row two		mmmm	mmm
Row three		mmmmm	mmmmm
Row four		mmmmm	mmmm
Totals		mmmmm	mmmmm

Example
11-3-23

Another interesting aspect in this example is the use of \hhline to achieve a partial rule. The ~ notation generates no rule segment coloring the space in \doublerulesepcolor. So, by setting this color to the background color, we achieve the desired result. An alternative solution, which comes in handy if you need even more complicated arrangements, is the use of the > notation for \hhline. This extension is provided by colortbl and is not available with the original package; it allows you to set the \arrayrulecolor for further rule segments. The rule in the previous example could have been achieved by this method with

```
\hhline{>{\arrayrulecolor{Dark}}--%
        >{\arrayrulecolor{black}}--%
        >{\arrayrulecolor{Dark}}-}
```

We hope these examples have shown how flexible the color commands are in creating almost any possible layout. The only caveat is that you should not get carried away by the wealth of options. The purpose of using color is to help the reader understand material better—don't let your use of color stand in the way of comprehension.

11.4 Color slides with LaTeX — The beamer class

Many LaTeX users want to take advantage of TeX's high-quality typesetting to produce slides for a presentation. This facility was originally provided by a separate package, SliTeX, but it had a number of disadvantages. In this section we discuss the powerful **beamer** class which can be used to make presentation slides with a huge variety of facilities. It is just one of a number of LaTeX packages for presentations—we do not have enough space here to describe them all.

beamer is a LaTeX class that can be used with almost all other LaTeX packages, such as those to change fonts, include graphics, or add mathematical facilities. It's main job is to produce slides for display using a data projector, but it can also generate output for printing or a handout from the same source file.

The main features of **beamer** are as follows:

- You can create PDF slides with **pdflatex** or **dvips** and **ps2pdf**.

- You can use nearly all LaTeX macros inside **beamer** e.g., `\tableofcontents`.

- Predefined themes let you produce professional-looking slides without knowing too much of the internals of the package.

- You can change most color and font options globally or locally.

- You can take advantage of a special style file to use a source in an article or book document class.

- You can write **beamer** files with a special layout file for the LyX (`http://www.lyx.org`) document processor.

11.4.1 Using the beamer class

To create your first slides, begin your document in the usual way with **beamer** as the document class name, perhaps with some optional arguments from those listed in Table 11.3. You can load additional packages e.g., **fontenc**, **inputenc**, or **amsmath** as usual.

```
\documentclass[ class options ]{beamer}
\usepackage[T1]{fontenc}
\usepackage[latin1]{inputenc}
\usepackage{amsmath}
  ...
```

You can use **beamer** to write a document with different modes from the same source—a presentation, an article or a handout. Due to space limitations, only the default presentation mode is used and described in following sections. The possible modes are listed in Table 11.3 and in Section 11.4.10 with examples showing how to switch between these modes.

Table 11.3: **beamer** class options and modes

Option Name	Meaning
ucs	Loads the package **ucs** and the Unicode pages 0 and 1. Also passes the correct options to the **hyperref** package.
utf8	Same as option ucs with an additional loading of the **inputenc** package with option utf8.
8pt ... 20pt	Uses the **extsizes** package for 8pt, 9pt,14pt,17pt, and 20pt.
smaller	Same as option 10pt.
bigger	Same as option 12pt.
draft	Replaces all headlines, footlines, and sidebars with empty rectangles, similar to the draft option of the **graphicx** package.
hyperref={...}	Options for the **hyperref** package.
usepdftitle={...}	true (default) or false. If false, the title is not passed into the information field of the generated PDF file.
xcolor={...}	Options for the **xcolor** package.
c	Makes text in a frame vertically centered.
t	Makes text in a frame top aligned.
compress	Makes navigation bars as small as possible.
trans	Uses the trans overlay specification.
noamsthm	Does not load the packages **amsthm** and **amsmath**. proof and theorem must be defined by another package or the user, if needed.
notheorems	Loads the packages **amsthm** and **amsmath**, but does not define the block style of the environments.
envcountsec	Sets the counting to depend on sections, so that a new section resets all counters.
ignoreonframetext	Ignores all text and code outside frames (same as executing the macro \mode*; see Section 11.4.10).
handout	Sets options to be suitable for a handout.
notes={...}	hide (default), show, only or onlyslideswithnotes. Defines how notes should be handled by **beamer**.

Mode Name	Meaning
beamer	Default mode.
handout	Create handouts.
trans	Create transparencies.
article	This is the mode when **beamer** creates the document with any other class than the **beamer** documentclass e.g., the book class.
presentation	Define sections for the article and handout mode.
all	Create all possible modes.

11.4.2 Your first slides

The **beamer** class comes with lengthy documentation, example files, and a lot of ready-made templates for different colors and layouts. The following example shows the default output. It is difficult to choose the right layout for the presentation—when people are more impressed by the fancy layout than by the contents, then there is something wrong! For a first-time user, it is sensible to use some of the predefined themes of **beamer**, and to attempt to write your own only after gaining some experience with this class.

Let us start with a simple pair of slides:

```
\documentclass{beamer}
\title{The Declaration of Independence of
       the Thirteen Colonies.}
\author{by Thomas Jefferson et al.}
\date{July 4, 1776}
\frame{\maketitle}

\section{The unanimous Declaration}
\begin{frame}
 \frametitle{Self-evident truths.}
 We hold these truths to be self-evident,
 \begin{itemize}
  \item \textbf{that} all men are created equal,
  \item \textbf{that} they are endowed by their
        Creator with certain inalienable rights,
  \item \textbf{that} among these are Life,
        Liberty and the Pursuit of Happiness.
  \item \textbf{That}, to secure these rights,
Governments are instituted among Men, deriving
their just powers from the consent of the governed.
  \item \textbf{That}, when any form of government
becomes destructive of these ends, it is the Right
of the People to alter or abolish it.
 \end{itemize}
\end{frame}
```

Example
11-4-1

We can change appearance of the slides by choosing variants in five style levels for **beamer**: the theme, the outer layout, the inner layout, the color theme, and the font theme. In each case you can use the standard LaTeX \usepackage mechanism by preceding the style name with the word beamertheme, beameroutertheme, beamerinnertheme, beamercolortheme, or beamerfonttheme respectively.

Table 11.4 lists the predefined styles that come with **beamer**. These themes are not official, and their contents and layout depend on what users have contributed to the community.

In the next step we choose the Malmoe main theme; this is just a name for the theme and not the official layout of the Swedish university!

Table 11.4: Predefined themes and layouts in **beamer**

Type	*Name*
themes	Antibes, Bergen, Berkeley, Berlin, Boadilla, boxes, Copenhagen, Darmstadt, default, Dresden, Frankfurt, Goettingen, Hannover, Ilmenau, JuanLesPins, Luebeck, Madrid, Malmoe, Marburg, Montpellier, PaloAlto, Pittsburgh, Rochester, Singapore, Szeged, Warsaw
outer themes	default, infolines, miniframes, shadow, sidebar, smoothbars, smoothtree, split, tree
inner layouts	circles, default, inmargin, rectangles, rounded
color themes	albatross, beetle, crane, default, dolphin, dove, fly, lily, orchid, rose, seagull, seahorse, sidebartab, structure, whale
font themes	default, professionalfonts, serif, structurebold, structureitalicserif, structuresmallcapsserif

The example shows the second slide of our simple presentation. The contents are the same, the view different:

Example
11-4-2

```
\documentclass{beamer}
\usepackage{beamerthemeMalmoe}
\title{The Declaration of Independence of
       the Thirteen Colonies.}
\author{by Thomas Jefferson et al.}
\date{July 4, 1776}
\frame{\maketitle}
\section{The unanimous Declaration}
\begin{frame}
 \frametitle{Self-evident truths.}
 We hold these truths to be self-evident,
 \begin{itemize}
  \item \textbf{that} all men are created equal,
... further code omitted ...
```

The outer theme, or layout, styles control everything to do with the frame layout:

- The head- and footline.
- The sidebars.
- The logo.
- The frame title.

Since we often use a rectangular display with a width greater than the height (in general, a proportion of 4:3), it is often a good idea to have a menu on the side. The theme "sidebar" in the next example demonstrates this:

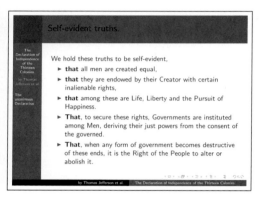

```
\documentclass{beamer}
\usepackage{beamerthemeMalmoe}
\usepackage{beamerouterthemesidebar}
\title{The Declaration of Independence of
       the Thirteen Colonies.}
\author{by Thomas Jefferson et al.}
\date{July 4, 1776}
\frame{\maketitle}

\section{The unanimous Declaration}
\begin{frame}
 \frametitle{Self-evident truths.}
 We hold these truths to be self-evident,
 ... further code omitted ...
```

Example
11-4-3

Choosing the right colors for a presentation is not easy and often comes down to personal preference. Try to avoid choosing a color for its own sake, and focus on the information in the slide. We show the "dove" color theme in the next example:

```
\documentclass{beamer}
\usepackage{beamerthemeMalmoe}
\usepackage{beamerouterthemesidebar}
\usepackage{beamercolorthemedove}
\title{The Declaration of Independence of
       the Thirteen Colonies.}
\author{by Thomas Jefferson et al.}
\date{July 4, 1776}
\frame{\maketitle}

\section{The unanimous Declaration}
\begin{frame}
 \frametitle{Self-evident truths.}
 We hold these truths to be self-evident,
 ... further code omitted ...
```

Example
11-4-4

The inner theme controls the layout of the frame contents. It implements the following features:

- Title and part pages.
- Itemize environments.
- Enumerate environments.
- Description environments.

- Block environments.
- Theorem and proof environments.
- Figures and tables.
- Footnotes.
- Bibliography entries.

In the next example we demonstrate the user of the "rounded" inner theme (notice the change in the bullets):

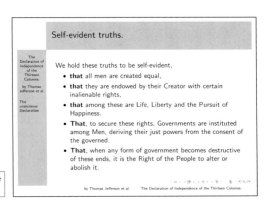

Example
11-4-5

```
\documentclass{beamer}
\usepackage{beamerthemeMalmoe}
\usepackage{beamerouterthemesidebar}
\usepackage{beamercolorthemedove}
\usepackage{beamerinnerthemecircles}
\title{The Declaration of Independence of
      the Thirteen Colonies.}
\author{by Thomas Jefferson et al.}
\date{July 4, 1776}
\frame{\maketitle}

\section{The unanimous Declaration}
\begin{frame}
 \frametitle{Self-evident truths.}
 We hold these truths to be self-evident,
... further code omitted ...
```

Finally, we can vary the font setup. Here we demonstrate the "structureitalicserif" style:

Example
11-4-6

```
\documentclass{beamer}
\usepackage{beamerthemeMalmoe}
\usepackage{beamerouterthemesidebar}
\usepackage{beamercolorthemedove}
\usepackage{beamerinnerthemecircles}
\usepackage{beamerfontthemestructureitalicserif}
\title{The Declaration of Independence of
      the Thirteen Colonies.}
\author{by Thomas Jefferson et al.}
\date{July 4, 1776}
\frame{\maketitle}

\section{The unanimous Declaration}
\begin{frame}
 \frametitle{Self-evident truths.}
 We hold these truths to be self-evident,
... further code omitted ...
```

Instead of loading the style packages with `\usepackage`, you also can use the following macros in the preamble:

```
\usetheme [options] {theme name}
\usefonttheme [options] {font theme name}
\usecolortheme [options] {color theme name}
\useinnertheme [options] {inner theme name}
\useoutertheme [options] {outer theme name}
```

In the following examples we often use

```
\usetheme{Malmoe}      \useoutertheme{sidebar}
\usecolortheme{dove}
```

which is equivalent to

```
\usepackage{beamerthemeMalmoe,beamerouterthemesidebar,%
            beamercolorthemedove}
```

11.4.3 The structure of a presentation

A presentation consists of a series of "frames". Inside a frame there can be one or more slides; thus, for example, a presentation with a six item list that is revealed point by point will be regarded in **beamer** as one frame containing six slides. There is no limit to the number of frames and slides. However, you should not make one frame with hundreds of slides in it.

Frames are created in **beamer** with the `\frame` macro or `frame` environment:

```
\frame <overlay spec.> [ <default overlay spec. >] [keyword list] {... }
\begin{frame} <overlay spec.> [ <default overlay spec. >] [keyword list]
    ...
\end{frame}
```

By default, the frame is in landscape mode for slides, with a dimension of $128\mathrm{mm} \times 96\mathrm{mm}$, which is a ratio of 4:3 and should be optimal for modern data projectors.

Each frame may have one or more of the following components:

- A headline and a footline.
- Left and a right sidebars.
- A navigation bar.
- Navigation symbols.
- A logo.
- A frame title.
- A background.
- Usually some frame contents.

Table 11.5: Keywords for the `frame` environment of **beamer**

Name	Values	Default	Meaning
allowdisplaybreaks	0 ... 4	4	The value is passed to the `\allowdisplaybreaks` command of **amsmath**. This keyword makes sense only when it is used together with the `allowsframebreaks` keyword and, of course, **amsmath**.
allowframebreaks	0 ... 1	0.95	This keyword controls the amount of material that appears on the slide until a page break is inserted and a new frame created. The default of 0.95 starts a new page when 95% of the free vertical space is filled. See the package documentation for the details and the restrictions of this keyword.
b, c or t	-	c	Vertical alignment of the frames, maybe bottom/center/top. This overrides the placement setting by the class option.
fragile	singleslide	-	Handling fragile macros. This is especially important for verbatim text, which causes special problems in processing. With this keyword **beamer** writes the contents of a frame to a file named `jobname.vrb` and reads it back.
environment	<name>	-	This keyword makes sense only when it is used in conjunction with `fragile`. The environment <name> is used to detect the end of the scanning when gathering the frame contents. This is important when the `frame` environment is part of another environment.
label	<name>	-	The frame contents are saved under the given name and can be used again later with the macro `\againframe`.
plain	-	-	Headlines, footlines, and sidebars of this frame are suppressed.
shrink	0 ... 100	0	If the text of the frame is too large to fit on the frame, it can be shrunk by a minimum of the `shrink` percentage.
squeeze	-	-	All vertical space in the text is minimized as much as possible.

Most frames will have a title, set by `\frametitle`, and a subtitle, set by `\framesubtitle`. The short form of the main title is not used by **beamer** itself, but rather is accessed via `\insertshortframetitle`. There is no short form for the subtitle.

```
\begin{frame} <overlay spec.> [ <default overlay spec. >] {keyword list}
  \frametitle <overlay spec.> [short title] {long title}
  \framesubtitle <overlay spec.> {long subtitle}
  ...
\end{frame}
```

Commonly used keywords for the `frame` environment are `allowframebreaks`, and `allowdisplaybreaks`, especially for a bibliography or large equations that do not fit on a single slide. Table 11.5 shows the keywords available for `frame`.

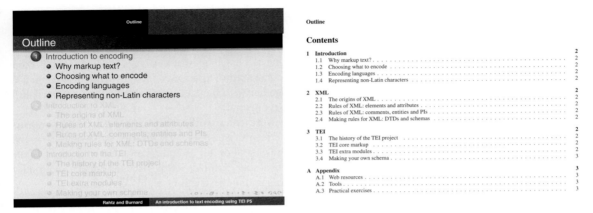

Figure 11.1: Table of contents in presentation and article display

Let us look at some practical examples of how to change **beamer**'s behavior with commands in the preamble.

```
\documentclass[xcolor=tables]{beamer}
\mode<article>{
  \usepackage{fullpage}
  \usepackage{hyperref}}
\mode<presentation>{
  \setbeamertemplate{background canvas}[vertical shading]
                                       [bottom=red!10,top=blue!10]
  \usetheme{Warsaw}
  \usefonttheme[onlysmall]{structurebold}}
\setbeamercolor{math text}{fg=green!50!black}
\setbeamercolor{normal text in math text}{parent=math text}
\setbeamercovered{dynamic}
  ...
```

The option `xcolor=table` is an example of **beamer**'s way of passing options to other packages. **beamer** itself loads the extended color package by default, but without any options set.

One powerful feature of **beamer** is the ability to set different options depending on the output mode. If you have set the class options to make a printable version of the slides, the "article" `\mode` macro is activated, which can load additional packages. The "presentation" mode is the default.

Figure 11.1 shows how the table of contents is typeset differently in the presentation and article versions.

Overlay specifications   Another very important tool is the *overlay specification*, which determines which slide components of a frame to typeset. In the simplest case, it consists simply of a slide number (e.g., 3). This causes **beamer** to show only the third slide of that frame. There are many other ways to use overlays, as described in more detail in Section 11.4.4 on page 762.

Creating a title page

A title is normally placed in its own frame, and the `\titlepage` macro puts it in a frame if you have not already done so. Thus the following two statements are equivalent:

```
\titlepage
\frame{\titlepage}
```

For compatibility with other packages, the macro `\maketitle` is also supported, with the same effect.

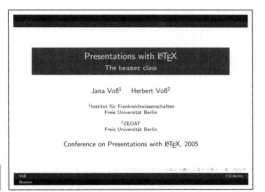

```
\documentclass{beamer}
\usepackage{beamerthemeBerlin}
\title[Beamer]{Presentations with \LaTeX}
\subtitle{The \texttt{beamer} class}
\author[Vo\ss]{Jana Vo\ss\inst{1} \and
        Herbert Vo\ss\inst{2}}
\institute[FU-Berlin]{
  \inst{1}%
  Institut f\"ur Frankreichwissenschaften\\
  Freie Universit\"at Berlin
  \and
  \inst{2}%
  ZEDAT\\
  Freie Universit\"at Berlin}
\date[\TeX\ 2005]{Conference on Presentations
                 with \LaTeX, 2005}

\frame{\titlepage}
```

Saving and reusing a frame

A frame can be saved and used again, as an alternative to putting in links to allow the reader to jump back and forth. The optional argument to `frame` provides a way to name a frame and refer to it later.

In the following example we label the first frame with the label `FrameI` and give it the overlay specification `<1-2>`, which says that only the first two slides are to be shown in this frame. The second frame has some simple text. The third frame reloads `FrameI` and starts with the third slide. The output shows the first slide of each frame. The `\alert` macro is used to create multiple slides within one frame; it is explained in Section 11.4.4.

```
\documentclass{beamer}
\usetheme{Malmoe}
\useoutertheme{sidebar}
\usecolortheme{dove}
\begin{frame}<1-2>[label=FrameI]
  \frametitle{A demonstration of saving and
              reusing frames.}
  \framesubtitle{This is the first frame.}
```

```
\begin{itemize}[<+->]
  \item<alert@+> First item.
  \item<alert@+> Second item.
  \item<alert@+> Third item.
  \item<alert@+> Fourth item.
\end{itemize}
\end{frame}
\begin{frame}
  This is the second frame in a series of three.
\end{frame}
\againframe<3->{FrameI}
```

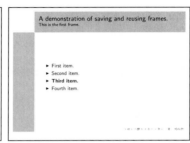

Example
11-4-8

11.4.4 Hiding and showing material on slides — overlays

An important facility you can use in creating presentation slides is making "overlays"; this may mean adding successive bullets to a list, superimposing graphics, or highlighting words and phrases. It is implemented as a set of separate slides within a frame, and the user can step back and forth through successive slides with a mouse or keyboard.

    beamer supports several ways of creating such overlays. Recall that in **beamer** a frame is what we would call a page in other styles; inside a frame we can have none or several overlays, which may be thought of as a kind of sub-page.

    Here are some examples of overlay specifications:

`\frame<0>`	Show no slides
`\frame<1>`	Show only slide 1
`\frame<2->`	Show slide 2 and following
`\frame<-4>`	Show all slides up to 4
`\frame<1,3-5>`	Show slides 1 and 3, 4, 5
`\only<+>`	Show only the current slide
`\only<+->`	Show only the current slide and those following
`\only<article:2>`	Show slide 2, but only in the article mode
`\begin{frame}<all:2-3>`	Show slides 2 and 3 only in all modes

$$\boxed{\texttt{\textbackslash pause}<\textit{overlay spec.>}}$$

The \pause command is the easiest way to create overlays. It stops the presentation of a frame and waits for a "continue" command, such as pressing the Enter key or clicking the mouse on the continue button. The following example shows what it looks on the second and fourth slides of the sequence. The effect of the \onslide macro is to make items visible from the very beginning; thus the phrase "this is the cycle of the seasons" appears on all slides.

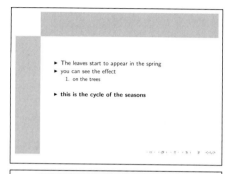

Example 11-4-9

```
\documentclass{beamer}
\usetheme{Malmoe}
\useoutertheme{sidebar}
\usecolortheme{dove}
\begin{frame}
 \begin{itemize}
 \item The leaves start to appear in the spring \pause
 \item you can see the effect
   \begin{enumerate}
   \item on the trees \pause
   \item and on the flowers
   \end{enumerate}
 \onslide % to make it visible for the first slide
 \item \textbf{this is the cycle of the seasons}
 \pause
 \item The leaves are at their strongest in the summer
 \pause
 \item The leaves start to turn color in the autumn
 \pause
 \item The leaves fall off the trees in the winter
 \end{itemize}
\end{frame}
```

The second example shows how the \pause macro can be used inside a table. It is useful only when the rows of the table are colored, because it cannot work with horizontal and vertical lines separating rows, since they are not drawn at the same time as a row is colored. You will have to learn to work with colors instead of horizontal and vertical lines in your presentation tables.

```
\documentclass[xcolor=table]{beamer}
\usetheme{Malmoe}
\useoutertheme{sidebar}
\usecolortheme{dove}
\newcommand\bfrm[1]{\textbf{\textrm{\textcolor{white}{#1}}}}
\section{Reveal a table row by row}
\begin{frame}
  \frametitle{Reveal rows and columns in a table}
  \framesubtitle{Using the pause macro}
```

```
\rowcolors[]{1}{blue!40}{blue!10}
\begin{tabular}{>{\ttfamily}l|>{\ttfamily}ll}
  \rowcolor{gray}\bfrm{package} & \bfrm{date} & \bfrm{function}\\
  pstricks.tex & 2004 & basic package          \pause \\
  pst-3d.tex   & 1999 & basic 3-D macros       \pause \\
  pst-char.tex & 1999 & character manipulation \pause \\
  pst-coil.tex & 1999 & coils and zig zags     \pause \\
  pst-eps.tex  & 1999 & EPS export             \pause \\
  pst-fill.tex & 2004 & filling and tiling     \pause \\
  pst-grad.tex & 2004 & color gradients        \pause \\
  pst-xkey.tex & 2005 & key setting            \pause \\
  pst-node.tex & 2001 & nodes and connections  \pause \\
  pst-plot.tex & 2000 & plotting functions     \pause \\
  pst-text.tex & 1999 & text manipulations     \pause \\
  pst-tree.tex & 2004 & trees
\end{tabular}
\end{frame}
... further code omitted ...
```

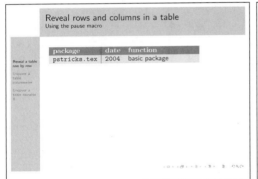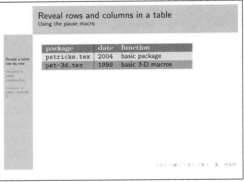

Example
11-4-10

Alternatively, we can use \onslide instead of \pause, and uncover successive columns rather than rows.

\onslide modifier <*overlay spec.*> {*text*}

The behavior of this macro depends on whether the optional argument {text} is present. If it is present, the modifier can be either + or *; if not present, all text following the macro will be shown only on the specified slides. If no slide specification is given, then the text is shown on all slides, as in the previous example. The text still occupies space on all slides, whether it is shown or not.

In the following example, the table header is used to insert \onslide commands, one for each column, using the array package, which is automatically loaded by beamer. >{\ttfamily}l<{\onslide<2->} produces a a left-aligned column (l) with the macro \ttfamily run before (>) the column definition, and the macro \onslide<2-> after (<) that. The effect is that the column, typeset in a monospace font, appears only on slide 2. At the end of the last column, the use of \onslide without a specification ensures that the first column on the next row is once more shown normally, so that the whole first column is seen (the last slide is also shown in Color Plate XVI x).

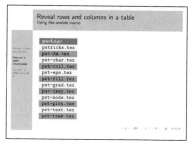

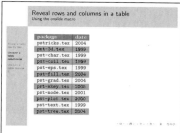

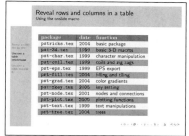

Example
11-4-11

```
\documentclass[xcolor=table]{beamer}
\usetheme{Malmoe}
\useoutertheme{sidebar}
\usecolortheme{dove}
\newcommand\bfrm[1]
            {\textbf{\textrm{\textcolor{white}{#1}}}}
\section{Reveal a table row by row}
\begin{frame}
  \frametitle{Reveal rows and columns in a table}
  \framesubtitle{Using the pause macro}
  ...
\end{frame}
\section{Uncover a table columnwise}
\begin{frame}
  \frametitle{Reveal rows and columns in a table}
  \framesubtitle{Using the onslide macro}
  \rowcolors[]{1}{blue!40}{yellow!20}
  \begin{tabular}{>{\ttfamily}l<{\onslide<2->}|%
    >{\ttfamily}l<{\onslide<3->}l<{\onslide}@{}}
  \rowcolor{gray}
    \bfrm{package}&\bfrm{date}&\bfrm{function} \\
  pstricks.tex & 2004 & basic package       \\
  pst-3d.tex    & 1999 & basic 3-D macros    \\
  pst-char.tex & 1999 & character manipulation\\
  pst-coil.tex & 1999 & coils and zig zags  \\
  pst-eps.tex   & 1999 & EPS export          \\
  pst-fill.tex & 2004 & filling and tiling  \\
... further code omitted ...
```

\onslide can also be used to show specific rows of a table, as we saw earlier with \pause. The following example shows the third and fifth slides of the frame. Note that in the example the \onslide commands are added at the end of the rows (affecting the next) and not at the beginning, as that would trigger the coloring of the row.

```
\documentclass[xcolor=table]{beamer}
\usetheme{Malmoe}   \useoutertheme{sidebar}   \usecolortheme{dove}
\newcommand\bfrm[1]{\textbf{\textrm{\textcolor{white}{#1}}}}
\section{Reveal a table row by row}      \begin{frame}  ... \end{frame}
\section{Uncover a table columnwise}     \begin{frame}  ... \end{frame}
\section{Uncover a table rowwise II}
\begin{frame}
  \frametitle{Reveal rows and columns in a table}
```

```
    \framesubtitle{Using the onslide macro}
    \rowcolors[]{1}{blue!40}{blue!10}
    \begin{tabular}{>{\ttfamily}l|>{\ttfamily}ll}
     \rowcolor{gray}\bfrm{package} & \bfrm{date} & \bfrm{function}   \\
       pstricks.tex & 2004 & basic package          \onslide<2->    \\
       pst-3d.tex   & 1999 & basic 3-D macros       \onslide<3->    \\
       pst-char.tex & 1999 & character manipulation \onslide<4>     \\
       pst-coil.tex & 1999 & coils and zig zags     \onslide<5->    \\
       pst-eps.tex  & 1999 & EPS export             \onslide<6,4>   \\
       pst-fill.tex & 2004 & filling and tiling     \onslide<7->    \\
       pst-grad.tex & 2004 & color gradients        \onslide<2-8>   \\
       pst-xkey.tex & 2005 & key setting            \onslide<9->    \\
       pst-node.tex & 2001 & nodes and connections  \onslide<1,5,10->\\
       pst-plot.tex & 2000 & plotting functions     \onslide<11->   \\
       pst-text.tex & 1999 & text manipulations     \onslide<12->   \\
       pst-tree.tex & 2004 & trees
    \end{tabular}
  \end{frame}
```

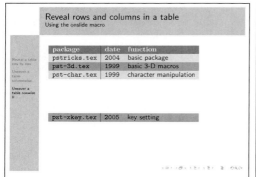
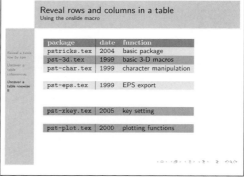

Example
11-4-12

The \only macro provides a way to hide and reveal material within the body of the slide.

> \only<*overlay spec.*>{*text*}

The first argument determines the slide numbers on which the contents of the second argument appear. Almost any combination is possible:

- An absolute number for a single slide.

- Absolute numbers for different slides, separated by commas.

- A range for an interval of slides.

- An open range for a defined start/end of the slides.

The output shows the third and sixth slides. Note that the words have not yet been revealed.

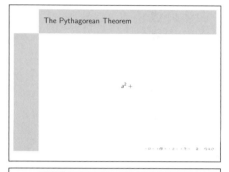

```
\documentclass{beamer}
\usetheme{Malmoe}
\useoutertheme{sidebar}
\usecolortheme{dove}
\begin{frame}
  \frametitle{The Pythagorean Theorem}
  \only<1,8>{OK, let's start \ldots}

  \[ \only<2->{a^2} \only<3->{ + }
     \only<4->{b^2} \only<5->{ = }
     \only<6->{c^2} \]

  \only<7>{Or in words:}\par
  \only<8>{The Pythagorean Theorem asserts that
    for a \textbf{right} triangle, the square
    of the hypotenuse is equal to the sum of
    the squares of the other two sides!}
\end{frame}
```

Example
11-4-13

Opaqueness

In addition to simply hiding or showing slides, you can show them partially, with a degree of transparency.

```
\uncover<overlay spec.>{text}
\setbeamercovered{argument}
\opaqueness<overlay spec.>{percentage of opaqueness}
```

Like \only and \onslide, \uncover shows some text under the conditions of the *overlay specification*. In this case text that is not being shown on the current slide is rendered opaquely. The background is rendered in a transparent way, determined by \setbeamercovered. This command can take the following values:

invisible   The default; the text is visible or not.

transparent=⟨*value*⟩   Typesets the inactive material in a "transparent" way with a opaqueness of $0..100\%$, where 0 is totally transparent.

dynamic   Defines the value for the opaqueness depending on the slide number.

highly dynamic   Same with stronger differences in the slides.

still covered=⟨*opaqueness list*⟩ Lets the user define the opaqueness.

again covered=⟨*opaqueness list*⟩ Lets the user define the opaqueness of slides, which are again covered.

The degree of opaqueness is set by \opaqueness. The following example shows the fourth slide. The [-15pt] spacing is used here to force text to overlap and demonstrate how the transparency works.

```
\documentclass{beamer}
\usetheme{Malmoe}
\useoutertheme{sidebar}
\usecolortheme{dove}
\newcommand\HText{\Huge Getting started}
\begin{frame}
  \frametitle{The transparent
                    \texttt{uncover} macro}
  \setbeamercovered{transparent}
  \uncover<1>{\HText}              \\[-15pt]
  \uncover<2>{\color{red}\HText}   \\[-15pt]
  \uncover<3>{\color{green}\HText}\\[-15pt]
  \uncover<4>{\color{blue}\HText}  \\[-15pt]
  \uncover<5>{\color{cyan}\HText}
\end{frame}
```

Example
11-4-14

\visible<*overlay spec.*>{*text*}
\invisible<*overlay spec.*>{*text*}

\visible is similar to \uncover, except that the opaqueness setting has no effect. \invisible is the other way round.

Sometimes you want to change some text in a frame depending on which slide is being shown.

\alt<*overlay spec.*>{*default text*}{*alternative text*}<*overlay spec.*>

On the slide determined by the *overlay specification*, the *default text* is shown; otherwise, the *alternative* is shown. The *overlay specification* can appear only once, before or after the text arguments.

You can also display different text before and after a particular slide.

\temporal<*overlay spec.*>{*before text*}{*default text*}{*after text*}

The arguments do not have to be just text, but can contain anything that is legal LaTeX, such as color definitions:

    \temporal<3>{\color{red}}{\color{green}}{\color{blue}}

Overlays using existing LaTeX environments

Some commonly used LaTeX constructs are redefined as follows in the **beamer** class, allowing for overlays to be used with them.

```
\begin{theorem} <overlay spec.> [optional text] <overlay spec.>     ...\end{theorem}
\begin{corollory} <overlay spec.> [optional text] <overlay spec.>    ...\end{corollory}
\begin{definition} <overlay spec.> [optional text] <overlay spec.>  ...\end{definition}
\begin{definitions} <overlay spec.> [optional text] <overlay spec.> ...\end{definitions}
\begin{fact} <overlay spec.> [optional text] <overlay spec.>         ...\end{fact}
\begin{proof} <overlay spec.> [optional text] <overlay spec.>        ...\end{proof}
\begin{example} <overlay spec.> [optional text] <overlay spec.>      ...\end{example}
```

An example of the usefulness of the changes is shown below, where parts of a theorem are revealed in successive slides. The top picture is the third slide of the first frame. You can see that the proof environment is invisible but still takes up space. In the third slide of the second frame the space has vanished due to the use of the \onlyenv environment.

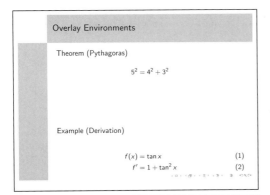

```
\documentclass{beamer}
\usetheme{Malmoe} \usecolortheme{dove}
\useoutertheme{sidebar}

\begin{frame}
  \frametitle{Overlay Environments}
  \begin{theorem}<1->[Pythagoras]
    \[ 5^2 = 4^2 + 3^2 \]
  \end{theorem}
  \begin{proof}<2>
    \[ 25 = 16 + 9 = 25 \]
  \end{proof}
  \begin{example}<3>[Derivation]
    \begin{align}
      f(x)      &= \tan x\\
      f^\prime &= 1+\tan^2 x
    \end{align}
  \end{example}
\end{frame}
\begin{frame}
  \frametitle{Overlay Environments}
  \begin{theorem}<1->[Pythagoras]
    \[ 5^2 = 4^2 + 3^2 \]
  \end{theorem}
  \begin{onlyenv}<2>
  \begin{proof}
    \[ 25 = 16 + 9 = 25 \]
  \end{proof}
  \end{onlyenv}
... further code omitted ...
```

Example
11-4-15

The **beamer** class also includes the following new environments `onlyenv`, `altenv`, `visibleenv`, `uncoverenv`, and `invisibleenv` which have the same effect as the macros defined earlier. An example of `onlyenv` appears in the second frame of the previous example (bottom picture).

Overlay areas

When the text changes dynamically, it can be annoying when text that appears on every slide moves to a different position on different slides within the same frame. **beamer** has two environments to hold such texts in a static way.

```
\begin{overlayarea}{area width}{area height}   ...   \end{overlayarea}
\begin{overprint}{area width}                  ...   \end{overprint}
```

Actions on overlays

Every overlay specification can have an additional action specification with the following syntax:

```
<overlay specification| ⟨action⟩@overlay specification>
```

The space after the | character is important. The *action* can have one of five values:

`uncover` Uncovers the text item or text block (default).

`alert` Changes the appearance of the text item or text block (the default is bold).

`only` The text item or text block is inserted only in the specified slide(s).

`visible` Makes the item or text block visible for the specified slide(s).

`invisible` The other way round.

In the following example, the first item must appear at the start of the list to ensure that the `enumerate` starts with the number 0. We see here all three slides in the frame, showing the sequence in which items appear.

```
\documentclass{beamer}
\usetheme{Malmoe}
\useoutertheme{sidebar}
\usecolortheme{dove}
\begin{frame}
  \frametitle{Alerted text}
  \begin{enumerate}
  \item<3-| alert@3>[0.]
      The last item to be shown, even though it is
      at the top of the list.
  \item<1-| alert@1>
      The first main item, alerted only on slide 1,
      but appearing on all slides.
```

```
\item<2| alert@2>
   The second item, shown and alerted only on slide 2.
\end{enumerate}
\end{frame}
```

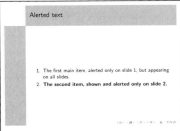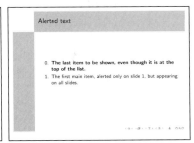

Example
11-4-16

It is also possible to use the alert option as a macro in its own right to highlight parts of an item. In the following example, the first and last slides are shown; the text "important" is highlighted only on the first slide. For the meaning of the overlay specification < . >, see Section 11.4.7 on page 786. It uses the value of the beamerpause counter without incrementing it. This makes it possible to synchronize the alert with the item.

```
\documentclass{beamer}
\usetheme{Malmoe}
\useoutertheme{sidebar}
\usecolortheme{dove}
\begin{frame}
  \frametitle{Optional increment with alerted text}
  \begin{itemize}[<+->]
    \item This is \alert<.>{important}.
    \item We want to \alert<2->{highlight} not this but \alert<.>{that}.
    \item Where is the \alert<.>{sense}?
  \end{itemize}
\end{frame}
\end{document}
```

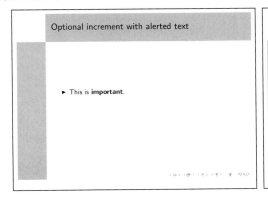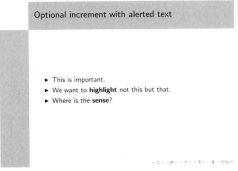

Example
11-4-17

Often an itemized list should have every active item highlighted, which is possible with the optional argument of the `itemize` environment. This example shows the third slide of the frame:

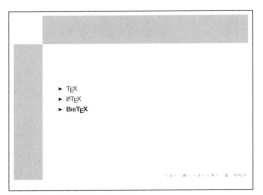

```
\documentclass{beamer}
\usetheme{Malmoe}
\useoutertheme{sidebar}
\usecolortheme{dove}
\begin{frame}
  \begin{itemize}[<+-| alert@+>]
  \item \TeX
  \item \LaTeX
  \item \BibTeX
  \item and so on
  \end{itemize}
\end{frame}
\end{document}
```

Example
11-4-18

11.4.5 Additional facilities in beamer

Navigation bar

In most of the examples we have seen in this chapter, an area of navigation symbols has appeared in the lower-right corner of the slides, which is seen enlarged in Figure 11.2. The symbols are as follows:

- A *slide* icon as a single rectangle with left and right arrows
- A *frame* icon as three slide icons stacked on top of one another, with left and right arrows
- A *subsection* icon as a highlighted subsection entry in a table of contents with left and right arrows
- A *section* icon as a highlighted section entry (together with all subsections) in a table of contents with left and right arrows
- A *presentation* icon as a completely highlighted table of contents
- An *appendix* icon as a highlighted table of contents consisting of only one section (this icon is shown only if there is an appendix)
- *Back* and *forward* icons as circular arrows
- A *search/find* icon as a magnifier

Figure 11.2: The default navigation bar with the symbols for (from left to right) slide, frame, subsection, section, document, and back/search/forward navigation

The navigation bar can be modified. For instance, you can suppress all the symbols with the following command:

```
\setbeamertemplate{navigation symbols}{}
```

The predefined symbols are available through these macros:

- \insertslidenavigationsymbol (slide navigation symbol with hyperlinked left and right arrows)
- \insertframenavigationsymbol (frame navigation symbol with hyperlinked left and right arrows)
- \insertsubsectionnavigationsymbol (subsection navigation symbol with hyperlinked left and right arrows)
- \insertsectionnavigationsymbol (section navigation symbol with hyperlinked left and right arrows)
- \insertdocnavigationsymbol (presentation navigation symbol and, if needed, the appendix navigation symbol)
- \insertbackfindforwardnavigationsymbol (back, find, and forward navigation symbol)

It is also possible to define your own symbols or to resize the existing ones. The following example first deletes the default navigation bar and then puts the first two navigation symbols for the slides and the frames at the bottom of the left sidebar. These two navigation symbols should meet most of your needs for a presentation. The example shows the last slide in the first frame.

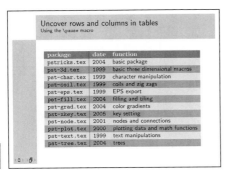

Example
11-4-19

```
\documentclass[xcolor=table]{beamer}
\usetheme{Malmoe}
\useoutertheme[width=42pt,left]{sidebar}
\usecolortheme{dove}
\setbeamertemplate{footline}{}
\setbeamertemplate{navigation symbols}{}
\setbeamertemplate{sidebar left}{%
  \vspace*{\fill}
  \scalebox{1}[2]{\insertslidenavigationsymbol}
  \scalebox{1}[2]{\insertframenavigationsymbol}
}
\newcommand\bfrm[1]
        {\textbf{\textrm{\textcolor{white}{#1}}}}
\section{Uncover a table rowwise}
\begin{frame}
  \frametitle{Uncover rows and columns in tables}
... further code omitted ...
```

Here, the optional argument of the style package **beamerouterthemesidebar** determines the position and size of the sidebar. One \setbeamertemplate suppresses the default navigation bar, and another creates a new navigation bar inside the left sidebar. \scalebox is used to stretch existing symbols in the vertical direction.

Animation, sound, and movies

The **beamer** class comes with **multimedia**, a style file for using sound or video in a presentation. These kinds of effects obviously depend on which PDF viewer you use when playing sounds or viewing movies. If your viewer supports sound and video, you would load the package as usual with

```
\usepackage{multimedia}
```

The multimedia package provides the following macros:

```
\animate<overlay spec.>
\animatevalue<start slide>-<end slide>{name}{start value}{end value}
\movie [key/vals] {poster text}{file name}
\hyperlinkmovie [key/vals] {movie label}{text}
\sound [key/vals] {poster text}{file name}
\hyperlinksound [key/vals] {sound label}{text}
\hyperlinkmute{text}
```

Transitions

Presentations can look nicer if a slide seems to dissolve slightly while a new one appears, instead of making an abrupt change from one slide to the next. You can set this preference with the following macros:

```
\transblindshorizontal<overlay spec.> {key/vals}
\transblindsvertical<overlay spec.> {key/vals}
\transboxin<overlay spec.> {key/vals}
\transboxout<overlay spec.> {key/vals}
\transdissolve<overlay spec.> {key/vals}
\transduration<overlay spec.> {key/vals}
\transglitter<overlay spec.> {key/vals}
\transsplitverticalin<overlay spec.> {key/vals}
\transsplitverticalout<overlay spec.> {key/vals}
\transsplithorizontalin<overlay spec.> {key/vals}
\transsplithorizontalout<overlay spec.> {key/vals}
\transwipe<overlay spec.> {key/vals}
```

Table 11.6: Keywords for \transdissolve

Keyword	Meaning
duration=⟨*time*⟩	Time in seconds for the transition effect. The default is 1s, but smaller values may be better.
direction=⟨*degree*⟩	Allowed values are 0, 90, 180, 270, and, for a glitter effect, 315.

The possible keywords for dissolving are listed in Table 11.6. The following example shows the second slide of the first frame when its first slide dissolves and the second appears. It shows only how the macro \transdissolve works, because it is not really possible to demonstrate this kind of animation in a static book.

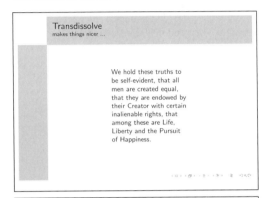

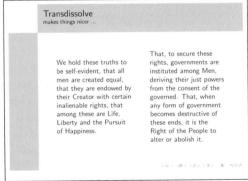

```
\documentclass{beamer}
\usetheme{Malmoe} \usecolortheme{dove}
\useoutertheme{sidebar}
\begin{frame}
  \transdissolve<2>[duration=0.74]
  \frametitle{Transdissolve}
  \framesubtitle{makes things nicer ...}
  \begin{columns}
    \only<1->{\begin{column}{.4\textwidth}
We hold these truths to be self-evident,
that all men are created equal,
that they are endowed by their
Creator with certain inalienable rights,
that among these are Life,
Liberty and the Pursuit of Happiness.
    \end{column}}
    \only<2->{\begin{column}{.4\textwidth}
That, to secure these rights, governments are
instituted among Men, deriving their just
powers from the consent of the governed.
That, when any form of government becomes
destructive of these ends, it is  the Right
of the People to alter or abolish it.
    \end{column}}
  \end{columns}
\end{frame}
```

Boxed and colored text

In addition to the standard LʌTEX macros for framing or boxing text, beamer provides two new environments for this purpose:

```
\begin{beamercolorbox} [key/vals] {beamer color} ... \end{beamercolorbox}
\begin{beamerboxesrounded} [key/vals] {title} ... \end{beamerboxesrounded}
```

There are a lot of keywords for `beamercolorbox`, which are shown in Table 11.7. The keywords for `beamerboxesrounded` are shown in Table 11.8 on page 778.

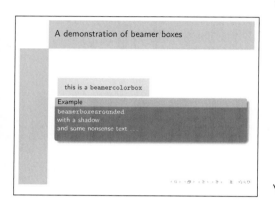

```
\documentclass{beamer}
\usetheme{Malmoe} \usecolortheme{dove}
\useoutertheme{sidebar}

\begin{frame}
 \frametitle{A demonstration of beamer boxes}
 \setbeamercolor{postit}{fg=black,bg=yellow}
 \begin{beamercolorbox}[sep=1em,wd=5cm]{postit}
   this is a \texttt{beamercolorbox}
 \end{beamercolorbox}
 \setbeamercolor{headerCol}{fg=black,bg=lightgray}
 \setbeamercolor{bodyCol}{fg=white,bg=gray}
 \begin{beamerboxesrounded}[upper=headerCol,%
         lower=bodyCol,shadow=true]{Example}
  \texttt{beamerboxesrounded}\\
  with a shadow\\ and some nonsense text \ldots\\
 \end{beamerboxesrounded}
\end{frame}
```

Example
11-4-21

Logos

Often the corporate layout design for a company, university, or institute includes a logo, which can be easily defined:

`\logo{`*object*`}`

The *object* can be anything—maybe some text or more often a graphic. It is placed by the theme packages using the `\insertlogo` macro; there are no optional arguments to position the logo, as it is always set at TEX's current point. Unlike all other frame objects, the logo must be defined *before* the `frame` environment, usually in the preamble. In the following example, the logo is placed by the theme package in the upper-left corner; in other themes, such as the Malmoe theme we use elsewhere, it goes to the lower-left corner.

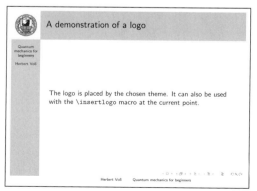

```
\documentclass{beamer}
\usetheme{Malmoe}    \useoutertheme{sidebar}
\usecolortheme{dove}
\pgfdeclareimage[width=1.5cm]{uni-logo}{fu-berlin}
\logo{\pgfuseimage{uni-logo}}

\title{Quantum mechanics for beginners}
\author{Herbert Vo\ss}
\institute{ZEDAT} \date{\today}
\begin{frame}{A demonstration of a logo}
The logo is placed by the chosen theme. It can
also be used with the \texttt{\textbackslash
insertlogo} macro at the current point.
\end{frame}
```

Example
11-4-22

Table 11.7: Keywords for the beamercolorbox environment

Keyword	Meaning
wd=⟨*dimen*⟩	The width of the box. Using a minipage inside this environment may be a good idea, if you have problems with the box width. If the dimension is greater than \textwidth, then **beamer** does wd=\textwidth.
dp=⟨*dimen*⟩	The depth of the box.
ht=⟨*dimen*⟩	The height of the box.
left	Typesets the box text left-aligned and with a ragged right border. This is the default. To get a better ragged right border, use the rightskip keyword.
right	Typesets the box text right-aligned with a (very) ragged left border.
center	Centers the text inside the box.
leftskip=⟨*dimen*⟩	TEX's left skip is a glue that is inserted at the left end of every line.
rightskip=⟨*dimen*⟩	Same for the right skip. A good value may be rightskip=0pt plus 4em.
sep=⟨*dimen*⟩	Separation between text and border.
colsep=⟨*dimen*⟩	Separation between text and border for a colored background.
colsep*=⟨*dimen*⟩	Adds some space if the box text is greater than the defined width.
shadow=⟨*bool*⟩	Draws a shadow behind the box.
rounded=⟨*bool*⟩	Causes the borders of the box to be rounded off if there is a background installed.
ignorebg	Ignores the background color.
vmode	Causes TEX to be in vertical mode when the box starts.

Inserting a second logo is not possible with the \insertlogo macro. You can instead tweak the theme, as we do in the following example, where we override the template's sidebar left, use footline to position the second logo, and make sidebar right empty.

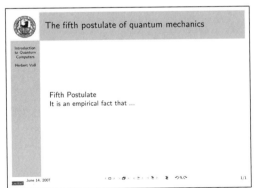

Example
11-4-23

```
\documentclass{beamer}
\usetheme{Malmoe} \usecolortheme{dove}
\useoutertheme{sidebar}
\pgfdeclareimage[height=2.25ex,
    width=2.5\baselineskip]{institute-logo}{zedat}
\pgfdeclareimage[height=1.3cm]{uni}{fu-berlin}
\logo{\pgfuseimage{uni}}
\setbeamertemplate{footline}{%
    \raisebox{-2ex}{\pgfuseimage{institute-logo}}
    \usebeamerfont{date in head/foot}
    \insertshortdate{}\hfill
    \usebeamertemplate{navigation symbols}\hfill
    \insertframenumber{}/\inserttotalframenumber}
\setbeamertemplate{sidebar right}{}
\title{Introduction to Quantum Computers}
... further code omitted ...
```

The two logos—one for the university and one for the institute—are declared with the \pgfdeclareimage macro. The main logo is passed to the internal template with the macro \logo. Then the footline is defined as a horizontal line with the objects "institute logo – date – navigation symbols – framenumber/totalnumber".

Table 11.8: Keywords for the `beamerboxesrounded` environment

Keyword	Meaning
lower=⟨*beamer color*⟩	Sets the color to be used for the lower (main) part of the box.
upper=⟨*beamer color*⟩	Same for the header.
width=⟨*dimen*⟩	The width of the text inside the box.
shadow=⟨*bool*⟩	If set to true, a shadow will be drawn.

Block environments

A special `block` environments is defined for **beamer**, containing a header and a frame. The syntax is

```
\begin{block}<action specification>{header text}<action specification>
  ...
\end{block}
```

Only one of the two action specifications is possible. The following example shows two block environments. The first one has the default layout; the second one has a modified template, colors, and font because of the declarations placed in front of it. Section 11.4.8 provides more information about the details of template style setting.

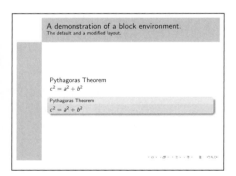

```
\documentclass{beamer}
\usetheme{Malmoe}
\useoutertheme{sidebar}
\usecolortheme{dove}
\begin{frame}
\frametitle{A demonstration of a block environment.}
\framesubtitle{The default and a modified layout.}
\begin{block}<1->{Pythagoras Theorem}
  $c^2=a^2 + b^2$
\end{block}
\setbeamertemplate{blocks}[rounded][shadow=true]
\setbeamercolor{block body}{bg=normal text.bg!90!black}
\setbeamercolor{block title}{bg=normal text.bg!90!red}
\setbeamerfont{block title}{size=\footnotesize,
                           parent={structure,block body}}
\begin{block}<2->{Pythagoras Theorem}
  $c^2=a^2 + b^2$
\end{block}
\end{frame}
```

Example
11-4-24

There are two more block environments apart from `block`, called `alertblock` and `exampleblock`. All of these environments can be modified in different ways and are shown in the following example, which uses the Berkeley theme with predefined block environments (the next example is also shown in Color Plate XVI y)

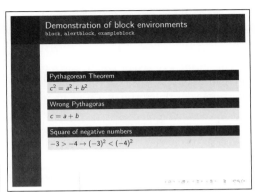

Example
11-4-25

```
\documentclass{beamer}
\usetheme{Berkeley}
\begin{frame}
 \frametitle{Demonstration of block environments}
 \framesubtitle{\texttt{block},
     \texttt{alertblock}, \texttt{exampleblock}}
 \begin{block}{Pythagorean Theorem}
   $c^2=a^2 + b^2$
 \end{block}
 \begin{alertblock}{Wrong Pythagoras}
   $c=a + b$
 \end{alertblock}
 \begin{exampleblock}{Square of negative numbers}
   $-3>-4\rightarrow (-3)^2<(-4)^2$
 \end{exampleblock}
\end{frame}
```

11.4.6 Using LaTeX structural components in beamer

Sectioning commands

The normal LaTeX sectioning (\section, \subsection etc) commands can be used *out-side* the frame environment, but do not generate any visible slides. They do have an effect on the table of contents and some title layouts, depending on the style requested. Perhaps surprisingly, the normal effect of the section macros is reversed, with the optional argument appearing on screen and the default one going into the table of contents file. The normal macros are redefined as follows:

\section *<mode specification>* [*navigation bar name*] {*frame name*}
\subsection *<mode specification>* [*navigation bar name*] {*frame name*}
\section *<mode specification>* * {*navigation bar name*}
\subsection *<mode specification>* * {*navigation bar name*}

The starred versions create no entry in the table of contents file and no heading title, only a possible entry in the navigation bar.

The philosophy of **beamer** is that an appendix in not shown in a presentation, but can be useful to answer questions at the end of the talk. The \appendix command therefore starts a new part.

In general, there is no real need for parts in a presentation. However, you can use the \part macro with the following syntax if needed:

\part *<mode specification>* * [*navigation bar name*] {*frame name*}

The starred version creates no entry in the table of contents file and no heading.

```
\AtBeginPart{...}
```

This is a special declaration to insert some code before each part.

Figures and tables

beamer supports figures and tables in the usual way, except that they cannot float. This makes it possible to use all the overlay facilities inside the `figure` or `table` environment.

It usually looks strange to see captions on figures or tables in a presentation. However, if you are going to print a handout or an article from your slides, you may want to put them in.

Multiple columns

Often one needs to place text and an image or a table side by side. This positioning can be achieved as usual in LaTeX with two minipages or parboxes, but beamer offers a better and easier solution—the `column` environment.

```
\begin{columns} [key/vals]
  \begin{column} [placement] <column width>  ...  \end{column}
  \begin{column} [placement] <column width>  ...  \end{column}
  ...
\end{columns}
```

The number of columns inside the main `columns` environment is limited only by the frame size. The following examples show the first and third slides of a frame. The `column` environments can be inside an `\only` macro (first and last columns) or the other way round (middle column).

```
\documentclass{beamer}
\usetheme{Malmoe} \usecolortheme{dove} \useoutertheme{sidebar}
\setlength\unitlength{1mm}

\begin{frame}
 \frametitle{Multiple columns in a frame}
 \framesubtitle{\texttt{columns} and \texttt{column}}
 \begin{columns}[b] % bottom aligned
   \only<1->{%
    \begin{column}{.4\textwidth}
     \TeX\ is the world's premi\`ere markup-based typesetting system,
       and PostScript is the leading language for describing the printed
       page. We describe how they can produce even more beautiful results
       when they work together.
    \end{column}}
   \begin{column}{.2\textwidth}
     \only<2->{\rule{20mm}{25mm}
     \put(-13,20){{\color{white}\TeX}}}
   \end{column}
```

```
    \only<3>{%
      \begin{column}{.2\textwidth}
        {\color{red}\rule{20mm}{40mm}}
        \put(-13,20){\LaTeX}
      \end{column}}
  \end{columns}
\end{frame}
```

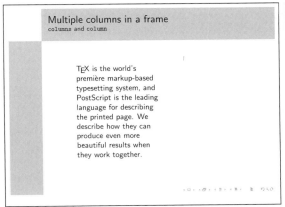 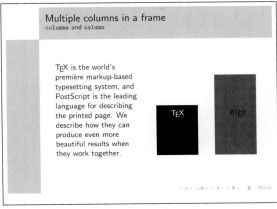

In addition to the `column` environment, there is a `\column` macro, which starts a new column that remains active until another column macro or environment appears, or until the end of the main column. The keywords for the `columns` and `column` environments are listed in Table 11.9.

Bibliography

A bibliography in a presentation looks a little odd. However, sometimes it may be useful to refer to additional literature or if the presentation will be printed as an article or handout.

Table 11.9: Keywords for the `columns` environment

Keyword	Meaning
b	Aligned at the bottom line of the columns.
c	Vertically centered relative to each column. The default, unless the global option t is used.
onlytextwidth	Same as `totalwidth=\textwidth`.
t	Aligned at the baseline of the first line. The default if the global option t is used.
T	Similar to the t keyword, except that it is really aligned at the top of the first line and not only the baseline.
totalwidth=⟨dimen⟩	Total width of all columns.

| `\beamertemplatebookbibitems` | `\beamertemplatearticlebibitems` |

The following example demonstrates some useful commands for inserting icons in a bibliography.

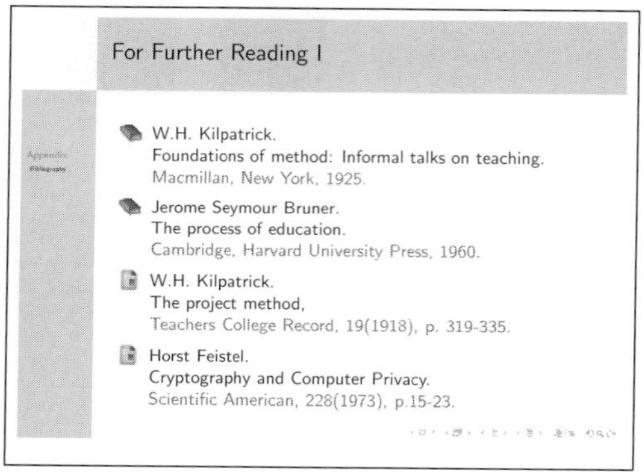

```
\documentclass{beamer}   \usetheme{Malmoe}
\useoutertheme{sidebar}  \usecolortheme{dove}
\appendix
\section<presentation>*{\appendixname}
\subsection<presentation>*{Bibliography}

\begin{frame}[allowframebreaks]
 \frametitle<presentation>{For Further Reading}
 \begin{thebibliography}{10}
 \beamertemplatebookbibitems
 \bibitem{kilp:1925}
   W.H. Kilpatrick.
   \newblock Foundations of method: Informal
   talks on teaching.
   \newblock Macmillan, New York, 1925.
 \bibitem{bruner:1960}
   Jerome Seymour Bruner.
   \newblock The process of education.
   \newblock Cambridge,
   Harvard University Press, 1960.
 \beamertemplatearticlebibitems
 \bibitem{Kilp:1918}
   W.H. Kilpatrick.
... further code omitted ...
```

Example
11-4-27

Table of contents

The table of contents for a presentation can be generated as usual with the macro `\tableofcontents` placed in its own frame:

```
\begin{frame}
  \frametitle{Table of contents}  \tableofcontents
\end{frame}
```

The **beamer** class adds optional arguments for `\tableofcontents`, all of which are listed in Table 11.10. The following example shows how to code a table of contents with a pause between the section entries.

```
\section*{Table of contents}
\begin{frame}
  \frametitle{Table of contents}
  \tableofcontents[part=1,pausesections]
\end{frame}
```

Table 11.10: Keywords for the `\tableofcontents` command

Keyword	*Meaning*
`currentsection`	Causes all sections except the current one to be shown in a semi-transparent way. Also, all subsections except those in the current section are shown in the semi-transparent way. This command is a shorthand for specifying the following keywords: `sectionstyle=show/shaded,subsectionstyle=show/show/shaded`.
`currentsubsection`	Similar to `currentsection`.
`firstsection=`⟨*section number*⟩	Specifies which section should be numbered as section "1". This is useful if you have a first section (like an overview section) that should not be numbered. Section numbers are not shown by default. To show them, you must use a different table of contents template.
`hideallsubsections`	Causes all subsections to be hidden.
`hideothersubsections`	Causes the subsections of sections other than the current one to be hidden.
`part=`⟨*part number*⟩	Causes the table of contents of part `<part number>` to be shown, instead of the table of contents of the current part (which is the default).
`pausesections`	Causes a `\pause` command to be issued before each section. This is useful if you wish to show the table of contents in an incremental way.
`pausesubsections`	Same for subsections.
`sections=`⟨*overlay specification*⟩	Causes only the sections mentioned in the overlay specification to be shown.
`sectionstyle=`⟨*current/other*⟩	Specifies how sections should be displayed. Possible styles are `show`, `shaded`, and `hide`.
`subsectionstyle=`⟨*current/other/subsections in other sections*⟩	Specifies how subsections should be displayed.

11.4.7 Using LaTeX inline components in beamer

All of the usual LaTeX macros can be used inside beamer frames, but many of them are redefined to add extra power.

Hyperlinks

beamer loads the hyperref package by default, except when the presentation mode is set to "article". In the latter case the package must be loaded manually in the preamble via `\usepackage{hyperref}`.

A target for a hyperlink can be created in the normal way by a `\hypertarget` or `\label` command. This is no problem when writing an article, where all targets are permanently visible. In a presentation, however, a target may be invisible or in a transparent mode, so a jump to it may be possible but meaningless. This makes it tricky to create hyperlinks in a presentation which uses the overlay technique.

In the following example the frame starts with the first item and buttons for jumping to the second and third items. The first button becomes invisible when slide 2 is visible, as seen in the second screenshot, where a new link appears as the second item. In the third screenshot the third item appears, and the link reappears at the bottom of the second item.

```
\documentclass{beamer}
\usetheme{Malmoe} \useoutertheme{sidebar} \usecolortheme{dove}
\begin{frame}
  \frametitle{Hyperlinks and -targets}
  \begin{itemize}
  \item<1-> First item.
  \item<2> \hyperlink{jumptofourth}
                    {\beamergotobutton{Jump to fourth item}}
          \hypertarget<4>{jumptofourth}{}
  \item<3-> Third item.  \item<4-> Fourth item.
  \end{itemize}
  \invisible<2>{\hyperlink{jumptosecond}
                    {\beamergotobutton{Jump to second item}}}
  \invisible<3>{\hyperlink{jumptothird}
                    {\beamergotobutton{Jump to third item}}}
  \hypertarget<2>{jumptosecond}{}
  \hypertarget<3>{jumptothird}{}
  \hyperlink{frameII<2>}{\beamergotobutton{Jump to next frame}}
\end{frame}
```

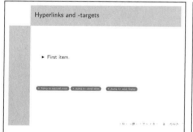
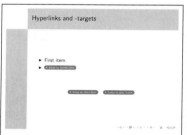
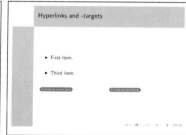

Example
11-4-28

To make it simpler for you to do hyperlinking, the frame environment has an optional argument for labels (see Table 11.5 on page 759). The beamer class constructs targets for each slide in labelled frames. Thus, for a frame with the label frameII, a target frameII<2> is created automatically for the second slide of the frame, which we can link to as follows:

```
\hyperlink{frameII<2>}{\beamergotobutton{Jump to second frame}}
```

beamer knows about a lot of predefined targets (shown in Table 11.11 on page 786), which makes hyperlinking very easy. The links are created for sections and subsections as well as for frames, with the frame in the macro name simply being replaced with the `section` or `subsection`. All of these macros also accept an overlay specification at the end, rather than at the beginning.

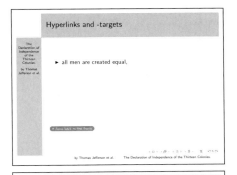

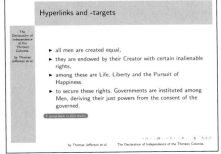

Example
11-4-29

```
\documentclass{beamer}  \usetheme{Malmoe}
\useoutertheme{sidebar} \usecolortheme{dove}
\title{The Declaration of Independence of
         the Thirteen Colonies.}
\author{by Thomas Jefferson et al.}
\date{July 4, 1776}
\begin{frame}
  \frametitle{Hyperlinks and -targets}
  \begin{itemize}
  \item<1-> all men are created equal,
  \item<2-> they are endowed by their
          Creator with certain inalienable rights,
  \item<3-> among these are Life,
          Liberty and the Pursuit of Happiness.
  \item<4-> to secure these rights,
Governments are instituted among Men, deriving
their just powers from the consent of the governed.
  \end{itemize}
  \hyperlink{jumptoI}
          {\beamergotobutton{Jump back to first frame}}
  \hypertarget<2>{jumptoI}{}
\end{frame}
```

Targets are defined for a frame with the name `jumpto` followed by the number of the frame.

Labels

> `\label`*<overlay spec.>* *{label name}*

Without an overlay specification, only the active slide gets the label. This behavior is important when you are jumping from a reference point to a slide. In this case it makes sense only when the text referring to the label is visible.

```
\begin{frame}
  \begin{align}
    c^2 &= a^2 + b^2              \label{Pythagoras}\\
    c^2 &= a^2 + b^2-2ab\cos\gamma \label{cosin-theorem}
  \end{align}
  Start \uncover<2>{end}

  \only<3>{The specification is needed now.\label<3>{mylabel}}
\end{frame}
```

Table 11.11: Hyperlink commands

Command	Meaning

`\hyperlinkslideprev` *<overlay spec.>* {*object*}
 Mouse click on the object jumps one slide back.
`\hyperlinkslidenext` *<overlay spec.>* {*objeLargbct*}
 Mouse click on the object jumps one slide forward.
`\hyperlinkframestart` *<overlay spec.>* {*object*}
 Mouse click on the object jumps to the first slide of the current frame.
`\hyperlinkframeend` *<overlay spec.>* {*object*}
 Mouse click on the object jumps to the last slide of the current frame.
`\hyperlinkframestartnext` *<overlay spec.>* {*object*}
 Mouse click on the object jumps to the first slide of the next frame.
`\hyperlinkframeendprev` *<overlay spec.>* {*object*}
 Mouse click on the object jumps to the last slide of the previous frame.
`\hyperlinkpresentationstart` *<overlay spec.>* {*object*}
 Mouse click on the object jumps to the first slide of the presentation.
`\hyperlinkpresentationend` *<overlay spec.>* {*object*}
 Mouse click on the object jumps to the last slide of the presentation. This *excludes* the appendix.
`\hyperlinkappendixstart` *<overlay spec.>* {*object*}
 Mouse click on the object jumps to the first slide of the appendix. If there is no appendix, this will jump to the last slide of the document.
`\hyperlinkappendixend` *<overlay spec.>* {*object*}
 Mouse click on the object jumps to the last slide of the appendix.
`\hyperlinkdocumentstart` *<overlay spec.>* {*object*}
 Mouse click on the object jumps to the first slide of the presentation.
`\hyperlinkdocumentend` *<overlay spec.>* {*object*}
 Mouse click on the object jumps to the last slide of the presentation or, if an appendix is present, to the last slide of the appendix.

List items

Items in the list environments `enumerate`, `description` and `itemize` are, in general, a good choice for a presentation, as a lot of useful information can be presented in an easy and effective way. As usual, `\item` is extended to support overlays.

`\item` *<overlay spec.>* *[item label]* *<overlay spec.>*

The redefinition of the `\item` macro makes it easy to affect the sequence of slides, without needing to use the `\only` macro.

```
\begin{frame}
  \begin{itemize}
  \item<1-> First item, shown on all slides.
```

```
  \item<2-> Second item, shown on slide 2 and following.
  \item<2-> Third item, also shown on slide 2 and following.
  \item<3-> Fourth item, shown on slide 3.
  \end{itemize}
\end{frame}
```

The problem with this macro is that the overlap specifications force us to effectively perform a manual enumeration. Luckily, beamer supports a more practical way to increment the overlay numbers.

```
\item<+->[item label]
```

Here beamer accesses the counter beamerpauses, increments it, and then uses its value. The itemized list can now be edited in an easy way, so that adding or deleting an item is no longer a problem.

```
\begin{frame}
  \begin{itemize}
  \item<+-> First item, shown on all slides.
  \item<+-> Second item, shown on slide 2 and following.
  \item<+-> Third item, shown on slide 3 and following.
  \item<+-> Fourth item, shown on slide 4.
  \end{itemize}
\end{frame}
```

In the following example all items have the same overlay specification. In this case the short form can be used.

```
\begin{frame}
  \begin{itemize}[<+->]
  \item First item, shown on all slides.
  \item Second item, shown on slide 2 and following.
  \item Third item, shown on slide 3 and following.
  \item Fourth item, shown on slide 4.
  \end{itemize}
\end{frame}
```

Coming back to the original definition of the first itemized example, where the third item should appear on the second slide, the automatic increment can be avoided with a dot:

```
\item<.->[item label]
```

In this case the counter beamerpauses will not be incremented for the third item, but is also active for the second slide.

```
\begin{frame}
  \begin{itemize}
```

```
  \item<+-> First item, shown on all slides.
  \item<+-> Second item, shown on slide 2 and following.
  \item<.-> Third item, also shown on slide 2 and following.
  \item<+-> Fourth item, shown on slide 3.
  \end{itemize}
\end{frame}
```

The dot symbol merely stops the counter from being incremented; it cannot be used for the case "fourth item shown together with the first one". The counter has to be decreased or the increment must be a negative number in such cases. beamer supports this behavior with an optional increment:

```
\item<+(<increment>)->[item label]

\begin{frame}
  \begin{itemize}
  \item<+-> First item, shown on all slides.
  \item<+>  Second item, shown only on slide 2.
  \item<+>  Third item, shown only on slide 3.
  \item<+(-\value{beamerpauses})-> Fourth item,
          shown on slide 1 and following.
  \end{itemize}
\end{frame}
```

This demonstrates elegantly how to make the last item visible at the same time as the first one without knowing how many items are in the list. The second and third items are shown only on one specific slide; on all other slides they are invisible (but do occupy space).

Text styles

As expected, the standard macros for changing the text style are redefined to support overlays:

```
\textbf <overlay spec.> {text}
\textit <overlay spec.> {text}
\textsl <overlay spec.> {text}
\textrm <overlay spec.> {text}
\textsf <overlay spec.> {text}
\color <overlay spec.> [color model] {value(s)}{text}
\structure <overlay spec.> {text}
```

The effect is the same on all of these macros. If there is an overlay specification, the text style is changed for only the specified slide(s), but has no effect on the other slides. Thus \textit<3>{This is in italic} causes the text to appear in italic on the third slide. The \structure macro provides a generic facility, which sets the style for the specified slides to whatever is defined by \setbeamerfont. The display of the following example shows the last slide of the frame.

```
\documentclass{beamer}
\usetheme{Malmoe} \usecolortheme{dove}
\useoutertheme{sidebar}
\setbeamerfont{structure}{shape=\scshape}

\begin{frame}
  \frametitle{Text macros}
  \framesubtitle{Other text macros}
  Start. \textbf<1->{This is in bold font.}   Finish\\
  Start. \textit<2->{This is in italic font.} Finish\\
  Start. \textsl<3->{This is slanted.}        Finish\\
  Start. \textrm<4->{This is in Roman font.}  Finish\\
  Start. \textsf<5->{This is sans serif.}     Finish\\
  Start. {\color<6->[rgb]{0,0,1}Colorized}    Finish\\
  Start. \structure<7>{This is structured.}   Finish\\
  Start. This is only text. Finish
\end{frame}
```

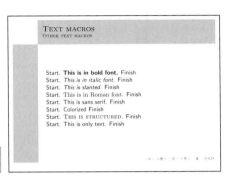

Example 11-4-30

Footnotes

Having footnotes in a presentation is usually unwise, and they should be used with caution. As usual, the macro is redefined to support overlays.

> \footnote *<overlay spec.>* [*key*] {*text*}

Footnotes appear at the bottom of the current frame and cannot be moved to another frame. There is only one keyword possible, `frame`, which causes **beamer** to typeset the footnote right at the bottom of the frame. This is important for minipages, where the footnote is normally placed at the bottom of the minipage itself.

```
\documentclass{beamer}
\usetheme{Malmoe} \useoutertheme{sidebar} \usecolortheme{dove}
\begin{frame}  \frametitle{A demonstration of footnotes}
               \framesubtitle{A bad idea in presentations}
 \only<1->{Cats, dogs and lions\footnote<1>{all carnivores} are scary}\\[4ex]
 \only<2->{\fbox{\begin{minipage}[t]{0.4\linewidth}sheep
          and goats\footnote[frame]{herbivores} are dull \end{minipage}}}
 \only<3->{\fbox{\begin{minipage}[t]{0.45\linewidth}
          pigs and men\footnote{omnivores} are interesting \end{minipage}}}
\end{frame}
```

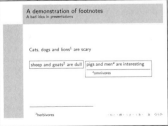

Example 11-4-31

On the third slide of the previous example you see that the first footnotemark is still there, while the footnote text has disappeared. Nevertheless, it still occupies the vertical space. The last footnote has no `frame` keyword, so it is placed inside the minipage with an alpha footnote mark.

Verbatim text

Verbatim text written with the `\verb` macro or the `verbatim` environment cannot be used directly inside a frame. You must use `fragile` keyword on the frame, which comes with some restrictions:

- `frame` must be used as an environment and not as a macro.
- `\end{frame}` must be in a single line.
- `\alert<1>` and similar macros are not allowed inside the `verbatim` environment.

The `fragile` keyword causes **beamer** to write the content of the `frame` environment to a file and read it back. Typically the `verbatim` mode is used to typeset fragments of code, which can often be done in a better way by packages such as **alltt** and **listings**. However, **beamer** offers a limited verbatim environment called `semiverbatim` without any optional arguments, which removes the third restriction above:

```
\begin{semiverbatim} ... \end{semiverbatim}
```

```
\documentclass{beamer}
\usetheme{Malmoe}
\useoutertheme{sidebar}
\usecolortheme{dove}
\begin{frame}[fragile]
  \setbeamercovered{transparent=25}
  \frametitle{A demonstration of verbatim text}
  \framesubtitle{Which needs special code}
  \uncover<1->{A demo of semiverbatim:}
  \begin{semiverbatim}
    \uncover<2->{<xd:cvsId>$Id: sprits_totest.xsl
    2007-01-11 rahtz $</xd:cvsId>}
  \end{semiverbatim}

  A demo of verbatim:
  \begin{verbatim}
    This is verbatim text:
    <xd:cvsId>$Id: sprits_totest.xsl
      2007-01-11 rahtz $</xd:cvsId>
  \end{verbatim}
\end{frame}
```

Example
11-4-32

The `semiverbatim` environment does a good job for a presentation of source code, when parts of it should be uncovered and alerted. The next example shows the second slide of a frame. It is easy to change the alert color—in this case, blue (see also Color Plate XVI z).

```
\documentclass{beamer}
\usetheme{Malmoe}
\useoutertheme{sidebar}
\usecolortheme{dove}
\begin{frame}[fragile]
 \frametitle{An Algorithm For Finding Prime Numbers.}
 \framesubtitle{Use of semiverbatim}
 \setbeamercolor{alerted text}{fg=blue}
 \begin{semiverbatim}
  \uncover<1->{\alert<0>{int main (void)}}
  \uncover<1->{\alert<0>{\{}}
  \uncover<1->{\alert<1>{  \alert<4>{\color{red}std::}vector<bool> is_prime (100, true);}}
  \uncover<1->{\alert<1>{  for (int i = 2; i < 100; i++)}}
  \uncover<2->{\alert<2>{    if (is_prime[i])}}
  \uncover<2->{\alert<0>{      \{}}
  \uncover<3->{\alert<3>{        \alert<4>{\color{red}std::}cout << i << " ";}}
  \uncover<3->{\alert<3>{        for (int j = i; j < 100;}}
  \uncover<3->{\alert<3>{          is_prime [j] = false, j+=i);}}
  \uncover<2->{\alert<0>{      \}}}
  \uncover<1->{\alert<0>{  return 0;}}
  \uncover<1->{\alert<0>{\}}}
 \end{semiverbatim}
 \visible<4>{Note the use of \alert{\color{red}\textttt{std::}}.}
\end{frame}
```

Example
11-4-33

Graphics

Images can be created and manipulated in the usual way of LaTeX with the **graphics** package. In addition, **beamer** comes with a basic drawing facility, the **pgf** package (Portable Graphics Format), which is similar to the picture macros and can be used with pdfTeX as well as ordinary TeX. It also has some macros to save and reuse images, which have the advantage that some transparency is possible. The `\includegraphics` macro is redefined by **beamer** to get the additional argument for the overlay specifications.

```
\includegraphics<overlay spec.> [key/vals] {file name}
\pgfdeclareimage{key/vals}{beamer name }{file name}
\pgfuseimage{key/vals}{beamer name}
```

The following example shows both ways of using a graphic. The screenshot is the thirteenth slide, which is easy to control because each line has five pictures. The automatic slide control is done by the option <+-> together with the \only and \includegraphics macros.

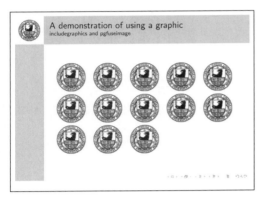

```
\documentclass{beamer}   \usetheme{Malmoe}
\useoutertheme{sidebar}  \usecolortheme{dove}
\pgfdeclareimage[width=2cm]{fu}{fu-berlin}
\newcommand\FU{\only<+->{\pgfuseimage{fu}}}
\newcommand\fu
    {\includegraphics<+->[width=2cm]{fu-berlin}}
\logo{\includegraphics[width=1.5cm]{fu-berlin}}
\begin{frame}
\frametitle{A demonstration of using a graphic}
\framesubtitle{includegraphics and pgfuseimage}
\FU \fu \FU \fu \FU\par \fu \FU \fu \FU \fu\par
\FU \fu \FU \fu \FU
\end{frame}
```

Example
11-4-34

Often a full-screen graphic is needed, which is possible with an empty frame (keyword plain) and filling the background canvas with the graphic.

```
\documentclass{beamer}   \usetheme{Malmoe}
\useoutertheme{sidebar}  \usecolortheme{dove}
\setbeamertemplate{background canvas}{%
    \includegraphics[width=\paperwidth]%
                    {fu-berlin-air}}
\begin{frame}[plain]
\end{frame}
```

Example
11-4-35

This image shows the main campus of the Free University of Berlin and is courtesy of Foster & Partners.

11.4.8 Managing your templates

The **beamer** class is totally driven by templates, and nearly everything can be overwritten or simply defined by the user. In general there are three kinds of templates:

Table 11.12: Font attributes for **beamer**

Keyword	Meaning

`size=`⟨*LATEX font size*⟩

Sets the size of the **beamer** font. The `font size` must be a standard LATEX command (`\tiny`, `\scriptsize`, `\footnotesize`, `\small`, `\normalsize`, `\large`, `\Large`, `\huge`, and `\Huge`.) used for setting the font size; otherwise it should be empty. **beamer** itself defines two more font sizes, `\Tiny` and `\TINY`, for very small text. Note that an empty definition is different than `\normalsize`. An empty definition doesn't change anything, the current font setting is valid.

`size*={`⟨*size in pt*⟩`}{`⟨*baselineskip*⟩`}`

Sets the size attribute of the font to the given size in points and the baseline skip to the given value. Note that not all font sizes are available.

`shape=`⟨*font shape*⟩

Sets the shape attribute of the font. The command must be a default LATEX shape: `\itshape`, `\slshape`, `\scshape`, or `\upshape`.

`shape*=`⟨*LATEX abbreviation*⟩

Sets the shape attribute of the font using the LATEX's abbreviations for attributes (`n`, `it`, `sl`, `sc`, `u`), which is the same as `shape=\fontshape {...}`.

`series=`⟨*LATEX series name*⟩

Sets the series attribute of the font; it must be `\bfseries` or `\mdseries`.

`series*=`⟨*LATEX abbreviation*⟩

Same effect as `series=\fontseries {...}`.

`family=`⟨*LATEX font family*⟩

Sets the font family attribute, which must be either `\rmfamily`, `\ttfamily`, or `\sffamily`.

`family*=`⟨*LATEX abbreviation*⟩

Same effect as `family=\fontfamily {...}`.

`parent=`⟨*parent list*⟩

Specifies a list of parent fonts.

```
\setbeamertemplate{beamer element} [predefined keywords] [...]{⟨definition⟩}
\setbeamercolor* {beamer element}{definition}
\setbeamerfont* {beamer element}{attributes}
```

The starred versions reset all attributes to the default values to make only the new definitions active. The default is, in general, the empty definition.

With the optional argument for the `\setbeamertemplate` macro, you can use predefined values e.g., a circle or a square for itemized lists. The package documentation describes all of the **beamer** elements (there are a lot of them!). Here we show only a few examples to see how it works.

Table 11.12 shows all attributes that are possible when setting the fonts.

The next example defines its own title header for the main-title and sub-title of the frame. The first **beamer** element, which is redefined with default values, is the `background`. With `\setbeamercolor`, the element `frametitle` gets the foreground color white and the background color gray. With `\setbeamerfont`, the element `frametitle` gets the

font series \bfseries and the element framesubtitle, then the size small and the
\bfseries. Finally, the template frametitle is redefined. To make the header independent of the normal font size, the width and the height are hard-coded; both titles in the examples are of the same height. The logo is defined and positioned by the default theme.

Not all templates can be easily changed like the one for the frame title; others are more complex and need some experience to modify them effectively.

```
\documentclass{beamer}
\setbeamertemplate{background}[grid][0.5cm]
\setbeamercolor{frametitle}{fg=white,bg=gray}
\setbeamerfont{frametitle}{series=\bfseries}
\setbeamerfont{framesubtitle}{size=\small,series=\bfseries}
\setbeamertemplate{frametitle}{%
  \begin{beamercolorbox}[wd=\paperwidth,ht=5.2ex,leftskip=.3cm,%
      rightskip=.3cm plus1fil,vmode]{frametitle}
    \usebeamerfont*{frametitle}\insertframetitle\strut
      \hfill\Huge\raisebox{-1ex}{FU}%
      \ifx\insertframesubtitle\empty\else\par
        {\usebeamerfont*{framesubtitle}{%
          \usebeamercolor[fg]{framesubtitle}%
          \insertframesubtitle}\strut\par}%
      \fi
  \end{beamercolorbox}}
\logo{\includegraphics[width=1.5cm]{fu-berlin}}

\begin{frame}[fragile]
  \frametitle{The macro \texttt{\textbackslash setbeamertemplate}}
  \framesubtitle{how it works ...}
... further code omitted ...
```

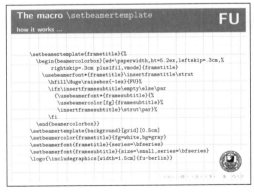 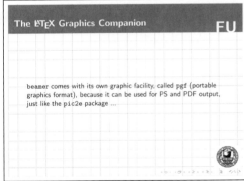

Example
11-4-36

11.4.9 Backgrounds and colors

Each frame has a background, which can consist of anything: an image, some text, or nothing. Superimposed on that element is a background canvas, which appears before the normal slide components are built up on top. The next example shows the specific background canvas, a background with a grid, and the effect of changing the default text color.

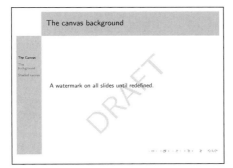

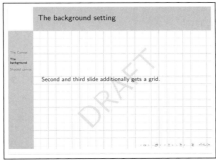

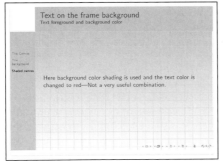

```
\usepackage{beamerthemeMalmoe}
\usepackage{beamerouterthemesidebar}
\usepackage{beamercolorthemedove}
\section{The Canvas}
\setbeamertemplate{background canvas}
   {\put(120,-230){\rotatebox{45}
        {\scalebox{5}{\textcolor{gray!20}{DRAFT}}}}}
\begin{frame}
  \frametitle{The canvas background}
  A watermark on all slides until redefined.
\end{frame}

\section{The background}
\setbeamertemplate{background}[grid]
                 [step=0.5cm,color=red!20]
\begin{frame}
  \frametitle{The background setting}
  Second and third slide additionally gets a grid.
\end{frame}

\section{Shaded canvas}
\setbeamertemplate{background canvas}
               [vertical shading][top=blue!25]
\setbeamercolor{normal text}{fg=red}
\usebeamercolor[fg]{normal text}
\begin{frame}
  \frametitle{Text on the frame background}
  \framesubtitle{Text foreground and background color}
  Here background color shading is used and the
  text color is changed to red---Not a very
  useful combination.
\end{frame}
\end{document}
```

Example
11-4-37

This example includes three frames. The first slide has a watermark for the canvas background, defined before the first frame, which means that it will persist until a new global or local redefinition of the canvas happens.

For the second and third slides, a grid is defined for the background.

On the third slide the background canvas is changed to a color shading and the default text color to red. This requires the use of two commands: one to define the "normal text" color and one to use it.

11.4.10 Document modes

Table 11.3 listed the possible modes of a document. Switching between these different modes is possible with the \mode macro:

> \mode<*mode specification*>{*object*}   \mode<*mode specification*>   \mode*

In the first case the object, which can be simple text or anything else, is set in the specified mode. For example,

```
\mode<article>{This text is printed only in the article mode}
```

The other cases are more sophisticated, working more like switches. The second macro form allows you to switch between the different modes.

```
\mode<article>

This text is typeset only in \verb+article+ mode.
\verb!verbatim text is ok {!

\mode
<presentation>
{ % this text is inserted only in presentation mode
\frame{\tableofcontents[currentsection]}}

Here we are back to article mode. This text is not inserted in
presentation mode.

\mode
<presentation>

This text is inserted only in presentation mode.
[ ... ]
```

The final usage pattern for the \mode macro, with a star, causes **beamer**, if in presentation mode, to ignore all text and code outside of a \frame macro or environment. In the article mode, the starred version has no effect. There is also a class option to activate this behavior right from the beginning of a document (see Table 11.3).

11.4.11 The beamer **project**

In this book we have merely been able to give an overview of **beamer**, which is a hugely complex package. If we have whetted your appetite for learning more, the main Web page at https://sourceforge.net/projects/latex-beamer has many more details; you can also subscribe to the **beamer** mailing list there to keep up-to-date with changes.

Producing PDF from Various Sources

The only graphical object that LATEX can handle internally is the `picture` environment, which is very easy to use but rather restrictive. All other graphical material must be encapsulated in `\special` commands and later extracted by the DVI processor (e.g., dvips), and transformed into PostScript code. Alternatively, we can use an extended TEX, such as pdf-tex, in which we can directly embed PDF code. Packages such as pstricks can produce the `\special` commands for DVI, but this method does not work with pdflatex. Depending on whether you need to include EPS graphics files in your LATEX document, one or more strategies can be used to obtain PDF output:

- latex creates a DVI file, which is read by dvips, which creates a PostScript file, which is finally translated into PDF by ps2pdf or Acrobat Distiller (this is the traditional way).

- The package pst-pdf is used.

- dvipdfm creates the DVI file and generates PDF directly.

- pdflatex, or another TEX variant such as Michael Vulis's VTeX,[1] reads the LATEX source and creates PDF directly.

In this appendix we first describe the dvipdfm and dvipdfmx programs, which generate PDF from a DVI file. Then we turn our attention to the pst-pdf package, which automates the translation of EPS images and PSTricks PostScript code into PDF. The final part of the appendix looks at an example of a LATEX file that is translated into PDF using each of the first four alternatives mentioned above.

---

[1] *Visual TEX*: see `http://www.micropress-inc.com/`

A.1 dvipdfm and dvipdfmx

Mark A. Wicks's program dvipdfm (`http://gaspra.kettering.edu/dvipdfm/`) supports the following features:

- Bookmarks, named destinations, and annotations (many of Acrobat Distiller's `pdfmark` features)
- dvips specials
- Inclusion of METAPOST output and of arbitrary PostScript files with help from an external program
- Thumbnails (generated by ghostscript)
- Arbitrary, nested linear transformations (including scaling and rotation) of typeset material
- Inclusion of PDF images, including cropping by supplying a bounding box
- Inclusion of JPEG and PNG images
- A color stack for keeping track of the current color
- Partial font embedding and Flate compression to reduce file size
- Balancing of page and destination trees to speed up reader access for very large documents

A detailed description of how these functions are supported can be found in the program documentation (CTAN: `dviware/dvipdfm/dvipdfm-0.13.2c.pdf`). To take advantage of these functions when running dvipdfm on a DVI file, you must specify the `dvipdfm` option with LATEX (and hyperref).

Shunsaku Hirata and Jin-Hwan Cho extended dvipdfm to enhance its Unicode capabilities, adding support for multibyte character encodings and large character sets for East Asian languages by CID-keyed fonts. Their dvipdfmx program (`http://project.ktug.or.kr/dvipdfmx/`) also has support for many features of Hàn Thế Thành's pdfTEX program.

dvipdfmx is a must if you want to deal with large character sets, since all traditional methods—especially pdftex—cannot handle those natively. For instance, dvipdfmx lets you extract and search 16-bit characters. Full support for PostScript Type 1, TrueType, and Open-Type is provided, and if the font resides on the system you can instruct dvipdfmx not to embed it. dvipdfmx is used by the TEX variant xetex. PDF encryption and multiple page sizes in a single document are possible.

The following command-line options are available for dvipdfm:

-c   *Disable color specials.*
         This option forces all color commands to be ignored. Useful for printing a color document on a black-and-white printer.

-e   *Disable partial font embedding.*
         Useful for forms that need complete fonts, or for PFB files that dvipdfm cannot parse.

`-f`   *Set font map file name* (default `t1fonts.map`).

`-l`   *Select landscape.* Only meaningful for paper sizes specified on the command line.

`-m` *number*   *Specify additional magnification for document.*

`-o` *filename*   *Output PDF file name* (default `dvifile.pdf`).

`-p` *papersize*   *Output paper size* (default "`letter`").
        Possible other values are "`legal`", "`ledger`", "`tabloid`", "`a4`", and "`a3`";
        papersize can also be specified as *w*`<unit>`,*h*`<unit>` (e.g., "`20cm,30cm`").

`-s` *page_ranges*   *Select a subset of pages from the DVI file.*
        Similar to dvips's `-pp` option, but with the colon range indicator replaced by a hyphen; e.g., `dvipdfm -s 10,21,73-92` prints pages 10, 21, and 73 through 92. If the first page in a range is empty, PDF generation starts at the beginning of the document (`dvipdfm -s -20`). If the last page in a range is empty, the end of the document is taken (`dvipdfm -s 97-`).

`-t`   *Embed thumbnail images.* Thumbnails must be generated by a separate program.

`-d`   *Delete thumbnail images after embedding.*

`-x` *number*   *Horizontal offset for document* (default 1 in).

`-y` *number*   *Vertical offset for document* (default 1 in).

`-z` *number*   *zlib compression level.*
        The value of *number* must be in the range 0 (no compression) to 9 (maximal compression, the default).

`-v`   *Verbose.* Display complete file.

`-vv`   *Superverbose.* Display maximal log messages.

To the preceding options, **dvipdfmx** adds the following options:

`-d` *number*   *PDF decimal digits.* The value of *number* must be in the range 0–5 (default 2).

`-r` *number*   *Resolution for raster fonts.* In DPI (default 600).

`-C` *number*   *Option flags* (default 0).

    `0x0001`   Reserved.
    `0x0002`   Use semi-transparent filling for tpic shading command, instead of opaque gray color (requires PDF 1.4).
    `0x0004`   Treat all CID Fonts as fixed-pitch fonts.
    `0x0008`   Do not replace duplicate font map entries.

    Positive values are always *ORed* with previously given flags, while negative values replace old values.

`-O` *number*   *Maximum depth of open bookmark items* (default 0).

-P *number*   *Permission flags for PDF encryption* (default 0x003C).

-S *Enable PDF encryption.*

-T *Embed thumbnail images.* Like -t, but image files are removed when finished.

-V *number*   *PDF minor version* (default 3).

A.2 pst-pdf—From PostScript to PDF

The pst-pdf package uses the LaTeX package preview, which is part of the preview [66, 88] bundle. The preview package extracts all "marked" parts in a LaTeX document into a DVI file, in which each such part is saved on a separate page. This makes it easy to convert the DVI file into PDF format and then include these parts in a subsequent pdflatex run.

A.2.1 Package options

active   Enables the extraction modus of the preview package; the DVI output collects only the images (default).

inactive   Only the packages pstricks and graphicx are loaded; all macros are disabled.

pstricks   The package pstricks is loaded (default).

nopstricks   The package pstricks is not loaded; however, if the macro detects any PSTricks macro, then pstricks will be loaded automatically nevertheless.

draft   Same meaning as for package graphicx, but only valid for the last pdflatex run.

final   In the last pdflatex mode the container file is used (default).

tightpage   White space around images is cut (default).

notightpage White space around images is not cut.

displaymath Treats displaymath, eqnarray, equation, and $$ or \(...\) as images.

other   All other options are passed to the package pstricks.

When you specify the inactive option, all the pst-pdf macros will be disabled, apart from the trimming function, so that latex can be run in the usual way and PostScript output can be generated (with dvips), if desired.

A.2.2 Usage

pst-pdf was originally designed for PSTricks. This fact explains why it supports by default the pspicture and psmatrix environments, as well as all commands that are internally defined through \pst@object. The pst-pdf package works with the help of the package preview completely in the background; you simply have to load the package in the preamble of a document.

The process of generating a PDF file from a LaTeX source consists of two stages: the creation of the graphics container and the subsequent **pdflatex** run to create the PDF. These stages are described next.

Creation of the graphics container

latex *file*.tex

> Initial run of **latex**, where **preview** extracts all known objects and saves them into *file*.dvi, where each object is on its own page. The DVI file created in this way has a special internal format and is unsuited for user purposes, such as viewing the file with a DVI viewer.

dvips -Ppdf -o *file-pics*.ps *file*.dvi

> **dvips** run to convert the DVI file to PostScript, where the -Ppdf option tells **dvips** to load the config file for PDF-related output. **dvips** creates the new file *file-pics*.ps.

ps2pdf *file-pics*.ps *file-pics*.pdf

> **ps2pdf** run to convert the PostScript file to PDF, with each image on a separate page.

Creation of the final PDF output document

pdflatex *file*.tex   First run of **pdflatex** run, where **pst-pdf** is not active.

bibtex *file*   **bibtex** run.

. . .   Any other additional runs (e.g., index, glossary).

pdflatex *file*.tex   Ultimate **pdflatex** run, where all generated PDF images are included.

A simple example with **PSTricks** follows.

This is a **PDF**–document!

```
\usepackage{pst-plot,pst-text}
\usepackage{pst-pdf}
This is a \textbf{PDF}--document!

\begin{pspicture}(-0.25,-2.25)(6.25,2.5)
  \pstextpath[linestyle=none]%
    {\psplot[linewidth=1pt,%
      linestyle=dotted,%
      plotpoints=300,%
      xunit=0.015,%
      yunit=2]{0}{400}{x sin}}
    {\large The \LaTeX\ Graphics
    Companion, $2^{nd}$ Edition}
\end{pspicture}%
```

Example
A-2-1

pst-pdf provides a macro called \PreviewEnvironment that lets you define additional environments, which are then scanned by the **preview** package and also written as an image into the DVI file. In the following example, **PSTricks** is used to connect some nodes in a tabular format. With the command \PreviewEnvironment{tabular}, this environment is also written into the DVI file. There are no restrictions in declaring environments for preview.

```
\usepackage{bigdelim,multirow,array}
\usepackage[table]{pstricks}    \usepackage{pst-node,pst-pdf}
\PreviewEnvironment{tabular}
\definecolor{Gray}{gray}{0.1}
\renewcommand\arraystretch{1.1}
\begin{tabular}{c|c|l} \multicolumn{1}{c}{\textbf{Segments}}
 & \multicolumn{1}{c}{\textbf{Usage}}             & \\\cline{2-2}
0x0  & \cellcolor{gray}Kernel text and data       & \\\cline{2-2}
0x1  & \cellcolor{gray}User text                   & \\\cline{2-2}
0x2  & \cellcolor{red}User stack, data             & \\\cline{2-2}
0x3  & \pnode{A}
     & \rdelim\}{5}{5.5cm}[\parbox{7.5cm}{Available for the user process\\
            \hspace*{0.25cm}\pnode{A2}~if \texttt{shmat()}or
\texttt{mmap()} is called]]\\\cline{2-2}
0x4  &    & \\\cline{2-2}  0x5--0xA &               & \\\cline{2-2}
0xB  &    & \\\cline{2-2}  0xC      & \pnode{B}  & \\\cline{2-2}
0xD  & \cellcolor{gray}Shared library text         & \\\cline{2-2}
0xE  &                          & \pnode{B2}       \\\cline{2-2}
\ncline[arrows=->,linewidth=2pt,linecolor=blue,doubleline=true]{A}{B}%
\ncdiag[arrows=->,linewidth=1.25pt,linearc=0.2,%
  angleA=180,angleB=0,armA=0.2cm,nodesepB=-0.25cm,armB=0.625cm]{A2}{B2}%
0xF      & \cellcolor{gray}\footnotesize Per-process shared library data
                                          & \\\cline{2-2}
\end{tabular}
```

Example
A-2-2

The package pst-pdf also supports EPS images with the help of a postscript environment, whose contents are scanned by preview, written into the DVI file, and then converted to PDF. This approach is sometimes easier to use than ps2pdf, because the conversion of the EPS image occurs in the background.

It is important to realize that pst-pdf numbers all images consecutively. If anything changes in the order of the images, when an image is added, deleted, or just edited, the first three runs for building the graphics image container must be repeated. By contrast, if only the text was edited, then rerunning pdflatex once is sufficient, as long as the PDF image container exists, since all images are taken from there.

A.3 Generating PDF from LaTeX

As explained at the beginning of this appendix, a PDF file may be generated from a LaTeX source in several different ways. The route that you should follow depends mostly on the graphics material that you want to include. If most of it is in EPS format, the easiest way is to use latex, followed by dvips and finally ps2pdf. If all of your graphics files are already in PDF format, with some JPEG and PNG images, the more direct route is to run pdflatex. You can also combine both approaches by running latex and the dvipdfmx program. The xetex TeX variant, which is designed to work with Unicode text internally, depends on dvipdfmx.

If you make a lot of use of PSTricks, you should look at the technique introduced in Section A.2 based on the pst-pdf package.

As an example of these four possibilities, we will use a medium-size file exa.tex, where we also are interested in taking advantage of PDF's hypertext capabilities by loading the hyperref package in the LaTeX source. Given that the way the LaTeX structural information is translated into PDF hypertext commands differs for each program (dvips, dvipdfm, and pdflatex), we have to indicate which program will generate the final PostScript or PDF output (see the three first lines of the LaTeX source of the file exa.tex).[1]

```
\documentclass[a4paper,dvipdfm]{article}   % using dvipdfm
%\documentclass[a4paper,dvips]{article}     % using dvips & ps2pdf
%\documentclass[a4paper,pdftex]{article}    % using pdflatex with pdf graphics
\usepackage{graphicx}
\usepackage{url}
\usepackage{makeidx}
\usepackage[backref]{hyperref}
\makeindex
\title{Simulation of  Energy Loss  Straggling}
\author{Maria Physicist}
\begin{document}
\maketitle
\tableofcontents
\section{Introduction} ...
```

Running the example with latex and dvipdfmx

For the first run we use dvipdfmx to generate the PDF. Therefore we must ensure that we have the images also available as .pdf files and that each image is accompanied by a small

---

[1] This example is more or less identical—a few hyperref and PDF-related lines have been added—to the LaTeX code described in Appendix A of the *LaTeX Web Companion*[35] and is available as info/examples/lwc/apa/latexexa.tex on CTAN.

text file that specifies its bounding box (dvipdfmx assumes that for each image *fig*.pdf there exists a file *fig*.bb). For transforming EPS files into PDF, we can use the script epstopdf (part of the TEX Live distribution). Information about the resulting PDF file can be obtained with the pdfinfo utility (part of the xpdf distribution).

```
> ls *.eps
phys332-1.eps   phys332-2.eps
> more phys332-1.bb
%%BoundingBox: 0 0 567 567
> epstopdf phys332-1.eps
> pdfinfo phys332-1.pdf
Producer:      GNU Ghostscript 7.05
Tagged:        no
Pages:         1
Encrypted:     no
Page size:     567 x 567 pts
File size:     11549 bytes
Optimized:     no
PDF version:   1.3
```

We observe that the bounding box of the PDF corresponds to the bounding box of the EPS source. If this were not the case, the PDF image could be cropped to the correct size with the pdfcrop utility, which is part of the TEX Live distribution (see Appendix B).

Next we run the LATEX source exa.tex the correct number of times through latex, before generating the PDF file with dvipdfmx.

```
> latex exa
> latex exa
> makeindex exa
> latex exa
> dvipdfmx -o exadvipdfmx.pdf exa
exa.dvi -> exadvipdfmx.pdf
[1] [2] [3] [4] [5] [6] [7] [8] [9] [10] [11]
130030 bytes written
```

The resulting file is written to exadvipdfmx.pdf and can be viewed with ghostview, Adobe Reader, etc. Since we activated the hyperref package in the LATEX source, the viewer can navigate conveniently through the document.

Running the example with latex, dvips, and ps2pdf

If we activate the dvips option on the \documentclass command in the LATEX source and run latex the correct number of times, we can use dvips and ps2pdf (or its explicit variant ps2pdf13) to obtain the PDF output file exadvips.pdf. This file has the same (hypertext) characteristics as exadvipdfmx.pdf in the previous example.

```
> rm *.aux         # get rid of program-specific entries in aux file
> latex exa
> latex exa
> makeindex exa
> latex exa
> dvips -j0 exa -oexadvips.ps
> ps2pdf13 -sPAPERSIZE=a4 exadvips.ps
```

Running the example with pdflatex

Since we already have all images in PDF format, we can run **pdflatex** directly and obtain the file exapdflatex.pdf, which is functionally equivalent to the PDF output files generated in the two previous cases.

```
> rm *.aux         # get rid of program-specific entries in aux file
> pdflatex exa
> pdflatex exa
> makeindex exa
> pdflatex exa
> mv exa.pdf exapdflatex.pdf
```

Running the example with pdflatex, using the pst-pdf package

As the fourth alternative for generating PDF, we load the **pst-pdf** package in the preamble of our example LaTeX file exa.tex (see page 803).

```
\documentclass[a4paper,dvips]{article}
%\documentclass[a4paper,pdftex]{article}  % .. once graphics are in pdf
\usepackage{graphicx}
\usepackage{url}
\usepackage{makeidx}
\usepackage{pst-pdf}%<<<<<< line added
\usepackage[backref]{hyperref}
```

First we produce the PDF version of the EPS images by running the example with the dvips option for the hyperlinks (see Section A.2 for the details of the procedure).

```
> latex exa
...
Output written on exa.dvi (2 pages, 3344 bytes).
Transcript written on exa.log.
> dvips -Ppdf -o exa-pics.ps exa.dvi
This is dvips(k) 5.95b Copyright 2005 Radical Eye Software
' TeX output 2006.05.30:1632' -> exa-pics.ps
<tex.pro><alt-rule.pro><pstricks.pro><pst-dots.pro><special.pro>.
[1<phys332-1.eps>] [2<phys332-2.eps>]
> ps2pdf exa-pics.ps  exa-pics.pdf
```

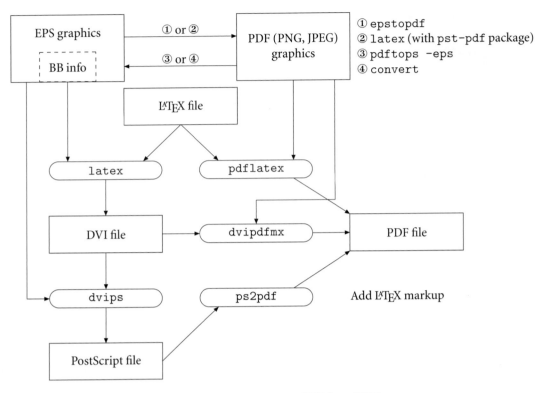

Figure A.1: Four ways to generate PDF from LaTeX

The file `exa-pics` contains the PDF instances of the two EPS pictures referenced in the example document. So that we can run this file with **pdflatex**, we activate the line with the `pdftex` option on the `\documentclass` command, and process the file `exa.tex` the relevant number of times, with, if needed, runs of **makeindex** and **bibtex** interspersed to generate index and bibliographic references.

```
> pdflatex exa
> makeindex exa
> pdflatex exa
> pdflatex exa
```

In summary (see Figure A.1), when deciding which method to use to generate PDF output when starting from a LaTeX source file, the latex → dvips → ps2pdf route is appropriate for cases where most of the external graphics files are in EPS format. When a lot of **PSTricks** images are present in the source, the use of the **pst-pdf** package and **pdflatex** is to be seriously considered. The more direct **pdflatex** route seems more attractive if the graphics files are available as .pdf, .jpeg, or .png files. Finally, the choice of **dvipdfmx** seems necessary

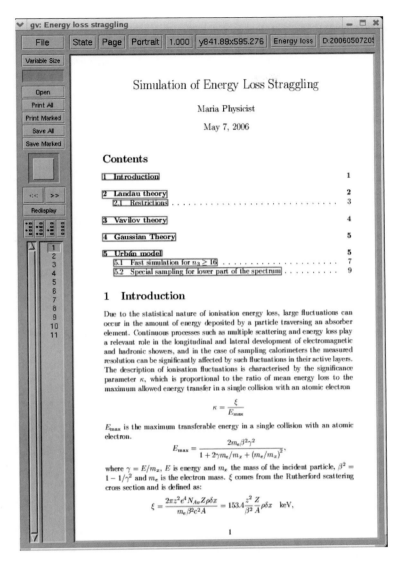

Figure A.2: Hypertext document generated with pdflatex

only if large, multibyte font sets (e.g., for handling Far-East Asian languages) are required.

The PDF files generated by the four methods discussed in this section are completely functionally equivalent. Figure A.2 shows the first page of the PDF file `exapdflatex.pdf` as displayed by a PDF viewer. The hyperlinks (surrounded by boxes) allow you to jump from the various entries in the table of contents to the start of the corresponding sections in the document body.

L^AT_EX Software and User Group Information

We hope that, when reading this book, you will actually be tempted to get one or more of the packages and programs we describe onto your computer and try them out yourself, see how useful they are to your work—or perhaps just have some fun.

The files and packages that are described in this book are available in most TEX distributions, such as the TEX Live DVD or on the TEX Collection DVD of DANTE. The newest versions can also be downloaded directly from the Internet. The aim of this appendix is to provide you with the information necessary to obtain current releases of these DVDs (CD-ROMs are available on demand) and to give hints on how to locate and get the files you need directly from the Internet.

B.1 Getting help

While we certainly hope that your questions have been answered in this book, we know that this cannot be the case for all of them. For additional information related to specific packages discussed in the book, it can be helpful to read the original documentation provided with the package. Appendix B.4 suggests ways to find that documentation on your system.

The existing "Frequently Asked Questions" (FAQ) documents are particularly valuable resources. The most important one is the UK-TUG FAQ by Robin Fairbairns, which is available at `http://www.tex.ac.uk/faq` (or `http://faq.tug.org`).

If precomposed answers are not enough to answer your questions, several news groups are devoted to general TEX and LATEX questions: `news://comp.text.tex` is perhaps the most important one, with usually more than 100 messages posted each day. Many of the authors mentioned in this book are regular contributors on the news groups and help with answering questions and requests. Thus there is a vast amount of helpful material on the Internet that can be conveniently searched using any search engine that indexes news entries.

If you post to any of these news groups, please adhere to basic netiquette. The community is friendly but sometimes direct and expects you to have done some research of your own first (e.g., read the FAQ first and searched the archived news, such as via `google.groups`) and not ask questions that have been answered several hundred times before. You should perhaps read Eric Raymond's "How To Ask Questions The Smart Way", available at `http://www.catb.org/~esr/faqs/smart-questions.html`, as a starter. Also, if applicable, provide a minimal *and* usable example of your problem that allows others to easily reproduce the symptoms you experience—this will save others time and might get you a faster reply.

B.2 How to get those TEX files?

A useful entry point to the TEX world is the TUG home page (`http://www.tug.org`; see Figure B.1). From there you can reach most information sources about TEX worldwide.

In particular, from the TUG home page you can go to one of the CTAN (Comprehensive TEX Archive Network) nodes. CTAN is a collaborative effort initiated in 1992 by the TUG Technical Working Group on TEX Archive Guidelines and is currently maintained by Jim Hefferon, Robin Fairbairns, and Rainer Schöpf (as of early 2007). Its main aim is to provide easy access to up-to-date copies of all nonproprietary versions of TEX, LATEX, METAFONT, and ancillary programs, as well as their associated files.

Presently, three backbone machines act as FTP servers: in the United Kingdom (`cam.ctan.org`), in Germany (`dante.ctan.org`), and in the United States (`tug.ctan.org`). These sites are mirrored worldwide and all have a Web interface (see Figure B.2).

The material on CTAN is regularly (currently on a yearly basis) made available on a DVD and and distributed by various TEX user groups to their members (if needed, the corresponding material is also available on several CD-ROMs). These days this DVD also contains ready-to-run distributions of TEX for various platforms. One is the TEX Live distribution (see `www.tug.org/texlive`). TEX Live CD-ROMs have been developed since 1996 through a collaboration between various TEX user groups.

B.3 Using CTAN

In Section B.2, we described TEX Live and the CTAN DVD. Obtaining the latest version of this DVD is an optimal way to gain access to recent versions of LATEX software.

Nevertheless, for readers with an Internet connection, it makes sense to query one of the CTAN nodes every now and then to see whether one of the LATEX components you need has been updated. In particular, the TUG home page includes an area that gives a list of the latest updates available on CTAN (see Figure B.1, bottom oval). If you find updates, you can

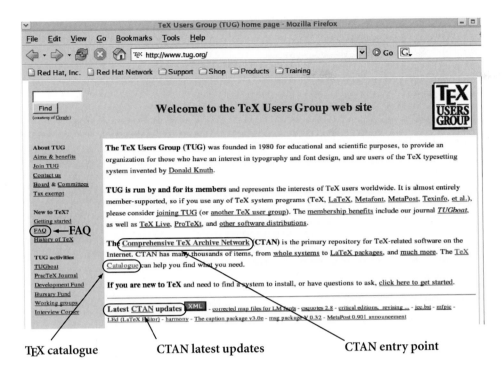

Figure B.1: The TUG Web home page

download the latest version of the package of interest directly from a CTAN archive (see Section B.3.2 for how this can be done).

Although network connections get faster all the time, it is often wise to connect to a site that is not too distant geographically from your location (consult the Web page `http://www.tug.org/tex-archive/CTAN.sites` for a list of mirror sites for the CTAN nodes).

B.3.1 Using the TeX file catalogue

A catalogue of TeX- and LaTeX-related packages maintained by Graham Williams can be consulted at `http://texcatalogue.sarovar.org/`. The catalogue is also directly reachable from the TUG home page (see the second oval in Figure B.1).

Moreover, the TeX catalogue is directly searchable from the CTAN interface (e.g., `http://www.tug.org/ctan.html`). In Figure B.2 we show how, after typing the string "`graphicx`" in the "Search Catalogue" area, we get the page shown in the bottom part of that figure. From this second page we can choose directly which of the proposed entries we want to investigate further (left side of the page) or we can follow a link to the associated CTAN directory (right side of the page).

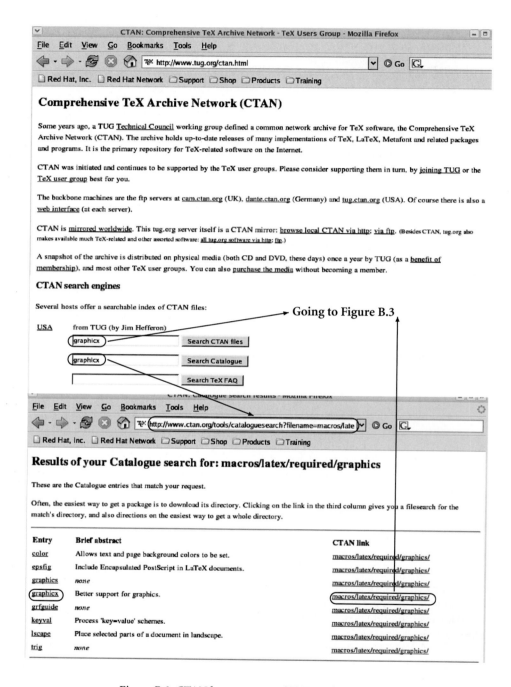

Figure B.2: CTAN home page and TeX catalogue entry

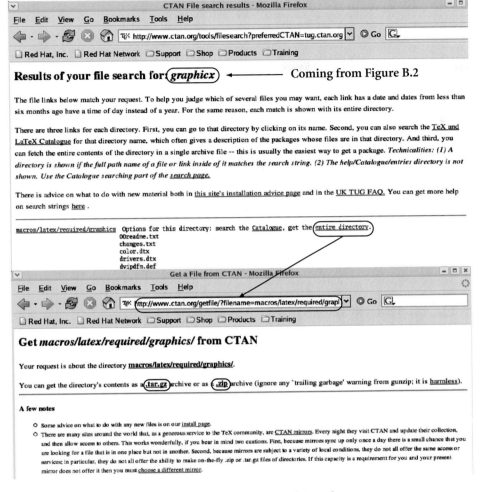

Figure B.3: Using the CTAN Web interface

B.3.2 Finding files on the archive and transferring them

Returning to Figure B.2, we see that an easy way to find a file on CTAN is to use the Web interface. Indeed, we merely have to type our search string in the CTAN search area. In this case, we specified the string "graphicx" (top oval in Figure B.2). The search engine returns the list of all files in the CTAN archive matching the given search criterion (see top part of Figure B.3). We can now browse this directory and decide to get one file. We can also transfer a complete directory by clicking on the link "entire directory" (rightmost oval in Figure B.3), which leads us to the page shown in the bottom part of Figure B.3. Here we are given the choice between a gzipped tar or a zip archive. By right-clicking on one of the two pointers (bottom ovals in Figure B.3), we download the archive in the desired format to our local machine so that we can install the files.

These search facilities are actively maintained and updated and, in fact, differ in look and feel between different CTAN nodes or mirrors. By the time you read this book, they may show different output compared to the figures in the book. However, they all follow a similar logic, so you should not find it difficult to obtain the desired information.

B.3.3 Getting files from the command line

If you know the Internet address of the package that you want to transfer (for instance from a Web search), it is perhaps more convenient to access the archive from the command line, without going through a Web interface. In this case you can use FTP or the **wget** program. The latter program allows you to download files from the Web non-interactively. It supports the HTTP, HTTPS, and FTP protocols, and CTAN offers zipped archives of the packages. An example follows (commands input by the user are underlined).

```
> wget ftp://ftp.dante.de/tex-archive/macros/latex/required/graphics.zip
--18:13:27--  ftp://ftp.dante.de/tex-archive/macros/latex/required/graphics.zip
           => 'graphics.zip'
Resolving ftp.dante.de... 80.237.210.73
Connecting to ftp.dante.de[80.237.210.73]:21... connected.
Logging in as anonymous ... Logged in!
==> SYST ... done.     ==> PWD ... done.
==> TYPE I ... done.   ==> CWD /tex-archive/macros/latex/required ... done.
==> PASV ... done.     ==> RETR graphics.zip ... done.
Length: 361,065 (unauthoritative)

100%[=====================================>] 361,065       378.48K/s

18:13:28 (377.84 KB/s) - 'graphics.zip' saved [361,065]
```

Alternatively, you can use the FTP protocol. To demonstrate this technique, we first connect to the CTAN site (`ftp.dante.de`) and specify `ftp` as a login name. The password *should be* your e-mail address. As we decided to transfer the **graphics** package, we first position ourselves in the directory where the file resides (`cd tex-archive/macros/latex/required`). We have a look at the files in that directory (`ls`), transfer the zip archive, and close the FTP session (`quit`).

```
> ftp ftp.dante.de
Connected to ftp.dante.de (80.237.210.73).
220 ProFTPD 1.2.10 Server (CTAN) [80.237.210.73]
Name (ftp.dante.de:goossens): ftp
331 Guest login ok, send your complete e-mail address as password.
Password: uuu.vvv@xxx.zz (use your email address here!)
230 Anonymous access granted, restrictions apply.
Remote system type is UNIX.
Using binary mode to transfer files.
ftp> cd tex-archive/macros/latex/required
250 CWD command successful
ftp> ls
```

```
227 Entering Passive Mode (80,237,210,73,145,185).
150 Opening ASCII mode data connection for file list
drwxrwxr-x   6 ftpmaint server       94 Oct 22  2004 amslatex
-rw-rw-r--   1 ftpmaint server  2121853 May  1 17:26 amslatex.zip
drwxrwxr-x   2 ftpmaint server     4096 Apr  1 22:03 babel
-rw-rw-r--   1 ftpmaint server  3098120 May  1 17:25 babel.zip
drwxrwsr-x   2 ftpmaint server     4096 Mar  1  2004 cyrillic
-rw-rw-r--   1 ftpmaint server    37586 May  1 17:25 cyrillic.zip
drwxrwsr-x   2 ftpmaint server     4096 Dec 20 14:43 graphics
-rw-rw-r--   1 ftpmaint server   361065 May  1 17:25 graphics.zip
drwxrwxr-x   2 ftpmaint server     4096 Apr 12 15:26 psnfss
-rw-rw-r--   1 ftpmaint server  1068096 May  1 17:25 psnfss.zip
drwxrwsr-x   2 ftpmaint server     4096 Mar  1  2004 tools
-rw-rw-r--   1 ftpmaint server   280673 May  1 17:25 tools.zip
226 Transfer complete.
ftp> get graphics.zip
local: graphics.zip remote: graphics.zip
227 Entering Passive Mode (80,237,210,73,145,193).
150 Opening BINARY mode data connection for graphics.zip (361065 bytes)
226 Transfer complete.
361065 bytes received in 0.832 secs (4.2e+02 Kbytes/sec)
ftp> quit
221 Goodbye.
```

B.4 Finding the documentation on your TₑX system

When you want to use a LaTeX package, it would be nice if you could study the documentation without having to remember where the relevant files are located on your TₑX system. Two ways exist to help you in your search: **texdoc** and its derivative **texdoctk**.

B.4.1 texdoc—Command-line interface for a search by name

Thomas Esser developed the program **texdoc**, which is part of the TₑX Live distribution. If you know the name of the file describing a package, you can find the relevant documentation files as follows:

```
texdoc -l pspicture
/TeXlive/tl7/texmf/doc/latex/carlisle/pspicture.dvi
/TeXlive/tl7/texmf/doc/html/catalogue/entries/pspicture.html
```

The `-l` option tells **texdoc** to list only the paths to the files that fulfill the selection criterion (in this case, files called `pspicture` regardless of their extension). If you do not specify the `-l` option, **texdoc** will show you the entire contents of the documentation file (in this case, `pspicture.dvi`) with the help of the relevant display program (for instance, **xdvi** or **Windvi**).

If you do not know the precise name of the file, you can specify the `-s` option and provide a wildcard-like specification as a search pattern.

```
texdoc -s *picture*
/TeXlive/tl7/texmf/doc/generic/mfpic/examples/lapictures.tex
```

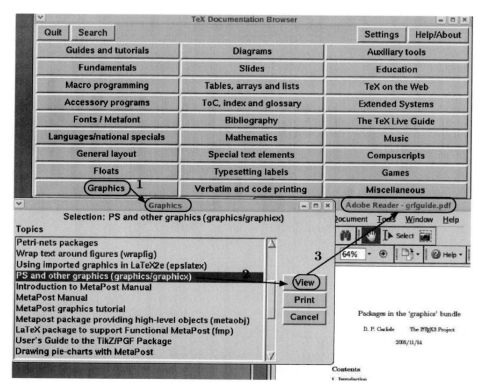

Figure B.4: Finding documentation with the **texdoctk** program

```
/TeXlive/tl7/texmf/doc/generic/mfpic/examples/pictures.tex
/TeXlive/tl7/texmf/doc/latex/carlisle/pspicture.dvi
/TeXlive/tl7/texmf/doc/html/catalogue/entries/pspicture.html
/TeXlive/tl7/texmf/doc/html/catalogue/entries/pspicture.xml
```

Here we have picked up files that have the string `picture` in their name—among them the "pspicture" files we found previously.

The **texdoc** utility is quite useful, but it has a drawback: you must know the name of the file describing the package that you want to use. This is not always just the name of the package itself (as with **pspicture** in the previous examples).

B.4.2 texdoctk—Panel interface for a search by subject

Thomas Ruedas took a somewhat different approach to provide easy access to the documentation for files present on your TEX system. His **texdoctk** program uses a graphical user interface based on **perl** and **Tk**. It relies on a database that groups documentation files included in Thomas Esser's `tetex` distribution (TEX Live uses some components of `tetex`) into a number of categories. As with **texdoc**, the display or print programs present on the system will be used for viewing (e.g., **xdvi**, **dvips**).

Figure B.4 on the facing page shows how we used the **texdoctk** system to display the documentation for the **graphics** package. We navigated from the main panel, where we chose the "Graphics" category (1), which opened the "Graphics" menu (lower left), where we selected "PS and other graphics (graphics/graphicx)". We then clicked the "View" button (2), which called the PostScript viewer Adobe Reader (3), which displayed the text of the documentation.

Figure B.4 on the preceding page also shows all available documentation categories (note the button labeled "Miscellaneous" in the lower-right corner for special cases) as well as the "Search", "Settings", and "Help/About" buttons for more advanced use.

B.5 TEX user groups

TEX users in several countries have set up TEX user groups, mostly based on language affinities. If you need help, you should contact your local user group first, since its members might be able to come up with an answer that is most suited to your language-dependent working environment. Here we give some information about groups that have a formal existence (see http://www.tug.org/usergroups.html for up-to-date and more complete lists). They can help you obtain TEX-related material on DVDs or other publications.

cn:	**China PR**
name:	Chinese TeX Users Group
language:	Chinese
Web site:	www.rons.net.cn
e-mail:	info@mail.rons.net.cn
cz:	**Czech Republic**
language:	Czech
name:	CsTUG
e-mail:	cstug@cstug.cz
Web site:	www.cstug.cz
de:	**Germany**
name:	DANTE e.V.
language:	German
e-mail:	dante@dante.de
Web site:	www.dante.de
dk:	**Denmark**
name:	DK-TUG
language:	Danish
e-mail:	board@tug.dk
Web site:	www.tug.dk
ee:	**Estonia**
name:	Estonian User Group
e-mail:	saar@aai.ee
es:	**Spain (CervanTeX)**
name:	CervanTeX
language:	Spanish
e-mail:	secretario@cervantex.org
Web site:	www.cervantex.org

esc:	**Spain (Catalan)**
name:	Catalan TeX Users Group
language:	Catalan
e-mail:	valiente@lsi.upc.es
Web site:	www-lsi.upc.es/~valiente/tug-catalan.html
fr:	**France**
name:	GUTenberg
language:	French
e-mail:	gut@irisa.fr
Web site:	www.gutenberg.eu.org
fra:	**France (Astex)**
short name:	AsTEX
language:	French
e-mail:	astex-admin@univ-orleans.fr
Web site:	www.univ-orleans.fr/EXT/ASTEX/astex/doc/en/web/html/astex000.htm
gr:	**Greece**
name:	Greek TeX Friends Group
language:	Greek
e-mail:	eft@ocean1.ee.duth.gr
Web site:	obelix.ee.duth.gr/eft/
hu:	**Hungary**
name:	MaTeX
language:	Hungarian
e-mail:	matex@math.klte.hu
Web site:	www.math.klte.hu/~matex/

in:	**India**
name:	TUGIndia
e-mail:	tugindia@river-valley.com
Web site:	www.river-valley.com/tug/
kr:	**Korea**
name:	KTUG
language:	Korean
e-mail:	info@mail.ktug.or.kr
Web site:	www.ktug.or.kr
lt:	**Lithuania**
name:	Lietuvos TeX'o Vartotojų Grupė
e-mail:	vytass@ktl.mii.lt
mx:	**Mexico**
name:	TeX México
e-mail:	tex@ciencia.dcc.umich.mx
Web site:	ciencia.dcc.umich.mx./tex/
nl:	**Netherlands, Belgium (Flemish part)**
name:	NTG
language:	Dutch
e-mail:	info@ntg.nl
Web site:	www.ntg.nl
no:	**Nordic countries**
name:	NTUG
language:	Scandinavian languages
e-mail:	dag@ifi.uio.no
Web site:	www.ifi.uio.no/~dag/ntug/
discussion:	nordictex@ifi.uio.no
ph:	**Philippines**
name:	TUG-Philippines
e-mail:	fpmuga@admu.edu.ph
pl:	**Poland**
name:	GUST
language:	Polish
e-mail:	sekretariat@gust.org.pl
Web site:	www.GUST.org.pl

pt:	**Portugal**
name:	GUTpt
language:	Portuguese
e-mail:	GUTpt@hilbert.mat.uc.pt
Web site:	http://hilbert.mat.uc.pt/~GUTpt/
ru:	**Russia**
name:	CyrTUG
e-mail:	cyrtug@mir.msk.su
Web site:	www.cemi.rssi.ru/cyrtug/
discussion:	CyrTeX-en@vsu.ru
subscription:	CyrTeX-en-on@vsu.ru
si:	**Slovenia**
name:	TeXCeH
e-mail:	Tex.Ceh@fmf.uni-lj.si
Web site:	vlado.fmf.uni-lj.si/texceh/texceh.htm
uk:	**United Kingdom**
name:	UKTUG
language:	British English
e-mail:	uktug-enquiries@tex.ac.uk
Web site:	uk.tug.org
e-mail:	enxtw1@nottingham.ac.uk
us:	**TeX User Group (international)**
name:	TUG
e-mail:	office@tug.org
Web site:	www.tug.org
vn:	**Vietnam**
name:	ViêtTUG
e-mail:	kyanh@o2.pl
Web site:	www.viettug.org

Bibliography

[1] Adobe Systems Inc. (Glenn C. Reid). PostScript Language Program Design. Addison-Wesley, Reading, MA, 1988.

This so-called "Green Book" introduces programming techniques for designing efficient PostScript programs with the help of examples in the areas of typesetting text, constructing graphics, writing calculators, debugging programs, etc. These directly usable examples accomplish specific practical tasks and have been carefully designed and debugged to show in detail how the language works. Each of the fifteen chapters addresses a specific aspect of top-to-bottom program design or problem solving and contains some useful advice. Available electronically from
`http://partners.adobe.com/public/developer/ps/sdk/sample/index_psbooks.html`

[2] Adobe Systems Inc. PostScript Language Tutorial and Cookbook. Addison-Wesley, Reading, MA, 1985.

This so-called "Blue Book" has a *Tutorial* section with numerous annotated examples and short programs, and a *Cookbook* section which is a collection of useful techniques and procedures for the PostScript language. Available electronically from
`http://partners.adobe.com/public/developer/ps/sdk/sample/index_psbooks.html`

[3] Adobe Systems Inc. "Encapsulated PostScript File Format Specification (Version 3.0)". Technical Note 5002, 1992.

This technical note details the Encapsulated PostScript file (EPSF) format, a standard format for importing and exporting PostScript language files among applications in a variety of heterogeneous environments. The EPSF format is based on and conforms to the document structuring conventions (DSC) [4].
`http://partners.adobe.com/public/developer/en/ps/5002.EPSF_Spec.pdf`

[4] Adobe Systems Inc. "PostScript Document Structuring Conventions Specification (Version 3.0)". Technical Note 5001, 1992.

This technical note defines a standard set of document structuring conventions (DSC), which will help ensure that a PostScript document is device independent. DSC allows PostScript language programs to communicate their document structure and printing requirements to document managers in a way that does not affect the PostScript language page description.
`http://partners.adobe.com/public/developer/en/ps/5001.DSC_Spec.pdf`

[5]   Adobe Systems Inc. PostScript Language Reference Manual, Third Edition. Addison-Wesley, Reading, MA, 1999.

This so-called "Red Book" describes the syntax and semantics of the complete PostScript language. The book documents the imaging model and the graphics, fonts, device, and rendering operators. Available electronically from   http://www.adobe.com/products/postscript/pdfs/PLRM.pdf

[6]   Adobe Systems Inc. PDF Reference (Version 1.6), Fifth Edition. Addison-Wesley, Reading, MA, 2005.

This is the specification of Adobe's Portable Document Format (PDF). The book introduces and explains all aspects of the PDF format, including its architecture and imaging model (allowing transparency and opacity for text, images, and graphics), the command syntax, the graphics operators, fonts, and rendering, and the relation between PostScript and PDF.
                                        http://partners.adobe.com/public/developer/en/pdf/PDFReference16.pdf

[7]   Alfred V. Aho, Monica S. Lam, Ravi Sethi, and Jeffrey D. Ullman. Compilers: Principles, Techniques and Tools, Second Edition. Addison-Wesley, Reading, MA, 2007.

This book is the standard reference about compiler construction and is widely regarded as the classic definitive compiler technology text. It not only provides a thorough introduction to compiler design but it also shows how to apply compiler technology to a broad range of problems in software design and development. This second edition includes the most recent developments in compiling. See also
                                        http://en.wikipedia.org/wiki/Compilers:_Principles,_Techniques_and_Tools

[8]   Dwight Aplevich. "Circuit_macros". MAPS, 31:19–24, 2005.

This article describes macros for drawing electrical circuits.   On CTAN at: graphics/circuit_macros

[9]   Wolfgang Appelt. "Typesetting chess". TUGboat, 9(3):284–287, 1988.

This article describes how TEX can be used to typeset chess games and chess diagrams.
                                        http://www.tug.org/TUGboat/Articles/tb09-3/tb22appelt.pdf

[10] Gustavo S. Bustamante Argañaraz. makecirc: A METAPOST library for electrical circuit diagrams drawing.

This manual is the documentation of makecirk, a METAPOST library containing diverse symbols for use in (electric) circuit diagrams. The system can be easily integrated in LATEX documents and combined with other METAPOST drawings and graphics.
                                        On CTAN at: graphics/metapost/contrib/macros/makecirc/MakeCirc-en.pdf

[11] Jon Bentley and Brian Kernighan. "Grap — a language for typesetting graphs". Computing Science Technical Report 114, AT&T Bell Laboratories, Murray Hill, NJ, 1984.

Grap is a language for describing graphical displays of data. It provides automatic scaling, labeling of axes, some programming constructs, and a macro facility. It is intended primarily for including graphs in documents prepared for the Unix operating system. Document available electronically as:
                                        http://cm.bell-labs.com/cm/cs/cstr/114.ps.gz

[12] Piotr Bolek. "METAPOST and patterns". TUGboat, 19(3):276–283, 1998.

This article presents METAPOST macros for defining and using patterns.
                                        http://www.tug.org/TUGboat/Articles/tb19-3/tb60bolek.pdf
                                        On CTAN at: graphics/metapost/contrib/macros/mpattern

[13] Anne Brüggemann-Klein and Derrick Wood. "Drawing trees nicely with TEX". Electronic publishing — origin, dissemination and design, 2(2), 1989.

This article describes a solution to the tree-drawing problem that integrates an excellent tree-drawing algorithm implemented as a TEX package (TreeTEX). Also available on pages 185–206 of [18].

[14] Włodzimierz Bzyl. "The Tao of fonts". TUGboat, 23(1):27–40, 2002.

This article presents a new technique for creating fonts. It is based on METAPOST, and is able to produce Type 1 and Type 3 fonts.   http://www.tug.org/TUGboat/Articles/tb23-1/bzyl.pdf

[15] David Carlisle. "Packages in the "graphics" bundle (The LaTeX3 Project)", 2006.
Part of the LaTeX distribution, the documentation describes a collection of LaTeX packages for: producing color, including graphics (e.g., PostScript) files and how to rotate and scale objects.
On CTAN at: `latex/required/graphics/grfguide.pdf`

[16] Bill Casselman. Mathematical Illustrations. A manual of geometry and PostScript. Cambridge University Press, Cambridge, United Kingdom, 2005.
This book shows how to use PostScript for producing mathematical graphics at several levels of sophistication. It discusses some of the mathematics involved in computer graphics and gives some hints about good style in mathematical illustration. After providing a short introduction to the basic features of the PostScript language, the author describes several 2-D and 3-D graphics techniques and algorithms. The appendices deal with more technical matters (see `http://www.ams.org/notices/200701/rev-roegel.pdf` for a detailed review).   `http://www.math.ubc.ca/~cass/graphics/manual/`

[17] Adrian F. Clark. "Halftone Output from TeX". *TUGboat*, 8(3):270–274, 1987.
This article presents results that the author obtained while doing experiments with halftone production on an early laser printer device.   `http://www.tug.org/TUGboat/Articles/tb08-3/tb19clark.pdf`

[18] Malcolm Clark, editor. TeX Applications, Uses, Methods. Ellis Horwood, Chichester, 1990.
Papers from the 1988 TeXeter Conference.

[19] Pierre Duplan, Roger Jauneau, and Jean-Pierre Jauneau. Maquette et mise en page, Fifth Edition. Electre - Éditions du Cercle de la Librairie, Paris, 2004.
This book (in French) presents the results of an analysis by the authors of the layout of over 400 documents—on paper as well as on screen. From this study they derive a set of fundamental rules for making a graphical composition look well balanced geometrically and color-wise. The importance of fully integrating image and text is emphasized. When designing for the Internet its space- and timeless communication aspects should be fully integrated from the start.

[20] Hagen Eck and Sepp Küblbeck. "Generating Feynman graphs and amplitudes with FeynArts 3". *Computer Physics Communications*, 140:418–431, 2001.
This article describes FeynArts (`http://www.feynarts.de/`), a Mathematica package that can be used for the generation and visualization of Feynman diagrams and amplitudes. The main features of version 3 are: generation of diagrams at three levels, user-definable model files, support for supersymmetric models, and publication-quality Feynman diagrams in PostScript or LaTeX.
`http://arxiv.org/abs/hep-ph/0012260`

[21] Philippe Esperet and Denis Girou. "Coloriage du pavage dit « de Truchet »". *Cahiers GUTenberg*, 31:5–18, 1998.
This article presents the results of a contest to solve an algorithmic problem on tiling of a plane. A presentation of the main answers received is followed by an implementation of the algorithms in METAPOST and PSTricks.   `http://www.gutenberg.eu.org/pub/GUTenberg/publicationsPDF/31-girou.pdf`

[22] James D. Foley, Andries van Dam, Steven K. Feiner, and John F. Hughes. Computer Graphics, Principles and Practice, Second Edition. Addison-Wesley, Reading, MA, 1990.
This standard reference work is one of the most comprehensive and authoritative in the field of computer graphics. Current concepts as well as practical applications are dealt with. The text also provides a thorough presentation of the mathematical principles of geometric transformations and viewing. Lecture notes on computer graphics are available from van Dam's web site   `http://www.cs.brown.edu/courses/cs123/lectures.shtml`

[23] Shinsaku Fujita and Nobuya Tanaka. "XyMTeX (Version 2.00) as Implementation of the XyM Notation and the XyM Markup Language". *TUGboat*, 21(1):7–14, 2000.
This article presents some of the new features added in versions 1.01 and 2 of XyMTeX. Version 2 implements the XyM notation, a linear notation for representing organic structures. The XyM notation removes layout data by virtue of the newly introduced concepts of yl-function, substitution derivation, atom derivation, and bond derivation. The article also describes the XyMMML markup language. It shows how XyMMML markup can be used for representing organic structures and how it translates into the XyM notation, which, in turn, can be typeset with XyMTeX.   `http://www.tug.org/TUGboat/Articles/tb21-1/tb66fuji.pdf`

[24]   Shinsaku Fujita and Nobuya Tanaka. "Size reduction of chemical structural
       formulas in XΥMTEX (Version 3.00)". *TUGboat*, 22(4):285–289, 2001.
       This article shows how XΥMTEX system (Version 3.00) provides a method for permitting the size reduction of
       structural formulas within the scope of the LATEX picture environment and the epic package.
                                          http://www.tug.org/TUGboat/Articles/tb22-4/tb72fuji.pdf

[25]   Shinsaku Fujita. "XΥMTEX for drawing chemical structural formulas". *TUGboat*,
       16(1):80–88, 1995.
       This article introduces XΥMTEX, a package consisting of a set of LATEX style files. The package has been devel-
       oped for drawing a wide variety of chemical structural formulas. Its commands offer an ensemble of system-
       atic arguments for specifying substituents and their positions, endocyclic double bonds, and bond patterns.
       In some cases, they have an additional argument for specifying hetero-atoms on the vertices of heterocy-
       cles. As a result of this systematic feature, XΥMTEX fits perfectly well in the device-independent concept of
       TEX.   http://www.tug.org/TUGboat/Articles/tb16-1/tb46fuji.pdf

[26]   Shinsaku Fujita. "XΥMTEX: a macro package for typesetting chemical structural
       formulas", 2006.
       The manual of successive XΥMTEX versions as well as information about the latest developments are available
       from the URL   http://imt.chem.kit.ac.jp/fujita/fujitas3/xymtex/indexe.html

[27]   Federico Garcia. "On musical typesetting: Sonata for TEX and METAFONT, Op. 2".
       TUGboat, 24(2):169–182, 2003.
       In this article the author explains why he thinks that existing typesetting systems for music cannot cope with
       several aspects of music compostion, such as new musical and its non-standard representation, musicology,
       which needs some parts of a score to be circled, highlighted, tied together, etc. He first details the nature of
       musical typesetting with the problem of horizontal spacing, line breaking, and the use of glue. He then shows
       how his program TEX*muse* deals with the challenges mentioned and ends with a description of its implemen-
       tation.   http://www.tug.org/TUGboat/Articles/tb24-2/tb77garcia.pdf

[28]   Hubert Gäßlein and Rolf Niepraschk. The pict2e - package, 2004.
       This new package extends the existing LATEX picture environment, using the familiar technique of driver
       files.   On CTAN at: macros/latex/contrib/pict2e/

[29]   Frans Gerritsen. Evolution in Color. Schiffer Publishing Ltd, West Chester, PA,
       1988.
       This book is an overview of the theory of color from antiquity to the present. Thanks to its many illustrations
       the book clearly explains how the concept of color perception evolved over the ages. More information on
       color is on Bruce MacEvoy's Web page (http://www.handprint.com/HP/WCL/wcolor.html) or Charles
       Poynton's color Web page (http://www.poynton.com/ColorFAQ.html).

[30]   Ovidiu Gheorghieş. "An Introduction to MetaUML: Exquisite UML Diagrams in
       METAPOST". *MAPS*, 32:2–15, 2005.
       This article provides an introduction to the MetaUML package, a METAPOST for drawing UML diagrams.
                                          On CTAN at: graphics/metapost/contrib/macros/metauml

[31]   Denis Girou. pst-fill—A PSTricks package for filling and tiling, 2006.
       This is the documentation of a PSTricks-based package for filling and tiling areas or characters.
                                          On CTAN at: graphics/pstricks/contrib/pst-fill/

[32]   Luís Nobre Gonçalves. "FEATPOST and a Review of 3D METAPOST Packages".
       volume 3130 of *Lecture Notes in computer Science*, pp. 112–124. Springer-Verlag,
       Berlin, Germany / Heidelberg, Germany / London, UK / etc., 2004.
       This article is a description of FEATPOST, a METAPOST package for 3-D graphics.
                                          On CTAN at: graphics/metapost/contrib/macros/featpost/doc

[33]   Luís Nobre Gonçalves. "FEATPOST macros", 2004.
       Manual of the METAPOST FEATPOST macros for 3-D graphics.
                                          On CTAN at: graphics/metapost/contrib/macros/featpost/latex/macroMan.tex

[34] Michel Goossens and Eric van Herwijnen. "The elementary Particle Entity Notation (PEN) scheme". *TUGboat*, 13(2):201–207, 1992.

This article introduces a scheme for marking up elementary particle names in LaTeX and SGML. The scheme assures the typographic correctness of the printed symbols. It also allows automatic extraction of information about the entities used in the text.
http://www.tug.org/TUGboat/Articles/tb13-2/tb35goossens.pdf

[35] Michel Goossens, Sebastian Rahtz, Eitan M. Gurai, Ross Moore, and Robert S. Sutor. The LaTeX Web Companion: Integrating TeX, HTML, and XML. Addison-Wesley, Reading, MA, 1999.

This book teaches (scientific) authors how to publish on the Web or other hypertext presentation systems, building on their experience with LaTeX and taking into account their specific needs in fields such as mathematics, non-European languages, and algorithmic graphics. The book explains how to make full use of the Adobe Acrobat format from LaTeX, convert legacy documents to HTML or XML, make use of math in Web applications, use LaTeX as a tool in preparing Web pages, read and write simple XML/SGML, and produce high-quality printed pages from Web-hosted XML or HTML pages using TeX or PDF.

[36] Michel Goossens and Vesa Sivunen. "LaTeX, SVG, Fonts". *TUGboat*, 22(4):269–280, 2001.

This article gives a short overview of SVG and points out its advantages for describing in a portable way the graphics content of electronic documents. The conversion of Type 1 font instances into SVG outlines is described, and it is shown how these SVG font glyphs can be used in SVG instances of documents typeset with TeX.
http://www.tug.org/TUGboat/Articles/tb22-4/tb72goos.pdf

[37] Timothy G. Greenwood. "International cultural differences in software". *Digital Technical Journal*, 5(16):8–20, 1993.

Throughout the world, computer users approach a computer system with a specific set of cultural requirements. In all cultures, they expect computer systems to accommodate their needs, including when interacting with computers through written language where culture influences the way computer systems must operate. The article gives examples of various national conventions for the presentation of date, time, and numbers. It then explains how the design of an adequate user interface must take into account these conventions in the way it uses images, color, sound, and in the overall layout of the screen. The author concludes that successful computer systems must respond to the multicultural needs of users.
http://www.hpl.hp.com/hpjournal/dtj/vol5num3/vol5num3art1.pdf

[38] Branko Grünbaum and Geoffrey Sheppard. Tilings and Patterns. W.H. Freeman, New York, 1987.

This is the definitive book on ways to tile the two-dimensional plane. The authors treat well-known periodic tilings such as those in a bathroom, the patterns of bricks on walls, or the wonderful geometries created by Islamic artists. They also describe aperiodic tilings, such as Penrose tiles, which use a five-way symmetry to cover the plane without ever repeating; Amman constructs using a four-way plan to define tiles that forever create new patterns; and spiral tiles, which are perfectly regular, but different at every scale. For more on tilings see:
http://en.wikipedia.org/wiki/Category:Tiling

[39] Eitan M Gurari. TeX and LaTeX: Drawing and Literate Programming. McGraw-Hill, New York, 1994.

This book describes device-independent tools for drawing figures with (LA)TeX. Supported are drawing basic shapes, such as lines, rectangles and Bézier curves, as well as utilities for producing more complex graphs, such as charts and diagrams. Also described are packages that allow (LA)TeX to support literate programming.

[40] Eckhart Guthörlein. "Object-Oriented Graphics with MetaObj". *MAPS*, 31:77–86, 2005.

This article is an introduction to the METAOBJ package, and provides some interesting examples.

[41] Roswitha T. Haas and Kevin C. O'Kane. "Typesetting chemical structure formulas with the text formatter TeX/LaTeX". *Computers and Chemistry*, 11(4):251–271, 1987.

This article describes how to incorporate chemical structure diagrams into compuscripts prepared with LaTeX. With the help of some 30 LaTeX macros it is easy to typeset common structural fragments such as branching patterns and alicyclic and heterocyclic rings. These macros permit optional substituents and multiple bonds. Fragments from different macros can be combined.

[42] Hans Hagen. "Pretty printing TeX, MetaPost, Perl and JavaScript". *MAPS*, 20:286–289, 1998.

> This article explains that, although one has to use CWEB-like environments for real pretty printing of sources, TeX can also do a rather good job. CONTeXT's verbatim environment has pretty printing built in, and either specific colors or fonts can be used.   http://www.ntg.nl/maps/pdf/20_43.pdf

[43] Hans Hagen. metafun, 2002.

> This is the metafun manual. The metafun system provides an interface between METAPOST and TeX. The required TeX macros are included in CONTeXT, and the METAPOST code comes with metafun. Thanks to metafun, METAPOST definitions can be easily integrated in TeX code, thus adding large graphics capabilities to TeX. Available electronically from
>   http://www.pragma-ade.com/general/manuals/metafun-p.pdf

[44] J. Hagen and A. F. Otten. "PPCHTeX: typesetting chemical formulas in TeX". *TUGboat*, 17(1):54–66, 1996.

> This article describes PPCHTeX, a package for typesetting chemical formulas with a multi-lingual interface. The manual is at the URL http://www.pragma-ade.com/general/manuals/mp-ch-en.pdf. The package can use PiCTeX or PSTricks, is compatible with other macro packages, and falls back on a few generic context modules. It supports typesetting chemical structure formulas like six-rings at different sizes, parts of which can be reused. It also can deal with reaction mechanisms.
>   http://www.tug.org/TUGboat/Articles/tb17-1/tb50hage.pdf

[45] Brian Hamilton Kelly. "Some macros to draw crosswords". *TUGboat*, 11(1):103–119, 1990.

> This is a description of a package to typeset crossword diagrams.
>   http://www.tug.org/TUGboat/Articles/tb11-1/tb27kelly.pdf

[46] Andy Hammerlindl, John Bowman, and Tom Prince. Asymptote, 2005. Version 0.76.

> The manual of the Asymptote system, a system similar to METAPOST, is available electronically from
>   http://asymptote.sourceforge.net

[47] John D. Hobby. "A user's manual for METAPOST". Computing Science Technical Report 162, AT&T Bell Laboratories, 1992.

> The METAPOST system implements a picture-drawing language very much like Knuth's METAFONT except that it outputs PostScript commands instead of bitmaps. METAPOST is a powerful language for producing figures for documents targetted to PostScript output devices. It provides easy access to all features of PostScript and it includes facilities for integrating text and graphics. The appendix of this user's manual explains the differences between METAPOST and METAFONT. The document is available electronically as: http://cm.bell-labs.com/cm/cs/cstr/162.ps.gz

[48] John D. Hobby. "Drawing graphs with METAPOST". Computing Science Technical Report 164, AT&T Bell Laboratories, 1993.

> This report describes a graph-drawing package that has been implemented as an extension to the METAPOST graphics language, which has a powerful macro facility for implementing such extensions. A few new language features to support the graph macros are introduced. The proposed features for generating and manipulating pictures allow the user to perform actions that would be difficult to achieve in a stand-alone package. The document is available electronically as:
>   http://cm.bell-labs.com/cm/cs/cstr/164.ps.gz

[49] Alan Hoenig. TeX Unbound: Strategies for Fonts, Graphics, and More. Oxford University Press, New York, 1998.

> This book describes how to produce good typography with LaTeX, in particular how to set up and make proper use of PostScript fonts, and create high-quality graphics illustrations with TeX-friendly methods. It contains many examples and summaries of procedures to follow. The book starts with a good overview of TeX, LaTeX, METAFONT, and METAPOST, explaining how they all fit together. The second part of the book describes TeX's font mechanisms. The author does not limit himself to a description of how to set up a standard font family, but includes a lot of more advanced material. Examples included are using special effect fonts, specifying font families that contain alternate character sets or symbols, integrating high-quality commercial fonts, and typesetting mathematics with fonts other than the original TeXfonts (there is a 30-page overview on how to combine available mathematics font families with various often-used typefaces). The final part of

the book discusses graphics applications, in particular METAFONT, METAPOST, PSTricks, P$_I$CT$_E$X, and mfpic.

[50] Jan Holeček and Petr Sojka. "Animations in pdfTEX-generated PDF: A new method for directly embedding animation into PDF". volume 3130 of *Lecture Notes in computer Science*, pp. 179–191. Springer-Verlag, Berlin, Germany / Heidelberg, Germany / London, UK / etc., 2004.
This article describes a method for producing real animations within a PDF file.

[51] Andrew D. Hwang. "ePiX: A utility for creating mathematically accurate figures". *TUGboat*, 25(2):172–176, 2004.
This article describes ePiX, a collection of command line utilities for creating mathematically accurate, logically structured, camera-quality 2- and 3-dimensional figures and animations in LATEX. ePiX provides a bridge between the powerful numerical capabilities of C++ and the high-quality typesetting of LATEX.
http://www.tug.org/TUGboat/Articles/tb25-2/tb81hwang.pdf

[52] International Organization for Standardization, Geneva, Switzerland. Quantities and Units (Parts 0 to 13), 1992. International Standard ISO 31-0:1992.
Part 0: General principles (1992, Amd 1:1998, Amd 2:2005); Part 1: Space and time (1992, Amd 1:1998); Part 2: Periodic and related phenomena (1992, Amd 1:1998); Part 3: Mechanics (1992, Amd 1:1998); Part 4: Heat (1992, Amd 1:1998); Part 5: Electricity and magnetism (1992, Amd 1:1998); Part 6: Light and related electromagnetic (1992, Amd 1:1998); Part 7: Acoustics (1992, Amd 1:1998); Part 8: Physical chemistry and molecular (1992, Amd 1:1998); Part 9: Atomic and nuclear physics (1992, Amd 1:1998); Part 10: Nuclear reactions and ionizing (1992, Amd 1:1998); Part 11: Mathematical signs and symbols for for use in the physical sciences and technology (1992, Amd 1:1998); Part 12: Characteristic numbers (1992, Amd 1:1998); Part 13: Solid state physics (1992, Amd 1:1998).

[53] International Organization for Standardization, Geneva, Switzerland. SI Units and Recommendations for the Use of their Multiples and of Certain Other Units, 1992. International Standard ISO 1000:1992.

[54] International Organization for Standardization, Geneva, Switzerland. Information Technology—Computer graphics – Metafile for the Storage and Transfer of Picture Description Information, 1999. International Standard ISO 8632:1999.
Part 1: Functional specification (1999, Cor 1:2006); Part 2: Character Encoding (1999); Part 3: Binary encoding (1999); Part 4: Clear text encoding (1999). In part freely downloadable from http://isotc.iso.org/livelink/livelink/fetch/2000/2489/Ittf_Home/PubliclyAvailableStandards.htm

[55] International Union of Pure and Applied Chemistry. Nomenclature of Organic Chemistry. Pergamon, Oxford, 1979.
Many recommendations on organic and biochemical nomenclature, symbols and terminology, etc. are available at the IUPAP Web site: http://www.chem.qmul.ac.uk/iupac/

[56] International Union of Pure and Applied Physics. "Symbols, units, nomenclature and fundamental constants in physics". *Physica*, 146A:1–67, 1987.
Information is available on the IUPAP Web site (www.iupap.org). The IUPAP Report number is 25. For the latest on the values of fundamental constants consult the NIST website:
http://physics.nist.gov/cuu/Constants

[57] Johannes Itten. The Art of Color: The Subjective Experience and Objective Rationale of Color. Wiley, New York, 1974.
The author introduces two approaches to understanding the art of color. Subjective feelings and objective color principles are described in detail and clarified by color reproductions.

[58] Bogusław Jackowski. "A METAFONT-eps interface". *TUGboat*, 16(4):388–395, 1995.

    This article explains that one of the best features of the TEX/METAFONT system is its openness, i.e., its capability of collaboration with other systems. This is illustrated by presenting a METAFONT-to-PostScript interface, mftoeps, based on a METAFONT kernel with the necessary definitions for translating the description of graphic objects from METAFONT to PostScript. The PostScript output code is written to a file from which it can be extracted. Two utilities that address the task of further manipulation of METAFONT graphics objects in PostScript are described.

    `http://www.tug.org/TUGboat/Articles/tb16-4/tb49jack.pdf`

[59] Laura E. Jackson and Herbert Voß. "Die mathematischen Funktionen von Post-Script". *Die TEXnische Komödie*, 1/02:40–47, 2002.

    This article summarizes all PostScript functions that can be used to calculate mathematical expressions and can be used with the `\psplot` macro from the PSTricks package bundle.

[60] Laura E. Jackson and Herbert Voß. "Die plot-funktionen von `pst-plot`". *Die TEXnische Komödie*, 2/02:27–34, 2002.

    This article describes the use of the plotting macros of pst-plot from the PSTricks package bundle. It gives examples for plotting mathematical functions and external data files that can be read by a special macro.

[61] Richard Jackson, Lindsay MacDonald, and Ken Freeman. Computer Generated Color: A Practical Guide to Presentation and Display. Wiley, New York, 1994.

    This book offers practical advice on how to use color effectively for presentation on computer screens and for printing on paper.

[62] François Jalbert. "MuTEX user's guide", 1989.

    MuTEX, based on work for their Master's Thesis by Andrea Steinbach and Angelika Schofer, is a set of macros allowing TEX to typeset beautiful music.   `http://icking-music-archive.org/software/mutex/`

[63] Christophe Jorssen and Herbert Voß. The `pst-circ`-package, 2004.

    pst-circ is a package built above PSTricks and, in particular, pst-node. It can easily draw current dipoles, some tripoles, and quadrupoles used in elecronic or electric theory.

    On CTAN at: `graphics/pstricks/contrib/pst-circ/`

[64] Christophe Jorssen. `pst-math`- a PSTricks package for mathematical function, 2004.

    PostScript lacks a lot of basic operators. pst-math provides all the operators in a PostScript-header file. In addition, sinc, gauss, gammaln, and bessel are implemented (only partially for the latter). pst-math is designed essentially to work with pst-plot but can be used in whatever PostScript code.

    On CTAN at: `graphics/pstricks/contrib/pst-math/`

[65] Deane B. Judd and Günter Wyszecki. Color in Business, Science, and Industry, Second Edition. Wiley, New York, 1963.

    The perception of color permeates our daily lives. The color of soil, vegetables, fruit, meat, textiles, minerals, the sky, or a human face, informs us about their value or state. Color management is an essential tool to effectively control all aspects of color in the commercial process.

[66] David Kastrup. `preview-latex`, 2003.

    preview-latex allows appropriately selected parts of a LATEX document to be formatted and displayed within your Emacs editor, allowing you to view what it looks like while still allowing you to edit it.

    On CTAN at: `support/preview-latex/`

[67] Brian Kernighan. "PIC — a graphics language for typesetting". Computing Science Technical Report 116, AT&T Bell Laboratories, Murray Hill, NJ, 1984.

    Pic is a language for drawing simple figures on a typesetter. The basic objects in pic are boxes, ellipses, lines, arrows, arcs, spline curves, and text. These may be placed anywhere, at positions specified absolutely or in terms of previous objects. Pic is a troff preprocessor.

    Document available electronically as: `http://cm.bell-labs.com/cm/cs/cstr/116.ps.gz`

[68]   Uwe Kern. Color extensions with the `xcolor` package, 2006.
       Provides easy driver-independent access to several kinds of color tints, shades, tones, and mixes of arbitrary
       colors. It allows a user to select a document-wide target color model and offers complete tools for conversion
       between eight color models. Additionally, there is a command for alternating row colors and repeated non-
       aligned material (like horizontal lines) in tables.   On CTAN at: `macros/latex/contrib/xcolor/`

[69]   Jörg Knappen. "Changing the appearance of math". In Zlatuška [140], pp. 212–216.
       Mathematical typesetting is based on many conventions, which can vary by country and by area of scientific
       activity. In particular American and European mathematics and physics journals often use different nota-
       tions for identical items. The author presents his "European math" package, which makes it easy to adapt the
       notation needed for publishing in a given journal.

[70]   Donald E. Knuth. The TEXbook, volume A of *Computers and Typesetting*. Addison-
       Wesley, Reading, MA, 1986.
       This book is the definitive user's guide and complete reference manual for TEX.

[71]   Donald E. Knuth. TEX: The Program, volume B of *Computers and Typesetting*.
       Addison-Wesley, Reading, MA, 1986.
       This book contains the complete source code for the TEX program, typeset with several indices.

[72]   Donald E. Knuth. The METAFONT Book, volume C of *Computers and Typesetting*.
       Addison-Wesley, Reading, MA, 1986.
       This is the user's guide and reference manual for METAFONT, the companion program to TEX for designing
       fonts.

[73]   Donald E. Knuth. METAFONT: The Program, volume D of *Computers and
       Typesetting*. Addison-Wesley, Reading, MA, 1986.
       This book contains the complete source code listing of the METAFONT program.

[74]   Donald E. Knuth. Computer Modern Typefaces, volume E of *Computers and
       Typesetting*. Addison-Wesley, Reading, MA, 1986.
       This book depicts graphically more than 500 Greek and Roman letterforms, together with punctuation marks,
       numerals, and many mathematical symbols. The METAFONT code to generate each glyph is given and
       it is explained how, by changing the parameters in the METAFONT code, all characters in the Computer
       Modern family of typefaces can be obtained.

[75]   Donald E. Knuth. "Fonts for digital halftones". *TUGboat*, 8(2):135–160, 1987.
       This article explains how small pictures can be "typeset" on raster devices in a way that simulates the screens
       used to print fine books on photography. This article describes an experiment with METAFONT to generate
       halftone fonts to create such pictures on laser printers.
                                            http://www.tug.org/TUGboat/Articles/tb08-2/tb18knut.pdf

[76]   Helmut Kopka and Patrick W. Daly. Guide to LATEX, Fourth Edition. Addison-Wes-
       ley, Reading, MA, 2004.
       This introductory book, which shows how to begin using LATEX to create high-quality documents, serves also
       as a handy reference for all LATEX users. The book covers the LATEX 2_ε standard and provides many details,
       examples, exercises, tips, and tricks. It goes beyond the base installation by describing important contributed
       packages that have become essential to LATEX processing. This book can be advantageously complemented by
       The LATEX Companion [83].

[77]   Gerard Kunkel. Graphic Design with PostScript. Scott, Foresman, Glenview, IL,
       1990.
       This book is a hands-on guide to using PostScript containing complete coded examples for many practically
       relevant applications, including (pseudo) 3-D effects for graphs, etc.

[78]   Leslie Lamport. LATEX: A Document Preparation System, Second Edition. Addison-
       Wesley, Reading, MA, 1994.
       This book is the definitive user's guide and reference manual for LATEX 2_ε written by LATEX's original author.

[79] Michael J. S. Levine. "A LaTeX graphics routine for drawing feynman diagrams". *Computer Physics Communications*, 58:181–198, 1990.

This article describes a package that uses LaTeX's picture environment for drawing Feynman diagrams. The package and its manual are available   On CTAN at: `macros/latex209/contrib/feynman`

[80] Manuel Luque. The `pst-vue3d`-package, 2004.

Three-dimensional objects like cubes, spheres, and others can be viewed from different points. The distribution includes a comprehensive set of examples of usage.

On CTAN at: `graphics/pstricks/contrib/pst-vue3d/`

[81] M. P. Maclenan and G. M. Burns. "An approach to drawing circuit diagrams for text books". *TUGboat*, 12(1):66–69, 1991.

This article describes a library of pictograms, which are defined using macros embodied in PICTEX. These pictograms are used to create applications that enable high-definition circuit diagrams to be easily included in TeX documents.   `http://www.tug.org/TUGboat/Articles/tb12-1/tb31maclenan.pdf`

[82] Henry McGilton and Mary Campione. PostScript by Example. Addison-Wesley, Reading, MA, 1992.

This book first introduces the basic concepts of PostScript language (paths, graphic states, text, clipping, transformations, arcs, curves, and images). It then presents a set of tools to construct fonts, patterns, forms, and manage your printing environment. PostScript Level 2 issues such as patterns, forms, images, composite fonts, halftones, and color models are covered. With its many hands-on exercises and step-by-step instructions, this book becomes a genuine toolkit, for building effective PostScript programs.

[83] Frank Mittelbach, Michel Goossens, Johannes Braams, David Carlisle, and Chris Rowley. The LaTeX Companion, Second Edition. Addison-Wesley, Reading, MA, 2004.

This book describes over 200 LaTeX packages and presents a whole series of tips and tricks for using LaTeX in both traditional and modern typesetting, in particular how to customize layout features to your own needs—from phrases and paragraphs to headings, lists, and pages. It provides expert advice on using LaTeX's basic formatting tools to create all types of publication, from memos to encyclopedias. It covers in depth important extension packages for tabular and technical typesetting, floats and captions, multi-column layouts, including reference guides and discussion of the underlying typographic concepts. It details techniques for generating and typesetting indexes, glossaries, and bibliographies, with their associated citations.

[84] Alun Moon. "Digital Illumination". *TUGboat*, 24(1):18–22, 2003.

This article explains how Donald Knuth's programs TeX and METAFONT (METAPOST) have made digital typography and calligraphy a reality. The author, an amateur calligrapher in Celtic artwork, explores how these tools can be used for digital illumination. He shows some nice examples of knotwork and keypatterns that he was able to draw.   `http://www.tug.org/TUGboat/Articles/tb24-1/moon-celtic.pdf`

[85] Jens-Uwe Morawski. piechartMP: Drawing pie-charts with MetaPost, 2002.

This is the manual for the `piechartMP` METAPOST package.

On CTAN at: `graphics/metapost/contrib/macros/piechartmp`

[86] Santiago Muelas. "A macro routine for writing text along a path in MetaPost". *MAPS*, pp. 103–113, 2000.

This article describes a general macro written in pure METAPOST for putting any text using any font over any path. The routine is explained in detail and some graphics examples are given.

`http://www.ntg.nl/maps/pdf/25_14.pdf`
On CTAN at: `graphics/metapost/contrib/macros/txp`

[87] Antal Nemcsics. Colour Dynamics: Environmental Colour Design. Prentice Hall, New York, 1993.

The book defines color dynamics and their effects on the environment. After explaining the fundamentals of chromatics (color spaces, color vision, color harmony) the psychosomatic effects of color, such as the relation between color and space, color and function, and color and illumination, are discussed.

[88] Rolf Niepraschk. "Anwendungen des LaTeX-pakets preview". *Die TeXnische Komödie*, 1/2003:60–65, 2003.

This article describes how PostScript-related code can be integrated into sources, which will be compiled with pdfLaTeX.

[89] Jan Nieuwenhuizen and Han-Wen Nienhuys. "MusiXTEX pre-processor—using TEX and the MusiXTEX macro package to write parts and scores of music", 1996.
Deprecated package, replaced by LilyPond. http://icking-music-archive.org/software/mpp/

[90] A. C. Norris and A. L. Oakley. "Electronic publishing and chemical text processing". In Clark [18], pp. 207–225.
This article describes strategies to combine high-quality computer-based scientific typesetting of chemical structures with low cost. Results are reported of how to interface an interactive chemical editor with PostScript and TEX.

[91] Thorsten Ohl. "Drawing feynman diagrams with LATEX and METAFONT". *Computer Physics Communications*, 90:340–354, 1995.
This article describes FeynMF, a package for easy drawing of professional-quality Feynman diagrams with METAFONT (or METAPOST). Most diagrams are drawn satisfactorily from the structure of the graph without need for manual intervention. Nevertheless all the power of METAFONT (or METAPOST) is available for the more complicated cases or for fine tuning the layout. http://www.cpc.cs.qub.ac.uk/summaries/ADCD_v1_0.html

[92] Thorsten Ohl. "feynMF, Drawing Feynman Diagrams with LATEX and METAFONT", 1996.
Some information is available at the URL http://xml.cern.ch/textproc/feynmf.html.
On CTAN at: macros/latex/contrib/feynmf

[93] Premshree Pillai. infix-postfix.py, 2003.
This package provides a solution with Python for an Infix–Postfix converter.
http://aspn.activestate.com/ASPN/Cookbook/Python/Recipe/228915

[94] Sunil Podar. "Enhancements to the picture environment of LATEX". Technical Report 86-17, Dept. of Computer Science, State University of New York, Stony Brook, NY, 1986.
This report describes the epic macros, which extend the capabilities of LATEX picture without requiring new facilities. On CTAN at: macros/latex/contrib/epic/picman.tex

[95] Sebastian Rahtz. "The Protestant Cemetery, Rome". *Opuscula Romana*, 16:149–167, 1987.
This article discusses a study undertaken under the auspices of the Unione Internazionale degli Istituti di Archeologia, Storia e Storia dell'Arte in Roma.

[96] Michael Ramek. "Chemical structure formulae and x/y diagrams with TEX". In Clark [18], pp. 227–258.
Macros are presented to easily generate chemical structure formulae and x/y diagrams. Plain TEX and a DVI driver that can handle rules are sufficient to generate the graphics output.

[97] Denis Roegel. "Creating 3D animations with METAPOST". *TUGboat*, 18(4):274–283, 1997.
This article describes the METAPOST 3d package for representing and animating objects in space.
http://www.tug.org/TUGboat/Articles/tb18-4/tb57roeg.pdf
On CTAN at: graphics/metapost/contrib/macros/3d

[98] Denis Roegel. "METAPOST, l'intelligence graphique". *Cahiers GUTenberg*, 41:5–16, 2001.
This article, in French, explains the advantages of a text-oriented approach to graphics, as provided by the METAPOST language.
http://www.gutenberg.eu.org/pub/GUTenberg/publicationsPDF/41-roegel.pdf

[99] Denis Roegel. "Space geometry with METAPOST". *TUGboat*, 22(4):298–314, 2001.
This article describes the author's package for drawing space geometry figures in METAPOST.
http://www.tug.org/TUGboat/Articles/tb22-4/tb72roeg.pdf

[100] Denis Roegel. "METAOBJ: Very high-level objects in METAPOST". *TUGboat*, 23(1):93–100, 2002.

This article summarizes the main features of METAOBJ, a METAPOST package for manipulating graphics in a structured way.   http://www.tug.org/TUGboat/Articles/tb23-1/roegel.pdf
On CTAN at: graphics/metapost/contrib/macros/metaobj

[101] Denis Roegel. "Kissing Circles: A French Romance in METAPOST". *TUGboat*, 26(1):10–17, 2005.

This article describes METAPOST macros for drawing the Apollonian gasket, a well known fractal.
http://www.tug.org/TUGboat/Articles/tb26-1/tb82roegel.pdf

[102] Denis Roegel. The METAOBJ tutorial and reference manual, 2007.

This is the METAOBJ manual, describing a METAPOST package for the manipulation of structured objects, boxes, trees, matrices, connections, etc.
On CTAN at: graphics/metapost/contrib/macros/metaobj

[103] Tom Rokicki. "Driver Support for Color in TEX: Proposal and Implementation". *TUGboat*, 15(3):205–212, 1994.

This article presents a new implementation of color support, with a proposal for an initial standard for color and color-like specials. Examples show the difficulties to be addressed when supporting color. An implementation of a driver providing a solution to these problems is described.
http://www.tug.org/TUGboat/Articles/tb15-3/tb44rokicki.pdf

[104] Kristoffer H. Rose and Ross Moore. "XY-pic reference manual. version 3.7", 1999.

This document describes in detail the capabilities of the XY-pic package for typesetting graphs and diagrams in TEX. The package works with most TEX formats, including plain TEX, LATEX, and $\mathcal{A}\mathcal{M}\mathcal{S}$-LATEX. Several styles of input for various diagram types are supported; they all share a mnemonic notation based on the logical composition of visual components. The electronic version of the manual is distributed with the package.
On CTAN at: macros/generic/diagrams/xypic/xy-3.7/doc/xyrefer.pdf

[105] Kristoffer H. Rose. "How to typeset pretty diagram arrows with TEX—design decisions used in XY-pic". In Zlatuška [140], pp. 183–190.

This article gives a non-technical overview of how to draw arrows with TEX, and in particular with the author's XY-pic system. The article shows how a large variety of arrows can be obtained by combining a few special fonts.

[106] Kristoffer H. Rose. "XY-pic user's guide. version 3.7", 1999.

XY-pic is a package for typesetting graphs and diagrams with TEX. This user guide concentrates on how to typeset matrix-like diagrams. The electronic version of the manual is distributed with the package.
On CTAN at: macros/generic/diagrams/xypic/xy-3.7/doc/xyguide.pdf

[107] Zalman Rubinstein. "Chess printing via METAFONT and TEX". *TUGboat*, 10(2):170–172, 1989.

This article presents a METAFONT-TEX system to enable printing chess positions with ease by incorporating them in arbitrary TEX output. The chess board is integrated with the chess pieces.
http://www.tug.org/TUGboat/Articles/tb10-2/tb24rubinstein.pdf

[108] Rod Salmon and Mel Slater. Computer Graphics — Systems & Concepts. Addison-Wesley Europe, Amsterdam, 1987.

A practical guide to the construction and implementation of computer graphics systems. The basic principles for building such systems for a range of 2-D and 3-D applications are explained. The Graphical Kernel System (GKS) is treated in detail and its characteristics are compared with those of other systems, including PostScript. Aspects of human–computer interaction, equipment, and systems design are discussed.

[109] Andreas Scherer. "Smoothing *augmented* paths in METAPOST". *TUGboat*, 20(2):142, 1999.

This article shows a slight change to the METAPOST graph package in order to produce smooth curves in graphs drawn from data.   http://www.tug.org/TUGboat/Articles/tb20-2/tb63gibb.pdf

[110] Angelika Schofer and Andreas Steinbach. "Automatisierter Notensatz mit TEX". Technical report, Rheinische Friedrich-Wilhelms-Universität, Bonn, 1987.

This report, which combined and updated the content of the masters theses of both authors, demonstrated that music typesetting was possible. Their mutex package was rather limited, and is hardly ever used nowadays. However, it inspired Daniel Taupin, who took up the baton, and developed MusixTEX (see Ref. [116]).

On CTAN at: `macros/mtex`

[111] Claus Schönleber and Frank Klinkenberg-Haaß. "Goldene Schnittmuster". *mc-Extra*, 2:21–25, 1995.

This article covers metalic alloys, non-periodic tilings and Penrose-tilings.

[112] Don Simons. "PMX, a preprocessor for MusiXTEX. Version 0.92", 1995.

PMX facilitates typesetting music scores and parts that have an almost professional appearance. It is easier to learn than MusiXTEX, of which it is a preprocessor. PMX automatically takes care of grouping notes, selecting groups of notes to be beamed, defining beam heights and slopes, spreading the entire piece evenly over specified numbers of systems and pages, and inserting extra spaces where needed to make room for accidentals, flags, dots, and new clefs. Note values, rests, ornaments, slurs, and limited text strings can be specified. Every voice in every bar must have exactly the correct number of beats in the current meter, but you may change the meter at the beginning of any measure, with or without printing the new time signature. PMX checks the timings and other aspects of the input for consistency before generating its output. `http://icking-music-archive.org/software/pmx/pmx250.pdf`

[113] Ian Stewart. "Ungewöhnliche Kachelungen". *Spektrum der Wissenschaft*, p. 114, 2001.

This article explains how, starting with a very simple construction, one can get very complicated tilings and patterns. `http://www.wissenschaft-online.de/spektrum/index.php?action=rubrik_detail&artikel_id=5811`

[114] Sebastian Tannert and Andreas Tille. "The CIRC package", 2005.

This is a description of CIRC, a tool for typesetting circuit diagrams and block schematics. The package defines a large set of electrical symbols including resistors, capacitors, and transistors, which can be connected with wires in a very easy way. All symbols are drawn with METAFONT and the symbol set can be easily extended by the user. On CTAN at: `macros/generic/diagrams/circ/circ.pdf`

[115] Till Tantau. The Ti*k*Z and PGF Packages.

PGF is a TEX macro package for generating graphics. It is platform- and format-independent. It comes with a user-friendly syntax layer called Ti*k*Z. It is somewhat less powerful than PSTricks, which can use the full power of the PostScript language (e.g., for inline function plotting) and has a nice library of extra packages for specific application areas. However, it works together with most important TEX backend drivers, including pdftex (which is not directly possible with PSTricks) and dvips. Moreover, since it is a recent development, its syntax is somewhat more consistent that PSTricks'. The home page is at `http://sourceforge.net/projects/pgf/`. On CTAN at: `graphics/pgf/doc/generic/pgf/version-for-pdftex/en/pgfmanual.pdf`

[116] Daniel Taupin, Ross Mitchell, and Andreas Egler. "MusiXTEX, using TEX to write polyphonic or instrumental music, Version T.113", 2005.

MusiXTEX is a set of TEX macros to typeset orchestral or polyphonic music. This guide contains a technical and detailed description of all features of the system. The main author of MusiXTEX, Daniel Taupin, passed away in 2003. Two years later the MusiXTEX community decided to help keep his excellent work alive and current by assembling a new release (T.113), correcting various minor bugs, updating some references and providing dynamic links to archived versions where possible. No new functionality was introduced but a few additional packages were added to the basic distribution.

`http://icking-music-archive.org/software/musixtex/musixdoc.pdf`

[117] Daniel Taupin. "MusicTEX: using TEX to write polyphonic or instrumental music". In Zlatuška [140], pp. 257–272.

This article gives a short overview of MusicTEX, a set of (LA)TEX macros to nicely typeset polyphonic, instrumental, or orchestral music. Many voices or instrument lines, as well as up to four staffs per voice are supported. Several note sizes, most usual ornaments, and such features as grace notes and cadenzas are also available. It is explained that the major typesetting difficulty resides in the handling of glue and of breaking lines when meeting irregular music and slurs.

[118]   Daniel Taupin. "MusicTEX: using TEX to write polyphonic or instrumental music".
        TUGboat, 14(3):203–211, 1993.
        This article is a short introduction to MusicTEX, a set of TEX and LaTEX macros to typeset polyphonic, in-
        strumental or orchestral music. It handles an important number of instruments or voices (up to nine) and
        staffs (up to four for each instrument). Most usual ornaments are available, including several note sizes, grace
        notes, and cadenzas. Several staff sizes can coexist in the same score to combine full-size staffs with smaller
        "reminder" staffs. The LaTEX version is not suited for producing full scores but it can be used to typeset mu-
        sic excerpts in musicographic texts. Special attention has to be given to glue and line breaking in the case of
        irregular music and slurs.   http://www.tug.org/TUGboat/Articles/tb14-3/tb40musictex.pdf

[119]   Daniel Taupin. "Using TEX and METAFONT to build complicated maps". *TUG-
        boat*, 14(3):196–202, 1993.
        The article descibes the procedure to publish a catalog of 1500 crags and climbable rocks in France. All relevant
        information, such as name, location, and importance, are stored in a large TEX master file. The marks and their
        associated text, as well as their optimal position are calculated from these data and are superimposed on a map
        generated in METAFONT.
                                    http://www.tug.org/TUGboat/Articles/tb14-3/tb40taupin-maps.pdf

[120]   Daniel Taupin. "MusiXTEX, even more beautiful than MusicTEX for music type-
        setting". In Wietse Dol, editor, "Proceedings of the 9th European TEX Conference,
        September 4–8 1995, Arnhem, The Netherlands", pp. 351–358. Nederlandstalige
        TEX Gebruikersgroep, 1995.
        This article is a description of MusiXTEX as a new music typesetting package derived from MusicTEX.
        MusiXTEX is a three-pass system and produces more beautiful scores than MusicTEX, which was a one-pass
        system. The first pass performs a rough TEXing which reports the spacings of each music section, the sec-
        ond pass uses an external program to compute optimal note spacings, and the third pass lets TEX include
        this information to typeset the final score. This results in more visually attractive slurs and regularly spaced
        notes.   http://www.ntg.nl/maps/pdf/E_23.pdf

[121]   Daniel Taupin. "MusicTEX, using TEX to write polyphonic and instrumental music,
        Version 5.17", 1996.
        This is a deprecated package. Use MusiXTEX instead. Old files are still available at the URL
                                    http://icking-music-archive.org/software/musictex/

[122]   Piet Tutelaers. "A font and a style for typesetting chess using LaTEX or TEX". *TUG-
        boat*, 13(1):85–90, 1992.
        The author describes how he built a 26-character chess font with METAFONT. The font consists of a chess
        board and separate sets of black and white chess pieces and empty squares. The TEX macros for typesetting
        chess using the font are described.
                                    http://www.tug.org/TUGboat/Articles/tb13-1/tb34tutelaers.pdf

[123]   Gabriel Valiente Feruglio. "Typesetting commutative diagrams". *TUGboat*,
        15(4):466–484, 1994.
        This article presents a review of macro packages for typesetting commutative diagrams, which are compared
        according to several criteria, such as capability to produce complex diagrams, ease of use, quality of the output
        diagrams, readability of the documentation, installation procedures, resource requirements, availability, and
        portability. The compatibility of the different macro packages is also analyzed.
                                    http://www.tug.org/TUGboat/Articles/tb15-4/tb45vali.pdf

[124]   Kees van der Laan. "Typesetting bridge via LaTEX". *TUGboat*, 10(1):113–116, 1989.
        Macros and a bidding environment for typesetting bridge card distributions and bidding sequences are de-
        scribed complemeted by examples borrowed from the bridge literature.
                                    http://www.tug.org/TUGboat/Articles/tb10-1/tb23laan.pdf

[125]   Kees van der Laan. "Tiling in PostScript and METAFONT — Escher's wink".
        MAPS, 19:39–67, 1997.
        This article describes programs for various tilings, both in METAFONT and in PostScript.
                                    http://www.ntg.nl/maps/pdf/19_12.pdf

[126] Timothy Van Zandt and Denis Girou. "Inside PSTricks". *TUGboat*, 15(3):239–246, 1994.

> The macro-commands of the PSTricks package offer impressive additional capabilities to (LA)TEX users, by giving them direct access to much of the power of PostScript, including full support for color. The article describes the implementation of a few of the features of PSTricks (version 0.94).
>
> http://www.tug.org/TUGboat/Articles/tb15-3/tb44tvz.pdf

[127] Timothy Van Zandt. "PSTricks user's guide", 1993.

> This is the official PSTricks documentation.   http://tug.org/PSTricks/doc/pst-usrfull.pdf

[128] Timothy Van Zandt. PSTricks - PostScript macros for Generic TEX, Documented Code, 1997.

> PSTricks is a collection of PostScript macros that is compatible with most TEX macro packages, including Plain TEX and LATEX. Included are macros for color, graphics, rotation, and overlays. This is the documented code. There is also a *User's Guide* and a read-me file.
>
> On CTAN at: graphics/pstricks/doc/code/pst-code.pdf

[129] Timothy Van Zandt. The multido package, 2004.

> Fixed-point arithmetic is used when working on the loop variable, so that the package is equally applicable in graphics applications like PSTricks as it is with the more common integer loops.
>
> On CTAN at: graphics/pstricks/base/generic/

[130] Boris Veytsman and Leila Akhmadeeva. "Drawing Medical Pedigree Trees with TEX and PSTricks". *The PracTEX Journal*, 2006(4).

> The package provides a set of macros based on PSTricks to draw medical pedigrees according to the recommendations for standardized human pedigree nomenclature. The drawing commands place the symbols on a pspicture canvas. An interface for making trees is also provided.
>
> http://tug.org/pracjourn/2006-4/veytsman

[131] Herbert Voß and Jana Voß. "The plot functions of pst-plot". *TUGboat*, 22-4:314–318, 2001.

> Plotting of external data records is one of the standard problems of technical–industrial publications. Very often the data files are imported into gnuplot, provided with axes of coordinates and further references and finally exported to LATEX. This article explains ways to get proper data plotting without using external applications.   http://www.tug.org/TUGboat/Articles/tb22-4/tb72vossplot.pdf

[132] Herbert Voß. "Three-dimensional plots with pst-3dplot". *TUGboat*, 22-4:319–329, 2001.

> There exist several packages for plotting three-dimensional graphical objects. This article describes pst-3dplot, which is similiar to the pst-plot package for two dimensional objects, mathematical functions and datafiles.   http://www.tug.org/TUGboat/Articles/tb22-4/tb72voss3d.pdf

[133] Herbert Voß. The pstricks-add - package, 2006.

> This package collects together examples that have been posted to the PSTricks mailing list, together with some additional features for PSTricks . The package also includes additions and bugfixes for PSTricks, pst-plot, pst-node and pst-tree.   On CTAN at: graphics/pstricks/contrib/pstricks-add/

[134] Herbert Voß. The pst-3dplot - package, 2006.

> A package using PSTricks to draw a large variety of graphs and plots, including 3-D math functions. Data can be read from external data files, making this package a generic tool for graphing within TEX/LATEX without the need for external tools.   On CTAN at: graphics/pstricks/contrib/pst-3dplot/

[135] Herbert Voß. PSTricks: Grafik für TEX und LATEX, Fourth Edition. DANTE – Lehmanns, Heidelberg/Hamburg, 2007.

> This book explains all keywords and macros of the basic packages of the PSTricks bundle uing examples. A lot of the additional packages including pst-vue3d, pst-3dplot or pst-eucl, are also mentioned.

[136] Helene Wanske. "Notenproduktion im Umbruch. Gedanken zur gegenwärtigen und zukünftigen Musikalienherstellung". In Hans-Joachim Koppitz, editor, "Gutenberg-Jahrbuch 1990", pp. 237–243. Gutenberg-Gesellschaft, Internationale Vereinigung für Geschichte und Gegenwart der Druckkunst e.V., Mainz, Germany, 1990.

[137] Jan V. White. Color for the Electronic Age. Watson-Guptil Publications, New York, 1990.

This book is about the functional use of color in charts, graphs, typography, and pictures. It shows how color can be used as a practical and efficient tool to focus attention, explain relationships, and analyze data; how color helps the reader comprehend information faster; and how it can establish identity by associating a certain color with a given element thus easing recognition and turning information into knowledge. Colors can have psychological and emotional effects, carry cultural connotations, and must thus be used with great care. With the help of hundreds of "right" and "wrong" examples the author shows practically and clearly what works and what does not in many of the important areas of written communication.

Useful rules about color patterns can also be found on the Web in Susan Fowler's "Color and patterns" (http://www.fast-consulting.com/color/cp_toc.htm), Jan White's "Full color" (http://www.insideoutdesign.com/full_color.pdf), Ann L. Wiley's "Effective color" (http://www.tec.ufl.edu/~kdtn/effcol.pdf), or Aries Arditi's "Effective color contrast" (http://www.lighthouse.org/color_contrast.htm).

[138] Michael J. Wichura. The PICTEX Manual. Number 6 in TEXniques: publications for the TEX community. TEX Users Group, Providence, RI, 1987.

This book describes the PICTEX language. The syntax of each command is fully detailed. With the help of many examples it is explained how to setup a graph, draw rules, lines, curves, dots and dashes, and generate shadings. Inclusion of PICTEX pictures in a page, the rotation of images, and how to use LATEX and PICTEX together are described. The level of reader understanding can be tested with the help of several dozen exercises, whose answers are included in an appendix.

[139] Michael J. Wichura. "Macros for drawing PiCtures". TUGboat, 9(2):193–197, 1988.

This article is a short overview of PICTEX, a collection of TEX macros that let TEX users easily instruct TEX to typeset beautiful pictures, and in particular mathematical figures, as a part of their books.
                                    http://www.tug.org/TUGboat/Articles/tb09-2/tb21wichura-pictex.pdf

[140] Jiří Zlatuška, editor. EuroTEX '92: Proceedings of the 7th European TEX Conference, Prague, Czechoslovakia, September 14–18, 1992. Masarykova Universita, Brno, 1992.

Indexes

The index has been split into five parts. We start with a general index that covers all entries apart from those of the three large graphics languages, METAPOST, PSTricks, and Xy-pic, that are described in chapters 3, 5, and 7 respectively. These three languages each have their own separate index, in order to do justice to the specific terms they use to denote their native constructs. This also helps the reader to avoid mistakenly finding a solution offered by one language when creating a graphic in one of the other languages. Important general concepts are additionally cross-referenced from the general index. We end with an index of authors.

To make the indexes easier to use, the entries are distinguished by their "type", and this is often indicated by one of the following "type words" at the beginning of the main entry or a sub-entry:

boolean, counter, document class, env., file, file extension, font, key, key value, option, package, program, rigid length, or syntax.

The absence of an explicit "type word" means that the "type" is either a LaTeX "command" or simply a "concept".

Use by, or in connection with, a particular package is indicated by adding the package name (in parentheses) to an entry or sub-entry. There is one "virtual" package name, tlgc, that indicates commands introduced only for illustrative purposes in this book.

A *blue italic* page number indicates that the command or concept is demonstrated in an example on that page.

When there are several page numbers listed, **bold** face indicates a page containing important information about an entry, such as a definition or basic usage.

When looking for the position of an entry in the index, you need to realize that, when they come at the start of a command or file extension, both the characters \ and . are ignored. All symbols come before all letters and everything that starts with the @ character will appear immediately before A.

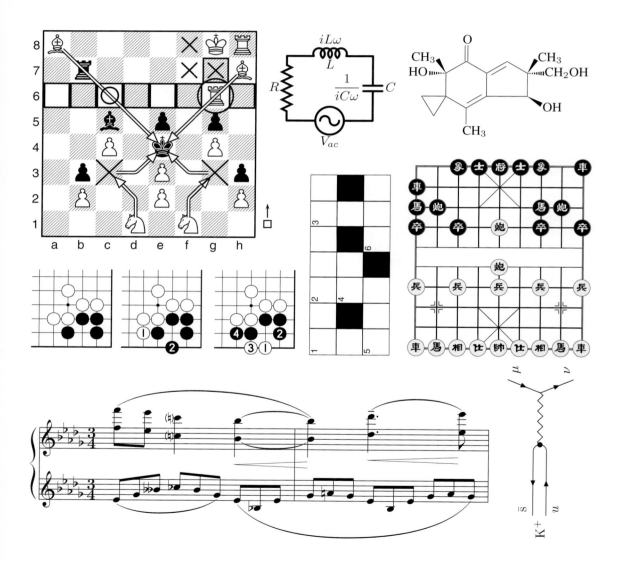

General Index

D

I

M

\protect (igo), 695
\providecolor (xcolor), **726**, *727*, 728
\providecolorset (xcolor), **727**, *728*
.ps file extension (graphics/graphicx), 35
ps option (skak), *676*
.ps.bb file extension (graphics/graphicx), 35
.ps.gz file extension (graphics/graphicx), 35
ps2eps program, 615
ps2epsi program, 615
ps2pdf program, 797, 801–806
ps2pdf13 program, 804, 805
psfrag package, 5
\psframebox (xcolor), *733*
psgo package, 691
psmatrix env. (pst-pdf), 800
pspicture env. (pst-pdf), 800
pspicture package, 47, 511
pst-eucl package, VIII
pst-pdf package, 797, **800–803**, 805, 806
\pst@object (pst-pdf), 800
pstarrows option (pict2e), *44*
PSTricks, *see* PSTricks *index*
pstricks option (pst-pdf), 800
pstricks package, 515, 797, 800
\pt (MusiXTEX), 594
\pteridinev (hetarom), 530
\pteridinevi (hetarom), 530
\PText (axodraw), 559
.ptx file extension, xxxi
\purinev (hetarom), 520, 530
\purinevi (hetarom), 530
purity of color, 718
purple syntax (xcolor), 726
\put
        (curve2e), *48, 49*
        (cwpuzzle), *705*
    Puzzle env. (cwpuzzle), *704*, *705*, *707, 708*
\PuzzleBlackBox (cwpuzzle), 708
\PuzzleClueFont (cwpuzzle), *708*
    PuzzleClues env. (cwpuzzle), *705*
\PuzzleFont (cwpuzzle), 708
\PuzzleHook (cwpuzzle), 705, **708**
\PuzzleLetters (cwpuzzle), *708*
\PuzzleLettersText (cwpuzzle), *708*
\PuzzleNumberFont (cwpuzzle), *708*
\PuzzleNumbers (cwpuzzle), *708*
    puzzles, *see* crosswords, *see* Sudoku
\PuzzleSolution (cwpuzzle), **705**, *706, 708*
\PuzzleUnitlength rigid length (cwpuzzle), *708*
\PuzzleUnsolved (cwpuzzle), 705
    PuzzleWords env. (cwpuzzle), *707*
\PuzzleWordsText (cwpuzzle), *707*
\pvmos (circ), *577*
\pyranose (hcycle), *532*
    pyranoses derivatives, *532*

\pyrazinev (hetarom), *524*, 530
\pyrazolev (hetarom), 530
\pyrazolevi (hetarom), 530
\pyridazinev (hetarom), 530
\pyridazinevi (hetarom), 530
\pyridinev (hetarom), 530
\pyridinevi (hetarom), 530
\pyrimidinev (hetarom), 530
\pyrimidinevi (hetarom), 530
\pyrrolev (hetarom), 530
\pyrrolevi (hetarom), 530
Python program, 661

Q

\Q (circ), *577*
    Q: syntax (abc), 602, *610*
\qa (MusiXTEX), **593**, *594, 595*
\qb (MusiXTEX), *596*, **597**, *599*
\qbezier, 46, *47*
        (pict2e), 46, *47*
\qbeziermax, 46
\ql (MusiXTEX), 592, **593**, *596*, 597, *599*
\qlp (MusiXTEX), *599*
\qp (MusiXTEX), 592, **594**, *599*
\qqs (MusiXTEX), 592
\qs (MusiXTEX), 592
\qu (MusiXTEX), 592, **593**, *594–596*, 597
    quadratic Bézier curves, 46, *47*
    quadruplets (musical), *605*
\queen (chessfss), 672
\quinazolinev (hetarom), 530
\quinazolinevi (hetarom), 530
\quinolinev (hetarom), 530
\quinolinevi (hetarom), 530
\quinoxalinev (hetarom), 530
\qupp (MusiXTEX), 592

R

R syntax
        (PMX), 639
        (m-ch-en), 542, 544
\R (circ), *577*, *581*
    r syntax (PMX), **625**, *626*, **628**
\r... (MusiXTEX), 594
    R: syntax (abc), *608*
    radii, specifying, 45, *46*
    rand (pic), 19
\rarw (timing), 575
\rawboard (bg), 697
    Rb syntax (PMX), **639**, *640*
    rb syntax (PMX), 625, *626*
    RD syntax (PMX), **639**, *640*
    Rd syntax (PMX), **639**, *640*
    Rdl syntax (PMX), *640*

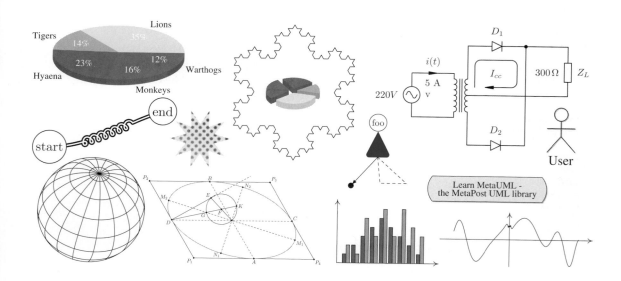

METAFONT **and** METAPOST

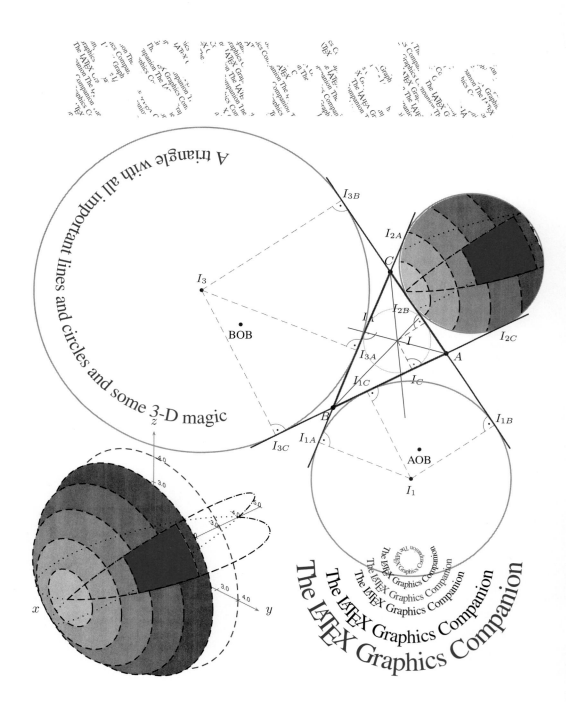

PSTricks

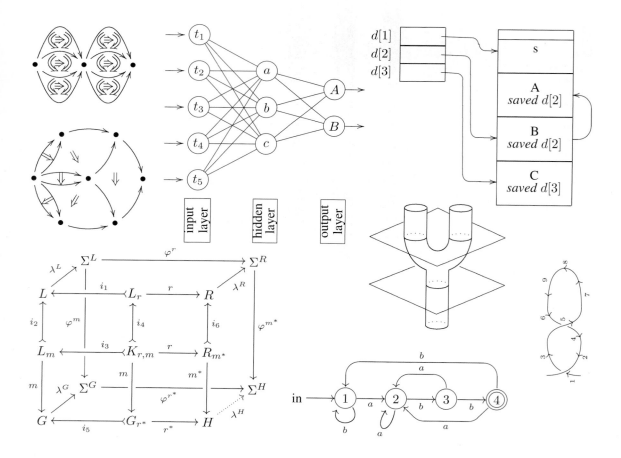

Xy-pic

People

TOOLS AND TECHNIQUES FOR COMPUTER TYPESETTING

Frank Mittelbach, Series Editor

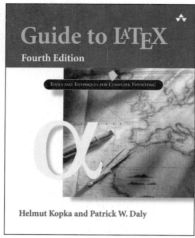

ISBN: 0-321-17385-6

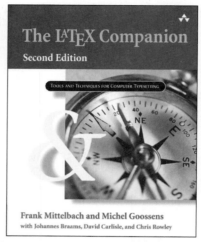

ISBN: 0-201-36299-6

ISBN: 0-201-43311-7

ISBN: 0-321-50892-0

All four books also available in a handsome boxed set (ISBN: 0321514432)

For additional information, including free sample chapters, please visit
www.awprofessional.com